Berlin-Brandenburg

Ein Architekturführer
An Architectural Guid

herausgegeben vom / edited by
Institut für Regionalentwicklung und
Strukturplanung
gemeinsam mit dem / with
Architekten- und Ingenieur-Verein
zu Berlin

BERLIN BRANDENBURG

Ein Architekturführer
An Architectural Guide

Peter Güttler
Joachim Schulz
Ingrid Bartmann-Kompa
Klaus-Dieter Schulz
Karl Kohlschütter
Arnold Jacoby

Ernst & Sohn

ISBN 3-433-02407-3

Texte/Texts:
Güttler (Berlin B 13, 16-17, 23-37, 39-40, C-E, F 1-6, F 20, 27-32, G 12-16, H-K, M 7, N 16-17, 20-24, O, R 12-20, Land Brandenburg S 11-12, 26, 28, U 2, 18-24, 27, W 21, X 15, Y 10-12, Z 11-12, Z 17-20),
J. Schulz (Berlin A, B 1-12, 14-15, 18–22, 38, F 7-19, 21-26, G 1-11, L, M 1-6, 8-12, N 1-15, 18-19, Land Brandenburg Y 1-9, Z 21-32),
Bartmann-Kompa (Potsdam, Stadt Brandenburg),
K.-D. Schulz (Land Brandenburg V, W 1-20, 25-32, X 1-14, 16, Z 1-10, 13-16),
Kohlschütter (Land Brandenburg S 1-10, 13-25, 27, U 1, 3-17, 25-26, 28-48, W 22-24)

Übersetzung/Translation: Michael Robinson, London, und Hans H. Harbort, Berlin
Satz/Type-setting: FRD GmbH, Berlin
Reproduktionen/Reproductions: Reprowerkstatt Rink, Berlin;
Reprogesellschaft L. Wahl, Berlin
Druck/Printing: Mercedes-Druck GmbH, Berlin
Bindearbeiten/Binding: Lüderitz & Bauer GmbH, Berlin

Printed in Germany

Inhalt
Content

Geleitwort
Preface

Vor drei Jahren erschien die erste Auflage dieses Architekturführers in einer Zeit grundlegender politischer Veränderungen in Deutschland. Als eines der ersten gemeinsamen Projekte von Herausgebern und Autoren aus Ost und West dokumentierte er, was zusammengehört und erfolgreich zusammenwirken kann.
Über drei Jahre der neuen Gemeinsamkeit liegen nun hinter uns – für den Architekturführer war es Grund genug, sich in einer aktualisierten Form vorzustellen mit zeitbedingten Änderungen, Neubauten, großen Projekten der wiedergefundenen deutschen Hauptstadt und mit der im inzwischen geschaffenen Bundesland Brandenburg weiter gefaßten Region. Geblieben aber ist die Darstellung der geschlossenen Kulturlandschaft Brandenburg mit Berlin in seiner Mitte, eine Landschaft, die nun wieder ohne innere Grenzen gesehen und erlebt werden kann und die in dem jungen Prozeß des Wiederzusammenwachsens nach ihrer Identität sucht. Gleichfalls geblieben ist in dieser bewegten Zeit die Notwendigkeit gegenseitigen Kennenlernens, zu dem der Architekturführer seinen Beitrag leisten kann. Der Titel »Berlin-Brandenburg« stand vor drei Jahren für die neue grenzenlose Zusammengehörigkeit. Inzwischen gibt es Pläne eines Verschmelzens beider bisher noch politisch selbständigen Einheiten, womit »Berlin-Brandenburg« eine neue Bedeutung gewinnt. Berlin als wichtiger Wohn- und Industriestandort war immer mit dem Land Brandenburg und seinen Traditionen eng verflochten. Wie eng beides verwoben ist, läßt sich nirgends so deutlich ablesen wie am baugeschichtlichen Werdegang dieses »Berlin-Brandenburg« mit seinen Kirchen und Schlössern, Fabriken und Wohnbauten, Gärten, Theatern oder Schulen.
Seine Architektur in den übergeordneten Zusammenhängen verständlich zu machen und Kenntnisse über die berlin-brandenburgischen Bauten zu vermitteln, ist daher Aufgabe des vorliegenden Architekturführers.

Three years ago the first edition of this Architectural Guide was published in a period of fundamental political changes in Germany. As one of the first joint projects of editors and authors from east and west, the Guide served to document the fact that it is indeed possible to join together what belongs together.
Today, more than three years have passed since reunification – reason enough to update the Architectural Guide. A second edition is presented here with numerous new entries, including alterations and conversions, new buildings, large-scale projects relating to the old and new capital, and also a larger excursion into the surrounding area of the newly created Land Brandenburg. As before, the Guide attemps to cover the entire cultural region of Brandenburg with Berlin at the centre. This region, which can now be seen and experienced as a whole and without borders, is looking to find a new identity in the still young process of growing together. At the same time, there is a continuing need in these eventful times to learn more about each other. The Architectural Guide is designed to make an important contribution to this process. Three years ago, the heading «Berlin-Brandenburg» underscored the new-found unity without intervening borders. Today, plans are being made to merge these two separate political entities, thus lending new meaning to the title «Berlin-Brandenburg». As a major industrial and residential centre, Berlin always had close ties with the Brandenburg and its traditions. How close these ties actually are is nowhere more apparent than in the architectural history of «Berlin-Brandenburg» with its churches and castles, factories and dwellings, gardens, theatres, and schools.
It will be the task of this Architectural Guide to promote a better understanding of this unified architectural context and to impart a better knowledge about the buildings in Berlin and Brandenburg.

Jochen Wolf
Minister für Stadtentwicklung, Wohnen
und Verkehr des Landes Brandenburg

Wolfgang Nagel
Senator für Bau- und Wohnungswesen
von Berlin

Geschichte, Bedingungen, Ereignisse
History, conditions, events

Die Mark Brandenburg mit ihren Städten Berlin, Potsdam, Frankfurt/Oder und Brandenburg hat in tausend Jahren Geschichte nahezu alle Phasen politischer Entwicklung erlebt – Kolonisation und Reformation, Kleinstaaterei und militärisches Erstarken, Großmacht und Niederlage, Revolution und Diktatur, Teilung und Wiedervereinigung. Mit Preußens Übernahme der führenden Rolle in der deutschen Geschichte wurde Berlin-Potsdam auch kultureller Angelpunkt in Mitteleuropa, zeitweise beherbergte die junge Millionenstadt sogar die Weltelite der Architekten.
Die Architektur wird von Menschen gemacht. Ihre schöpferische Kraft beziehen diese aus Strömungen der Zeit, in der sie leben: politische Verhältnisse, Religion, Wissenschaft, Technik. Diese Einflüsse schlagen sich in allen Bereichen der Kunst und des geistigen Lebens nieder und sie wirken aufeinander, auf Malerei, Literatur, Musik, Bildhauerei, Baukunst.

In sechs für Berlin-Brandenburg wichtigen geschichtlichen Abschnitten soll wie im Zeitraffer die Abfolge der Ereignisse komprimiert und reduziert werden – auf Zufälliges, vielleicht auch auf Wesentliches. Weltgeschichte steht neben Regionalgeschichte, Dinge aus der Kunst neben Technik. Alles zusammen kann einen flüchtigen Eindruck vermitteln von der Zeit, in der das Schloß oder die Kirche entstand, die uns später begegnen wird. Umgekehrt mag auch die Brücke, der Turm oder das Haus, welches wir sehen, dazu verleiten, in dieser knappen Aufstellung nach deren geschichtlichen Begleitumständen zu suchen. Auf lehrmeisterhafte Ausführlichkeit kommt es dann nicht an, wenn durch wenige Stichworte der gedankliche Anstoß gegeben werden kann, Gebautes – unsere tägliche Umwelt – in das logische Raster unseres Verständnisses einzugliedern und zu begreifen.

Das Wort »Zeitgeist« steht heute für das Motiv der Ereignisse, und nur aus der Gegenüberstellung der Ereignisse kann der Zeitgeist verstanden werden. Das ist ein Teil des Anliegens dieses Buches. Fachwissen wollen wir dabei nicht voraussetzen. Denn Architektur und Baukunst geht alle an.

The Mark Brandenburg with its cities of Berlin, Potsdam, Frankfurt an der Oder and Brandenburg has run the gamut of political development in its thousand-year history – colonialization and Reformation, small-statehood and military build-up, great power status and defeat, revolution and dictatorship, division and reunification. When Prussia adopted its leading role in German history, Berlin-Potsdam became a political focus in Europe, and for a time the youthful city of millions was home to the world's architectural elite.
Architecture is made by man, drawing creative force from the forces of the period in which he lives: political conditions, religion, science, technology. These affect all fields of art and intellectual and spiritual life, and they are in their turn interdependent: painting, literature, music, sculpture, architecture.

We have chosen six periods of history important for Berlin and Brandenburg, with the intention of compressing and reducing the sequence of events, as in a time-lapse film. World history is set alongside regional history, art alongside technology. Together all this conveys a fleeting impression of the time in which a palace or church we come across later was built. Conversely, it may be that a bridge, tower or house we are looking at makes us want to familiarize ourselves with its historical context by consulting this short survey. But we are not aiming for schoolmasterly thoroughness: we use a few key words to give a stimulus as an aid to categorizing and grasping things built – our daily environment – and assimilating them within the logical framework of our understanding.

The word «Zeitgeist» suggests the driving force behind events, and it is only by juxtaposing events that the Zeitgeist can be understood. This is one of the aims of this book. But no specialist knowledge is required. Architecture and the art of building concern everybody.

Mittelalter

Das junge deutsche Reich sucht seine Stärkung im Einrichten von Markgrafschaften zwischen Elbe und Oder. Während des Machtkampfes zwischen König und Herzögen gewinnt die Kirche zunehmend politischen Einfluß. Der Papst zerstört das universale Kaisertum und die abendländische Einheit. Das deutsche Reich erhält seinen föderativen Charakter.
Unter dem Einfluß des antik-römischen Vorbildes setzt sich nördlich der Alpen der romanische Stil durch und wird kultiviert. Im Streben nach Höhe und im Ausdruck der Dynamik bildet sich aus ihm die Gotik – im Kirchenbau Sinnbild der weltentsagenden mittelalterlichen Frömmigkeit.

750 Hevellerburg in Spandau.
928 Heinrich I. erobert Brandenburg.
948 Brandenburg wird Bischofssitz.
962 Krönung Otto I. in Rom zum Kaiser.
968 Erzbistum Magdeburg.
983 Aufstand der West-Slawen.
1077 Heinrich IV. geht nach Canossa.
1096 Erster Kreuzzug.
1134 Albrecht der Bär erhält vom Kaiser die Nordmark.
1140 Westfront der Abteikirche in Saint-Denis vollendet – Beginn der Gotik.
1150 Der slawische Fürst Jaxa von Köpenick tritt zum Christentum über.
1152 Friedrich Barbarossa wird König, er gibt Heinrich dem Löwen Sachsen und Bayern.
1170 Gründung von Kloster Zinna.
1200 Deutsche Besiedlung des Teltow und Barnim, Gründung von Cölln-Berlin.
1210 Wolfram v. Eschenbach schreibt den Parzifal.
1213 Pommern und die Niederlausitz kommen zu Brandenburg.
1241 Die Mongolen stehen vor Liegnitz.
1248 Kölner Dom begonnen.

Middle Ages

The new German Empire seeks to reinforce its strength by setting up margravates between Elbe and Oder rivers. The church gains increasing political influence in the power struggle between king and dukes. The Pope abolishes the concept of universal empire, and with it the unity of the West. The German Empire becomes federal.
Under the influence of the ancient Roman model, the Romanesque style is generally accepted north of the Alps and spreads rapidly. Striving for height and dynamics leads to the development of Gothic from it – in church building the symbol of world-renouncing medieval piety.

750 Hevel castle in Spandau.
928 Heinrich I conquers Brandenburg.
948 Brandenburg becomes a bishopric.
962 Coronation of Otto I as emperor in Rome.
968 Magdeburg archbishopric.
983 Revolt of Western Slavs.
1077 Heinrich IV goes to Canossa.
1096 First Crusade.
1134 Albrecht the Bear receives the Nordmark from the emperor.
1140 West front of the abbey of Saint-Denis completed – beginning of the Gothic period.
1150 Slavic prince Jaxa von Köpenick converts to Christianity.
1152 Frederick Barbarossa becomes king, and presents Saxony and Bavaria to Henry the Lion.
1170 Foundation of the monastery of Zinna.
1200 German settlement of Teltow and Barnim, foundation of Cölln-Berlin.
1210 Wolfram von Eschenbach writes Parzival.
1213 Brandenburg acquires Pomerania and Niederlausitz.

1254 Das Interregnum beginnt.
1261 Markgräflicher Hof in Berlin.
1300 Erfindung des Schießpulvers.
1307 Vereinigung von Berlin und Cölln.
1309 Marienburg wird Sitz des Hochmeisters.
1320 Das brandenburg-askanische Geschlecht stirbt aus.
1321 Dante stirbt.
Mittelmärkischer Städtebund.
1345 Erster allgemeiner Landtag der Mark in Berlin.
1348 Die Pest kommt nach Europa.
1354 In Berlin werden Juden zu Mitbürgern.
1356 Brandenburg wird Kurfürstentum.
1358 Die Hanse wird zum Begriff.
1359 Berlin zur Hanse eingeladen.
1380 Berlin brennt.
1410 Schlacht bei Tannenberg.
1411 Die Hohenzollern kommen nach Brandenburg.
1414 Erstürmung der Quitzowburgen und Ende der Raubritterzeit.
1419 Brunelleschi beginnt in Florenz den Bau des Findelhauses – erster Renaissancebau.
1431 Jeanne d'Arc auf dem Scheiterhaufen.
1448 Niederwerfung des »Berliner Unwillens«.
1450 Erfindung des Buchdrucks.
1486 Berlin kurfürstliche Residenz.
1492 Kolumbus erreicht Westindien.
1495 Reichsreform Maximilians I. scheitert.

1241 Mongols outside the gates of Liegnitz.
1248 Cologne cathedral started.
1254 Beginning of Interregnum.
1261 Margrave's court in Berlin.
1300 Invention of gunpowder.
1307 Unification of Berlin and Cölln.
1309 Marienburg becomes seat of the Grand Master.
1320 The Brandenburg-Ascanian tribe dies out.
1321 Death of Dante.
Federation of the towns of the central Mark.
1345 First general parliament of the Mark in Berlin.
1348 Plague comes to Europe.
1354 Jews acquire citizenship in Berlin.
1356 Brandenburg becomes an Electorate.
1358 Beginning of Hanseatic League.
1359 Berlin invited to join Hanseatic League.
1380 Fire of Berlin.
1410 Battle of Tannenberg.
1411 Hohenzollerns come to Brandenburg.
1414 Storming of Quitzow castles and end of age of robber barons.
1419 Brunelleschi starts work on the Foundling Hospital in Florence – first Renaissance building.
1431 Joan of Arc burned at the stake.
1448 Suppression of the «Berliner Unwillen».
1450 Invention of printing.
1486 Berlin Electoral residence.
1492 Columbus reaches the West Indies.
1495 Failure of Maximilian I's imperial reforms.

Reformation und Absolutismus

Zwischen hellenistisch-heidnischem Humanismus und antik verwurzelter Wissenschaftlichkeit setzt als religiöses Bedürfnis die Reformation der in mittelalterlicher Machtfülle verschlissenen Kirche ein Ende. Dem Aufbruch folgt die Krise. Doch dem in Handel und Handwerk selbstbewußten Bürgertum kann nur noch eine absolutistische Politik entgegengesetzt werden, wie sie in den Fürstenstaaten zum Ausdruck kommt.

Die Renaissance – schon vor einem Jahrhundert in den italienischen Stadtstaaten geboren – wird in Deutschland als bürgerliche Kunst adaptiert und weiterentwickelt. Üppiger und plastischer geht aus der Renaissance das Barock hervor und verkörpert auf seinem Höhepunkt fürstliche und höfische Macht- und Prachtentfaltung.

1502 Erste brandenburgische Druckwerkstatt Viadrina in Frankfurt.
1506 Kurfürst Joachim I. gründet in Frankfurt/Oder die erste brandenburgische Universität.
1514 Kopernikus behauptet, die Erde drehe sich um die Sonne.
1517 Luthers Thesenanschlag in Wittenberg.
1519 Magalhäes umsegelt den Erdball.
1524 Bauernkrieg.
1529 Die Türken belagern Wien.
1534 Die anglikanische Kirche fällt von Rom ab.
1538 Schloßbau in Berlin.
1539 Berlin wird protestantisch.

Reformation and Absolutism

Moving between hellenistic-heathen humanism and an academic approach rooted in antiquity, the Reformation expresses a profound religious need, and puts an end to a church threadbare in the fullness of its medieval might. This new departure is followed by crisis. But only absolutist politics can be set against a bourgeoisie self-confident in trade and craft, as expressed in the prince-states.

The Renaissance – born a century before in the city states of Italy – is adapted and further developed as bourgeois art in Germany. The Renaissance is followed by the more lavish plasticity of the Baroque, which at its peak embodied the unfolding of princely power and splendour.

1502 First Brandenburg press, Viadrina, in Frankfurt an der Oder.
1506 Elector Joachim I founds the first Brandenburg university in Frankfurt an der Oder.
1514 Copernicus asserts that the Earth revolves around the sun.
1517 Luther nails up the 95 Theses in Wittenberg.
1519 Magellan sails round the world.
1524 Peasant Wars.
1529 Turks besiege Vienna.
1534 The Anglican Church secedes from Rome.
1538 Schloss built in Berlin.
1539 Berlin becomes Protestant.
1540 St. Ignatius Loyola founds the

1540 Ignatius v. Loyola gründet den Jesuitenorden.
1548 Die Kartoffel kommt nach Europa.
1550 Rechenbuch von Adam Riese.
1562 Beginn der Hugenottenkriege in Frankreich.
1563 Konzil von Trient beendet – Gegenreformation.
1568 Niederländischer Freiheitskampf.
1570 Gründung der Börse in London.
1582 Gregorianischer Kalender.
1588 Erste deutsche Zeitung in Köln.
1618 Dreißigjähriger Krieg beginnt.
1620 Finowkanal als neuer Handelsweg.
1633 Galilei: »Sie bewegt sich doch!«
1640 Der Große Kurfürst.
1648 Ende des Dreißigjährigen Krieges: Die Mark Brandenburg ist strichweise entvölkert, Berlin verlor über die Hälfte seiner Einwohner.
Westfälischer Friede: Brandenburg erhält Hinterpommern, Minden, Halberstadt und Magdeburg.
1649 England wird für elf Jahre Republik.
1660 Friede von Oliva – Souveränität in Preußen.
1661 »Sonnenkönig« Ludwig XIV. in Frankreich: »Der Staat, das bin ich!«
1670 Die ersten Hugenotten werden in Altlandsberg angesiedelt.
1685 Edikt von Potsdam.
1694 Akademie der Künste in Berlin gegründet.
1701 Königreich Preußen.
1721 Johann Sebastian Bach: 6 »Brandenburgische Konzerte«.
1735 Erster Kokshochofen.
1740 Friedrich II. besteigt den preußischen Thron.
Maria Theresia wird Kaiserin.
1742 1. Schlesischer Krieg beendet.
1744 2. Schlesischer Krieg.
1747 Regulierung des Oderbruchs.
1748 Lessing kommt nach Berlin.
Montesquieu: »L'Esprit des Lois«.
1750 Voltaire wird Gesinnungsfreund und Gesellschafter Friedrichs II.
1756 Siebenjähriger Krieg beginnt.
1762 Deutsche Bauern wandern nach Osteuropa aus.
1769 Watt baut die erste Dampfmaschine.
1772 Beginn der Polnischen Teilung.
1775 Letzte Hexenverbrennung.

1540 Ignatius Loyola founds the Jesuit Order.
1548 The potato comes to Europe.
1550 Adam Riese's arithmetic book.
1562 Beginning of the Huguenot wars in France.
1563 End of the Council of Trent – Counter-Reformation.
1568 Dutch Wars of Independence.
1570 London Stock Exchange founded.
1582 Gregorian calendar.
1588 First German newspaper in Cologne.
1618 Start of the Thirty Years War.
1620 Finow canal as a new trade route.
1633 Galileo: «But it does move!»
1640 The Great Elector.
1648 End of the Thirty Years War: Mark Brandenburg is depopulated in places, Berlin lost over half its inhabitants.
Peace of Westphalia: Brandenburg acquires Eastern Pomerania, Minden, Halberstadt and Magdeburg.
1649 England a republic for eleven years.
1660 Peace of Oliva – sovereignty in Prussia.
1661 «Roi Soleil» Louis XIV in France: «L'état, c'est moi!»
1670 First Huguenots settled in Altlandsberg.
1685 Edict of Potsdam.
1694 Academy of Arts founded in Berlin.
1701 Kingdom of Prussia.
1721 Johann Sebastian Bach: 6 «Brandenburg Concertos».
1735 First coke-fired blast furnace.
1740 Frederick II ascends Prussian throne.
Maria Theresa becomes Empress.
1742 End of 1st Silesian War.
1744 2nd Silesian War.
1747 Marshes of the Oderbruch drained.
1748 Lessing comes to Berlin.
Montesquieu: «L'Esprit des Lois».
1750 Voltaire becomes kindred spirit and companion of Frederick II.
1756 Seven Years war begins.
1762 German peasants emigrate to Eastern Europe.
1769 Watt builds first steam engine.
1771 Beginning of division of Poland.
1775 Last witch burned.

Aufklärung und Restauration

Das Wissenschaft und Wirtschaft tragende Bürgertum verlangt, durch die Idee der Aufklärung in seiner Mündigkeit bestärkt, nach einem Anteil an der politischen Macht. Die Revolution wird zum Mittel der gesellschaftlichen Veränderung. In den Wirren neuer Verhältnisse läßt sich anfänglicher Idealismus zu einem immer pragmatischeren Nationalismus verbiegen, der die Macht der alten Herrscher wiederherstellt.
In der Kunst werden Ideale der griechischen Antike zu Maß und geistiger Grundlage der Gestaltung. Dieser neue Klassizismus bemächtigt sich auch des Vorbildes Italien. Die schwärmerische Übersetzung des Klassizismus ins Abendländisch-Religiöse fördert die Neugotik zutage, die den gesamten stilistischen Formenkatalog abrundet und einer beliebigen Anwendung öffnet.

1776 Unabhängigkeitserklärung der Vereinigten Staaten von Nordamerika.
Friedrich II. gründet die »Ecole de Génie et d'Architecture«.
1781 Die ersten englischen Spinnereimaschinen treffen in Berlin ein.
1784 Immanuel Kant: »Was ist Aufklärung?«
1785 Erste preußische Dampfmaschine in Hettstedt.
1788 Goethe kehrt von seiner ersten Italienreise heim.
1789 Revolution in Frankreich.
1791 Daniel Itzig erster Jude mit Berliner Bürgerrecht.
1792 Erste preußische Chaussee zwischen Berlin und Potsdam.
1799 Napoleon übernimmt die Macht in Frankreich.
Gründung der Berliner Bauakademie.
1800 Einrichtung einer Stadtpost in Berlin.
1803 Erste Straßenbeleuchtung in Berlin.

Enlightenment and Restoration

The educated and commercial bourgeoisie, strengthened in its responsibility by the idea of the Enlightenment, demands a share of political power. Revolution becomes a tool of social change. In new and confused circumstances, initial idealism is distorted into an ever more pragmatic nationalism, restoring the power of the old rulers.
In art, ideals of Greek antiquity become the standard, intellectual and spiritual basis of creativity. This new classicism also adopts Italian models. Enthusiastic translation of classicism into Western religiosity produces the neo-Gothic movement, which takes the entire catalogue of style and form and opens them up to any kind of application.

1776 Declaration of Independence by the United States of America.
Frederick II founds the «Ecole de Génie et d'Architecture».
1781 First English weaving machines arrive in Berlin.
1748 Immanuel Kant: «What is Enlightenment?»
1785 First Prussian steam engine in Hettstedt.
1788 Goethe returns from his first Italian journey.
1789 French Revolution.
1791 Daniel Itzig first Jew with Berlin citizenship.
1792 First Prussian Chaussee between Berlin and Potsdam.
1799 Napoleon comes to power in France.
Foundation of the Berliner Bauakademie.
1800 City post office founded in Berlin.
1803 First street lighting in Berlin.

1806 Das »Heilige Römische Reich Deutscher Nation« zerbricht, Niederlage Preußens, Napoleons Einzug in Berlin.
1808 Goethes »Faust«.
1809 Gründung der Berliner Universität.
1810 Caspar David Friedrich stellt in Berlin aus.
»Turnvater Jahn« eröffnet in der Berliner Hasenheide den ersten deutschen Turnplatz.
Gewerbefreiheit in Preußen.
1813 Völkerschlacht bei Leipzig.
1814 Beethovens Fidelio uraufgeführt.
1815 Napoleon bei Waterloo endgültig geschlagen.
Im Wiener Kongreß wird der Deutsche Bund geschaffen.
»Heilige Allianz« Rußland – Österreich – Preußen.
E.T.A. Hoffmann schreibt: »Die Elixiere des Teufels«.
1816 Stapellauf des ersten Raddampfers in Pichelsdorf.
1817 Wartburgfest.
1818 Aufhebung der Binnenzölle in Preußen.
1821 Aufstände der Griechen.
1822 Der englische Dichter Lord Byron geht als Freiheitskämpfer nach Griechenland.
1824 Architekten-Verein zu Berlin.
1826 Eichendorff: »Aus dem Leben eines Taugenichts«.
1832 Hambacher Fest.
Goethe stirbt.
1835 Der Vatikan zieht die Verurteilung der kopernikanischen Schriften zurück.
1838 Berlin–Potsdamer Bahn eröffnet.
Borsig gründet Maschinenbauanstalt.
1839 Preußen verbietet Kinder-Nachtarbeit und begrenzt die tägliche Arbeitszeit für Kinder auf zehn Stunden.
1840 Friedrich Wilhelm IV. auf dem Thron.
1842 Ferdinand v. Quast wird erster preußischer Denkmalpfleger.
1843 Richard Wagners »Tannhäuser« uraufgeführt.
1844 Liebig führt den Kunstdünger ein.
1847 Neugründungen: Meteorologisches Institut, Städtische Gasanstalt Berlin, Gemeinnützige Baugesellschaft.
1848 Marx: »Kommunistisches Manifest«.
Revolution in Preußen.
1850 Oktroyierte Verfassung in Preußen.
1853 Berliner Bauordnung.
1862 Theodor Fontane: »Wanderungen durch die Mark Brandenburg«.
1863 Abschaffung der Sklaverei in Amerika.
1864 Deutsch-dänischer Krieg.
1866 Preußen besiegt Osterreich.
Werner v. Siemens entwickelt die Dynamomaschine.
1870 Deutsch-französischer Krieg.

1806 Collapse of the «Heiliges Römisches Reich Deutscher Nation», defeat of Prussia, Napoleon enters Berlin.
1808 Goethe's «Faust».
1809 Berlin University founded.
1810 Caspar David Friedrich exhibition in Berlin.
«Turnvater Jahn» opens the first German open-air gymnastics area in Hasenheide.
Freedom of trade in Prussia.
1813 Battle of the Nations at Leipzig.
1814 First performance of Beethoven's Fidelio.
1815 Napoleon finally defeated at Waterloo.
German Federation created at the Congress of Vienna.
«Holy Alliance» of Russia, Austria, Prussia.
E.T.A. Hoffmann writes «Die Elixiere des Teufels».
1816 Launch of the first paddle steamer in Pichelsdorf.
1817 Wartburg festival.
1818 Internal tolls revoked in Prussia.
1821 Greek uprising.
1822 Lord Byron goes to Greece as a freedom fighter.
1824 Architekten-Verein in Berlin.
1836 Eichendorff: «Aus dem Leben eines Taugenichts».
1832 Hambach festival.
Death of Goethe.
1835 Vatican withdraws condemnation of writings of Copernicus.
1838 Berlin-Potsdam railway opened.
Borsig founds heavy engineering plant.
1839 Prussia forbids night work for children and limits children's daytime working hours to ten.
1840 Friedrich Wilhelm IV on the throne.
1842 Ferdinand von Quast becomes first Prussian keeper of monuments.
1843 First performance of Richard Wagner's «Tannhäuser».
1844 Liebig introduces artificial fertilizer.
1847 New foundations: meteorological institute, Berlin municipal gasworks, Gemeinnützige Baugesellschaft.
1848 Marx: «Communist Manifesto».
Revolution in Prussia.
1850 Imposed constitution in Prussia.
1853 Berlin building regulations.
1862 Theodor Fontane: «Wanderungen durch die Mark Brandenburg».
1863 Abolition of slavery in America.
1864 German-Danish War.
1866 Prussia defeats Austria.
Werner von Siemens develops the dynamo.
1870 Franco-Prussian War.

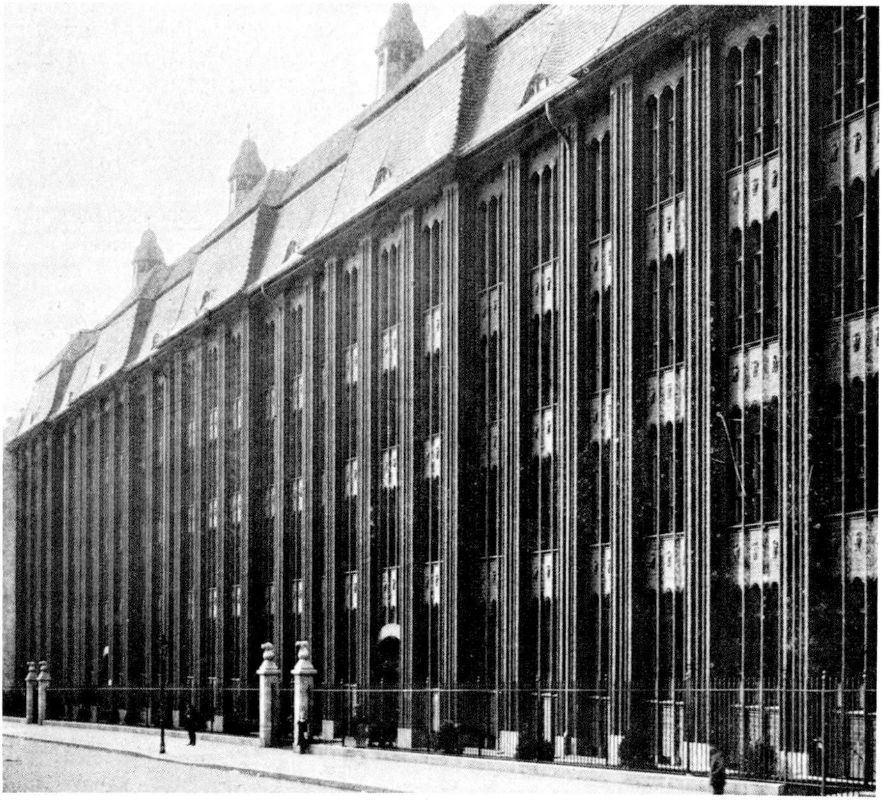

Kaiserreich

Deutschland knüpft an die Geschichte seiner Kaiser im Mittelalter an. Die Großmacht zitiert gerne das historische Erbe. Reformbestrebungen verhindern nicht, daß Nationalstolz und Machtanspruch in Chauvinismus und Weltkrieg münden.
In der Architektur klingt der Einfluß der Schinkelzeit aus. Der Historismus, das Nachahmen alter Stilformen, beherrscht bis zur Jahrhundertwende das Bauen, dann wird im Jugendstil, im Landhausstil oder in der Beginnenden Moderne Neues gewagt.

1871 Kaiserproklamation Wilhelms I. in Versailles.
Berlin wird Hauptstadt des deutschen Reiches.
1872 Demonstrationen gegen Mietwucher und Wohnungsnot.
In Berlin werden 174 Aktiengesellschaften gegründet.
1873 Börsenkrach.
1876 Auguste Renoir malt »Die Badende«.
Der erste Teil des Berliner Entwässerungssystems geht in Betrieb.
1877 Berlin wird Millionenstadt.
Erstes Telefongespräch Berlin–Magdeburg.
1878 Sozialistengesetz.
1880 Wirtschaftsdepression hält an.

Empire

Germany looks back to the time of its medieval emperors. Great powers like to cite an historic legacy. Efforts at reform fail to prevent nationalist pride and assertion of power degenerating into chauvinism and the First World War.
In architecture the influence of the Schinkel period fades. Historicism, the imitation of older styles, dominates building until the turn of the century, then new approaches are risked in Jugendstil, the country house style or the beginnings of Modernism.

1871 Wilhelm I proclaimed emperor in Versailles.
Berlin becomes capital of Germany.
1872 Demonstrations against extortionate rents and housing shortage.
174 joint-stock companies founded in Berlin.
1873 Stock Exchange crash.
1876 Auguste Renoir paints «Les Baigneuses».
Berlin sewerage system starts to operate.
1877 Berlin's population reaches one million.
First telephone conversation between Berlin and Magdeburg.
1878 Law against socialists.

1882 Die Berliner Stadtbahn nimmt den Betrieb auf.
1883 Hygieneausstellung in Berlin.
1884 Deutschland erwirbt die ersten Kolonien.
1885 Zwei Elektrizitätswerke in Berlin.
1887 Verstaatlichung aller Eisenbahnen.
1888 Bismarck: »Wir Deutsche fürchten Gott, aber sonst nichts in der Welt«.
1889 Unzensierte »Freie Bühne« führt in Berlin Ibsens »Gespenster« auf. Gerhart Hauptmanns naturalistisches Drama »Vor Sonnenaufgang« löst einen politischen Skandal aus.
1890 Bismarck entlassen.
Aufhebung des Sozialistengesetzes.
1894 Gustav Mahlers 2. Sinfonie.
Uraufführung der »Weber« von Hauptmann – Kaiser kündigt Hofloge.
1895 Lenin in Berlin.
1896 Otto Lilienthal verunglückt tödlich.
Röntgen führt in Berlin die von ihm entdeckten Strahlen vor.
In Berlin leben auf einem Grundstück durchschnittlich 72 Menschen.
1898 Gründung der »Berliner Sezession«.
Gründung des »Wandervogel«.
1899 Das erste Kino in Berlin.
1901 Pergamonmuseum eröffnet.
Thomas Manns »Buddenbrooks«.
1902 Erste U-Bahnstrecke in Berlin
1904 Im Grunewald statt Hofjagd jetzt Erholung für Bürger.
1905 Nobelpreis für Robert Koch.
1906 Pablo Picasso: »Die beiden Brüder«.
Kaufhaus KaDeWe in Berlin eröffnet.
1907 Hermann Muthesius gründet den Deutschen Werkbund.
Preußisches Gesetz gegen Verunstaltung von Ortschaften und Landschaften.
1910 Igor Strawinski: »Der Feuervogel«.
Erstes Motorflugzeug über Berlin.
1913 Thomas Mann veröffentlicht »Der Tod in Venedig«.
1914 Der Erste Weltkrieg bricht aus.
Franz Kafka schreibt »Der Prozeß«.
1915 Brot wird rationiert.
1916 Friedensdemonstration in Berlin, Liebknecht verhaftet.
1918 Militärischer Zusammenbruch Kaiser-Deutschlands

1880 Continuing economic depression.
1882 The Berlin inner railway (Stadtbahn) goes into service.
1883 Hygiene exhibition in Berlin.
1884 Germany acquires first colonies.
1885 Two power stations in Berlin.
1887 All railways nationalized.
1888 Bismarck: «We Germans fear God, but nothing else in the world».
1889 Uncensored «Freie Bühne» stages Ibsen's «Ghosts». Gerhart Hauptmann's naturalistic drama «Vor Sonnenaufgang» unleashes a political scandal.
1890 Bismarck dismissed.
Repeal of law against socialists.
1894 Gustav Mahler's 2nd symphony.
First performance of Hauptmann's «Weavers» – emperor cancels royal box.
1895 Lenin in Berlin.
1896 Otto Lilienthal fatally injured in attempt to fly.
Röntgen demonstrates his X-rays in Berlin.
An average of 72 people live on one building plot in Berlin.
1898 Foundation of the «Berliner Sezession».
Foundation of the «Wandervogel» movement.
1899 First cinema in Berlin.
1901 Pergamon Museum opens. Thomas Mann's «Buddenbrooks».
1902 First underground line in Berlin.
1904 Grunewald used for popular recreation rather than for hunting by the court.
1905 Nobel Prize for Robert Koch.
1906 Pablo Picasso: «The Two Brothers».
Kaufhaus des Westens opens in Berlin.
1907 Hermann Muthesius founds Deutscher Werkbund.
Prussian law against disfigurement of towns, villages and countryside.
1910 Igor Stravinsky: «The Firebird».
First motor-powered flight over Berlin.
1913 Thomas Mann publishes «Death in Venice».
1914 Outbreak of First World War.
Franz Kafka writes «The Trial».
1915 Bread rationing.
1916 Peace demonstrations in Berlin, Liebknecht arrested.
1918 Military collapse of imperial Germany.

Zwanziger und dreißiger Jahre

Die junge Deutsche Republik leidet an den Nachkriegsfolgen. Auch die Verständigung mit dem Ausland kann eine Hinwendung zum Nationalismus nicht verhindern. Allgemein unterschätzt, gelingt es Hitler, an die Macht zu kommen. Er stürzt die Welt in eine neue Katastrophe.

Der geistigen Unruhe und Gärung vor und nach dem Ersten Weltkrieg entspringt der Expressionismus. Liberalität und Weltoffenheit fördern den internationalen Stil der Sachlichkeit, der vom Bauhaus verkörpert wird. Nach 1933 behauptet sich neben einer kraftlos-kleinlichen Verhärtung und Verflachung des sachlichen Stils ein größenwahnsinniger neoklassizistischer Monumentalismus ideologischer Färbung.

1918 Philipp Scheidemann ruft in Berlin die Republik aus.
Straßenkämpfe in Berlin.
1919 Versailler Vertrag.
Wahl der Nationalversammlung von Weimar.
Walter Gropius gründet das Bauhaus in Weimar.
1920 Völkerbund in Genf.
Bildung von Groß-Berlin.
In Berlin fehlen über 100 000 Wohnungen.
Kapp-Putsch.
1921 Albert Einstein erhält den Nobelpreis.
1923 Hermann Oberths Theorie zur Weltraumfahrt.
Inflation: Ein Brot kostet eine Billion Mark.
1924 In Italien setzt sich mit Mussolini der Faschismus durch.
Bruno Taut schreibt: »Die neue Wohnung«.
1925 Locarno-Vertrag.

Twenties and Thirties

The new German Republic suffers from the consequences of the war and the Treaty of Versailles. Rapprochement with other nations is not enough to prevent a turn to Nationalism. Hitler is generally underestimated, and manages to seize power. He throws the world into a new catastrophe.

Expressionism springs from intellectual unrest and ferment before and after the First World War. Liberality and openness encourage the international style of functionality embodied by the Bauhaus. After 1933 the functional style is weakened and trivialized, and a megalomaniac neo-classical monumentalism with ideological colouring predominates.

1918 Philipp Scheidemann proclaims the Republic in Berlin.
Street fighting in Berlin.
1919 Treaty of Versailles.
Weimar National Assembly elected.
Walter Gropius founds the Bauhaus in Weimar.
1920 League of Nations in Geneva.
Formation of Greater Berlin.
Over 100,000 homes short in Berlin.
Kapp putsch.
1921 Albert Einstein awarded Nobel prize.
1923 Hermann Oberth's theory on space travel.
Inflation: a loaf of bread costs one billion marks.
1924 Mussolini established Fascism in Italy.
Bruno Taut writes «Die Neue Wohnung».
1925 Treaty of Locarno.

1926 Fritz Lang dreht »Metropolis«.
Deutschland wird in den Völkerbund aufgenommen.
Heinrich Zille publiziert seine Zeichnungen in drei Bänden.
Am Kurfürstendamm feiert man die »Goldenen Zwanziger«.
1927 Bertolt Brecht schreibt die »Dreigroschenoper«.
1928 Alexander Fleming entdeckt Penicillin.
1929 Gustav Stresemann stirbt.
Erste Fernsehsendung in Berlin.
»Bankenkrach« in den USA.
1930 Fünfmillionen Arbeitslose in Deutschland.
1931 Deutsche Bauausstellung in Berlin.
1932 Das Bauhaus eröffnet als Privatschule in Berlin.
1933 Hindenburg beruft Hitler als Kanzler.
Max Liebermann erklärt seinen Austritt aus der Akademie der Künste.
Öffentliche Bücherverbrennungen.
Thomas Mann, Bruno Walter und andere verlassen Deutschland.
Auflösung des Bauhauses in Berlin.
1935 Kurt Tucholsky begeht Selbstmord in der Emigration.
Hitler verkündet Wehrpflicht.
1936 Olympische Spiele in Berlin.
1937 Albert Speer General-Bauinspektor für die Neugestaltung der Reichshauptstadt.
1938 Österreich tritt dem Deutschen Reich bei.
Hans Steinhoff dreht mit Gustav Gründgens »Tanz auf dem Vulkan«.
Judenpogrome, Kristallnacht.
1939 Deutschland greift Polen an und löst den Zweiten Weltkrieg aus.
Anna Seghers schreibt »Das 7. Kreuz«.
1942 Wannseekonferenz.
1943 Kriegswende in Stalingrad.
Die ersten schweren Luftangriffe auf Berlin.
1944 Mißglücktes Attentat auf Hitler.
1945 Deutsche Kapitulation.
»Atombombe« zerstört Hiroshima.

1926 Fritz Lang films «Metropolis».
Germany joins the League of Nations.
Heinrich Zille publishes his drawings in three volumes.
«Golden Twenties» celebrated on the Kurfürstendamm.
1927 Bertolt Brecht writes «The Threepenny Opera».
1928 Alexander Fleming discovers penicillin.
1929 Death of Gustav Stresemann.
First television broadcast in Berlin.
Bank collapse «Wall Street crash».
1930 5 million unemployed in Germany.
1931 German Building Exhibition in Berlin.
1932 Bauhaus opens as a private school in Berlin.
1933 Hindenburg appoints Hitler Chancellor.
Max Liebermann resigns from Academy of Arts.
Books burned in public.
Thomas Mann, Bruno Walter and others leave Germany.
Bauhaus dissolved in Berlin.
1935 Kurt Tucholsky commits suicide in emigration.
Hitler proclaims compulsory military service.
1936 Olympic Games in Berlin.
1937 Albert Speer put in charge of redesigning the imperial capital.
1938 Austria joins the German Reich.
Hans Steinhoff makes «Dance on the Volcano» with Gustav Gründgens.
Jewish pogroms, Kristallnacht.
1939 Germany seizes Poland and starts the Second World War.
Anna Seghers writes «Das 7. Kreuz».
1942 Wannsee conference.
1943 Watershed in war at Stalingrad.
First severe air raids on Berlin.
1944 Unsuccessful attempt to assassinate Hitler.
1945 German capitulation.
«Atom bomb» destroys Hiroshima.

Nach dem Zweiten Weltkrieg

Der Zerschlagung Hitler-Deutschlands folgt eine territoriale Neuordnung Europas, die in eine globale Ost-West-Konfrontation und schließlich in den »Kalten Krieg« mündet. Ideologische Gegensätze, internationale Bemühungen um einen menschenrechtlichen Ausgleich und die zunehmende Polarisierung zwischen armen und reichen Ländern – unter denen die Bundesrepublik Deutschland eine führende Rolle gewinnt – bestimmen die politische Entwicklung über Jahrzehnte. Eine neue sowjetische Politik hebt alte Feindbilder auf und gibt Hoffnung auf eine friedliche Zukunft.
Ratlosigkeit und Suche nach verbindlichen Traditionen der Moderne kennzeichnen Kunst und Architektur der Nachkriegsjahre. Das Besinnen auf Wurzeln in den dreißiger Jahren festigt den Plastischen Stil der Fünfziger, neben dem der nochmals bemühte Neoklassizismus in den Ostblockländern wie zeitlich verirrt erscheint. Die folgenden Jahre der Nüchternheit und Zweckmäßigkeit ebnen dem industriellen Bauen den Weg. Zeitweise unterdrückte ästhetische Ansprüche beantwortet nun eine neue phantasievolle Gestaltungsweise, für die vielfach der Begriff »Postmoderne« steht.

1945 Gründung der UNO.
Potsdamer Abkommen.
1946 Wolfgang Borchert: »Draußen vor der Tür«.
1947 Hans Werner Richter gründet die literarische »Gruppe 47«.
1948 West-deutsche Währungsreform.
Spaltung Berlins.
Berliner Blockade.
1949 Bildung der Bundesrepublik Deutschland und der Deutschen Demokratischen Republik.
1950 Le Corbusier beginnt mit dem Bau der Kirche Notre Dame du Haut bei Ronchamp.

After the Second World War

Defeat of Hitler's Germany is followed by territorial reorganization in Europe leading to global East-West confrontation and finally the «Cold War». Ideological conflicts, international striving for balance in terms of human rights and increasing polarization of poor and rich countries – among which latter West Germany gains a leading role – determine political development for decades. New Soviet policy revokes all inimical images and gives hope of a peaceful future.
Post-war architecture is at a loss in its search for a reliable Modern tradition. A return to thirties roots produces the Plastic Style of the fifties, in comparison with which the Eastern bloc's striving for neoclassicism seems to have lost its way. Subsequent years of sobriety and functionality clear the way for industrial building. Aesthetic demands, suppressed for a time, are now met with a new and imaginative way of building, largely covered by the label «post-Modernism».

1945 Foundation of UNO.
Potsdam accord.
1946 Wolfgang Borchert: «Draussen vor der Tür».
1947 Hans Werner Richter founds the literary «Gruppe 47».
1948 West German currency reform. Division of Berlin.
Berlin blockade.
1949 Formation of German Federal Republic and German Democratic Republic.
1950 Le Corbusier starts to build Notre Dame du Haut near Ronchamp.
1951 European Coal and Steel Community.
Start of National Reconstruction Plan in GDR.
1952 Uprising in GDR and East Berlin.

1951 Montan-Union.
Beginn des Nationalen Aufbauprogramms in der DDR.
1953 Volksaufstand in der DDR und Ost-Berlin.
1955 Beide deutsche Staaten werden souverän.
Herbert v. Karajan wird Leiter der Berliner Philharmoniker.
1957 Willy Brandt wird Regierender Bürgermeister von West-Berlin.
Beginn der Raumfahrt: Sputnik 1.
1958 Chruschtschow-Ultimatum.
1959 Günter Grass: »Die Blechtrommel«.
1961 Bau der »Mauer«.
1966 Berliner Studenten demonstrieren gegen den Vietnamkrieg.
1967 Barnard: erste Herzverpflanzung.
1968 DDR führt Visumpflicht ein.
1969 Die ersten Menschen auf dem Mond.
1971 Berlin-Abkommen.
1974 Club of Rome in Berlin: »Menschheit am Wendepunkt«.
1975 Unterzeichnung der KSZE-Schlußakte in Helsinki.
1985 Heinrich Böll: »Frauen vor Flußlandschaft«.
1987 Internationale Bauaustellung in West-Berlin.
750-Jahrfeiern in Berlin.
1989 Öffnung der »Mauer«.
1990 Deutsche Wiedervereinigung.
Gorbatschow erhält den Friedens-Nobelpreis.
1991 Berlin wird deutsche Hauptstadt.
Die Sowjetunion zerfällt.
1992 Berlin bewirbt sich für die Olympischen Spiele 2000.
Willy Brandt stirbt.
1993 1000-Jahrfeier in Potsdam.

1955 German states become sovereign.
Herbert von Karajan becomes chief conductor of Berlin Philharmonic.
1957 Willy Brandt becomes Governing Mayor of West Berlin.
Space travel begins: Sputnik I.
1958 Khrushchev ultimatum.
1959 Günter Grass: «The Tin Drum».
1961 Building of the «Wall».
1966 Berlin students demonstrate against Vietnam War.
1967 Barnard: first heart transplant.
1968 GDR introduces compulsory visas.
1969 First men on the moon.
1971 Berlin accord.
1974 Club of Rome in Berlin: «Mankind at the turning point».
1975 Signature of CSCE accords in Helsinki.
1985 Heinrich Böll: «Frauen vor Flusslandschaft».
1987 Internationale Bauausstellung in West Berlin.
Berlin celebrates 750th anniversary.
1989 Opening of the «Wall».
1990 German reunification.
Gorbachev wins Nobel Peace Prize.
1991 Berlin becomes capital of Germany.
Soviet Union dissolved.
1992 Berlin nominated to host Olympic Games 2000.
Willy Brandt dies.
1993 Potsdam celebrates 1000th anniversary.

Abbildungen:
Seite 8 Wittstock; Stadtmauer und Amtshof; 13. Jahrhundert und später
Seite 10 Potsdam; Schloß Sanssouci; 1745-47 von Georg Wenzeslaus v. Knobelsdorff
Seite 12 Berlin-Wannsee; Kasino des Schlosses Klein-Glienicke; 1824-25 von Karl Friedrich Schinkel
Seite 14 Berlin-Prenzlauer Berg; Gemeindeschule Christburger Straße; 1907-08 von Ludwig Hoffmann
Seite 16 Berlin-Rummelsburg; Großkraftwerk Klingenberg; 1925-26 von Walter Klingenberg und Werner Issel
Seite 18 Berlin-Tegel; Humboldtbibliothek; 1985-88 von Charles Moore, John Ruble und Buzz Yudell

A
Berlin
Alter Stadtkern

Der alte Kern der großen Berliner Stadtagglomeration liegt seit dem Mittelalter beiderseits der Spree in den Gründungsstädten Kölln und Berlin, umfaßt aber auch die seit 1250 entstandene Neustadt mit der Marienkirche. Im Südwesten reicht der Altstadtkern bis zum Spreekanal zwischen Kupfergraben und Friedrichsgracht, an der früher die Köllnische Stadtmauer stand. Die nordöstliche Grenze der Berliner Stadterweiterung markiert heute der Stadtbahnbogen zwischen Alexanderplatz und Friedrichstraße, der dem zugeschütteten Graben der barocken Festungswerke folgt. Wie Vorwerke lagen das Gertraudenspital am Spittelmarkt und das Georgenhospital am Alexanderplatz vor den Toren der Stadt. Nach den schweren Zerstörungen im Zweiten Weltkrieg sind in diesem Altstadtkern nur wenige Zeugen der verschiedenen Kulturepochen erhalten geblieben. Am Molkenmarkt, dem Gründungsort Berlins, wurde die spätgotische Hallenkirche St. Nicolai wiederaufgebaut und als Museum und Konzerthalle hergerichtet; im ehemaligen Kölln zeugen Ribbeckhaus und Alter Marstall von Renaissance- und Barockbaukunst. Aus dem vorigen Jahrhundert sind das Rote Rathaus und die Bauten der weltberühmten Museumsinsel wieder zu besichtigen. Mit der Neuordnung des Altberliner Stadtzentrums entstand ein Straßenzug, der sich vom Brandenburger Tor bis zur Frankfurter Allee erstreckt, und auch mit dem Durchbruch der Grunerstraße am Alexanderplatz wurde das innerstädtische Verkehrsgerüst in diesem Stadtteil von Grund auf verändert. Eine Vielzahl von Neubauten säumen seit den sechziger Jahren die neuen, weitgefaßten Straßen- und Platzräume. Als neue, weithin sichtbare Dominante entstand in unmittelbarer Nähe von Marienkirche und Rotem Rathaus der 365 Meter hohe Fernsehturm.

Since the Middle Ages the old center of the Berlin urban agglomeration has been on either side of the Spree in the foundation centres, Kölln and Berlin, but it also includes the new town, which came into being from 1250 onwards, with the Marienkirche. In the south-west, the core of the old town extends to the Spree canal between Kupfergraben and Friedrichsgracht, formerly the line of the Kölln town wall. The north-eastern boundary of the extending town of Berlin is marked today by the curve of the S-Bahn between Alexanderplatz and Friedrichstrasse. This follows the line of the baroque fortifications, which have been filled in. The Gertraudenspital in Spittelmarkt and the Georgenhospital in Alexanderplatz were like outworks outside the town gates. Very little evidence of the various cultural epochs has survived in this core area of the old town. St. Nicolai, a late Gothic hall church, has been rebuilt in Molkenmarkt, the point at which Berlin was originally founded; the church is used as a museum and concert hall. In what was formerly Kölln, Ribbeckhaus and Alter Marstall represent Renaissance and baroque architecture. The Rotes Rathaus and the buildings on the world-famous Museumsinsel can now be seen again: they date from the nineteenth century. When the old Berlin town centre was redesigned, a street was created that stretched from the Brandenburg Gate to Frankfurter Allee, and when Grunerstrasse cut through at Alexanderplatz the inner city traffic framework in this part of the town was fundamentally changed. A large number of new buildings dating from the sixties are set on the new broad streets and spacious squares. The 356 metre Fernsehturm was built as a new dominant feature near Marienkirche and Rotes Rathaus.

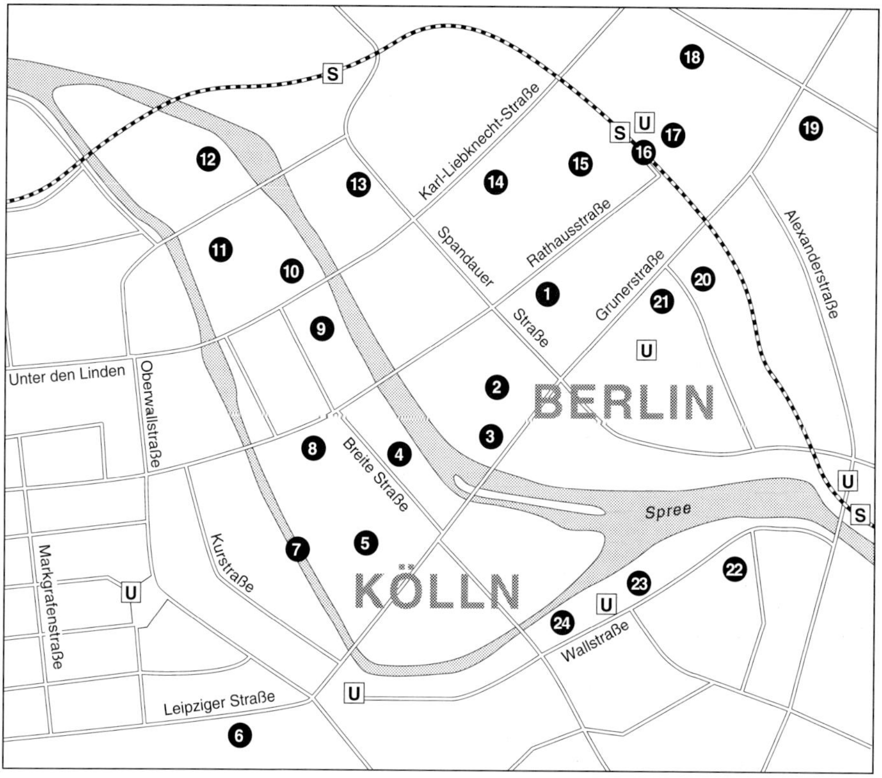

A 1 Berliner Rathaus
A 2 Nikolaikirche
A 3 Ephraimpalais
A 4 Ribbeckhaus
A 5 Nicolaihaus
A 6 Spittelkolonnaden
A 7 Jungfernbrücke
A 8 Portal IV des Berliner Stadtschlosses
A 9 Palast der Republik
A 10 Dom
A 11 Altes Museum
A 12 Nationalgalerie
A 13 Heiliggeistkapelle
A 14 Marienkirche
A 15 Fernseh- und UKW-Turm
A 16 Bahnhof Alexanderplatz
A 17 Berolinahaus und Alexanderhaus
A 18 Forum-Hotel Berlin
A 19 Haus des Lehrers und Kongreßhalle
A 20 Gerichtsgebäude
A 21 Klosterkirche der Franziskaner
A 22 Märkisches Museum
A 23 Gewerkschaftshaus
A 24 Ermelerhaus

A 1 Berliner Rathaus
Berlin-Mitte; Rathausstraße 15-18, Jüdenstraße 1-3
1861-69 • Hermann Friedrich Waesemann

Schon der Vorgängerbau aus der Zeit um 1300 lag hier, auf halbem Wege zwischen dem Molkenmarkt, dem Ursprungsort der Stadt, und dem 1250 angelegten Neumarkt. Die alte, nach drei Seiten offene Gerichtslaube steht seit 1871 im Park von Babelsberg. Seinen Namen »Rotes Rathaus« verdankt der Neubau den roten Klinkern, dem typischen Baustoff der Mark, dieser eiszeitlich entstandenen »Streusandbüchse des Heiligen Römischen Reiches deutscher Nation«. Ein Relieffries aus den Jahren 1876-79, die Steinerne Chronik, aus 36 roten Terrakottatafeln schildert die Geschichte der Stadt von den Anfängen bis zu Bismarcks Reichsgründung 1871. Der 97 Meter hohe Turm – wie das Haus im Stil der oberitalienischen Renaissance erbaut – war schon damals ein markantes Zeichen der neuen Hauptstadt Berlin. Obwohl auf einem ganzen Baublock der Altstadt mit drei Innenhöfen errichtet, wurde bereits nach 50 Jahren das Stadthaus als Erweiterung nötig, dem dann nach weiteren zwei Jahrzehnten die Verwaltungsgebäude am Rolandufer folgen mußten.

The earlier building dating from c. 1300 was on this site as well, half way between the Molkenmarkt, where the town first came into being, and the Neumarkt, established in 1250. The old law court, open on three sides, has stood in Babelsberg park since 1871. The new building gets its nickname «Rotes Rathaus» («Red Town Hall») from its red clinker brick, the typical building material of the Mark Brandenburg, that «sandpit of the Holy Roman Empire» created in the ice age. A relief frieze dating from 1876-9, a stone chronicle of 36 red terra-cotta panels, depicts the history of the city until the foundation of the empire by Bismarck in 1871. The tower, 97 metres high and like the rest of the building in High Renaissance style, was a striking symbol of Berlin as the new capital even then. Although it was built over an entire block of the old town and had three courtyards, the Stadthaus became necessary as an extension after 50 years, and then two decades later more administrative buildings were needed on the Rolandufer.

in der Nähe/nearby:
Stadthaus; Jüdenstraße 34-42, Klosterstraße 47
1902-11 • Ludwig Hoffmann
Städtische Feuersozietät; Parochialstraße 1/3
1937-39 • Franz Arnous, Kurt Starck
Rathauspassagen; Rathausstraße 7/13, Jüdenstraße
1967-73 • Heinz Graffunder, Lothar Köhler

A 2 Nikolaikirche
Berlin-Mitte; Nikolaikirchplatz, Probststraße
Nach 1380, bis 2. Hälfte 15. Jahrhundert

An dem aus einer Straßengabelung am Spreeübergang entstandenen Molkenmarkt liegt die älteste Pfarrkirche Berlins. Von der um 1230 begonnenen spätromanischen Feldsteinbasilika ist nur der viergeschossig abgestufte Westbau mit dem abgetreppten spitzbogigen Hauptportal erhalten. Einer Umwandlung noch im 13. Jahrhundert zur frühgotischen Hallenkirche folgte nach dem Stadtbrand 1380 der Neubau einer spätgotischen Halle. Vollendet wurde der Hallenumgangschor mit den Randkapellen um 1400, in seiner Art das früheste Beispiel in der Mark, und erst in der zweiten Hälfte des 15. Jahrhunderts folgte das Langhaus. Gleichzeitig entstand seit 1452 die Liebfrauenkapelle mit den Staffelgiebeln. 1876 wuchs nach Hermann Blankensteins Plan der neugotische Turmaufsatz mit zwei Spitzhelmen. 1944/45 wurde das Bauwerk zerstört, 1977-87 rekonstruiert und als Museum und Konzerthalle eingerichtet.

This is the oldest parish church in Berlin. It stands in the Molkenmarkt, which came into being at a fork in the streets by the Spree bridge. All that has survived of the late Romanesque stone basilica started c. 1230 is the four storey stepped west section with ribbed and pointed-arched main portal. In the thirteenth century it was rebuilt as an early Gothic hall church, and after the great fire of 1380 it was again rebuilt, this time as a late Gothic hall church. The hall ambulatory with chapels was completed c. 1400, the earliest example of the type in the Mark Brandenburg, and the nave was not added until the second half of the fifteenth century. The Lady Chapel with pinnacled gables was built at the same time, from 1452. The neo-Gothic top section of the tower with two spires was added in 1876 to designs by Hermann Blankenstein. The building was destroyed 1944/45, rebuilt 1977/87 and equipped as a museum and concert hall.

in der Nähe/nearby:
Alt-Berliner Bürgerhäuser; Mühlendamm
1977-87 • Heinz Mehlan, Rolf Ricken
Wohnhäuser, Gerichtslaube, Haus am Nußbaum;
Rathausstraße, Poststraße, Probststraße
1977-87 • Günter Stahn, Wolfgang Woigk
Marx-Engels-Denkmal; Rathausstraße
1985-86 • Ludwig Engelhardt

A 3 Ephraimpalais
Berlin-Mitte; Poststraße 15, Mühlendamm
1761-64 • Friedrich Wilhelm Dietrichs

Als eines der schönsten Barockhäuser des friderizianischen Berlins wurde das Palais im Auftrage des Münzpächters und Hofjuweliers Nathan Veitel Ephraim erbaut. Im Zuge der Erweiterung von Mühlendammschleuse und Mühlendammbrücke ist das Haus 1935 abgetragen worden. Die Sandstein-Fassadenteile fanden Asyl auf verschiedenen Lagerplätzen, kamen dann aber 1985 aus West-Berlin zurück. Weitgehend original konnte das Palais nahe seinem alten Platz wiederaufgebaut werden. In diesem Gebäude fand auch eine barocke Decke aus dem Wartenbergpalais Verwendung, sie wird Andreas Schlüter zugeschrieben. Das Haus ist heute eingebunden in erhaltene Bauten an der Poststraße und die Neubauten an der umgestalteten Spreeuferpromenade.

This palace, commissioned by court jeweller and coiner Nathan Veitel Ephraim, is one of the most beautiful buildings in Frederick the Great's Berlin. The building was pulled down in 1935 when the Mühlendamm lock and bridge were being extended. Parts of the sandstone façade found a home in various storage sites, and returned from West Berlin in 1985. It was possible to rebuild the palace near its own site, and to a large extent as it used to be. A baroque ceiling attributed to Andreas Schlüter from the Wartenburgpalais was also used in this building. The building blends with surviving buildings dating from the nineteenth and twentieth centuries, and buildings in Poststrasse, and with new buildings in the redesigned Spreeuferpromenade.

in der Nähe/nearby:
Knoblauchsches Haus; Poststraße 23
1759 (verändert um 1800)
Kurfürstenhaus; Spreeufer 5, Poststraße 4-5
1895 • Carl Gause
Berliner Münze; Molkenmarkt 1-2
1936 • Fritz Keibel
(Fries um 1800 • Gottfried Schadow)
Palais Schwerin; Molkenmarkt 3
1704 • Jean de Bodt

A 4 Ribbeckhaus
Berlin-Mitte; Breite Straße 35
1624

Dieser heute einzig erhaltene Bau der Spätrenaissance in Berlin ist für den kurfürstlichen Kammerrat Hans Georg v. Ribbeck durch Zusammenlegung zweier kreuzgratgewölbter Häuser errichtet worden. 1629-30 durch Balthasar Benzelt aus Dresden erneut umgebaut, gehörte er schon 1660 zum benachbarten Alten Marstall; dieser wiederum ist der einzig erhaltene frühbarocke Bau Berlins. Architektonisch unterscheiden sich die beiden Häuser vor allem auch durch ihre Dachaufbauten: vier gleiche Zwerchgiebel in Renaissanceformen stehen dem einen flachen Dreiecksgiebel gegenüber, der den barocken Risalit betont. Aber auch die rundbogigen Portale sind unterschiedlich gestaltet: Unter dem Wappen Ribbecks und dem seiner Frau findet sich eine leichte und bewegte Knorpelwerkeinfassung, dagegen beim frühbarocken Marstall streng rustizierte Quaderung und plastisch hervortretende Löwenkopfkonsolen. In Teilen des neuen Marstalles und an der Stelle der ehemaligen Ritterakademie und des Tattersalles ist die Stadtbibliothek untergebracht. In deren Portal finden sich 117 Varianten des Buchstaben A, geschmiedet und beschmolzen von Fritz Kühn.

This is the only surviving late Renaissance building in modern Berlin. It was built for Electoral Kammerrat Hans Georg v. Ribbeck by combining two cross-vaulted buildings. It was again modified by Balthasar Benzelt of Dresden 1629-30, and in 1660 it was already part of the neighbouring Alter Marstall; these royal stables are the only survivng early baroque building in Berlin. The two buildings differ architecturally, particularly in their roof structures: four identical gables of Renaissance design confront a shallow triangular gable emphasizing the baroque projection. But the round-arched portals are also differently designed: under the coats of arms of Ribbeck and his wife is a light and lively gnarled border, while the early baroque stables have severely rusticated ashlars and three-dimensional lion corbels. The municipal library is accommodated in parts of the Neuer Marstall and on the site of the Ritterakademie and the Tattersall. Its portal shows 117 variants of the letter A, forged and with a melted metalwork design by Fritz Kühn.

in der Nähe/nearby:
Alter Marstall; Breite Straße 36-37
1666-70 • Michael Mathias Smids
Neuer Marstall; Marx-Engels-Platz 7
1898-1900 • Ernst v. Ihne
Stadtbibliothek; Breite Straße 32-34
1964-66 • Heinz Mehlan, Erwin Kussat

A 5 Nicolaihaus
Berlin-Mitte; Brüderstraße 13
1710; 1787 • Karl Friedrich Zelter

Die Brüderstraße, heute nur bis zur Sperlingsgasse erhalten, vermittelte früher zwischen der Stadtpfarrkirche am Köllnischen Fischmarkt und dem Kloster der Brüder vom Dominikanerorden, nach dem sie benannt worden war. Die Grundstücke der westlichen Seite reichten bis zur Stadtmauer an der späteren Friedrichsgracht. Als einziges barockes Bürgerhaus ist das kulturhistorisch bedeutende Nicolaihaus erhalten. 1670 auf zwei mittelalterlichen Grundstücken errichtet, erhielt es 1710 seine heutige Gestalt und wurde 1787 für den Verleger Friedrich Nicolai mit neuer Fassade umgebaut. Erwähnenswert sind die geschnitzten eichenen Geländer der Haupttreppe, um 1710, der begrünte und durch Galerien belebte Hof sowie der Einbau einer klassizistischen Treppe aus dem Weydingerhaus im Quergebäude.

Brüderstrasse, which has survived only as far as the Sperlingsgasse, used to connect the town parish church on the Köllnischer Fischmarkt and the monastery of the Brothers of the Dominican Order, from which it got its name. The building plots on the western side stretched down to the city wall on what was later to become the Friedrichsgracht. The only baroque town house to survive is the Nicolaihaus, which is of art-historical importance. It was built in 1670 on two medieval plots, rebuilt in its present form in 1710 and modified with a new façade for Friedrich Nicolai, the publisher, in 1787. The carved oak banisters, c. 1710, of the main staircase are a notable feature, as are the courtyard, planted and enlivened with galleries, and also the neoclassical staircase from the Weydingerhaus installed in the transverse building.

in der Nähe/nearby:
Galgenhaus; Brüderstraße 10
1688 (Umbau 1805)
Kaufhaus Rudolf Hertzog; Brüderstraße 26
1910
Geschäftshaus; Gertraudenstraße 10-11
1898 • Max Jacob, Georg Roensch

A 6 Spittelkolonnaden
Berlin-Mitte; Leipziger Straße (zwischen 47 und 48)
1776 • Karl v. Gontard

Seit dem 13. Jahrhundert lag unmittelbar vor dem westlichen Stadttor in der mittelalterlichen Köllnischen Stadtbefestigung nahe der heutigen Gertraudenbrücke das Gertraudenhospital. Da die Memhardtschen Festungswerke seit 1658 auf Köllnischer Seite teilweise beträchtlich vor die alte Stadtmauer verlegt wurden, lag das Spital seitdem auf der Bastion IV, dem späteren Spittelmarkt. Mit dem Schleifen der Anlagen wurden über den verbliebenen Festungsgräben mehrere Brücken zur Friedrichstadt geschlagen. Die Spittelkolonnaden sind zur Begrenzung der zur Leipziger Straße führenden Brücke beidseitig errichtet worden. Die südliche Kolonnade 1929 abgetragen und eingelagert, steht seit 1980 als Kopie auf etwas verändertem Standort zusammen mit einem Meilenstein vom ehemaligen Dönhoffplatz in der Bebauung der Leipziger Straße.

The Gertraudenhospital was directly in front of the western city gate in the medieval Kölln town fortification near the present Gertraudenbrücke from the thirteenth century. As the Memhardt fortifications on the Kölln side were partially but substantially moved to stand in front of the old city wall, the hospital was then on Bastion IV, later to be Spittelmarkt. When the defensive buildings were abandoned, several bridges leading to Friedrichstadt were built over the remaining moats. The Spittelkolonnaden were built to border both sides of the bridge leading to Leipziger Strasse. The southern colonnade was pulled down and stored in 1929, and was rebuilt on a slightly different site as a copy in 1980 with a milestone from the former Dönhoffplatz in the Leipziger Strasse development.

in der Nähe/nearby:
Wohnbebauung; Leipziger Straße 40-49, 54-66
1972-77 • Joachim Näther, Peter Schweizer
Boutique Spittelmarkt; Leipziger Straße 50
1979-81 • Eckardt Schmidt
Wohngebäude; Wallstraße 88 a-90
1982-84 • Michael Limberg

A 7 Jungfernbrücke
Berlin-Mitte; Friedrichsgracht, Oberwasserstraße
1798

Der grachtenartige Straßenzug am westlichen Spreearm zwischen Gertraudenbrücke am Spittelmarkt und der Schleusenbrücke am Werderschen Markt wird durch die Gebäude der ehemaligen Reichshauptbank an der Ober- und Unterwasserstraße einerseits und auf der anderen Seite von den Wohnbauten an der Friedrichsgracht gebildet. Beide Straßen verbindet die fußgängige Jungfernbrücke. Das 1789 errichtete Bauwerk ist die letzte original erhaltene von neun Brücken über Spreekanal und Kupfergraben. Sie verbanden Kölln im 18. Jahrhundert mit den westlichen Vorstädten: Neukölln am Wasser (1680), Dorotheenstadt (1674), Friedrichswerder (1662). Der Übergang vermittelte seit dem letzten Viertel des 17. Jahrhunderts vom Leipziger Tor, zwischen den Bastionen des späteren Hausvogteiplatzes und der des Spittelmarktes gelegen, vorbei an den Häusern der Friedrichsgracht nach Kölln. – Die unterschiedlich breiten Durchlässe des Bauwerks sind aus rotem Sandstein gearbeitet. Nur der mittlere von acht Meter Breite öffnet sich der Schiffahrt als Sinusoiden-Zugbrücke, also über halbkreisförmige Zahnräder hochklappbar.

The gracht-like set of streets on the western arm of the Spree between the Gertraudenbrücke on the Spittelmarkt and the Schleusenbrücke on the Werderscher Markt is formed by the former Reichshauptbank buildings on the Ober- and Unterwasserstrasse on one side and by residential buildings on the other. The two streets are connected by the pedestrian Jungfernbrücke. It dates from 1789 and is the last of nine bridges over the Spree and the Kupferkanal to survive in its orignal form. In the eighteenth century they connected Kölln with the western suburbs: Neukölln am Wasser (1680), Dorotheenstadt (1674), Friedrichswerder (1662). From the last quarter of the seventeenth century the bridge formed a link from the Leipziger Tor, placed between the bastions of what was later to become Hauptvogteiplatz and that of Spittelmarkt, past the buildings on Friedrichsgracht to Kölln. – The arches of the bridge are in red sandstone and of different widths, and only the central one, which is eight metres wide, is open to shipping: it can be raised on semicircular gearwheels, and is thus a sinusoidal drawbridge.

in der Nähe/nearby:
Verwaltungsgebäude; Oberwasserstraße 12
1912-15 • Ferdinand Schopp, Wilhelm Vortmann
Appartementhäuser; Friedrichsgracht 53-58
1964-67 • Heinz Graffunder, Manfred Prasser
Gertraudenbrücke; Spittelmarkt, Gertraudenstraße
1894-95 • Otto Stahn

A 8 Portal IV des Berliner Stadtschlosses
Berlin-Mitte; Marx-Engels-Platz 1
1706-13 • Johann Friedrich v. Eosander

Vom Balkon dieses Portalrisalites hatte Karl Liebknecht am 9. November 1918 – allerdings einige Stunden später als Scheidemann – die sozialistische Republik ausgerufen. In Erinnerung daran wurde dieser Portikus in das 1962-64 von Roland Korn und Hans-Erich Bogatzky entworfene Staatsratsgebäude einbezogen. Das Berliner Stadtschloß war nach schweren Kriegsschäden in den Jahren 1950-51 auf Beschluß der DDR-Staats- und der SED-Parteiführung gesprengt und abgerissen worden. Ulbricht selbst hatte diesen Akt initiiert und sich über viele Einsprüche und Proteste im eigenen Lande und erst recht von westlicher Seite hinweggesetzt. Der Portalrisalit war eine Wiederholung des 1698-1706 nach Entwürfen von Andreas Schlüter entstandenen Portals V durch dessen Nachfolger Eosander, der das Schloß auf das Doppelte erweitert hatte. Das heutige Portal ist zwischen Breiter Straße und Spreekanal Bestandteil der den Marx-Engels-Platz südlich abschließenden Fassade, asymmetrisch vor das Treppenhaus eingefügt. Hier endete ursprünglich die Brüderstraße. Der von Atlantenhermen getragene Balkon der Hauptetage stammt von Balthasar Permoser; der plastische Schmuck besteht aus restaurierten Originalen.

It was from the balcony of this projecting portal that Karl Liebknecht proclaimed the socialist Republic on 9 November 1918 – albeit several hours after Scheidemann. In memory of this event the portico was incorporated into the Staatsratsgebäude designed by Roland Kern and Hans-Erich Bogatzky in 1962-64. After suffering severe damages in the war, the ruins of the Berliner Stadtschloss had been blown-up and dismantled in 1950-51 on the basis of the decision by the GDR government and party leaders. It was Ulbricht himself who had initiated this move, ignoring numerous objections and protests in his own country and, even more so, in the west. The present portal between the Breite Strasse and the Spreekanal is a component of the façade forming the southern side of Marx-Engels-Platz. It is placed asymmetrically in front of the staircase. This was originally the end of Brüderstrasse. The balcony of the principal storey is supported by atlantes, and was designed by Balthasar Permoser; the sculptural decoration consists of restored originals.

in der Nähe/nearby:
Schleusenbrücke; Werderstraße
1914-15 • Kritzler, Tischer (äußere Medaillons: Robert Schirmer, Markert; innere Medaillons: 1937, Kurt Schumacher)

A 9 Palast der Republik
Berlin-Mitte; Marx-Engels-Platz
1973-76 • Heinz Graffunder, Karl-Ernst Swora

Für DDR-Volkskammer, zentrale Tagungen und kulturelle Großveranstaltungen war dieser Gebäudekomplex auf dem östlichen Terrain des 1950-51 abgetragenen ehemaligen Berliner Stadtschlosses errichtet worden. 1443 hatte der Hohenzoller, Kurfürst Friedrich II., nach Niederwerfung des Berliner Unwillens und der erneuten Teilung der Städte Kölln und Berlin in diesem Bereich eine Zwingburg errichten lassen. 1538 wurde sie unter Joachim II. durch Caspar Theiß nach dem Vorbild sächsischer Schlösser in einen stattlichen Renaissancebau verwandelt. Der Ausbau zum Barockschloß erfolgte 1698-1716 nach Entwürfen von Andreas Schlüter und Johann Friedrich v. Eosander; 1845-53 wurde er durch Friedrich August Stüler um die Kuppel nach einer Idee von Karl Friedrich Schinkel ergänzt. Bis in die dreißiger Jahre durfte kein Gebäude der Innenstadt höher als die Laterne auf der Kuppel des kaiserlichen Schlosses aufragen. Auf einer Fläche von 1,5 Hektar errichtet, bildet der Palast der Republik heute mit seiner 180 Meter langen Westfront den östlichen Abschluß des Marx-Engels-Platzes. Die Einbindung des 25 und 32 Meter hohen Gebäudes in die Platz- und Straßenflächen vermitteln teils begrünte Terrassen und die Untergeschosse in der Spreeuferzone. Beteiligt am Ausbau des Hauses war eine große Zahl von Fachleuten: an Volkskammer und Hauptrestaurants Günter Kunert, Großer Saal Manfred Prasser, Foyer Wolf-Rüdiger Eisentraut, Außenhülle Dieter Bankert, gastronomische Einrichtungen Gerd Pieper, Technologie der Einrichtungen Klaus Wever sowie Terrassen und Spreeuferzone Heinz Aust.

The Palast der Republik was built to house the GDR-Volkskammer, central conferences, and large-scale cultural events on the eastern part of the site of the former Berliner Stadtschloss, pulled down 1950-1. In 1443 the Hohenzollern Elector Friedrich II, after suppressing the angry Berliners and re-establishing Kölln and Berlin as separate towns, built a stronghold in this area. In 1538, under Joachim II, this was transformed into a magnificent Renaissance building by Caspar Theiss on the model of the palaces of Saxony. It was further extended as a Baroque palace in 1698-1716 to designs by Andreas Schlüter and Johann Friedrich von Eosander; in 1845-53 Friedrich August Stüler added the dome, based on an idea by Karl Friedrich Schinkel. Right into the 1930s no building in the city centre was allowed to be higher than the lantern on the dome of the Imperial Palace. The present Palast der Republik extends over an area of 1.5 hectares; its west façade is 180 metres long, and forms the eastern extremity of Marx-Engels-Platz. The sections of the building are 25 and 32 metres high, and tied into the square and streets by planted terraces, and by the lower storeys in the area along the banks of the Spree. A large number of experts were involved in constructing the building: Volkskammer and main restaurants Günter Kunert, Great Hall Manfred Prasser, Foyer Wolf-Rüdiger Eisentraut, outer shell Dieter Bankert, catering equipment Gerd Pieper, equipment technology Klaus Wever and terraces and area on the bank of the Spree by Heinz Aust.

A 10 Dom
Berlin-Mitte; Karl-Liebknecht-Straße, Lustgarten
1894-1905 • Julius Carl Raschdorff und Otto Raschdorff

Als erster Dom wurde die Kirche des 1297 gegründeten Dominikanerklosters genutzt, ehemals zwischen Breiter Straße und Brüderstraße gelegen. 1747 ließ Friedrich II. einen Dom am Lustgarten errichten, der 1817 von Schinkel umgestaltet wurde. Der jetzige überdimensionale, viertürmige Zentralbau, anknüpfend an Formen des römischen Barock, war zugleich Staats- und Hofkirche und sollte nach dem Willen der Hohenzollern auch Hauptkirche des Protestantismus werden. Im Zusammenhang damit steht auch der Skulpturen- und Reliefschmuck: Christus und die Evangelisten, Heilige des Alten und Neuen Bundes und die Reformatoren. Unter der Kuppel liegt die Fest- und Predigtkirche, südlich davon die Tauf- und Traukirche. In der Domgruft stehen 90 Sarkophage, darunter solche von Peter Vischer aus dem Jahre 1530 und der Prunksarg für König Friedrich I. nach Andreas Schlüter.

The church of the Dominican monastery founded in 1297, formerly sited between Breite Strasse and Brüderstrasse, served as the first cathedral. In 1747 Friedrich II had a cathedral built by the Lustgarten, and this was rebuilt by Schinkel in 1817. The present enormous, centrally-planned building with four towers, based on Roman baroque forms, was a church for both state and court, and the will of the Hohenzollerns was that it should be the principal Protestant church. Sculptural and relief decoration should be seen in this context: Christ and the Evangelists, Old and New Covenant Saints and the Reformers. Under the dome is a church for ceremonial and preaching, south of this a church for baptisms and weddings. In the cathedral crypt are 90 sarcophagi, including some by Peter Vischer dating from 1530 and the state coffin for King Friedrich I after Andreas Schlüter.

in der Nähe/nearby:
Liebknechtbrücke; Karl-Liebknecht-Straße
1886
Gedenkstein für Herbert Baum; Lustgarten
1981 • Jürgen Raue

A 11 Altes Museum
Berlin-Mitte; Lustgarten
1823-28 • Karl Friedrich Schinkel

Von 1645 an ließ der Große Kurfürst vor seinem Schloß auf der sumpfigen Nordspitze der Spreeinsel einen Lustgarten anlegen. Seit 1817 ordnete Schinkel diesen städtebaulichen Raum neu, durch Umbau des alten Doms, mit den Neubauten von Museum und Schloßbrücke und schließlich 1830 durch die Bepflanzung unter Mitwirkung von Lenné. Schinkels Museum, 1822-23 entworfen, zählt besonders auch wegen des plastischen und malerischen Schmuckes neben dem vier Jahre älteren Schauspielhaus zu den Hauptwerken des romantischen Klassizismus. Der breit gelagerte zweigeschossige Vierflügelbau hat zwei Innenhöfe beidseitig der schönen Rotunde, die in Anlehnung an das römische Pantheon in das Programm aufgenommen wurde. Die von 18 ionischen Säulen getragene 87 Meter lange Vorhalle des eigentlich zweigeschossigen Gebäudes begrenzt den städtebaulichen Raum eindrucksvoller als der gewaltige Bau des Doms. Zwei hochaufragende Plastiken auf den Wangen der Freitreppe, die kämpfende Amazone, 1842 von August Kiss, und der Löwenkämpfer, 1854 von Albert Wolff, unterstützen den Eindruck eines eingeschossigen Baus. Gleichermaßen ist daran die knapp sieben Meter messende Granitschale beteiligt, gehauen aus dem größeren der beiden Markgrafensteine, eiszeitlichen Findlingen aus der Nähe von Fürstenwalde.

The Great Elector had a Lustgarten, or pleasance, built in front of his palace on the marshy northern extremity of the island in the Spree from 1645 onwards. Schinkel redesigned this urban space from 1817, by rebuilding the old cathedral, producing new buildings for the museum and a new Schlossbrücke over the Spree, and finally in 1830 by planting the gardens, in co-operation with Lenné. Schinkel's museum was designed 1822-3. Its sculptural and painted decoration in particular make it, along with the Schauspielhaus, which is four years older, one of the principal works of romantic classicism. The broad two-storey building with four wings has two inner courtyards on both sides of the fine rotunda, which imitates the Pantheon in Rome. The portico of the building, which actually has two storeys, is 87 metres long and supported by 18 Ionic columns, and makes a more impressive effect within the urban space than the massive cathedral building. Two towering statues on the open staircase, the fighting Amazon, 1842 by August Kiss, and the Fight with the Lion, 1854 by Hubert Wolff, reinforce the impression of a single-storey building. The granite shell is equally involved in this: it was created from the larger of the two Markgrafensteine, ice age erratics from the neighbourhood of Fürstenwalde, and measures almost seven metres.

in der Nähe/nearby:
Granitschale; Lustgarten
1828 • Christian Gottlieb Cantian
Friedrichsbrücke; Bodestraße, Burgstraße
1981 (mit Formen von 1892) • Rolf Ricken
Eiserne Brücke; Bodestraße, Am Kupfergraben
1914-16 • Walter Köppen

A 12 Nationalgalerie
Berlin-Mitte; Bodestraße
1866-76 • Friedrich August Stüler

1841 bestimmte König Friedrich Wilhelm IV., das Gelände auf der Nordspitze Köllns zu einem »der Kunst und der Altertums-Wissenschaft geweihten Bezirk«. Im Verlauf von fast neunzig Jahren entstand daraus die weltberühmte Museumsinsel. 1843-55 hatte Stüler das Neue Museum für die ägyptische Sammlung geschaffen und 1862-65 die Nationalgalerie entworfen; ausgeführt wurde sie durch Johann Heinrich Strack. Tempelartig über zweigeschossigem Unterbau mit breit vorgelagerter Freitreppe und dem Reiterstandbild des Königs, 1886 von Alexander Calandrelli, wirkt sie wie ein einziger Block. Das Bodemuseum entstand auf dreieckigem Grundriß an der Spitze der Spreeinsel 1897 als neubarocker Gebäudekomplex mit fünf Höfen: in der Mittelachse liegen das ovale Treppenhaus unter der Kuppel mit der Nachbildung des Reiterstandbildes des Großen Kurfürsten von Andreas Schlüter, dann eine Basilika nach Art florentinischer Renaissancekirchen und das Nebentreppenhaus unter kleiner Kuppel im Stil Knobelsdorffs gehalten. Von 1912 bis 1930 wurde das Pergamonmuseum für die berühmte Antikensammlung mit der Westseite des Altars von Pergamon aus dem 2. Jahrhundert v. Chr. erbaut.

In 1841 King Friedrich Wilhelm IV designated the site at the northern extremity of Kölln an «area dedicated to art and the knowledge of antiquity», and over 90 years it became the world-famous Museumsinsel. In 1843-55 Stühler created the Neues Museum for the Egyptian collection and designed the Nationalgalerie 1862-5; it was built by Johann Heinrich Strack. It is built like a temple over a two-storey lower section with a broad open staircase and the equestrian statue of the king, by Alexander Calandrelli, 1897, in front of it, and gives the impression of being a single block. The Bodemuseum came into being on a triangular ground plan at the tip of the Spree island in 1897 as a set of neobaroque buildings with five courtyards: in the central axis are the oval staircase under the dome with the copy of Andreas Schlüter's equestrian statue of the Great Elector, then a basilica in the manner of Florentine Renaissance churches and the side staircase under a small dome in the style of Knobelsdorff. The Pergamon Museum for the celebrated collection of antiquities including the west side of the Pergamon altar dating from the second century BC was built from 1912 to 1930.

in der Nähe/nearby:
Neues Museum; Bodestraße 5
1843-55 • Friedrich August Stüler
Pergamonmuseum; Am Kupfergraben
1912-30 • Alfred Messel, Ludwig Hoffmann
Bodemuseum; Monbijoubrücke
1898-1904 • Ernst v. Ihne

A 13 Heiliggeistkapelle
Berlin-Mitte; Spandauer Straße 1
13. Jahrhundert

Das Heiliggeistspital, 1272 genannt und 1825 bis auf die Kapelle abgebrochen, lag ursprünglich am Rande der Stadt, im Zuge der heutigen Burg- und Rochstraße, direkt an der mittelalterlichen Stadtmauer, wie auch das Franziskanerkloster; im Gegensatz dazu waren das ehemalige Gertraudenkrankenhaus am Spittelmarkt oder das seinerzeitige Georgenhospital am heutigen Alexanderplatz unmittelbar vor den Toren der Stadt angesiedelt worden. Die Heiliggeistkapelle stammt wohl aus dem 13. Jahrhundert, ein Backsteinbau über einem Feldsteinsockel. 1476 erhielt sie ein Sterngewölbe, aus dieser Zeit rühren auch die Ostfassade und weitere spätgotische Veränderungen her. Bis 1905 katholische Kapelle, war sie dann Hörsaal einer Handelshochschule, die Cremer & Wolffenstein 1905–06 auf dem ehemaligen Spitalgelände erbauten. Die Bauplastik stammt von Ernst Westphal; im Foyer steht ein Hermes, Gott des Handels, der Diebe und der Redekunst, 1907 in Marmor von Fritz Klimsch.

The Heiliggeistspital, mentioned in 1272 and pulled down in 1825 with the exception of the chapel, was originally on the outskirts of the town, on the route of the modern Burg- and Rochstrasse, directly on the medieval city wall, like the Franziskanerkloster as well; in contrast with this the former Gertraudenkrankenhaus in Spittelmarkt and what was then the Georgenhospital in the present Alexanderplatz were built immediately outside the town gates. The Heiliggeistkapelle probably dates from the thirteenth century, and is a brick building on a rubble masonry base. The stellar vaulting was added in 1476, and the east façade and other late Gothic accretions also date from this period. Until 1905 it was a Catholic chapel, and then became a lecture theatre for a business college built on the site of the former hospital by Cremer & Wolffenstein 1905-6. Architectural sculpture is by Ernst Westphal; in the foyer stands Hermes, the god of trade, thieves and oratory, carved in marble by Franz Klimsch in 1907.

in der Nähe/nearby:
Pfarrhaus der Garnisonskirche; Burgstraße 21
Ende 18. Jh.
Punkthochhaus »Windmühle«; Rochstraße 9
1968-70 • Wolfgang Radke, Hans-Peter Schmiedel, Manfred Zumpe
Radisson-Plaza-Hotel; Karl-Liebknecht-Straße 5
1976-79 • Ferenz Kiss

A 14 Marienkirche
Berlin-Mitte; Karl-Liebknecht-Straße 8
Nach 1380

Wie eine Insel liegt die Pfarrkirche der seit 1250 entstandenen mittelalterlichen Neustadt heute in ihrer baulichen Umgebung, entblößt von den einst sie eng umstehenden Häusern. Sie ist gegründet auf einem eiszeitlichen Talsander, auf dem auch noch der Fernsehturm Platz fand. Dessen rhombenförmige Umbauung nimmt Bezug auf die Längsachse der Kirche. Das umgebende rechtwinklige Straßenraster widerspiegelt noch deutlich das System der planmäßig angelegten Bürgerstadt. Deren Straßen wurden bewußt diagonal zu den Himmelsrichtungen angeordnet, so daß die ost-west-orientierten Kirchen dazu in Divergenz stehen. St. Marien, wohl 1270 begonnen, nach dem Stadtbrand 1380 als dreischiffige Hallenkirche mit einschiffigem Chor erneuert, erhielt 1418 die Vorhalle, 1466 darüber nach Steffen Boxthude den hochaufragenden Turm und 1789 durch Carl Gotthard Langhans den gotisierenden Aufsatz. Von der reichen Ausstattung sind zu nennen der »Totentanz«, ein Fries von 1485, die Marmorkanzel, 1703 von Andreas Schlüter, und der Orgelprospekt nach Johann Georg Glume, 1742 von Paul de Ritter fertiggestellt.

The parish church of the medieval new town, built from 1250, stands like an island in its present architectural surroundings, stripped of the buildings that once huddled so tightly around it. It is founded on an ice age sand outwash, on which the television tower also stands: the buildings forming a rhombus around the latter relates to the longitudinal axis of the church. The surrounding network of streets at right angles still clearly reflects the system of the meticulously planned medieval town, with streets running consciously diagonal to the points of the compass and thus inevitably diverging from the east-west orientation of the churches. St. Marien was probably started in 1270, then rebuilt after the great fire of 1380 as a hall church with nave and two aisles and single-aisled choir; the vestibule was added in 1418, the high tower above it after Steffen Boxthude in 1466 and the neo-Gothic upper section by Carl Gotthard in 1789. Notable among the lavish decorations and furnishings are the «Dance of Death», a frieze dating from 1485, the marble pulpit, 1703 by Andreas Schlüter and the organ front after Johann Georg Glume, completed by Paul de Ritter in 1742.

in der Nähe/nearby:
Martin-Luther-Denkmal; Karl-Liebknecht-Straße 8
1895 • Paul Otto, Robert Toberentz
Berliner Markthalle; Karl-Liebknecht-Straße 11
1968-69 • Wolfgang Radke, Gerhard Hoelke
Geschäftshaus; Rosenstraße 19, Rochstraße
1895 • Otto March

A 15 Fernseh- und UKW-Turm
Berlin-Mitte; Panoramastraße
1965-69 • Fritz Dieter, Günter Franke

Dieser Turm, nach einer Idee von Hermann Henselmann und Jörg Streitparth, ist mit seinen 365 Metern Höhe im Zentrum der Stadt Blick- und Aussichtspunkt zugleich. Er ist sichtbar aus allen Teilen Berlins und Drehpunkt der radialen Überlandstraßen im Weichbild der großen Stadt-Agglomeration. Von den beiden Panoramaetagen im kugelförmigen Turmkopf erkennt man bei einem Rundblick den Flughafen Tempelhof, das Rathaus Schöneberg, das Europa-Center am Kurfürstendamm, aber auch das Märkische Viertel, die Bauten in Pankow, am Prenzlauer Berg und in den durchgrünten Stadtgebieten bis hin zum Müggelturm in Köpenick. Die Bebauung vom Reichstag bis zum Strausberger Platz liegt dem Betrachter zu Füßen, so wie er sie unten in der Umbauung des Turmes am Stadtmodell sehen kann.

This tower, based on an idea by Hermann Henselmann and Jörg Streitparth, is 365 metres high, a focal point and a viewing point as well. It is visible from all over Berlin and a pivot for the radial long-distance roads as they reach the precincts of the city. From the two panoramic viewing platforms in the spherical head of the tower there is a view of Tempelhof airfield, Rathaus Schöneberg and the Europa-Center on the Kurfürstendamm, but also out to the Märkisches Viertel, the buildings of Pankow and the Prenzlauer Berg, then over the townscape livened up by greens and parks to the Müggelturm in Köpenick. The centre, from the Reichstag to Strausberger Platz is at the viewer's feet, and it looks just as it does down below in the building around the base of the tower, where its miniature version rises over the model of the town.

in der Nähe/nearby:
Fernsehturm-Umbauung; Panoramastraße
1969-72 • Walter Herzog, Herbert Aust, Rolf Heider
Freiflächen und Wasserspiele; Rathausstraße
1969-72 • Hubert Matthes, Eberhard Horn, Rolf Rühle; Gottfried Funeck, Werner Stockmann
Neptunbrunnen; Rathausstraße
1886 • Reinhold Begas

A 16 Bahnhof Alexanderplatz
Berlin-Mitte; Dircksenstraße, Gontardstraße
1963-64 • Hans-Joachim May, Günter Andrich

Seit dem ausgehenden 19. Jahrhundert mauserte sich der »Alex« zu einem der bedeutendsten innerstädtischen Verkehrsplätze im Osten Berlins. Unter der Kreuzung Rathausstraße-Dirksenstraße am ehemaligen Königstor liegt das Kernstück der Anlage, die fünf Ebenen umfaßt: die als Hochbahn im Zuge des zugeschütteten Memhardtschen Festungsgrabens geführten Trassen der Fern- und S-Bahn; ebenerdig der Fußgänger- und Bus- sowie ehemals der Straßenbahnverkehr; über den zwei niveauverschiedenen, sich kreuzenden drei U-Bahnlinien liegt ein Laden-Passagensystem im Zwischengeschoß mit Zugängen zur S-Bahn und zu Straßenunterführungen. Dort findet man Wandplatten der Porzellanmanufakturen Berlin und Meißen mit acht Darstellungen der historischen Entwicklung des Alexanderplatzes. Ein Bild von 1785 zeigt die Königsbrücke über dem Festungsgraben mit den Königskolonnaden, die jetzt am Kleistpark stehen. Zu Beginn des 19. Jahrhunderts diente der Alex vor dem Georgentor, das nach 1701 Königstor hieß, als Vieh- und Wollmarkt, aber auch als Exerzier- und Paradeplatz. Hier trafen sich die nach ihren Zielorten benannten Überlandwege, die Landsberger, Greifswalder, Prenzlauer und Schönhauser Straße.

From the late nineteenth century the «Alex» blossomed as one of the most important inner city traffic intersections in the eastern part of Berlin. Under the Rathausstrasse-Dirksenstrasse junction by the former Königstor is the core of the complex, which operates on five levels: the long-distance and S-Bahn, or inner city railway, lines run on elevated tracks along the line of the filled-in Memhardt moat; pedestrian and bus traffic run at ground level, as the trams used to do; above the three underground lines, crossing over each other on two different levels, is a system of shopping arcades in the mezzanine with access to the S-Bahn and pedestrian subways. Here there are wall plaques from the Berlin and Meissen porcelain manufactories showing eight scenes of the historical development of Alexanderplatz. A picture dating from 1785 shows the Königsbrücke over the moat with the Königskolonnaden, now in the Kleistpark. In the early nineteenth century it served as a wool and cattle market, but also as a drill and parade ground, outside the Georgentor, called Königstor after 1701. Here the overland routes named after their destinations met: Landsberger, Greifswalder, Prenzlauer and Schönhauser Strasse.

in der Nähe/nearby:
U-Bahnhof Alexanderplatz (Linie U 2)
1911-13 • Alfred Grenander
U-Bahnhof Alexanderplatz (Linie U 8)
1927-30 • Alfred Grenander, Alfred Fehse
U-Bahnhof Alexanderplatz (Linie U 5)
1927-30 • Alfred Grenander
Fußgängerpassagen zum U-Bahnhof
1968-69

A 17 Berolinahaus und Alexanderhaus
Berlin-Mitte; Alexanderplatz 1 und 2
1928-31 • Peter Behrens

Diese Torbauten sind ein klassisches Spätwerk des Hausarchitekten der AEG. Sie liegen unmittelbar vor den ehemaligen Stadtbefestigungen mit dem barocken Königstor und verweisen damit auch auf das mittelalterliche Georgentor. Für die Formfindung seiner Büro- und Geschäftshäuser nutzt Behrens diese historisch-räumlichen Besonderheiten des Ortes und steigert sie durch die symmetrische Gegenüberstellung der beiden auch nachts erhellten, weiß verglasten Treppenhäuser, im Wettbewerbsentwurf noch als asymmetrische Glasturmvariante ausgelegt. Nach Kriegszerstörungen bis 1952 rekonstruiert, zählt die Baugruppe zu den herausragenden Zeugnissen der neuen Lichtarchitektur der zwanziger Jahre. Die Winkelform des Alexanderhauses folgte dem Kreisverkehr des nach einer Idee von Stadtbaurat Martin Wagner seit 1928 umzugestaltenden Platzes, dessen einheitliche Umbauung aber nicht zustande kam. Quadratische Fenster, quadratisch geteilt, in allen oberen Geschossen der Skelettfassaden kehren später in Formprinzipien von Oswald Mathias Ungers wieder, die gestuften Fensterleibungen erinnern an Formen Schinkels, wie man sie auch am Alten Leuchtturm auf Kap Arkona sehen kann. Solche Bezüge sind nicht versatzstückhaft verarbeitet, sondern räumlich zu einer Meisterleistung der Neuen Sachlichkeit komponiert.

These gate buildings are a classic late work by AEG's house architect Peter Behrens. They are directly outside the section of the former town fortifications containing the baroque Königstor, and thus also a reference to the medieval Georgentor. Behrens used these particular historical and spatial features of the site to find a suitable form for his office and commercial buildings, and enhanced them by the symmetrical juxtaposition of two white-glazed staircases, also illuminated at night; these appeared in the competition drawing as asymmetrical variations on the glass tower theme. They were rebuilt after being destroyed in the war, and completed in 1952, and as a group are considered to be one of the outstanding manifestations of the new twenties light architecture. The angle of the Alexanderhaus follows the line of the traffic roundabout in the square, redesigned from 1928 on the basis of an idea by Stadtbaurat Martin Wagner, but the uniform plan was not finally realized. Square windows, subdivided into squares, in all the upper storeys of the exposed concrete façades, later recur in Oswald Mathias Ungers' formal vocabulary, the staggered window soffits are reminiscent of Schinkel, as seen in the Old Lighthouse on Cape Arcona. These references are not used as set pieces, but blend to create a masterpiece of Neue Sachlichkeit.

in der Nähe/nearby:
Urania-Weltzeituhr; Alexanderplatz
1969 • Erich John
Berliner Kaffeehaus; Alexanderplatz
1981 • Gerd Pieper

A 18 Forum-Hotel Berlin
Berlin-Mitte; Alexanderplatz 8
1967-70 • Roland Korn, Heinz Scharlipp

Fast 125 Meter hoch ist das Bettenhaus des einstigen »Interhotel Stadt Berlin«, weithin sichtbar, auch außerhalb der Stadt. Es markiert zugleich einen wichtigen Drehpunkt der Innenstadt am Knick jener sonst so schnurgeraden Ost-West-Magistrale, die seit 1960, durch die neue Karl-Marx-Allee verlängert, bis zur Frankfurter Allee verläuft und sich in anderer Richtung vorbei am »Alex«, entlang den »Linden« durch das Brandenburger Tor, über den Stern im Tiergarten, den Ernst-Reuter- und Theodor-Heuss-Platz bis zur alten Heerstraße erstreckt. Das Hochhaus umschließt zusammen mit dem dreigeschossigen Flachbau, dem Warenhaus und dem Berolinahaus einen geräumigen Platz; er ist beliebter Treffpunkt meist jüngerer Leute. So ist der zentral gelegene Brunnen mit seinen 17 wassertragenden Kupferschalen von Walter Womacka oft umlagert. Die spiralförmige Komposition des Brunnens wird im Pflasterbelag des inneren Platzraumes fortgeführt und entspricht damit auch der Höhenentwicklung der Gebäude vom Berolinahaus über das Haus des Lehrers, das Haus des Reisens und das Hotel bis zum Fernsehturm.

This hotel is almost 125 metres high, and visible for miles, even outside the city. It also marks an important pivot of the inner city, standing as it does at the kink in the East-West axis, a street which otherwise runs so absolutely dead straight to the Frankfurter Allee, after the addition of the new Karl-Marx-Allee from 1960 onwards, and just as straight in the other direction past Alexanderplatz, along Unter den Linden, through the Brandenburg Gate, over the «Stern» roundabout in the Tiergarten, through Ernst-Reuter-Platz, Theodor-Heuss-Platz and on to the old Heerstrasse, the military road. The high-rise hotel, particularly its broad side, with the three-storey lower building, the Centrum department store and the Berolina building form a spacious square which is a popular meeting place, especially for young people. Thus Walter Womacka's central fountain with its 17 water-filled copper bowls is often completely surrounded, almost besieged. The spiral composition of the fountain is continued in the pavement of the inner part of the square and thus also corresponds with the way in which the height of the buildings develops from the Berolina building via the Haus des Lehrers, the Haus des Reisens and the hotel, then on to the television tower.

in der Nähe/nearby:
Warenhaus; Alexanderplatz 9
1967-70 • Josef Kaiser, Günter Kunert
Haus der Berliner Verlage; Karl-Liebknecht-Straße 29
1970-73 • Karl-Ernst Swora
Berliner Verkehrsbetriebe; Dircksenstraße 32-35
1929-30 • Alfred Grenander

A 19 Haus des Lehrers und Kongreßhalle
Berlin-Mitte; Alexanderplatz 3-4, Karl-Marx-Allee 2
1961-64 • Hermann Henselmann, Bernhard Geyer

An der Stelle des zerstörten Lehrervereinshauses von 1908 hat dieses Haus ein Jahrzehnt lang im Blickpunkt zweier Magistralen gestanden. Es beendete jene eklektische Architekturperiode, die Henselmann 1951 mit dem Hochhaus an der Weberwiese selbst eröffnen durfte, und es war damit auch zugleich das neue Leitbild für die sechziger Jahre mit seiner klaren Trennung der funktional bedingten Rohbaukonstruktionen: ein zwölfgeschossiger Hochkörper aus stapelbaren Büros neben einem Saal im Flachbau mit 1000 Plätzen von einer Schalenfertigteilkuppel überdacht, anknüpfend an den Funktionalismus der zwanziger Jahre. Der sieben Meter hohe Bildfries Walter Womackas ist ein schwacher Abglanz jener ursprünglichen Idee, diese Bauchbinde mit neuen technischen Mitteln als Informations- und Werbeträger zu nutzen. Als jüngere, höhere Dominante an dieser Kreuzung und auch als Leitbild für die siebziger Jahre ist das Haus des Reisens mit stärkerer Plastizität der Rohbaustrukturen und engerer Verknüpfung von Supplement und Hochkörper ausgelegt.

This building on the site of the destroyed teachers' association building dating from 1908 stood at the visual axis of two major thoroughfares for a decade. It marks the end of the period of eclectic architecture opened in 1951 by Henselmann himself with the high-rise building on the Weberwiese; it was thus also a model for the sixties, with the clear separation offered by a functionally determined shell structure: a twelve storey high-rise section with offices stacked one above the other alongside a flat hall building with 1,000 seats under a prefabricated shell dome, linking back to the functionalism of the twenties. Walter Womacka's seven metre high pictorial frieze is a pale reflection of the original idea of using this binding link to carry information and advertising using new technical resources. A more recent and even taller dominant feature of this junction, this time a model for the seventies, is the Haus des Reisens, showing a stronger sense of the three-dimensional in construction and closer connection of the high-rise with the lower one.

in der Nähe/nearby:
Haus des Reisens; Alexanderplatz 5
1969-71 • Roland Korn, Johannes Brieske
Haus der Elektroindustrie; Alexanderplatz 6
1967-69 • Heinz Mehlan, Peter Skujin
Verwaltungsgebäude; Hans-Beimler-Straße 27/37
1930-31 • Philipp Schaefer

A 20 Gerichtsgebäude
Berlin-Mitte; Littenstraße 16-17, Grunerstraße
1896-1904 • Rudolf Mönnich, Otto Schmalz

Die Littenstraße verlief früher durchgehend von der Friedrichsbrücke an der Burgstraße bis zur Spree am Stralauer Tor auf dem Terrain zwischen der mittelalterlichen Stadtmauer und den hier nur mäßig vorverlegt errichteten Memhardtschen Festungswerken. Deren Bastionen waren im 18. Jahrhundert mit Militärbauten besetzt, so an der Spandauer Brücke mit der Garnisonskirche und an der Klosterkirche mit dem Kadettenhaus. Dort entstand nach einem Vorentwurf von Paul Thoemer (1894) ein Justizpalast mit elf Höfen. Das Haupttreppenhaus, ein phantasievoll bewegtes Raumgebilde, ist in Jugendstilformen gehalten und entstand wohl unter Einfluß böhmischer Barockgotik nach Entwurf von Otto Schmalz.

Littenstrasse used to run through from the Friedrichsbrücke in Burgstrasse to the Spree at the Stralauer Tor on the land between the medieval city wall and the Memhardt fortifications, which here protruded only a moderate distance. In the eighteenth century its bastions were occupied by military buildings, for example the garrison church at the Spandauer Brücke and the cadet house at the Klosterkirche. It was here that a Palace of Justice with eleven courtyards was built in 1894, to an original design by Paul Thoemer. The main staircase, an imaginative and lively spatial construction, is Jugendstil in form and was probably created under the influence of Bohemian Baroque Gothic, to a design by Otto Schmalz.

in der Nähe/nearby:
Stadtmauer; Waisenstraße
A. 14. Jh.
Gaststätte »Zur letzten Instanz«, Wohnhäuser; Waisenstraße, Parochialstraße
18. Jh.
Verwaltungsgebäude; Littenstraße 109, Rolandufer
1911 • Ludwig Hoffmann

A 21 Klosterkirche der Franziskaner
Berlin-Mitte; Klosterstraße 73 a
Mitte 13. Jahrhundert

Im 13. Jahrhundert war die Klosterstraße der dritte der halbkreisförmig um den Berliner Molkenmarkt geführten Wege und lag wahrscheinlich auf exterritorialem Gebiet der Markgrafen, die hier im »Hohen Hause« zeitweilig residierten, direkt an der Stadtmauer. Als Vorgängerbau der heutigen Ruine wird eine Saalkirche aus Feldsteinen für den 1249 gegründeten Konvent vermutet. Mitte des 13. Jahrhunderts entstand die Backsteinbasilika durch eine Brandenburger Bauhütte und unter dem Einfluß von Chorin Ende des 13. Jahrhunderts der einschiffige Chor, geschlossen durch sieben Seiten des Zehnecks und dadurch erweitert. Nach der Säkularisation 1574 wurde das »Graue Kloster« in ein Gymnasium umgewandelt. Nach Kriegszerstörungen erfolgte 1968 mit der Verbreiterung der Grunerstraße der Abbruch der Ruine. In der Grünanlage auf dem ehemaligen Klostergebäude sind zwei Säulenkapitelle vom Eosanderportal (Portal III, 1706-13) des Berliner Stadtschlosses aufgestellt.

In the thirteenth century Klosterstrasse was the third of the ways leading in a semicircle round the Molkenmarkt in Berlin. It was probably extraterritorial to the Margraves, who sometimes lived here in the «Hohes Haus», directly by the city wall. It is thought that the present ruin was preceded by a single-aisled church built in rubble masonry for the monastery founded in 1249. In the mid-thirteenth century the brick basilica was built by a Brandenburg church masons' guild and under the influence of Chorin in the late thirteenth century the single-aisled choir, enclosed by seven sides of the decagon and extended by it. After secularization in 1574 the «Grey Monastery» was turned into a grammar school. After being damaged in the war the ruin was pulled down when Grunerstrasse was being widened. Two column capitals from the Eosanderportal (Portal III, 1706-13) of the Berliner Stadtschloss have been set up in the park where the monastery used to stand.

in der Nähe/nearby:
Podewils'sches Palais; Klosterstraße 68-70
1701-04 • Jean de Bodt
Parochialkirche; Klosterstraße 66-67
1695-1703 • Johann Arnold Nering, Martin Grünberg
Geschäftshaus; Klosterstraße 64
1904-06 • Georg Lewy

A 22 Märkisches Museum
Berlin-Mitte; Am Köllnischen Park 5
1901-07 • Ludwig Hoffmann

Das 1874 gegründete märkische Provinzialmuseum geht auf eine Initiative von Rudolf Virchow und Ernst Friedel zurück. Nach einem Wettbewerbsentwurf entstand unter Anlehnung an heimatliche Architekturmotive, so die Katharinenkapelle in Brandenburg, die Bischofsburg in Wittstock und andere Denkmale der Backsteingotik und Renaissance, dieser Museumskomplex, der bis heute größtes Heimatmuseum der märkischen Region blieb. Beabsichtigt war der Zusammenklang von Sammlung und der sie bewahrenden Architektur, hier war das zuvor errichtete Bayerische Nationalmuseum in München Vorbild. Neben der Treppenhalle des Haupteingangs steht die Kopie des Brandenburger Rolands, 1905 in Muschelkalk gefertigt. Die malerisch-romantische Wirkung dieser Ensembles wird gesteigert durch den landschaftlichen Rahmen, den Spreeufer und Köllnischer Park bieten. Diese Grünanlage entstand 1873 aus der Bastion VII der barocken Befestigung und beherbergt ein Architektur-Lapidarium, so seit 1893 den »Wusterhauser Bär«, einen Turm von der Bastion VI und seit den zwanziger Jahren einen Zwinger für einige Vertreter des Berliner Wappentiers.

This museum of the Mark Brandenburg stemmed from 1874, an initiative by Rudolf Virchow and Ernst Friedel. The museum complex, still the largest local history museum in the region, was built after a competition. It borrows local architectural motifs like the Katharinenkapelle in Brandenburg, the Bishofsburg in Wittstock and other brick-Gothic and Renaissance buildings. The intention was that the collection should blend with the architecture that housed it, on the model of the earlier Bayerisches Nationalmuseum in Munich. By the stairwell of the main entrance is a copy of the Brandenburg Roland, made in muschelkalk in 1905. The picturesque and romantic effect of this ensemble is further enhanced by the surrounding landscape of the bank of the Spree and the Kölln park. This green area was created in 1873 from Bastion VII of the baroque fortifications and houses a collection of architectural monuments, like the «Wüsterhauser Bär», acquired in 1893, a tower from Bastion VI, and since the twenties a bear-pit to house a few representatives of the animal on the Berlin coat of arms.

in der Nähe/nearby:
Köllnischer Park
1969-71 • Eberhard Jaenisch, Stefan Ranner
Landesversicherungsanstalt; Am Köllnischen Park 3
1903-04 • Alfred Messel
Zentralverwaltung der AOK Berlin; Rungestraße 3-7
1930-32 • Albert Gottheiner

A 23 Gewerkschaftshaus
Berlin-Mitte; Inselstraße 6, Wallstraße 65
1922-23 • Max Taut, Franz Hoffmann

Dieses Büro- und Verwaltungsgebäude für den Allgemeinen Deutschen Gewerkschaftsbund ist für die Entwicklung der modernen Architektur von wegweisender Bedeutung. Es ist eines der ersten Beispiele, bei dem die Stahlbeton-Rahmenkonstruktion unverkleidet als bestimmender Architekturausdruck gestalterisch zur Wirkung kommt. Gleichzeitig dokumentiert der Bau die Tendenz einer Wende von den mitunter kristallinen Strukturen expressionistischer Architektur zu Formen der Neuen Sachlichkeit. Die das strenge Raster durchbrechenden, schräg verformten und vertikal orientierten Bauteile an der Inselstraße mit zwerchgiebelartigen Abdachungen sowie die bis zur Rekonstruktion 1964 rhomboidisch ausgeformten Stützen der Betonrahmen erinnern an das Grabmal Wissinger Max Tauts von 1920 auf dem Stahnsdorfer Friedhof. Der Erweiterungsbau 1930-31 von Walter Würzbach ist besonders am Märkischen Ufer von betonter Sachlichkeit bestimmt.

The office and administrative building for the trade union organization is of revolutionary importance for the development of modern architecture. It is one of the first examples in which a reinforced-concrete frame construction is used unclad to make a quite specific architectural effect. At the same time the building marks the tendency to a change from the occasionally crystal-clear structures of expressionist architecture to the forms of Neue Sachlichkeit. The strict grid pattern is broken by the obliquely distorted and vertically oriented parts of the building on Inselstrasse with high gables, and the rhomboid supports of the concrete frame are reminiscent of Max Taut's 1920 memorial in the Stahnsdorf Cemetery. Walter Würzbach's extension of 1930-31 is notably functional, especially on the Märkisches Ufer.

in der Nähe/nearby:
U-Bahnhof Märkisches Museum; Wallstraße
1911-13 • Alfred Grenander
Verlagshaus; Wallstraße 76-79
1912 • Fritz Crzellitzer
Geschäftshaus; Wallstraße 27, Neue Roßstraße 14-15
1913 • Hoeninger & Sedelmeier
1979-80 (Erweiterung) • Georg Krause

A 24 Ermelerhaus
Berlin-Mitte; Märkisches Ufer 10
1760-62 • Friedrich Wilhelm Dietrichs

Das Märkische Ufer gehörte einstmals zu Neukölln am Wasser. Die Bebauung zwischen Roßstraßen- und Inselbrücke ermöglicht noch heute eine Vorstellung von dem grachtenartigen Charakter beiderseits des westlichen Spreearms, besonders nach den Kriegszerstörungen der gegenüberliegenden Friedrichsgracht. Das Ermelerhaus, hierher 1968-69 translociert, stand ursprünglich in der Breiten Straße 11 und hatte von Carl Friedrich Fechhelm und Johann Christoph Frisch seine Rokokoausschmückung erhalten; erwähnenswert sind Rosen-, Vogel- und Florazimmer sowie die Treppenanlage des Weydingerhauses am Schleusengraben. Das benachbarte Wohnhaus von 1740, ehemals an der Friedrichsgracht stehend, ist mit der Gaststätte des Ermelerhauses verbunden. Die beiden barocken Wohnhäuser Nr.16 und 18 vom Ende und Anfang des 18. Jahrhunderts sind heute zu einem Museum, dem Otto-Nagel-Haus zusammengefaßt.

The Märkisches Ufer was once part of Neukölln am Wasser. The development between Rosstrassenbrücke and Inselbrücke still allows one to imagine the gracht-like character of the area on both sides of the western arm of the Spree, especially after war damage to the Friedrichsgracht opposite. The Ermelerhaus, moved here 1968-69, was originally at 11 Breite Strasse and was given its rococo decoration by Carl Friedrich Fechhelm and Johann Christoph Frisch; notable features are rose, bird and floral rooms and the staircase from the Weydingerhaus on the Schleusengraben. The two baroque residential buildings at numbers 16 and 18 dating from the late and early eighteenth century have been joined to make a museum, the Otto-Nagel-Haus.

in der Nähe/nearby:
Wohngebiet Fischerinsel; Fischerinsel 1-12
1967-70 • Joachim Näther, Peter Schweizer
Gaststätte Ahornblatt; Fischerinsel 12
1971-73 • Helmut Stingl, Gerhard Lehmann
Ministerium für Bauwesen; Breite Straße 12, Scharrenstraße 2-3, Neumannsgasse 1
1967-68 • Rolf Göpfert

B
Berlin
Unter den Linden und Friedrichstadt

Die »Linden« entstanden mit dem Bau der Hundebrücke 1573 zunächst nur als kurfürstlicher Reitweg vom Schloß zum Tiergarten. Erst 1674 wurde der Weg sechsreihig mit den Bäumen bepflanzt, die der Straße dann den Namen »Unter den Linden« gaben. Den sechzig Meter breiten Straßenzug säumen seit 1680 etliche Palais, später folgte eine mehrgeschossige geschlossene Bebauung. Unter Friedrich dem Großen schuf Knobelsdorff am Ostende der Linden das Forum Fridericianum, aus dem sich beginnend mit dem Opernhaus ein kulturelles Zentrum entwickelte. Die Gründerjahre ließen die Prachtstraße mit großen Bank- und Hotelbauten entstehen. Noch vor Vollendung der Memhardtschen Festungswerke war 1674 nördlich der Linden die zweite barocke Neustadt gegründet und nach der Gemahlin des Großen Kurfürsten Dorotheenstadt benannt worden. Sie reichte nur bis zur Mauerstraße. Die Friedrichstraße, zunächst nur eine Querstraße der Dorotheenstadt, bildete dann 1688 in ihrer Verlängerung bis zur Zimmerstraße das Rückgrat der Friedrichstadt, der dritten barocken Stadterweiterung. Vorwiegend Hugenotten bewohnten diese Vorstädte. Nach Pariser Vorbild entstanden seit 1732 mit der Erweiterung bis zur Akzisemauer Schmuckplätze: das Quarré, der spätere Pariser Platz am Brandenburger Tor, das Oktogon am Potsdamer Tor und das Rondell am Halleschen Tor, der heutige Mehringplatz. Im 19. und 20. Jahrhundert entwickelte sich die Friedrichstadt zwischen Friedrichswerderschem Markt und Leipziger Platz zum Regierungs-, Banken- und Zeitungsviertel und zur Berliner City. Der Zweite Weltkrieg schlug viele Wunden, und die taktlose Abbruch- und Neubaumentalität der fünfziger und sechziger Jahre setzte das Zerstörungswerk fort. Zwar wurden die wichtigsten historischen Gebäude dieses Stadtteils, so die der Linden und die des Gendarmenmarktes, der Gropiusbau und das ehemalige Kammergericht wiederaufgebaut, doch ganze Viertel verloren ihren Charakter, versanken in der Gesichtslosigkeit oder verödeten wie die südliche Friedrichstadt, der erst die Pläne der Internationalen Bauausstellung 1984/87 wieder zu einer eigenen Identität verhelfen sollten.

When the Hundebrücke was built in 1573 the «Linden» was at first just a bridle path for the use of the Elector, leading from his palace to the Tiergarten. It was not until 1674 that six rows of lime trees were planted and the street acquired the name «Unter den Linden». The street is sixty metres wide, and was bordered by a number of palaces from 1680, later followed by an unbroken run of buildings with several storeys. Under Frederick the Great, Knobelsdorff created the Forum Fridericianum at the eastern end of the Linden; this developed into a cultural centre, starting with the opera house. Rapid development in the late nineteenth century saw the emergence of a magnificent boulevard with large banks and hotels. Even before the Memhardt fortifications were complete, a second baroque new town had been established north of the Linden in 1674, called Dorotheenstadt after the Great Elector's consort. It extended only as far as Mauerstrasse. Friedrichstrasse, at first only a Dorotheenstadt side street, was extended to Zimmerstrasse in 1688, thus forming the backbone of Friedrichstadt, the city's third baroque expansion. These suburbs were occupied mainly by Huguenots. On the Parisian model, decorative squares were created with extensions towards the excise wall from 1732: the Quarré, later to be Pariser Platz by the Brandenburg Gate, the Oktogon at Potsdamer Tor and the Rondell at Hallesches Tor, the present Mehringplatz. In the nineteenth and twentieth centuries Friedrichstadt between Friedrichswerder Markt and Leipziger Platz developed into an administrative, banking and newspaper centre, the heart of the city. The Second World War inflicted many wounds, and rash demolition and rebuilding in the fifties and sixties continued the work of destruction. The most important historic buildings in this part of the city, like those on the Linden and the Gendarmenmarkt, the Gropius building and the former Kammergericht were rebuilt, but the character of entire districts was lost, or they became faceless, or wildernesses like southern Friedrichstadt, which was not to regain an identity of its own until work was done by the Internationale Bauausstellung in 1984-7.

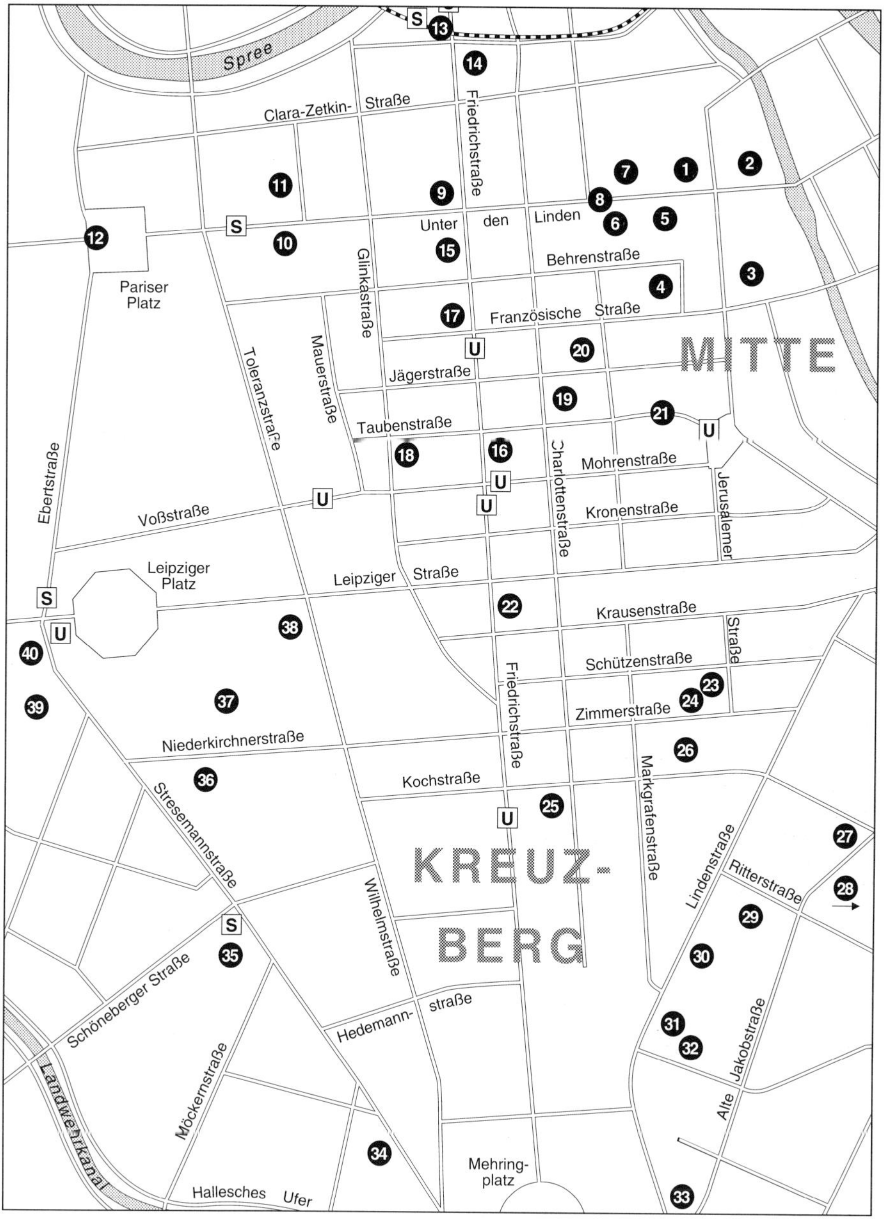

B 1 Neue Wache
B 2 Zeughaus
B 3 Friedrichswerdersche Kirche
B 4 St. Hedwigskathedrale
B 5 Deutsche Staatsoper
B 6 Alte Bibliothek
B 7 Humboldt-Universität
B 8 Denkmal Friedrichs II.
B 9 Haus der Schweiz
B 10 Botschaft der UdSSR
B 11 Schadowhaus
B 12 Brandenburger Tor
B 13 Bahnhof Friedrichstraße
B 14 Internationales Handelszentrum
B 15 Grandhotel
B 16 Friedrichstadtpassagen
B 17 Geschäftshaus Automat
B 18 Pfarrhäuser
B 19 Schauspielhaus
B 20 Französische Kirche
B 21 Mohrenkolonnaden
B 22 Geschäftshaus am »Checkpoint Charlie«
B 23 Mossehaus
B 24 Mossezentrum
B 25 Redaktionsgebäude der »taz«
B 26 Springerhaus
B 27 Reichsschuldenverwaltung
B 28 St. Jacobi
B 29 Wohnpark Ritterstraße
B 30 Viktoria-Versicherung
B 31 Kollegienhaus (Berlin-Museum)
B 32 Jüdisches Museum
B 33 Deutscher Metallarbeiter-Verband
B 34 Hebbel-Theater
B 35 Anhalter Bahnhof
B 36 Kunstgewerbemuseum (Martin-Gropius-Bau)
B 37 Preußischer Landtag
B 38 Luftfahrtministerium
B 39 Debis-Zentrum
B 40 Sony-Gebäude

B 1 Neue Wache
Berlin-Mitte; Unter den Linden 4
1816-18 • Karl Friedrich Schinkel

Die ehemalige Königswache ist Schinkels erstes Meisterwerk, ein Hauptwerk des deutschen Klassizismus und zugleich das monumentalste Gebäude dieser Straße. Der durch den dorischen Portikus eingeschossig wirkende Bau ist aber nach den Fenstern der Seitenfront zweigeschossig angelegt und als quadratischer, würfelförmiger Baukörper mit vier Eckrisaliten »einem römischen Castrum ungefähr nachgeformt«, wie Schinkel es beschrieb. Er war zu den vorhandenen Nachbargebäuden in günstige Beziehung gesetzt worden durch die flankierenden Denkmäler der Feldherren Scharnhorst und Bülow, überlebensgroß auf hohe Postamente gestellt, aber auch durch die nach romantischem Empfinden um das Gebäude gepflanzten Bäume des Kastanienwäldchens. Die zehn Viktorien im Gebälk schuf Gottfried Schadow, die Allegorien auf Kampf und Sieg, Flucht und Niederlage im Giebelfeld 1842-46 von August Kiß. 1931 gestaltete Heinrich Tessenow den inneren Hof zu einem Gefallenenehrenmal mit offenem Oberlicht um. 1956-57 wurde der 1945 schwer beschädigte Bau unter Heinz Mehlan wiederaufgebaut, 1969 erfolgte eine neuerliche Umgestaltung. Eine Neufassung als Gedenkstätte für die Kriegsgefallenen und die Opfer der Gewaltherrschaft ist vorgesehen.

This former royal guardhouse is Schinkel's first masterpiece, a major work of German classicism and also the most monumental building in this street. The Doric portico gives the impression of a single storey, but the windows of the side façade show that there are two, a cuboid building with four corner towers, «shaped roughly like a Roman castrum», as Schinkel put it. It related well to existing neighbouring buildings because of the flanking monuments to Field Marshals Scharnhorst and Bülow, larger than life size and on high pedestals, and also because of the little chestnut wood planted around the building, a response to Romantic sensibilities. The ten Victories in the entabulature are the work of Gottfried Schadow, the allegories of Struggle and Victory, Flight and Defeat in the tympanum by August Kiss, 1842-6. In 1931 Heinrich Tessenow made the inner courtyard into a war memorial with open upper light. Following heavy damages in 1945, the building was reconstructed by Heinz Mehlan and once again redesigned in 1969. It is now scheduled to be converted to a memorial for the victims of the War and of the time of tyranny.

in der Nähe/nearby:
Scharnhorst-Denkmal; Unter den Linden
1822 • Christian Daniel Rauch
Maxim-Gorki-Theater; Am Festungsgraben 2
1825-27 • Karl Theodor Ottmer
Palais; Am Festungsgraben 1
1751;1861 • Christian Friedrich Feldmann; Heinrich Bürde, Hermann v. der Hude

B 2 Zeughaus
Berlin-Mitte; Unter den Linden 2, Kupfergraben
1695-1706 • Johann Arnold Nering,

Das Zeughaus, Berlins schönster Barockbau, geht auf Planungen aus dem Jahre 1688 und vermutlich auf einen Vorentwurf des 1686 verstorbenen französischen Architekten François Blondel zurück. Der Bau des Waffenarsenals zwischen Spree und den Festungswerken wurde von Nering begonnen, nach seinem Tode von Martin Grünberg und dann von Andreas Schlüter fortgeführt. Fertiggestellt war es 1706, der Innenausbau zog sich aber bis 1730 hin. Schlüter arbeitete daran auch als Bildhauer, von ihm stammen die Helme an der Außenfront und im quadratischen Innenhof die 22 Masken sterbender Krieger, ein Hauptwerk europäischer Barockskulptur. Jean de Bodt wirkte an der Lindenfassade, so der großen Portalnische; der plastische Schmuck stammt von Guillaume Hulot. Über den allegorischen Sandsteinfiguren am Hauptzugang findet man das Bronzerelief des Bauherren, König Friedrich I., eine Wappenkartusche, und im Giebelfeld Minerva, ihre Jünger in der Kriegskunst unterrichtend. In der Gaststätte am Kupfergraben sind Gipsabgüsse von Schlüters Sklavenskulpturen aus dem Stadtschloß zu sehen. Friedrich Hitzig leitete 1877-80 den Umbau zum Waffenmuseum und Otto Haesler die 1965 abgeschlossene Beseitigung der Kriegsschäden.

The Zeughaus, Berlin's most beautiful baroque building, is based on plans made in 1688 and presumably on a preliminary design by the French architect François Blondel, who died in 1686. Nering started work on this arsenal between the Spree and the fortifications, and it was taken over by Martin Grünberg and Andreas Schlüter after his death. It was completed in 1706, but interior work continued until 1730. Schlüter also worked on the building as a sculptor; he was responsible for the statuary on the outer façade and the 22 masks of dying warriors in the square inner courtyard, a major work of European baroque sculpture. Jean de Bodt worked on the Linden façade and great portal niche; sculptural decoration is by Guillaume Hulot. Above the allegorical sandstone figures on the main entrance is a bronze relief of King Frederick I, who commissioned the building, a heraldic cartouche and Minerva in the tympanum, instructing her disciples in the art of war. There are copies of Schlüter's slave sculptures from the Stadtschloss in the restaurant on the Kupfergraben. Friedrich Hitzig directed the conversion to an arms museum in 1877-80 and Otto Haesler was responsible for completing repairs to war damage in 1965.

in der Nähe/nearby:
Schloßbrücke; Unter den Linden
1821-24 • Karl Friedrich Schinkel
(1852-57 Siegesgöttinnen mit Kriegern)
Freiherr-von-Stein-Denkmal; Unter den Linden
1867 • Hermann Schievelbein, Hugo Hagen

B 3 Friedrichswerdersche Kirche
Berlin-Mitte; Werderscher Markt
1824-30 • Karl Friedrich Schinkel

Die Stadt Friedrichswerder entstand seit 1662, als die neuen Festungswerke hier besonders weit vor die alte Stadtgrenze verlegt wurden, und reichte von der Gertraudenbrücke über die heutigen »Linden« hinaus bis zur Gießhausgasse hinter dem Zeughaus. Erster Bürgermeister wurde 1669 der Festungsbaumeister Johann Gregor Memhardt, der auch die Anlage der Straßen geplant hatte. Der Vorgängerbau der Kirche am Werderschen Markt stammte von 1700. Schinkels Neubau, erst 1830 fertiggestellt, gilt als erster neugotischer Backsteinbau Berlins. Es ist ein Versuch der Verschmelzung des deutschen Klassizismus mit gotischen Stilelementen. Strebepfeiler enden über dem durchbrochenen Fries in Fialen; dagegen steht die horizontale Gliederung der Zweiturmfront. Aufeinandergesetzte Würfel bilden helmlose Türme. Das spitzbogige Doppelportal ist zum Markt gewendet. Im Inneren ist 1987 ein Schinkelmuseum eingerichtet worden.

The town of Friedrichswerder was built from 1662, when the new fortifications were moved here, a considerable distance from the old city boundary; Friedrichswerder extended from the Gertraudenbrücke across the modern »Linden« and out to Giesshausgasse behind the Zeughaus. The first mayor was Johann Gregor Memhardt, architect of the fortifications, in 1669; he was also responsible for the layout of the streets. The previous church in the Werderscher Markt dated from 1700. Schinkel's new building, not completed until 1830, is Berlin's first neo-Gothic brick building. It attempts to blend German Classicism with Gothic elements. Buttresses terminate in pinnacles above the broken frieze, contrasting with the horizontal articulation of the twin-towered façade. Cubes set one on top of the other form towers without spires. The pointed-arched double portal faces the market. A Schinkel museum was established in the church in 1987.

in der Nähe/nearby:
Reichsbank; Kurstraße 36-51, Werderscher Markt
1932-38 • Heinrich Wolff
Außenministerium; Marx-Engels-Platz 2
1964-67 • Josef Kaiser, Heinz Aust, Gerhard Lehmann
Haupttelegraphenamt; Jägerstraße 43-44
1877-78 • Carl Schwatlo, Kessler
Konfektionshaus Mannheimer; Jägerstraße 33
Gegen 1909 • Salinger & Schmohl

B 4 St. Hedwigskathedrale
Berlin-Mitte; Bebelplatz
1747-73 • Jean Legeay, Johann Boumann d.Ä.

Mit dem Baubeginn des Zeughauses, vielleicht aber schon 1690, nur wenige Jahre nach ihrer Vollendung, war das Schleifen der Festungswerke beschlossene Sache; aber erst 1740 waren die Wälle soweit abgetragen, daß mit dem Bau der Oper die Anlage des Forum Fridericianum begonnen werden konnte. Als zweiter Bau entstand nach Ideen des jungen Königs Friedrich II. in Anlehnung an das Pantheon in Rom nach Skizzen von Knobelsdorff und in der Ausführung von Johann Boumann d.Ä. eine Kirche für die katholische Gemeinde. Sie lag am Rande des Terrains einer Bastion aber noch jenseits des nun schmaleren Festungsgrabens und war auch daher schräg zum Forum gestellt. 1952-63 erfolgte nach Entwürfen von Hans Schwippert die Erneuerung des kreisrunden Zentralbaus durch eine Fertigteil-Betonschalenkonstruktion für die Kuppel. In der Krypta befindet sich unter den Gräbern der Berliner Bischöfe auch das des Domprobstes Bernhard Lichtenberg.

A firm decision to pull down the fortifications had been made when building work started on the Zeughaus, but perhaps minds were made up as early as 1690, only a few years after they were completed; but it was not until 1740 that enough of the ramparts had been pulled down for a start to be made on the Forum Fridericianum by building the opera house. It was followed by a church for the Catholic community, based on ideas by the young King Frederick II derived from the Pantheon in Rome; Knobelsdorff provided sketches and it was executed by Johann Boumann the Elder. The church was on the edge of a rampart area but still beyond the fortification moat, and thus diagonal to the Forum. The circular centrally-planned building was rebuilt 1952-63 to designs by Hans Schwippert using a prefabricated concrete shell structure for the dome. In the crypt the tomb of Domprobst Bernhard Lichtenberg is to be found among those of the Berlin bishops.

in der Nähe/nearby:
Kronprinzenpalais; Unter den Linden 3
1732; 1856 • Philipp Gerlach; Johann Heinrich Strack
1968 (Neuaufbau) • Richard Paulick, Werner Prendel
Prinzessinnengarten; Unter den Linden (5/7)
1964 • Rolf Rühle, nach Ideen von Heinz Mehlan
Blücher-, Gneisenau-, Yorckdenkmal; Unter den Linden (5/7) • 1826/55 • Christian Daniel Rauch

B 5 Deutsche Staatsoper
Berlin-Mitte; Unter den Linden 7
1741-43 • Georg Wenzeslaus v. Knobelsdorff

Als den »neuesten, längsten und breitesten« Theaterbau hat der König seinen »Apollotempel« 1742 bekannt machen lassen, zu einer Zeit, als bereits Architekten und Sänger weit gereist waren, um das halbfertige Opernhaus zu bewundern. Beeindruckend war der klassische Giebelportikus mit den seitlichen Aufgängen, beeinflußt von englischer Architektur. Zusammen mit den anderen drei Risaliten erinnerte der Bau an Palladios Villa Rotonda. Das entscheidend Neue aber war die räumliche Trennung dieser Hofoper vom Schloß, ihre allseitige Freistellung, und das Innere als Folge von drei Haupträumen: Apollosaal, Theaterparkett und korinthischer Saal als Bühnenraum. Das Parkett konnte durch Winden angehoben und so die Oper zusätzlich als Redoutensaal genutzt werden. Nach einem Brand baute 1843-44 Carl Ferdinand Langhans das Haus wieder auf, 1926-28 vergrößerte Eduard Fürstenau trotz heftiger Kritik das Bühnenhaus und nach den Zerstörungen von 1945 folgten Wiederaufbau und Umbau durch Richard Paulick und Kurt Hemmerling. Der reiche plastische Schmuck, das Programm war Apoll und den Musen gewidmet, entstand unter der Leitung von Johann August Nahl, auch durch Friedrich Christian Glume und Benjamin Griese.

The king proclaimed his «Temple of Apollo» to be the «newest, longest and widest» theatre building in 1742, at a time when architects and singers had already travelled great distances to admire the half-completed opera house. The pedimented portico with side access, influenced by English architecture, made a great impression. With three other projections the building was reminiscent of Palladio's Villa Rotonda. But the decisive new feature was the spatial separation of this court opera house from the palace, the fact that it was open on all sides, and that the interior was a sequence of three principal spaces, Apollo room, theatre stalls and a Corinthian hall as stage area. The stalls could be raised on winches and the opera thus also used as a ballroom. It was rebuilt 1843-4 by Carl Ferdinand Langhans after a fire, and the stage area was enlarged by Eduard Fürstenau 1926-8, despite vehement protests, and after severe damage in 1945 it was rebuilt and altered by Richard Paulick and Kurt Hemmerling. The lavish sculptural decoration, on the theme of Apollo and the Muses, was created under the direction of Johann August Nahl, and also by Christian Glume and Benjamin Griese.

in der Nähe/nearby:
Prinzessinnenpalais; Unter den Linden 5, Oberwallstraße 1-2
1733 • Friedrich Wilhelm Dietrichs
1810 (Eckbau) • Heinrich Gentz
1963-64 (Rekonstruktion) • Richard Paulick

B 6 Alte Bibliothek
Berlin-Mitte; Bebelplatz
1775-80 • Georg Christian Unger

Als letzter Bau des »Forum Fridericianum« war die Königliche Bibliothek der Abschluß der kleineren Variante der Schloßbaupläne Friedrich des Großen. Die stark geschwungene Hauptfront, die dem Gebäude den Beinamen »Kommode« einbrachte, ist nicht nur barockes Gegenstück zum frühklassizistischen Opernhaus, sondern in ihrem Aufbau mit dominierendem Mittelteil und kräftigen Seitenrisaliten auch bezeichnend für den konservativen Spätstil der friderizianischen Architektur. Der plastische Schmuck auf der Attika stammt von Wilhelm Christian Meyer d.Ä. Der Bau wuchs bis 1780 unter der Leitung von Georg Friedrich Boumann d.J. nach Plänen von Unger, der sich wiederum auf einen 1725 entstandenen Entwurf von Joseph Emanuel Fischer von Erlach für den begonnenen Michaelertrakt der Wiener Hofburg stützen mußte. Dieser konnte aber erst 1893 vollendet werden, und so stand die preußische Kopie früher als das Wiener Vorbild – ein kleiner Triumph Friedrichs II. über seine Kontrahentin Maria Theresia. Seit 1914 ist die Alte Bibliothek Institutsgebäude der Universität, zu der auch seit 1963, rekonstruiert durch Fritz Meinhardt, das Alte Palais und das Gouverneurshaus gehören.

This royal library – the old library – was the last building in the «Forum Fridericianum» and concluded the smaller variant of Frederick the Great's palace-building plan. The sweeping curves of the façade gave the building the nickname «commode»; it is not just a baroque counterpoint to the early classicism of the opera house, but also typical of the conservative late style of architecture of Frederick's period, with its dominant central section and massive side projections. The sculpture on the attic storey is by Wilhelm Christian Meyer the Elder. The building was under construction until 1780 under the direction of Georg Friedrich Boumann the Younger to plans by Unger, who for his part was instructed to base his work on a design dating from 1725 by Joseph Emanuel Fischer von Erlach for the Michaelertrakt that had been started at the Hofburg in Vienna. This was however not completed until 1893, and thus the Prussian copy was completed before the Viennese model – a small triumph by Frederick II over his rival Maria Theresia. From 1914 the Alte Bibliothek was part of the university, to which the Altes Palais and the Gouverneurshaus, rebuilt from 1963 by Fritz Meinhardt, also belong.

in der Nähe/nearby:
Dresdener Bank; Behrenstraße 37-39
1887-89 • Ludwig Heim
Berliner Handelsgesellschaft; Behrenstraße 32-33
1899-1900 • Alfred Messel
1911 • Heinrich Schweitzer
Altes Palais; Unter den Linden 9
1834-37 • Carl Ferdinand Langhans
Gouverneurgebäude (Kopie); Unter den Linden 11
1721 • Friedrich Wilhelm Dietrichs

B 7 Humboldt-Universität
Berlin-Mitte; Unter den Linden 6
1748-53 • Johann Boumann d.Ä.

In Anlehnung an Ideenskizzen des Königs für ein großes Forum, dessen Achse in der heutigen Universitätsstraße gelegen hätte, sowie unter Verwendung der darauf bezogenen Schloßbaupläne von Knobelsdorff entstand als dritter Bau des Forum Fridericianum das Stadtpalais für den Prinzen Heinrich, den Bruder Friedrichs II. Erst 1766 waren die um den lindenseitigen Ehrenhof gelegenen Bauten fertiggestellt. 1810 gehörten sie der neuen Universität. 1913-20 war dieser Teil unter Ludwig Hoffmann in den Formen des friderizianischen Klassizismus bis zum Hegelplatz erweitert worden. Die Attikaplastiken schufen Johann Peter Benckert und Johann Gottlieb Heymüller, die Figuren über den Seitenrisaliten stammen vom Potsdamer Stadtschloß und sind Werke von Johann August Nahl aus dem Jahre 1745. Die Marmorstatuen der Brüder Alexander und Wilhelm v. Humboldt von den Bildhauern Reinhold Begas und Otto Paul wurden erst 1883 beiderseits des Eingangsportals aufgestellt. Denkmäler für Hermann Helmholtz und Theodor Mommsen stehen vor der Westfassade gegenüber der Staatsbibliothek, ein Bronzestandbild für Eilhardt Mitscherlich am Festungsgraben.

The third building in the Forum Fridericianum was the town palace for Prince Heinrich, Frederick II's brother, based on the king's ideas for a great forum the axis of which would have lain on the present Universitätsstrasse, using Knobelsdorff's palace plans, which also related to this project. The buildings around the courtyard on the Linden side were not completed until 1766. From 1810 they were part of the new university. From 1913-20 this section was extended to Hegelplatz under Ludwig Hoffmann in the style of the classicism of Frederick's period. The attic storey sculptures were the work of Johann Peter Benckert and Johann Gottlieb Heymüller, the figures above the side projections came from the Stadtschloss in Potsdam and are the work of Johann August Nahl, dating from 1745. The marble statues of the brothers Alexander and Wilhelm v. Humboldt by sculptors Reinhold Begas and Otto Paul were not erected on either side of the entrance portal until 1883. Memorials to Hermann Helmholtz and Theodor Mommsen stand in front of the west façade opposite the Staatsbibliothek, and a bronze statue in memory of Eilhardt Mitscherlich by the moat.

in der Nähe/nearby:
Hegel-Denkmal; Hegelplatz
1872 • Gustav Bläser
Handelshaus Hermes (Mitropa-Verwaltung); Universitätsstraße 2-3 a
1913-14 • Johann Emil Schaudt
Universitätsbibliothek; Clara-Zetkin-Straße 28
1871-74 • Paul Spieker

B 8 Denkmal Friedrichs II.
Berlin-Mitte; Unter den Linden
1840-51 • Christian Daniel Rauch

Die Planungen für dieses Denkmal begannen schon zu Lebzeiten des Monarchen, blieben aber lange ohne Ergebnis. Viele Künstler, unter ihnen Langhans, Gilly und Schinkel, lieferten Entwürfe für verschiedene Standorte. 1836 erhielt der Schadowschüler Christian Daniel Rauch den Auftrag für ein Reiterstandbild; 1840 erfolgte die Grundsteinlegung, aber erst 1851 die Enthüllung. Nun aber war es Vorbild für zahlreiche Fürstenstandbilder bis ins 20. Jahrhundert. Beispielhaft war der pyramidal gegliederte Aufbau, ein dreistufig thematisch gestaltetes Postament mit Darstellungen bedeutender Zeitgenossen aus des Königs Umgebung und als Bekrönung das Reiterbild des Königs in Uniform, gleichsam in sein Forum einreitend. 1951 nach Potsdam verbracht, stand das Denkmal 1962 dort im Hippodrom, 1980 kehrte es nach Berlin zurück und wurde etwa sechs Meter östlich vom alten Standort wieder aufgestellt.

Planning for this monument was under way even when the monarch was still alive, but for a long time nothing was produced. Many artists, including Langhans, Gilly and Schinkel, provided designs for various sites. In 1836 an equestrian statue was commissioned from Schadow's pupil Christian Daniel Rauch; the foundation stone was laid in 1840; the work was not unveiled until 1851, but from then it was a model for statues of royalty well into the twentieth century. An exemplary feature was the pyramidic structure, a pedestal in three sections on separate themes showing important contemporaries from the king's entourage, topped by the equestrian statue of the king in uniform, riding into his Forum, as it were. It was taken to Potsdam in 1951, and stood as a monument in the Hippodrom there in 1962, in 1980 it returned to Berlin and was re-erected about six metres east of its former position.

in der Nähe/nearby:
Deutsche Staatsbibliothek; Unter den Linden 8
1903-14 • Ernst v. Ihne
Geschäftshaus; Unter den Linden 10
1910 • Kurt Berndt, A. F. M. Lange
Geschäftshaus; Unter den Linden 12
1909-10 • Max Grünfeld
Hotel Unter den Linden; Unter den Linden 14
1964-66 • Heinz Scharlipp, Günter Boy

B 9 Haus der Schweiz
Berlin-Mitte; Unter den Linden 24
1935-36 • Hennig Meier-Appenzell

Das Eckhaus schließt eine Bebauung aus den ersten Jahrzehnten des 20. Jahrhunderts zwischen Friedrich-, Mittel- und Neustädtischer Kirchstraße. Dieser Baublock war schon vor mehr als dreihundert Jahren mit dem Entstehen der Dorotheenstadt angelegt worden. Die Grundstücke der Geschäftshäuser reichen oft bis zur Mittelstraße und sind fast vollständig überbaut. Meist reich dekorierte sechsgeschossige Werksteinfassaden wurden durch Kolossalpilaster oder Wandsäulen gegliedert. Die Erdgeschoßzone ist repräsentativen Geschäften vorbehalten. Das Haus der Schweiz besitzt an der Friedrichstraße rundbogige Kolonnaden, ist wie der »Zollernhof« ein Stahlskelettbau und gleichfalls mit Naturstein verkleidet. Die Friedrichstraße war einst nur Querachse der Dorotheenstadt. 1688 wurde sie bis zum Halleschen Tor als Rückgrat der Friedrichstadt verlängert. Seitdem, besonders aber im 20. Jahrhundert, lag die Kreuzung mit den Linden an exponierter Stelle innerhalb der Stadt.

This corner building concludes an early twentieth century development between Friedrich-, Mittel- and Neustädtischer Kirchstrasse. The block had been started over three hundred years before, when Dorotheenstadt was built. The plots of these business premises often extend to Mittelstrasse, and are almost completely built up. Most of them have lavishly decorated, six-storey ashlar façades, articulated by colossal pilasters. The ground floor is reserved for smart shops. The Haus der Schweiz has round-arched colonnades on Friedrichstrasse, and like the «Zollernhof» is a stone-clad steel-framed building. Friedrichstrasse was once just a side road in Dorotheenstadt, until it was extended to Hallesches Tor to form the spine of Friedrichstadt in 1688. From then onwards, but particularly in the twentieth century, the junction with the Linden was a key point in the city.

in der Nähe/nearby:
Geschäftshaus; Unter den Linden 26
1914 • Bielenberg & Moser
Bürohaus Zollernhof; Unter den Linden 36/38
1910-11 • Kurt Berndt, Bruno Paul
Geschäftshaus; Unter den Linden 40
1907-08 • A. F. M. Lange
Bürohaus Pietzsch mit Galerie; Unter den Linden 42
1992-94 • Jürgen Sawade
Warenhaus für Armee und Marine (später Botschaft der USA); Neustädtische Kirchstraße 4-5
1886-87 • Hermann v. der Hude, Julius Hennicke
Außenhandelsministerium (Bürogebäude für Bundestagsabgeordnete); Unter den Linden 44/60
1962-65 • Emil Leibold, Herbert Boos, Hanno Walther

B 10 Botschaft der UdSSR (Russische Botschaft)
Berlin-Mitte; Unter den Linden 63/65
1950-53 • A. Stryshewski, F. Skujin

Auf dem Gelände der im Zweiten Weltkrieg zerstörten sowjetischen Botschaft wurde nach Gründung der DDR unter Hinzunahme weiterer Grundstücke ein großer Komplex errichtet, der später jenseits der Behrenstraße noch eine Erweiterung erfuhr. Der Vorgängerbau, ein 1765 von Johann Boumann errichtetes Palais, war seit 1837 russische Gesandtschaft. Der Neubau besteht aus viergeschossigen Trakten in der Bauflucht der Linden, wobei der Hauptflügel mit seinem blockhaften Mittelteil und der kubischen Laterne hinter die Straßenfront zurücktritt, um einen Ehrenhof zu bilden. 1963 entstand an der Glinkastraße nach Entwurf von Wolfgang Ortmann ein Bürogebäude für Nachrichtenagentur, Reisebüro und Luftfahrtgesellschaft der UdSSR. Klubhaus und Schwimmhalle wurden 1975-82 an der Behrenstraße nach Entwürfen von Dieter Bankert, Karl-Ernst Swora und Gerd Pieper als zwei- bis dreigeschossige Anlage um einen Gartenhof errichtet.

A large complex was built on the site of the Soviet Embassy, destroyed in the Second World War, after the foundation of the GDR; it included several other plots, and was later extended beyond Behrenstrasse. The earlier building, a palace built by Johann Boumann in 1765, was the Russian embassy from 1837. The new building consists of four-storey tracts on the Linden building line, with the central wing with block-like middle section and cubic lantern set back from the street façade to form a courtyard. In 1963 Wolfgang Ortmann designed an office block for the Soviet news agency, travel agency and airline in Glinkastrasse. Club house and indoor swimming pool were built as a three-storey complex around a garden court in Behrenstrasse to designs by Dieter Bankert, Karl-Ernst Swora and Gerd Pieper from 1975-82.

in der Nähe/nearby:
Polnische Botschaft; Unter den Linden 70/72
1963-64 • Emil Leibold, Christian Seyfarth
Ungarische Botschaft; Unter den Linden 74/76
1965-66 • Karl-Ernst Swora, Rainer Hanslick
Ministerium für Bildung (Bürogebäude für Bundestagsabgeordnete); Unter den Linden 69/73
1962-64 • Manfred Hörner
1992-94 • Gehrmann & Partner (Wiesbaden)
Schaffhausenscher Bankverein; Behrenstraße 21-22
1912 • Bielenberg & Moser
Deutsche Bank; Mauerstraße 29-32 (I.) u. 25-28 (II.)
1896-98 (I.) u. 1908 (II.) • Wilhelm Martens

B 11 Schadowhaus
Berlin-Mitte; Schadowstraße 10-11
1805

In dieser Straße endete die Dorotheenstadt, bevor sie 1742 bis zum Brandenburger Tor erweitert wurde. Anfangs hieß sie auch Mauerstraße, so wie ihre südliche Fortführung noch heute in der Friedrichstadt. In diesem einst zweigeschossigen klassizistischen Haus wohnte der Bildhauer Johann Gottfried Schadow. Neben dem nördlichen Seitenflügel gab es ein quergestelltes Werkstattgebäude auf dem Hof. 1851 erhöhte der Sohn Felix Schadow alle diese Hausteile um ein Geschoß und schloß den Hof mit dem Südflügel. Die Stuckreliefs am Erdgeschoß stammen von Gottfried Schadow, die am Obergeschoß aus dem Jahre 1851 von Hermann Schievelbein. In der Wohnung im ersten Geschoß befindet sich ein Fresko »Der Brunnen des Lebens«, gemalt 1837 von Eduard Bendemann, dem Schwiegersohn Schadows.

Dorotheenstadt ended in this street until it was extended to the Brandenburg Gate in 1742. It was originally called Mauerstrasse as well, like its southern continuation in Friedrichstadt. The classical building formerly had only two storeys, and was the home of sculptor Johann Gottfried Schadow. Alongside the north side wing was a transverse studio building in the courtyard. In 1851 his son Felix Schadow added a storey to all parts of the building, and closed the courtyard with the south wing. The stucco reliefs on the ground floor are by Gottfried Schadow, those on the upper storey by Herrmann Schievelbein, 1851. In the first-floor flat is a fresco «The Fountain of Life», painted in 1837 by Eduard Bendemann, Schadow's son-in-law.

In der Nähe/nearby:
Bürogebäude; Unter den Linden 62/68
1962-64 • Peter Senf
Gaststätte; Clara-Zetkin-Straße 74, Reichstagsufer
1964-65 • Heinz Mehlan, Harry Reichert
Institutsgebäude; Clara-Zetkin-Straße 94/96
1873-83 • Paul Spieker

B 12 Brandenburger Tor
Berlin-Mitte; Pariser Platz
1788 • Carl Gotthard Langhans

Dieser Ort ist heute mehr denn je weltweites Symbol der Stadt Berlin. Vorgängerbau war ein einfaches Stadttor in der »Linie«. Der Soldatenkönig Friedrich Wilhelm hatte diese »Linie« seit 1735 um Berlin errichten lassen als Akzisemauer, aber auch um Desertionen zu unterbinden. Als der neue, vielbestaunte Torbau 1789-91 errichtet wurde, war er Abschluß der barocken Schloßachse, zugleich aber auch ein erstes Werk des romantischen Klassizismus. Teile der Bauplastik und die bronzene Quadriga mit der Siegesgöttin als Friedensbringerin wurden nach Entwürfen von Johann Gottfried Schadow erst 1793 fertiggestellt. Dieses letzte der Berliner Stadttore entstand nach dem Vorbild der Propyläen auf der Athener Akropolis, der Parthenontempel lieferte die Motive für die Metopen im dorischen Gebälk mit den Kentaurenkämpfen. 20 Reliefs nach Christian Bernhard Rode stellen die Taten des Herkules und seine Heimkehr dar. Die Statue des Mars zeigt den Gott, sein Schwert in die Scheide steckend. Dieses bildkünstlerische Programm charakterisiert das Ende der durch Kriege gekennzeichneten friderizianischen Epoche und spiegelt die Friedenssehnsucht des deutschen Volkes zu Beginn der Romantik wider. Mit dem Abbruch der Stadtmauer sind die flankierenden Anbauten 1867 durch Johann Heinrich Strack umgestaltet worden. Nach starken Kriegsschäden erfolgte 1956 die Wiederherstellung unter Theodor Voissem.

Now more than ever this is the symbol of Berlin, all over the world. Its predecessor was a simple town gate in the «Linie». Friedrich Wilhelm, the soldier king, established this «Linie» around Berlin from 1735, as an excise wall in the first place, but also to prevent desertion. When the new and much admired gate was built from 1789-91 it concluded the baroque palace axis, but was also an early work of Romantic classicism. Some of the sculpture on the building and the bronze quadriga with victory goddess as bringer of peace were not completed until 1793, to designs by Gottfried Schadow. This last Berlin city gate was modelled on the Propylaeum on the Acropolis in Athens, the Parthenon provided motifs for the metopes in the Doric entabulature with the Battle of the Centaurs. 20 reliefs after Christian Bernhard Rode show the Labours of Hercules and his homecoming. The statue of Mars shows the god putting his sword into its sheath. This pictorial programme is typical of the period of Frederick, in which there were many wars, and reflects the people's longing for peace at the beginning of the Romantic period. The side buildings were redesigned by Johann Heinrich Strack when the town wall was pulled down in 1867. Severe war damage was repaired under Theodor Voissem in 1956.

B 13 Bahnhof Friedrichstraße
Berlin-Mitte; Friedrichstraße 98-99 und 141 a-142
1919-25 • Carl Theodor Brodführer

Die sich seit 1882 auf einem Viadukt im West-Ost-Verlauf durch Berlin schlängelnde Stadtbahn sollte sowohl dem Nahverkehr dienen als auch die Durchführung von Fernzügen ermöglichen, die sonst grundsätzlich in den Kopfbahnhöfen endeten. Der Bahnhof Friedrichstraße übernahm schnell die Funktion des zentralen Berliner Bahnhofs, der mit der seit 1906 geforderten und 1934-38 gebauten Nord-Süd-S-Bahn in den Schnittpunkt des inneren Berliner Streckenkreuzes rückte. Zur Erweiterung des oberirdischen Bahnhofs auf sechs Gleise kam es 1919, etwa gleichzeitig mit dem Bau einer U-Bahn im Verlauf der Friedrichstraße. Die neue Bahnsteighalle mußte zweischiffig und streckenbedingt gekrümmt angelegt werden. Als Charakteristikum erhielt sie Stahlvollwandbinder mit flachen und zeitgemäß spitzbogigen Untergurten. Auch die Architektur des Sockelbaus gibt sich bedingt expressionistisch mit späten Einflüssen des Pfeilerstils. Das Material: violettbraune Eisenklinker und schwarze Terrakotta. Als Bildhauer wirkte Felix Kupsch. Nach 1961 wurde die Bahnsteighalle durch eine hohe Drahtglaswand längsgeteilt, und später kam auf der Bahnhofnordseite noch als deutsch-deutsches Grenzkontrollgebäude der »Tränenpalast« hinzu. Mit der Wiedervereinigung ist der grenznahe Dämmerschlaf des Bahnhofs Friedrichstraße vorbei. 1993 wurde ein städtebaulicher Wettbewerb zugunsten eines Entwurfs des Architektenpaares Nalbach entschieden.

The Stadtbahn which weaves its way through the city on an elevated viaduct running from west to east was meant to facilitate local traffic and to create a new right-of-way for long-distance trains which until then had ended in stub-end terminals. With the opening of the new north-south line of the S-Bahn which had been called for since 1906 and was finally built in 1934-38, the Friedrichstrasse station assumed the role of a central interchange for Berlin, being located at the hub of a variety of inner-city transport lines. The elevated station was extended in 1919 to house a total of six tracks; at the same time a new U-Bahn (underground) was built along Friedrichstrasse. For technical reasons the new platform shed had to be a curving two-bay structure. Its characteristic features are plain-webbed girders with modern-type undergirders in the shape of low pointed arches. The architecture of the base building is moderately expressionist in style with some late reflections of the so-called pillar style. The materials are violet-brownish iron clinker and black terracotta. The sculptural work is by Felix Kupsch. After 1961 the platform shed was divided lengthwise with a high wire-glass wall, and later an inner-German border control building was added to the north of the station, soon nicknamed the «palace of tears». Following reunification, the Friedrichstrasse station awakened from its half-sleep near the Wall. The urban design competition for this area was won in 1993 by the Nalbach office, a husband-and-wife team of architects.

B 14 Internationales Handelszentrum Berlin
Berlin-Mitte; Friedrichstraße 95
1976-78

Direkt am Bahnhof Friedrichstraße, auf kleinstem Terrain zwischen Clara-Zetkin-, Charlotten- und Georgenstraße liegt dieser mächtige Gebäudekomplex. Damit wurde das Internationale Handelszentrum an einem der wichtigsten Verkehrsknotenpunkte der Stadt lokalisiert. Hier schneiden Fern-, S- und U-Bahnlinien die große Berliner Ost-West-Straßenachse. Das Hochhaus dominiert mit seinen 93 Metern im Stadtbild auch an manch ungewollter Stelle. Zum Bahnhofsvorplatz vermittelt das zwei- bis dreigeschossige Komplement; das Kongreßzentrum besitzt Ausstellungsräume und einen Saal mit 250 Plätzen; im Einkaufszentrum an der Friedrichstraße befinden sich auch Spezialläden und drei Restaurants. Ein Parkhaus wurde zusätzlich 1988-90 an der Charlottenstraße errichtet. Auf der gegenüberliegenden Seite an der Friedrichstraße steht seit 1979 ein Brunnen von Achim Kühn.

This massive building is on a tiny site directly by Friedrichstrasse station, between Clara-Zetkin-, Charlotten- and Georgenstrasse, thus placing the International Trade Centre at one of the city's most important junctions, where main line, S-Bahn and U-Bahn intersect with the great east-west road axis. The building is 93 metres high, and is visually dominant in many places where this is less than welcome. The two- and three-storey section forms a link with the station approach; the congress centre has exhibition galleries and a hall seating 250; the shopping centre in Friedrichstrasse has specialist shops and three restaurants. A multi-storey car park was added in Charlottenstrasse in 1988-90. There has been a fountain by Achim Kühn on the opposite side of Friedrichstrasse since 1979.

in der Nähe/nearby:
Admiralspalast (Metropoltheater); Friedrichstraße 101
1911 • Heinrich Schweitzer
Grenzübergangsstelle (Tränenpalast); Reichstagufer
1961-62
Polnische Apotheke; Friedrichstraße 153 a
1898-1900 • Alfred Breslauer
Hotel Splendid (Bank); Clara-Zetkin-Straße 37
1904 • Gronau & Graul

B 15 Maritim-Grandhotel
Berlin-Mitte; Friedrichstraße 158-164
1985-87

Das Grandhotel steht an jener Stelle, wo 1871-73 die Kaisergalerie errichtet worden war, eine Verbindung zwischen den Linden und der Behrenstraße, um die Ecke an der Friedrichstraße zu entlasten. Gerade noch vor dem Gründerkrach fertiggestellt, war sie anfangs Mittelpunkt der eleganten Welt. Der heutige Hotelkomplex mit 600 Betten umfaßt einen winkelförmigen Baukörper. Der Innenhof ist zweigeschossig überbaut und trägt eine begrünte Dachterrasse. Die gastronomischen Einrichtungen bieten 900 Gästen Platz. Neben den Hotelrestaurants gibt es ein Konzertcafé mit einer Terrasse unter den erdgeschossigen Arkaden. Dort liegen auch mehrere Spezialitätenrestaurants. In den oberen Geschossen findet man ein Dachrestaurant und den Wintergarten. Darüber hinaus gibt es einen Fitnessbereich mit Schwimmbecken, Friseur und Boutiquen. Die Fassaden, mit Lisenen und Gesimsen plastisch gegliedert, bestehen aus vorgefertigten Beton-Außenwandelementen; nur das Erdgeschoß ist mit Sandstein verkleidet.

The Grandhotel is on the site where the Kaisergalerie was built in 1871-3, a link between the Linden and Behrenstrasse, intended to relieve the Friedrichstrasse corner. It was completed just before rapid industrial and commercial expansion exploded in the late nineteenth century, and was initially a centre for the elegant world. The present 600 bedroom hotel complex contains another building. The inner courtyard is built on to a height of two storeys, with planted roof terraces. There are gastronomic facilities for 900 people. Aside from the hotel restaurants there is a concert café with a terrace under the ground-floor arcades. There are also several speciality restaurants here. In the upper storeys are a roof restaurant and a conservatory. Additionally, there is a keep-fit area with swimming pool, hairdresser and boutiques. The façades are articulated with pilaster strips and cornices, and consist of prefabricated concrete outer wall sections; only the ground floor is clad in sandstone.

in der Nähe/nearby:
Pschorrhaus; Friedrichstraße 165
1887-88 • Kayser & Großheim
Geschäftshaus; Friedrichstraße 166
1898-99 • Ferdinand Wendelstadt und Max Welsch
Reichsbahn-Kreditgesellschaft; Friedrichstraße 169-170
1898-99 • Ferdinand Wendelstadt und Max Welsch
Komische Oper; Behrenstraße 54-57
1891-92 • F. Fellner, H. Helmer
1966 • Kunz Nierade

B 16 Friedrichstadtpassagen
Berlin-Mitte; Friedrichstraße 66-70
1993-95 • Oswald Mathias Ungers

Die Friedrichstadtpassagen standen bereits im Rohbau mit ihren vorgehängten Fassaden, als sie die politische und damit auch wirtschaftliche Wende überraschte. Den drei neuen Investoren aus Frankreich, USA und Deutschland genügte das Vorgefundene nicht, sie ließen es wieder abreißen. Für die drei Blöcke entstanden neue Entwürfe, nun in neuer Gestaltung und mit Rücksicht auf den Standort von international renommierten Architekten: Nördlich errichtet Jean Nouvel aus Paris das Nobel-Warenhaus Galeries Lafayette, den mittleren Block bebauen Pei, Cobb & Freed aus New York mit einem Büro- und Geschäftshaus und südlich anschließend folgt ein weiterer Geschäftshauskomplex, den Oswald Mathias Ungers entwarf. Schlechte Erfahrungen mit reinen Gewerbekomplexen führten zu einem größeren Anteil an Wohnungen, deren Mieter das Viertel auch außerhalb der Geschäftszeiten mit Leben füllen sollen. Ob die Friedrichstraße wieder zur belebtesten Einkaufsstraße Berlins wird, muß sich zeigen. Die Internationalität der hier entstehenden Architektur verspricht zumindest Spannung.

Rough construction of the Friedrichstadtpassagen had already been completed when the political and economic situation changed. The three new investors from France, USA and Germany were not satisfied with what they found here and simply had everything demolished. New designs were developed for the three city-blocks involved: On the northernmost block, Jean Nouvel (Paris) is building a fashionable department store for the Galeries Lafayette; the central block will house an office and commercial building designed by Pei, Cobb and Freed (New York); and on the block to the south another complex of commercial buildings will be erected to designs by Oswald Mathias Ungers (Cologne). In view of negative experiences with purely commercial complexes of this size, a larger number of apartments will be included in the hope that the tenants may provide a certain degree of urban life outside of store hours as well. It remains to be seen if Friedrichstrasse will once again become the busiest shopping street in Berlin. The international character of the architecture being realized here will at least create a certain kind of tension.

in der Nähe/nearby:
Friedrichstadtpassagen; Friedrichstraße 71-75
1993-95 • Pei, Cobb & Freed
Friedrichstadtpassagen; Friedrichstraße 76-78
1993-95 • Jean Nouvel
Weinhandlung Borchardt; Französische Straße 47
1895 • Carl Gause
Hotel Charlottenhof; Charlottenstraße 52
1980 • Manfred Prasser, Ernst Wallis
Jacob-Kaiser-Haus; Charlottenstraße 53-54
1980 • Manfred Prasser, Günter Boy

B 17 Geschäftshaus Automat
Berlin-Mitte; Friedrichstraße 167-168
1904-05 • Bruno Schmitz

Bruno Schmitz ist der Architekt der großen Nationaldenkmale und der monumentalen Geschäftshäuser. Sein Stil wird aus dieser Sicht auch gern als der teutonische Stil bezeichnet. Die Pfeilerfronten und schweren Gesimse hat er mit Messel gemeinsam, der diese Elemente am augenfälligsten im Wertheimbau am Leipziger Platz entwickelte. Die vorgewölbten Fenster sind ein seit dem Ende des 19. Jahrhunderts besonders im Berliner Geschäftshausbau beliebtes Motiv. Die Ornamentik und die formale Ausgestaltung der architektonischen Glieder folgen schließlich dem Kanon des Jugendstils, der etwa bis 1905 noch Gültigkeit besaß. Bruno Schmitz verband all diese Elemente zu einer wirkungsvollen und dabei gestalterisch geschlossen Fassade. Das moderne Geschäftshaus mußte sich auch – das war Forderung der Hauptgeschäftsstraße – gegenüber den Nachbarhäusern durchsetzen. So vermittelte schließlich das namengebende Automatenrestaurant im Erdgeschoß einen Eindruck der modernen Zeiten, wenn der eilige Gast gegen Münzeinwurf aus Automaten Speisen und Getränke entnehmen konnte.

Bruno Schmitz is the architect of the great national monuments and stately commercial buildings. As a result, his style has frequently come to be dubbed the teutonic style. His predilection for pillars and heavy cornices was also shared by Messel who used these elements in a highly conspicuous way at the Wertheim building on Leipziger Platz. The vaulted windows have become a popular motif especially in commercial architecture since the late nineteenth century. The ornamentation and formal expression of the structural elements adhere to the canon of the Jugendstil which continued to be valid until c. 1905. Bruno Schmitz combined all these elements in his striking and formally consistent façade design. Modern commercial buildings were expected, at least along major shopping streets, to stand out from the neigbouring buildings. Thus the automated restaurants at ground floor which gave the building its name projected an image of modern times, allowing customers to have a quick meal, food and drink being sold from automatic dispensers.

B 18 Pfarrhäuser
Berlin-Mitte; Taubenstraße 3, Glinkastraße 16
1738-39

Unter der Oberaufsicht von Johann Arnold Nering kam die Bebauung der Friedrichstadt gut voran, so daß diese Neustadt in sieben Jahren mit etwa dreihundert Häusern besetzt war. Johann Heinrich Behr hatte die Absteckung des Straßenplanes besorgt – die Behrenstraße ist nach ihm benannt. Eine Vielzahl rechtwinklig aufeinander bezogener Querstraßen der sich in Nord-Süd-Richtung erstreckenden Friedrichstraße bildet ein Straßenraster mit gestreckten Karrees. Dieses System war nur gestört durch die gekrümmt verlaufende Mauerstraße; sie war bis 1732 die westliche Grenze der Friedrichstadt. Auf zwei sich dadurch bildenden Dreieckplätzen lagen seit 1735 die Böhmische und seit 1737 die Dreifaltigkeitskirche inmitten der ein- bis dreigeschossigen Bebauung. Die Pfarrhäuser gehörten zur heute zerstörten Dreifaltigkeitskirche. Nach einheitlichem Plan errichtet lag diese Gruppe von drei Wohnhäusern auf einem Eckgrundstück um einen großen begrünten Innenhof. Das Schleiermacherhaus Glinkastraße 16 wurde 1945 zerstört. Im Hof finden sich zwei Reliefs mit den Stiftern der Dorotheenstädtischen Kirche, der Große Kurfürst und Kurfürstin Dorothea, 1904 von Albert Moritz-Wolff.

Building proceeded quickly in Friedrichstadt under the supervision of Johann Arnold Nering, with the result that this new town had about three hundred houses within seven years. The street plan was marked out by Johann Heinrich Behr – Behrenstrasse is named after him. A street grid of extended rectangles is formed by a large number of streets set at right angles to each other off Friedrichstrasse, which runs north-south. This system was spoiled only by the crooked Mauerstrasse, until 1732 the western border of Friedrichstadt. This formed two triangular sites on which the Böhmische and the Dreifaltigkeitskirche had stood amidst the two- and three-storey buildings since 1735 and 1737 respectively. The priests' houses belonged to the Dreifaltigkeitskirche, which no longer exists. The three residential buildings were built to a uniform plan on a corner plot around a large, planted courtyard. The Schleiermacherhaus at 16 Glinkastrasse was destroyed in 1945. In the courtyard are two reliefs showing the founders of the church in Dorotheenstadt, the Great Elector and Electress Dorothea, by Albert Moritz-Wolff, 1904.

in der Nähe/nearby:
Zürich-Haus; Taubenstraße 4-6
1913-14 • Bielenberg & Moser
Geschäftshaus Patzenhofer; Taubenstraße 10
1906-07 • Hermann Dernburg
Deutsche Bau- und Bodenbank; Taubenstraße 48-49
1928-29 • Hans Jessen
»Club von Berlin«; Jägerstraße 2-3
1892-93 • Kayser & Großheim

B 19 Schauspielhaus
Berlin-Mitte; Gendarmenmarkt 3-4
1818-21 • Karl Friedrich Schinkel

Der Friedrichstädtische Markt, später Gendarmenmarkt genannt, liegt im regelmäßigen Straßenraster der 1688 gegründeten Friedrichstadt. Er besteht aus drei Karrees, von denen jedes mit einem Monumentalgebäude besetzt ist. Seit 1701 standen hier die Französische und die Deutsche Kirche, beide 1780 mit den Gontardschen Türmen ergänzt, und seit 1801 das Nationaltheater von Langhans. Nach dessen Brand errichtete Schinkel hier unter Verwendung von Mauerresten und sechs Portikussäulen das Königliche Schauspielhaus, ein Hauptwerk des romantischen Klassizismus in Berlin. So wie das alte Gebäude liegt das neue Haus in Nord-Süd-Richtung, ist aber von einem erhöhten Mittelbau durchdrungen, welcher Zuschauerraum und Bühne aufnahm und in dem heute der neue große Konzertsaal liegt. Während der Adel einstmals unter der großen Freitreppe vorfuhr, war sie selbst mehr für die bürgerlichen Fußgänger gedacht. Der König dagegen betrat das Haus über eine seitliche Halle.

Friedrichstädtischer Markt, then also called Gendarmenmarkt, is within the regular grid of streets of Friedrichstadt, founded in 1688. It consists of three rectangles, upon each of which a monumental building stands. The French and German churches have stood on the site since 1701, both with towers by Gontard added in 1780. Langhans' National Theatre joined them in 1801. When this burned down, Schinkel built the Königliches Schauspielhaus here, a major work of Romantic classicism in Berlin, using remains of walls and six portico columns. Like the old building the new one is north-south oriented, but has a raised central section running through it which used to contain stage and auditorium and now houses the new concert hall. The nobility used to drive up underneath the great flight of steps which it was intended more for bourgeois pedestrians. The king entered the building through a side hall.

in der Nähe/nearby:
Schillerdenkmal; Gendarmenmarkt
1871 • Reinhold Begas
Hilton-Hotel; Mohrenstraße 24-31
1988-90 • Karl-Heinz Bäthge, Bernd Seidel
Geschäftshaus; Mohrenstraße 22-23
Gegen 1908 • Cremer & Wolffenstein

B 20 Französische Kirche
Berlin-Mitte; Gendarmenmarkt 5
1701; 1780 • Louis Gayard; Karl v. Gontard

Die Französische Kirche wurde für die französisch-reformierte Gemeinde der in der Friedrichstadt angesiedelten Refugés erbaut. Vorbild war die 1685 zerstörte Hauptkirche der Hugenotten im französischen Charenton. Gleichzeitig entstand als Pendant an der Mohrenstraße nach Entwurf von Martin Grünberg die Deutsche Kirche. Friedrich II. veranlaßte 1780 die Umgestaltung des Gendarmenmarktes. Nach Plänen von Gontard erfolgte der Bau von repräsentativen Kuppeltürmen vor beiden Kirchen, wohl nach dem Vorbild der Piazza del Popolo in Rom. Der untere Zentralbau – in Anlehnung an Palladios Villa Rotonda – wird von einem Peripteros bekrönt. Der Bau ist ein letztes Hauptwerk des spätbarocken Klassizismus. Der figürliche Schmuck am Turm entstand nach Zeichnungen von Daniel Chodowiecki. Der Wiederaufbau von Turm und Kirche erfolgte 1978-83 nach Entwürfen von Manfred Prasser, Roland Steiger und Uwe Karl, gleichzeitig wurde das auf 1926 zurückgehende Hugenottenmuseum wiedereröffnet.

The Französische Kirche (French Church) was built for the French-Reformed community of refugees who had settled in Friedrichstadt. It was modelled on the Huguenot mother church in Charenton in France, destroyed in 1685. The Deutsche Kirche (German Church) was built at the same time in Mohrenstrasse to balance it, to designs by Martin Grünberg. In 1780 Frederick II had what was then the Gendarmenmarkt redesigned. Stately domed towers were built in front of both churches to plans by Gontard, probably on the model of the Piazza del Popolo in Rome. The lower centrally-planned building – imitating Palladio's Villa Rotonda – is topped by a peripteros. The building is a last major work of late baroque classicism. The sculptural decoration on the tower was designed by Daniel Chodowiecki. Tower and church were rebuilt from 1978-83 to designs by Manfred Prasser, Roland Steiger and Uwe Karl, and the Huguenot museum, dating from 1926, was reopened at the same time.

in der Nähe/nearby:
Deutsche Kirche; Gendarmenmarkt 2
1701-08 • Martin Grünberg
Handelshaus; Taubenstraße 26
1913-14 • Max Reichhelm & Co.

B 21 Mohrenkolonnaden
Berlin-Mitte; Mohrenstraße 37 b und 40-41
1787 • Carl Gotthard Langhans

Die 1688 vor den Memhardtschen Festungswerken angelegte Friedrichstadt reichte zunächst nur bis zur Mauer- und Zimmerstraße. Mit ihrer Erweiterung und dem Bau der Akzisemauer seit 1732 konnten die Festungswälle abgetragen werden. Die Querstraßen der Friedrichstadt wurden nun über den begradigten Graben geführt und mit dem Straßennetz von Friedrichswerder durch die Oberwall- und die Niederwallstraße verbunden. 1742 entstand so in der Mohrenstraße die erste Brücke und erleichterte den Verkehr und damit auch den Handel zwischen beiden Stadtteilen. Neben den Mohrenkolonnaden gab es noch drei andere dieser Art. Die Königskolonnaden am Alexanderplatz, die im Kleistpark erhalten sind, und die Spittelkolonnaden, deren eine Seite jetzt in der Leipziger Straße steht. Die Kolonnaden auf dem Mühlendamm bestanden bis 1892. Die Kolonnaden in der Mohrenstraße sind die einzigen, die an Ort und Stelle erhalten geblieben sind. Die Plastiken verweisen auf den Reichtum durch Land- und Seehandel und auf vier Erdteile; sie entstanden wohl nach Entwürfen von Christian Bernhard Rode. Das Motiv der Arkaden auf gekuppelten toskanischen Säulen kehrt im Haus Charlottenstraße 54 wieder.

From its foundation in 1688, Friedrichstadt was outside Memhardt's fortifications and originally extended only to Mauer- and Zimmerstrasse. It became possible to remove the fortified ramparts when Friedrichstadt expanded and the excise wall was built from 1732. Friedrichstadt's side streets were now taken across the straightened moat and linked to the Friedrichswerder street network by Oberwall- and Niederwallstrasse. The first bridge was built in Mohrenstrasse in 1742, making traffic and thus trade between the two parts of the town easier. There were three other sets of colonnades other than the Mohrenkolonnaden. The Königskolonnaden in Alexanderplatz, now to be seen in Kleistpark, and the Spittelkolonnaden, one side of which is now in Leipziger Strasse. The Mühlendamm colonnades survived until 1892. The Mohrenstrasse colonnades are the only ones to have survived on their original site. The sculptures refer to the wealth of trade by land and sea, and to the four corners of the earth; they were probably designed by Christian Bernhard Rode. The motif of an arcade on coupled Tuscan columns recurs at 54 Charlottenstrasse.

in der Nähe/nearby:
Konfektionshaus; Hausvogteiplatz 1
1925-26 • Hans Sbrzesny
Geschäftshaus Am Bullenwinkel; Hausvogteiplatz 3-4
1894-95 • Alterthum & Zadek
Haus »Zur Berolina«; Hausvogteiplatz 12
Gegen 1898 • Alterthum & Zadek
St. Joseph-Krankenhaus; Niederwallstraße 8-9
1890-92 • Max Hasak

B 22 Geschäftshaus am »Checkpoint Charlie«
Berlin-Mitte; Friedrichstraße 56
1986-88 • Peter Meyer

Abseits vom Baugeschehen zwischen Platz der Akademie und Leipziger Platz, nicht zufällig unmittelbar am ehemaligen Ausländerübergang »Checkpoint Charlie«, schließt dieses Haus eine Baulücke. Das Haus entstand zwar in der üblichen Montage-Plattenbauweise und folgt teilweise der »Wohnungsbauserie 70«, in der Grundrißlösung und in der Fassadengestaltung weicht es aber auffällig vom typisierten und normierten DDR-Wohnungsbau der siebziger und achtziger Jahre ab. Die beiden unteren Etagen werden traditionell von Läden und Büros genutzt. In den darüberliegenden sechs Geschossen ordnete Meyer 24 Zwei- und Vierraumwohnungen mit sechs Meter breiten Loggien und kleinen Wintergärten an. Die quadratisch geteilten Glasflächen orientieren sich an Motiven der Nachbargebäude. Hof- wie Straßenfassade sind gleichermaßen durchgebildet. Zum Gelb der Großplatten steht das Blau der Wintergärten und Zimmerfenster und das Rot der Stahlgeländer in frischem Kontrast. Die mittige Treppenhauspartie in der Straße nimmt Bezug auf das Erkermotiv des Nachbarhauses, ist auch asymmetrisch strukturiert und in seinen Teilen ausgewogen wie eine griechische Plastik.

This building closes a gap away from all the construction work between Platz der Akademie and Leipziger Platz, not unintentionally close to the former «Checkpoint Charlie» crossing point for foreigners. It was built by the usual slab erection method, and partially follows «residential building series 70», but in ground plan and façade design it is strikingly different from standardized, stylized GDR residential building of the seventies and eighties in that it shows individual architectural features. The two lower storeys are used in the traditional way for shops and offices. Meyer put 24 one- and three-bedroom flats with six metre wide loggias and small conservatories in the upper six storeys. The square areas of glass echo motifs from neighbouring buildings. The yellow of the large slabs forms a lively contrast with the blue of the conservatories and room windows and the red of the steel railings. The central staircase section in the street relates to the bay window in the adjoining building, and is also asymmetrically structured and balanced in its sections like a Greek sculpture.

in der Nähe/nearby:
Geschäftshaus Mädler; Friedrichstraße 58
1908-09 • Robert Leibnitz
1987-89 • Gerd Pieper, Wolf-Dieter Halbach
Geschäftshaus Kersten & Tuteur; Leipziger Straße 36
1912-13 • Hermann Muthesius
Geschäftshaus; Krausenstraße 9-10
1908 • Salinger & Schmohl

B 23 Mossehaus
Berlin-Mitte; Schützenstraße 18-25
1901-03 • Cremer & Wolffenstein
1921-22 • Erich Mendelsohn und Richard Neutra
1992-93 • Peter Kolb, Bernd Kemper, Dieter Schneider

Rudolf Mosse, Berliner Zeitungsmagnat, der schon 1867 eine erfolgreiche Annoncenexpedition gegründet hatte und in dessen Verlag unter anderen das Berliner Tageblatt erschien, leitete hier, in der Friedrichstadt, seinen Konzern. Der deutlich konservativ gehaltene erste Bau von Cremer & Wolffenstein erlitt während der Revolution an der Hausecke arge Blessuren. Der Wiederaufbau sollte zugleich eine Erweiterung werden. Mit ihr wurde Mendelsohn betraut, der die Aufgabe nun avantgardistisch löste. Wie die überdimensionale Kühlerfigur eines windschnittigen Sportwagens pfropfte er dem starren Altbau die neue Ecke auf. Wie Chromleisten laufen die Gesimse zwischen den Fensterbändern, und zackige Abrißkanten unterstreichen die dynamische Architektur in ihrer perspektivischen Dehnung. Verkehr, Geschwindigkeit und pulsierendes Leben waren Mendelsohn Vorbilder für seine Großstadtarchitektur, wie viele seiner elegant hingeworfenen Entwurfsskizzen gleichsam Fahrtwind andeutende Schattenstriche enthalten. Der Zweite Weltkrieg hat dem Mossehaus übel mitgespielt. Heute, fünfzig Jahre später, wird der Bau als Keimzelle eines neuen Verlagszentrums denkmalpflegerisch wiederhergestellt, nur auf die verlorengegangene Ostfassade von 1903 wird zugunsten eines neutralen Überganges zum Neubau verzichtet.

The Berlin newspaper tycoon Rudolf Mosse, who had founded a highly successful dispatch office for small advertising in 1867 and who published, among other papers, the Berliner Tageblatt, directed his empire from this headquarters here in the Friedrichstadt. During the Revolution, the highly conventional original building by Cremer & Wolffenstein suffered substantial damage at the corner. When the building was reconstructed, it was expanded at the same time. The commission was given to Mendelsohn who presented a more avant-garde solution, grafting onto the rigid old structure a new corner resembling the over-sized hood ornament of a streamlined sports-car. Like so many chrome mouldings, the cornices are run between the strip windows, and jagged edges serve to emphasize the dynamic architecture which appears elongated in perspective. Traffic, speed and pulsing life provided the models for Mendelsohn's urban architecture, and many of his elegantly executed sketches are marked by lines of shadows which seem to indicate the power of the airstream, as it were. During World War II the Mossehaus suffered heavy damages. Today, fifty years later, the building is being reconstructed by conservationists as the germ cell of a new publishing district, sacrificing only the no longer extant former east façade of 1903 in order to achieve a neutral transition to the new structure.

B 24 Mossezentrum (Neubau)
Berlin-Mitte; Zimmerstraße 54-65, Jerusalemer Straße 48-51, Schützenstraße 15-17
1993-95 • Jürgen Fissler und Hans-Christof Ernst

Für das »Druckhaus Berlin Mitte« entsteht auf dem einstigen Mauerstreifen und ausgehend vom wiederhergestellten legendären Mossehaus ein neuer Bürohauskomplex mit Tiefgaragen. Städtebaulich orientiert sich der Neubau an der ursprünglichen Blockbebauung mit taktvoller Traufhöhe. Das mag zu einer Beruhigung des in den Nachkriegsjahren auf beiden Seiten der Mauer leichtsinnig zerstörten Stadtgrundrisses und Straßenrasters der Friedrichstadt führen. Formal enthält sich der Neubau neben der dominierenden Mendelsohn-Ecke bewußt jeder auftrumpfenden Geste. Vielmehr bezieht er sich auf traditionell vertraute und bewährte Gestaltungsmuster. Der zweigeschossigen Ladenzone als Sockel folgt die breite Obergeschoßzone, abgeschlossen durch das eigenständige Band des obersten Stockwerkes. Das ist der Fassadenrhythmus des Berliner Geschäftshauses. Fensterbänder lassen die zwanziger Jahre anklingen. Aus der Front vorgewölbte Portalachsen vermitteln Reminiszenzen an Mendelsohn, der dieses Motiv im Vorprojekt zu den Woga-Bauten am Kurfürstendamm bzw. in den Hoffronten seiner Wohnhäuser in der Cicerostraße verwendete.

In conjunction with the restoration of the legendary Mossehaus, a new office complex with underground parking is being built on the former site of the Wall. It will house the «Druckhaus Berlin Mitte». In terms of urban design, the new structure takes conforms with the original block development of moderate eaves height. This may help to recompose the old urban framework and grid of streets of the Friedrichstadt that was so carelessly destroyed on both sides of the Wall after the War. The formal expression of the new structure is intentionally modest and unspectacular vis-à-vis the dominating corner designed by Mendelsohn, relying instead on familiar and traditional patterns and elements. Above the two storeys of shopping which form the base of the building, the broad upper storey is crowned by the independent ribbon of the top floor. This is the typical formal rhythm of Berlin commercial building façades. The strip windows evoke memories of 1920s architecture. The convex projections above the portals are reminiscent of Mendelsohn who employed this motif in the early projects for the Woga buildings on Kurfürstendamm and also in the court façades of his residential buildings in Cicerostrasse.

in der Nähe/nearby:
Geschäftshaus Wolf; Krausenstraße 17-18, Schützenstraße 65-66
1907-09 • Friedrich Kristeller
Geschäftshaus Piesbergen; Krausenstraße 19-20
1910-11 • Nentwich & Simon
Geschäftshaus Tischbein & Mendel; B-Kreuzberg; Lindenstraße 44-47
1908-09 • Hans Bernoulli

B 25 Redaktionsgebäude der »taz«
Berlin-Kreuzberg; Kochstraße 19
1990-91 • Gerhard Spangenberg

Ein Zeitungsgebäude für das Zeitungsviertel, das war die Aufgabe. Vorbild war das Geschäftshaus der Jahrhundertwende, das einst das Viertel geprägt hatte; ein Vertreter dieses Bautyps stand als Nachbar da und wurde bereits von der Redaktion genutzt. Wesentliches Gestaltungsmittel wurden die Balkone; sie sind in der verkehrsreichen Straße kaum funktional, jedoch ästhetisch zu verstehen, sie leiten nämlich geschickt zur ostwärts zurückspringenden Bauflucht aus einer veralteten Schnellstraßenplanung über. Die Übersetzung formaler Elemente ins Moderne erfolgte nicht planmäßig. Die einen fühlen sich an den sowjetischen Konstruktivismus der zwanziger Jahre erinnert, andere an die dynamische Architektur Erich Mendelsohns, der 1921 in der Nähe für Mosse ein Zeitungshaus gestaltet hatte. Wozu Spangenberg sich bekennt, ist die Umsetzung des Zeitungs-Ideals in die architektonische Sprache: Transparenz. Die ruppige, und doch fragile Fassade ist ebenso als Gleichnis zu sehen wie die Sparsamkeit, mit der hier Klarheit dargestellt wird.

The brief called for a newspaper building in this newspaper district. It was to be modeled on the commercial buildings built around the turn of the century which once dominated this part of town. A traditional building of this kind immediately adjoining the site was already being used by the newspaper. An essential element of design were the balconies which, although perhaps not quite functional in view of this busy street, serve an aesthetic purpose by cleverly providing a transition to the set-back in the street alignment which was the result of earlier, long-abandoned plans for an expressway. The translation of formal elements into modern architecture is anything but consistent. Some observers are reminded of the Soviet Constructivism of the nineteen-twenties, while others have noted a certain similarity with the dynamic architecture of Erich Mendelsohn who designed another newspaper building for Mosse not far from here in 1921. Spangenberg makes a conscious effort to translate the newspaper ideal into the language of architecture, thus creating transparency. Like the economy which is used here to achieve clarity, the rude and at the same time fragile façade must be seen as a kind of allegory.

in der Nähe/nearby:
Geschäftshaus; Kochstraße 18
1906

B 26 Springerhaus
Berlin-Kreuzberg; Kochstraße 50
1959-66 • Bega & Franzi, Sobotka & Müller

Nahe dem alten Berliner Zeitungsviertel setzte der Verleger der Bild-Zeitung hier ein durchaus politisch zu verstehendes Signal. Wenn der Bau der »Mauer« 1961 auch die Wirtschaftlichkeit eines solchen Verlagshausriesen plötzlich in Frage stellte, wurde er deshalb doch vollendet. Jenseits der Grenze, wo derzeit noch weite Teile des Bezirks Mitte Nachkriegsbrache waren, verstellte nichts den Blick auf das neue Hochhaus. Erst ein Jahrzehnt später folgte im Sinne des »kalten Architektur-Krieges« die Antwort in Form der Hochhauskette in der Leipziger Straße. Als Bauwerk reiht sich das Springerhaus ein in die Büro- und Geschäftshäuser der sechziger Jahre, die mit ihren Skelettkonstruktionen und verglasten Vorhangfassaden, mit Hochhausscheiben über Flachbautrakten und mit dem stets zitierten Attribut »Dominante« doch eine Uniformität nicht verleugnen können.

The publisher of Bild-Zeitung put out a signal with clear political significance near the old Berlin newspaper quarter. When the building of the «Wall» in 1961 made the viability of a giant publishing building on this site suddenly questionable, Springer still went ahead. On the other side of the border, where large areas of the Mitte district were still a post-war desert, there was nothing to block the view of the new high-rise building. It was not until a decade later that the answer came, in the spirit of the «cold architecture war» and in the form of the chain of high-rise buildings in Leipziger Strasse. The Springer building is typical of sixties office and commercial building: skeleton structure and glazed curtain façades, with high-rise sections above a lower tract, cannot deny the charge of uniformity, despite the attribute of a «dominant factor» that is always cited.

in der Nähe/nearby:
Wohnhaus; Kochstraße 59
1984-85 • Hans Kammerer, Walter Belz, Klaus Kucher
Wohn- und Geschäftshaus; Kochstraße 62-63
1985-86 • Peter Eisenman, Jaquelin Robertson
Wohnhaus am Checkpoint C; Friedrichstraße 207-208
1987-90 • Elia Zenghelis, Rem Koolhaas, Mathias Sauerbruch (Office for Metropolitan Architecture)
Landesarbeitsamt; Friedrichstraße 34-37 a
1940 • Hans Fritsche
Wohn- und Geschäftshaus; Friedrichstraße 32-33
1986-87 • Raimund Abraham
Wohnhäuser und Atelierturm; Charlottenstraße 96-98
1986-88 • John Hejduk, Moritz Müller

B 27 Reichsschuldenverwaltung
Berlin-Kreuzberg; Oranienstraße 106-109
1919-24 • German Bestelmeyer

Daß die Reichsschuldenverwaltung ausgerechnet in den Inflationsjahren einen repräsentativen Neubau errichtete, mag verwundern oder nicht. Bestelmeyers Honorarprofessur im Fache Theologie ist jedenfalls eine weitere Merkwürdigkeit. Doch beides tritt in den Hintergrund angesichts der wohlgelungenen architektonischen und städtebaulichen Leistung. Mit einer Rundung bewältigt Bestelmeyer den spitzen Winkel zwischen Oranienstraße und Alter Jakobstraße. Monumentalität verleiht er den Fronten allein durch die Reihung der Wandpfeiler, die im auskragenden Hauptgesims einen zwingenden Abschluß finden – das fand sich so schon bei Messel oder Behrens. Anderthalb Jahrzehnte später lebt dieser Formenkanon nochmals in der nahen Möckernstraße beim Briefverteilamt SW 11 auf. Ähnlichkeiten mit Hamburger Kontorhäusern fallen auf, das machen auch die roten Ziegelflächen und die reliefartig verwandten Spitzgiebelverdachungen über den Erdgeschoßfenstern. Fast alles am Hause wirkt konventionell, norddeutsch-reserviert, nichts drängt sich auf, sieht man von Hugo Lederers Terracotta-Skulpturen ab.

It may or may not be surprising that the Imperial Debt Administration service was given a striking new building in the years of massive inflation. Bestelmeyer's honorary professorship in theology is another oddity. But both fade into the background in the face of this enormously successful architectural and town planning achievement. The rounded end enables Bestelmeyer to manage the acute angle between Oranienstrasse and Alte Jakobstrasse. He gives a monumental quality to the façades simply by the arrangement of the pilasters, compellingly concluded in the projecting cornice – that is the sort of thing that Messel and Behrens did. Fifteen years later this formal canon found a new lease of life in the SW 11 Postal Sorting Office in nearby Möckernstrasse. There are similarities with office buildings in Hamburg, emphasized by the red brick surfaces and the relief-like related pointed gable roofings of the ground floor windows. Almost everything about the building is north German and conservative, nothing forces itself upon the attention, with the exception of Hugo Lederer's terra-cotta carvings.

in der Nähe/nearby:
Bundesdruckerei; Oranienstraße 90-96
1956-82 • Prosper Lemoine, Eberhard Kobe u.a.m.

B 28 St. Jacobi
Berlin-Kreuzberg; Oranienstraße 132-134
1844-45 • Friedrich August Stüler

Italien in Kreuzberg – romantische Architektur in einem durch und durch unromantischen Gewerbe-, Arbeits- und Wohnviertel zwischen Friedrich- und Luisenstadt. Mit ihren flach geneigten Dächern atmet die Basilika südliche Leichtigkeit, der zarte Campanile aus gelben Ziegeln läßt vergeblich nach dem Ruf der Zikaden lauschen. Seit 1857-59 und 1865-66 rahmen ein Pfarr- und ein Predigerhaus den Hof vor der zurückgesetzten Kirche ein, bilden mit Arkaden den schattigen Kreuzgang in einer Zeit, die bald durch Krieg, Gründerjahre und Industrialisierung aus jeder Italiensehnsucht herausgerissen wird. 1979-82 fügten Dieter Frowein und Gerhard Spangenberg der Anlage zwei Pfarrhäuser hinzu. Behutsam nahmen sie Maß und Gestalt der Kirche auf, ohne in gedankenlosen Historismus zu verfallen. Die Pfarrhäuser stehen am architektonischen Neuanfang dieses durch städtebauliche Sünden der fünfziger und sechziger Jahre geschundenen Stadtbezirks.

Italy in Kreuzberg – romantic architecture in an utterly unromantic trade, working and residential area between Friedrich- and Luisenstadt. The shallow sloping roofs make the basilica breathe southern lightness, the delicate yellow brick campanile makes one listen in vain for the rustle of cicadas. From 1857-9 and 1865-6 a parish and a preacher's house framed the courtyard in front of the church, which is set back from the street; their arcades joined to form a shady cloister at a time that was about to be rudely awakened from any longing for Italy by war, rapid expansion in the late nineteenth century and industrialization. From 1979-82 Dieter Frowein and Gerhard Spangenberg added two houses for the clergy to the complex. They carefully accepted scale and shape of the church, without lapsing into mindless historicism. These houses signalled a new architectural beginning for a district that had suffered so wretchedly from the town planning sins of the fifties and sixties.

in der Nähe/nearby:
Springsiedlung; Alexandrinenstraße 115-124
1959-62 u. 1966-67 • Wils Ebert
St. Agnes; Alexandrinenstraße 118-121
1964-66 • Werner Düttmann

B 29 Wohnpark Ritterstraße
Berlin-Kreuzberg; Ritterstraße 63-64
1979-81 • Rob Krier

Die Versachlichung der Architektur und die ästhetische Bedürfnislosigkeit des Wohnungsbaus zwischen Nachkriegszeit und siebziger Jahren hatte mit den großen Trabantenstädten endgültig offenen Widerstand provoziert. Zudem war die stadträumliche Reparatur alter Wohnviertel schmählich vernachlässigt worden. Rob Kriers Häuser an der Ritterstraße mußten deshalb gefallen. Die städtebauliche Referenz an die traditionelle Blockbebauung verband sich mit einer Architektur zum Hinsehen und einem Wohnen als Erlebnis. Ein gewölbter Durchgang öffnet den Innenhof, der sich auch nicht zu verstecken braucht. Plastischer Schmuck belebt die Baugruppe, die an sich bereits plastisch in ihren Elementen geformt und in eigenständige Glieder individueller Prägung geschieden ist. Damit findet Krier Anschluß an die große Zeit des Wohnungsbaus in den zwanziger Jahren.

Objectification of architecture and the modest aesthetic demands made by residential building between the post-war period and the seventies finally produced open resistance when it came to large satellite towns. Additionally, repair and renewal of older residential areas had been shamefully neglected. It was thus no surprise that Rob Krier's buildings in Ritterstrasse met with approval. Reference in urban planning terms to traditional block development was combined with architecture intended to be looked at, and living as an experience. A vaulted passageway leads into the courtyard, and this certainly has no need to hide coyly away. The group of buildings is enlivened with sculptural decoration, indeed the elements of the group are shaped sculpturally and divided into individual sections, each bearing an individual stamp. In this way Krier finds a link with the great residential building period of the twenties.

in der Nähe/nearby:
Wohnhäuser; Ritterstraße 62 u. 65, Lindenstraße 28
1979-81 • Horst Hielscher, Georg-Peter Mügge
Wohnhäuser; Ritterstraße 61 u. 66, Lindenstraße 26-27
1979-81 • Gruppe 67
Wohnhäuser; Alte Jakobstraße 122-123, Lindenstraße 29
1979-81 • Planungskollektiv Nr. 1
Wohnanlage Ritterstraße-Nord; Ritterstraße 55-60 b, Lindenstraße 30-31 u. 36-37, Alte Jakobstraße 120 a-121, Feilnerstraße 1-4 u. 7-15, Oranienstraße 99-105
1982-83, 1986-88 • Rob Krier; Dietrich Bangert, Bernd Jansen, Stefan Scholz, Axel Schultes; Axel Liepe, Hartmut Steigelmann, Andreas Brandt, Thomas Heiß; Feddersen, Herder & Partner; Ganz & Rolfes; Müller, Rhode & Partner

B 30 Viktoria-Versicherung
Berlin-Kreuzberg; Lindenstraße 20-25
1906-13 • Wilhelm Walther

Einen ersten Bau für die Viktoria errichtete Walther bereits 1902-04 in der Alten Jakobstraße, er fiel dem Krieg zum Opfer. Zusammen mit dem erhaltenen Erweiterungsbau durchgehend zur Lindenstraße war dann kurz vor dem Weltkrieg ein Komplex entstanden, der mit zwölf Innenhöfen und einer 130 m langen Monumentalfront als typischer Vertreter einer schreienden architektonischen Repräsentationssucht in einem chauvinistischen Klima kaiserzeitlicher Kraftprotzerei gelten kann. Wilhelm Walther war nicht der Architekt, der sich grundsätzlich Reformgedanken hingegeben oder frei einer beginnenden Moderne zugewendet hätte. Sein Metier war die Übersteigerung des eigentlich schon überwundenen Historismus des ausgehenden 19. Jahrhunderts ins Komisch-Kolossale. Ein konservativer Bauherr war sicher die Voraussetzung für diese Haltung.

Walther built his first building for the Viktoria insurance company in Alte Jakobstrasse in 1902-4, but it was destroyed by war. Then, shortly before the World War, a complex was built to include the surviving extension through to Lindenstrasse. It had twelve courtyards and a monumental façade 130 m long, and can be considered a typical specimen of blatant architectural megalomania in the chauvinistic climate of imperial sabre-rattling. Wilhelm Walther was not an architect to embrace fundamentally reformist thinking or to turn to the modern movement, which was just beginning, of his own free will. His métier was trying to push late nineteenth century historicism, actually already a thing of the past, into the realms of the cosmic and the colossal, an approach for which a conservative client was essential.

in der Nähe/nearby:
Wohnhaus; Lindenstraße 79-80
1979-81 • Hans Heidenreich, Michael Polensky, Reinhard Vogel, Helmut Zeumer
Wohnhof; Lindenstraße 81-84
1984-86 • Herman Hertzberger

B 31 Kollegienhaus (Berlin-Museum)
Berlin-Kreuzberg; Lindenstraße 14
1734-35 • Philipp Gerlach

Das königliche Kollegienhaus, Sitz der Regierungsbehörden und auch des Kammergerichts, ist das erste Verwaltungsgebäude, das in Berlin entstand. Gerlach, der Architekt der Potsdamer Garnisonkirche und Planer der südlichen Friedrichstadt, hatte vom König und seinem Kanzler Samuel v. Cocceji hierzu den Auftrag erhalten. Die allegorischen Figuren der Gerechtigkeit und der Barmherzigkeit auf dem Giebelfeld künden noch von der Bedeutung des Hauses. Hier taten schon E. T. A. Hoffmann und Willibald Alexis ihren Dienst. Vor der ausgewogenen Barockfassade führt eine symmetrische Rampe zum Portal, ein Merkmal, das in Berlin den Bautypus der Palais bestimmte. Ähnlichkeiten mit dem ebenfalls von Gerlach umgebauten Kronprinzenpalais fallen auf, deuten aber auch eine architektonische Entwicklung in Preußen an, die sich zunehmend von ausländischen Vorbildern löst. Seit 1969 beherbergt das nach Kriegsschäden wiederhergestellte Gerichtsgebäude das Berlin-Museum, das auf westlicher Seite die Tradition des Märkischen Museums mit einer breit angelegten Sammlung zur Geschichte und zum Leben in Berlin fortführen sollte.

The royal Kollegienhaus, seat of government departments and also the supreme court, was the first administrative building to emerge in Berlin. Gerlach, architect of the Garnisonkirche in Potsdam and planner of southern Friedrichstadt, was commissioned by the king and his chancellor Samuel v. Cocceji. The allegorical figures of Justice and Mercy over the pediment are further evidence of the importance of the building. E.T.A. Hoffmann and Willibald Alexis performed their duties here. In front of the balanced baroque façade a symmetrical ramp leads to the portal, a typical Berlin palace feature. There are striking similarities with the Kronprinzenpalais, also rebuilt by Gerlach, but they also indicate that Prussia was increasingly detaching itself from foreign architectural models. The building was restored after war damage and since 1969 has housed the Berlin-Museum, intended to continue the tradition of the Märkisches Museum on the western side, with a broadly based collection devoted to history and life in Berlin.

in der Nähe/nearby:
Wohnpark am Berlin-Museum; Lindenstraße 15-19, Alte Jakobstraße 129-136
1984-86 • Hans Kollhoff, Arthur Ovaska; Franz C. Demblin; Dieter Frowein, Gerhard Spangenberg; Horst Hielscher, Georg Peter Mügge; Arata Isozaki; Jochem Jourdan, Bernhard Müller, Sven Albrecht; Werner Kreis, Peter Schaad, Ulrich Schaad; John Eisler, Emil Prikryl, Jiri Suchomel

B 32 Jüdisches Museum
Berlin-Kreuzberg; Lindenstraße 13
1993-95 • Daniel Libeskind

Berliner Geschichte ist ohne die Berliner Juden nicht denkbar, ihr beträchtlicher Anteil an Kultur und Geistesleben offenkundig. Diese Verwobenheit zu zeigen neben der eigenen jüdischen Welt, ist Aufgabe dieses Museums, welches neben und eng verbunden mit dem Berlin-Museum bestehen muß. Liebeskind nannte das Projekt »Zwischen den Linien« –, er sah darin zwei Strömungen von Gedanken und Beziehungen: eine gerade, aber in Fragmente zersplitterte und eine gewundene, unendliche. Dazwischen definiert er architektonisch und programmatisch die Folge von Raum und Leere. Den Ursprung sucht er im Irrationalen. Der Entwurf ist voller Gleichnisse. So führt Libeskind die Matrix der Dreiecke auf das Muster eines komprimierten und verzerrten Sternes zurück. Aber auch andere Gedanken flossen in die Gestaltung ein: Arnold Schönbergs unvollendete Oper »Moses und Aron«, das »Gedenkbuch« mit den Namen der deportierten Berliner und auch Walter Benjamins städtische Apokalypse entlang der »Einbahnstraße«. Innen werden die Brüche zwischen Logik und Realität der gesellschaftlichen Integration von Menschen anderer Religion und Abstammung, wie sie gerade angesichts der Tradition des aufgeklärten Preußen außer Frage stehen müßte, zum architektonischen Motiv. »Voids«, den Raum verstellende Wände, versinnbildlichen diese Brüche. Die Fülle der Gedanken, die sich hier nicht nur dem Architekten aufdrängen, muß auch bei allen späteren Besuchern zur lebhaften Auseinandersetzung mit Thema und Gebäude führen.

The history of Berlin would be nothing if not for the Berlin Jews; their contribution to cultural and intellectual life is considerable. To demonstrate this close interweaving as well as the characteristic features of Jewish life is the task of this museum which is closely connected to the neighbouring Berlin Museum. Libeskind called his project «Between the Lines», seeing it as a combination of two flows of thoughts and relations: one straightforward, although broken up into fragments, the other winding and endless. It is between the two that he programmatically and architecturally defines the sequence of space and voids. For him, the original source lies in the irrational. His design is full of allegories. For example, the matrix of triangles is traced back by Libeskind to the pattern of a compressed and distorted star. Other ideas also entered into the design, from Arnold Schönberg's unfinished opera »Moses and Aaron« to the «Book of Remembrance» with the names of those Berliners who were deported, to Walter Benjamin's urban apocalypse down the »One-Way Street«. Inside the museum, the ruptures between logic and reality of the social integration of people of different religion and descent – something that should be taken for granted considering the traditions of enlightened Prussia – are turned into an architectural motif. «Voids», walls which block and obscure the space, are used to symbolize these ruptures. The wealth of ideas and associations which flood not only the architect himself will certainly cause future visitors of the museum to enter into a lively debate with the subject-matter as well as the building.

B 33 Deutscher Metallarbeiter-Verband
Berlin-Kreuzberg; Alte Jakobstraße 148-155
1929-30 • Erich Mendelsohn

Es ist die Übersetzung des expressionistischen Hamburger Chilehauses in die Formensprache der Neuen Sachlichkeit, die zu dieser nicht minder genialen Architektur führte. Das Expressive ist geblieben, der Ausruf in den Straßenraum hinein: »Hier stehe ich!« Das Dynamische der Schiffsarchitektur ist geblieben, nicht mehr Bug, aber Kommandobrücke mit vorgehaltenem Fahnenmast. Alles, was die Neue Sachlichkeit der Jahre 1928/30 ausmacht, ist in diesem Gebäude vereinigt und zur Formvollendung gebracht: die stereometrische Blockhaftigkeit, die abstrakte Wandfläche, die knappe Kante, das betont Horizontale, das Material von Glas, Metall und Travertin. Das Gewerkschaftshaus steht mit dem untergegangenen Columbushaus am Potsdamer Platz am Ende einer Reihe von Großbauten Mendelsohns in Berlin. Der tödlichen Bedrohung wich Mendelsohn 1933 aus und emigrierte, mit ihm verließ einer der eigenwilligsten und genialsten Architekten des Jahrhunderts das Land.

The translation of the Expressionist Chilehaus in Hamburg into the formal language of Neue Sachlichkeit led to this equally dazzling piece of architecture. Expressive features have been retained, and the building still shouts «Here I am!» into the street. The dynamic element derived from marine architecture is still here, this time not the bow of a ship, but the bridge with flagstaff in front of it. Everything that was involved in Neue Sachklichkeit from 1928-30 is united in this building and brought to formal perfection: a stereometric block-like quality, abstract wall surfaces, thin edges, emphasis on the horizontal, and materials like glass, metal and travertine. The metal-workers' union building and the Columbushaus, which was destroyed, on Potsdamer Platz, were the last of a series of major buildings by Mendelsohn in Berlin. Mendelsohn gave way to death threats in 1933 and emigrated; the country lost one of the most original and brilliant architects of the century.

in der Nähe/nearby:
Patentamt; Gitschiner Straße 97-103
1903-05 • Solf & Wichards
Wohnbauten; Mehringplatz
1968-75 • Werner Düttmann
Amerika-Gedenkbibliothek; Blücherplatz 1
1951-53 • Gerhard Jobst, Willy Kreuer, Fritz Bornemann, Hartmut Wille
Kirche zum Heiligen Kreuz; Blücherstraße
1885-88 • Johannes Otzen

B 34 Hebbeltheater
Berlin-Kreuzberg; Stresemannstraße 29
1907-08 • Oskar Kaufmann

Kaufmann ist eine schillernde Gestalt deutscher und Berliner Theaterbaukunst. Eugen Robert, der erste Direktor des Hebbeltheaters, hatte aus einer Laune heraus dem bis dahin glücklosen jungen Architekten den Auftrag erteilt. Kaufmann erntete Kopfschütteln und Begeisterung zugleich. An Aufträgen fehlte es ihm aber fortan nicht mehr. Das Hebbeltheater nimmt mit seinen teigigen Konturen Elemente des Jugendstils auf, die rauhe Quaderung der Front folgt dem teutonischen Stil der damals in Mode geratenen Nationaldenkmale – man denke etwa an das Leipziger Völkerschlachtdenkmal –, und es zeigt beispielsweise in den Okuli Merkmale des Rokoko. Diese Mischung aus dramatischer Architekturinszenierung außen und intim-verspielter Innengestaltung behält Kaufmann bei all seinen Theaterbauten bis in die späten zwanziger Jahre bei. Das Hebbeltheater ist der letzte dieser Kaufmann-Bauten, der unzerstört und ohne verändernde Umbauten bis heute erhalten blieb.

Kaufmann is an enigmatic figure in the theatre, in Germany and in Berlin. Eugen Robert, the first director of the Hebbeltheater, gave the hitherto hapless young architect the contract on a whim. Kaufmann's reward was a mixture of headshaking and a great deal of enthusiasm. He had no lack of contracts after this. The doughy contours of the Hebbeltheater adopt some elements of Jugendstil, and the rough ashlar rectangles of the façade follow the Teutonic style of national monuments that had become fashionable at the time – like the Leipzig Battle of the Nations monument – and there are also rococo features, the oculi, for example. This mixture of architectural drama outside and an intimate and playful interior was retained by Kaufmann in all his theatres down to the late twenties. The Hebbeltheater is the last of these buildings by Kaufmann to have survived undamaged and unaltered to the present day.

in der Nähe/nearby:
Grund- und Sonderschule; Friedrichstraße 13
1988-90 • Gino Valle, Mario Broggi, Michael Burckhardt
Postgiroamt; Hallesches Ufer 40-60
1965-71 • Prosper Lemoine
Wohn- und Geschäftshaus; Hallesches Ufer 24-28
1968-70 • Hermann Fehling, Daniel Gogel

B 35 Anhalter Bahnhof
Berlin-Kreuzberg; Askanischer Platz 6-7
1876-80 • Franz Schwechten

Schwechtens Anhalter Bahnhof gehörte architektonisch zu den bemerkenswerten Schöpfungen des Berliner Rundbogenstils, konnte aber auch in den großen Segmentbogen-Doppelbindern eine beachtliche Ingenieurleistung aufweisen. Als Kopfbahnhof mit sechs Gleisen ist der Anhalter Bahnhof gemessen an den späteren großen Hallen in Köln, Hamburg oder Leipzig eher bescheiden gewesen. Da aber die Größe Berlins es verhinderte, daß für die zwölf sternförmig auf die Stadt zulaufenden Bahnlinien eine geeignete Streckenverlegung gefunden wurde, welche die Einfädelung in einen gemeinsamen Hauptbahnhof erlaubt hätte, blieb es bei der Vielzahl kleinerer Bahnhöfe. Dem Reisenden war dies kaum lästig, da er das Umsteigen gerne zum Anlaß für eine Übernachtung in der Hauptstadt nahm. Im Zweiten Weltkrieg wurde der Bahnhof beschädigt, die politische Abriegelung West-Berlins führte dann 1952 zur Stillegung, 1959/60 folgten trotz vieler Proteste Sprengung und Abbruch. Erhalten blieb der Portikus, heute Reliquie eines verspäteten denkmalpflegerischen Verständnisses.

Schwechten's Anhalter Bahnhof was architecturally one of the most remarkable creations of the Berlin round-arched style, but the great double-truss segmental arch also represents a considerable engineering achievement. The Anhalt station was a terminus with six platforms, modest in comparison with the great halls in Cologne, Hamburg or Leipzig. But as the size of Berlin prevented the twelve lines running into Berlin in the shape of a star to swing round and terminate in a common central station, it was necessary to use a large number of smaller stations. This was scarcely a problem for travellers: they enjoyed using the change as an opportunity to spend a night in the capital. The station was damaged in the Second World War, then closed in 1952 as a result of Berlin's political isolation, and it was blown up and pulled down, despite much protest, in 1959/60. The portico survived, a gesture towards understanding the necessity to preserve monuments, unfortunately rather a belated one.

in der Nähe/nearby:
Briefabfertigungsamt SW 11; Möckernstraße 135-138
1933-36 • Werner, Kurt Kuhlow
Abwasser-Pumpwerk; Hallesches Ufer 78
1873-76 • James Hobrecht
Schule am Anhalter Park; Schöneberger Straße 21-34
1988-90 • Wolfgang Scharlach, Rainer Wischhusen

B 36 Kunstgewerbemuseum (Martin-Gropius-Bau)
Berlin-Kreuzberg; Stresemannstraße 110
1877-81 • Martin Gropius, Heino Schmieden

Überdeutlich war hier Schinkels vier Jahrzehnte zuvor errichtete Bauakademie Vorbild: die quadratische Baukörperverteilung, die horizontale Schichtung, die Proportionen der gereihten Fenster und der Bauschmuck. Doch stärker leben nun Elemente italienischer Renaissance auf, die der Idee des Palazzos entspringen. Nach dem Kriege ruinös und seit 1961 in bedrängender Randlage, kam der Wiederaufbau erst 1979 in Gang. Winnetou Kampmann und Ute Weström nahmen ihre Aufgabe recht frei wahr, manches geriet üppiger als ursprünglich, doch beim Publikum kam es an. Heute dient das Haus vorrangig wechselnden Ausstellungen. Die Verlegung des Haupteinganges auf die Südseite war eine Konsequenz der nördlich einst dicht vorbeiführenden »Mauer«.

It is more than clear that the model here was Schinkel's Bauakademie, built four decades earlier: the square shape of the building, horizontal layering, the proportions of the rows of windows and the decorative features. But now Italian Renaissance elements start to make their presence more strongly felt, derived from the idea of the palazzo. The building was in ruins after the war, and from 1961 in a dire position on the fringe, and so rebuilding did not start until 1979. Winnetou Kampmann and Ute Weström interpreted their task very freely, and many features turned out more lavish than the original, but the public liked it. The building is used mainly for temporary exhibitions. The main entrance was moved to the southern side because the «Wall» used to be very close to the northern side.

in der Nähe/nearby:
Wohnhäuser; Köthener Straße 39-43
1984-85 • Hans-Christian Müller
Wohnhäuser mit Pflanzenkläranlage; Bernburger Straße 22-23 und 26, Dessauer Straße 9-17
1985-87 • Jan Rave, Rolf Rave; Borck, Boye & Schaefer; Christoph Langhof; Grötzebach, Plessow & Ehlers
Wohnhäuser; Dessauer Straße 30-31
1986-87 • Klaus Effenberger
Lukaskirche; Bernburger Straße 3-5
1859-61 • Gustav Möller
Wohn- und Geschäftshäuser; Kochstraße 1-4
1986-88 • Aldo Rossi, Gianni Braghieri
Wohn- und Geschäftshäuser; Kochstraße 67-74
1986-92 • Josep Martorell, Oriol Bohigas, David Mackay (Torhäuser); Christian Muschalek, Jörg Pampe, Hermann Schröder, Peter Faller (Zwischenzeilen)
Gartenhaus; Kochstraße 65
1986-92 • Josep Martorell, Oriol Bohigas, David Mackay
Wohnhäuser; Wilhelmstraße 119-120
1986-88 • Dietrich v. Beulwitz, Pietro Derossi

B 37 Preußischer Landtag (Abgeordnetenhaus von Berlin)
Berlin-Mitte; Niederkirchnerstraße 3-5
1892-98 • Friedrich Schulze
1991-93 • Rolf Rave, Jan Rave und Marina Stankovic

Seit 1850 ist Preußen ein konstitutioneller Staat mit zwei Kammern. Für das Herrenhaus wurde ein Wohngebäude in der Leipziger Straße umgebaut, für die Abgeordneten ein Haus am Dönhoffplatz. Der provisorische Charakter der Bauten erwies sich schon bald, und 1882 empfahl der Landtag Neubauten. Die Planung zog sich aber über ein Jahrzehnt hin, bis durch den Landbauinspektor Friedrich Schulze mit den Arbeiten begonnen wurde. Es entstand auf dem von der Leipziger bis zur damaligen Prinz-Albrecht-Straße durchgehenden Grundstück eine gemeinsame Bauanlage für den Landtag im Süden und für das Herrenhaus im nördlichen Gelände. Während das Herrenhaus mit zwei flankierenden Präsidenten-Wohnhäusern eine tiefe Dreiflügelanlage bildet, erhielt der Landtag eine kompakte, fast quadratische Form mit vier Innenhöfen. Als Stilfassung zitierte Schulze die italienische Hochrenaissance – das war für Preußen nicht gerade bezugsreich, aber es war Mode. Der Neubau des kriegszerstörten Plenarsaals für das Berliner Abgeordnetenhaus folgte dem heutigen Formenkanon.

Ever since 1850, Prussia had been a constitutional state with two chambers of parliament. A former residential building in Leipziger Strasse was remodeled to take up the Herrenhaus (House of Lords), likewise a building at Dönhoffplatz for the Abgeordnetenhaus (House of Representatives). It did not take long before these buildings proved insufficient, however, and in 1882 parliament recommended the construction of new facilities. Planning continued for more than a decade, before work was finally begun by Landbauinspektor Friedrich Schulze. On the site extending from Leipziger Strasse to what used to be Prinz-Albrecht-Strasse a new complex was built including the Landtag in the southern part of the lot and the Herrenhaus to the north. Whereas the Herrenhaus consists of a deep-plan three-wing structure, being flanked by two presidential residences, a more compact, almost square plan with four interior courtyards was selected for the Landtag. In terms of style, Schulze's designs were based on the Italian High Renaissance – highly fashionable at the time, although it had little in common with Prussian tradition. The new building which replaced the old plenary hall of the Berlin parliament that was destroyed in the war adheres to today's canon of forms.

in der Nähe/nearby:
Herrenhaus; Leipziger Straße 3-4
1899-1903 • Friedrich Schulze
Tschechoslowakische Botschaft; Toleranzstraße 21
1975-78 • Vera Machoninova, Vladimir Machonin

B 38 Luftfahrtministerium
Berlin-Mitte; Leipziger Straße 5-7
1935-36 • Ernst Sagebiel

Mit der Entwicklung der Berliner City zwischen Tiergartenviertel und dem Friedrichswerder siedelten sich in der Wilhelmstraße seit dem späten 19. Jahrhundert hohe Regierungsstellen an: das Auswärtige Amt, das Reichskanzleramt, das Justizministerium. Nahe dem Potsdamer Platz waren schon seit der Mitte des 19. Jahrhunderts Abgeordnetenhäuser eingerichtet worden. Die Leipziger Straße hatte sich zudem in eine der wichtigsten Hauptgeschäftsstraßen verwandelt, an ihrem Eingang stand Messels legendäres Warenhaus Wertheim – es wurde nach Kriegsschäden von 1953 bis 1957 abgetragen. Mitten in diesem städtischen Brennpunkt, unweit der Reichskanzlei, erhielt das Reichsluftfahrtministerium sein neues Domizil. Lage und Größe dieses bis zur Niederkirchnerstraße reichenden Komplexes dokumentieren die Bedeutung ziviler und besonders militärischer Luftfahrt in jenen Jahren. Durch seine massive Bauweise überstand das Gebäude den Krieg und wurde zum Haus der Ministerien. Im anschließenden Park befindet sich eine Gedenktafel für die Widerstandsgruppe um Schulze-Boysen und Harnack.

As the area between Tiergarten and Friedrichswerder grew to be the key district of Berlin, the major government bodies moved into Wilhelmstrasse from the late nineteenth century onwards: Foreign Office, Chancellor's Office, Ministry of Justice. There had been houses for members of parliament near Potsdamer Platz since the mid nineteenth century. Leipziger Strasse had also been transformed into one of the most important shopping streets, with Messel's legendary Wertheim department store at the top – it was pulled down from 1953-7 as a result of war damage. In the middle of this urban focal point, not far from the Reichskanzlei, the Air Ministry found a new home. The site and size of this complex extending to Niederkirchner Strasse are testimony to the importance of civil and particularly military air travel in those years. The building survived the war because it was so solidly built, and became the Haus der Ministerien. There is a memorial plaque to the resistance group around Schulze-Boysen and Harnack in the adjacent park.

in der Nähe/nearby:
Nordkoreanische Botschaft; Glinkastraße 5/7
1972-74 • Manfred Jäckel, Gerhard Schubring
Allianz-Versicherung; Mohrenstraße 63-64
1916 • Bodo Ebhardt
Bankhaus v. d. Heydt (Kleisthaus); Mauerstraße 53
1913 • Bodo Ebhardt (Schmuck: Georg Kolbe)
Möbelhaus Trunck; Kronenstraße 10
1901-02 • Hart & Lesser
Postmuseum; Leipziger Straße 18, Mauerstraße 69-75
1892-97 • E. Hake
Geschäftshaus; Mauerstraße 76
1909

B 39 Debis-Zentrum
Berlin-Tiergarten; Potsdamer Platz
1994-97 • Renzo Piano

Der Potsdamer Platz, einst verkehrsreichster Platz Berlins, im Zweiten Weltkrieg in eine Ruinenlandschaft verwandelt, zuletzt mit dem Mauerbau zum Todesstreifen planiert, öffnete sich nach der Wiedervereinigung dem eiligen Zugriff von Interessenten und Planern. Nach dem Willen des Berliner Senates wird Debis – Daimler-Benz Interservices – nun das Gelände zwischen Potsdamer Platz, Staatsbibliothek und Landwehrkanal bebauen. Vorgesehen ist ein Komplex aus zwei Bürohochhäusern, mehreren Geschäfts- und Wohnhäusern, Kaufhäusern und einem Theater. Hilmer & Sattler lieferten mit einem Wettbewerbsentwurf die städtebaulichen Rahmenbedingungen, Renzo Piano gewann im folgenden Wettbewerb den Auftrag zur architektonischen Ausgestaltung. Der Anspruch ist hoch angesetzt. Das Drei-Milliarden-Vorhaben soll der wiedergewonnenen Hauptstadtrolle Berlins gerecht werden und es soll menschliche Züge bewahren. Daß an so hervorragender Stelle in einem stadträumlich weitgehend undefinierten Gebiet bei noch strittiger Verkehrslösung in kürzester Zeit ein so großer Bau verwirklicht werden muß, geschieht nicht oft. Die Zerrissenheit des Meinungsbildes, das berufene und unberufene Fachleute wie auch mehr oder weniger ernst zu nehmende Laien in der öffentlichen Diskussion vermitteln, spiegelt den hohen Stellenwert des Projektes wider.

Potsdamer Platz, once the busiest spot in all of Berlin, was turned into a landscape of ruins during the Second World War and later razed to become a «death strip» in conjunction with the building of the Wall. Following reunification of the city, it immediately became an object of greatest interest to developers and planners. According to the decision of the Berlin Senate, the area between Potsdamer Platz, Staatsbibliothek and Landwehrkanal will now be developed by Debis – Daimler Benz Interservices. The programme calls for a huge complex consisting of two office towers, several commercial and residential buildings, department stores and a theatre. Hilmer & Sattler established a framework for urban development with their prize-winning masterplan, and Renzo Piano prevailed in the subsequent architectural competition and was commissioned to design the buildings. The expectations are high. The three billion dollar project is to reflect the new role of Berlin as capital of Germany and still maintain human dimensions. It is not very often that a huge complex like this is erected in an area still largely undefined in terms of urban development and infrastructural planning. The highly controversial and widely publicized debate among both concerned and unconcerned professionals as well as more or less competent laymen reflects the crucial importance of the project.

in der Nähe/nearby:
Weinhaus Huth; Potsdamer Straße 5, Linkstraße 45
1912 • Heidenreich & Michel

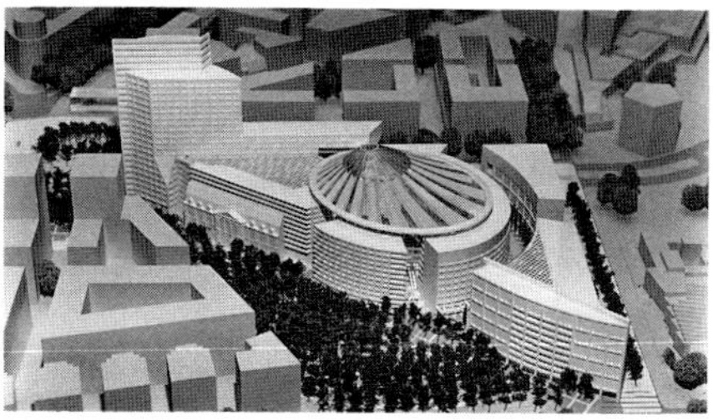

B 40 Sony-Gebäude
Berlin-Tiergarten; Potsdamer Platz
1994-97 • Helmut Jahn

Wie beim Daimler-Areal ließ man sich auch beim Verkauf des zweiten großen Geländestücks am Potsdamer Platz an Sony von dem Gedanken leiten, daß eine seriöse und durch ihre Produkte weltbekannte Firma der sicherste Investor sei und mit ihrem Namen für die architektonische Qualität wie den Erfolg des Projektes bürge. Vorgaben waren einerseits der Masterplan von Hilmer & Sattler zum anderen das Ziel, nicht nur der Europa- und Deutschlandzentrale des Konzerns einen Sitz von hohem baukünstlerischem Wert zu schaffen, sondern dem Ort auch die Urbanität eines »lebendigen öffentlichen Raumes« zu geben. Was Jahn, der erste Preisträger des Sony-Wettbewerbes, vorsieht, ist eine Baugruppe mit nicht einmal hälftigem Büroanteil, die aufgelockert und belebt wird durch Wohnungen, Läden, Restaurants, Kino, Hotel und ein Filmhaus für die Deutsche Film- und Fernsehakademie mit angeschlossenen Einrichtungen. Mittelpunkt der Bauanlage ist ein überdachtes Forum, Jahn stellt es sich als einen High-Tech-Dorfplatz vor: Gartenelemente, weltstädtische Geschäftigkeit, Kommunikation, Information. Die Reste des einstigen Esplanade-Hotels werden auch verwendet, als Illusionsfront eines neuen Hotels. Baulicher Ausklang des Ganzen wird ein kleiner Park, der sich zum Tiergarten hin öffnet, barock und regelmäßig, ein Kontrast zur Architektur des 21. Jahrhunderts.

As in the case of the Daimler-Benz complex, the sale of the second large area at Potsdamer Platz to the Sony Corporation was also motivated by the idea that a respected company, well-known internationally for its line of products, would be the most reliable investor whose name would guarantee architectural quality as well as economic success of the project. Based on the masterplan by Hilmer & Sattler, the objective was not only to provide the company with a German and European headquarters of outstanding architectural quality but also to lend the area some of the urbanism of a «public space full of life». Helmut Jahn, the winner of the Sony competition, is designing a complex of buildings consisting of office space (less than half of the total floor space) in combination with dwellings as well as a wide range of shops and restaurants, a cinema, a hotel and a «Filmhaus» for the German Film and Television Academy, complete with additional facilities. At the centre of the complex is a covered forum which Jahn envisions as a kind of high-tech village square with garden elements, internationally oriented activities, communication and information. The surviving remnants of the former Esplanade Hotel will also be incorporated to serve as illusionary front of the new hotel. The architectural epilogue will consist of a small park on a baroque, regular plan facing the Tiergarten – in interesting contrast to the architecture of the twenty-first century.

in der Nähe/nearby:
Hotel Esplanade (Teilruine); Bellevuestraße 16-18 a
1907-12 • Otto Rehnig

C
Berlin
Der Tiergarten

Bereits im 16. Jahrhundert waren die Wald- und Auenflächen südlich der Spree zwischen Berlin und dem Dorf Lietzow kurfürstliches Jagdgebiet. Nach wechselvollem Schicksal ging daraus der heutige Tiergarten hervor, der seine Gestalt als Landschaftspark im 19. Jahrhundert durch Peter Joseph Lenné erhielt. Die wachsende Stadt Berlin hatte im Laufe der Zeit mit ihren Häusern den Tiergarten umwuchert, und von Westen war die Residenzstadt Charlottenburg an den Park herangerückt. Begonnen hatte das Baugeschehen nach dem Potsdamer Edikt von 1685 mit der Ansiedlung französischer Glaubensflüchtlinge vor den Toren der Stadt. Diesen »Refugiés« wurden Viertel in den neuen Stadtteilen Dorotheenstadt und Friedrichstadt zugewiesen. Einige von ihnen begannen zwischen dem Tiergarten und dem Schafgraben mit Gartenbau, sie kultivierten die sumpfigen Wiesen. Hierher drängte es dann um 1800 auch den natursuchenden Städter, der am Rande des beliebten Ausflugsziels Tiergarten in der Ruhe der Gärten und stiller Straßen die Erfüllung seiner romantischen Sehnsucht fand. Sommer- und Landhäuser entstanden, gänzlich im Gegensatz zu den neueren Massenquartieren der Vorstädte. Damit war der Charakter des Tiergartenviertels als vornehme Wohngegend festgelegt, die zeitweise noch anzutreffenden Ausflugslokale wurden zur Spree hin verdrängt, der Bau von Fabriken polizeilich verboten. Mit der Anlage von Landwehrkanal und Zoologischem Garten grenzte sich das Gebiet in den vierziger Jahren des vorigen Jahrhunderts endgültig ab. Ein Wandel setzte im Kaiserreich ein. Als Hauptstadt wurde Berlin auch Verwaltungsmittelpunkt, und Ämter sowie Firmenzentralen wählten das Tiergartenviertel wegen seiner städtebaulichen Güte und seiner Nähe zum Regierungssitz als Standort. Hinzu kamen Botschaften und ausländische Vertretungen, denen das repräsentative Domizil als unumgänglich galt. Bis zum Zweiten Weltkrieg hielt diese Entwicklung an, dann ging alles in Schutt und Asche unter. Nur langsam entstanden an den Rändern neue Bauten, wichtigster Schauplatz wurde das neue Kulturforum, dessen später heiß umstrittene Konzeption von der Schaffung einer kulturellen Mitte eines vereinten Berlins ausging.

The areas of wood and meadow south of the Spree between Berlin and the village of Lietzow were the Elector's hunting ground from the sixteenth century onwards. It passed through various phases before the present Tiergarten grew up from it; it was laid out as a landscape park by Peter Josef Lenné in the nineteenth century. The growing city of Berlin had gradually surrounded the Tiergarten with its buildings, and the residential town of Charlottenburg had started to encroach on the park from the west. Building had started after the Potsdam edict of 1685 with the settlement of French religious refugees before the gates of the town. These «refugiés» had areas in the new districts of Dorotheenstadt and Friedrichstadt allotted to them. Some of them started to cultivate the marshy meadows between the Tiergarten and the Schafgraben. Then around 1800 city-dwellers in search of nature started to come out here, looking for fulfilment of their Romantic longings in the quiet of the gardens and quiet streets on the edge of the popular Tiergarten excursion area. Summerhouses and country houses were built, in complete contrast with the newer mass quarters in the suburbs. This established the character of the Tiergarten as an exclusive residential area, surviving restaurants and cafés for trippers were forced down to the Spree, and it was forbidden by law to build factories. Construction of Landwehrkanal and Zoo meant the boundaries of the area were finally established in the 1840s. The empire began to change. Berlin was a capital, and therefore also an administrative centre, and government departments as well as companies chose the Tiergarten for their officers because of its high quality of urban life and proximity to the seat of government. Then came embassies and consulates, for whom prestigious residences were essential. This development continued up to the Second World War, then everything was reduced to ashes and rubble. New buildings appeared only slowly on the fringes, the most important centre of activity was the new Kulturforum. This was a concept that was later hotly contested, intended to create a cultural centre for a united Berlin.

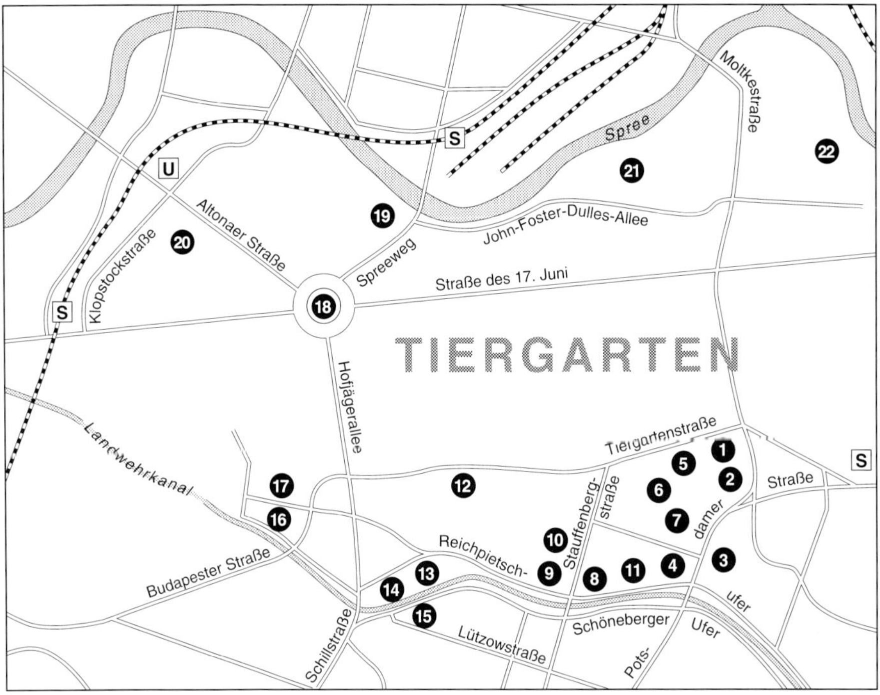

C 1 Philharmonie
C 2 Kammermusiksaal
C 3 Staatsbibliothek
C 4 Neue Nationalgalerie
C 5 Kunstgewerbemuseum
C 6 Eingangshalle der Museen Europäischer Kunst
C 7 Matthäikirche
C 8 Shellhaus
C 9 Reichsmarineamt
C 10 Bendlerblock
C 11 Wissenschaftszentrum
C 12 Japanische Botschaft
C 13 Villa Von der Heydt
C 14 Bauhaus-Archiv
C 15 Hotel Esplanade
C 16 Ökohaus
C 17 Stadtvillen
C 18 Siegessäule
C 19 Schloß Bellevue
C 20 Hansaviertel
C 21 Kongreßhalle
C 22 Reichstag

C 1 Philharmonie
Berlin-Tiergarten; Matthäikirchstraße 1
1960-63 • Hans Scharoun

Als Ersatz für die im Kriege zerstörte alte Philharmonie in der Bernburger Straße entstand ein Bauwerk von Weltgeltung. Ohne eine Schaufassade im klassischen Sinne wurde hier von innen nach außen gebaut. Aus drei sich unregelmäßig umschreibenden Fünfecken entwickelt sich der Grundriß. Der Zuschauerraum mit dem zentralen Orchesterpodium ist die moderne Umsetzung der alten Idee der Arena. Die Ränge sind in einzelne Blöcke aufgelöst und neigen sich wie die Rabatten eines Weinberges der Mitte zu. Herbert v. Karajan, Chefdirigent des Berliner Philharmonischen Orchesters, kommentierte Scharouns Entwurf: »Ich kenne keinen bestehenden Konzertsaal, in dem das Sitzproblem so ideal gelöst ist.« Das Äußere der Philharmonie war jahrelang – durchaus in märkischer Tradition – ein schlichter ockerfarbener Anstrich des Betons, wirkungsvoll hob sich aber die bizarre Silhouette vor den Bäumen des Tiergartens ab. Erst 1978-81 erhielt das Bauwerk seine endgültige Haut aus goldeloxierten Lochblechen.

This world-class building came into being to replace the old Philharmonie in Bernburger Strasse, which was destroyed in the war. It has no show façade in the classical manner: it was built from the inside outwards. The ground plan was developed from five pentagons placed around each other in an irregular pattern. The auditorium with central platform for the orchestra is a modern version of the old idea of the arena. The rows of seats are broken up into individual blocks and run down towards the middle like the tiers of a vineyard. Herbert von Karajan, then conductor-in-chief of the Berlin Philharmonic, said of Scharoun's design: «I know of no existing concert hall in which the seating problem has been so well solved.» For years the exterior of the Philharmonie – absolutely within the tradition of the Mark – was plain ochre-painted concrete, but the bizarre silhouette stood effectively against the trees of the Tiergarten. It was not until 1978-81 that the building acquired its final skin of perforated plate anodized in gold.

in der Nähe/nearby:
Musikinstrumentenmuseum; Tiergartenstraße 1
1981-84 • Hans Scharoun, Edgar Wisniewski

C 2 Kammermusiksaal
Berlin-Tiergarten; Matthäikirchstraße 3
1984-87 • Hans Scharoun, Edgar Wisniewski

Zu Scharouns Gesamtkonzept für das Kulturforum gehörte auch der Kammermusiksaal. Über zwei Jahrzehnte nach dem Bau der Philharmonie konnte nach vielen Startschwierigkeiten auch dieses Projekt verwirklicht werden. Entscheidenden Einfluß sowohl auf die Ausarbeitung des Entwurfs als auch auf die Überwindung der behördlichen und finanziellen Hürden hatte der Schüler Scharouns, Edgar Wisniewski. Grundgedanke des Kammermusiksaals war wiederum das Prinzip »Musik im Mittelpunkt«. Fast regelmäßig, aber dadurch auch starrer ordnen sich die Zuschauerblöcke um das zentrale Podium. Was bei der Philharmonie noch Experiment war, übernimmt der Kammermusiksaal als Selbstverständlichkeit. Das musikalische Experiment aber geht weiter: Ein breiter Umgang in mittlerer Höhe der Parkettgruppen ermöglicht Wandelkonzerte, drei Musikeremporen dienen der Raummusik. Philharmonie und Kammermusiksaal sind räumlich und gestalterisch miteinander verwachsen, wie sie auch – trotz unterschiedlicher Bauzeit – einer Idee entspringen.

The Kammermusiksaal (chamber music hall) was also part of Scharoun's overall concept for the Kulturforum. This project was finally realized, after many problems in the initial stages, over two decades after the building of the Philharmonie. Edgar Wisniewski, a pupil of Scharoun, had a decisive influence both on working out the design and on getting over red tape and financial hurdles. The guiding idea behind the Kammermusiksaal was the principle of «music at the centre». The blocks of spectators are arranged around the central platform almost regularly, but also rather rigidly. Something that in the Philharmonie was still an experiment is taken for granted in the Kammermusiksaal. But the musical experiment goes further: a broad aisle runs round the groups of seats halfway up, making concerts with moving ensembles possible, and three music galleries can be used for experimental music. Philharmonie and Kammermusiksaal have grown together spatially and in terms of design – just as they are based on a single idea, despite being built at different times.

C 3 Staatsbibliothek
Berlin-Tiergarten; Potsdamer Straße 33
1967-78 • Hans Scharoun, Edgar Wisniewski

Die Staatsbibliothek sollte das Kulturforum nach Osten hin abschließen. So sind auch Magazine und Cafeteria auf dieser Rückseite angeordnet, um die Lesesäle gegen den Lärm der dort geplanten Stadtautobahn abzuschirmen. Den Benutzerräumen vorgelagert ist das ibero-amerikanische Institut. Ähnlich dem Philharmoniefoyer klingt in dem für die Benutzer bestimmten Bereich wieder das Motiv des durchgehenden Raumes mit verschiedenen Ebenen großer und kleiner Niveauunterschiede an, dessen Reiz in der Vielfalt der räumlichen Eindrücke liegt. Diese bewußte Zergliederung teilt sich nach außen durch einen geometrisch unbestimmten Baukörper mit. Lediglich in dem hohen fensterlosen Magazintrakt findet das Auge Halt. Darüberhinaus liefert die eigenwillige Silhouette das unerläßliche Charakteristikum eines Gebäudes, das sich über jede Mittelmäßigkeit erheben soll. Die Parallelität zur Philharmonie ist hierin ebenso gegeben wie in der gemeinsamen goldeloxierten Verkleidung, die Scharouns Bauten des Kulturforums ausweist.

The Staatsbibliothek was intended to form the eastern conclusion of the Kulturforum. Thus stacks and cafeteria are placed at the rear, to protect reading rooms from the noise of the planned city autobahn. In front of the users' rooms is the Ibero-American Institute. In a similar way to the Philharmonie there is also a motif of continuous space with various areas showing large and small differences of level in sections intended for users, the charm of which lies in the variety of spatial impressions it conveys. This conscious articulation is also communicated outside by the fact that the building is geometrically indeterminate. The eye only comes to rest in the high, windowless stack block. Beyond this the unconventional silhouette presents the imperative characteristic of a building intended to rise above any mediocrity. A parallel with the Philharmonie is present in this just as much as in the anodized gold cladding they have in common, a characteristic of Scharoun's buildings in the Kulturforum.

in der Nähe/nearby:
Wohn- und Geschäftshaus; Potsdamer Straße 101
1987-89 • Hinrich Baller, Inken Baller
Wohnhäuser; Potsdamer Straße 43/49
1984-85 • Georg Heinrichs
Wohnhaus; Am Karlsbad 1
1984-85 • Jürgen Sawade
Wohnhaus; Am Karlsbad 2
1984-85 • Heinz Hilmer, Christoph Sattler
Verwaltung der Feuersozietät; Am Karlsbad 4-5
1934-35 • Mebes & Emmerich
EAB-Großwärmepumpe; Flottwellstraße 4-5
1986-87 • Mario Maedebach, Werner Redeleit

C 4 Neue Nationalgalerie
Berlin-Tiergarten; Potsdamer Straße 50
1965-68 • Ludwig Mies van der Rohe

Im Nebeneinander von Philharmonie und Neuer Nationalgalerie kommen die beiden Architekturauffassungen der fünfziger und sechziger Jahre zum Ausdruck. Hier in spielerischer Phantasie plastische Verformung des Werkstoffes Beton, da klassische Strenge in einem zur architektonischen Ehrlichkeit stilisierten Konstruktivismus. Mies stellte seinen Entwurf auf die moderne Auffassung vom Museum als Innenraum ab. Unter einer weiten Terrasse hinter fensterlosen Mauern verbirgt sich die Galerie. Darüber aus Dachplatte, Stützen und Glas entsteht in transzendenter Schwebe ein Raum, der nur wechselnden Ausstellungen dient. Mies berief sich – vollkommen zu Recht – auf Schinkel, der in seinem Museum am Lustgarten ebenfalls eine Schaufront aus Säulen und Dachbalken schuf, die wenig oder keinen Bezug zum eigentlichen Museumsraum hat. Der Nationalgalerie als dem großen Pendant zum Barcelona-Pavillon von 1929 zollte die Fachwelt einhellig Beifall. Daß in dieser baulichen Abstraktion aber auch die Grenze des architektonisch Sinnvollen erreicht ist, bleibt nicht zu übersehen.

The juxtaposition of Philharmonie and Neue Nationalgalerie expresses the architectural views of the fifties and the sixties. In the first case consummate imagination in the use of three-dimensionally moulded concrete as a working material, and in the second, classical austerity in a Constructivism stylized into architectonic honesty. Mies geared his design to the modern view of the museum as interior. The gallery is hidden under a broad terrace behind windowless walls. Above this roof slab, supports and glass hover transcendentally to form a space used only for temporary exhibitions. Mies invoked – with complete justification – Schinkel, who also created a show façade of columns and roof beams in his Museum am Lustgarten, with little or no reference to the actual museum space. The specialist world applauded the Nationalgalerie unanimously as the great counterpart to the Barcelona-Pavillon, dating from 1929. It cannot be overlooked however that this structural abstraction is on the border of what is architecturally sensible.

in der Nähe/nearby:
Geschäftshaus Loeser & Wolff; Potsdamer Straße 56
1929 • Albert Biebendt

C 5 Kunstgewerbemuseum
Berlin-Tiergarten; Tiergartenstraße 5-11
1978-85 • Rolf Gutbrod

Mit der zementierten Teilung der Stadt Berlin 1961 wurde der nun unausweichliche Bedarf neuer Museumsbauten im Westteil erkennbar. Eine Rückgabe der während des Krieges in die späteren Westzonen ausgelagerten Bestände an die Institutionen der Museumsinsel in Ost-Berlin kam nun erst recht nicht in Frage, im Dahlemer Ausweichquartier herrschte andererseit bedrohliche Enge. In der Erweiterung des Kulturforums um fünf Museen der Europäischen Kunst sah man Abhilfe. 1965/66 brachten zwei Wettbewerbe kein greifbares Ergebnis, keinen Sieger. Rolf Gutbrod erhielt schließlich den Auftrag, seine Tätigkeit wurde aber an der Erfüllung von Raumprogrammen gemessen und nicht an architektonischen Qualitäten. Das führte in der Nachbarschaft von Mies van der Rohes Nationalgalerie und Scharouns Philharmonie zu einem Ergebnis, welches einen Wettstreit gar nicht erst aufnahm. Die nicht erfüllten Erwartungen einer nicht erfüllten Architektursensation führten zu herber Kritik, die auch eine mangelnde städtebauliche Konzeption beklagte: Von »Kulturghetto« und »Stadtbrache mit Kulturtempeln« war die Rede. 1985 konnte das Kunstgewerbemuseum eröffnet werden, äußerlich modisch, aber neben den Nachbarn belanglos, im Inneren großzügig und für eine zeitgemäße Inszenierung der Exponate geeignet.

When the division of Berlin was cemented in 1961 it was obvious that the West was inevitably going to need more museum space. It was now clear that the items from collections that had been stored in what were later to be the western zones could not possibly be returned to the Museumsinsel in East Berlin, but the temporary quarters in Dahlem were becoming seriously cramped. A solution was seen in extending the Kulturforum by building five museums of European art. Two competitions in 1965/6 brought no tangible result, no victor. Finally Rolf Gutbrodt was commissioned to carry out the work, but his activity was restricted to providing space, and not concerned with architectural quality. This meant a building that offered no competition to Mies van der Rohe's Nationalgalerie and Scharoun's Philharmonie. Unfulfilled expectations of an architectural sensation that was never produced led to bitter criticism, and lack of planning in terms of urban space was also complained about. People were talking about a «cultural ghetto» and «urban wasteland with cultural temples». The Kunstgewerbemuseum was opened in in 1985; it has a fashionable but inconsequential exterior, but the interior is spacious, and well suited to displaying the exhibits in a manner appropriate to the times.

in der Nähe/nearby:
Cafeteria; Matthäikirchstraße 2
1993-94 • Hilmer & Sattler
Gemäldegalerie; Stauffenbergstraße 3-4
1991-96 • Hilmer & Sattler

C 6 Eingangsbau der Museen Europäischer Kunst
Berlin-Tiergarten; Matthäikirchstraße 4
1985-92 • Rolf Gutbrod; Hilmer & Sattler

Nach Fertigstellung des Kunstgewerbemuseums kam der Bau der weiteren vier Museen ins Stocken. Ein städtebaulicher Entwurf Hans Holleins sorgte für gänzliche Verwirrung. Der Streit zwischen den Gralshütern des Scharounerbes und den arglosen Neuerern blockierte besonders die politische Entscheidungsebene. Erst 1987 ließ die Beauftragung der Architekten Hilmer und Sattler mit einer Überarbeitung der inzwischen angestaubten Vorentwürfe Hoffnungen auf eine würdige Vollendung der Bauaufgabe zu. Im Hintergrund der noch von Scharoun erdachten, schräg ansteigenden Piazzetta wurde nun vorab die große Eingangshalle fertiggestellt, die mit ihren Baugliedern Anschluß an zeitgemäße Architektur sucht. Im Vordergrund stand das Ziel, für die nun nicht mehr veränderbaren Baukörper und Grundrisse wenigstens eine architektonische Beruhigung durchzuführen: Homogenisierung der Oberflächen, Beschränkung auf wenige Materialien, Änderungen in Details wie schlankeren Säulen. Die eigenen Entwürfe von Hilmer & Sattler wenden sich endgültig dem Prinzip selbstbewußter Museumsarchitektur zu – nicht mehr Hülle für die Kunst, sondern Kunst für die Kunst. Fassade und Raum werden geprägt von Transparenz und Licht. Die edle Zurückhaltung in Form und Material dient nur der Steigerung der inszenierten Architektur, die für sich schon zum Erlebnis wird.

Following completion of the Kunstgewerbemuseum, construction of the other four museums of this complex was halted. A master-plan by Hans Hollein for new urban development served only to complicate things even more. The controversy between the custodians of the Scharoun legacy and unsuspecting innovators also blocked things at the level of political decision-making. It was not until 1987 and the commissioning of architects Hilmer & Sattler to revise the somewhat dusty preliminary designs that hopes for a worthy completion of the task returned. In the background of the slightly graded piazetta originally envisioned by Scharoun at least the great entrance hall has now been completed, making an effort to establish a link with contemporary architecture. The main objective was to achieve a minimum of composure in order to unify the existing volumes and plans which can of course no longer be changed. This was to be achieved by a homogenization of the surfaces, a limitation to only a few materials, and alteration of details such as more slender columns. Hilmer & Sattler's own designs are clearly oriented to the idea of an assertive museum architecture – one that no longer provides merely a container or shell for the arts but becomes a form of art itself. Façade and space are characterized by transparency and light. The precious yet unobtrusive forms and materials serve only to enhance the dramatic effect of the architecture which provides an experience in itself.

C 7 Matthäikirche
Berlin-Tiergarten; Matthäikirchplatz
1844-46 • Friedrich August Stüler

Als einen »Gruß aus alter Zeit« bezeichnete der Berliner Bauhistoriker Günther Kühne diese Kirche. Einsam und fremd steht sie heute zwischen all den Neubauten des Kulturforums, und nur die Ortsansässigen haben sich an das bizarre Nebeneinander von Alt und Neu gewöhnt. Die dreischiffige Langhaus-Hallenkirche mit Konchenchor und zwei Nebenapsiden wirkt ein wenig starr. Vielleicht liegt das an dem regelmäßigen Aneinanderfügen geometrischer Bauglieder, das an alte Steinbaukästen erinnert. Diese schon spürbare akademische Gestaltungshaltung und das Nachklingen italienisch-römischer Elemente sind typisch für Stüler und typisch für die Bauzeit.

The Berlin architectural historian Günther Kühne called this church a «greeting from olden times». Today it stands, lonely and alien, among the new buildings in the Kulturforum, and only local people have accustomed themselves to this bizarre juxtaposition of old and new. The hall church with nave and two aisles, conch choir and two side apses seems a little stiff. This is perhaps because of the regular way in which geometrical structural sections are fitted together, reminiscent of stone-built boxes. This clearly discernible attitude to design, the echoes of Italian and Roman elements are typical of Stüler and of the period at which the church was built.

in der Nähe/nearby:
Kupferstichkabinett und Kunstbibliothek; Matthäikirchstraße 6/8
1985-93 • Rolf Gutbrod; Hilmer & Sattler
Wohnhäuser am Kulturforum; Hitzigallee 17-21
1984-85 • Kurt Ackermann & Partner

C 8 Shellhaus
Berlin-Tiergarten; Reichpietschufer 60/62
1930-31 • Emil Fahrenkamp

Neben dem Hamburger Chilehaus ist das Berliner Shellhaus eine der großen architektonischen Bürohausschöpfungen seiner Zeit in Europa. In keinem baugeschichtlichen Fachbuch fehlt es, und fast jede zeitgenössische Architekturzeitschrift berichtete in mehreren Artikeln. Nur der Architekt hatte seine Not mit dem kühnen Entwurf – 324 Besuche bei den Baubehörden beklagte er. Die charakteristische Silhouette erhält der Bau durch die abgestaffelte Höhe entlang dem Kanalufer und durch die in regelmäßigen Rücksprüngen gewellte Front. Auch wenn diese Wellenlinie mit dem schrägen Verlauf der Uferstraße erklärbar sein mag, ist der gestalterische Wille doch zu vordergründig, der Geist des Expressionismus spürbar. Hierin ergibt sich auch eine Gemeinsamkeit mit Erich Mendelsohns Einsteinturm in Potsdam oder dessen Universum-Kino am Kudamm, deren plastisch-dynamische Formen in den schwingenden Fensterbändern Fahrenkamps anklingen.

Along with the Chilehaus in Hamburg, the Shellhaus in Berlin is one of the great architectural creations in the field of office buildings of its period in Europe. It features in every textbook on architectural history, and almost every contemporary architectural magazine carried several articles on it. But the architect had trouble with his bold design – he complained of 324 visits to the building authorities. The building gains its characteristic silhouette from its staggered height along the bank of the canal and the waves of the façade, moving backwards at regular intervals. Even if this wavy line is explicable in terms of the oblique run of the road along the bank, the creative will is still too superficial, the spirit of Expressionism detectable. The building also has something in common with Erich Mendelsohn's Einstein Tower in Potsdam or his Universum cinema on the Ku-Damm, the plastic and dynamic forms of which are hinted at in Fahrenkamp's curving runs of windows.

in der Nähe/nearby:
Bewag-Verwaltung; Stauffenbergstraße 27-34
1965-67 • Paul Baumgarten
Eckwohnhaus; Kluckstraße 18
1984-85 • Antoine Grumbach, Klaus Kammann

C 9 Reichsmarineamt
Berlin-Tiergarten; Reichpietschufer 72-76
1911-14 • Reinhardt & Süßenguth

Zu den hochtrabenden Lieblingsplänen Wilhelms II. gehörte, mit einer großen Flotte reichsdeutsches Machtbewußtsein sichtbar zum Ausdruck zu bringen und – in imperialer Selbstüberschätzung – der englischen Seeüberlegenheit die Stirn zu bieten. 1898 setzte unter Tirpitz, dem neuen Leiter des Marineamtes, das auf 16 Jahre bemessene Bauprogramm für 34 Schlachtschiffe mit den zugehörigen Verbänden ein. Dem entsprach auch der Neubau eines Reichsmarineamtes. Mit dem Entwurf für die Mammutanlage wurde die renommierte Architektenfirma Reinhardt & Süßenguth beauftragt, die im Bau derartig umfangreicher Vorhaben erfahren war. Hinter den schlicht konservativen Fassaden liegen 800 Büroräume. Nach dem Ersten Weltkrieg war das Gebäude Sitz des Reichswehr-Ministeriums, in der NS-Zeit hieß es dann Oberkommando der Wehrmacht, des Heeres und der Marine. Ein gigantischer Neubau für diese Dienststellen war Bestandteil der Speerschen Planung entlang der großen Nord-Süd-Achse. Ihm sollte das gesamte Tiergartenviertel zwischen Stauffenbergstraße und Potsdamer Straße geopfert werden, es kam aber nie zur Ausführung.

One of Wilhelm II's favourite grandiose schemes was to have a large fleet to express German imperial power and – in a mood of imperial self-delusion – to defy English naval supremacy. In 1898, under Tirpitz, the new director of the naval office, a 16 year programme was set up for building 34 battleships and the necessary support ships. This also meant building a new naval office. The famous firm of Reinhardt and Süssenguth was commissioned to carry out the work, as they had experience with projects of this kind. There are 800 offices behind the plain, conservative façade. After the First World War the building housed the imperial defence ministry, under the Nazis it was the Wehrmacht headquarters, including both the army and the navy. A gigantic new building for these services was an element of Speer's planning for the north-south axis. The entire area of the Tiergarten between Stauffenbergstrasse and Potsdamer Strasse was to be sacrificed to it, but it was never built.

C 10 Bendlerblock
Berlin-Tiergarten; Stauffenbergstraße 11-13
1938

In den Jahren NS-deutscher Kriegsvorbereitung wurde eine Erweiterung des Oberkommando der Wehrmacht, des Heeres und der Marine notwendig. Die nach der damaligen Bendlerstraße – heute Stauffenbergstraße – als Bendlerblock bezeichnete nordseitige Fortsetzung des ehemaligen Reichsmarineamt-Gebäudes verzichtete auf äußeren Glanz und folgte militärisch-nüchterner Zweckmäßigkeit. Im Westflügel war die Nachrichtenzentrale untergebracht. Sie wurde 1942 überbunkert, nach dem Kriege aber geschleift. Im Hof befindet sich seit 1952 eine Gedenkstätte. Hier wurden am 20. Juli 1944, dem Tage des mißglückten Bombenattentats auf Hitler, noch in der Nacht Claus Schenk Graf v. Stauffenberg und die beteiligten Offiziere standrechtlich erschossen, Generaloberst Beck kam den Henkern durch Selbstmord zuvor. Das 1953 aufgestellte Standbild schuf Richard Scheibe.

In the years of Nazi preparation for war it became necessary to extend the Wehrmacht, army and navy, headquarters. The building, extending the former imperial naval building on the northern side, named after what was then the Bendlerstrasse – now Stauffenbergstrasse – made no claims to splendour, but was sober and purposeful in a military fashion. It was made into a bunker in 1942, then pulled down after the war. There has been a memorial in the courtyard since 1952. On 20 July 1944, the day of the unsuccessful attempt to assassinate Hitler with a bomb, Claus Schenk Graf von Stauffenberg and the officers involved were shot by firing squad the same night; General Beck avoided the executioners by committing suicide. Richard Scheibe was responsible for the statue set up in 1953.

in der Nähe/nearby:
Wohnhaus Parey; Sigismundstraße 4 a
1895-96 • Kayser & Großheim
Wohnhaus Gontard; Stauffenbergstraße 41
1906-07 • Cremer & Wolffenstein

C 11 Wissenschaftszentrum
Berlin-Tiergarten; Reichpietschufer 50/54
1984-87 • James Stirling, Michael Wilford

»Mit dem Konzept verschiedener Einzelgebäude jeweils anderer Form, ohne starre Beziehung zum Garten und zum bestehenden Haus hoffen wir einen freundlichen, ansprechenden und unbürokratischen Ort ohne Institutsatmosphäre zu schaffen.« So schrieben die Architekten in ihrem Erläuterungsbericht. Die Einbeziehung des Kopfbaues des ehemaligen Reichsversicherungsamtes am Landwehrkanal – 1891-94 von August Busse – läßt ein Gefüge von Bauten entstehen, deren Zusammenhalt nur schwer zu bewältigen ist. Äußerlich verbindet eine auffällige, einheitliche Farbgebung nur die Neubauten. Deren jeweils körperliche Eigenständigkeit mildert den Übergang zum Altbau. Da das Wissenschaftszentrum als anwendungsbezogene sozialwissenschaftliche Einrichtung sich aus Instituten zusammensetzt, die recht unabhängig voneinander arbeiten, war auch die Lösung der selbständigen Baukörper tragbar; trotzdem ermöglichen Übergänge in allen Geschossen den Verkehr zwischen den Bauten, den Austausch von Gedanken und Informationen.

«With the concept of several buildings, each of differing form, informally related to gardens and to the existing building we hope to make a friendly, charming, unbureaucratic place – the opposite of an institutional environment.» This is what the architects said in their explanatory report. Inclusion of the end section of the former Reichsversicherungsamt on the Landwehrkanal – 1891-4 by August Busse – produces a set of buildings which it is not easy to grasp as an entity. Externally only the new buildings are linked by a striking and uniform colour scheme. Their physical independence alleviates the transition to the old building. As the Wissenschaftszentrum as an application-based social and scientific facility is made up of institutions working independently of one another, the solution using independent building sections is tolerable; despite this, crossing points in all parts of the building make it possible to move between the sections and exchange ideas and information.

C 12 Japanische Botschaft
Berlin-Tiergarten; Tiergartenstraße 26-27
1938-42 • Ludwig Moshamer
1986-88 • Kisho Kurokawa, Taiji Yamaguchi

Dem bis zur Jahrhundertwende eher unüblichen Bedarf eigener Gebäude für ausländische Vertretungen folgten die Jahre der Aufwertung von Gesandtschaften und Botschaften. Vorwiegend in der Nähe des Reichstages oder im Tiergartenviertel nahe den Ministerien in der Wilhelmstraße mieteten oder kauften sie nun Häuser. Spanien besaß in der Hitzigstraße schon 1898 ein Haus, die USA erwarben 1910 in der Rauchstraße ihre Residenz. Neubauten entstanden aber erst Ende der dreißiger Jahre. Ausgelöst durch die städtebaulichen Pläne Speers und der Partei mußten nämlich Häuser im Bereich der geplanten Nord-Süd-Achse geräumt werden, und etliche Staaten erhielten als Entschädigung großzügige Grundstücke am südlichen Tiergartenrand. Die neuen Botschaftsgebäude sollten in ihrer »künstlerischen Gestaltung der im repräsentativen Neuaufbau Berlins verkörperten Baugesinnung angepaßt werden«. So war ein verhärteter, fast lebloser Neoklassizismus angesagt, wie er allen staatlichen Bauten jener Jahre eigen ist. Eine besondere Note bekamen die Gebäude durch landestypische Zutaten. Die Japanische Botschaft erhielt im Attikaband ein Feld mit dem Sonnenrad, zwischen den Hofflügeln entstand ein Garten von fernöstlicher Kargheit.

Until the turn of the century it was unusual to have special buildings for the representatives of foreign powers, but then came a period in which embassies were given considerably enhanced status. They bought or rented buildings principally near the Reichstag or the Tiergarten area, near the ministries in Wilhelmstrasse. Spain had a building in Hitzigstrasse as early as 1898, and the USA acquired its residence in Rauchstrasse in 1910, but there were no custom-built buildings until the late thirties. Because of Speer's and the party's plans for the development of the city, buildings in the area of the north-south axis had to be cleared, and several states were given generous plots on the southern edge of the Tiergarten in compensation. New embassy buildings were to be «adapted in their artistic design to an attitude to building concomitant with rebuilding Berlin in prestigious style». This led to a hard, almost lifeless neoclassicism, of the kind common to all the buildings of that period. The buildings were given some elements of personal style as a result of additions typical of the country concerned. The Japanese embassy's attic strip has a field containing the wheel of the sun, and a garden of far-eastern austerity was planted between the courtyard wings.

in der Nähe/nearby:
Italienische Botschaft; Tiergartenstraße 21 a-23
1938-41 • Friedrich Hetzelt
Krupphaus; Tiergartenstraße 30-31
1937-38 • Mebes & Emmerich

C 13 Villa Von der Heydt
Berlin-Tiergarten; Von-der-Heydt-Straße 16
1860-62 • Hermann Ende

Gebaut als Palais eines Ministers, lange Jahre Ruine, ist das Haus heute Sitz des Präsidenten der Stiftung Preußischer Kulturbesitz. Hermann Ende mußte sich hier deutlich an der Idee orientieren, wie Schinkel ein kleines Schlößchen gebaut hätte. Die griechische Antike ist damit präsent. Die Art der Interpretation nimmt aber die Renaissance zum Vorbild, wie diese Stilphase für den Historismus im Berlin des letzten Jahrhundertdrittels überhaupt bestimmend blieb. Äußerliche Repräsentation und der Zwang, Nutzung des Hauses und Wohnen dem Gleichmaß des Baukörpers zu unterwerfen, lassen sich hier vorzüglich ablesen. Der Unterschied etwa zum Landhaus des zwanzigsten Jahrhunderts im Sinne von Muthesius liegt in der Zweckbestimmung, die sich architektonisch manifestiert: symmetrische Fassade, Achse, Portikus, hier für das gesellige Leben und seine Spielregeln – Asymmetrie, Wohnlichkeit, Naturnähe, dort für ein Leben in der Familie.

This was built as a ministerial palace, was in ruins for years, and is now the base of the Stiftung Preussischer Kulturbesitz. Clearly Hermann Ende's guideline here was the thought of how Schinkel would have handled a building of this kind. Thus Greek antiquity is a key element. However, the way in which it is interpreted is modelled on the Renaissance, the stylistic phase that was to determine historicism in Berlin in the last third of the century. A need to impress, and to subordinate use of the building and living to evenness of proportion can be clearly seen here. The difference between this and country houses of the twenties in the manner of Muthesius can be seen in the different purposes expressed by the architecture: here a symmetrical façade, axis, portico for social life with all the rules of that particular game – there asymmetry, homeliness, closeness to nature, all features stressing family life.

in der Nähe/nearby:
Hiroshima-Steg; Lützowufer, Reichpietschufer
1985-87 • Klaus Theo Brenner, Benedict Tonon
Energiesparhäuser; Lützowufer 1 a-5 a
1983-85 • Gerkan, Marg & Partner; Pysall, Jensen & Stahrenberg; Bernd Faskel, Vladimir Nikolic; Manfred Schiedhelm, Karin Axelrad; Kilpper & Partner
Stadthäuser; Lützowstraße 45, 47, 49, 51
1981-84 • Andreas Brandt, Thomas Heiß, Axel Liepe, Hartmut Steigelmann; Otto Steidle; Gerkan, Marg & Partner; Oefelein & Freund; Manfred Schiedhelm
Torhäuser; Lützowstraße 44, 46, 48, 50
1984-86 • Gregotti Associati

C 14 Bauhaus-Archiv
Berlin-Tiergarten; Klingelhöferstraße 13-14
1976-78 • Walter Gropius, Alexander Cvijanovic

Für die Hinterlassenschaft des 1919 in Weimar gegründeten, dann in Dessau und zuletzt bis zur Auflösung 1933 in Berlin ansässigen Bauhauses schuf der einstige Mitbegründer Walter Gropius den Entwurf eines Archives. Standort sollte ursprünglich Darmstadt sein, in den siebziger Jahren fiel dann die Entscheidung für Berlin. Alexander Cvijanovic mußte den Gropius-Entwurf von 1964 für den Berliner Bauplatz umdeuten: aus Hangschräge wurde flaches Gelände, aus der idyllischen Darmstädter Rosenhöhe wurde die Verkehrsinsel am Landwehrkanal, aus Nordlage wurde Südlage. Die Führung der Wege und Betonrampen lassen noch die Schwierigkeiten und Folgen der Umplanung ahnen. Das wesentliche Gestaltungselement blieb aber erhalten, die charakteristischen Shedoberlichte. Sie drängen sich in enger Reihung, wachsen von der Seite gesehen wie freie Baukörper aus dem Boden. Damit gewinnt das Gebäude seine Unverwechselbarkeit, und es versteht sich neben Neuer Nationalgalerie und Philharmonie als drittes Architekturdenkmal eines der großen Baumeister des 20. Jahrhunderts in Berlin.

Walter Gropius, cofounder of the Bauhaus founded in Weimar in 1919, which then moved to Dessau and finally to Berlin where it was dissolved in 1933, designed the Bauhausarchiv to accommodate the material it left behind. It was originally intended to be in Darmstadt, but in the seventies Berlin was chosen instead. Alexander Cvijanovic had to reinterpret Gropius' 1964 design for the Berlin site: the site was flat rather than sloping, the idyllic Rosenhöhe in Darmstadt gave way to the Verkehrsinsel on the Landwehrkanal, and the site was north-facing rather than south-facing. The way in which the paths and ramps are handled shows the difficulties and consequences of the replanning. The essential design element was retained, however: the characteristic shed skylights. They are set very close together, and seem to grow out of the floor like independent blocks when seen from the side. This gives the building its unmistakable quality, and along with Neue Nationalgalerie and Philharmonie it is the third architectural monument to a great twentieth century architect in Berlin.

in der Nähe/nearby:
Wohn- und Geschäftshaus; Lützowplatz 1
1988-90 • Mario Botta
Wohnhaus »Archigram«; Lützowplatz 3
1988-90 • Peter Cook
Wohnhaus; Lützowplatz 5
1988-90 • Axel Schultes
Bar am Lützowplatz; Lützowplatz 7
1990 • Jürgen Sawade
Wohnanlage; Lützowplatz 2-16
1982-83 • Oswald Mathias Ungers

C 15 Hotel Esplanade
Berlin-Tiergarten; Lützowufer 15-19 b
1986-88 • Jürgen Sawade

Während noch in den Siebzigern Architektur zur gemauerten oder betonierten Raumumgrenzung unter Berücksichtigung funktionaler Anforderungen zu verkommen drohte, herrscht im letzten Jahrzehnt ein neuer Geist. Dies gilt auch für Hotelbauten. Sawade präsentiert das neue Grand Hotel als diagonal halbierten Baublock mit spitzwinkligen Schnittkanten. Die Restfläche zwischen den beiden hohen Flügeln nehmen Flachtrakte und die glasüberdachte Vorfahrt ein, die in ihrer Geschlossenheit wie ein Innenraum wirkt. Durch eine »Wasserwand« wird sie zur Straße abgeschirmt. Damit ist schon viel Neues gewagt, ungewöhnlich viel für den Bautyp Hotel, der sich in Berlin von jeher aller avantgardistischen Experimente enthielt, allenfalls auf einst Bewährtes zurückgriff und seinen Gästen eher prunkende Schnörkel bot. Beim Esplanade ging man nicht nur in den Fassaden mit grauem polierten Granit und weißen glasierten Verblendern einen eigenen Weg, auch die Innenräume verschreiben sich einem ausgesucht zeitgemäßen Design nach der Losung des Architekten »Wahrheit des Raumes, Ehrlichkeit der Raumgestaltung«.

In the seventies, architecture threatened to degenerate into brick or concrete as definition of enclosed space, but a new spirit started to make its presence felt in the last decade. This is also true of hotel buildings. Sawade presents the new Grand Hotel as a building block cut in half on the diagonal, with acute-angled sectional edges. The space between the two high sections is occupied by flat sections and the glass-roofed approach, which has the feel of an interior because of its enclosed quality. It is shielded from the street by a «water-wall». A great deal that is very new has been risked here, particularly for an hotel, a type of building that in Berlin has avoided avant-garde experiments, at the most using tried and tested solutions and then offering its visitors showy scrolls and flourishes. The Esplanade not only goes its own way with façades of grey polished granite and white glazed facings, but the interior is also designed in a carefully up to date manner, in keeping with the architect's slogan «truthful space, honesty in the creation of space».

in der Nähe/nearby:
Hotel Berlin; Kurfürstenstraße 62-69
1957-58 • Paul Schwebes, Hans Schoßberger
1986-87 (Erweiterung) • Klaus Theo Brenner, Benedict Tonon

C 16 Ökohaus
Berlin-Tiergarten; Corneliusstraße 11-12
1988-90 • Frei Otto (Idee)

18 Bauherren planen mit ihren Architekten ein Haus, in dem sie selbst wohnen wollen. Dabei haben sie sich etliche Leitsätze auferlegt: schonungsvoller Umgang mit dem kostbaren innerstädtischen Bauplatz, Begrünung von Terrassen, Fassaden und Dächern, Anwendung ökologisch einwandfreier Baustoffe, sparsamer Umgang mit Wasser und Energie, Abwasser-Wärmerückgewinnung, Regenwassersammlung, Bau einer Pflanzenkläranlage. Gefördert wird das Projekt im Rahmen eines Bundes- und Landesprogramms für experimentellen Wohnungs- und Städtebau. Das Erstaunen vieler Fachleute, daß das Ökohaus auch nicht anders aussehe als gewöhnliche Häuser, kann umgemünzt werden in die Erkenntnis, daß es sich ökologisch vertretbar bauen läßt ohne gestalterische Nachteile für die Architektur eines Hauses.

18 clients and their architects planned a house in which they wished to live themselves. They laid down a considerable number of guidelines: careful use of the expensive, inner-city site, planted terraces, façades and roofs, use of ecologically sound building materials, economical use of water and electricity, recovery of heat from waste water, rainwater collection, construction of a botanical clarification plant. The project was supported by Federal and Land programmes for experimental residential and urban building. The astonishment of a number of experts that the Ökohaus does not look any different from any other house can be reinterpreted as a perception that is is possible to build in an ecologically sound fashion without disadvantages in terms of architectural design.

in der Nähe/nearby:
Jugoslawische Gesandtschaft; Rauchstraße 17-18
1938-40 • Werner March
Dänische Gesandtschaft; Drakestraße 1
1938-40 • Johann Emil Schaudt

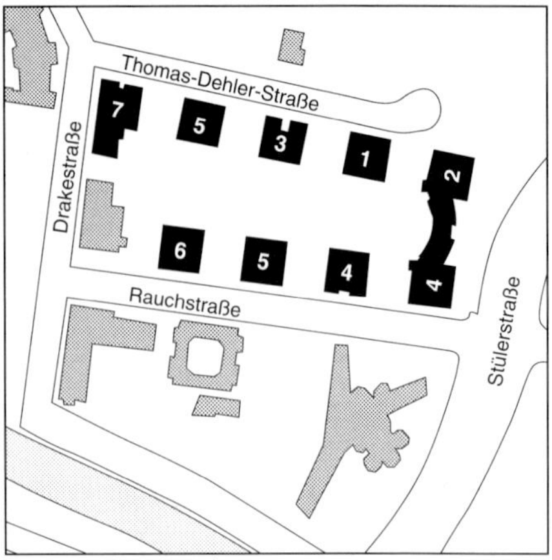

Rauchstraße 6 • Rob Krier
Rauchstraße 5 • Hans Hollein
Rauchstraße 4 • Francy Valentiny, Hubert Hermann
Stülerstraße 2/4 • Rob Krier
Thomas-Dehler-Straße 1 • Klaus Theo Brenner, Benedict Tonon
Thomas-Dehler-Straße 3 • Giorgio Grassi, Edoardo Guazzoni
Thomas-Dehler-Straße 5 • Henry Nielebock
Thomas-Dehler-Straße 7 • Aldo Rossi, Gianni Braghieri

C 17 Stadtvillen
Berlin-Tiergarten; Rauchstraße
1983-84

Die Planung im Rahmen der Internationalen Bauausstellung Berlin 1984/1987 hatte als Baugebiet auch das Tiergartenviertel erkoren. Für dessen Westzipfel, im Bereich der Rauchstraße, am Rande zwischen Zentrum und Parklandschaft sollte »attraktives und verschiedenartiges Wohnen« demonstriert werden. Der internationale Wettbewerb sah vor, daß die wenigen Gebäude nach neuem städtebaulichen Konzept und ohne einengende Vorgaben zu einer hohen Wohnqualität führen. Unmittelbarer Zugang, eigene Gärten, deren ungestörte Nutzung, freie Entscheidung über den Kontakt mit Nachbarn, das alles gehörte mit zu den Forderungen. Rob Krier aus Luxemburg, der den Wettbewerb gewann, sah von Anfang an isolierte Häuser mittlerer Größe nach Entwürfen verschiedener Architekten vor. In zwei Reihen ordnen sich neun Villen für jeweils mehrere Familien an, das Hauspaar an der Stirnseite riegelartig verbunden. Bezug nehmen die Häuser in Größe und Funktion auf die im Kriege zerstörte, die verbliebene und die neue Bebauung in der Umgebung, besonders auf die »Stadtvilla«. Diese erste Stadtvilla entstand in den Jahren 1980-81 südlich der Rauchstraße nach dem Entwurf der Architekten Dietrich Bangert, Bernd Jansen, Stefan Scholz und Axel Schultes, sie nimmt die Idee des Wohnens in individueller Abgeschlossenheit bei gleichzeitiger Nähe der Nachbarn vorweg. Das Schicksal der ersten Stadtvilla, der der Bauherr aus finanziellen Gründen die Großzügigkeit nahm, teilten im übertragenen Sinne auch die neuen Häuser. Hier war es die Bürokratie, die den Lauf des architektonischen Experiments in das Dickicht der Vorschriften lenkte. Mario Botta, der an dem Gemeinschaftsunternehmen beteiligt werden sollte, rückte deshalb frühzeitig von seinem Auftrag ab. Insgesamt beteiligten sich schließlich sieben Architekten und Gruppen aus mehreren Ländern, Rob Krier mit zwei Bauten, die übrigen mit je einem Bau. Bei aller grundrißlichen Kargheit entstanden zumindest äußerlich anspruchsvolle Gebäude: Rossi setzt auf das Treppenhaus ein Türmchen, Nielebock und Hollein geizten nicht mit Farben, Krier gab dem Hofdurchgang des Kopfbaues eine pathetische Plastik. – Das phantasievolle Ensemble fand nicht nur zur Bauaustellung reichlich Beachtung.

Planners of the Internationale Bauausstellung Berlin 1984/7 selected the Tiergarten as one of its areas. The western tip, the Rauchstrasse district, an extremity between the centre and parkland, was intended to demonstrate «attractive and varied ways of living». The international competition provided for a small number of buildings following a new urban planning concept with nothing to hamper a high quality of life. Direct access, gardens of their own, undisturbed use of these, freedom to decide about contact with neighbours were all part of the conditions laid down. Rob Krier from Luxemburg, who won the competition, saw the project in terms of isolated middle-sized buildings designed by various architects. This produced nine villas in two rows, each for several families, with the front pair of houses connected together. Size and function of the buildings relate to buildings on the site destroyed in the war, to those that remain and to new developments in the area, particularly the «urban villa». The first urban villa was built in 1980-1, south of Rauchstrasse, to a design by Dietrich Bangert, Bernd Jansen, Stefan Scholz and Axel Schultes, and anticipated the idea of living in a way that is both self-contained and yet close to neighbours. The first villa had its generous qualities reduced by the client for financial reasons, and the others shared this fate, though figuratively: here bureaucracy lured architectural experiment into a thicket of regulations. Mario Botta, who should have been involved in the communal project, thus withdrew from his contract at an early stage. A total of seven architects and groups from several countries were involved in the project. Rob Krier was responsible for two buildings, and the rest one each. Despite scant space in terms of ground plan, all the buildings were impressive at least in terms of their exterior: Rossi put a little tower on the stairwell, Nielebock and Hollein were generous with colour, Krier provided a dramatic sculpture for the courtyard entrance of the end building. The imaginative ensemble has continued to attract considerable attention outside the context of the building exhibition.

C 18 Siegessäule
Berlin-Tiergarten; Großer Stern
1873 • Johann Heinrich Strack

Ursprünglich stand die Siegessäule auf dem Königsplatz gegenüber dem Reichstag. Von dort wurde sie 1938 auf die zur Paradestraße ausgebaute Ost-West-Achse transloziert und zur monumentalen Wirkung die untere 6,5 m hohe Trommel eingefügt. Anlaß für die Aufstellung des Denkmals waren die Feldzüge zwischen 1864 und 1871. So schmücken bedeutungsvoll auch erbeutete Kanonenrohre den Säulenschaft, in dessen Innerem 285 Stufen zur Aussichtsplattform am Fuße der vergoldeten Siegesgöttin führen, ein Werk des Bildhauers Friedrich Drake.

Originally the Siegessäule was in Königsplatz opposite the Reichstag. It was transferred to the East-West axis in 1938, when the street had been developed for the purpose of military parades, and the 6.5 metre high drum was added to enhance its monumental effect. It was originally built to commemorate military campaigns between 1864 and 1871. Thus the shaft of the column is significantly decorated with captured cannons. Inside, 285 steps lead to the viewing platform at the feet of the gilded victory goddess, a work of sculptor Friedrich Drake.

in der Nähe/nearby:
Tiergarten; Straße des 17. Juni, Hofjägerallee
1833-38 • Peter Joseph Lenné
Bismarckdenkmal; Großer Stern
1901 • Reinhold Begas
Moltkedenkmal; Großer Stern
1904 • J. Uphues
Roondenkmal; Großer Stern
1904 • H. Magnussen
Sowjetisches Ehrenmal; Straße des 17. Juni
1945
Löwenbrücke; südlicher Tiergarten
1838 (Löwen) • Christian Daniel Rauch

C 19 Schloß Bellevue
Berlin-Tiergarten; Spreeweg
1785-86 • Michael Philipp Boumann

Für Prinz Ferdinand von Preußen, den jüngsten Bruder Friedrich des Großen, wurde dieses Schloß errichtet. Es ist der früheste Bau des Hofes, der den Regeln klassizistischer Architektur folgt. Das Grundmuster des Barockschlosses mit dem großen Ehrenhof ist zwar unverkennbar, doch werden die Risalite nur noch angedeutet, die Fassade ist flächiger, die Fenster reihen sich schlicht und das Dach schließt das Ganze beruhigend einheitlich ab. In der Zeit der Republik diente das Haus zunächst wechselnden Ausstellungen, dann war es Museum. 1938-39 gestaltete es Paul Baumgarten im Sinne der NS-Machthaber zum Gästehaus des Reiches um. Nach den Wiederherstellungsarbeiten bis 1959 ist es nun Amtssitz des Bundespräsidenten. Von den Innenräumen blieb nur der ovale Festsaal, 1790 von Carl Gotthard Langhans, in seiner ursprünglichen Gestalt erhalten.

This palace was built for Prince Ferdinand of Prussia, the youngest brother of Frederick the Great. It is the first court building to follow the rules of classical architecture. The basic pattern of a baroque place with large cour d'honneur is unmistakable, but the protruding sections are merely hinted at, the façade is flatter, the rows of windows plain, and the roof lends a comforting unity to the building as a whole. Under the Weimar Republic the building was used for temporary exhibitions, then it became a museum. In 1938-9 Paul Baumgartner adapted it for the use of guests of the Reich in conformity with the style of the ruling Nazi party. After restoration completed in 1959 it became the official seat of the Federal President. In the interior only the oval ballroom, 1790 by Carl Gotthard Langhans, has survived in its original form.

in der Nähe/nearby:
Schloßpark; Spreeweg
1787 • Johann August Eyserbeck
1958-59 • Reinhard Besserer
Englischer Garten; Altonaer Straße
1952 • Wilhelm Alverdes
Gerickesteg; Calvinstraße
1913-14 • Bruno Möhring

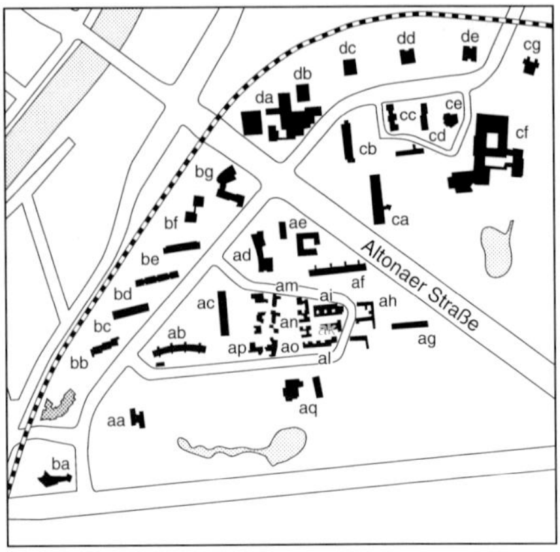

C 20 Hansaviertel
Berlin-Tiergarten; Klopstockstraße, Bartnigallee
1955-57

Als Ergebnis gründerzeitlichen Spekulationsgeistes entstand am Nordwestrande des Tiergartens seit den siebziger Jahren des vorigen Jahrhunderts eine dichte vier- bis fünfgeschossige Wohnbebauung für wohlsituierte Bürger in den Vorderhäusern und ärmere Mieter in den Hofflügeln. Die Hanseatische Erschließungsgesellschaft gab dem Viertel den Namen. Nach dem Zweiten Weltkrieg waren von 161 Gebäuden noch 21 bedingt bewohnbar, alle anderen zerstört. Ein Wettbewerb im Jahre 1953 bereitete die Neubebauung des Hansaviertels vor; Gerhard Jobst und Willy Kreuer erhielten den ersten Preis. Es folgte der Plan, den Wiederaufbau zum Kernstück einer internationalen Bauausstellung zu machen, die dann 1957 in Berlin stattfand. 53 Architekten aus 14 Ländern sowie 10 Gartengestalter sorgten für ein buntes Bild aus niedrigen Zeilen, Punkthäusern, Bungalows und hohen Hausscheiben, eingebettet in viel Grün und aufgelockert durch zwei Kirchen, den U-Bahnhof, ein kleines Einkaufszentrum mit einem Kino, eine Bücherei und einen Kindergarten. Hier konnten nun 5000 Menschen nach den Prinzipien des modernen Städte- und Wohnungsbaus »im Herzen einer Weltstadt in Licht, Luft und Sonne leben«. Zu verstehen ist das Hansaviertel als baulicher Ausdruck des westdeutschen Wirtschaftswunders sowie als Antwort auf den hölzernen Neoklassizismus der dreißiger Jahre und die pompösen Neubauten der ein halbes Jahrzehnt zuvor entstandenen Stalinallee im Ostteil der Stadt.

In the 1870s, as a result of speculation at the time of rapid industrial expansion, a great deal of residential accommodation in four to five storey buildings sprang up on the north-western edge of the Tiergarten. Comfortably-off middle class residents lived in the front buildings and poorer tenants in the courtyard sections. The district got its name from the Hanseatische Erschliessungsgesellschaft, which was responsible for a lot of the building. After the Second World War, 21 of what had originally been 161 buildings were still habitable, all the rest were destroyed. A competition in 1953 prepared for rebuilding the Hansaviertel; Gerhard Jobst and Willy Kreuer won the first prize. Then came the plan to make rebuilding the core of the Internationale Bauausstellung, which took place in Berlin in 1957. 53 architects from 14 countries, and 10 garden designers created a colourful picture with low terraces, point blocks, bungalows and tall slabs of building, set in a great deal of green and broken up by two churches, underground station, small shopping centre with cinema, library and kindergarten. It was now possible for 5,000 people to live here according to the principles of modern urban and residential building «at the heart of a metropolis in light, air and sun». The Hansaviertel is best understood as an expression of the West German economic miracle and as a reply to the wooden neoclassicism of the thirties, and to the bombastic new buildings that had sprung up half a decade earlier in Stalinallee in the eastern part of the city.

östlich der Klopstockstraße
(aa) Hochhaus »Giraffe«, Klopstockstraße 2 • Klaus Müller-Rehm, Gerhard Siegmann
(ab) Händelallee 3/9 • Walter Gropius
(ac) Klopstockstraße 14/18 • Pierre Vago
(ad) Klopstockstraße 30/32 • Alvar Aalto
(ae) Stadtbibliothek; Altonaer Straße 15 • Werner Düttmann
(af) Altonaer Straße 3/9 • Fritz Jaenecke, Sten Samuelson
(ag) Altonaer Straße 1 • Paul Baumgarten
(ah) Händelallee 26/34 • Eduard Ludwig
(ai) Händelallee 33/39 • Arne Jacobsen
(ak) Händelallee 29 und 41 • Gerhard Weber
(al) Händelallee 43/47 • Alois Giefer, Hermann Mäckler
(am) Händelallee 49/53 • Johannes Krahn
(an) Händelallee 55/57 • Sep Ruf
(ao) Händelallee 59 • Sergius Ruegenberg, Wolf v. Möllendorff
(ap) Händelallee 63 • Günter Hönow
(aq) Kaiser-Friedrich-Gedächtnis-Kirche; Händelallee 20/22 • Ludwig Lemmer

westlich der Klopstockstraße
(ba) Berlin-Pavillon; Straße des 17. Juni • Hermann Fehling, Daniel Gogel, Peter Pfankuch
(bb) Klopstockstraße 7/11 • Hans Müller
(bc) Klopstockstraße 13/17 • Günther Gottwald
(bd) Klopstockstraße 19/23 • Wassili Luckhardt, Hubert Hoffmann
(be) Klopstockstraße 25/27 • Paul Schneider-Esleben
(bf) Kindergarten; Klopstockstraße 29 • Hochbauamt Tiergarten
(bg) St.-Ansgar-Kirche; Klopstockstraße 31 • Willy Kreuer

südlich der Bartnigallee
(ca) Altonaer Straße 4/14 • Oscar Niemeyer
(cb) Bartnigallee 2/4 • Egon Eiermann
(cc) Hanseatenweg 1/3 • Max Taut
(cd) Bartnigallee 10 a-d • Kay Fisker
(ce) Bartnigallee 12 • Otto H. Senn
(cf) Akademie der Künste (1960); Hanseatenweg 10 • Werner Düttmann
(cg) Bartnigallee 16 • Hans Schwippert

nördlich der Bartnigallee
(da) Einkaufszentrum; Altonaer Straße 18/20 • Hansrudolf Plarre, Ernst Zinsser
(db) Bartnigallee 5 • Luciano Baldessari
(dc) Bartnigallee 7 • J. H. van den Broek, J. B. Bakema
(dd) Bartnigallee 9 • Gustav Hassenpflug
(de) Bartnigallee 11/13 • Eugène Beaudoin, Raymond Lopez

C 21 Kongreßhalle
Berlin-Tiergarten; John-Foster-Dulles-Allee 10
1956-57 • Hugh A. Stubbins

Anläßlich der »Interbau 1957« wurde die Kongreßhalle als Symbol der Deutsch-Amerikanischen Freundschaft errichtet. Die eigens ins Leben gerufene Benjamin-Franklin-Stiftung stand hinter dem Vorhaben. Es sollte ein Tagungsort entstehen für literarische, wissenschaftliche und andere kulturelle Gesellschaften, und der Bau sollte die Höchstleistung im Bauschaffen der Epoche zum Ausdruck bringen. Das erste Ziel ließ sich in einer geschickten Raumfolge erreichen und darüber hinaus die Funktion des Gebäudes durch die Betonung des Auditoriums unmißverständlich in den Vordergrund rücken. Das zweite Ziel löste der Architekt durch die Wahl einer Hängedachkonstruktion, die in den fünfziger Jahren als Novum der Ingenieurbaukunst für Aufsehen sorgte. Die beiden kühn geschwungenen Stahlbetonträger des Daches schweben gleichsam in der Luft, ruhen lediglich auf den beiden äußeren Widerlagern, und die großen Glasflächen der Halle leugnen scheinbar jede statische Unterstützung der Dachkonstruktion. Die bedingungslose Zuversicht in den modernen Werkstoff Stahlbeton verschaffte der Kongreßhalle den Ruhm des Wahrzeichens, wurde ihr aber auch 1980 zum Verhängnis, als Teile des Daches einstürzten. Bis 1987 dauerte der Wiederaufbau des inzwischen zum Baudenkmal erhobenen Gebäudes.

The Kongresshalle was built as a symbol of German-American friendship on the occasion of «Interbau 1957». The Benjamin Franklin Foundation, set up specifically for the purpose, was behind the project. The aim was to provide a conference centre for literary, scientific and other cultural societies, and the building was intended to represent the limits of achievement as far as the architecture of the period was concerned. The first goal was achieved in a skilful sequence of rooms, and beyond this the function of the building was unmistakably brought into the foreground by the stress laid upon the auditorium. The second aim was solved by the architect by choosing a suspended roof structure, which caused quite a stir as a novelty in fifties architecture. The two bold curves of the roof support seem to hover in the air, and are supported only by the two outer abutment piers, and the great glass areas of the hall seem to deny any static support of the roof structure. Unquestioning faith in reinforced concrete as a modern material brought the Kongresshalle fame and the distinction of becoming a symbol, but was also its undoing in 1980, when parts of the roof collapsed. It took until 1987 to restore the building, which in the meantime had been listed as an architectural monument.

in der Nähe/nearby:
Carillon; John-Foster-Dulles-Allee
1986-87 • Dietrich Bangert, Bernd Jansen, Stefan Scholz, Axel Schultes

C 22 Reichstag
Berlin-Tiergarten; Platz der Republik 1
1884-94 • Paul Wallot

Erst ein Jahrzehnt nach Schaffung des Kaiserreiches war man sich über den Bau eines Reichstagsgebäudes einig. Am Wettbewerb nahmen 183 Architekten teil, Paul Wallot erhielt den Vorrang. 1884 konnte mit dem Bau begonnen werden, der sich über zehn Jahre hinzog. Mehr als 26 Millionen Mark verschlang das Projekt einschließlich der üppigen Ausstattung. Bereits 30 Jahre später galt das Bauwerk als erweiterungsbedürftig. Ein neuer Wettbewerb blieb aber ohne bauliches Ergebnis, bis 1933 die Geschichte des Reichstages vorläufig durch Brandstiftung endete. In den folgenden Jahren war dann auch ein Ort des Parlamentarismus überflüssig. Weiteren Schäden im Weltkrieg folgten Jahre der Ungewißheit. Nach der bis 1972 währenden Wiederherstellung tagten von Zeit zu Zeit Bundesgremien im alten Haus; in der gesamtdeutschen Hauptstadt Berlin wird der Reichstag nun wieder Sitz des Parlamentes. Norman Foster, Santiago Calatrava und Piet de Bruyn sind für den Umbau favorisiert. Verändern wird sich auch die gesamte Umgebung des Reichstags im Spreebogen. Axel Schultes, Gewinner des städtebaulichen Wettbewerbs, schlägt als Pendant zum Reichstag das Bundesratsgebäude vor, das in einer gemeinsamen Achse neben der Kongreßhalle angeordnet wird. Nach Norden schließt ein Riegel mit Kanzleramt und Regierungsgebäuden an, jenseits der Spree folgen Blöcke unterschiedlicher Nutzung.

A mere decade after the creation of the Reich, agreement was reached about a building to house the Reichstag, or parliament. 183 architects took part in the competition, which was won by Paul Wallot. Building eventually started in 1884, and took ten years. The project swallowed over 26 million marks, including the lavish interior, but as early as the twenties it was felt that the building should be extended. A new competition failed to produce a suitable building, and the history of the Reichstag came to a temporary end when it was set on fire in 1933. In subsequent years a building in which parliament met was superfluous. After additional damages in the Second World War came years of uncertainty. Following reconstruction which took until 1972, various committees of the Federal Government met in the building from time to time. As Berlin has become the German capital once again, the Reichstag is scheduled to become the seat of Parliament. Norman Foster, Santiago Calatrava and Piet de Bruyn shared first prize in the competition for the conversion. The entire surroundings of the Reichstag, the so-called Spreebogen area, will also be redesigned. Axel Schultes, the winner of the urban design competition, has proposed to complement the Reichstag with a new building for the Bundesrat, to be placed next to the Kongresshalle along the same axis. To the north a new complex consisting of the Kanzleramt and various government buildings will be erected, followed by mixed use development on the other bank of the Spree.

D
Berlin
Westliche City

In der Kreuzung des 1863 festgeschriebenen Ringstraßenabschnittes von Charlottenburg zur Hasenheide mit dem Reitweg von Berlin zum Grunewald an der damaligen Rückseite des 1844 eröffneten Zoologischen Gartens war städtebaulich ein Punkt markiert, der 1882 durch die neue Stadtbahn noch aufgewertet wurde. Hierhin zielte die bauliche Entwicklung Berlins außerhalb seiner alten Mauern mit dem Stadtviertel südlich des Tiergartens, dem später so genannten »Alten Westen«. Hier war auch die erste bauliche Berührung mit der Residenzstadt Charlottenburg zu erwarten. Ab 1882 baute eine Tochtergesellschaft der Deutschen Bank den Kurfürstendamm zur Prachtstraße aus. Auf deren Drängen wurde 1890 auch der Bau der Kaiser-Wilhelm-Gedächtniskirche als »monumentaler Anziehungspunkt« beschlossen. Ihr gegenüber baute Schwechten das Romanische Haus und später das Neue Romanische Haus. Das Romanische Café und das Café des Westens waren bald Treffpunkt von Intellektuellen und Künstlern. Theater, Kinos, Ausstellungsgebäude bildeten den Hintergrund. Das, was hier um die Jahrhundertwende gedanklich bewegt wurde, war in den zwanziger Jahren selbstverständliche Grundlage einer weltstädtisch-modernen City, die Abkehr von kaiserzeitlichen Traditionen war vorweggenommen. Auch die Voraussetzungen für die vornehme Geschäftsstraße Tauentzien-Kurfürstendamm reichen in die Zeit nach der Jahrhundertwende zurück. Am Wittenbergplatz öffnete 1907 das Kaufhaus des Westens und begründete eine Welle von Laden- und Geschäftshausbauten. Publikum und Käufer brachte von 1902 an die neue Untergrundbahn, für die 1913 die Station Wittenbergplatz zum Knotenpunkt weiterer Linien, zur Uhlandstraße, nach Wilmersdorf und Dahlem sowie zur Innenstadt ausgebaut wurde. Die Spaltung der Stadt nach 1945 ließ den Bereich um den Bahnhof Zoo und die Gedächtniskirche zum unangefochtenen Zentrum West-Berlins aufrücken, zur Drehscheibe geschäftlichen und kulturellen Lebens. Diesen Rang wird die Westliche City wohl auch im wiedervereinigten Berlin behaupten.

The junction of the ring road section from Charlottenburg to Hasenheide fixed in 1863 and the bridleway from Berlin to the Grunewald at what was then the back of the Zoological Garden, opened in 1844, marked a key point in urban development terms, and it was further enhanced by the new Stadtbahn in 1882. This area now became crucial for building development in Berlin outside its old walls, along with the part of the town south of the Tiergarten, later known as the «Old West». Here too the first structural contact with the residence town of Charlottenburg was to be expected. A daughter company of the Deutsche Bank extended the Kurfürstendamm as a show street from 1882. Pressure from this source also led to the building of the Kaiser-Wilhelm-Gedächtniskirche as a «monumental point of attraction», in 1890. Opposite it Schwechten built the Romanisches Haus and later the Neues Romanisches Haus. The Romanisches Café and the Café des Westens soon became meeting places for intellectuals and artists, with theatres, cinemas and exhibition centres forming the background. Things that were thought about here at the turn of the century were to be taken for granted as the basis of a modern cosmopolitan city in the twenties; a turn away from the traditions of the imperial period was anticipated. The necessary conditions for Tauentzienstrasse-Kurfürstendamm as a fashionable shopping street go back to the time just after the turn of the century. The Kaufhaus des Westens opened in Wittenbergplatz in 1907, the first in a wave of shop and office buildings. Public and buyers were brought here from 1902 by the new underground railway, and in 1913 the station in Wittenbergplatz was extended as a junction for new lines, to Uhlandstrasse, Wilmersdorf and Dahlem, and to the inner city. Division of the city in 1945 promoted the area around Bahnhof Zoo and the Gedächtniskirche to be the undisputed centre of West Berlin, the heart of its business and cultural life, and it will probably assert its claim to this status in a reunified Berlin.

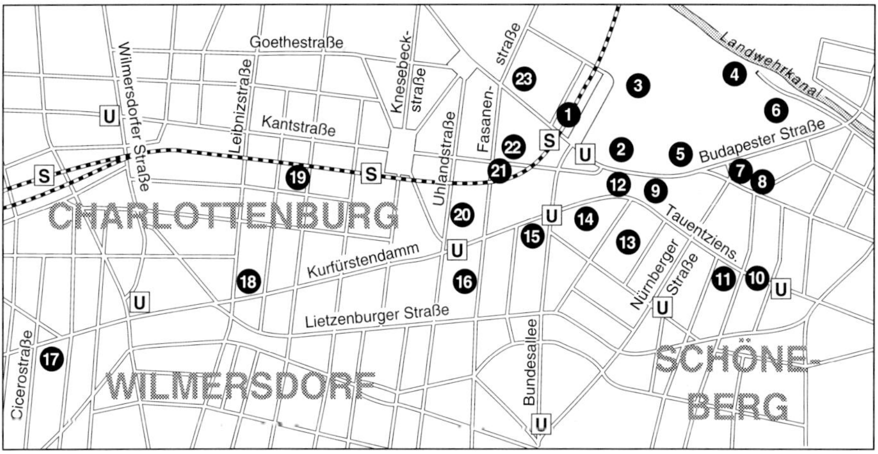

D 1 Bahnhof Zoologischer Garten
D 2 Zentrum am Zoo mit Zoopalast
D 3 Zoologischer Garten
D 4 Beamtenwohnhaus
D 5 Aquarium
D 6 Hilton-Hotel (Intercontinental)
D 7 Grundkreditbank
D 8 Lenzhaus
D 9 Europa-Center
D 10 U-Bahnhof Wittenbergplatz
D 11 Kaufhaus des Westens (KaDeWe)
D 12 Gedächtniskirche
D 13 Hotel Steigenberger
D 14 Marmorhaus
D 15 Allianzversicherung
D 16 Villa Grisebach
D 17 Universum (Schaubühne)
D 18 Wohnhaus
D 19 Kindertagesstätte
D 20 Kempinski-Plaza
D 21 Kantdreieck
D 22 Theater des Westens
D 23 Berliner Bank

D 1 Bahnhof Zoologischer Garten
Berlin-Charlottenburg; Hardenbergstraße 30
1934-40 • Fritz Hane

Mit dem Bau der Stadtbahn entstand 1880-81 zunächst eine Haltestelle für Vorortzüge, das Hinterland für den großen Bahnhof fehlte damals, der Kurfürstendamm war dem Zustand des Reitweges noch nicht entwachsen. Um die Jahrhundertwende änderte sich aber die Situation: Die neue elektrische Schnellbahn kreuzte am Bahnhof »Zoo« als Untergrundbahn die alte Viadukttrasse, der »Neue Westen« erblühte mit Gedächtniskirche, Romanischem Haus, Kaufhaus des Westens, Cafés, Restaurants, Theatern und Galerien. Es dauerte aber noch bis in die dreißiger Jahre, daß mit zwei Hallen – einer wegen des Rauchs der Dampflokomotiven hohen Fernbahnhalle und einer für die elektrisch betriebenen Züge niedrigen S-Bahnhalle – ein neuer Bahnhofsbau entstand. Unmittelbarer Anlaß waren die olympischen Spiele, für die sich die Stadt herausputzte und die für den Nahverkehr eine besondere Herausforderung darstellten. Zwischen Abdrosselung des Eisenbahnverkehrs und Aufblühen des westlichen Zentrums vollzog sich die Nachkriegsgeschichte des Bahnhofs Zoo. Nach 1984, mit dem Besitzwechsel bei der S-Bahn und motiviert durch die 750-Jahr-Feier Berlins, kam der Bahnhof in den Genuß einer Grunderneuerung und Modernisierung, dabei wurde die Gestalt von 1935 denkmalpflegerisch wiederhergestellt.

When the Stadtbahn was built in 1880-1 there was only a halt for local trains here, there being no hinterland for a major station: the Kurfürstendamm was still only a bridle path. The situation changed quickly about the turn of the century: the new electric express railway ran under the old viaduct line at Bahnhof Zoo, the «New West» was flourishing with Gedächtniskirche, Romanisches Haus, Kaufhaus des Westens, cafés, restaurants, theatres and galleries. But it was not until the thirties that a new station was built, with two halls – a high hall for long distance trains, because of the smokey steam locomotives, and a low one for the electric S-Bahn trains. The immediate reason was the Olympic games, for which the city was smartening itself up, and which were a particular challenge to local traffic. Post-war history of the station was played out against a background of much reduced rail traffic and the increasing importance of the western centre. After 1984, when the S-Bahn changed hands, and motivated by the 750th anniversary of Berlin, the station was thoroughly rebuilt and modernized, retaining its 1935 design, with the status of an ancient monument.

in der Nähe/nearby:
Heereswaffenamt; Jebensstraße 1
1928-29 • Otto Rudolf Salvisberg
Landwehrkasino; Jebensstraße 2
1908-09 • Schmieden & Boethke
Oberverwaltungsgericht; Hardenbergstraße 31
1905-07 • Paul Kieschke, Eduard Fürstenau

D 2 Zentrum am Zoo mit Zoopalast
Berlin-Charlottenburg; Hardenbergstraße 29 b
1956-57 • Schwebes, Schoßberger & Fritsche

Die Randbebauung des Zoo nördlich der Gedächtniskirche mit den Ausstellungshallen, dem Haus Gourmenia und Poelzigs Capitol mit der Ladenzeile war nach 1945 unrettbar zerstört. Nach der Spaltung der Stadt erfuhr die westliche City um den Bahnhof Zoo ihre Aufwertung zum neuen Zentrum, und die Bebauung des Ruinenstreifens rückte in den Brennpunkt städtebaulichen Interesses. Die Bandstadt-Vision jener Jahre gab der Reihung von Gebäuden den Vorzug vor einer mehr zentrierten Ausrichtung auf den Platzmittelpunkt mit der Gedächtniskirche. So entstand bis 1957 die Baufolge von Hochhaus, Zoopalast, Langhaus und kleinem Hochhaus, die in der Tiefen- und Höhenstaffelung bewußt jeden Eindruck einer geschlossenen Bebauung vermeidet, wenn schon bei dem wertvollen Baugrund die in den fünfziger Jahren bevorzugte aufgelockerte Anordnung freistehender Gebäude nicht in Frage kam. Die Fassadengestaltung erhebt keinen weiteren Anspruch, als schlicht-modern zu sein. Die Belanglosigkeit der Rasterfronten wird hier und da durch eine dekorativ wirksame Rhythmisierung durchbrochen.

Peripheral development around the Zoo north of the Gedächtniskirche with exhibition halls, Haus Gourmenia and Poelzig's Capitol with row of shops were damaged beyond repair after 1945. After the division of the city the western area around the Zoo acquired enhanced status as the new centre, and development of the ruined strip became a focus of interest for town planners. The ribbon city vision of those years preferred rows of buildings to a centred arrangement with the Gedächtniskirche as the focal point. Thus until 1957 the sequence of high-rise block, Zoopalast, long block and lower high-rise building in their staggering of high and lower buildings consciously avoided any impression of completed development, since on a site of this value the broken up arrangement of free-standing buildings preferred in the fifties was out of the question. Façade design does not try to do anything more than be plain and modern. The triviality of the grid façades is occasionally broken by a decoratively effective rhythmic element.

in der Nähe/nearby:
Platzbauten; Hardenbergplatz
1986-87 • Arno Bonanni, Klaus Lattermann

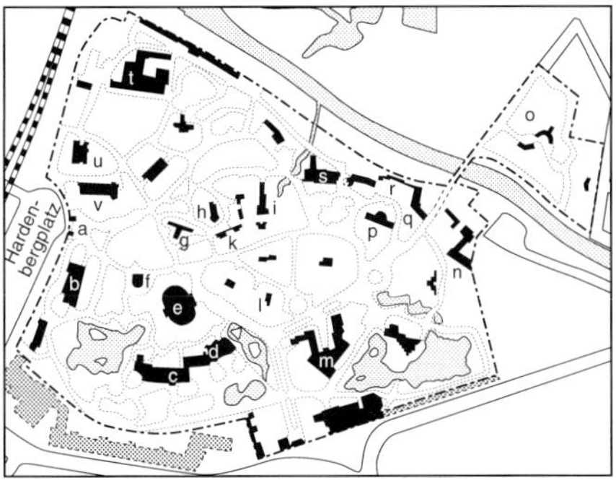

D 3 Zoologischer Garten
Berlin-Tiergarten; Hardenbergplatz
1841-44 • Peter Joseph Lenné

Nach Paris, London, Amsterdam und Antwerpen erhielt 1844 auch Deutschland seinen ersten Zoologischen Garten vor den Toren von Berlin. Zuvor existierte bereits unter Friedrich Wilhelm III. eine ansehnliche Sammlung von 850 Tieren auf der Pfaueninsel, die dessen Sohn nach Übernahme des Thrones der neuen Zoo-Aktiengesellschaft stiftete, zusammen mit dem Fasaneriegelände am Südrand des Tiergartens. Kein Geringerer als Lenné gestaltete den Landschaftspark, den die Tiergehege und Käfige bereicherten. Erst als die wachsende Stadt um 1870 den Zoologischen Garten einholte, stellte sich auch eine solide wirtschaftliche Situation ein. Eine neue Generation von Tierhäusern wurde geschaffen, die alle in folkloristischer Weise auf die Herkunft der Tiere eingingen, das Antilopenhaus ist als solches Beispiel erhalten. Bis zum Ersten Weltkrieg blieb diese Gestaltungsidee – zuletzt unter den Architekten Zaar & Vahl – bestehen, dann traten eher sachliche Bauten hinzu. Im Zweiten Weltkrieg wurden Garten und Tierhäuser verwüstet, die Tiere starben oder verwilderten. Nach 1945 konnte durch mühevollen Wiederaufbau und Neubau der Anschluß an die Tradition des Zoo gefunden werden, der sich nun im Herzen der aufstrebenden Westlichen City veränderten Gegebenheiten stellen mußte. Der Wandel in der Auffassung von artgerechter Tierhaltung und ein nostalgisch gefärbtes Streben nach den malerischen Bildern der alten Tore und Bauten geben der heutigen Anlage ihr Gesicht.

After Paris, London, Amsterdam and Antwerp, Germany acquired its first Zoological Garden, outside the gates of Berlin, in 1844. Before this, under Friedrich Wilhelm III, there was a sizeable collection of 850 animals on the Pfaueninsel, and these were presented by his son after his accession to the new Zoo-Aktiengesellschaft, along with the pheasant-run area on the southern edge of the Tiergarten. Lenné himself designed the landscaped park, which was then enhanced by the addition of animal enclosures and cages. It was not until the rapidly growing city absorbed the Zoo in 1870 that the economic situation became a little more sound. A new generation of animal houses was created, all alluding through folklore to the animals' country of origin; the antelope house is a surviving example of this approach. This design idea persisted until the First World War, finally under architects Zaar and Vahl, then after this rather more neutral buildings were added. In the Second World War the gardens and animal houses were devastated, and the animals died or returned to the wild state. After 1945 laborious rebuilding and new buildings re-established contact with the old tradition of the Zoo, which now had to face changed conditions in the up-and-coming western centre. The present appearance of the Zoo derives from a changed view of keeping animals in a way that is fair to species, and a nostalgic striving after the picturesque image of the old gates and buildings.

(a) Löwentor • 1987-88 • Schaefers & Löffler
(b) Elefantenhaus • 1987-88 • Stockhaus, Srp & Hafemann
(c) Affenhaus • 1958-65 • Heinz Diesing
(d) Tropenhaus • 1974-75 • Schaefers
(e) Antilopenhaus • 1871-72 • Ende & Böckmann
(f) Hühner- und Taubenhaus • 1909-10 • Zoo-Baubüro
(g) Großkäfige • 1936-37
(h) Schweinehaus • 1906-07 • Zaar & Vahl
(i) Wildrindhaus • 1937
(k) Büffelhaus • 1904-05 • Zaar & Vahl
(l) Hirschhaus • 1899-1900 • Fritz Schultze
(m) Raubtierhaus • 1970-75 • Schaefers
(n) Nashornhaus • 1986-87 • Schaefers & Löffler
(o) Erdteilanlagen • 1984-87 • Schaefers & Löffler
(p) Wildpferdehaus • 1909 • Zaar & Vahl
(q) Eselhaus • 1909-10 • Zaar & Vahl
(r) Pferdehaus • 1969-70 • Zoo-Baubüro
(s) Flußpferdhaus • 1955-56 • Heinz Diesing
(t) Vogelhaus • 1961-62 • Heinz Diesing
(u) Kamelhaus • 1960-61 • Heinz Diesing
(v) Nashornhaus • 1962-64 • Heinz Diesing

D 4 Beamtenwohnhaus
Berlin-Tiergarten; Lützowufer 36
1928-29 • Fritz Höger

Fritz Höger, der berühmte Hamburger Architekt, dessen Chilehaus symbolhaft für expressionistische Architektur steht, ist mit wenigen Bauten auch in Berlin präsent. Einer ist das Beamtenwohnhaus des Zoologischen Gartens am Landwehrkanal. Der Virtuose der Ziegelbaukunst ließ auch hier keine Gelegenheit aus, zu zeigen, welche plastischen Möglichkeiten in den kleinen roten Quadern stecken. Der Baukörper besteht zunächst schlicht aus zwei ineinandergeschobenen Kuben, die dem Gesetz der Zeit folgend ein weit auskragendes Flachdach deckt. Soweit möchte man schon an einen Bau der Neuen Sachlichkeit glauben, wären da nicht die Wände mit ihrem abstrakten textilen Muster und dem Fries laufender Hasen. Tierdarstellungen aus einfachen Verblendziegeln überziehen auch die Mauer, die zum Kassenhäuschen des einstigen Nordeingangs führt. Die Tierbilder gipfeln in einem vollplastischen Bären. Er ist nicht das einzige Ziegel-Tier Högers in Berlin. So läßt sich in der Rudolstädter Straße auch ein meisterhaft gemauerter Schafbock bewundern.

Fritz Höger, the famous Hamburg architect, whose Chilehaus stands as a symbol of Expressionist architecture, is also represented by a few buildings in Berlin. One of these is the house for officials of the Zoologischer Garten on the Landwehrkanal. The virtuoso of brick building missed no opportunities to show what three-dimensional effects these little red rectangles can make. The building consists essentially of two cubes pushed into one another, with a protruding flat roof, as was the custom at the time. So far the building could be taken as an example of Neue Sachlichkeit, if it were not for the walls, with their abstract textile pattern, and the frieze of running hares. The wall that led to the entrance building and ticket desk for the former northern entrance is also covered with representations of animals in simple facing bricks. The animal pictures culminate in a three-dimensional bear. It is not Höger's only brick animal in Berlin. There is a masterly ram to be admired in Rudolstädter Strasse.

in der Nähe/nearby:
Rosa-Luxemburg-Denkmal; Lützowufer, Lichtensteinbrücke
1987 • Ralf Schüler, Ursulina Schüler-Witte

D 5 Aquarium
Berlin-Tiergarten; Budapester Straße 30 a/32
1911-13 • Zaar & Vahl

Seit 1869 besaß Berlin im Hof eines Wohnhauses Unter den Linden Ecke Schadowstraße ein Aquarium – beliebt beim Publikum, doch mit seinen labyrinthischen Gängen nicht mehr zeitgemäß, verschwand es um die Jahrhundertwende. Dafür wuchs am Südrand des Zoologischen Gartens ein ansehnlicher Neubau aus dem Boden. Neben Fischen waren hier auch Insekten, Spinnen, Amphibien, Schlangen und Reptilien zu sehen. Die seltene Bauaufgabe lösten die Architekten in einer logischen horizontalen und vertikalen Abfolge der Räume: Ringförmig ordnen sich von außen nach innen Futtergang, Aquarien, Schaugang, Aquarien, Futtergang und in der Mitte ein großes Becken. Im Keller befinden sich die Betriebsräume mit der Süß- und Seewasseraufbereitung, das oberste Geschoß ist zur Belichtung der dortigen Terrarien mit Glasdächern versehen. Der Kopfbau mit Eingangshalle und Treppen ist um ein Geschoß für das Insektarium höhergeführt. Äußerlich erhielt der Bau in seinen fensterlosen Wandfeldern Reliefschmuck in Form von Saurierbildern, da sich hierauf durch jüngste Ausgrabungen und Funde das zeitgenössische Interesse in besonderem Maße richtete. Im Jahre 1980 konnte ein Erweiterungsbau von Schaefers & Löffler mit Landschaftsaquarien eröffnet werden.

Berlin had an aquarium in the courtyard of a residential building in Unter den Linden at the corner of Schadowstrasse from 1869. It was very popular with the public, but its labyrinthine corridors were no longer up to date, and it disappeared around the turn of the century. It was replaced by a handsome new building on the southern edge of the Zoological Garden. This housed insects, spiders, amphibians, snakes and reptiles, as well as fish. The architects solved this unusual structural problem in a logical horizontal and vertical sequence of space: feeding walk, aquariums, spectator walk, aquariums, feeding walk are arranged in a circle around a large central pool. In the cellar are the machine rooms for preparing fresh and salt water, and the upper storey has glass roofs to provide light for the terrariums there. The end of the building containing entrance hall and stairs is a storey higher, to house the insect department. The exterior walls have no windows, but are broken into areas with relief sculpture in the form of pictures of dinosaurs, as these were a particular focus of contemporary interest because of recent excavations and finds. In 1980 an extension housing landscape aquaria, designed by Schaefers & Löffler, was opened.

in der Nähe/nearby:
Elefantentor; Budapester Straße 34
1984-85 • Hans Schaefers, Hans-Jürgen Löffler, Jochen Ihle

D 6 Hilton-Hotel (Inter-Continental)
Berlin-Tiergarten; Budapester Straße 2
1957-58 • William Pereira, Luckman

Der Untergang der großen Berliner Hotelpaläste im Zweiten Weltkrieg verlangte den Neubau repräsentativer Häuser. Mit der wirtschaftlichen Spaltung der Stadt zeichnete sich seit Anfang der fünfziger Jahre die Entwicklung der Zoogegend zur neuen City ab, und das Band Kurfürstendamm–Budapester Straße–Kurfürstenstraße wurde bevorzugter Standort neuer Hotels – der »Kudamm« als Pulsader großstädtischen Lebens, die Straßen östlich der Gedächtniskirche wegen ihrer attraktiven Nähe zum Tiergarten. Auf dem Gelände der zerstörten Zoogaststätten baute man 1957-58 ein großes 600-Betten-Hotel, das an die amerikanische Hilton-Kette verpachtet wurde. Die Kombination von Hochhaus und Flachbau entspricht der seinerzeit für Großbauten üblichen Baumasseverteilung. Die Außengestaltung im schachbrettartigen Raster stellte das Äußerste an ornamentalem Aufwand dar in einer Zeit ambitionsloser Sachlichkeit. Die frühere Prachtentfaltung im Hotelbau ersetzte nun die Großzügigkeit in Gliederung und Anordnung der Bauteile. Lange Jahre blieb das »Berlin Hilton« größtes und komfortabelstes Hotel in Berlin. Seit 1979 heißt das Haus Inter-Continental. Den hohen Ansprüchen an ein Luxushotel trug inzwischen eine Modernisierung Rechnung.

As Berlin's great palace hotels had been destroyed in the Second World War, new and imposing buildings had to be provided. When the city was divided the area around the Zoo began to develop as the new centre from the fifties onwards, and the strip running from the Kurfürstendamm via Budapester Strasse to Kurfürstenstrasse became the preferred site for new hotels – the Kudamm as the artery of cosmopolitan life, and the streets east of the Gedächtniskirche because of their attractive proximity to the Tiergarten. In 1957-8 a large hotel with 600 beds was built on the site of the Zoo restaurants that had been destroyed, and this was leased to the American Hilton chain. The combination of high-rise and lower building was in keeping with the massing for large buildings that was usual at the time. The façade design with its chessboard grid shows an extreme degree of ornamental effort for the unambitious neutrality of its period. The splendour that used to be customary in hotel buildings is replaced here by lavishness in articulating and arranging the parts of the building. For years the «Berlin Hilton» was the largest and most comfortable hotel in Berlin. Since 1979 the building has been called Inter-Continental. The high expectations of a luxury hotel have in the meantime been met by modernization.

in der Nähe/nearby:
Hotel Schweizerhof; Budapester Straße 21/31
1964-66, 1971-77 • Schwebes & Schoßberger uam.

D 7 Grundkreditbank
Berlin-Tiergarten; Budapester Straße 35
1984-85 • Hans Joachim Pysall, Peter Otto Stahrenberg

Das kaiserzeitliche Berlin liebte architektonische Lösungen für Ecken. Spitz, abgerundet oder abgestumpft, mit Türmchen, mit Erkern oder mit Kuppeln – alle Register baukünstlerischen Formenschatzes wurden gezogen. In den fünfziger und sechziger Jahren ließ das Diktat puritanischer Sachlichkeit solche Gestaltung nicht zu, das Ergebnis waren aus Verlegenheit fehlende Eckbauten, wie heute im Stadtbild vielfach zu beobachten ist. Erst die phantasiebetonte Architektur der achtziger Jahre fand wieder zur Prägung des Straßenraumes durch die Hervorhebung von Eckgebäuden zurück. Der Neubau für die Grundkreditbank überbrückt den spitzen Winkel zwischen Kurfürstenstraße und Budapester Straße durch einen Kreisbogen. Die Starrheit des Kreisbogens verleiht dem Bau etwas Statisches, Monumentales. Diese Haltung verträgt sich aber gut mit der Stellung des Hauses zur platzartig erweiterten Straßenkreuzung und als asymmetrischer Schlußpunkt der Nürnberger Straße, die dem Blick von Süden zuvor mit den flachen Zoorandbauten keinerlei Halt bot.

Imperial Berlin was fond of architectural solutions for corners. Pointed, rounded or blunt, with oriels or domes – all the stops in the architectural canon of form were pulled out. In the fifties and sixties the dictates of puritanical neutrality did not allow for such creativity, and the result was that corner buildings were simply left out in embarrassment, as can be seen today in many parts of Berlin. It was not until the more imaginative approach to architecture that came with the eighties that street space began to be enlivened by stress placed on corner buildings. The new Kreditbank building bridges the acute angle between Kurfürstenstrasse and Budapester Strasse by using an arc of a circle. The frozen quality of the circle gives the building a static, monumental quality, but this goes well with its position on the junction, which has been developed as an urban square, and as an asymmetrical close for Nürnberger Strasse, where previously no focus was offered when looking from the south, as the eye met only the flat buildings on the periphery of the Zoo.

in der Nähe/nearby:
Penta-Hotel; B-Schöneberg; Nürnberger Straße 63-66
1979-80 • Ullrich Krüger, Jan Rave, Rolf Rave
Haus Nürnberg; B-Schöneberg; Nürnberger Straße 50-55
1928-31 • Bielenberg & Moser

D 8 Lenzhaus
Berlin-Tiergarten; Kurfürstenstraße 87
1928-29 • Heinrich Straumer

Die Fassade des Lenzhauses verrät, daß zwischen Entwurf und Bauausführung wohl mehrere Jahre gelegen haben. Das bevorzugt vertikale Gliederungssystem der Front paßt zu Bauten der Jahre 1924/25, es mag als abstrakte Übersetzung des gotisch verklärten Expressionismus gelten. Die Kunsthistorikerin Irmgard Wirth sprach einmal von »einer in den sachlichen Geschäftsbau unbewußt als Gefühlsmoment einbezogenen heimlichen Gotik«. Die enge Verknüpfung von Gotik und Sakralbau läßt in diesem Sinne den Geschäftshausbau des 20. Jahrhunderts in einem besonderen Licht erscheinen. Zwar ersetzen in der Berliner Stadtsilhouette Hochhäuser nicht generell die Kirchtürme, doch wurde spätestens in den zwanziger Jahren ein Trend zum Hochhaus im Stadtbild ablesbar. Auch das Lenzhaus rechnet nach Berliner Baurecht dazu, liegt es doch mit seinen acht Geschossen bereits weit über der zulässigen Geschoßzahl. Das führte für eines der ersten Berliner »Hochhäuser« letztlich zu Auseinandersetzungen mit der Genehmigungsbehörde und zu der Bauverzögerung.

The façade of the Lenzhaus shows that there were probably several years between the time the building was designed and the time when it was built. The vertical system of articulation for the façade is in keeping with buildings dating from 1924 and 1925, and may be considered an abstract translation of Expressionism transfigured by Gothic. Art historian Irmgard Wirth once spoke of «a secret Gothic, unwittingly included in the neutral office building as a moment of feeling». The close link between Gothic and ecclesiastical building put twentieth century office building in a particular light. It is not true to say that high-rise blocks replace church towers in the urban silhouette of Berlin, but by the twenties at the latest there was a clear trend towards high-rise building in the townscape. The Lenzhaus is included here as far as Berlin building regulations are concerned, as its eight floors put it well above the permitted number of storeys. This led to clashes with the authorities, and thus the delay in putting up the building.

in der Nähe/nearby:
Landesversicherungsanstalt; Keithstraße 28/32
1908-09 • Hermann Rohde

D 9 Europa-Center
Berlin-Charlottenburg; Tauentzienstraße 9
1963-65 • Helmut Hentrich, Hubert Petschnigg

Der Kalte Krieg hatte in West-Berlin über lange Jahre Investoren verschreckt. Selbst das einer Großbank gehörende abgeräumte Ruinengelände des Neuen Romanischen Hauses in bester Citylage beherbergte noch zehn Jahre nach dem Wirtschaftswunder lediglich eine Reihe von Kiosken und gelegentlich ein Zirkus- oder Boxkampfzelt. Erst die Mauer in ihrer Zweideutigkeit schuf klare Verhältnisse. Zu einer der wichtigsten Neuplanungen der sechziger Jahre wurde dann das Europa-Center. Um den immer wieder erörterten Urbanitätsansprüchen zu genügen, sah der Bauherr eine bunte Mischung verschiedener Nutzungen vor: über hundert Läden, eine Ausstellung, zwei Großkinos, ein Kabarett, zwölf Gaststätten, mehrere Bars und Cafés, eine Eisbahn, ein 86-m-Hochhaus für Büros. Eine Unterführung der damals noch bestehenden Verbindungsfahrbahn östlich der Gedächtniskirche und zwei Fußgängerbrücken über die angrenzenden Straßen vermittelten den Verkehr zu den Geschäften und Einrichtungen im Unter- und 1. Obergeschoß des Flachbaues – beides ist inzwischen beseitigt. Ivan Krusnik baute 1974 und 1982 den unteren Komplex um, ersetzte die Eisbahn durch ein überdachtes Gartencafé und schloß auch zum Vorteil der Ladenzeilen den zweiten Hof und die Gänge mit Dach und Türen.

For many years the Cold War frightened investors away from West Berlin. The site, belonging to a major bank, of the Neues Romanisches Haus, in an ideal central position, was cleared of ruins, but still housed nothing but a row of kiosks and the occasional tent for boxing matches or a circus, even ten years after the economic miracle. It was the ambiguity of the Wall that was to clarify the situation. The Europa-Center then became one of the most important planning projects of the sixties. In order to fulfil much-mentioned urban needs, the client intended a colourful mixture of various functions: over a hundred shops, an exhibition, two large cinemas, a cabaret, twelve restaurants, several bars and cafés, a skating rink, and an 86 metre high-rise building for offices. An underpass under the connecting carriageway that still existed east of the Gedächtniskirche and two pedestrian bridges over adjacent streets gave access to the shops and facilities in the basement and first floor of the low building; both have since been removed. In 1974 and 1982 Ivan Krusnik rebuilt the lower complex, replaced the ice rink with a roofed garden café and also closed off the second courtyard and the passageways with roof and doors, to the great benefit of the shops.

in der Nähe/nearby:
Palace-Hotel; Budapester Straße 45
1966-68 • Helmut Hentrich, Hubert Petschnigg; Schwebes & Schoßberger, Peter Hartwig, Franz Ott

D 10 U-Bahnhof Wittenbergplatz
Berlin-Schöneberg; Wittenbergplatz
1911-13 • Alfred Grenander

Als im Jahre 1902 die erste elektrische Schnellbahn zwischen Warschauer Brücke und dem heutigen Ernst-Reuter-Platz eröffnet wurde, verlangte die Stadt Charlottenburg – städtebaulich weitsichtig – die Verlegung der Strecke unter die Straße. Wittenbergplatz war die erste der Untergrundstationen. Die schnelle Entwicklung des U-Bahnnetzes brachte dem Wittenbergplatz 1913 einen großen Bahnhofsneubau für drei Linien. Es zeichnete sich schon damals der bevorstehende Wandel des Bereichs Tauentzienstraße-Kurfürstendamm von der ruhigen Wohngegend zum weltstädtischen Geschäfts- und Amüsierzentrum ab. Ganz im Gegensatz zu den sonst oberirdisch eher unscheinbaren U-Bahnhöfen erhielt das Bahnhofsgebäude in der Mitte des Platzes eine vorrangig repräsentative Aufgabe, sozusagen als stadtraumgestaltender Torbau zum Neuen Westen. Insofern vermied Grenander auch jedes architektonische Experiment, er knüpfte mit einem Kreuzbau von klassischer Klarheit stilistisch an die Zeit um 1800 an und richtete sich im Sinne Schinkels mit geschmackvollem Dekor am Charakter des Standortes aus. Damit lag er gänzlich im Trend der Zeit. Was an Bauschmuck des Bahnhofs den Krieg überlebt hatte, fiel dem puritanischen Kehraus der fünfziger Jahre zum Opfer. In jüngster Zeit hat man versucht, nach denkmalpflegerischen Gesichtspunkten möglichst weitgehend den Originalzustand wiederherzustellen.

In 1902, when the first electric express railway was opened between Warschauer Brücke and what is now Ernst-Reuter-Platz, the town of Charlottenburg – with considerable foresight in town planning terms – demanded that the line should run under the road. Wittenbergplatz was the first of the underground stations. Rapid development of the underground network brought Wittenbergplatz a large new station for three lines in 1913. The area around Tauentzienstrasse and Kurfürstendamm was already showing signs of its forthcoming transformation from quiet residential area to cosmopolitan business and amusement centre. In complete contrast with the other underground stations, which were essentially inconspicuous above ground, the station building in the middle of the square acquired a predominantly representative status, almost as though it was a gateway to the new West, marking the edge of the town. To this extent Grenander also avoided any attempt at architectural experimentation; he referred back to the period around 1800 with a cruciform building of classical clarity, and in the spirit of Schinkel used tasteful decoration directed at the character of the site. In doing this he was very much in tune with his times. Much of the architectural decoration that survived the War fell victim to the puritanical clearout of the fifties. More recently an attempt has been made to restore the building to its original condition, following principles for the preservation of ancient monuments.

D 11 Kaufhaus des Westens (KaDeWe)
Berlin-Schöneberg; Tauentzienstraße 21-24
1906-07 • Johann Emil Schaudt

Als der Jandorf-Konzern 1906 daranging, im Neuen Westen ein Warenhaus zu bauen, verwunderte dieses. Ob es das kaufmännische Gespür für den kommenden Aufschwung des Geschäftslebens in diesem Viertel war oder die Einsicht in die Dezentralisierung zur Entlastung der überfüllten Innenstadt, wird sich kaum noch klären lassen. Daß das KaDeWe einmal zu den wenigen weltweit führenden Warenhäusern gehören würde, war aber sicher nicht vorhersehbar. Schaudt nahm mit dem Äußeren des Hauses behutsam Rücksicht auf die hier überwiegende Wohnbebauung. Kleinere Fenster, Gliederung in Stockwerke und Betonung der Mittelrisalite stehen nicht für die Warenhausarchitektur der Jahrhundertwende mit schwermütigen Pfeilerfronten oder reklameschreienden Glasflächen wie bei Wertheim oder Tietz in der Leipziger Straße. Auch im Inneren wirkt das KaDeWe bedächtiger, es verzichtet auf überdimensionale Lichthöfe, begnügt sich mit einer zweigeschossigen Treppenhalle. Alles gibt sich zurückhaltender und vornehmer, statt Laufkundschaft wird der Stammkunde angesprochen. Über die doppelte Aufstockung 1929-30 und den Wiederaufbau 1950 hinweg hat das Haus diesen Charakter behalten, ihn sogar kultiviert. Mit einem neuen, für den Gebäudecharakter wichtigen Walmdach und dem verglasten Bogenabschluß des Mittelrisalites wurden 1992 ursprüngliche architektonische Gestaltungselemente zum Vorteil des Hauses zitiert.

A great deal of surprise was expressed when the Jandorf concern decided to build a new department store in the New West in 1906. Whether it was a businessman's sense of the coming upsurge of the economy of the district, or an insight into decentralization to take pressure off the overfull city centre, we are now never likely to know. It was certainly not foreseeable, however, that KaDeWe was destined to become one of the few leading department stores with a world-wide reputation. The exterior of Schaudt's building took the preponderantly residential nature of the district at the time carefully into account. Smaller windows, articulation into storeys and emphasis of central protrusions are not usual features of department store architecture at the turn of the century, which tended to be all melancholy pillared façades or areas of noisily advertising glass, as is the case with Wertheim or Tietz in Leipziger Strasse. KaDeWe is more moderate inside as well, going without outsize air wells, and making do with a two-storey stairwell. Everything is more restrained and refined, appealing to regular rather than casual customers. Despite additional storeys added in 1929-30 and rebuilding in 1950 the house has retained, even cultivated, this character. The new hipped roof, which is so important for the character of the building, and the glazed arch crowning the central projection, both added in 1992, mark a return to the original design elements and do much to enhance the appearance of the building.

D 12 Gedächtniskirche
Berlin-Charlottenburg; Breitscheidplatz
1891-95 • Franz Schwechten
1961-63 • Egon Eiermann

Nach dem Tode Wilhelms I. regten einflußreiche Kreise den Bau einer Gedächtniskirche an. Die aus ganz Deutschland reichlich fließenden Spenden erlaubten eine für evangelische Kirchen ungewöhnliche Prachtentfaltung. Unter Schwechten entstand ein sechstürmiger Bau im Stile der rheinischen Spätgotik, in dem an Ausstattung und vergoldeten Details nichts fehlte, dafür sorgte allein schon die Mitsprache des Kaisers. Ganz im Sinne des blühenden Nationalismus weihte man die Kirche am »Sedantag« 1895 ein. Es gab also Gründe genug, daß sie heftiger Kritik ausgesetzt war. Zwischen 1943 und 1945 wurde sie weitgehend zerstört. Um Wiederaufbau und Abriß entbrannte eine heftige Diskussion. Schließlich blieb der Turmstumpf als Mahnung an Krieg und Zerstörung stehen, und Egon Eiermann erstellte einen Neubau aus fünf freien Baukörpern als Stahlskelett, ausgekleidet mit Betonwaben und farbiger Verglasung.

After the death of Kaiser Wilhelm I, influential circles pressed for the building of a memorial church. Lavish donations from all over Germany made it possible to build on a splendid scale unusual for Protestant churches. Schwechten created a church with six towers in the style of Rhenish late Gothic, with no lack of decoration and lavish detail: the fact that the Emperor had a say was enough to make that certain. In the spirit of flourishing nationalism the church was consecrated on «Sedan Day» in 1895. There were thus ample reasons for its being the subject of violent criticism. It was largely destroyed between 1943 and 1945. There was fierce discussion about rebuilding or demolition. Finally the stump of the tower remained as a reminder of war and destruction and Eiermann created a new building consisting of five steel-frame, free-standing elements, clad in concrete honeycombs and coloured glass.

in der Nähe/nearby:
Brunnen; Breitscheidplatz
1982-84 • Joachim Schmettau

D 13 Hotel Steigenberger
Berlin-Charlottenburg; Los-Angeles-Platz
1979-81 • Manfred Pechtold, Hans Jürgen Ruprecht, Wolfgang Schlicht, Jakob Schulze-Rohr

Das Hotel Steigenberger entstand im Zuge des dritten Förderungsprogramms des Berliner Senats für den Hotelbau. Mit den Veranstaltungen im 1979 fertiggestellten Kongreßzentrum war ein Mehrbedarf an Hotelbetten zu erwarten, dem eine Reihe von Neubauten Rechnung trugen. Als innerstädtisches Hotel hatte das »Steigenberger« den seltenen Vorzug, einen Straßenblock vollständig abzuschließen, also gleichsam freistehend zu wirken. Außerdem blieb vor seiner Hauptfront eine unbebaute Fläche, die eine Tiefgarage erhielt und darüber als architektonisch und gärtnerisch gegliederter Stadtplatz gefaßt wurde, mit Spielplatz und Granada-Lustgarten, heckengeschütztem Theatron und Pergolagarten. Äußerlich hält sich der Bau bescheiden zurück, verläßt sich gänzlich auf innere Ausstattung und verdeckte Eleganz.

Hotel Steigenberger was built in the context of the Berlin Senate's third programme for the promotion of hotel building. Events in the Kongresszentrum, completed in 1979, meant that more hotel beds were needed, and a series of new buildings helped to meet this need. The «Steigenberger» has the rare advantage for an inner-city hotel of completely closing off an urban block, thus giving the impression of being free-standing. Also there was an area in front of its main façade that had not been built on; an underground car park was built under it, and it was then developed as an urban square in both architectural and horticultural terms, with playground and Granada pleasure garden, a theatron protected by hedges, and a pergola garden. The exterior of the building is modestly withdrawn, relying entirely on interior decoration and concealed elegance.

in der Nähe/nearby:
Tiefgarage und Architekturplatz; Los-Angeles-Platz
1981-82 • Urs Müller, Thomas Rhode
Hochschule der Künste; Lietzenburger Straße 43/47
1985-88 • Dieter Hundertmark, Dieter Ketterer
Wohnanlage; Lietzenburger Straße 16/18, Passauer Straße, Ansbacher Straße
1986-87 • Jan C. Bassenge, Kay Puhan-Schulz; Dietrich Bangert, Bernd Jansen, Stefan Scholz, Axel Schultes; Hans-Christian Müller
Wohnhochhaus; Lietzenburger Straße 2
1985-86 • Hans-Peter Störl

D 14 Marmorhaus
Berlin-Charlottenburg; Kurfürstendamm 236
1912-13 • Hugo Pál

1895 zeigten die Brüder Max und Emil Skladanowsky dem erstaunten Publikum im Berliner Wintergarten ihre ersten »laufenden Bilder«. Im Hause Unter den Linden 21 entstand bald das erste Lichtbildtheater, ein notdürftig hergerichteter Raumschlauch. So sahen die Kinos aus bis 1911, als im neuen Admiralspalast ein großes Lichtspieltheater eröffnete. Nun entdeckte auch das vornehmere Publikum den Film. Wie Pilze schossen die neuen Theater aus dem Boden, fast alle im teuren Westen, auch das Marmorhaus. Der weißgraue schlesische Marmor der Fassade gab ihm den Namen. Der Marmor versinnbildlichte aber auch die Gewinne, die man aus dem neuen Kunst- und Unterhaltungsmedium zu ziehen hoffte. Eine phantastisch-stimmungsvolle Ausstattung voller Farben und Lichteffekte, dazu bizarre Formen von Lampen und Wandschmuck, alles war auf Effekt und Überraschung aufgebaut. Von den frühexpressionistischen Innenräumen ist keiner erhalten, dazu war das Kino immer zu stark den modischen Strömungen unterworfen.

In 1895 the brothers Max and Emil Skladanowsky presented their first «running pictures» to an astonished public in the Berlin Wintergarten. The first cinema was soon built at Unter den Linden 21; this was a miserable tube of a room. Cinemas tended to look like this until 1911, when a large one opened in the new Admiralspalast. Now films started to attract a better class of audience. New cinemas shot up like mushrooms, almost all in the expensive West, and these included the Marmorhaus. It took its name from the whitish-grey Silesian marble from which the façade was made. But the marble also symbolized the profits that people hoped to draw from the new art and entertainment medium. A fantastic and atmospheric decor full of colour and light effects, and also bizarre shapes for lamps and wall decoration, all aimed at effect and surprise. None of the early Expressionist interiors has survived, the cinema has always been too much subject to fashionable trends for that.

in der Nähe/nearby:
Geschäftshaus; Kurfürstendamm 235
1983-87 • Graaf, Schweger & Partner
Wertheim; Kurfürstendamm 230-233
1971-72 • Hans Soll
1984 (Umbau) • Haus-Rucker-Co, Laurids Ortner, Gunter Zamp Kelp, Manfred Ortner
Gloria-Passage; Kurfürstendamm 13
1985-87 • Helge Sypereck, Frank Metz, Volker Kranz
Kaisereck (Michelshaus); Kurfürstendamm 237
1914-15 • Johann Emil Schaudt

D 15 Allianzversicherung
Berlin-Charlottenburg; Joachimstaler Straße 10-12
1953-55 • Alfred Gunzenhauser, Paul Schwebes

Am Schnittpunkt von Kurfürstendamm, Joachimstaler Straße und Augsburger Straße ist ein kleiner Platz ausgespart, der zur Stadtbildgestaltung herausfordert. Als hier Anfang der fünfziger Jahre eines der ersten großen Nachkriegs-Bürohäuser gebaut wurde, stand deshalb auch fest, daß es in den Blickachsen von Augsburger Straße, von Joachimstaler Straße und Bundesallee als Hochhaus dominieren müsse. Die Platzgestaltung hatte unter Wahrung des straßenräumlichen Maßstabes ein langgezogener sechsgeschossiger Trakt zu vermitteln, der mit einem schüchternen leichten Schwung – ganz zeitgemäß – Gefälligkeit und Eleganz ausdrücken und jeden Verdacht der Monumentalität vermeiden sollte. Auch das Hochhaus ist unmerklich geschwungen, ein Gestaltungsmerkmal, das bei vielen Bauten jener Jahre zu beobachten ist, Ausdruck des ideologischen Bruchs mit der jüngsten deutschen Vergangenheit, deren Hang zu harten symmetrischen Formen, erdrückender Größe und pomphaften architektonischen Gesten noch zu gut erinnerlich war. Verdacht erregte bereits die Fassadenverkleidung des Allianzhauses aus Travertin. Sie erinnere an die dreißiger Jahre, wurde bemängelt, und andere Architekten flüchteten deshalb scheu in die modische Allüre der Kachelfassade.

At the junction of Kurfürstendamm, Augsburger Strasse and Joachimstaler Strasse is a small square that cries out to be designed into the townscape. And so when one of the first post-war office buildings was built here in the early fifties it was also decided that it should be a high-rise building, dominating the axes of view from Augsburger Strasse, Joachimstaler Strasse and Bundesallee. The design of the square had to preserve the urban scale of the site and provide a long six-storey section, intended to express pleasantness and elegance and avoid any element of monumentality with its shy and gentle curve – quite in keeping with the spirit of the times. The high-rise building is slightly curved as well, a design feature that can be seen in many buildings of that period, an expression of an ideological break with the most recent German past: its inclination towards hard, symmetrical forms, oppressive size and pompous architectural gestures could be remembered all too clearly. Even the Allianz building's Travertine cladding aroused suspicions. It was said to be reminiscent of the thirties, and was criticized, and thus other architects timorously sought refuge in the fashionable allure of the tiled façade.

in der Nähe/nearby:
Café Kranzler; Kurfürstendamm 18-19
1957-58 • Hanns Dustmann
Union-Palast (Filmbühne Wien); Kurfürstendamm 26
1912-13 • Nentwich & Simon

D 16 Villa Grisebach
Berlin-Charlottenburg; Fasanenstraße 25
1891-95 • Hans Grisebach

Bevor die fünfgeschossige Bebauung auch auf die Kudamm-Seitenstraßen übergriff, galten diese als bevorzugter Ort verträumter Stadtvillen. Sie lagen zurückgesetzt im Garten wie das Haus Fasanenstraße 23. Daneben rückten aber manche Bauten auch vor an die Straße, wurden schmaler und höher, behielten aber doch noch den Charakter des Einfamilienhauses. Der Architekt Grisebach nutzte das obere Stockwerk als Atelier, die beiden unteren Geschosse verband eine durchgehende Diele, und vor der Front lag ein Treppenturm, als handele es sich um ein freistehendes Haus. In Zeiten hoher Grundstückspreise sind Häuser wie diese vom Abriß bedroht. Auch in der Fasanenstraße ging vor Jahren dieses Gespenst um, bis Bürger und Denkmalpfleger eine andere Lösung erzwangen. Gefördert durch die Deutsche Bank wurde ein kleines kulturelles Zentrum geschaffen: ein Literaturhaus in der Nr. 23, das Käthe-Kollwitz-Museum in der Nr. 24, eine Galerie in der Grisebach-Villa.

Before the building of five-storey blocks started to dominate the side streets of the Kurfürstendamm as well, these were the preferred site for idyllic urban villas. Some were set back in gardens, like the house at Fasanenstrasse 23, but others stood close to the street, were narrower and higher, but still maintained the character of detached houses. Architect Grisebach used the top floor as a studio, the two lower storeys were connected by a through hall, and there was a staircase tower in front of the façade, just as though this were a free-standing building. At times of high prices for building land, houses like this are threatened with demolition. This ghost haunted Fasanenstrasse as well, until townspeople and curators of monuments found another solution. A small cultural centre was set up, supported by the Deutsche Bank: a literature house at no. 23, the Käthe Kollwitz Museum in no. 24 and a gallery in the Grisebach villa.

in der Nähe/nearby:
Wohn- und Geschäftshaus; Fasanenstraße 31
1984-86 • Bernhard Binder

D 17 Universum (Schaubühne)
Berlin-Wilmersdorf; Kurfürstendamm 153
1927-28 • Erich Mendelsohn

Nicht mehr das Theater war Vorbild für diesen Kinobau, sondern das Medium Film gestaltete. »Filmspiel, Theater der Bewegung! Bewegung ist Leben«, rief Mendelsohn aus. Der Bau sperrt sein Maul auf, verschluckt sein Publikum. Der Reklameturm greift in den Straßenraum des Boulevards. Dynamische Architektur aus Geometrie und Licht war die Devise, die Mendelsohn mit der Meisterschaft eines Artisten beherrschte. Kriegsschäden und entstellende Umbauten leiteten zum Niedergang des Hauses über. 1978 wurde es schließlich weitgehend abgetragen, um dann bis 1981 durch Jürgen Sawade als Kopie wiederzuerstehen für die Schaubühne. Entspricht das Äußere noch Mendelsohns Universum, ist innen etwas vollkommen Neues entstanden: der wandelbare Theatersaal. Ob Arena, Guckkastenbühne, Kabuki-Theater, ob großer Saal oder dreigeteilt, ob Orchestergraben oder Rundhorizont, alles läßt sich unter dem neuen Dach einrichten, und so nutzt die Schaubühne auch diese »Raummaschine«. In ihr erfüllt sich spät Gropius' Idee vom Totaltheater.

Theatre architecture was no longer the model for this cinema, film as medium was the driving force behind the design. «Film, theatre of movement! Movement is life!» exclaimed Mendelsohn. The building opens its mouth and swallows its audience. The tower, for advertisements, impinges on the street image of the boulevard. Dynamic architecture of geometry and space was the currency, and Mendelsohn controlled it with the mastery of an artist. War damage and disfiguring rebuilding led to the decline of the building. Finally in 1978 it was largely pulled down and then rebuilt as a copy for the Schaubühne by Jürgen Sawade, completion in 1981. The exterior still corresponds to Mendelsohn's Universum, but inside something completely new has been created: a convertible theatre auditorium. Arena, proscenium stage, Kabuki theatre, one large space or divided into three, orchestra pit or cyclorama, all this is possible in the new building, and the Schaubühne makes full use of this «space machine». It is a late fulfilment of Gropius' idea of «total theatre».

in der Nähe/nearby:
Kabarett der Komiker; Kurfürstendamm 156
1926-28 • Erich Mendelsohn
Woga-Park; Kurfürstendamm 154-155 b
1926-28 • Erich Mendelsohn
Wohn- und Geschäftshaus; Kurfürstendamm 74
1980-82 • Rainer Oefelein, Bernhard Freund

D 18 Wohnhaus
Berlin-Charlottenburg; Kurfürstendamm 60
1905-07 • Hans Toebelmann, Henry Groß

Das Gebäude gehört zu einer Gruppe von vier gemeinsam geplanten und ausgeführten Mietwohnhäusern, die in einer Zeit entstanden, als der Kurfürstendamm bereits als »erste Adresse« galt. Die Palastarchitektur war somit vorgegeben, zumal es als Eckhaus besonders hervorgehoben werden konnte. Über der abgeschrägten Ecke thront nicht nur eine große Kuppel, die stumpfen Winkel sind als polygonale Turmachsen mit eigenen Kuppeln ausgebildet, was zur Steigerung der Gesamtwirkung beitrug. Streifenquaderung, Prunkerker, eine große Korbbogenloggia mit Säulen und reichlicher bildhauerischer Schmuck sichern den kolossalen Eindruck des Ganzen. Jugendstilelemente treten in den teigigen und wuchernden Formen der Kuppeln, Zwerchgiebel und Konsolen zutage, nur als unorganische Applikation, nicht als Teil eines stilistisch durchdrungenen Gesamtwerkes. Hinter der Schaufassade entwickelte sich dennoch – wie auch bei anderen »Kurfürstendammpalästen« – Großzügigkeit. Jedes Geschoß war in eine 11- und eine 8-Zimmer-Wohnung aufgeteilt mit 575 m² bzw. 410 m² Wohnfläche. Inzwischen sind diese herrschaftlichen Wohnungen längst in kleine Appartements aufgeteilt, das Erdgeschoß erhielt Läden, die Vorgärten sind verschwunden.

The building is one of a group of four blocks of rented accommodation, planned and built together at a time when the Kurfürstendamm was already «the best address». Thus a palatial style of architecture was essential, especially as it could be a particular feature in a corner building. The chamfered corner not only has a dome at the top, the obtuse angles are made into polygonal tower axes with domes of their own, enhancing the overall impression. Ashlar strips, show oriels, a large basket-arched loggia and lavish sculptural decoration ensure the colossal impression made by the whole. Jugendstil elements can be seen in the doughy and rampant shapes of the domes, gables and corbels, merely as an inorganic application, not as part of a style in which the whole building is steeped. Nevertheless behind the show façade – as in other «Kurfürstendamm palaces» – there was a great deal of generosity. Each floor was divided into one eleven- and one eight-room apartment, with an area of 575 and 410 square metres respectively. These magnificent apartments have since been split up into smaller flats, the ground floor given over to shops, and the front gardens have disappeared.

in der Nähe/nearby:
Boarding-Palast (Hotel); Kurfürstendamm 193-194
1911-12 • Robert Leibnitz

D 19 Kindertagesstätte
Berlin-Charlottenburg; Schlüterstraße 25
1989-92 • Karl Manfred Pflitsch

»Das ist unser Haus«, sollen die Kinder sagen und sich in »ihrer« Tagesstätte wohlfühlen. Der Not des innerstädtischen Bauplatzes ausweichend schuf der Architekt eine kleine Baugruppe, die – eingezwängt zwischen hohe Miethäuser und die Stadtbahntrasse – sich durch ein auffälliges Äußeres zu behaupten sucht. Mit der Dreigeschossigkeit wahrt das Gebäude für Kinder überschaubare Maßstäbe und ermöglicht eine ausreichende Belichtung des großen Spielhofes, zu dem sich auch die Gruppenräume in einem halbkreisförmigen Baukörper öffnen. Der Südflügel präsentiert sich weitgehend symmetrisch mit Eingangsnischen und einem im flachen Kreisbogen geführten Erker. Der Nordflügel in seiner kindlich abstrahierten Baugestalt mit bündig abschließendem Satteldach weist mit dem Giebel zur Straße. Der Vorstellungswelt des Kindes entspringen auch Details wie die einfachen Fensterkreuze, der verzierte Dachfirst oder die wie Sterntaler in die rotbraune Klinkerfassade eingestreuten weißen Platten.

The aim was to make the children feel at home in «their» day-care centre, enabling them to say: «This is our house.» Responding to the constraints of the inner-city site, the architect designed a small group of buildings which, although crowded by neighbouring multi-storey tenements and the railway line, assert themselves with a highly conspicuous appearance. The buildings are limited to three storeys, thus maintaining a proper scale for children and ensuring sufficient lighting of the large playground enclosed by the semicircular wing of group facilities. The south wing is largely symmetrical with entrance niches and the small oriel forming a shallow circular arch. The north wing resembles a child's abstract version of a house with flush gable roof and is oriented with its gable facing the street. The detailing was also designed with a child's perception in mind and includes such features as simple windows with crossbars, decorated roof ridges, and the white tiles inserted in the reddish-brown clinker façade like so many stars fallen from the sky.

in der Nähe/nearby:
Mietwohnhaus; Mommsenstraße 5-6
1903-05 • Albert Geßner
Abspannwerk Leibniz; Leibnizstraße 65-68 a
1928-29 • Hans Müller
Büro- und Geschäftshaus der Apotheker- und Ärztebank; Kantstraße 128
1991-93 • Henry Nielebock und Klaus Meier-Hartmann

D 20 Kempinski-Plaza
Berlin-Charlottenburg; Uhlandstraße 181-183
1990-93 • Rave & Partner

Seit den zwanziger Jahren entwickelte sich der Kurfürstendamm zum Bummel-Boulevard mit Läden und Gaststätten der oberen Kategorie. Die lineare Aufreihung von Schaufenstern und Schankveranden reichte aber bald nicht mehr aus, und die Seitenstraßen wurden auf 50 oder 100 Meter mit in das Geschäftsleben einbezogen. In jüngster Zeit wird nun auch das Blockinnere mit Durchgängen und öffentlichen Höfen erschlossen. Eine dieser Schöpfungen ist das Kempinski-Plaza. Mit dem glasüberdeckten Innenhof knüpft der Bau an die Tradition der Passagen an. Als Durchgang zum angrenzenden Hotel Kempinski führt dieses Bauglied zu einer gegenseitigen Aufwertung. Eine sinnvolle Mischung aus Läden, Büros und Wohnungen in horizontaler Schichtung vermeidet stadtplanerische Monokultur. Der architektonische Maßstab der im Kudammviertel üblichen Gebäudeabmessungen bleibt dabei gewahrt: Die Traufhöhe wird nicht überschritten, und im Takt der Parzellenbreite wechselt das Fassadenmaterial.

Ever since the nineteen-twenties the Kurfürstendamm has become a widely popular boulevard with high-end shops and restaurants. The long alignment of display windows and sidewalk verandahs did not provide sufficient space, however, and so the side streets were increasingly utilized commercially to a depth of up to a hundred meters. Most recently the interior of the city blocks is also being developed by creating passages and public courts. One of these new creations is the Kempinski-Plaza. The building with its glazed interior courtyard continues the tradition of the galleries. By providing a passage to the adjoining Hotel Kempinski both complexes are given new attractiveness. A balanced mix of shops, offices and apartments, all layered horizontally, serves to prevent any uniformity in terms of urban development and at the same time maintains the architectural scale of the traditional building dimensions around the Kurfürstendamm, conforming with the established eaves height and alternating the façade materials in rhythm with the width of the individual lots.

in der Nähe/nearby:
Hotel Kempinski; Kurfürstendamm 27
1951-67 • Schwebes & Schoßberger
Union-Palast (Film-Bühne Wien); Kurfürstendamm 26
1912-13 • Nentwich & Simon
Hotel am Zoo; Kurfürstendamm 25
1891-92 • Alfred Messel
1910-11 • Wittling & Güldner
1956-57 • Paul Baumgarten

D 21 Kantdreieck
Berlin-Charlottenburg; Kantstraße 155
1992-94 • Josef Paul Kleihues

Die Bebauung des von der Stadtbahnkurve abgeschnittenen Dreieckgeländes hat – wie in den letzten zwei Jahrzehnten fast jedes größere Berliner Bauprojekt – eine komplizierte Vorgeschichte mit Wettbewerben, öffentlichem Widerstreit der Meinungen und Interessen sowie langwierigen Entscheidungsfindungen. Josef Paul Kleihues, der als Planungsdirektor des Neubaubereichs der Internationalen Bauausstellung Berlin 1984/1987 sein Konzept der »Kritischen Rekonstruktion von Stadt« schon umsetzen und so dokumentieren konnte, macht hier eine besondere Idee zur Entwurfsgrundlage. Vor einem dreieckigen Bauteil der üblichen Berliner Gebäudehöhe steht ein schlankes Turmhaus, dessen Abschluß eine riesige, flossenförmige Wetterfahne bildet. Kleihues setzt hier nach seinen Worten »bewußt eine spielerische Attitüde« ein. Das »in der bildhaften Symbolik erlebbare Maß unkonventionellen Verhaltens« steht für das Individuelle, das er aus der baukünstlerischen Umsetzung einer Inspiration durch das Leben der Josephine Baker sieht. Diese Widmung bezieht Kleihues aus einer vielschichtigen Besinnung auf örtliche und zeitliche Bezüge des Kantdreieckes.

Like almost any large-scale construction project in Berlin in the last two decades, development of this triangular site cut off by the bend of the Stadtbahn went through a complicated pre-history of competitions, clashing public opinions and interests, and a protracted process of decision-making. Josef Paul Kleihues, who successfully realized and documented his concept of a «critical reconstruction of the city» as director of planning for the new buildings section of the Internationale Bauausstellung Berlin 1984-87, prevailed here with a highly unique project. Placed in front of a triangular building conforming with the traditional eaves height is a slender tower crowned with a huge, fin-shaped weathervane. In his design, Kleihues was, in his own words, «consciously experimenting with a playful approach.» For him, the «degree of unconventional behaviour to be experienced in the symbolic imagery» represents the individuality which he draws from the architectural translation of an inspiration he found in the life of Josephine Baker. Kleihues derives this dedication from a careful and complex consideration of the spatial and temporal correlations of the Kantdreieck.

in der Nähe/nearby:
Jüdisches Gemeindehaus; Fasanenstraße 79-80
1958-60 • Dieter Knoblauch, Hans Heise

D 22 Theater des Westens
Berlin Charlottenburg; Kantstraße 12
1895-96 • Bernhard Sehring

»Hanc domum artis colendae causa condidit Bernhard Sehring« steht auf dem Attikafries – »Dieses Haus zur Pflege der Kunst baute Bernhard Sehring«. Die Pflege der Baukunst fiel jedenfalls sehr konservativ aus. Nichts ist spürbar vom Reformtheater nach Bayreuther Verständnis oder vom beginnenden Jugendstil, der Sehrings Cottbusser Theater so eindringlich prägen sollte. Eher originell kann das Theater des Westens genannt werden mit seiner historistischen Renaissancefassade französischer Spielart und dem Bühnenhaus im Aussehen einer mittelalterlichen Burg. Es ist der Schlußpunkt für das Theaterverständnis des 19. Jahrhunderts und auch für eine Epoche der Theaterarchitektur, die in erster Linie das Repräsentative für den Bau und auch das Publikum zum Maßstab machte. Aber auch wenn die Kritik es einmal als »eine der Architektursünden der Kaiserzeit« bezeichnete, verhalf die Nostalgie der siebziger Jahre dem Theater zu einer liebevollen Restaurierung, die eklektischen Schnörkel wurden wieder gesellschaftsfähig.

«Hanc domum artis colendae causa condidit Bernhard Sehring» it says on the attic frieze – «this building for the care of art was built by Bernhard Sehring». Care of architecture turned out very conservatively, however. There is no sense of reform theatre as understood in Bayreuth or the early days of Jugendstil, which was to have such an effect on Sehring's Cottbus theatre. A better word for the Theater des Westens is unusual, with its historical Renaissance façade of the French variety and fly tower like a medieval castle. It represents the full stop at the end of the nineteenth century's perception of theatre, and also for a period of theatre architecture in which the main concern for building and public was that it should be imposing. But even though it was once criticized as «one of the architectural sins of the imperial period», the nostalgia of the seventies helped the theatre to affectionate restoration: its eclectic flourishes were socially acceptable once more.

in der Nähe/nearby:
Geschäfts- und Wohnhaus; Uhlandstraße 15
1991-93 • Patzschke & Partner
Geschäftshaus; Uhlandstraße 14
1993-94 • Patzschke & Partner

D 23 Berliner Bank
Berlin-Charlottenburg; Hardenbergstraße 32
1952-53 • Gerhard Siegmann

Nach der Berliner Blockade kam es zum Neuaufbau des West-Berliner Bankwesens. Eine der ersten privatrechtlichen Gründungen war die Berliner Bank. Sie wählte ihren Standort in der Nähe der neuen Westlichen City und bezog dort 1953 einen repräsentativen Neubau. Siegmann, der aus dem Wettbewerb mit 200 Architekten als Sieger hervorgegangen war, verfolgte im Grundriß ein Konzept abseits der alten Lösungen. Hatte man bisher die Obergeschosse als Flügel um die zentrale Kassenhalle herumgelegt und so einen häßlichen Innenhof über dem Glasdach der Halle erhalten, machte er die Kassenhalle zum Herzstück des Baues. Die Belichtung übernimmt ein hochliegendes Fensterband, und die stützenfreie Überspannung der Halle trägt die sieben Obergeschosse mit den Geschäftsräumen. Erst die moderne Spannbetonkonstruktion erlaubte eine solche Lösung. Schon ein Jahr später baute auf der gegenüberliegenden Straßenseite die Industrie- und Handelskammer einen neuen Gebäudekomplex, es folgten die Börse, nahe in der Uhlandstraße die Bank für Handel und Industrie und später am Ernst-Reuter-Platz die Berliner Disconto-Bank. Damit hatte West-Berlin ein eigenes Bankenzentrum.

Banking in Berlin started to be built up again after the blockade. One of the first private foundations was the Berliner Bank. It chose a site near to the new western centre, and moved into a prestigious new building there in 1953. Siegmann won a competition with 200 architects and used a ground plan that departed from old solutions. Previously the upper storeys had been laid out as wings around the central banking hall, thus creating an ugly inner courtyard above the glass roof of the hall. Instead of this he made the banking hall the heart of the building. Light is provided by a row of high windows, and the support-free span over the hall carries the seven upper storeys containing the offices. A solution of this kind is only possible with modern prestressed concrete. As little as a year later the Chamber of Commerce and Industry built a new complex of buildings on the other side of the road, then came the Stock Exchange, and in nearby Uhlandstrasse the Bank für Handel und Industrie and later in Ernst-Reuter-Platz the Berliner Disconto-Bank. Thus West Berlin had a banking centre of its own.

in der Nähe/nearby:
Industrie- und Handelskammer; Hardenbergstraße 16
1953-54 • Sobotka & Müller
Börse; Fasanenstraße 85-86
1954-55 • Sobotka & Müller
Hotel Excelsior; Hardenbergstraße 13-14
1978-79 • Georg Heinrichs & Partner

E
Berlin Charlottenburg

Das mittelalterliche Dorf Lützow ist Ausgangspunkt des heutigen Charlottenburgs, auch wenn es den städtebaulichen Charakter dieses Stadtgebietes kaum beeinflußt hat. Entscheidend war vielmehr die Wahl des Sommersitzes Lützenburg für Sophie Charlotte, die Gemahlin des Kurfürsten Friedrich III., kurz vor 1700. Das 1695 begonnene Schloß und die axial darauf zulaufende Schloßstraße bilden die städtebauliche Keimzelle der Residenzstadt Charlottenburg. Endpunkt der Schloßstraße war ein Karpfenteich, Schnittpunkt mit der großen Achse, die von Berlin durch den Tiergarten nach Westen führte. Von dieser Achse zweigte am Knie – heute Ernst-Reuter-Platz – die Verkehrsverbindung Berlin–Charlottenburg ab und lief gerade auf das Schloß zu. Nach 1705 setzte der Bau einer regelmäßigen Stadtanlage östlich der Schloßstraße und beiderseits der Berliner Straße ein, zunächst noch sorgfältig überwacht von Eosander, dem Baumeister am Schloß. Bereits 1720 erfolgte die Eingemeindung Lützows, das weitere Wachstum des Ortes setzte sich bevorzugt nach Osten, in Richtung Berlin fort. Dem trug 1862 der »Bebauungsplan von der Umgebung Berlins und Charlottenburgs« Rechnung. Die Fortsetzung der Berliner Straße im »Generalszug« Hardenberg-, Tauentzien-, Kleist-, Bülow-, Yorck- und Gneisenaustraße als Teil einer Ringstraße um Berlin rührt daher. Der wiederum schnitt den später zum Kurfürstendamm ausgebauten Feld- und Reitweg von Berlin zum Grunewald. Hier nahm der »Neue Westen« in den achtziger Jahren des 19. Jahrhunderts seinen Ausgang, der dann die bauliche Verbindung Berlin–Charlottenburg herstellte und die gesamte südliche Ausdehnung Charlottenburgs als großbürgerliches Wohngebiet prägte. 1877 die Ringbahn, 1882 die Stadtbahn und 1902 die erste U-Bahn vermittelten die verkehrliche Anbindung an Berlin und beeinflußten entscheidend städtisches Wachstum und Baugeschehen, ebenso wie die 1884 eröffnete Technische Hochschule. Mit dem Anschluß an Groß-Berlin 1920 verwischten sich die Unterschiede zwischen Berlin und Charlottenburg weiterhin und schließlich gänzlich mit der Übernahme der Funktion als neues Zentrum der westlichen Stadthälfte durch die Spaltung der Stadt in den Jahren west-östlicher Gegensätze.

The medieval village of Lützow was the starting point for modern Charlottenburg, even though it had scarcely any influence on the urban character of this district. Far more crucial was the choice of the summer palace of Lützenburg for Sophie Charlotte, the consort of Elector Friedrich III, shortly before 1700. Work started on the palace in 1695, and this and the Schlosstrasse, which runs axially towards it, form the germ cell in terms of urban design of the residence town of Charlottenburg. The Schlosstrasse ended at a carp pool, at the point of intersection with the great axis leading from Berlin through the Tiergarten to the west. At the Knie – now Ernst-Reuter-Platz – the road connecting Berlin and Charlottenburg branched off, and ran directly towards the palace. After 1705 work started on a regular urban complex east of Schlosstrasse and on either side of Berliner Strasse, at first under the careful supervision of Eosander, the architect of the palace. Lützow was incorporated into the town in 1720, which continued to grow predominantly to the east, in the direction of Berlin. The 1862 «Development plan for the environs of Berlin and Charlottenburg» took this into account. The continuation of Berliner Strasse in the «general run» of Hardenberg-, Tauentzien-, Kleist-, Bülow-, Yorck- and Gneisenaustrasse as part of the ring road around Berlin goes back to this. This was again cut by the field and bridle path, later upgraded as the Kurfürstendamm, from Berlin to the Grunewald. This was where the «New West» started in the 1880s, which then formed a link between Berlin and Charlottenburg in terms of buildings and made the whole southern section of Charlottenburg into an upper-middle-class residential area. The Ringbahn, or ring railway, in 1877, the S-Bahn in 1882 and the first underground railway in 1902 provided a public transport link with Berlin and had a decisive influence on the growth of the city and its buildings, and the same was true of the Technische Hochschule, which opened in 1884. When Charlottenburg became part of Greater Berlin in 1920, distinctions between the two began to be blurred, and disappeared entirely when it took over the function of a new centre for the western half of the city after the division of Berlin during the years of conflict between East and West.

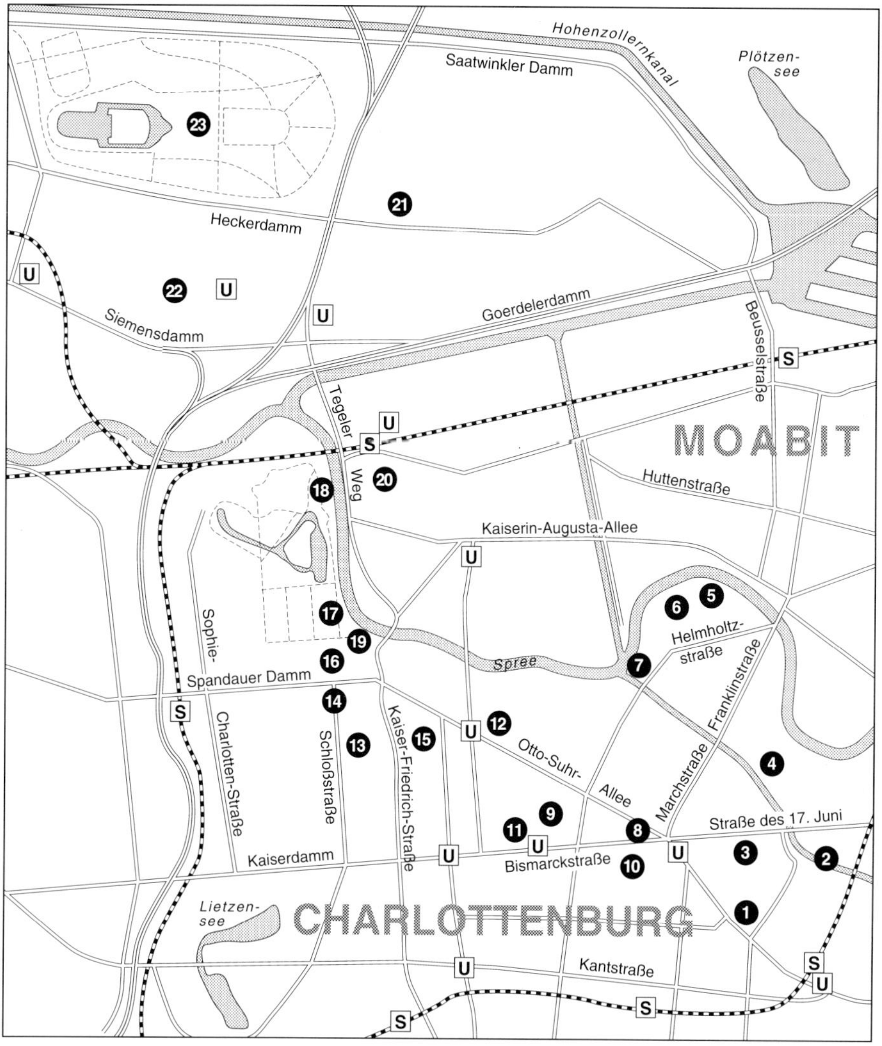

E 1 Konzertsaal der Hochschule für Musik
E 2 Umlaufkanal
E 3 Technische Universität – Hauptgebäude
E 4 Zwietuschwerk (Siemens)
E 5 Doppelinstitut
E 6 Spreebogen-Plaza
E 7 Müllverladebahnhof
E 8 Telefunken-Hochhaus
E 9 Abspannwerk Zauritzweg
E 10 Schillertheater
E 11 Deutsche Oper
E 12 Rathaus Charlottenburg
E 13 Sporthalle
E 14 Kaserne der »Garde du corps«
E 15 Luisenkirche
E 16 Schloß Charlottenburg
E 17 Schloßpark
E 18 Schinkelpavillon
E 19 Belvedere
E 20 Gustav-Adolf-Kirche
E 21 Kirche Maria Regina Martyrum
E 22 Siedlungen Charlottenburg-Nord
E 23 Volkspark Jungfernheide

E 1 Konzertsaal der Hochschule für Musik
Berlin-Charlottenburg; Fasanenstraße 1
1953-54 • Paul Baumgarten

Der Konzertsaal ersetzt den vorderen zerstörten Bauteil der gleichzeitig mit der benachbarten Hochschule der Künste entstandenen Musikhochschule. Wie wenig die fünfziger Jahre mit älteren Gebäuden anzufangen wußten und wie wenig sie auf ein harmonisches Nebeneinander von Altem und Neuem eingehen wollten, offenbart dieses Gebäude. Unbeirrt geht Baumgarten in der Gestaltung seine eigenen Wege, als stünde der Saal ohne Nachbarn da. Die Zeit spricht aus der spiegelnden Glasfront, die Transparenz und Leichtigkeit zur Devise hatte. Ihre volle Wirkung entfaltet die Fassade erst bei Dunkelheit, wenn das Licht aus dem Foyer auf die Straße flutet und das bunte Treiben während der Pause den Blick des Passanten auf die Fenster lenkt. Über dem Foyertrakt erhebt sich das flach geschwungene Saaldach. Seiner Linie entspricht spiegelbildlich der sanfte Bogen der Fensterfolge in der Fasanenstraße, welcher die Kontur des Parkettbodens nachzeichnet. Auch die Saalwände verlaufen nicht parallel, sie divergieren leicht, verjüngen sich zur Bühne hin. Das ist menschlich belangvoll und eine Abkehr von zwanghafter Rechtwinkligkeit, die man noch ein oder zwei Jahrzehnte zuvor unheilvoll erleben mußte.

The concert hall replaces the destroyed front part of the building of the Musikhochschule, which was built at the same time as the adjacent Hochschule der Künste. This building shows how little the fifties knew about handling older buildings, and how little they were prepared to attempt a harmonious juxtaposition of old and new. Baumgarten calmly goes his own way with the design, as though the neighbouring buildings were not even there. The period speaks out of the reflecting glass façade, the motto of which was transparency and lightness. It does not make its full effect until night-time, when light from the foyer streams out into the street and the colourful comings and goings of the interval draw the attention of passers-by to the foyer. Above the foyer section is the shallow curve of the hall roof. Its line mirrors the gentle arch of the sequence of windows in Fasanenstrasse, which follows the contour of the parquet floor. The walls of the hall do not run parallel either, they diverge slightly, narrowing towards the platform. This is relevant in human terms, and a departure from the compulsive rectangularity that prevailed so disastrously one or two decades before.

in der Nähe/nearby:
Hochschule der Künste; Hardenbergstraße 33
1898-1902 • Kayser & Großheim
Haus am Steinplatz; Steinplatz 4
1906-07 • August Endell
Goethe-Institut; Hardenbergstraße 7
1988 • Wolf-Rüdiger Borchardt

E 2 Umlaufkanal
Berlin-Tiergarten; Müller-Breslau-Straße
1975-76 • Ludwig Leo

Auf der Schleuseninsel, dem Gelände der ehemaligen Versuchsanstalt für Wasserkraftmaschinen, erhielt das Institut für Wasserbau und Schiffbau der Technischen Universität eine Versuchsanlage, die durch ihre Höhe weit über die Baumwipfel des Tiergartens hinausragt. Der beengte Platz ließ es geraten erscheinen, den üblicherweise in der Fläche angeordneten Umlaufkanal in die Vertikale aufzurichten. Dem unübersehbaren Gebäude gab Ludwig Leo ein betont technisches Aussehen: dicke Rohre, gehalten von einem unverkleideten Stahlgerüst, und ein kastenartiger Aufbau für die Meßlabore. Die auffällige Farbgebung in kräftigen Rosa-, Blau- und Grüntönen läßt das Ganze wie eine Großplastik erscheinen.

The Institut für Wasserbau und Schiffsbau of the Technische Universität acquired a research plant on the Schleuseninsel, the site of the former testing station for water power machines. The building towers high above the tops of the trees in the Tiergarten. The cramped site made it seem advisable to move the circulation channel, usually on the level, on to the vertical. Ludwig Leo made the highly conspicuous building look very technical: fat pipes, supported by an unclad steel framework, and a box-like structure on top for the measurement laboratories. The striking colouring in strong shades of pink, blue and green make the whole thing seem like a gigantic sculpture.

in der Nähe/nearby:
Unterschleuse; B-Tiergarten; Müller-Breslau-Straße
1936-40 (Kammer); 1953-54 (Wärterhaus)
Porzellan-Manufaktur; B-Charlottenburg; Wegelystraße 1
1868-72 • Gustav Möller
Ernst-Reuter-Haus; B-Charlottenburg; Straße des 17. Juni 110/114
1938-40 • Walter Schlempp, Karl Elkart
Charlottenburger Brücke; B-Charlottenburg; Straße des 17. Juni
1905-09 • Bernhard Schaede

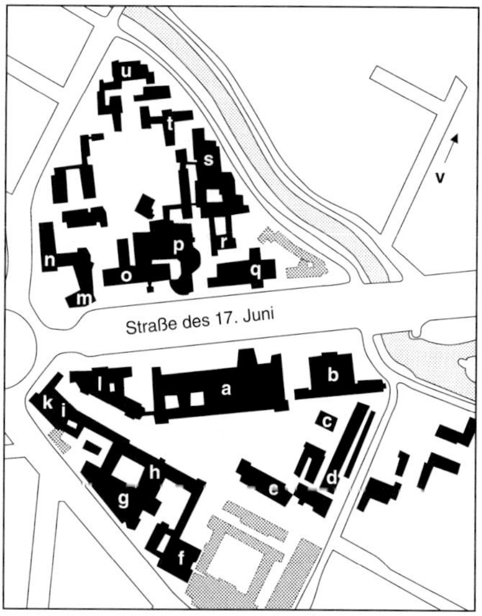

E 3 Technische Universität – Hauptgebäude
Berlin-Charlottenburg; Straße des 17. Juni 135
1878-84 • Richard Lucae, Friedrich Hitzig, Julius Carl Raschdorff
1961-68 • Kurt Dübbers, Karl-Heinz Schwennicke

Aus Bauakademie und Gewerbeakademie ging 1879 die Technische Hochschule Charlottenburg hervor. Westlich des Tiergartens hatte die neue Einrichtung bereits ein Baugelände erhalten, und 1884 stand der fertige Neubau. Das imposante Gebäude von 228 m Länge verlangte als Hochschule eine Würde vermittelnde Gestaltung. Quaderung im Erdgeschoß, Säulenordnungen in den Obergeschossen, endlose Reihen von Rundbogenfenstern und ein mächtiges Kranzgesims mit Skulpturen, Attika und Geländer kamen dem nach. Den Zerstörungen des Zweiten Weltkrieges entging nur die Rückfront. Seit 1968 ergänzen eine schlichte Hochhausscheibe und das vorgelagerte Auditorium maximum die Reste des Altbaues. Erweiterung erhielt die spätere Technische Universität zunächst auf ihrem Stammgelände. Das 1882 errichtete Chemiegebäude nahm noch die Gestaltung des Hauptgebäudes auf, spätere Bauten folgten dem Geschmack der Zeit, deutlich ablesbar am 1932 fertiggestellten Physikgebäude. Mitte der fünfziger Jahre setzte eine umfangreiche Erweiterung ein, zunächst östlich der Fasanenstraße mit kleineren, anspruchslos nüchternen Institutsbauten. Eine Chance zu städtebaulich bedeutsamer Bebauung bot sich beim Nordgelände entlang dem Landwehrkanal. Es blieb aber bei einem unverbindlichen Nebeneinander zweckmäßig-moderner Bauten, die den föderativen Charakter der heutigen Hochschule zum Ausdruck bringen. Seit etwa 1980 versucht man, mit einer baulichen Verdichtung des Geländes städtebaulichen Zusammenhalt zu finden.

The Technische Hochschule Charlottenburg grew out of the Bauakadamie and the Gewerbeakademie in 1879. The new institution had already acquired a site west of the Tiergarten, and the new building was completed in 1884. The imposing building is 228 metres long, and as an institute of higher education demanded a design suggesting dignity. Rustication on the ground floor, column orders in the upper storeys, endless rows of round-arched windows and a massive cornice with sculptures, attica and balustrade provided this. Only the rear façade escaped damage in the Second World War. The remains of the old building have been complemented by a plain high-rise block and the auditorium maximum in front of it, since 1968. The later Technische Universität was extended at first on its traditional site. The chemistry building, dating from 1882, followed the design of the main building, and subsequent buildings followed the taste of the period concerned, as can be seen clearly in the physics building, completed in 1932. In the mid fifties considerable expansion began, at first east of Fasanenstrasse with small, unassuming, sober institute buildings. An opportunity for development that was significant in town planning terms was offered by the northern site on the Landwehrkanal. But it remained a non-committal juxtaposition of functional modern buildings, expressing the federal nature of the modern university. Since about 1980 an attempt has been made to produce some urban impact by compacting the buildings to an extent.

(a) Hauptgebäude
(b) Chemiegebäude • 1882 • Julius Carl Raschdorff
(c) Mechanisch-technische Versuchsanstalt • 1884
(d) Prüfungsanstalt für Heizungs- und Lüftungseinrichtungen • 1906-07
(e) Institut für Umwelttechnik • 1980-81 • Johann Friedrich Geist, Helmut Maier, Hans Heinrich Moldenschardt, Peter Voigt, Hans Wehrhahn
(f) Mensa • 1964-67 • Werner Düttmann
(g) Institut für Physik • 1978-84 • Dieter Hundertmark, Bruno Lambart
(h) Institut für Physik • 1930-32 • Otto Weißgerber, Fritz Schirmer
(i) Metallhüttenmännisches Institut • 1914-20 • Rackebrandt
(k) Institut für Bergbau und Hüttenwesen • 1955-59 • Willy Kreuer
(l) Erweiterungsbau • 1900-02 • Eggert, Leibnitz
(m) Städtebauinstitut • 1967-69 • Hans Scharoun, Bernhard Hermkes
(n) Institut für Architektur • 1963-68 • Bernhard Hermkes
(o) Institut für Wasserbau • 1958/59 • Hellmut Bressler
(p) Institut für Mathematik • 1976-80 • Barna v. Sartory, Georg Kohlmaier
(q) Institut für Technische Chemie • 1963-69 • Willy Kreuer
(r) Institut für Elektrotechnik • 1959-62 • Ochs
(s) Institut für Elektrotechnik • 1981-88 • Gerd Fesel, Peter Bayerer
(t) Institut für Nachrichtentechnik • 1963-69 • Werner March
(u) Heinrich-Hertz-Institut für Schwingungsforschung • 1964-68 • Karl-Heinz Schwennicke
(v) Institut für Werkstoffkunde • 1971-72 • Peter Brinkert

in der Nähe/nearby:
Berliner Disconto-Bank; Otto-Suhr-Allee 6-16
1966-67 • Günter Hönow
Marchbrücke; Marchstraße
1911-12 • Heinrich Seeling

E 4 Zwietuschwerk (Siemens)
Berlin-Charlottenburg; Salzufer 6-7
1925-26 • Hans Hertlein

Die Zwietuschwerke, ein Tochterunternehmen von Siemens, behielten bei der Erweiterung des Betriebes in den zwanziger Jahren den alten Standort bei, folgten als kleinere Firma nicht der allgemeinen Randwanderung der Industrie. Hier am Landwehrkanal war noch genügend Platz, dem Altbau zwei neue Flügel anzufügen. Hertlein, der Hausarchitekt von Siemens, löste die Aufgabe auf seine Weise. Ein möglichst hohes, zweckmäßig gegliedertes Haus kleidet sich in eine widerstandsfähige Klinkerhaut. Die städtebaulichen Belange nimmt die Ausrichtung des vorderen Baukörpers parallel zum Kanal auf, und der vom Charlottenburger Tor her sichtbare Giebel wird zur Schauseite gestaltet. Höhe und bestmögliche Ausnutzung des Gebäudes gewann Hertlein durch die bauamtliche Genehmigung von drei Staffelgeschossen anstelle eines steilen Satteldaches. Die Stirnseite geriet so zum dekorativen Stufengiebel, der in einer Zeit sachlichen Bauens als organische Schmuckform gebilligt war. Umbau und Erweiterung des Fabrikgebäudes 1976 nahmen Rücksicht auf die alte Gestaltung.

The Zwietusch works, a daughter firm of Siemens, retained their old site when the firm expanded in the twenties, and as a small firm did not take part in the general migration to the periphery. There was still plenty of room here on the Landwehrkanal to add two new wings to the old building. Hertlein, Siemens' house architect, found a solution that was typical of his approach. The building is as high as possible, functional, and has a skin of resistant clinker. The orientation of the end section of the building parallel to the canal takes care of urban development requirements, and the gable, visible from the Charlottenburger Tor, becomes the show façade. Hertlein gained height and the best possible use of the building by getting planning permission for three staggered storeys instead of a saddle roof. Thus the front side became a decorative stepped gable, which was permitted as an organic decoration at a time of functional building. The old design was taken into account when the building was rebuilt and extended in 1976.

E 5 Doppelinstitut
Berlin-Charlottenburg; Pascalstraße
1983-86 • Gerd Fesel, Peter Bayerer

Das Institut für Werkzeugmaschinen und Fertigungstechnik der TU und das Fraunhofer-Institut für Produktionsanlagen und Konstruktionstechnik haben im Spreebogen, dem jüngsten Erweiterungsgelände der Technischen Universität einen aufsehenerregenden Neubau erhalten. Als ließe der Lauf der Spree keine andere Lösung zu, wurde der Kreis zum baukörperlich bestimmenden Element. Gestalterisch, aber auch bautechnisch von Bedeutung ist das kreisrunde Technikum mit seinen 64 Metern Durchmesser. Ohne Innenstützen überspannt die filigrane Konstruktion die Halle und bietet der wechselnden Aufstellung von Geräten und Anlagen jegliche Entfaltungsmöglichkeit. Abgeleitet wurde die Form vom Rundlauf eines mittig aufgehängten Kranes und dem Vorzug des größten Raumes bei geringster Außenfläche. Als konzentrischer Dreiviertelring legen sich in mehreren Geschossen Verwaltungs- und Arbeitsräume um das zentrale Technikum. Sie schirmen die gläserne Halle gegen die Sonnenstrahlung ab, öffnen aber die Nordseite dem indirekten Licht. Wie hier Trennung von Produktion und Verwaltung und jede Hierarchie vermieden wurden, so kann sich daraus eine neue, menschliche Art der Arbeitsorganisation auch für die industrielle Fertigung ableiten. Als Prototyp einer ästhetisch befriedigenden und städtebaulich verträglichen Industriebaukultur mag der Komplex außerdem gelten.

The Technical University's institute of tools and manufacturing technology and the Fraunhofer institute for production plants and construction technique have acquired a building that has attracted a lot of attention, on the bend of the Spree, the TU's latest site for expansion. A circle was chosen as the determining element for the design, as though the bend in the Spree would not permit any other. This circular institution with a diameter of 64 metres is significant in terms of both design and building techniques. The filigree construction spans the hall without internal supports, and offers every possible form of arrangement for the changing installation of equipment and machines. The form was derived from the swing of a crane suspended in the middle, and the advantage of the largest amount of space with the smallest exterior surface. The offices and workrooms surround the central technical area as a concentric three-quarter circle, in several storeys. They protect the glass hall from the sun, but leave the north side open to indirect light. Here separation of production and administration, and any sort of hierarchy, were avoided, and from this a new, humane way of organized work can be derived for industrial production as well. The complex is also valid as a prototype of aesthetically satisfying and tolerable industrial building culture in urban development terms.

E 6 Spreebogen-Plaza
Berlin-Charlottenburg; Pascalstraße 10
1993-94 • Jürgen Fissler und Hans-Christof Ernst

Seit den achtziger Jahren mausert sich das bisher eher desolate Gelände am Charlottenburger Spreebogen zu einem Forschungs- und Verwaltungszentrum. Mit dem 1983-86 errichteten Doppelinstitut wurden architektonische Maßstäbe gesetzt, die auch spätere Bauherren herausforderten, ihren Investitionen nicht nur wirtschaftliche, sondern auch baukünstlerische Aspekte abzugewinnen. Zu einer der gestalterischen Vorbedingungen für das Spreebogen-Plaza wurde die Absicht, sich städtebaulich einzupassen und dabei doch eigenständig zu bleiben. Glas und das Weiß des Granits sind offensichtliche Zugeständnisse an den älteren Nachbarn, dessen Rundung findet dagegen kaum merklich, doch wohltuend einen reziproken Anklang in der konkaven Front des Plaza. Mit der Abtreppung des Komplexes zum Spreeufer hin, mit der unaufdringlichen Dachlösung und mit der Flankierung der begrünten Innenhöfe durch transparente Glastrakte wird unmißverständlich dokumentiert, daß im Bürohausbau Bedarfsdeckung durch Baukunst abgelöst wurde. Sachlichkeit und individueller Charakter vereinigen sich wieder zu einer architektonischen Haltung, wie sie die späten zwanziger Jahre prägte.

Beginning in the nineteen-eighties, this formerly desolate area at the crescent of the Spree in Charlottenburg has been turned into a centre for research and administration. The twin institutions established here in 1983-86 set architectural standards which inspired subsequent developers to see to it that their investments conformed not only to considerations of economic feasibility but also presented certain aesthetic qualities. One of the design criteria for the Spreebogen-Plaza was to adapt to the urban situation and at the same time maintain a unique character. The glazing and the white granite are obvious concessions to the older neighbour whose curvature is echoed almost unnoticeably but harmoniously in the concave form of the plaza. The stepping of the complex towards the banks of the Spree, the unobtrusive solution for the roof, and the flanking of the green interior courts with transparent glazed wings can be taken as an indication that mere provision of office space has given way to true architecture. Functionality and individual character are once again merging in an architectural approach reminiscent of that which marked the late nineteen-twenties.

in der Nähe/nearby:
Kraftwerk Charlottenburg; Am Spreebord 5-8
1899-1900 • Georg Klingenberg (Erweiterung ab 1902)

E 7 Müllverladebahnhof
Berlin-Charlottenburg; Helmholtzstraße 42
1936-37 • Paul Baumgarten

Die Feststellung, daß sich die täglich 2500 t Berliner Hausmüll zur Aufbesserung karger märkischer Sumpfböden eignen, ließ diese Anlage entstehen. Da der Transport nur mit Lastkähnen in Frage kam, entwickelte Baumgarten eine Brückenrampe, die einen kontinuierlichen und weitgehend vereinfachten Abladevorgang gewährleistet. Über einer mit Spundwänden gefaßten Wasserhalle erhebt sich das Eisengerüst der Brücke, die Massivdecken und klinkerausgefachte Aufbauten trägt. Vier Fuhrwerke konnten sich gleichzeitig in einer wettergeschützten Halle ihrer Ladung entledigen. Automatische Tore der Abladehalle und der Wasserhalle sowie eine Absauganlage an den Schüttrichtern beugten der Staubentwicklung vor, die der hohe Aschegehalt des Hausmülls mit sich brachte. Nach außen gestalterisch wirksam wurde die glatte Brüstung der gekurvten Abfahrtsrampe für die entladenen Fuhrwerke. Damit steht das Bauwerk noch ganz in der Tradition des sachlichen Bauens, das um 1936 in Deutschland schon allgemein verpönt war, doch bei einem Bauwerk für den Stadtmüll offenbar nicht dem »repräsentativen« offiziellen Stil weichen mußte.

This building came into being when it was established that Berlin's daily 2,500 tons of domestic rubbish could be used to improve barren marshland in the Mark. As barges were the only possible means of transport, Baumgarten developed a bridge ramp that guaranteed a continuous and largely simplified loading process. The iron framework of the bridge, supported by solid ceilings, rises above a water hall framed with bulkheads and superstructures clad in clinker. Four vehicles could be unloaded here at the same time, in a weatherproof hall. Automatic doors on unloading hall and water hall, and the suction plant on the rubbish funnels, prevented the spread of dust which the high ash content of the domestic rubbish brought with it. The curved ramp for the unloaded vehicles with its smooth parapet is an effective external design feature. Thus the building is completely in the functional building style that was generally frowned upon in Germany even in 1936, but apparently a building dealing with refuse did not have to abandon it in favour of the official «prestigious» style.

in der Nähe/nearby:
Autobusbetriebshof; Helmholtzstraße 41
1925-26 • Franz Ahrens
Dovebrücke; Dovestraße
1908-09 • Heinrich Seeling
Wohnanlage; Pascalstraße 5-8
1984-85 • Henry Nielebock

E 8 Telefunken-Hochhaus
Berlin-Charlottenburg; Ernst-Reuter-Platz 7
1958-60 • Schwebes & Schoßberger

Bernhard Hermkes wies 1955 im Ergebnis eines städtebaulichen Wettbewerbs den Weg für die bauliche Entwicklung des nun in Citynähe gerückten Ernst-Reuter-Platzes. Im Zeitgeschmack lag die locker-beschwingte Anordnung von Gebäuden. Acht- bis zehngeschossige Scheiben, in Gruppen parallel ausgerichtet, weisen mit den Stirnseiten zum Platz. Abwechslung vermittelt ein Hochhaus von 22 Geschossen, seinerseits aber mit der Breitseite zum Platz gewandt. Dazwischen gewähren ein weites Platzrund und breite Straßen dem Autoverkehr sein noch unbestrittenes Vorrecht. In diesem Sinnbild des »modernen« großstädtischen Ensembles bot sich den Architekten des Telefunkenhauses nur geringer Gestaltungsspielraum. Immerhin durchbrachen sie die Rechtwinkligkeit durch ein dezentes Aufbauchen des Baukörpers und gaben dem Sockel mit konischen Stützen einen besonderen Akzent.

In 1955, as a result of an urban development competition, Bernhard Hermkes defined architectural development in Ernst-Reuter-Platz, now near the city centre. The relaxed and vibrant arrangement of the buildings was appropriate to the taste of the times. Eight- to ten-storey slabs are arranged in parallel groups with their ends to the square. A 22 storey high-rise building provides variety, and this turns its broad side to the square. Between them a large area of square and broad streets afford motor traffic its as yet undisputed privilege. In this symbol of the «modern» big-city ensemble the architects of the Telefunken building were left very little leeway. Nevertheless they broke up the dominant rectangularity by allowing the building to bulge a little, and gave the base area with its conical supports a particular accent.

in der Nähe/nearby:
IBM-Haus; Ernst-Reuter-Platz 2
1960-62 • Rolf Gutbrod, Hermann Kiess, Bernhard Binder
Deutsche Bank; Otto-Suhr-Allee 6-16
1966-67 • Günter Hönow

E 9 Abspannwerk Zauritzweg
Berlin-Charlottenburg; Zauritzweg 13-17
1922-24 • Walter Klingenberg, Werner Issel

Das Abspannwerk steht am Anfang einer neuen Generation von Verteilerwerken für die Elektrizitätsversorgung in Berlin. Durch die Vereinheitlichung des Netzes im 1920 geschaffenen Groß-Berlin entstand eine Reihe solcher Stationen, welche die 30-kV-Hochspannung aus den Elektrizitätswerken auf 3000 Volt transformieren und auf die kleineren Netzstationen verteilen, wo schließlich in einer weiteren Transformationsstufe die Haushaltsspannung von 380 bzw. 220 Volt erzeugt wird. Die großen Energiemengen, die durch dieses Gebäude geleitet werden, stellten auch Anforderungen an die Sicherheit und an die Architektur. So waren das hohe Transformatorenhaus, der Schalthaustrakt mit den brand- und explosionsgefährlichen Ölschaltern und die Bedienungswarte im halbrunden Anbau klar geschieden. Klingenberg und Issel, die späteren Architekten des Großkraftwerks Klingenberg – benannt nicht nach dem Architekten sondern nach dem Direktor der AEG Georg Klingenberg –, benutzten den Formenkatalog des expressionistischen Industriebaues, um zwischen banaler Zweckmäßigkeit und falschem Pathos der kleinen Baugruppe ein gefälliges Äußeres zu geben. Als Ersatz für das inzwischen abgetragene Trafohaus wurden 1979-80 von Helge Pitz drei neue Transformatorkapseln vor die Ostwand gesetzt.

The transformer station is one of the first of a new generation of distribution stations for Berlin's electricity supply. When the network was standardized in Greater Berlin, created in 1920, a series of such stations was built to transform the 30 kV high tension current from the generators to 3,000 volts and distribute it to the smaller network stations, where it went through a final transformer stage to 380 or 220 volts. The large quantities of energy that passed through this building made heavy demands in terms of safety and architecture. Thus a clear distinction was made between the high transformer house, the distribution hall with oil switches, which were susceptible to fire and explosion, and the service observation point in the semicircular extension. Klingenberg and Issel, later to be the architects of the large Klingenberg power station – named not after the architect but after AEG director Georg Klingenberg – used the formal catalogue of Expressionist industrial building to give the little group of buildings a pleasing exterior, somewhere between banal functionality and false drama. The transformer house has been pulled down, and was replaced by three new transformer capsules in front of the east wall, designed by Helge Pitz, in 1979-80.

in der Nähe/nearby:
Arbeitsschutzmuseum; Frauenhoferstraße 11-12
1900-06 • Hückels

E 10 Schillertheater
Berlin-Charlottenburg; Bismarckstraße 110
1950-51 • Völker & Grosse

Unter dem Münchener Architekten Max Littmann entstand hier 1905-06, in der Zeit der großen Volkstheater, ein Amphitheater für 1350 Zuschauer. Wie viele andere Bühnen wurde es 1937-38 im Sinne jener Jahre nach den Gesetzen einer Pseudotradition umgebaut, im Kriege dann zerstört. Der Neubau von 1950 nahm im Zuschauerraum etwas halbherzig die Idee des Reformtheaters wieder auf. In der Fassade dagegen offenbarte sich die ganze Ziellosigkeit der Nachkriegsjahre. Die Härte der kantigen Baukörper, gepaart mit der glatten Travertinwand, setzt eine architektonische Haltung der dreißiger Jahre fort. Unvermittelt bricht daraus das Rund des Foyerfensters hervor, das trotz Größe in seiner Teilung kleinlich und provinziell wirkt. Das Aufgesetzte – es teilte sich auch innen in manchem Detail mit – und die Bereitschaft zu improvisieren sind so charakteristisch für die Bauzeit, daß der bekannte Berliner Architekturkritiker Günther Kühne Jahre später erkennt, es sei »die Sichtbarmachung geschichtlicher Abläufe im gebauten Raum«.

An amphitheatre for 1350 spectators was built here in 1905-6, in the period of the great popular theatres, by Munich architect Max Littmann. Like many other buildings it was rebuilt in 1937-8 in the spirit of those years according to the laws of a pseudo-tradition and later destroyed in the war. In the auditorium of the new building dating from 1950 the idea of reform theatre was somewhat half-heartedly taken up again. The façade on the other hand revealed all the lack of purpose of the postwar years. The hardness of the angular building, paired with the smooth Travertine wall, continues an architectural approach of the thirties. The circular section of the foyer window breaks through it unexpectedly, and despite its size seems petty and provincial, because of the way it is broken up. The way things are simply added on – this shows in many of the interior details as well – and the readiness to improvise, are so typical of the building period that the well-known Berlin architecture critic Günther Kühne wrote ten years later that it «made historical processes visible in architectural space.»

E 11 Deutsche Oper
Berlin-Charlottenburg; Bismarckstraße 34-37
1957-61 • Fritz Bornemann

Wenn beim Wiederaufbau des nahen Schillertheaters der Blick zurück noch formgebend wurde, geht Bornemann bei der Deutschen Oper eigene Wege. Kein belastendes Erbe des zerstörten Seeling-Baues schränkt den Architekten ein. »Modern« mußte in jenen Jahren gebaut werden, und das sollte man auch sehen. So ist der krasse Wechsel von geschlossener Betonwand und lichtdurchfluteter Glasfläche zu verstehen. Das statische Wagnis wurde zum Leitfaden der Architektur, das äußert sich bei der Oper im Schweben des massigen Kubus auf fast unsichtbaren zurückgesetzten Stützen. Tektonische Kräfte werden fast geleugnet. Dies gilt auch für den Balanceakt der Großplastik von Hans Uhlmann, die ohne falschen Symbolismus mit der Wandfläche hinter ihr eine enge Symbiose eingeht. Verblüffen mußte 1961 auch der Zuschauerraum, der ganz ohne Pomp und Zierrat auskommt. Alles konzentriert er auf die Bühne. In der Anordnung der Ränge und Logen schafft er eine von der Sehbarkeit diktierte ranglos-demokratische Theatergemeinde, wie sie schon vom Reformtheater des ausgehenden 19. Jahrhunderts gefordert wurde.

When the nearby Schiller Theatre was rebuilt the architects looked backwards, but for the Deutsche Oper Bornemann went his own way. He was not inhibited by the burden of the legacy of the building by Seeling that had been destroyed. Now buildings had to be «modern», and it had to show. This is the idea behind the stark contrast of closed concrete wall and a wall of glass flooded with light. Static daring became the guideline for architecture, and this is expressed in the opera house by the way the massive cube hovers on almost invisible supports. Tectonic forces are almost completely denied. This is also true of the balancing act performed by Hans Uhlmann's enormous sculpture, which enters into close symbiosis with the wall behind it without false symbolism. In 1961 the auditorium must have been amazing as well, as it is completely free of pomp and decoration. It concentrates everything on the stage. The balconies and boxes are arranged in such a way as to create a theatre audience that is without rank, and democratic, with the ability to see well as the main aim, as demanded by the reform theatre movement in the late nineteenth century.

in der Nähe/nearby:
Geschäftshaus Hardenberg mit Buchhandlung Kiepert; Hardenbergstraße 4-5
1955-56 • Paul Schwebes
Renaissance-Theater; Hardenbergstraße 6
1926-27 • Oskar Kaufmann
Entenbrunnen; Hardenbergstraße 6
1911 • August Gaul

in der Nähe/nearby:
VDE-Haus; Bismarckstraße 33
1930-31 • Hans Hertlein
Stadtbad; Krumme Straße 9-10
1896-98 • Paul Bratring
Wohn- und Geschäftshaus; Bismarckstraße 79-80
1905-06 • Otto March

E 12 Rathaus Charlottenburg
Berlin-Charlottenburg; Otto-Suhr-Allee 96-102
1899-1905 • Reinhardt & Süßenguth

Galt Charlottenburg um die Jahrhundertwende als wohlhabendste Stadt im Kaiserreich, so kommt dieses in Größe und künstlerischer Ausprägung des neuen Rathauses unzweifelhaft zum Ausdruck. In altbewährter Weise wurden Säle und andere repräsentative Räume in den Vorderflügel gelegt. Geschoßhöhen und Fenstermaße korrespondieren deshalb gut mit dem gewaltigen Turm. Wirkung wurde auch im Material gesucht. Rauhe, unregelmäßige Sandsteinquader bilden die Grundlage der Fassadenausformung in einer ernsten Spielart des Jugendstils. Fern jeder Sparsamkeit bereichert ein üppiger plastischer Schmuck das Gebäude. Im Sinne der Zeit prägt die Werke von Ernst Westphal, H. Giesecke, Riegelmann, August Vogel und anderen ein Symbolismus, auf den auch Wandmalereien und Mosaik nicht verzichten wollen. Zwar wird in den Einzelformen der Bruch mit dem zuletzt gedankenlosen Historismus des 19. Jahrhunderts deutlich, doch bleibt das Neue an der Oberfläche, ein Wandel in der Fassung des Baukörpers ist noch nicht spürbar. – Bereits 1911-15 war eine Erweiterung nötig, die Heinrich Seeling besorgte.

At the turn of the century Charlottenburg was considered the most prosperous town in the empire, and this is expressed in the size and artistic flourishes of the town hall. In the tried and tested fashion, halls and other prestigious public rooms were placed in the front section. Thus the height of the storeys and the proportions of the windows are appropriate to the massive tower. Materials were also chosen for the sake of effect. The basis of the façade design is rough, regular sandstone ashlar, in a serious variation on Jugendstil. The building is decorated with lavish sculpture rejecting any sense of economy. In the spirit of the times these works by Ernst Westphal, H. Giesecke, Riegelmann, August Vogel and others are steeped in symbolism, and this is also true of the paintings and mosaics. Individual forms do show a break with the ultimately mindless historicism of the nineteenth century, but the innovations are superficial, there is still no sign of a change in the organization of the body of the building. An extension was needed as early as 1911-15, and this was provided by Heinrich Seeling.

E 13 Sporthalle
Berlin-Charlottenburg; Schloßstraße 56
1988 • Inken Baller, Hinrich Baller

Fern von genormter Kargheit und nüchterner Zweckmäßgkeits-Ideologie schwelgen Inken und Hinrich Baller in von ihnen erfundenen lindgrünen filigranen Schwüngen. Sie provozieren naturgemäß die Frage nach Gründen und Herkunft solcher Formen. Wartete der Jugendstil noch mit floralen Vorbildern auf oder verwies der Expressionismus auf gotisches Empfinden, gilt hier offenbar nur architektonischer Mutwille, der dem erregten Kritiker zum Trotz menschlich nach Traumbildern baut und der Schaulust des Benutzers und der Passanten etwas zu sehen gibt. So ist auch Hinrich Ballers Ausspruch zu verstehen: »Normale Turnhallen sehen aus wie für die Schweinezucht gebaut«. Doch der Vorzug dieser Halle erschöpft sich nicht im Aussehen. Mit der Raumaufteilung und -ausnutzung konnte das anfangs für unmöglich Erachtete gelöst werden, auf engem Grundstück eine Halle in der Größe eines Handballfeldes und darüber eine weitere Halle in den Maßen der Olympianorm unterzubringen. Da das spielerische Lineament des Hallenbaues nicht bloße Dekoration ist, sondern auch tragende Funktionen hat, werden an den Statiker besondere Anforderungen gestellt, die nur im Zeitalter elektronischer Rechenprogramme zu bewältigen sind.

Inken and Hinrich Baller, far away from standardized meagreness and sober functionality as ideologies, revel in the lime-green filigree curves they invented. Naturally they provoke questions about the reasons for and origins of forms of this kind. Jugendstil was able to point to floral models, and Expressionism could invoke Gothic sensibility, but what we have here seems to be architectural mischievousness, which in defiance of the excited critic builds humanly in accordance with dream pictures, and offers some satisfaction to the curiosity of passers-by and users like. Hinrich Baller's statement is also to be understood in this way: «Normal gymnasia look as though they were built for pig-breeding.» But the advantages of this building are not exhausted in its appearance. The way in which space is distributed and exploited made it possible to achieve something at first thought to be out of the question, and to provide on a cramped plot both a hall the size of a handball court and above that another hall of standard Olympic proportions. As the playful lines of the gymnasium are not mere decoration, but also distribute the thrust of the building, particular demands were made on the structural engineers, which in the last resort can only be met in the age of the computer.

in der Nähe/nearby:
Wohnhaus; Schloßstraße 45-47
1985-86 • Hinrich Baller, Inken Baller
Boschhaus; Bismarckstraße 71
1916-17 • Bielenberg & Moser

E 14 Kaserne der »Garde du corps«
Berlin-Charlottenburg; Schloßstraße 1 und 70
1852-59 • Friedrich August Stüler

Auf eine Idee von Friedrich Wilhelm IV. gehen die beiden Eckbauten beiderseits der Schloßstraße zurück. Sie sollten die auf das Schloß zuführende Hauptachse und den Luisenplatz aufwerten. Als Nutzung der beiden Gebäude fand sich die recht preußische Lösung, daraus Kasernen für die Garde zu machen. Stüler vermied aber mit Quadersockel, Risaliten, Pilastern, Giebeln, Attika und säulengetragenen Kuppeln jeden spartanischen Eindruck und schuf zwei Bauten, die sich als würdiges Gegenüber für das Schloß erwiesen. In der Formensprache ergab sich eine unzeitgemäße Mischung aus Barock und Zopfstil, die man nur als Zugeständnis an den formal beherrschenden Schloßbau verstehen kann. Heute beherbergen die beiden Gebäude das Antikenmuseum und das Ägyptische Museum. In einer Zeit, als auf West-Berliner Gebiet dringend Museumsräume benötigt wurden, ergab sich dieser Behelf, der dann später auch durch Umbauten gefestigt wurde und sich nun in das museale Ensemble des Schlosses einfügt.

The two corner buildings on either side of Schlossstrasse go back to an idea of Friedrich Wilhelm IV's. They were intended to enhance the main axis leading to the palace and Luisenplatz. An extremely Prussian solution was found by using the buildings as barracks for the guards. But Stüler avoided any spartan impression by giving them ashlar bases, protruding sections, pilasters, gables, attica and domes supported on columns, thus creating a pair of buildings that are a worthy counterpart to the palace. The formal language is an untimely mixture of baroque and rococo style, which can only be understood as a concession to the prevalent style of palace building. Today the two buildings house the museum of antiquities and the Egyptian museum. This makeshift solution came about at a time when museum space was desperately needed in West Berlin, but later the buildings were suitably modified, and now form part of a museum ensemble with the palace.

in der Nähe/nearby:
Denkmal des Großen Kurfürsten; Luisenplatz
1696-1700 • Andreas Schlüter
Bahnhof Westend; Spandauer Damm 89
1883-84 • Kayser & Großheim
Wohnbauten; Otto-Suhr-Allee 144
1988 • Hans Kollhoff

E 15 Luisenkirche
Berlin-Charlottenburg; Gierkeplatz
1712-16 • Martin Heinrich Böhme

Ein erster Entwurf von Philipp Gerlach war der neuen Gemeinde Charlottenburg offenbar zu kostspielig, Martin Böhme vereinfachte und baute die Kirche für nur 6100 Taler. Preußisch-einfach geriet der Neubau: Als griechisches Kreuz durchschneiden sich zwei kurze Schiffe, im Schnittpunkt der flachen Walmdächer als einziger Schmuck ein Dachreiter, der die ersten hundert Jahre nicht erlebte. Schinkel schlug schließlich vor, den puritanischen Bau zu restaurieren und der Kirche einen Turm zu geben. Nach langem Zögern bewilligte der sparsame König Friedrich Wilhelm III. diese Maßnahme, vielleicht gab die Bitte der Gemeinde den Ausschlag, das Gotteshaus nach der im Volk beliebten und 1810 verstorbenen Königin Luise benennen zu dürfen. Nach den schweren Zerstörungen im Zweiten Weltkrieg wurde das Kirchlein bis 1956 wieder aufgebaut. Für den Ostflügel entwarf Ludwig Peter Kowalski Glasfenster, zu deren Stiftern auch der vor den Nazis nach London emigrierte Berliner Bauunternehmer Heinrich Mendelssohn gehörte.

Philipp Gerlach's first design was apparently too expensive for the people of Charlottenburg, Martin Böhme simplifed it and built the church for only 6,100 talers. The new building was Prussian and plain. Nave and transept, both small, intersect as a Greek cross, and the only decoration was a ridge turret at the point of intersection of the hipped roofs, but this did not survive the first hundred years. Finally Schinkel suggested that the puritanical building should be restored, and that the church should have a tower. After much hesitation, the thrifty King Friedrich Wilhelm III agreed to this measure; it is possible that the decisive factor was the congregation's request that the church should be called after Queen Luise, who was popular with the people, and who had died in 1810. After severe damage in the Second World War the little church was rebuilt, and completed by 1956. Ludwig Peter Kowalski designed the windows for the east wing; one of the donors was the Berlin building contractor Heinrich Mendelssohn, who had emigrated to London when the Nazis came to power.

in der Nähe/nearby:
Wohnhaus; Haubachstraße 33
1983-84 • Johannes Uhl
Wohnhof am Goethepark; Kaiser-Friedrich-Straße 68
1980-82 • Oswald Mathias Ungers

E 16 Schloß Charlottenburg
Berlin-Charlottenburg; Luisenplatz
1695-1712 • Johann Arnold Nering; Johann Friedrich v. Eosander

Wenig westlich vom Dorf Lützow, reizvoll an einer Biegung der Spree, wählte Kurfürst Friedrich III. für seine Gemahlin Sophie Charlotte, die »philosophische Königin« und Freundin von Leibniz, den Bauplatz für ein kleines Landschloß. Nering begann den Bau, verstarb jedoch im selben Jahr. Es wäre zunächst auch bei der kleinen Anlage aus Mittelpavillon und zwei vierachsigen Flügeln geblieben, doch 1701 arrivierte Preußen zum Königreich und der Kurfürst zum König Friedrich I. Nun war Repräsentation geboten. Schloß Lietzenburg – wie es bis zum Tode der Königin hieß – mußte getreu der neuen Würde erweitert werden. Die vom Hofe Ludwigs XIV. mitgebrachten Reiseerfahrungen des Schweden Eosander schienen den gesuchten architektonischen Erfolg zu verheißen. Aus dem Neringbau und einem Seitenflügel von 1698 wurde eine große Dreiflügelanlage, die westlich noch einen langgestreckten Orangerietrakt erhielt. In der Mittelachse bekam auch die Ehrenhofseite einen Risalitvorbau, der höhergeführt wurde zu Turm und Kuppel. Nach dem Tode Friedrichs I. stellte dessen Sohn, der Soldatenkönig, den Weiterbau ein. Ihm waren die philosophische Neigung der Mutter und der Pomp des Vaters ohnehin fremd. Erst Friedrich II. beauftragte 1740 Knobelsdorff, auch auf der Ostseite einen Flügelbau auszuführen, symmetrisch zur Orangerie. Seine letzte Erweiterung erfuhr das Schloß 1788-90 durch einen Theaterbau von Carl Gotthard Langhans.

Elector Friedrich III chose a site a little to the west of the village of Lützow, charmingly placed on a bend in the Spree, for a country palace for his consort Sophie Charlotte, the «philosophical queen» and friend of Leibniz. Nering started the building, but died in the same year. It could have remained a small building with central pavilion and two wings with four axes, but in 1701 Prussia became a kingdom and the Elector King Frederick I. Now something more prestigious was needed. Schloss Lietzenburg, as it was called until the death of the queen, had to be extended in keeping with this new-found dignity. The experience that Swedish architect Eosander had brought back from his travels to the court of Louis XIV seemed to promise the architectural success required. Nering's building and a side wing added in 1698 were extended to form a large building in three sections, with a long orangery to the west. In the central axis the cour d'honneur side also acquired a projecting section, rising to tower and dome. After the death of Frederick I, his son, the soldier king, stopped further building. In any case his mother's philosophical inclinations and his father's liking for pomp were alien to him. It was Frederick II who in 1740 commissioned Knobelsdorff to build a wing on the east side as well, symmetrical with the orangery. The last expansion was the theatre added by Carl Gotthard Langhans in 1788-90.

E 17 Schloßpark
Berlin-Charlottenburg; Luisenplatz
1701 • Johann Friedrich v. Eosander, Siméon Godeau

Wie viele Gartenanlagen war der Charlottenburger Schloßpark nicht nur den Veränderungen durch das Wachstum der Pflanzen, sondern auch geschmäcklerischen Umgestaltungen ausgesetzt. Die barocke Anlage mit den großen Parterres und ihren ornamentalen Broderien, gefolgt vom rechteckigen Wasserbassin, auslaufend in einer weiten Schneise mit dem »unendlichen« Blick über Spree und Jungfernheide hinweg, wurde schon 1788 von Johann August Eyserbeck in einen Naturpark umgewandelt. Aus diesem Garten machte dann Peter Joseph Lenné 1819-28 einen romantischen Landschaftspark, behielt aber etliche alte Teile bei. Nach den Verwüstungen des Krieges nahm sich Joachim Kaiser 1950 des Parks an und führte ihn in freier Interpretation auf seine barocke Gestalt zurück. Nur im Nordteil wurde von Walter Hilzheimer ein Teil als Erholungsgelände abgesetzt.

Like many gardens the Schlosspark at Charlottenburg was subject to reshaping as a result of changing taste as well as the growth of plants. The baroque layout with large parterres and ornamental embroidery, followed by the rectangular pool and finishing in a broad break with the «endless» view over the Spree and Jungfernheide, was changed into a nature park by Johann August Eyserbeck as early as 1788. In 1819-28 Peter Joseph Lenné made this garden into a romantic landscaped park, but retained many of the older features. After devastation during the war, Joachim Kaiser took over the park in 1950, and returned it to a free interpretation of its baroque design. Only a small section in the north was set aside as a recreation area, by Walter Hilzheimer.

in der Nähe/nearby:
Neuer Flügel (Schloß-Ostflügel); Luisenplatz
1740-47 • Georg Wenzeslaus v. Knobelsdorff
Theaterbau (veräng. Orangerieflügel); Luisenplatz
1787-91 • Carl Gotthard Langhans
Kleine Orangerie; Luisenplatz
1790 • (vielleicht) Georg Friedrich Boumann

E 18 Belvedere
Berlin-Charlottenburg; Schloßpark
1789-90 • Carl Gotthard Langhans

Der in der Zeit der Empfindsamkeit umgestaltete Schloßpark hatte in der Hauptachse hinter dem großen Bassin zwischen den Armen der Alten und der Neuen Spree eine Insel behalten, deren günstige Lage zum Bau eines Belvederes genutzt wurde. In der schon zur Barockzeit geschätzten Blickschneise zur Jungfernheide, aber doch weit genug entfernt vom Schloß baute Langhans diesen schlichten, ovalen Pavillon, dessen recht konservative Formen noch auffällig der verflossenen Rokokophase folgen. Friedrich Wilhelm II. nutzte die Abgeschiedenheit des Belvedere für seine mystisch-spiritistischen Sitzungen der »Rosenkreuzer«. Bis heute hat sich die Umgebung des Bauwerkes erheblich verändert. Durch die Kanalisierung der Spree sind die Wasserläufe verlandet, die Insellage ist verschwunden, und der Damm der Hamburger Eisenbahn verdeckt den Blick nach Norden in die Weite der Landschaft.

When the Schlosspark was redesigned in the age of sentimentalism it retained, in the main axis between the arms of the Old and the New Spree, an island whose favourable position was used for the construction of a belvedere. Langhans built his plain, oval pavilion, to a conservative design still strikingly following the superceded rococo phase, in the break providing a view of Jungfernheide that had been highly thought of even in the baroque period, but far enough away from the palace. Friedrich Wilhelm II used the seclusion of the belvedere for the mystical-spiritual meetings of his «Rosicrucians». The building's surroundings have now changed considerably. Canalization of the Spree has meant that the water courses silted up, the island site has disappeared, and the Hamburg railway embankment blocks the view over the landscape to the north.

in der Nähe/nearby:
Inselbrücke; Schloßpark
1801
Mausoleum; Schloßpark
1810 • Heinrich Gentz

E 19 Schinkelpavillon
Berlin-Charlottenburg; Luisenplatz
1824 • Karl Friedrich Schinkel

Italienreisen waren in der Zeit des romantischen Biedermeier nicht nur das Recht eines von Eichendorff erfundenen »Taugenichts«, sie gehörten ebenso zum gesellschaftlichen Muß der »besseren Leute«. Auch Friedrich Wilhelm III. reiste nach Italien, sah am Meer bei Neapel eine Villa und ließ sie, zurückgekehrt nach Berlin, von Schinkel architektonisch nachempfinden. Das Sommerhaus entstand gleich seitwärts der Charlottenburger Schloßanlage. Einen krasseren Gegensatz mag es nicht geben, so glaubt man: feudales Barockschloß und schlichter Biedermeierbau – eine 500 m lange Schloßfront und ein zierlicher Hauswürfel. Aber gute Architektur verträgt sich, und der neue Pavillon ordnete sich dem bereits Vorhandenen bedingungslos unter.

In the romantic Biedermeier period, journeys to Italy were not just the prerogative of the kind of «good-for-nothing» invented by Eichendorff, they were also a social must for the «better classes». Friedrich Wilhelm III also travelled to Italy, saw a villa by the sea in Naples and on his return to Berlin had Schinkel make an architectural copy of it. The summerhouse was built immediately adjacent to Schloss Charlottenburg. One would think that there could hardly be a more blatant architectural contrast – a 500 hundred metre palace façade and a delicate cubic house. But good architecture can live with good architecture, and the new pavilion subordinated itself unreservedly to the existing buildings.

in der Nähe/nearby:
Schloßbrücke; Luisenplatz
1926-28
Mierendorff-Grundschule; Mierendorffstraße 20-26
1976-78 • Rolf D. Weisse
Mariae-Himmelfahrt-Kirche; Mindener Straße 1
1964-66 • Alfons Bocklage

E 20 Gustav-Adolf-Kirche
Berlin-Charlottenburg; Herschelstraße 14-15
1932-34 • Otto Bartning

Kaum eine Berliner Kirche der Zeit nach dem Ersten Weltkrieg verdeutlicht die Abkehr von traditionellen Formen und deutschtümelnder Stileinengung so sehr wie Bartnings Gustav-Adolf-Kirche. Aus neun konzentrischen Sektoren unterschiedlicher Tiefe baut sich der Grundriß auf, die Raumsegmente verjüngen sich zum Altar hin, steigen dabei aber auch zu größerer Höhe auf. Symbolhaft teilt sich das auch im Äußeren mit, wo Flächen und Linien auf den schlanken, pfeilartigen Turm zulaufen, aus dem das Kreuz herauswächst. Stahlbeton und Stahl sind die konstruktiven Elemente der Kirche, Turm und rückwärtiger Emporenring der statische Halt für die sechs großen Längsrahmen. Unorthodox ist auch die Inneneinrichtung gewählt. Die Bankreihen folgen den Kreislinien der Grundrißsektoren und deuten die für evangelische Predigtkirchen gewünschte Zentralisierung an.

There is hardly a church in Berlin built in the period after the First World War that so clearly shows the departure from traditional form and Germanicizing unity of style as Bartning's Gustav-Adolf-Kirche. The ground plan is built up of nine concentric sectors of different depth, and the spatial segments narrow as they approach the altar, but rise to a greater height. Symbolically this is also conveyed in the exterior, where the surfaces and lines run towards the slender, arrow-like tower, out of which the cross grows. The church is built of reinforced concrete and steel, and the tower and rear ring of galleries provide static support for the six large longitudinal frames. The rows of pews follow the circular lines of the ground plan sectors, and provide the central plan required in a church laying emphasis on preaching.

in der Nähe/nearby:
Landgericht III; Tegeler Weg 17-20
1901-06 und 1912-15 • Paul Thoemer, Rudolf Mönnich

E 21 Kirche Maria Regina Martyrum
Berlin-Charlottenburg; Heckerdamm 230
1960-63 • Hans Schädel, Friedrich Ebert

In der Nähe des ehemaligen Gefängnisses Plötzensee, wo während der Hitler-Diktatur aus rassistischen und politischen Gründen Menschen gequält und gemordet wurden, entstanden eine Gedenkstätte und die den Opfern geweihte Kirche. So befinden sich auch in der Krypta drei Gräber: Erich Klausener, Domprobst Bernhard Lichtenberg und ein symbolisches Grab für die Blutzeugen, denen ein Begräbnis verweigert wurde. Feierhof und Freialtar sind von hohen schwarzgrauen »Gefängnismauern« aus Basaltplatten umgeben. Der Glockenturm bildet weit abgerückt von der Kirche das Eingangstor. Kunstwerke wie Fritz Koenigs Portalplastik «Apokalyptisches Weib» und seine Pietà, O. H. Hajeks Kreuzwegbronzen oder Georg Meistermanns Altarwandfresco der Vision des Himmlischen Jerusalem nehmen eindeutig auf das Gedenken Bezug.

Near the former prison in Plötzensee, where people were tortured and murdered for racial and political reasons under Hitler's dictatorship, a memorial was created, and a church dedicated to the victims. Thus there are also three tombs in the crypt: Erich Klausener, dean Bernhard Lichtenberg and a symbolic tomb for the martyrs who were denied burial. The ceremonial courtyard and open-air altar are surrounded by high, grey-black «prison walls» in basalt slabs. The bell tower, set well away form the church, provides an entrance. Works of art like Fritz Koenig's portal sculpture «Apocalyptic Woman» and his Pietà, O. H. Hajek's bronzes of the Stations of the Cross and Georg Meistermann's altar wall fresco of the Vision of the Heavenly Jerusalem are all clearly associated with remembrance.

in der Nähe/nearby:
Jugendstrafanstalt (Gedenkstätte Plötzensee); Hüttigpfad
1868 • Herrmann, Spieker

E 22 Siedlungen Charlottenburg-Nord
Berlin-Charlottenburg; Heilmannring
1956-61 • Hans Scharoun, Werner Weber uam.

Die Wohnungsnot der Nachkriegszeit führte zur Fortsetzung des Großsiedlungsgedankens der zwanziger Jahre. Östlich der Siemensstadt hatte man bereits vor dem Krieg eine Kanalisation angelegt, die nun zur Grundlage einer weiteren Siedlungsplanung wurde. Hans Scharoun arbeitete am Institut für Städtebau der TU einen Plan aus, der nach dem Prinzip der Strukturmischung »Wohngehöfte« vorsah. Strukturmischung hieß für ihn, daß sich abhängig vom wirtschaftlichen und städtischen Umfeld eine statistische Verteilung in Berufsbild, Lebensgewohnheit und Familiengröße ergibt, die sich in einer kleinsten gesellschaftlichen Gruppe, sozusagen einer Grundeinheit großstädtischer Symbiose, widerspiegelt, für deren individuellen Bedarf das Wohngehöft als analoge Wohneinheit geschaffen wird. Der theoretische Ansatz ergab für Berlin 310 Wohnungen nach 36 Typen je Wohngehöft. Im südwestlichen Bereich des Heilmannringes sind solche, wenn auch mit planerischen Abstrichen, verwirklicht. Für den übrigen Teil der Siedlung setzte sich aber eine regelmäßige Bebauung durch, die sich an vordergründiger Bedarfsdeckung orientierte und schon bald dem Vorwurf eines »rechteckigen Manierismus« und der »trostlosen Langeweile« ausgesetzt war.

Acute housing shortage in the post-war period led to a continuation of the twenties tradition of large estates. A sewerage system had been laid down east of Siemensstadt even before the war, and this now formed the basis of planning for a new estate. Hans Scharoun, at the Technical University's urban development institute, devised a plan which provided for «residential farmsteads» on the principle of mixed structure. For him structural mixture meant a statistical division into professional image, life style and size of family, dependent on the urban and economic environment; this was to be reflected in the smallest possible social group, as it were a basic unit of metropolitan symbiosis, and the residential farmstead is created for their individual needs, as an analogous residential unit. This theoretical approach required 310 residential units of 36 types per residential farmstead for Berlin, and some of these were built, with some planning cutbacks, in the south-western area of the Heilmannring. But more normal development was the order of the day elsewhere in the estate, simply meeting superficial requirements; it was soon subject to reproach for «rectangular mannerism» and «desperate boredom».

in der Nähe/nearby:
Paul-Hertz-Siedlung; Reichweindamm, Bernhard-Lichtenberg-Straße
1961-65 • Wils Ebert, Werner Weber

E 23 Volkspark Jungfernheide
Berlin-Charlottenburg; Heckerdamm
1920-23 • Erwin Barth

Dem Flußlauf der Spree folgt ein Wirtschaftsband, dann Eisenbahn und Verkehrsstraßen, weiter ein Wohnband und schließlich ein Erholungsband. Diesem Bandstadt-Gedanken begegnet man nach 1945 immer wieder, er sollte Prinzip einer städtebaulichen Neuordnung Berlins werden. Im Bereich der Siemensstadt sah man ihn bereits angelegt, Kernstück des Erholungsbandes war die Jungfernheide. Dieser große Volkspark stand zwar in der Tradition von älteren Anlagen wie Friedrichshain, Humboldthain oder Treptower Park, er erfuhr aber als erster Volkspark der republikanischen Zeit eine neue Ausrichtung. Sport und Freizeitgestaltung erhielten größeren Raum, und statt des früheren Spielplatzes gab es nun Liege- und Spielwiesen, Sportplätze, Freibad, Teich mit Ruderbooten und eine Freilichtbühne. Vieles am Park mutet noch an wie die Gartengestaltung nach der Jahrhundertwende: die Hufeisenform des großen Weges oder die Insel, ein typisches Jugendstilelement. Selbst der 1926 von Walter Helmcke errichtete Wasserturm mit seinen frühexpressionistischen Ziegelmustern ließe sich ein Jahrzehnt früher datieren.

The line of the Spree is followed by a commercial band, then railway and roads, then a residential band, and finally a recreational band. This idea of banding in towns kept cropping up after 1945, and was intended to be the urban development principle behind a new order for Berlin. In Siemensstadt it was already established, and the core of the recreational band was Jungfernheide. This great public park was in the tradition of Friedrichshain, Humboldthain and Treptower Park, but was the first public park in the Republican era to be organized on a different basis. More space was allotted to sport and leisure activities, and instead of the earlier playgrounds there were lawns for sunbathing and games, sports grounds, open air pool. boating lake and an open-air theatre. Much in the park is reminiscent of garden design in the early years of the century: the horseshoe shape of the main path and the island are typical Jugendstil elements. Even the water tower built by Walter Helmcke in 1926 with its early Expressionist brick patterns could be dated a decade earlier.

in der Nähe/nearby:
Wasserturm; Volkspark Jungfernheide
1926 • Walter Helmcke

F
Der alte Berliner Norden

Dieser Bereich der Stadt umfaßt historisch unterschiedlich gewachsene Teile des nördlichen Berlins: Alt- und Neu-Moabit, die heute zum Stadtbezirk Berlin-Tiergarten gehören, der Wedding, die Friedrich-Wilhelm-Stadt und die Spandauer Vorstadt sowie das äußere Spandauer Revier, Teile, die heute zu den Stadtbezirken Mitte und Prenzlauer Berg gehören. Außer der seit 1670 besiedelten Spandauer Vorstadt – auch Sophienvorstadt – entstanden die anderen Stadtteile vorwiegend erst im 19. und 20. Jahrhundert. Nach der Bauordnung von 1853/60 kam es zu einer sehr dichten Bebauung, nachdem die Weichbildgrenze 1861 fast bis nach Weißensee hinausverlegt worden war. Sie verlief entlang der nördlichen Ringstraße, dem heutigen Zug Seestraße, Bornholmer Straße und Ostseestraße. Diese neuen Terrains waren in James Hobrechts Bebauungsplan von 1858/62 nach dem Vorbild der Altberliner Stadterweiterungen, aber mit großen Blöcken ausgelegt worden. Verbunden waren diese Stadtteile seit 1871 durch die Ringbahn zwischen den Bahnhöfen Moabit und Weißensee an der Greifswalder Straße. Als Querverbindungen dienten seit 1876 Pferdebahnen, so zwischen Neu-Weißensee und dem Alexanderplatz, ab 1895 elektrifizierte Straßenbahnen und seit 1913 die Hoch- und Untergrundbahn in der Schönhauser Allee. Der alte Berliner Norden ist hervorgegangen aus der Erweiterung des bürgerlichen Altstadtkerns; er war daher auch immer ein Standort großer Betriebe und der damit verbundenen Arbeiterwohngebiete. Selbst nach der Randwanderung der Industrie blieb dieser Charakter erhalten, noch heute erinnern das Stammhaus der Firma Borsig in der Chausseestraße oder die AEG-Turbinenhalle in Moabit an die stürmische Entwicklung des Schwermaschinenbaus in der Stadt. Nun siedeln sich neue Nutzer in den alten Industriequartieren an, so führt seit 1988 an der Lessingbrücke ein Dienstleistungszentrum der Computer- und Elektronikbranche die örtlichen Traditionen der Leichtindustrie fort.

This area of the city includes parts of northern Berlin that developed historically in different ways: Alt- and Neu-Moabit, which now belong to the Tiergarten district, Wedding, Friedrich-Wilhelm-Stadt and the Spandauer Vorstadt, as well as outer Spandau, areas which now belong to the districts of Mitte and Prenzlauer Berg. With the exception of the Spandauer Vorstadt – also called Sophienvorstadt – which had been settled since 1670, the other parts of the town came into being predominantly in the nineteenth and twentieth centuries. In accordance with the 1853/60 regulations building was very dense after the city border had been moved out almost to Weissensee in 1861. It ran along the northern ring road, the present run of Seestrasse, Bornholmer Strasse and Ostseestrasse. In James Hobrecht's 1858/62 development plan, these new areas were laid out on the model of the Old Berlin town extensions, but in large blocks. These districts were linked from 1871 by the ring railway between stations in Moabit and Weissensee in Greifswalder Strasse. Connecting links were provided by horse-drawn trams from 1876, between Neu-Weissensee and Alexanderplatz, for example, from 1895 by electric trams and from 1913 by the overhead and underground railway in Schönhauser Allee. The old north of Berlin grew out of the extension of the bourgeois core of the city; it was thus always a site for large-scale industry and the workers' residential areas associated with this. Even after industry migrated to the edges of the town this character was retained, and even today the original Borsig works in Chausseestrasse or the AEG turbine hall in Moabit are a reminder of the ultra-rapid development of heavy engineering in the city. Now new users are moving into the old industrial quarters, for example since 1988 a computer and electronics service centre has been carrying on the local tradition of light industry by the Lessing bridge.

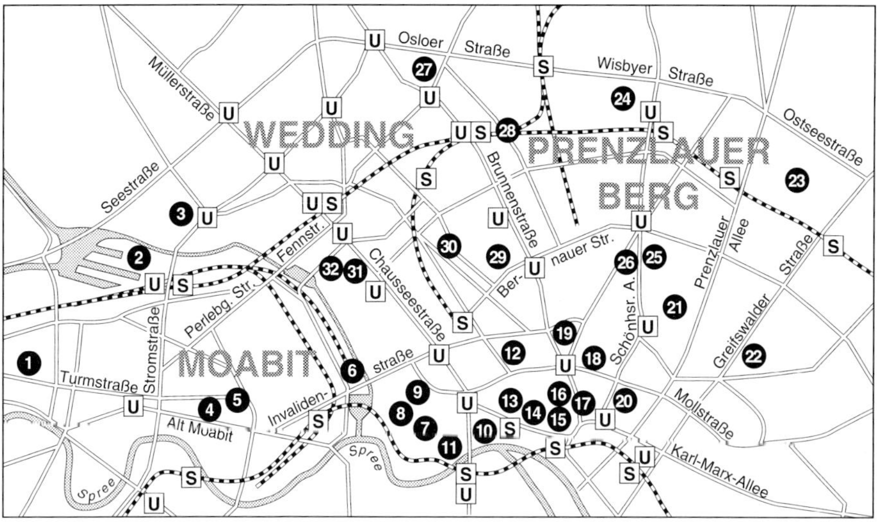

F 1 AEG-Turbinenfabrik
F 2 Westhafen
F 3 Virchowkrankenhaus
F 4 Johanniskirche
F 5 Kriminalgericht
F 6 Hamburger Bahnhof
F 7 Miethäuser
F 8 Charité – Chirurgisch orientiertes Zentrum
F 9 Altes Anatomiegebäude
F 10 Friedrichstadtpalast
F 11 Berliner Ensemble am Schiffbauerdamm
F 12 Stadtbad Mitte
F 13 Postfuhramt
F 14 Neue Synagoge
F 15 Alter Jüdischer Friedhof
F 16 Sophienkirche
F 17 Handwerkervereinshaus
F 18 Wohnbauten der Berliner Baugesellschaft
F 19 Volkspark am Weinberg
F 20 Volksbühne
F 21 Wasserturm
F 22 Miethäuser mit Läden
F 23 Wohnstadt Carl Legien
F 24 Wohnquartier
F 25 Schultheissbrauerei
F 26 Stadtbad Prenzlauer Berg
F 27 Groterjanbrauerei
F 28 Swinemünder Brücke
F 29 Versöhnungs-Privatstraße
F 30 AEG-Apparatefabrik
F 31 Eisstadion
F 32 Abspannwerk Scharnhorst

F 1 AEG-Turbinenfabrik
Berlin-Tiergarten; Huttenstraße 12-19
1908-09 • Peter Behrens

Die Konstruktion als gestaltendes Element, das war die Devise der Ingenieurbaukunst um die Jahrhundertwende. Völlig vom Ornament und von bezugslosem Zierrat befreit, dennoch in monumentaler Eindringlichkeit stellt sich diese Halle dar als Aufbruch einer neuen Stilphase. Ungewöhnlich die Stirnseite, die den Umriß des polygonal gebrochenen Daches unverhüllt zeigt, ungewöhnlich auch die sichtbare Basis der Binder in der 110 m langen Längsfront. Glas, Stahl und Beton sind die Baustoffe, welche die Gestaltung des Äußeren bestimmen. Die Turbinenhalle ist aus der Entwicklung moderner Industriearchitektur nicht hinwegzudenken. Peter Behrens wurde 1907 Hausarchitekt der AEG. Außer Industrieanlagen erhielt er auch andere Bauaufgaben bis hin zum kleinen Laden für AEG-Erzeugnisse, und selbst bei der Formgebung der Waren wie Teekessel, Haartrockner und Bügeleisen sprach Behrens mit. Die Turbinenhalle wurde 1939 von Jacob Schallenberger und Schmidt nach Norden um fast 100 m verlängert. Sie ist eine der ersten Industrieanlagen, die unter Denkmalschutz gestellt wurde.

Structure as a creative element, that was the slogan of engineering architecture around the turn of the century. Completely free of ornament and non-referential decoration, yet monumentally insistent, the hall indicates the start of a new stylistic phase. The end wall is unusual, revealing the outline of the polygonal roof, and also unusual is the visible base of the trusses in the 110 m longitudinal façade. Glass, steel and concrete are the materials dominating the exterior design. It is impossible to think of the history of modern industrial design without the turbine hall. Peter Behrens became AEG's house architect in 1907. Aside from industrial plants he was also commissioned to design other buildings, right down to a little shop for AEG products, and was also involved in the design of goods like tea kettles, hairdryers and irons. The turbine hall was lengthened to the north by almost 100 m by Jacob Schallenberger and Schmidt in 1939. It is one of the earliest industrial buildings to have been listed.

in der Nähe/nearby:
Maschinenfabrik Ludwig Loewe; Huttenstraße 17-20
1897-98 • Arnold Vogt
1907-08 • Alfred Grenander
Telefunken-Röhrenfabrik; Sickingenstraße 71
1905-11 • Viktor Kühn, Gustav Teske
Gotzkowskybrücke; Gotzkowskystraße
1910-11 • Alfred Grenander
Kleistschule; Levetzowstraße 1-4
1927-29 • Rudolf Kolweß, Freiberg

F 2 Westhafen
Berlin-Tiergarten; Westhafenstraße 13
1914-23 • Richard Wolffenstein, Lorenz, Friedrich Krause

Berlin, seine Wasserläufe und der Schiffsverkehr gehören eng zusammen. 1906 rückt Berlin zum zweitgrößten deutschen Binnenhafen auf, ohne über eine größere Hafenanlage zu verfügen. Pläne für einen Ost- und einen Westhafen folgen. Der Osthafen wird noch 1913 fertig, der größere Westhafen erst nach dem Weltkrieg. Abseits der überlasteten Spree liegt er im Schnittpunkt dreier Kanäle, Charlottenburger Verbindungskanal zur Havel, Hohenzollernkanal zur Oder und Spandauer Schiffahrtskanal zur Spree. Benachbart dem damals bereits projektierten Großmarkt und angeschlossen an das ausgedehnte Gütergleisnetz der nördlichen Ringbahn waren günstigste Verkehrsbedingungen geschaffen. Als Wahrzeichen ragt der Turm des Verwaltungsgebäudes auf. Ihn verbindet mit den anderen Bauten im Hafen eine einheitliche Gestaltung, die einfach und sachlich bleibt, doch mit Blenden, gebrochenen Dächern, Erkern, Halbkreisfenstern und Gauben die damals beliebten Bezüge zur Zeit »Um 1800« schafft. Die Gruppierung der Bauten ist eine städtebauliche Leistung von Rang.

Waterways and shipping have always been important to Berlin. In 1906 Berlin became the second-largest inland harbour in Germany, but had no large dock complex. Plans for an east and a west harbour followed. The east harbour was completed in 1913, but the larger west harbour not until after the World War. It is off the overloaded Spree, at the intersection of three canals, the Charlottenburg canal connecting to the Havel, the Hohenzollernkanal to the Oder and the Spandau Shipping Canal to the Spree. Outstanding transport conditions were created by proximity to the Grossmarkt, which was already planned, and links with the extensive goods rail network of the northern ring railway. Emblem of the complex is the tall tower of the office building. It is linked with other buildings in the harbour by uniform design which remains simple and unadorned, but still uses blind windows, broken roofs, oriels, semi-circular windows and dormers to create the references, popular at the time, to the period «around 1800». The way in which the buildings are grouped is a major urban development achievement.

in der Nähe/nearby:
Kraftwerk Moabit; Friedrich-Krause-Ufer 10-13
1899-1900 • Franz Schwechten
Großmarkt; Beusselstraße 44 n-q
1963-65 • Bruno Grimmek

F 3 Virchowkrankenhaus
Berlin-Wedding; Augustenburger Platz 1
1899-1906 • Ludwig Hoffmann

Kein geringerer als Robert Koch bestätigte, er habe in den Städten der verschiedenen Weltteile die großen Krankenhäuser besichtigt und auch das Rudolf-Virchow-Krankenhaus, er könne nur sagen, daß weder in hygienischer noch in architektonischer Hinsicht irgendein Krankenhaus auch nur entfernt hieran reiche, so erinnert sich Ludwig Hoffmann in seinem Tagebuch. In einer Mischung aus mehrgeschossigen Trakten im Korridorsystem und einer regelmäßigen Folge von licht- und luftdurchfluteten Pavillonbauten war kurz nach der Jahrhundertwende eine Anlage entstanden, die gerade in einem so ungesunden und unwohnlichen Arbeiterbezirk wie dem Wedding eine hoffnungsfrohe Signalwirkung haben mußte. 2100 Betten standen zur Verfügung, und das gesamte Gelände umfaßte mehr als einen viertel Quadratkilometer. Zu 75% wurde das Krankenhaus im letzten Krieg zerstört, teilweise wieder aufgebaut, teilweise kamen Neubauten hinzu. Nach neuester Planung wird es nun Universitätsklinikum, nicht ohne Proteste aus Fachkreisen.

No less a person than Robert Koch confirmed that he had visited large hospitals in cities in various parts of the world, including the Rudolf Virchow Hospital, he could only say that there wasn't a hospital to touch it, in terms of either hygiene or architecture. The hospital is a mixture of multi-storey tracts built on the corridor system, with a regular sequence of pavilion buildings flooded with light and air. It dates from shortly after the turn of the century, and it must have struck a note of hope in an unhealthy and inhospitable area like Wedding. It offered 2,100 beds and the whole site covered over a quarter of a square kilometre. 75% of the hospital was destroyed in the last war, some of it was rebuilt, and some new buildings were added. The most recent plans will make it a university clinic, not without some resistance in specialist circles.

in der Nähe/nearby:
Osterkirche; Sprengelstraße 34
1910-11 • August Dinklage, Ernst Paulus, Olaf Lilloe
Gemeindeschule; Tegeler Straße 18-20
1909-10 • Ludwig Hoffmann
Gemeindeschule; Müllerstraße 158, Triftstraße 71-73
1891-93 • Hermann Blankenstein
Josephskirche; Müllerstraße 161
1909 • Wilhelm Frydag

F 4 Johanniskirche
Berlin-Tiergarten; Alt-Moabit 25
1832-35 • Karl Friedrich Schinkel

Für den kirchlich schlecht versorgten Nordwesten Berlins entwarf Schinkel in den dreißiger Jahren des 19. Jahrhunderts vier Gotteshäuser, eines davon war die Johanniskirche. Es war zunächst nur ein einschiffiger turmloser Rechteckbau, welcher der schnell wachsenden Gemeinde bald schon nicht mehr genügte. Bis 1853 fügte Friedrich August Stüler dem Kirchlein einen Portikus mit Säulengang an und baute auch ein Schulhaus und einen freistehenden Glockenturm. Der architektonisch interessierte Friedrich Wilhelm IV. war auch hier in der gewohnten Weise beteiligt. Gegen Ende des Jahrhunderts erfuhr das von der Romantik geprägte Ensemble eine neuerliche Erweiterung durch Max Spitta: Die Kirche erhielt mit verlängertem Hauptschiff, Querschiff, Chor und Apsis fast die dreifache Grundfläche.

North-west Berlin was poorly provided with churches, and Schinkel designed four in the 1830s, one of which was the Johanniskirche. At first it was just a single-aisled rectangular building without a tower, but this was soon inadequate for the rapidly growing congregation. By 1853 Friedrich August Stüler had added a portico with colonnade, and also built a school house and a free-standing bell tower. Friedrich Wilhelm IV was interested in architecture, and was involved here in the usual way. Towards the end of the century the essentially Romantic ensemble gained a new extension by Max Spitta: the area of the church was increased almost three-fold by the addition of an extended nave, transept, choir and apse.

in der Nähe/nearby:
Lessingbrücke; Lessingstraße, Stromstraße
1901-03 • Ludwig Hoffmann
Business-Center; Stromstraße 1-2 a
1987-90 • Joachim Ganz, Walter Rolfes
Schultheiss-Brauerei; Stromstraße 11-17
1871-77 • Friedrich Koch
1880-1900 • Overbeck & Lüdicke
Heilandskirche; Tusneldaallee
1892-94 • Friedrich Schulze
Rathaus Tiergarten; Turmstraße 35
1935-36 • Richard Ermisch

F 5 Kriminalgericht
Berlin-Tiergarten; Turmstraße 91
1902-06 • Paul Thoemer

Berlins Justizpalast – so wie er sich heute dem Betrachter präsentiert – ist der Erweiterungsbau eines 1877 begonnenen Erstbaus, der im Krieg zerstört wurde. Hochragende Türme und ein maßloses Treppenhaus mahnen mit erdrückender Bedeutsamkeit an die Macht der Gerichte. Mit virtuoser Bedenkenlosigkeit wurden hier besonders barocke Stilmittel, aber auch Anleihen bei Gotik, Renaissance und Jugendstil zur Steigerung der monumentalen Wirkung eingesetzt. Das Kriminalgericht ist insofern vergleichbar den vielen Gerichtsneubauten Berlins vom Anfang des 20. Jahrhunderts, die meist unter der architektonischen Leitung von Paul Thoemer und Rudolf Mönnich nach gleichem Geist und in ähnlicher Gestaltung entstanden. Von 1957 an gab es mehrere Erweiterungen, von denen keine neben dem dominierenden Altbau ins Gewicht fällt.

Berlin's Palace of Justice – as it is today – is an extension to a first building started in 1877 that was destroyed in the war. Massive towers and an immoderate stairwell are oppressively eloquent reminders of the might of the courts. Baroque features in particular, but also loans from Gothic, Renaissance and Jugendstil, are used with virtuoso lack of scruple to enhance the monumental effect. Thus the Criminal Court is comparable with many new court buildings in early twentieth century Berlin, which were mainly built under the architectural direction of Paul Thoemer and Rudolf Mönnich, in the same spirit and to a similar design. From 1957 onwards there were many extensions, none of which makes any impression at the side of the dominant old building.

in der Nähe/nearby:
Wohnhaus; Turmstraße 5
1976-77 • Hasso Windeck
Jugendzentrum; Rathenower Straße 15-18
1974-78 • Neumann, Grötzebach & Plessow
Heinrich-Zille-Siedlung; Rathenower Straße 1-8
1979-82 • Volker Theissen, Georg Heinrichs, Fleischer & Hübscher, Hanebutt, Benze, Hasso Windeck
Wohnhauszeile mit Kindertagesstätte; Lüneburger Straße 14-18
1991-92 • Jürgen Fissler und Hans-Christof Ernst

F 6 Hamburger Bahnhof
Berlin-Tiergarten; Invalidenstraße 50-51
1845-47 • Friedrich Neuhaus, Ferdinand Wilhelm Holz

Nach dem Potsdamer und dem Frankfurter Bahnhof war der Hamburger der dritte Bahnhof in Berlin. Von diesen Bahnhofsbauten der ersten Generation steht er noch als einziger. Der viergleisige Kopfbahnhof hatte zwei Seitenbahnsteige, einen für die Ankunft, einen für die Abfahrt. Die Fassade wird beherrscht von zwei Türmen, die beiderseits eines hohen Doppelportals aus der Wand wachsen. Die beiden Tore dienten ursprünglich der Lokomotive des ankommenden Zuges zur Durchfahrt auf den Vorplatz, wo eine Drehscheibe sie wieder in Fahrtrichtung wendete. Bereits 1884 wurde der Bahnhof für den Personenverkehr geschlossen. Der preußische Staat hatte die Bahn übernommen und leitete die Hamburger Züge nun zum jüngeren und größeren Lehrter Bahnhof, der auch über einen Anschluß an die Ringbahn verfügte. 1905-06 bauten Schwarz und Doerge das lange Zeit nur für den Güterverkehr genutzte Gebäude zum Verkehrs- und Baumuseum um. Eine dreischiffige geschlossene Halle ersetzte die längst abgerissene alte Bahnsteighalle.

The Hamburg Station was the third in Berlin, after the Potsdam and Frankfurt stations, and is the only survivor of this first generation. This terminus had four tracks and two platforms, one for arrivals and one for departures. The façade is dominated by two towers growing out of the wall on either side of a high double portal. The two gateways were originally intended to allow a locomotive that had just arrived to pass through on to the forecourt, where a turntable swung it back into the direction of travel. The station was closed for passenger traffic as early as 1884. The Prussian state had taken over the railway and directed Hamburg traffic via the more recent Lehrter Bahnhof, which also had a connection to the ring line. In 1905-6 Schwarz and Doerge rebuilt the station, which had for a long time been used only for goods traffic, as a transport and building museum. The old platform area had long since been pulled down, and was replaced by a closed hall with three aisles.

in der Nähe/nearby:
Lehrter Stadtbahnhof; Friedrich-List-Ufer
1880-82
Poststadion; Lehrter Straße 59
Gegen 1926 • Georg Demmler und Kleefeld

F 7 Miethäuser
Berlin-Mitte; Schumannstraße 14-17
1830/40

Die Schumannstraße hieß ursprünglich Schumanns Straße, benannt nach dem Seifensieder Schumann, der hier seit 1823 Häuser bauen ließ. Sie gehörte später zur 1827 planmäßig angelegten Friedrich-Wilhelm-Stadt, die bis zur Hannoverschen Straße reichte, der ehemaligen »Communikation« zwischen dem Oranienburger und dem Neuen Tor. Dieser Stadtteil entstand nördlich des Schiffbauerdamms um Kristallisationspunkte wie Kasernen und Exerzierplätze, Charité (1710) oder Tierarzneischule (1790). Er wurde vorwiegend von Beamten, Offizieren und Studenten bewohnt. Die Friedrich-Wilhelm-Stadt galt daher als »Quartier Latin Berlins«. Denn auch als Theaterviertel war sie bekannt; bis 1944 gab es hier sechs Spielstätten. Die Biedermeier-Wohnhäuser Schumannstraße 14-17 stammen aus der Entstehungszeit der Friedrich-Wilhelm-Stadt zwischen 1830 und 1840. Die dreigeschossigen schlichten Putzbauten haben große Durchfahrten und Seitenflügel an den Höfen. Sie wurden in den letzten Jahren wieder instandgesetzt.

Schumannstrasse was originally called Schumanns Strasse, after Schumann the soapboiler, who had houses built here from 1823. It later became part of Friedrich-Wilhelm-Stadt, planned in 1827, and extending to Hannoversche Strasse, the former «Communikation» between Oranienburger Tor and the Neues Tor. This part of the city came into being north of the Schiffbauerdamm around crystallization points like barracks and parade grounds, the Charité (1710) and the School of Veterinary Medicine (1790). It was occupied mainly by civil servants, officers and students. Thus Friedrich-Wilhelm-Stadt was considered the «Quartier Latin» of Berlin. It was also known as a theatre district; there were six here by 1944. The Biedermeier houses at 14-17 Schumannstrasse date from the period in which Friedrich-Wilhelm-Stadt came into being between 1830 and 1840. The plain, three-storey rendered buildings have large gateways and side wings in the yards. They were restored within the last few years.

in der Nähe/nearby:
Denkmal für Rudolf Virchow; Am Karlplatz
1906-10 • Fritz Klimsch
Deutsches Theater; Schumannstraße 12-13
1849-50 • Eduard Titz
Kammerspiele; Schumannstraße 14
1906 • William Müller

F 8 Charité – Chirurgisch orientiertes Zentrum
Berlin-Mitte; Schumannstraße 20-21
1897-13 • Kurt Diestel; 1976-82 • Karl-Ernst Swora

Die Charité, ein Klinikenviertel der Innenstadt, erstreckt sich von der Schumannstraße bis zum Robert-Koch-Platz am ehemaligen Neuen Tor. Es ist aus einem Pesthaus von 1710 hervorgegangen und gehört seit 1810 zur Universität. Auf Initiative von Friedrich Althoff, dessen Büste 1902 von Ferdinand Harzer geschaffen am Haupteingang steht, entstand eine stark durchgrünte Gebäudefolge aus Spezialkliniken, deren Klinkerfassaden und laubengangartige Loggien Reformbautendenzen der Jahrhundertwende zeigen. Das Chirurgische Zentrum ist ein 1976-82 errichteter Klinikkomplex für jährlich 30 000 stationär zu behandelnde Patienten. Er entstand nach einem Funktionsplan von Peter Korneli. Das Bettenhochhaus von Christian Schulz umfaßt 30 Stationen und 24 Operationssäle, die Friedrich Kalusche ausbaute. Vorgelagert ist ein viergeschossiger Trakt für Röntgen- und Labordiagnostik von Günter Kunert und Heinz Aust. Davor steht das Denkmal für Robert Koch, 1916 geschaffen von Louis Tuaillon. Eine Versorgungseinrichtung mit zweigeschossiger Betriebsgaststätte entstand 1976-78 nach Entwürfen von Gerd Pieper und Gunter Derdau.

The Charité, an inner-city hospital complex, extends from Schumannstrasse to Robert-Koch-Platz by the former Neues Tor. It developed from a plague house dating from 1710 and has belonged to the university since 1810. On the initiative of Friedrich Althoff, whose bust, carved by Ferdinand Harzer in 1902, is at the main entrance, a sequence of buildings separated by planted areas came into being. It is made up of specialist clinics, whose clinker façades and arbour-like loggias show the building reform tendencies of the turn of the century. The Chirurgisches Zentrum (surgical centre) is a complex of clinics built from 1976-82 for 30,000 in-patients per year. It was built to a functional design by Peter Korneli. Christian Schulz' high-rise building contains 30 wards and 24 operating theatres, extended by Friedrich Kalusche. In front of this is a four-storey wing containing X-ray and laboratory facilities, by Günter Kunert and Heinz Aust. In front of this is the Robert Koch monument, created by Louis Tuaillon in 1916. A catering facility with two-storey staff canteen was built 1976-8, to plans by Gerd Pieper and Gunter Derdau.

in der Nähe/nearby:
Landwirtschaftliche Hochschule; Invalidenstraße 42
1876-80 • August Tiede
Museum für Naturkunde; Invalidenstraße 43
1883-89 • August Tiede
Geologische Landesanstalt; Invalidenstraße 44
1875-78 • August Tiede
Akademie (Krankenhaus); Invalidenstraße 48-49
1905-10 • Cremer & Wolffenstein

F 9 Altes Anatomiegebäude
Berlin-Mitte; Reinhardtstraße 24 (Zugang)
1789-90 • Carl Gotthard Langhans

Nach dem Bau der Marschallbrücke, die seit 1821 den Zugang von der Dorotheenstadt ermöglichte, wurde die Luisenstraße zur Hauptachse dieser Vorstadt bestimmt. Sie war nach der Gemahlin Friedrich Wilhelms III. benannt worden. Die Friedrich-Wilhelm-Stadt entstand auf einem Terrain, das bereits durch ältere Gründungen teilweise erschlossen war, so mit der Charité seit 1710 und durch die Tierarzneischule ab 1790. Für diese Anstalt wurde seit 1789 das Anatomische Theater errichtet, das heute in dem parkartigen, von der Panke durchflossenen Gelände neben veterinärmedizinischen Instituten der Humboldt-Universität liegt. Der frühklassizistische Bau mit dem Grundriß in Form eines griechischen Kreuzes wurde auch bezeichnenderweise »Trichinentempel« genannt. Die Schlußsteine der Rundbogenfenster sind als Tierschädel gestaltet. Der Hörsaal im Zentrum des Hauses ist ein Kuppelraum, amphitheatralisch mit steil ansteigenden Sitzreihen und gotisierenden Brüstungen. In seiner Mitte befand sich ehemals ein durch hölzernes Räderwerk in den Keller zu versenkender Seziertisch. Das Wandgemälde, Hirten und Landleute mit Haustieren, stammt von Eduard Rode; es wurde 1970 von Rudolf Weinrich restauriert.

After the building of the Marschallbrücke, which gave access from Dorotheenstadt from 1821, the Luisenstrasse became the main axis of this suburb. It was named after the consort of Friedrich Wilhelm III. Friedrich-Wilhelm-Stadt was built on terrain that had been partly opened up by older foundations, like the Charité from 1710 and the School of Veterinary Medicine from 1790. The Anatomy Theatre was built for this institution from 1789; the theatre now stands on a park-like site through which the Panke flows, alongside the Humboldt Univerity's veterinary institutions. This early classical building with a Greek cross ground plan was also typically called «Trichinosis Temple». The keystones of the round-arched windows are carved as animal skulls. The lecture room at the centre of the building is a domed amphitheatre with steep rows of seats and Gothic-style balustrades. In the middle there used to be a dissecting table that could be lowered into the cellar by a mechanism of wooden wheels. The wall painting, shepherds and country folk with pets, is by Eduard Rode, and was restored by Rudolf Weinrich in 1970.

in der Nähe/nearby:
Tierarzneischule; Luisenstraße 56
1839-40 • Ludwig Ferdinand Hesse
Club »Die Möwe«; Luisenstraße 18
Um 1840 • ehemaliges Palais Bülow
Wohnhäuser; Marienstraße
1830-1900

F 10 Friedrichstadtpalast
Berlin-Mitte; Friedrichstraße 107
1981-84 • Walter Schwarz, Manfred Prasser

Unmittelbar neben dem Theater am Schiffbauerdamm, in der Straße Am Zirkus, stand bis 1985 der alte Friedrichstadtpalast. Hervorgegangen war er aus einer von Friedrich Hitzig entworfenen Markthalle, die 1873 zum Zirkus umgerüstet und 1918-19 unter Hans Poelzig für Max Reinhardt zum Großen Schauspielhaus, einem Hauptwerk expressionistischer Lichtarchitektur umgestaltet worden war. Der Neubau entstand als Revue- und Varietétheater seit 1981 auf dem historischen Standort des Zirkus Barlay zwischen der Friedrich-, Ziegel-, Kalkscheunen- und Johannisstraße. Werner Hoffmann schuf den großen Saal mit 1900 Plätzen, Haupt-, Seiten-, Hinter- und Vorbühne mit Eisparkett, Wasserbecken und Manege. Das Bühnenhaus mit 32 Meter hohem Turm und 24 Meter breitem Bühnenportal stammt von Werner Schön, von Michael Ulbricht das Tanzkabarett »Kleine Revue«. Das Foyer von Horst Meyer liegt an der Friedrichstraße hinter der von Werner Knopf gestalteten Fassade aus geschoßhohen, in Matrizen vorgefertigten Betonelementen.

The old Friedrichstadtpalast was immediately adjacent to the Theater am Schiffbauerdamm, in the Strasse am Zirkus, until 1985. It evolved from a market hall designed by Friedrich Hitzig, re-equipped as a circus in 1873 and redesigned from 1918-19 under Hans Poelzig as the Grosses Schauspielhaus for Max Reinhardt; this was a major work of Expressionist light architecture. The new building was built from 1981 as a revue and variety theatre on the historic site of the Zirkus Barlay between Friedrich-, Ziegel-, Kalkscheunen- and Johannisstrasse. Werner Hoffmann created the great hall with ice rink, main, side, rear and front stage, pool and ring. The fly tower, 32 metres high, and the 24 metre wide stage portal are by Werner Schön, and the «Kleine Revue» dance-cabaret by Michael Ulbricht. Horst Meyer's foyer is on Friedrichstrasse behind the façade designed by Werner Knopf using storey-high premoulded concrete elements.

in der Nähe/nearby:
Verwaltungsgebäude Borsig; Chausseestraße 13
1899 • Reimer & Körte
Bertolt-Brecht-Haus; Chausseestraße 125
1840/50
Dorotheenstädtischer und französisch-reformierter Friedhof; Chausseestraße
1762; 1780
Wohn- und Geschäftshaus; Friedrichstraße 129-130
1985-87 • Karl-Ernst Swora, Gunter Derdau

F 11 Berliner Ensemble am Schiffbauerdamm
Berlin-Mitte; Bertolt-Brecht-Platz 1
1891-92 • Heinrich Seeling

Als Querachse zu den Linden reichte die Friedrichstraße in ihrem nördlichen Teil zunächst nur als ein weidenbestandener Damm bis zur Spree. Durch den Bau der Brücke am Weidendamm war die Dorotheenstadt seit 1685 mit dem unbebauten Acker jenseits der Spree verbunden. Das Land gehörte zum Vorwerk der Kurfürstin Dorothea in der Spandauer Vorstadt, dem Standort des späteren Schlosses Monbijou. Erst 1827, mit Beginn der planmäßigen Bebauung der Friedrich-Wilhelm-Stadt, reichte die Friedrichstraße vom Halleschen bis zum Oranienburger Tor und war damit die damals längste Straße Berlins. Hier auf dem Damm westlich der Weidendammer Brücke, wo die Berliner Schiffbauer 1738 die Erlaubnis erhielten, ihre Werkstätten anzulegen, entstand 1891 ein reich ausgestattetes Theater, in dem seit 1954 das »Berliner Ensemble am Schiffbauerdamm« Weltgeltung errang. Die Grabstätten der Begründer dieses Theaterensembles, Helene Weigel und Bertolt Brecht, liegen auf dem Dorotheenstädtischen Friedhof, auf dem sich auch die Gräber von Karl Friedrich Schinkel (die Stele ausgeführt von August Kiss) und anderer Persönlichkeiten befinden.

The northern section of Friedrichstrasse, which crosses Unter den Linden at right angles, was at first just an embankment planted with willows leading down to the Spree. From 1685, when the Brücke am Weidendamm was built, Dorotheenstadt was connected with the open fields on the other side of the Spree. The land belonged to the outlying estate of Electress Dorothea in the Spandauer Vorstadt, site of the later Schloss Monbijou. It was not until 1827, when planned development of Friedrich-Wilhelm-Stadt began, that Friedrichstrasse extended from Hallesches Tor to Oranienburger Tor, making it the longest street in Berlin. Here on the embankment west of the Weidendamm bridge, where Berlin shipbuilders were given permission to set up their workshops in 1738, a lavishly decorated theatre was built in 1891, in which the «Berliner Ensemble» achieved their world-wide reputation from 1954 onwards. The tombs of the founders of this ensemble, Helene Weigel and Bertolt Brecht, are in the Dorotheenstädtischer Friedhof, where Karl Friedrich Schinkel (stela by August Kiss) and other public figures are buried.

in der Nähe/nearby:
Weidendammer Brücke; Friedrichstraße
1894-97 • Puls, Langer, Fabian, Krüger
Augenklinik; Ziegelstraße 5-9
1878-83 • Martin Gropius, Heino Schmieden
Frauenklinik; Ziegelstraße 14-19
1927-33 • Heinrich Wolff

F 12 Stadtbad Mitte
Berlin-Mitte; Gartenstraße 56
1929-30 • Carlo Jelkmann, Heinrich Tessenow

Zum äußeren Spandauer Revier gehörten um 1871 die Oranienburger, die Schönhauser und die Rosenthaler Vorstadt, die sich seit 1752 aus einer königlichen Ansiedlung sächsischer Bauleute entwickelt hatte. Dieses »Voigtland«, zwischen Rosenthaler und Hamburger Tor umfaßte die Acker-, Berg- und Gartenstraße und war 1843 zu einer Armenkolonie verkommen, über die Bettina von Arnim in ihrer Schrift dem König berichtet hat. Die Rosenthaler Vorstadt in ihrer heutigen Gestalt entstand nach städtebaulichen Planungen von James Hobrecht in der zweiten Hälfte des 19. Jahrhunderts und wurde sehr dicht bebaut. 1832 war für diesen bereits damals volkreichen Stadtteil nach Entwurf Schinkels die Elisabethkirche an der Invalidenstraße errichtet worden. Letztere verband die Schönhauser mit der Oranienburger Vorstadt, wo die Maschinenbauanstalten von Borsig und Egells lagen, die wie später auch die AEG viele Arbeiter anzogen. Bereits im Jahre 1888 entstand hier ein erstes Bad für dieses nördliche Arbeiterwohnviertel. Das neue Bad wurde im Innern von Heinrich Tessenow gestaltet; die Bronzefigur einer Badenden in der Eingangshalle schuf 1939 Ernst Hermann Grämer.

Around 1871 the Oranienburger, Schönhauser and Rosenthaler Vorstadt were part of the outer Spandau district. The Rosenthaler Vorstadt developed from 1752 from a royal colony of Saxon farmers. This «steward's land» between the Rosenthaler and Hamburg gates included Acker-, Berg- and Gartenstrasse, and by 1843 had been reduced to a pauper colony reported to the king in the writings of Bettina von Arnim. The Rosenthaler Vorstadt in its present form evolved from urban planning by James Hobrecht in the second half of the nineteenth century, and was very densely built up. In 1832 the Elisabethkirche was built by Schinkel in Invalidenstrasse for this already populous part of the town. Invalidenstrasse connected the Schönhauser with the Oranienburger Vorstadt, where Borsig and Egells' mechanical engineering plants were situated. Like AEG after them, they attracted large numbers of workers. The first bath for this northern working quarter was built as early as 1888. The interior of the new bath was designed by Heinrich Tessenow; the bronze figure of a bather in the entrance hall was created by Ernst Hermann Grämer in 1939.

in der Nähe/nearby:
Scharnhorst-Grabmal; Invalidenfriedhof
1824/34 • Karl Friedrich Schinkel, Christian Friedrich Tieck, Christian Daniel Rauch
Wohnbauten; Wilhelm-Pieck-Straße 194-210
1985-86 • Iris Grund, Manfred Hartung, Klaus Wolf
St. Adalbert-Kirche; Linienstraße 100
1933• Clemens Holzmeister

F 13 Postfuhramt
Berlin-Mitte; Oranienburger Straße 35-36
1875-81 • Carl Schwatlo, Wilhelm Tuckermann

Ein Vorgängerbau, das »Postillonhaus«, wurde als Wohnunterkunft für Postillone mit Ställen und Remisen an gleicher Stelle bereits 1705-13 in der Spandauer Vorstadt errichtet. Seit dem Mittelalter verliefen hier durch die Berliner Feldmark ausgehend vom Spandauer Tor eine Reihe von Überlandstraßen: die Oranienburger Straße nach Spandau, nach Neuruppin und Hamburg die Große und Kleine Hamburger Straße und darüberhinaus die Rosenthaler sowie die Alte und Neue Schönhauser Straße nach Pankow. Diese alten Überlandwege waren das Gerüst der sich seit 1670 entwickelnden Spandauer Vorstadt. Sie reichte von der Friedrichstraße bis zum Scheunenviertel am heutigen Luxemburgplatz nahe dem Schönhauser Tor. 1875 wurde das Postillonhaus in der Oranienburger Ecke Tucholskystraße durch ein neues bis zur Auguststraße reichendes Gebäude ersetzt, das verschiedenen Einrichtungen der Post diente und heute ein Institut beherbergt. Im hofseitigen Stall konnten in zwei Geschossen 200 Pferde untergebracht werden. Dort befindet sich auch ein großes Flachrelief mit einer Postkutsche, 1878 von Hermann Steinemann geschaffen.

An earlier building on the site, the «Postillonhaus» was built as accommodation for postilions, with stables and coach houses, in the Spandauer Vorstadt as early as 1705-13. A series of overland routes ran through Berlin territory from the Spandau Gate: Oranienburger Strasse to Spandau, Grosse and Kleine Hamburger Strasse to Neuruppin and Hamburg, and also Rosenthaler and Alte and Neue Schönhauser Strasse to Pankow. These old overland routes were the framework of the Spandauer Vorstadt, which developed from 1670. It extended from Friedrichstrasse to the Scheunenviertel by the present Luxemburger Platz near the Schönhauser Gate. In 1875 the Postillonhaus at the corner of Oranienburger and Tucholskystrasse was replaced by a new building extending to Auguststrasse, serving various postal institutions and now housing an institute. 200 horses could be accommodated in two storeys in the stables on the courtyard side. There is also a large bas-relief there of a post coach, created by Hermann Steinemann in 1878.

in der Nähe/nearby:
Wohnhaus; Auguststraße 69
A. 19. Jh.
Jüdisches Krankenhaus; Auguststraße 14-16
1858-60 • Eduard Knoblauch
St. Johannes Evangelist; Auguststraße 90
1895-1900 • Max Spitta

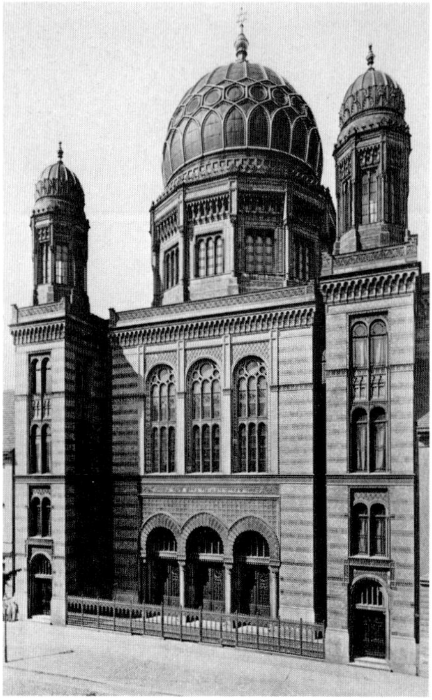

F 14 Neue Synagoge
Berlin-Mitte; Oranienburger Straße 30
1859-66 • Eduard Knoblauch

An der Oranienburger Straße, schräg gegenüber dem im Zweiten Weltkrieg schwer beschädigten und 1960 abgetragenen Schloß Monbijou, wurde die Hauptsynagoge der im 19. Jahrhundert rasch anwachsenden Jüdischen Gemeinde erbaut. Nach der Erkrankung Knoblauchs von Friedrich August Stüler fortgeführt, entstand ein Bau, der wegen seiner spätromantischen Gestaltung in Verbindung mit modernen Glas-Eisen-Konstruktionen im 19. Jahrhundert ein vielbeachtetes Gebäude war. In der Kristallnacht 1938 in Brand gesteckt, 1943 im Krieg stark beschädigt, ist jetzt ein Teilwiederaufbau in die Wege geleitet worden.

The main synagogue for the rapidly expanding nineteenth century Jewish community was built in Oranienburger Strasse diagonally opposite Schloss Monbijou, which was badly damaged in the Second World War and pulled down in 1960. When Knoblauch fell ill, work continued under Friedrich August Stüler, who produced a building that because of its late-Romantic design combined with modern glass and iron construction was highly esteemed in the nineteenth century. It was set on fire on Kristallnacht in 1938, badly damaged in the war in 1943, and partial rebuilding has now begun.

in der Nähe/nearby:
Monbijoupark mit Freibad; Oranienburger Straße 80
1960 • Walter Hinkefuß, Heinz Graffunder
Denkmal Adelbert v. Chamisso; Präsidentenstraße 6
1888 • Julius Moser
Bahnhof Börse (Hackescher Markt); Am Zwirngraben
1878-82 • Johannes Vollmer

F 15 Alter Jüdischer Friedhof
Berlin-Mitte; Große Hamburger Straße 26
1672

Dieser ehemalige Friedhof wurde 1943 von der Gestapo zerstört, zusammen mit dem an der Straße gelegenen Altersheim, dem Sammelpunkt für jüdische Bürger vor ihrem Abtransport 1942/43 in die KZ-Lager. »Mißtraut den Grünanlagen«, sagt Heinz Knobloch Besuchern dieses nach 1945 angelegten kleinen Parkes, an dessen hinterer Wand von den wenigen erhaltenen Grabsteinen noch der für Gumpericht Jechiel Aschkenasi – es war die erste Beisetzung – und ein Gedenkstein für den Stifter des Friedhofes Model Ries stehen. In der Nähe liegt aus der Zeit nach 1945 das Grabmal für Moses Mendelssohn (1729-1786). Auf einem Gedenkstein liest man die Worte: »Vergeßt das nie!« Nach Norden grenzt die einstige Knabenschule der Jüdischen Gemeinde an, zur Oranienburger Straße lag seit 1756 das Jüdische Krankenhaus. In der Nähe gab es neben der Hauptsynagoge auch Synagogen in der Johannis- und Tucholskystraße sowie für Adass Jisroël in der Gipsstraße. Etwa 12 000 Tote sollen in 155 Jahren bis zu seiner Schließung auf dem ersten Jüdischen Friedhof bestattet worden sein; mehr als 50 000 Juden wurden allein in Berlin 1942/43 zum Transport in die Vernichtungslager zusammengetrieben.

This former cemetery was destroyed by the Gestapo in 1943, along with the old people's home by the street, an assembly point for Jewish citizens before they were taken to concentration camps in 1942/43. «Mistrust green open spaces» was what Heinz Knobloch said to visitors to the little park laid out after 1945, by the rear wall of which only a few tombstones have survived, like that of the first committal of Gumpericht Jechiel Aschkenasi and a memorial stone for Model Ries, who endowed the cemetery. The tomb of Moses Mendelssohn (1729-86), dating from after 1945, is nearby. The words «Never forget that!» are inscribed on a memorial tablet. The Jewish Hospital stood by the end wall of the cemetery, in Oranienburger Strasse, from 1756. Nearby, as well as the main synagogue, there were synagogues in Johannis- and Tucholskystrasse and for Adass Jisroël in Gipsstrasse. About 120,000 people were buried in the first cemetery over a period of 155 years until it was closed; in 1942/3 over 50,000 Jews were herded together for transport to the concentration camps.

in der Nähe/nearby:
Denkmal; Große Hamburger Straße 26
1957 (1984 aufgestellt) • Will Lammert
Jüdische Knabenschule; Große Hamburger Straße 27
1906
Hedwigskrankenhaus; Große Hamburger Straße 5-11
1851-55 (Kernbau) • Vinzenz Statz, Albert Kinel
1888-89 (Hospital) • Max Hasak
1905 (Josefshaus) • Carl Moritz
1926-27 (Aufstockung) • Wilhelm Fahlbusch

F 16 Sophienkirche
Berlin-Mitte; Große Hamburger Straße 29-31
1712-34 • Johann Friedrich Grael

1712 stiftete Königin Sophie Luise diese Pfarrkirche für die Spandauer Vorstadt. Sie lag auf einem Grundstück zwischen der Sophien- und der Großen Hamburger Straße, unmittelbar an den Jüdischen Friedhof grenzend. Das Schiff war zunächst ein schlichter Emporenraum vom Typ der Berliner protestantischen Predigtkirchen. Erst spät, 1732-34, wurde der Turm nach dem Vorbild des Schlüterschen Münzturmes hinzugefügt. Aus der Erbauungszeit ist die Kanzel erhalten. 1892 wurde das Innere neubarock nach Entwürfen von Adolf Heyden und Kurt Berndt verändert. Auf dem Sophienkirchhof sind Grabdenkmale für den Historiker Leopold v. Ranke (1795-1886), den Baumeister Karl Friedrich Zelter (1758-1832), und Erinnerungstafeln für die Dichterin Anna Louisa Karschin († 1791) und den Dichter Karl Wilhelm Ramler († 1796) erhalten.

Queen Sophie Luise endowed this parish church for the Spandauer Vorstadt in 1712. It was on a plot of land between Sophien- and Grosse Hamburger Strasse, directly adjacent to the Jewish Cemetery. At first the nave was a plain room with a gallery, like Protestant preaching churches in Berlin. The tower, modelled on Schlüter's Münzturm, was not added until 1732-4. The original pulpit has survived. The interior was refurbished in neo-baroque style by Adolf Heyden and Kurt Berndt in 1892. The churchyard contains memorial tombs of historian Leopold von Ranke (1795-1886), architect Karl Friedrich Zelter (1758-1832), and memorial plaques for poetess Anna Louisa Karschin (d. 1791) and poet Karl Wilhelm Ramler (d. 1796).

in der Nähe/nearby:
Wohnhaus mit Gaststätte; Große Hamburger Straße 37
Nach 1890
Altersheim; Linienstraße 163-165, Koppenplatz 11
1835
Denkmal für Christian Koppe; Koppenplatz 12
1855 • Friedrich August Stüler
Garnisonsfriedhof; Kleine Rosenthaler Straße 37
1722

F 17 Handwerkervereinshaus
Berlin-Mitte; Sophienstraße 18
1904 • Joseph Franckel, Theodor Kampfmeyer

Der Berliner Handwerkerverein wurde 1844 gegründet. Er tagte zunächst in der Oranienburger Straße 18 und in der Johannisstraße 4. Von 1850 bis 1859 war er verboten, danach fand er sich an den Königskolonnaden nahe dem Alexanderplatz oder in der Blumenstraße zusammen. 1864 wurde in der Sophienstraße 15 »das erste eigens dazu erbaute Vereinshaus für Arbeiterbildungszwecke in Deutschland« errichtet. Bei Gründungsarbeiten für den benachbarten Wertheim-Erweiterungsbau waren die Sophiensäle baufällig geworden. Unweit wurde das neue Handwerkervereinshaus 1905 eingeweiht. Auf dem Grundstück stehen heute zwei Vorderhäuser wohl um 1800 und 1850 mit dem neuen Portal und einer gewölbten Durchfahrt, zwei Seitenflügel wohl um 1885 erbaut, und fünf neuerrichtete Hofflügel. Der Querflügel enthält die Fest- und Gesellschaftsräume; an zwei Höfen schließen sich vier Seitenflügel an. Seit 1933 ist das Gebäude zunehmend verwahrlost; es wird als Magazin und für Werkstätten genutzt. Von der Innenausstattung sind fast nur noch Beschreibungen erhalten und einige Fotos: Virchowsaal, Hochzeitssaal, Bibliothek.

The Berlin Craftsmen's Association was founded in 1844. At first it met at 18 Oranienburger Strasse and 4 Johannisstrasse. It was banned from 1850 to 1859, then met in the Königskolonnaden near Alexanderplatz or in Blumenstrasse. In 1864 «the first club house specially built for the purpose of educating workers in Germany» went up at 15 Sophienstrasse. The rooms in Sophienstrasse became unsafe as a result of work on the foundations for the nearby Wertheim extension. The new Craft Association building was opened in 1905, not far away. Today there are two front-facing buildings on the site, probably c. 1800 and 1850, with the new portal and an arched entrance, two side wings probably built c. 1855 and five rebuilt courtyard wings. The wing at right angles contains the rooms for celebrations and other social purposes; there are four side wings around two courtyards. The building has been increasingly neglected since 1933; it is used for storage, and as workshops. Only descriptions and a few photographs have survived of the interior: Virchow hall, wedding hall, library.

in der Nähe/nearby:
Warenhaus Wertheim; Sophienstraße 12-15
1903-06 • Alfred Messel
Wohnhaus; Sophienstraße 11
E. 18. Jh.

F 18 Wohnbauten der Berliner Baugesellschaft
Berlin-Prenzlauer Berg; Wilhelm-Pieck-Straße 85
1849 • Carl Wilhelm Hoffmann

Diese Wohnhäuser entstanden durch die 1847 gegründete Berliner Gemeinnützige Baugesellschaft. Versuche Carl Wilhelm Hoffmanns seit 1841 zur Gründung von Vereinen zur Verbesserung der Arbeiterwohnungen gelangen erst auf der Grundlage der Ideen des christlichen Sozialreformers Victor Aimé Huber von 1844. Durch »Innere Kolonisation« wollte er Häuser und Werkstätten für Handwerker und Kleinbürger bauen. Zu den Mitbegründern und Vorstandsmitgliedern dieser ersten Berliner Baugesellschaft zählten neben Hohenzollernprinzen, Bankiers und Industriellen auch Alexander v. Humboldt und Friedrich August Stüler. Die ersten zwei Wohnbauten an der ehemaligen Wollankstraße wurden 1849-50 wohl nach einem Entwurf von Hoffmann errichtet, und zwar unter Verzicht auf Kellerwohnungen und bewohnte Hinterhäuser. 1887 entstanden die Klinkerverblendbauten an der rückwärtigen Zehdenicker Straße 26-27. Und erst 1914 sind die fünfgeschossigen, neubarocken Seitengebäude zur besseren Ausnutzung des Grundstücks am begrünten Hof errichtet worden. Weitere Wohnanlagen dieser Gesellschaft befinden sich in der Schönhauser Allee.

This accommodation was built for the Berliner Gemeinnützige Baugesellschaft, a building society founded in 1847. Attempts from 1841 by Carl Wilhelm Hoffmann to found an association for the improvement of workers' accommodation were not successful until they were developed on the basis of ideas conceived by Christian social reformer Victor Aimé Huber, dating from 1844. He wanted to build houses and workshops for workmen and the petty bourgeoisie by means of «inner colonization». The co-founders and board members of this first Berlin building society included not only Hohenzollern princes, bankers and industrialists, but also Alexander von Humboldt and Friedrich August Stüler. The first two residential buildings in what was then Wollankstrasse were built in 1849-50, probably to a design by Hoffmann, without basement flats or occupied rear buildings. The clinker-faced buildings in Zehdenicker Strasse behind, numbers 26-27 were built in 1887. The five-storey, neo-baroque side buildings using the plot on the planted courtyard were not added until 1914. There is more accommodation built by this society in Schönhauser Allee.

in der Nähe/nearby:
Wohnhaus mit Läden; Wilhelm-Pieck-Straße 83
1851
Herz-Jesu-Kirche; Fehrbelliner Straße 98-99
1897-99 • Christoph Hehl
Teutoburger Platz; Templiner Straße, Zionskirchstraße
1862 • James Hobrecht

F 19 Volkspark am Weinberg
Berlin-Mitte; Brunnenstraße, Veteranenstraße
1954-57 • Helmut Kruse

Seit dem 18. Jahrhundert lag nordöstlich der Brunnenstraße ein vom Barnimplateau nach Süden abfallender Weinberg, der zuletzt der Familie Wollank gehörte. Er erstreckte sich von der Wollankschen Mühle, an der Stelle der heutigen Zionskirche, bis zur Lohmühle am Teutoburger Platz und reichte fast bis zum Schönhauser Tor. Vom Rosenthaler Tor führte ein Weg zu dem kleinen Weingut. Im letzten Drittel des 19. Jahrhunderts wurde dieses Gebiet mit Miethäusern bebaut. Hier konnte 1954-56 auf dem Terrain zerstörter Häuser zwischen Weinbergsweg und Veteranenstraße zur Auflockerung des dicht besiedelten Gebietes ein Park angelegt werden. Um große Liegewiesen, die zu einem Teich an der Brunnenstraße abfallen, gruppieren sich Stauden- und Rosengärten mit Ruhebänken, Sitzgruppen für Unterhaltungsspiele und ein Kinderspielplatz. Das Café Weinberg wurde nach Plänen von Hans Jährig und Max Kowohl auf einem zehn Meter über der Brunnenstraße angelegten Hügel erbaut. Der gekrümmte Gastraum öffnet sich mit großen Glastüren zur Terrasse. An der Veteranenstraße steht seit 1958 das Heinrich-Heine-Denkmal von Waldemar Grzimek.

From the eighteenth century onwards, north-east of Brunnenstrasse, a vineyard sloped south from the Barnim plateau. It finally came into the possession of the Wollank family. It extended from the Wollank mill, on the site of the present Zionskirche, to the Lohmühle on Teutoburger Platz, and out almost to the Schönhauser Gate. There was a lane leading to the little vineyard from the Rosenthal Gate. In the last third of the nineteenth century rented accommodation was built in the area. In 1954-6 it became possible to establish a park for leisure and recreation on the bomb site between Veteranenstrasse and Weinbergsweg, to break up this heavily built-up urban area. Large grassy areas slope down to a pond by Brunnenstrasse, and around them are flowerbeds, shrubberies and rose gardens with benches, and seats where games can be played; there is a children's playground by Fehrbelliner Strasse. Café Weinberg was built to plans by Hans Jährig and Max Kowohl on an artificial mound ten metres above Brunnenstrasse. The large glass doors of the curved interior open on to a terrace. Waldemar Grzimek's Heinrich Heine monument has stood on Veteranenstrasse since 1958.

in der Nähe/nearby:
Warenhaus (Modeinstitut); Brunnenstraße 19-21
1903-04 • Lachmann & Zauber
Elisabethkirche; Invalidenstraße 3
1832-34 • Karl Friedrich Schinkel
Ackerhalle; Invalidenstraße 158, Ackerstraße 23
1886-88 • Hermann Blankenstein
Zionskirche; Zionskirchplatz
1866-73 • Gustav Möller, August Orth

F 20 Volksbühne
Berlin-Mitte; Luxemburgplatz 2-3
1913-14 • Oskar Kaufmann

Nicht Erzieher, sondern Illusionist wollte Oskar Kaufmann als Architekt sein. So baute er sein Volkstheater nicht als Arena nach altgriechisch-demokratischem Verständnis, sondern als Rangtheater. Die Öffnung des Theaters für alle Bevölkerungsschichten dokumentierte nur die Zahl von fast 2000 Plätzen. Kaufmann bekannte einmal, daß er als Architekt auf die Bedürfnisse der Zeit eingehen wolle. Das ist hier wie auch bei anderen Kaufmann-Theatern geschehen: Er bot dem Zuschauer die Flucht aus der Gegenwart, und das ist aus dem Empfinden jener Zeit heraus zu verstehen. Kaufmann ging noch weiter, er beschränkte sich nicht nur auf die Wechselwirkung Zuschauer–Bühne, er bezog auch den Raum in seiner intimen Wirkung und die Fassade als erhebendes Element in die Illusion ein. Der Theaterbesucher wurde in eine gesellschaftliche Welt entführt, die es schon nicht mehr gab. 1939 wurde die Volksbühne von Paul Baumgarten umgebaut. Im Sinne der kulturpolitischen Gleichschaltung erfolgte die innenarchitektonische Gleichschaltung, der in diesen Jahren fast alle individuell geprägten Berliner Theaterräume zum Opfer fielen. Das Rezept: Weißer Lack, roter Plüsch, etwas Gold und Kristall sowie die »Führerloge«.

As an architect, Oskar Kaufmann preferred to be an illusionist instead of an educator. Hence he designed this people's theatre not as an arena reflecting the democratic principles of the ancient Greeks, but as a tiered structure. The seating capacity of almost 2,000 makes it clear that the theatre was open to all strata of the population. Kaufmann once stated that he wanted his architecture to respond to the needs of the time, and that is what he did in this as in other theatre buildings. When he offered the audience an escape from reality, he certainly conformed to the spirit of the time. But Kaufmann did not limit himself to the relationship between stage and audience: the intimate atmosphere of the space and the solemn façade are also part of the illusion. The theatre-goers were carried off into a kind of society that had long since ceased to exist. In 1939 the Volksbühne was remodeled by Paul Baumgarten. In keeping with the general policy of eliminating all opposition, the interior design of the theatre was also streamlined and unified – a fate shared by almost all the individually designed theatres in Berlin at the time. The recipe was simple: white varnish, red plush, some gold and crystal and, of course, the «Führer's box».

in der Nähe/nearby:
Wohnhäuser; Rosa-Luxemburg-Straße, Weydingerstraße
1928-30 • Hans Poelzig

F 21 Wasserturm
Berlin-Prenzlauer Berg; Knaackstraße 29
1877

1853 wurde von einer englischen Privatgesellschaft vor dem Stralauer Tor an der Spree das erste Berliner Wasserwerk errichtet. Der Hochbehälter als Teil dieser Anlage für die tiefer gelegenen Stadtteile bestand zunächst aus einem offenen, später aber überwölbten Reinwasser-Erdbehälter mit schlankem Standrohr für das Sicherheitsventil. Er wurde nach dem Plan von Henry Gill auf dem Windmühlenberg angelegt. Zur Versorgung der Hochstadt auf dem Barnimplateau wurden 1873-77 zwei Maschinenhäuser, ein zweiter überwölbter Wasserbehälter und der Wasserturm, dieser zugleich mit einigen Wohnungen errichtet. Obwohl seit 1914 und 1952 in Teilen stillgelegt, bestimmt die Anlage noch heute das Bild der umliegenden Straßen. Ein Gedenkstein an der Knaackstraße erinnert daran, daß in den Kellern und Maschinenhäusern dieser Wassertürme zu Beginn der Hitlerdiktatur Regimegegner inhaftiert, mißhandelt und getötet wurden.

The first Berlin waterworks were built in 1853 by a private English company outside the Stralau Gate by the Spree. The reservoir, which was the part of the plant serving lower-lying parts of the town, was initially an open earth container for pure water, later covered, with a slender safety valve tower. It was built on the Windmühlenberg, to a plan by Henry Gill. Two machine houses, a second covered reservoir and the water tower, which contained accommodation, were built from 1873-7 to supply the high-lying town on the Barnim plateau. Although some parts were shut down in 1914 and 1952, the plant still dominates the surrounding streets. A memorial slab on Knaackstrasse commemorates the fact that at the beginning of Hitler's dictatorship opponents of the regime were imprisoned, maltreated and murdered in the cellars and machine houses.

in der Nähe/nearby:
Denkmal für Käthe Kollwitz; Kollwitzplatz
1955-58 • Gustav Seitz
Frisierplatz im Friseurmuseum; Husemannstraße 8
1901 • Henry van de Velde
Synagoge; Rykestraße 53
1903-04 • Johann Hoeniger

F 22 Miethäuser mit Läden
Berlin-Prenzlauer Berg; Greifswalder Straße 9-12
1879 • Wilhelm Koch

Diese Wohnhausreihe mit hinteren Seitenflügeln ist eine geschlossene Baugruppe in Neurenaissanceformen. Mit großen Läden und repräsentativen Hauseingängen liegt sie an einer wichtigen Hauptstraße, der Greifswalder Straße. Diese ist die mittlere der drei Ausfallstraßen, die seit dem Mittelalter ausgehend vom Georgentor am späteren Alexanderplatz durch die Berliner Feldmark führten. Heute ist dieser Straßenzug Teil einer wichtigen Verkehrsader, die sich vom Potsdamer Platz über das Dorf Malchow bis zum Autobahnring erstreckt. In den Miethäusern Greifswalder Straße 15-19 hat sich eine um 1863 erbaute Gruppe spätklassizistischer Bauten von jeweils sieben Achsen mit mittleren oder seitlichen Durchfahrten und einst auch hofseitigen Ställen erhalten. Durch Mittebetonungen, aber auch durch seitenrisalitartige Fensterkopplungen sind die Fassaden reicher gegliedert als die gleichzeitigen Bauten der Lottumstraße.

This row of buildings with rear side wings is a complete group of dwellings in neo-Renaissance style. It contains large shops, the entrances are imposing, and it is in an important thoroughfare, Greifswalder Strasse. This is the middle of the three arterial roads which from the Middle Ages have run from the Georgentor in what was later Alexanderplatz through the territory of Berlin. Today Greifswalder Strasse is part of a route from Potsdamer Platz through the village of Malchow to the autobahn ring. The rented accommodation at 15-19 Greifswalder Strasse has survived from a group of late classical buildings dating from about 1863. Each has seven axes with central or side entrances, and formerly stables on the courtyard side as well. Emphasis on the centre of the building and also the horizontal projections linking the windows articulate the façades more richly than those of their contemporaries in Lottumstrasse.

in der Nähe/nearby:
Oberschule; Greifswalder Straße 25
1913-14 • Ludwig Hoffmann
Schule (Krankenhaus); Christburger Straße 7
1907-08 • Ludwig Hoffmann
Miethaus; Prenzlauer Allee 222
1890-91 • Erich Herkewitz

F 23 Wohnstadt Carl Legien
Berlin-Prenzlauer Berg; Friedländer Straße
1929-30 • Bruno Taut, Franz Hillinger

Diese Wohnanlage wurde nach einem 1925 entstandenen Entwurf durch die Gehag mit 1150 Wohnungen in einem Gebiet mit hoher Wohndichte zwischen der Gubitz- und der Sültstraße errichtet. Vorbild war eine Siedlung von J. J. Pieter Oud in Rotterdam. Beiderseits einer Durchgangsstraße sind recht breite baumbestandene Grünflächen angeordnet. Zum Straßenraum öffnen sich die Wohnhöfe mit ihren aneinandergereihten Loggien der Eineinhalb- bis Dreieinhalb-Zimmerwohnungen. Dunkelrote und ockerfarbene Putzflächen wechselten an kubisch geschnittenen Baukörpern mit dem Fächer teils hellgrün verglaster, gerundeter Balkone. Die originelle Teilung der Küchenfenster an den Nebenstraßen in Beziehung zu den Luftschlitzen und den Bad- sowie Treppenhausfenstern läßt deutlich den Einfluß des Neoplastizismus der niederländischen De-Stijl-Gruppe erkennen, der vermittelt durch die Vorträge des holländischen Architekten Theo van Doesburg 1922 in Deutschland nicht ohne Bedeutung auch für die künstlerische Entwicklung des Weimarer Bauhauses geblieben war.

This residential complex was built to a design dating from 1925 by Gehag (Gemeinnützige Heimstätten-Aktien-Gesellschaft), a building society, with 1,150 flats in a high-density residential area between Gubitz- and Sültstrasse. It was modelled on an estate by J. J. Pieter Oud in Rotterdam. Broad green areas with trees are set on both sides of a through road. The residential courtyards open on to the street with the rows of balconies of the single-room to two-bedroom flats. Areas of dark red and ochre plaster alternate on the cube-based buildings with flights of rounded balconies, partially glazed in light green. The unusual division of the kitchen windows in the side streets relating to the air slits and bathroom and staircase windows shows clearly the influence of the De Stijl group in the Netherlands, passed on by Dutch architect Theo van Doesburg's lectures in Germany in 1922 and also not without significance for the development of the Weimar Bauhaus.

in der Nähe/nearby:
Wohnanlage; Naugarder Straße 46/54, Grellstraße
1927-28 • Bruno Taut
Wohnbauten am Ernst-Thälmann-Park
1983-86 • Helmut Stingl, Manfred Zumpe
Zeiss-Planetarium; Prenzlauer Allee 77
1987 • Gottfried Hein
Wohnkomplex; Greifswalder Straße, Michelangelostraße
1973-83 • Roland Korn, Karin Maaß, Harald Hanspach

F 24 Wohnquartier
Berlin-Prenzlauer Berg; Arnimplatz
Seit 1973 • Manfred Zache; Dorothea Krause

Das Stadtviertel um den Arnimplatz, zwischen Schönhauser Allee, Bornholmer Straße und dem S-Bahnbogen an der Dänenstraße gelegen, ist ein intensiv genutztes Wohnmischgebiet mit 8 300 Wohnungen für 17 200 Einwohner mit einer Fläche von 40 Hektar. Mit der fünfgeschossigen Bebauung aus der Zeit nach 1905 und nach der sozialen Struktur seiner Bewohner war es immer eines der dichtbesiedeltsten Arbeiterwohngebiete Berlins. Vom Verkehr ist es günstig erschlossen: neben U-Bahn und S-Bahn bieten vier Straßenbahnlinien eine günstige Anbindung an das Stadtzentrum und zu den Arbeits- und Erholungsstätten sowie zu den Fernbahnhöfen. Die Modernisierung des ersten Bauabschnittes zwischen Paul-Robeson-, Willi-Bredel- und Seelower Straße begann 1973. Zu den Baumaßnahmen gehörten die Veränderung der Wohnungsgrundrisse, die Zusammenlegung von Einraumwohnungen, Entkernungsabrisse und Beseitigung überflüssiger Hofbebauung sowie Neugestaltung der Hof- und Grünflächen. 1976 waren 1500 Wohnungen fertiggestellt. Mit dem zweiten Bauabschnitt erhielt das Gebiet eine Kaufhalle, einen Kindergarten, Klubs und Reparaturzentren; störende Betriebe wurden verlagert und der Arnimplatz als Grünplatz rekonstruiert.

The district around Arnimplatz, between Schönhauser Allee, Bornholmer Strasse and the bend in the S-Bahn at Dänenstrasse, is an intensively used mixed residential area with 8,300 dwellings for 17,200 inhabitants on an area of 40 hectares. With its five-storey development from the period after 1905 and because of the social structure of the population it was always one of the most densely populated working-class districts in Berlin. It has good transport facilities: U-Bahn and S-Bahn and also four tram routes link it with city centre, places of work and recreation and the main-line stations. Modernization of the first section to be built, between Paul-Robeson-, Willi-Bredel- and Seelowerstrasse, started in 1973. The project included alteration of the ground plan of the flats, knocking single-room flats together, demolishing to reduce density and removal of superfluous building in the yards, and redesign of yards and green areas. 1,500 flats were completed in 1976. The second building phase gave the area a department store, children's facilities, clubs and repair centres; disruptive businesses were moved and Arnimplatz was reconstructed as a green area.

in der Nähe/nearby:
Augustinuskirche; Dänenstraße 17-18
1927-28 • Josef Bachem, Heinrich Horvatin
Hoch-Bahnhof Schönhauser Allee (U 2)
1911-13 • Alfred Grenander
Gethsemanekirche; Stargarder Straße 77
1891-93 • August Orth
Mietwohnhaus; Schönhauser Allee 59 a-b
1870-71

F 25 Schultheissbrauerei
Berlin-Prenzlauer Berg; Schönhauser Allee 36-39
Bis 1891 • Franz Schwechten

Die ehemalige Brauerei, in romanischen Formen erbaut, war nicht die einzige in dieser Gegend. Sie ist heute unter eine Reihe verschiedener Nutzer aufgeteilt: Jugendklub »Erich Franz« im ehemaligen Restaurant, Trainingsräume mit Sportkasino und ein Möbelgeschäft. Während die übrigen Bauteile eher einen behäbigen Eindruck hinterlassen, erscheint der übereck gestellte, fast zu hoch geratene Turm über dem Gaststätteneingang wie ein Fanal, werbend und nicht ohne stadträumliche Wirkung in der Schönhauser Allee. Diese schon im Mittelalter bestehende, vom Spandauer Tor ausgehende wichtige Verbindung zu den Dörfern Pankow und Niederschönhausen war später auch Zufahrtsweg zum Schloß Niederschönhausen, der Residenz der Gemahlin Friedrichs II., und ist in unserer Zeit eine der nördlichen Ausfallstraßen.

This former brewery, borrowing Romanesque features, was not the only one in this area. It is now divided between a number of different users: the «Erich Franz» youth club in the former restaurant, training rooms and sports club and a furniture shop. While the other parts of the building make an essentially solid impression, the tower set diagonally over the restaurant is almost too high and seems like a beacon, proclaiming its presence and making quite an impression on the urban pattern of Schönhauser Allee. This important link, which existed even in the Middle Ages, from the Spandau Gate to the villages of Pankow and Niederschönhausen was later also the access to Schloss Niederschönhausen, the residence of Frederick II's consort, and is today one of the main arterial roads to north Berlin.

in der Nähe/nearby:
Jüdischer Friedhof; Schönhauser Allee 23-25
1827 • Friedrich Wilhelm Langerhans
Jüdisches Altersheim; Schönhauser Allee 23-25
1883-87 • Carl Schwatlo
Denkmal für Alois Senefelder; Senefelder Platz
1892 • Rudolf Pohle

F 26 Stadtbad Prenzlauer Berg
Berlin-Prenzlauer Berg; Oderberger Straße 57-59
1899-1902 • Ludwig Hoffmann

Dieses Bad mit seiner schönen Neorenaissancefassade liegt zwischen Schönhauser Allee und Kastanienallee. Der Besitzer des Vorwerkes am Schönhauser Tor, Griebenow, hatte seit 1861 Kastanien- und Pappelallee anlegen lassen, dem Militärfiskus das Gelände für den Exerzierplatz an der Kantianstraße verkauft, und konnte daher 1866 auch den Grund und Boden für des Königs Votivkirche am Zionskirchplatz stiften. Mit Ausnahme der 1865 erbauten Schule am Arkonaplatz mußten fast alle kommunalen Gebäude, so auch Bad und Schule an der Oderberger Straße, wegen der hohen Bodenpreise ins Blockinnere gelegt werden. Links und rechts des Bades sind daher die Eingänge zur ehemaligen Knaben- und Mädchen-Gemeindeschule angelegt worden. Die bildhauerischen Arbeiten stammen von Otto Lessing.

These baths with their fine neo-Renaissance façade are between Schönhauser Allee and Kastanienallee. Griebenow, the owner of the estate beginning at Schönhauser Tor, had a chestnut and poplar avenue planted from 1861, sold the site for the parade ground on Kantianstrasse to the army and was thus able to donate land for the king's votive church at Zionsplatz in 1866. With the exception of the school on Arkonaplatz built in 1865, almost all public buildings, including baths and school in Oderberger Strasse, had to be sited inside blocks because of the high price of land. For this reason the entrances to the former boys' and girls' schools can be seen to the right and left of the baths. Sculpture is by Otto Lessing.

in der Nähe/nearby:
Segenskirche; Schönhauser Allee 161
1905-08 • August Dinklage, Ernst Paulus, Olaf Lilloe
Miethaus; Kastanienallee 10
1910-11 • Siegfried Löwenstein
Freilichtbühne Prater; Kastanienallee 79
1963 • Wladimir Rubinow, Udo Schulz

F 27 Groterjanbrauerei
Berlin-Wedding; Prinzenallee 78-79
1928-29 • Bruno Buch

Auf obergäriges Karamelbier war die Groterjan-Brauerei spezialisiert, bis sie 1957 aufgekauft und 1960 stillgelegt wurde. Die Bauten aus den zwanziger Jahren waren damit vom Verfall bedroht. Denkmalpflege und Denkmalschutz konnten nicht den Abbruch des großen Stall- und Garagengebäudes verhindern, und bis sich 1983 endlich ein neuer Nutzer fand, war vieles von der Originalausstattung aus den verbliebenen Bauteilen verschwunden. Bruno Buch, der als Industriearchitekt etwa seit 1910 in allen Berliner Bezirken schöpferisch tätig war, hat mit diesem seinem Spätwerk Stetigkeit in der Güte einer soliden und doch ästhetisch befriedigenden Gestaltung bewiesen. Klingen in der Straßenfront ein maßvoller Expressionismus und zaghafte Sachlichkeit gleichermaßen an, diktiert die Zweckmäßigkeit bei der Rückfront und dem Produktionstrakt klare, knappe Formen, die ohne jedes dekorative Element auskommen.

The Groterjan brewery specialized in top-fermented caramel beer until it was bought up in 1957 and closed in 1960. This meant that the buildings, dating from the 1920s, were likely to fall into disrepair. Regulations protecting historic buildings were not able to prevent demolition of the large stables and garages, and by the time a new user was at last found in 1983, much of the original interior of the remaining parts of the building had disappeared. Bruno Buch worked as an industrial architect in most districts of Berlin from 1910, and this late work proves his consistency by its solid and yet aesthetically satisfying design. The street façade may have equal notes of moderate Expressionism and timid functionalism, but the purposefulness of rear façade and production wing produces clear, concise forms that manage without any decorative element.

in der Nähe/nearby:
Stützpunkt Prinzenallee; Osloer Straße 16-17
1928-29 • Hans Müller
Amtsgericht Wedding; Brunnenplatz 1
1901-06 • Paul Thoemer, Rudolf Mönnich
Paulskirche; Badstraße 50
1832-35 • Karl Friedrich Schinkel

F 28 Swinemünder Brücke
Berlin-Wedding; Swinemünder Straße
1905 • Bruno Möhring, Friedrich Krause

Millionenbrücke hieß dieses neue Bauwerk sehr bald, da es die erste Berliner Brücke war, deren Bau mehr als eine Million Goldmark verschlang. Nötig war sie zur Anbindung des neuen Siedlungsgebietes nordöstlich vom Gesundbrunnen, überbrückt wurden fünf Hauptgleispaare der Stettiner Bahn, der Nord- und der Ringbahn sowie eine Reihe von Neben- und Abstellgleisen des Güterbahnhofs. 228 Meter mußten überspannt werden bei geringem Niveauunterschied, bei schrägwinkliger Kreuzung von Straße und Gleisen und mit der Auflage, den Bahnbetrieb möglichst nicht mit Pfeilern und Auflagern zu stören. Die Lösung lag in einer hängebrückenartigen Konstruktion mit zwei Mittelpfeilern, verwendet wurden 1700 t Flußeisen und Gußstahl. Die künstlerische Ausgestaltung oblag Bruno Möhring, der wenige Jahre zuvor beim Hochbahnviadukt in der Bülowstraße bereits Erfahrungen mit Eisentragwerk gemacht hatte. Er griff nur auf Schmiedeeisen zurück, beschränkte sich aber auf die Portale, die Geländer und die Trägerenden an den Brückenköpfen. Formal zitierte Möhring den Jugendstil.

This was very quickly called the million bridge, as it was the first Berlin bridge to cost over a million gold marks. It was needed to form a link with the new residential area north-east of Gesundbrunnen, and bridged five pairs of main lines of the Stettin railway, the northern and ring lines and a series of side and shunting lines belonging to the goods station. 228 metres had to be spanned, with little height difference, with road and rails intersecting diagonally and with the additional requirement of disturbing rail traffic as little as possible with piers and supports. The solution was a kind of suspension bridge with two central piers, using 1,700 tons of low-carbon iron and cast steel. Bruno Möhring, who a few years before had had experience with iron supports in the Bülowstrasse overhead railway viaduct, was responsible for artistic decoration. He fell back on wrought iron, but limited himself to the portals and railings, and the bearer ends at the bridgeheads. The formal language is Jugendstil.

in der Nähe/nearby:
Altenheim; Graunstraße 12-13
1977-79 • Jan Rave, Rolf Rave
Berufsfachschule; Badstraße 10, Grüntaler Straße 4-5
1913-15 • Ludwig Hoffmann
Bahnhof Humboldthain; Wiesenstraße
1934-35 • Richard Brademann
Gemeindeschule; Grenzstraße 8, Wiesenstraße 65-66
1899-1900 • Ludwig Hoffmann
Unterführung Liesenstraße; Liesenstraße
1890-92
Friedhofskapelle (ehem. Dankeskirche); Grenzstraße
1950-51 • Otto Bartning

F 29 Versöhnungs-Privatstraße
Berlin-Wedding; Hussitenstraße 4-5, Strelitzer Straße 43
1903-04 • Schwartzkopff

Der christlich-nationale »Vaterländische Bauverein« entstand in einer Zeit der Einsicht in soziale Reformen. Genossenschaftliche Selbsthilfe sollte sich mit großmütiger Gönnerschaft vereinen. So ist auch die Namensfindung für das erste größere Bauprojekt zu verstehen, mit dem etwa 1000 Menschen ein neues Obdach gegeben werden konnte. Aus dem sparsamen Rückgriff auf preiswertes Bauland im Blockinneren wurde die Idee geboren, durch anheimelnde und wechselvolle Gestaltung der Höfe dem Wohnen neue Reize zu vermitteln. Der Raumfolge von sechs Höfen legte Schwartzkopff die geschichtliche Entwicklung Berlins vom Fischerdorf zur Weltstadt als Programm zugrunde. Die pseudostilgeschichtliche Absicht im Sinne des Historismus läßt hintereinander Romanischen Hof, Gotischen Hof, Renaissancehof, Barockhof und wilhelminischen Hof erleben.

The Christian-National «Vaterländischer Bauverein» came into being at a time of enlightened interest in social reform. Co-operative self-help was to be combined with generous patronage. This is the reason for the name – reconciliation-private road – of the first large building project, intended to provide new homes for about 1,000 people. By thrifty use of cheap building land inside a block the idea was born of giving the flats new charm by familiar and changing design of the courtyards. Schwarzkopff based the spatial sequence of six courtyards on Berlin's historical development from fishing village to metropolis. A pseudo style-historical intention in the spirit of historicism produced a Romanesque Courtyard, a Gothic courtyard, a Renaissance Courtyard and a Wilhelminian Courtyard, one after the other.

in der Nähe/nearby:
Autobus-Betriebshof; Usedomer Straße 24-25
1909-12, 1929–30 • Franz Ahrens
Jugendfreizeitheim; Demminer Straße 30
1987-88 • Hans Kollhoff, Helga Timmermann
Block 270; Vinetaplatz
1971-76 • Josef Paul Kleihues

F 30 AEG-Apparatefabrik
Berlin-Wedding; Ackerstraße
1888-90 • Franz Schwechten, Paul Tropp

Mit der weitreichenden Erfindung der Dynamomaschine durch Siemens im Jahre 1866 und den weiteren Entwicklungen in der Elektrotechnik setzte sich zum Ende des 19. Jahrhunderts die Elektrizität als Energieform durch und bedingte das Aufblühen eines neuen Industriezweiges, der gerade für Berlin mit den weltweiten Konzernen Siemens und AEG prägend werden sollte. Die Fabrik in der Ackerstraße ist die erste einer ganzen Reihe von Großanlagen der AEG. Sie entstand zwar noch auf Stadtgebiet innerhalb der Ringbahntrasse, verfügte aber doch über einen ganzen Baublock, in dem die Bauten nach funktionalen Gesichtspunkten ohne Rücksicht auf bestehende Häuser angeordnet werden konnten. Doch nicht nur die bauliche Hülle für Maschinen und Arbeitsplätze war gefragt, auch die Selbstdarstellung der jungen Industrie wurde bedacht. Franz Schwechten, der Architekt von Anhalter Bahnhof und Kaiser-Wilhelm-Gedächtniskirche, erhielt den Auftrag zur Gestaltung der Fassaden. Er blieb gänzlich verhaftet dem Geschmack der Zeit, schuf Fronten von historistischer Weihe und inhaltlicher Bezugslosigkeit. Die bahnbrechende Übertragung des Funktionalen in die Industriearchitektur blieb etliche Jahre später Baumeistern wie Behrens vorbehalten.

The epoch-making invention of the dynamo by Siemens in 1866 and further development in electrical technology established electricity as a form of energy in the late nineteenth century and caused the rise of a new branch of industry which was to have a particular impact on Berlin through the world-wide businesses of AEG and Siemens. The factory in Ackerstrasse was the first of a series of large AEG plants. It was still on city territory within the Ringbahnstrasse, but covered a whole building block, in which the buildings could be arranged for functional purposes without regard to existing buildings. But it was not just a question of a shell to house machines and working space, but also self-representation by the young architects. Franz Schwechten, architect of the Anhalter Bahnhof and the Kaiser-Wilhelm-Gedächtniskirche, was commissioned to design the façades. He remained completely attached to the taste of the time, and produced façades of historicist devotion, unrelated to function. Pioneering work in translating function into industrial architecture was left to architects like Behrens, many years later.

in der Nähe/nearby:
AEG-Beamtentor; Brunnenstraße 107-111 a
1896 • Franz Schwechten
AEG-Kleinmotorenfabrik; Voltastraße 8-9
1910-13 • Peter Behrens
AEG-Hochspannungsfabrik; Hussitenstraße 23-33
1909-13 • Peter Behrens
Himmelfahrtkirche; Gustav-Meyer-Allee 2
1954-56 • Otto Bartning

F 31 Eisstadion
Berlin-Wedding; Müllerstraße 185
1965-67, 1983-85 • Od Arnold

Unbedachte Sparsamkeit haben der Weddinger Eissporthalle eine bewegte Baugeschichte beschert. Zunächst nur als Freiluftanlage gedacht, leiteten die Planer bald aus einer Überdachung größere Wirtschaftlichkeit ab. Nach dem Abbruch des Schöneberger Sportpalastes galt es noch während der ersten Bauphase, dessen bisherige Aufgaben teilweise zu übernehmen – eine Kapazitätserweiterung auf 3700 Plätze rührt daher. Für eine räumliche Schließung der Halle reichte das Geld aber nicht, sie mußte in den achtziger Jahren nachgeholt werden. Fünf Gruppen von Stahlbetonbindern, die wie Zeltstangen zu Pyramiden zusammengestellt sind, tragen in halber Höhe die auskragende kräftige Dachplatte von 55 m × 65 m. Mit der Schließung des Hallenraumes hat die Ästhetik der Konstruktion an Reiz eingebüßt, auch wenn Schrägen in den Wänden die Neigung der Binder aufzunehmen suchen.

Unthinking thrift meant that the Wedding sports hall had a chequered building history. At first it was intended to be an open-air project, but planners soon made it more productive by adding a roof. When the Schöneberg Sportpalast was pulled down some of its functions had to be taken over in the first building phase – this was the reason for an increase in capacity to 3,700 seats. But there was not enough money to allow the hall to be completely covered, this had to wait for the eighties. Five groups of reinforced concrete trusses, forming pyramids like tent poles, carry the massive 55 m × 65 m roof slab at half height. Enclosure has detracted from the attractiveness of the structure, even though diagonals in the walls attempt to reflect the inclination of the trusses.

in der Nähe/nearby:
Dankeskirche; Weddingplatz
1970-72 • Fritz Bornemann
Postamt 65; Gerichtstraße 50-51
1926-28 • Tietze
Krematorium; Gerichtstraße 37-38
1909-15 • William Müller

F 32 Abspannwerk Scharnhorst
Berlin-Wedding; Sellerstraße 16-26
1928-29 • Hans Müller

Das in den zwanziger Jahren zwischen den Berliner Kraftwerken vereinheitlichte 30-kV-Netz machte eine ganze Reihe von Anlagen für die Energieverteilung nötig. Jeweils für ein größeres Stadtviertel mußte die Hochspannung auf eine Mittelspannung von 3000 Volt transformiert werden. Die Entwürfe für diese Abspannwerke lieferte der damalige Chefarchitekt der Bewag, Hans Müller. Er sagte einmal, sein Schaffen habe die Ziegelbauweise des Vorderen Orients und die gotische Baukunst der Mark Brandenburg am stärksten beeinflußt. Die dunklen Klinkerfronten seiner Bauten im Verein mit exotisch-expressionistischen Schmuckformen und sakralen Pfeilerbögen wurden zu einem Markenzeichen. Beim Werk Scharnhorst tritt ein weiteres Merkmal hinzu, dreieckig vorspringende Wandvorlagen – sie enthalten Kabelschächte – verkörpern in ihrer Zickzacklinie symbolhaft die Elektrizität und spannen den Bogen zum Lieblingsmotiv des Expressionismus.

The 30 kV network agreed between the Berlin power stations in the twenties necessitated a whole series of equipment for energy distribution. In each case high voltage had to be transformed to a medium high voltage of 3,000 volts for a relatively large district of the city. These transformer stations were designed by Berlin electricity's then chief architect Hans Müller. He once said that his way of building was most influenced by brick architecture in the Near East and Gothic architecture in the Mark Brandenburg. The dark clinker façades of his buildings, combined with exotic-Expressionist decoration and ecclesiastical pier arches became a trade mark. Another characteristic feature appeared in the Scharnhorst building: triangular wall projections – they contain cable shafts – represent electricity symbolically by their zig-zag line and form a link with a favourite Expressionist motif.

in der Nähe/nearby:
Schering-Verwaltung; Müllerstraße 175-181
1970-78 • Dietrich Kolb, Reinhart Steinweg; Kiemle, Kreidt & Partner
Schering-Schulungszentrum; Sellerstraße 1-13
1985 • Alfons Hiergeist
Schering-Verwaltung; Sellerstraße 31
1991-93 • BHLM (Düsseldorf)
Schering-Laboratorium; Fennstraße 9-10
1871-72 • Erdmann

G
Berlin
Vom Friedrichshain zur Luisenstadt

Die Königsstadt, die Stralauer Vorstadt und die Luisenstadt waren beiderseits der Spree seit 1690/95 die südöstlichen Erweiterungsgebiete vor den Toren der damals gerade fertiggestellten barocken Festungswerke. Diese Areale wurden begrenzt durch die 1734 bis 1869 bestehende Akzisemauer, die hier vom Wassertor über den Oberbaum an der Spree und über das Frankfurter Tor bis zum Königstor verlief. Weite Teile dieser Vorstädte trugen bis ins 19. Jahrhundert den Charakter einer Landstadt. Auf dem Köpenicker Feld beiderseits des Kottbusser Tores wurde innerhalb und außerhalb der Mauer Ackerbau betrieben, an den sich ländliche Gewerbe anschlossen. 1848-52 hatte Lenné hier den Luisenstädtischen Kanal anlegen lassen, eine schiffbare Verbindung zwischen Spree und Landwehrkanal, über die vornehmlich das Baumaterial für die Luisenstadt antransportiert wurde. Der bald wieder bedeutungslose Kanal wurde 1926-27 beim Bau der U-Bahn Neukölln–Gesundbrunnen wieder zugeschüttet. Nur das Engelbecken und die Uferstraßen im Zuge vom Bethaniendamm bis zum Wassertorplatz blieben. Die Bebauungspläne, 1825 von Carl Ludwig Schmid und 1841 von Peter Joseph Lenné, teilten das Köpenicker Feld in größere Baublöcke auf, um auch Großbetrieben wegen der günstigen Transportmöglichkeiten die Ansiedlung am neuen Kanal zu ermöglichen. Mit den verschiedenartig angelegten Plätzen war die Bebauung beispielgebend für die Hobrechtschen Stadterweiterungsplanungen von 1862. In dieser Weise wurden dann auch außerhalb der Akzisemauer Stadtgebiete wie Friedrichshain und Kreuzberg bebaut; sie erstreckten sich insbesondere beiderseits der Frankfurter Allee bis zur Trasse des 1871 eröffneten Ostrings. Gegen Ende des 19. Jahrhunderts waren neben dicht bebauten Wohnquartieren eine Reihe von Großbetrieben entstanden, so die Deutsche Gas-Glühlicht-AG oder die Musikinstrumentenfirma Bechstein, und seit 1877 der Vieh- und Schlachthof unmittelbar an der Ringbahn zwischen dem Dorf Lichtenberg und dem Friedrichshain. Im Zweiten Weltkrieg sind besonders die Wohngebiete beiderseits der Frankfurter Allee schwer zerstört worden. Sie wurden seit den fünfziger Jahren neu aufgebaut.

Königsstadt, Stralauer Vorstadt and Luisenstadt are set on both sides of the Spree, and were from 1690-5 the main expansion areas to the south-east, outside the gates of the baroque fortifications, which had just been completed. The excise wall, which existed from 1734 to 1869, formed the boundary of this area, and here it ran from the Wassertor (watergate) via the Oberbaum on the Spree and the Frankfurter Tor to the Königstor. Until the nineteenth century, large areas of these towns were essentially rural in character. Arable cultivation took place on the Köpenicker Feld on either side of the Kottbusser Tor inside and outside the wall, and country crafts established themselves as a result of this. From 1848-52 Lenné built the Luisenstädtischer Kanal here, a navigable connection between the Spree and the Landwehrkanal, used mainly to transport building materials for Luisenstadt. The canal soon lost its significance, and in 1926-7 it was filled in, when the underground railway from Neukölln to Gesundbrunnen was being built. Only the Engelbecken and the streets along the bank from Bethaniendamm to Wassertorplatz remained. Development plans by Carl Ludwig Schmidt in 1825 and Peter Joseph Lenné in 1841 divided the Köpenicker Feld into large building blocks, to allow industrial operations to establish themselves on the new canal. The development structure with squares laid out in different ways stood as an example for Hobrecht's plans for expanding the city in 1862. In this way districts outside the excise wall like Friedrichshain and Kreuzberg were developed; they extended in particular on both sides of Frankfurter Allee to the Ostring, which opened in 1871. Towards the end of the nineteenth century a number of industrial operations had established themselves here, alongside densely developed residential areas; they included the Deutsche Gas-Glühlicht AG and Bechstein, the musical instrument manufacturers, and from 1877 the stockyards and slaughterhouse directly on the Ringbahn between the villages of Lichtenberg and Friedrichshain. In the Second World War the residential areas on either side of Frankfurter Allee were particularly badly damaged. They were built up again from the fifties.

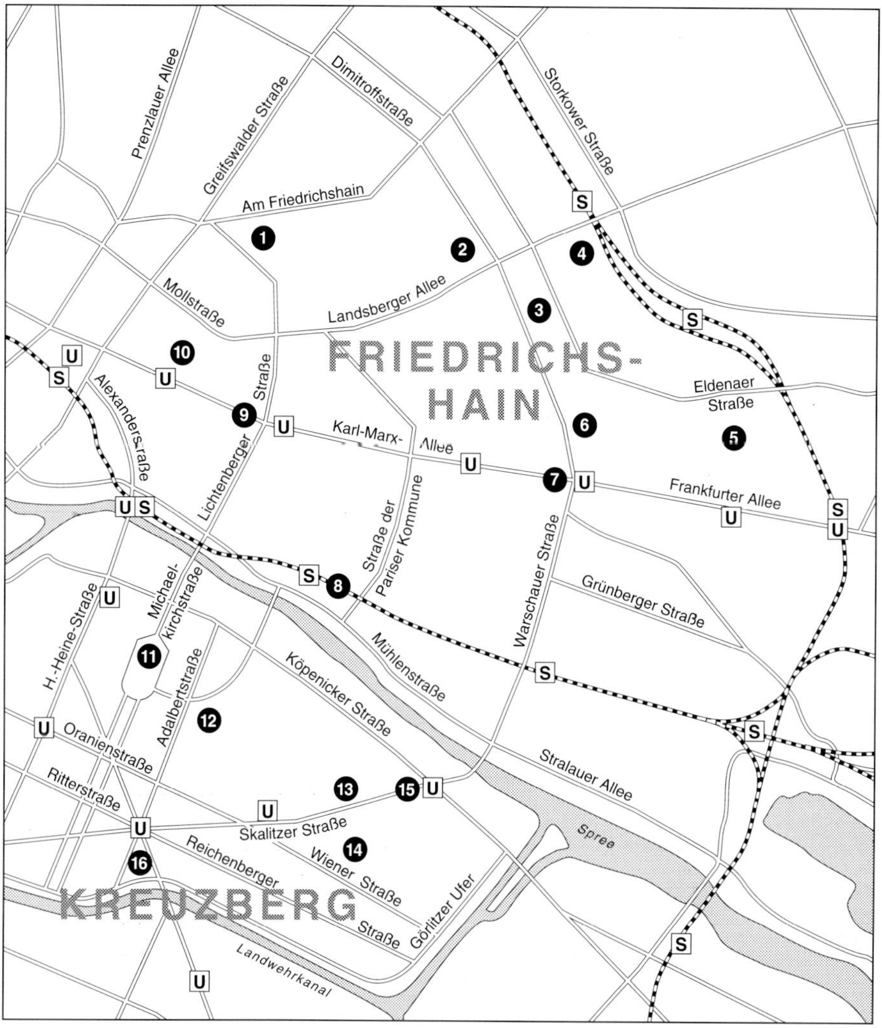

G 1 Volkspark Friedrichshain
G 2 Sport- und Erholungszentrum
G 3 Wohnanlage »Weisbachgruppe«
G 4 Zentralviehhof
G 5 Samariterkirche
G 6 Wohnbebauung
G 7 Turmbauten am Frankfurter Tor
G 8 Hauptbahnhof
G 9 Haus Berlin und Haus des Kindes
G 10 Interhotel Berolina
G 11 Michaelkirche
G 12 Diakonissenkrankenhaus Bethanien
G 13 Postamt SO 36
G 14 Spreewaldbad
G 15 U-Bahnhof Schlesisches Tor
G 16 Wohn- und Geschäftshaus

G 1 Volkspark Friedrichshain
Berlin-Friedrichshain; Friedenstraße
1846-48 • Gustav Meyer

Nach einer Idee von Peter Joseph Lenné beschloß die Berliner Stadtverordnetenversammlung, zwischen dem Königstor und dem Landsberger Tor anläßlich des hundertsten Jahrestages der Thronbesteigung Friedrichs des Großen im Jahre 1840 für die umliegenden dicht besiedelten Arbeiterwohngebiete im Osten Berlins einen Erholungspark einzurichten, und ließ einen Wettbewerb ausschreiben. Nach verzögertem Ankauf des Geländes wurde die Anlage 1846-48 errichtet, nahm kurz vor ihrer Fertigstellung den Friedhof der Märzgefallenen auf sowie 1868 ein erstes städtisches Krankenhaus, um dann 1874-75 mit dem »Neuen Hain« östlich der Virchowstraße erweitert zu werden. Ohne den Märchenbrunnen, eine 1913 von Ludwig Hoffmann mit den Bildhauern Georg Wrba und Ignatius Taschner errichtete neubarocke Schauarchitektur, ist für die Berliner der Friedrichshain nicht denkbar. Als Gegenstück schuf 1985 Achim Kühn einen modernen begehbaren Springbrunnen. Wegen der schweren Zerstörungen im Zweiten Weltkrieg mußte ein großer Teil des Parkes neu angelegt werden; nach einer Idee von Reinhold Lingner entstanden um zwei Flakbunker die beiden Trümmerberge, wie im Volkspark Humboldthain und am Prenzlauer Berg.

On the occasion of the hundredth anniversary of Frederick the Great's accession to the throne in 1840, the Berlin authorities decided to lay out a park in the densely populated residential areas of eastern Berlin. A competition was announced for the realization of this idea for extra recreational facilities, which was based on a suggestion made by Peter Joseph Lenné. After delays in acquiring the land, the park was laid out in 1846-8, and shortly before completion the cemetery for the victims of the 1848 revolution was also included in the project, followed by an early municipal hospital in 1868; it was then extended by the addition of the «Neuer Hain» east of Virchowstrasse in 1874-5. Berliners cannot imagine Friedrichshain without the Märchenbrunnen, a neo-baroque show design built in 1913 to designs by Ludwig Hoffmann with sculptors Georg Wrba and Ignatius Taschner. Achim Kühn provided a counterpart in the form of a modern fountain intended to be walked on in 1985. As a result of severe damage in the Second World War a large part of the park had to be laid out again; the two rubble mounds were built around two flak bunkers, based on an idea by Reinhold Lingner, as in the people's parks in Humboldthain and at Prenzlauer Berg.

in der Nähe/nearby:
Bartholomäuskirche; Friedenstraße 1
1854-58 • Friedrich August Stüler
Denkmal für Alexander Freiherr v. Blomberg
1913 • Otto Kuhlmann
Denkmal für Rosa Luxemburg; Weinstraße
1977 • Günter Junge

G 2 Sport- und Erholungszentrum
Berlin-Friedrichshain; Landsberger Allee 77
1978 • Bernd Fundel, Günter Reiß, Klaus Tröger

Dieser Erholungskomplex wurde 1978-81 an der Stelle alter Miethäuser an einem wichtigen Verkehrsknoten in der Nähe eines S-Bahnhofes und mit Straßenbahnverbindungen zu zentralen und peripheren Wohngebieten der Stadt errichtet. Am Rande des »Neuen Hains« gelegen, ergänzt diese Anlage zusammen mit dem Schwimmstadion »Karl-Friedrich Friesen« die Sportstätten des Volksparkes Friedrichshain. Drei voneinander abgesetzte Baukörper für die unterschiedlichsten Sportarten sind winkelförmig an einer Straßenkreuzung angeordnet. Diagonal gestellt bildet die 95 Meter tiefe Schwimmhalle das Kernstück der Gebäudegruppe, daneben dehnt sich der 117 Meter lange Trakt der Eislaufhalle mit Gaststätten, spiegelbildlich dazu liegt der Sport- und Spielbereich mit mehreren Hallen und einer Bowlingbahn. Hinter den Gebäuden schließen sich Freianlagen an; eine Liegewiese leitet zu Kleinsportplätzen über. Gestalterisches Wesensmerkmal ist die räumliche Durchdringung der drei Hauptbereiche sowie der Außen- und Innenräume, vermittelt durch fachwerkartige Stahlkonstruktionen und großflächige Verglasungen der Außenwände.

This recreational complex was built in 1978-81 on the site of old tenements at an important traffic junction, near an S-Bahn station and with road connections to central and peripheral residential areas. It is on the edge of the «Neuer Hain», and with the «Karl-Friedrich Friesen» swimming stadium complements sports facilities in the park at Friedrichshain. The three separate buildings for different kinds of sport are set at an angle to a road junction. The 95 metre deep building for the indoor pool is placed diagonally, and forms the core of the building; next to it is the 117 metre long run of the ice-skating hall with restaurants, and as a mirror image of this the sport and games area, with several halls and a bowling alley. There are open-air facilities behind the buildings; lawns for sun-bathing lead to a little sports field. The essential design feature is the three-dimensional penetration of the three main areas and the outdoor and indoor spaces, achieved by lattice-like steel construction and large glazed areas in the outer walls.

in der Nähe/nearby:
Adventskirche; B-Prenzlauer Berg; Dimitroffstraße 201
1910-11 • Ernst Paulus, August Dinklage
Wohnanlage; B-Prenzl. B.; Heinz-Bartsch-Straße 11-15
1927-28 • Mebes & Emmerich
Wohnanlage; B-Prenzl. B.; Paul-Heyse-Straße 3/17
1926-27 • Bruno Taut
Friesenstadion; B-Friedrichshain; Werneuchener Straße
1951 • Karl Souradny
Fruchtbarkeitsbrunnen; B-Friedrichshain; Arnswalder Platz
1927/34 • Hugo Lederer

G 3 Wohnanlage »Weisbachgruppe«
Berlin-Friedrichshain; Weisbachstraße 1-8
1898-1904 • Alfred Messel

Diese Wohnanlage des »Vereins zur Verbesserung der kleinen Wohnungen in Berlin« war besonders auch wegen ihrer Gemeinschaftseinrichtungen programmatisch für den reformierten Miethausbau der Jahrhundertwende. Der Vorsitzende des Vereins, Valentin Weisbach, nach dem bereits 1901 die Weisbachstraße benannt wurde, erwarb schon 1890 recht günstig unbebautes Gelände, das später noch durch Zukauf vergrößert wurde. Ursprünglich sollten ganz im Sinne des Vereins vierhundert Wohnungen mit achtzehn Läden errichtet werden. Vorausgegangen war diesem Projekt 1897-98 die Wohnhausgruppe des »Berliner Spar- und Bauvereins« in der Proskauer Straße, auch nach einem Entwurf Alfred Messels und ebenfalls in fünfgeschossiger Bauweise mit Läden, aber ohne Quer- und Seitengebäude im Gartenhof. Die in dem zwischen Kochhahn-, Ebeling- und Ebertystraße gelegenen Hof 1905-06 errichteten Gesellschaftsräume, die Badeanstalt und der Kindergarten sind nicht mehr vorhanden.

These flats built by the «Association for the improvement of small flats in Berlin» was typical of the reformed rented accommodation building programme around the turn of the century, especially because of its community facilities. The chairman of the association, Valentin Weisbach, after whom Weisbachstrasse had been named as early as 1901, acquired land which had not been built on in 1890, and enlarged the site by additional purchases at a later date. The original intention was to build four hundred flats with eighteen shops, completely within the spirit of the association. This project had been preceded by the residential group built by the «Berliner Spar- und Bauverein» in 1897-8 in Proskauer Strasse, also to a design by Alfred Messel, and also with five storeys and shops, but without transverse and side buildings in the garden courtyard. The social rooms, baths and kindergarten built in the courtyard between Kochhahn-, Ebeling- and Ebertysstrasse in 1905-6 are no longer in existence.

in der Nähe/nearby:
Wohnhausgruppe; Proskauer Straße 14-17, Schreinerstraße 63-64, Bänschstraße 28/30
1897-98 • Alfred Messel

G 4 Zentralviehhof
Berlin-Prenzlauer Berg; Thaerstraße
1878-81 • Hermann Blankenstein

Der ehemalige städtische Zentral-Vieh- und Schlachthof ist ein mehrstufig errichteter Industriekomplex. Von der Eldenaer Brücke bei Lichtenberg erstreckte er sich entlang der Ringbahn bis zur Paul-Heyse-Straße im Stadtbezirk Prenzlauer Berg. Ursprünglich gehörte auch das Gelände der heutigen Werner-Seelenbinder-Sporthalle dazu. Der erste Bauabschnitt mit dem Zugang Eldenaer Straße 37 wurde 1878-81 nach Plänen von Blankenstein unter Mitwirkung von August Lindemann errichtet. Die zweite Baugruppe zwischen Thaerstraße und der Landsberger Allee entstand nach Entwürfen von Lindemann in den neunziger Jahren. 1930 baute Richard Ermisch noch ein Rinderschlachthaus. Überwiegend von Ermisch stammt auch der zwischen 1914 und 1929 nördlich der Landsberger Allee errichtete Fleischgroßmarkt. Im Zweiten Weltkrieg wurde die Anlage teilweise zerstört und verkürzt sowie mit neuen Gebäuden wiederaufgebaut. Die gelben Klinkerverblendbauten mit Terrakottenschmuck in Form von Rosetten und Rankenwerk sowie Symbolen des Fleischerhandwerks treten besonders an den Verwaltungsgebäuden hervor.

The former municipal central stockyard and slaughterhouse is an industrial complex built in several stages. It extended along the Ringbahn from the Eldena road bridge in Lichtenberg to Paul-Heyse-Strasse in Prenzlauer Berg. Originally the site of the present Werner Seelenbinder sports hall belonged to it as well. The first building phase with access at Eldenaer Strasse 37 was built 1878-81, to plans by Blankenstein, in association with August Lindemann. The second group of buildings, between Thaerstrasse and Landsberger Allee was built to designs by Lindemann in the nineties. In 1930 Richard Ermisch added another beef slaughterhouse. The meat wholesale market built between 1914 and 1929 north of Landsberger Allee is also predominantly the work of Ermisch. Parts of the complex were destroyed in the Second World War, and rebuilt in reduced form with new buildings. Yellow clinker cladding with terracotta decoration in the form of rosettes, tendrils and symbols of the butcher's craft are a particular feature of the office buildings.

in der Nähe/nearby:
Corpus-Christi-Kirche; Thorner Straße 64
1904, 1908, 1916-20 • Max Hasak
Krankenhaus Friedrichshain; Landsberger Allee 49
1868-74 • Martin Gropius, Heino Schmieden
Grabstätte Francke; Friedenstraße 80 (Friedhof)
1903 • Werner Lundt, Georg Kallmorgen
Friedhofskapelle; St. Petri-Friedhof
1910-11 • Walter Köppen

G 5 Samariterkirche
Berlin-Friedrichshain; Samariterplatz
1892-94 • Gotthilf Ludwig Möckel

Möckels Bauten findet man in Sachsen, Brandenburg und Mecklenburg. Eigene Wohnhäuser baute er sich in Zwickau, Dresden und in Bad Doberan. Neben Kirchen hat er auch eine Reihe zum Teil bedeutender Profanbauten entworfen. Der stolze Westturm der Samariterkirche mit dem hohen Helm muß wie ein mächtiger Zeigefinger gewirkt haben, als dieser neugotische Bau in dem 1892 noch unbebauten Gelände emporwuchs; erst 1895 erhielt der Platz seinen Namen nach der schon errichteten evangelischen Kirche. Im Inneren bewirkte Möckel mit der Verbreiterung der Vierung eine Zentralisierung des Predigtraumes, ganz im Sinne protestantischer Kirchenräume; so versuchte er eine Kombination der barocken Zentralbauideen mit den christlichen Formen der gotischen Basiliken.

Buildings by Möckel are to be found in Saxony, Brandenburg and Mecklenburg. He built houses for himself in Zwickau, Dresden and Bad Doberan. He was responsible for a series of important secular buildings as well as churches. The proud west tower of the Samariterkirche with its tall spire must have looked like a massive index finger when this neo-Gothic building grew up on the site, which had not been built upon in 1892; it was not until 1895 that the area was named after the existing Protestant church. In the interior Möckel broadened the crossing to centralize the preaching area, in the best Protestant tradition, and thus attempts a combination of the baroque idea of a centrally-planned building with the Christian shape of the Gothic basilica.

in der Nähe/nearby:
Wohnanlage; Proskauer Straße 15-17, Schreinerstraße 63-64
1897-98 • Alfred Messel
Oberschule; Rigaer Straße 81-82
1901-02 • Ludwig Hoffmann
Wohngebäude; Frankfurter Allee 104-106
1986 • Till Dorst

G 6 Wohnbebauung
Berlin-Friedrichshain; Bersarinplatz
1985-87 • Georg Timme, Feldmann

Dieser Platz liegt an einem leichten Knick jener tangentialen Ringverbindung, die ausgehend von der Mühlenstraße am ehemaligen Oberbaum der Spree die Radialstraßen bis zur Schönhauser Allee miteinander verbindet. Der Bersarinplatz war einer der schwer zerstörten Plätze im Stadtbezirk Friedrichshain. Er erhielt seinen Namen nach dem sowjetischen Stadtkommandanten, der hier 1946 bei einem Verkehrsunfall tödlich verunglückte. Mit der Neugestaltung sollte auch der Kreisverkehr aufgehoben werden, und eine veränderte Freiraumgestaltung war vorgesehen. Die Platzwände des ehemals siebenstrahligen Verkehrsknotens wurden mit achtgeschossigen Wohngebäuden besetzt, wobei in die Erdgeschoßzone Läden, Gaststätten und Dienstleistungseinrichtungen eingefügt wurden. Auffallend ist die starke Gliederung der Fassaden durch Loggien, die dem Platz einen unverwechselbaren Akzent im Stadtbild verleihen.

This square is on a slight bend of the tangential ring road starting in Mühlenstrasse at the former upper boom on the Spree, and connecting radial roads as far as Schönhauser Allee. Bersarinplatz was one of the worst-damaged squares in the Friedrichshain district. It was named after the Soviet town commandant who was killed here in a traffic accident in 1946. When it was redesigned, the intention was to remove the traffic roundabout and alter the shape of the open space. The peripheral buildings at this junction, formerly of seven streets, were eight-storey residential blocks, with shops, restaurants and service facilities on the ground floor. The façades are strikingly articulated with loggias, which give the square an unmistakable accent within the townscape as a whole.

in der Nähe/nearby:
Schulkomplex; Straßmannstraße 14
Um 1901 • Ludwig Hoffmann
Gemeindehaus; Petersburger Platz 5 (Hof)
1927-29 • Walter Erdmann
Wohnbauten; Frankfurter Allee
1984-88 • Ernst Kristen, Thomas Neudert

G 7 Turmbauten am Frankfurter Tor
Berlin-Friedrichshain; Karl-Marx-Allee 130 u. 131
1957-61 • Hermann Henselmann

Durch die Stralauer Vorstadt führte die mittelalterliche Handelsstraße nach Frankfurt/Oder, die seit 1701 als »Frankfurter Linden« auch Zufahrtsstraße zum königlichen Schloß in Friedrichsfelde war. Das Frankfurter Tor lag damals am heutigen Strausberger Platz, gleich neben dem Hochgericht und später nahe der heutigen Marchlewskistraße im Zuge der Akzisemauer. Vor diesem Tor lag die Weberwiese, später ein Stadtpark. Die noch weiter außerhalb gelegen Kreuzung mit der neuen Ringstraße heißt heute Frankfurter Tor. Jeweils zwei Hochhäuser am Strausberger Platz und am Frankfurter Tor markieren den 1949 bis 1961 nach fast völliger Kriegszerstörung neubebauten und auf 90 Meter verbreiterten Straßenzug der damaligen Stalinallee bis zur Proskauer Straße. Die beiden gegenüberliegenden Turmhochhäuser mit aufgesetzten und kuppelbekrönten Rotunden knüpfen an die Gontardschen Türme am Gendarmenmarkt von 1780 an, die schon für Ludwig Hoffmanns Stadthausturm Pate gestanden hatten. An der Nordostecke des Platzes liegt ein Kaufhaus. In der Frankfurter Allee bis zur Proskauer Straße schließen Neubauten an, die nach Entwürfen von Hanns Hopp errichtet wurden.

The medieval trading route to Frankfurt an der Oder led through the Stralauer Vorstadt, and from 1701 it was also the road to the royal palace in Friedrichsfelde, and known as the «Frankfurter Linden». At that time the Frankfurter Tor was on what is now Strausberger Platz, immediately adjacent to the high court and later near to what is now Marchlewskistrasse, on the line of the excise wall. Beyond this gate lay the Weberwiese which was later turned into a municipal park. Still further outside the town, the road crossed the new ring road at what is now called Frankfurter Tor. Two tower buildings at both Strausberger Platz and at the Frankfurter Tor mark the run of what was then called Stalinallee to Proskauer Strasse. It was rebuilt and extended to a width of 90 metres in 1949 to 1961, after being almost completely destroyed in the war. The two facing tower blocks, topped with domed rotundas, link back to Gontard's church towers in the Gendarmenmarkt of 1780, which had already served as model for Ludwig Hoffmann's Stadthaus tower. There is a department store in the north-eastern corner of the square. There are new buildings in Frankfurter Allee running up to Proskauer Strasse, built to designs by Hanns Hopp.

in der Nähe/nearby:
Hochhaus an der Weberwiese; Marchlewskistraße 25
1951-52 • Hermann Henselmann
Laubenganghaus; Karl-Marx-Allee 102/104, 126/128
1949 • Hans Scharoun, Ludmilla Herzenstein
Filmtheater Kosmos; Karl-Marx-Allee 131 a
1960-62 • Josef Kaiser, Herbert Aust

G 8 Hauptbahnhof
Berlin-Friedrichshain; Stralauer Platz
1985-89 • Karl-Ernst Swora, Heinz Aust

Mit der Entwicklung des Eisenbahnnetzes zwischen den deutschen Ländern entstanden in vielen Großstädten vor der Mitte des 19. Jahrhunderts, so auch in Berlin, eine Reihe von Kopfbahnhöfen. Im Osten der Stadt lag seit 1842 an der Stelle des heutigen Hauptbahnhofs die Endhaltestelle der Frankfurter Eisenbahn. Ab 1867 gab es nördlich davon am heutigen Franz-Mehring-Platz den Bahnhof der Ostbahn, der aber 1882 schon wieder geschlossen wurde, und seit 1898 zwischen diesen beiden noch das Provisorium des Wriezener Bahnhofs. Der Frankfurter Bahnhof machte 1867-69 einem Neubau Platz und wurde 1878-82 mit dem Bau der Stadtbahn zum Durchgangsbahnhof, hieß dann Schlesischer Bahnhof und von 1950 an Ostbahnhof. Im Vorfeld aller drei Bahnhöfe lagen großflächige Güterbahnhöfe; hinzu kam noch die Hauptwerkstatt der Ostbahn, das heutige Ausbesserungswerk am Bahnhof Warschauer Straße. Seit 1985 wird das 300 Meter lange Empfangsgebäude des Hauptbahnhofs mit der Abfertigungshalle, den Gaststätten, Service- und Verkaufseinrichtungen und einem Zeitkino erneuert, Bahnsteige und Bahnhofshallen werden rekonstruiert. Ein Teil der alten Rundbogenarchitektur ist von einem Lichthof aus noch erkennbar.

As the railway network between the various German countries developed in the mid nineteenth century, many major cities, including Berlin, acquired a series of terminus stations. The last stop on the Frankfurt railway was in the east of the town from 1842, on the site of the modern Hauptbahnhof. From 1867, north of this, in the present Franz-Mehring-Platz, was the Ostbahn station, but this was closed again in 1882, and from 1898 between these two was the provisional Wriezen station. In 1867-9 the Frankfurt station was replaced by a new building, which became a through station in 1878-82 when the S-Bahn was built; it was then renamed Schlesischer Bahnhof and from 1950 Ostbahnhof. All three stations were preceded by large goods stations; in addition to this there were the main workshops of the Ostbahn, the present repair works at Warschauer Strasse stations. Work has been going on since 1985 on the three hundred metre long reception building at the Hauptbahnhof with ticket hall, restaurants, service and sales facilities and a cinema; platforms and station halls are being rebuilt. A section of the old round-arched architecture can still be made out from an air well.

in der Nähe/nearby:
U-Bahnhof Warschauer Brücke; Warschauer Straße
1900-02 • Konstruktionsbüro Siemens & Halske
Osthafen; Stralauer Allee 1-16
1907-13 • Friedrich Krause, Zaar, Kritzler & Tischer
Eierkühlhaus; Stralauer Allee, Am Oberbaum
1928-29 • Oskar Pusch

G 9 Haus Berlin und Haus des Kindes
Berlin-Mitte; Strausberger Platz 1 und 19
1951-53 • Hermann Henselmann, Rolf Göpfert, Emil Leibold

Hatte Henselmann 1957 für die Hochhäuser am Frankfurter Tor wieder die Gontard-Türme der Friedrichstadt zum Vorbild genommen und damit entsprechend der Architektur- und Städtebautheorie der vorangegangenen Jahre an die nationalen Traditionen der Berliner Baukunst angeknüpft, so war er 1951 mit den Hochhäusern am Strausberger Platz noch jüngeren Vorschlägen gefolgt. Diese gestaffelte Baukörperbildung hatte Bruno Möhring im Jahre 1920 als Idealentwurf zweier Hochhäuser an einer Straßenkreuzung in der Zeitschrift »Stadtbaukunst in alter und neuer Zeit« veröffentlicht. Spannungsreich wurde diese Komposition aber erst durch den leichten Knick der großen Magistrale an dieser Stelle, denn in der Hauptblickrichtung auf das Zentrum tritt zunächst nur das Haus des Kindes allein und damit auch nur asymmetrisch in Erscheinung, ehe der sich nahende Betrachter auf diesem oval gestalteten Platz die Symmetrie der Torsituation wahrnimmt. Der Ringbrunnen mit verkupferten Zierkörpern über einem Wasserbecken von 30 Meter Durchmesser wurde 1967 auf der bepflanzten Verkehrsinsel nach Entwürfen von Achim Kühn, Heinz Graffunder und Rolf Rühle errichtet.

In 1957 Henselmann took Gontard's Friedrichstadt towers as his model for the high-rise buildings on Frankfurter Allee, thus forming a link back to the national tradition of Berlin architecture, in accordance with the architectural and urban development theories of previous years, but in 1951 he followed more recent suggestions when designing the high-rise buildings in Strausberger Platz. These have a staggered design published in 1920 by Bruno Möhring in the magazine «Stadtbaukunst in alter und neuer Zeit» as an ideal solution for two high-rise buildings at a junction. But this composition really gains its tension from the slight bend in the great main street at this point, for on the principal view line at first only the Haus des Kindes can be seen in the centre, and then only asymmetrically, before the approaching observer suddenly perceives the symmetry of the gate situation in this oval square. The circular fountain with copper-plated decorative elements over a pool 30 metres in diameter was constructed on the traffic island with gardens in 1967, to designs by Achim Kühn, Heinz Graffunder and Rolf Rühle.

in der Nähe/nearby:
Wohngebäude Block B-Süd; Karl-Marx-Allee
1952 • Egon Hartmann
Wohngebäude Block C-Nord; Karl-Marx-Allee 77/85
1952 • Richard Paulick
Seniorenheim; Andreasstraße 21
1958-59 • Heinz Bärhold

G 10 Interhotel Berolina
Berlin-Mitte; Karl-Marx-Allee 31
1961-63 • Josef Kaiser, Günter Kunert

In diesem zweiten Bauabschnitt der Karl-Marx-Allee, der 1959-65 nach Entwürfen von Edmund Collein und Werner Dutschke entstand, sind einige städtebauliche Elemente des ersten Bauabschnittes, der ehemaligen Stalinallee, übernommen worden. Durch das Zurücksetzen der Wohngebäude wurde zwar der Straßenraum von 90 auf 125 Meter verbreitert, durch die vorgezogenen Ladenbauten jedoch und durch das Kino International sowie das Restaurant Moskau blieb die Straßenflucht erhalten. Im alten Teil dieses fast zwei Kilometer langen Straßenabschnittes wurden einzelne öffentliche Gebäude, wie das Filmtheater Kosmos, in ausgesparte Platzräume eingefügt, offenbar nach einer städtebaulichen Idee, zu der die Schloßstraße in Ludwigslust als Vorbild gedient hat. Im neueren Abschnitt unterbricht die Schillingstraße den 700 Meter langen Straßenzug und gab als Querachse den Anlaß für eine ähnliche Raumbildung. Diese einprägsame asymmetrische Komposition, die Hotel, Kino und Restaurant miteinander bilden, ist besonders gut von der Fußgängerverbindung zum S- und U-Bahnhof Jannowitzbrücke erlebbar.

This second building phase of the Karl-Marx-Allee, built 1959-65 to designs by Edmund Collein and Werner Dutschke, adopted some urban planning elements of the first building phase, the former Stalinallee. The residential buildings were set back, thus widening the street from 90 to 125 metres, but the line of the street was retained by pulling the shop buildings forward, and by the Kino International and the Restaurant Moskau. In the old area of this section of the street, almost two kilometers long, some public buildings, like the Kosmos cinema were placed in spaces like urban squares, clearly based on planning ideas taking their cue from Schlosstrasse in Ludwigslust. In the newer section Schillingstrasse breaks up the 700 metre long street and as a transverse axis gave a reason for similar spatial organization. This striking asymmetrical composition formed by hotel, cinema and restaurant can be seen to particular advantage from the footbridge leading to Jannowitzbrücke S-Bahn station.

in der Nähe/nearby:
Kino International; Karl-Marx-Allee 29
1961-63 • Josef Kaiser, Heinz Aust
Restaurant Moskau; Karl-Marx-Allee 34
1961-64 • Josef Kaiser, Horst Bauer
Wohnhochhaus; Platz der Vereinten Nationen 1-3
1968-70 • Heinz Mehlan, Egon Kreißl, Erwin Kussat

G 11 Michaelkirche
Berlin-Mitte; Michaelkirchplatz 3
1851-56 • August Soller

Mit dem Ausbau der schmalen Vorstadt »Neu-Cölln am Wasser« entstand seit 1695 die Köpenicker Vorstadt, die seit 1802 Luisenstadt hieß. Dieser Stadtteil erhielt mit den Erweiterungsplanungen von 1840 durch Peter Joseph Lenné ein städtebauliches Zentrum in der Achse des Luisenstädtischen Kanals, einen großen Platz, auf dem die Michaelkirche als katholische Garnisonskirche und zugleich als bedeutendster Kirchenbau der Schinkelnachfolge errichtet wurde. Stilistisch folgt sie der oberitalienischen Renaissance und bricht so mit der Gestaltungstradition der ersten Jahrhunderthälfte. Bezeichnend ist die Ablösung einer feinsinnigen Ausbildung durch selbstbewußte Monumentalität. Hierin kündigt sich schon der neue Geist an, der Kunst und Architektur später in den Historismus einmünden läßt.

The Köpenicker Vorstadt came into being from 1695, with the expansion of the little suburb of «Neu-Cölln am Wasser»; it was called Luisenstadt from 1802. Peter Joseph Lenné's expansion plans gave this part of the town an urban centre on the axis of the Luisenstadt canal in 1840. This was a large square in which St. Michael's church was built as a Catholic garrison church, and at the same time the most important church building by Schinkel's successors. Stylistically it follows northern Italian Renaissance models, and thus breaks with the design tradition of the first half of the century. A characteristic feature is the replacement of delicate form by self-confident monumentality. This is a precursor of the new spirit that was to lead art and architecture into historicism.

in der Nähe/nearby:
Gewerkschaftshaus; Engeldamm 70
1927-30 • Bruno Taut, Max Taut
Zigarettenfabrik Josetti; Rungestraße 22-24
1905/10
S-Bahnhof Jannowitzbrücke; Brückenstraße
1927-32 • Hugo Röttcher

G 12 Diakonissenkrankenhaus Bethanien
Berlin-Kreuzberg; Mariannenplatz 1-3
1845-47 • Theodor Stein, Römer

Als große symmetrische Dreiflügelanlage im Flurgangsystem mit einem rückwärtigen Kirchenanbau in der Hauptachse, so wurde Bethanien gebaut zu einer Zeit, da die Krankenpflege noch reine Angelegenheit der Kirche war oder anderen barmherzigen Helfern überlassen blieb. Der maßvolle Rundbogenstil war als altchristliches Merkmal damals allein dem kirchlichen Bauen vorbehalten. Der Aufgabe gemäß und als Stiftung der Sparsamkeit verpflichtet, gibt sich das Äußere schlicht, nur der Mittelrisalit mit zwei schlanken Türmen, die ausdrücklich von Friedrich Wilhelm IV. gefordert wurden, hebt sich aus der Front zum Mariannenplatz ab. Über 400 Betten verfügte das Krankenhaus, immer 10 bis 14 in einem Saal, zwischen den Sälen abwechselnd Teeküchen oder Doppelzimmer für die Schwestern und Toiletten. So war immer eine Schwester für einen Saal zuständig, wohnte im Verständnis des Ur-Christentums bei ihren Kranken. Die Anstalt erhielt als Nebenbauten Leichenhaus, Predigerhaus, Beamtenwohnhaus und Feierabendhaus, bis 1930 kamen noch Erweiterungsbauten hinzu. Im Kriege ging einiges davon unter, das Haupthaus blieb aber bestehen, bis man in den sechziger Jahren glaubte, es abreißen zu müssen. Reger Widerstand aus allen Kreisen der Bevölkerung verhinderte dies, und es fand sich auch die neue Nutzung für kulturelle Veranstaltungen.

Bethanien is a large symmetrical building in three sections on the corridor system with a church in the principal axis at the rear, built at a time when care for the sick was still purely a matter for the church or other charitable organizations. The controlled round-arched style was at the time reserved for ecclesiastical buildings as an ancient Christian characteristic. The exterior is plain, as is fitting for its purpose and for an institution committed to economy, and only the central protruding section, expressly demanded by Friedrich Wilhelm IV, stands out in the façade on Mariannenplatz. The hospital had 400 beds, with 10 to 14 in each ward, and between the wards were alternately small kitchens or double rooms for the nurses, and toilets. Thus one nurse was always responsible for one ward, and lived with the sick people in her care, in the manner of the earliest Christians. Outbuildings included a mortuary, house for a preacher, accommodation for officials and a recreation building, and additional buildings were added until 1930; some of this was destroyed in the war, but the main building survived until it was thought that it would have to be pulled down in the sixties. This was prevented by fierce opposition from all circles of the population, and it is now used for cultural events.

in der Nähe/nearby:
Thomaskirche; Mariannenplatz
1864-69 • Friedrich Adler
Bürohaus (ehem. Warenhaus); Oranienplatz 4-10
1930-32 • Max Taut, Franz Hoffmann

G 13 Postamt SO 36
Berlin-Kreuzberg; Skalitzer Straße 84-92
1925-27 • Jakob, Nissle

Während bis zum Ersten Weltkrieg kaum ein größeres Postamt errichtet werden konnte, ohne daß der Kaiser persönlich Entwurf und Gestaltung begutachtete, hier und da »etwas mehr Gotik« verlangte und darüber wachte, daß alles recht stilvoll aussah, befreiten sich die Postbaumeister in den zwanziger Jahren von solchem gestelzten Architekturspuk. Willy Hoffmann steht in Berlin für den baukünstlerischen Neubeginn, aus seinem Amt stammen auch die von den Postbauräten Jakob und Nissle ausgearbeiteten Pläne für das Postamt SO 36. Seine beeindruckende Größe verdankt es – wie manches andere Postamt jener Jahre – dem schnellen Anwachsen des Telefonverkehrs, denn die oberen Etagen waren den Einrichtungen des Fensprechamtes Südost und den neuen Selbstwählvermittlungen »Moritzplatz« und »Oberbaum« vorbehalten. Die endlose Front von 118 Metern mit 43 Fensterachsen wirkt durch die regelmäßige Reihung der dreieckig vorspringenden Wandpfeiler fast wie ein Industriebau. Die Zickzacklinie der Pfeiler, textile Ziegelmuster und viele Details, von denen viele in früheren Jahren einer unbedachten Purifizierung zum Opfer gefallen sind, zeigen den maßgeblichen Einfluß des Expressionismus.

Until the First World War it was not possible to build a post office of any size without having plans and design approved by the Kaiser in person, who would ask for «a bit more Gothic» here and there and make sure that everything was nice and stylish, but postmasters shook off stilted architectural haunting of this kind in the twenties. Willy Hoffmann is the leading figure of this new architectural start in Berlin, and these plans for the SO 36 post-office by postal building officers Jakob and Nissle also came from his office. Like many other post office buildings of its period it owes its impressive size to the rapid growth of the telephone service at the time: the upper storeys were reserved for the south-eastern telephone district's facilities and the new «Moritzplatz» and «Oberbaum» subscriber-dialling exchanges. The endless 118 metre façade with 43 window axes seems almost like an industrial building because of the regular arrangement of pilasters protruding in triangular sections. The zig-zag line of the piers, textile brick patterns and many details of which some fell victim to thoughtless purification in earlier years, show the decisive influence of Expressionism.

in der Nähe/nearby:
Markthalle; Eisenbahnstraße 42-43, Pücklerstraße 34
1890-91 • Hermann Blankenstein
Gewerbehof; Zeughofstraße 20
1902 • Paul Überholz

G 14 Spreewaldbad
Berlin-Kreuzberg; Spreewaldplatz
1984-87 • Christoph Langhof, Thomas M. Hänni, Herbert Meerstein

Lange Zeit wurde der Osten Kreuzbergs städtebaulich vernachlässigt, nachdem der Krieg hier so viele Wunden geschlagen hatte, die Teilung Berlins den Stadtteil zum Randgebiet machte und Spekulation und Flächensanierung hier den sozialen Frieden zerstörten. Für die Nutzung des ruinösen Görlitzer Bahnhofsgeländes, eine der großen Stadtbrachen, gab es unterschiedliche Konzepte. Stadtbad und Park wurden schließlich als städtebauliche Strategie für »SO 36« – so nannte sich der Kreuzberger Osten nach seinem Zustellpostamt – favorisiert. Langhof gestaltete eine hügelige Landschaft, in die sich das Bad einfügt und die das Bad durchdringt. Innenräume, Wände und Dächer sind in diese Durchdringung einbezogen. Die neuen Ideen und der Mut zu Wellenbad, Wasserkaskaden und Sauna in einem städtischen Hallenbad kommen nicht von ungefähr, sie sind die Antwort auf das zuvor in Britz eröffnete private »Freizeitbad blub«, welches sich bewußt der bisher gepflegten puritanischen Hallenbad-Freudlosigkeit enthielt.

For a long time the eastern part of Kreuzberg was neglected in urban development terms; the war had inflicted terrible damage, the district was marginalized by the division of Berlin, and social peace was disturbed by speculation and redevelopment by demolition. There were various plans for the use of the ruined Görlitzer Bahnhof site, a great fallow urban area. Finally it was decided that municipal baths and a park were the favoured urban plan for «SO 36», as eastern Kreuzberg is called after its district post office. New ideas and the courage to build a pool with waves, water cascades and a sauna in a municipal swimming baths did not come about by chance, they are a response to the private «Freizeitbad blub», which had previously opened in Britz, and which deliberately eschewed the puritanical joylessness of swimming pools that had predominated hitherto.

in der Nähe/nearby:
Schule; Waldemarstraße 118
1900-02 • Ludwig Hoffmann
Turm der Emmauskirche; Lausitzer Platz
1890-93 • August Orth
Schule; Görlitzer Ufer 2, Taborstraße 12-13
1900-02 • Ludwig Hoffmann
Abspannwerk; Paul-Lincke-Ufer 20-22
1925-26 • Hans Müller
Erdmannshof; Paul-Lincke-Ufer 39-40
1909 • Ernst Schneckenberg

G 15 U-Bahnhof Schlesisches Tor
Berlin-Kreuzberg; Skalitzer Straße
1899-1901 • Hans Grisebach, Georg Dinklage

Seinen Ausgang nahm das Berliner U-Bahnnetz von der Hochbahnstrecke zwischen Warschauer Brücke und dem »Knie«, dem heutigen Ernst-Reuter-Platz. Nur Charlottenburg hatte sich gegen eine oberirdische Schnellbahn gewehrt. Durch die Straßen der damaligen Berliner Vorstädte verläuft die Bahn auf straßenräumlich störenden Brücken und Viadukten. Von 1896 bis 1902 baute die Firma Siemens & Halske die Strecke und einige Bahnhöfe in schmucklos sachlicher Form. Doch der sonst so ornamentierfreudigen Zeit mußten Zugeständnisse gemacht werden: Einige Bahnhöfe wurden von freien Architekten entworfen und gestaltet, nicht nach einem gemeinsamen Konzept, sondern jeder nach seinen Vorstellungen. Unterschiedliche Jugendstilschöpfungen kamen dabei heraus, aber auch historistisch-konservative Bauten wie der Bahnhof Schlesisches Tor. Seine etwas verzwickte Lage zwischen den sich kreuzenden Straßen und vor der Kurve zur Oberbaumbrücke teilt sich dem Gebäude mit und verhilft ihm zu einer recht reizvollen verwinkelten Vielfalt. Das gibt Platz für Läden, eine Bahnhofswirtschaft, ein paar Säulchen und einen Turm, schafft also die vertraute Bahnhofsatmosphäre.

The Berlin underground system started from the overhead railway section between Warschauer Brücke and the «Knie», now Ernst-Reuter-Platz. Only Charlottenburg resisted an overground railway. The railway runs through the streets of the former suburbs of Berlin on bridges and viaducts that are an undesirable imposition on the urban space. The firm of Siemens & Halske built the line and some stations in an undecorated and functional style from 1896 to 1902. But some concession had to be made to a period that otherwise took such joy in ornament: some stations were designed by independent architects, not following any common plan, but each expressing his own ideas. This produced various Jugendstil creations, but also conservative historicist buildings like Schlesisches Tor station. The somewhat tricky site between intersecting streets and in front of the curve of the Oberbaum bridge communicated itself to the building and helped to give it a charming variety, with a great number of corners. This gives space for shops, a station café, a few little columns and a tower, thus creating the familiar station atmosphere.

in der Nähe/nearby:
Lagerhaus Südost; Pfuehlstraße 5
1906-07 • Kurt Berndt
»Bonjour Tristesse«; Schlesische Straße 8
1982-83 • Alvaro Siza Vieira
Industriehaus; Schlesische Straße 26
1912 • Wilhelm Peters, Alfred Grenander

G 16 Wohn- und Geschäftshaus
Berlin-Kreuzberg; Kottbusser Damm 2-3
1910-11 • Bruno Taut

Über dreißig Jahre hat es gedauert, bis man sich endlich 1978 der Kriegsruine dieses frühen Baues von Bruno Taut annahm. Unter denkmalpflegerischen Aspekten wurde gerettet, was zu retten war, nämlich die Fassade. Sechs Meter dahinter beginnt ein Neubau. Daß ausgerechnet Hinrich und Inken Baller mit der schwierigen Aufgabe einer Verbindung von denkmalgeschütztem Altbau und wirtschaftlich vertretbarem Neubau betraut wurden, hat insofern seinen Reiz, da sowohl Taut mit dieser Fassade gestalterisch ein Wagnis beging, als auch das Architektenpaar Baller für eigenwillige Architektur bürgt. Straßen- und Hoffront sind aber säuberlich voneinander geschieden, und so stellt sich auch nicht die Frage, ob beides zusammenpaßt. Interessant sind die Lösungen für die Wohnungsschnitte. Im flachen Vorderteil des Hauses sind die alten Raumhöhen von 3,80 m erhalten, im rückwärtigen Bauteil gelten die geringeren Neubauhöhen. Das führt zu unterschiedlichen Höhenstufen von Raum zu Raum und zu einem unkonventionellen »Wohnerlebnis«.

Thirty years passed before a decision was made to do something about the wartime ruin of Bruno Taut's building in 1978. What could be rescued in terms of care for ancient monuments was rescued, and that was the façade. The new building starts six metres behind it. There is a certain charm in the fact that Hinrich and Inken Baller were entrusted with the difficult architectural task of linking the old listed building with a new building that was economically acceptable, as Taut himself took a risk with the design of the façade, and the Ballers can be relied upon to produce unconventional architecture. But street and courtyard façade are neatly separated, and so the question of whether they suit each other is never raised. Interesting solutions were found for the cross-section of the flats. In the shallow front part of the building the old room height of 3.8 metres has been retained, and the rear sections keep to the lower height for modern buildings. This gives different heights from room to room, and makes for an unconventional «living experience».

in der Nähe/nearby:
Wohnhaus; B-Neukölln; Bürknerstraße 13-14
1910 • Bruno Taut
Wohnhäuser; B-Kreuzberg; Fraenkelufer 38 u. 44
1982-84 • Hinrich Baller, Inken Baller
Wohnhaus; B-Kreuzberg; Fraenkelufer 26
1983-84 • Hinrich Baller, Inken Baller
»Wohnregal«; B-Kreuzberg; Admiralstraße 16
1984-86 • Nylund, Puttfarken & Stürzebecher
Bahnhof Kottbusser Tor; B-Kreuzberg; Skalitzer Straße
1927-29 • Alfred Grenander

H
Berlin
Vom Kreuzberg nach Wilmersdorf

Die in den sechziger Jahren des 19. Jahrhunderts stürmisch einsetzenden Stadterweiterungen griffen im Süden nun über den Landwehrkanal. Der Fall der Akzisemauer 1865 gab Neubauten den Raum, der Hobrechtplan von 1862 den rechtlichen Rahmen, der bei wachsenden Bodenpreisen dennoch durch die hohe Ausnutzung des Grundstücks bei Investitionen reichliche Gewinne versprach. Die später von Werner Hegemann zitierte »größte Mietkasernenstadt der Welt« konnte entstehen. Bis an den Rand des Höhenrückens Teltow schoben sich die Häuser heran, dann hemmte ein ausgedehntes Militärgelände die fortschreitende Erschließung. Nach Westen begrenzten die Gleisnetze der Anhalter und der Potsdamer Bahn die neuen Viertel. Jenseits regte sich der »Neue Westen«. Beiderseits der Straße nach Potsdam wuchsen Geschäftshäuser aus dem Boden, in den Seitenstraßen Wohnhäuser. Bis zur Jahrhundertwende reichte die Bebauung schon an das Dorf Schöneberg heran, das nun seinerseits begann, Ackerland in Bauland umzuwandeln. Auch für Wilmersdorf kam nun der Aufschwung zur Stadt. Seit 1877 markierte bereits die Ringbahn die vorläufige Ziellinie städtischer Expansion. Mit dem Bayerischen Viertel wurde dann von 1895 an die Lücke geschlossen zwischen Berlin, Schöneberg, Wilmersdorf und Charlottenburg. 1910 fuhr der erste U-Bahnzug zum Innsbrucker Platz und 1913 durch Wilmersdorf nach Dahlem. Als 1920 Groß-Berlin gebildet wurde, lebten in Schöneberg wie auch in Wilmersdorf bereits über 100 000 Einwohner. Die zwanziger Jahre brachten manche städtebauliche Neuordnung. Südlich von Kreuzberg stellte das Siedlungsgebiet Neu-Tempelhof die Verbindung her zur früheren Landgemeinde Tempelhof. Einen großen Teil des ehemaligen Militärgeländes rüstete man zum Flughafen her. Die Randwanderung der Industrie bescherte dem Süd- und Westrand Tempelhofs entlang dem Teltowkanal und den Bahnlinien Fabrikansiedlungen. Der Südwesten Schönebergs mit dem alten Villengebiet Friedenau und Wilmersdorf bewahrten sich aber einen eher vornehmen Charakter, daran änderte auch die spätere Geschichte nichts mit Zerstörung und Wiederaufbau.

The city was growing at an enormous pace in the 1860s, and development started beyond the Landwehrkanal in the south. Removal of the excise wall in 1865 made room for new building, and the 1862 Hobrecht Plan provided the legal framework; although the price of land was rising, investors could expect large profits because of the high level of plot exploitation. The moment had come for the emergence of what Werner Hegemann was later to call «the biggest tenement city in the world». Building advanced as far as the Teltow ridge, then further development was blocked by an extensive military site. The new district was confined on the western side by the track networks of the Potsdam and Anhalt railways. Beyond this the «New West» was stirring. Big shops proliferated on both sides of the road to Potsdam, and residential buildings shot up in the side streets. Development had reached the village of Schöneberg by the turn of the century, where a start had already been made on turning agricultural land into building land. Wilmersdorf now began to turn into a town as well. The Ringbahn, the railway encircling the city, had marked the provisional limit for urban expansion since 1877. The gap between Berlin, Schöneberg, Wilmersdorf and Charlottenburg was closed by the building of the Bayerisches Viertel from 1895. In 1910 the first underground train ran to Innsbrucker Platz and in 1913 through Wilmersdorf to Dahlem. When Greater Berlin was formed in 1920, there were already 100,000 inhabitants in both Schöneberg and Wilmersdorf. The twenties brought a good deal of urban redevelopment. The Neu-Tempelhof settlement area established a connection with the former rural community of Tempelhof. A large part of the former military site was developed as an airport. Industry's migration to the periphery brought workers' estates to the southern and western edge of Tempelhof along the Teltow canal and the railway line. South-western Schöneberg with the old villa district of Friedenau and Wilmersdorf maintained their exclusive character, however, and this was not changed by the destruction and rebuilding later history was to bring.

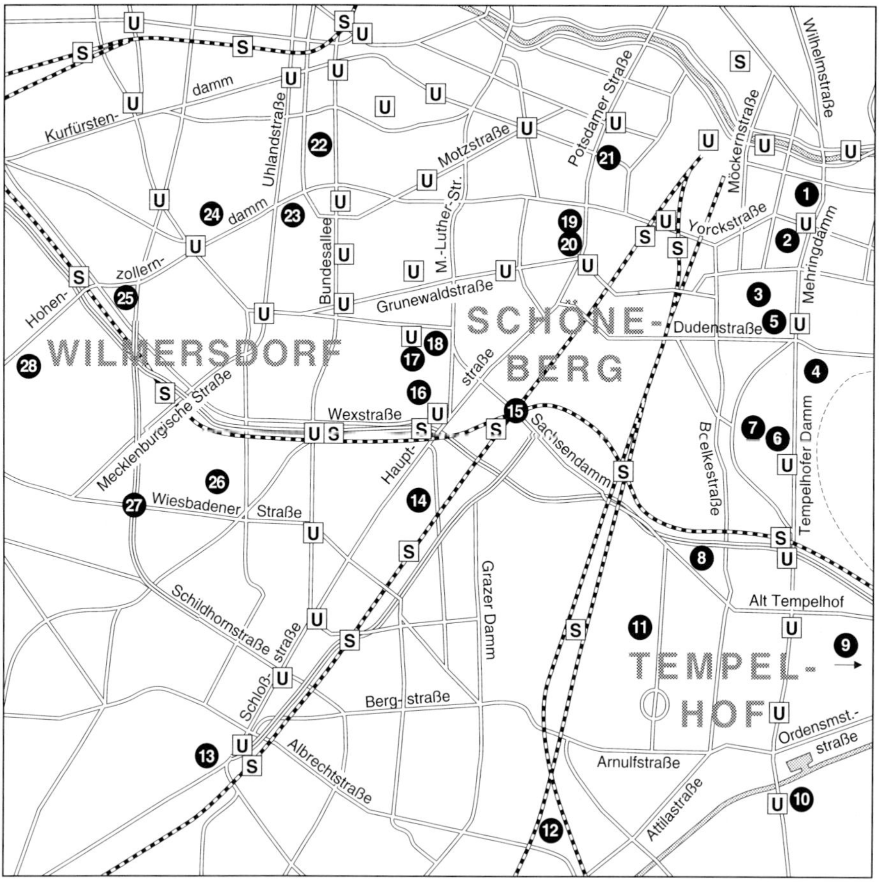

H 1 Kaserne des 1. Garde-Dragoner-Regiments
H 2 Riehmers Hofgarten
H 3 Befreiungsdenkmal
H 4 Zentralflughafen Tempelhof
H 5 Verbandshaus der Buchdrucker
H 6 Wohnhäuser Paradestraße
H 7 Siedlung Neutempelhof
H 8 Reichspostzentralamt
H 9 Dampfwaschwerk Reibedanz
H 10 Ullsteinhaus
H 11 Fabrik Schwarzkopf
H 12 Fabrik Scherk
H 13 Bürohaus Schloßstraße
H 14 Ceciliengärten
H 15 S-Bahnhof Schöneberg
H 16 Deutsche Krankenversicherung
H 17 U-Bahnhof Rathaus Schöneberg
H 18 Rathaus Schöneberg
H 19 Kathreiner-Hochhaus
H 20 Kolonnaden am Kleistpark
H 21 Hochbahnhof Bülowstraße
H 22 Joachimsthaler Gymnasium
H 23 Kirche am Hohenzollernplatz
H 24 Senatsverwaltung für Bau- und Wohnungswesen
H 25 Russische Kirche
H 26 Rheinisches Viertel
H 27 Autobahnüberbauung
H 28 Kreuzkirche

H 1 Kaserne des 1. Garde-Dragoner-Regiments
Berlin-Kreuzberg; Mehringdamm 20/24
1850-53 • Fleischinger, Drewitz, Becker

Die romantische Begeisterung für verfallene Burgzinnen und die in Mode gekommene englische Tudorgotik, wie sie sich im Schloß Babelsberg zeigte, mögen Antrieb für eine Kasernengestaltung gewesen sein, die bis etwa 1850 in Berlin und Potsdam mehrfach zu beobachten ist. Die Kreuzberger Kaserne gleicht der vier Jahre zuvor in Moabit errichteten Ulanenkaserne, der Stülersche Skizzen zugrunde lagen, aber auch Schinkels Gardehusarenkaserne in Potsdam. Es sind alle langgezogene Trakte, die durch einen Mittelbau und zwei Kopfbauten gegliedert sind. Putzquader müssen als preiswerte, aber dekorative Fassadenlösung genügen. Was bei Schinkel noch schlichte Rechteckfenster waren, sind nun bei den späteren Bauten Rundbogenfenster, die zwecks wirtschaftlicher Beheizung recht klein ausfallen. Auf dem rückwärtigen Gelände befanden sich die schlichten Nebenbauten für Reitbahn und Pferdeställe, die zum Teil noch erhalten sind. Mit der Entmilitarisierung Deutschlands nach dem Ersten Weltkrieg wurde die Kaserne dem Finanzamt Kreuzberg zugewiesen.

Romantic enthusiasm for ancient castle battlements and the increasingly fashionable English Tudor style, as seen in the palace at Babelsberg, may have been the inspiration for a barracks design that appeared in several places in Berlin and Potsdam until about 1850. The barracks in Kreuzberg was like the Ulanenkaserne built four years before in Moabit, based on sketches by Stüler, but also on Schinkel's barracks for the Hussar Guards in Potsdam. They are all long buildings, articulated by taller sections in the middle and at each end. Rectangular rendering had to serve as an economical but decorative solution for the façade. Schinkel had used plain rectangular windows, but in later buildings they have round arches, kept small to reduce heating bills. Plain outbuildings for riding school and stables were provided at the rear of the site, and some of these have survived. When Germany was demilitarized after the First World War the barracks was allotted to the Kreuzberg finance department.

in der Nähe/nearby:
Kirchhof; Mehringdamm 21
1819
Museum für Verkehr und Technik; Trebbiner Straße 8
1983-85 • Ulrich Wolff, Wolfgang Peters

H 2 Riehmers Hofgarten
Berlin-Kreuzberg; Hagelberger Straße 9-12, Großbeerenstraße 56-57, Yorckstraße 83-86
1881-92 • Wilhelm Ferdinand August Riehmer, Otto Moesk

Der intensive Wohnungsbau zum Ausgang des 19. Jahrhunderts führte bei später unterschiedlicher Schuldzuweisung zur bekannten Berliner Mietkasernen-Misere. Letztlich lag der Grund in einer zu dichten Bebauung schmaler, aber tiefer Grundstücke in zu großen Straßenblöcken. Dunkle, stickige Hinterhöfe mit minderwertigen Wohnungen waren die Folge. Es ist das Verdienst einiger Vereine und Gesellschaften zur Besserung des Berliner Wohnungselends, aber auch weniger privater Bauherren, wenn bauliche Lösungen entstanden, die solchen Mißständen vorbeugten. Der Maurermeister Riehmer zeigte, wie durch eine kleine Wohnstraße das Blockinnere aufgeschlossen werden kann und man so ruhige und menschenwürdige Wohnungen gewinnt. Rund zwanzig Häuser sind hier als intimes Viertel zusammengefaßt, ein Beispiel, das noch mehrfach aufgegriffen wurde, bevor der Wohnungsbau in den Siedlungen der zwanziger Jahre gänzlich neue Wege ging.

Intensive building of residential accommodation at the end of the nineteenth century later led to Berlin's celebrated tenement troubles, for which various causes have been identified. In the last resort the reason was excessively dense development of narrow but deep plots, using street blocks that were too large. Credit is due to some associations and companies concerned to alleviate the wretchedness of accommodation in Berlin, but also to a few private developers who found architectural solutions that prevented such unfortunate states of affairs from coming about. Master builder Riehmer showed how a small residential street can be used to open up the interior of a block and thus create quiet and dignified living conditions. About twenty buildings join to form an intimate little district here, an example that was often followed before residential building started to move in quite different directions in the twenties.

in der Nähe/nearby:
Rathaus Kreuzberg; Yorckstraße 4-11
1952-58 • Willy Kreuer
Bonifatiuskirche; Yorckstraße 88-89
1906-07 • Max Hasak
Schultheiss-Schankhaus; Methfesselstraße 28
1900-01 • Carl Teichen
Wasserhebewerk Kreuzberg; Fidicinstraße 32
1887-88 • Hugo Hartung, Richard Schultze

H 3 Befreiungsdenkmal
Berlin-Kreuzberg; Kreuzbergstraße
1818-21 • Karl Friedrich Schinkel

Zur Erinnerung an die Befreiungskriege 1813-15 und zur Ehrung der Gefallenen ließ Friedrich Wilhelm III. dieses Denkmal auf einer Erhebung vor dem Tempelhofer Exerzierfeld errichten. Das Eiserne Kreuz auf der Spitze des Monumentes gab dem Hügel fortan den Namen Kreuzberg. Das Kreuz wurde auch zur Grundfläche des Denkmals, das dem Turmhelm eines gotischen Domes nachempfunden ist. Die Romantik und gerade Schinkel hatten zur Gotik ein inniges Verhältnis, und so muß sich dieser fälschlich als »deutsch« bevorzugte Stil für ein Nationaldenkmal zur Erinnerung an den Sieg über Napoleon besonders geeignet haben. Das in Eisenguß hergestellte Gebilde trägt zwölf Standbilder von Rauch, Tieck und Wichmann sowie Tafeln mit Namen der entscheidenden Schlachten. 1878-79 wurde es auf eine 8 m hohe Bastei gestellt und auf die Großbeerenstraße ausgerichtet. Seit 1893 ist zu seinen Füßen ein Wasserfall dem Zackenfall im Riesengebirge nachgebildet.

Friedrich Wilhelm III had this monument built on an eminence outside the Tempelhof parade ground in memory of the Wars of Liberation, 1813-5. The iron cross at the top of the monument gave the hill the name Kreuzberg (cross hill) from then on. The shape of the cross also provided the ground plan of the monument, which is like the spire of a Gothic cathedral. The Romantics, and Schinkel in particular, had an intimate relationship with Gothic, and thus this style, wrongly preferred because it was «German», must have seemed particularly suitable for a national monument in memory of the victory over Napoleon. The structure is in cast iron and carries twelve statues by Rauch, Tieck and Wichmann, and also plaques bearing the names of the decisive battles. In 1878-9 it was placed on a plinth 8 metres high, and aligned with Grossbeerenstrasse. Since 1893 there has been a waterfall below it, modelled on the Zackenfall in the Riesengebirge.

in der Nähe/nearby:
Viktoriapark; Kreuzbergstraße
1888-94 • Hermann Mächtig

H 4 Zentralflughafen Tempelhof
Berlin-Tempelhof; Platz der Luftbrücke
1936-41 • Ernst Sagebiel

Im Jahre 1922 hatte man das bisherige Exerzierfeld in Tempelhof zum Rollfeld eingeebnet, und 1924 entstanden südlich der Hasenheide, weit in das Gelände vorgeschoben, die ersten Flugzeughallen, denen bis 1925-29 ein Abfertigungsgebäude folgte. In den dreißiger Jahren rückte Tempelhof zum verkehrsreichsten Flugplatz Europas auf. Die dringenden Erweiterungen und die Vergrößerung des Rollfeldes machten eine bauliche Neuordnung notwendig, mit der Sagebiel, der Architekt des Luftfahrtministeriums, betraut wurde. Abgestimmt auf die Speerschen Pläne der Neugestaltung Berlins und im Stil gigantomanischer Repräsentationssucht begann 1936 der Bau eines Viertelrundes von 380 m Länge, das sich mit einer 49 m tiefen Überdachung zum Flugfeld öffnet. Im Scheitel schließt ein Komplex von 14 Flügeln an, der sich symmetrisch und in monumentaler Höhensteigerung einem geplanten runden Platz angleicht und jenseits in einer diagonalen Parkachse auf das Kreuzbergdenkmal ausrichten sollte. In den vorgesehenen drei Jahren konnten die Arbeiten nicht abgeschlossen werden, manche Teile standen erst im Rohbau, als der Krieg einen Baustopp diktierte. Nach 1945 zunächst Militärflugplatz, wurde Tempelhof von 1951 bis 1959 nach und nach zum Zivilflughafen ausgebaut, bis die Beengtheit des Platzes zum Ausweichen nach Tegel zwang.

In 1922 the former parade ground in Tempelhof was levelled to form a runway, and in 1924 the first airport buildings appeared, pushing deep into the site; these were followed by a terminal building in 1925-9. In the thirties Tempelhof became the busiest airport in Europe. Urgent need to extend and enlarge the runway meant re-arrangement of the buildings, and this was entrusted to Sagebiel, the Air Ministry architect. Work started in 1936 on building a quarter circle 380 metres long, opening on to the airfield with a roofed area 49 metres deep, absolutely in tune with Speer's plans for redesigning Berlin and showing megalomaniac obsession with building for the sake of prestige. At the vertex is a complex of buildings in fourteen sections, symmetrical and with monumental emphasis on height, like a strictly planned, rounded urban square, and beyond this a diagonal park axis intended to align the whole complex with the Kreuzberg monument. It proved impossible to complete the work in the anticipated three years, and many parts existed only as shells when the war put a stop to building. After 1945 Tempelhof was at first a military airfield, then gradually extended as a civilian airport from 1951 to 1959, until restricted space forced the move to Tegel.

in der Nähe/nearby:
Luftbrückendenkmal; Platz der Luftbrücke
1951 • Eduard Ludwig

H 5 Verbandshaus der Buchdrucker
Berlin-Kreuzberg; Dudenstraße 10
1925-26 • Max Taut, Franz Hoffmann

Durch Spenden von Gewerkschaftsmitgliedern konnte der Bau des Verbandshauses ermöglicht werden. Im Vorderhaus befinden sich Wohnungen der Verbandsleitung und Läden, im Hof ein Druckereigebäude. Die Anlage sucht einerseits Anschluß an die großen Berliner Industriehöfe des 19. Jahrhunderts, andererseits folgt Max Taut der wirtschaftlichen Notwendigkeit, das ungünstig tiefe Grundstück sinnvoll auszunutzen. Während die Straßenfront noch mit gelben Klinkern verblendet wurde, wählte man für das Druckereigebäude ein Stahlbetonskelett, dessen außenliegende Stützen wie auch die Brüstungen sich in Sichtbeton geben. Adolf Behne betrachtete deshalb das Buchdruckerhaus »als den entscheidenden Bau am Beginn der Neuen Sachlichkeit«.

Donations from trade unions members made it possible to build this association building. The front section contains accommodation for the directors of the association, and shops, and there is a printing shop in the courtyard. On the one hand the building looks back to the great landmarks in Berlin industrial architecture of the nineteenth century, and on the other Max Taut follows the economic necessity of making sensible use of the unsuitably deep plot. The street façade was clad in yellow clinker, but a reinfoced concrete skeleton was chosen for the printing shop, and its outer supports and also the window breasts were in exposed concrete. For this reason Adolf Behne considered the book printers' building to be «the key building at the beginning of Neue Sachlichkeit».

in der Nähe/nearby:
Wohnhauszeile mit Läden und Wohnhochhaus; B-Kreuzberg; Dudenstraße 12/20, Methfesselstraße 49
1955-56 • Max Taut
Wohnhausgruppe; B-Kreuzberg; Dudenstraße 26/38
1913-14 • Adolf Matheus
Oberstufenzentrum; B-Tempelhof; Dudenstraße 23-55
1977-79 • Dietrich Bangert, Bernd Jansen, Stefan Scholz, Axel Schultes

H 6 Wohnhäuser Paradestraße
Berlin-Tempelhof; Tempelhofer Damm 44, 44 a, 46
1990-91 • Rebecca Chestnutt und Robert Niess

»Es galt, die vorgegebene stadträumliche Situation im Wesentlichen aufzunehmen und zu unterstützen«, heißt es bei den Architekten. In diesem Satz ist die nahezu unmögliche Forderung an den Wettbewerbsentwurf verschlüsselt, zwischen dem Kolossalbau des Flughafengebäudes und der beschaulichen Siedlung Neutempelhof eine architektonische Vermittlung zu bewerkstelligen. Was hier stadtplanerische Unfähigkeit um 1910 und städtebaulicher Größenwahn in der Nazizeit an Ungereimtheiten hinterlassen hatten, das wurde zwei Neubauten arglos als erdrückende Erblast aufgebürdet. Allein wenn die spektakulären Fronten der Neubauten den Blick vom umgebenden Dilemma ablenken, erfüllen sie schon die gestellte Aufgabe. Darüberhinaus vereinen sie aber auch Blockhaftigkeit mit Kleinteiligkeit und scheinen so tatsächlich hierher zu passen. Daß dem Mietwohnungsbau in einer klaren Absage an gestalterische Langeweile Individualität zugestanden wird, reiht die Häuser in die erfreulichen Beispiele neuerer Baugesinnung ein.

«The objective was essentially to take up and support the urbanistic situation», as the architects put it. This statement paraphrases the almost impossible demand formulated in the competition brief, calling for an architecture which would mediate between the colossal structure of the airport complex and the contemplative residential estate Neutempelhof. The incongruities caused by urbanist failures around 1910 and by the megalomania of the Nazis were simply placed as a suffocating historical burden on two new buildings. If the spectacular façades of the new buildings distract from the surrounding dilemma, they are already answering to their task. In addition they also combine a block structure with careful detailing and thus seem to fit quite well. The fact that this housing architecture places individualism above designed boredom makes these buildings true models of a refreshing new approach.

in der Nähe/nearby:
Wohn- und Geschäftshaus; Kaiserkorso 155
1912-13 • Bruno Möhring
Wohnhäuser; Tempelhofer Damm 32/102
1927-28 • Eduard Jobst Siedler

H 8 Reichspostzentralamt
Berlin-Tempelhof; Ringbahnstraße 126-134
1925-28 • Pfuhl

H 7 Siedlung Neutempelhof
Berlin-Tempelhof; Manfred-von-Richthofen-Straße 34/218 u. 35/217, Paradestraße 3-72 usw.
1920-28 • Fritz Bräuning

Der erste Plan zur Bebauung des Tempelhofer Feldes kam 1909 auf. Er sah noch die übliche tiefe Blockbebauung vor. Dem folgte 1911 ein Plan von Hermann Jansen mit fünfgeschossigen Häusern entlang den Blockrändern und einem breiten Parkgürtel. Im Tauziehen um das Gelände zwischen Militärfiskus und der Stadt Berlin gesellte sich nun auch eine Verwertungs-Gesellschaft hinzu, die einem Plan von Fritz Bräuning den Vorzug gab. Er schlug die später weitgehend ausgeführten zweigeschossigen Reihen- und Einzelhäuser vor, die ein Ring höherer Bauten umgeben sollte. So machte das Projekt innerhalb von zwei Jahren die gesamte Entwicklung vom Mietkasernenviertel bis zur Gartenstadt durch. Die dann in den zwanziger Jahren fertiggestellte Siedlung wurde von Bräuning durch Kirche und Schule ergänzt, die Randbebauung im Osten stammt von Eduard Jobst Siedler, an den Bauten im Norden beteiligten sich Walter Borchard sowie Ernst und Günther Paulus. Einige Gevierte blieben lange Zeit frei, bis sie in den fünfziger Jahren dem Wohnungsneubau zur Verfügung standen.

The first plan for development of the Tempelhofer Feld was produced in 1909, and intended to keep to the usual deep block development. This was followed in 1911 by a plan by Hermann Jansen suggesting five-storey buildings at the block peripheries and a broad park belt. In the course of the tug-of-war over the site between the military finance department and the city of Berlin a land-use company also became involved, and they opted for a plan submitted by Fritz Bräuning. He suggested the pattern of twin-storey terraced and detached buildings that was later much used; they were to be surrounded by a ring of taller buildings. Thus in two years the project developed from tenement district to garden city. Bräuning added a church and a school to the estate, which was finally completed in the twenties; peripheral development in the east is by Eduard Jobst Siedler, and Walter Borchard and Ernst and Günter Paulus were involved with the buildings in the north. Some plots remained vacant for a long time, and were made available for new building in the fifties.

in der Nähe/nearby:
Schule Tempelhofer Feld; Boelckestraße 58
1927-28 • Fritz Bräuning
Kirche auf dem Tempelhofer Feld; Wolffring 72
1927-28 • Fritz Bräuning

In den zwanziger Jahren machte die rasche technische Entwicklung auch bei den zentralen Behörden der Post eine Neuorganisation notwendig. Für das neu geschaffene Telegraphentechnische Reichsamt, das spätere Reichspostzentralamt, wurden zunächst Lagergebäude des Militärs in Tempelhof freigemacht. Als diese nicht ausreichten, begann man einen Neubau. Er enthielt eine Fülle von Verwaltungsräumen und Labors, aber auch eine Bibliothek und einen Hörsaal. Wegen der funktechnischen Versuche waren alle Eisenteile des Baues über aufgeschweißte Drähte an eine Erdung angeschlossen. Äußerlich gab sich der Komplex zeitgemäß in blauroten Klinkern, sie hatten zudem den Vorteil einer pflegeleichten und widerstandsfähigen Haut, zumal das Gelände in der rußigen Luft zwischen dem Tempelhofer Industriegebiet und am Schnittpunkt der Anhalter Bahn und der Ringbahn liegt. Ging im Krieg der expressionistische Zinnenkranz verloren, büßte die Fassade 1970 durch »Modernisierung« der Sprossenfenster viel von ihrem Charakter ein. Trotzdem bleibt der in seiner Masse sorgfältig gegliederte Komplex mit seinen textilen Klinkerflächen und den überraschenden Details in Portalen oder auch in Treppen und Lichthöfen ein Architekturerlebnis besonderer Art.

In the twenties, rapid technical development necessitated reorganization in central post offices. At first military warehouses were made available for the newly-created Telegraphentechnisches Reichsamt, later the Reichspostzentralamt. When these were no longer adequate, a new building was started. It contained a lavish number of storerooms and labs, but also library and lecture theatre. As radio experiments were conducted, all the iron components of the building were earthed with welded wires. The exterior was clad in bluish-red clinker, as was customary at the time. This gave the added advantage of providing a resistant skin that was easy to maintain, especially as the site was in the sooty atmosphere of the industrial area of Tempelhof, and at the junction of the Anhalt railway and the Ringbahn. The Expressionist façade was destroyed in the war, and the building sacrificed a great deal of its character when the transom windows were «modernized» in 1970. Nevertheless the carefully articulated mass of the complex with its textile clinker surfaces and surprising detail in portals, stairs and air wells remains a very special architectural experience.

in der Nähe/nearby:
BSR-Hauptwerkstatt; Ringbahnstraße 96
1971-73 • Josef Paul Kleihues
Dorfkirche Tempelhof; Reinhardtplatz
Um 1250

H 9 Dampfwaschwerk Reibedanz
Berlin-Tempelhof; Teilestraße 23
1911-14 • Bruno Taut und Franz Hoffmann

Diese kleine, ziervolle Front eines ehemals weit ins Hintergelände reichenden Flachbaues nimmt die stilistischen Merkmale des Bauens um 1925 vorweg. Spitz vorspringende Pfeiler, Sägefriesfelder und plastische Ziegelschichten sind hier frühexpressionistische Gestaltungsmittel, ebenso wie der kontrastreiche Wechsel gelber und schwarzer Klinker. Bruno Taut, dem der Entwurf wohl überwiegend zugeschrieben werden kann, hatte um 1911 bereits an mehreren Häusern expressionistische Merkmale anklingen lassen, hier paart sich der neue Stil jedoch nicht mehr mit herkömmlicher Baukunst, vielmehr leitet er bedingt durch den Industriebau über zu einer sachlichen Architektur. Das steht in Einklang mit Tauts damaligem Streben nach einer Erneuerung der Kunst und dem unbedingten Bruch mit kraftlos-historistischer Baukunst. Ängstlichen Architekturphilistern muß damals die Wäschereifassade als Provokation erschienen sein.

The delicate, ornamented front of a low-rise building which once extended far into the depth of the site anticipates the building style of the mid nineteen-twenties. Sharply projecting pillars, sawn frieses and sculptural brickwork represent early expressionist forms of design, as does the contrastive combination of yellow and black clinker. As early as 1911, Bruno Taut, to whom the design may largely be attributed, had already toyed with expressionist elements in several of his buildings. In this case, however, the new style is not associated with traditional architecture but rather with a new, functional type of architecture based on the design of industrial buildings. This corresponds with Taut's striving, at the time, for a renewal in the arts and the unqualified break with a historical architecture sapped of all strength. For timid Philistines of architecture, the façade of this commercial laundry must have come as a provocative shock.

in der Nähe/nearby:
Rathaus Tempelhof; Tempelhofer Damm 165/169
1936-38 • Hellmut Delius
Bürogebäude; Germaniastraße 14-17
1993-94 • Bauch & Tatic
Monopolverwaltung; Ringbahnstraße 10-14
1928 • Paul Renner

H 10 Ullsteinhaus
Berlin-Tempelhof; Mariendorfer Damm 1-3
1925-26 • Eugen Schmohl

Das Ullsteinhaus entstand als »Repräsentationsgebäude des größten Zeitungs- und Zeitschriftenverlages Europas, dessen Haus augenfälliges Wahrzeichen seiner Größe und kulturellen Bedeutung sein sollte«. Die Größe des Baukörpers und die strenge Vertikalität der Gliederung verleihen ihm in der Tat Monumentalität, und der Turm betont die Bedeutung des Gebäudes. Dekorative Parabelbögen, phantasievoll geformte Treppentürme und Portalbauten, ausschwingende Eckstützen und ein reicher bildhauerischer Schmuck – für den man allein ein Zehntel der Bausumme ausgab – unterstreichen das für einen Industriebau untypische Repräsentationsgebaren. Schmohl, der es ablehnte, nur zweckmäßig zu bauen, verkleidete diesen Stahlbetonbau mit Klinkern. Das war am Vorabend der »Neuen Sachlichkeit« ein Wagnis, welches er nur im Schutz des ausdrücklichen Wunsches des Bauherrn eingehen konnte. Funktionalität war Nebensache – Schmohl mußte sogar ohne einen Aufstellungsplan für die Maschinen bauen, was nachträglich wochenlange Stemmarbeiten nötig machte. Der städtebauliche Wert des Ullsteinhauses an der Kreuzung des Teltowkanals mit der großen Berliner Südachse bleibt aber unbestritten.

The Ullstein building came into being as «a prestigious home for the largest publisher of newspapers and magazines in Europe, whose building is intended to be a striking symbol of the greatness and cultural significance of the house». The size of the building and the rigorous verticality of its articulation do indeed give it a monumental quality, and the tower emphasizes its significance. Decorative parabolic arches, imaginatively shaped staircase towers and portal structures, corner piers curving outwards and lavish sculptural decoration – costing a tenth of the total budget for the building – emphasize the need to project a prestigious image atypical in an industrial building. Schmohl refused to build in a way that was merely functional and expedient, and clad this reinforced concrete building with clinker. This was a risk on the eve of «Neue Sachlichkeit», and he could only take that risk under the protection of the client's express wish. The latter had not even provided his architect with complete information about the position of the machines, with the result that weeks of retrospective bracing work were needed. But there is no controversy about the value of the Ullsteinhaus as part of the planned townscape at the point where the Teltow canal meets the great southern axis of Berlin.

in der Nähe/nearby:
Gewerbezentrum am Ullsteinhaus; Ullsteinstraße 114
1991-93 • Johanne Nalbach und Gernot Nalbach
Siedlung; B-Mariendorf; Monopolstraße 12-37 u. 46-87
1922-23 • Binder

H 11 Fabrik Schwarzkopf
Berlin-Schöneberg; Alboinstraße 36-42
1928-30 • Carl Mackensen

Der starke Einfluß von Högers Scherkfabrik in gestalterischer Hinsicht ist bei Mackensens Schwarzkopfwerk unübersehbar. Auch die Tatsache, daß noch 1928 der expressionistische Formenkanon für einen Industriebau zitiert wird, da sich doch bereits die Sachlichkeit als stilistisches Vorbild etabliert hat, weist auf das Motiv der Konkurrenz zwischen zwei Parfümerie-Unternehmen hin. Das soll aber Mackensens Leistung nicht schmälern. In der Verteilung der Baumassen ging er eigene Wege, gruppierte den hohen Fabrikationstrakt im Hintergrund, versteckte die häßlichen Liefervorgänge in einem Innenhof, den er mit umgreifenden niedrigen Flügeln und einer symmetrischen Toranlage faßte. Dem Reklamebedürfnis der Firma und der Repräsentationsabsicht des Gebäudes gab er einen Turm, dessen gläserner Aufbau von innen erleuchtet das Markenzeichen weithin kündet. Die Aufstockung der niedrigen Trakte 1936 und Modernisierungen der Nachkriegszeit haben die baukünstlerisch wertvolle Substanz weitgehend geschont.

It is impossible to overlook the influence of Höger's Scherk factory on the design of Mackensen's building for Schwarzkopf. And the fact that the formal canon of Expressionism was still being used for an industrial building in 1928, when Neue Sachlichkeit had already established itself as the style model, suggests a whiff of competition between the two perfume companies. But this is not to decry Mackensen's achievement. He went his own way as far as the distribution of building masses was concerned, grouping the high factory wing in the background and hiding the ugly delivery process in an inner courtyard, which he surrounded with low wings and a symmetrical gatehouse. The firm's need to advertise itself and the prestigious nature of the building he met with a tower, with the trade mark visible over long distances in the glass structure at the top; this was illuminated from within. Additional storeys added to the low wings in 1936 and post-war modernization largely maintained the architectural value of the building.

in der Nähe/nearby:
Schultheiss-Mälzerei; Bessemerstraße 2-14
1914-17 • Schlüter
Isophon-Werke; Eresburgstraße 22-23
1923-24 • Otto Schröder
Brotfabrik; Eresburgstraße 24-27
1927-28 • Bruno Buch

H 12 Fabrik Scherk
Berlin-Südende; Kelchstraße 31
1926 • Fritz Höger

Das Gebäude entstand als erster Abschnitt einer weit größer geplanten Anlage, die sich mit gestaffelt angesetzten Baugliedern zu einem großen Dreieck entsprechend den durch die nahen Bahnlinien vorgezeichneten Fluchten ergänzen sollte. »Dreieck« und »Höger« assoziieren sofort »Chilehaus«, und diesem Hamburger Kontorhaus ist die Scherkfabrik auch gestalterisch verwandt. Mit den Mitteln des Expressionismus versteht es Höger, dem zweckmäßig regelmäßigen Baukörper Charakter zu geben. Das textile Ziegelmuster, die Rautenfenster und die Kontrastierung dunkler Klinker und weißer Rahmen beleben den Bau und machten ihn durch viele weitere Einzelheiten, die inzwischen unverständlicherweise beseitigt wurden, zu einem architektonischen Kleinod. Heute läßt sich nur noch erahnen, welchen Eindruck die Fassade mit der Eingangspagode und den wohlabgestimmten Sprossenfenstern gemacht hat.

This building was the first stage of a complex intended to be much larger; staggered elements were to be arranged in a large triangle corresponding with the lines dictated by the nearby railway tracks. «Triangle» and «Höger» immediately suggest «Chilehaus», and the Scherk factory is indeed related to the celebrated Hamburg office building in its design. Höger uses the medium of Expressionism to give character to the inevitably regular building. A textile brick pattern, lozenge windows and the contrast of dark clinker with white frames enliven the building, and together with other details that have in the meantime for some incomprehensible reason been removed, make it an architectural jewel. Today one can only imagine the impression the façade must have made with entrance pagoda and perfectly harmonized transom windows.

in der Nähe/nearby:
Rathaus Lankwitz; B-Lankwitz; Leonorenstraße 70
1910-11 • Gebr. Ratz
Sternwarte; B-Schöneberg; Munsterdamm 86-90
1962-63 • Carl Bassen
Rauchlose Siedlung; B-Steglitz; Munsterdamm 1/15
1931-32 • Mebes & Emmerich
Wasserturm Steglitz; B-Steglitz; Bergstraße 34-38
1914 • Hans Müller

H 13 Bürohaus
Berlin-Steglitz; Schloßstraße 40
1991-92 • Assmann, Salomon und Scheidt

Im Schlagschatten des umstrittenen Steglitzer Kreisels liegt zwischen Grenzburg- und Muthesiusstraße ein Gebiet, das den Folgen des letzten Krieges und dem bizarren Wechsel stadtplanerischer Ideologien seine städtebauliche Heterogenität verdankt. Als Wiedergutmachung wurde 1987 unter dem Titel »Steglitzer Kulturviertel« ein Ideenwettbewerb ausgeschrieben. Gewinner waren die Architekten Assmann, Salomon und Scheidt. Als eine erste Stufe der Realisation entstand das Geschäftshaus Schloßstraße 40. Mit einem hohen Maß an Eigenwilligkeit wird hier den vielfältigen Forderungen nach stilistischer Rücksichtnahme begegnet, eine häßliche Brandwand versteckt und ein Keim für architektonische Stadtreparatur gelegt.

Located in the shadow of the controversial Steglitzer Kreisel, the area between Grenzburgstrasse and Muthesiusstrasse owes much of its homogeneity in terms of urban development to the consequences of the last war and the sometimes bizarre shifts in town-planning ideologies. In order to make amends, a competition was held in 1987 under the heading of «Steglitzer Kulturviertel.» It was won by architects Assmann, Salomon and Scheidt. In a first phase of construction, a commercial building was erected at Schlosstrasse 40. With a marked degree of individuality this building responds to the various demands for stylistic discretion, at the same time succeeding in hiding an ugly fire-wall and laying the foundations for architectural repair of the city.

in der Nähe/nearby:
Rathaus Steglitz; Schloßstraße 37
1896-97 • Reinhardt & Süßenguth
Ausstellungspavillon Winter; Schloßstraße 38
1951 • Curt Hans Fritzsche
Steglitzer Kreisel; Schloßstraße 78-82
1969-75 • Sigrid Kreszmann-Zschach
Matthäus-Gemeindehaus; Schloßstraße 44 a-e
1928-30 • Otto Rudolf Salvisberg
Wrangelschlößchen; Schloßstraße 48
1804 • David Gilly, Heinrich Gentz
Wasserturm Fichtenberg; Schmidt-Ott-Straße 13
1894

H 14 Ceciliengärten
Berlin-Schöneberg; Rubensstraße 14/50
1924-26 • Heinrich Lassen

Nach dem Prinzip der aufgelockerten Blockbebauung hatte Paul Wolf 1912 einen Entwurf für eine Wohnanlage »In den Ceciliengärten« geliefert, auf den Lassen dann ein Jahrzehnt später weitgehend zurückgriff. Kennzeichnend ist der Verzicht auf Hinterhäuser und die Schaffung weiter begrünter Innenhöfe. So ist auch die Wohnstraße Ceciliengärten größtenteils angerartig aufgeweitet und als stiller Wohnplatz gestaltet. Die Baukörper variieren in der Höhe, setzen mit ihren höheren Kopfbauten straßenräumliche Betonungen. Die Fassaden zeigen in ihrer lebhaften Gliederung einen maßvollen Expressionismus, der sich wechselnder Formen und Farben bedient. Alle Wohnungen haben Küche, Bad sowie eine kleine Loggia, und selbst die Zweizimmerwohnungen sind mit 72 m² Nutzfläche noch recht geräumig.

Paul Wolf presented a design for a development «In den Ceciliengärten» on the principle of broken-up block building in 1912, and Lassen had recourse to this a decade later. Characteristic features are the lack of rear building and the creation of spacious, planted inner courtyards. Thus Ceciliengärten as a residential street is largely broadened in village green style, and designed as a quiet square in which to live. The buildings vary in height, and the larger sections at the end of each block set accents in the street picture. The lively articulation of the façades is moderately Expressionist, using alternating shapes and colours. All the flats have bathroom, kitchen and a little loggia, and even the one-bedroom flats are quite spacious, with 72 square metres of usable floor space.

in der Nähe/nearby:
Rathaus Friedenau; B-Friedenau; Breslauer Platz
1914-16 • Hans Altmann
Roxy-Palast; B-Friedenau; Hauptstraße 78-79
1929 • Martin Punitzer
Bauklempnerei; B-Friedenau; Bennigsenstraße 23-24
1904-07 • Peter Vogler

H 15 S-Bahnhof Schöneberg
Berlin-Schöneberg; Dominicusstraße 56
1930-33 • Carl Heinz Schwennecke, Erich Zimmermann
1991-93 • Orlando Figallo & Peter Rottwinkel

Im Zusammenhang mit der Elektrifizierung der S-Bahn wurde die Kreuzung der Wannseebahn mit der Ringbahn zu einem Bahnhof ausgebaut. Gleichzeitig wurde das Verkehrshindernis der engen Straßenunterführung beseitigt und neue Brückenträger eingezogen. Der zweigeschossige Bahnhof erhielt für den oberen Bahnsteig eine allseits verglaste Halle, für den unteren Bahnsteig, der im Windschatten der oberen Halle liegt, genügte eine ein- und teils zweistielige Überdachung mit offenen Seiten. Breite Bahnsteige und breite Treppen charakterisieren den wichtigen Umsteigebahnhof. Die anschließenden Brückenbauwerke über den Straßenzug Dominicusstraße–Sachsendamm verdeutlichen die Schwierigkeiten bei der Konstruktion innerstädtischer Bahnüberführungen. Die Breite der teils spitzwinklig unterführten Hauptverkehrsstraße, die Forderung nach einer für Straßenbahn und Doppelstockbus ausreichenden lichten Durchfahrtshöhe und die zusätzlichen Lasten durch das Bremsen und Anfahren der S-Bahnzüge in unmittelbarer Nähe des Bahnhofs verlangten eine sorgfältige Ausbildung von Trägern und Widerlagern. Während für die oben liegenden Ringbahngleise stützenfreie Vollwandträger der imposanten Höhe von vier Metern eingesetzt werden konnten, bedurfte es bei den tieferen Wannseebahngleisen einer Mittelstützenreihe, da hier nur schwächere Träger Platz fanden.

When the S-Bahn was electrified, the point at which the Ringbahn crossed the S-Bahn was developed as a station. At the same time the narrow road underpass, a traffic bottleneck, was removed, and new bridge girders installed. The station is on two levels, and a hall glazed on all sides was provided for the upper platform, while for the lower platform, protected from the wind by the upper hall, an open-sided shelter, supported sometimes on one and sometimes on two shafts, was sufficient. This is an important interchange station, and so had wide platforms and stairs. The adjacent bridges over Dominicusstrasse and Sachsendamm make clear the difficulties of building railway bridges in towns. The fact that the main road passes underneath at an acute angle in places, the need for sufficient height for tram and double-decker buses to pass through, and additional strain caused by the braking and pulling away of S-Bahn trains so near the station required a careful arrangement of girders and abutments. For the upper Ringbahn track it was possible to use unpropped plate girders of the impressive height of four metres, but the lower Wannsee railway tracks needed a central row of supports, as there was room only for weaker girders.

in der Nähe/nearby:
Schaltwerk Ebersstraße; Werdauer Weg 6
1927-28 • Richard Brademann
Sport- und Lehrschwimmhalle; Sachsendamm 11
1963-67 • Hansrudolf Plarre

H 16 Haus der Deutschen Krankenversicherung
Berlin-Schöneberg; Innsbrucker Straße 26-27
1929-30 • Otto Rudolf Salvisberg

Eines der hervorragenden Beispiele für den Bürohausbau um 1930 ist das DKV-Gebäude in Schöneberg. Salvisberg präsentiert diesen Bau der Neuen Sachlichkeit hinter einer Travertinfassade mit waagerechten Fensterbändern in den Bürogeschossen und senkrechten Bändern im Treppenhaus. Der Eingang schwingt gerundet zum Vestibül ein und schafft in der Gestaltung das Gegengewicht zu der Kantigkeit der übrigen Details, ein Kunstgriff, der damals auch von Architekten wie Bruno Taut, Erich Mendelsohn oder Hans Scharoun gerne verwendet wurde. Von welcher entscheidenden Bedeutung Details für das Erscheinungsbild eines Hauses sein können, zeigt der spätere Ersatz der ehemals quergeteilten Fenster durch neue längsgeteilte – die Fassade hat viel von ihrem eleganten Schwung verloren.

The DKV's (health insurance) building in Schöneberg is an outstanding example of office building around 1930. Salvisberg presents this example of Neue Sachlichkeit behind a Travertine façade with horizontal strips of windows in the office storeys and vertical strips for the stairwells. The entrance curves in to the vestibule, and its design creates a counterweight to the angular nature of the rest of the details, a trick that architects like Bruno Taut, Erich Mendelsohn and Hans Scharoun enjoyed using at the time. The windows were originally divided crossways, and later replacement with windows divided longways show the crucial importance of such details for the appearance of a building – the façade has lost a great deal of its elegant zest.

in der Nähe/nearby:
Hochhaus am Innsbrucker Platz; Innsbrucker Platz 4
1927-28 • Mebes & Emmerich
Dorfkirche Schöneberg; Hauptstraße 46
1764-66
Paul-Gerhardt-Kirche; Hauptstraße 47-48
1961-62 • Hermann Fehling, Daniel Gogel, Peter Pfankuch
Büro- und Geschäftshaus; Hauptstraße 117
1993-94 • Josef Paul Kleihues
Norbertkirche; Dominicusstraße 15/17
1918 • Carl Kühn
1962 • Hermann Fehling, Daniel Gogel, Peter Pfankuch
Verwaltungsgebäude (RIAS); Kufsteiner Straße 69
1931 • Walter Borchard
»Wohnen am Volkspark«; B-Wilmersdorf; Durlacher Straße 26/46
1978-80 • Christine Jachmann, Klaus D. Krebs, Monika Krebs

H 17 U-Bahnhof Rathaus Schöneberg
Berlin-Schöneberg; Innsbrucker Straße
1909-10 • Johann Emil Schaudt

Zwischen Bayerischem Viertel, Alt-Schöneberg und Ringbahn wurde gegen 1910 Ackerland zur Bebauung und Erweiterung des Stadtgebietes erschlossen. Die Planung war umfassend, Stadtbaurat Friedrich Gerlach war maßgeblich daran beteiligt. Gleichzeitig entstanden neue Wohnviertel, das Rathaus, eine Schule, Verwaltungsbauten wie das Nordsternhaus, der Stadtpark und die U-Bahnlinie – bis heute ein einzigartiges Architekturensemble. Als besondere Bauaufgabe erwies sich die Überquerung des Fenngrabens durch die U-Bahn. Da die Berliner U-Bahn wegen des hohen Grundwasserstandes als Unterpflasterbahn konzipiert war, mußte sie hier zutage treten. Gerlach und der Architekt Schaudt nutzten diese Situation zum Bau einer Station, die durch verglaste Wände einen überraschenden Blick in den Stadtpark freigibt, andererseits diesen architektonisch faßt und zudem – sozusagen auf dem Dach – der Innsbrucker Straße als Brücke über den Graben dient. Im östlichen Parkrund wird die Architektur des Bahnhofs von Mauern und Brunnen aufgenommen. Auf einer Brunnensäule steht eine der besten Schöpfungen des Bildhauers August Gaul, der »Goldene Hirsch«. Von den städtebaulich wertvollen Wohnstraßen lassen südlich des Parks noch die Hewaldstraße und die Nymphenburger Straße die großzügige Planung jener Zeit erkennen.

Agricultural land between the Bayerisches Viertel, Alt-Schöneberg and the Ringbahn was released for city expansion in about 1910. It was planned down to the last detail, and Friedrich Gerlach, an official in the municipal building department, was heavily involved in this. New residential areas were built at the same time, and also the town hall, a school, office buildings like the Nordsternhaus, a municipal park and the underground railway – still a unique architectural ensemble today. A particular engineering problem was posed by the need for the underground to pass over the Fenngraben, a drainage ditch. As the Berlin underground was planned to run immediately under the road surface, because of the high groundwater level, it had to come to the surface here. Gerlach and the architect, Staudt, exploited this situation, and built a station that gives a surprising view into the municipal park through its glazed walls, and also provides an architectural frame for the park and additionally – on the roof, as it were – takes Innsbrucker Strasse over the ditch. In the eastern part of the park the architecture of the station is picked up in walls and fountain. The «Golden Stag», one of sculptor August Gaul's best works, stands on one of the fountain columns. Of the finely designed residential streets south of the park, Hewaldstrasse and Nymphenburger Strasse are two that show the generous planning of the period.

H 18 Rathaus Schöneberg
Berlin-Schöneberg; John-F.-Kennedy-Platz
1911-14 • Jürgensen & Bachmann

Seit dem frühen Mittelalter führte Schöneberg – 1264 urkundlich als Sconenberghe erwähnt – seinen Dornröschenschlaf als märkisches Dorf am Wege von Berlin nach Potsdam. Um 1900 wurde der Ort dann von der Berliner Flächenexpansion erfaßt. Der 1898 zur Stadt erhobene Vorort Berlins wuchs und brauchte ein Rathaus, das er 1911-15 wie in dieser Zeit viele der Vorstädte als großes repräsentatives Gebäude durch die auf dem Gebiet der Großbauten erfahrenen Architekten Jürgensen und Bachmann erhielt. Im Kriege wurde die Turmhaube zerstört, seitdem hat der Turm seinen inzwischen charakteristischen geraden Abschluß. 1950 schenkten Amerikaner der Stadt Berlin die Freiheitsglocke, eine Nachbildung der »Liberty-Bell« aus den nordamerikanischen Unabhängigkeitskriegen. Sie ertönt nun jeden Tag um 12 Uhr vom Schöneberger Rathausturm. Bis zur Wiedervereinigung der vier Jahrzehnte geteilten Stadt war das Rathaus Schöneberg Sitz des Regierenden Bürgermeisters von West-Berlin.

From the early Middle Ages Schöneberg – mentioned as Sconenberghe in 1264 – slumbered like Sleeping Beauty as a Mark village on the way from Berlin to Potsdam. It was then swallowed as Berlin expanded around 1900. As a suburb of Berlin, raised to the status of town in 1898, it grew, and needed a town hall, and acquired one in 1911-15, like many other suburbs at the time. It is a large and imposing building by architects Jürgensen and Bachmann, who were experienced in the field of large-scale buildings. The dome on the tower was destroyed in the war, and the present straight top has since become a characteristic feature. In 1950 the Americans presented the city of Berlin with the Freiheitsglocke, a copy of the «Liberty Bell» from the American War of Independence. It now sounds every day at 12 o'clock from the tower of Schöneberg town hall. Until the city, divided for four decades, was reunited, Rathaus Schöneberg was the seat of the Mayor of West Berlin.

in der Nähe/nearby:
Olexhaus (Senator für Wirtschaft); Martin-Luther-Straße 105
1916-22 • Bielenberg & Moser
Nordsternhaus; Badensche Straße 2
1913-14 • Mebes & Emmerich
Amtsgericht Schöneberg; Grunewaldstraße 66-67
1901-06 • Paul Thoemer, Rudolf Mönnich

H 19 Kathreiner-Hochhaus
Berlin-Schöneberg; Potsdamer Straße 186
1929-30 • Bruno Paul

Schon vor dem Ersten Weltkrieg gab es in Berlin Pläne für »Turmhäuser«. Entwürfe für ein Hotelhochhaus am Bahnhof Friedrichstraße gingen durch die Presse. Doch nicht allein der Berliner Sandboden verhinderte, daß Bauten in den Himmel wuchsen. Der Internationalismus der zwanziger Jahre bescherte Berlin dann endlich doch die Hochhäuser nach amerikanischem Vorbild. Das Kathreinerhaus fiel mit seinen zwölf Geschossen vergleichsweise bescheiden aus, es besitzt aber eine zeitgemäße Stahlskelett-Konstruktion. Mit den kubischen Baugliedern, den Fensterbändern und der Travertinfassade folgt es dem Geschmack jener Jahre.

Even before the First World War there were plans for «tower houses» in Berlin. Designs for a high-rise hotel by Bahnhof Friedrichstrasse were published in the press. But it was not Berlin's sandy ground alone that prevented such buildings rising into the sky. Finally the internationalism of the twenties gave Berlin high-rise buildings on the American pattern. The Kathreiner building with its twelve storeys turned out relatively modest, but it has the steel frame structure customary at the time. It follows the taste of the period with its cubic sections, banded windows and Travertine façade.

in der Nähe/nearby:
Fernamt; Winterfeldtstraße 19/23
1923-29 • Otto Spalding, Kurt Kuhlow
Zentralvermittlungsstelle; Winterfeldtstraße 27/29
1985-89 • Bassenge, Puhan-Schulz & Partner

H 20 Kolonnaden am Kleistpark
Berlin-Schöneberg; Kleistpark
1777-80 • Karl v. Gontard

Monumentale Brückenhallen mit anschließenden Verkaufsräumen als Fortführung der geschlossenen Bebauung über Spree oder Seitenkanäle hinweg haben in Berlin Tradition. Erhalten geblieben sind nur wenige Beispiele, diese mußten zwar Brücken- und Straßenerweiterungen weichen, erhielten aber neue Standorte, wo sie wieder aufgebaut wurden. Der Name Königskolonnaden verweist auf eine solche Translozierung, sie standen ursprünglich in der Königstraße nahe dem Bahnhof Alexanderplatz, mußten dort 1910 einem Warenhausbau weichen und wurden dann zur Zierde des nach Auflösung des alten Botanischen Gartens neugestalteten Kleistparkes.

Monumental halls offering shopping facilities as a continuation of enclosed bridges over the Spree or side canals were traditional in Berlin. Only a few examples have survived; they had to make way for bridge or road widening, but were rebuilt at new sites. The name Königskolonnaden suggests a relocation of this kind: they were originally in Königstrasse near Alexanderplatz station, but had to make way for a department store there in 1910, and became a decorative feature in the newly designed Kleistpark after it relinquished its former role as botanical garden.

in der Nähe/nearby:
Kammergericht (Kontrollrat); B-Schöneberg; Elßholzstraße 31-32
1909-13 • Paul Thoemer, Rudolf Mönnich
Neues Schauspielhaus (Metropol); B-Schöneberg; Nollendorfplatz 5
1906 • Albert Fröhlich
Stadtvilla; B-Tiergarten; Kurfürstenstraße 59
1987-89 • Heinz Hilmer, Christoph Sattler
Maggi-Haus; B-Tiergarten; Lützowstraße 102-104
1910 • R. Schubring

H 21 Hochbahnhof Bülowstraße
Berlin-Schöneberg; Bülowstraße, Potsdamer Straße
1900-01 • Bruno Möhring

Die sichere Hand eines Bruno Möhring ließ aus der Eisenskeletthalle des Hochbahnhofs ein Jugendstilbauwerk von bestechender Vielfalt der Einzelheiten werden. Genaugenommen unsinnig in mancher Ausformung und überflüssig in der Dekoration ist der Bahnhof doch ein Gewinn, betrachtet man ihn als Stilerlebnis. Die zeitgenössische Begeisterung, die sich in der Aussage »überwältigende Kraft in der Wahrheit des formalen Ausdrucks« niederschlug, ist allein aus der damaligen Abkehr vom Historismus und der ermüdenden Strapazierung historischer Stile im ausgehenden 19. Jahrhundert zu verstehen. Möhring schwelgte in phantasievollen Details und in eigenwilliger Linienführung. Spargelförmige Pfeilerköpfe, kurvige Stützen und florale Verzierungen entstehen ohne die Belastung gotischer oder barocker Vorbilder. Vorausschauend bildete Möhring die nach Osten der Halle folgenden Pfeiler bereits so aus, daß ohne Mühe eine Erweiterung der Station vorgenommen werden konnte. 1928 war es dann auch soweit. Taktvollerweise beauftragte man den Sohn, Rudolf Möhring, mit dieser Aufgabe. Er setzte eine moderne Halle an, aber mehr im Stil der Neuen Sachlichkeit als im Jugendstil, im ganzen doch unauffällig passend.

The sure hand of Bruno Möhring made the iron-frame hall of this elevated railway station into a Jugendstil building with a captivating multiplicity of detail. Strictly speaking some of the shapes make little sense, and the decoration of the station could be said to be superfluous, but it is an overall gain if seen as a stylistic experience. Contemporary enthusiasm, expressed in the statement «overwhelming force in the truth of formal expression», can be seen in the turn away from historicism that was occurring at the time, and from the wearying over-use of historical styles in the late nineteenth century. Möhring revelled in imaginative detail and wilful line. Piers shaped like asparagus, curved supports and floral decorations appear, without the strain of Gothic or baroque models. With an eye for the future, Möhring designed the piers east of the hall so that the station could be extended without difficulty, and this was indeed necessary in 1928. Tactfully, the contract was awarded to Möhring's son Rudolf. He built a modern hall, more in the style of Neue Sachlichkeit than Jugendstil, but unobtrusively fitting overall.

in der Nähe/nearby:
Wohnanlage; Bülowstraße 12-13
1986-87 • Dietrich v. Beulwitz

H 22 Joachimsthaler Gymnasium
Berlin-Wilmersdorf; Bundesallee 1-12
1875-79 • Ludwig Giersberg, Johann Heinrich Strack

Im 19. Jahrhundert mußte das seit 1604 in Joachimsthal am Werbellinsee bestehende Gymnasium aufgegeben werden, und es entstand in der Wilmersdorfer Feldmark, damals weit vor den Toren Berlins, ein Neubau nach dem Entwurf von Strack, den Giersberg ausführte. Das Gymnasium war das erste monumentale Gebäude im Berliner Westen. Seit 1912 wird es anderweitig genutzt: als Stadthaus, als Museum, als Verwaltungsgebäude. Die meisten Nebengebäude des Internats sind im Kriege untergegangen.

In the nineteenth century the grammar school that had existed in Joachimsthal on the Werbellinsee since 1604 had to be given up and new premises were designed by Strack and built by Giersberg in the parish of Wilmersdorf. The school was the first monumental building in western Berlin. It has been used for various purposes since 1912: as local government offices, as a museum, as an office building. Most of the extra buildings for the boarding school were destroyed in the war.

in der Nähe/nearby:
Freie Volksbühne; Schaperstraße 24-25
1961-63 • Fritz Bornemann
Wohnhaus; Fasanenstraße 62, Fasanenplatz
1982-83 • Gottfried Böhm
Wohnhäuser; Fasanenstraße 35 a-36
1979-81 • Hasso v. Werder, Uwe Pompinon, Klaus Beyersdorff
Wohnhaus; Prager Platz 4
1987-89 • Gottfried Böhm

H 23 Kirche am Hohenzollernplatz
Berlin-Wilmersdorf; Hohenzollerndamm 202-203
1930-33 • Fritz Höger

Diese Kirche ist Fritz Högers bedeutendster Sakralbau. Er, der eigentlich für Kontorhäuser und Industriebauten prädestiniert schien, mußte sich hier auf eine vielschichtige Bauaufgabe einstellen. Das Grundstück schloß einen spitz zulaufenden Baublock ab, es lag am platzartig erweiterten Hohenzollerndamm, und der Kirchenbau suchte in jenen Jahren eine neue Identität. Daß es Höger gelang, die Kirche unmerklich und ohne Verlust an Monumentalität an die geschlossene Bebauung anzusetzen, versteht sich, ebenso daß sie am Platz und in den Blickachsen der Straßen zum baulichen Höhepunkt geriet. Den gestalterischen Erwartungen begegnete er mit zwei aus Vertikalen gebündelten Baukörpern – Turm und Schiff –, die ernst und feierlich zwischen religiösem Expressionismus und bescheidener Sachlichkeit verharren. Gotische Tradition in norddeutschem Sinne nimmt der Backstein auf, dem Höger untrennbar verbunden ist.

This church is Fritz Höger's most important ecclesiastical building. As a man predestined to work on offices and industrial buildings, he was faced here with a multi-layered architectural task. The plot concluded a block of buildings that ran to a point. Hohenzollerndamm widened to form a square here, and church building in those years was looking for a new identity. It will come as no surprise that Höger managed to fit the church into the completed development unobtrusively and without loss of monumental quality, and also that it became the architectural climax of the square and on the lines of vision of the streets. He met design expectations by creating two buildings – tower and nave – focussed by verticals; they hover, seriously and ceremoniously, between religious Expressionism and modest functionality. The use of brick, a material to which Höger was inextricably bound, takes up the Gothic tradition in the spirit of North Germany.

in der Nähe/nearby:
Wohn- und Geschäftshaus; Uhlandstraße 150
1982-83 • Regina Poly, Dieter Steinebach, Friedrich Weber
Technisches Zentrum der Landesbank Berlin; Badensche Straße 21-23
1986-89 • Rave und Partner

H 24 Senatsverwaltung für Bau- und Wohnungswesen
Berlin-Wilmersdorf; Württembergische Straße 6-10
1954-56 • Werry Roth

Der größte Nachkriegs-Behördenbau in Berlin und zunächst auch das höchste Bürogebäude entstand gegenüber dem Preußenpark. Die Änderung der Bauordnung ließ in der Innenstadt nun solche Bauten zu, da für die Bauklasse Va nicht mehr die Geschoßzahl 6 bei halber Grundflächenausnutzung als Obergrenze galt, sondern das Produkt aus Geschoßzahl und Flächenausnutzung, nämlich die Geschoßflächenzahl 3. Die Kombination von Hochhaustrakten und Flachtrakten wurde damit zu einem beliebten Motiv baukörperlicher Ordnung. Als bautechnischer Einfluß machte sich geltend, daß der Stahlbetonskelettbau herkömmliche Konstruktionsweisen verdrängte. Ihm ist die Rasterfassade zuzuschreiben. Hochhauswände sind nur mit großem Aufwand zu reinigen oder zu streichen, dem trug eine pflegeleichte Kachelverkleidung Rechnung. Somit konnte das neue Haus des Bausenators in einer Zeit verhaltener baukünstlerischer Ambitionen als vorbildlich gelten.

The largest official building in post-war Berlin, also the highest office building at first, was built opposite Preussenpark. Altered building regulations now permitted such structures in the inner city, as six was no longer the maximum number of storeys for buildings in class Va if half the usable area was to be exploited, but the product of the number of storeys and area to be exploited, in other words storey area figure three. A combination of high-rise and lower sections thus became a popular motif for the organization of buildings. A technical influence on architecture that was making itself felt was that reinforced concrete frame construction was displacing more traditional methods. This is the reason for the grid façade. The walls of high-rise buildings can only be cleaned or painted with great difficulty, and tile cladding, which is easy to look after, took account of this. Thus the building senator's new offices can be considered exemplary for a time of modest architectural ambition.

in der Nähe/nearby:
Kontorhaus Karstadt; Fehrbelliner Platz 1
1935-36 • Philipp Schaefer
Rathaus Wilmersdorf; Fehrbelliner Platz 4
1941-43 • Remmelmann

H 25 Russische Kirche
Berlin-Wilmersdorf; Hohenzollerndamm 166
1937-38 • Schellberg

Als fremdartiger, aber doch reizvoller Bau steht die russisch-orthodoxe Christi-Auferstehungs-Kathedrale auf einem kleinen, von breiten Fahrbahnen umschlossenen Straßendreieck. Mit ihrer gedrungenen kurzen Kreuzform, dem weißen Putz sowie Zwiebelhaube und Zwiebeltürmchen folgt sie ganz dem heimischen Baustil. Die Bezeichnung Kathedrale verdient sie nicht etwa wegen ihrer Größe, sondern als Bischofssitz für Berlin und Mitteleuropa. Das kleine Kirchlein diente wie sein Vorgängerbau am Fehrbelliner Platz der Gemeinde russischer Emigranten, die nach der Oktoberrevolution in Berlin Zuflucht gefunden hatten.

The Russian Orthodox cathedral of Christ's Ascension is an alien but charming building on a small street triangle surrounded by broad carriageways. Its square, short-armed cruciform shape, white rendering and onion dome and turrets follow the building style of its homeland completely. It is not designated a cathedral because of factors like its size, but as the seat of a bishop for Berlin and Central Europe. Like its predecessor in Fehrbelliner Platz, the little church served the community of Russian emigrants who sought refuge in Berlin after the October Revolution.

in der Nähe/nearby:
Moschee; Brienner Straße 7-8
1923 • K. A. Herrmann
Versicherungskonzern; Hohenzollerndamm 174-177
1930, 1935 • Emil Fahrenkamp
BfA-Gebäude; Westfälische Straße 90
1921 • Georg Reuter
BfA-Gebäude; Fehrbelliner Platz 5
1970-73 • Jan Rave, Rolf Rave
Wohnanlage; Eisenzahnstraße 56-59
1984-86 • Rob Krier; Pysall, Jensen & Stahrenberg; Christine Jachmann; Grundei; Ganz & Rolfes
Fußgängersteg Hoher Bogen; Rudolstädter Straße
1974 • Bauabteilung der Senatsverwaltung für Bau- und Wohnungswesen

H 26 Rheinisches Viertel
Berlin-Wilmersdorf; Landauer Straße
1910-14 • Paul Jatzow

Individuell gestaltete Häuser verschiedener Bauherren auf Einzelgrundstücken, allenfalls nach einem gemeinsamen Konzept gleichzeitig erbaut, das war bis zum Ersten Weltkrieg die gängige Art des Mietwohnungsbaues. Auch die Gartenterrassenstadt im Rheinischen Viertel um den Rüdesheimer Platz, in der Landauer Straße und weiteren Seitenstraßen folgte diesem Prinzip. Die Gemeinsamkeiten der Häuser gingen hier aber schon sehr weit. Gartenstadt und Landhausstil galten um 1910 als unerläßliche Bestandteile einer anerkannten Planung. Das Grün vor den Häusern – ohne einen Zaun! – setzt sich mit Kletterrosen in einem feinen Stabwerk bis zum ersten Stockwerk fort. Erker, Balkone, Giebel mit Kaminen, Zwerchhäuser und Gauben erzeugen den malerischen Eindruck englischer Landsitze als Übersetzung ins städtische Wohnen.

Until the First World War the usual style of building for rented residential accommodation was individually designed buildings for various clients on individual plots, though they were built at the same time, and with an overriding concept. The terraced garden city in the Rheinisches Viertel around Rüdesheimer Platz, in Landauer Strasse and other side streets followed this principle. However, in this case the houses had many common features. Around 1910 garden cities and the country house style were considered essential when planning townscapes. The green spaces in front of the houses – unfenced! – were continued with rambler roses on fine trellises rising to the height of the first storey. Bay windows, balconies, gables with chimneys, dormers and attics give the impression of English country houses adapted for urban living.

in der Nähe/nearby:
U-Bahnhof Rüdesheimer Platz; Rüdesheimer Straße
1911-13 • Wilhelm Leitgebel
Internationales Begegnungszentrum; Wiesbadener Straße 18-23
1980-83 • Otto Steidle, Sigwart Geiger

H 27 Autobahnüberbauung
Berlin-Wilmersdorf; Schlangenbader Straße 12-36
1976-81 • Georg Heinrichs

Die Idee, städtebaulich störende Autobahnabschnitte zu überbauen und zu dem ökologischen Vorteil noch eine hohe Ausnutzung wertvollen innerstädtischen Baulandes zu gewinnen, wurde allgemein begrüßt. Das Ergebnis eines der locker bebauten Umgebung aufgezwungenen Hochhausriegels gewaltigen Ausmaßes dagegen nährte die Kritik. Unglücklicherweise begann sich das Bauwerk bald nach seiner Fertigstellung im weichen Baugrund zu senken und konnte nur mit hohen Kosten aufgefangen werden. Damit war das Urteil »Zu groß!« schnell gesprochen. Wie das Märkische Viertel oder das Congress-Centrum geht aber die Planung auch dieses Projektes auf eine Zeit zurück, in der maßstablose Größe noch kein Unbehagen hervorrief und Superlative noch begeistern konnten. Diese Wohnmaschine für 4000 Menschen türmt sich mit ihren Terrassen und 15 Geschossen wie ein Gebirge über den beiden Tunnelröhren, ohne mit ihnen in Verbindung zu stehen. So können Vibrationen und Geräusche nicht übertragen werden. Parkpaletten und reichlich Ladenflächen sind in den Komplex integriert.

The idea of building over intrusive sections of motorway, thus gaining an advantage in town planning terms as well as ecologically, was generally welcomed. But there was loud criticism when a gigantic high-rise block was imposed upon the lightly built-up surroundings. Unhappily the building began to sink into the soft site shortly after it was completed, and this process could only be halted at great expense. And so the verdict of «too big!» was quickly pronounced. But like the Märkisches Viertel or the Congress-Centrum, planning for this project goes back to a time when size that disregarded scale caused no particular misgivings, and could still evince enthusiastic superlatives. This living machine for 4,000 people with its terraces and fifteen storeys towers like a mountain range over the two tunnels, without being in any way connected to them. In this way vibration and noise cannot be communicated. Parking spaces and lavish shopping facilities form an integral part of the complex.

in der Nähe/nearby:
Elektrizitätswerk Südwest; Forckenbeckstraße 3-6
1911-12 • Hans Liepe (Erweiterung 1924-29 • Stanke)
U-Bahnhof Heidelberger Platz; Heidelberger Platz
1911-13 • Wilhelm Leitgebel
Haus der Zahnärzte; Heidelberger Platz 3
1936 • Emil Rüster

H 28 Kreuzkirche
Berlin-Schmargendorf; Hohenzollerndamm 130 a
1927-29 • Ernst Paulus, Günther Paulus

Ausdruck einer ringenden, gottsucherischen Religiosität sollte diese Kirche sein. Darin nahm sie das wesentliche geistige Element der Gotik auf, wie die Gotik überhaupt in der expressionistischen Architektur eine wichtige Rolle spielte. Beeindruckend ist die phantasievolle Eigenwilligkeit der Formgebung im gesamten Baukörper wie auch im Detail. Voller Spannung stehen der geschlossene Turmbau und der polygonal zergliederte Saalbau nebeneinander. Hervorstechend lenkt der Portalbaldachin asiatischer Prägung in blau glasierter Keramik den Blick auf sich, dann die schraubenförmigen Rippen der Strebepfeiler, die Zickzackbänder der abkippenden Attika, darüber die Dreifaltigkeit der Turmspitzen. Auch das Innere wartet mit Überraschungen auf, dazu trugen die bekannten Bildhauer Felix Kupsch und Max Esser ihren Teil bei. Die Kreuzkirche stellt eines der großartigen Beispiele expressionistischer Baukunst dar.

This church was intended to express religiosity struggling in its search for God. To this end it adopted the essential spiritual element of Gothic, which anyway played an important role in Expressionist architecture. The design of the building as a whole and the detail are impressive in their imaginative originality. The separate tower and polygonal hall building stand side by side, exuding tension. The protruding portal baldacchino in blue-glazed ceramic tiles draws attention to itself, then the eye is drawn to screw-shaped ribs of the buttresses, the zig-zag bands on the attic storey, which slopes outwards, and above that the three-fold spires. The interior also has a few surprises to offer, and sculptors Felix Kupsch and Max Esser played their part in this. The Kreuzkirche is one of the most splendid examples of Expressionist architecture.

in der Nähe/nearby:
Generalkommando des 3. Armeekorps (heute AEG);
Hohenzollerndamm 150-152
1936-37 • Rudolf Klar (Heeresbauverwaltung)
Rathaus Schmargendorf; Berkaer Platz
1900-02 • Otto Kerwien

J
Berlin
Westend und Spandau

Westlich von Charlottenburg begann 1866 die Erschließung einer Villenkolonie. Wirtschaftliche Nöte ließen eine rege Bautätigkeit in Westend jedoch erst nach 1905 aufkommen, dann aber in einer Mischung aus Miet- und Landhausbebauung. Auf freien Arealen siedelten sich Messebauten und Sportanlagen an, später ein Zentrum für Rundfunk und Fernsehen. Eine eigene Entwicklung nahm Spandau. Im sumpfigen Bereich der Spreemündung gründeten Slawen gegen Ende des 4. Jahrhunderts auf einigen Havelinseln eine Dorfgemeinschaft von Jägern und Fischern. Vom 8. bis 12. Jahrhundert als Burgwallsiedlung mehrmals abgebrannt, wandelte sich der Ort zur deutschen Kaufmannssiedlung, bis er gegen 1200 weiter nach Norden an die Kante der seeartigen Havelausweitung verlegt wurde. Um 1230 erhielt Spandau Stadtrecht, und in seiner Umgebung gründeten Siedler die Dörfer Gatow, Kladow und Staaken. Auf einer Insel entstand die Burg, Keimzelle der im 16. Jahrhundert angelegten mächtigen Zitadelle. Festung und strategisch wichtige Lage bestimmten die weitere Entwicklung. Der enge Mauerkreis der Altstadt blieb lange aus militärischen Gründen erhalten und behinderte ein homogenes städtebauliches Wachstum. Die Vorstädte – im Schußfeld der Festungskanonen – waren als Bauland risikoreich und so zur Bedeutungslosigkeit verurteilt. Die Anfang des 18. Jahrhunderts östlich der Zitadelle angesiedelte Rüstungsindustrie mit eigenen Befestigungen veränderte das Bild, verschwand aber wieder während der napoleonischen Besatzungszeit. Erst das Jahr 1903 brachte eine Lockerung der militärtechnischen Bauauflagen. Aus den Wällen entstand damals ein Grüngürtel. Entlang Spree und Havel dominierte Industrie, ebenso beiderseits der Bahnstrecken nach Hannover und Hamburg. Entscheidend für Spandau wurde die Ansiedlung der Firma Siemens, für die an der Grenze zu Charlottenburg im Laufe der Zeit ein eigener großer Stadtteil entstand. An der Peripherie Spandaus kam es nach 1910 zum Bau von Wohnsiedlungen, darunter vorbildliche Anlagen wie die Gartenstadt Staaken, aber auch die Trabantenstadt auf dem Falkenhagener Feld. Gatow und Kladow behielten weitgehend ihren ländlichen Charakter und boten vielfach Platz für kleine Einfamilienhäuser.

The Westend villa district started to be developed in 1866. The first real spurt in building did not come until 1905 however, as a result of economic pressure, and this was a mixture of tenanted and country house accommodation. Exhibition buildings and sports facilities established themselves in open areas, and later a radio and television centre. Spandau developed independently. Towards the end of the fourth century, Slavic tribes founded a hunting and fishing village in the marshy territory of an island in the Havel near the confluence with the Spree. This fortified settlement burned down several times from the eighth to the twelfth century, then became a base for German merchants, and then moved further north to the edge of the lake-like Havel widening around 1200. Spandau was granted a charter in about 1230, and settlers founded the surrounding villages of Gatow, Kladow and Staaken. The castle was built on an island and was to form the core of the massive citadel that grew up in the sixteenth century. Further development was determined by the fortress and the strategically important position of the site. The tight wall around the old town retained its military significance for a long time and prevented homogeneous growth in urban development terms. The suburbs were within range of the fortress cannons, thus risky building territory and reduced to insignificance. The picture changed when the arms industry was established east of the citadel, with its own fortifications, in the early eighteenth century, but it disappeared again during the period of Napoleonic occupation. It was not until 1903 that the military installations began to be demolished, and the ramparts became a green belt. Industry dominated the banks of the Spree and the Havel, and also both sides of the railway lines to Hannover and Hamburg. The arrival of the Siemens factory had a crucial effect on Spandau; in the course of time a large town in its own right grew up to service it on the border with Charlottenburg. Residential estates were built on the periphery of Spandau after 1910, including model developments like the Staaken garden city, but also the satellite town on the Falkenhagener Feld. Gatow and Kladow largely retained their rural character, with space available for small detached houses.

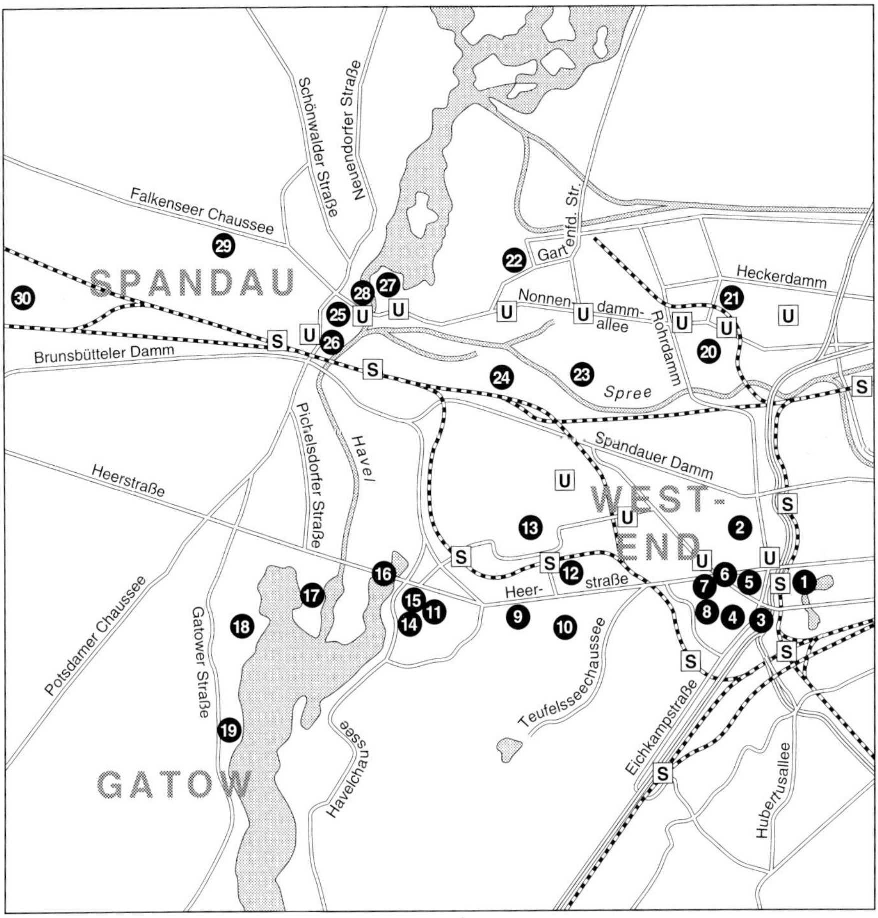

J 1 Lietzenseepark
J 2 Bürogebäude
J 3 Internationales Congress-Centrum ICC
J 4 Funkturm
J 5 Haus des Rundfunks
J 6 Fernsehzentrum des Senders Freies Berlin
J 7 Deutschlandhaus, Amerikahaus
J 8 Doppelvilla Heymann-Mendelsohn
J 9 Haus Sternefeld
J 10 Haus Poelzig
J 11 Britischer Kriegerfriedhof
J 12 »Unité d'Habitation Typ Berlin«
J 13 Olympiastadion
J 14 Haus Mendelsohn
J 15 Zwei Einfamilienhäuser
J 16 Stößenseebrücke
J 17 DLRG-Rettungsturm
J 18 Haus Baensch
J 19 Haus Wagner
J 20 Siemenswerke
J 21 Großsiedlung Siemensstadt
J 22 Reichsforschungssiedlung Haselhorst
J 23 Kraftwerk Reuter
J 24 Klärwerk Ruhleben
J 25 Nikolaikirche
J 26 Rathaus Spandau
J 27 Zitadelle
J 28 Schleuse Spandau
J 29 Siedlung Zeppelinstraße
J 30 Gartenstadt Staaken

J 1 Lietzenseepark
Berlin-Charlottenburg; Lietzenseeufer, Wundtstraße
1919-20 • Erwin Barth

Bereits 1912 hatte Barth, vermutlich gemeinsam mit Heinrich Seeling, die Kaskade am Dernburgplatz, dem Südende des Sees angelegt. Als kleiner Architekturgarten von neuklassizistischer Prägung hatte er sich in eine größere Anlage einzufügen, die dann nach 1919 insgesamt neugestaltet wurde. Kleine regelmäßige Partien, wie sie städtischen Schmuckplätzen entsprechen, sind eingebettet in einen Landschaftspark – sofern man davon überhaupt bei dem schmalen Streifen am West- und Nordrand des Sees sprechen kann. Der Reiz besteht offensichtlich im gewundenen Band des Sees selbst und in den hohen Uferhängen, die sich geschickt zur Bildung von Baumkulissen ausnutzen lassen. Einbezogen wurde auch die 1904 aus rotem Sandstein erbaute Lietzenseebrücke, die mit der Neuen Kantstraße See und Park teilt.

The cascade on Dernburgplatz, at the southern end of the lake, had been laid out by Barth, presumably in cooperation with Heinrich Seeling, as early as 1912. It had to fit into a larger park as a small neoclassical landscaped architectural garden, then the whole area was redesigned after 1919. Small regular areas, corresponding to decorative urban squares, are set in a landscaped park – to the extent that this term can sensibly be used for the narrow strip on the western and northern edge of the lake. Its charm obviously lies in the winding band of the lake itself and in the high banks, which are highly suitable for artful tree-planting. The red sandstone Lietzenseebrücke, which with the Neue Kantstrasse divides lake and park, was also included in 1904.

in der Nähe/nearby:
Hotel Seehof; Lietzenseeufer 11
1964-66 • Rudolf Fuchs-Henel
Petrus-Canisius-Kirche; Witzlebenstraße 27-29
1954-56 • Reinhard Hofbauer
Reichsmilitärgericht; Witzlebenstraße 4-5
1908-10 • Kayser & Großheim
Knappschaftshaus; Kuno-Fischer-Straße 8
1929-30 • Rudolf Hartmann
Lietzenseekirche; Herbarthstraße 5
1957-59 • Paul Baumgarten
Oberpostdirektion; Dernburgstraße 40-54
1926-28 • Willy Hoffmann
Bahnhof Witzleben; Neue Kantstraße
1913-16 • August Bredtschneider
Bahnhof Westkreuz; Am Westkreuz
126-28 • Richard Brademann
Schaltwerk Halensee; Halenseestraße 26-30
1927-28 • Richard Brademann

J 2 Bürogebäude
Berlin-Westend; Soorstraße 80-81
1987-88 • Karl-Heinz Steinebach, Friedrich Weber

Die Kunst, einem Bürohaus mit wenig gestalterischen Mitteln oder mit einer Idee Unverwechselbarkeit zu geben, beherrschten die Architekten der zwanziger Jahre hervorragend. Nach einer Zeit zwingender Funktionalität und bauwirtschaftlicher Optimierung hat eine neuerliche Rückbesinnung auf die Baukunst zu beachtenswerten Lösungen geführt. Für das Bürogebäude in Westend war 1987 ein Wettbewerb ausgeschrieben, dessen Sieger noch im gleichen Jahr den Auftrag zum Bau erhielten. Das Gebäude verfügt mit 29 000 m^2 vermietbarer Fläche über eine imponierende Größe. Nach außen bleibt die Gestaltung aber eher zaghaft und ohne laute Töne, setzt den geschlossenen Blockrand fort, beschränkt sich auf polierten roten Granit und schlicht eingeschnittene Fenster. Nur die Eingänge heben sich als deutliche Nischen ab, und die Fensterbänder der obersten Geschosse vermeiden jene Langeweile früherer »Endlosfassaden«. Die Anlage umschließt symmetrisch einen »Pocketpark«. Hier steht auch ein burgartiger Solitär mit den Service-Einrichtungen für das Bürohaus. Park und Solitär bilden mit der gläsernen Eingangshalle als Raumfolge eine Einheit. Sie steht für das Lebensgefühl der achtziger Jahre: phantasievolle Kreativität gepaart mit Sinn für das Exklusive und mit ökologischem Bewußtsein.

The architects of the twenties were masters of the art of making an office block highly distinctive with limited design resources, or simply by hitting upon a particularly striking idea. After a period of necessary functionality and optimum use of building funds, a new return to building as an art led to some striking solutions. A competition was announced for the office building in Westend in 1987, and the winners were commissioned to build in the same year. The building is of impressive size, with 29,000 square metres of space available for renting. Externally the design is rather hesitant, without any louder tones, continuing the complete block edge and restricting itself to polished red granite with plain windows cut into it. Only the entrances are differentiated as clear niches, and the rows of windows in the uppermost storeys avoid the tedium of «infinite façades». The complex is surrounded by a symmetrical «pocket park». Here there is also a castle-like detached building containing service facilities for the offices. Park and detached building form a unit with the glazed entrance hall, as a spatial sequence. They show the sensibility of the eighties: imagination and creativity paired with a sense of the exclusive, and ecological awareness.

in der Nähe/nearby:
BVG-Betriebshof; Königin-Elisabeth-Straße 9/29
1928-30 • Jean Krämer
Wohnanlage; Knobelsdorffstraße 94/122
1927-30 • Otto Rudolf Salvisberg, Jean Krämer

J 3 Internationales Congress-Centrum ICC
Berlin-Westend; Messedamm
1973-79 • Ralf Schüler, Ursulina Schüler-Witte

Wie eine überdimensionale Maschine mutet dieses Bauwerk an, das in der Zeit zunehmenden Wissenschafts- und Polit-Tourismus Berlin als Kongreß- und Tagungsort Attraktivität verleihen sollte. Eine Anbindung an das Messegelände ergab sich zwingend. Der Anschluß an die Stadtautobahn mit eigener Ab- und Auffahrt löste durch ein 600-Plätze-Parkhaus das Problem der verkehrsmäßigen Erreichbarkeit. Zwei Großsäle sind enthalten, die neueste und aufwendige Technik bieten, um für Kongreß, Bühnenveranstaltung oder Ball variabel herrichtbar zu sein. Fast 80 weitere Räume stehen zu Verfügung, und ein elektronisches Leitsystem vom Eingang bis zum Sitzplatz »verarbeitet« die bis zu 20 000 Besucher. Die vorzügliche Schallisolierung erreicht eine aus der Haus-in-Haus-Technik abgeleitete Konstruktion mit außenliegenden Stahlbindern und einer zweiten Lamellenhülle. Die silbrig eloxierte Haut unterstreicht den maschinellen Charakter, der auch von der schiffsbugartig ausgebildeten Stirnseite nicht gemildert wird. Dem Kolossalen des Baugebildes folgen nicht nur die Kosten von rund einer Milliarde Mark, sondern ebenso die mutige Monumentalplastik »Alexander der Große vor Ekbatana« von Jean Ipoustéguy.

This building like a colossal machine was intended to make Berlin attractive as a congress and conference centre in the period when Berlin was increasingly a centre of academic and political tourism. A link-up with the exhibition area was clearly the solution. Connection to the city motorway, with its own entrances and exits, solved the problem of road access, and parking for 600 vehicles was provided. The complex contains two large-scale halls offering the most recent and lavish technology, so that it can be adapted for congresses, stage presentations and balls. Almost 80 other rooms are available, and a system of electronic signs «processes» up to 20,000 visitors from entrance to individual seat. Outstanding soundproofing is achieved by a structure derived from the building-within-a-building technique, with external truss beams and a second envelope of slats. The silvery anodized skin underlines the machine-like character of the building, and this impression is not softened by the end façade, which is like the prow of a ship. The colossal element in the structure of the building is reflected not only in the cost, around a thousand million marks, but also in Jean Ipoustéguy's monumental sculpture of «Alexander the Great before Ekbatana».

in der Nähe/nearby:
AVUS-Turm; B-Westend; Avus-Nordkurve
1935-36 • Walter Bettenstaedt

J 4 Funkturm
Berlin-Westend; Messedamm
1925-26 • Heinrich Straumer

Als Ausstellungs- und Betriebsgebäude hatte Straumer 1924 für die Erste Große Funkausstellung in Berlin die Funkhalle gebaut. Über einem als Erdung verlegten Kupfernetz führte er ohne alles Metall eine reine Holzbinderhalle auf, transparent für die elektromagnetische Strahlung der Sender. 1935 wurde dieser Bau durch Feuer zerstört. Als Ergänzung zu dieser Halle war aber rechtzeitig vor der Funkausstellung des Jahres 1926 ein Sendeturm errichtet, der für Berlin wahrzeichenhafte Funkturm. Seine einstige Funktion verraten noch die mächtigen Porzellanisolatoren, auf denen seine 400 t Stahl stehen. Die Höhe von 138 Metern zeugt von voreiliger Bescheidenheit und falscher Sparsamkeit, denn schon 1932 reichte der Turm als Sendemast nicht mehr aus, und in Tegel entstand ein höherer. Geblieben ist aber das Wahrzeichen mit Aussichtsplattform und Restaurantkanzel.

Straumer built the Funkhalle as an exhibition and service building for the first great radio exhibition in Berlin in 1924. He produced a hall built entirely using wooden trusses, set on a network of copper for earthing purposes, which did not affect the transmitters' electromagnetic waves. This building was destroyed by fire in 1935. But well before the 1926 radio exhibition the hall had been complemented by a transmitter tower, the Funkturm, which was to become the emblem of Berlin. Its former function is revealed by the massive porcelain insulators on which its 400 tons of steel stand. Its height, 138 metres, is a sign of excessive haste, undue modesty and false economy, as the tower was already inadequate as a transmitter by 1932, and a taller one was built in Tegel. But the emblem has remained, with its viewing platform and restaurant floor.

in der Nähe/nearby:
Messehallen 12-20; Masurenallee, Messedamm
1935-37 • Richard Ermisch
Messehallen 7-11, 21-22; Masurenallee, Messedamm
1950 • Alfred Roth, Franz Heinrich Sobotka, Georg Müller

J 5 Haus des Rundfunks
Berlin-Westend; Masurenallee 10-14
1929-31 • Hans Poelzig

Ende 1923 meldete sich erstmals die »Radio-Stunde« als erster offizieller Rundfunksender aus dem Voxhaus in der Potsdamer Straße. Nur wenige Räume waren provisorisch hergerichtet. Die technische Entwicklung überschlug sich aber in den folgenden Jahren gleichsam, und bereits 1927 stand fest, daß ein eigenes Haus des Rundfunks zu bauen sei. Der Blick richtete sich auf den Westen, wo seit kurzem bereits Funkhalle und Funkturm standen. Nach einem Wettbewerb erhielt Poelzig den Auftrag und baute unter größten planerischen Schwierigkeiten eine gewaltige Dreiflügelanlage, deren Innenhof drei Quertrakte für Sendesäle durchschneiden. Bei einer Nutzfläche von 30 000 m^2 entwickelt der Bau entlang der Masurenallee eine Frontlänge von über 155 m. Diese ästhetisch zu beherrschen, gelang nur mit einer vertikalen Blendengliederung und einem symmetrisch höhenabgestuften Baukörper, der bei der unumgänglichen Monumentalität wenigstens übertriebenes Pathos vermeidet. Der Wechsel zwischen rotbraunen Keramikplatten und blauschwarz schimmernden Klinkern verstärkt den unverwechselbaren Charakter des Gebäudes. Ein baukünstlerisch wertvoller Bestandteil des Hauses ist die große Treppenhalle. Die weitgehend originalgetreue Wiederherstellung jüngeren Datums machte die Entstellungen der Nachkriegsmodernisierung rückgängig.

In late 1923 «Radio-Stunde» broadcast for the first time as the first official radio station from the Voxhaus in Potsdamer Strasse. But technical developments came thick and fast in subsequent years, and by 1927 it was clear that the broadcasting service would need a building of its own. Eyes turned west, where Funkhalle and Funkturm were already established. Poelzig acquired the commission as a result of a competition, and built a massive building in three sections despite enormous planning difficulties; the courtyard had three transverse sections for studios. The building had 30,000 square metres of usable space, with a façade on Masurenallee 155 metres long. The only way to handle this in aesthetic terms was to use blind vertical articulation and symmetrical organization in terms of height differentials, which at least avoids exaggerated drama, despite the inevitable monumentality of the building. The great staircase is a valuable component of the building in artistic terms. Recent reconstruction, largely faithful to the original, has removed the disfigurements of postwar modernization.

in der Nähe/nearby:
Appartementhaus; Kaiserdamm 25/25 a
1928-29 • Hans Scharoun
Haus Kallmann; Ahornallee 33
1912 • Karl Stahl
Haus Beheim; Ebereschenallee 18
1918 • Paul Schultze-Naumburg

J 6 Fernsehzentrum des Senders Freies Berlin
Berlin-Westend; Theodor-Heuss-Platz 1-3
1966-68 • Robert Tepez

Hatte in den Nachkriegsjahren das Deutschlandhaus noch dem Berliner Fernsehsendebetrieb genügt, machte sich Ende der fünfziger Jahre der zunehmende Wohlstand bemerkbar. Die sprunghaft steigende Zahl von Fernsehern und die damit verbundenen Gebühren-Mehreinnahmen, die Ausweitung der Sendezeit und das bevorstehende Farbfernsehen, das waren Gründe für den Neubau eines größeren Sendehauses. Beratende Hilfe kam von der BBC in London, deren Erfahrungen mit dem Fernsehbetrieb für das bauliche Konzept den Ausschlag gaben. Für modernste Sendetechnik entstand ein Komplex, dessen städtebauliche Dominanz durch die erhöhte Lage am Theodor-Heuss-Platz noch hervorgehoben wird. Es entsprach nicht dem unbefangen zukunftsorientierten Denken der Bauzeit, auf die Umgebung Rücksicht zu nehmen. Nur so erklärt sich der auffällige Kontrast zu Poelzigs Haus des Rundfunks, die Konkurrenz in der Höhe zum Funkturm und der fehlende Bezug zum übrigen Rand des Platzes. Dem eigenwilligen Solitär ist das für heutige Sendehäuser typische Mischen verschiedener Funktionen ablesbar. Verwaltung und Redaktionen finden zweckmäßig Platz in einem Hochhaus, Repräsentation und Berührung mit Publikum wird auf einen Flachbauteil beschränkt, die Produktion erhält geschlossene Haus-in-Haus-Baukörper, deren Schallisolierung Vorrang vor der Gestaltung haben muß.

In the years immediately after the war the Deutschlandhaus proved adequate to meet Berlin's television needs, but in the late fifties increasing prosperity was making itself felt. Rapidly increasing numbers of television sets, and thus increasing income from fees, a longer broadcasting day and the imminence of colour television were all reasons for a new television centre. Advice came from the BBC in London, and their experience with running a television service determined the architectural concept. A complex was built to house the most modern broadcasting technology, and its dominance of the urban space was further stressed by its raised site on Theodor-Heuss-Platz. Uninhibited and futuristic thinking in the period in which it was built was not inclined to take the immediate surroundings into consideration; this is the only way in which the marked contrast to Poelzig's Haus des Rundfunks can be explained, and also competition with the Funkturm as far as height is concerned and a complete lack of reference to the rest of this side of the square. This wilful solitaire shows the mixture of various functions typical of today's broadcasting buildings. Offices and editors are housed in a functional high-rise building, matters of prestige and contact with the public are confined to a low section, and production is given a self-contained building within a building in which soundproofing is more important than design.

J 7 Deutschlandhaus, Amerikahaus
Berlin-Westend; Theodor-Heuss-Platz 7-11, Heerstraße 1-3
1929-31 • Heinrich Straumer

Der Bankier Heinrich Mendelssohn hatte bereits mit Bauten am Zoo und mit dem Europahaus in der Stresemannstraße bewiesen, daß er Gespür für wertsteigernde Investitionen besaß. Am höchsten Punkt Charlottenburgs und optischen Endpunkt der Berliner Westachse, dem damaligen Reichskanzlerplatz, sah er kommende wirtschaftliche Aufwertung und beauftragte Straumer mit dem Bau von zwei Geschäftshäusern. Ihr sachliches Äußeres lag im Geschmack der Zeit begründet. Der Name »Amerikahaus« deutet bereits Vorbilder an, die der Bauherr in den reklamestrotzenden Geschäftshäusern New Yorks sah und als modern und zeitgemäß empfand. Der Turmvorbau als Träger eines überdimensionalen Reklamegerüstes war das Ergebnis. Beiden Bauten war zunächst ein wechselvolles Schicksal beschert. Im Deutschlandhaus wurde dann 1936 das erste Fensehstudio eingerichtet, bis heute dient das Haus dem SFB. Das Amerikahaus richteten nach 1945 die Briten als Naafi-Club her.

The banker Heinrich Mendelssohn had already shown that he had a nose for lucrative investment with buildings at the Zoo and the Europahaus in Stresemannstrasse. He anticipated the increasing economic importance of the highest point in Charlottenburg, the visual conclusion of Berlin's east-west axis, and commissioned Straumer to build two office blocks. Their functional exterior stems from the taste of the period. The name «Amerikahaus» hints at the fact that Mendelssohn had seen the glittering flood of advertising on buildings in New York, and found it up to date, and in keeping with the times. The tower with its colossal scaffolding for advertising was a result of this. At first both buildings had varied fates in store. Then the first television studio was set up in the Deutschlandhaus in 1936, and the building is still used by Sender Freies Berlin. The British established their Naafi-Club in the Amerikahaus after 1945.

in der Nähe/nearby:
Hildegard-Krankenhaus; Thüringer Allee 12
1898-1901 • Pauly, Luedecke
U-Bahnhof; Theodor-Heuss-Platz
1907-08 • Alfred Grenander

J 8 Doppelvilla Heymann-Mendelsohn
Berlin-Westend; Karolingerplatz 5-5 a
1922 • Erich Mendelsohn

»Eckhaus einer gedachten Platzwand am Kreuzungspunkt zweier Straßen. Betonung der Wirkungsdiagonalen. Spiegelbildanlage.« Das war Mendelsohns Beschreibung. Unverkennbar ging es dem Architekten um die Ecklösung und dabei – sonst wäre es nicht Mendelsohn – um die dynamische Wirkung. Allein die Verteilung der Farbwerte mit der Verkehrung von Hell unten und Dunkel oben schafft Spannung, dann natürlich die Staffelung zu drei Eckkanten und letztlich die unvermittelte Höherführung der Mauern an den Ecken. In stark abstrahierter Form ist hier Expressionismus spürbar: etwa in der sich aus der Staffelung ergebenden Zackenlinie oder in der bewegten Ziegelschichtung der Obergeschosse.

«Corner house for a proposed square at the intersection of two streets. Emphasis of the effective diagonals. Mirror complex.» This was Mendelsohn's description. The architect was unmistakably concerned with the corner solution and also – otherwise it would not be Mendelsohn – with dynamic effect. The distribution of colour values alone, with its reversal of light below and dark above, creates tension in itself, and so of course does the staggering of the building to produce three corner edges, and finally the unexpected raising of the height of the walls at the corners. Here there is a sense of Expressionism in a highly abstract form: in the jagged line produced by the staggering, for instance, or in the lively layering of the bricks in the upper storeys.

in der Nähe/nearby:
Haus G. Klingenberg; B-Westend; Alemannenallee 6
1922 • Walter Klingenberg, Werner Issel
Mommsen-Stadion; B-Eichkamp; Waldschulallee 34
1930 • Fred Forbat
Bahnhof Eichkamp; B-Eichkamp; Waldschulallee
1928-29 • Richard Brademann
Siedlung Eichkamp; B-Eichkamp; Eichkampstraße 8/136, Eichkatzweg 1/77 u. 2/70 usw.
1919-24 • Max Taut & Hoffmann
Atelierhaus Arnold Zweig; B-Eichkamp; Kühler Weg 9
1929-30 • Harry Rosenthal

J 9 Haus Sternefeld
Berlin-Westend; Heerstraße 109
1923-24 • Erich Mendelsohn

Wegweisend für die Entwicklung der Architektur in Berlin und auch über Berlin hinaus waren Anfang der zwanziger Jahre die Bauten von Erich Mendelsohn. Das Haus Sternefeld ist mit dem Doppelhaus am Karolingerplatz der erste kubische Flachbau der Stadt. Nicht die große historistische Geste, nicht malerische Kleinteiligkeit und nicht expressionistischer Formenschatz kennzeichnen das Haus, sondern es beeindruckt durch die einfache Gestalt und erlaubt sich lediglich eine dynamische Gruppierung der Bauglieder. Der geschlossene Wandblock über dem vertieften Fensterband spielt dabei die entscheidende Rolle. Diese Spannung kündigt sich bereits in der schwer über der Eingangsnische lastenden blockhaften Terrassenbrüstung an und wiederholt sich in den fensterlosen Mauern des Sonnendachs. »Ornament und Verbrechen« setzte der österreichische Architekt Adolf Loos 1908 gleich. Hier zeichnet sich die Erfüllung seines Postulates ab.

Erich Mendelsohn's buildings showed the way forward for the development of architecture in Berlin and beyond in the early twenties. The Sternefeld house, along with the semi-detached house in Karolinger Platz, was the first flat-roofed cubic building in the city. The characterisitic features of this house are not the grand historical gesture, not picturesque attention to detail, and not the formal vocabulary of Expressionism: it is impressive because of its simple design, and only permits itself dynamic grouping of the individual parts of the building. The decisive role here is played by the unified block of wall above the sunken row of windows. This tension is already heralded by the block-like terrace parapet above the entrance niche and continues in the windowless walls of the sun roof. The Austrian architect Adolf Loos equated «Ornament and Crime» in 1908. Here we see the fulfilment of this postulate.

in der Nähe/nearby:
Haus Steingroever; Stallupöner Allee 37
1937 • Egon Eiermann

J 10 Haus Poelzig
Berlin-Westend; Tannenbergallee 28
1930 • Marlene Poelzig

Daß sich der berühmte Hans Poelzig nicht selbst am Entwurf des eigenen Hauses beteiligte, sondern dieses gänzlich seiner Frau – selbst Architektin und zeitweise Mitarbeiterin von Hans Poelzig – überließ, löste selbst noch am Ende der zwanziger Jahre Verwunderung aus. Marlene Poelzig hielt sich an die Prinzipien der Sachlichkeit. Der hell verputzte Flachbau mit Fensterbändern und einem betonten Dachüberstand wurde sorgfältig gegliedert. Die Vorderfront verrät die Dreiteilung in Atelier, Chauffeurwohnung und privaten Wohnbereich, der sich fast ausschließlich zum Garten wendet und diesen auch in das Wohnprogramm einbezieht. Karl Förster und Hermann Mattern gestalteten ihn kinderfreundlich mit Spielplatz und Spielwiese.

Even in the late twenties it was a source of some amazement when the famous Hans Poelzig took no part in the design of his own house, but left it entirely to his wife, herself an architect and for a time Hans Poelzig's working colleague. Marlene Poelzig kept to the principles of functionality. The building has light-coloured rendering, with rows of windows and markedly protruding roof, and was carefully articulated. The front façade shows a division into three for studio, chauffeur's accommodation and private residential area, which almost entirely faces the garden and also includes this as part of the programme for living the house offers. Karl Förster and Hermann Mattern designed it to be appealing to children, with playground and lawns.

in der Nähe/nearby:
Haus Klingholz; Lyckallee 6
1912-14 • Fritz Klingholz
Haus Meyer; Tannenbergallee 11
1913-14 • Alfred Lesser

J 11 Britischer Kriegerfriedhof
Berlin-Pichelsberge; Heerstraße
1955-57 • Philip Dalton Hepworth

Die Anlage folgt allgemeingültigen Überlieferungen, die für britische Kriegerfriedhöfe gelten. Weitläufig und übersichtlich entwickelt sich die Rasenfläche, auf der in militärischer Ordnung Felder gleicher Grabzeichen aus weißem Sandstein mit Namen und Regimentswappen stehen. Ein Hochkreuz, gleichfalls aus weißem Stein, bildet den Blickpunkt des Gräberfeldes. Knapp gefaßt wird das Ganze durch einen dreibogigen Torbau mit schmiedeeiserner Pforte im Osten und eine siebenjochige Bogenreihe gegenüber am Westrand. Der Verzicht auf Wege und die dunkle Einfassung mit immergrünen Gehölzen vermitteln eine ernste Würde, welche die Gleichartigkeit der Steine unterstreicht. Dieser Eindruck bleibt das Vorrecht eines Kriegerfriedhofes, da hier individuelle Grabgestaltung nicht möglich und persönliche Grabpflege nicht erwünscht sind.

The cemetery follows the traditional pattern for British war graves. The lawns are extensive and open, with identical white sandstone gravestones bearing name and regimental coat of arms, drawn up in military array. A tall cross, also in white stone, is the predominant visual feature of the cemetery. The whole area is sparely framed by a three-arched structure with wrought-iron gate to the east and seven bays of arches opposite it, at the western extremity. The lack of paths, and the evergreens on the periphery, convey a solemn dignity, underlined by the identical nature of the stones. This impression is the privilege of the military cemetery, as it is not possible to design individual graves here, nor is individual care for them desirable.

in der Nähe/nearby:
Friedhof der Jüdischen Gemeinde; B-Pichelsberge; Scholzplatz
1954-56 • Hermann Guttmann, Bernhard Kynast
Friedhof Heerstraße; B-Westend; Trakehner Allee 1
1921-24 • Erwin Barth, Richard Köhler
Feierhalle; B-Westend; Trakehner Allee 1
1923-24 • Erich Blunck

J 12 »Unité d'Habitation Typ Berlin«
Berlin-Westend; Reichssportfeldstraße 16
1956-59 • Le Corbusier

Dieses Wohngebilde mit 530 Wohnungen in 17 Etagen, eigener Heiz-Kraft-Anlage, Läden und Postamt im Erdgeschoß ist nicht das einzige dieser Art. Le Corbusier wandelte den Typ in mehreren französischen Städten ab. Dort enthalten die Häuser noch Kindergärten, Arztpraxen und Hotelzimmer. Dieses Berliner Beispiel zeichnet sich jedoch durch etwas vergrößerte Raumabmessungen aus. Auch wenn es überwiegend Maisonnettewohnungen sind, erschien die Raumhöhe von 2,26 m doch zu gering. Zu einem Schwachpunkt der Anlage wurden die neun Innenstraßen, also die langen fensterlosen Flure von 130 m beklemmender Länge. Die »Unité d'Habitation« leitet sich von Le Corbusiers 1922 entwickelter Vision der »Ville Contemporaine« ab, einer Millionenstadt aus gewaltigen Wohnblöcken in weiten Grünflächen. Der in sich architektonisch geschlossene, aber lebensfähige Wohn- und Versorgungsorganismus ist das Kernstück seiner »Stadt der Gegenwart«.

This residential machine with 530 units on 17 floors, its own co-generation plant, shops and post office on the ground floor is not the only one of its kind. Le Corbusier produced variations on the type in several French towns. There the buildings also contain kindergartens, medical practices and hotel rooms. But this Berlin example is different because of the rather more generous dimensions of its rooms. Even though they are predominantly maisonette flats, a room height of 2.26 metres still seemed too low. The nine internal streets are a weak point of the building, long windowless corridors an oppressive 130 metres long. The «Unité d'Habitation» derives from Le Corbusier's vision of a «Ville Contemporaine», developed in 1922: a city for millions of people made up of massive residential blocks in spacious green areas. These architecturally self-contained but viable residential and supply organisms are the core of his «Contemporary City».

in der Nähe/nearby:
Polizeirevier; Reichssportfeldstraße 22
1930-31 • Richard Scheibner
Atelierhaus Georg Kolbe; Sensburger Allee 25-26
1928-29 • Ernst Rentsch

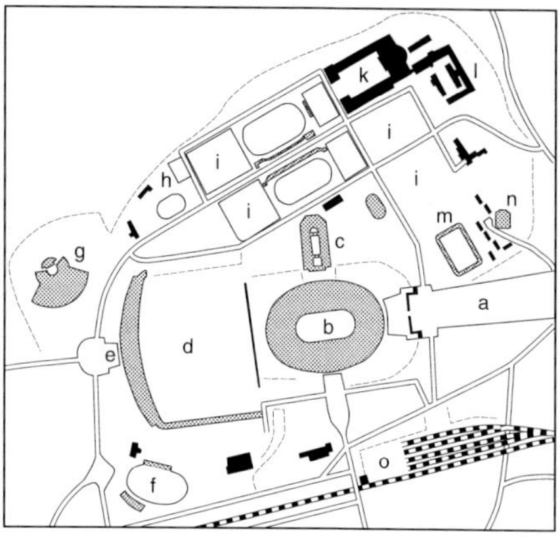

J 13 Olympiastadion
Berlin-Westend; Olympischer Platz, Trakehner Allee
1934-36 • Werner March

Seit 1909 gab es im äußersten Westend bereits eine Pferderennbahn und ab 1913 ein »Deutsches Stadion«, das den baulichen Rahmen für die 1916 in Berlin geplanten Olympischen Spiele abgeben sollte. Der Krieg vereitelte die Pläne. In den zwanziger Jahren begann dann der Ausbau zu einem Sportforum, mußte aber aus Geldmangel eingestellt werden. 1928 erfolgte endlich wieder die internationale Zulassung deutscher Sportler, und Berlin wurde zum Austragungsort der Olympischen Spiele 1936 bestimmt. Die Nazis sahen hierin ihre große propagandistische Chance und inszenierten eine großartige Veranstaltung zum Beweis ihrer Friedensliebe, aber auch zur Dokumentation deutscher Kraft. Das Reichssportfeld wurde vollkommen neugestaltet. Monumentalität hatte Disziplin und Stärke zum Ausdruck zu bringen, religiös-feierliche Weihe gehörte als Einstimmung auf Verführung und Massenpsychose dazu. Mittelpunkt wurde das gigantische Stadion mit 120 000 Plätzen. Seine Eisenbetonkonstruktion verkleiden Muschelkalkplatten, der Boden ist mit Granit belegt. In der Gliederung der Außenansicht ist bewußt jede Unterteilung oder Rhythmisierung vermieden, nur die endlose Reihung hart umrissener Pfeiler und der Abschluß der tiefen Arkaden mit einem ununterbrochenen, schweren Hauptgesims sichern die gesuchte kraftvolle Größe. Aufmarschflächen, geometrische Pfeilertürme, überlebensgroße Plastiken von Kämpfern und ein Maifeld für 500 000 Menschen setzen das Programm politisch-ideologischer Machtdemonstration fort, in das sich der Staatssport einzufügen hatte. Der 77 m hohe Glockenturm sorgte mit dem monotonen Klang der fast 10 t schweren Olympiaglocke für die ehrfürchtigen Schauer der unmerklichen, aber beabsichtigten Einschüchterung. Selbst die im Nordwesten in einen Talkessel gesenkte Freilichtbühne geriet mit 20 000 Plätzen hinreichend groß, um auch ohne Bühnenhandlung Ergriffenheit zu vermitteln. Heute werden die weitläufigen und im Gebrauchswert nicht zu unterschätzenden Sportanlagen, das große Stadion und auch die Waldbühne unbefangen besucht und genutzt. Trotzdem sollte der politische Mißbrauch der monumentalen Architektur mahnend in der Erinnerung wach bleiben.

There had been a racecourse on the periphery of Westend from 1909 and a «Deutsches Stadion» from 1913, and these were intended to provide the architectural framework for the planned Berlin Olympics in 1916, which never took place because of the war. In the twenties work started on expanding it into a sports forum, but money ran out. In 1928 German sportsmen were at last re-admitted to international competition, and Berlin was chosen to host the 1936 Olympics. The Nazis saw an opportunity for propaganda here, and laid on a tremendous event to show their love of peace, but also as a demonstration of German strength. The Reichssportfeld was completely redesigned. Monumentality was required to express discipline and strength, and religious solemnity set the mood for seduction to mass psychosis. At the centre of the complex was the gigantic stadium to seat 120,000. Its iron-frame structure is clad with muschelkalk slabs, and the floor is laid with granite. The exterior articulation consciously avoids any subdivision or establishment of rhythm, only an endless sequence of hard-edged piers and an unbroken, heavy cornice over the deep arcade secure the required power and size. Parade areas, geometrical buttress towers, larger-than-life statues of warriors and an assembly area for 500,000 people continue the programme of a political and ideological show of power into which the international games had to be fitted. The 77 metre high bell-tower with the monotonous sound of the Olympic bell, weighing almost 10 tons, provided the reverent shudder of imperceptible but intentional intimidation. Even the open-air theatre in the north-west, seating 20,000, was sufficiently large to convey emotion without anything happening on the stage at all. Today these extensive sports facilities – and their value as such should not be underestimated – the great stadium and the open-air theatre are uninhibitedly visited and used. Nevertheless the political abuse of monumental architecture should be kept in mind, as a warning.

(a) Vorplatz • 1934-36 • Werner March
(b) Stadion • 1934-36 • Werner March
(c) Schwimmstadion • 1934-36 • Werner March
(d) Maifeld • 1934-36 • Werner March
(e) Glockenturm • 1934-36 • Werner March
(f) Reitturniergelände • 1934-36 • Werner March
(g) Waldbühne • 1934-36 • Werner March
(h) Tennisplätze • 1934-36 • Werner March
(i) Sportplätze • 1934-36 • Werner March
(k) Haus des Sports mit Schwimmhalle und Sporthalle 1926-28 • Werner March
(l) Friesenhaus • 1934-36 • Werner March
(m) Hockeystadion • 1934-36 • Werner March
(n) Tennisstadion • 1934-36 • Werner March
(o) Bahnhofsgebäude • 1908-09 • Ernst Schwartz
Bahnhofsanlage • 1935-36 • Fritz Hane

in der Nähe/nearby:
Horst-Korber-Sporthalle; Glockenturmstraße 2-4
1988-90 • Christoph Langhof, Thomas M. Hänni, Herbert Meerstein
Pension Westend; Kastanienallee 32
1912 • August Endell
Wasserturm Westend; Spandauer Damm 165-167
1908-10 • Heinrich Seeling

J 14 Haus Mendelsohn
Berlin-Pichelsberge; Am Rupenhorn 6
1929 • Erich Mendelsohn

Gegenüber Mendelsohns frühen Bauten läßt sich eine Stilberuhigung feststellen, die Dynamik ist gebändigt. Unter dem Einfluß der Neuen Sachlichkeit gibt sich das Haus ruhig lagernd, die Horizontale wird stärker betont, und nur in einem zum Hang hin vorspringenden Bauteil wirkt das geschlossene Obergeschoß mit dem Studio über dem verglasten Eßzimmer im Erdgeschoß wie ein Erker, vergleichbar dem Haus Sternefeld. Den Vorzug der Lage nutzte Mendelsohn weitgehend aus. Nicht nur die Verschmelzung von Haus und Garten durch verbindende architektonische Elemente wie Terrassen, Mauern und Treppen, auch der weite Blick über die Havel hatte einen starken Einfluß auf die Grundrißdisposition und die Gestalt der Fenster. Die Straßenseite bleibt eher geschlossen, nur ein hochliegendes Fensterband gehört zu den Schlafräumen im Obergeschoß. Zur Wasserseite öffnen sich alle Räume in tief angesetzten, teils versenkbaren Fenstern, die jedoch die greifbar nahe Natur immer rahmen und für eine letzte Distanz zwischen architektonisch definiertem Raum und Außenwelt sorgen.

In comparison with Mendelsohn's earlier buildings this house is calm and still; its dynamism has been tamed. Under the influence of Neue Sachlichkeit the building lies quietly, horizontals are more strongly emphasized and only in a section of the building that protrudes towards the slope does the self-contained upper storey with the studio over the glazed dining room on the ground floor give the effect of a bay, comparable with the Sternefeld house. Mendelsohn made great play with the eminence of the site. Both the blending of house and garden by the use of linking architectual elements like terraces, walls and steps, and the sweeping view over the Havel had a profound influence on the layout of the ground plan and the shape of the windows. The street side is essentially closed, showing only a high row of windows in the bedroom area. On the water side all the rooms have low windows that can be lowered, but they always provide a frame for nature, with which the house is in close contact, and put a final distance between architecturally defined space and the outside world.

in der Nähe/nearby:
Haus Lindemann; Am Rupenhorn 5
1929 • Bruno Paul
Wohnhaus; Am Rupenhorn 9
1935 • Ludwig Hilberseimer

J 15 Einfamilienhäuser
Berlin-Pichelsberge; Am Rupenhorn 24 und 25
1928 • Hans Luckhardt, Wassili Luckhardt, Alfons Anker

»Neue Sachlichkeit« verstanden viele Architekten nicht nur als Maßstab einer neuen Gestaltung, es war ein grundlegend neues Denken im Bauen, unbelastet von Traditionen und Gewohnheiten. Für die Konstruktion ergaben die technischen Möglichkeiten der Stahlskelett- und Stahlbetonskelettbauweise ein willkommenes Instrument, Häuser mit freier Inneneinteilung und großzügig verglasten Fronten zu entwerfen. Die beiden Häuser am Rupenhorn erhielten ein Stahltragwerk. Die untere Etage wurde zum ungeteilten Wohnraum, der sich mit geschoßhohen Fenstern zur weit in die Waldlandschaft hinausschwingenden Terrasse öffnet. Mehr als zwei Jahrzehnte zuvor hatte das Landhaus schon einmal die Beziehung Wohnen und Landschaft aufgenommen, damals aber in einem anderen Verständnis. Hatte einst das Kunstwerk »Landhaus« als Ausdruck eines Lebensgefühls im Vordergrund gestanden, so wird nun das Haus zum Mittel, um das Programm eines neuen Wohnens zu erfüllen.

Many architects saw «Neue Sachlichkeit» not just as a standard for a new kind of design, it was fundamentally new thinking about building, unburdened by tradition and custom. The technical possibilities afforded by steel-frame and reinforced concrete structures provided a welcome instrument for constructing buildings with open distribution of interior space and generously glazed façades. The two houses Am Rupenhorn had steel frames. The lower floor became an undivided living space, opening through floor-to-ceiling windows on to the terrace, which swung into the wooded countryside in sweeping curves. More than two decades previously the country house had taken up the relationship of living and landscape again, but then on a different basis. Then the expression «country house» came to the fore as an expression of a feeling about life, but now the house is the means by which a new way of living can be created.

in der Nähe/nearby:
Reihenhäuser; Am Rupenhorn 1
1955 • Norman Braun

J 16 Stößenseebrücke
Berlin-Pichelsdorf; Heerstraße
1908-09 • Carl Bernhard, Johann Emil Schaudt

Die Deutsche Bank, die nach der Gründerkrise des Jahres 1874 große Teile im Westen Charlottenburgs erworben hatte, nutzte ihren politischen Einfluß, um die Erschließung des Geländes voranzubringen. In einem Vertrag mit der Stadt Charlottenburg im Jahre 1901 trat die Bank das Straßenland an die Stadt ab, die sich ihrerseits zur Erschließung verpflichtete und statt der Landhausbebauung eine fünfgeschossige Blockbebauung erlaubte. Zur weiteren Wertsteigerung des Baugeländes wurde der seit 1893 bestehende Plan gefördert, den vom Brandenburger Tor nach Westen führenden Straßenzug zu verlängern und Anschluß an die Döberitzer Heerstraße zu gewinnen, um den Truppen der Berliner Garnison den Anmarsch zu den Manöverplätzen zu erleichtern. Selbst Wilhelm II. begeisterte sich für den Plan einer solchen »monumentalen, wahrhaft imperialen Prachtstraße«. Als Teil dieser Planung entstand die Brücke über den Stößensee. Westseitig mußte ein Damm aufgeschüttet werden, bis die Höhe des östlichen Uferhanges erreicht war. Der unsichere sandige Grund der Widerlager zwang zum Bau einer eisernen Hochbrücke mit zwei Halbbögen auf einem Mittelpfeiler, in dessen Auflager fast die gesamte Brückenlast von über 2300 t abgeleitet wird. Die ingenieurtechnisch interessante und für den märkischen Raum seltene Konstruktion wird durch die von Schaudt stammenden architektonischen Zutaten in den Brückenköpfen bereichert.

The Deutsche Bank, after the crisis of 1874, acquired large tracts of west Charlottenburg. It used its political influence to hurry along the opening up of the area. It made a contract with Charlottenburg in 1901 in which the bank surrendered the street land to the town, which for its part committed itself to development, and permitted the building of five-storey blocks rather than country houses. The land again increased in value when a plan dating from 1893 to extend the street leading west from the Brandenburg Gate was implemented, giving access to the Döberitzer Heerstrasse and making it easier for troops of the Berlin garrison to march to their manoeuvres. Even Wilhelm II was enthusiastic about this plan for such a «monumental, truly imperial show street». The bridge over the Stössensee was built as part of this plan. An embankment was raised on the western side to match the height of the eastern bank. The insecure sand on which the abutment piers were built called for the construction of an iron viaduct with two arches on a central pier, with a bearer carrying almost the full thrust of the bridge's 2,300 tons. This is an unusual structure for the Mark, and of technical interest to engineers; it is enriched by the architectural additions made by Schaudt to the bridgeheads.

in der Nähe/nearby:
Gemeindezentrum; B-Pichelsberge; Angerburger Allee 56
1974-75 • Peter Lehrecke, Reinald Neumann

J 17 DLRG-Rettungsturm
Berlin-Pichelsdorf; Am Pichelssee 20-21
1970-72 • Ludwig Leo

Platzmangel oder teurer Baugrund als Vater einer Idee – so mag man dieses Bauwerk kommentieren. Zu den Aufgaben der Zentrale der Deutschen Lebensrettungsgesellschaft gehört die Unterbringung von mindestens 30 Booten, Werkstätten, Nachrichtenzentrale, Ausbildungs- und Schulungsräumen sowie die Unterkunft für 72 Personen. Sie verfügt über eine Station für Erste Hilfe und übernimmt die technische Versorgung der untergeordneten Rettungsstationen an der Havel. Aus der Unterbringung der Boote leitet sich die merkwürdige Bauform ab. Über einen Kanal erreichen sie den Turmbau, und der Schrägaufzug befördert sie in die einzelnen Lagerebenen. Der Turm ermöglichte aber auch den Einbau einer Tauchanlage. Diese unterscheidet sich zwar mit einer Wassertiefe von 8,50 m nicht wesentlich von den flachen Berliner Gewässern, durch Druckerhöhung in der geschlossenen Tauchkammer können aber Tauchtiefen von 158 m simuliert werden.

Lack of space or expensive building land as the father of an idea – that is the comment to be made about this building. Among the duties of the DLRG (life-saving association) are accommodating at least 30 boats, workshops, news facilities and training- and classrooms as well as accommodation for 72 people. It has a first aid station and is responsible for techncial facilities for the subsidiary rescue stations on the Havel. The unusual shape of the building arises from the fact that it has to accommodate boats, They reach the tower via a canal, and the diagonal lift carries them to their individual pens. But the tower also meant that it was possible to include diving facilities. As the water is only 8.5 metres deep this is not substantially different from other shallow Berlin waterways, but increased pressure in the sealed diving chamber can simulate depths of up to 158 metres.

in der Nähe/nearby:
Haus Plettner; Scharfe Lanke 51
1970-71 • Jan Rave, Rolf Rave

J 18 Haus Baensch
Berlin-Gatow; Höhenweg 19
1934-35 • Hans Scharoun

Auf der Haveldune der Weinmeisterhöhe liegt ein Einfamilienhaus, das die Frage der Herkunft des Baustils der fünfziger Jahre beantwortet. Als konsequente Fortführung des Wohnprogrammes, wie es die Luckhardt-Häuser am Rupenhorn 1928 zum Ausdruck brachten, wird die wechselseitige Entsprechung von Innen und Außen gesucht. Scharoun steigert diese Idee durch das Auffächern des Grundrisses: Die divergierenden Linien untermalen das gefühlsmäßige Verströmen beim Blick vom Hausinneren in die Natur, umgekehrt verdichten sie die von außen kommenden Eindrücke. Damit erschöpfen sich aber bereits die formalen Vorgaben, alles weitere unterliegt einem einsichtigen Funktionalismus. Der Wohnraum war ursprünglich in zwei Ebenen angelegt – hier klingt Scharouns Idee von der Terrassierung an, die alle seine Bauten bis hin zur Philharmonie begleitet.

On a Havel dune on the Weinmeiserhöhe is a detached house that may hold the solution to the question of where the building style of the fifties came from. As a logical extension of the living programme expressed by the Luckhardt houses am Rupenhorn in 1928, the architect is looking for mutual correspondence between inside and outside. Scharoun further enhances this idea by fanning out the ground plan: the diverging lines underline the stream of feeling when looking at nature from the inside, and conversely they condense impressions when coming in from the outside. This exhausts the formal requirements however, everything else is consistently functional. The living space was originally arranged on two levels – this gives a hint of Scharoun's ideas of terracing, which is to be found in all his buildings right through to the Philharmonie.

in der Nähe/nearby:
Haus Goedel-Dreising; Gotenweg 17
1937 • Hans A. Pfeffer

J 19 Haus Wagner
Berlin-Gatow; Rothenbücher Weg 56
1959-60 • Heinz Schudnagies

Die freie Hausform, wie sie Scharoun bereits in den dreißiger Jahren vorführte, blieb auch nach dem Kriege aktuell. Schudnagies ist einer der wesentlichen Verfechter der sich daraus ableitenden neuen Form des Wohnens. Seine Formel lautet: Der Wohnraum dominiert, alle Räume und Wege im Haus sind auf ihn bezogen; drei Ebenen sind jeweils um ein halbes Geschoß versetzt; die Räume von mindestens zwei Ebenen bilden ein zusammenhängendes Gefüge; der Raum wird lebendig geformt; ausgreifende Pultdächer schneiden Fenster oder Terrassenverglasungen oben ab. Mit diagonalen Raumachsen, sich neigenden Decken, unorthodoxen Höhenstufen und Abkehr vom rechten Winkel ergeben sich Spannungen, die auf den Bewohner übergehen und Wohnen zu einem aktiven Vorgang machen. Es offenbart sich die heiter-unbeschwerte Lebenshaltung der späten fünfziger Jahre, sie mündet ein in den Akt der »Befreiung des Menschen«, wie schon ein halbes Jahrhundert zuvor in der Landhaus-Ideologie.

Free design for houses was introduced by Scharoun in the thirties, and it remained up to date after the war. Schudnagies is one of the fundamental proponents of the new style of living that grew out of this. His formula runs: the living room is the dominant space, and all spaces and paths within the house refer to it; in each case three levels are placed around a half-floor; the rooms on at least two levels form a coherent structure; space is shaped in a lively fashion; overhanging penthouse roofs cut off windows or terrace glazing at the top. Diagonal room axes, sloping ceilings, unorthodox height relationships and rejection of right angles create tensions that are communicated to the occupants and make living an active process. This is symptomatic of the cheerful and unencumbered life style of the late fifties, leading to the notion of «freeing the human being» that had been part of the country house ideology half a century before.

in der Nähe/nearby:
Dorfkirche; Alt-Gatow 30-38
Ab 14. Jh.

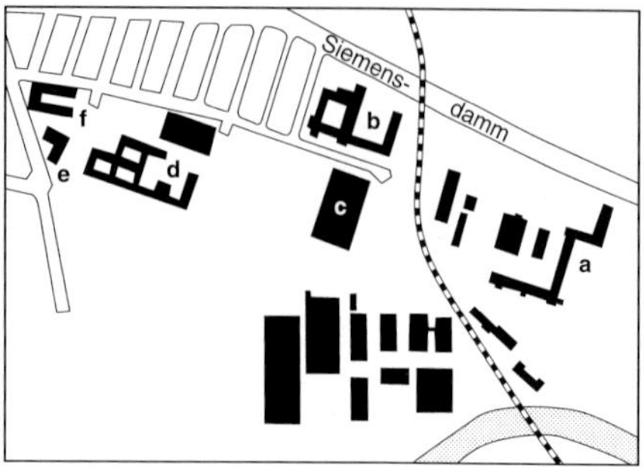

J 20 Siemenswerke
Berlin-Siemensstadt; Siemensdamm, Nonnendammallee
Ab 1906 • Karl Janisch, Hans Hertlein uam.

Am Unterlauf der Spree, außerhalb der Ringbahn, erwarb Siemens 1897 ein erstes Grundstück, das zur Keimzelle eines riesigen Industrieareals mit eigener Wohn- und Geschäftsstadt werden sollte. Das Wachstum der Siemensstadt vollzog sich kontinuierlich und führte zu einem harmonischen Nebeneinander aller Funktionen bei einer geordneten städtebaulichen Entwicklung. Stand die Zeit bis in die dreißiger Jahre noch unter dem Zeichen der industriellen Expansion, kennzeichnen Wiederaufbau und Umstrukturierung die Nachkriegsgeschichte. Wenn auch die meisten Bauten des ersten Jahrzehnts bereits verschwunden sind, prägen doch nach wie vor die hohen Komplexe der zehner, zwanziger und dreißiger Jahre die Silhouette. Jüngere Neubauten fallen im Einklang mit modernen Fertigungstechniken als Flachbauten, meist sogar eingeschossig aus. Industriebauten unterliegen stets neuen Anforderungen in dem Maße, wie Produkte, Märkte oder Techniken wechseln. Umbauten und Erweiterungen stehen damit auf der Tagesordnung. Diese stetige bauliche Veränderung ist auch an den Siemensbauten ablesbar. Verantwortlich waren die jeweiligen Chefarchitekten, zunächst Karl Janisch, ab 1915 dann Hans Hertlein. Die zeitabhängigen Gestaltungsmerkmale, wie sie durch die Fülle der Bauten dem Betrachter mitgeteilt werden, offenbaren die Chronologie eines Industrie-Baugeschehens. Überdeutlich wird aber die gestalterische Bindung an eine maßvolle Beschränkung auf sachliche Zweckmäßigkeit, die sich in Anbetracht der monumentalen Wirkung einer so großen Anlage jeder überflüssigen stilistischen Dekoration enthält.

Siemens acquired their first plot on the lower reaches of the Spree, beyond the Ringbahn in 1897, and this became the core of a gigantic industrial area with its own residential and commercial centre. Siemensstadt grew continuously, and led to a harmonious juxtaposition of all functions within an ordered urban development. Industrial expansion continued until the thirties, but post-war history is more a matter of rebuilding and restructuring. Most of the buildings of the first decade have disappeared, but the silhouette is still dominated by high complexes dating from the tens, twenties and thirties. More recent new building is usually low, very often even single-storey, to accommodate modern manufacturing techniques. Industrial buildings are always having new demands made upon them as products, markets and techniques change. This means that rebuilding and extension are always on the agenda. This constant structural change can also be seen in the Siemens buildings. Siemens' chief architects of the period were responsible, first Karl Janisch, then Hans Hertlein from 1915. The building chronology is revealed by period design features conveyed to the observer by the mass of buildings.

Spreegelände
(a) Wernerwerk XV • 1924-25 • Hans Hertlein
(b) Wernerwerk X • 1928-30 • Hans Hertlein
(c) Blockwerk • 1906 • Karl Janisch, Pfeil
(d) Wernerwerk M • 1914-21 • Karl Janisch
(e) Feuerwache • 1912 • Karl Janisch
(f) Forschungslabor • 1914-22 • Hans Hertlein

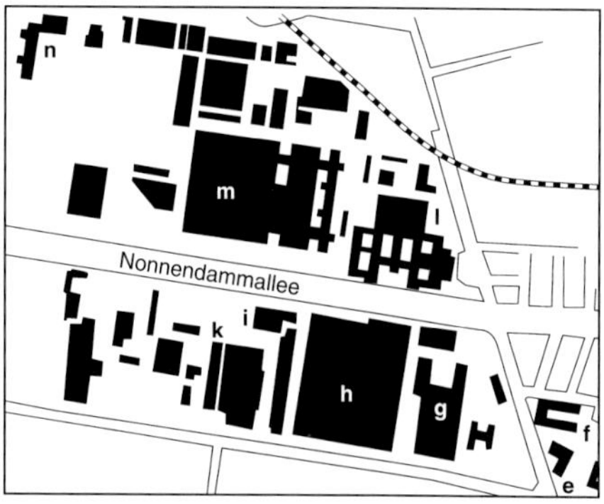

Bereich Nonnendammallee
(g) Automobilwerk • 1906 • Karl Janisch
(h) Dynamowerk • 1906-07 • Karl Janisch, Carl Diehlmann
(i) Heizwerk • 1910 • Karl Janisch
(k) Großschweißerei • 1938-39 • Hans Hertlein
(l) Verwaltung • 1910-13 • Karl Janisch, Friedrich Blume
(m) Schaltwerk • 1916-28 • Hans Hertlein
(n) Hochspannungsprüffeld • 1958-59 • Walter Henn

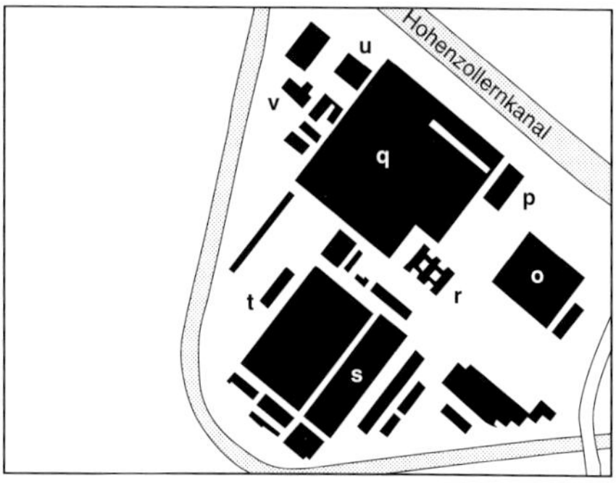

Bereich Gartenfeld
(o) Metallwerk • 1917-18
(p) Prüffeldhalle • 1942-43 • Hans Hertlein
(q) Kabelwerk • 1911-12 • Karl Janisch
(r) Verwaltung • 1911-12 • Karl Janisch
(s) Vorfertigungshalle • 1935-36 • Hans Hertlein
(t) Chemisch-technisches Labor • 1937 • Hans Hertlein
(u) Hochspannungslabor • 1925-27 • Hans Hertlein
(v) Heizwerk • 1927 • Hans Hertlein

J 21 Großsiedlung Siemensstadt
Berlin-Siemensstadt und Berlin-Charlottenburg; Goebelstraße 2/122 u. 21/113, Jungfernheideweg 1/45 u. 4/30 usw.
1929-32 • Hans Scharoun, Walter Gropius, Hugo Häring, Fred Forbat, Paul Rudolf Henning, Otto Bartning

Die Firma Siemens war derart gewachsen, daß täglich über 50 000 Menschen den Werken zuströmten. So lag es nahe, bei dem ohnehin in Berlin bestehenden Wohnungsmangel eine neue Großsiedlung in der Nähe dieser Arbeitsplätze zu schaffen. Am Südrand der Jungfernheide bot sich ein passendes Gelände an, somit unmittelbar neben den Erholungs- und Sportflächen. Nach Süden schloß die geplante Trasse der Siemensbahn an, die für die verkehrsmäßige Anbindung sorgte. Auf Empfehlung von Baustadtrat Martin Wagner wurden sechs Architekten aus der Gruppe »Der Ring« ausgewählt, die Entwürfe und Bauten liefern sollten. Scharoun erarbeitete die städtebauliche Ordnung und errichtete südlich der Bahnlinie, sozusagen als Eingangsbau, aus drei Flügeln eine Häusergruppe, die trichterartig zur eigentlichen Siedlung führt. Dort erkennt man das Überwiegen der streng parallelen Nord-Süd-Zeilen, die den Vorzug ausgewogener Besonnung und Belüftung bieten, zwar viergeschossig, aber mit gehörigem Abstand. Eine Ausnahme macht der von Bartning gebaute »lange Jammer«, der in einem leichten Schwung von West nach Ost den Abschluß der Siedlung zur Bahntrasse bildet.

Siemens had grown to such an extent that over 50,000 people a day were pouring into the factories. It was thus necessary, as Berlin had a housing shortage anyway, to build a new large-scale estate near these factories. There was a suitable site on the southern edge of Jungfernheide, thus with direct access to recreation and sports facilities. The southern boundary was the projected Siemens railway line, which provided the transport infrastructure. On the recommendation of Martin Wagner, a building official, six architects from the group known as «Der Ring» were chosen to provide designs and buildings on a co-operative basis. Scharoun was responsible for town-planning arrangements, and built a group of houses in three sections south of the railway line, as an entrance building as it were, to lead into the actual estate like a funnel. Here one is very aware of the dominance of the strictly parallel north-south rows, offering the advantage of balanced sunlight and air, with four storeys, but a suitable distance apart. An exception was the «long misery» built by Bartning, which finished off the estate with a gentle curve along the railway line.

in der Nähe/nearby:
Siedlung Heimat; Quellweg, Schuckertdamm
1930-34 • Hans Hertlein

J 22 Reichsforschungssiedlung Haselhorst
Berlin-Haselhorst; Gartenfelder Straße 104/140, Burscheider Weg 11/61, Daumstraße 2/10, Haselhorster Damm 1/25 und Burscheider Weg 1/5 g u. 4/10 g, Haselhorster Damm 2/48, Riensbergstraße 61/77
1931-32 • Fred Forbat; Mebes & Emmerich

Die Baugesellschaft »Heimag« erwarb 1928 ein Gelände von 360 000 m^2 aus Reichsbesitz mit der Auflage, dort eine Forschungssiedlung mit 3000 Wohnungen zu errichten. Das Programm der »Reichsforschungsgesellschaft für Wirtschaftlichkeit im Bau- und Wohnungswesen« sah vor: Untersuchungen des Nord-Süd-Zeilenbaus, Vergleich verschiedener Bauweisen, Untersuchungen des Baubetriebes und Arbeitsstudien. Der Wettbewerb lieferte bei den engen Vorgaben sehr ähnliche Ergebnisse, den ersten Preis erhielten Walter Gropius und Stephan Fischer. Die architektonische Überarbeitung und Ausführung des ersten Bauabschnittes wurde Fred Forbat übertragen. Im Jahre 1930 löste sich die Reichsforschungsgesellschaft auf, und die Heimag baute nun in eigener Verantwortung, jedoch mit reduziertem Programm. Als mageres Ergebnis läßt sich zusammenfassen, daß sich ein Verzicht auf Blockrandbebauung ergab, daß sich daraus ein eigenes System der Straßenführung ableitete mit Wegen zwischen den Zeilen, Sammelstraßen an den Köpfen der Zeilen und Hauptstraßen möglichst fern oder abgeschirmt vom Wohnen, schließlich daß Wohnungen mit Querlüftung bevorzugt wurden. Erkennbar ist aber auch die Tendenz zum einfachen Reihenbau, einer Voraussetzung für industrielles Bauen.

In 1928 the «Heimag» building society acquired a site of 360,000 square metres from the state, with the condition that they should build a research estate with 3,000 residential units. The building research unit intended to conduct a programme of research into building in rows running north-south, comparison of various building methods, examination of the building industry and work studies. Given the very precise requirements, the competition produced very similar results; the first prize was won by Walter Gropius and Stephan Fischer. Architectural revision and execution of the first building phase were handed over to Fred Forbat. In 1930 the building research society was dissolved, and Heimag continued to build independently, but with a reduced programme. The slender result produced can be summed up as follows: building on all the edges of the block was abandoned, and this led to a new system of street arrangement with paths between the rows, collective streets at the heads of the rows and main roads as far away as possible or protected from residential areas, and finally that residential units with transverse ventilation were preferred. But a tendency towards simple terraced buildings can be seen, a prerequisite for industrial building.

J 23 Kraftwerk Reuter
Berlin-Siemensstadt; Otternbuchtstraße 11-27
1929-30 • W. Dohme, Tratt

Der wachsende Strombedarf der Stadt in den zwanziger Jahren, nicht zuletzt durch die Elektrifizierung der S-Bahn, machte den Bau neuer Kraftwerke nötig. Die Schaffung von Groß-Berlin erlaubte nun auch den Bau von Großkraftwerken. Als erstes war 1926 das Werk Klingenberg fertiggestellt. Ihm folgte bis 1930 das Kraftwerk West, das in den fünfziger Jahren zur Ehrung Ernst Reuters umbenannt wurde. Dohme, ein Schüler des Siemens-Architekten Hans Hertlein, brachte im Einklang mit der gültigen architektonischen Auffassung viel Sachlichkeit in den Entwurf ein. Er gestaltete das Gebäude als zweckmäßige Hülle für die Maschinen und Kessel, so entstand ein riesiger Kubus mit einzeln angefügten Baugliedern. Einziges stadtbildprägendes Element sind die Schornsteine. – Im Kriege stark zerstört, danach demontiert, erlebte das Kraftwerk einen denkwürdigen Wiederaufbau, nachdem die Militärregierung 1948 diesen als unverzichtbar für die Energieversorgung eines isolierten West-Berlin erkannt und verfügt hatten. Kaum waren die Arbeiten aufgenommen, begann die Blockade. Fast die gesamte technische Ausrüstung – insgesamt 1500 t Güter – mußte zerlegt mit Flugzeugen transportiert werden, eine geschichtemachende Leistung.

The city's increased electricity requirements in the twenties, not least because of the electrification of the S-Bahn, meant that new power stations were needed. The creation of Greater Berlin permitted the construction of large-scale power stations. Dohme, a pupil of Siemens' architect Hans Hertlein, brought a great deal of functionality into the design, in harmony with the prevalent architectural attitude. He designed the building as a functional envelope for turbines and boilers, resulting in a gigantic cube with additional sections. The only element to impinge on the cityscape is the chimney design. The power station was badly damaged in the war, then demolished, but memorably rebuilt when in 1948 the military government decided this was essential for energy provision in an isolated West Berlin and gave orders that the work should be carried out. It had hardly started when the blockade began. Almost all the technical equipment – a total of 1,500 tons of materials – had to be flown in, an achievement of historic proportions.

in der Nähe/nearby:
Wasserwerk Jungfernheide; B-Siemensstadt; Motardstraße 1-59
1961-63 • Krems

J 24 Klärwerk Ruhleben
Berlin-Ruhleben; Freiheit 17-19
1956-58 • Berliner Entwässerungswerke

Nach einer langen Zeit der Vernachlässigung und einer Zuspitzung zu unerträglichen hygienischen Zuständen arbeitete James Hobrecht 1872 für Berlin einen Plan zur Abwasserbeseitigung aus, der ein in zwölf Bereiche unterteiltes unterirdisches Kanalsystem vorsah. Jedem Bereich war ein Pumpwerk zugeordnet, welches die Abwässer radial weit in das Berliner Vorland förderte, wo es auf »Rieselfeldern« eigens eingerichteter Güter versickerte und deren Düngung diente. Noch vor der Jahrhundertwende waren die Anlagen fast vollständig eingerichtet, aber in den dreißiger Jahren war die Abwassermenge bereits derart angestiegen, daß die Verrieselung nicht mehr ausreichte, in Stahnsdorf entstand das erste Großklärwerk. Als erstes innerstädtisches Klärwerk folgte Ruhleben. Es arbeitet nach dem Belebungsverfahren: Zunächst wird das Abwasser zur Geruchsbeseitigung mit Chlor versetzt, feste Bestandteile werden ausgesiebt, dann folgen Sand- und Schlammabsetzbecken, bei anschließender Belüftung wird die Bildung weiterer Schlammflocken durch Mikroorganismen gefördert. Nach einem weiteren Durchgang durch Absetztrichter verläßt klares Wasser die Anlage, das zur Abtötung von Keimen nochmals gechlort wird, doch noch eine erhebliche Salzlast führt. In statisch bedingt birnenförmigen Faulbehältern setzt sich der Schlamm in hochwertige Düngemittel um.

In 1872, after a long period of neglect and deterioration to intolerable hygienic conditions, James Hobrecht drew up a plan for sewage disposal for Berlin, with an underground sewerage system divided into twelve districts. Each district had a pumping station which pumped the sewage radially into the countryside outside Berlin, where it was processed at specially established «sewage farms», and used by them as fertilizer. These were almost completely set up even before the turn of the century, but in the thirties the quantity of sewage had risen to the extent that the sewage farm technique was no longer adequate, and the first large-scale sewage plant was established in Stahnsdorf. Ruhleben came next, as the first inner-city sewage plant. It worked on the activated sludge process: first the sewage is treated with chlorine to remove odours, solid components are sieved out, it then passes through sand and sludge sedimentation tanks, and the formation of further sludge is encouraged by subsequent aeration. After passing through sedimentation funnels again, clear water flows out of the plant, after first being treated with chlorine again to kill germs. Statically designed septic containers are used to convert the sludge into high-grade fertilizer.

in der Nähe/nearby:
Müllverbrennungsanlage; Freiheit 24
1964-68 • Hendel & Haseloff

J 25 Nikolaikirche
Berlin-Spandau; Reformationsplatz
Um 1400

Neben den Alt-Berliner Kirchen ist die Spandauer Nikolaikirche die einzige mittelalterliche Stadtkirche auf heutigem Berliner Gebiet. Ihr massiger quadratischer Westturm war lange Zeit höchster Kirchturm der Mark. Entsprechend der Bauzeit – im Übergang zur Spätgotik – wurde sie als dreischiffige Hallenkirche mit kreuzrippengewölbten Langhausjochen errichtet. Auch die flachgedrückten Spitzbögen weisen auf die Zeit um 1400 hin, wie überhaupt das Kircheninnere nicht dem ur-gotischen Streben nach Höhe, sondern eher nach Weite nachzukommen scheint. Schlichter in der Ausformung und in der architektonischen Dekoration, unterscheidet sich die Nikolaikirche etwa von der zeitgleichen Brandenburger Katharinenkirche. Reich ist dagegen ihre Ausstattung mit Stücken aus Mittelalter, Renaissance und Barockzeit. Ihre geschichtliche Bedeutung bezieht die Kirche aus dem Jahre 1539, als in ihr Kurfürst Joachim II. zum lutherischen Glauben übertrat und mit ihm sein Land. Ein Denkmal auf dem Kirchvorplatz, 1889 von Erdmann Encke, erinnert an dieses für Brandenburg-Preußen wichtige Ereignis.

With the exception of the churches in Old Berlin the Nikolaikirche in Spandau is the only medieval parish church in Berlin. For a long time its massive square west tower was the highest church tower in the Mark. Appropriately for the period in which it was built – the transition to late Gothic – it emerged as a hall church with nave and two aisles with rib-vaulted bays in the nave. The shallow pointed arches also suggest the period c. 1400, just as the entire interior seems not to show the primal Gothic striving for height, but rather more for breadth. The Nikolaikirche is plainer in shape and in its architectural decoration than the roughly contemporary Katharinenkirche in Brandenburg. Its furnishings are lavish, however, with items from the Middle Ages and the Renaissance and baroque periods. The church's historical importance arises from the year 1539, when Elector Joachim II converted to Protestantism in the building, taking his Land with him. A monument in the square outside the church, 1889 by Erdmann Encke, is a reminder of this important event in the history of Brandenburg and Prussia.

J 26 Rathaus Spandau
Berlin-Spandau; Carl-Schurz-Straße 2-6
1910-13 • Reinhardt & Süßenguth

Spandaus Geschichte reicht ins 4. Jahrhundert zurück. In der Zeit der Völkerwanderung gründeten Slawen hier ein Dorf, dem später Burganlagen und Kaufmannssiedlung folgten. Verkehrsmäßig und strategisch wichtig erschienen die Talinseln am Zusammenfluß von Havel und Spree. Die deutsche Kolonisation der Mark bescherte Spandau weiteren Aufschwung, 1230 erhält es – noch vor Berlin – das Stadtrecht. Doch im Mittelalter und in der Neuzeit bleibt Spandau Handwerker- und Ackerbürgerstadt. Die Sogwirkung des aufstrebenden Berlins dämpft jedes Wachstum. Erst die letzte Jahrhundertwende ändert die Situation. Die Randwanderung der Berliner Industrie und der damit einhergehende Wohnungsbau und Ausbau des Nahverkehrsnetzes bringen Spandau schließlich den Status des selbstbewußten Vorortes einer Millionenstadt. Mit dem Rathausbau wird dieses Selbstverständnis repräsentativ zum Ausdruck gebracht. Zehn Jahre später wird Spandau zu einem der großen Außenbezirke von Groß-Berlin.

The history of Spandau goes back to the fourth century. At the time of the migration of the peoples, Slavic tribes founded a village here, later followed by a castle and a merchants' settlement. The islands at the confluence of Havel and Spree seemed important in terms of transport, and strategically. German colonization of the Mark gave Spandau another boost. It was granted a charter in 1230, even before Berlin. But in the Middle Ages and the modern period Spandau remained a town of craftsmen and agricultural workers. The suction effect of up-and-coming Berlin damped down all further growth. The situation did not change until the turn of the present century. Berlin industry was moving to the periphery, and the associated building of housing and expansion of the city transport network brought Spandau the status of a self-confident suburb in a city with millions of inhabitants. This self-view was expressed to the world by the building of the town hall. Ten years later Spandau became one of the major outer districts of Greater Berlin.

in der Nähe/nearby:
Büro- und Hotelgebäude; Freiheit 7-8
1991-93 • Herbert Gergs und Siegfried Gergs
Siemens-Luftfahrtgerätewerk; Streitstraße 5-17
1936-37 • Hans Hertlein
Brauerei-Gebäude; Neuendorfer Straße 20-30
1927-29 • Hermann Dernburg
Geschützgießerei; Schürstraße 5-7
1871-74 • Wevel
Wohnblock; Wilhelmstraße 134-136
1928-29 • Richard Ermisch
Hilfsschule Spandau; Askanierring 42
1926-27 • Ludorf

J 27 Zitadelle
Berlin-Spandau; Am Juliusturm
1560-94 • Christoph Römer, Francesco Chiaramella da Gandino, Rochus Guerrini Graf zu Lynar

Der Juliusturm zeugt von einer askanischen Burg, die hier im Mittelalter unter Albrecht dem Bären errichtet wurde, an strategisch günstiger Stelle. Auch Kurfürst Joachim II. erkannte die Vorzüge der Lage und ließ die Burg zu einer zeitgemäßen Festungsanlage ausbauen. Daran waren mehrere Baumeister tätig, zuletzt Graf zu Lynar, er stammte aus Norditalien, trat in den Dienst des französischen Königs, floh aber bei den ersten Hugenottenverfolgungen nach Sachsen, wo er die Umwallung von Dresden leitete. Er vollendete diese typische Renaissancefestung mit ihren vier spitzwinklig zulaufenden Bastionen. Den Verbindungswegen zwischen den Bastionen gaben die zurückspringenden Flanken des Kurtinenmauerwerks Feuerschutz. Gegenüber dem einfachen mittelalterlichen Mauerwerk hielten diese tiefen Basteien auch einer Kanonade stand. Ihre Stellung und Neigung leitete sich – ganz im Sinne des beginnenden naturwissenschaftlichen Zeitalters – aus der ballistischen Gesetzmäßigkeit ab. Die Bastion König läßt noch heute den inneren Aufbau erkennen: unten der Minengang, dann die Hauptfeuergalerie mit dem Wechsel der Stellungen für Geschütze und Handfeuerwaffen, darüber das ungedeckte Plateau.

The name Juliusturm is evidence of an Ascanian castle built here in the Middle Ages under Albrecht the Bear, on a strategically important site. Elector Joachim II also recognized the advantages of the situation and had the castle rebuilt as an up-to-date fortress. Several architects were involved in this, and lastly Graf zu Lynar, who came from northern Italy, entered the service of the French king, but fled to Saxony at the time of the first Huguenot persecutions, where he directed the construction of the ramparts around Dresden. He completed this typical Renaissance fortress with its four bastions running together at acute angles. The paths connecting the bastions gave additional protection from firepower to the set-back flanks of the curtain wall. Unlike the simple medieval masonry, these deep bastions would withstand cannon-fire. Their position and inclination were derived – as was appropriate to the beginning of the scientific age – from the laws of ballistics. The König bastion still shows the internal structure: the mine passage is below, then the main gallery with alternating positions for artillery and hand-held firearms, and above this the uncovered plateau.

in der Nähe/nearby:
Abspannwerk Uklei; B-Haselhorst; Am Juliusturm 2/8
1929-30 • Hans Müller

J 28 Schleuse Spandau
Berlin-Spandau; Möllentordamm
1908-11

In den ersten Jahren nach 1900 wurde das Berliner Wasserstraßennetz erheblich ausgebaut. 1906 wurde im Süden der Stadt der Teltowkanal fertiggestellt, gleichzeitig der Prinz-Leopold-Kanal als Abzweig zum Wannsee und der Neuköllner Schiffahrtskanal, und mit dem Bau des Hohenzollernkanals begonnen, der als Großschiffahrtsweg Berlin–Stettin 1913 dem Verkehr übergeben wurde. In der Folge dieser Neubauten kam es auch zur Modernisierung bestehender veralteter Anlagen wie etwa der Spandauer Havelschleuse, die den Verkehr der neuen 600-t-Schiffe zwischen Hohenzollernkanal und Unterhavel vermitteln mußte. Von beiden Seiten hart bedrängt durch den Spandauer Ortsteil Behnitz westlich und die Zitadelle östlich, gestaltete sich zudem die nördliche Ein- und Ausfahrt der Schiffe in einer engen Kurve des Havellaufs schwierig. Für die Planung der siebziger Jahre, eine zweite Schleusenkammer für 1350-t-Regelschiffe, sogenannte Europaschiffe, zu bauen, wurden diese Beengtheit und die nicht geduldeten Eingriffe in die Substanz der denkmalgeschützten Zitadelle zur unüberwindlichen Hürde. Mit dem Wegfall der deutsch-deutschen Grenzen bieten sich bisher versperrte Wasserwege im Nordwesten der Stadt an, und der kleinen Spandauer Schleuse scheint die Zukunft gesichert.

The network of Berlin waterways was considerably expanded after 1900. In 1906 the Teltow canal was completed in the south of the town, and so at the same time were the Prinz-Leopold-Kanal as a branch to Wannsee and the Neukölln shipping canal, and building started on the Hohenzollernkanal, which was opened to traffic in 1913 as the great shipping route from Berlin to Stettin. A consequence of this new building was modernization of existing antiquated plant like the lock on the Havel at Spandau, which had to handle the new 600 ton ships passing from the Hohenzollernkanal to the lower Havel. Cramped on both sides by Behnitz, a district of Spandau to the west, and the citadel to the east, ingress and egress of ships to the north into a narrow curve of the Havel was additionally difficult. Planning in the seventies foresaw the building of a second lock in Spandau for regulation 1,350 ton ships, so-called Europaschiffe, but the narrowness of the river and the fact that it was not permissible to impinge on the citadel, which is a listed building, were an insurmountable hurdle. When the German-German frontier was removed the waterways in the north-west of the town that had hitherto been closed, became available, and so the future of the little lock in Spandau seems assured.

in der Nähe/nearby:
St. Marien am Behnitz; B-Spandau; Behnitz
1848 • Julius Manger, Friedrich Wilhelm IV.

J 29 Siedlung
Berlin-Spandau; Zeppelinstraße 12-27 u. 76-110
1926 • Richard Ermisch, Adolf Steil

Kaum eine andere Baugruppe dokumentiert den Formenreichtum des Expressionismus so eindringlich wie diese Siedlung. Die abgetreppten Turmhelme der Eckbauten mit dem Zickzackband der Ladenoberlichter sind für sich schon sehenswert. In den langen Hauszeilen wiederholen sich Dreiecke, Spitzen und Zacken in allen Baugliedern und Details, die Formen werden aber vielfältig abgewandelt in den Profilen der Gesimse oder auch in der Farbigkeit. Dieser ekstatische Expressionismus erweist sich getreu dem französischen Begriff »art deco« hier als reines Dekorieren. Unter dem äußeren Schmuck verbergen sich ganz normale Baukörper. Wenn auch die organische Verbindung einer durchgehend architektonischen Haltung, etwa in Grundriß und Gestalt, fehlt, so bleibt immerhin die Wirkung der Häuser im Stadtbild. Gärung und Revolution können mit dem Expressionismus besser in Verbindung gebracht werden als eine fertige Ideologie, die sich dann im zeitlich nachfolgenden Stil der Neuen Sachlichkeit äußert.

There is scarcely another group of buildings that demonstrates the formal wealth of Expressionism as well as this estate. The ribbed steeples on the corner buildings with the zig-zag line of the shop skylights are worth seeing in themselves. In the long rows of houses, triangles, points and indentations are repeated in all parts of the buildings and in every detail, but the shapes are varied a great deal in the profiles of the ledges or in the colour schemes. This ecstatic Expressionism shows itself true to the French notion of «art deco», as pure decoration. This external decoration conceals quite ordinary buildings. Organic connection is not made in terms of a coherent architectural attitude, in outline and design, for example, but despite this the effect the buildings make in the townscape remains. Fermentation and revolution are easier to link with Expressionism than a complete ideology of the kind expressed in the style that was to follow, Neue Sachlichkeit.

in der Nähe/nearby:
Miethaus Steil; Falkenhagener Straße 37
1927 • Richard Ermisch
Doppelwohnhaus; Marwitzer Straße 37-37 a
1979-81 • Johanne Nalbach, Gernot Nalbach
Stadthauspark; Spandauer Straße 100-105
1982-84 • Hans-Peter Störl
Fort Hahneberg; Hahnebergweg
1884

J 30 Gartenstadt Staaken
Berlin-Staaken; Heidebergplan, Am Heideberg, Torweg, Zwischen den Giebeln usw.
1913-17 • Paul Schmitthenner

Antwort auf die Vermassung der Städte und auf verantwortungslose Baudichte zum Ende des 19. Jahrhunderts war die Gartenstadtbewegung. Eine hervorragende Umsetzung ihrer Gedanken lieferte Paul Schmitthenner mit der Gartenstadt Staaken. Zwei-, höchstens dreigeschossige Häuserreihen teils in Ziegeln, teils in Putz, kurvige Straßen, kleine Plätze, stille Winkel, steile Dächer, kleine Treppchen, Blumenerker, Gauben – das alles soll Erinnerungen an verträumte Städtchen der »guten alten Zeit« wachrufen. Großstädtischer Anonymität wird menschliche Maßstäblichkeit, Nutzquartieren wird Heimat entgegengesetzt. Zwar decken sich zeitlich die Anfänge der Bewegung, das 1898 erschienene Buch »Tomorrow« des Engländers Howard, mit dem reformbewußten Jugendstil, die Gartenstadt folgt ihm aber nicht formal, entwickelt vielmehr den eigenen Stil, der deutlich rückblickend Gefühle und Sehnsüchte auszudrücken sucht, sich dabei klar bestimmbarer Gestaltungselemente bedient und deshalb bevorzugt mit dem Begriff »Expressiver Realismus« belegt wird.

The garden city movement was a response to the stereotyping of towns and irresponsible building density in the late nineteenth century. Paul Schmitthenner's garden city in Staaken was an outstanding support for these ideas. Rows of two-, at the most three-storey houses, some in brick, some rendered, curving streets, small squares, quiet corners, steep roofs, little flights of steps, flower bays, dormers – all this is intended to be a reminder of sleepy little towns in the «good old days». The anonymity of the city is exchanged for humanity of scale, and the idea of home is set against commercial properties. It is true that the beginnings of the movement, which started with the appearance of the book «Tomorrow» by Sir Ebenezer Howard in 1898, correspond with reform-conscious Jugendstil in terms of time, but the garden city does not follow this formally; it develops a style of its own, clearly looking back and trying to express feelings and longings, using design elements that can clearly be determined and therefore best described by the term «Expressive Realism».

K
Berlin
Nordwestliche Vororte

Dörfer und Gutsbezirke kennzeichneten bis zu Beginn unseres Jahrhunderts den Nordwesten Berlins. Lediglich Tegel war bekannt als Wohnstätte Wilhelm v. Humboldts und erfreute sich im bürgerlichen Berlin schon lange großer Beliebtheit als Ausflugsort. Einige Landhäuser entstanden hier, zumal seit 1893 die Kremmener Bahn gute Verbindungen nach Berlin gewährleistete. Im Jahre 1896 ließ sich die Maschinen- und Lokomotivbaufirma Borsig in Tegel nieder, nachdem das bisherige Gelände in Moabit und zuvor schon vor dem Oranienburger Tor zu eng geworden war. 1908 erhielt Tegel einen kleinen Hafen und schließlich eine Industriebahn, die im weiten Bogen die Verbindung zu den Vororten östlich Berlins herstellte. Im Süden von Tegel baute von 1902 an die Stadt Berlin ihr sechstes großes Gaswerk. Aber auch andere Einrichtungen verlegte Berlin weit vor seine Tore: 1877 die Irrenanstalt Dalldorf – die späteren Karl-Bonhoeffer-Heilstätten Wittenau – und 1896 die Haftanstalt Tegel. Als reine Villenkolonie wurde 1910 Frohnau parzelliert und fortan bebaut. Eine städtische Entwicklung für den Nordwesten brachten dann die zwanziger Jahre. Im neugeschaffenen Groß-Berlin drängten die Siedlungen nun in die unbebauten Gelände nördlich der Ringbahn. Wedding dehnte sich nochmals beiderseits der Müllerstraße bis nach Reinickendorf aus, der Volkspark Rehberge wurde angelegt. In einem breiten Gürtel füllten Siedlungen auch das Gebiet zwischen Reinickendorf und Tegel auf, stellenweise durchsetzt mit Industrieanlagen. Zwischen Tegel und Waidmannslust erweiterte die Baugesellschaft »Freie Scholle« ihre 1895 dort begonnene Siedlung. Der Wohnungsbau nach 1945 sorgte dann endgültig für ein lockeres Zusammenwachsen der alten Vororte. Die Idee der Trabantenstädte hinterließ auch hier ihre Spuren, im Jahre 1963 war Baubeginn für das Märkische Viertel, in welchem 50000 Menschen Wohnung finden sollten. – Heute prägen Gegensätze den Berliner Nordwesten, es fehlt das ordnende städtebauliche Konzept einheitlicher Planung oder der Charme eines langsamen historischen Wachsens. Hochhäuser stehen nun neben Kleingärten, die Wittenauer Industrie muß sich mit dem ländlichen Idyll von Lübars vertragen, ein moderner Flughafen grenzt an die Wälder des Tegeler Sees.

Until the beginning of the present century the characteristic feature of north-western Berlin was villages and country estates. Only Tegel was well known; it was the place where Wilhelm von Humboldt had lived, and had long been popular throughout Berlin as an excursion destination. Some country houses were built here, especially after the Kremmen railway provided good connections with Berlin from 1893. In 1896 Borsig, the machine and locomotive building firm, established itself in Tegel, after its former sites in Moabit and before that in Oranienburger Tor had become too cramped. In 1908 Tegel acquired a little harbour and finally an industrial railway, which in a wide curve established a connection with the suburbs in the east of Berlin. From 1902 the city of Berlin built its sixth large gasworks in the south of Tegel. But Berlin put other institutions well outside its gates: in 1877 the Dalldorf lunatic asylum – later the Karl Bonhoeffer establishment in Wittenau – and in 1896 Tegel jail. Frohnau was parcelled and developed as a pure villa district from 1910. The twenties then brought municipal development to the north-west. In what was now Greater Berlin, settlement was beginning in the undeveloped area north of the Ringbahn, the ring railway. Wedding again extended on both sides of Müllerstrasse to Reinickendorf, and the people's park in Rehberge was laid out. A broad settlement belt also filled the area between Reinickendorf and Tegel, including some industrial complexes. The «Freie Scholle» building company extended the estate it had started between Reinickendorf and Waidmannslust in 1895. Finally, residential accommodation built after 1945 led to the old suburbs growing loosely together. The idea of satellite towns also made its mark: work started on the Märkisches Viertel in 1963, intended to provide accommodation for 50,000 people. Today the north-west of Berlin is full of contrasts, it lacks both ordered planning and the charm of slow historic growth. High-rise buildings stand next to allotments, industry in Wittenau has to coexist with the rural idyll of Lübars, and a modern airport encroaches upon the woods around the Tegeler See.

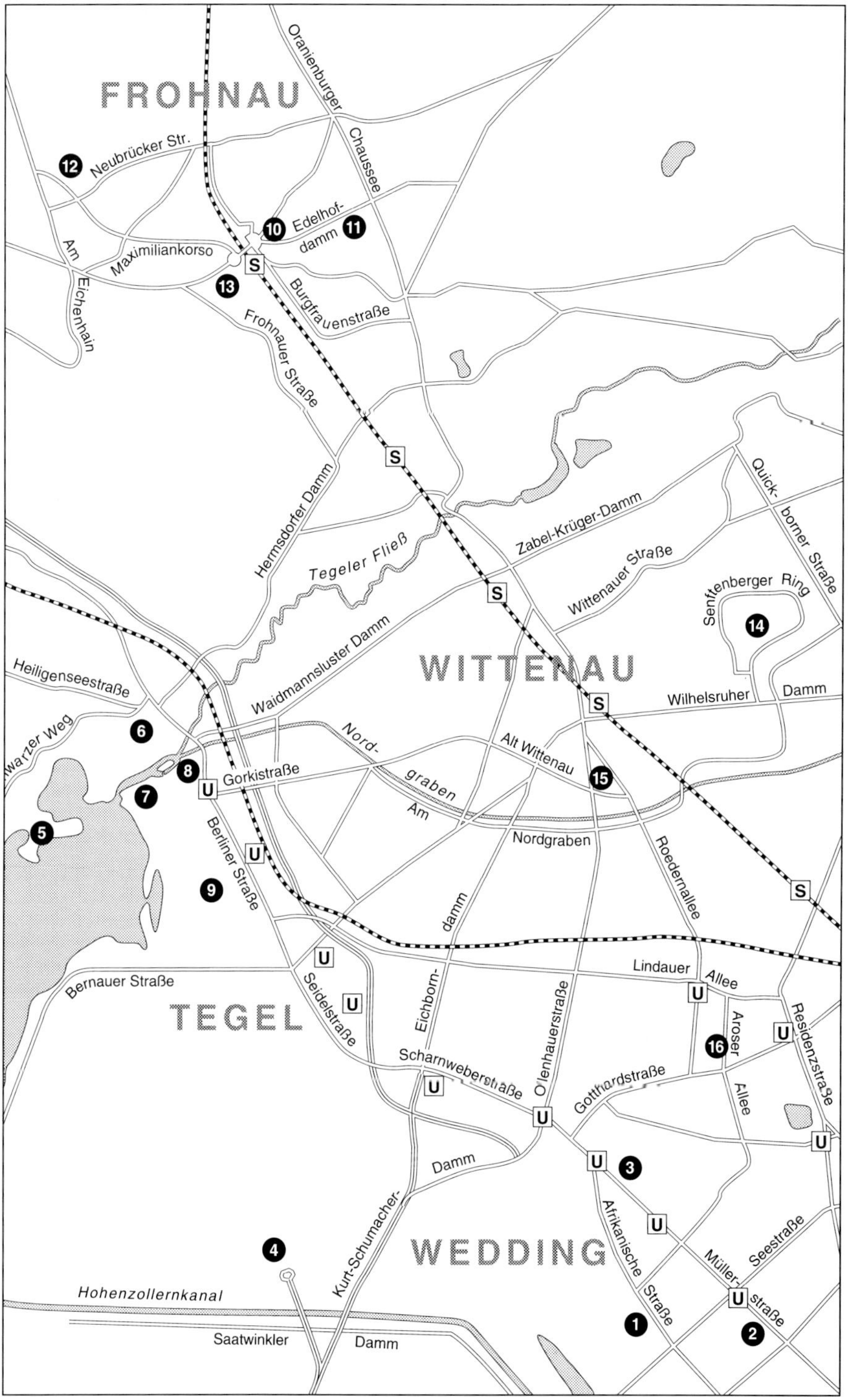

K 1 Wohnzeilen Afrikanische Straße
K 2 Rathaus Wedding
K 3 Betriebsbahnhof Müllerstraße
K 4 Flughafen Tegel
K 5 Villa Borsig
K 6 Humboldtschloß
K 7 Wohnbauten am Tegeler Hafen
K 8 Phosphateliminierungsanlage PEA
K 9 Borsigturm
K 10 Johanneskirche
K 11 Buddhistisches Haus
K 12 Friedhofskapelle Frohnau
K 13 Häuser an der Buche
K 14 Wohnstadt Märkisches Viertel
K 15 Schule Wittenau
K 16 Weiße Stadt

K 1 Wohnzeilen
Berlin-Wedding; Afrikanische Straße 14-41
1926-27 • Ludwig Mies van der Rohe

Die als Abschluß der Kleinsiedlung Jungfernheide von Mies erbauten vier Wohnblöcke bringen unmißverständlich die Formensprache der Neuen Sachlichkeit zum Ausdruck, die in der kurzen Phase von 1926 bis 1932 das Bauen prägte. Die Häuser erscheinen als abstrakte, stereometrische Blöcke mit glatten Wandflächen. Scharfe Umrisse, eine betont waagerechte Gliederung und flache Dächer kennzeichnen die neue asketische Haltung, die mit der noch ein oder zwei Jahrzehnte zuvor propagierten Wohnlichkeit oder malerischen Behaglichkeit nichts gemein hat. Der formale Wille beherrscht als vergeistigtes, fast ideologisches Element derart die Gestaltung, daß für Details kein Raum bleibt. Wenn Mies aber dennoch mit dem graphischen Muster der Fensteranordnung oder den wie Scharniere zwischen die Blockflügel gespannten Balkonen aus der auferlegten Sterilität ausbricht, mag dieses als Zeichen gelten, wie schwer der Umgang mit der Sachlichkeit in der Architektur ist. Daß es in Berlin eine Fülle hervorragender Bauten dieser Stilrichtung gibt, liegt nicht zuletzt daran, daß sich in den zwanziger Jahren die Elite der Architekten hier versammelt hatte.

These four residential blocks built by Mies as a conclusion to the little Jungfernheide estate unmistakably express the formal language of Neue Sachlichkeit, which put its stamp on building for the short phase from 1926 to 1932. The buildings appear as abstract, stereometric blocks with smooth wall surfaces. Sharp outlines, emphatically horizontal articulation and flat roofs are the characteristic features of this new ascetic attitude, which has nothing in common with the cosiness or picturesque homeliness that was all the rage a decade or two earlier. Formal will dominates the design as a cerebral, almost ideological element to the extent that there is no room for detail. But when Mies uses the graphic pattern of the window arrangement or the balconies placed like hinges between the sections of the block to break away from the sterility the style imposes, this may be a sign for the difficulty of handling functionality in architecture. The fact that Berlin has a large number of outstanding buildings in this style is not least due to the fact that the architectural élite collected here in the twenties.

in der Nähe/nearby:
E-Stützpunkt Zeppelin; Brüsseler Straße 32
1928 • Hans Müller
Kapernaumkirche; Seestraße 34
1897-1902 • Siebold
Friedrich-Ebert-Siedlung; Afrikanische Straße 140/146 d und 139/153 e usw.
1929-31 • Mebes & Emmerich, Bruno Taut
Volkspark Rehberge; Transvaalstraße
1926-29 • Erwin Barth

K 2 Rathaus Wedding
Berlin-Wedding; Müllerstraße 146-147
1928-30 • Friedrich Hellwig (Hochbauamt Wedding)

In Ablehnung alles Monumentalen, in seiner Sachlichkeit eher als Fabrikbau zu verstehen, weicht das Weddinger Rathaus von allen früheren Rezepturen für eine solche Bauaufgabe auffällig ab. In einer Zeit sozialen Verständnisses hätte jeder Repräsentationsbau gerade im Arbeiterbezirk Wedding wie eine Verhöhnung der an dunklen Hinterhöfen wohnenden Bevölkerung gewirkt. Deshalb bleibt es bei einer zaghaften Betonung der straßenräumlich wichtigen Ecke an der Müllerstraße durch eine Wappentafel und durch die Höherführung der Wände um ein Halbgeschoß. Mit den im Erdgeschoß eingebauten Läden wird weiterhin Nähe zum Bürger versinnbildlicht, ähnlich wie in mittelalterlichen Rathäusern. Überhaupt war die Entmystifizierung der Behörden ein wesentliches Anliegen der Weimarer Zeit.

Wedding town hall, with its rejection of anything monumental, more like a factory building in its functionality, is a striking departure from all previous prescriptions for a building of this kind. At a time of enhanced social understanding any markedly prestigious building, in a working district like Wedding in particular, would have seemed like a mockery of the population living in its dark back yards. For this reason it goes no further than a hesitant emphasis of the important corner on Müllerstrasse with a plaque bearing a coat of arms, and by increasing the height of the walls by half a storey. Shops built into the ground floor further emphasize closeness to the people, in a similar way to the medieval town hall. The demystification of authority was a matter of fundamental concern under the Weimar Republic.

in der Nähe/nearby:
Alte Nazarethkirche; Leopoldplatz
1832-35 • Karl Friedrich Schinkel

K 3 Betriebsbahnhof Müllerstraße
Berlin-Wedding; Müllerstraße 77-81
1925-27 • Jean Krämer

Der heutige Omnibus-Betriebshof diente bis 1957 der Straßenbahn, und nur so ist die Weiträumigkeit des Platzes vor den Hallen zu erklären, da hier die Gleisanlagen mit Weichen und Wendeschleifen unterzubringen waren. Die Rationalisierung bei der Straßenbahngesellschaft – erst seit 1929 gibt es die Berliner Verkehrs-Aktiengesellschaft BVG – verlangte nach einem Betriebshof in Innenstadtnähe, um lange Leerfahrten in die Vorortanlagen zu vermeiden. Die Einpassung einer großen Fahrzeughalle in die geschlossene städtische Bebauung erforderte nun aber städtebauliches Feingefühl. Jean Krämer gelang es, im Neubaugebiet von Wedding eine ganze Straßenbahnerstadt zu schaffen, bei der ein Ring von Hauszeilen mit 380 Wohnungen die Halle für 320 Straßenbahnwagen umgibt. Mit den hohen Torbauten setzte er in der Straße sogar einen Akzent, der das Stadtbild bereichert. Krämers maßvoller Expressionismus äußert sich zudem in vielen Einzelformen und begründet den baugeschichtlichen Wert der Anlage.

The present bus garage was used for trams until 1957, which explains the spaciousness of the area in front of the garage: it formerly accommodated tracks with points and turning loops. Rationalization by the Berlin tram company – BVG as an umbrella transport company did not exist until 1929 – required a depot near the city centre, to avoid long empty journeys into the suburbs. Fitting a large vehicle depot into a heavily built-up area needed sensitive planning, however. Jean Krämer succeeded in creating an entire tramworkers' city in the Wedding new building area, with a ring of buildings providing 380 residential units around the hall for 320 trams. Indeed the tall building with its great entrances to the depot sets an accent that actually enriches the look of the street. Krämer's restrained Expressionism is additionally expressed in many individual forms, confirming the value of the complex in terms of architectural history.

in der Nähe/nearby:
Siedlung am Schillerpark; Bristolstraße 1/23
1926-28 • Bruno Taut

K 4 Flughafen Tegel
Berlin-Tegel; Kurt-Schumacher-Damm
1969-74 • Meinhard v. Gerkan, Volkwin Marg, Klaus Nickels

Bereits in den fünfziger Jahren zeigte sich, daß der Flughafen Tempelhof nicht mehr auf Dauer den steigenden Fluggastzahlen gewachsen war und die Startbahn dem kommenden Düsenflugverkehr nicht genügte. Der Ausbau des seit der Blockade bestehenden Flugfeldes in Tegel wurde 1966 schließlich durch einen Wettbewerb eingeleitet. Die Idee der Hamburger Preisträger bestand in der funktionalen Anordnung der Bereiche Vorfahrt, Abfertigung, Warten und Abflug in radialer Folge von innen nach außen. Das brachte kürzeste Wege mit sich und bei der Fächerform der Sektoren die günstigste Flächennutzung in Anbetracht des unterschiedlichen Platzbedarfs von PKW oder Bus einerseits und Flugzeug andererseits. Die Dezentralisierung und Reihung der Abfertigungseinheiten macht den Flughafen zudem übersichtlich und erleichtert Erweiterungen und Umbauten, wie sie der ständige technische Wandel mit sich bringt. Projektiert war eine Anlage aus zwei sechseckigen Abfertigungsringen, die ein Zentralgebäude mit dem Tower verbindet, der zweite Ring blieb der späteren zweiten Ausbaustufe vorbehalten. Vierzehn Fluggastbrücken vermitteln ein reibungsloses Ein- und Aussteigen und reichten aus, über anderthalb Jahrzehnte nahezu den gesamten West-Berliner Flugverkehr abzuwickeln.

Even in the fifties it became clear that Tempelhof airport was in the long run not going to be adequate for increasing passenger numbers, and that the runway was too short to accommodate the new jet planes. Tegel airport had existed since the blockade, and was finally extended in 1966 on the basis of a design produced in a competition. The Hamburg prizewinners' idea was to arrange the areas for approach, checking in and customs clearance, waiting and departure in a functional radial sequence, working from the inside outwards. This meant that distances to be covered were reduced to a minimum, and that best use was made of the area in terms of the different spatial needs of private cars and buses on the one hand and aircraft on the other. Decentralization and sequential arrangement of check-in and customs clearance units additionally make the layout of the airport clear, and make it easy to extend and to accommodate the modifications required by constant technical change. The complex was projected as consisting of two hexagonal check-in and clearance rings, connected to the tower by a central building, but the second ring was finally reserved for the second development stage. Fourteen passenger gates allow for trouble-free passage to and from aircraft and proved adequate to handle almost all West Berlin's air traffic for one and a half decades.

in der Nähe/nearby:
Wohnblöcke; B-Reinickendorf; Ollenhauerstraße 45-51
1927 • Erwin Gutkind

K 5 Villa Borsig
Berlin-Tegel; Reiherwerder
1908-13 • Eugen Schmohl, Alfred Salinger

Reiherwerder entstand nach 1898 durch Sandaufschüttung aus zwei kleinen natürlichen Inseln. Auf der so gebildeten künstlichen Halbinsel ließ sich Ernst v. Borsig ein Landhaus bauen, das in mancherlei Hinsicht eher als Schloß angesehen werden kann. Sowohl die Größe des Baues als auch die Weitläufigkeit des Parkes mit den Nebengebäuden deuten die Veränderung in der Gesellschaft an und dokumentieren den Führungsanspruch des neuen Industrieadels. Passend zum Schloß wählten die Architekten die neubarocke Gestaltung, die sich in der Verteilung der Baumassen wie in den formalen Details niederschlägt. Ein Hauch von »Sanssouci« prägt die Fassade, und das sicher nicht ohne Absicht. Bezeichnenderweise greift in jenen Jahren das Bürgertum auf die Formensprache höfischer Baukunst zurück, während der Hof modern baut, etwa Cecilienhof bei Potsdam im englischen Landhausstil.

Reiherwerder was created after 1898 by filling in the area between two small natural islands with sand to form a small artificial peninsula, upon which Ernst von Borsig built a country house that could in many ways be considered a palace. Both the size of the building and the spaciousness of the park containing other buildings are signs of social change, documenting the new industrial aristocracy's claim to leadership. The architects chose a neo-baroque style suitable for a palace, and this shows in both the distribution of building masses and formal details. The façade carries a hint of «Sanssouci», and this is certainly not unintentional. It was characteristic of the period that the upper middle class looked back to the formal language of court architecture, while the court adopted a modern style, as for example in the Cecilienhof near Potsdam, in the English country house style.

in der Nähe/nearby:
Garten Borsig; Reiherwerder
1908-13 • Körner & Brodersen
Hafenbrücke; Greenwichpromenade
1908
Wohnanlage Neptun und Nixe; Wilkestraße 1/15 a
1965-67 • Montag & Druschke, Heinz Schudnagies
Kirche; Alt-Tegel
1911-12 • Jürgen Kröger

K 6 Humboldtschloß
Berlin-Tegel; Adelheidallee 17/23
1821-24 • Karl Friedrich Schinkel

Seit dem Einzug der Römer in germanisches Gebiet wurde immer wieder selbst in klimatisch aussichtslosen Lagen versucht, Wein anzubauen. Auch Tegel besaß ein »Weingut«, 1765 kam es in den Besitz der Familie Humboldt. Für Wilhelm und Caroline v. Humboldt baute Schinkel das Gutshaus zu einem ländlichen Schloß um. Ganz im Sinne der von Humboldt vertretenen Synthese aus humanistischer Bildung und moderner Wissenschaft übersetzte Schinkel dieses geistige Ideal in eine ideale Architektur. Klassisch in seiner Klarheit, modern in seiner Schlichtheit gibt sich das Schlößchen. Die vier Ecktürme tragen aus der Werkstatt von Christian Daniel Rauch antikische Reliefs nach Vorbildern des Turms der Winde in Athen. In Wandnischen stehen Kopien antiker Marmorskulpturen. Schinkel selbst schrieb: »Mit seiner heiteren Mauerfarbe und den hellen bläulichen Zinkdächern ist das Gebäude in der Umgebung der dunklen Baumgruppen von der freundlichsten Wirkung und aus weiter Ferne bemerkbar.«

Ever since the Romans arrived on German soil, attempts have been made to grow vines, even in situations with an entirely unsuitable climate. Tegel too had a «vineyard», and this came into the possession of the Humboldt family in 1765. Schinkel rebuilt the house as a country residence for Wilhelm and Caroline von Humboldt. Schinkel translated von Humboldt's intellectual ideal of a synthesis of humanist education and modern science into idealized architecture. The house is classical in its clarity and modern in its plainness. The four corner towers carry ancient reliefs modelled on the Tower of the Winds in Athens, from the studio of Christian Daniel Rauch. Copies of ancient marble statues stand in wall niches. Schinkel himself wrote: «With its bright wall paint and light roofs in blueish zinc, the building, which is surrounded by a group of trees, makes a most pleasing impression, and can be seen from a great distance.»

in der Nähe/nearby:
Humboldtsäule; Schloßpark
1829-31 • Karl Friedrich Schinkel, Christian Friedrich Tieck
Haus Heinz; Gabrielenstraße 35
1900 • A. Witt
Sorat-Hotel Humboldt-Mühle; An der Mühle 5-9
Um 1875; 1906; 1911; 1912-13; 1939-40;
1989-92 • Karl-Heinz Steinebach, Friedrich Weber

K 7 Wohnbauten am Tegeler Hafen
Berlin-Tegel; Am Tegeler Hafen
1985-88 • Charles Moore, John Ruble, Buzz Yudell

Mehr in der städtebaulichen Güte als im Wohnkomfort ist der Wert dieses Projektes der Internationalen Bauausstellung 1987 zu sehen. Baukastenartig setzt sich dieses phantasievolle Gebilde zusammen. Gemessen an den nüchternen Siedlungen der vergangenen drei Jahrzehnte kommt die Häuserkulisse dem Betrachter wie eine Traumwelt vor. Der Begriff »Postmoderne« steht hier für eine architektonische Haltung, die menschlich-ästhetischen Bedürfnissen mit ausdrücklicher Individualität und nicht mit Maximen der Zweckmäßigkeit oder Wirtschaftlichkeit gerecht werden möchte. Die gesamte neue Umbauung des Tegeler Hafens atmet diesen Geist.

The value of this project of the Internationale Bauausstellung 1987 lies more in its pleasing impact in urban development terms than in comfortable living. The imaginative structure is put together to an almost modular scheme. Seen against the sober estates of the past three decades the building seems like a dream world to the observer. The concept post-modern here stands for an architectural attitude that tries to do justice to human and aesthetic requirements with express individuality and not with maxims of expediency or economy. All the new building around Tegel harbour is imbued with this spirit.

in der Nähe/nearby:
Wohnzeilen; Am Tegeler Hafen 13-13 d u. 15-15 d
1985-88 • Dietrich Bangert, Bernd Jansen, Stefan Scholz, Axel Schultes
Wohnzeilen; Am Tegeler Hafen 14-14 d
1985-88 • Regina Poly, Karl-Heinz Steinebach, Friedrich Weber
Wohnhaus; Am Tegeler Hafen 15 a
1985-88 • Antoine Grumbach
Wohnhaus; Am Tegeler Hafen 16
1985-88 • John Hejduk, Moritz Müller
Wohnhaus; Am Tegeler Hafen 16 b
1985-88 • Paolo Portoghesi
Wohnhaus; Am Tegeler Hafen 16 c
1985-88 • Stanley Tigerman, Fugman, McCurry
Wohnhaus; Am Tegeler Hafen 16 d
1985-88 • Robert Stern
Doppelhaus; Am Tegeler Hafen 17
1985-88 • Karl-Heinz Steinebach, Friedrich Weber
Wohnhaus; Am Tegeler Hafen 18
1985-88 • Charles Moore, John Ruble, Buzz Yudell
Humboldtbibliothek; Karolinenstraße 19
1985-88 • Charles Moore, John Ruble, Buzz Yudell

K 8 Phosphateliminierungsanlage PEA
Berlin-Tegel; Buddestraße
1982-85 • Gustav Peichl

Rieselfelder und Kläranlagen älterer Bauart vermögen nicht, dem Abwasser die gelösten Salze zu entziehen. Besonders Phosphate, die mit Waschmitteln ins Wasser gelangen, bedrohen das biologische Gleichgewicht in Seen und Flüssen. Tegeler Fließ und Nordgraben, Zuflüsse des Tegeler Sees, führen als Entwässerung der nördlichen Rieselfelder eine besonders hohe Salzlast, unter welcher der See erheblich litt. Die PEA hat die Aufgabe, Phosphate aus dem Nordgrabenwasser auf chemischem Wege auszuflocken und so durch einen biologisch einwandfreien Wasserzulauf die Veralgung des Sees zu verhindern und damit auch die Trinkwasserversorgung des Berliner Nordens zu sichern. Die im Dreieck angeordneten kreisförmigen Flocker sind in eine übergrünte Erdschüttung eingebettet. Wie ein Schiff steuert auf deren Mittelpunkt das Betriebsgebäude, das in seiner baukörperlichen Gliederung die Maßstäbe der nahen Vorortbebauung aufnimmt. Die PEA ist Pilotprojekt eines neuen ökologiebedingten Bauens. Darüber hinaus weist der Komplex auch Alternativen zu den gesichtslosen Fabrikhallen aus Fertigteilen, vermittelt einen Anschluß an bewährte Berliner Industriebaukultur.

Old-style sewage farms and purification plants cannot remove salts in solution from sewage. Phosphates in particular, which get into water from detergents, threaten the biological balance of lakes and rivers. The Tegeler Fliess and the Nordgraben flow into the Tegeler See, and carry high quantities of salt as they drain the sewage farms to the north, and this is deleterious to the lake. The Phosphate Elimination Plant uses a chemical process to separate the salts from the Nordgraben water as a flocculent precipitation, and thus to prevent the lake from clogging up with algae by allowing water that is biologically sound to flow into it, thus also securing drinking water provision for northern Berlin. The circular flocculation tanks are arranged in a triangle, on an artificial mound of grassed earth. The plant building steers towards their centre point like a ship; its architectural articulation takes up the scale of the nearby suburban buildings. The PEP is a pilot-project for new, ecology-conscious building, and beyond this indicates alternatives to faceless factory halls made of prefabricated parts, and forms a link to tried and tested Berlin industrial architecture.

in der Nähe/nearby:
Gleichrichterwerk Tegel; Buddestraße 24-26
1925-26 • Richard Brademann
Humboldt-Realschule; Hatzfeldtstraße 2/4
1910-11 • Fischer
Wohnanlage; Gorkistraße 28/70
1929-30 • Erwin Gutkind

K 9 Borsigturm
Berlin-Tegel; Berliner Straße 29
1922-24 • Eugen Schmohl

Das Attribut »erstes Hochhaus von Berlin« steht dem Borsigturm zu. Auf dem dicht bebauten Werksgelände bot das elfgeschossige Gebäude dringend benötigten Büros Platz. Sowohl konstruktiv wie auch gestalterisch gab es in Deutschland keine Erfahrungen im Hochhausbau. So erstellte Schmohl den Turm in einer Mischung aus Mauerwerk in Hartbrandsteinen und inneren Stahlstützen und Stahlrahmen. Die Fronten bildete er im bewährten Pfeilerstil aus, der wie die Kombination des Fassadenmaterials aus Ziegeln und Werkstein bereits zwei Jahrzehnte zuvor Anwendung fand. Neu waren allenfalls die expressionistischen Details in den Konturen des Turmaufbaues, in dessen parabelförmigen Fensterblenden oder in den abgetreppten Gesimsen, welche die Vertikale in drei mal drei Geschosse teilen, als fürchte man sich vor der optischen Wirkung der Gebäudehöhe. Im Ullsteinhaus in Tempelhof fand die architektonische Idee des Borsigturmes ihre Fortsetzung.

The Borsig tower can claim to be «the first high-rise building in Berlin». The eleven-storey building provided much-needed office space on the highly built up works site. Germany had no experience of either designing or building high-rise structures, and so Schmohl constructed his tower in a mixture of hard burnt brick with inner steel supports and frames. He built the façades in the tried and tested pier style, which like the combination of brick and ashlar for the façade had been applied two decades before. But certainly the Expressionist details in the contours of the top of the tower were new: its parabolic blind windows or the curved cornices cutting the vertical into three times three storeys, as though afraid of the visual impact of the building's height. The architectural idea of the Borsig tower is continued in the Ullsteinhaus in Tempelhof.

in der Nähe/nearby:
Germaniahalle; Berliner Straße 19-37
1872/1915
Borsig-Werktor und Hallen; Berliner Straße 19-37
1896-98 • Friedrich Reimer & Konrad Körte

K 10 Johanneskirche
Berlin-Frohnau; Zeltinger Platz 17-18
1934-36 • Walter Krüger, Johannes Krüger

Die planmäßige Anlage von Frohnau, die auf den 1908 für Brix und Genzmer entschiedenen städtebaulichen Wettbewerb zurückgeht, läßt als Mittelpunkt klar den Bahnhof und zu beiden Seiten der Eisenbahn je einen Schmuckplatz erkennen. Im Laufe der Jahre entstanden hier Ladenzeilen, Gaststätten und die Post. Als städtebaulich besonders wirksamen Bau errichteten die Brüder Walter und Johannes Krüger am östlichen Ende der Querachse eine evangelische Kirche, die in ihrer Gestaltung vorzüglich den Ortscharakter der in den märkischen Wald eingebetteten Kolonie widergibt. In Material und Dimension bezieht sich die als Blickpunkt konzipierte mächtige Turmfront auf norddeutsche Westwerke wie etwa Havelberg. Wenn sich auch der Saaltrakt konstruktiv der Stahlbetonbinder bedient, füllen Holzdecken seine Felder aus. Bewußt sollte damit das Gefühl »Heimat« angesprochen werden, wohl in ideologiefreier Harmlosigkeit, wenn auch die Bauzeit einen Verdacht aufkommen läßt.

The centre of the planned town of Frohnau, based on the urban development competition won by Brix and Genzmer in 1908, can be seen clearly to be the station and an elegant square on either side of the railway. Over the years shops, restaurants and a post office have come into being here. The brothers Walter and Johannes Krüger built their Protestant church at the eastern end of the transverse axis, and it is particularly effective as part of the urban scene; its design reflects the character of this place deep in the forest of the Mark in a most excellent fashion. The materials and dimensions of the massive tower façade, clearly conceived as to be a central visual feature, is reminiscent of north German westworks like Havelberg, for instance. The hall section does make structural use of reinforced concrete trusses, but the areas between them are filled with wooden ceilings. This is clearly intended to evoke the idea of «Heimat», probably harmlessly and without ideological content, although the time at which the church was built does arouse some suspicions on this head.

in der Nähe/nearby:
Haus Weydemann; Im Fischgrund 1
1913 • Wilhelm Koban

K 11 Buddhistisches Haus
Berlin-Frohnau; Edelhofdamm 54
1924 • Max Meyer

Der Anlaß für diesen ortsfremden Bau ist einfach: Der Bauherr war zum Buddhismus übergetreten. Und doch klingt in diesem fernöstlichen Bauwerk mehr als das Vordergründige an. Der Anfang der zwanziger Jahre war prädestiniert, eine solche Schöpfung hervorzubringen. Diese Zeit der Unruhe, der zerrissenen Bindungen, des gesellschaftlichen Umbruchs fand ihre geistig-künstlerische Äußerung im Expressionismus, der in seiner Suche nach einer Grundform beispielsweise den gotischen Spitzbogen fand. So wie das Element der Gotik sich auf das gottsucherische Mittelalter bezieht und dabei einer abendländischen Prägung entspringt, wirken auch andere religiöse Kräfte und fließen teils unbewußt in den Stil der Zeit ein. Der weltlichen Entsagung des mittelalterlichen Menschen verwandt ist der Buddhismus. Was etwa beim Portal der Schmargendorfer Kreuzkirche als Nebeneinander von gotischen und fernöstlichen Motiven zu beobachten ist, tritt beim Buddhistischen Haus als Reinform in Erscheinung.

There is a simple reason for the existence of this alien building: the man who commissioned it had converted to Buddhism. And yet this house is not just superficially oriental. The early twenties were predestined to produce a creation of this kind. This time of unrest, of broken connections, of radical social change made its spiritual and artistic statements through Expressionism, which in its search for fundamental form found, for example, the Gothic pointed arch. The Gothic element invokes to the God-seeking Middle Ages, and thus arises from an occidental source, but other religious forces were beginning to make themselves felt, and melt, to an extent unconsciously, with contemporary style. Buddhism is related to medieval man's renunciation of the world. Something that in the Kreuzkirche in Schmargendorf can be observed as a juxtaposition of Gothic and oriental motifs appears in the Buddhist house as pure form.

in der Nähe/nearby:
Victor-Gollancz-Schule; Gollanczstraße 18-24
1928-29 • Fritz Beyer
Haus Trapp; Hohenheimer Straße 31
1910-11 • Heinrich Straumer
Haus Kersten; Wiltinger Straße 15
1958 • Heinz Schudnagies
Haus Janson; Zeltinger Straße 53
1909 • Heinrich Straumer
Haus Ludwig; Mehringer Straße 5/7
1921-24 • Paul Poser
360-m-Fernmeldemast; Jägerstieg 1
1977-82

K 12 Friedhofskapelle Frohnau
Berlin-Frohnau; Hainbuchenstraße 64-76
1910-11 • Carl Stahl-Urach

Das Landhaus und der sich damit anbahnende Stil hatten bald nach der Jahrhundertwende gezeigt, welch starke geistige Strömung sich in dem neuen »Zurück zur Natur« offenbarte. Die Kolonie Frohnau entstand ganz unter diesem Einfluß. Nirgends sonst findet man so viele Bauten, die mit malerischer Kleinteiligkeit unter Verwendung von Holz und Fachwerk eine fast ortstypische Bauweise hervorbringen, wie in Frohnau. Sowohl aus der Gestaltung wie aus der Wirkung leitet sich der Begriff »Heimatstil« ab, der in den dreißiger Jahren dann zur mißverständlichen Aussage wird. Details und Materialien der Dorfkirche werden auch bei der Frohnauer Friedhofskapelle zu etwas Neuem verarbeitet – »ohne Künstelei und sentimentale Absichten«, wie der Kunstgeschichtler Karl Stahl feststellt. Die nordisch anmutenden geschnitzten Holzsäulen der umlaufenden Laube müssen 25 Jahre später die Architekten der Frohnauer Johanneskirche bei ihrer Vorhalle inspiriert haben.

The country house and the style for which it was preparing the way had shown shortly after the turn of the century what a strong spiritual current was revealed in the new «back to nature» movement. The Frohnau colony came into being under this influence. Nowhere else one can find so many buildings creating a style almost typical of the immediate locality, with picturesque attention to detail, using wood and timber frame, than in Frohnau. The concept of «Heimatstil» derives both from design and effect, but was to become a statement open to misinterpretation in the thirties. Details and material from the village church are reworked to create something new in the Frohnau cemetery chapel – «without affectation and sentimental intentions», as art historian Karl Stahl states. The carved wooden columns of the arcade running round the building have a Nordic feel, and must have inspired the architects of the Johanneskirche in Frohnau when they came to build their porch.

in der Nähe/nearby:
Friedhof Frohnau; Hainbuchenstraße 64-76
1910-11 • Ludwig Lesser
Bahnhof und Casino Frohnau; Ludolfingerplatz
1908-10 • Hart & Lesser

K 13 Häuser an der Buche
Berlin-Frohnau; An der Buche 17/19/21 und 18
1910-11 • Heinrich Straumer

Die Berliner Terrain-Zentrale gab hier Straumer Gelegenheit, vier Häuser zu bauen, die später verkauft werden sollten, für Einfamilienhäuser ein sehr ungewöhnliches Verfahren. Für den Architekten war es eine Herausforderung, denn nur selten läßt sich bei dieser Bauaufgabe ohne die vielen kleinen Wünsche des Bauherrn planen. Bei aller Individualität der vier Landhäuser schuf Straumer doch eine einheitliche Baugruppe – einheitlich durch die gleiche Formensprache und durch die geschickte Bildung eines Ensembles um die »Buche« und einen kleinen Brunnen, die beide durch Feldsteinmauern, Hecke und Treppe malerisch verbunden sind. Gerade das Unregelmäßige der gekrümmten Straße, der Geländeschräge mit dem ansteigenden Fußweg, der verwinkelten und versetzten Dach- und Giebel-Unordnung erhöht den Zauber dieser ländlichen Szene.

The Berlin land office gave Straumer the opportunity to build four detached houses here, intended for later sale. It was a challenge to the architect, as he was very rarely allowed to get on with planning these buildings without having to take the client's many little wishes into account. The four country houses are very individual, and yet Straumer succeeded in creating a unified group of buildings, unified because of the fact that they used the same formal language and by the skilful formation of an ensemble around the «beech» and a little well, picturesquely connected by rubblestone walls, hedge and steps. The magic of this rural scene is enhanced by the irregularity of the twisty street, the sloping site with footpath climbing up it, and the many corners and displaced untidiness of the gables.

in der Nähe/nearby:
Haus Rudolphson; Ludolfingerweg 35
1911-12 • Heinrich Straumer
Haus Corts; Sigismundkorso 82
1910 • Leo Nachtlicht
Wasserturm Frohnau; Frohnauer Straße 112-122
1908-09 • Carl Francke

K 14 Wohnstadt Märkisches Viertel
Berlin-Wittenau; Wilhelmsruher Damm usw.
1963-74 • Werner Düttmann, Hans Müller, Georg Heinrichs uam.

Das Märkische Viertel gilt heute als Schulbeispiel für die Widersprüchlichkeit zwischen Planungen und Konsequenzen des Städtebaus der sechziger Jahre. Aus der wohlmeinenden Absicht, in großen Zügen neue Wohnungen zu schaffen, der Beengung der Innenstadt zu entfliehen und ein modernes Wohnumfeld zu schaffen, verselbständigte sich ein Moloch. Das Märkische Viertel wurde in einer Zeit geplant, in der die Begeisterung am technischen Aufschwung noch ungebrochen war, der Glaube an immerwährenden Fortschritt noch die Skepsis gegenüber der Großform vernebelte und empirischer Städtebau sich noch vom Pioniergeist der Nachkriegsjahre mit ihren großen Aufgaben nährte. Heute versucht man mit Nachbesserungen den augenscheinlichen Mängeln beizukommen: anonyme Hauseingänge und Treppen, typisierte Fassaden, fehlende Gemeinschaftseinrichtungen, liebloses Straßenland, verstellte städtebauliche Entwicklung. Verbesserungen erhofft man sich von dem spät als notwendig erkannten Wechselspiel zwischen Planer und Betroffenem, dessen Mündigkeit nicht erstickt werden darf.

The Märkisches Viertel is now considered a perfect example of the contradiction between planning and the consequences of planning in the sixties. The well-meaning intention of providing new accommodation on a large scale, fleeing from the cramped inner city and creating a modern residential environment in fact brought a Moloch into being. The Märkisches Viertel was planned at a time when enthusiasm for surging technical development was still unbroken, when faith in ever-continuing progress still obscured scepticism about large scale forms, and empirical town planning was still fuelled by the pioneering spirit of the post-war years and the enormous tasks they posed. Nowadays attempts are made to deal with the most obvious faults by retrospective improvement: work on anonymous entrances and staircases, blankly standardized façades, lack of social facilities, loveless streetscapes, misplaced urban development. Improvements are hoped from dialogue between planners and those affected by it, something recognized all too late as necessary. The latter group's responsible comment must not be suppressed.

in der Nähe/nearby:
Adalbert-v.-Chamisso-Schule; Senftenberger Ring 27
1968-70 • Karl Fleig
Wilhelm-Raabe-Schule; Senftenberger Ring 97
1966-69 • Stephan Heise

K 15 Schule Wittenau
Berlin-Wittenau; Alt-Wittenau 8-13
1928-31 • Jean Krämer

Die überall in Reinickendorf aus dem Boden schießenden Siedlungsbauten führten bald zu einer krisenhaften Schulraumnot im Bezirk. Neubauten wurden geplant, auch im Ortsteil Wittenau. Der pädagogische Wandel der zwanziger Jahre von der Lernschule weg, hin zur Erziehungs- und Lebensschule griff auch auf die Schularchitektur über. Daß die Zukunft des demokratischen Staates nur von einer gebildeten Jugend abhänge, war damals in aller Munde. Krämers Bau mangelt es nicht an der architektonischen Geste, er erscheint sogar wie das Glaubensbekenntnis einer neuen Schulbaulehre. Die weit ausladende Flügelanlage schafft sich Raum, um Licht und Sonne aufzufangen, die den innerstädtischen Schulen in ihren beengten Hinterhoflagen oft fehlen. Es ist die Zeit, da ernsthaft diskutiert wurde, alle Berliner Schulen an den Stadtrand zu verlegen. Die bewußt großzügige Planung litt bald am üblichen Geldmangel, und die anfängliche Begeisterung schlug in Kritik an dem neuen Schulpalast um. Trotzdem konnte 1931 eine Schule eingeweiht werden, deren vorbildliches Raumprogramm eine Fülle von Fachklassen und Sonderräumen anbot und mit modernster technischer Ausstattung den Schulalltag erleichterte.

Estates were springing up all over Reinickendorf, and this soon led to a crisis over school places. New buildings were planned, in areas including Wittenau. The educational change in the twenties away from learning-centred schools to education and schooling for life also had an effect on school architecture. The fact that the future of the democratic state demanded well-educated young people was on every lip. Krämer's building is not lacking in architectural gestures, in fact it seems like a credo for a new theory of school building. The spaciously sectioned building creates space to catch light and sun, often not the case in inner-city schools built in cramped back yards. This was the period in which there was serious discussion of whether to move all Berlin schools to the outskirts. This consciously expansive planning suffered from the usual lack of money, and early enthusiasm soon gave way to criticism of the new school palaces. Despite all this a school was opened in 1931 which used space in an exemplary fashion and offered a vast range of specialist classes and rooms, easing the school day with the most modern technical equipment.

in der Nähe/nearby:
Dorfkirche Wittenau; Alt-Wittenau
15. Jh.
Rathaus Wittenau; Eichborndamm 215-239
1909-11 • Fritz Beyer
Lindner-Verwaltungsgebäude; Lübarser Straße 8-38
1932-33 • Martin Punitzer
Fahrzeugfabrik Dittmann; Lübarser Straße 40-46
1913-14 • Bruno Buch

K 16 Weiße Stadt
Berlin-Reinickendorf; Aroser Allee, Emmentaler Straße, Schillerring usw.
1929-31 • Otto Rudolf Salvisberg, Wilhelm Büning, Bruno Ahrends

Über 1200 Wohnungen wurden in dieser Siedlung erstellt, die ihren Namen vom einheitlich weißen Anstrich der glatt verputzten Häuser erhielt. In der Aroser Allee mit dem markanten Brückenhaus baute Salvisberg, die Häuser in der Emmentaler Straße stammen überwiegend von Büning, die am Schillerring von Ahrends. Der Wechsel von Blockrandbebauung und freien Zeilen sowie die großzügigen Grünflächen entsprachen dem damaligen Ideal vom Wohnen in Licht, Luft und Sonne. So folgt auch die Gestaltung gänzlich der Neuen Sachlichkeit, sieht man einmal von den expressiven Kunstgriffen der als straßenräumlicher Auftakt zu verstehenden Torbauten von Ahrends oder dem straßenraumbildenden Brückenbau von Salvisberg ab. Wie auch bei Bruno Taut leuchten hier und da Farbtupfer auf in Türen, Fensterrahmen, Rohren und Gesimsen – wiederum ein Relikt des Expressionismus. Zeitgemäß aber gibt sich der dynamische Schwung der Häuserfolge in der Aroser Allee. Etwa zwanzig Läden waren von Anfang an berücksichtigt, ebenso ein Kindergarten und Sonnenterrassen. Das abseits gelegene Heizwerk ist inzwischen abgerissen.

This estate provided over 1,200 residential units. It takes its name from the uniform white paint of the smoothly rendered buildings. Salvisberg was the architect of Aroser Allee, where the striking bridge feature is to be found, Büning was largely responsible for work in Emmentaler Strasse, and Ahrends handled the Schillerring. Alternate building on the block periphery and free-standing rows and the generous green areas were entirely in harmony with the period's ideal of living in light, air and sun. Thus the design is also completely within the canons of Neue Sachlichkeit, with the exception of expressive tricks like Ahrends' gate buildings, like an upbeat in the street space, or Salvisberg's streetscape-creating bridge. As is the case with the work of Bruno Taut there are occasional dabs of colour on doors, window frames, pipes and ledges – again features lingering on from Expressionism. But the dynamic flourish of the sequence of buildings in Aroser Allee is completely up to date. About twenty shops were written into the plan, and also a kindergarten and sun terraces. The heating plant was set a little apart, and has since been pulled down.

in der Nähe/nearby:
Humboldtkrankenhaus; Teichstraße 65
1908-10 • Mohr & Weidner
Dorfkirche Reinickendorf; Alt-Reinickendorf
15. Jh.
Haus der Jugend; Thurgauer Straße 66
1944/51 • Boris v. Bodisco
Lutherhaus; Baseler Straße 18
1928-29 • Werner Gregor

L
Berlin
Pankow und Weißensee

Dieser weit nach Norden reichende Teil des Berliner Stadtgebietes liegt zwischen dem Märkischen Viertel und dem Neubaugebiet Hohenschönhausen-Wartenberg; er wird im Süden durch die inneren Stadtbezirke Prenzlauer Berg und Lichtenberg und im Norden durch den Landkreis Bernau begrenzt. Die Stadtbezirke Pankow und Weißensee wurden im Jahre 1920 aus Dörfern gebildet, deren Entstehung auf die deutsche Besiedlung des Barnim im 13. Jahrhundert zurückgeht und von denen sich als älteste Denkmale meist die Dorfkirchen oder auch die Umrisse der Dorfanger erhalten haben. Auf die slawische Ortsbezeichnung »pania«, das bedeutet »Flachmoor«, gehen die Namen Pankow und Panke zurück. Der kleine Fluß Panke entspringt bei Bernau. Bei Buchholz gibt er einen Teil des Wassers in den Nordgraben ab, der durch Reinickendorf zum Tegeler See führt. Teils kanalisiert durchfließt die Panke den Wedding und mündet gegenüber dem Bahnhof Friedrichstraße in die Spree. Der Weiße See dagegen ist abflußlos, ein Relikt der letzten Eiszeit, an dem vor 10 000 Jahren steinzeitliche Fischer und Jäger gelebt haben. Während Pankow, Niederschönhausen und Rosenthal heute trotz unterschiedlich dichter Bebauung in ein geschlossenes Siedlungsband von Reinickendorf bis Hohenschönhausen eingebettet sind, blieben die Ortsteile Blankenburg, Karow und Buch bisher räumlich eigenständig. Trotz industrieller Ansiedlung sind Pankow und Weißensee vorwiegend Wohnbezirke, so auch die Neubaugebiete der achtziger Jahre zwischen den ehemaligen Gutsbezirken und Landgemeinden Malchow, Wartenberg, Falkenberg und Hohenschönhausen. Erschlossen wird dieses Stadtgebiet durch die seit dem Mittelalter vom Spandauer und Oderberger Tor ausgehenden radialen Verkehrswege, die Schönhauser und Prenzlauer Allee, flankiert durch Rosenthaler und Greifswalder Straße. Alle diese ehemaligen Überlandwege wurden im 18. Jahrhundert beidseitig bepflanzt, zu Beginn des 19. Jahrhunderts gepflastert, später kamen Straßenbahnen hinzu. Allerdings fehlen in Pankow und Weißensee zügig durchgehende Ringverbindungen, wie sie James Hobrecht für die innerstädtischen Erweiterungsgebiete in seinen Planungen Mitte des 19. Jahrhunderts vorgesehen hatte.

This part of Berlin extends a long way north; it lies between the Märkisches Viertel and the newly built-up area of Hohenschönhausen-Wartenberg; it is bordered to the south by the inner city areas of Prenzlauer Berg and Lichtenberg, and to the north by the country district of Bernau. The urban districts of Pankow and Weissensee were formed in 1920 from villages going back to German settlement of the Barnim in the thirteenth century; the oldest monuments to have survived are usually the village churches, or the outline patterns of village greens. The names Pankow and Panke go back to the Slavic place name «pania», meaning «flat moor». The little river Panke rises near Bernau. At Buchholz some of its water flows into the Nordgraben, which passes through Reinickendorf to the Tegeler See. Partially canalized, the Panke flows through Wedding and joins the Spree opposite Bahnhof Friedrichstrasse. The Weisser See on the other hand has no outflow; it is a relic of the last ice age; stone age fishermen and hunters lived beside it 10,000 years ago. While Pankow, Niederschönhausen and Rosenthal are today part of a closed band of settlement of uneven density stretching from Reinickendorf to Hohenschönhausen, so far Blankenburg, Karow and Buch have remained isolated. Despite industrial settlement Pankow and Weissensee are predominantly residential, and so too are the new eighties' development areas between the former country estates and communities of Malchow, Wartenberg, Falkenberg and Hohenschönhausen. Access to this area is via Schönhauser and Prenzlauer Allee, flanked by Rosenthaler and Greifswalder Strasse, radial traffic routes that have led out from the Spandau and Oderberg Gates since the Middle Ages. All these former overland routes were planted on both sides in the eighteenth century, paved in the early nineteenth century, with trams as a later addition. Pankow and Weissensee are however still without the fast ring road connections planned by James Hobrecht for inner city development areas in the mid nineteenth century.

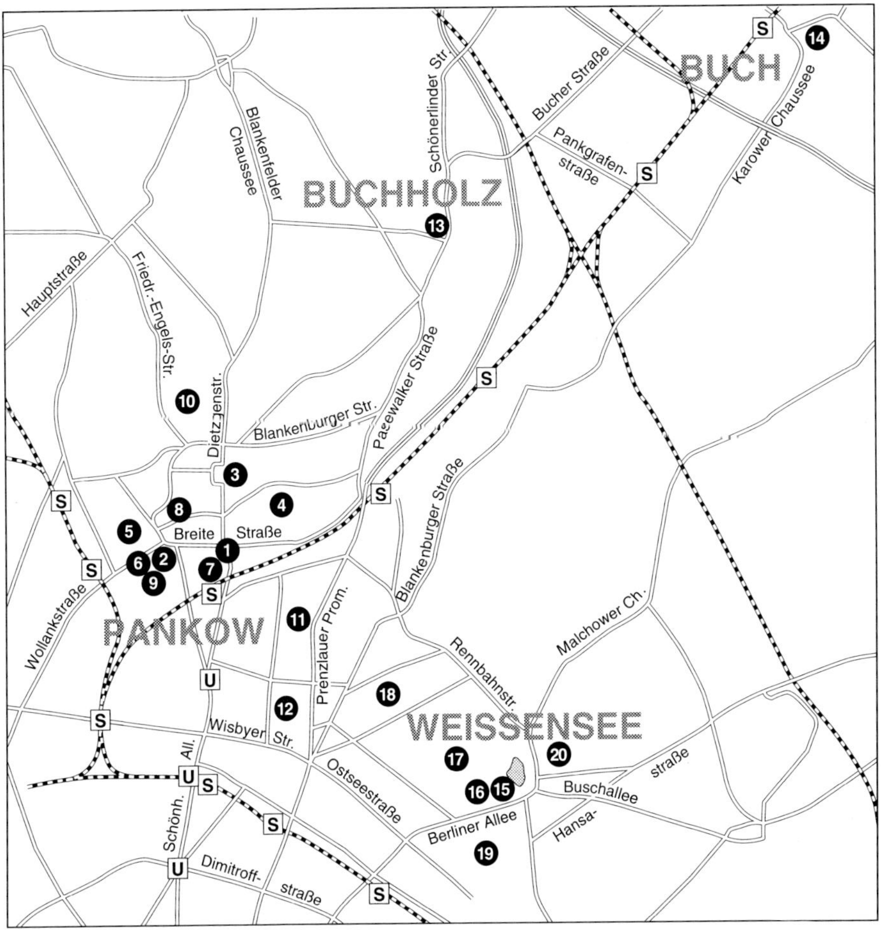

L 1 Pfarrkirche Pankow
L 2 Rathaus Pankow
L 3 Schloß Niederschönhausen
L 4 Freibad Pankow
L 5 Bürgerpark
L 6 Vorstadtvilla
L 7 Gesundheitshaus
L 8 Wohnanlage Grabbeallee
L 9 Schulkomplex (Gymnasium)
L 10 Maria-Magdalenen-Kirche
L 11 Wohnbebauung »Zeppelinhäuser«
L 12 Wohnanlage Thulestraße
L 13 Dorfkirche Buchholz
L 14 Hufelandkrankenhaus (Städtisches Klinikum)
L 15 Park am Weißen See
L 16 Wohnhaus mit Flora-Apotheke
L 17 Gemeindeforum am Kreuzpfuhl
L 18 Kunsthochschule Berlin
L 19 Jüdischer Friedhof
L 20 Wohnzeile Trierer Straße

L 1 Pfarrkirche Pankow
Berlin-Pankow; Breite Straße
1858-59 • Friedrich August Stüler

Der alte Dorfanger zwischen Rathaus und Dorfkirche ist in ganzer Breite und Länge noch ablesbar. Das Dorf erstreckte sich über etwa 800 Meter von der Neuen Schönholzer Straße bis zum Stiftsweg. Die Dorfaue mit dem Dorfteich an der Mühlenstraße und mit dem Lehnschulzengut an Berliner Straße und Schulstraße waren Teil einer breiten und sandigen, von Bäumen gesäumten Dorfstraße, an deren beiden Enden Verbindungswege zum benachbarten Heinersdorf und nach Gesundbrunnen führten. In der Mitte der langen Dorfstraße lagen um 1800 Kirche, Schule, Spritzenhaus und ein Amtshaus mit Räumen für den Fleischbeschauer und Gefängniszellen. Die Dorfkirche war wohl um 1230 mit dem Vordringen deutscher Siedler auf den Barnim von Zisterziensermönchen begründet worden. Ihre heutige Gestalt als Stadtpfarrkirche erhielt sie in vier Etappen: im 15. Jahrhundert ein rechteckiger Feldsteinbau mit steingewölbtem Chorjoch; 1832 Erneuerung durch Redtel und Schinkel; 1858 Erweiterung um neugotisches dreischiffiges Hallenlanghaus mit dreiseitiger Empore und zwei schlanken Türmen, die alte Kirche als Chor einbezogen; 1906-08 entstand der gotisierende Westbau.

The full width and length of the old village green between town hall and village church can still be discerned. The village extended over about 800 metres from Neue Schönholzer Strasse to Stiftsweg. The village pasture with village pond on Mühlenstrasse and the former feudal estate on Berliner Strasse and Schulstrasse were part of a broad, sandy, tree-lined village street, at the ends of which connecting routes went off to nearby Heinersdorf and Gesundbrunnen. In about 1800, church, school, fire station and an official building containing rooms for the meat inspector and prison cells were in the middle of the long village street. The village church was probably founded c. 1230 by Cistercian monks, when German settlers began to thrust through into the Barnim. It achieved its present parish church shape in four stages: in the fifteenth century a rectangular rubble stone building with stone-vaulted choir bay; rebuilt by Redtel and Schinkel in 1832; in 1858 it was extended by adding a neo-Gothic hall with nave with two aisles and gallery on three sides and two slender towers, including the old church as choir; the Gothic-style west building was added 1906-8.

in der Nähe/nearby:
Villa mit kleinem Park; Breite Straße 32
Um 1850/60
Hildebrandsche Villa; Breite Straße 45
M. 18. Jh.

L 2 Rathaus Pankow
Berlin-Pankow; Breite Straße 24-26
1901-03 • Wilhelm Joho

Im 19. Jahrhundert war die lockere Reihe der Bauern- und Kossätenhöfe bereits durch Landhäuser unterbrochen, von denen die Bleichrödersche Villa in der Breite Straße 33 a noch erhalten ist. Um 1800 hatte Pankow 286 Einwohner, 1870 waren es schon 2000. Seit 1857 gibt es den beliebten Wochenmarkt auf dem Anger. Mit der Residenzstadt war Pankow damals durch Pferdeomnibusse verbunden. Der erste Bauteil des Pankower Rathauses wurde für die Verwaltung der stark wachsenden Gemeinde mit ihren inzwischen 21 000 Einwohnern errichtet. Bis 1914 stieg die Zahl der Einwohner auf 57 000, so daß bald eine Erweiterung des Rathauses erforderlich war. Der zweite Bauteil folgte 1927 nach Plänen von Albert Pöschke und Rudolf Klante in der Neuen Schönhauser Straße als Anbau. Im Erdgeschoß wurde 1979 ein Trauzimmer eingebaut, das aus dem von Ludwig Hoffmann 1899-1901 errichteten Standesamt an der Fischerbrücke stammt. Die Schnitzereien der Wandverkleidungen und der Kassettendecke in Formen des Barock und Jugendstils stammen von Ernst Westphal, die Gemälde spielender Kinder von Ludwig v. Hoffmann.

As early as the nineteenth century the loose series of farm and cottagers' houses was interrupted by country houses, of which the Bleichrod villa at 33a Breite Strasse has survived. Around 1800 Pankow had 286 inhabitants, rising to 2,000 in 1870. The popular weekly market has been held on the green since 1857. At that time a horse-bus service connected Pankow with the city. The first section of Pankow town hall was built for a rapidly increasing community already 21,000 strong. By 1914 the number of inhabitants had risen to 57,000, meaning that an extension to the town hall was needed. The second section of the building, designed by Albert Pöschke and Rudolf Klante followed in 1927, as an extension in Neue Schönhauser Strasse. In 1979 a marriage room was installed on the ground floor; this came from the registry office on the Fischerbrücke, built by Ludwig Hoffmann 1899-1901. The carvings on wall panels and coffered ceiling with baroque and Jugendstil designs are by Ernst Westphal, and the paintings of children playing by Ludwig von Hoffmann.

in der Nähe/nearby:
Wohnhofanlage; Mühlenstraße 2-2 a
1906 • M. Scheiding
Botschaftsgebäude; Mühlenstraße 80
1968 • Eckardt Schmidt
Mälzerei der Schultheiss-Brauerei; Mühlenstraße 11
1881-87
Wohnhäuser; Florastraße 63-64, Dusekestraße 1-8
Vor 1930 • Vielleicht Ludwig Mies van der Rohe

L 3 Schloß Niederschönhausen
Berlin-Niederschönhausen; Ossietzkystraße, Dietzgenstraße
1704 • Johann Friedrich v. Eosander

Das Angerdorf und der Rittersitz »Nedern Schonhuszen« sind wie Pankow wohl um 1230 begründet und bereits 1370 von den Städten Berlin und Cölln erworben worden. Aus dem Jahre 1718 sind 23 vermessene Grundstücke an der Dorfstraße, der heutigen Dietzgenstraße bekannt, darunter befanden sich 18 Bauern- und Kossätenhöfe und somit offenbar auch fünf Landhäuser. Kurfürst Friedrich III., der spätere König Friedrich I., erwarb 1691 Pankow und Niederschönhausen zurück und ließ den 1664 angelegten Landsitz der Gräfin v. Dohna zunächst vermutlich durch Johann Arnold Nering, seit 1704 dann durch Johann Friedrich v. Eosander zu einer Dreiflügelanlage ausbauen. 1763 wurde das Schloß, von 1740 bis 1796 Sommersitz der Gemahlin Friedrichs II., unter Johann Boumann d.Ä. zu einem Rechteckbau erweitert; der Treppenrisalit steht jetzt an der Stelle des Ehrenhofes und ist so in Formen der Schule von Knobelsdorff gehalten. Der Park war ursprünglich eine Anlage im holländischen Stil, er wurde seit 1680 erweitert und zunehmend zu einem französischen Garten verändert, 1828-31 gestaltete ihn dann Peter Joseph Lenné zu einem englischen Landschaftspark mit seltenen Bäumen um.

The village with green and the manor house of «Nedern Schonhuszen» were probably, like Pankow, founded c. 1230 and acquired by the towns of Berlin and Cölln as early as 1370. In 1718 there were 23 known surveyed plots in the village street, now Dietzgenstrasse, including 18 farm and cottagers' houses and apparently five country houses as well. Elector Frederick III, later King Frederick I, bought Pankow and Niederschönhausen back in 1691 and had the country seat, established in 1664 by Gräfin von Dohna, extended, at first presumably by Johann Arnold Nering, then from 1704 by Johann Friedrich von Eosander as a building in three sections. In 1763 the Schloss, summer seat of Frederick II's consort from 1740 to 1796, was extended as a rectangular building by Johann Boumann the Elder; now the staircase projection replaces the principal courtyard, thus retaining the school of Knobelsdorff design. The park was originally laid out in Dutch style, extended from 1680 and gradually changed into a French garden, then in 1828-31 Peter Joseph Lenné turned it into an English landscape park with rare trees.

in der Nähe/nearby:
Villa; Majakowskiring 2
1900
Friedenskirche; Ossietzkyplatz
1869-71
Holländerhaus; Dietzgenstraße 51-53
1852 • Ludwig Schulz

L 4 Freibad Pankow
Berlin-Pankow; Wolfshagener Straße
1958-60 • Walter Hinkefuß, Heinz Graffunder, Joachim Streichhahn

Durch den Schloßpark von Niederschönhausen fließt die Panke, jener kleine Fluß, der dem mittelalterlichen Nachbardorf den Namen gab. Am Ende des 19. Jahrhunderts unterhielt man an der Schloßstraße eine Flußbadeanstalt, aber mit den Verunreinigungen der Panke durch die Rieselfelder und durch Gerbereien mußte dieses Bad ebenso geschlossen werden, wie 1925 der Freibadestrand im Volkspark an der Leonard-Frank-Straße. Der Wunsch nach einer Badeanstalt wurde seit Beginn des Jahrhunderts immer wieder von Bürgern und Sportlern vorgetragen, ihm konnte erst in den fünfziger Jahren entsprochen werden. Am Schloßpark entstand nach der Freiflächen- und Hochbauplanung von Hinkefuß und Graffunder und Entwürfen für Turm und Becken von Joachim Streichhahn unter der Mitwirkung der Pankower Bevölkerung ein Volks- und Erholungsbad für den dicht besiedelten Norden Berlins. 1973-74 ergänzten Karl-Ernst Swora und Gunter Derdau die Anlage durch eine Schwimmhalle.

The Panke, the little river that gave the neighbouring medieval village its name, flows through the park of Schloss Niederschönhausen. In the late nineteenth century there was a river bathing pool in Schlosstrasse, but when the Panke became polluted from sewage farms and tanneries the baths had to be shut again, and so did the open air bathing beach in the Volkspark in Leonard-Frank-Strasse in 1925. Ordinary people and sportsmen pressed for a swimming pool from the early years of the century, but none was provided until the fifties. A people's and recreational pool for the denselypopulated north of Berlin was built by the Schlosspark, to open-space and structural engineering plans by Hinkefuss und Graffunder and designs for diving towers and pool by Joachim Streichhahn, with assistance from the residents of Pankow. In 1973-4 an indoor pool was added by Karl-Ernst Swora and Gunter Derdau.

in der Nähe/nearby:
Städtisches Krankenhaus Pankow; Galenusstraße 60
1905-06 • Wilhelm Joho
Wohnhäuser; Galenusstraße 6-26, Klaustaler Straße 21
Nach 1906
Wohnhäuser mit Ladenbauten; Prießnitzstraße 11-18
1927 • Joseph Tiedemann
Wohnhausgruppe Amalienpark; Breite Straße 2-2 a
1896-97 • Otto March

L 5 Bürgerpark
Berlin-Pankow; Cottastraße, Wilhelm-Kuhr-Straße
1854 • Wilhelm Perring

Die Schönholzer Heide und der Bürgerpark sind Endpunkte eines langen Großgrünzuges, der als »Grüne Lunge« von Wilhelmsruh bis nach Pankow reicht. Mit der Zerstörung einer Papiermühle durch Hochwasser entstand seit 1854 neben einem kleinen Schloß der Bürgerpark durch den Industriellen und Begründer der Berliner Börsenzeitung Baron Killisch v. Horn. Die Anlage befindet sich seit 1907 durch Ankauf unter dem Bürgermeister Wilhelm Kuhr in städtischem Besitz und war damit der Terrainspekulation entzogen. Von den Bauten sind nur erhalten: das Eingangstor, nach italienischem Vorbild, das Kastellanhaus und die Gärtnerei. Seit 1910 gibt es den Teich mit der Brücke zwischen zwei Hügeln, das heutige Tiergehege. 1912 kam die Parkgaststätte mit dem Musikpavillon hinzu und 1964 mit der Neugestaltung die Parkbücherei an der Liegewiese. Die Steinbüste von Heinrich Mann schuf 1954 Gustav Seitz.

Schönholzer Heide and the Bürgerpark mark the end of a long run of green stretching as a «green lung» from Wilhelmsruh to Pankow. The Bürgerpark was laid out from 1854 next to a little country seat, because a paper mill had been destroyed by flooding. It was endowed by the industrialist and founder of the Berliner Börsenzeitung Baron Killisch von Horn. The park has been owned by the town since 1907, when it was purchased by Mayor Wilhelm Kuhr, and thus removed from land speculation. Of the buildings all that have survived are: the main gate, on the Italian model, castellan's house and nursery garden. The pool with the bridge between two mounds, the present animal enclosure, has existed since 1910. The park restaurant with bandstand was added in 1912 and the park library by the sun-bathing lawns was redesigned in 1964. The stone bust of Heinrich Mann was carved by Gustav Seitz in 1954.

in der Nähe/nearby:
Friedhof I; Wilhelm-Kuhr-Straße, Kreuzstraße
1841 (Grabmale: Baron Killisch v. Horn • Um 1886; N. Scherel • Um 1925 • D. Diesch)
Wohnhaus; Wilhelm-Kuhr-Straße 1
Um 1860

L 6 Vorstadtvilla
Berlin-Pankow; Kreuzstraße 16
1870-80

Von 1370 bis 1680 gehörten Pankow und Niederschönhausen dem Rat der Städte Berlin und Cölln. In dieser Zeit befand sich das Lehnschulzengut oft im Besitz von Berliner Patrizierfamilien. 1486-99 besaß an der Stelle des heutigen Krankenhauses in der Galenusstraße der Kurfürst Johann Cicero einen Landsitz mit einem Vogelherd. Im 18. und 19. Jahrhundert werden die Orte durch wohlhabende Berliner Familien zunehmend als Sommeraufenthalte genutzt. Landhäuser entstehen und etliche private Parkanlagen, von denen der Brosepark an der Dietzgenstraße erhalten blieb. Aus der zweiten Hälfte des 19. Jahrhunderts sind eine Reihe von Vorstadtvillen erhalten, die mit seitlichem Turm nach Art der italienisierenden Landhäuser von Persius angelegt wurden. Der ländlichen Situation der Häuser entsprechen solche Namen wie »Haus Horidoh« oder die Stuckplastik einer Flora mit Ährenkranz und Sichel.

From 1370 to 1680 Pankow and Niederschönhausen belonged to the Berlin and Cölln town councils. At this time feudal land was often owned by patrician families from Berlin. In 1486-99 Elector Johann Cicero had a country seat with fowling floor on the site of the present hospital in Galenusstrasse. In the eighteenth and nineteenth century these places were increasingly used as summer resorts by well-to-do Berlin families. Country houses were built and numerous private parks laid out, of which Brosepark in Dietzgenstrasse has survived. A series of suburban villas dating from the second half of the nineteenth century have survived, built with side towers like Persius' Italienate country houses. House names like «Haus Horidoh» or the carved stucco of flora with garland of ears of corn and sickle are appropriate to the rural situation.

in der Nähe/nearby:
Wohnhaus; Wollankstraße 131 a
Um 1860
Wohn- und Bankgebäude; Wollankstraße 132
1906
Lutherhaus; Pradelstraße 11
1930 • Rudolf Klante, Ernst Christian Pfannschmidt

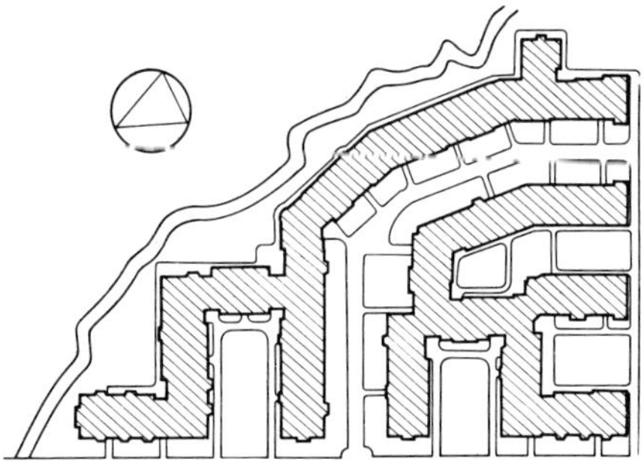

L 7 Gesundheitshaus
Berlin-Pankow; Grunowstraße 8-11
1926-28 • Eilert Franzen

Obwohl Pankow kein bedeutender Industriestandort ist, gab es in Buchholz seit 1857 eine Lederfabrik, 1907 in Wilhelmsruh die Bergmann-Elektrizitäts-Werke und 1906 die Zigarettenfabrik Garbaty. Daneben entwickelten sich andere Betriebe, auch solche der Genußmittelindustrie, wie Brauereien. Aber Pankow blieb vorwiegend ein Wohnstandort, begünstigt durch die 1880 eingerichtete Bahnstation der seit 1842 bestehenden Berlin-Stettiner Eisenbahn. Einem ersten Bahnhof von 1892 folgte das heutige Gebäude von 1925. In der Nähe zweier Stadtbahnhöfe an Wollank- und Berliner Straße entstand beidseits der Florastraße ein Arbeiterwohngebiet. 1893 hatte Pankow mit einem Wasserwerk und eigener Kanalisation die stadthygienischen Bedingungen wesentlich verbessert. Das Gesundheitsamt von Franzen zeigt spätexpressionistische Formen und Allegorien auf das Gesundheitswesen.

Although Pankow is not important industrially speaking, there was a leather factory in Buchholz from 1857, the Bergmann power station was in Wilhelmsruh from 1907, and the Garbaty cigarette factory was built in 1906. Alongside these other businesses grew up, semi-luxury industries like breweries, for example. But Pankow remained predominantly a residential area, benefiting from the halt established in 1880 on the Berlin-Stettin railway, which had been in existence since 1842. The first station was built in 1892, followed by the present building dating from 1925. A workers' residential area grew up on either side of Florastrasse, served by nearby S-Bahn stations at Wollank- and Berliner Strasse. In 1893 Pankow considerably improved its urban hygiene with a water works and its own sewerage system. Franzen's health department is late Expressionist in design, with allegories of health care.

in der Nähe/nearby:
Bahnhof Berlin-Pankow; Florastraße 52
1909-14 • Ernst Schwartz, Karl Cornelius, Lücking
Jüdisches Waisenhaus; Berliner Straße 120-121
1912 • Alexander Beer
Zigarettenfabrik Garbaty; Hadlichstraße 44
1930-31 • Fritz Höger

L 8 Wohnanlage Grabbeallee
Berlin-Niederschönhausen; Grabbeallee 14/26
1908-09 • Paul Mebes

Diese einheitliche Anlage aus der Zeit des Reformmiethauses wurde für den Beamten-Wohnungsverein am Zingergraben auf einem dreieckigen Restgrundstück errichtet. Zwei äußerst differenzierte Bauteile sind durch eine Privatstraße getrennt. Die Auflockerung der damals üblichen Hinterhofbebauung gelang durch Erschließung des Geländes mit Hilfe dieser Wohnstraße und durch weitere Wohnwege und Wohnhöfe. Bei den mit Loggien und Erkern ausgestatteten Bauten sind die Küchen, Bäder und Treppenhäuser fast ausschließlich nach Norden und Osten orientiert, die Wohnräume dagegen fast immer nach Süden und Westen. Damit ist das Prinzip der Zeilenbauweise bereits hier in dieser schon damals ausgezeichneten Wohnanlage vorweggenommen worden.

This uniform complex from the period of the reform tenement was built for the civil servants' accommodation association in Zingergraben on a triangular leftover plot. Two extremely differentiated building sections are divided by a private road. The back-yard building customary at the time was relieved by giving access to the site via this residential street and by further residential alleys and courtyards. The buildings have balconies and bay windows, and inside the kitchens, bathrooms and stairwells face almost exclusively north and east, but the living rooms almost always south and west. Thus the principle of terrace development has been anticipated in this residential complex, outstanding for its period.

in der Nähe/nearby:
Vorstadtvillen; Grabbeallee 35, 39, 41, 45 und 67
2. H. 19. Jh.
Altersheim; Heinrich-Mann-Straße 31, Cottastraße
1929-31 • Mebes & Emmerich
Botschaftsresidenz; Tschaikowskistraße 45-51
1974 • Horst Bauer

L 9 Schulkomplex (Gymnasium)
Berlin-Pankow; Görschstraße 43-44
1909-10 • Carl Fenten, Rudolf Klante, Eilert Franzen

Eine große Anzahl sehenswerter Bauten entstand seit der Gründung des Deutschen Reiches 1871 und der sich zur Weltstadt entwickelnden Reichshauptstadt. Dieser Prozeß erfaßte auch die außerhalb der Weichbildgrenze liegenden Gemeinden wie Schöneberg, Wilmersdorf, Weißensee oder Pankow. Neben neuen Wohnvierteln entstanden auch Rathäuser, Kirchen, Gerichtsgebäude und Schulen. Die Reihe hoher Kunststile von der Romanik über Gotik und Renaissance zum Barock entsprach dem Repräsentationsbedürfnis dieser Zeit und ganz besonders einigen wohlhabenden Vorortgemeinden. Der Schulkomplex in der Görschstraße, unter der Leitung von Carl Fenten durch Rudolf Klante und Eilert Franzen in Formen der deutschen Spätrenaissance ausgeführt, bildet durch seine Turmhauben und die mächtigen Erker zusammen mit dem Rathausturm zugleich auch eine Betonung des Zentrums in der Silhouette des Ortes.

A large number of fine buildings appeared in the period after the establishment of the German Empire in 1871, as the imperial capital developed into a metropolis. This process also included parishes outside the city area like Schöneberg, Wilmersdorf, Weissensee or Pankow. Town halls, churches, court buildings and schools grew up alongside the new residential areas. The series of high art styles extending from Romanesque via Gothic and Renaissance to Baroque was appropriate to the period's need for official prestige, most particularly in some prosperous suburban communities. The school complex in Görschstrasse, built under the direction of Carl Fenten using late German Renaissance design characteristics by Rudolf Klante and Eilert Franzen, has spires and a massive oriel. Together with the town hall tower, it helps to form a central focus in the townscape.

in der Nähe/nearby:
Wohnhäuser; Florastraße 74 und 27
Um 1900 und gegen 1910
Verwaltungsgebäude; Florapromenade 4
1926-27 • Rudolf Klante
Jüdisches Lehrlingsheim (Bibliothek); Mühlenstraße 24
1896

L 10 Maria-Magdalenen-Kirche
Berlin-Niederschönhausen; Platanenstraße 20-21
1929-30 • Felix Sturm

Die Platanenstraße durchquert ein Kleinhausgebiet und verbindet die Dietzgenstraße in Niederschönhausen mit dem Ortsteil Schönholz. Dieser entstand aus einer Ansiedlung böhmischer Kolonisten, die der Königin dienstbar waren, im Schloßpark Niederschönhausen und auf der 1753 angelegten Maulbeerplantage, die dann zur Schönholzer Heide wurde. Die katholische Maria-Magdalenenkirche besteht aus einer zur Straße gewandten Turmfront in spätexpressionistischen Formen, einem basilikalen Schiff mit querschiffartigen Seitenkapellen und der polygonalen Apsis. Die Supraporte, ein Terrakottarelief mit der Darstellung des »Noli me tangere«, schuf W. Halbhuber.

Platanenstrasse cuts through an area of small buildings and connects Dietzgenstrasse in Niederschönhausen with the district called Schönholz. This grew up from a settlement of Bohemian colonists subject to the queen in Schlosspark Niederschönhausen, and on the mulberry plantation laid out in 1753, which then became Schönholzer Heide. The Catholic Maria-Magdalenenkirche consists of a tower in late Expressionist style facing the street, a basilican nave with transept-like side chapels and polygonal apse. The sopraporta, a terra-cotta relief of the «Noli me tangere», is the work of W. Halbhuber.

in der Nähe/nearby:
Schützenhaus Schönholz; B-Niederschönhausen; Pastor-Niemöller-Straße 82 • 1884
Sowjetisches Ehrenmal; B-Wilhelmsruh; Germanenstraße (Volkspark Schönholzer Heide)
1947-49 • K. A. Soboljew
Straßenbahn-Betriebshof; B-Niederschönhausen; Blankenfelder Straße 1-7
1900-01 • Joseph Fischer-Dick
1924 • Jean Krämer

L 11 Wohnbebauung »Zeppelinhäuser«
Berlin-Pankow; Prenzlauer Promenade 129-143
1930-31 • Walter Borchard

Die Berlin-Stettiner Eisenbahn ist durch die Anlage der Bahnhöfe Pankow und Heinersdorf auch für diese Ortsteile zu einem wichtigen Nahverkehrsmittel geworden. Obwohl das Gelände außerhalb des Ortskerns und beiderseits der Bahnlinie bereits seit 1900 erschlossen wurde, ist es in den folgenden Jahrzehnten nur sehr zögerlich bebaut worden. Nach dem Ersten Weltkrieg hat dann aber allein die 1919 gegründete gemeinnützige Siedlungsgesellschaft »Pankower Heimstätten« 250 Häuser errichten lassen. So entstanden das »Krankenhausviertel« um die Galenustraße, Teile des »Harzer Viertels« in der Klausthaler Straße, alle nördlich der Bahnlinie, oder das südlich davon gelegene »Kissingenviertel« mit seinen begrünten Innenhöfen zwischen Berliner Straße und Prenzlauer Promenade. An dieser Hauptausfallstraße liegen die sogenannten Zeppelin-Häuser, benannt nach der Form ihrer runden Dächer, die aus einer nur 4 cm dünnen, materialsparenden, weil gekrümmten Stahlbeton-Schale bestehen.

When stations were opened at Pankow and Heinersdorf the Berlin-Stettin railway became an important local transport service for these places as well. Although there was access to the area outside the centre and on both sides of the railway from as early as 1900, building proceeded only in fits and starts in subsequent decades. After the First World War only «Pankower Heimstätten», a non-profit-making association founded in 1919, built 250 houses here. These formed the «Krankenhausviertel» around Galenusstrasse, parts of the «Harzer Viertel» in Klausthaler Strasse, all north of the railway line, or the «Kissingenviertel» south of it, with its planted inner courtyards between Berliner Strasse and Prenzlauer Promenade. On this main road are the so-called Zeppelin-Häuser, named after the shape of their vaulted roof consisting of a reinforced concrete shell of only 4 cm which was curved in order to save on material.

in der Nähe/nearby:
Amtsgericht; Kissingenstraße 5-6
1902-06 • Paul Thoemer, Rudolf Mönnich
Wohnhauszeile; Gemündener Straße 24/42
Um 1925/30 • Jakobus Goettel
Wohnanlage; Kissingenstraße 7-10
1928-30 • Otto Rudolf Salvisberg

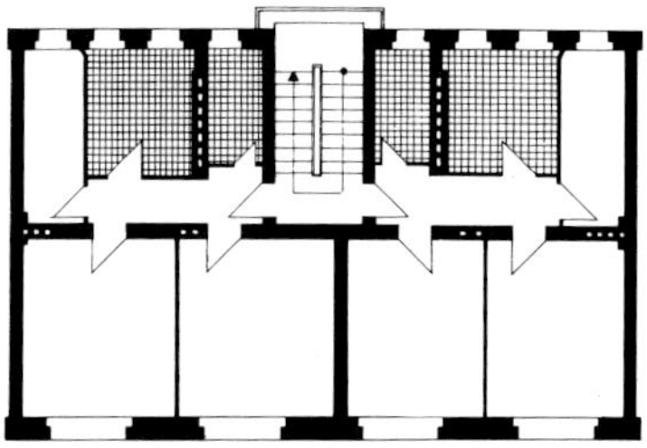

L 12 Wohnanlage Thulestraße
Berlin-Pankow; Thulestraße 61/63, Talstraße 1-2a, Hardangerstraße 1-5, Eschegraben 54
1925 • Erwin Gutkind

Pankow blieb auch in den zwanziger Jahren vorwiegend ein Wohnbezirk. Es wuchs seit 1920 mit der Bildung der Einheitsgemeinde Groß-Berlin an der Wisbyer Straße mit dem Stadtbezirk Prenzlauer Berg langsam zusammen, nicht zuletzt durch die Bautätigkeit verschiedener Wohnungsbaugesellschaften. Der Wohnblock an der Thulestraße mit seinen Zwei- bis Dreizimmerwohnungen ist in den Fassaden mit dem Wechsel von Glas, Stahlbeton, Klinkern und Putzflächen in betonter Sachlichkeit gehalten.

Pankow remained predominantly residential in the twenties as well. From 1920, when Greater Berlin was formed, it slowly joined on to the urban district of Prenzlauer Berg at Wisbyer Strasse, not least because of building activities by various housing companies. The residential block in Thulestrasse with its one- and two-bedroom residential units has façades kept emphatically functional with their alternating glass, reinforced concrete, brick and rendered surfaces.

in der Nähe/nearby:
Wohnbebauung; Elsa-Brandström-Straße 30
1925-30
Hoffnungskirche; Elsa-Brandström-Straße 51
1912-13 • Walter Köppen
Wohnhausgruppe; Max-Koska-Straße 7-12, Wisbyer Straße 41
1909-10 • Paul Mebes

L 13 Dorfkirche Buchholz
Berlin-Buchholz; Hauptstraße, Mühlenstraße
13. Jahrhundert

Der Ortsteil Buchholz ist sechs Kilometer lang und an der Fernstraße 109 aufgefädelt. Ein Buchholzer Wald, wie der Bucher Wald 1375 verzeichnet, stand bis ins 19. Jahrhundert zwischen der Panke und dem Straßenangerdorf. 1688 siedelten hier sechs hugenottische Gärtner- und zehn Kossätenfamilien aus Frankreich auf Höfen, die seit dem Dreißigjährigen Krieg leer standen. Bis 1913 hieß der Ort auch Französisch-Buchholz. Die Glaubensflüchtlinge hatten aus ihrer Heimat nicht nur französische Sitten und Bräuche, sondern auch handwerkliche Fertigkeiten und neue Gemüsesorten mitgebracht. Mitten auf dem Anger des ehemaligen Lehnschulzendorfes steht die Dorfkirche. Der rechteckige Granitquaderbau aus der zweiten Hälfte des 13. Jahrhunderts, um 1600 mit Kreuzrippengewölben versehen, erhielt 1852 anstelle des Chores ein Querschiff und 1886 den Turm.

The district of Buchholz is six kilometres long, strung together on trunk road 109. There was a Buchholz forest, recorded in 1375 like the Bucher Wald, until the nineteenth century between the Panke and the linear, village-green style village. In 1688 six families of Huguenot gardeners and ten of cottagers settled here in farms that had been empty since the Thirty Years War. The place was called Französisch-Buchholz until 1913. The religious refugees brought craft skills and new kinds of vegetables with them from their homes, as well as French customs and traditions. In the middle of the green of the former feudal village is the village church, a rectangular granite ashlar building dating from the second half of the thirteenth century, provided with ribbed vaulting in 1600, a transept to replace the choir in 1852 and the tower in 1886.

in der Nähe/nearby:
Schule; Hauptstraße 58
Um 1852
Bauerngehöft; Hauptstraße 5
A. 19. Jh.
Apotheke; Hauptstraße 14
Um 1890
Oberschule; Berliner Straße 19
1908
Miethaus; Berliner Straße 7
Nach 1900
Gewächshaus; Berliner Straße 45
1965 • G. Hänelt

L 14 Hufelandkrankenhaus (Städtisches Klinikum)
Berlin-Buch; Karower Straße 11
1901-06 • Ludwig Hoffmann

Alt-Buch war ein großes Straßendorf mit einem Rittergut, aus dem später das Schloß mit dem noch bestehenden Park hervorging. An der Stelle der Dorfkirche entstand die Schloßkirche als barocker Zentralbau und wurde zur schönsten Landkirche der Mark. Sie enthält ein Marmorepitaph von 1763, das letzte Werk des Schlüterschülers Glume. 1898 erwarb die Stadt das Gut zur Anlage von Rieselfeldern und zum Bau von Wohlfahrtseinrichtungen. Die ehemaligen Anstalten für unheilbare Leiden, im Pavillonsystem errichtet, entstanden bis 1926 in fünf Komplexen. Nach 1945 sind sie für die Behandlungen akuter Krankheiten zum Städtischen Klinikum Berlin-Buch umgebaut worden. Das Hufelandkrankenhaus wurde als Irrenanstalt erbaut. Es besteht aus einer Vielzahl von Backsteinbauten mit Sandsteingliederungen und ist architektonisch in Formen des holländischen Frühbarock angelegt worden. Die Skulpturen stammen von Ignatius Taschner, der Brunnen von Georg Wrba. Die Bronzeplastik von Christoph Wilhelm Hufeland am Haupteingang schuf 1833 Christian Daniel Rauch.

Alt-Buch was a large linear village with a manor house, from which the Schloss and the park, which still exists, developed. The Schloss church was built on the site of the village church as a centrally planned building, and became the most beautiful country church in the Mark. The marble memorial stone dating from 1763 was the last work of Glume, a pupil of Schlüter. In 1898 the town acquired the estate in order to establish sewage farms and build charitable institutions. The former institutes for incurable diseases, built using the pavilion system, were built in five sections to 1926. After 1945 they were rebuilt as Städtisches Klinikum Berlin-Buch for the treatment of acute illness. The Hufeland hospital was built as a lunatic asylum. It consists of a number of brick buildings with sandstone articulation, in early Dutch baroque style. Sculptures are by Ignatius Taschner, the fountain by Georg Wrba. The bronze of Christoph Wilhelm Hufeland at the main entrance is by Christian Daniel Rauch, 1833.

in der Nähe/nearby:
Robert-Rössle-Klinik; Lindenberger Weg
1961-68 • Roland Jaenisch
Schloßkirche; Alt-Buch (Schloßpark)
1731-36 • Friedrich Wilhelm Dietrichs
Taubenturm im Gutshof; Alt-Buch
2. H. 19. Jh.
Schloßkrug; Alt-Buch, Karower Straße 1
Nach 1823

L 15 Park am Weißen See
Berlin-Weißensee; Berliner Allee
1860

1859 entstand am »Großen See« ein inzwischen zerstörtes schloßähnliches Landhaus. Der dazugehörige Park, seinerzeit fern der Großstadt in idyllischer Lage, ist inzwischen zu einer weitläufigen Parklandschaft mit Pappeln, Weiden und Robinien umgestaltet worden und vereinigt eine Reihe unterschiedlicher Einrichtungen der Naherholung: Dazu gehören der Rosengarten, die Freilichtbühne, das Damwildgehege und der benachbarte Kinderspielplatz mit großem Planschbecken wie auch die ausgedehnte Liegewiese mit der Parkbücherei. Das Freibad, dem Frischwasser aus Tiefbrunnen zugeführt wird, hat einen künstlichen Strand. Am Wasser befinden sich ein Bootsverleih und eine Aussichtsplattform, von der man den See, das Bad und die Uferlandschaft überblicken kann; die Tritonengruppen, Mann und Frau mit Fischleibern, schuf 1908 Hans Schellhorn. Die Gaststätte »Milchhäuschen« liegt mit offener Terrasse direkt am See. Der Hauptzugang zum Park befindet sich gegenüber der Indira-Ghandi-Straße.

In 1859 a palatial country house, since destroyed, was built on the «Great Lake». The adjoining parkland, at the time in an idyllic situation well out of the city, has in the meantime been redesigned as an extensive landscaped park with poplars, willows and robinias, and a number of local recreational facilities have been incorporated in it. These include rose garden, open air theatre, fallow deer enclosure and neighbouring children's playground with large paddling pool, and also extensive sun-bathing lawns and park library. The open-air pool is fed with fresh water from underground wells and has an artificial beach. By the lake are a boat hire firm and a viewing platform from which lake, bathing pool and the landscape on the bank can be seen; the triton group, man and woman with the bodies of fish, was created by Hans Schellhorn in 1908. The «Milchhäuschen» restaurant with open terrace is right by the lake. The main entrance to the park is opposite Indira-Gandhi-Strasse.

in der Nähe/nearby:
Wohnhäuser; Parkstraße 62-63 und 64-65
1875-80
Amtsgericht; Parkstraße 71
1902-06 • Paul Thoemer, Rudolf Mönnich
Oberschule; Amalienstraße 5-8
1930-31 • Reinhold Mettmann

L 16 Wohnhaus mit Flora-Apotheke
Berlin-Weißensee; Berliner Allee 109
Um 1880

Das Rückgrat von Weißensee ist die Bundesstraße 2. Sie durchzieht den Stadtteil von der Greifswalder Straße an der Grenze zum Stadtbezirk Prenzlauer Berg bis zur Malchower Chaussee, wo dieser Straßenzug die bebauten Teile der Stadtrandzone verläßt und in die offene Feldmark hinaustritt. Als 1873 beiderseits der Langhansstraße die Siedlung Neu-Weißensee gegründet und zugleich zwischen dem Alexanderplatz und dem Antonplatz ein Pferdeomnibus eingerichtet wurde, entstand die heutige Berliner Allee in Verlängerung der Greifswalder Straße als Geschäftsstraße. Heute durchfahren diesen Hauptstraßenzug auch Omnibus- und Straßenbahnlinien. Er ist ein Einkaufsboulevard ganz eigener Prägung. Diesen Charakter trägt er von der Kreuzung an der Rennbahnstraße bis zur Grünanlage am Antonplatz. Bauten wie die Flora-Apotheke, Häuser im ländlichen oder Vorstadtstil, wechseln mit Geschäftsbauten des ausgehenden 19. und beginnenden 20. Jahrhunderts.

Trunk road 2 is the backbone of this district. It runs through Weissensee on the border with the district of Prenzlauer Berg to Malchower Chaussee, where this street leaves the built-up area of the city periphery and runs out into open land. In 1873, when the settlement of Neu-Weissensee was established and at the same time a horse-bus service set up between Alexanderplatz and Antonplatz, the present Berliner Allee was built as a shopping street and extension of Greifswalder Strasse. Today this main street is a bus and tram route, and a shopping boulevard of distinctive appearance from the Rennbahnstrasse junction to the little park at Antonplatz. Buildings like the Floraapotheke, in rural or suburban style, alternate with late nineteenth and early twentieth century commercial buildings.

in der Nähe/nearby:
Villa; Berliner Allee 185
Um 1860/70
Dorfkirche; Berliner Allee, Falkenberger Straße
15. Jh. (1830 Turmfront verändert)
Wohnhausgruppe; Graacher Straße, Wehlener Straße
Um 1925/30

L 17 Gemeindeforum am Kreuzpfuhl
Berlin-Weißensee; Woelckpromenade
1908-12 • Carl James Bühring

1870/71 brachte ein Hamburger Großkaufmann die Ländereien des Gutes Weißensee in seinen Besitz. Er verkaufte dann wieder größere und kleinere Flächen und setzte damit die Miethausbebauung im späteren Ortsteil Neu-Weißensee in Gang. So entstand seit 1872 das heutige »Komponisten-Viertel« um die Meyerbeerstraße südlich des Weißen Sees. Westlich davon entwickelte sich ein ebensolches, etwas größeres Wohngebiet um die Langhansstraße, das bis zur Prenzlauer Promenade reicht. Bereits 1879 wurde Neu-Weißensee eine selbständige Landgemeinde, die 1905 dann mit dem Dorf Alt-Weißensee vereinigt wurde. Nun bemächtigte sich die Miethausbebauung auch des alten Dorfes. Auf Initiative des Bürgermeisters Carl Woelk wurde 1908 versucht, den sich entwickelnden Ortsteilen ein gemeinsames neues Zentrum zu geben. So entstand um den Kreuzpfuhl ein stark durchgrüntes »Munizipalviertel« zunächst mit Wohnbauten an der Tassostraße, dem Zugang zu diesem Gemeindeviertel sowie in der Paul-Oestreich- und Pistoriusstraße in dekorativen Formen des Materialstils. Im Mittelpunkt steht ein repräsentatives Schulgebäude; die Bauplastik stammt von Hans Schellhorn. Das benachbarte Festsaal- und Turnhallengebäude wurde im letzten Krieg zerstört. Das Abwasserpumpwerk ist erhalten. 1925-28 ist die Bebauung durch Wohnhäuser zwischen Woelkpromenade 25/35 und Schönstraße 18/28 nach Entwürfen von Joseph Tiedemann ergänzt worden.

In 1870/1 a wealthy Hamburg merchant bought the Weissensee estates. He then resold larger and smaller areas, and thus started the building of rented accommodation in what was later to be Neu-Weissensee. The present «composers' district» around Meyerbeerstrasse south of the Weissensee started in 1872. West of this, around Langhansstrasse, a similar, somewhat larger residential area developed, extending to Prenzlauer Promenade. Neu-Weissensee became an independent district as early as 1879, and in 1905 it was combined with the village of Alt-Weissensee. Now rented accommodation started to take over the old village as well. On the initiative of mayor Carl Woelk an attempt was made in 1908 to give the developing areas a communal centre. Thus a heavily-planted «municipal quarter» grew up around the Kreuzpfuhl, firstly with residential buildings in Tassostrasse, the access road to this district, then in Paul-Oestreich- and Pistoriusstrasse, using the decorative forms of the Material style. The centre is taken up by an imposing school building, with sculptural decoration by Hans Schellhorn. The neighbouring ballroom and gymnasium building was destroyed in the last war. The sewage pump works has survived. The development was completed by the building of houses between Woelkpromenade 23/25 and Schönstrasse 18/28 to designs by Joseph Tiedemann in 1925-8.

L 18 Kunsthochschule Berlin
Berlin-Weißensee; Straße 203 Nr. 20
1956 • Selman Selmanagic, Peter Flierl

Auf dem nordöstlich der Pistoriusstraße gelegenen Bauterrain der ehemaligen Ländereien des Weißenseer Gutes zwischen Park- und Gustav-Adolf-Straße konnte sich eine Miethausbebauung nicht durchsetzen. Hier liegen Friedhöfe, Sportplätze und Kleinhaussiedlungen. An der Rennbahnstraße erwarb der »Berliner Traber-Klub« ein etwa 20 Hektar großes Gelände und ließ eine Trabrennbahn einrichten, die von 1878 bis 1912 betrieben worden ist. 1950 wurde dann dort in Erweiterung einer Sportanlage die Radrennbahn Weißensee mit 9000 Tribühnenplätzen errichtet. In der Straße 203 entstand 1956 durch Nutzung eines bestehenden Verwaltungsgebäudes als vorübergehender Sitz der Hochschule für bildende und angewandte Kunst ein Gebäudekomplex für 240 Studenten. Er ist später durch Werkstatträume ergänzt worden und kann gegebenenfalls auch durch eine 20-Klassenschule genutzt werden. Um einen Innenhof gruppieren sich das viergeschossige Seminargebäude, der zweigeschossige Aula- und Mensabau und ein flacher Eingangstrakt für Ausstellungen. Die Reliefbilder schuf Jürgen v. Woyski, den Fries Toni Mau.

The building of rented accommodation did not take off on the plots from the former lands of the Weissensee estate north-east of Pistoriusstrasse between Park- and Gustav-Adolf-Strasse. It is an area of cemeteries, sports grounds and estates of small houses. The «Berliner Traber-Klub» acquired a site of about 20 hectares on Rennbahnstrasse and set up a trotting course which operated from 1878 to 1912. In 1950, when a sports complex was being extended, the Weissensee racecourse was built with stand accommodation for 9,000. In 1956, temporary accommodation was provided for 240 students of the Hochschule für bildende und angewandte Kunst by using an existing office building in road number 203. It was later extended by the addition of workshops and can be used by a school with 20 classes if the need arises. The four-storey teaching buildings, two-storey hall and refectory facilities and a low entrance section for exhibitions are grouped around an inner courtyard. The relief pictures are by Jürgen von Woyski, the frieze by Toni Mau.

in der Nähe/nearby:
Bethanienkirche; Mirbachplatz
1900-02 • Ludwig v. Tiedemann, Robert Leibnitz
Friedhofstore; Roelckestraße 48-51, Schönstraße
1915 • Carl James Bühring, Hans Schellhorn
Wohnhäuser; Rennbahnstraße 119-136
1930-31 • Paul Mebes, Paul Emmerich

L 19 Jüdischer Friedhof
Berlin-Weißensee; Herbert-Baum-Straße 45
1880 • Hugo Licht

Im Jahre 1875 war die Zahl der Mitglieder der Jüdischen Gemeinde zu Berlin auf 65 000 angewachsen. Wie bei den Friedhöfen in der Großen Hamburger Straße von 1672 und dem in der Schönhauser Allee von 1827 erwarb man nun auch für diesen großen Friedhof ein Terrain weit »vor den Toren der Stadt«. Es erstreckt sich vom Haupteingang an der Herbert-Baum-Straße über eine Fläche von etwa 40 Hektar bis zu den Stadtbezirken Hohenschönhausen und Prenzlauer Berg. Gleich hinter dem Eingangsportal, um ein Rondell gruppiert, liegt der Gebäudekomplex mit der Trauerhalle, die als Zentralbau auf quadratischem Grundriß mit einer halbrunden Apsis errichtet worden ist. Die Gebäude im Eingangsbereich wurden mit gelben Verblendziegeln und in Formen der italienischen Renaissance ausgestattet. Die Gärtnerei und die 1910 errichtete zweite Trauerhalle sind 1944 durch Bomben stark zerstört worden. Dieser Friedhof der Jüdischen Gemeinde in Weißenssee ist ein bedeutendes Geschichts- und Kulturdenkmal, Ruhestätte namhafter Personen und zugleich Erinnerungsmal an die unmenschliche Verfolgung und Tötung der Juden in Konzentrationslagern und Gefängnissen während der Jahre 1933 bis 1945.

In 1875 the number of members of the Jewish community in Berlin had risen to 65,000. As had been the case with the cemeteries in Grosse Hamburger Strasse in 1672 and then in Schönhauser Allee in 1827 a site «far beyond the town gates» was acquired for this great cemetery as well. It extends from the entrance in Herbert-Baum-Strasse over an area of about 40 hectares to the districts of Hohenschönhausen and Prenzlauer Berg. Immediately behind the entrance portal, grouped around a circular flowerbed, is the complex of buildings with mourning hall, a centrally planned building on a square gound plan with semi-circular apse. The buildings at the entrance were decorated with yellow facing tiles in Italian Renaissance style. The nursery garden and second mourning hall built in 1910 were badly damaged by bombing in 1944. This Jewish cemetery in Weissensee is an important historical and cultural monument, the resting place of many famous men and women and also a memorial to the inhuman persecution and killing of Jews in concentration camps and prisons from 1933 to 1945.

in der Nähe/nearby:
Wohnhäuser; Smetanastraße 16, 18, 20
Um 1880/90
Kindl-Brauerei; Indira-Ghandi-Straße 66-92
E. 19. Jh.; 1929 • Hans Claus, Richard Schepke
Sportkomplex; B-Hohenschönhausen; Konrad-Wolf-Straße
1954-89 • Walter Schmidt, Erwin Zitzke

L 20 Wohnzeile
Berlin-Weißensee; Trierer Straße 8/18
1926-27 • Bruno Taut

Hoch- oder Flachbau, das waren zwei programmatische Schlagworte in der Auseinandersetzung um eine Reformierung des Städtebaus der zwanziger Jahre. Anhänger der Gartenstadtbewegung versuchten zunächst den Bau ein- und zweigeschossiger Einzel-, Doppel- oder Reihenhäuser durch Bodenpreisregulative durchzusetzen. Aber zumindest an bereits erschlossenen Straßen oder in der Nähe bestehender Siedlungskerne mußten dann doch mehrgeschossige Miethäuser errichtet werden. Die Wohnzeile in der Trierer Straße lebt von dem alternierenden Wechsel zweier Haustypen mit Anderthalb- und Zweieinhalb-Zimmerwohnungen sowie einem Farbvorschlag Karl Schmidt-Rottluffs von 1919.
Das Haus Lemke hingegen, für den Besitzer einer lithographischen Anstalt gebaut, ist nach dem Prinzip des fließenden Raumes organisiert.

High or low buildings, these were two catchwords in the discussion about urban building reform in the twenties. Supporters of the garden city movement first tried to put through the building of one- and two-storey detached, semi-detached or terraced houses by regulating land prices. But at least in streets that had already been developed or were near the centre of existing settlements multi-storey rented accommodation had to be built. The flats in Triererstrasse draw life from the alternation of two types of building with studio and one-bedroom flats and a colour-scheme by Karl Schmitt-Rottluff proposed in 1919.
The Lemke building on the other hand, built for the owner of a lithographic institution, is organized on the principle of fluid space.

in der Nähe/nearby:
Haus Lemke; B-Hohenschönhausen; Oberseestraße 60
1932 • Ludwig Mies van der Rohe
Dorfkirche; B-Hohenschönhausen; Hauptstraße
13./15. Jahrhundert
Wohnanlage; B-Hohenschönhausen; Große-Leege-Straße 68-82, Goeckestraße 11-23
1932 • Paul Mebes, Paul Emmerich

M
Berlin
Östliche Vororte

Diese Stadtteile liegen östlich des Stadtbahnringes und sind damit außerhalb des kompakt bebauten Kerngebietes von Berlin lokalisiert. Als Vororte erstrecken sie sich entlang der Bundesstraße 1 von Lichtenberg über Biesdorf bis nach Mahlsdorf. Sie umfassen heute im Norden die Stadtbezirke Marzahn und Hellersdorf und reichen im Süden bis an den Rummelsburger See und bis an die Spree. Kristallisationspunkte der Besiedlung waren auch hier Straßenangerdörfer wie Lichtenberg, Biesdorf, Friedrichsfelde oder aber auch Marzahn, das in seiner dörflichen Bebauung noch am originalsten erhalten ist. Obwohl bereits 1772 in Neu-Marzahn auf Gutsländereien 46 pfälzische Familien angesiedelt worden waren, hatte dieser Ort 1920 nur 750 Einwohner. In Lichtenberg dagegen stieg die Bevölkerung seit 1870 mit der Industrieansiedlung um die jetzige Herzbergstraße auf dem Rittergutsland in 40 Jahren auf 60 000 Einwohner. Nach der Vereinigung mit dem Industrieort Boxhagen-Rummelsburg konnte Lichtenberg im Jahre 1912 sogar schon zu den Großstädten gerechnet werden. Als Auswirkung dieser unterschiedlichen Entwicklungstendenzen besitzen die östlichen Vororte eine sehr differenzierte und zum Teil recht heterogene Besiedlungsstruktur. Schon auf einem normalen Stadtplan unterscheidet man deutlich die geschlossenen Miethausgebiete um den Bahnhof Lichtenberg von den großen zusammenhängenden Industriearealen östlich der Vulkanstraße oder von den kleineren in Rummelsburg und an den Ufern entlang der Spree. Überspielt werden diese verschieden genutzten Flächen allerdings von den großen Industrie- und Wohngebieten, die sich in Marzahn von der Allee der Kosmonauten bandartig bis nach Falkenberg und Ahrensfelde erstrecken. Zwischen diese geschlossenen Bauareale der Vororte sind wiederum einige große Grünzüge eingestreut, vor allen der Tierpark Berlin um das Schloß Friedrichsfelde, der Zentralfriedhof am Bahnhof Lichtenberg, aber auch die Stadtparke in Biesdorf und Hellersdorf sowie die Baumassive anderer großer Friedhöfe und Krankenanstalten.

These parts of the city are east of the S-Bahn ring, and thus outside the densely built-up heart of Berlin. As suburbs they extend along trunk road 1 from Lichtenberg via Biesdorf as far as Mahlsdorf. Today they include the districts of Marzahn and Hellersdorf in the north, and in the south go down as far as the Rummelsburger See and the Spree. Here too settlement crystallization points were linear villages on the village green pattern like Lichtenberg, Biesdorf, Friedrichsfelde or indeed Marzahn as well, where the shape of the original village has survived to the greatest extent. Although 46 families from the Pfalz were settled on estates in Neu-Marzahn as early as 1772, the place only had 750 inhabitants in 1920. In Lichtenberg on the other hand the population on the former manorial territory grew from 1870 as industry began to be established around the present Herzbergstrasse; it had 60,000 inhabitants 40 years later. After joining up with industrial Boxhagen-Rummelsburg, Lichtenberg could have been considered a city in its own right from 1912. As a result of these different development tendencies, the eastern suburbs have a very varied and in places quite heterogeneous settlement structure. Even on a normal town plan it is possible to distinguish between closed tenement areas around Lichtenberg station serving the great, linked industrial areas east of Vulkanstrasse or the smaller ones in Rummelsburg and on the banks of the Spree. However, these varied areas are outdone by the great industrial and residential areas extending as a band from the Allee der Kosmonauten in Marzahn to Falkenberg and Ahrensfelde. Between these built-up areas in the suburbs there is a scattering of green, above all Tierpark Berlin around Schloss Friedrichsfelde, the Zentralfriedhof at Lichtenberg station, and also the municipal parks in Biesdorf and Hellersdorf, and the green areas round other great cemeteries and hospitals.

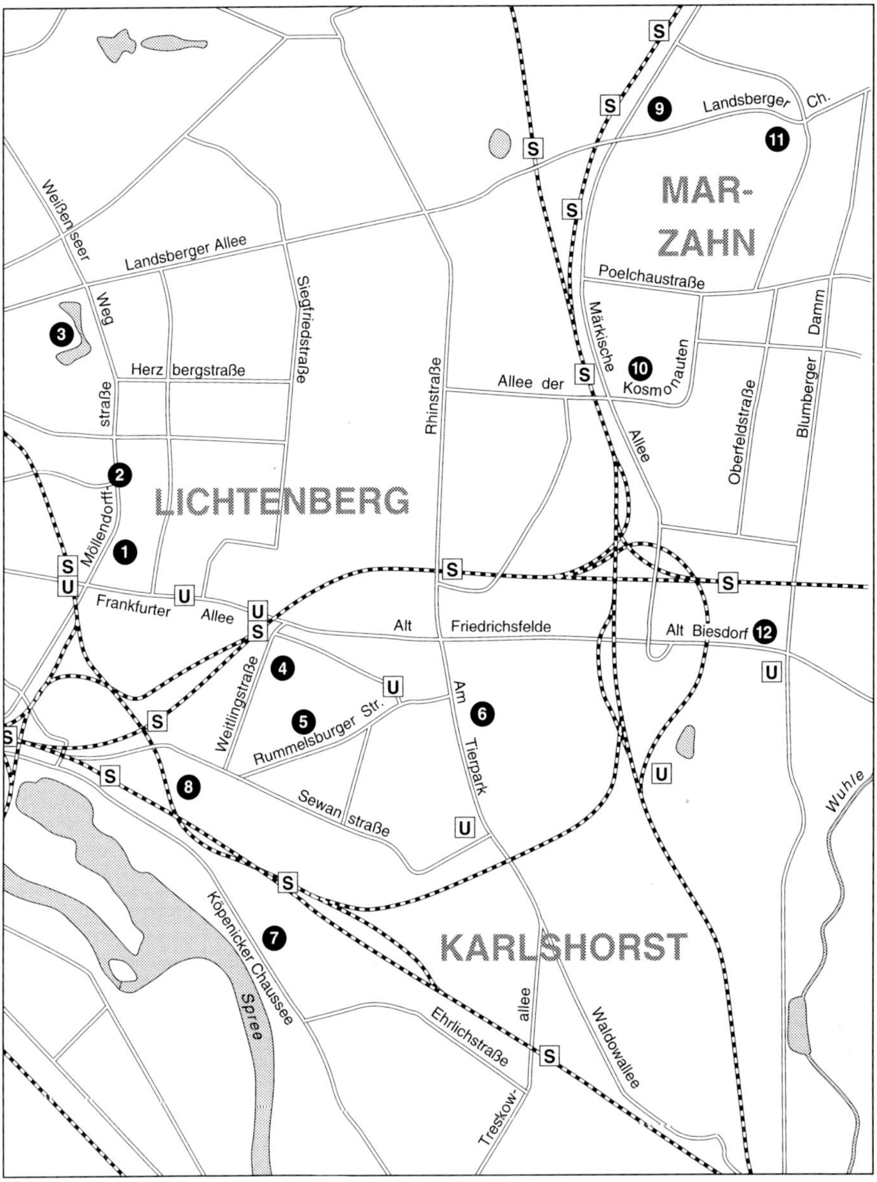

M 1 Rathaus Lichtenberg
M 2 Dorfkirche Lichtenberg
M 3 Gaststätte Seeterrasse am Fennpfuhl
M 4 Miethäuser Margaretenstraße
M 5 Wohnanlage Sonnenhof
M 6 Schloß Friedrichsfelde
M 7 Großkraftwerk Klingenberg
M 8 Schulkomplex am Nöldnerplatz
M 9 »Hauptzentrum« Marzahn
M 10 Wohngebiet am Springpfuhl
M 11 Dorfkirche Marzahn
M 12 Schloß Biesdorf

M 1 Rathaus Lichtenberg
Berlin-Lichtenberg; Möllendorfstraße 6
1897-98 • Knipping

Noch kurz vor der Jahrhundertwende und noch vor Pankow und Köpenick erhielt Lichtenberg sein imponierendes Rathaus. An der Kreuzung von drei Straßen beherrscht dieser Gebäudekomplex mit seinem spitzen Türmchen den Verkehrsweg von Weißensee nach Boxhagen-Rummelsburg und Stralau. Aber er kündet gleichzeitig auch mit seiner spätgotischen Backsteinarchitektur, dem großen stolzen Staffelgiebel mit den hohen Ratssaalfenstern und den anderen gewichtigen Gebäudefronten von der gewachsenen Bedeutung dieser damaligen Landgemeinde. Lichtenberg wurde 1907 zur Stadt erklärt und besaß 1912 über 100 000 Einwohner. Um dieses Rathaus wurden dann auch andere öffentliche Gebäude gruppiert. So entstand das heutige Jugendtheater als Realgymnasium an der Stelle des Möllendorfschen Landhauses. Dessen englischer Garten war 1907 durch die Gemeinde zum Stadtpark umgewandelt worden.

Lichtenberg's impressive town hall was built shortly before the turn of the century, before its fellows in Pankow and Köpenick. The complex of buildings with pointed towers stands at the junction of three roads and dominates the route from Weissensee to Boxhagen-Rummelsburg and Stralau. At the same time its late Gothic brick architecture, large, proud stepped gable, high council chamber windows and other weighty façades proclaim the growing importance of what was then a country community. In 1907 Lichtenberg was given town status, and by 1912 had over 100,000 inhabitants. Other public buildings were then grouped around this town hall. The present youth theatre was built as a school on the site of Möllendorf country house. Its English garden was turned into a municipal park by the community in 1907.

in der Nähe/nearby:
Postamt; Dottistraße 12-16
1925-30
Oberschule; Rathausstraße 8, Rudolf-Reusch-Straße
1910-11 • Wilhelm Grimme
Gebäude der Allgemeinen Ortskrankenkasse; Parkaue 3/9, Deutschmeisterstraße 16/24
1925
Wohnbauten; Scheffelstraße 15-16, Paul-Junius-Straße 2-12
1926-27 • Hans Kraffert

M 2 Dorfkirche Lichtenberg
Berlin-Lichtenberg; Loeperplatz
2. Viertel 13. Jahrhundert

Vom frühgotischen Feldsteinbau aus der Gründungszeit sind die Umfassungswände erhalten geblieben. Der massive Dachturm und auch die Strebepfeiler stammen aus dem 18. Jahrhundert. Nach Kriegszerstörungen erhielt das Schiff 1950-54 einen modernen Ausbau, der Turm wurde 1965 mit einem spitzen Helm verändert wiederhergestellt. Die Kirche liegt an einem sanften Geländebruch, am Rande des Barnimplateaus, das hier sichtbar zur Spreeniederung abfällt. Die Kirche ist in Ost-West-Richtung orientiert und erscheint in den beiden sie umflutenden Verkehrsströmen als quergestellt, da sich die Dorfaue des um 1230 als deutsche Siedlung gegründeten Straßenangerdorfes in Nord-Süd-Richtung erstreckt. Der innere Teil des ehemaligen Angers ist jetzt eine Grünanlage. Obwohl im 18. Jahrhundert zwei Kolonistensiedlungen und nach 1870 mit der Industrieansiedlung auf den Gutsländereien zwei Arbeiterkolonien und dann auch ausgedehnte Arbeiterwohnquartiere gebildet worden waren, blieb der ländliche Charakter dieses Straßenangerdorfes fast bis zum Ende des 19. Jahrhunderts erhalten.

The exterior walls of the original rubble-stone building have survived. The massive tower and buttresses date from the eighteenth century. The nave was rebuilt in modern style in 1950-4 after war damage, and the tower was redesigned with a spire in 1965. The church is set on a gentle break in the terrain, on the edge of the Barnim plateau, which here drops visibly to the Spree marshes. The church is oriented east-west, and seems to be set at right angles to the two streams of traffic that flow round it, as the village green runs north-south. The linear German settlement on the village green pattern was founded c. 1230. The inner section of the former green is now a little park. Although two settlements of colonists were established here in the eighteenth century, followed after 1870 by industrial development on the estate lands, and then by extensive residential areas for workers as well, the rural character of the village was maintained almost until the end of the nineteenth century.

in der Nähe/nearby:
Pfarrhaus; Möllendorfstraße 33
1848
Körperbehindertenschule; Paul-Junius-Straße 15
1976-77 • Wolf-Rüdiger Eisentraut, Erhard Rimek, Dieter Bierwisch
Pumpwerk Lichtenberg; Landsberger Allee 230
1893 • Henry Gill

M 3 Gaststätte Seeterrasse am Fennpfuhl
Berlin-Lichtenberg; Anton-Saefkow-Platz 6
1983 • Wolf-Rüdiger Eisentraut, Thomas Weber

Die Gaststätte liegt zwischen dem Zentrum des Wohnkomplexes und dem zu einem See gefaßten Fennpfuhl. Ihr räumlicher Aufbau ist ganz aus diesen landschaftlichen Gegebenheiten entwickelt worden. Das Grillrestaurant und das Café im Erdgeschoß und auch die obere Tanzgaststätte, die Bar und zwei Freiterrassen haben alle Blickbeziehungen zum See und sind über ein zentrales Foyer erschlossen. Nur die Bierstube ist vom Anton-Saefkow-Platz unmittelbar erreichbar. Dieses Wohngebiet ist ein um den Fennpfuhl und zwischen der Storkower Straße, Hohenschönhauser Straße und Vulkanstraße in den Jahren 1970-80 unter der Gesamtleitung von Joachim Näther, Heinz Graffunder, Roland Korn und nach Entwürfen von Peter Schweizer, Thorleif Neuer und Lothar Köhler errichteter großer Neubaukomplex mit etwa 16000 Wohnungen. Er ist in fünf Bereiche untergliedert, von denen jeder ein eigenes Versorgungszentrum mit einer Kaufhalle, Gaststätten und anderen Gemeinschaftseinrichtungen wie Schulen, Kindergärten oder Schwimmhallen besitzt, die wie die Wohnbauten fast ausschließlich aus Fertigbauteilen errichtet worden sind.

The restaurant is between the centre of the residential complex and the marshy pool that has been made into a lake. Its design derives entirely from this rural context. The grill restaurant and café on the ground floor, and also the upper restaurant with dancing, bar and two open-air terraces, all have views to the lake; access is from a central foyer. Only the beer bar can be reached directly from Anton-Saefkow-Platz. This residential area newly built around the marsh pool between Storkower Strasse, Hohenschönhauser Strasse and Vulkanstrasse in 1970-80 under the overall direction of Joachim Näther, Heinz Graffunder and Roland Korn, to designs by Peter Schweizer, Thorleif Neuer and Lothar Köhler is a large complex with about 16,000 residential units. It breaks down into five areas, each with its own centre including supermarket, restaurants and other community facilities such as schools, kindergartens or swimming pools, which like the residential buildings are almost entirely prefabricated.

in der Nähe/nearby:
Wohngebiet; Herzbergstraße
1972 • Dieter Rühle
Wohngebiet; Hohenschönhauser Straße
1973 • Jörg Piesel
Wohngebiet; Karl-Lade-Straße
1975• Walter Wenzel, Herbert Knopf
Wohnbereichszentrum; Storkower Straße
1972-77 • Friedrich Kalusche

M 4 Miethäuser
Berlin-Lichtenberg; Margaretenstraße 5-6
Um 1890

Diese Miethäuser aus der »Gründerzeit« erhielten keine Hinterhäuser. Diesen Vorzug haben sie sicher der Vorortlage und den hier preiswerten Grundstücken zu verdanken. Auch an den Fassaden sparte der Bauherr nicht. Sie sind von der für die Bauzeit charakteristischen Üppigkeit. Die viergeschossigen Klinkerfronten tragen schweren Schmuck und sind durch Halbsäulen und Pilaster gegliedert. Sie scheinen einer historischen Tradition des Ortes verpflichtet. Schon im 18. Jahrhundert war Lichtenberg beliebter Sommeraufenthalt und Villenvorort Berlins. So ließ sich Generalleutnant v. Möllendorf, Gouverneur von Berlin, 1786 in der Nähe des heutigen Stadtparkes ein schloßähnliches Landhaus errichten. Auch im 19. Jahrhundert war der Landort ein sonntägliches Ausflugsziel der Berliner. Erst seit 1870 mit der industriellen Ansiedlung auf dem Terrain des Gutsbezirkes östlich der Vulkanstraße entwickelte sich Lichtenberg sprunghaft zu einem dicht besiedelten Arbeiterwohnbezirk. Hierher legte man 1881 den ersten großen kommunalen Friedhof Berlins. Er wurde Ruhestätte bedeutender Arbeiterführer. 1926 entstand dort das Revolutionsmonument nach einem Entwurf von Ludwig Mies van der Rohe, das dann 1935 von den Nationalsozialisten zerstört worden ist.

These late nineteenth century tenements had nothing built behind them, an advantage for which they have to thank their suburban situation and the low price of land out here. They have the lavishness typical of the period in which they were built. The four-storey clinker façades are heavily decorated and articulated with half columns and pilasters, and seem to acknowledge a historical tradition of the place. Even in the eighteenth century, Lichtenberg was a popular summer resort and villa suburb of Berlin, and so Lieutenant General von Möllendorf, the governor of Berlin, built a palace-like country house near the present municipal park in 1786. The country town was a destination for Berliners' Sunday outings in the nineteenth century as well. It was not until 1870, when industrial settlement began on the estate terrain east of Vulkanstrasse, that Lichtenberg suddenly developed into a densely populated residential district for workers. Berlin's first large communal cemetery was established here in 1881, and important workers' leaders were buried here. In 1926 Ludwig Mies van der Rohe designed a monument here that was destroyed by the Nazis in 1935.

in der Nähe/nearby:
Zentralfriedhof Friedrichsfelde; Gudrunstraße
1881 • Hermann Mächtig
Gedenkstätte der Sozialisten; Gudrunstraße
1951 • Richard Jenner, Hans Mucke, Reinhold Lingner
Wohnblock; Irenenstraße 8-13, Friedastraße, Metastraße
1930-33 • Adolf Rading

M 5 Wohnanlage Sonnenhof
Berlin-Lichtenberg; Archenholdstraße, Delbrückstraße, Marie-Curie-Allee, Bietzkestraße
1926-27 • Erwin Gutkind

Dieser Wohnhof ist das klassische Beispiel einer hinterhoflosen Randbebauung des Reform-Wohnungsbaus der zwanziger Jahre. Der eingeschobene eingeschossige Kindergarten teilt den langgestreckten Hof wohltuend, so daß seine Wohnlichkeit erhalten bleibt, die sich aus einheitlicher, aber gegliederter Begrünung und durch die Öffnung der Wohnräume über loggienartige Balkone ergibt. Die Straßenfassaden mit ihrer hervorgehobenen waagerechten Gliederung haben dagegen etwas Abschließendes. Ursprünglich besaß die Anlage 264 Wohnungen in drei- bis viergeschossiger Bebauung. Das darüberliegende Dachgeschoß, ehemals mit kleinen Bodenfenstern, wurde 1972-73 zu Wohnzwecken ausgebaut. Der Eindruck der nunmehr vier- bis fünfgeschossigen Anlage ist dadurch sehr beeinträchtigt worden, denn ein fünftes Geschoß war geradezu verpönt für den Wohnungsbau einer »Stadt- und Land«-Siedlungsgesellschaft.

This is a classic example of a peripheral development without rear courtyard, dating from the residential reform building movement of the twenties. The single-storey kindergarten that has been inserted divides the extended courtyard pleasingly, and a feeling of homeliness, arising from uniform but articulated planting and the fact that living rooms open on to loggia-like balconies, is retained. The street façades, on the other hand, have emphatic horizontal articulation, giving a somewhat forbidding quality. Originally the complex contained 264 residential units, and was three or four storeys high. The attic storey above them, originally with small dormer windows, was added to provide further accommodation in 1972-3. This means the complex is now four- to five-storeyed, which is considerably to its disadvantage, as a fifth storey had been definitely frowned upon for residential building under the auspices of a «town and country» estate-building company.

in der Nähe/nearby:
Ulmenhof, Pappelhof, Erlenhof; B-Friedrichsfelde; Kraetkestraße, Ribbecker Straße, Rummelsburger Straße
1929-31 • Jakobus Goettel
Wohnzeilen; B-Friedrichsfelde; Sewanstraße 213-248
1961-66 • Leopold Wiel, Günter Kabus
Plattenbauten; B-Friedrichsfelde; Splanemannstraße
1926 • Martin Wagner
Großblockbauten; B-Karlshorst; Ilsestraße
1956-57 • Leopold Wiel
Waldsiedlung Wuhlheide; B-Karlshorst; Hegemeisterweg 18-30
1915 (Entwurf); 1919-20 • Peter Behrens

M 6 Schloß Friedrichsfelde
Berlin-Friedrichsfelde; Am Tierpark
1719 • Martin Heinrich Böhme

Einen mehrfachen Wechsel der Nutzung haben Schloß und Park Friedrichsfelde erlebt. Vom einfachen Lusthaus, 1695 für den Generaldirektor der kurfürstlichen Marine in Rosenfelde erbaut, wandelte sich der Bau 1719 nach Plänen von Martin Heinrich Böhme zum Schloß. Der ehemals holländische Garten wurde ständig erweitert und 1821 durch Peter Joseph Lenné zu einem großzügigen englischen Landschaftspark umgestaltet. 1954-64 entstand auf einer 160 Hektar großen Fläche nach Plänen von Heinz Graffunder, Editha Bendig und Oskar Köster in mehreren Abschnitten der Tierpark Berlin. Eine Reihe größerer Bauten bilden wie die Gehege und Gewässer wirkungsvolle Blickpunkte im weitläufigen Park. Dabei wechseln streng gefaßte Bauteile mit frei gestalteten Felspartien, wie am Bärenschaufenster oder an der Eisbärenanlage. Das Alfred-Brehm-Haus, ein Universal-Warmhaus mit Tropenhalle, wurde 1963-65 von Heinz Graffunder und Lothar Köhler für Großkatzen, Kleinsäuger, aber auch für Vögel und Reptilien eingerichtet. Imponierend sind die beiden Felsenhallen mit den anschließenden Freigehegen. 1989 konnte das neue Elefantenhaus eröffnet werden; es ist nach Entwürfen von Wolf-Rüdiger Eisentraut errichtet worden.

The Friedrichsfelde Schloss and park have been used for various purposes. Originally a summer residence built in 1695 for the director general of the Electors' navy in Rosenfelde, the building was converted into a palace to plans by Martin Heinrich Böhme in 1719. The former Dutch garden was constantly extended, then redesigned as a spacious English park by Peter Joseph Lenné in 1821. In 1954-64 Tierpark Berlin, a zoo, was established in several phases on an area of 160 hectares to plans by Heinz Graffunder, Editha Bendig and Oskar Köster. Enclosures, pools, lakes and a series of larger buildings form effective viewpoints in the extensive park. Rigorously designed buildings alternate with freer rocky areas, like the viewing window for the bears, or the polar bears' enclosure. The Alfred-Brehm-Haus, a general hothouse with tropical hall, was designed in 1963-5 by Heinz Graffunder and Lothar Köhler for big cats and small mammals, but also for birds and reptiles. The two rock halls with adjacent open-air enclosures are impressive. The new elephant house was opened in 1989, built to designs by Wolf-Rüdiger Eisentraut.

in der Nähe/nearby:
Wohngebiet am Tierpark; B-Friedrichsfelde; Alfred-Kowalke-Straße
1975-82 • Solveig Steller, Marianne Batke, Edith Diehl
Marienkirche; B-Karlshorst; Gundelfinger Straße 36
1935-37 • Clemens Lohmer
Ev. Kirche; B-Karlshorst; Weseler Straße 6
1909-10 • Jürgensen & Bachmann

M 7 Großkraftwerk Klingenberg
Berlin-Rummelsburg; Köpenicker Chaussee 24-39
1925-26 • Walter Klingenberg und Werner Issel

Seit der Einführung des Drehstroms um die Jahrhundertwende hatte der Stromverbrauch stetig zugenommen, neue Werke wurden in der städtischen Peripherie gebaut und regelmäßig erweitert. Mit der planmäßigen Umstellung der Berliner S-Bahn auf elektrischen Betrieb von 1924 an stieg der Bedarf schließlich so stark an, daß der Bau eines Großkraftwerkes nötig wurde, wollte man sich vom damals auch schon möglichen Fernstrombezug nicht zu abhängig machen. In Rummelsburg – unweit eines älteren Werkes – fand sich ein geeignetes Gelände an der Spree, die das notwendige Kühlwasser lieferte und die Anlage eines eigenen Hafens zur Kohleanlieferung erlaubte. Der Grundriß des Werkes deckt sich mit einer hervorragenden betrieblichen Organisation, läßt aber auch die städtebauliche Wirkung nicht außer acht. Die architektonische Gestaltung der Stahlskelettbauten folgt dort, wo Fassaden vom Wasser oder von der Straße einsehbar sind, klaren dekorativen Absichten und wird besonders beim Verwaltungshochhaus ins Theatralische gesteigert. Sonst beschränken sich die Architekten auf eine mehr sachliche, doch dabei ästhetisch beständige Verkleidung der technischen Bauteile, ganz im Sinne des damals verinnerlichten Zusammenhanges Technik – Kultur – Kunst.

Ever since the introduction of three-phase electrical current around the turn of the century the consumption of electricity had steadily increased. New power stations were erected on the periphery of the city and regularly expanded. With the scheduled electrification of the Berlin S-Bahn system after 1924 the huge eletricity requirements required construction of a new large-scale power station in order to avoid dependence on a long-distance power supply which had become technically possible. In Rummelsburg, close to an existing older power station, a suitable site was found near the Spree which provided the necessary water for cooling and also allowed construction of a special harbour for shipping coal. The plan of the station follows functional requirements and at the same time makes allowance for the effects on the cityscape. Wherever the façades are visible from the river or from the street, the architectural design of the steel skeleton structures clearly displays decorative elements, becoming particularly dramatic in the case of the tall administration building. In all other areas the architects preferred a rather functional if aesthetically consistent cladding of the technical installations much in conformity with the contemporary understanding of the relationship between technology, culture and the arts.

in der Nähe/nearby:
Gaswerksiedlung; Köpenicker Chaussee 24-39
Um 1925 • Ernst Engelmann

M 8 Schulkomplex am Nöldnerplatz
Berlin-Rummelsburg; Fischerstraße 32-35
1929-32 • Max Taut

1783 ließ der Pächter des Lichtenberger Guts im Bereich der Lückstraße eine Kolonie für acht Tagelöhner, den Lichtenberger Kietz, anlegen. Nach 1871 entstanden in der Kolonie Victoriastadt um den heutigen Tuchollaplatz 75 Doppel- und Reihenhäuser der »Cement-Bau AG« in Gußbeton. Der Schulkomplex an der Fischerstraße und Schlichtallee wurde nach einem Wettbewerb im Jahre 1927 errichtet und in Teilen erst 1935 fertiggestellt. Er war für ein Lyzeum, eine Mittel-, eine Grund- und eine Berufsschule erbaut worden. Die überaus schlichte Architektur bedient sich einer Stahlbetonkonstruktion und wirkt allein durch die großzügig bewegten Baukörper. Die Aula, im Krieg stark beschädigt, ist im Gegensatz zum sonst gelben Klinkermauerwerk durch rote Ziegel hervorgehoben. Anders als Bruno Taut beim Projekt der Aufbauschule am Neuköllner Dammweg, verfolgte hier Max Taut nicht besondere sozialpädagogische Ziele. Lediglich eine freie Nutzbarkeit der Schulbereiche je nach Bevölkerungsentwicklung stand im Vordergrund; damit hängt auch die ungewöhnliche Zusammenfassung von vier Schulen zum damals größten Berliner Schulkomplex zusammen.

1783 the lessee of the Lichtenberg estate established a colony for eight day-labourers, the Lichtenberger Kietz, in the Lückstrasse area. After 1871, 75 semi-detached and terraced houses were built in cast concrete by «Cement-Bau AG» in the Victoriastadt colony around the present Tuchollaplatz. The school complex in Fischerstrasse and Schlichtallee was built in 1927 after a competition, and parts of it were not completed until 1935. It was built to accommodate a girls' grammar school, a middle, a primary, and a vocational training school. The architecture is very plain, built of reinforced concrete, and makes its effect simply because of the vigorous rhythm of the buildings. The school hall, badly damaged in the war, is in red brick, contrasting with the rest of the yellow clinker masonry. Unlike Bruno Taut with the Aufbauschule in Neuköllner Dammweg, Max Taut had no particular social and educational aims. The main thing was simply flexibility of school premises according to the development of the population, and this was the reason for the unusual grouping together of four schools, making it the largest Berlin school complex of is period.

in der Nähe/nearby:
Schrotturm der Bleischmelze; Nöldnerstraße 16
1908
Erlöserkirche; Nöldnerstraße 43
1890-92 • Max Spitta, Conrad Wilhelm Hase
Gußbeton-Wohnhaus; Spittastraße 40
Um 1871/75 • Türrschmidt
Berliner Bremsenwerk; Hirschbergstraße 4
1922-27 • Alfred Grenander

M 9 »Hauptzentrum« Marzahn
Berlin-Marzahn; Marzahner Promenade
1984-90 • Wolf-Rüdiger Eisentraut, Heinz Graffunder

Auf einer Gesamtfläche von 600 Hektar entstand seit 1975 nach Plänen von Roland Korn, Peter Schweizer und anderen Architekten eine sechs Kilometer lange und mehr als zwei Kilometer breite Wohnstadt mit einer Industriezone entlang der S-Bahntrasse und einem Park am Flüßchen Wuhle. Die städtebauliche Gliederung ergab sich durch nacheinander entstehende Wohngebiete entlang dem Industriegebiet, aber auch mit der planmäßigen Anlage verschiedenartiger Zentren. Das Hauptzentrum liegt zwischen dem alten Dorf und dem Marzahner Friedhof. Es ist angeschlossen an den Bus- und S-Bahnhof und erstreckt sich vom »Marzahner Tor« über die Einkaufspromenade mit eingeschossigen Ladenbauten bis zum Kultur- und Sportkomplex gegenüber der Paul-Dessau-Straße. Hier findet man neben einer Schwimm- und Sporthalle unter anderem die Bibliothek und ein Kulturhaus. Neben diesem Hauptzentrum gibt es in der Wohnstadt Marzahn mit ihren nunmehr über 150 000 Einwohnern am Helene-Weigel-Platz und an der Ludwig-Renn-Straße zwei Nebenzentren. Weitere kleine Versorgungszentren mit Kaufhallen sind den einzelnen Wohnvierteln zugeordnet.

This residential town with industrial zone, six kilometres long and over two kilometres wide, occupying a total area of 600 hectares, was built from 1975 to plans by Roland Korn, Peter Schweizer and other architects along the S-Bahn line and the little Wuhle river. The urban articulation followed from the series of new residential districts established consecutively along the industrial area as well as from the system of planned new centres. The principal centre is between the old village and the Marzahn cemetery. It is linked to bus and railway stations and extends from the «Marzahn Gate» via the shopping mall with single-storey shop buildings to the culture and sports centre opposite Paul-Dessau-Strasse. Here, as well as an indoor swimming pool and sports hall, are library and culture house, among other things. As well as this main centre, Marzahn, now with a population of over 150,000, has two subsidiary centres in Helene-Weigel-Platz and Ludwig-Renn-Strasse. The individual residential areas have a number of additional smaller supply centres with shops and markets.

in der Nähe/nearby:
Hauptpostamt Marzahn; Marzahner Promenade 2
1984-87 • Wolf-Rüdiger Eisentraut, Michael Kny
Katholisches Gemeindezentrum; Rebhuhnweg
1983-87 • Hermann Korneli
Backwarenfabrik; Wolfener Straße 38
1981-84 • Lothar Arzt, Hans Gott, Ulrich Balke

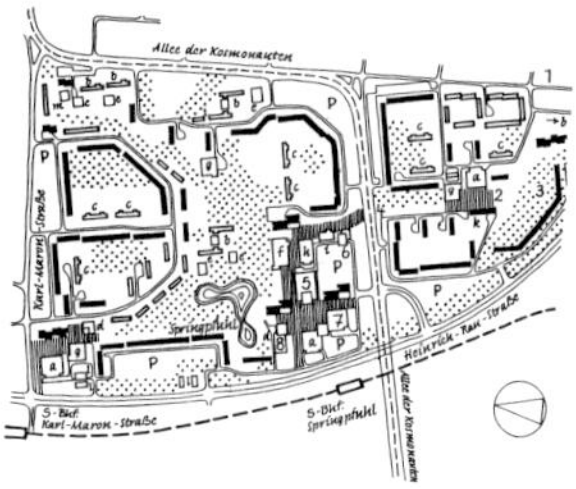

M 10 Wohngebiet am Springpfuhl
Berlin-Marzahn; Allee der Kosmonauten
1976-86 • Dieter Schulze, Thorleif Neuer, Jörg Piesel

Rings um den Springpfuhl entstand beiderseits der Allee der Kosmonauten das erste der Marzahner Wohngebiete nach städtebaulichem Entwurf von Edith Diehl und Joachim Felke. In der Mitte der südlichsten Wohngruppe ist ein kleines Einkaufs- und Versorgungszentrum mit einer Gaststätte, einer Kaufhalle und einer Dienstleistungsstelle untergebracht. Hier steht auch ein Altersheim nahe einem großen Kinderspielplatz. Er besitzt als Attraktion für den Sommer eine »Sprühplansche«, das ist eine mit Duschen besetzte Steinplattenfläche, auf der man im Frühjahr und im Herbst auch Rollschuh laufen kann. Der hier beginnende Fußgängerbereich führt durch eine Unterführung vorbei an dem Kino »Sojus«, einer Apotheke, der Poliklinik, einer Schwimmhalle zum Springpfuhl. Neben dem Rathaus, der Post, der Kaufhalle und Läden beleben ambulante Händler den Platz.

The first of Marzahn's residential areas, designed by urban planners Edith Diehl and Joachim Felke, grew up around the Springpfuhl on both sides of the Allee der Kosmonauten. In the middle of the southernmost residential group is a small shopping and supply centre with restaurant, supermarket and service centre. There is also an old people's home near a large children's playground. One of its summer attractions is a «spray splash», a stone-flagged area with showers that can also be used for roller-skating in spring and autumn. The pedestrian precinct begins here and leads via a subway past the «Sojus» cinema, a chemist's, the outpatients' clinic to the Springpfuhl. The square accommodates town hall, post office, department store and shops, and occasional mobile traders.

in der Nähe/nearby:
Wohngebietszentrum; Helene-Weigel-Platz
1981-86 • Heinz Graffunder, Wolf-Rüdiger Eisentraut, Michael Kny
Rathaus Marzahn; Helene-Weigel-Platz
1983-88 • Wolf-Rüdiger Eisentraut, Karin Bock
Filmtheater »Sojus«; Helene-Weigel-Platz 12
1984 • Wolf-Rüdiger Eisentraut, Dietrich Kabisch

M 11 Dorfkirche Marzahn
Berlin-Marzahn; Alt-Marzahn
1870-71 • Friedrich August Stüler

Wie ein trutziger Fels in der stürmischen See steht in der Längsachse des spindelförmigen Dorfangers heute Stülers neugotische Backsteinkirche; ihr mußte 1874 die alte Dorfkirche weichen. Im 2. Viertel des 13. Jahrhunderts wurde das an der Straße nach Landsberg liegende Dorf gegründet und als »Mortzane« um 1300 erstmals erwähnt. 1412 befand sich der Ort mit »Äckern, Obst- und Hopfengärten, mit Holzungen und einem großen Weinberg, mit Schäfereien, Fischereien und allen Untertanen« im erblichen Besitz des Rittergutes. Die Gemarkung ist seit dem 19. Jahrhundert immer wieder parzelliert worden.1866 wurden Rieselfelder angelegt, 1898 die Bahnlinie nach Werneuchen und Wriezen eröffnet und um das Dorf entstanden seit 1900 die verschiedensten Siedlungen. Der dörfliche Kern, seit 1982 vom Durchgangsverkehr befreit, ist mit seinen ehemaligen Vierseithöfen in den Grundzügen erhalten geblieben, wird als Fußgängerzentrum eingerichtet und behutsam mit neuen Einrichtungen in maßstabgerechten Neubauten ergänzt.

Stüler's neo-Gothic brick church stands on the longitudinal axis of the spindle-shaped village green like a defiant rock in a stormy sea; it was built on the site of the old village church in 1874. This village on the road to Landsberg was founded in the third quarter of the thirteenth century and first mentioned as «Mortzane» c. 1300. In 1412 it was hereditary property of the manor, with «fields, orchards and hop gardens, woods and a large vineyard, with sheep farms, fish farms and all subjects». The territory has been frequently parcelled since the nineteenth century. In 1866 sewage farms were established, the railway line to Werneuchen and Wriezen opened in 1898, and various settlements grew up around the village from 1900. The core of the village, closed to through traffic since 1982, has essentially survived with its former buildings on four sides. It is being made into a pedestrian area and carefully provided with new facilities and new buildings on an appropriate scale.

in der Nähe/nearby:
Bauernhäuser; Alt-Marzahn 61 und 66
Um 1830/40 und um 1800
Städtischer Friedhof Marzahn; Wiesenburger Weg
1908
Straßenbahn-Betriebshof; Landsberger Allee 565
1981-85 • Helga Hartenfeld

M 12 Schloß Biesdorf
Berlin-Biesdorf; Alt-Biesdorf 55
1868 • Martin Gropius, Heino Schmieden

Biesdorf liegt an der alten Handelsstraße Berlin–Frankfurt (Oder), wurde wohl als Straßenangerdorf wie andere märkische Dörfer in der 2. Hälfte des 13. Jahrhunderts gegründet und blieb bis ins 19. Jahrhundert in seiner Gestalt fast unberührt. 1868 ließ der Besitzer des Biesdorfer Gutes, Freiherr von Rüxleben, sein Wohnhaus nördlich des Dorfangers durch ein schloßähnliches Gebäude ersetzen und auch einen ausgedehnten Park anlegen. 1887 erwarb der Industrielle Werner v. Siemens das Grundstück. Vom Turm des Schlosses erfolgten erste Versuche für drahtlose Telegraphie. Seit 1927 sind Haus und Park in städtischem Besitz. Gropius und Schmieden schufen mit diesem Schloßbau eine reizvolle italianisierende Anlage. Der spätklassizistische Putzbau, gegenüber der Straße leicht überhöht, wurde über einem T-förmigen Grundriß entwickelt und hatte früher zwei Hauptgeschosse über dem hohen Sockelgeschoß. Der oktogonale Turm mit abschließendem Belvedere ist asymmetrisch angeordnet. 1891-98 wurde der Park erweitert und von Albert Brodersen landschaftlich gestaltet.

Biesdorf is on the old trade route from Berlin to Frankfurt an der Oder. It was probably founded as a linear settlement on the village green pattern like other villages in the Mark in the second half of the thirteenth century, and remained virtually undisturbed in design terms until the nineteenth century. In 1868, Freiherr von Rüxleben, owner of the Biesdorf estate, replaced his residence north of the village green with a palace-like building, and also had an extensive park laid out. In 1887 Werner von Siemens, the industrialist, acquired the plot, and early experiments in wireless telegraphy were made from the tower. House and park have been owned by the city since 1927. Gropius and Schmieden created a delightful Italianate complex. The late-classical rendered building, slightly raised vis-à-vis the street, was developed on a T-shaped ground plan and formerly had two main storeys over the high base storey. The octagonal tower with belvedere is arranged asymmetrically. The park was extended in 1891-8 and landscaped by Albert Brodersen.

in der Nähe/nearby:
Wilhelm-Griesinger-Krankenhaus; Brebacher Weg
1890-93 • Hermann Blankenstein
Gutshaus (Gründerzeit-Museum); B-Mahlsdorf; Hultschiner Damm 333 • E. 18. Jh.
Kreuzkirche; Albrecht-Dürer-Straße, Pfarrhufenweg
1935 • Otto Risse (Glasmaler: Hans Uhl)

N
Berlin
Köpenick, Treptow, Neukölln

Über weite Strecken gliedern Spree und Teltowkanal heute den Südosten Berlins in die Bezirke Köpenick, Treptow und Neukölln. Die Spree fließt hier in einem Einbruchstal, einem Teil des späteren Berliner Urstromtales, das sich auf der Höhe von Altglienicke und Köpenick von zehn Kilometer auf nur fünf bei Alttreptow verengt und mit Talsandinseln durchsetzt ist. Sie ist in ihrem geraden Verlauf von Köpenick bis Berlin einst durch den Rummelsburger See geflossen, war in Höhe der heutigen Mühlendammbrücke durch einen quergelagerten Talsander angestaut, auf dem die Doppelstadt Cölln/Berlin gegründet wurde, und verlief danach weiter gewunden wie ein normaler Fluß. Mit den Spreeüberschwemmungen wurde die lange Talsohle und damit auch die Cöllnische Heide besonders unwegsam. Dann mußten die Fuhrleute ihren Weg nach Köpenick über Tempelhof oder Rixdorf, das spätere Neukölln, nehmen. 1589 ließ daher der Kurfürst den mittelalterlichen Weg von Berlin nach Köpenick mit dem »Neuen Damm« aufschütten, der später über das Adlergestell nach Schmöckwitz und weiter bis nach Königs Wusterhausen geführt wurde. Erst lange nach dem Bau der Frankfurter und Görlitzer Eisenbahnen, der Anlage von Bahnstationen und dem Anschluß an den Ringbahnverkehr begann nach 1896 die Industrieansiedlung in diesen Stadtteilen. Von der Oberspree bis zum Rummelsburger See, besonders aber in Oberschöneweide entstanden Großbetriebe, die in der Innenstadt keine Erweiterungsmöglichkeiten mehr hatten. Hier fanden sie billiges Bauland vor. Der Lauf von Spree und Dahme, die neuen Kanäle sowie eigene Gleisanschlüsse schufen recht gute Voraussetzungen für den Massengütertransport. Der Industrie folgten bald nach der Jahrhundertwende kleinere Wohnanlagen, in den zwanziger Jahren die großen Wohnsiedlungen, von denen manche zu weltbekannten Beispielen vorbildlicher Städtebaukultur wurden.

Long stretches of the Spree and the Teltow canal today divide the south-east of Berlin into the districts of Köpenick, Treptow and Neukölln. Here the Spree flows into a rift valley, part of the later Berlin glacial valley, which narrows down from ten kilometres at Altglienicke and Köpenick to only five in Alttreptow, with many sandy islands. In its straight run from Köpenick to Berlin it once flowed through the Rummelsburger See, and at the point where the Mühlendammbrücke now is it was once dammed by a transverse valley outwash, on which the double towns of Cölln/Berlin were founded. After that it flowed twisting on like a normal river. Spree floods made the valley bottom and thus the Cöllnische Heide as well particularly impassable, and carters had to make their way to Köpenick via Tempelhof or Rixdorf, later Neukölln. For this reason the Elector had the medieval route from Berlin to Neukölln raised as the Neuer Damm in 1589, later continued via the Adlergestell to Schmöckwitz and on to Königs Wusterhausen. It was long after the building of the Frankfurt and Görlitz railways, construction of stations, and a link with the ring line that industry began to establish itself in these districts after 1896. From the Upper Spree to the Rummelsburger See, but particularly in Oberschöneweide, large concerns grew up that had no further possibility of expansion in the inner city. Here they found cheap building land. The Spree and the Dahme, the new canals and their own rail connections created excellent conditions for the mass transport of goods. Industry was followed by small residential areas shortly after the turn of the century, and in the twenties by the great residential estates, some of which became world-famous specimens of exemplary urban culture.

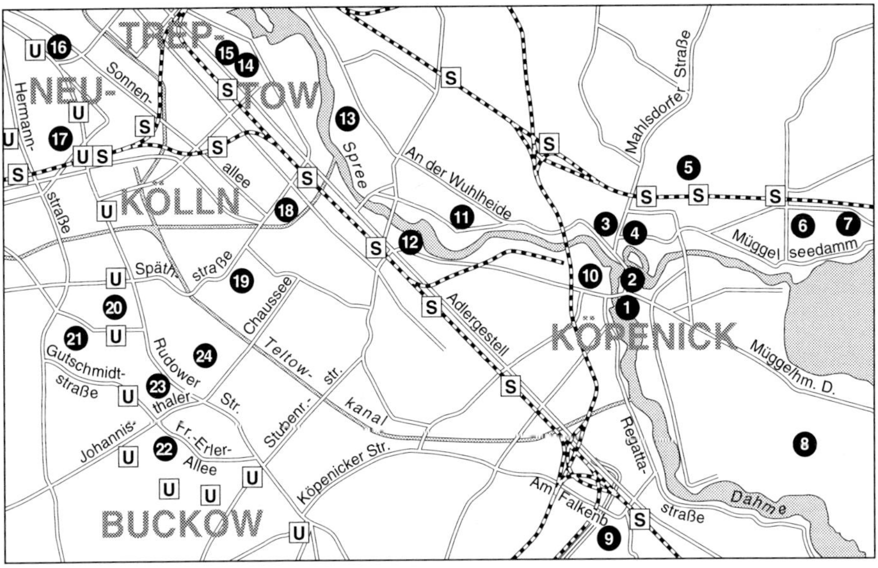

N 1 Schloß Köpenick
N 2 Rathaus Köpenick
N 3 Realgymnasium Köpenick
N 4 Evangelisches Gemeindehaus
N 5 Siedlung Elsengrund
N 6 Christopheruskirche
N 7 Wasserwerk Friedrichshagen
N 8 Müggelturm
N 9 Gartenvorstadt Falkenberg
N 10 Dorotheen-Lyzeum
N 11 NAG-Fabrikgebäude
N 12 Spreesiedlung
N 13 Rundfunkgebäude
N 14 Rathaus Treptow
N 15 Treptower Park
N 16 Rathaus Neukölln
N 17 Körnerpark
N 18 Einfamilien-Reihenhäuser Radenzer Straße
N 19 Wohnhaus der Familie Späth
N 20 Hufeisensiedlung
N 21 Albert-Einstein-Schule
N 22 Walter-Gropius-Schule
N 23 Krankenhaus Neukölln (Neubau)
N 24 Gemeinschafts-Wohnhäuser

N 1 Schloß Köpenick
Berlin-Köpenick; Schloßinsel
1677-81 • Rutger van Langefelt

Die Schloßinsel, ein frühgeschichtlicher Siedlungskern der jüngeren Steinzeit, beherbergt heute im Schloß des Kurprinzen Friedrich, des späteren ersten Königs in Preußen, das staatliche Kunstgewerbemuseum. Im südlichen Teil, an der Stelle des heutigen Schloßparks, bestand seit dem neunten Jahrhundert eine slawische Burg; ihr Besitzer um 1150, Fürst Jaxa de Copnic, ist durch Münzfunde nachgewiesen. 1245 ist ein Voigt der nach Osten vorgedrungenen Askanier erwähnt. Das Schloß ist in Formen des holländischen Barocks errichtet und der bedeutendste Profanbau der Mark Brandenburg aus der Zeit vor Schlüter. Die Innenräume mit farbigen Stuckdekorationen sind von Giovanni Caroveri und Giovanni Simonetti zwischen 1684 und 1690 ausgeschmückt worden. Im großen Saal des zweiten Obergeschosses tragen Hermen Wappenschilde brandenburgischer Besitzungen. Die Deckengemälde in 15 Räumen stammen wohl von Jacques Vaillant und seiner Werkstatt. Die dem Schloß gegenüberliegende, von Wirtschaftsgebäuden gerahmte intime Kapelle entstand 1682-85 nach Plänen von Johann Arnold Nering; er baute ebenfalls das 1682 datierte Torhaus und das 1688 am Ehrenhof errichtete Galeriegebäude.

The Schlossinsel, a centre of neolithic settlement, now houses the state museum of applied art in the palace of the Elector Friedrich, later first king of Prussia. In the southern section, on the site of the present park, a Slavic castle stood from the ninth century; its owner c. 1150, Fürst Jaxa de Copnic, has been authenticated by numismatic finds. There is mention of an Ascanian official who had penetrated east in 1245. The Schloss is of Dutch baroque design, and is the most important secular building in the Mark Brandenburg of the period before Schlüter. The coloured stucco interiors were decorated by Giovanni Caroveri and Giovanni Simonetti between 1684 and 1690. In the great hall on the second floor herms carry coats of arms of Brandenburg possessions. Ceiling paintings in 15 rooms are probably by Jacques Vaillant and his studio. The intimate chapel is opposite the main section and surrounded by domestic buildings. It was built from 1682-5 to plans by Johann Arnold Nering, who also built the gatehouse dated 1682 and the gallery erected in 1688 in the main courtyard.

in der Nähe/nearby:
Wohnhaus; Kietz 8
18. Jh.; 1. H. 19. Jh.
Siedlung Kietzer Feld; Wendenschloßstraße 307/323
1930-32 • Paul Schmidt
Gaststätte; B-Wendenschloß; Niebergallstraße 20
1893
Landhaus; B-Wendenschloß; Slevogtweg 5/7
1914 • Kurt Schramm

N 2 Rathaus Köpenick
Berlin-Köpenick; Alt Köpenick 21
1901-04 • Hans Schütte, Hugo Kinzer

Die vom Schloß zur Dammvorstadt verlaufende Straße »Alt Köpenick« entstand mit der im 13. Jahrhundert gegründeten Siedlung, die nach 1300 in Richtung »Alter Markt« erweitert und 1705 um die »Freiheit« zum Bau von Häusern für französische Wollweber ergänzt wurde. Südlich davon lag am Frauentrog als slawisches Fischerdorf seit Mitte des 13. Jahrhunderts der Kietz; er war bis 1898 selbständig. Fast gleichzeitig mit vielen anderen Berliner Vororten erhielt Köpenick 1904 sein neues Rathaus mit dem stolzen Turm und der nach Westen gerichteten Fassade in Formen märkischer Backsteingotik mit teils farbigen Glasur- und Formsteinen. 1906 war das Rathaus Schauplatz der weltberühmten »Köpenickiade«, als der Schumacher Voigt in geborgter Uniform eines preußischen Hauptmanns die Stadtkasse aus den Händen des Bürgermeisters an sich brachte – ein Lehrstück kaiserzeitlichen Untertanengeistes.

The road that runs from the Schloss to the suburb on the dyke, «Alt-Köpenick» came into being with the settlement founded in the thirteenth century; after 1300 it was extended in the direction of the «Alter Markt» and in 1705 by the addition of the «Freiheit» for the building of houses for French wool weavers. South of this was the Kietz, a Slavic fishing village on the Frauentrog from the mid thirteenth century; it was independent until 1898. Köpenick acquired its new town hall in 1904, at almost the same time as other Berlin suburbs. It has a proud tower and west-facing façade, and is a Mark brick Gothic design with some glazed and shaped bricks. In 1906 the famous «Köpenickiade» took place in the town hall: shoemaker Voigt, in the borrowed uniform of a Prussian captain, took the city treasury out of the mayor's hands – an exemplary demonstration of the subservient spirit of the imperial period.

in der Nähe/nearby:
Laurentiuskirche; Alt Köpenick, Kirchstraße
1838-41 • Butzke
Amtsgericht; Freiheit 16
1878-79
Schötzes Hof; Alter Markt 2
Vermutlich 1712

N 3 Realgymnasium Köpenick
Berlin-Köpenick; Lindenstraße 1, Bahnhofstraße
1909-10 • Hugo Kinzer

In der Köpenicker Feldmark zwischen der Altstadt und der 1843 angelegten Trasse der Frankfurter Eisenbahn lagen 1860 etwa 70 Wohnhäuser, Wirtschaftsgebäude und Scheunen. Nach 1881 entwickelte sich hier an der Verbindungsstraße nach Mahlsdorf zwischen dem Bahnhof und der Lindenstrasse die Dammvorstadt. Seit der Jahrhundertwende entstand auch eine Reihe öffentlicher Gebäude wie Post, katholische Kirche und Schule. Das Realgymnasium, die heutige Fachschule für Kindergärtnerinnen, wurde als betont repräsentativer Bau in der Mode der Stilmischung ausgeführt. An der Straßenkreuzung im Blickpunkt der Dammbrücke liegt das Aulagebäude, im Erdgeschoß die Turnhalle. Hohe Fenster in übersteigerten spätgotischen Formen mit Kielbögen und reichem Fialenbesatz finden ihre Fortsetzung in polygonalen Dacherkern mit spitzen Helmen. In der Gebäudeflucht an der Lindenstraße steht das Rektorenwohnhaus, es gibt sich ländlich mit Fachwerk und Krüppelwalmdach. Dazwischen liegt der Klassentrakt mit großem Renaissancegiebel und Treppenturm, abgeschlossen von einer Doppelhaube über einem Umgang – Versatzstücke aus einer alten deutschen Reichsstadt als Schmuck des aufstrebenden Köpenick.

In the parish of Köpenick between the old town and the Frankfurt railway line, built in 1843, there were about 70 homes, working quarters and barns in 1860. The Dammvorstadt developed here on the road to Mahlsdorf between the station and Lindenstrasse after 1881. From the turn of the century a series of public buildings like post-office, Catholic church and school were built. The Realgymnasium, the present training school for kindergarten teachers, is an emphatically representative building in mixed styles. The building containing the hall is on the junction seen from the Dammbrücke, with the gymnasium on the ground floor. Tall windows of exaggerated Gothic design with ogee arches and lavish pinnacles are continued by polygonal roof oriels with spires. In the section on Lindenstrasse is the rector's residence, rural, with half-timbering and half-hip roof. Between them is the classroom section with large Renaissance gable and staircase tower concluding in a double cupola above an ambulatory, set-pieces from an old German imperial town as decoration for up-and-coming Köpenick.

in der Nähe/nearby:
Villa; Lindenstraße 44
1875; 1880 • C. Schubert
Postamt; Lindenstraße 42
1892-93 • E. W. J. Zimmermann
Wohnbebauung; Oettingstraße, Cardinalstraße
1922-24 • Willy Wagenknecht, Heinrich Peter Kaiser

N 4 Evangelisches Gemeindehaus
Berlin-Köpenick; Am Generalshof 1 a
1927-28 • Otto Firle

Auf dem ehemaligen Heuplatz und dem Areal für die Scheunen der Köpenicker Ackerbürger entstand Anfang des 20. Jahrhunderts der Stadtpark an der Alten Spree gegenüber der Baumgarteninsel. Dort steht auch das 1966-70 von Walter Sutkowski gestaltete Mahnmahl für die Opfer der Köpenicker Blutwoche vom Juni 1933. Gegenüber am Generalshof wurde 1927-28 ein evangelisches Gemeindehaus errichtet. Stilistisch folgt es der Neuen Sachlichkeit. Der spannungsreiche Wechsel von hellem Putz und dunklen Ziegeln, von glatter Wand und plastischen Gesimsen, Pfeilern oder Fensterrahmungen, die bewegte Anordnung streng kubischer Baukörper lassen ein im Sinne des Bauhauses typisches, doch unverwechselbares Bild entstehen.

The municipal park on the Alte Spree opposite Baumgarten island came into being in the early twentieth century on the former Heuplatz and the area used by Köpenick farmers for their barns. Here also stands the memorial designed by Walter Sutkowski in 1966 70 for the victims of Köpenick's week of blood in June 1933. A Protestant parish house was built opposite in Generalshof in 1927-8, in the the style of Neue Sachlichkeit. The exciting alternation of light rendering and dark brick, smooth walls and three-dimensional moulding, piers or window framing, the vigorous juxtaposition of austerely cubic sections, all this produces an image typical of the Bauhaus, but unmistakable.

in der Nähe/nearby:
Umformerstation; Bahnhofstraße, Lindenstraße
1904 • Hugo Kinzer
Gericht; Mandrellaplatz 5-6, Puchanstraße
1899-1901 • Paul Thoemer
Wohnbebauung; Seelenbinderstraße 61/69
1926-30 • Willy Wagenknecht, Heinrich Peter Kaiser
Polizeidienstgebäude; Seelenbinderstraße 83
1930-31 • Conrad Beckmann

N 5 Siedlung Elsengrund
Berlin-Köpenick; Stellingdamm, Heidekrugstraße
1919-28 • Otto Rudolf Salvisberg

Nördlich der S-Bahnlinie nach Erkner zwischen dem Waldgelände Mittelheide und dem Flüßchen Wuhle entstanden beiderseits der Mahlsdorfer Straße nach 1910 auf bewaldetem Gebiet die Vorstadtsiedlungen Elsengrund, Wolfsgarten, Uhlenhorst und Dammfeld. Salvisberg erbaute 1919-20 die Doppel- und Reihenhaussiedlung Elsengrund zwischen Wolfsgartenstraße und Essenplatz, im zweiten Bauabschnitt zwischen 1921 und 1928 kamen um die Heidekrugstraße auch Miethäuser hinzu, ebenfalls für die Gemeinnützige Baugesellschaft Berlin-Ost. 400 Wohnungen sind in drei verschiedenen Einfamilienhaustypen sowie in Mehrfamilienhäusern errichtet worden. Im Zentrum der Anlage liegt der Lindenhof mit Grünanlagen unter Beibehaltung des alten Kiefernbestandes und wie bei allen anderen Wohnungen auch mit Hausgärten. Am Essenplatz steht der Gedenkstein für die 91 Opfer der Köpenicker Blutwoche, sozialdemokratische und kommunistische Bewohner dieser Vorstadtsiedlungen, die von den Nationalsozialisten nach deren Machtübernahme im Juni 1933 ermordet wurden.

The suburban estates in Elsengrund, Wolfsgarten, Uhlenhorst and Dammfeld were built after 1910 on both sides of Mahlsdorfer Strasse in a wooded area north of the S-Bahn line to Erkner, between the woods of Mittelheide and the little river Wuhle. Salvisberg built the Elsengrund estate of semi-detached and terraced houses in 1919-20, between Wolfsgartenstrasse and Essenplatz, and rented accommodation around Heidekrugstrasse was added in the second building phase between 1921 and 1928, also for the Gemeinnützige Baugesellschaft Berlin-Ost. 400 residential units were built, three different types of house for single families, and some buildings to accommodate a number of families. At the centre of the complex is the Lindenhof with green spaces retaining the old pines, and gardens for each house, as with all the other residential units. The memorial for the 91 victims of the Köpenick week of blood is in Essenplatz. These were social-democrat and communist citizens of Köpenick murdered by the Nazis after their seizure of power in June 1933.

in der Nähe/nearby:
Landhauskolonie Uhlenhorst; Pflanzengartenplatz 1-6
1910-18 • Wilhelm Liefert, Erich Peters
Stadtrandsiedlung Mittelheide; Mittelheide 5-108 a
1928-29 • Otto Rudolf Salvisberg
Wohnbebauung; Mahlsdorfer Straße 16-25, Hirtestraße
1926-27 • Ernst Engelmann, Emil Fangmeyer
Wohnbebauung; Mahlsdorfer Straße 54-61
1928 • Hans Kraffert

N 6 Christopheruskirche
Berlin-Friedrichshagen; Bölschestraße
1901-03 • Jürgen Kröger

Friedrichshagen wurde 1753 als friderizianische Kolonie für hundert böhmische und sächsische Baumwoll- und Seidenspinner gegründet und entstand zunächst als Einstraßenanlage im Verlauf der heutigen Bölschestraße mit dem Lehnschulzengut am südlichen Ende, dort, wo heute die Gaststätte »Bräustübl« liegt. Die parallele Scharnweberstraße und vier verbindende Querstraßen bildeten seit dem frühen 19. Jahrhundert mit der Hauptstraße ein leiterartiges Straßensystem. In dessen Mitte liegt an einer platzartigen Erweiterung die Christopheruskirche an der Stelle eines Vorgängerbaus. Der Neubau ist kompakt gestaltet, aber lebhaft gruppiert. Der hohe quadratische Turm hatte ursprünglich noch einen schlanken Spitzhelm; er wurde nach Sturmschäden 1972 vereinfacht wiederhergestellt. Das Ganze ist in Stilformen der märkischen Backsteingotik eindrucksvoll gestaltet.

Friedrichshagen was founded in 1753 under Frederick the Great as a colony for a hundred Bohemian and Saxon cotton and silk spinners. It started as a single street on the present Bölschestrasse with the feudal estate at the southern end, where the «Bräustübl» restaurant is today. Scharnweberstrasse, which is parallel, and the four connecting side roads have formed a ladder-like system of streets with the main road since the early nineteenth century. The Christopheruskirche is in the middle of this on the site of a predecessor, at a point at which the streets broaden almost into a square. The new building is compact in design, but composed in a lively fashion. The tall square tower originally had a slender spire; it was rebuilt in simplified form after storm damage in 1972. The whole building is an impressive example of the brick Gothic style of the Mark.

in der Nähe/nearby:
Wohn- und Geschäftshaus; Bölschestraße 74
1875
Rathaus; Bölschestraße 87
1897-99 • Peter Groth
Gemeindehaus; Peter-Hille-Straße 47
1928-29 • Friedrich Brinkmann

N 7 Wasserwerk Friedrichshagen
Berlin-Friedrichshagen; Müggelseedamm 301
1889-93 • Henry Gill

Dieses Wasserwerk am Müggelsee konnte zusammen mit dem bereits 1877 eröffneten Werk Tegel und seinem Zwischenpumpwerk Charlottenburg die Wasserversorgung Berlins nach damaligen Erfordernissen hinreichend sicherstellen. Gleichzeitig wurde daher das 1853 auch schon von Gill erbaute Wasserwerk vor dem Stralauer Tor stillgelegt und planmäßig das Zwischenpumpwerk Lichtenberg in Betrieb genommen. Das Friedrichshagener Werk hat auf einer Fläche von 35 Hektar eine klare technologische Gliederung: Die Schöpfmaschinenhäuser sowie ein Sammelbrunnen, dem das Grundwasser aus rings um den Müggelsee verteilten Tiefbrunnen zugeführt wird, liegen unmittelbar am Ufer. Es folgen langgestreckte Rieselhäuser, in denen durch Oxidation mit Luftsauerstoff die im Berliner Grundwasser reichlich gelösten Eisensalze gefällt werden, und mit Erde abgedeckte Langsamfilter. Dazwischen sind Maschinenhäuser angeordnet, die das Reinwasser zum Zwischenpumpwerk Lichtenberg befördern. Von dort wird es unter Druckerhöhung in das Trinkwasserrohrnetz der nördlichen Berliner Hochstadt und der Berliner Tiefstadt geleitet. 1977-82 erfolgte die Erweiterung des Wasserwerkes nach Entwurf von Wolf-Rüdiger Eisentraut.

This water works on the Müggelsee, the works that opened in Tegel in 1877 and the intermediary pumping station in Charlottenburg, covered all Berlin's water requirements at that time. For this reason the water works by the Stralauer Tor, also built by Gill as early as 1853, was closed down, and the Lichtenberg intermediary pumping station became operative as planned. The Friedrichshagen works occupies an area of 35 hectares, and is clearly laid out in terms of industrial design: the pumping houses and a small reservoir to receive ground water from the deep wells around the Müggelsee, are directly by the bank. These are followed by long treatment plants, in which the iron salts, present in solution in large quantities in Berlin's ground water, are removed by oxidation with atmospheric oxygen and by slow filters covered with earth. Between these are the machine houses which convey the purified water to the Lichtenberg pumping station. From there it is pumped, with raised pressure, into the drinking water pipes of the high areas of Berlin in the north, and to low-lying areas of Berlin. The waterworks were extended to a design by Wolf-Rüdiger Eisentraut in 1977-82.

in der Nähe/nearby:
Villa; Müggelseedamm 10
1874 • vermutlich Eduard Titz
Strandbad Müggelsee; Fürstenwalder Damm 838/844
1929-30 • Martin Wagner, Richard Ermisch, Hennings
Dorfkirche Rahnsdorf; Dorfstraße
1887 • Kappen, Friedrich Adler

N 8 Müggelturm
Berlin-Müggelheim; Müggelberge
1960-61• Jörg Streitparth, Siegfried Wagner, Klaus Weißhaupt

Der weithin sichtbare Berliner Müggelturm liegt im Landschaftsschutzgebiet »Berliner Stadtwald« in der Bürgerheide neben den Müggelbergen zwischen Teufelssee und dem Aussichtspunkt an der Müggelbaude, die zusammen durch einen Naturlehrpfad verbunden sind. Der Vorgängerbau, ein Ende des 19. Jahrhunderts errichteter Aussichtsturm in Holzkonstruktion, war schon immer ein Festpunkt im belebten wald- und wasserreichen Ausflugsgebiet zwischen dem Großen Müggelsee und den Gewässern um Grünau; er wurde 1958 durch Brand zerstört. Nach dem Wettbewerbsentwurf einer Studentengruppe entstand der neue Aussichtsturm mit vier großen Restaurants. In drei Ebenen finden 240 Personen Platz und 500 auf den Terrassen. Der Turm wurde als Stahlbetonkonstruktion mit verglasten Treppenpodesten sowie überdachter Aussichtsplattform erbaut.

The Berlin Müggelturm, visible over great distances, is in the «Berliner Stadtwald» nature reserve, in the Bürgerheide near the Müggelberge between Teufelssee and the viewpoint on the Müggelbaude, which are connected by an educational nature trail. The earlier building, a wooden lookout tower built in the late nineteenth century, was always an attraction in this lively excursion area with woods and lakes between the Grosser Müggelsee and the stretches of water around Grünau; the tower was destroyed by fire in 1958. The new lookout tower with four large restaurants was built to a competition design by a group of students. There is seating for 240 people on three levels and for 500 on the terraces. The tower is built in reinforced concrete with glazed stair-heads and roofed viewing platform.

in der Nähe/nearby:
Gaststätte Müggelseeperle; Müggelheimer Damm
1980-81 • Achim Wolff
Dorfkirche Müggelheim; Alt-Müggelheim
1803-04 • Berger
Denkmal für Johann Jacob Baeyer; Alt-Müggelheim
1962 • Hans Füssel

N 9 Gartenvorstadt Falkenberg
Berlin-Altglienicke; Akazienhof, Gartenstadtweg
1913-15 • Bruno Taut

In gleicher Weise wie die Großbetriebe aus der dicht bebauten Innenstadt auszogen und sich über den Stadtrand hinaus in die Weichgebiete der großen Berliner Agglomeration verlagerten, wo sie bessere Produktionsbedingungen und preiswertes Bauland vorfanden, siedelten auch gemeinnützige Baugesellschaften in der Nähe von Vorortbahnhöfen auf noch weithin unbebauten Terrains, ganz im Sinne der 1908 gegründeten deutschen Gartenstadtgesellschaft. Der erste Bauabschnitt der Genossenschaftssiedlung am Falkenberg umfaßt zweigeschossige Reihenhäuser am Akazienhof und am Gartenstadtweg nach Bruno Taut und ein Wohnhaus Am Falkenberg 119 von Heinrich Tessenow. Im Gegensatz zu den vorangegangenen Jahren des »Materialstils« und unter dem Einfluß des Expressionismus verselbständigte Taut die Farbe gegenüber dem Baustoff. Konservative Zeitgenossen sprachen abwertend von einer »Tuschkasten-Siedlung«. Doch Taut blieb auch bei späteren Siedlungen dem Prinzip der kräftigen Farbe treu, andere Architekten folgten ihm.

Heavy industry moved out of the heavily built-up inner city and moved beyond the city boundary into Greater Berlin, where they found better production conditions and cheap building land, and in just the same way non-profit-making building associations moved into terrain that was still largely not built up near to suburban stations, precisely in the spirit of the German garden city society, founded in 1908. The first phase of the estate on Falkenberg includes two-storey terraced houses in Akazienhof and in Gartenstadtweg after Bruno Taut, and a house Am Falkenberg 119 by Heinrich Tessenow. In contrast with the preceding years of «material aesthetics» under the influence of the Expressionists, Taut emancipated colour from building materials. Conservative contemporaries decried it as a «paint-box estate». But Taut remained faithful to the principle of strong colours in later estates as well, and other architects followed suit.

in der Nähe/nearby:
Wasserturm; B-Altglienicke; Schirnerstraße 17/19
1905-06 • Heinrich Scheven
Kleinhaussiedlung; B-Altglienicke; Preußenstraße 41
1912-14 • Hermann Muthesius
Fischerdorf-Rundling; B-Grünau; Alt-Schmöckwitz
13. Jh. (Anlage); 1866 (Wohnhäuser)

N 10 Dorotheen-Lyzeum (Gymnasium)
Berlin-Köpenick; Oberspreestraße 173/181
1928-29 • Max Taut

Die Köllnische Vorstadt mit dem Friedhof der Laurentiusgemeinde liegt zwischen Spree, Dahme und Köllnischer Heide beiderseits der Oberspreestraße. Ab 1872 entwickelte sich mit der chemischen Reinigung, Wäscherei und Färberei der Fabrikanten Spindler im Anschluß an eine Werksiedlung der Ortsteil Spindlersfeld, der seit 1892 durch eine Eisenbahnlinie mit Niederschöneweide verbunden ist. Das Dorotheen-Lyzeum mit dem an der Flemmingstraße gelegenen Direktorenwohnhaus ist eines der Hauptwerke des Architekten Max Taut. Der winkelförmig angelegte Komplex besteht aus dem fünfgeschossigen Klassentrakt mit der Doppelturnhalle an der Mentzelstraße und dem Gebäudeteil für Aula und Verwaltung an der Oberspreestraße, zwischen die das viertelrunde Haupttreppenhaus eingespannt ist. Das Keramik-Relief »Die Heilige Dorothea verteilt Brot an Flüchtlinge« stammt von Rudolf Belling. Wesentlicher Bestandteil der Gestaltung war die ursprüngliche Verkleidung der Fassaden mit Siegersdorfer Tonplatten, sie wurden inzwischen leider durch Putz ersetzt.

The Köllnische Vorstadt with the Laurentinus cemetery is between Spree, Dahme and Köllnische Heide, on both sides of Oberspreestrasse. The district of Spindlersfeld, which has had a rail connection with Niederschöneweide since 1892, developed from 1872, linked with a factory estate, along with the Spindlers' dry-cleaning, laundry and dyeing business. The Dorotheen-Lyzeum with head teacher's house in Flemmingstrasse, is one of architect Max Taut's major works. The angled complex consists of a five-storey classroom section with double gymnasium in Mentzelstrasse and a section for hall and adminstration in Oberspreestrasse; the quarter circle of the main stairwell is between them. The ceramic relief «St. Dorothy distributes bread to refugees» is by Rudolf Belling. An essential part of the design was the original cladding with Siegersdorf earthenware slabs, unfortunately since replaced with plaster.

in der Nähe/nearby:
Werksiedlung; Mentzelstraße 12-24
1873
Wohnhaus; Färberstraße 17-19
1887
Friedhof; Rudower Straße 23-35 und 39-49
1831/1891

N 11 NAG-Fabrikgebäude
Berlin-Oberschöneweide; Ostendstraße 1-5
1914-17 • Peter Behrens

Oberschöneweide und Niederschöneweide am nördlichen und südlichen Ufer der Spree haben »auf der schönen Weide« die gleiche Wurzel, werden amtlich seit 1871 unterschieden und gehören seit 1939 getrennt zu den Stadtbezirken Köpenick und Treptow. Mit der Ende des 19. Jahrhunderts einsetzenden Industrialisierung etablierten sich am Nordufer der Spree von Rummelsburg bis Schöneweide bedeutende Großbetriebe, so die Allgemeine Elektrizitätsgesellschaft AEG. Das Fabrikgebäude an der Wilhelminenhofstraße, das während des Ersten Weltkrieges für die Nationale Automobilgesellschaft errichtet wurde, war ein wichtiges Beispiel moderner Industriearchitektur. Wie bei der Turbinenhalle in Moabit und anderen Fabrikbauten benutzt Behrens auch hier weitgehend das Fassadensystem aus Pfeilern und Fensterachsen, wie es sich aus der Synthese von Konstruktion und Funktion ergab. Nur der Verwaltungstrakt erhält mit Giebel und Turm eine Betonung im Sinne der nach 1910 durchaus erwünschten belebten Baugruppe. Beeindruckend ist auch die viergeschossige Treppen- und Eingangshalle mit umlaufenden Galerien und Oberlicht.

Oberschöneweide and Niederschöneweide on the north and south banks of the Spree both have their roots «auf der schönen Weide», but have been officially distinct since 1871 and have belonged separately to the urban districts of Köpenick and Treptow since 1939. With the onset of industrialization in the late nineteenth century, important industries established themselves on the north bank of the Spree from Rummelsburg to Schöneweide, including AEG (Allgemeine Elektrizitätsgesellschaft). The factory building in Wilhelminenhofstrasse, built during the First World War for the Nationale Automobilgesellschaft, was an important piece of modern industrial architecture. As in the turbine hall in Moabit and other factory buildings, here again Behrens used a façade system of piers and window axes arising from the synthesis of construction and function. Only the office section was accentuated with gable and tower in the spirit of the enlivened building group, so much in demand after 1910. The four-storey staircase and entrance hall with surrounding galleries and skylight is also impressive.

in der Nähe/nearby:
Bootshaus Elektra; An der Wuhlheide 192-194
1910 • Peter Behrens
Kraftwerk Oberspree; Wilhelminenhofstraße 77-78
1895-97; um 1927

N 12 Spreesiedlung
Berlin-Niederschöneweide; Hainstraße 1/55 u. 6/56
1930-32 • Paul Mebes, Paul Emmerich

Am Abzweig der mittelalterlichen Köpenicker Landstraße vom barocken Adlergestell entstand 1763 etwa am heutigen S-Bahnhof Oberspree in der Nähe eines 1697 genannten Teerofens die Siedlung »auf der schönen Weide«. 1858 lebten hier nur 20 Menschen; die industrielle Entwicklung seit Ende des 19. Jahrhunderts führte jedoch zu einem intensiven Miethausbau. Die Wohnanlage in der Hainstraße ist für den sozialen Wohnungsbau der späten zwanziger Jahre ein hervorragendes Zeugnis geschickter straßenräumlicher Anpassung und bleibt beispielhaft über seine örtliche Bedeutung hinaus. Die in Kammstellung angelegte Zeilenbauweise ist durch die angerartige Bebauung und die Orientierung der Wohnhöfe zur Spree und auf das zum Park gestaltete Ufergelände zu einer abwechslungsreichen räumlichen Komposition entwickelt worden.

In 1763, at the point where the medieval Köpenicker Landstrasse branches off from the baroque Adlergestell, an estate called «auf der schönen Weide» (on the beautiful pasture) was built at the present Oberspree S-Bahn station near a tar boiler mentioned in 1697. In 1858 only 20 people lived here, but industrial development from the late nineteenth century led to intensive building of rented accommodation. The residential complex in Hainstrasse is, as publicly funded residential building dating from the late twenties, an outstanding example of skilful adaptation of street space, and remains exemplary beyond its significance for the immediate area. The houses are built in rows arranged like a comb, and a village green style of development and orientation of residential courtyards to the Spree and the area on the banks laid out as a park made it a varied spatial composition.

in der Nähe/nearby:
Versicherungsgebäude; Fennstraße 5-6
1929-30 • Kurt Vogeler
Postamt; Fennstraße 9-11
1925-26 • Willy Hoffmann
Feuerwache; Grünauer Straße 8
1908 • K. A. Herrmann
Friedenskirche; Britzer Straße 1
1928-30 • Fritz Schupp, Martin Kremmer

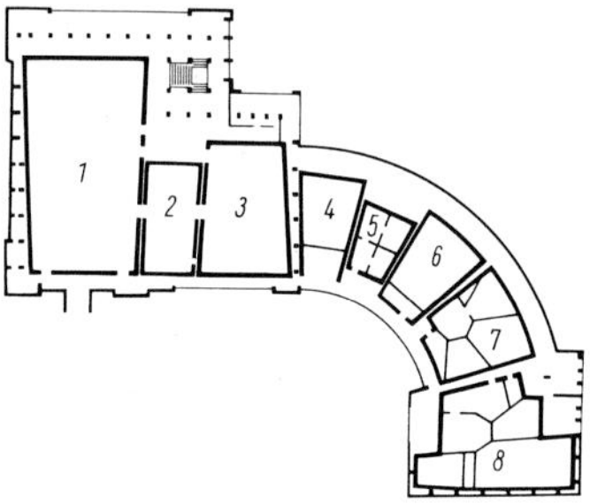

N 13 Rundfunkgebäude
Berlin-Oberschöneweide; Nalepastraße 18-50
1951-56 • Franz Ehrlich

Rummelsburg verdankt seinen Namen einer Ratsziegelei und Meierei von 1699, die später dem Weinschenken Rummel gehörte. Von Rummelsburg bis Schöneweide sind die Spreeufer meist mit Industriebetrieben besetzt. Eine im Krieg teilzerstörte Furnierfabrik in Nobelshof an der Spree mußte 1951 eilig zu einem Rundfunkgebäude umgebaut werden, da Radio DDR mit der baldigen Verwehrung des Zuganges zum Berliner Sendegebäude in Westend rechnete. Daneben entstanden 1952-56 das Aufnahme- und Studiogebäude. Zur unerläßlichen Schallisolation während der Aufnahmen baute man die Studios als Haus im Haus, eine für Rundfunkgebäude übliche Konstruktionsweise. Zwischen den Außenwänden und den acht trapezförmigen Räumen verlaufen beiderseits Gänge. Nicht nur die Fassade in Klinkern und Werkstein, auch die formale Ausbildung verweist noch deutlich auf die Architektursprache der frühen dreißiger Jahre.

Rummelsburg gets its name from a municipal brickworks and dairy dating from 1699, which later belonged to a wine merchant called Rummel. The banks of the Spree are largely industrialized from Rummelsburg to Schöneweide. A veneer factory that had been partially destroyed in the war in Nobelshof on the Spree had to be hastily converted into a radio station in 1951, as Radio DDR anticipated that it would soon be refused access to the Berlin transmitter in Westend. The recording and studio buildings were erected next to it in 1952-6. The studios are a building within a building to provide the essential soundproofing, a customary construction method for broadcasting purposes. There are corridors on both sides between the outer walls and the eight trapezoid rooms. Both the clinker and ashlar façade and the general design are clearly part of the architectural language of the thirties.

in der Nähe/nearby:
Wohnhaus mit Atelier; Helmholtzstraße 5
1903 • Max Sutterheim
AEG-Siedlung; Zeppelinstraße 11/71
1919-21 • Peter Behrens

N 14 Rathaus Treptow
Berlin-Treptow; Neue Krugallee 2-6
1909-10 • Reinhardt & Süßenguth

Seit 1707 gab es in Treptow, der einst letzten Station für Postkutsche und reitende Boten auf der Köpenicker Landstraße in Richtung Berlin, ein Gasthaus und später auch verschiedene Gartenlokale. Östlich gelangte man zum Neuen Krug, der vor Schöneweide in der Nähe der heutigen Stubenrauchbrücke lag. Auch wenn die Köllnische Heide ein beliebtes Ausflugsziel der Berliner war, so zählte Treptow zu Beginn des 19. Jahrhunderts nur 60 Einwohner. Erst zum Ende des Jahrhunderts entstanden auch hier große Industriebetriebe und in deren Folge zwischen Ringbahn und Landwehrkanal die üblichen Mietkasernen. Um 1910 setzte dann entlang dem Treptower Park eine ganz andere Bautätigkeit ein: Vornehme Miethäuser mit prunkenden Fassaden und großen Wohnungen sollten wohlhabendes Bürgertum herbeiziehen. Dem hatte auch das neue Rathaus zu entsprechen. Es ist auf winkelförmigem Grundriß als asymmetrische Anlage mit bewegter Baukörpergruppierung errichtet worden. Stilistisch folgt es somit ganz der malerischen Vielfalt, wie sie der Landhausstil aufbrachte, in Einzelheiten wie der Pilastergliederung klingen aber auch Reminiszenzen an den Klassizismus an.

Treptow, once the last staging post for post coaches and mounted messengers on the Köpenick Road before Berlin, had a guest house and later various garden cafés from 1707. Further east came the Neuer Krug, before Schöneweide and near the present Stubenrauchbrücke. Even though Köllnische Heide was a popular excursion destination for Berliners, Treptow had only 60 inhabitants at the beginning of the nineteenth century. It was not until the end of the century that large industrial areas grew up here as well, accompanied by the usual tenement housing between the ring railway and the Landwehr canal. Then in about 1920 a quite different kind of building started along Treptower Park: high-class residential accommodation with magnificent façades and spacious accommodation, intended to attract the wealthy middle classes. And the new town hall had to reflect this. It is built asymmetrically on an angled ground plan, with a lively composition of individual elements. Stylistically it is completely at one with the picturesque variety thrown up by the country-house style, but details like the articulation of the pilasters are reminiscent of classicism.

in der Nähe/nearby:
Fischerbrunnen; Bulgarische Straße
1916; 1925 • Reinhold Felderhoff
Wohnbebauung; Neue Krugallee 32/52
1928 • Paul Krebs
Gaststätte Eierhäuschen; Kiehnwerderallee
1890

N 15 Treptower Park
Berlin-Treptow; Puschkin-Allee
1876-88 • Gustav Meyer, Hermann Mächtig

Die Cöllnische Heide, seit 1261 im Besitz der Stadt, um 1780 durch Quer- und Längsgestelle unterteilt – daher der Straßenname Adlergestell –, war seit 1840 zum Leidwesen der Berliner bis auf den Schlesischen Busch und den Alten Treptower Park abgeholzt. Der neue Park wurde neben dem Humboldt- und Friedrichshain zum dritten von Meyer und Mächtig angelegten Volkspark. Von 1894 bis 1896 mußte er die Gewerbeausstellung aufnehmen, war dann aber auch eine wichtige Versammlungsstätte der Berliner Sozialdemokraten; 1911 sprachen hier gleichzeitig zehn Redner, darunter August Bebel und Karl Liebknecht, gegen die drohende Kriegsgefahr. Die spätere Erweiterung zu einem großen Erholungspark von der Ringbahn bis zum Plänterwald auf einer Fläche von 230 Hektar erfolgte in mehreren Abschnitten mit Dampferanlegestation und Rosengarten. Eine 1916 errichtete Stahlbetonbrücke führt zur Gaststätte auf der Insel der Jugend. Ein Ehrenmal wurde 1946-49 nach Entwürfen von J. B. Belopolski für 5000 im Kampf um Berlin gefallene sowjetische Soldaten angelegt. Ein »Kulturpark« entstand seit 1969 nach Entwurf von Walter Hinkefuß.

To the distress of Berliners, Cöllnische Heide, owned by the city from 1261, divided by longitudinal and transverse streets called «Gestelle» from c. 1780 – hence the street name Adlergestell – had been deforested from 1840, with the exception of Schlesischer Busch and Alter Treptower Park. The new park, along with Humboldthain and Friedrichshain, was the third people's park laid out by Meyer and Mächtig. From 1894 to 1896 it had to play host to the industrial exhibition, and was then also an important assembly point for Berlin's social democrats; in 1911 ten speakers, including August Bebel and Karl Liebknecht, spoke here at the same rally against the rising danger of war. Subsequent development into a large recreational park extending from the ring railway to the Plänterwald, covering an area of 230 hectares, happened in several phases, with steamer berth and rose garden. A reinforced concrete bridge built in 1916 leads to the restaurant on the Insel der Jugend. A memorial to the 5,000 Soviet soldiers who fell in the battle for Berlin was built in 1946-9 to designs by J. B. Belopolski. A «culture park» was laid out from 1969 to a design by Walter Hinkefuss.

in der Nahe/nearby:
Archenhold-Sternwarte; Alt-Treptow 1
1896; 1908-09 • Reimer & Körte
Bus-Betriebshof Treptow; Eichenstraße 4
1925-28 • Franz Ahrens, Alfred Warthmüller
Bekenntniskirche; Plesser Straße 3-4
1930-31 • Curt Steinberg

N 16 Rathaus Neukölln
Berlin-Neukölln; Karl-Marx-Straße 83-85
1905-09 • Reinhold Kiehl

Eine der nach der Jahrhundertwende am schnellsten expandierenden Städte Deutschlands war Rixdorf – so hieß Neukölln bis 1912. Dem »Dorf« längst entwachsen, betrug 1909 die Einwohnerzahl schon weit über 200 000, gegenüber 90 000 im Jahre 1900. Der Bau eines neuen großen Rathauses war unabdingbar, als Reinhold Kiehl die Leitung des städtischen Hochbauamtes übernahm. Die Schwierigkeit des Bauplatzes, eingezwängt zwischen bestehenden Bauten am Knick einer engen Straße, ließ kaum eine beherrschende repräsentative Front zu. Kiehl, der mit viel Fleiß und Können Neukölln um so manchen öffentlichen Bau bereichert hat, verstand sein Handwerk zu gut, um nicht eine geschickte Lösung zu finden. Seine Idee, Repräsentationsräume und Verwaltungsräume baukörperlich zu trennen, kann als schöpferisch gelten. So vermochte er einen Kopfbau von stattlicher Höhe mit mächtigem Turm zu entwickeln, der auch auf kleinstem Raum wirkte. Bildhauer für den Bauschmuck war Josef Rauch. Erweiterungen folgten von Kiehl 1910-11 und 1913-14 sowie 1950-56 von Hans Eicheler und Hans Freese.

One of Germany's most rapidly expanding towns after the turn of the century was Rixdorf – Neukölln's name until 1912. It had long since ceased to be a «Dorf», or village: it had 200,000 inhabitants in 1909, as opposed to 90,000 in 1900. There was no avoiding building a new town hall when Reinhold Kiehl took over the municipal structural engineering department. The difficult nature of the site, cramped between existing buildings on a kink in a narrow street, hardly permitted a dominant and imposing façade. Kiehl enriched Neukölln with many public buildings, executed with much hard work and great ability, and was far too good at his job not to be able to find a skilful solution. His idea of separating administrative areas and rooms for public functions into separate parts of the building can be considered inspired. He was thus able to create a header building with a massive tower, to make an impact in a restricted space. Joseph Rauch was the sculptor responsible for the decoration of the building. Extensions were added in 1910-1 and 1913-4 by Kiehl, and 1950-6 by Hans Eicheler and Hans Freese.

N 17 Körnerpark
Berlin-Neukölln; Selkestraße
1912-16 • Hans Richard Küllenberg, Gutzeit

Aus Körners aufgelassener Kiesgrube entstand diese Anlage. Im Zusammenhang mit einem größeren Geländeverkauf an die Stadt Rixdorf/Neukölln stiftete er dieses Areal für eine öffentliche gärtnerische Anlage, die seinen Namen tragen sollte. Die fünf bis sieben Meter Höhendifferenz zu den umgebenden Straßen waren wohl der Grund, mit Terrassen und Treppen einen Architekturpark zu gestalten. Die Begrenztheit des Raumes und die Regelmäßigkeit des Straßengevierts wiesen den Weg zum Barockgarten, der allerdings zeitgemäße Abwandlungen erfuhr. Die axiale Abfolge von Kaskadenfall, Springbrunnen, Rasenparterre, mittlerer Terrasse, in die Böschung eingebauter Orangerie und oberer Terrasse entsprechen dem Parkprogramm des 17. und 18. Jahrhunderts. Größere Bäume blieben aber erhalten und stören allenfalls nach den strengen Regeln des Barock die Symmetrie der geometrischen Anlage. Auch mit dem Beschnitt der Bäume nimmt man es im 20. Jahrhundert nicht mehr so genau. In Gestaltung und Charakter ist der Körnerpark für Berlin ein Einzelfall.

This little park was laid out on the site of Körner's abandoned gravel pit. He had occasion to sell a great deal of land to the town of Rixdorf/Neukölln, and at that time endowed this area as a public garden, to be named after him. There is a difference of five to seven metres in height from the surrounding streets, and this was probably the reason for the creation of an architectural park with terraces and steps. The limited nature of the space and the regularity of the square of streets suggested a baroque garden, but certain modifications in keeping with the times were made. The axial sequence of cascade, fountain, lawns, central terrace, orangery built into the bank and upper terrace are totally appropriate to seventeenth and eighteenth century park design. However, larger trees were retained, and they disturb the symmetry of the geometrical layout, at any rate as far as the strict rules of baroque are concerned. The trees and shrubs are also not trimmed quite as precisely in the twentieth century. The Körnerpark is unique in Berlin in design and character.

in der Nähe/nearby:
S-Bahnhof Neukölln; Karl-Marx-Straße 229
1929-30
Böhmische Bethlehems-Kirche; Richardplatz 22
1639
Elektrizitätsstützpunkt; Richardstraße 20-21
1928-29 • Hans Müller
Stadtbad; Ganghoferstraße 3-5, Donaustraße 48
1913-14 • Heinrich Best
Postamt 44; Karl-Marx-Straße 97/99
1905-07 • Stuve
1979-82 • Christina Brommer

N 18 Einfamilien-Reihenhäuser
Berlin-Baumschulenweg; Radenzer Straße
1960-61 • Martin Wimmer, Wolfgang Kretschel

Wegen des hohen Grundwasserstandes waren die Areale beiderseits der Landstraße nach Köpenick sehr fruchtbar; trotzdem blieb die Cöllnische Heide jahrhundertelang unbewohnt. Erst Friedrich II. siedelte in Johannisthal, Adlershof und Schöneweide mehrere Meiereien und einige Kolonisten an, die wie in Neuglienicke Kristallisationspunkte neuer Ortsteile wurden. Mit dem Bau des Teltowkanals, besonders aber des Britzer Zweigkanals wurden die ehemaligen Rudower Wiesen in Baumschulenweg derart entwässert, daß etwa die Gartenbaufirma Späth Teile ihrer Kulturen aufgeben mußte. Trotzdem blieben die Areale um die Königsheide wenig begehrtes Bauland und dünn besiedelte Wohngebiete. Auch der »komplexe Wohnungsbau« der Nachkriegszeit nahm von den Freiflächen bisher nicht Besitz. Dagegen finden sich auf einem Restgrundstück am Britzer Zweigkanal fünf zweigeschossige Einfamilien-Reihenhäuser – für den Wohnungsbau der DDR eine ausgesprochene Seltenheit. Südseitige Balkone vor den Schlafräumen im Obergeschoß und Terrassen, die sich zum gemeinsamen Wohngarten öffnen, sind das Besondere an dieser Wohngruppe.

Because of high ground water levels, the areas on either side of the road to Köpenick were very fertile; nevertheless no-one lived on the Cöllnische Heide for centuries. Frederick II was the first to settle several dairies and some colonists in Johannisthal, Adlershof and Schöneweide, and as in Neuglienicke these then became crystallization points for new districts. When the Teltow canal, but more particularly the Britz branch canal were built, the former Rudow meadows in Baumschulenweg were drained to the extent that the Späth nursery business for example had to stop its operation there. Despite this the areas around Königsheide remained little in demand as building land, and thinly populated. Post-war «complex building of residential accommodation» has not yet impinged upon these open spaces. But there are five two-storey single-family terraced houses – a great rarity in the residential building of the GDR – on a remaining plot by the Britz branch canal. Special features of the group are balconies for the bedrooms in the upper storey and terraces opening on to the communal garden.

in der Nähe/nearby:
Wohnbebauung; Baumschulenstraße 39-55
1927-32 • Walter Kaas
Wohnbebauung; Baumschulenstraße 2-4
1929-30 • Paul Rudolf Henning
Wohnhaus; Ernststraße 5
1894-95 • Bruno Möhring
Wohnhäuser; Marienthaler Straße 3/23
1894 • Gabriel Wohlgemuth
Krematorium Baumschulenweg; Kiefholzstraße 211
1911 • Erich Bientz, Mathias Bardenheuer

N 19 Wohnhaus der Familie Späth
Berlin-Baumschulenweg; Späthstraße 80-81
1874

Den entscheidenden Anstoß zur Entwicklung des Ortsteiles Baumschulenweg gab der Gärtnereibetrieb Späth. Am Johannestisch vor dem Halleschen Tor 1720 gegründet, zog der Betrieb 1760 zur Köpenicker Straße an die Spree; er lag dem heutigen Hauptbahnhof gegenüber. Die Entwicklung zum Großunternehmen begann im Jahre 1864 auf den ehemaligen Kämmereiwiesen zwischen Alt-Treptow und Johannisthal. Es folgte dorthin die Gärtnerei-Firma Mosich; sie errichtete 1869 das erste Haus in der Baumschulenstraße 34. Nach 1870 kamen weitere Gärtnereien und ein Böttcher, der die chemischen Fabriken in Niederschöneweide mit Fässern versorgte. 1891 wurden mit der Eisenbahnhaltestelle an der Görlitzer Strecke und 1896 mit einem Anschlußgleis nach Neukölln zur Ringbahn weitere Entwicklungsmöglichkeiten eröffnet. Die 1908-10 gepflasterte Baumschulenstraße ist bis 1914 beidseitig bebaut worden. Das Wohnhaus der Familie Späth, zunächst nur mit sechs Achsen und einem Mittelrisalit errichtet, wurde 1891 auf zehn Achsen erweitert. Mehrere Nebengebäude von 1888 ergänzen die Anlage. Sehenswert ist das anschließende Arboretum, ein seit den siebziger Jahren des 19. Jahrhunderts landschaftlich angelegter Park.

The Späth nursery business gave a decisive boost to the development of the Baumschulenweg district. It was founded in 1720 on the Johannestisch outside Hallesches Tor, and moved to Köpenicker Strasse and the Spree in 1760; it used to be opposite the present main station. It started to develop into a large-scale business in 1864 on the former combing works meadows between Alt-Treptow and Johannisthal. It followed the Mosich garden business to the site; they built the first house in Baumschulenstrasse, no. 34, in 1869. After 1870 more garden businesses and a cooper came along; he supplied barrels to the chemical factories in Niederschöneweide. The railway halt on the Görlitz line in 1891 and the link to the ring line in Neukölln in 1896 opened up further development possibilities. Baumschulenstrasse was paved in 1908-10, and buildings were erected on both sides until 1914. The Späth family residence, built at first with only six axes and a central protruding section, was extended to ten axes in 1891. There are also various outbuildings dating from 1888. The adjacent arboretum is worth seeing, a landscaped park dating from the 1870s.

in der Nähe/nearby:
Bank- und Wohnhaus; Baumschulenstraße 92
1927-28 • Friedrich Brinkmann
Gemeindezentrum; Baumschulenstraße 79-83
1910-11 • Reinhardt & Süßenguth
Cohn-Zoellner-Werke; B-Neukölln; Neuköllnische Allee 60-74
1923-24 • Otto Rudolf Salvisberg

N 20 Hufeisensiedlung
Berlin-Britz; Fritz-Reuter-Allee 2/72, Lowise-Reuter-Ring 1/47 usw.
1925-27 • Bruno Taut, Martin Wagner

Die Wohnungsnot im Berlin der Jahre nach dem Ersten Weltkrieg und der Beginn des politisch und gewerkschaftlich unterstützten Wohnungsbaues ließen schon bald nach der Inflation große Wohnsiedlungen entstehen. Zusammenhängende Bauflächen zu vertretbaren Preisen fanden sich fast nur noch außerhalb des Ringbahngürtels wie hier in Britz. Die Siedlungs- und Wohnungskonzeption jener Jahre suchte den Kompromiß zwischen einer möglichst großen Zahl neuer Wohnungen, preiswertem Wohnraum und sozial sowie hygienisch angemessenem Wohnen. In der Sachlichkeit des Bauens der zwanziger Jahre muß insofern auch die Wechselwirkung zwischen wirtschaftlicher Einsicht und gestalterischem Wollen gesehen werden. Die Hufeisensiedlung mit ihren über 1000 Wohnungen ist heute ein Musterbeispiel des neuen Siedlungsbaus. Durch maßvolle Höhe, reichlich Gartenfläche, Wechsel in Farben und Formen, Vermeidung städtebaulicher Langeweile durch Kurvung, Knicken oder Staffeln von Baukörpern und Straßen war die Wohnlichkeit sichergestellt. Bruno Tauts Meisterschaft in der Vermittlung zwischen Sachlichkeit und optischer Harmonie zeigt sich in vielen Einzelheiten wie beispielsweise den immer wiederkehrenden Drempelgeschossen, die dem Übergang Fassade–Flachdach die Härte nehmen.

Shortage of accommodation in Berlin in the years after the First World War and the early stages of building residential accommodation with political and trade union support brought large residential estates into being shortly after the great inflation. However, coherent building areas at decent prices could be found almost exclusively outside the ring railway, as here in Britz. The estate building and residential concept of those years sought a compromise between the largest possible number of new homes, cheap living space and living that was socially and hygienically acceptable. To this extent the functionality of twenties building must be seen as an interaction of economic insight and creative will. The Hufeisen (horseshoe) estate with over 1,000 residential units is today a classic example of modern estate building. Comfortable living was assured by moderate height, lavish garden space, changing colours and forms, avoiding urban development boredom by the uses of curves, kinks and staggered buildings and streets. Bruno Taut's mastery in marrying functionalism and visual harmony is shown in numerous details like the recurrent aprons which soften transitions from façade to flat roof.

in der Nähe/nearby:
Siedlung; Fritz-Reuter-Allee 5/73 usw.
1925-27 • Engelmann & Fangmeyer
Miethausgruppe; Parchimer Allee 7/29 u. 10/32
1928-29 • Bruno Taut

N 21 Albert-Einstein-Schule
Berlin-Britz; Parchimer Allee 109-133
1988-90 • Stefan Scholz (in BJSS)

Die »Altbauten« dieser Schule stammen aus den Jahren 1954-57 und wurden in der damals bevorzugten lockeren Anordnung als simple Putzbauten quer zur Straße gestellt. Ob der Fachklassenneubau den Altbestand integrieren oder verstecken sollte oder wollte, mag offen bleiben. In seiner individuellen Dominanz besteht er aber auf unbedingter Beachtung. Als einprägsames Beispiel für eine gewandelte Architekturauffassung setzt sich die Fassade in Szene. Nichts ist mehr übrig von einem übermächtigen Diktat der Funktionalität oder von systemplanerischem Sektierertum – erlebbarer Raum wird geschaffen, der Eindruck steht im Vordergrund und nicht die Zweckerfüllung. So enden die umgebördelten Enden der Fassade im Nichts, mag der Betrachter sich auch wundern, das gehört hier mit dazu. Solches »Architekturerlebnis« ist zweifellos auch ein Motto der Bonner Kunsthalle von Axel Schultes, der neben Dietrich Bangert und Bernd Jansen der vierte im Bunde von BJSS ist.

The «old buildings» of this school date from the years 1954-57. In keeping with the loose arrangements preferred then, the simple rendered buildings were placed with their ends facing the street. It remains an open question whether the new classroom wing was to integrate or hide the existing structures – it certainly asserts its presence with an individual, dominating appearance. The dramatically staged façade stands out as an impressive example of a new understanding of architecture. There is nothing left of the overpowering dictate of functionality or the sectarianism of systems planners. What is created here is space to be experienced, with the emphasis on appearance and not on purpose. Thus the flanged edges of the façade point to nowhere – and if the beholder wonders at this, that is part of the game. To be sure, «experiencing architecture» was the motto for the Kunsthalle in Bonn by Axel Schultes as well – the fourth member of BJSS, along with Dietrich Bangert and Bernd Jansen.

in der Nähe/nearby:
Dorfkirche Britz; Backbergstraße 40
2. H. 13. Jh.
Gutshaus; Alt-Britz 79-81
1860 • Carl Busse
Gropiusstadt; Fritz-Erler-Allee, Lipschitzallee usw.
1962-72 • Wils Ebert, Wolfgang Dommer, Klaus H. Ernst, Rolf Gutbrod, Hans Bandel

N 22 Walter-Gropius-Schule
Berlin-Buckow; Fritz-Erler-Allee 66/96
1965-69 • Walter Gropius

Nachdem Bruno Taut als Architekt und Fritz Karsen als Pädagoge in den zwanziger Jahren vergeblich versucht hatten, in Berlin eine Aufbauschule zu errichten, erfuhr dieser Schultyp über drei Jahrzehnte später – abgewandelt unter dem Namen Gesamtschule – eine Neuauflage. Ziele waren gleiche Bildungschancen durch Transparenz zwischen den Zweigen mit unterschiedlichen Abschlüssen, gezielte Förderung des einzelnen Schülers und ökonomische Verbesserungen etwa durch Ganztagsbetrieb. Gropius' architektonische Lösung zeigte so auch eine gänzliche Abkehr vom herkömmlichen Schulbau. In sternförmigen Pavillons – äußerlich unterschieden nach Grund- und Oberstufe – sind die sechseckigen Stammklassenräume mit Arbeitsnische, Bücherzimmer und Gemeinschaftsraum untergebracht. In einem zentralen Gebäude befinden sich die Fachklassen, in denen der größte Teil des Unterrichts in Kursform stattfindet. Zur Schulanlage gehört auch ein Kindergarten mit einer Vorschulgruppe. Die großzügige Anordnung der Bauteile und die Nüchternheit der Betonarchitektur verweisen einerseits auf Amerika, die neue Heimat des Architekten, andererseits auf das Bauhaus, seine Herkunft.

After architect Bruno Taut and educator Fritz Karsen had tried in vain to establish an intermediate school in Berlin back in the nineteen-twenties, this type of school saw a revival more than three decades later, although under the new heading of a comprehensive school. The objective was to provide equal opportunities for all students by means of a transparent organization of the various study courses and diplomas as well as a direct fostering of individual students and economic improvements, for example through all-day classes. Correspondingly the architectural solution proposed by Gropius also represented a complete rejection of traditional school architecture. Star-shaped pavilions with different outsides for lower and upper levels house the hexagonal classrooms with study niches, library and communal spaces. The central building contains the special rooms in which most classes are taught as study courses. The school also includes a kindergarden with pre-school facilities. The generous layout of the various elements and the sobriety of the concrete architecture reflect the influences of both America, the new homeland of the architect, and the Bauhaus from which he came.

in der Nähe/nearby:
Walt-Disney-Schule; Fritz-Erler-Allee 123/151
1965-68 • Gerd Hänska und Magdalena Hänska
Martin-Luther-King-Kirche; Johannisthaler Chaussee 329
1966-68 • Karl Otto
Dominicuskirche; Lipschitzallee 74-76
1976-77 • Hans Schädel und Hermann Jünemann

N 23 Krankenhaus Neukölln (Neubau)
Berlin-Buckow; Rudower Straße 48
1977-85 • Josef Paul Kleihues, Jürgen König

Neben der älteren Krankenhausanlage von Reinhold Kiehl aus den Jahren 1906-09 sollte ein »moderner, leistungsfähiger und humaner« Neubau entstehen, so sah es die Planung bereits 1973 vor. Mehr als bei anderen Bauaufgaben muß aber beim Krankenhaus die Zweckmäßigkeit im Vordergrund stehen. Das setzt die nicht immer leichte Zusammenarbeit von Arzt und Architekt voraus. Kleihues selbst bedauerte den Verzicht auf das »Schinkelsche Ideal vom konstruktiv und formal ganz vollständig in sich geschlossenen Gebäude«. Eher attributiv fügen sich die Elemente äußerer Gestaltung zu dem 500 Meter langen Komplex. Der bandartige Grundriß mit den gerundeten Enden erinnert an den der wenige Jahre zuvor ebenfalls von Kleihues geschaffenen Hauptwerkstatt der Stadtreinigung, beweist aber auch das Diktat der Zweckmäßigkeit. So ist von dem »langen Haus der kurzen Wege« die Rede. Zusammenhalt schaffen die einheitlichen weißen Fassadenplatten und das schwarze Raster der Abdeckleisten, die nüchterne Farblosigkeit assoziiert klinische Reinheit. Auch die zentrale Halle nimmt diese Aussage auf mit weißem und grauem Marmor, weißem Lack für Brüstungen und Rahmen sowie dem geometrisch gebrochenen Oberlicht.

As early as 1970 planners were talking of a «modern, efficient and humane new building» to operate alongside the old hospital complex built by Reinhold Kiehl in 1906-9. But function had to be more in the foreground for a hospital than for many other buildings. This requires co-operation between architects and doctors, which is not always easy. Kleihues himself regretted having to forego the «Schinkelesque ideal of a building that was complete in itself both constructively and formally». The elements of external design in the complex, which is 500 metres long, are rather more attributive. The band-like ground plan with rounded ends is reminiscent of the main workshops of the city cleansing department, which Kleihues had designed a few years before, but does also confirm the dominance of functionality. Thus the hospital is called the «long building with short routes». Unity is created by uniform white façade sheets and a black grid of capping strips. The austere colourlessness suggests clinical purity. The white and grey marble of the central hall takes this up as well, along with white paint for breastwork and frames and the geometrical breakdown of the skylight.

in der Nähe/nearby:
Krankenhaus Neukölln; Rudower Straße 56
1906-09 • Reinhold Kiehl

N 24 Gemeinschafts-Wohnhäuser
Berlin-Buckow; Ortolanweg
1990 • Axel Liepe, Hartmut Steigelmann

Als »kommunikatives Modell« entstanden am Ortolanweg 120 Wohnungen im Auftrage der »Berliner Bau- und Wohnungsgenossenschaft von 1892 e.G.«. Der Bauherr steht für die Wiederauflage der ursprünglichen sozialreformerischen Idee, die in der nun hundertjährigen Geschichte nach und nach verlorenzugehen drohte. Das Zusammenleben der Generationen, das gemeinsame Wohnen mit Behinderten, therapeutisch betreute Wohngemeinschaften und das Angebot von Gästewohnungen, Werkräumen und Jugendräumen standen auf dem Programm, wenn auch für den heute Wohnungssuchenden das Wohnen schlechthin einziges Ziel sein mag. Selbst wenn so der Gemeinschaft die Voraussetzung der Freiwilligkeit fehlt, ist dieses Experiment im Rahmen des Sozialen Wohnungsbaues gerechtfertigt. Der Mieter findet im Inneren der dreiflügeligen Bauten eine große Glashalle vor, er hat Zugang zu mietfreien Gemeinschaftsräumen und ist damit aufgefordert, dem Begriff Nachbarschaft zu einer neuen Qualität zu verhelfen. Mehr als ein Versuch will das Projekt nicht sein, es lebt aber von der Hoffnung, etwas zu bewegen oder notwendige Veränderungen zu fördern.

The 120 apartments built by the «Berlin Building and Housing Cooperative of 1892» at Ortolanweg were to serve as a «communicative model.» The client stood for a revival of the original concept of social reform which had threatened to become lost in the hundred years since its inception. The idea was to have all generations living together, to include handicapped persons, to create therapist-guided co-ops and to provide guest apartments, workshops and youth facilities, although today most of those looking for housing are only looking for a place to live. Even if the community thus lacks the essential supposition of voluntary membership, this experiment within the framework of public housing is well justified. Inside the three-winged buildings the residents find themselves in a large glazed hall with access to communal facilities provided free of charge, inviting them to help lend a new meaning to the concept of neighbourhood. The project is not meant to be anything more than an experiment, but it lives on the hope of moving things and promoting necessary change.

in der Nähe/nearby:
Behindertenhaus; Parchimer Allee 6
1983-85 • Eckhard Feddersen und Wolfgang v. Herder

O
Der Berliner Südwesten

Zwischen Bäketal und Havel lagen seit dem Mittelalter die Dörfer Steglitz, Lichterfelde, Zehlendorf, Schönow und Stolpe, nach Norden hin grenzten Dahlem und Schmargendorf an. Aus solchen mittelalterlichen Ansiedlungen ist kein Haus überliefert, nur Dorfkirchen oder die Wege und Plätze der alten Dorfanger. Sie bildeten die einzigen Siedlungskerne und bestimmen die städtebaulichen Anlagen des 19. und 20. Jahrhunderts. Diese und die Neugründungen von Villenkolonien prägen heute den Berliner Südwesten, nicht zu vergessen die ausgedehnten Waldgebiete, die Havel und Havelseen begleiten. Erst mit den siebziger Jahren des vorigen Jahrhunderts begannen die Dörfer über ihre Grenzen hinauszuwachsen. Die Richtung gaben die bestehenden Verkehrswege an. Das waren die Straße Berlin–Steglitz–Zehlendorf–Potsdam, die Bahnlinie Berlin–Potsdam – 1838 als erste Berliner Eisenbahn eröffnet – und die 1879 fertiggestellte Wetzlarer Bahn, die von Charlottenburg durch den Grunewald über Wannsee und Potsdam nach Blankenheim und von dort weiter ins Hessische führte. Industriebetriebe zogen die Bahnen nicht an, dafür aber wurden sie zum überzeugenden Argument für die Villenkolonien, die in ihnen die wesentliche verkehrsmäßige Anbindung an Berlin sahen. So entstanden bis zur Jahrhundertwende im Süden die Kolonie Lichterfelde, im Norden Grunewald, im Westen Wannsee. 1901 begann die Aufteilung und Bebauung in Nikolassee, Schlachtensee und Dahlem. Um diese Zeit kam der Entwicklung auch die einsetzende Stadtflucht und die Sehnsucht nach dem »Haus im Grünen« zugute. Der Südwesten wurde zur gehobenen Wohngegend, und das blieb so. Der Bahnverkehr stellte sich darauf ein. 1900 richtete man den elektrischen Versuchsbetrieb auf der Vorortstrecke Berlin–Zehlendorf ein, die Wannseebahn war schon 1889-91 ausgebaut worden, 1913 kam die Wilmersdorf-Dahlemer U-Bahn hinzu. In den zwanziger Jahren setzt schließlich auch der Siedlungsbau ein, in Schmargendorf, im Norden von Lichterfelde, in Zehlendorf, dort beispielgebend in der Waldsiedlung.

The villages of Steglitz, Lichterfelde, Zehlendorf, Schönow and Stolpe, with Dahlem and Schmargendorf adjacent to the north, have existed between the Bäke valley and the Havel since the Middle Ages. No medieval buildings except village churches have survived, along with the paths and squares of the old village greens. These were the sole cores of the settlements, and impose themselves on nineteenth and twentieth century urban structure. These and newly founded villa colonies are characteristic of south-west Berlin, not forgetting the extensive wooded areas accompanying the Havel and its lakes. It was not until the 1870s that the villages started to grow out beyond their boundaries, following the lines of existing transport systems. These were the Berlin-Steglitz-Zehlendorf-Potsdam road, the Berlin-Potsdam railway line – opened in 1838 as the first Berlin railway – and the Wetzlar railway, completed in 1879, which ran from Charlottenburg through the Grunewald via Wannsee and Potsdam to Blankenheim and from there on into Hesse. The railways did not attract industry, but they were the clinching argument for the villa colonies, who saw them as the essential transport link with Berlin. Thus by the turn of the century villa districts had been established in Lichterfelde in the south, Grunewald in the north and Wannsee in the west. In 1901 parcelling out and development began in Nikolassee, Schlachtensee and Dahlem. At this time developments of this kind benefited from the start of flight from the city and longings for a «house in green surroundings». The south-west became a superior area in which to live, and it still is. The railways took this into account. In 1900 an experimental electric service was started on the suburban line from Berlin to Zehlendorf, the Wannsee railway had been extended in 1889-91, and the Wilmersdorf-Dahlem underground was added in 1913. And finally estate building started as well in the twenties, in Schmargendorf, in the north of Lichterfelde, and in Zehlendorf with the exemplary forest estate.

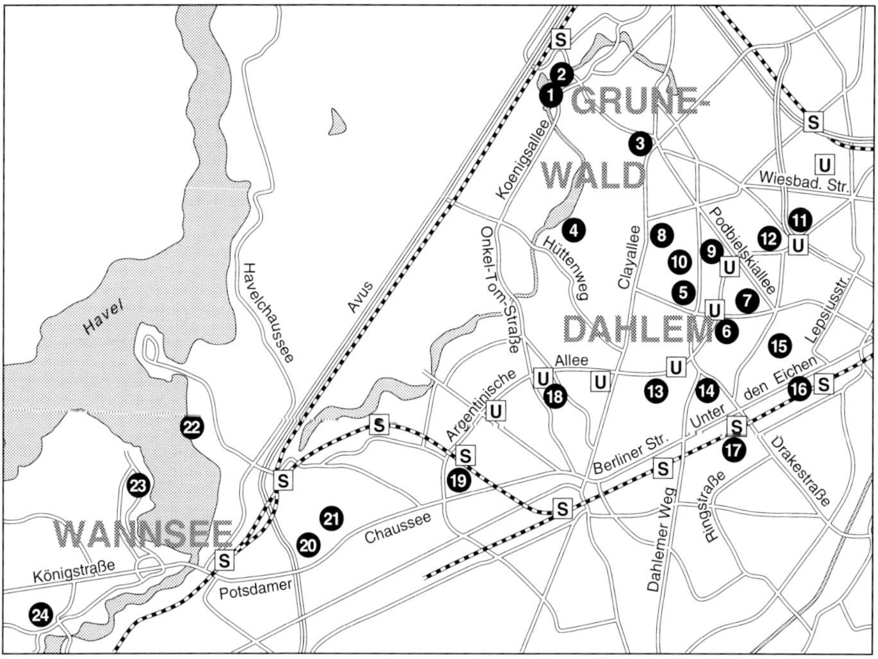

O 1 Villa Konschewski
O 2 Haus Flechtheim
O 3 Bank- und Geschäftshaus Roseneck
O 4 Jagdschloß Grunewald
O 5 Annenkirche
O 6 U-Bahnhof Dahlem Dorf
O 7 Haus Wiegand
O 8 Haus Auerbach
O 9 Haus Cramer
O 10 Botschaftsresidenz
O 11 Reichsknappschaftshaus
O 12 Reihenhäuser Schorlemerallee
O 13 Henry-Ford-Bau
O 14 Philosophisches Institut
O 15 Botanischer Garten
O 16 Wohnhäuser am Botanischen Garten
O 17 Bahnhof Lichterfelde West
O 18 Großsiedlung Onkel-Toms-Hütte
O 19 Haus Otte
O 20 Haus Freudenberg
O 21 Evangelische Kirche und Pfarrhaus
O 22 Strandbad Wannsee
O 23 Haus Springer
O 24 Dorfkirche Stolpe

O 1 Villa Konschewski
Berlin-Grunewald; Gottfried-v.-Cramm-Weg 33/37
1922-23 • Oskar Kaufmann

Mehr Schloß als Villa, so thront dieses Musterbeispiel des Kaufmannschen Expressionismus über dem Hundekehlesee. Wie fast allen späteren Bauten des bekannten Theaterarchitekten liegt der Villa baukörperlich und gestalterisch ein Rokokoschema zugrunde. Die im Mittelbau und in den beiden Seitenflügeln jeweils geschwungene Straßenfront und das anschließende Remisengebäude deuten einen »Cour d'honneur« an, den Ehrenhof, wie ihn Schlösser des 18. Jahrhunderts besitzen. Barock ist auch die Gartenseite, wo Freitreppen in symmetrischer Anordnung zum Seeufer hinabführen. Kulissenhaft leitet das Haus aus einer Zeit bewährter Stilistik in die bewegten zwanziger Jahre über. Spätestens die Inflationsjahre hatten auch gesellschaftliche Umschichtungen ausgelöst, und gerade die »Neureichen« mit ihrer verwaschenen und traditionslosen Vorstellung von Lebensart erlagen dieser theatralischen Repräsentation, wie sie Oskar Kaufmann hier vielleicht schmunzelnd darbot.

More a palace than a villa, this perfect specimen of Kaufmann's Expressionism lords it over the Hundekehlesee. Like almost all the theatre architect's later buildings, the villa is rococo-based in design and architecture. The central part of the building and the street façade, each curved, and the adjacent coach house suggest a cour d'honneur, like eighteenth century palaces. The garden side is also baroque, with symmetrically arranged steps leading down to the bank of the lake. The building leads in a theatrical fashion from a period of tried and tested style into the lively twenties. The years of inflation at the latest had unleashed social upheaval, and it was the «nouveaux riches» in particular with their woolly, traditionless ideas of living who were prone to the kind of melodrama that Oskar Kaufmann was offering them here, perhaps with his tongue in his cheek.

in der Nähe/nearby:
Wohnanlage; Koenigsallee 77
1991-92 • Arno Bonanni und Klaus Lattermann
Haus Wolfheim; Richard-Strauß-Straße 12
1910-12 • Oskar Kaufmann
Haus Andreae; Kronberger Straße 7/9
1912-13 • Breslauer & Salinger
Palais Pannwitz (Hotel Gerhus); Brahmsstraße 6-10
1912-14 • William Müller
Haus Vollberg; Delbrückstraße 29
1938-39 • Egon Eiermann
Haus Meyer; Seebergsteig 23
1897-98 • Arnold Hartmann
Haus Rose; Koenigsallee 49
1939 • Hugo Schellenberg

O 2 Haus Flechtheim
Berlin-Grunewald; Douglasstraße 12
1928 • Otto Rudolf Salvisberg

Im Fahrwasser der Neuen Sachlichkeit entstehen gegen Ende der zwanziger Jahre viele Einfamilienhäuser von gewollter Repräsentation. Die Sachlichkeit leitet sich hier nicht unbedingt aus einem tieferen geistigen Antrieb ab, vielmehr ist sie nur noch äußeres Gestaltungsmittel. In Größe und Wohnlichkeit entspricht ein Haus Flechtheim viel eher den späten Landhäusern der Zeit vor dem Ersten Weltkrieg. In den Jahren der vorübergehenden wirtschaftlichen Konsolidierung war bereits wieder die vom Geschmack her sichere Lösung gefragt, nicht das architektonische Experiment. Solide Oldenburger Klinker verblenden das Haus, edler Travertin ersetzt den billigen Putz. In dieser Mischung aus gediegener Moderne und eleganter Zurückhaltung war der über Jahre in Berlin ansässige Schweizer Architekt Salvisberg ein Meister. Sein Geschick für den Umgang mit dem Baukörper und mit dem sparsamen, aber wirkungsvollen Einsatz der wenigen Stilmittel der Zeit bewies er bei unterschiedlichsten Bauaufgaben.

Many intentionally imposing family houses were built in the late twenties in the wake of Neue Sachlichkeit. Here functionality is not necessarily derived from profound intellectual drive, but much more an exterior design device. In size and comfort the Flechtheim house is much more appropriate to late country houses in the period before the First World War. In the years of temporary economic consolidation what was demanded was the safe solution in terms of taste, not architectural experimentation. The house is clad in respectable Oldenburg clinker, with noble travertine instead of cheap rendering. The Swiss architect Salvisberg, who had lived in Berlin for years, was a master of this mixture of solid modernism and elegant restraint. He proved his skill in handling a building as a whole, and in economical but effective treatment of the few stylistic devices the period put at his disposal, in a number of buildings.

in der Nähe/nearby:
Haus Epstein; Douglasstraße 15/19
1923 • Oskar Kaufmann
Haus Erxleben; Douglasstraße 24/28
1907 • Hart & Lesser
Bahnhof Grunewald; Am Bahnhof Grunewald
Gegen 1899 • Karl Cornelius
Haus Noelle; Winklerstraße 10
1901 • Solf & Wichards
Haus Bernhard; Winklerstraße 11
1906 • Hermann Muthesius

O 3 Bank- und Geschäftshaus am Roseneck
Berlin-Grunewald; Hohenzollerndamm 130 a
1900-92 • Johanne Nalbach und Gernot Nalbach

Aufmerksamkeit als Werbung für ein Geschäftshaus ist hier architektonisch ausgeformt. Nicht die lauten Töne waren gefragt, sondern vornehme Gediegenheit glaubte man dem gehobenen Publikum aus den angrenzenden Villenvierteln schuldig zu sein. Dementsprechend stellt sich die weiße Front mit ihren großen Fensterblenden dar, ausklingend in einer Attika mit einer strengen Lochreihung. Der verglaste Abschlußkegel des Treppenturmes ragt darüber hervor als Mittelpunkt der darauf hinlaufenden Wandspiralen. Die äußere Gestaltung ist es wert, im Inneren fortgesetzt zu werden. Dem Selbstverständnis der Grundkreditbank als Mäzen ist es zu verdanken, daß im Sinne einer ganzheitlichen Auffassung der Baukunst – man erinnere sich an die Tendenzen um die Jahrhundertwende – auch die Innenarchitektur Nalbachsche Handschrift trägt. Eigens entworfene Arbeitsplatzmöbel nehmen Elemente der Außenarchitektur auf. Farben und Materialien der Böden, die Ausformung der Treppengeländer, die Wahl der Sessel und Bänke, nichts wird dem Zufall überlassen – Bau- und Raumkunst verschmelzen wohltuend.

The architecture of this commercial building is designed to draw attention to itself. The idea was not to make a loud noise but to reflect the kind of purity and noblesse which was thought to be suitable for the upper-class population of the adjoining residential areas. Hence the white façade with its huge windows and the perforated parapet. The glazed cone covering the stairwell rises above the roof and serves as the centre for the spiraling walls. The exterior design is continued in the interior as well. Thanks to the sponsorship of the client, the Grundkreditbank, the design of the interior also betrays Nalbach's handwriting, much in keeping with a holistic, comprehensive understanding of architecture that was associated with the concepts prevalent at the turn of the century. The specially designed office furniture takes up elements of the architecture of the exterior. In selecting the colour and material of the floors, the design of the stair railings, and the choice of chairs and benches, nothing was left to chance. The result is a pleasant harmony of architecture and interior design.

in der Nähe/nearby:
Haus am Roseneck; Hohenzollerndamm 88-88 a
1929 • Siegfried Kaprowski
Wohnhäuser; Teplitzer Straße 11 u. 13
1981-82 • Manfred Pechtold, Hans-Jürgen Ruprecht, Wolfgang Schlicht u. Jakob Schulze-Rohr
Wohnhäuser; Teplitzer Straße 20, Egerstraße 6
1930-31 • Kurt Heinrich Tischer

O 4 Jagdschloß Grunewald
Berlin-Dahlem; Hüttenweg
1542-43 • Caspar Theiß

Kurfürst Joachim II. ließ 1542 das kleine Jagdschloß »Zum Grunen Wald« errichten. Turm und Wendelstiege sind aus dieser Zeit noch erhalten. Vor und nach 1700 kamen Umbauten und Erweiterungen hinzu: Nering war beteiligt, aber auch Grünberg und Behr. Heute ist das Schloß mit seinen Wirtschaftsgebäuden zusammengenommen eine reizvolle Vierflügelanlage. Mit der Übernahme durch den Staat im Jahre 1928 wurde das Schlößchen überwiegend musealen Aufgaben zugeführt. Seine idyllische Lage büßte es am Rande einer ausufernden Millionenstadt schon lange ein, wurde zum Ausflugsziel der Großstädter. 1905-06 erbaute man neben dem Schloß die große Ausflugsgaststätte »Forsthaus Paulsborn«.

Elector Joachim II built this little hunting lodge «Zum Grunen Wald» in 1542. The tower and spiral staircase have survived from this period. Rebuilding and extension work took place before and after 1700: Nering was involved, and so were Grünberg and Behr. Today the lodge and its domestic buildings make a charming ensemble in four sections. It was taken over by the state in 1928, and used largely for museum purposes. It has long foregone its idyllic position on the edge of an overflowing city with millions of inhabitants, and has become a popular destination for outings. The large «Forsthaus Paulsborn» restaurant was built beside it in 1905-6.

in der Nähe/nearby:
Gaststätte »Forsthaus Paulsborn«; Hüttenweg
1905-06 • Friedrich Wilhelm Göhre
Brückemuseum; Bussardsteig 9
1966-67 • Werner Düttmann

O 5 Annenkirche
Berlin-Dahlem; Königin-Luise-Straße 55
14. Jahrhundert

Seitlich des Dorfangers von Dahlem liegt die Annenkirche. Im 14. Jahrhundert war es ein einfacher Bau, der dann im späten Mittelalter nach Osten verlängert wurde und einen polygonalen Chor erhielt. Die Einwölbung ist noch später zu datieren, und der Turmaufsatz kam im 19. Jahrhundert hinzu. Zunächst hatte dieser militärische Bedeutung: Auf seiner Plattform stand die zweite Station der optischen Telegraphenlinie Berlin–Koblenz, Sichtkontakt bestand zur Sternwarte der Akademie in Berlin und im Westen zum Brauhausberg bei Potsdam. Die Linie übermittelte Nachrichten zwischen der Hauptstadt und dem Kommando der Garnisonen in den Koblenzer Festungen, dem Vorposten zur französischen Grenze. Seit 1951 schließt ein kleiner Pyramidenhelm den Dachturm ab.

The Annenkirche stands beside the village green in Dahlem. In the fourteenth century it was a simple building which was then extended towards the east in the late Middle Ages, when a polygonal choir was added. The vaulting is even later in date, and the top of the tower was added in the nineteenth century. At first the latter had military significance: the second station of the optical telegraph line from Berlin to Koblenz was on its platform, with visual contact to the observatory at the Akademie in Berlin and west to the Brauhausberg in Potsdam. The line transmitted news between the capital and the commander of the garrisons in the Koblenz fortresses, the outpost nearest the French border. The small pyramid has topped the tower since 1951.

in der Nähe/nearby:
Pfarrhaus; Pacelliallee 61
1910 • Heinrich Straumer
Reihenhausgruppen; Im Gehege, Falkenried, Hohe Aehren, Am Hirschsprung
1912/1929 • Heinrich Schweitzer, Bruno Ahrends
Haus Huth; Bitterstraße 8/12
1914-17 • Heinrich Straumer
Haus Krahner; Auf dem Grat 26
1924-25 • Otto Rudolf Salvisberg
Haus Telschow; Auf dem Grat 50
1925-26 • Heinrich Straumer
Gutshaus; Königin-Luise-Straße 49
1678-80 (Kapelle um 1500)
Gasthaus »Alter Krug«; Königin-Luise-Straße 52
18./19. Jh.
Eiskeller; Königin-Luise-Straße (Dorfaue)
1709

O 6 U-Bahnhof Dahlem Dorf
Berlin-Dahlem; Königin-Luise-Straße
1912-13 • Friedrich Hennings, Wilhelm Hennings

Der 1909-13 gebauten U-Bahnlinie vom Wittenbergplatz durch Wilmersdorf und Dahlem zum Thielplatz sieht man an, daß sie durch wohlhabende Vororte führt. Alle Bahnhöfe wurden mit erheblichem gestalterischen Aufwand eingerichtet, voller Bezüge zu den Stationsnamen und den Eigenheiten des jeweiligen Ortes. »Dahlem Dorf« wurde zum idyllischen Bauern-Fachwerkhaus mit Reetdach. Es ist aber nicht die verkrampfte Nachäffung, sondern die schlicht ländlich aufgefaßte Bauaufgabe, die überzeugt. Funktional genügt das Bauwerk allen Anforderungen. Auch innen fügen sich die farbig bemalten Holzbalkendecken und die blau und grün gekachelten Wände in das Gesamtbild ein. Selbst der Übergang zum rein technisch aufgefaßten Bahnsteig, der wie die Strecke von der Station Podbielskiallee an im offenen Einschnitt liegt, wird bewältigt. Zur Bauzeit der Linie ging man davon aus, daß später mit dichterer Bebauung dieser Einschnitt einmal abgedeckt und damit die Linie zur richtigen Untergrundbahn würde. Bisher unterblieb dies aber, und inzwischen übernahmen dichte Büsche und Bäume die Abschirmung des Verkehrs von der ruhigen Wohnumgebung.

It is obvious that the underground line built in 1909-13 from Wittenbergplatz via Wilmersdorf and Dahlem to Thielplatz ran through well-to-do suburbs. No expense was spared in designing the stations, all of which make reference to the station names and characterisitics of the place in question. «Dahlem Dorf» became an idyllic rural half-timbered building with a thatched roof. But what is convincing is not the quality of desperate imitation, but the plain and rural interpretation of the building brief. Functionally the building fulfills every requirement. Inside as well the colourfully painted ceilings with wooden beams and blue and green tiled walls fit perfectly into the overall picture. Even the transition to the purely functional platform, which like the rest of the line from Podbielskiallee onwards is in an open cutting, is successful. At the time the line was built, the view was taken that if the area became more built up the cutting could be covered over to make the line a genuine underground. So far, however, this has not been done, and in the meantime dense bushes and trees have taken over the task of screening the peaceful residential area from noise.

in der Nähe/nearby:
Geheimes Staatsarchiv; Archivstraße 11-15
1914-20 • Kraecker, Büssow
Asiatisches Museum; Arnimallee 23-27
1914-23 • Bruno Paul
Völkerkundemuseum; Lansstraße 8-12
1965-70 • Wils Ebert, Fritz Bornemann

O 7 Haus Wiegand
Berlin-Dahlem; Peter-Lenné-Straße 28/30
1911-12 • Peter Behrens

Der neue Klassizismus der frühen zehner Jahre prägt das Haus des Archäologen Theodor Wiegand. Die Klarheit der hellenischen Antike spricht aus der Flächigkeit des ohne Mörtelfuge gemauerten Muschelkalks, aus dem abstrahierten Portikus, aus der Attika und dem flach geneigten Walmdach mit seinen griechischen Ludovici-Pfannen. Peter Behrens bildet mit seinem Haus Wiegand stilistisch den Angelpunkt zwischen Schinkel und Mies van der Rohe, der als einstiger Assistent von Behrens den Einfluß seines Lehrers nie leugnen konnte. Einzelformen des Hauses folgen einer sparsamen Geometrie, wie sie um 1800 als Antwort auf die feudale Barock- und Rokokoarchitektur gefunden wurde. Aus der strengen Knappheit ergibt sich wirksam eine stille und zeitlose Größe.

This house built for archaeologist Theodor Wiegand bears the stamp of the new classicism of the second decade of the twentieth century. The clarity of Greek antiquity speaks out of the flatness of the muschelkalk, built without mortar, in the abstract portico, the attic storey and the shallow slope of the hip roof with its Greek Ludovici pantiles. Peter Behrens' Wiegand house is the stylistic hinge between Schinkel and Mies van der Rohe, who as a former assistant of Behrens could never deny the influence of his teacher. Individual elements of the design follow an economical geometry of the kind current around 1800 as a reply to feudal baroque and rococo architecture. Austere conciseness produces an effective and timeless greatness.

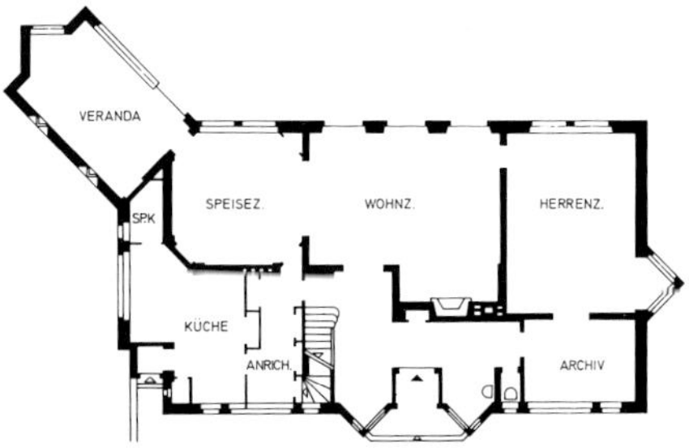

O 8 Haus Auerbach
Berlin-Dahlem; Clayallee 34
1924-25 • Bruno Paul

Einem maßvollen Expressionismus scheint Bruno Paul bei diesem Haus zu folgen. Doch eher unentschlossen bewegt er sich auch zwischen Landhausstil, Klassizismus und Sachlichkeit. »Voller frommer Lügen ... jedoch meisterhaft«, so charakterisierte es der bekannte Architekturtheoretiker Julius Posener einmal. Der Entwurf ist nur scheinbar axial, das Diktat der Fensterfolge aber so zwingend, daß hier und da selbst ein kleines Dilemma in der grundrißlichen Raumordnung hingenommen wird. Die Wohnlichkeit jedoch steht außer Frage, und so wirkt das Haus wieder überzeugend.

Bruno Paul seems to be using a moderate form of Expressionism in his design for this house. But he does show a certain indecision as he moves between country house style, classicism and functionalism. «Full of pious lies . . . but masterly», said famous architectural theorist Julius Posener once about this building. The design is only apparently axial, but the sequence of windows is so compulsive that small dilemmas in spatial organization of the ground plan are accepted here and there. But there is no question about its pleasantness to live in, and thus the house is again convincing.

in der Nähe/nearby:
Haus Heydenreich; Peter-Lenné-Straße 1/3
1915-16 • Ernst Paulus, Günther Paulus
Haus Hecht; Arnimallee 8
1910 • Paul Mebes
Haus Auhagen; Arnimallee 12
1911-12 • Heinrich Lassen
Botanisches Museum; Königin-Luise-Straße 6/8
1903-06 • Alfred Koerner
Haus Stolper; Englerallee 25
1929 • Bruno Ahrends
Haus Maurer; Am Erlenbusch 14 a
1933 • Walter Gropius
Haus Penzlin; Podbielskiallee 28
1928-29 • Otto Rudolf Salvisberg

in der Nähe/nearby:
Haus Scharf; B-Schmargendorf; Pücklerstraße 5
1938 • Hans Scharoun
Haus Riefenstahl; B-Schmargendorf; Heydenstraße 30
1936 • Albert Speer
Haus Breuhaus; B-Schmargendorf; Max-Eyth-Straße 12 a
1938 • Hans Scharoun
Haus Paulus; B-Schmargendorf; Rheinbabenallee 32
1907-10 • August Dinklage, Ernst Paulus, Olaf Lilloe
Haus Berkel; B-Schmargendorf; Rheinbabenallee 18
1927 • Peter Großmann
Haus Harkort; B-Schmargendorf; Rheinbabenallee 5
1913 • Heinrich Straumer

O 9 Haus Cramer
Berlin-Dahlem; Pacelliallee 18/20
1911-12 • Hermann Muthesius

Lange Zeit war der Fortbestand dieses Hauses gefährdet, denn große Grundstücke verlockten Spekulanten immer wieder, die alten Häuser abzubrechen – seien sie bauhistorisch noch so wertvoll – und gewinnbringend eine neue dichtere Bebauung mit Reihenhäusern oder größeren Wohnkomplexen vorzunehmen. Schwierig sind Nutzung und Erhalt eines Landhauses dieser Größe ohnehin. Nur mit einem ganzen Stab von Personal läßt sich ein solches bewirtschaften. Das Haus Kramer erweckt noch den Eindruck einer freien Gruppierung der Bauglieder zu einem malerischen Ganzen. Gegen 1910 war das die architektonische Auffassung, nicht nur bei Hermann Muthesius. Doch Anfang der zehner Jahre neigte der gestalterische Wille immer mehr zu einer strengen klassizistischen Formgebung. Sie äußert sich hier bereits in einer Erstarrung der Fassaden in grauem Bruchsteinmauerwerk, in einer versteckten Symmetrie.

For a long time the continuing existence of this house was under threat, as large plots continually tempted speculators to pull down old buildings – however great their interest in terms of architectural history – and to build more densely, using terraced houses or larger residential complexes. Use and maintenance of a house of this size are difficult anyway, and require a full domestic staff. The Kramer house still gives the impression of various parts of a building grouped freely to form a picturesque whole. This was the way architecture was interpreted around 1910, and not just by Hermann Muthesius. But early in the second decade of the twentieth century the designer's will inclined increasingly to austere classical shapes. Here it is expressed in the frozen façades in undressed grey stone, in concealed symmetry.

in der Nähe/nearby:
Haus Strauss; Pacelliallee 14/16
1914 • Cremer & Wolffenstein
Haus Neuhaus; Bernadottestraße 56/58
1906 • Hermann Muthesius
Haus Holler; Amselstraße 18
1937 • Fritz August Breuhaus
Haus Pircher; Wachtelstraße 4
1928 • Bruno Ahrends
Haus Paret; Vogelsang 12
1929 • Hans Ruhl

O 10 Botschaftsresidenz
Berlin-Dahlem; Im Dol 36/38
1988-89 • Steinebach & Weber

Wenn es heute noch den Bautyp »Schloß« gibt, dann ist er hier in freier Deutung verwirklicht. Allein die unmißverständliche Einfriedung des Geländes dokumentiert, daß sich dahinter wohl etwas Besonderes verbirgt, was nicht »jeden« etwas angeht. Drei Gebäude umstehen einen Vorplatz, der dem klassischen Ehrenhof entspricht. Die beiden seitlichen Häuser suchen in ihren fein abgestimmten Proportionen Anschluß an Schinkels Biedermeierbauten, etwa Charlottenhof in Potsdam. Der als Tempelgiebel gebildete Mittelrisalit, die maßvolle Zweigeschossigkeit, das Attikaband, die flachen Walm- und Satteldächer, das sind Elemente, die auch in der Zeit nach 1800 verwendet wurden. Der Verzicht auf jedes Ornament und die zum Balken verbreiterten Linien gehören dagegen ganz der Moderne an. Auch die asymmetrische Lage des mittleren Gebäudes – es weicht einer alten Buche aus – ist nur heute denkbar. Zwischen den Pfeilern seiner Stirnseite liegen durchgehende sprossengeteilte Glasflächen von Wintergärten. Damit drängt sich der Eindruck eines Gartenhauses oder einer Orangerie auf. Bleibt man beim Bild der Schloßanlage, fehlt nur die Wagenremise – sie ist zeitgemäß durch eine Tiefgarage ersetzt. Bewohnt wird dieser Herrensitz durch amerikanische Botschaftsangehörige.

If we still build palaces today, then this, freely interpreted, is one. The unmistakable enclosure of the site shows clearly that there is something special behind, which is not for «anybody». The buildings are set around a forecourt corresponding to the classical cour d'honneur. The two side buildings seek for a link with Schinkel's Biedermeier buildings, the Charlottenhof in Potsdam perhaps, in their finely tuned proportions. The central section in the form of a temple pediment, the moderate height of two storeys, the attic storey band, the shallow hip and saddle roofs, are all elements used in the post 1800 period as well. On the other hand the complete lack of ornament and lines broadened to bars are entirely Modern. The asymmetrical placing of the central building as well – it accommodates an ancient beech tree – could only be conceivable today. Between the piers of the end wall are a run of mullioned glass panes belonging to the conservatories. This gives the impression of a garden house or orangery. If one returns to the image of the palace, the only thing that is missing is a coachhouse – this is replaced by an underground garage, in keeping with the times. This stately home is occupied by staff of the American embassy.

in der Nähe/nearby:
Haus Oesten; Im Dol 50
1923 • Otto Rudolf Salvisberg

O 11 Reichsknappschaftshaus
Berlin-Wilmersdorf; Breitenbachplatz 2
1929-30 • Max Taut, Franz Hoffmann

Max Taut war neben dem Franzosen Perret der erste Architekt des Neuen Bauens, der die Konstruktion so zeigt, wie sie ist. Nicht die Verfremdung im vertikal betonten Pfeilerstil oder in der Schichtung horizontaler Bänder, sondern die Darstellung des Rahmens prägte die äußere Gestaltung. Dem frühen Rasterbau des Gewerkschaftshauses in der Wallstraße folgten weitere Beispiele, auch das Knappschaftshaus am Breitenbachplatz. Sein Stahlskelett steht in der Wand, und es wird nachgezeichnet mit großen Keramikplatten, die Füllung der Gefache ist dagegen mit schmalen Klinkern verblendet. Die Nüchternheit scheint bei Max Taut aus einer allzu berechtigten Skepsis gegenüber modischen Strömungen herzurühren. Trotzdem ist beim Knappschaftshaus noch die formende Kraft des Architekten erkennbar, er überläßt die Gestalt nicht allein der Konstruktion oder der Funktion.

With the French architect Perret, Max Taut was the first proponent of Neues Bauen, which showed construction as it is: the exterior is not alienated by the use of vertically accentuated piers or layered with horizontal bands, but simply represents the frame. Further examples followed suit from the early grid structure of the trade union building in Wallstrasse, including the miners' guild building in Breitenbachplatz. Its steel skeleton is set in the wall, with large ceramic slabs following its line, and filling panels clad with narrow clinker. Max Taut's sobriety seems to stem from an entirely justifiable scepticism about fashionable trends. Despite this the architect's creative power still comes over in the miners' guild building, and design is not entirely subordinated to structure or function.

in der Nähe/nearby:
Elektronen-Speicherringanlage Bessy; Lentzeallee 100
1978-81 • Gerd Hänska
Institut für Bildungsforschung; Lentzeallee 94
1972-74 • Hermann Fehling, Daniel Gogel
Landwirtschaftliche Hochschule; B-Dahlem; Lentzeallee 45/75
1922-25 • Heinrich Straumer
Kleinhaus-Siedlung; B-Schmargendorf; Lentzeallee 16/74, Zoppoter Straße 36/64, Misdroyer Straße 1/27
1920 • Heinrich Schweitzer
Dorfkirche; B-Schmargendorf; Breite Straße 38
13./14. Jh.

O 12 Reihenhäuser
Berlin-Dahlem; Schorlemerallee 13/23 a
1925 • Luckhardt & Anker

»Rhythmische Verschiebungen« waren das Motto dieser Reihenhäuser. Während die Brüder Luckhardt noch einige Jahre zuvor in der »Gläsernen Kette« verwegene Architekturgedanken und -entwürfe verfolgten, brachte die praktische Arbeit – wie immer – eine stilistische Beruhigung mit sich. Trotzdem enthielt diese keilförmig von der Straße weggestaffelte Häuserzeile noch genügend Revolutionäres, bedenkt man, wie noch ein Jahrzehnt zuvor gebaut wurde. Der Materialwechsel Hell-Dunkel, die Schatten in der Staffelung, das sind deutliche Relikte des Expressionismus. Die Argumentation der Architekten war dagegen funktional geführt: Belichtung, Sichtschutz, Wärmetechnik. Die kubischen Bauglieder und ornamentlosen Flächen weisen schon auf die strengere Sachlichkeit, den Funktionalismus der späteren Bauten hin. Und dort hat die Architektengemeinschaft von Wassili und Hans Luckhardt mit Alfons Anker in Berlin Beispielhaftes geleistet, dazu gehören auch die 1929 fertiggestellten weiteren Reihen- und Einzelhäuser in der Schorlemerallee.

«Rhythmic displacement» was the motto for these terraced houses. A few years before, the Luckhardt brothers had been disciples of the «Gläserne Kette» (glass chain) movement with its rash architectural approach and designs, but practical work – as always – concentrated the stylistic mind wonderfully. Nevertheless this row of houses, staggered away from the street in wedge shapes, had quite enough revolutionary features, if one thinks how people built a decade earlier. The alternation of dark and light materials, shadows caused by the staggering, these are clear relics of Expressionism. But on the other hand the architectural argument was conducted functionally: lighting, sight protection, heat engineering. The cubic sections of the building and unornamented surfaces already point forward to the more austere objectivity, the functionality of the later buildings. In this field the architectural association of Wassili and Hans Luckhardt with Alfons Anker produced some exemplary work in Berlin, including other terraced and detached houses in Schorlemerallee, completed in 1929.

in der Nähe/nearby:
Stahlskeletthaus Luckhardt; Schorlemerallee 7/7 a
1929 • Luckhardt & Anker
Reihenhäuser; Schorlemerallee 12/12 c
1928-29 • Luckhardt & Anker
Reihenhäuser; Schweinfurthstraße 58/72, Schorlemerallee 32/40
1912-14 • Paul Imberg
U-Bahnhof Podbielskiallee; Podbielskiallee
1911-13 • Heinrich Schweitzer

O 13 Henry-Ford-Bau
Berlin-Dahlem; Garystraße 35/39
1952-54 • Franz Heinrich Sobotka, Gustav Müller

Nachdem 1948 die ersten Studenten aus politischen Gründen vom Studium an der Berliner Universität im damaligen Ostteil der Stadt ausgeschlossen wurden, regte sich der Wille, im Westteil eine »freie« Universität zu gründen. Dafür bot sich Dahlem an. Schon seit den zehner Jahren waren hier Institute der einstigen Kaiser-Wilhelm-Gesellschaft angesiedelt, neben dem Botanischen Garten auch Institute der Universität. Angemietete Villen dienten und dienen noch der Unterbringung von Lehr- und Forschungseinrichtungen der Freien Universität – kurz FU. Erster Neubau war 1949-51 das Anatomische Institut von Günter Kalesky, dann die Mensa von Hermann Fehling. Mit Geldern der amerikanischen Ford-Stiftung konnte nach vier Jahren endlich mit dem Bau eines Hauptgebäudes begonnen werden. Von den vielen weiteren Bauten machte ein Flächenbau der Architekten Georges Candilis, Alexis Josic, Shadrach Woods und Manfred Schiedhelm von 1967-73 für die Geisteswissenschaftlichen Institute von sich reden. Die Fassadenteile aus »edelrostenden« Corten-Stahlplatten verhalfen dem Bau zu dem treffsicheren Namen »Rostlaube«. Allen FU-Bauten in Dahlem ist eines gemeinsam: Auch wenn sie sich als Flachbauten der Umgebung anzupassen suchen, werden sie von den Dahlemer Villenbewohnern nicht geliebt.

In 1948, after the first students had been prevented for political reasons from attending Berlin University in what was then the eastern part of the city, the idea formed in the western part of founding a «free» university. Dahlem was the obvious place for this. Institutions of the former Kaiser-Wilhelm-Gesellschaft had been based here since the second decade of the present century, including the Botanical Garden and university departments. Rented villas served and indeed still serve to accommodate teaching and research facilities for the Free University – FU for short. The first new building was Günter Kalesky's Anatomical Institute, built in 1949-51, then the Refectory by Hermann Fehling. It finally became possible to start work on a main building with funding from the American Ford Foundation four years later. The arts building by architects Georges Candilis, Alexis Josic, Shadrach Woods and Manfred Schiedhelm, dating from 1967-73, was one of the later buildings to cause a stir. The façade sections in «stainless rusting» Corten steel sheets gave the building its accurate nickname «rust arbour». The FU buildings in Dahlem have one thing in common: even when they try to fit in with the area by restricting their height, they are not popular with Dahlem's villa residents.

in der Nähe/nearby:
Luftgaukommando; Clayallee 170
1937 • Fritz Fuß

O 14 Philosophisches Institut
Berlin-Dahlem; Habelschwerdter Allee 30
1981-83 • Hinrich Baller, Inken Baller

An Gaudis verwegene Linienführung erinnert dieses Gebäude mit seinen filigranen Stützen und den Schwüngen des Daches. Das Gebiet rechtwinkliger Universitätsbauten wird verlassen, und das Neue erscheint wie die Antwort auf eine Zeit, die glaubte, mit Zweckmäßigkeit und Funktion als Gestaltungsmoment für immer und überall auskommen zu können. Es ist nicht das Einladende der malerischen Architektur um 1910, es ist nicht das klinisch Sterile der Bauten um 1930, es ist so, daß man hinsieht und etwas zu sehen hat, mit dem Auge auf die Suche nach einer Überraschung geht. Hinrich und Inken Baller haben inzwischen schon etliche Bauten in der ihnen eigenen Gestaltungsweise geliefert – wo auch immer sie stehen, sorgen sie für Aufsehen.

The filigree pillars and roof curves of this building are reminiscent of Gaudi's daring line. The territory of university buildings with right angles is abandoned, and the new appears like a reply to a time which believed that it would always and everywhere survive with fitness for purpose and function as the driving force behind design. This does not have the inviting quality of picturesque architecture c. 1910, not the clinical sterility of buildings c. 1930, it is design of a kind that catches the eye and gives it something to look at, sends it searching for a surprise. In the meantime Hinrich and Inken Baller have produced many buildings, all designed in this way that they have made their own – and wherever they are, they attract attention.

in der Nähe/nearby:
Haus Borchert; Habelschwerdter Allee 17
1911 • Heinrich Straumer
Häuser Jessen und Rosenstein; Hittorfstraße 12/14
1914 • Hans Jessen
Jesus-Christus-Kirche; Hittorfstraße 21/23
1930-31 • Jürgen Bachmann
Haus Gesky; Faradayweg 15
1923-24 • Walter Klingenberg, Werner Issel
Entomologisches Museum; Ehrenbergstraße 26
1910-11 • Heinrich Straumer
Haus Wiertz; Patschkauer Weg 56
1927-28 • Otto Rudolf Salvisberg
Haus Möller; B-Lichterfelde; Altensteinstraße 66
1921 • Heinrich Möller

O 15 Botanischer Garten
Berlin-Lichterfelde; Unter den Eichen 5
1897-1907 • Alfred Koerner

Einen Vorläufer hatte der »Botanische Garten« seit 1573 an der Stelle des späteren Lustgartens. Von 1679 an gab es einen solchen dann zwischen Berlin und Schöneberg, der heutige Kleistpark. Ende des 19. Jahrhunderts war auch dieser Garten zu klein, und am Westhang des Steglitzer Fichtenberges wurde ein Gelände erworben, welches genügend groß war für einen wissenschaftlichen Garten mit Arboretum, Teiche, flache und bergig modellierte Gelände für typische Anpflanzungen und lebende Sammlungen der heimischen und fremdländischen Vegetation. Gewächshäuser helfen dort, wo das hiesige Klima kein Gedeihen erlaubt – sie entstanden zuletzt, und zwar in den Jahren 1906-07, noch nach dem 1903-06 erbauten Museumsgebäude. Erhöht über dem Garten beherrschen die Gewächshäuser mit ihrer Glas-Eisen-Konstruktion das Ostgelände. Beträchtliches Aufsehen erregte seinerzeit das Große Tropenhaus, dessen freitragende Konstruktion über 36 000 m^3 Luftraum umschloß. 1984-87 wurden die Pflanzenhäuser von Engelbert Kremser und Manfred Korthals restauriert und baulich ergänzt. Einen Museumsanbau errichtete gleichzeitig Rainer Gerhard Rümmler.

The «Botanical Garden» had a predecessor dating from 1573 on the site of the later Lustgarten. From 1679 there was one between Berlin and Schöneberg, the present Kleistpark. In the late nineteenth century this became too small as well, and a site was acquired on the western slope of the Fichtenberg in Steglitz. This was large enough for a scientific garden with arboretum, pools, flat and hilly areas for typical planting and living collections of native and foreign vegetation. Glasshouses lend a hand when the climate here does permit specimens to flourish – they were the last things to be built, in 1906-7, even after the museum building, which dates from 1903-6. The iron and glass greenhouses dominate the eastern section from a slight eminence. The Great Tropical House attracted much attention at the time, its cantilever construction enclosing over 36,000 cubic metres of air space. In 1984-7 Engelbert Kremser's and Manfred Korthal's plant houses were restored and extended. Rainer Gerhard Rümmler put up a museum building at the same time.

in der Nähe/nearby:
Stubenrauch-Krankenhaus (Bundesanstalt für Materialprüfung); Unter den Eichen 44-46
1891-1900 • Heino Schmieden
Martin-Luther-Kirche; Tulpenstraße 1
1930-36 • Fritz Schupp und Martin Kremmer
Bahnhof Botanischer Garten; Hortensienstraße 28 a
1908-09 • Erdmann & Spindler
Laubenganghaus; Neuchateller Straße 19-20
1929-30 • Anton Brenner, Mebes & Emmerich

O 16 Wohnhäuser am Botanischen Garten
Berlin-Lichterfelde; Hortensienstraße 34-63
1924-26 • Otto Rudolf Salvisberg

Dieser Reihenhauszeile merkt man an, daß ihr Architekt Schweizer Herkunft ist. Erinnerungen an die heimatlichen Städtchen beeinflußten die Gestaltung: solide Schlichtheit der Häuser, abfallende Höhe der Zeile, wechselnde Farbigkeit der Fassaden, kleine Fenster, auskragende Dächer, ein Torbau. Salvisberg hielt sich kaum an den derzeit gültigen Expressionismus, vielmehr vermittelt er noch einmal die Idee eines deutlich auf Heimat und Bodenständigkeit gerichteten Realismus, wie er etwa auch beim Heidehof von Mebes & Emmerich in Zehlendorf auftaucht. Doch während solche Kriterien auf das Unterbewußte des Zeitgenossen gewirkt haben mögen, mußten um so mehr die Farben ins Auge fallen. Die Farbgebung folgte einem Wechsel von leuchtenden und matten Tönen, von Hell und Dunkel, wobei die Häuser, mit denen jeweils eine neue Firstlinie beginnt, immer durch tiefere, schwere Farben hervorgehoben sind. – Reihenhäuser leiden grundsätzlich unter der Diskrepanz zwischen einheitlich durchdachter Planung und vom jeweiligen Besitzer unbedachter Veränderung. Ausnahmen bestätigen die Regel.

You can tell from this row of terraced houses that the architect is Swiss. The design is influenced by reminiscences of the small towns of his homeland: the buildings are respectably plain, the houses decrease in height along the row, the façades are in different colours, the windows are small, the roofs protrude and there is a gatehouse. Salvisberg almost completely ignores the Expressionism of his period, but prefers again to convey the idea of realism directed clearly at home and a feeling of being rooted in one's native soil, as also seen in Mebes' and Emmerich's Heidehof in Zehlendorf. But while such criteria may haved worked on the subconscious of contemporaries, the colours must have been all the more striking. The colour scheme followed an alternating sequence of gleaming and dull tones, of light and dark, and the houses at which a new roof height begins are always picked out with deeper, darker colours. – Terraced houses always suffer from a discrepancy between planning thought through in a unified fashion and alterations carried out without careful thought by current owners. Exceptions prove the rule.

in der Nähe/nearby:
Wohnhausgruppe; Hortensienplatz 1-3
1924-26 • Otto Rudolf Salvisberg

O 17 Bahnhof Lichterfelde West
Berlin-Lichterfelde; Hans-Sachs-Straße
1871-72

Der Bahnhof liegt an Berlins erster Eisenbahnstrecke, der 1837-38 gebauten Potsdamer Bahn. Damals lag das Dorf Lichterfelde noch unbeachtet abseits der Trasse. Doch mit der Gründung der Villenkolonie Lichterfelde durch Carstenn rückte die Bebauung an die Bahn heran und verlangte nach einem Bahnhof. Dieser wurde dann auch unter Berücksichtigung des Stils der Lichterfelder Villen erbaut. Das italienische Landhaus wurde zitiert, entsprechend etwa den Häusern in der nahen Curtiusstraße. In nachromantischem Empfinden ziert ein Uhrturm den Bau als sinnfälliges Signal für die Bedeutung des Gebäudes. 1889-91 erhielt der Bahnhof im Zuge des Ausbaus der Wannseebahn einen Mittelbahnsteig mit Überdachung und eine Unterführung mit verglasten Treppenhäusern. Gegen die Jahrhundertwende wird auch der Vorplatz architektonisch gefaßt. Ladenbauten lassen ein kleines städtisches Zentrum entstehen.

This station is on Berlin's first railway line, the Potsdam Railway, built in 1837-8. At that time the village of Lichterfelde was unnoticed at the side of the line. But when Carstenn established the Lichterfelde villa colony, the development came close to the railway and demanded a station. This was then built with regard for the style of the Lichterfelde villas. Italian country houses were quoted, roughly corresponding with the houses in nearby Curtiusstrasse. Post-Romantic sensibility requires the building to be decorated with a clock tower as an obvious signal of the importance of the building. In 1889-91, when the Wannsee railway was being extended, a central platform was added, with roof and subway with glazed staircases. Around the turn of the century the square in front of the station was also framed architecturally. Shops created a small urban centre.

in der Nähe/nearby:
»Westbazar«; Baseler Straße 2-4
1896-97 • Georg Böhme
Haus Lilienthal; Weddigenweg 17
1893 • Gustav Lilienthal
Töchterheim; Kommandantenstraße 9-12
1896-98 • Alfred Koerner
Bahnhof Lichterfelde-Ost; Bahnhofstraße
1915-16 • Karl Cornelius
Villa; Königsberger Straße 29
1871 • Herold & Hinze

O 18 Großsiedlung Onkel-Toms-Hütte
Berlin-Zehlendorf; Argentinische Allee, Riemeisterstraße, Onkel-Tom-Straße und Nebenstraßen
1926-31 • Bruno Taut, Otto Rudolf Salvisberg, Hugo Häring

Im Wald- und Heidegebiet nördlich des alten Zehlendorf entstand von 1926 bis 1931 eine Siedlung nach den Prinzipien des Neuen Bauens. Bruno Taut, Salvisberg und Häring stehen für die architektonische Qualität. In einer gelungenen Mischung aus langen und kurzen Hauszeilen, Reihenhäusern, Blockrandbebauung und aufgelockerter Anordnung ist die Wohnstadt durchgrünt, voller Licht und Luft. Die Häuser bleiben in maßvoller Höhe grundsätzlich unter den Kronen der märkischen Kiefern und lassen selbst in den längsten Zeilen durch baukörperliche und farbliche Gliederung keinesfalls den Eindruck von Eintönigkeit aufkommen. Überhaupt spielt die Farbgebung eine große Rolle wie bei allen Häusern von Taut. Etwa 15 000 Menschen fanden hier Wohnung. Durch die Verlängerung der Dahlemer U-Bahn fand die Siedlung 1929 Anschluß an das städtische Schnellbahnnetz. Im Herzen der Siedlung umbaute Salvisberg 1931 den Bahnhof »Onkel Toms Hütte« mit einer Ladenzeile, in der auch Postamt und Kino untergebracht wurden.

An estate built on the principles of Neues Bauen was built in the area of wood and heath north of old Zehlendorf from 1926 to 1931. Bruno Taut, Salvisberg and Häring were responsible for the quality of the architecture. The residential town is planted with grass and trees, full of air and light, a successful mixture of long and short rows of houses, terraced houses, development on the edge of blocks and generally free arrangement. The houses are of moderate height, lower than the pines of the Mark as a matter of principle, and even in the longest rows their architectural and colour articulation never permits the slightest hint of monotony. Colour schemes are an important factor everywhere, as in all Taut's buildings. About 15,000 people were accommodated here. When the Dahlem underground line was extended in 1929 the estate was connected to the express railway network. At the heart of the estate, Salvisberg rebuilt «Onkel Toms Hütte» station in 1931 with a row of shops including a post office and a cinema.

in der Nähe/nearby:
Reihenhäuser; Riemeisterstraße 135/185 usw.
1929 • Bruno Taut
Haus Blumenthal; Wilskistraße 66
1932 • Ludwig Hilberseimer
»Sommerfelds Aue«; Onkel-Tom-Straße 85/91
1923 • Richard Neutra
Versuchssiedlung Fischtal; Am Fischtal 2/90
1928-29 • Heinrich Tessenow, Hans Poelzig, Fritz Schopohl, Paul Schmitthenner u.a.m.
Siedlung »Krumme Lanke«; Argentinische Allee 51/83
1938-40 • Hans Gerlach
Wasserwerk Riemeisterfenn; Jagen 27
1953-55 • Johannes Krüger

O 19 Haus Otte
Berlin-Zehlendorf; Wolzogenstraße 17
1922 • Walter Gropius

Im Grunde genommen ist das Haus nur noch Wallfahrtsort für Gropius-Anhänger oder andere Berufene, denn die entscheidenden äußeren wie inneren Merkmale des Hauses sind inzwischen verändert und entstellt. Neben dem zerstörten Blockhaus Sommerfeld ist es eine der expressionistischen Schöpfungen von Walter Gropius, der doch eher als Bauhaus-Architekt von sich reden machte und in die Baugeschichte einging. Nur der weiße Putz verbindet das Haus Otte etwa mit dem Haus Lewin in der Fischerhüttenstraße 106 aus dem Jahre 1928. Alles andere wäre später verpönt gewesen, besonders das »Gesicht« des Hauses Otte mit Mund, Nase, Augen und Ohren. In seiner witzigen Art hat es Gemeinsamkeiten mit der sogenannten Postmoderne der achtziger Jahre.

Fundamentally this house is only a place of pilgrimage for Gropius disciples or others with a mission, as the essential interior and exterior features of the house have been changed and disfigured. Along with the Sommerfeld Blockhaus, which has been destroyed, this is one of Gropius' most Expressionist creations. Walter Gropius of course attracted most attention as a Bauhaus architect, and earned his place in building history as such. Only the white rendering links the Otte house with the Lewin house at Fischerhüttenstrasse 106, dating from 1928. Everything else would have been frowned upon later, especially the «face» of the Otte house, with mouth, nose, ears and eyes. In its witty way is has something in common with the so-called post-Modernism of the eighties.

in der Nähe/nearby:
Siedlung Heidehof; Am Heidehof 1-54
1923-24 • Mebes & Emmerich
Wohnhäuser; Mexikoplatz
1905-10 • Otto Kuhlmann
Bahnhof Lindenthaler Allee; Mexikoplatz
1904-05 • Hart & Lesser
Haus Fiedler; Argentinische Allee 28
1911 • Felix Lindhorst
Haus Lewin; Fischerhüttenstraße 106
1928 • Walter Gropius
Haus Elly Jahn; Fürstenstraße 11
1924 • Otto Rudolf Salvisberg
Reihenhäuser; Beerenstraße 45/59
1927 • Rudolf Prömmel, Wilhelm Keller
Haus Abraham; Beerenstraße 64
1927-28 • Arthur Korn, Siegfried Weitzmann
Haus Dreike; Beerenstraße 44/46
1923 • Leo Lottermoser
Haus Wagner; Beerenstraße 36
1924-25 • Heinrich Lassen
Haus Kern; Beerenstraße 31
1927-28 • Bruno Ahrends

O 20 Haus Freudenberg
Berlin-Nikolassee; Potsdamer Chaussee 48
1907-08 • Hermann Muthesius

Das Buch des schwedischen Malers Karl Larsson »Das Haus in der Sonne« versinnbildlicht die »Freuden des Landlebens«, drückt die Stimmung jener Jahre aus. In Berlin wird der »Trend« zum Landhaus wesentlich gefördert durch die Rückkehr des Architekten Hermann Muthesius aus England, seine Schriften und seine ersten Bauten. Als Attaché in London hatte Muthesius auf Weisung des Kaisers das englische Bauwesen und besonders den Landhausbau untersucht. Seine Erfahrungen ließen ihn zum Propagandisten des Landhauses werden. Am Rande der Rehwiese in Nikolassee baute er sein eigenes Haus und das des befreundeten Hermann Freudenberg. Beide Häuser sind ungewöhnlich groß, sie gehören aber zu den besten Wohnhausbauten ihrer Zeit. Alles bringt die Hinwendung zur ländlichen Beschaulichkeit und das Verwachsen mit der Landschaft zum Ausdruck. Ebenerdig sind die unteren Räume, kein trennender Sockel, die Linie tief herabgezogener Dächer leitet zur Wiese über, die Kleinteiligkeit der Fenstersprossen nimmt die filigrane Beschaffenheit der Natur auf: Architektur als Lebensgefühl.

The book by the Swedish painter Karl Larsson called «The House in the Sun» introduces the «joys of country life» and expresses the mood of the early years of the century. In Berlin the «trend» towards country houses was greatly encouraged by the return of architect Hermann Muthesius from England, his writings and his first buildings. As attaché in London, Muthesius had, on the Kaiser's instructions, done some research into English architecture and especially the building of country houses. His experience made him a propagandist for the country house. At the edge of the Rehwiese in Nikolassee he built a house for himself and one for his friend Hermann Freudenberg. Both houses are unusually large, but are among the best residential buildings of their period. Everything about them expresses an inclination towards rural tranquility and blending with the landscape. The downstairs rooms are at ground level, there is no dividing base, the line of the roofs, which come down very low, forms a transition to the meadow, and the tiny mullions pick up the filigree quality of nature. This is architecture as joie de vivre.

in der Nähe/nearby:
Haus Muthesius; Potsdamer Chaussee 49
1906-07 • Hermann Muthesius
Haus Bondi; An der Rehwiese 13
1912 • Bruno Schmitz
Haus Bousset; Libellenstraße 15-16
1909 • Alfred Grenander
»Villa Rosenburg«; Libellenstraße 17
1902 • G. Vohl

O 21 Evangelische Kirche und Pfarrhaus
Berlin-Nikolassee; Kirchweg 19/21
1909-10 • Erich Blunck

Der dörfliche Charakter fehlt der Villenkolonie Nikolassee gänzlich. Das hinderte Blunck jedoch nicht, für das Ensemble von Kirche und Pfarrhaus ländliche Motive heranzuziehen. Ein wehrhafter Turm mit übersteigert spitzem Helm, schlichte geometrische Körper für Schiff und Chor, einfacher Putz, steile Satteldächer, Pergola und eingeschossig geducktes Pfarrhaus mit Mansarde und Dachreiter stehen für neue stilistische Absichten. Ausgelöst wohl durch den Landhausstil, der sich von 1905 an bemerkbar macht, und ähnlich der Sehnsucht nach ländlich-einfachem Leben, die zu Beginn des 19. Jahrhunderts schon einmal Kunst und auch Baukunst geprägt hat, setzen sich kurz vor dem Ersten Weltkrieg neuromantische Strömungen durch, die sich wie hier überdeutlich in einem »Heimatstil« niederschlagen. Die Baugruppe schmiegt sich an den Hang zur Rehwiese. Die innige Verbindung von Architektur und Landschaft ist Blunk bei dieser Baugruppe wie bei keinem anderen Beispiel gelungen.

The Nikolassee colony has no village character at all, but this did not prevent Blunck from using rural motifs for church and vicarage. A sturdy tower with exaggeratedly pointed spire, plain geometrical design for nave and choir, plain rendering, steep saddle roofs, pergola and low, single-storey vicarage with mansard and ridge turret show new stylistic intentions. Probably unleashed by the country house style, which began to impinge from 1905, and in tune with the longing for a simple country life, which had made its mark on architecture once before, in the early nineteenth century, neo-Romantic tendencies were successfully establishing themselves in the period immediately before the First World War; here they make their presence felt all too clearly in a «Heimatstil». The group of buildings hugs the slope to the Rehwiese. Here Blunck achieved intimate linking of architecture and landscape more successfully than in any other project.

in der Nähe/nearby:
Haus Wild; Kirchweg 25
1914 • Hermann Muthesius
»Der Mittelhof«; Kirchweg 33
1914-15 • Hermann Muthesius
Haus van Heteren; Kirchweg 57
1922 • Heinrich Straumer

O 22 Strandbad Wannsee
Berlin-Nikolassee; Strandbadweg 25
1929-30 • Martin Wagner, Richard Ermisch

Noch zur Jahrhundertwende war das Baden im Freien bei Strafe verboten. 1907 endlich stellte der Kreis Teltow am Wannsee einen 400 m langen Uferstreifen für Badelustige zur Verfügung. Die Prüderie der Zeit verfügte zwar noch zwei durch Bretterwände gesonderte Abteilungen für Damen und Herren und ein großes Umkleidezelt, aber ein Anfang war gemacht. Die zwanziger Jahre ließen das Baden in einem neuen Licht erscheinen: Soziale Aspekte galten nun mehr, Sport hatte einen hohen Stellenwert, und das alles wurde in die Förderung der Volksgesundheit einbezogen. Nun entstand eine langgestreckte Anlage aus vier zweigeschossigen Umkleidehallen mit Terrassen, davor ein überdachter Wandelgang mit Läden und allen Nebeneinrichtungen, südlich eine große Gaststätte mit Gartenbetrieb. Die Stahlskelettbauten haben nichts Provisorisches mehr, verblendet sind sie mit roten Tonplatten. Mit 1300 Metern Strandlänge für 20 000 Badegäste wurde das Strandbad Wannsee zum größten und modernsten Binnenfreibad Europas.

As late as the turn of the century bathing in the open air was prohibited by law. Finally in 1907 the district of Teltow placed a 400 m stretch of the bank of the Wannsee at the disposal of keen bathers. However, the prudishness of the period insisted on separate fenced-off sections for men and women, and a large tent for changing, but a start had been made. The twenties put bathing in a new light: social aspects were now more important, sport was highly thought of and all this came under the heading of the health of the people. A long complex was now built, with four two-storey changing rooms with terraces, a roofed walkway with shops and other facilities beneath them and to the south a large restaurant with garden service. The steel-framed buildings no longer had a provisional feel; they were clad in red earthenware slabs. With 1,300 hundred metres of beach for 20,000 bathers, Strandbad Wannsee became the largest and most modern inland open air bathing facility in Europe.

in der Nähe/nearby:
Raststätte Grunewald; Kronprinzessinnenweg 48
1966-68 • Neumann, Grötzebach & Plessow
Bahnhof Nikolassee; Hohenzollernplatz
1901-02 • Fritz Brüning, Paul Vogler
Rathaus Nikolassee; Hohenzollernplatz
1912 • Bruno Möhring
Bahnhof Wannsee; Kronprinzessinnenweg
1927-28 • Richard Brademann
Villa; Am Sandwerder 21-23
1906-07 • Friedrich Kristeller

O 23 Haus Springer
Berlin-Wannsee; Am Großen Wannsee 39/41
1901 • Alfred Messel

Der Name Alfred Messel verbindet sich eher mit Monumentalbauten wie Warenhäusern oder Museen. Seine architektonische Sprache ist bestimmt von Pfeilerfronten und sakralen Lichthöfen. Um so mehr mußte das Haus Springer überraschen, das für Berlin recht früh Elemente des englischen Landhauses aufnimmt und konsequent in vollkommener Abkehr von historisierender Stilarchitektur umsetzt. Der rauhe Natursteinsockel, die mit Schindeln verblendeten Giebel und Brüstungen, das hohe haubenartige Dach – es erinnert an den späteren Wertheim-Eckbau am Leipziger Platz – und die aufragenden Kamine lassen den Wunsch nach ländlicher Wohnlichkeit und inniger Naturverbundenheit erahnen. Die Räume sind frei um die Diele gruppiert, haben jeweils einen eigenen Charakter, wobei jedoch die gestaltende Durchbildung längst nicht mit der Perfektion späterer Jahre betrieben wird.

The name of Alfred Messel is more usually associated with monumental buildings like department stores or museums, and his architectural language is all pillared façades and ecclesiastical air wells. Thus the Springer house was all the more surprising: it takes up, at a very early stage for Berlin, elements of the English country house style and implements them consistently, turning away completely from an architecture of historical styles. A rough base in natural stone, gables and breastwork clad in shingles, the tall, hood-like roof – all this is reminiscent of the later Wertheim corner building in Leipziger Platz – and the towering chimney suggests an increasing desire for rural comfort and intimate connection with nature. The rooms are grouped freely around the hall, but each has a character of its own, although the design is not carried through with the perfection characteristic of later years.

in der Nähe/nearby:
Haus Oppenheim; Am Großen Wannsee 43/45
1908 • Alfred Messel
Haus Max Liebermann; Am Großen Wannsee 42
1909-10 • Paul Baumgarten
Haus Langenscheidt; Am Großen Wannsee 44
1901 • Bodo Ebhardt
Haus Collignon (Krankenhaus); Am Großen Wannsee 80
1923 • Bruno Paul
Haus Endell; Am Großen Wannsee 30 b
1939-40 • Hans Scharoun
Haus Jeidels (Don-Bosco-Heim); Straße zum Löwen 11
1922-23 • German Bestelmeyer
Haus Leo; Am Großen Wannsee 5
1875/80 • Kyllmann & Heyden

O 24 Dorfkirche Stolpe
Berlin-Wannsee; Wilhelmplatz
1858-59 • Friedrich August Stüler, Gärtner

Das mittelalterliche Fachwerkkirchlein, das hier stand, war schon lange baufällig, als endlich unter Einschaltung von Friedrich Wilhelm IV. eine größere, neue Kirche errichtet wurde. Weit über den Bedarf des kleinen Dorfes Stolpe hinaus setzte der König wieder einmal eine künstlerisch wertvolle Lösung durch, mußte sich aber auch mit einem Drittel an den Kosten beteiligen. Die kreuzförmige Anlage mit dem einschiffigen Langhaus und der als Turm fortgesetzten Vierung wirken wuchtig und beherrschen das Ortsbild. Das bemerkte auch Fontane und sprach von einer »pittoresken Wirkung«. Drei polygonale Apsiden erhielt der Bau, die ebenfalls die Abkehr von der romantischen Baukunst und ihren italienischen Vorbildern spüren lassen. Die gelben Ziegel und profilierten rundbogigen Fenster gehören zum Schinkelschen Rundbogenstil.

The little medieval half-timbered church that used to stand here had been in need of repair for a long time when finally Friedrich Wilhelm IV's intervention led to the building of a larger, new church. Once more the king succeeded in achieving an artistically valid solution well beyond the needs of the village, but had to take on a third of the cost. The cruciform complex with single-aisled nave and crossing tower makes a massive impression, and dominates the village. Fontane noticed this as well and spoke of a «picturesque effect». The building was provided with three polygonal apses, which also suggest a turning away from Romantic architecture and its Italian models. The yellow bricks and ribbed, round-arched windows are in the round-arched style of Schinkel.

in der Nähe/nearby:
Rathaus Wannsee; Königstraße 42
1900-01 • Otto Stahn
St. Michael-Kirche; Königstraße 43
1926-27 • Wilhelm Fahlbusch
Haus Pallat; Otto-Erich-Straße 9
1905-07 • Erich Blunck
Gemeindehaus; Schuchardtweg 5
1927-28 • Bruno Ahrends
Haus Schönberg; Bismarckstraße 30-30 a
1923-24 • Alfred Breslauer

P
Potsdam
Stadt

Am 3. Juli 993 werden die Orte Geliti (Geltow) und Poztupimi (Potsdam) erstmals urkundlich erwähnt. Kaiser Otto III. schenkte beide Orte seiner Tante, der Äbtissin Mathilde v. Quedlinburg. Eine slawische Burg befand sich gegenüber der Nuthemündung auf einer Havelinsel, die im 18. Jahrhundert durch Aufschüttung mit der Burgstraße verbunden wurde. Albrecht der Bär, seit 1134 Markgraf der Nordmark, sicherte um 1150 den Havelübergang Potsdam; die deutsche Besiedlung setzte dann Anfang des 13. Jahrhunderts ein. Im Landbuch Kaiser Karls IV. wird 1375 die landesherrliche Burg im Bereich des heutigen Alten Marktes erwähnt. Ein Brand verwüstete im Jahre 1536 die Stadt. Die Kurfürstin Katharina errichtete im Jahre 1598 innerhalb des Burgbezirkes einen Neubau. Für das spätere Gesicht Potsdams bestimmend, legte ab 1660 Kurfürst Friedrich Wilhelm nach Plan von Johann Gregor Memhardt die Residenz an. Unter König Friedrich Wilhelm I. erfolgte die Erweiterung mit zwei planmäßig angelegten Neustädten und der Ausbau zur Garnisonsstadt. Im Nordwesten errichtete ab 1744 Friedrich II. Schloß und Park Sanssouci als Sommerresidenz. Vor den Toren entstanden seit der Mitte des 18. Jahrhunderts fünf Vorstädte: Jägervorstadt, Nauener, Berliner, Teltower und Brandenburger Vorstadt. Im 17./18. Jahrhundert entwickelt sich Potsdam zur Manufakturstadt, die Fertigung umfaßte Drell und Damast, Kristallglas, Gewehre, Tabakwaren sowie Schiffe. Seit 1809 ist Potsdam selbständiger Stadtkreis und Sitz der kurmärkischen Regierung. 1838 wurde die Berlin-Potsdamer Bahn als erste Eisenbahn der Region eröffnet. Bis 1918 war Potsdam dauernde Residenz der Hohenzollern. Am 14. April 1945 – drei Wochen vor Kriegsende – zerstörte ein Bombenangriff das Zentrum der Barockstadt. Der Wiederaufbau begann 1958 und war durch industrielle Serienbauweise bestimmt. In einem städtebaulichen Wettbewerb von 1960 wurden als Dominanten im Stadtzentrum neben der Nikolaikirche die Neubauten von Theater, Kaufhaus, Stadthalle, Hotel, Hochschulbibliothek und Hochhaus ausgeschrieben.

Geliti (Geltow) and Poztupimi (Potsdam) were first documented on 3 July 993. Emperor Otto III presented both places to his aunt, Abbess Mathilde von Quedlinburg. There was a Slavic castle opposite the mouth of the Nuthe on an island in the Havel, which was connected to the Burgstrasse by the building of an embankment in the eighteenth century. Albrecht the Bear, margrave of the Nordmark from 1134, secured the Potsdam Havel crossing c. 1150, and German settlement started in the early thirteenth century. The local ruler's castle in the area of the present Alter Markt was mentioned in Emperor Charles IV's land register in 1375. The town was devastated by fire in 1536. Electress Katharina built a new castle in the precinct in 1598. Elector Friedrich Wilhelm started to lay out the residence to plans by Johann Gregor Memhardt from 1660, and this was to have a decisive effect on the later appearance of Potsdam. Further building followed under King Friedrich Wilhelm I with two new towns built to strict plans and fortification as a garrison town. Friedrich II built the palace and laid out the park at Sanssouci as a summer residence in the north-west from 1744. Five suburbs were created outside the gates from the mid eighteenth century: Jägervorstadt, Nauener, Berliner, Teltower and Brandenburger Vorstadt. In the seventeenth and eighteenth centuries Potsdam developed into a manufacturing town, with products including drill and damask, crystal glass, guns, tobacco goods and ships. Potsdam was a district in its own right and seat of local government from 1809. In 1838 the Berlin-Potsdam railway was opened, the first in the region. Potsdam was the permanent residence of the Hohenzollerns until 1918. On 14 April 1945 – three weeks before the end of the war – the centre of the baroque town was destroyed by bombing. Rebuilding began in 1958, using an industrial mass production system. Plans were invited for the Nikolaikirche as a dominant feature of the town centre, and also for new buildings for theatre, department store, city hall, hotel, university library and high-rise building as part of a municipal competition in 1960.

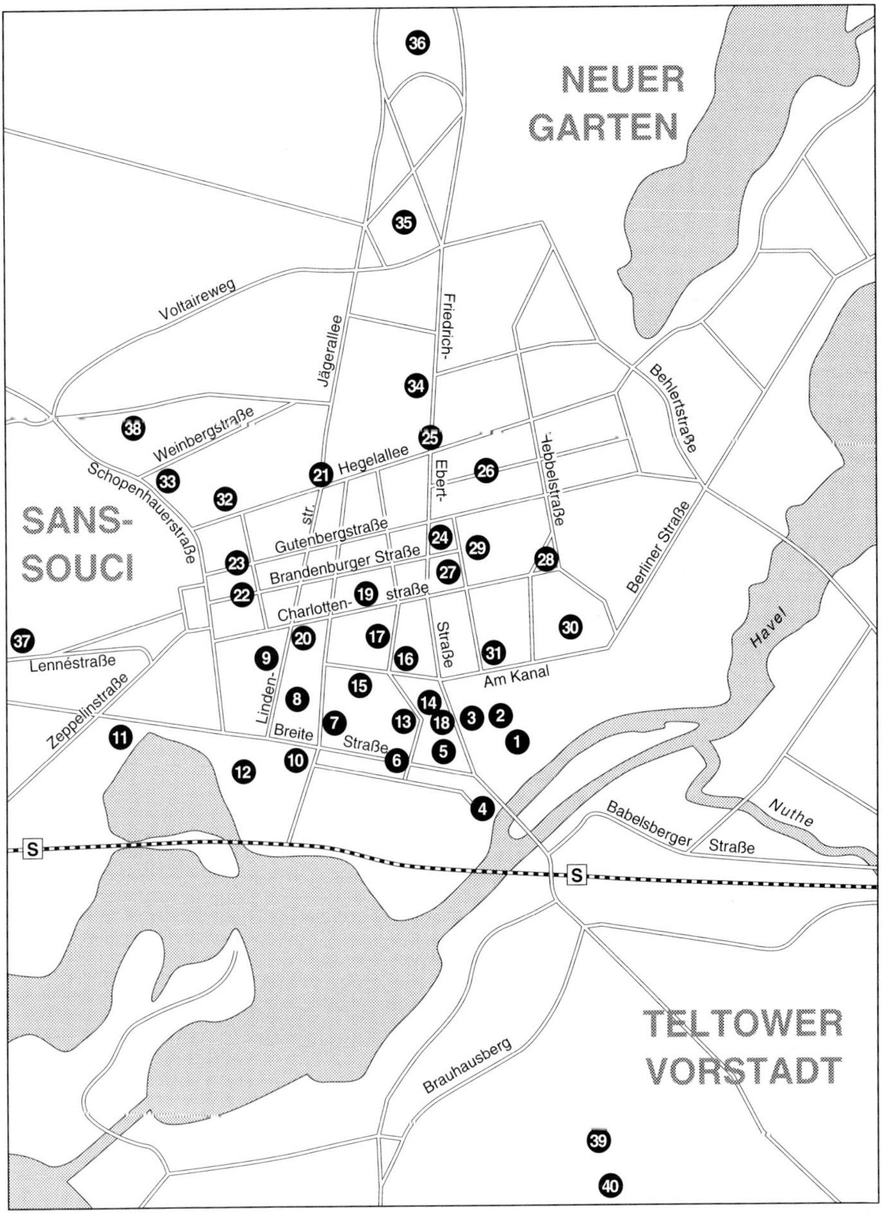

P 1 Altes Rathaus
P 2 Nikolaikirche
P 3 Institut für Lehrerbildung
P 4 Havelkolonnade des Stadtschlosses
P 5 Marstall (Filmmuseum)
P 6 Knobelsdorffhäuser
P 7 Datenverarbeitungszentrum
P 8 Militärwaisenhaus
P 9 Lazarett des Regiments Leibfußgarde
P 10 Hiller-Brandtsche Häuser
P 11 Pumpwerk
P 12 Wohnhäuser Kiezstraße
P 13 Kutschstall
P 14 Wohnhaus am Neuen Markt
P 15 Wohnhaus Brockes (Oberrechnungskammer)
P 16 Typenhaus der ersten Neustadt
P 17 Wohnhaus Wilhelm-Staab-Straße
P 18 »Acht-Ecken-Haus«
P 19 Wohnhaus Wilhelm-Pieck-Straße
P 20 Alte Wache
P 21 Jägertor
P 22 Zweite barocke Neustadt
P 23 Wohnhäuser Gutenbergstraße
P 24 Große Stadtschule
P 25 Nauener Tor
P 26 Holländisches Viertel
P 27 Wohnhäuser am Bassin
P 28 Französische Kirche
P 29 Katholische Kirche St. Peter und Paul
P 30 Schauspielerkaserne
P 31 Hauptpostamt
P 32 Werner-Alfred-Bad
P 33 Villa Arnim
P 34 Regierungsgebäude
P 35 Russische Kolonie Alexandrowka
P 36 Russische Kirche Hl. Alexander Newsky
P 37 Lordmarschallhaus
P 38 Winzerhaus auf dem Mühlenberg
P 39 Astrophysikalisches Observatorium
P 40 Einsteinturm

P 1 Altes Rathaus
Potsdam; Am Alten Markt 1-2
1753-55 • Johann Boumann, Carl Ludwig Hildebrandt

An der Stelle des mittelalterlichen Ratsgebäudes von 1536 und seinem Nachfolgebau von 1720 entstand auf Befehl König Friedrichs II. das neue Rathaus. Es war Teil der Umgestaltung des Alten Marktes zu einem repräsentativen Platz nach römischem Muster. Als Vorbild diente dem Architekten Johann Boumann ein nicht ausgeführter Entwurf des Architekten Andrea Palladio für den Palazzo Angarano in Vicenza. Die Schaufassade wird durch korinthische Dreiviertelsäulen gegliedert, die Mitte der Attika erhielt eine Wappenkartusche aus Sandstein mit dem Potsdamer Stadtwappen. Den überkuppelten Mittelturm ziert seit 1777 ein vergoldeter Atlas, als Wahrzeichen der Last, die auf den Schultern der Stadtregierung ruht. Das 1945 stark beschädigte Haus wurde erst 1963-66 wiederhergestellt, ebenso wie das benachbarte Knobelsdorffhaus. Die Lücke des zerstörten Windelbandtschen Hauses schlossen die Architekten Horst Görl und Ernst Pfrogner mit einem Neubau.

The new town hall was built on the site of the medieval council building dating from 1536 and a successor building dating from 1720, on the instructions of King Frederick II. It was part of the restructuring of the Alter Markt as an imposing square in Roman style. Architect Johann Boumann based his work on an unbuilt design for the Palazzo Angarano in Vincenza by Andrea Palladio. The main façade was articulated with Corinthian three-quarter columns, and the centre of the attica had a sandstone armorial cartouche with the town arms of Potsdam. The domed central tower has been topped with a gilded Atlas since 1777, as a symbol of the burden resting on the shoulders of the town government. The building was badly damaged in 1945, and not restored until 1963-6, along with the neighbouring building by Knobelsdorff. The gap left by the destruction of the Windelbandt building was filled in with a new design by architects Horst Görl and Ernst Pfrogner.

in der Nähe/nearby:
Knobelsdorffhaus; Am Alten Markt, Brauerstraße 10
1750 • Georg Wenzeslaus v. Knobelsdorff
Obelisk; Am Alten Markt
1753-55 • Georg Wenzeslaus v. Knobelsdorff

P 2 Nikolaikirche
Potsdam; Am Alten Markt
1830-37 • Karl Friedrich Schinkel, Ludwig Persius

Die Nikolaikirche zählt zu den bedeutendsten Bauten des Klassizismus. Ihre hohe Kuppel bestimmt die Stadtsilhouette, ähnlich wie schon die Fassade des Vorgängerbaues die Nordseite der barocken Platzanlage bestimmte. Auch hier war die architektonische Gestaltung einem römischen Vorbild gefolgt, der Kirche S. Maria Maggiore. Der Brand vom 3. September 1795 vernichtete das Hauptgebäude sowie die Platzwände der Nord- und Westseite des Alten Marktes. Zwischen 1796 und 1829 entstand für den Wiederaufbau eine Vielzahl von Entwürfen, bis Ludwig Persius 1830-37 nach einem Entwurf Schinkels den Zentralbau mit Satteldach und Portikus errichtete. Die von Schinkel geplante Kuppel nach dem Vorbild der Londoner Paulskirche wurde erst 1843-49 unter der Leitung von Friedrich August Stüler und Gustav Emil Prüfer aufgesetzt. Aus statischen Gründen erhielt der Bau an den Ecken vier Glockentürme als Verstärkung gegen den Druck der Kuppellast. Die schweren Schäden des Zweiten Weltkrieges wurden bis 1962 äußerlich beseitigt, 1974-75 wurde der Portikus versetzt, 1981 fand die feierliche Wiedereinweihung statt.

The Nicolaikirche is one of the most important buildings of the classical period. Its high dome dominates the silhouette of the town, just as the façade of its predecessor was the principal feature of the northern side of the baroque square. Here too the architect followed a Roman model: the church of Santa Maria Maggiore. The fire of 3 September 1795 destroyed the main building and the north and west sides of the Alter Markt. A number of designs for rebuilding emerged between 1796 and 1829; finally Ludwig Persius built the centrally planned church with saddleback roof and portico in 1830-7, to a design by Schinkel. The dome planned by Schinkel, modelled on St. Paul's in London, was not added until 1843-9, under the direction of Friedrich August Stüler and Gustav Emil Prüfer. The four bell towers at the corners were added as reinforcement against the thrust of the dome. Heavy damage caused in the Second World War was repaired externally until 1962, the portico was moved in 1974-5 and the building was solemnly rededicated in 1981.

in der Nähe/nearby:
Wohngebiet Zentrum-Süd; Am Kanal
1961-75 • Hans-Jürgen Kluge, Hermann Poetzsch

P 3 Institut für Lehrerbildung
Potsdam; Friedrich-Ebert-Straße 4
1971-77 • Sepp Weber, Wolfgang Merz

Der englische Luftangriff vom 14. April 1945 hatte die wertvolle Bebauung des Alten Marktes, wie das Stadtschloß, den Palast Barberini, das Rathaus und die Nikolaikirche zerstört. Auch die alte Wohnbebauung des Platzes und der angrenzenden Straßen und die Lange Brücke waren vernichtet. Bis 1961 entstand eine neue Brücke. Mit ihr ergab sich nach dem Abriß der Schloßruine eine neue innerstädtische Verkehrssituation. Gänzlich im Verständnis der Zeit erhielten breite Straßenzüge und eine großzügige Kreuzungsanlage den Vorzug vor dem städtebaulichen Erbe einer Barockstadt. Dem Diktat der »Modernen Stadt« hatten sich auch die Hochbauten zu beugen. Hochaufragende Solitäre wie das Interhotel und langgestreckte Raster- oder Bandfassaden bestimmten das Bild. So ersetzt seit 1977 das dreigeschossige Institut für Lehrerbildung als Montagebau aus industriell vorgefertigten Platten die ehemals kleinteilige Wohnbebauung, überbaut die Schwertfegerstraße mit ihrer einst berühmten Kreuzung der »Acht Ecken« und schneidet den Alten Markt von der neuen Hauptstraße ab. Durch die Gliederung in vier Kompartimente mit Innenhöfen und die Auflösung der Erdgeschoß-Ladenzone in einer Stützenreihe wurde der zaghafte Versuch einer Wahrung straßenräumlicher Maßstäblichkeit unternommen.

Fine buildings in the Alter Markt like the Stadtschloss, the Barberini Palace, the Town Hall and the Nicolaikirche were destroyed in the English air raid on 14 April 1945. Old residential building in the square and adjacent streets and the Lange Brücke were also destroyed. A new bridge was completed in 1961. This and the demolition of the ruined Schloss meant a completely new inner city traffic situation. Broad streets and a generous amount of space for the junction were given preference over the urban heritage of a baroque town, entirely within the spirit of the times. The high-rise buildings also had to bow to the requirements of the «modern town». The overall picture was dominated by towering individual buildings like the Interhotel, and extended grid or strip façades. Thus the former small units of residential accommodation were replaced by the three-storey teacher-training establishment from 1977. This is a building assembled from industrially prefabricated slabs, built over Schwertfegerstrasse with its formerly famous «Eight Corners» junction, and cutting off the Alter Markt from the Hauptstrasse. A tentative attempt at preserving street scale was made by articulation into four section with inner courtyards, and by breaking up the ground floor shop area with a series of pillars.

P 4 Havelkolonnade des Stadtschlosses
Potsdam; Breite Straße, Heinrich-v.-Treskow-Straße
1745-46 • Georg Wenzeslaus v. Knobelsdorff

Nach dem Bau des Interhotels begann nach 1969 die Gestaltung der Freiflächen bis zum Havelufer mit der Schiffsanlegestelle. Fragmente des zerstörten und 1960-61 abgetragenen Stadtschlosses wurden hier in einer Art Lapidarium aufgestellt, auch die Reste der Ringer- und Fechterkolonnaden, die fortan Havelkolonnaden hießen. Diese von Knobelsdorff herrührenden Kolonnaden aus korinthischen Sandsteinsäulen verbanden ursprünglich das Stadtschloß mit dem Marstall. Besondere Beachtung verdienen die qualitätvollen Rokokoplastiken der berühmten Potsdamer Bildhauer Friedrich Christian Glume, Georg Franz Ebenhech und Johann August Nahl. Als weitere Fragmente finden sich an: das 1751 von Johann Gottlieb Heymüller geschaffene Tympanonrelief »Friedensopfer« vom Giebel des westlichen Seitenflügels oder der »Blasende Triton« aus einer ehemaligen Brunnengruppe des Lustgartens, 1746-48 vom Potsdamer Bildhauer Johann Peter Benckert.

After the Interhotel was built a start was made in 1969 on organizing the open spaces running down to the bank of the Havel and the shipping pier. Fragments of the ruined Stadtschloss, demolished in 1960-1, were set up here in a kind of lapidarium, and also fragments of the wrestlers' and fighters' colonnades, which were then called Havel colonnades. These colonnades by Knobelsdorff consisted of sandstone columns, and originally connected the Stadtschloss with the stables. Particularly striking are the fine rococo sculptures by famous Potsdam sculptors Friedrich Christian Glume, Georg Franz Ebenhech and Johann August Nahl. Other fragments are: the tympanum relief from the gable of the west side wing «Peace Offering» by Gottlieb Heymüller, 1751, or the «Triton Blowing» from a former fountain group in the Lustgarten, 1746-8, by Potsdam sculptor Johann Peter Benckert.

in der Nähe/nearby:
Hotel Potsdam; Heinrich-v.-Treskow-Straße
1967-69 • Sepp Weber, Helmut Töpfer, Herbert Gödicke
Karl-Liebknecht-Forum; Breite Straße
1979-81 • Michael Kranz, Walter Funcke, Barbara Schwabe
Freundschaftsinsel; zwischen Alter und Neuer Fahrt
1935-36 • Hermann Mattern (Umgestaltung 1964-65)
Scheibenwohnhaus; Albert-Klink-Straße 19-22
1970-71 • Dietrich Schreiner

P 5 Marstall (Filmmuseum)
Potsdam; Schloßstraße 15
1685 • Johann Arnold Nering

Der Marstall ist heute das älteste Baudenkmal der Stadt. Der langgestreckte Putzbau wurde 1685 von Nering als Orangerie erbaut. Auf seiner Nordseite ist das ursprüngliche Gartenportal von 1679-82 erhalten, als dessen Architekt Johann Gregor Memhardt gilt. 1746 wurde das ehemalige Orangeriegebäude unter der Leitung des Baumeisters Andreas Ludwig Krüger nach einem Entwurf von Knobelsdorff zum Marstall umgebaut, nachdem es schon seit 1714 als solcher diente. Der alte Trakt wurde nach Westen verlängert und das obere Halbgeschoß ausgebaut. Die nur zehn Meter breiten westlichen und östlichen Stirnseiten erhielten je einen Mittelrisalit mit skulpturengeschmückter Attika. Die Südfront ist dagegen über 130 Meter lang. Sie gliedern zwei Risalite, deren Attika bewegte Pferde- und Reitergruppen aus Sandstein schmücken und auf die Nutzung des Gebäudes hinweisen. Geschaffen hat die wertvollen Plastiken Friedrich Christian Glume. 1977-80 wurde der Marstall durch die Polnischen Staatlichen Werkstätten für Denkmalpflege baulich wiederhergestellt. Nach dem Umbau der Innenräume durch den polnischen Architekten Zdzislaw Hejger dient er seit 1982 als Filmmuseum mit 750 Quadratmetern Ausstellungsfläche, Kinosaal und Café.

The royal stables are now the oldest monumental building in the town. The long rendered building was originally built by Nering as an orangery in 1685. The original garden portal dating from 1679-82 has survived on the northern side, said to have been designed by Johann Gregor Memhardt. The former orangery was rebuilt as a stables under the direction of architect Andreas Ludwig Krüger to a design by Knobelsdorff in 1746, having been used as such since 1714. The old building was extended to the west and the upper half-storey completed. The east and west ends were only ten metres wide, and each was given a central projection with attica decorated with sculpture. The south façade on the other hand is over 130 metres long. It is articulated with two projections with atticas decorated with lively sandstone figures of horses and riders, indicating the function of the building. The fine sculpture is the work of Friedrich Christian Glume. In 1977-80 the fabric of the stables was restored by the Polish State Department of Ancient Monuments. The interior was rebuilt by Polish architect Zdzislaw Hejger, and has been used as a film museum since 1982, with 750 square metres of exhibition space, cinema and café.

in der Nähe/nearby:
Wohnhaus; Schloßstraße 9 a-11, Am Neuen Markt 10-11
1752 • Georg Wenzeslaus v. Knobelsdorff

P 6 Knobelsdorffhäuser
Potsdam; Schloßstraße 13-14
1748 • Georg Wenzeslaus v. Knobelsdorff

Die beiden wohlproportionierten Bürgerhäuser an der Ecke Schloßstraße und Breite Straße entstanden 1748 als Pendantbauten und flankierten torartig den Eingang zur einstigen Prachtstraße der Stadt am Westrand des Lustgartens. Sie zählen, wie der Chronist Heinrich Ludwig Manger 1789 berichtete, zu den drei erstmals auf königliche Kosten gebauten Bürgerhäusern. »Beide hatten nicht so gar hohe Stockwerke, wie man an denen in folgenden Jahren erbaueten bemerket. Doch hatten sie wie jene über dem Hauptgesims Attiken und zwischen diesen und dem Dach hölzerne mit Bley ausgeschlagene Rinnen, welche den Einwohnern in der Folge sehr lästig fielen...« Manger verweist hier auf die Disproportionen der Potsdamer Bürgerhäuser mit ihren Palastfassaden. Bei der Umgestaltung der Breiten Straße zur sozialistischen Magistrale ab 1975 wurden die noch vorhandenen Altbauten »aufgewertet und ihre neue gesellschaftliche Nutzung geplant«. So restaurierte man die Bürgerhäuser äußerlich und baute ihr Inneres modernisierend um für ein Jugendklubhaus und einen Klub für Künstler und Architekten.

The two well-proportioned town houses at the corner of Schlosstrasse and Breite Strasse date from 1748. They were built as a pair to form a gate-like beginning to the town's former show street at the western edge of the Lustgarten. As chronicler Heinrich Ludwig Manger reported in 1789, these two and one other were town houses built at the king's expense for the first time. «Both had storeys that were not so high, unlike the ones in houses built in subsequent years. But like those they had attic storeys, and between these and the roof, wooden gutters lined with lead, which were a source of great annoyance to the residents...» Here Manger is referring to the poor proportions of Potsdam town houses with their palace façades. When Breite Strasse was redesigned as a principal socialist thoroughfare from 1975 the existing old buildings were «enhanced and their new social use planned». So the exteriors of the town houses were restored and the interiors rebuilt in modern style as a youth club and a club for artists and architects.

in der Nähe/nearby:
Garnisonschule; Bauhofstraße 11
1722, 1787
Predigerhaus; Bauhofstraße 12
1777 • Georg Christian Unger
Kommandantur; Bauhofstraße 13
1752 • Georg Wenzeslaus v. Knobelsdorff
Lustgartenmauer; Schloßstraße
1745 • Georg Wenzeslaus v. Knobelsdorff

P 7 Datenverarbeitungszentrum
Potsdam; Dortustraße 46
1969-71 • Sepp Weber

Auf dem Grundstück der zerstörten und 1968 abgetragenen Garnisonkirche, deren 90 Meter hoher schlanker Turm einst das Wahrzeichen der Stadt war, steht heute das Bürogebäude des Rechenzentrums. Der viergeschossige Hauptbau wurde in der üblichen Montagebauweise errichtet. Ein monumentales Mosaikband von Fritz Eisel umzieht den Baukörper, dessen fortschrittsgläubiges Thema ist »Der Mensch bezwingt den Kosmos«. Bescheidener erklang einst von der Barockkirche seit Ende des 18. Jahrhunderts das berühmte Glockenspiel des Holländers Albert de Graave mit »Lobe den Herren« und im halbstündigen Wechsel »Üb' immer Treu und Redlichkeit«.

The computer centre office building now stands on the site of the ruined Garnisonkirche, demolished in 1968: its slender tower, 90 metres high, was once the symbol of the town. The four-storey main building was built in the way customary at the time, using prefabricated materials. A monumental mosaic strip by Fritz Eisel runs round the building. It is built around the theme of «Man Conquers the Cosmos», showing a grandiose faith in the future. The famous glockenspiel by Dutchman Albert de Graave used to sound a rather more modest note from the baroque church from the late eighteenth century as it played tunes like «Praise to the Lord», and, alternating every half hour, «Always show faith and honesty».

in der Nähe/nearby:
Rechnungshof; Dortusstraße 30/34
1907
Oberrechnungskammer; Yorckstraße 19-20
1776 • Karl v. Gontard
Langer Stall (Kopfbau); Werner-Seelenbinder-Straße 7
1781 Georg Christian Unger

P 8 Militärwaisenhaus
Potsdam; Dortustraße 36
1771-78 • Karl v. Gontard

Das Große Militärwaisenhaus gilt als bedeutendes Bauwerk der Barockzeit. Gontard verwendete im Westflügel Teile eines Vorgängerbaues von 1724. Die ausgedehnte viergeschossige Vierflügelanlage – neben dem Schloß damals größter Bau Potsdams – läßt das Ausmaß des durch die Schlesischen Kriege ausgelösten Elends erahnen. Architektonisch am wirkungsvollsten ist der Flügel an der Lindenstraße. Skulpturen schmücken den Mittelrisalit, eine Inschrift nennt das Jahr 1773. Das Giebelrelief stammt von Rudolf Kaplunger. 1945 zerstört und danach nicht mehr aufgebaut wurde das den Mittelrisalit bekrönende Belvedere. Im Mittelbau befindet sich ein originelles Treppenhaus, das aus drei übereinandergestellten Kuppelräumen besteht, die Läufe der Treppen führen spiralförmig um die Lichtöffnungen dieser Kuppelräume.

The great military orphanage is considered an important work of baroque architecture. Karl von Gontard incorporated parts of an earlier building dating from 1724 into the west wing. The extensive four-storey building with four wings – along with the Schloss the largest building in Potsdam at the time – is an indication of the misery caused by the Silesian War. The most effective architecture is seen in the wing in Lindenstrasse. The central projection is decorated with sculpture, and an inscription names the year as 1773. The gable relief is the work of Rudolf Kaplunger. The belvedere that was formerly on top of the central projection was destroyed in 1945, and has not been restored. The central section contains an unusual staircase consisting of three domed spaces one above the other, with the stairs running in spirals around the openings that let light into the domes.

in der Nähe/nearby:
Landschaftshaus; Breite Straße 9
1724 • Peter v. Gayette
Ständehaus (Museum); Breite Straße 11
1770 • Georg Christian Unger
Obelisk vom Neustädter Tor; Breite Straße
1753 • Georg Wenzeslaus v. Knobelsdorff

P 9 Lazarett des Regiments Leibfußgarde
Potsdam; Lindenstraße 25
1772 • Georg Christian Unger

Auf Befehl König Friedrichs II. errichtete der aus Bayreuth stammende Georg Christian Unger in der Nähe der Hauptwache ein neues steinernes Lazarettgebäude von drei Geschossen. Es ersetzte ein Fachwerkgebäude aus der Zeit des Soldatenkönigs, das als Lazarett für dessen Leibgarde gedient hatte. Im Neubau befand sich auch die Wohnung des Regimentsfeldschers, des Militärsanitäters. Seitlich des übergiebelten Mittelrisalits befinden sich zwei bezeichnende Sandsteingruppen, eine mit Klistierspritze und die andere mit Arzeneiglas, Arbeiten des Bildhauers Philipp Gottfried Jenner, die den kranken Gardisten wohl eher abschrecken als einladen sollten. Das Militärarztwesen hatte während des Siebenjährigen Krieges immer mehr an Bedeutung gewonnen. Die vernichtende Niederlage des preußischen Heeres am 12. August 1759 in der Schlacht bei Kunersdorf forderte allein 19 000 Tote und Verwundete, unter ihnen auch der Dichter und Offizier Ewald Christian v. Kleist.

Georg Christian Unger, an architect from Bayreuth, built a new three-storey military hospital in stone near the Hauptwache on the orders of King Frederick II. It replaced a half-timbered building from the time of the Soldier King that had been used as a military hospital for his bodyguard. The regimental medical orderly was also provided with accommodation in the new building. On either side of the pedimented central projection are two sandstone groups that help to identify the building, one holding an enema and the other a medicine glass. These are the work of sculptor Philipp Gottfried Jenner, and were probably more likely to alarm sick guards than to entice them in. Military medicine had become increasingly important in the course of the Seven Years' War. The Prussian Army's devastating defeat at the Battle of Kunersdorf on 12 August 1759 alone yielded 19,000 dead and wounded, including Ewald Christian von Kleist, poet and officer.

in der Nähe/nearby:
Kaserne des Regiments Prinz Heinrich; Lindenstraße 35-39
1764-65 • Heinrich Ludwig Manger
Kaserne für beweibte Grenadiere; Lindenstraße 28-29
1753 • Johann Boumann
Infanteriekaserne; Schopenhauerstraße 2/4
1754 • Johann Boumann
Kaserne des Regiments Prinz v. Preußen; Kleine Gasse 1/3
1773 • Georg Christian Unger

P 10 Hiller-Brandtsche Häuser
Potsdam; Breite Straße 26-27
1769 • Georg Christian Unger

Der Architekt Georg Christian Unger erhielt 1769 von König Friedrich II. den Auftrag, in der Breiten Straße, der Prachtstraße der Stadt, ein repräsentatives Bürgerhaus mit einer Palastfassade zu errichten. Zur Vorgabe machte der königliche Bauherr einen Fassadenentwurf für Schloß Whitehall in London, den Inigo Jones im Jahre 1619 erarbeitet hatte. Unger veränderte die Proportionen und paßte sie der städtebaulichen Situation in Potsdam an. Das Doppelhaus wurde für den Kaufmann Johann Friedrich Hiller und den Schneider Johann Gerhard Brandt gebaut. Die beiden Wohntrakte bilden dreigeschossige Eckbauten, dazwischen liegt ein niedrigerer Verbindungsbau als Kasernentrakt für die Einquartierung. Die Hausgruppe ist heute einziges Potsdamer Beispiel des palladianischen Klassizismus, auffallend seine üppige plastische Gliederung und die mythologischen Figuren aus der römischen Antike auf der Dachbalustrade. Gesichert ist inzwischen die Originalfarbgebung als roter Putz mit weißen Fugen, ockergelbe Ädikulapilaster und schwarze Blindfenster mit weißen Sprossen.

In 1769 architect Georg Christian Unger was commissioned by King Frederick II to build an imposing town house with a palace façade in Breite Strasse, the town's ceremonial thoroughfare. The royal architect based himself on a façade design dating from 1619 by Inigo Jones for Whitehall Palace in London. Unger altered the proportions and adapted them to the urban situation of Potsdam. The pair of houses were built for merchant Johann Friedrich Hiller and tailor Johann Gerhard Brandt. The two residential sections are in three-storey corner buildings, and between then is a lower connecting building as a barracks section for billetting. This building is now the only example of Palladian classicism in Potsdam, with strikingly lavish three-dimensional articulation and mythological figures from Roman antiquity on the roof balustrade. It has been established that the original colour scheme was red plaster with white joints, yellow ochre aedicule pilasters and black blind windows with white bars.

in der Nähe/nearby:
Predigerwitwenhaus; Breite Straße 25
1826-27 • Carl Wilhelm Redtel
Punkthäuser; Wall am Kiez
1980 • Dietrich Schreiner, Hans-Joachim Engmann
Café Seerose; Breite Straße
1983 • Diether Athing

P 11 Pumpwerk
Potsdam; Zeppelinstraße 176
1841-42 • Ludwig Persius

Einem profanen Maschinenhaus die Form einer orientalischen Moschee zu geben, sie mit der Vielfalt maurischer Ornamentik und Polychromie auszustatten, um gleichzeitig noch mit diesem bunten Akzent die Landschaft zu bereichern, das macht den besonderen Reiz dieses für nordische Verhältnisse wohl einzigartigen Bauwerks aus. Die vergoldeten Spitzen von Minarett und Kuppel spiegeln sich im trüben Wasser der Havel. Die mehrfarbigen Fassaden sind mit Bändern glasierter Ziegel durchzogen. Die weißen Steine wurden mit Ölfarbe mehrfach gestrichen und mit heißem Ölfirnis überzogen – so ist es den Tagebuchaufzeichnungen des Rudolf Wilhelm Gottgetreu zu entnehmen. Die Technik der einheimischen Ziegelfabrikation stand erst an ihrem Anfang. Bis 1972 war die Schönheit der Moschee hinter Häusern verborgen, die dann dem Durchbruch der Breiten Straße weichen mußten. Die 1841 von der Berliner Firma Borsig angefertigte Dampfmaschine wurde 1985 umfassend restauriert und seitdem von einem Elektromotor zu Schauzwecken in Bewegung gesetzt. Sie ist ein technisches Denkmal aus der Frühzeit deutschen Maschinenbaus.

The notion of building a secular machine house in the form of an oriental mosque, and decorating it with all the trappings of Moorish ornament and colour, in order at the same time to enhance the area with this decorative accent, is the special charm of this building, which is probably unique in the world of northern Europe. The gilded tips of minaret and dome are reflected in the murky waters of the Havel. The multi-coloured façades are lined with bands of glazed brick. The white stones were painted with several coats of oil paint and covered with hot oil varnish – as we discover from entries in Rudolf Wilhelm Gottgetreu's diary. Local brick-making technology was in its infancy. Until 1972 the beauties of the mosque were hidden behind other buildings, but these were demolished when way was made for Breite Strasse. The steam engine built by the Berlin firm of Borsig in 1841 was thoroughly restored in 1985 and has since then been run by an electric motor for demonstration purposes. It is a technical monument from the early days of German mechanical engineering.

P 12 Wohnhäuser
Potsdam; Kiezstraße 1-20
1777-88 • Georg Christian Unger, Johann Rudolf Heinrich Richter

Mit dem Bau der askanischen Burg entstand um 1220 eine slawische Dienstsiedlung, und im Jahre 1349 wird der »Kytz zu Postamp« erstmals erwähnt. Bis zur Einbeziehung in die Stadterweiterung der ersten Neustadt 1721 war der Kiez eine selbständige Fischersiedlung mit einem eigenen Lehnschulzen. Die bescheidenen Häuser deckte zum großen Teil Stroh. Im Zuge des Ausbaus der ersten barocken Neustadt wurde der Anger begradigt, den 200 Meter langen Straßenzug säumten nun Kastanien und Linden, 1777 folgten die Häuser. Sie bilden mit ihren ausgewogenen Maßen und der sparsamen Rokoko-Ornamentik eine geschlossene Bebauung der Straßenwände. Das Haus der Freimaurerloge Minerva erhielt 1844-45 einen Neubau von Ludwig Persius, heute ist es Gemeindehaus der ehemaligen Garnisonkirche »Zum Heiligen Kreuz«.

When the Ascanian castle was built a Slavic service settlement grew up c. 1220, and the «Kytz zu Postamp» was first mentioned in 1349. Until is was made part of the extended town at the time of the first new town in 1721, the Kiez was an independent fishing settlement with its own governing official. The modest houses were largely roofed with straw. When the first baroque new town was being built the village green was straightened, and the 200 metres run of street lined with chestnuts and limes; the houses were built in 1777. Their balanced proportions and sparse rococo ornament make them a self-contained section of the street. The Minerva lodge of Freemasons acquired a new building by Ludwig Persius in 1844-5, and this is now the parish house of the former garrison church «Zum Heiligen Kreuz».

in der Nähe/nearby:
Villa mit Belvedere; Zeppelinstraße 172
1850 • Ferdinand v. Arnim
Erlöserkirche; Meistersingerstraße 19
1896-98 • Gotthilf Ludwig Möckel
Wohnsiedlung; Schillerplatz
1935-36 • G. Fritsch
Bahnhof Potsdam-West; Stiftstraße
1909 • Ernst Schwartz
Proviantamt; Zeppelinstraße 136
1841-42 • Ludwig Persius
Villa Ingenheim; Zeppelinstraße 126-127
Um 1830
Siedlung Stadtheide; Zeppelinstraße, Im Bogen
1919-22 • Sepp Kaiser
Sanssoucitor; Hegemeisterweg
1841-42 • Ludwig Persius
Wildmeisterei; Hegemeisterweg
1841-42 • Ludwig Persius
Bayerisches Haus; Schäfereiberg
1847 • Ludwig Ferdinand Hesse

P 13 Kutschstall
Potsdam; Am Neuen Markt 9
1787-91 • Andreas Ludwig Krüger

Wo zur Zeit des Großen Kurfürsten noch ein Baumgarten stand und 1671 ein flacher Stallbau Kutschen und Kutschpferden Schutz bot, ließ Friedrich Wilhelm II. durch Krüger ein solides Gebäude errichten, das der Residenzstadt würdig war. Die frühklassizistische Fassade zeigt eine straffe toskanische Ordnung, im Kontrast dazu steht der mächtige triumphbogenartige Portalrisalit. Eine bewegte Figurengruppe stellt Friedrichs II. Leibkutscher Pfundt dar, der mit Dreispitz auf dem Kopf in der Haltung des Sonnengottes Helios den vierspännigen Phätonwagen lenkt. So spielt die Plastik in der Symbolik von Aufgang und Untergang der Sonne auf die Vergänglichkeit des Lebens und in dem fast heiteren persönlichen Bezug auf das Ende des friderizianischen Zeitalters an. Seitlich des Gespannes sind Stalldiener in zeitgenössischer Tracht und mit Zöpfen wiedergegeben, die Sättel und Zaumzeug reinigen. Die Arbeiten stammen von Johann Christoph und Michael Christoph Wohler sowie Johannes Eckstein. Von überraschender Wirkung sind auch die Innenräume, die mit massigen Gewölben an römische Thermen und Markthallen erinnern.

Friedrich Wilhelm II had Krüger put up a solid building worthy of a residence on a site where at the time of the Great Elector there had been a garden with trees, and where in 1671 coaches and horses were still sheltered only by a low stable building. The early classical façade shows strict Tuscan organization, with a massive portal section, like a triumphal arch, contrasting with it. A lively set of sculptures shows Fredrick II's personal coachman Pfundt driving the sun-god Helios' four-horse chariot, his tricorn hat on his head. Thus the sculpture alludes symbolically, through the rising and setting of the sun, to the transitory nature of life, and almost playfully to the end of the age of Frederick the Great. On either side of the equipage are pigtailed stable boys in contemporary costume, cleaning saddles and bridles. The sculpture is by Johann Christoph and Michael Christoph Wohler with Johannes Eckstein. The interiors are also somewhat surprising, with massive vaults reminiscent of Roman baths and markets.

in der Nähe/nearby:
Ratswaage; Neuer Markt 12
1836 • Christian Heinrich Ziller

P 14 Wohnhaus
Potsdam; Am Neuen Markt 1-2
1753 • Friedrich Wilhelm Dietrichs

Im Jahre 1670 entstand ein quadratischer Platz nach holländischem Vorbild, der von 1740 an als Neuer Markt bezeichnet wird, auch wenn auf ihm nie Markt gehalten wurde. Seit 1735 war in einem Fachwerkhaus in der Platzmitte die königliche Waage untergebracht, 1836 erhielt sie einen Neubau. Auch die den Platz umstehenden Häuser wurden teils durch Neubauten ersetzt wie das alte Haus des Predigers Krumbholz. Aus dem Jahre 1753 stammt der repräsentative Neubau an der Ecke zur Schloßstraße; den Entwurf lieferte vermutlich Dietrichs. Die symmetrische Fassade betont die Mittelachse durch einen von Hermenpilastern getragenen Balkon sowie ein großes Rundbogenfenster mit Oberlicht und atmet den Geist barocker Architektur. Dem Haus war eine wechselvolle Geschichte beschieden. Von 1765 bis 1786 wohnte hier Kronprinz Friedrich Wilhelm, der spätere König Friedrich Wilhelm II. Bis 1806 befand sich im Gebäude die preußische Ingenieurakademie, ab 1833 wird es königliches Kabinettshaus. Hier soll auch am 22. Juni 1767 Wilhelm v. Humboldt, der berühmte preußische Gelehrte und Staatsmann, geboren sein.

In 1670 a square was built on a Dutch model, called the Neuer Markt from 1740, although a market was never held there. The royal weights and measures department was housed in a half-timbered building in the middle of the square from 1735, and this was rehoused in 1836. Some of the buildings around the square were also replaced, including the house of preacher Krumbholz. The imposing new building on the Schlosstrasse corner dates from 1753; it is thought to have been designed by Dietrichs. The central axis of the main façade is marked with a balcony borne by herm pilasters and a large round-arched window with upper light, all imbued with the spirit of baroque architecture. The house had a chequered history. Crown Prince Friedrich Wilhelm, later King Friedrich Wilhelm II, lived here from 1765 to 1786. Until 1806 it housed the Prussian engineering academy, and from 1833 the royal collections. It is said that Wilhelm von Humboldt, the famous Prussian scholar and statesman, was born here on 22 June 1767.

in der Nähe/nearby:
Doppelhaus; Am Neuen Markt 3
1773 • Georg Christian Unger
Wohnhäuser; Am Neuen Markt 6-8
1773 • Georg Christian Unger

P 15 Wohnhaus Brockes (Oberrechnungskammer)
Potsdam; Yorckstraße 19-20
1776 • Karl v. Gontard

Die Yorckstraße – einst Straße Am Kanal – war im 18. Jahrhundert die vornehmste Straße der Stadt und die bevorzugte Wohngegend für Minister und hohe Beamte. Der ehemalige Stadtkanal war 1673 anstelle des alten Stadtgrabens in der Art holländischer Grachten ausgebaut worden, seit 1965 ist er zugeschüttet. Das Haus des Glasschleifers Brockes zählt zu den schönsten Potsdamer Barockhäusern. Es war für den Bauplatz zwischen Nauener Brücke und Waisenbrücke bereits seit 1770 geplant, aber erst 1776 wurde es unter der Leitung des Baukondukteurs Titel nach dem Entwurf Karl v. Gontards errichtet. Der dreigeschossige Bau ist durch Mittel- und Eckrisalite gegliedert, eine Attika schließt die Front nach oben ab. Am Giebel des Mittelrisalits verweisen zwei Puttengruppen mit Retorten, Attributen des Glasmachens, auf den Beruf des Besitzers.

Yorckstrasse – formerly Strasse am Kanal – was the smartest street in the town in the eighteenth century, and the preferred residential area for ministers and high-grade civil servants. The former Stadtkanal had been laid out in the manner of a Dutch gracht in 1673, to replace the old town moat; the canal was filled in in 1965. Glasscutter Brockes' house is one of the finest baroque buildings in Potsdam. It was planned for the site between Nauener Brücke and Waisenbrücke as early as 1770, but was not built until 1776, under Baukondukteur Titel, to a design by Karl von Gontard. The three-storey building has central and corner projections, with an attica on the façade side. The owner's profession is indicated by two groups of putti with retorts, the attributes of glass-making, on the pediment of the central projection.

in der Nähe/nearby:
Happe-Röhrichtsche Häuser; Yorckstraße 3-4
1822-23 • Karl Friedrich Schinkel, Christian Heinrich Ziller
Max-Dortu-Oberschule; Dortustraße 28-29
1771 • Georg Christian Unger

P 16 Typenhaus der ersten Neustadt
Potsdam; Yorckstraße 5
1722-28 • Peter v. Gayette

Nördlich des Alten Marktes erstreckte sich im 18. Jahrhundert bis zum Ufer des Heiligen Sees sumpfiges Gebiet, das zum Teil durch den Stadtgraben entwässert wurde. 1673 hatte der Ausbau des Stadtkanals begonnen, er zog sich bis etwa 1720 hin. Im Memhardtschen Stadtplan fällt sein gerader, regelmäßiger Verlauf ins Auge. Auf der Nordseite des Kanals, der bislang die Stadtgrenze bildete, wurde die erste barocke Neustadt angelegt. Die 45 Meter breite Straße Am Kanal erhielt vornehme barocke Häuser, nach einheitlichem Plan als Typenbauten errichtet. Die zweigeschossigen Bürgerhäuser zeigen in der Front sieben Fensterachsen bei einer ansehnlichen Stockwerkshöhe von 4,50 Metern. Die in offener Bauweise mit Mansartdächern versehenen Häuser variieren nur in der Breite und in der Gliederung mit Lisenen. Zwischen zwei benachbarte Häuser schiebt sich jeweils ein kleineres vom gleichen Bautyp zur Unterbringung von Soldaten. Freitreppen mit schmiedeeisernen Geländern vervollständigen den vornehmen Eindruck. Einige Gruppen dieser Typenhäuser sind in der Yorckstraße 5, 6 und 7 sowie in der Straße Am Kanal 4, 4a und 7 erhalten.

In the eighteenth century a marshy area partially drained by the town moat extended from north of the Alter Markt to the bank of the Heiliger See. Construction of the Stadtkanal started in 1673, and continued until about 1720. Its straight, regular course is a striking feature of Memhardt's town plan. The first baroque new town was built on the north side of the canal, which had hitherto marked the town boundary. The Strasse am Kanal was 45 metres wide, and lined with elegant baroque houses, built to a uniform plan as model buildings. The two-storey town houses have seven window axes on the façade side, with each storey an impressive 4.5 metres high. The detached houses have mansard roofs and vary only in their width and pilaster strip articulation. Adjacent houses are separated by a smaller one on the same model to accommodate soldiers. The elegant impression is completed by flights of steps with wrought-iron banisters. Some groups of these model houses have survived at Yorckstrasse 5, 6 and 7, and at Strasse am Kanal 4, 4a and 7.

P 17 Wohnhaus
Potsdam; Wilhelm-Staab-Straße 7-8
1956-57

Im Zuge des Ausbaus der ersten barocken Neustadt entstand die 200 Meter lange Kleine Jägerstraße mit ihren zweigeschossigen Fachwerkhäusern. Friedrich II. verlieh dem Straßenzug ein repräsentatives Aussehen, indem er zwischen 1771 und 1785 insgesamt 23 Häuser durch die Architekten Karl v. Gontard, Georg Christian Unger und Andreas Ludwig Krüger auf königliche Kosten neu erbauen ließ. Der Historiograph Hans Kania schrieb über die Straße: »... für den Kenner einer der Glanzpunkte des friderizianischen Potsdam, sie ist reich und schwer an kulturhistorischen Erinnerungen und künstlerischen Werten.« Im Haus Nr. 9 wohnte der Kunsttischler Johann Melchior Kambly, im Haus Nr. 8 wurde der Physiker Hermann v. Helmholtz geboren, und im Hause Nr. 10-11 war der junge Bismarck Gast bei seiner Großmutter. Im Zweiten Weltkrieg gingen die Häuser unter, von einigen waren nur noch die Umfassungsmauern erhalten. Bis 1957 wurde das barocke Stadtbild nach denkmalpflegerischen Gesichtspunkten wiederhergestellt. Die Häuser Nr. 7 und 8 ersetzte dabei ein moderner Neubau mit barocken Fassadenelementen – ein herausragendes Beispiel für eine qualitätvolle Bauleistung der fünfziger Jahre.

The 200 metre long Kleine Jägerstrasse with its two-storey half-timbered houses came into being with the first baroque new town. Frederick II made the street look more imposing by rebuilding a total of 23 houses at his own expense between 1771 and 1785, designed by architects Karl von Gontard, Georg Christian Unger and Andreas Ludwig Krüger. On the subject of this street historiographer Hans Kania wrote: «... for the connoisseur this is one of the gems of Frederick's Potsdam, lavish and rich in cultural memories and artistic value.» Engraver Johann Melchior Kambly lived at no. 9, physicist Hermann von Helmholtz was born at no. 8, and the young Bismarck visited his grandmother at no. 10-11. The houses were destroyed in the Second World War, with only the outer walls of some left standing. By 1957 the baroque townscape had been restored on historical principles. In the course of this nos. 7 and 8 were replaced by a modern building with baroque elements in the façade – an outstanding example of building achievement in the fifties.

in der Nähe/nearby:
Wohnhaus; Wilhelm-Staab-Straße 6
1771 • Karl v. Gontard
Wohnhaus Mencken; Wilhelm-Staab-Straße 11-12
1777 • Georg Christian Unger
Wohnhaus; Wilhelm-Staab-Straße 19
1785 • Andreas Ludwig Krüger
Wohnhaus; Kupferschmiedgasse 4
1784 • Andreas Ludwig Krüger
Wohnhaus; Kupferschmiedgasse 8
1783 • Georg Christian Unger

P 18 »Acht-Ecken-Haus«
Potsdam; Friedrich-Ebert-Straße 122
1771 • Karl v. Gontard

Die Kreuzung der Schwertfegerstraße mit dem Hohen Weg, der 1950 zugunsten der verbreiterten Friedrich-Ebert-Straße aufgelassen wurde, war einst Glanzstück der Rokoko-Stadtbaukunst. Über die »Vier Häuser an den Ecken« schrieb Heinrich Ludwig Manger 1789 in seiner Potsdamer Baugeschichte: »... diese wurden nischenartig eingebogen, damit der Platz, den diese Kreuzwege formierten, etwas geräumiger wurde.« Aus vier wurden so acht Ecken. Drei der vier Eckhäuser sind den Kriegszerstörungen zum Opfer gefallen. Nur eines blieb erhalten und wurde bis 1956 restauriert. Die Beletagen besaßen in den Ecknischen jeweils einen Balkon mit schönen geschmiedeten Gittern. Zwei der Balkone ruhten auf skulpierten Konsolen, die anderen auf Schilden, Bildhauerarbeiten stammen von Martin Angermann. Besitzer der vier Häuser waren der italienische Kaufmann Boseri, der Glasschleifer Brocks, der Schwertfeger Zeunert und der Zimmermann Brendel.

The junction of Schwertfegerstrasse and Hoher Weg was left open in 1950 for the sake of the widened Friedrich-Ebert-Strasse. It was once a gem of rococo urban architecture. In 1789 Ludwig Manger wrote in his history of building in Potsdam on the subject of the «four houses on the corners»: «... these were indented like niches, so that the square formed by this crossroads became a little more spacious.» Thus the four corners became eight. Three of the four corner houses fell victim to the war. Only one survived, and this was restored, with completion in 1956. The bel-étage in each niche had a balcony with beautiful wrought-iron railings. Two of the balconies were supported by sculpted corbels, the others by shields, sculpture by Martin Angermann. The four buildings were owned by Boseri, an Italian merchant, glass-cutter Brockes, armourer Zeunert and carpenter Brendel.

in der Nähe/nearby:
Wohnhaus; Friedrich-Ebert-Straße 120-121
1770 • Karl v. Gontard
Wohnhochhaus; Friedrich-Ebert-Straße 115
1969 • Dietrich Schreiner

P 19 Wohnhaus
Potsdam; Charlottenstraße 102-103
1783 • Georg Christian Unger

Im Jahre 1722 war hier die Grenze der ersten barocken Neustadt. Die Häuser Nr. 16-55 führten die Bezeichnung »Hinter der Mauer«. Ab 1732 wurde dann die Akzisemauer beseitigt und die Stadt nach Norden erweitert. Nach dem Siebenjährigen Krieg war die Pflugstraße mit ihren 128 Häusern die längste Straße innerhalb der Stadt. Ab 1777 ließ Friedrich II. die Bebauung aus der Zeit des Soldatenkönigs durch repräsentative Neubauten ersetzen. Baumeister waren Karl v. Gontard, Georg Christian Unger, Andreas Ludwig Krüger, Johann Christian Valentin Schulze und Johann Rudolf Heinrich Richter. Der Zweite Weltkrieg hat den Bestand der historisch wertvollen Bauten reduziert; 1960 nahm sich die Denkmalpflege der Straße an. Entstellende Veränderungen der Fassaden wurden bereinigt, entstandene Lücken durch maßstäbliche Neubauten geschlossen. Das Haus Nr. 102-103 besitzt noch sein Puttirelief der vier Jahreszeiten von Michael Christoph Wohler, ein charakteristisches Beispiel für die Potsdamer Wohnhaus-Fassadendekoration der Rokokozeit.

In 1722 this was the boundary of the first baroque new town. Houses nos. 16-55 were said to be «beyond the wall». The excise wall was removed from 1732 and the town extended to the north. After the Seven Years' War, Pflugstrasse was the longest street in the town, with 128 houses. Frederick II had development dating from the time of the Soldier King replaced by imposing new buildings from 1777. These were designed by Karl von Gontard, Georg Christian Unger, Andreas Ludwig Krüger, Johann Christian Valentin Schulze and Johann Rudolf Heinrich Richter. The Second World War reduced the stock of buildings of historic value; in 1960 they were taken over by the town's department of ancient monuments. Alterations that had distorted the façades were corrected, and gaps closed by new building on the correct scale. No. 102-3 still has its putto relief of the four seasons by Michael Christoph Wohler, a typical example of rococo decoration in the residential architecture of Potsdam.

P 20 Alte Wache
Potsdam; Lindenstraße 45
1795-97 • Andreas Ludwig Krüger

Hier an der Stadtgrenze der ersten barocken Neustadt befand sich eine einfache Toranlage aus der Zeit des Soldatenkönigs. Sie wurde aber im Zuge einer repräsentativen Ausschmückung der Stadt Ende des 18. Jahrhunderts durch einen frühklassizistischen Neubau ersetzt. Die beiden Hauptfronten schmücken Bogenhallen auf gekuppelten Säulen. Die Attika zieren Sandsteinplastiken antiker Göttergestalten. Mars und Bellona mit allerlei Kriegsgerät und Trophäen symbolisieren die Kriegskunst und nehmen so auf die Nutzung des Gebäudes Bezug. In der Gestaltung orientierte sich Krüger an der kurz zuvor entstandenen Hauptwache in Posen und an den 1787 von Carl Gotthard Langhans errichteten Mohrenkolonnaden in Berlin.

Here, on the boundary of the first baroque new town, stood a simple gatehouse dating from the time of the Soldier King. This was however replaced by an early classical building when the town was being refurbished on a more impressive scale in the late eighteenth century. The two main façades have colonnades supported on coupled columns. The attic storeys have sandstone sculptures of ancient gods: Mars and Bellona in the full panoply of war and bearing trophies symbolizing the art of war, thus referring to the building's function. For the design Krüger based himself upon the Hauptwache in Posen, completed just previously, and on Carl Gotthard Langhans' Mohrenkolonnaden in Berlin, 1787.

in der Nähe/nearby:
Ordonnanzhaus (Schule); Charlottenstraße 31
1782 • Georg Christian Unger

P 21 Jägertor
Potsdam; Hegelallee
1733

Im Jahre 1733 wurde das Stadtgebiet nach Norden bis zum Schwarzen Graben, der heutigen Hegelallee, erweitert und mit einer Zoll- und Akzisemauer sowie Palisaden zum Havelufer versehen. Die Landseite erhielt sechs Stadttore, die Wasserseite vier Wassertore, so das Kellertor im Osten und im Südwesten einen Wall am Kiez. Von den sechs Landtoren sind das Berliner, das Brandenburger, das Nauener, das Neustädter und das Teltower Tor auf der Langen Brücke verschwunden oder ersetzt, lediglich das Jägertor blieb aus der Erbauungszeit erhalten. Der einfache Torpfeilerbau war mit einem Wach- und einem Zollhaus verbunden, die beide Ende des 19. Jahrhunderts abgerissen wurden. Das Tor bildet den Blickpunkt der barocken Achse der ehemaligen Lindenstraße, die bereits 1668 als Landschaftsallee zum kurfürstlichen Jägerhof vom holländischen Planteur Langelaar angelegt wurde. So steht die Toranlage schräg zur Hegelallee. Ihr plastischer Schmuck zeigt eine Jagdszene: Ein Hirsch wird von Hunden gestellt, zu beiden Seiten Trophäen.

In 1733 the area to the north of the town was extended as far as the Schwarzer Graben, the present Hegelallee, and acquired customs and excise wall and palisades down to the bank of the Havel. The land side had six city gates and the water side four water gates, the Kellertor in the east and a rampart along the Kiez in the south-west. Of the six land gates the Berlin, Brandenburg, Nauen, Neustadt and Teltow Gates, the last on the Lange Brücke, have disappeared or been replaced; only the Jägertor (Huntsman's Gate) has survived in its original form. The simple gatehouse with piers was connected with a guardhouse and a customs house, both of which were demolished in the late nineteenth century. The gate forms the focus of the baroque axis of what was formerly Lindenstrasse, laid out as early as 1668 as a landscaped avenue leading to the Elector's hunting lodge by Dutch planter Langelaar. Thus the gate is at an angle to the Hegelallee. The sculptural decoration is a hunting scene: a stag caught by dogs, with trophies on either side.

in der Nähe/nearby:
Kommandantenhaus; Lindenstraße 54-55
1737 • Philipp Gerlach
Villa Hacke; Jägerallee 1
1847 • Ferdinand v. Arnim
Unteroffiziersschule; Jägerallee 10-12
1824-25 • Karl Friedrich Schinkel, Karl Hampel
Jüdischer Friedhof; Puschkinallee 18
18. Jh.
Pomonatempel; Pfingstberg
1800-01 • Karl Friedrich Schinkel
Pfingstkapelle; Persiusstraße
1893 • Ludwig v. Tiedemann
Villa Henckel; Weinmeisterstraße 43
M. 19. Jh.

P 22 Zweite barocke Neustadt
Potsdam; Brandenburger Straße
1732-42 • Berger, Peter v. Gayette

Die Brandenburger Straße entstand nach 1734 als Ost-West-Achse der zweiten barocken Stadterweiterung des Soldatenkönigs Friedrich Wilhelm I. Beginnend am Brandenburger Tor, das bis 1769 wie das Jägertor ein einfacher Torpfeilerbau war, endete das Neubaugebiet am holländischen Bassin. Die planmäßige Anlage wurde unter der Leitung des Ingenieurkapitäns Berger und des Architekten Peter v. Gayette ausgeführt. Das geometrische Grundrißraster wurde durch rechtwinklig sich kreuzende Straßen in Quartiere oder Karrees geteilt, einige Karrees sind schiefwinklig geschnitten durch die 1668 kurfürstlich angelegte Landschaftsallee und die ihr angepaßten Straßenläufe. Von den insgesamt 21 neuen Stadtquartieren bilden die vier nordöstlichen das Holländische Viertel. Die übrigen wurden mit zweigeschossigen fünf- oder siebenachsigen Traufenhäusern bebaut. In der Gestaltung der Blockfronten bewirkt die Reihung gleicher oder verschiedenartiger Typenhäuser eine feine Rhythmisierung, die eine unterschiedliche Putzfärbung noch unterstreicht, bislang aber oft als Monotonie mißverstanden wurde.

Brandenburger Strasse was built after 1734 as the east-west axis of the second baroque extension of the town by Friedrich Wilhelm I, the Soldier King. The new building area started at the Brandenburg Gate, which like the Jägertor was a simple piered gate until 1769, and ended at the Holländisches Bassin. The planned district was laid out under the direction of Ingenieurkapitän Berger, with Peter von Gayette as architect. The basic geometrical grid was divided by streets intersecting at right angles into quarters or carrées, some of the latter being cut at oblique angles by the Landschaftsallee and the streets accompanying it, laid out by the Elector in 1668. The Holländisches Viertel is made up of the four north-eastern quarters of the twenty-one new quarters of the town. The rest had houses with their eaves to the street with two storeys and five or seven axes. The block façades are given a subtle rhythm by the juxtaposition of model houses of identical or different types. This is further underlined by different colouring for the rendering, although this was formerly misinterpreted as monotony.

in der Nähe/nearby:
Brandenburger Tor; Luisenplatz
1770 • Karl v. Gontard, Georg Christian Unger
Wohnhäuser; Brandenburger Straße 1 und 72
1785 • Johann Rudolf Heinrich Richter
Hofmarschallhaus; Allee nach Sanssouci 5
Um 1820
Zivilkabinett; Allee nach Sanssouci 6
1842-43 • Ludwig Persius

P 23 Wohnhäuser
Potsdam; Gutenbergstraße 1-6 und 109-114
1979-81

Die Straße war 1733 abgesteckt und vermessen worden. Ihre Bebauung mit zweigeschossigen Typenhäusern erfolgte in den Jahren 1736-37 durch Peter v. Gayette und Ingenieurkapitän Berger. Die Reihenhäuser errichteten sie teils in Fachwerkkonstruktion mit massiver Fassade und unter einheitlichem Walmdach. Als Besonderheit war in der betonten Mittelachse eine Giebelstube im Dacherker für vier bis sechs Soldaten Einquartierung vorgesehen. Die geschlossene barocke Bebauung hatte den Zweiten Weltkrieg ohne Zerstörung überstanden, erst zu Beginn der siebziger Jahre wurden drei verfallene Häuser abgerissen. Entscheidende Eingriffe in die historisch wertvolle Bausubstanz folgten, darauf formierten sich Bürgerinitiativen, die sich für den Erhalt der Häuser einsetzten. Zur Schließung der Lücken kam es 1979-81. In einer vom Wohnungsbaukombinat Potsdam entwickelten »leichten Plattenbauweise« entstanden aus industriell vorgefertigten Großbauteilen Neubauten, die sich der Gestalt der barocken Häuser anzupassen suchten. Die alte Traufhöhe, Mittelrisalite und Zwerchhäuser kehren bei ihnen wieder.

This street was staked out and surveyed in 1733. The two-storey model houses were built by Peter von Gayette and and Ingenieurkapitän Berger in 1736-7. The terraced houses were built partly as timber-frame structures with solid façades and a uniform hipped roof. A special feature was a room in the attic bay in the stressed central axis, intended as a billet for four to six soldiers. This uniform baroque development survived the Second World War undamaged; three houses that had fallen into disrepair were pulled down in the early seventies. This was followed by various things that impinged on the historically important building stock, and at this point pressure groups were formed to work for the preservation of the buildings. The gaps were filled in 1979-81. The Wohnungsbaukombinat Potsdam developed a «light slab-building technique» for the new buildings in prefabricated sections, and these attempted to adapt themselves to the design of the baroque buildings, retaining the old eaves height, central projections, and rooms in the attic bays.

in der Nähe/nearby:
Haus »Stadt Magdeburg«; Gutenbergstraße 108
1737-38
Haus »Zum güldenen Arm«; Hermann-Elflein-Straße 3
1737 • Berger
Wohnhaus; Hermann-Elflein-Straße 13-14
1832-33 • Christian Heinrich Ziller

P 24 Große Stadtschule
Potsdam; Friedrich-Ebert-Straße 17
1738-39 • Peter v. Gayette

Die Stadtschule ist einer der wenigen noch im originalen Zustand erhaltenen monumentalen Bauten aus der Zeit des Soldatenkönigs Friedrich Wilhelm I. Sie ist vergleichbar dem kurz zuvor von Gerlach in Berlin errichteten Kollegienhaus. Als zweigeschossiger Putzbau mit Mansartdach, Mittelrisalit, Segmentgiebel und Balkon, mit Ecklisenen und weiß abgesetzter Fassade in gelbem Ocker hebt es sich deutlich von den schlichteren Bürgerhäusern ab und vermittelt einen Eindruck von der Farbigkeit des Stadtbildes im ersten Drittel des 18. Jahrhunderts. Aus so manchem Schüler der Stadtschule wurde später ein berühmter Mann: August Friedrich Eisenhart, Heinrich v. Kleist, Moritz Hermann Jacobi, Carl Gustav Jacobi, Hermann Ludwig Ferdinand v. Helmholtz, Johann Maximilian Dortu und Wilhelm Windelband.

The Stadtschule is one of the few monumental buildings from the time of the Soldier King Friedrich Wilhelm I to have survived in its original condition. It is comparable with the Kollegienhaus, built shortly before by Gerlach in Berlin. It is a two-storey rendered building with mansard roof, central projection, segment gable, balcony, with corner pilaster strips and façade picked out in white on ochre, thus strikingly distinct from the plainer town houses and giving an impression of the colours of the townscape in the first third of the eighteenth century. Many pupils of the Stadtschule subsequently became famous: August Friedrich Eisenhart, Heinrich von Kleist, Moritz Hermann Jacobi, Carl Gustav Jacobi, Hermann Ludwig Ferdinand von Helmholtz, Johann Maximilian Dortu and Wilhelm Windelband.

in der Nähe/nearby:
Stadtsparkasse; Friedrich-Ebert-Straße 105
1768 • Karl v. Gontard
Wohnhäuser; Friedrich-Ebert-Straße 112-114
1765 • Karl v. Gontard
Wohnhaus; Friedrich-Ebert-Straße 117
1764 • Johann Gottfried Büring, Heinrich Ludwig Manger

P 25 Nauener Tor
Potsdam; Hegelallee, Friedrich-Ebert-Straße
1755 • Johann Gottfried Büring

König Friedrich II. ließ nach 1750 die einfachen Torbauten der Stadterweiterung von 1733, die im Typ dem Jägertor entsprachen, durch aufwendige Repräsentativbauten ersetzen. Als Bauherr bestimmte er deren Gestaltung und traf die Auswahl der Vorbilder. Nach einer Skizze des Königs aus dem Jahre 1754 und der Vorgabe »im gotischen Geschmack« errichtete Büring eine Toranlage in Formen der englischen Gotik. Seitlich schließen die Torhäuser an, die zur Stadt hin in drei Arkaden geöffnet sind, die Maskenköpfe an den Arkadenpfeilern stammen von Benjamin Giese. Erst 1867-68 wird das barocke Tor beseitigt und durch eine breitere spitzbogige Durchfahrt ersetzt, die Gesamtanlage erhält einen einheitlichen Zinnenkranz. Die Wiederverwendung gotischer Formen in der deutschen Architektur der zweiten Hälfte des 18. Jahrhunderts findet im Nauener Tor ihr frühestes Beispiel. Als Modeerscheinung neben dem Palladianismus konzentriert sich diese Neugotik im wesentlichen auf die Residenzen Berlin-Potsdam, Kassel, Dessau-Wörlitz, Weimar und Wien. Das Gestaltungsprogramm der Potsdamer Tore suchte Vielfalt: Das 1753 nach Knobelsdorffs Entwurf entstandene Neustädter Tor mit seinen beiden ägyptisierenden Obelisken ist der Wiener Barockarchitektur entlehnt, das antike Triumphbogenmotiv stand Pate für das im gleichen Jahr von Johann Boumann erbaute Berliner Tor und das 1770 nach Entwürfen Karl v. Gontards und Georg Christian Ungers errichtete Brandenburger Tor.

King Frederick II replaced the simple gates from the town extension of 1733, which were the same type as the Jägertor, with lavish and prestigious buildings after 1750. As he commissioned them he also decided on their design and selected the models upon which they were based. Büring built a gate in the English Gothic manner based on a sketch made by the king in 1754, and fulfilling the requirement «in Gothic style». The gates are attached at the sides; they have arcades on the town side, and the mask heads on the arcade piers are by Benjamin Giese. The baroque gate was not removed until 1867-8 and replaced with a broader entrance with pointed arches with battlements for the whole building. The Nauen Gate is the earliest example of the reappearance of Gothic forms in in German architecture in the second half of the eighteenth century. It was a fashionable phenomenon that occurred at about the same time as Palladianism, and largely concentrated in the residences of Berlin-Potsdam, Kassel, Dessau-Wörlitz, Weimar and Vienna. Variety was the key to the Potsdam gate programme: the Neustadt gate was built in 1753 to a design by Knobelsdorff, and has two Egyptian-style obelisks borrowed from Viennese baroque architecture; ancient triumphal arches were the inspiration for the Berlin Gate built by Johann Boumann in the same year, and behind the Brandenburg Gate, built in 1770 to designs by Karl von Gontard and Georg Christian Ungers.

P 26 Holländisches Viertel
Potsdam; Mittelstraße, Benkertstraße usw.
1732-42 • Johann Boumann

Das Holländische Viertel in Potsdam ist eine besondere städtebauliche Leistung des 18. Jahrhunderts. Es besteht aus vier Häuserkarrees mit ursprünglich 134 Häusern, davon wurden fünf im Zweiten Weltkrieg zerstört. Der Amsterdamer Johann Boumann, der die Zimmer-, Tischler- und Schiffsbaukunst erlernt hatte, wurde 1732 durch Friedrich Wilhelm I. nach Potsdam gerufen, was bei den einheimischen Bauleuten zunächst auf Ablehnung stieß. Boumann brachte die heimische Ziegelbauweise und bestimmte Bauelemente des holländischen Bürgerhauses mit, er entwickelte daraus Typenhäuser, die er in Anlehnung an die Blockbebauung der zweiten Stadterweiterung von Berger und Gayette nach neuen Gesichtspunkten gliederte und rhythmisierte. So wurde das Einzelhaus zum organischen Bestandteil der Blockseite, die eine Variation von drei Typenhäusern darstellt: dreiachsiges Giebelhaus, freistehendes fünfachsiges Haus, gereihtes Traufenhaus. Ein Ratsbeschluß von 1972 leitete die Wiederherstellung des Viertels mit Sanierung und Restaurierung ein: bis 1977 versuchsweise Mittelstraße 42 und 43, Friedrich-Ebert-Straße 27 und 28. Seit 1984 werden auch Häuser in der Gutenbergstraße überarbeitet, bis 1993 soll die Wiederherstellung des Viertels abgeschlossen sein.

The Holländisches Viertel in Potsdam is a particular achievement of eighteenth century urban architecture. It consists of four blocks originally containing 134 houses, of which five were destroyed in the Second World War. Johann Boumann of Amsterdam, who had trained as a carpenter, joiner and ship-builder, was summoned to Potsdam by Friedrich Wilhelm I in 1732; local builders and architects at first disapproved. Boumann brought his local style of building in brick with him, and certain elements of Dutch town houses, and from these developed model houses which he articulated and endowed with rhythm according to new points of view in the context of Berger and Gayette's second extension of the town. Thus the individual house became an organic part of the side of the block, with a range of three model houses: house with three axes set gable-on to the street, detached house with five axes, terraced houses set with eaves to the street. A local government decree in 1972 introduced restoration of the quarter with redevelopment and restoration: experimentally until 1977 this affected Mittelstrasse 42 and 43 and Friedrich-Ebert-Strasse 27 and 28. Houses in Gutenbergstrasse have also been part of the project since 1984, and by 1993 restoration of the quarter should be complete.

in der Nähe/nearby:
Wohnhaus; Friedrich-Ebert-Straße 89
1737 • Berger

P 27 Wohnhäuser
Potsdam; Am Bassin 7-12
1773-76 • Karl v. Gontard

Mit der Anlage der zweiten barocken Stadterweiterung in den dreißiger Jahren des 18. Jahrhunderts wurden auch die beiden Karrees am östlichen Stadtrand mit zweigeschossigen Typenhäusern bebaut. Lediglich die Seiten zu dem östlich angrenzenden Sumpf blieben offen. In den Jahren 1737-39 legte man die Gegend trocken und sammelte das Wasser in einem massiv eingefaßten »holländischen Bassin«. Inmitten des Bassins errichtete Johann Boumann 1739 auf einem Inselchen einen Pavillon, die Gloriette. Das Bassin hatte einen offenen Zufluß zum Heiligen See und einen unterirdischen zum Stadtkanal. Friedrich II. ließ dann die Westseite dieses Bassinplatzes mit schmuckvollen Giebelhäusern bebauen. Mit Rücksicht auf das Bassin schrieb er »holländischen Stil« vor. Die Häuser Nr. 2 und 6 wurden in Anlehnung an die Gontardschen Bauten erst 1780-85 errichtet, das Haus Nr. 18 entstand 1818 auf Kosten des »Immediatbaufonds«. Am Haus Nr. 10 erinnert eine Tafel an den Aufenthalt von Wolfgang Amadeus Mozart vom 25. April bis 28. Mai 1789 beim Hornisten Türrschmidt. Nach wiederholter Verschlammung wurde das Becken 1871-76 zugeschüttet. Peter Joseph Lenné hatte bis 1825 zehn Pläne für eine Verwandlung in eine Platzanlage vorgelegt. 1947 wurde die Gloriette abgetragen.

When the second baroque extension of the town started in the 1730s the two blocks on the eastern edge of the town were also developed with two-storey model houses. Only the sides facing the marsh to the east remained open. The area was drained in 1737-9 and the water collected in the solidly contained «holländisches Bassin». Johann Boumann built a pavilion, the Gloriette, on a little island in the middle of the Holländisches Bassin in 1739. The Bassin has an open outflow to the Heiliger See and an underground one to the Stadtkanal. Frederick II then built attractive gabled houses on the western side of the water. He asked for «Dutch style», because of the Bassin. Houses nos. 2 and 6 were not built until 1780-5, as an adjunct to Gontard's buildings, and no. 18 was built in 1818 and paid for by the «Immediatbaufonds». A plaque on no. 10 points out that Wolfgang Amadeus Mozart stayed here from 25 April to 28 May 1789, in the house of Türrschmidt, a horn-player. The pool was filled in in 1871-6, as it kept silting up. Peter Joseph Lenné had submitted ten plans for transformation into a square by 1825. The Gloriette was pulled down in 1947.

P 28 Französische Kirche
Potsdam; Bassinplatz
1751-53 • Johann Boumann

An der Südostseite des Bassinplatzes und als Blickpunkt der ehemaligen Französischen Straße wurde der Kirchenbau für die französisch-reformierte Gemeinde Potsdams errichtet. Die Entstehung dieser Gemeinde steht im Zusammenhang mit dem vom Kurfürsten Friedrich Wilhelm am 29. Oktober 1685 erlassenen Edikt von Potsdam, das den wegen ihres Glaubens vertriebenen Hugenotten, den Refugiés, in der Mark Brandenburg die Ansiedlung erlaubte. Nach dem Vorbild des Pantheon in Rom und ähnlich der Hedwigskirche in Berlin baute Boumann vermutlich nach einem Entwurf von Knobelsdorff diesen Zentralbau über einem querelliptischen Grundriß. Die Säulenvorhalle an der Südseite folgt der römisch-dorischen Ordnung. In den Portalnischen symbolisieren Sandsteinfiguren die christlichen Tugenden Glaube, Liebe und Hoffnung, darüber stellen zwei Reliefbilder »Zinsgroschen« und »Austreibung der Wechsler aus dem Tempel« dar. Die Bildhauerarbeiten stammen von Friedrich Christian Glume.

This church for the French-Reformed community in Potsdam was built on the south eastern side of the Bassinplatz and as a focus for the former Französische Strasse. This community came into being as a result of the Edict of Potsdam, issued by Elector Friedrich Wilhelm on 29 October 1685, permitting Huguenots who had been driven out of their homeland because of their faith, the so-called refugiés, to settle in the Mark Brandenburg. Based upon the Pantheon in Rome and similar to the Hedwigskirche in Berlin, this centrally-planned building on a transverse elliptical ground plan was built by Boumann, probably to a design by Knobelsdorff. The columned porch on the south side follows the Roman Doric order. Sandstone figures in the portal niches symbolize the Christian virtues of Faith, Hope and Love, and above this are two reliefs representing «Tribute Money» and «Driving the Moneychangers from the Temple». Sculptural work is by Friedrich Christian Glume.

in der Nähe/nearby:
Omnibusbetriebshof; Bassinplatz
1975-76 • Karl-Heinz Neumann
Sowjetischer Ehrenfriedhof; Bassinplatz
1949 • A. Brams

P 29 Katholische Kirche St. Peter und Paul
Potsdam; Am Bassin
1867-68 • Wilhelm Salzenberg

Die Kirche ist ein Beispiel für den Historismus in der Architektur der zweiten Hälfte des 19. Jahrhunderts, deren Verwendung von Bauformen auf der genauen Kenntnis der historischen Vorbilder beruht. Im Jahre 1847 hatte Wilhelm Salzenberg im Auftrage Friedrich Wilhelms IV. ein genaues Aufmaß der Kirche Hagia Sophia in Istanbul angefertig. Sein Tafelwerk »Altchristliche Baudenkmale von Konstantinopel« war epochemachend für die kunsthistorische Inventarisation. Seit 1865 war er nach Stülers Tod Dezernent für Kirchenbau und Denkmäler. Die Kirche beherrscht als »Point de vue« den östlichen Abschluß der barocken Achse der Brandenburger Straße. Sie ist ein Zentralbau über dem Grundriß eines griechischen Kreuzes mit kurzen Kreuzarmen und einem Dreikonchenchor. Die Zwerggalerien erinnern an die Hagia Sophia. Die Vorhalle im Westen mit dem 60 Meter hohen Turm entstand in Anlehnung an den Campanile von San Zeno Maggiore in Verona, einem der edelsten romanischen Bauten Oberitaliens, den der Architekt ebenfalls gezeichnet hatte. Rohziegelbauweise und Einzelgestaltung sind charakteristisch für die Spätphase des Berliner Rundbogenstils.

This church is an example of historicist architecture in the second half of the nineteenth century; this uses building forms dependent on precise knowledge of historical models. In 1847 Wilhelm Salzenberg had been commissioned by Friedrich Wilhelm IV to provide precise dimensions of Hagia Sophia in Constantinople. His book of plates called «Altchristliche Baudenkmale von Konstantinopel» was a landmark in the making of art-historical inventories. He had been in charge of church building and monuments since Stüler's death in 1865. The church is the point de vue dominating the eastern end of the baroque axis of Brandenburger Strasse. It is a centrally-planned building on a Greek cross ground plan with short cross arms and a choir with three conches. The dwarf galleries are reminiscent of Hagia Sophia. The west porch with tower sixty metres high was based on the campanile of San Zeno Maggiore in Verona, one of the finest Romanesque buildings in northern Italy, which the architect had also drawn. In the niches above the main portal are statues of the Madonna, Peter and Paul. Rough brick building and individual design are characteristic of the late phase of the Berlin round-arched style.

P 30 Schauspielerkaserne
Potsdam; Posthofstraße 17
1796 • Georg Friedrich Boumann

An das 1793-96 von Michael Philipp Boumann errichtete und im Zweiten Weltkrieg zerstörte frühklassizistische Schauspielhaus erinnert die ehemals an dessen Rückseite gelegene Schauspielerkaserne. In ihr hatten die Schauspieler ihre Wohnunterkünfte. Der stattliche Bau mit seinen drei Geschossen besitzt im segmentbogig vertieften Mittelrisalit ein Relief »Apoll mit den Musen«, das die Brüder Wohler nach einem Entwurf von Johann Gottfried Schadow ausführten. Ein Relief des gleichen Themas von der Front des zerstörten und 1966 abgetragenen Schauspielhauses ziert heute das Palais unter den Linden in Berlin. Ein Theaterneubau wurde noch vor dem 9. November 1989 auf dem Alten Markt begonnen. Dieser Standort war aber städtebaulich umstritten, und der erste Rohbauabschnitt wurde inzwischen wieder abgebrochen.

The «Schauspielerkaserne» (literally actors' barracks), where actors were housed, is reminiscent of the early classical Schauspielhaus, behind which it used to be. The Schauspielhaus was built 1793-6 by Michael Philipp Boumann and destroyed in the Second World War. The Schauspielerkaserne is a handsome building with three storeys and a relief of «Apollo with the Muses» in the segmented arch of the central projection. The relief is the work of the Wohler brothers, to a design by Johann Gottfried Schadow. A relief on the same subject from the façade of the ruined Schauspielhaus pulled down in 1966 can now be seen on the façade of the Palais Unter den Linden in Berlin. A new theatre was started before 9 November 1989 in the Alter Markt. The site is somewhat controversial in urban development terms, however, and the shell of the first building phase has already been demolished.

in der Nähe/nearby:
Krankenhaus; Türkstraße
1959-60 • Willi Schröder, Manfred Kärgel
Wohnzeilen; Joliot-Curie-Straße
1959-60 • Hans-Jürgen Kluge, Felix Hollesch
Bezirkskrankenhaus; Hebbelstraße
1961 • Manfred Kärgel

P 31 Hauptpostamt
Potsdam; Am Kanal
1897-1900 • Hacker

Auf dem Eckgrundstück am Wilhelmsplatz – zu DDR-Zeiten und heute zweideutig Platz der Einheit – errichtete die Oberpostdirektion an städtebaulich bevorzugter Stelle einen Neubau in den Stilformen des Wilhelminischen Barock. Der Baukörper wird durch Eckrisalite gegliedert, an der Hauptfront dominiert der übergiebelte Mittelrisalit. Blickfang waren Kuppeln über den Risaliten sowie die mit Vasen geschmückte Attika. Im Jahre 1936 beseitigte man die Kuppeln, um eine »städtebauliche Verbesserung des Platzbildes« zu erreichen. Die Postarchitektur der Jahrhundertwende galt nicht als historisches Dokument, und der Eingriff stand unter dem Motto »neue Sinngebung für das alte Potsdam«. Dieser »neuen Sinngebung« fiel 1938 auch die benachbarte Synagoge zum Opfer, eine Gedenktafel am neuen Gebäude erinnert heute daran.

On the corner plot at Wilhelmsplatz – now somewhat ambiguously Platz der Einheit (unity) – the post office built its new headquarters to a Wilhelminian baroque design. The building is articulated by corner projections, with the pedimented central projection dominating the main façade. The eye used to be caught by domes over the projections and urns on the attica, but the domes were removed in 1936 to «improve the square as part of the urban scene». Turn of the century post office architecture was not considered to be historically significant, and this intervention was made under the slogan «a new meaning for old Potsdam». The adjacent synagogue also fell victim to this «new meaning» in 1938, and a memorial plaque on the new building stands as reminder of this.

in der Nähe/nearby:
Bibliothek; Am Kanal 47
1970-74 • Sepp Weber
Staudenhof; Am Kanal
1977-78 • Hiltrud Berndt

P 32 Werner-Alfred-Bad
Potsdam; Hegelallee 23
1911-13 • Paul Baumgarten

Käte Pitschker, die Mutter eines tödlich verunglückten Sportfliegers, initiierte eine private Stiftung zur Errichtung einer Volksbadeanstalt, die den Namen des Sohnes vor dem Vergessen bewahren sollte. 1913 konnte das nach Plänen von Paul Baumgarten errichtete Hallenbad eröffnet werden. Es entstand in einer Zeit sozialhygienischer Einsicht und der Förderung der Verbindung von sportlicher Betätigung und körperlicher Reinhaltung. Auch Berlin und einige seiner Vororte erhielten bis zum Ersten Weltkrieg eine Reihe moderner Hallenbäder. Die Potsdamer Anlage hatte ein ovales Schwimmbecken mit 500 Kubikmetern Wasserinhalt, 18 Brause- und 26 Wannenbäder sowie russisch-römische Bäder und eine medizinische Badeabteilung. Die Sockelzone des dreigeschossigen Putzbaues ist zeitgemäß mit Muschelkalk verkleidet, ebenso das rustizierte Hauptportal, welches ein Relief mit den Naturgewalten schmückt. Die schlitzartigen Fenster entsprechen den schmalen Badezellen.

Käte Pitschker, the mother of an amateur pilot fatally injured in an accident, initiated a private fund to build a municipal baths in memory of her son. The indoor pool, designed by Paul Baumgarten, was opened in 1913. It was built at a time of great concern for social hygiene and the encouragement of a connection between sporting activity and bodily cleanliness. Berlin and its suburbs acquired a series of modern indoor pools up to the beginning of the First World War. The baths in Potsdam had an oval swimming pool containing 500 cubic metres of water, 18 showers and 26 bath tubs, and also Russian-Roman baths and a medical bathing section. The base area of the three-storey rendered building is clad with muschelkalk, as was fashionable at the time; the rusticated main portal is equally typical, and decorated with a relief showing natural forces. The slit-like windows correspond to cell-like rooms for the baths.

in der Nähe/nearby:
Thalia-Theater; Hegelallee 24
1865
Infanteriekaserne; Hegelallee 33-35
1782 • Heinrich Ludwig Manger

P 33 Villa Arnim
Potsdam; Weinbergstraße 20
1859-60 • Ferdinand v. Arnim

Erst unter der Regierung König Friedrich Wilhelms IV. entwickelte sich, seit die königlichen Unterstützungen für Privatbauten eingeschränkt wurden, eine selbständige Architektur im bürgerlichen Villenstil. Unter dem Einfluß der Architekten Persius, Hesse, Stüler, Schadow und Arnim entstanden nach 1840 in den Vorstädten Wohngebäude, die sich am Stil der italienischen Villen orientierten, so auch die eigene Villa Arnims. Der zweigeschossige kubische Baukörper mit flachem Walmdach ist durch Erker mit Eingangshalle und Balkon aufgelockert. Eine Mauer, teils zur Pergola geöffnet, faßt den Garten ein, an der Südostecke folgt ein Stibadium. Die Eingangshalle flankieren allegorische Relieftondi.

It was not until the reign of King Friedrich Wilhelm IV that independent architecture in the style of the bourgeois villa developed as a result of limited royal support for private building. Under the influence of architects Persius, Hesse, Stüler, Schadow and Arnim, residential buildings came into being in the suburbs after 1840 in the style of Italian villas, like the one that Arnim built for himself. The severity of the two-storey cubic building with a shallow hipped roof is broken by a bay containing entrance hall and balcony. The garden is enclosed by a wall partially open to the pergola, and a stibadium in the south-east corner. The entrance hall is flanked by allegorical relief tondi.

in der Nähe/nearby:
Elisabethhaus; Schopenhauerstraße 24
1843 • Ludwig Persius

P 34 Regierungsgebäude
Potsdam; Friedrich-Ebert-Straße 79-81
1902-08 • Paul Kieschke

Nach Paul Kieschkes Entwurf wurde das Regierungsgebäude unter der Bauleitung von Bohnstedt, Saran und Saltzwedel errichtet. Die Monumentalität des im Stil des Wilhelminischen Barock errichteten Gebäudes wird durch die Blockhaftigkeit der Sandsteinverblendung verstärkt. Eine kupfergedeckte Tambourkuppel mit einer Laterne über dem Mittelrisalit verleiht dem Bau als Regierungssitz das nötige Gewicht und die Würde. Dem entspricht auch die pavillonartige Fassung der Ecktrakte dieser weitläufigen Mehrflügelanlage. Der Gebäudekomplex besitzt vier Innenhöfe, im Mittelbau befindet sich die 16 Meter hohe überwölbte Treppenhalle in üppigen Jugendstilformen. Die Treppenwangen aus Cottaer Sandstein sollen entgegen aller preußischen Sparsamkeit von Reichtum und Größe des Kaiserreiches zeugen und kontrastieren zu den kunstgeschmiedeten Geländern.

The government building was built to a design by Paul Kieschke under the direction of Bohnstedt, Saran and Salzwedel. The monumental quality of this building in Wilhelminian baroque style is reinforced by the block-like nature of the sandstone cladding. A copper-covered drum dome with lantern over the central protruding section gives the building the necessary weight and dignity as a seat of government. The corner sections of this extensive building are designed like pavilions, which is also in keeping with the status it intends to project. The complex has four inner courtyards, and in the central section is a 16 metre high vaulted staircase in a lavish Jugendstil design. The Cotta sandstone stringboards were intended to testify to the wealth and greatness of the empire, against all sense of Prussian thrift, and contrast with the wrought-iron banisters.

in der Nähe/nearby:
Villa; Friedrich-Ebert-Straße 63
1860-61 • Ferdinand v. Arnim
Deutsche Lebens- und Rentenversicherungsgesellschaft; Friedrich-Ebert-Straße 32
1886-87 • Heinrich Schmieden
Villa Quistorp; Hegelallee 1
1872 • Ernst Petzholtz
Landgericht; Hegelallee 8
1880-83 • Karl Friedrich Endell
Landhaus Heydert; Friedrich-Ebert-Straße 83
1845 • Ludwig Ferdinand Hesse
Villa; Friedrich-Ebert-Straße 37
1874 • Reinhold Persius
Victoria-Gymnasium (Helmholtzschule); Straße der Jugend 53
1878

P 35 Russische Kolonie Alexandrowka
Potsdam; Russische Kolonie
1826-27 • Snethlage, Peter Joseph Lenné

Vom 10. April 1826 datiert die Urkunde Friedrich Wilhelms III. zur »Gründung einer russischen Kolonie vor dem Nauener Tor« als eine Memorialstiftung zu Ehren des russischen Zaren Alexander. Die Gesamtleitung für die Anlage der Kolonie lag in den Händen von Oberst Röder, Gartendirektor Lenné besorgte die Vermessung des Geländes auf der Bornstedter Flur und die Anfertigung eines Bebauungsplanes. Die Bauausführung leitete Hauptmann Snethlage, Kommandeur der Gardepionierabteilung. In den Häusern sollten ehemals russische Kriegsgefangene Wohnung finden, Mitglieder eines Soldatenchores, die später als Geschenk des Zaren in Potsdam verblieben und im 1. Garderegiment zu Fuß dienten. Für die zwölf verheirateten russischen Sänger entstanden zwölf Wohngebäude und ein Aufseherhaus in der Bauweise russischer Blockhäuser mit gesägten Giebelbrettern. Sie wurden an zwei sich in Form eines Andreaskreuzes schneidenden Alleen gruppiert und waren von Nutzland umgeben. Am 2. April 1827 bezogen die Kolonisten ihre vollständig eingerichteten Häuser, zusätzlich erhielten sie einen Stall mit einer Kuh und einen bereits bepflanzten Garten. Die nach dem Vorbild russischer Militärdörfer des 18. Jahrhunderts angelegte Kolonie ist heute das einzig erhaltene Beispiel dieser Art.

Friedrich Wilhelm III's declaration of «the foundation of a Russian colony outside the Nauen Gate» as a memorial to the Russian Tsar Alexander dates from 10 April 1826. Colonel Röder was in overall charge of the creation of the colony, garden director Lenné was responsible for surveying the site on the Bornstedter Flur and the preparation of a development plan. Hauptmann Snethlage, commander of the guard-pioneers, was in charge of building. The accommodation was formerly intended for Russian prisoners of war, members of a soldiers' chorus who later stayed in Potsdam as a gift from the Tsar and served in the 1st regiment of foot guards. Twelve residential buildings and an overseer's house were built for the twelve married Russian singers, in the style of Russian log cabins with serrated gable ends. They were grouped in two avenues in the form of a St. Andrew's cross and were surrounded by cultivated land. The Russians moved into their completely furnished houses on 2 April 1827. They were also given a cow in a stall and a ready-planted garden. The colony, laid out on the model of Russian military villages in the first half of the eighteenth century, is now the only surviving example of its kind.

in der Nähe/nearby:
Pfarrhaus Alexandrowka 14; Kapellenberg
1827 • Snethlage, Peter Joseph Lenné
Villa; Puschkinallee 5
1872-73 • Reinhold Persius

P 36 Russische Kirche Hl. Alexander Newsky
Potsdam; Kapellenberg
1826-29 • Snethlage, Karl Friedrich Schinkel

Am Südabhang des Kapellenberges, unweit der Russischen Kolonie, fand am 11. September 1826 die Grundsteinlegung für eine russisch-orthodoxe Kirche statt. Die Baupläne wurden am Zarenhof in Petersburg erarbeitet und von Schinkel begutachtet, von ihm stammen auch die Pläne für die Gestaltung des Innenraumes. Hauptmann Snethlage und Ingenieurleutnant Motz leiteten den Bau, der von Potsdamer Handwerkern ausgeführt wurde. Den Grundriß bildet ein griechisches Kreuz, das in ein Quadrat eingebunden ist und an der Ostseite mit halbrunder Apsis abschließt. Über einer Vierung mit breiten Gurtbögen erheben sich ein Tambour und die Hauptkuppel, die von vier Nebenkuppeln über den Eckräumen begleitet wird. Innen trennt eine Bilderwand (Ikonostas) den Altarraum (Bema) mit dem »Allerheiligsten« vom Gemeinderaum (Naos). Die Ikonen der Bilderwand entstanden während der Bauzeit in Rußland und wurden bis 1846 durch eine Stiftung ergänzt. Auf den Tag drei Jahre nach der Grundsteinlegung fand die feierliche Einweihung statt.

The foundation stone for a Russian Orthodox church was laid on 11 September 1826 on the southern slope of the Kapellenberg. The plans were drawn up at the Tsar's court in St. Petersburg and inspected by Schinkel, who was also responsible for the design of the interior. Hauptmann Snethlage and Ingenieurleutnant Motz were in charge of the building operation, which was carried out by workers from Potsdam. The ground plan is a Greek cross in square, concluding with a semi-circular apse to the east. Over the crossing with broad wall arches are a drum and the main dome, accompanied by four smaller domes over the corners. In the interior the iconostasis divides the altar room (bema) with the «holy of holies» from the congregation (naos). The icons on the iconostasis were painted in Russia while the church was being built, and more were added as the result of an endowment in 1846. The church was consecrated three years to the day after the foundation stone was laid.

P 37 Lordmarschallhaus
Potsdam; Lennéstraße 9
1764-65 • Heinrich Ludwig Manger

In der Brandenburger Vorstadt entstanden im 18. Jahrhundert in unmittelbarer Nähe von Park und Schloß Sanssouci adlige Landsitze, wie beispielsweise das Marquisat des Landgrafen Wilhelm v. Schwedt. Hier wohnten kurze Zeit der Marquis d'Argens und Voltaire, die Freunde Friedrichs II., sowie im Jahre 1755 Gotthold Ephraim Lessing. Für den 1763 nach Potsdam übergesiedelten Lord George Keith, kurz Lordmarschall genannt, ließ der König ein Haus im Stil eines englischen Landsitzes errichten. Auf königliche Kosten erhielt das Haus auch seine Möblierung, die 1766 abgeschlossen war. Lord Keith war seit 1747 im Dienste des Königs, zählte zu dessen engsten Vertrauten und gehörte zu seiner Tafelrunde. Am alten Eingang zum Marlygarten, in der Achse zum Schloß Sanssouci, errichtete Manger das Lordmarschallhaus als eingeschossige Dreiflügelanlage mit hohen Walmdächern um einen gepflasterten Ehrenhof. Ein dreiachsiger Mittelrisalit überragt das Gebäude an der Stadt- und Gartenfront um ein Geschoß. Freitreppenanlagen betonen den vornehmen Charakter des Hauses.

In the eighteenth century noble country seats, like for example that of landgrave Wilhelm von Schwedt, were built in the Brandenburger Vorstadt, very close to the park and palace of Sanssouci. The Marquis d'Argens and Voltaire, friends of Frederick II, lived here for a short time, and so did Gotthold Ephraim Lessing in 1755. In 1763 Lord George Keith moved to Potsdam. He was known as the Lordmarschall, and the king had a house built for him in the style of an English country seat. The house was also furnished at the king's expense, and completed in 1766. Lord Keith was in the king's service from 1747; he was one of his closest confidants, and also dined with him. At the old entrance to the Marly garden, on the axis of Sanssouci, Manger built the Lordmarschallhaus as a single-storey building with three sections and high hipped roofs, set around a paved courtyard. A central protruding section with three axes and an extra storey stands above the rest of the building in the town and garden façades. Flights of steps emphasize the exclusive character of the house.

in der Nähe/nearby:
Wohnhaus; Zeppelinstraße 189
1843 • Ludwig Persius
Villa Liegnitz; Am Grünen Gitter
1841 • Albert Dietrich Schadow
Villa Illaire; Am Grünen Gitter
1844-46 • Ludwig Persius, Ludwig Ferdinand Hesse

P 38 Winzerhaus auf dem Mühlenberg
Potsdam; Gregor-Mendel-Straße 25
1849 • Ludwig Ferdinand Hesse

Nördlich des Haupteingangs zum Schloßpark Sanssouci erhebt sich der Mühlenberg. Zum östlichen Teil der geplanten Triumphstraße wollte Persius hier eine architektonisch gestaltete Zufahrt schaffen, um dann Höhenstraße und Friedrichstempel über ein Viadukt mit dem Sanssouci-Plateau zu verbinden. Angelegt wurde schließlich nach Plänen von Friedrich Wilhelm IV. und Peter Joseph Lenné 1847 eine italienische Vigne mit Terrassen sowie Pergolen, und Hesse baute 1849 ein Winzerhaus in der Art einer Turmvilla mit einem von Koren getragenen Altan. Die Karyatiden aus Zinkguß stammen von August Kiss. Am Fuße des Weinberges entstand 1850-51 ebenfalls von Hesse das Triumphtor für den aus dem Badischen Feldzug heimkehrenden Prinzen Wilhelm (I.). Diese Nachbildung des römischen »Triumphbogens der Goldschmiede« in Terrakotta aus der Fabrik von Tobias Feilner beeinflußte wesentlich die Backstein-Terrakotta-Architektur in Berlin und Potsdam während der zweiten Hälfte des 19. Jahrhunderts, deutlich ablesbar am Roten Rathaus.

North of the entrance to the park of Sanssouci is the Mühlenberg. Here Persius wanted to create architecture providing an approach to the eastern section of the planned triumphal avenue, in order to connect the high road and Frederick's temple to the plateau of Sanssouci by means of a viaduct. Finally an Italian vigne with terraces and pergola was built in 1847 to plans by Friedrich Wilhelm IV and Lenné, and in 1849 Hesse built a wine-grower's house in the style of a villa with tower and balcony supported by caryatids cast in zinc by August Kiss. In 1850-1 a triumphal arch for Prince Wilhelm (I) was created by Hesse at the foot of the vineyard on the occasion of his return from the Baden campaign. This copy of the Roman «Goldsmiths' triumphal arch» in terracotta from the factory of Tobias Feilner greatly influenced brick and terracotta architecture in Berlin and Potsdam in the second half of the nineteenth century, as can clearly be seen in the Rotes Rathaus.

in der Nähe/nearby:
Villa; Gregor-Mendel-Straße 3
1846 • Häberlin
Villa; Gregor-Mendel-Straße 4
1844 • Häberlin
Villa Mertens; Gregor-Mendel-Straße 23
1873-74; 1911-12 • Peter Behrens

P 39 Astrophysikalisches Observatorium
Potsdam; Albert-Einstein-Straße
1876-77 • Paul Spieker

Auf dem 94 Meter hohen Telegrafenberg wurde 1832 eine optische Telegrafenstation errichtet, die vierte auf der mit 61 Stationen ausgerüsteten Strecke zur Nachrichtenübermittlung zwischen Berlin und Koblenz. Nach 1860 entstanden hier auch mehrere wissenschaftliche Einrichtungen: 1868 das Geodätische Institut, 1875 das Astrophysikalische und das Meteorologische Observatorium. Das Hauptgebäude des Astrophysikalischen Observatoriums wurde über einem T-förmigen Grundriß errichtet und mit farbigen Klinkern verblendet. Der Formsteinfries aus blauer Keramik ist ein Beispiel für die um 1870 einsetzenden Bestrebungen um eine polychrome Architektur. Die Hauptfront bilden drei Kuppelpavillons, die ursprünglich offene Arkaden verbanden. In den drehbaren und zu öffnenden Kuppeln befanden sich Refraktoren zur Sternbeobachtung. Benachbart entstand 1899 das Gebäude des großen Doppelrefraktors mit einem unteren Durchmesser von 25 Metern. Dieser diente der Himmelsbeobachtung und konnte gleichzeitig fotografische Aufnahmen machen. Das Instrument zählt heute noch zu den größten fotografischen Kameras der Welt, gemessen am Radius der Linse und der Brennweite des Objektivs.

An optical telegraph station was built on the 94 metre high Telegrafenberg in 1832, the fourth of 61 stations for transmitting news from Berlin to Koblenz. After 1860 several other scientific institutions were set up here: the Geodesic Institute in 1868, and the Astrophysical and Meteorologcal Observatory in 1875. The main building of the Astrophysical Observatory was built on a T-shaped ground plan and clad with coloured clinker. The shaped brick, blue ceramic frieze is an example of efforts to achieve polychrome architecture that started around 1870. The main façade is made up of three domed pavilions originally connected by open arcades. The domes could be turned and opened and contained refractors for observing the stars. The building containing the large double refractor with a lower diameter of 25 metres was built next door in 1899. This was used for observing the heavens and could also take photographs. The instrument is still one of the largest photographic cameras in the world as far as the radius and the focal length of the objective are concerned.

in der Nähe/nearby:
Kriegsschule; Brauhausberg
1899-1902 • Franz Schwechten
Proviantamt; Leipziger Straße 7-8
1843 • Ludwig Persius
Getreidemagazin; Leipziger Straße 7-8
1834-35 • Karl Hampel, Karl Friedrich Schinkel

P 40 Einsteinturm
Potsdam; Albert-Einstein-Straße
1920-24 • Erich Mendelsohn

1913 lernte Mendelsohn den Astrophysiker Erwin Finlay-Freundlich, den späteren Assistenten Albert Einsteins kennen. Er verschaffte 1917 dem jungen Architekten den Auftrag zum Bau eines Sonnenobservatoriums, in dem Voraussagen, die Einstein in Zusammenhang mit seiner Relativitätstheorie machte, praktisch überprüft werden sollten. 1920 konnten die Bauarbeiten beginnen, ein Jahr später stand der Rohbau, doch erst 1924 war die Inneneinrichtung abgeschlossen. Der entscheidende Versuch der Zerlegung eines im Turm gebündelten Sonnenlichtstrahls in die Spektrallinien und die Messung einer geringfügigen Rotverschiebung lieferten nur ungenaue und nicht befriedigende Ergebnisse. Dafür aber erlangte Mendelsohns architektonische Lösung Weltruhm – für Fachleute und Kenner wurde der Einsteinturm zum Kultgegenstand. Der plastisch modellierte Formkörper sollte zwar ein bauliches Bekenntnis zum neuen Werkstoff Beton sein, mußte wegen Schwierigkeiten mit der Schalung in Teilen aber doch gemauert werden. Stilistisch ist er im weiteren Sinne dem Expressionismus zuzuordnen, er kann aber auch als früher Vorläufer des Plastischen Stils der fünfziger Jahre gesehen werden.

In 1913 Mendelsohn met the astrophysicist Erwin Finlay-Freundlich, later to be Albert Einstein's assistant. In 1917 he got the young architect a contract to built a sun observatory in which statements that Einstein had made in his theory of relativity could be checked by practical experiment. Building started in 1920, the shell was completed a year later but the interior was not completed until 1924. The crucial experiment attempted to break down a beam of sunlight focused in the tower into spectral lines and to measure a slight red shift. The results were imprecise and unsatisfactory, but Mendelsohn's architectural solution became world famous – the Einstein Tower became a cult object for experts and connoisseurs. The three-dimensional modelling of the tower was intended to be a structural tribute to concrete as a new material, but brickwork had to be used in places because of difficulties with the shuttering. Stylistically it can be classified as Expressionist in the broadest sense, but can also be seen as a forerunner of the plastic style of the fifties.

in der Nähe/nearby:
Alter Friedhof; Heinrich-Mann-Allee
1851 • Ferdinand v. Arnim

Q
Potsdam
Sanssouci und Neuer Garten

Die ehemalige Sommerresidenz der preußischen Könige und deutschen Kaiser besteht aus einem einzigartigen Ensemble von Schlössern und Gärten des 18. und 19. Jahrhunderts. Bedeutende Baumeister, Gartengestalter, Künstler und Kunsthandwerker haben die Havelseenlandschaft in eine Kulturlandschaft verwandelt, in die die Architektur gleichsam hineinkomponiert ist. Gesamtbezüge zu den Berliner Schloßanlagen, die durch den Mauerbau seit 1961 erheblich gestört waren, werden jetzt durch die Aufhebung der Grenzen neu erschlossen. Der Park von Sanssouci umfaßt eine Gesamtfläche von 290 Hektar und entstand in zwei Bauperioden. Während der Regierungszeit Friedrichs II. zwischen 1740 und 1786, der Potsdam zu seiner Residenz wählte, beginnt mit der Anlage des Weinberges am 9. August 1744 die Geschichte des Parkes. Um den »Wüsten Berg« wird das Gelände der Brandenburger Vorstadt erschlossen. Es entstanden der östliche Lustgartenbezirk mit der Bildergalerie, die Weinbergterrasse mit Schloß Sanssouci und der westliche Lustgarten mit den Neuen Kammern. Der Rehgarten mit dem Neuen Palais rundet die Parkanlage des 18. Jahrhunderts ab. Erst Friedrich-Wilhelm IV. erweiterte den Park ab 1826 im Süden durch einen Landschaftspark mit Schloß Charlottenhof sowie den Marlygarten mit der Friedenskirche. Im Norden erfolgte mit dem Sizilianischen und dem Nordischen Garten eine Abrundung. Von den einzigartigen Planungen einer Triumphstraße legt das Orangerieschloß Zeugnis ab. Nordöstlich des Parkes Sanssouci entstand ab 1783 am Westufer des Heiligen Sees der Neue Garten als Sommerresidenz Friedrich-Wilhelms II. mit dem Marmorpalais. Der 74 Hektar große Garten wurde im 19. Jahrhundert durch Lenné überformt. Im nördlichen Bereich entstand bis 1916 Schloß Cecilienhof für den Kronprinzen Wilhelm von Preußen. Verknüpft mit diesem Schloß ist die vom 17. Juli bis 2. August 1945 tagende Potsdamer Konferenz der drei Siegermächte des Zweiten Weltkrieges, vertreten durch Präsident Truman, Generalissimus Stalin und Premierminister Attlee, die mit der Unterzeichnung des Potsdamer Abkommens ihren Abschluß fand.

The former summer residence of Prussian kings and German emperors consists of a single ensemble of eighteenth and nineteenth century palaces and gardens. Major architects, landscape gardeners, artists and craftsmen transformed the Havel landscape into a cultural composition controlled by the architecture. Links with Berlin palaces in general, significantly blurred by the building of the Wall in 1961, are now clarified again as the borders open. The park of Sanssouci covers a total area of 290 hectares, and was created in two building periods. Frederick II chose Potsdam as his residence, and in his reign, from 1740-1786, the history of the park began: the vineyard was laid out on 9 August 1744. The terrain of the Brandenburger Vorstadt was opened up around the «desolate hill». The eastern pleasure garden with picture gallery, the vineyard terrace and palace of Sanssouci, and the western pleasure garden with the Neue Kammern were built. Deer park and Neues Palais round off the eighteenth century park complex. Friedrich Wilhelm IV was the first to extend the park in the south from 1826 with a landscape park and the Charlottenhof palace, Marly Garden and Friedenskirche. The Sicilian and Nordic Gardens were the finishing touch in the north. Evidence of the unique plan for a triumphal road is provided by the Orangery Palace. North-east of the park of Sanssouci on the west bank of the Heiliger See, the Neuer Garten and Marmorpalais were built from 1783 as a summer residence for Friedrich Wilhelm II. The garden covered 74 hectares and was redesigned by Lenné in the nineteenth century. The Cecilienhof was built for Crown Prince Wilhelm of Prussia to 1916. This palace is associated with the Potsdam Conference at which the three victorious powers of the Second World War met from 17 July to 2 August 1945, represented by president Truman, Marshall Stalin and Prime Minister Attlee; it concluded with the signature of the Potsdam Agreement.

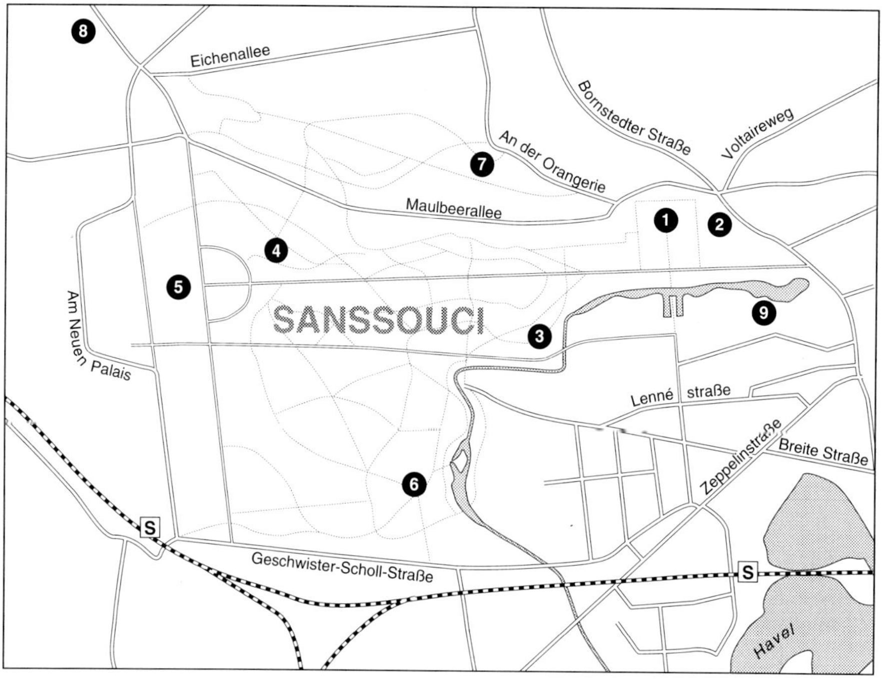

Q 1 Schloß Sanssouci
Q 2 Große Bildergalerie
Q 3 Chinesisches Teehaus
Q 4 Antikentempel und Freundschaftstempel
Q 5 Neues Palais
Q 6 Schloß Charlottenhof
Q 7 Neue Orangerie
Q 8 Schloß Lindstedt
Q 9 Friedenskirche

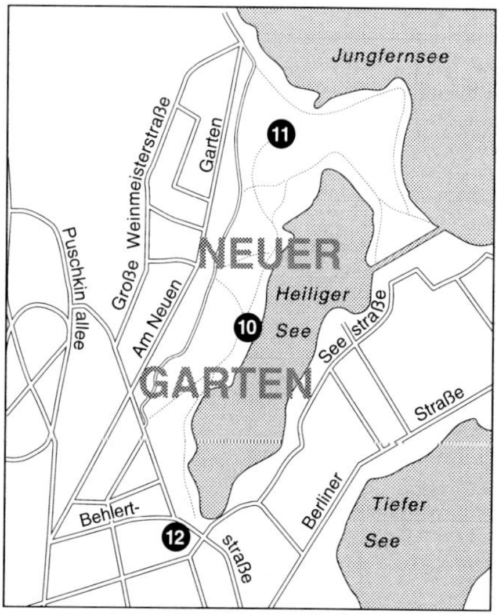

Q 10 Marmorpalais
Q 11 Schloß Cecilienhof
Q 12 Palais Lichtenau

Q 1 Schloß Sanssouci
Potsdam-Sanssouci; Zur historischen Mühle
1745-47 • Georg Wenzeslaus v. Knobelsdorff

König Friedrich II. hat durch seine Architekturideen und als Bauherr die bauliche Gestaltung Potsdams vielfältig bestimmt. Als bedeutendstes Beispiel des friderizianischen Rokoko gilt das westlich der Stadt entstandene Weinbergschloß mit seiner Terrassenanlage. Der aufgeklärte Monarch wollte sich hier, vor den Toren der Stadt, in der Art eines »Maison de plaisance« einen Ort schaffen, an dem er »ohne Sorge« in ländlicher Umgebung seinen privaten Neigungen nachgehen konnte. Eine Entwurfsskizze des Königs für die Terrassenanlage des damals noch »wüsten Berges« entstand im April des Jahres 1744. Gedacht waren sechs Terrassen am Südabhang des Hügels aus parabolisch geschwungenen Talutmauern. Am Fuße der Anlage war eine große Fontäne geplant, deren Bauausführung aber Friedrich II. versagt blieb, obwohl er in das Projekt viel Geld investierte. Erst im 19. Jahrhundert konnte mit dem Bau des Pumpenhauses und einer Dampfmaschine als Antrieb die Große Fontäne in Gang gesetzt werden. Die Gestaltung der Innenräume ist durch Gemälde Adolf v. Menzels wie die »Tafelrunde« und das »Flötenkonzert von Sanssouci« weltbekannt geworden. Zwischen den Fenstern der Parkfront tragen Pilaster 36 Sandsteinplastiken, Bacchanten und Bacchantinnen von Friedrich Christian Glume.

King Frederick II fixed the overall design of Potsdam with his architectural ideas and as patron of the project. The vineyard palace with its terraces is the most important example of the period's rococo. The enlightened monarch wanted to create for himself here outside the gates of the city a place that would be a kind of «maison de plaisance», in which he could follow his private inclinations «without cares» in rural surroundings. A design by the king for the terraces of what was then the «desolate hill» was produced in April 1744. The intention was to build six terraces on the southern slope of the hill with talus walls in parabolic curves. A large fountain was planned at the foot of the complex, but Frederick II never managed to build it, although he invested a lot of money in the project. The Great Fountain did not come on stream until the nineteenth century when the pump house was built, with a steam engine as power plant. The interior design is world famous because of paintings by Adolf von Menzel like the «Tafelrunde» and the «Flötenkonzert von Sanssouci». Between the windows of the park façade pilasters carry 36 sandstone sculptures, male and female bacchantes by Friedrich Christian Glume.

Q 2 Große Bildergalerie
Potsdam-Sanssouci; Schopenhauerstraße
1755-63 • Johann Gottfried Büring

Die westlich von Schloß Sanssouci gelegenen Neuen Kammern, ebenfalls nach Knobelsdorffs Entwurf 1747 errichtet, ursprünglich Orangerie und 1771-75 unter Karl v. Gontard und Georg Christian Unger zum Gästehaus umgestaltet, bilden mit der östlich gelegenen Großen Bildergalerie ein einzigartiges Architekturensemble. Das von Büring errichtete Gebäude ist als Bautyp der früheste erhaltene deutsche Museumsbau, zuvor waren Bildergalerien Bestandteil des jeweiligen Schlosses. Die Kuppelspitze des Mittelteils wird von Adler und Schlange bekrönt, eine Kupfertreibarbeit von Benjamin Giese und Friedrich Jury. Im festlichen Innenraum hingen ursprünglich 168 Bilder flämischer und italienischer Meister, ein Teil von ihnen bildete 1830 den Grundstock des neuen Berliner Museums, konnte aber ein Jahrhundert später wieder zurückgeführt werden. Heute ist nur noch ein Drittel des alten Bestandes vorhanden, die Lücken aus dem Zweiten Weltkrieg schließen inzwischen vergleichbare Bilder. Die Terrasse vor der Galerie mit dem »Holländischen Garten« legte 1764-66 Joachim Ludwig Heydert an. Von dem Flamen Franz Dusart stammen die um 1650 entstandenen acht Marmorbüsten, die 1702 als oranische Erbschaft an Preußen gingen und ihrem Standort nun den Namen »Oranienrondell« geben.

The Neue Kammern (New Chambers), west of the Sanssouci palace, also built in 1747 to Knobelsdorff's design, were originally an orangery, then redesigned as a guest house in 1771-5 by Karl von Gontard and Georg Christian Unger. They and the Great Picture Gallery to the east form a unique ensemble of buildings. Büring's gallery is the earliest surviving German museum building; earlier picture galleries were simply part of the palace. The point of the dome on the central section is topped by eagle and snake, a work in beaten copper by Benjamin Giese and Friedrich Jury. There were originally 168 pictures by Flemish and Italian masters in the festive interior; some of them formed the basic stock of the new Berlin Museum in 1830, but were returned a century later. Today only a third of the old stock is in existence, and gaps caused by the Second World War are being filled with comparable pictures. The terrace outside the gallery and the «Dutch Garden» were laid out by Joachim Ludwig Heydert in 1764-6. The eight marble busts that went to Prussia in 1702 as an Orange legacy and gave the name «Oranienrondell» to their site, are the work of the Flemish sculptor Franz Dusart, carved c. 1650.

in der Nähe/nearby:
Obelisk und Obeliskportal; Schopenhauerstraße
1747-48 • Georg Wenzeslaus v. Knobelsdorff

Q 3 Chinesisches Teehaus
Potsdam-Sanssouci; Ökonomieweg
1754-57 • Johann Gottfried Büring

Als eines der markantesten Architekturbeispiele für die Chinamode des 18. Jahrhunderts in Europa kann das Chinesische Teehaus am südöstlichen Zipfel des bis 1763 vom Lustgartenbezirk getrennten »Reh- und Fasanengartens« gelten. Als Vorbild diente das um 1740 von Héré errichtete Türkische Trèfle im Park von Luneville. Der runde Saal des Pavillons ist überkuppelt, auf der Spitze des Daches thront ein vergoldeter Mandarin von Benjamin Giese und Friedrich Jury. Von märchenhaft-fremdländischem Reiz lagern rings um das Haus Chinesengruppen. Die reiche Einrichtung der Kabinette konnte erst 1764 abgeschlossen werden, sie enthält eine wertvolle Sammlung japanischer, chinesischer und Meißener Porzellane. Die Tradition der Chinamode hatte bereits Friedrich I. im Berliner Stadtschloß mit einem »Chinesischen Zimmer« und ostasiatischen Lackmöbeln begründet, auch die Schlösser Monbijou und Charlottenburg erhielten zu Anfang des 18. Jahrhunderts ihre Porzellankabinette. Das Teehaus steht heute in einem Landschaftspark. Friedrich Zacharias Salzmann hatte das ursprüngliche Jagd- und Wildrevier 1763-72 umgestaltet, Peter Joseph Lenné gab ihm ab 1819 das endgültige Aussehen.

The Chinese teahouse at the south-eastern point of «deer and pheasant park», separate from the Lustgarten area until 1763, is one of the most striking examples of the China craze in eighteenth century Europe. It was modelled on the Turkish Trèfle built by Héré in the park at Luneville c. 1740. The round room of the pavilion is domed, with a gilded mandarin by Benjamin Giese and Friedrich Jury on top. The building is surrounded by groups of sculptures of Chinese people of fairy-tale, faraway charm. The lavish collections were not completed until 1764, and consist of valuable Japanese, Chinese and Meissen porcelain. Frederick I had already established the tradition of an interest in China in the Berliner Stadtschloss with a «Chinese room» and Far Eastern lacquer furniture, and the palaces of Monbijou and Charlottenburg acquired porcelain collections in the early eighteenth century. The tea house is now in a landscaped park. The original woodland and hunting reserve was originally redesigned by Friedrich Zacharias Salzmann in 1763-72, and given its final shape by Peter Joseph Lenné from 1819.

in der Nähe/nearby:
Chinesische Küche; (südöstl. des Teehauses)
1763 • Johann Gottfried Büring

Q 4 Antikentempel und Freundschaftstempel
Potsdam-Sanssouci; Hauptallee
1768 • Karl v. Gontard

Die 2,5 km lange Hauptallee führt in Ost-West-Richtung am Fuße der Hügelkette mit Bildergalerie, Schloß und Neuen Kammern entlang durch den Park von Sanssouci, parallel an den Bauten vorbei und nicht axial auf sie bezogen, wie es für eine strenge Barockanlage zu erwarten wäre. Erst das später erbaute Neue Palais nimmt die Axialität der Allee auf. Beiderseits des Halbrondells vor dem Palais stehen zwei Rundtempel: südlich der Freundschaftstempel, nördlich der Antikentempel (Bild). Die Idee und erste Skizzen stammen von Friedrich II. Als typologisches Vorbild diente der von Knobelsdorff im Tempelgarten von Neuruppin 1732-36 für den jungen Friedrich errichtete Apollotempel, ein Monopteros mit Kuppeldach. Die Wiederholung und Anknüpfung an bereits Geschaffenes entsprach der Lebenshaltung des Königs. Der Antikentempel entstand als architektonische Hülle für eine aus dem Nachlaß des Kardinals Polignac durch Friedrich II. erworbene Sammlung von 300 Marmorskulpturen und für die von Baron Philipp v. Stosch übernommene Gemmensammlung.

The main alley is 2.5 km long, and runs through the park of Sanssouci in an east-west direction at the foot of the chain of hills on which stand picture gallery, palace and Neue Kammern. It runs parallel with the buildings and does not relate to them axially, as one would anticipate in a strictly baroque complex. The axiality of the avenue was not taken up until later, when the Neues Palais was built. On either side of the half-rondell in front of the Palais are two round temples: to the south the Freundschaftstempel, and to the north the Antikentempel (picture). Idea and first sketches came from Frederick II. The typological model was the Temple of Apollo, a monopteros with domed roof, built by Knobelsdorff for the young Frederick in the Temple Garden of Neuruppin in 1732-6. Repeating and following existing ideas was in keeping with the king's attitude to life. The Antikentempel was built as an architectural setting for a collection of 300 sculptures acquired by Frederick II from the estate of Cardinal Polignac and for the gem collection taken over from Baron Philipp von Stosch.

in der Nähe/nearby:
Marmorstatuen im Halbrondell; Hauptallee
19. Jh. (Kopien) • Eduard Stützel (überwiegend)
Bronzefigur des Narziß; Hauptallee
1896 • Hubert Netzer
Rondell mit Apollo und Diana
1827 (Kopien antiker Vorbilder)

Q 5 Neues Palais
Potsdam-Sanssouci; Am Neuen Palais
1763-69 • Johann Gottfried Büring, Karl v. Gontard

Das repräsentative Wohnschloß ist die letzte bedeutende Anlage des friderizianischen Barock. Zwar bestand seit etwa 1750 die Absicht, Sanssouci zu erweitern, doch beeinflußte der Ausgang des Siebenjährigen Krieges ganz entscheidend Gestaltung und Größe der Anlage. Sie wurde zum Manifest des Erfolges und Selbstbewußtseins eines absolutistischen Herrschers und der jungen Großmacht Preußen. 213 m lang ist die Front des Schlosses. An den 428 Statuen der Fassade arbeiteten zwölf Bildhauer. Rückwärtig umschließt die Dreiflügelanlage einen Ehrenhof, der mit den zwei gegenüberliegenden Wirtschaftsgebäuden, den Communs, und dem zur Halbkreiskolonnade ergänzten Triumphbogen eine grandiose Architekturkulisse ergibt. Die Gestaltung der Innenräume im Rokokostil erfolgte von 1765 an unter der Leitung des aus Bayreuth stammenden Architekten Karl v. Gontard. In 200 Wohn- und Repräsentationsräumen hängen 259 Werke italienischer und niederländischer Maler des 16. bis 18. Jahrhunderts, aber auch Bilder der Berliner Schule. Höhepunkte der Raumfolge sind der Grottensaal und das Theater.

This imposing residential palace is the last important baroque building dating from Frederick's time. Certainly the intention to extend Sanssouci had been in the air since about 1750, but the outcome of the Seven Years' War considerably affected design and size of the complex. It became a manifestation of the success and self-confidence of an absolute ruler and of Prussia as a new great power. The façade is 213 m long, and twelve sculptors worked on the 428 statues. At the rear the three sections of the building surround a cour d'honneur, which together with the domestic buildings opposite, the Communs, and the triumphal arch extended into a semi-circular colonnade, forming a grandiose architectural backdrop. The interior is in rococo style, and was created from 1765 under the direction of Bayreuth architect Karl von Gontard. 259 works by sixteenth to eighteenth century Italian painters, and also pictures form the Berlin school, hang in 200 residential and public rooms. The high points of the sequence of rooms are the Grottensaal and the theatre.

in der Nähe/nearby:
Communs; Am Neuen Palais
1766-69 • Karl v. Gortard (nach Jean Legeay)

Q 6 Schloß Charlottenhof
Potsdam-Sanssouci; Geschwister-Scholl-Straße
1826-28 • Karl Friedrich Schinkel, Ludwig Persius

1826 kaufte König Friedrich Wilhelm III. das am Rande der Brandenburger Vorstadt gelegene Gut Charlottenhof für den Kronprinzen. In den folgenden Jahren entstand in schöpferischem Zusammenwirken des Bauherren, Kronprinz Wilhelm (IV.), des Baumeisters Schinkel und des Gartenarchitekten Peter Joseph Lenné ein vom Geiste des Klassizismus geprägtes Gesamtkunstwerk als Einheit von Architektur und Landschaft. In Lennés englischem Landschaftspark vereinen sich weite Rasenflächen, lockere Baumgruppen und künstliche Gewässer, geben wechselnde Blickachsen frei. Schinkel dagegen war an die Ausmaße des vorhandenen ehemals Büringschen Wohnhauses gebunden, das er in den Neubau einbeziehen sollte. So entstand ein Schloß in bürgerlichen Maßstäben – ganz im Sinne des Biedermeier. Die Formensprache orientiert sich am Stil der römischen Villa, des antiken Landsitzes. Von vornehmer Schlichtheit die Front, die Rückseite dagegen wendet sich mit einem dorischen Portikus zur künstlich aufgeschütteten Terrasse mit Fontäne, Exedra und seitlicher Pergola.

In 1826 King Friedrich Wilhelm III bought the Charlottenhof estate on the edge of the Brandenburger Vorstadt for the Crown Prince. In the following years a complete work of art steeped in the spirit of classicism, unified architecture and landscape, was created in creative co-operation between Crown Prince Wilhelm (IV) as patron, Schinkel as architect and Peter Joseph Lenné as landscape gardener. Lenné's English landscaped park combines broad areas of lawn, informal groups of trees and artificial pools, opening up varying axes of view. Schinkel however was bound by the dimensions of the existing building, formerly the Büring residence, which he had to incorporate into the new one. He thus created a palace of bourgeois dimensions – entirely in the spirit of Biedermeier. The formal language is guided by that of the Roman villa, the ancient country seat. The façade is elegant and plain, but the rear looks out from a Doric portico over the artificially raised terrace with fountain, exedra and side pergola.

in der Nähe/nearby:
Römische Bäder; Lennéstraße
1829-40 • Ludwig Persius
Hippodrom; Geschwister-Scholl-Straße
1836 • Peter Joseph Lenné
Fasanerie; Geschwister-Scholl-Straße
1844 • Ludwig Persius

Q 7 Neue Orangerie
Potsdam-Sanssouci; An der Orangerie
1851-60 • Ludwig Persius, Friedrich August Stüler, Ludwig Ferdinand Hesse

Bedeutende Impulse für die Gestaltung der Kulturlandschaft von Potsdam gingen von Friedrich Wilhelm IV. aus, wie viele Architekturskizzen von seiner Hand belegen. Das Projekt einer Triumphstraße lehnt sich an römische Vorbilder an und übersetzt sie in die neue Stilrichtung des romantischen Klassizismus. Nicht ohne Einfluß auf die Spätromantik bleiben Beispiele aus der italienischen Hochrenaissance. Ausgangspunkt des auf optischer Schauwirkung basierenden Projekts war die 1834/35 geborene Idee eines Ruhmestempels für Friedrich II. Sowohl Schinkel als auch sein Schüler Persius arbeiteten an Entwürfen, die aber nie gebaut wurden. Es folgten neue Pläne von immer gigantischeren Ausmaßen ohne jede Chance einer Realisierung. 1842 wird mit dem Bau der Straße begonnen. Doch die Prachtstraße über den Bornstedter Höhenzug mit ihren phantastischen Gebäuden bleibt Fragment, nicht zuletzt durch den Tod von Persius 1845. Als wichtigster Teil des Projektes entstand die Palastarchitektur der Neuen Orangerie. Mit 330 m Länge übertraf sie noch das Neue Palais. Der Mittelbau beherbergt den Raffaelsaal mit 67 wertvollen Gemäldekopien italienischer Renaissancemeister.

Friedrich Wilhelm IV provided important stimuli for Potsdam's cultural landscape, as is proved by many architectural sketches from his hand. The project for a triumphal avenue follows Roman models and translates them into the new style of Romantic classicism. Ideas stemming from the Italian High Renaissance were not without influence on late Romanticism. The starting point for the project, based on desire to make a visual show, was the idea of a temple of fame for Frederick II, conceived in 1834-5. Both Schinkel and his pupil Persius worked on designs that were never built. New plans of increasingly gigantic dimensions followed, without any chance of implementation. In 1842 work on the avenue began, but the show street running over the Bornstedt heights remains a fragment, not least because of Persius' death in 1845. The most important part of the project to be built was the palatial architecture of the New Orangery. It is longer than the Neues Palais, 330 m. The central building houses the Raphael room, with 67 valuable copies of paintings by Italian Renaissance masters.

in der Nähe/nearby:
Statue Friedrich Wilhelm IV.; An der Orangerie
1873 • Gustav Bläser
Jubiläumsterrasse; Maulbeerallee
1913
Botanischer Garten; Maulbeerallee
Ab 1844 • Ludwig Persius

Q 8 Schloß Lindstedt
Potsdam-Bornstedt; Lindstedter Chaussee
1859-60 • Ludwig Persius, Peter Joseph Lenné

Kronprinz Friedrich Wilhelm kaufte im Jahre 1828 das Gut Lindstedt, das sich im Nordwesten unmittelbar an den Park von Sanssouci anschließt. Im Sinne der Landesverschönerung zeichnete Lenné einen ersten Gartenplan, dem 1832 Entwürfe des Kronprinzen folgten. Weitere Grundstücksankäufe ließen mittlerweile das Krongut Bornstedt-Lindstedt entstehen. Die 1857 offenbar werdende unheilbare Geisteskrankheit Friedrich Wilhelms IV. beschleunigte die über Jahre verschleppte Bautätigkeit, da der Kranke einen Alterssitz in der Abgeschiedenheit brauchte. Der Bau wurde nach Plänen von Persius, Stüler, Hesse und Arnim erst nach dem Tode des Königs vollendet. Das bescheidene Schlößchen in spätklassizistischen Formen über asymmetrischem Grundriß erinnert mit seiner Pergola und dem Portikus an Charlottenhof. Den Bezug zur Landschaft stellt der Rundturm mit einem Belvedere her. Der Park wurde nach Lennés Projekt im Sinne antiker Gärten gestaltet und durch dichte Anpflanzungen zur Umgebung abgeschirmt.

In 1828 Crown Prince Friedrich Wilhelm bought the Lindstedt estate, which was immediately adjacent to the park of Sanssouci in the north-west. Lenné produced a first plan for the garden in the spirit of beautifying the countryside, and this was followed by designs by the Crown Prince in 1832. Further land acquisitions led to the emergence of the crown estate of Bornstedt-Lindstedt. In 1857 it became clear that Friedrich Wilhelm IV was incurably insane, and this accelerated building activity that had dragged on over years, as the invalid needed a solitary residence for his old age. The building was completed to plans by Persius, Stüler, Hesse and Arnim, but only after the king had died. This modest little palace with its asymmetrical ground plan, pergola and portico is reminiscent of Charlottenhof. The round tower with belvedere creates a point of reference to the countryside. The park was laid out like an ancient garden in accordance with Lenné's project and screened off from its surroundings by dense planting.

in der Nähe/nearby:
Kirche; P-Bornstedt; Ribbeckstraße
Ab 1842 • Ludwig Persius, Friedrich August Stüler
Alter Friedhof; P-Bornstedt; Ribbeckstraße
M. 18. Jh.
Belvedere auf dem Klausberg; P-Sanssouci; Maulbeerallee
1770-72
Drachenhaus; P-Sanssouci; Maulbeerallee
1770 • Karl v. Gontard

Q 9 Friedenskirche
Potsdam-Sanssouci; Am Grünen Gitter
1845-54 • Ludwig Persius, Ludwig Ferdinand Hesse, Ferdinand v. Arnim

Anläßlich des hundertjährigen Bestehens von Schloß Sanssouci wurde am 14. April 1845 der Grundstein zum Bau der Friedenskirche gelegt. Nach dem Vorbild der frühchristlichen Basilika S. Clemente in Rom entwarf Persius das Bauwerk nach einer Ideenkonzeption von Friedrich Wilhelm IV. Der siebengeschossige Campanile wiederum erfuhr Anregungen durch S. Maria di Cosmedin in Florenz und das anschließende Predigerhaus und Schulgebäude durch florentinische Villen. Julius Carl Raschdorff, der Architekt des Berliner Domes, ergänzte das Ensemble 1888-90 durch das Mausoleum für Friedrich III., eine Nachahmung der Grabkapelle zu Innichen in Tirol.

The foundation stone of the Friedenskirche was laid on 14 April 1845 to celebrate the one hundred years of Sanssouci. Persius designed the building on the basis of an idea by Friedrich Wilhelm IV on the model of the early Christian basilica of S. Clemente in Rome. The seven-storeyed campanile however drew upon S. Maria di Cosmedin in Florence, and the adjacent priest's house and school buildings followed the design of Florentine villas. Julius Carl Raschdorf, the architect of the Berlin Dom, completed the ensemble in 1888-90 with the mausoleum of Frederick III, an imitation of the funerary chapel at Innichen in the Tyrol.

in der Nähe/nearby:
Marlygarten; Am Grünen Gitter
Um 1850 • Peter Joseph Lenné
Eingangstor; Am Grünen Gitter
Um 1850

Q 10 Marmorpalais
Potsdam; Am Neuen Garten
1787-97 • Karl v. Gontard, Carl Gotthard Langhans

Im Jahre 1787 wurde mit der Anlage einer Sommerresidenz für König Friedrich Wilhelm II. am Westufer des Heiligen Sees begonnen. Die Anlagen von Dessau-Wörlitz beeinflußten und prägten deutlich die Gestaltung der weiträumigen Parklandschaft. Anregungen gehen auf Friedrich Wilhelm v. Erdmannsdorff zurück, Johann August Eyserbeck erweiterte den Neuen Garten bis zum Jungfernsee, und Peter Joseph Lenné überarbeitete ihn. Auf einer in den See vorgeschobenen Terrasse baute Gontard bis 1791 ein kleines quadratisches Schlößchen, das vermutlich Langhans bis 1797 zur Dreiflügelanlage ergänzte. Die Rohziegelfassade verweist auf holländische Vorbilder. Stilistisch kommt der Übergang vom Spätbarock zum Klassizismus zum Ausdruck, reicher plastischer Schmuck begleitet noch die Fronten. Die Innenräume sind wertvolle Zeugen der Raumkunst im Berliner Frühklassizismus. 1843-45 bauten Persius und Hesse die nur im Rohbau fertigen Erweiterungstrakte aus. Sie hielten sich dabei an den Stil der ersten Bauphase, so daß ein weitgehend einheitliches Bild erreicht wird.

In 1787 work started on a summer residence for King Friedrich Wilhelm II on the west bank of the Heiliger See. The Dessau-Wörlitz park clearly influenced and put its mark upon this spacious landscape design. Ideas were drawn from as far back as Friedrich Wilhelm von Erdmannsdorff. Johann August Eyserbeck extended the Neuer Garten to the Jungfernsee, and Peter Joseph Lenné reworked the concept. Gontard built a small, square palace on a terrace jutting out into the lake, completing it in 1791, and this was extended as a complex with three wings, presumably by Langhans, and completed in 1797. The rough brick façade suggests Dutch models. Style is transitional from late baroque to classicism, and the façades still have lavish sculptural decoration. The interiors are valuable evidence of early classical spatial design in Berlin. In 1843-5 Persius and Hesse built extension sections which were only completed as shells. They kept to the style of the first building phase, so that the overall picture is generally uniform.

in der Nähe/nearby:
Holländisches Etablissement; Am Neuen Garten
1789-90 • Karl v. Gontard, Andreas Ludwig Krüger
Orangerie; Am Neuen Garten
1791-92 • Carl Gotthard Langhans, Andreas Ludwig Krüger

Q 11 Schloß Cecilienhof
Potsdam; Am Neuen Garten
1913-16 • Paul Schultze-Naumburg

Im Norden des Neuen Gartens errichtete der Hofarchitekt Schultze-Naumburg im englischen Landhausstil das Schloß Cecilienhof als Landsitz des Kronprinzen Wilhelm. Der malerisch komponierte, um mehrere Innenhöfe angelegte Bau verwendet die Fachwerkkonstruktion als dekoratives Architekturelement. Entsprechend der Bauzeit fehlt Cecilienhof die große Geste, es ist mehr Landhaus als Schloß. Asymmetrie und Kleinteiligkeit herrschen vor, das Malerische und eine mit dem Äußeren durchaus harmonisierende Hinwendung zum Innenraum prägen das Bauwerk. Nur an der Hauptfront öffnet sich über zwei Geschosse eine verhalten repräsentative Halle. Cecilienhof war im Juli und August 1945 Tagungsort der Siegermächte des Zweiten Weltkrieges. In seinen Räumen wurde das Potsdamer Abkommen unterzeichnet.

Schultze-Naumburg, the court architect, built the Cecilienhof palace in the English country house style in the north of the Neuer Garten. The building is picturesquely composed and laid out around several inner courtyards, and uses half-timbering as a decorative architectural element. Appropriately to its building period, Cecilienhof makes no major gestures, is is more country house than palace. Asymmetry and breaking down into small areas are its hallmarks, along with picturesqueness and an emphasis on interior space that is entirely in harmony with the exterior. There is a hall, imposing but restrained, extending over two storeys, behind the main façade only. Cecilienhof was the meeting place of the victorious powers after the Second World War in July and August 1945. The Potsdam Accord was signed in its rooms.

in der Nähe/nearby:
Meierei; Neuer Garten
1844 • Ludwig Persius
Braunes, Weißes, Rotes und Grünes Haus;
Neuer Garten • 18. Jh.
Muschelgrotte; Neuer Garten
1792 • Andreas Ludwig Krüger
Pyramide; Neuer Garten
1791-92
Schindelhaus; Neuer Garten
Um 1792 • vermutlich Andreas Ludwig Krüger

Q 12 Palais Lichtenau
Potsdam; Behlertstraße 31
1796-97 • Michael Philipp Boumann, Carl Gotthard Langhans

Eines der besterhaltenen Beispiele frühklassizistischer Profanbaukunst in Potsdam ist das Palais Lichtenau. 1795 erwarben der Kämmerer Ritz und seine Gemahlin Gräfin Lichtenau, die bürgerliche Geliebte Friedrich Wilhelms II., das Grundstück am Südrand des Neuen Gartens. Die Entstehung des Hauses ist offenbar in enger Verbindung zum Schloß auf der Pfaueninsel zu sehen, das 1794 auf Anregung der Gräfin errichtet wurde. Das Palais schmücken im Fest- und Speisesaal so auch fünf ovale Wandgemälde mit Ansichten der Pfaueninsel. Der Raum selbst wurde nach Langhans' Entwurf durch Johann Carl Wilhelm Rosenberg dekoriert. Im Rosenholzzimmer sind die Wandpaneele von Angermann erhalten. Über den Türen finden sich noch originale geschnitzte Supraporten. Den Risalitgiebel der Straßenfront ziert ein segmentbogiges Relieffeld nach einem Entwurf von Johann Gottfried Schadow.

The Palais Lichtenau is one of the best-preserved examples of early classical secular architecture in Potsdam. Chamberlain Ritz and his consort Countess Lichtenau, the bourgeois mistress of Friedrich Wilhelm II, acquired this plot on the southern edge of the Neuer Garten in 1795. Clearly the emergence of the house has to be seen in close connection with the palace on the Pfaueninsel built at the suggestion of the Countess in 1794. Thus the ballroom and dining room of the Palais are decorated by five oval wall paintings with views of the Pfaueninsel. The room itself was decorated by Johann Carl Wilhelm Rosenberg to Langhans' design. Angermann's panels have survived in the rosewood room. There are original carved sopraportas over the doors. The pediment on the protruding section of the street façade is decorated with a segment-arched tympanum designed by Johann Gottfried Schadow.

in der Nähe/nearby:
Bibliothek; Neuer Garten
1792-94 • Carl Gotthard Langhans

R
Berlin/Potsdam
Babelsberg und Klein-Glienicke

Im Potsdamer Stadtteil Babelsberg sind noch heute drei Siedlungsbereiche deutlich zu erkennen: Neuendorf, Nowawes und die Villenkolonie Neubabelsberg. 1375 ist Neuendorf als »Nygendorp« im Landbuch Kaiser Karls IV. erstmals erwähnt. Aus einem slawischen Rundweiler entwickelte sich ein frühdeutsches Rundplatzdorf, wie Scherbenfunde bestätigen. 1750 muß Neuendorf das Gebiet der »Sandscholle« zur Errichtung des »Etablissements zu Potsdam« abgeben, und bis 1765 entsteht die planmäßig angelegte friderizianische Kolonistensiedlung Nowawes. »Nowa ves« ist die tschechische Bezeichnung für Neuendorf. Nach 1840 setzt die industrielle Entwicklung ein, begünstigt durch die Eröffnung der Eisenbahnlinie Potsdam–Berlin im Jahre 1838. Aus Dorf und Kolonie wurden nun stattliche Orte, 1880 besaß Nowawes 7000 Einwohner, 1907 bildete es mit Neuendorf eine Gemeinde, und 1924 wurde diese zur Stadt erhoben. Seit dem letzten Viertel des 19. Jahrhunderts entwickelte sich auch Neu-Babelsberg als Villenvorort, ihm wurde 1924 das Dorf Klein-Glienicke eingemeindet. 1938 und 1939 kommt es zu einer Neuordnung: zunächst wird aus Nowawes und Neu-Babelsberg die Stadt Babelsberg, diese wird dann Stadtteil von Potsdam. Eine eigene Entwicklung nahmen die Gelände des Babelsberges und nördlich des Dorfes Klein-Glienicke. Hier gab es ein Gut der Familie Schlabrendorf, das der Hof im 17. Jahrhundert erwarb und zum Jagdschloß umwandelte. Dieses war Ausgangspunkt weiterer Schloßbauten im 19. Jahrhundert. Nahe der Glienicker Brücke erhielt Prinz Karl ein Schloß, Prinz Wilhelm, der spätere König und Kaiser, gegenüber auf dem Babelsberg. Noch weiter nördlich, auf der wilden Insel »Großer Werder«, wurden nach dem Mittelalter zur Jagd Pfauen und dann Kaninchen gehalten, bis sich des Großen Kurfürsten Chemiker Kunkel hier niederließ. Friedrich Wilhelm II. entdeckte ein Jahrhundert später diese Einöde neu und baute auf ihr das Schloß Pfaueninsel, dem weitere Bauten folgten. 1934 kaufte die Stadt Berlin den Park Klein-Glienicke, später auch den Schloßbezirk. Schloß und Park Babelsberg dagegen fielen an Potsdam.

In the district of Potsdam known as Babelsberg there are still three distinct areas of settlement: Neuendorf, Nowawes and the villa colony of Neu-Babelsberg. Neuendorf was mentioned for the first time as «Nygendorp» in the land register of Emperor Charles IV in 1375. Pottery shards confirm that a Slavic radial village developed into an early German radial village with central square. In 1750 Neuendorf had to abandon the «Sandscholle» area so that the «Etablissements zu Potsdam» could be built, and Frederick's planned settlement for colonists, Nowawes, was completed by 1765. «Nowa ves» is the Czech term for Neuendorf. Industrial development started after 1840, boosted by the opening of the Potsdam-Berlin railway line in 1838. Village and colony now became handsome places; in 1880 Nowawes had 7,000 inhabitants, in 1907 it formed a parish with Neuendorf, and this was raised to the status of town in 1924. Neu-Babelsberg developed as a villa settlement from the last quarter of the nineteenth century, and in 1924 the village of Klein-Glienicke became part of the parish. In 1938 and 1939 came reorganization: first Nowawes and Neu-Babelsberg became the town of Babelsberg, and then this became a part of Potsdam. The territory of the Babelsberg hill itself, and to the north of the village of Klein-Glienicke, developed in their own way. In Klein-Glienecke the Schlabrendorf family owned an estate, acquired by the court in the seventeenth century and turned into a hunting lodge. This was the starting point for further palace building in the nineteenth century. Prinz Karl was given a palace near the Glienicker Brücke, and Prinz Wilhelm, later King and Kaiser, acquired one on the Babelsberg. Further north, on the wild island of «Grosser Werder», peacocks were kept for hunting surce the Middle Ages, and then rabbits, until the Great Elector's chemist, Kunkel, settled here. Friedrich Wilhelm II rediscovered this wilderness a century later and built the Pfaueninsel (peacock island) palace on it, and this was followed by other buildings. In 1934 the city of Berlin bought Klein-Gienicke park, then later the palace precincts. Palace and park in Babelsberg fell to Potsdam, however.

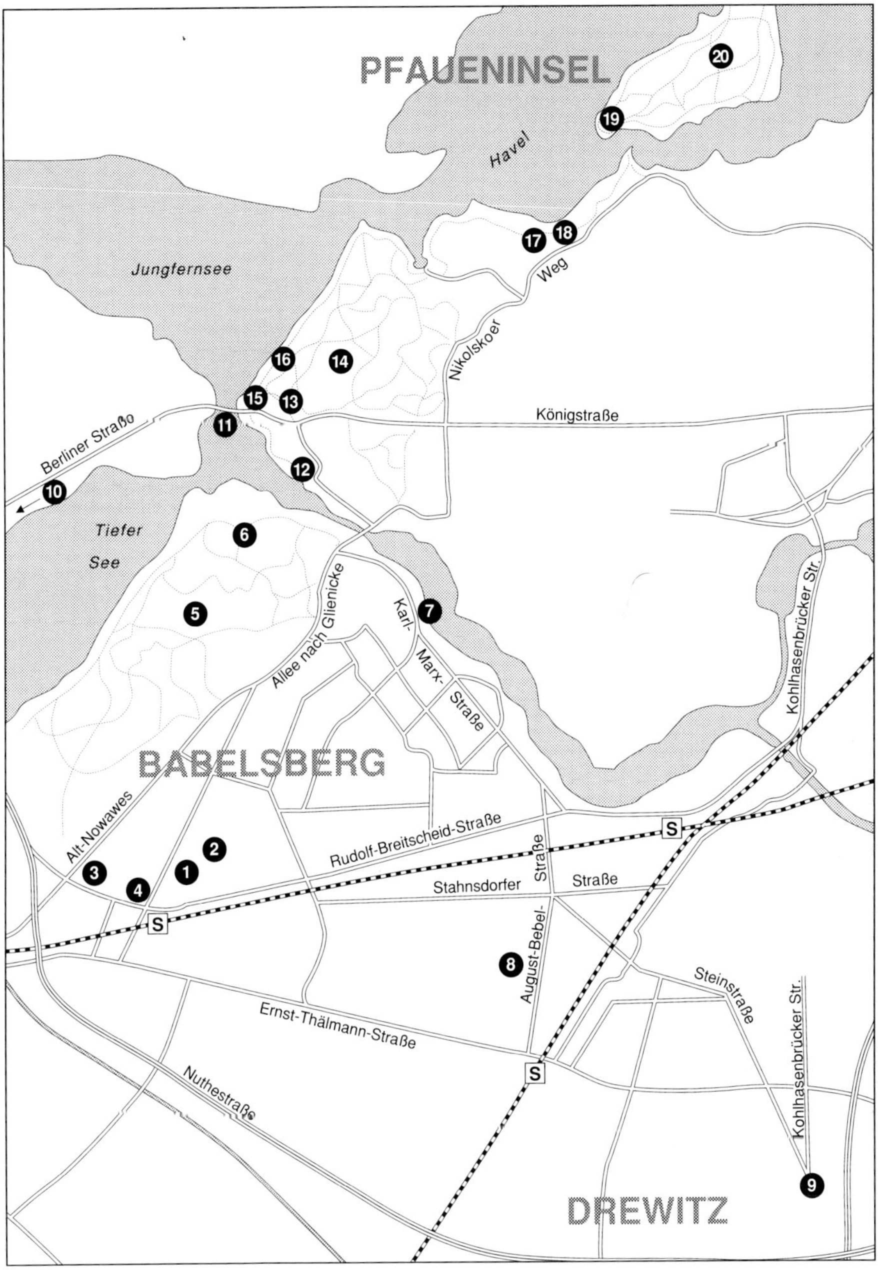

R 1 Weberkolonie Nowawes
R 2 Friedrichskirche
R 3 Oberlinhaus – Schwesternwohnheim
R 4 Rathaus Babelsberg
R 5 Park Babelsberg
R 6 Schloß Babelsberg
R 7 Haus Herpich
R 8 Filmatelier Neubabelsberg
R 9 Jagdschloß Stern
R 10 Leibgardehusaren-Kaserne
R 11 Glienicker Brücke (Brücke der Einheit)
R 12 Jagdschloß Glienicke
R 13 Schloß Glienicke
R 14 Park Klein-Glienicke
R 15 Große Neugierde
R 16 Kasino
R 17 Blockhaus Nikolskoe
R 18 St. Peter und Paul
R 19 Schloß Pfaueninsel
R 20 Kavalierhaus

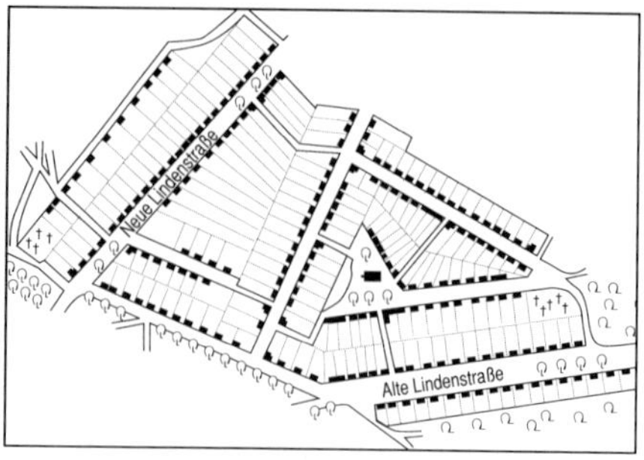

R 1 Weberkolonie Nowawes
Potsdam-Babelsberg; Karl-Liebknecht-Straße
1750-65 • v. Retzow, Heinrich Ludwig Manger

Durch Binnenkolonisation wollte Friedrich II. nach dem Zweiten Schlesischen Krieg die Verluste an Menschen ausgleichen. Er folgte der Devise seines Vaters »Wenn das Land gut peuplieret ist, das ist der rechte Reichtum des Landes«. Dem Aufruf des Generals v. Retzow vom 7. Oktober 1750 zur Ansiedlung in einem »Etablissement zu Potsdam« folgten 60 böhmische Familien evangelisch-lutherischen Glaubens. So entstand der östliche Teil der Siedlung um den dreieckigen Weberplatz 1751-54 unter Leitung v. Retzows, der bei der Kolonisation des Oderbruchs bereits Erfahrungen gesammelt hatte. Eingeschossige Doppelhäuser mit Gärten erhielten die Weber und Spinner. Wiederum mit Doppelhäusern wurde ab 1764 der nordwestliche Teil, der heutige Bereich zwischen Alt-Nowawes und Karl-Liebknecht-Straße, bebaut. Für diese Bauten war Manger verantwortlich. Maurer und Zimmerleute aus Württemberg und der Schweiz siedelte man hier an, die für den Bau des Neuen Palais dringend benötigt wurden. Die bis zu 70 m breite Straße säumten Maulbeerbäume für die Seidenraupenzucht. Im Originalzustand ist keines der Kolonistenhäuser, eine Sonderform des fränkischen Hauses, erhalten.

Frederick II intended to balance the loss of life incurred in the Second Silesian War by internal colonization. He followed his father's motto: «If the land is well peopled, that is the real riches of the land.» 60 Bohemian Lutheran-Protestant families responded to General Retzow's appeal of 7 October 1750 for settlement in an «Etablissement zu Potsdam». Thus the eastern section of the settlement around the triangular Weberplatz came into being in 1751-4 under the direction of Retzow, who had already gained experience from the colonization of the Oder marsh. The weavers and spinners were provided with single-storey semi-detached houses with gardens. The north-western section, the present area between Alt-Nowawes and Karl-Liebknecht-Strasse, was also developed by the building of semi-detached houses, from 1764. Manger was responsible for these buildings. Masons and carpenters from Württemberg and Switzerland, urgently needed to build the Neues Palais, were settled here. The road was up to 70 m wide, and bordered with mulberry trees for breeding silkworms. None of the colonists' houses, a particular version of the Franconian house, has survived in its original form.

R 2 Friedrichskirche
Potsdam-Babelsberg; Weberplatz
1752-53 • Johann Boumann

Gleichzeitig mit der Anlage der Weberkolonie Nowawes für die ihres Glaubens wegen verfolgten evangelisch-lutherischen Böhmen wurde eine Predigtkirche errichtet. Baumeister war der aus Amsterdam stammende königliche Bauinspektor Johann Boumann. Über einem achteckigen Grundriß erhebt sich der verputzte Saalbau mit einem niedrigen Turm an der westlichen Schmalseite. Die Wetterfahne am spitzen Turmhelm trägt die Jahreszahl 1752. Im Inneren der Kirche sind hufeisenförmige Emporen in zwei Geschossen angeordnet. Bemerkenswert ist auch die Ausstattung. Zwei Messingblaker sind aus Helmschilden des 1. Garderegiments zu Fuß, den sogenannten Langen Kerls, angefertigt. Erhalten ist auch das Kirchensiegel von 1753: Auf einem Schild ist ein Pilgrim mit Wanderstab abgebildet, darüber der preußische Adler, die Umschrift zweisprachig »Unter deinem Schutz, Kirche von Nowawes«.

A preaching church was built at the same time as the Nowawes weavers' colony for the Lutheran Bohemians, who had been persecuted for their faith. The architect was Royal building inspector Johann Boumann, originally from Amsterdam. The rendered single-room building has a low tower on the western narrow side, and is built on an octagonal ground plan. The weathercock on the spire carries the date 1752. The interior has horseshoe-shaped galleries on two levels. The interior decoration is also noteworthy. Two brass candlesticks were made from helmet-shields of the 1st Guard Foot-Regiment, the so-called Lange Kerls. The church seal dating from 1753 has also survived: a pilgrim with staff is depicted on a shield, with the Prussian eagle above him, and a bilingual inscription «Under your protection, church of Nowawes».

in der Nähe/nearby:
Kaufmännische Berufsschule; Weberplatz 13
M. 19. Jh.

R 3 Oberlinhaus – Schwesternwohnheim
Potsdam-Babelsberg; Rudolf-Breitscheid-Straße 24
1925-27 • Schleicher

Benannt nach dem aus den Vogesen stammenden Philanthropen und Pfarrer Johann Friedrich Oberlin wurde 1879 in Berlin auf Anregung des Freiherrn von Bissing-Beernberg der Oberlinverein gegründet. Zuvor, im Jahre 1874, hatte man bereits mit der Ausbildung von Kindergärtnerinnen begonnen und dafür 1877-78 ein erstes Haus in Nowawes errichtet. Neben dem dreigeschossigen Bau im Rundbogenstil entstanden weitere karitative Einrichtungen bis in die jüngste Vergangenheit: 1878-79 wurden das Diakonissenmutterhaus und die Poliklinik erbaut, 1883 die erste Kinderkrippe eingerichtet, 1886 erfolgte die Aufnahme körperbehinderter Kinder, 1906 wurde das erste deutsche Taubblindenheim errichtet. 1910 folgte das Kreiskrankenhaus, 1912 ein Altenheim, 1917 das Hortnerinnenseminar, 1928 Bäckerei und Schule, 1931 Lehrwerkstätten für Behinderte und eine orthopädische Klinik. 1954 entstanden ein Schwesternwohnheim, eine Jugendstation und eine Keramikwerkstatt. 1979-80 wurden ein Schwerstbehindertenwohnheim als Experimentalbau der Bauakademie nach dem Entwurf von Georg Krause errichtet.

The Oberlin association, named after Johann Friedrich Oberlin, a philanthropist and pastor from the Vosges, was founded in Berlin in 1879, at the suggestion of Freiherr von Bissing-Beernberg. Prior to this, in 1874, a start had already been made on training women kindergarden teachers, and a building had been erected in Nowawes for this purpose in 1877-8. Further charitable institutions have grown up beside the three-storey, round-arched building, until quite recently: deaconesses' training centre and outpatients' department date from 1878-9, the first crèche was set up in 1883, physically handicapped children were accepted from 1886, and the first home for the deaf and blind in Germany was built in 1906. The district hospital followed in 1910, an old people's home in 1912, the afternoon day-care seminar in 1917, bakery and school in 1928, training workshops for the handicapped and an orthopaedic clinic in 1931. In 1954 a nurses' home, a young people's ward and a ceramic workshop were built. A residential home for the severely handicapped was built in 1979-80 as an experimental building by the Bauakademie, to a design by Georg Krause.

in der Nähe/nearby:
Oberlinkirche; Rudolf-Breitscheid-Straße 24
1903-05 • Ludwig v. Tiedemann, Erich Riemasch
St. Antonius-Kirche; Goetheplatz
1933-34 • Wilhelm Fahlbusch

R 4 Rathaus
Potsdam-Babelsberg; Karl-Liebknecht-Straße 135
1898-99 • Otto Kerwien

Für die Industriegemeinde Nowawes wurde in den Jahren 1898-99 das Gebäude der Gemeindeverwaltung in den historisierenden Formen der märkischen Backsteingotik von Kerwien errichtet. Der stattliche dreigeschossige Klinkerbau ist durch Giebel, Erker, Loggien und einen hohen Turm gegliedert. 1924 wird der Bau zum städtischen Rathaus, nachdem die 1907 zu einer Gemeinde vereinigten Orte Nowawes und Neuendorf Stadtrecht erhielten. Heute dient das Gebäude als »Kulturhaus« und Bibliothek. Ähnlichkeiten mit dem ebenfalls von Kerwien erbauten Rathaus Schmargendorf in Berlin fallen auf.

This administrative building for the industrial community of Nowawes was built to a historicist design in the style of Mark Brandenburg brick Gothic in 1898-9. The handsome three-storey clinker building is articulated with gable, oriel, loggia and a tall tower. The building became a town hall in 1924, after Nowawes and Neuendorf, combined in 1907, were granted a charter. Today the building is used as «House of Culture» and library. There are striking similarities with Schmargendorf town hall in Berlin, also the work of Kerwien.

in der Nähe/nearby:
Postamt; Karl-Liebknecht-Straße 138
1966-69 • Wolfgang Müller

R 5 Park Babelsberg
Potsdam-Babelsberg; Allee nach Glienicke
1832-43 • Peter Joseph Lenné
1843-71 • Hermann v. Pückler-Muskau

Der Park umfaßt ein hügeliges, bewaldetes Gelände um den Babelsberg und einen flachen Wiesenteil im Westen. Die Fläche begrenzt im Nordwesten der Tiefe See, im Nordosten die Glienicker Lake. Die Gestaltung zu einem Landschaftspark durch Lenné begann noch vor dem Bau des Schlosses mit der Anlage eines Wegenetzes und der Pflanzung einheimischer Laubgehölze. 1841 erhält der Park eine Bewässerungsanlage für neue Fontänen, Seen und Wasserfälle. Historistische Gartenarchitektur und Erinnerungsmale wie das Matrosenhaus mit dem Staffelgiebel des Stendaler Rathauses beleben das Ganze. Nach 1843 übernimmt einer der bedeutendsten deutschen Gartenkünstler, Fürst Hermann v. Pückler-Muskau, die weitere Gestaltung. Seine Parks in Muskau und Branitz zählen zu den besten Schöpfungen des 19. Jahrhunderts. Babelsberg wird zu einem englischen Park, in dem weite Rasenflächen von Baumgruppen gerahmt werden und Blickachsen in die Ferne freigeben. Die einzelnen Höhen betonen Bauten. So entsteht der Flatowturm als Abbild des Eschenheimer Tores in Frankfurt/Main. Später wird auch die in Berlin abgetragene mittelalterliche Gerichtslaube im Park wieder aufgebaut.

The park consists of a hilly, wooded area around the Babelsberg and a flat grassy section in the north. The Tiefer See marks the limits of the park in the north-west, the Glienicker Lake in the north-east. Lenné's landscaping started even before the building of the palace when he laid out a network of paths and planted indigenous deciduous timber. In 1841 the park was provided with an irrigation plant for new fountains, lakes and waterfalls. The park as a whole is enlivened with historicist garden architecture and memorials like the Sailors' House with the staggered gable from Stendal town hall. After 1843 further design was taken over by one of Germany's most important garden artists, Fürst Hermann von Pückler-Muskau. Pückler's parks in Muskau and Branitz are among the best nineteenth century creations. Babelsberg became an English park, in which wide areas of grass are framed by groups of trees, and lines of view open up into the distance. Individual high points are accentuated with buildings. Thus the Flatow tower was modelled on the Eschenheim Gate in Frankfurt am Main. Later the medieval open-air court that had been demolished in Berlin was rebuilt in the park.

in der Nähe/nearby:
Matrosenhaus; Westteil des Parkes
1842 • Johann Heinrich Strack
Flatowturm; Westteil des Parkes
1853-56
Ehem. Berliner Gerichtslaube; Westteil des Parks
1871-72 • Johann Heinrich Strack
Maschinenhaus; Ufer Glienicker Lake
1843-45 • Ludwig Persius, Rudolf Wilhelm Gottgetreu

R 6 Schloß Babelsberg
Potsdam-Babelsberg; Allee nach Glienicke
1834-35 • Karl Friedrich Schinkel
1844-49 • Ludwig Persius, Johann Heinrich Strack

Bereits 1826 fertigte der Kronprinz Friedrich Wilhelm IV. für seinen Bruder Wilhelm erste Skizzen für einen Sommersitz auf dem Babelsberg. 1834 beginnt Schinkel nach weit umfangreicheren Plänen zu bauen. Der zweigeschossige Bau aus gelben Backsteinen ist im Stil der Tudorgotik konzipiert. Über asymmetrischem Grundriß erhebt sich auf einer Terrasse der mit Türmen, Erkern und Zinnenkränzen prächtig geschmückte Baukörper in der Gestalt spätromantischer Burganlagen. Bis 1835 entsteht der Ostflügel, 1844-49 der Westflügel. Für den zweiten Bauabschnitt wurden die Pläne von Persius und Strack unter der Einflußnahme des Bauherrn überarbeitet. Bindeglied zwischen den Flügeln wurde ein großer Oktogonbau mit einem durch zwei Geschosse reichenden Tanzsaal, das hohe Sterngewölbe »im altdeutschen Stil« ausgemalt. An altem und neuem Flügelbau ist der architektonische Stilwandel um die Mitte des 19. Jahrhunderts ablesbar. Von der ausgewogenen und wohlproportionierten Phase der Neugotik leitet die Überbetonung der Maßstäbe zum späteren Historismus über. Das Inventar des Schlosses ist heute weitgehend magaziniert.

Crown Prince Friedrich Wilhelm IV completed first sketches for a summer residence on the Babelsberg for his brother Wilhelm as early as 1826. Schinkel began to build in 1834, on a much larger scale. The two-storey, yellow-brick building is in Tudor-Gothic style. Magnificently decorated with towers, oriels and battlements, it soars up on a terrace on an asymmetrical ground plan in the form of a late-Romantic castle. The east wing was built by 1835, the west wing in 1844-9. For the second building phase, Persius' and Strack's plans were revised to accommodate the ideas of their client. The wings were linked by a large octagonal building with a ballroom rising through two storeys, with high stellar vaulting painted «in the old German style». The change in architectural style that took place in the mid nineteenth century is discernible in the old and new wings. Overaccentuation of scale leads from balanced and elegantly proportioned neo-Gothic to the later phase of historicism. The contents of the castle are now largely in store.

in der Nähe/nearby:
Kleines Schloß (Damenhaus); Nordwestteil des Parks
1841-42 • E. Gebhardt
Marstall; Nordwestteil des Parks
1842 • E. Gebhardt

R 7 Haus Herpich
Potsdam-Babelsberg; Karl-Marx-Straße 27
1910-11 • Alfred Grenander

1872 erwarb die Architektenfirma Ende & Böckmann ein 63 ha großes Gelände östlich des Babelsberger Parks an der Glienicker Lake für die Erschließung und spätere Bebauung als Villenkolonie. Begünstigt wurde die Anlage durch die Eröffnung eines Bahnhofs an der Berlin-Potsdamer Eisenbahnstrecke. Neben der Villenkolonie Grunewald gilt Neu-Babelsberg als bedeutendes Beispiel für den Villen- und Landhausbau des ausgehenden 19. Jahrhunderts und der beginnenden Moderne in der Potsdam-Berliner Architektur. Das Haus Herpich gehört zu den kurz vor dem Ersten Weltkrieg entstandenen Häusern, die sich nach Jugendstil und nach Landhausstil wieder deutlich an der Baukunst um 1800 orientieren. Dafür stehen die über beide Geschosse gehenden fein profilierten Rahmungen der Fensterachsen, der Brüstungsschmuck in abstrakt-floraler Zeichnung und das Mansartdach. Diese gestalterische Haltung ist gleichfalls bei Bauten von Ludwig Mies van der Rohe zu finden, die mehrfach in Neu-Babelsberg anzutreffen sind.

In 1872 architects Ende & Böckmann acquired 63 hectares east of Babelsberg Park on the Glienicker Lake, to be opened up and later developed as a villa colony. The idea was boosted by the opening of a station on the railway line from Berlin to Potsdam. With the Grunewald villa colony, Neu-Babelsberg is considered an important example of villa and country house building in the late nineteenth century and of the first stirrings of Modernism in the architecture of Potsdam and Berlin. The Herpich house was built shortly before the First World War, a period when houses were clearly orientated towards architecture of the period around 1800, after Jugendstil and the country house style. Signs of this are finely ribbed frames of the window axes rising through both storeys, abstract floral designs on the breasting and the mansard roof. This design approach can also be seen in a number of buildings by Mies van der Rohe to be found in Neu-Babelsberg.

in der Nähe/nearby:
Haus Mosler; Karl-Marx-Straße 28-29
1924-26 • Ludwig Mies van der Rohe
Haus Urbig; Virchowstraße 23
1915 • Ludwig Mies van der Rohe
Haus Riehl; Spitzweggasse 3
1907 • Ludwig Mies van der Rohe
Haus Mathies; Baldurstraße 6
1936 • Egon Eiermann
Sternwarte; Rosa-Luxemburg-Straße 17 a
1871-72 • Brüstlein, Thür

R 8 Filmatelier Neubabelsberg
Potsdam-Babelsberg; August-Bebel-Straße 26-53
1925-26 • Carl Stahl-Urach

Weltruf erlangte in den dreißiger Jahren die 1917 gegründete Universum-Film AG – kurz Ufa. In Neubabelsberg verfügte sie auf einem Gelände von 430 000 m^2 über den größten Atelierbetrieb in Europa. Aus bescheidenen Anfängen, einem 1911 von einem Kameramann eingerichteten »Photoatelier« auf der Sandscholle des Großen Heidefeldes und der Deutschen Bioskop-Gesellschaft, die zur gleichen Zeit eine leerstehende Kunstblumenfabrik bezog, entwickelte sich die Filmstadt. 1912 entstehen an der Stahnsdorfer Straße die ersten beiden Glashäuser für Filmaufnahmen, und der erste Stummfilm wird gedreht. 1925-26 baut Stahl-Urach die große Stummfilmhalle, überall wird nach amerikanischem Vorbild modernisiert, 1927-30 folgt der kreuzförmige Bau des Tonfilmstudios mit vier selbständigen Ateliers. Die fensterlosen Klinkerwände umschließen schalldichte Räume, die Türen sind als Schleusen gebaut. Um jeglichen Nachhall auszuschließen, wird in der Konstruktion auf die Verwendung von Stahl verzichtet. Nach 1945 wird in den Ateliers – nun unter der neugegründeten DEFA – weitergearbeitet. Erweiterungen und Neubauten kamen inzwischen hinzu.

Universum-Film AG – Ufa for short – was founded in 1917 and became world famous in the thirties. It has the largest studios in Europe, on a site covering 430,000 square metres. This film city developed from modest beginnings, a «photo-studio» started in 1911 by a cameraman on the sand outcrop of the Grosses Heidenfeld, and the Deutsche Bioskop-Gesellschaft, which moved into an empty artificial flower factory at the same time. The first glass buildings for shooting films were built in Stahnsdorfer Strasse in 1912, and the first silent film was made. Stahl-Urach built the great silent film hall in 1925-6; modernization on the American model took place everywhere: the cruciform sound studio building followed in 1927-30. The windowless clinker walls enclose soundproof spaces, and the doors are built as sound-locks. In order to exclude the possibilty of echo, no steel was used in the structure. Work continued in the studios after 1945, under the auspices of the newly-founded DEFA. There have been further additions and new buildings.

in der Nähe/nearby:
Tonfilmstudio; P-Babelsberg; August-Bebel-Straße 26-53
1930
Mischatelier; P-Babelsberg; August-Bebel-Straße 26-53
1964-66 • W. Pätzold
Haus Bejach; B-Steinstücken; Bernhard-Beyer-Straße 12
1926-27 • Erich Mendelsohn

R 9 Jagdschloß Stern
Potsdam-Drewitz; Kohlhasenbrücker Straße
1730-32

König Friedrich Wilhelm I. ließ 1724-29 die zum Amt Potsdam gehörende »Heide nach dem Teerofen« für Parforcejagden einhegen. Für die Hetze des von Hunden aufgespürten Wildes zu Pferd wurden Schneisen durch die Heide gezogen, die sich auf einem runden Sternplatz trafen. Neben dem achtstrahligen Wegeschnittpunkt entstand in holländischer Bauweise das bescheidene Jagdschloß »Stern«. Hinter der dreiachsigen, mit hohem, geschweiftem Giebel geschmückten Seitenfront verbirgt sich ein bis in den Dachraum reichender Jagdsaal mit Kuppelkassette, die einen bemalten Sternenhimmel trägt. Die Küche ist nach holländischem Geschmack mit Fliesen belegt. Das Jagdschloß zeigt die Vorliebe für holländische Ziegelbauweise, die in Potsdam während des 18. Jahrhunderts zu beobachten ist. Im Holländischen Viertel und den Bauten im Neuen Garten findet sie ihre Fortsetzung, und Schinkel knüpft im 19. Jahrhundert an diese traditionelle Bauweise an. Ein wirtschaftlicher Gesichtspunkt war auch immer die Belebung der heimischen Ziegelindustrie.

Friedrich Wilhelm I had the «heath beyond the tar-boiler», which belonged to Potsdam, enclosed for coursing in 1724-9. Paths meeting at a round, star-shaped centre were cut through the heath for horseback hunting of game tracked down by dogs. The modest «Stern» (star) hunting lodge was built in the Dutch style beside the centre point where the eight paths met. The side façade with three axes decorated with a curved gable conceals a hunting hall rising into the attic space with domed coffered ceiling painted with a starry sky. The kitchen is tiled in the Dutch fashion. This hunting lodge shows the preference for Dutch brick building which can be observed throughout eighteenth century Potsdam. It is continued in the Holländisches Viertel and the buildings in the Neuer Garten, and Schinkel kept up the tradition in the nineteenth century. Seen from the point of view of economics, this also stimulated the native brick industry.

in der Nähe/nearby:
Kastellanhaus (Gaststätte); Kohlhasenbrücker Straße
1730-32
Dorfkirche; Alt-Drewitz
1732
Wohngebiet Stern; Galileistraße, Ziolkowskistraße
1973-79 • Hermann Poetzsch, Hartwig Ebert u.a.m.

R 10 Leibgardehusaren-Kaserne
Potsdam; Berliner Straße 27
1839-42 • Karl Friedrich Schinkel, Karl Hampel

Unter dem Soldatenkönig Friedrich Wilhelm I. wurde Potsdam zur Garnisonsstadt. Zunächst bringt man die Soldaten in Bürgerquartieren unter, jedes Bürgerhaus erhält vier bis sechs Soldaten Einquartierung. Vor dem Siebenjährigen Krieg lagen in Potsdam 4630 Soldaten in 1083 Quartieren. Erst 1753/1754 entstehen die ersten selbständigen Kasernenbauten, hier werden bevorzugt »beweibte« Soldaten untergebracht. Im 19. Jahrhundert folgen mehrere repräsentative Kasernenbauten, darunter die Leibgardehusaren-Kaserne. Nach dem Entwurf Schinkels und Hampels erbaut sie der »Baukondukteur« Wilhelm Kreyher. Um ein Geschoß erhöhte Mittel- und Eckrisalite gliedern den monumentalen Putzbau. Die Bekrönung des Baues durch einen Zinnenkranz geht auf eine Zeichnung von Ludwig Persius zurück.

Potsdam became a garrison town under Friedrich Wilhelm I, the Soldier King. At first the soldiers were billeted in private houses, with each house taking four to six soldiers. Before the Seven Years' War there were 4,630 soldiers in 1,083 billets in Potsdam. The first independent barracks dates from 1753-4, preferably for the accommodation of «wedded» men. More imposing barracks followed in the nineteenth century, including the barracks for the lifeguards. They were built by «Baukondukteur» Wilhelm Kreyher to designs by Schinkel and Hampel. The monumental rendered building is articulated with central and corner protruding sections raised by a storey. The battlements go back to a drawing by Ludwig Persius.

in der Nähe/nearby:
Offiziersspeiseanstalt; Berliner Straße 28
1886-87
Haus Rahel Henriette Baranins; Berliner Straße 136
1798
Haus Hofmaurermeister Brendel; Berliner Straße 144
1790-92
Civil-Waisenhaus; Berliner Straße 148
1862

R 11 Glienicker Brücke (Brücke der Einheit)
Berlin-Wannsee/Potsdam; Königstraße
1905-07 • Born

Potsdam und Klein-Glienicke, die durch die Havel geographisch getrennt sind, werden seit dem 17. Jahrhundert durch die Glienicker Brücke verbunden. Die erste Holzbrücke von 1662 diente dem Zugang zum kurfürstlichen Jagdrevier östlich der Havel und später zum Jagdschloß Klein-Glienicke. 1693 wurde die alte Landstraße von Potsdam ausgebaut und mit Bäumen bepflanzt, hundert Jahre später geht über sie auch der Verkehr nach Berlin, der bisher den Weg über die Lange Brücke und die Teltower Vorstadt nahm. 1831-36 ersetzt Karl Friedrich Schinkel die Holzbrücke durch eine steinerne Bogenbrücke, die sich den nahen Schloßbauten würdig anpaßt. Aber auch sie genügt dem steigenden Verkehr bald nicht mehr, und der Bau des Teltowkanals verlangt schließlich den Durchlaß größerer Schiffe. So folgt ihr eine stählerne Hängebrücke, deren Konstruktion die notwendigen Durchfahrthöhen gewährleistet, ohne unnötig lange und hohe Anfahrtsrampen nach sich zu ziehen. Als besonderer Schmuck erhält das Bauwerk Kolonnaden an den Brückenköpfen. 1945 gesprengt und 1950 wiederhergestellt, blieb sie für Deutsche bald über Jahrzehnte gesperrt, nur gelegentlich machte sie von sich reden, wenn auf ihrer Mittelgrenze gegenseitig Spione oder andere menschliche Handelsobjekte ausgetauscht wurden.

Potsdam and Klein-Glienicke, which are separated geograpically by the Havel, have been connected by the Glienicker Brücke since the seventeenth century. The first wooden bridge, built in 1662, was used for access to the Elector's hunting ground east of the Havel, and later to the hunting lodge in Klein-Gleinicke. The old country road to Potsdam was made up and planted with trees in 1693, and a hundred years later traffic to Berlin used this route as well; previously it had gone across the Lange Brücke and through the Teltower Vorstadt. In 1831-6 Karl Friedrich Schinkel replaced the wooden bridge by a stone one with arches, a dignified complement to the nearby palace buildings. But soon this too was not adequate for the increasing traffic volume, and finally the building of the Teltow canal demanded the passage of larger ships. And so it was followed by a steel suspension bridge which permitted the necessary passage heights without needing unnecessarily long and high access ramps. Colonnades on the bridgeheads were a particular decorative feature. It was blown up in 1945, rebuilt in 1950, then closed to Germans for decades, only attracting attention when spies or other human «objects of trade» were exchanged in the middle.

in der Nähe/nearby:
Villa Schöningen; Potsdam; Berliner Straße 86
1843-45 • Ludwig Persius
Matrosenstation Kongsnaes; Potsdam; Schwanenallee
1896 • Henry Munthe

R 12 Jagdschloß Glienicke
Berlin-Wannsee; Königstraße, Mövenstraße
1889 • Albert Geyer

Im Landbuch Kaiser Karls IV. von 1375 ist Klein-Glienicke bereits als wendisches Dorf erwähnt. Im 16. Jahrhundert ging das Dorf an einen Herrn v. Schlabrendorf, der es in ein Gut umwandelte. Dieses erwarb schließlich der Große Kurfürst, der hier, östlich der Havel, gerne der Jagd nachging und 1682 von Charles Dieussart das Gutshaus zum Jagdschloß umbauen ließ. Friedrich I. ließ das Haus weiter ausbauen. Unter dem Soldatenkönig Friedrich Wilhelm I. wurde daraus ein Lazarett, dann verkam es zur Tapetenfabrik, zuletzt war es Waisenhaus. 1859 kaufte Prinz Karl – seit 1824 Besitzer von Schloß Klein-Glienicke – das ehemalige Jagdschloß und ließ es von Ferdinand v. Arnim im Sinne des französischen Barock neugestalten: Aus dem echten Barockschloß wurde ein nachgemachtes. Zwei Jahre später starb Karl, sein Enkel Friedrich Leopold gab dem Bau durch einen erneuten Umbau schließlich sein heutiges Aussehen – deutsche Renaissance war inzwischen als Architekturmode angesagt. Immerhin diente es so gelegentlich als Filmkulisse. Den letzten baulichen Eingriff verübte Max Taut 1963 mit einem gläsernen Vorbau.

Klein-Glienicke is mentioned as a Wendic village in Emperor Charles IV's land register of 1375. In the sixteenth century the village passed to a Herr von Schlabrendorf, who transformed it into a farm. This was finally acquired by the Great Elector, who liked hunting here, east of the Havel, and who commissioned Charles Dieussart to rebuild the farmhouse as a hunting lodge in 1682. Frederick I extended the building further. Under Soldier King Friedrich Wilhelm I it became a military hospital, then a wallpaper factory, and finally an orphanage. In 1859 Prinz Karl – owner of Schloss Klein-Glienicke from 1824 – bought the former hunting lodge and had it redesigned by Ferdinand von Arnim in French baroque style: the real baroque building became an imitation one. Karl died two years later, and his grandson Friedrich Leopold rebuilt again, and the building acquired its present appearance – German Renaissance was now the prevailing architectural fashion. It has often stood in for this as a background in films. The last architectural incursion was a glass porch added by Max Taut in 1963.

in der Nähe/nearby:
Schweizerhäuser; P-Babelsberg; Louis-Nathan-Straße
Um 1862 • Ferdinand v. Arnim
Loggia Alexandra; B-Wannsee; Böttcherberg
1869 • Ernst Petzholtz

R 13 Schloß Glienicke
Berlin-Wannsee; Königstraße
1824-27 • Karl Friedrich Schinkel

Für Prinz Karl v. Preußen baute Schinkel diesen Sommersitz. An seiner Stelle stand bereits seit dem 18. Jahrhundert ein Lustschlößchen, das zwischenzeitlich auch Fürst Hardenberg gehörte. Der Neubau bediente sich der Stilmittel des Biedermeier. In bürgerlicher Schlichtheit, aber dennoch in feinster Ausgewogenheit – dafür bürgte der Name des Baumeisters – paßt sich dieses Gebäude der stillen Parklandschaft ein. In seiner klassischen Symmetrie zitiert es griechisch-römische Traditionen, die auch hier und da als alte Fund- und Sammelstücke der neuen Architektur eingefügt sind. Nur wenige Jahre nach dem Auflodern der griechischen Befreiungsbewegung waren Philhellenismus und Begeisterung für das klassische Altertum in Deutschland und England allgemein verbreitet und schlugen sich allenthalben als »modisches« Element nieder.

Schinkel built this summer residence for Prince Karl of Prussia. There had been a small summer palace on the site since the eighteenth century, which for a time also belonged to Fürst Hardenberg. The new building is Biedermeier in style, and fits in with the park landscape in its bourgeois plainness, but it is also most delicately balanced – the architect's name guaranteed that. Its classical symmetry refers back to the tradition of Greece and Rome, with occasional additions from the finds and stock-in-trade of modern architecture. Only a few years after the Greek liberation movement philhellenism and enthusisam for classical antiquity were general in England and Germany and expressed themselves everywhere as a «fashionable» element.

in der Nähe/nearby:
Haupttorhaus; Königstraße
1849 • Ferdinand v. Arnim
Stibadium; Königstraße
1840 • Ludwig Persius
Wirtschaftshof; Königstraße
Um 1843 • Ludwig Persius
Portikus am Schloß; Königstraße
1840 • Ludwig Persius
Turm; nordwestlich des Schlosses
1832 • Karl Friedrich Schinkel
Kavalier- und Stallflügel; nordwestlich des Schlosses
1827 • Karl Friedrich Schinkel
Remise; nordwestlich des Schlosses
1828 • Karl Friedrich Schinkel
Klosterhof; nordwestlich des Schlosses
1850 • Ferdinand v. Arnim

R 14 Park Klein-Glienicke
Berlin-Wannsee; Königstraße
1816-22, 1824-50 • Peter Joseph Lenné

Bereits Hardenberg hatte seinen Besitz von Lenné gärtnerisch gestalten lassen, es ist heute der südwestliche Bereich des Parkes. Als Prinz Karl 1824 Glienicke erwarb, verpflichtete auch er Lenné, die nach Norden und Osten angrenzenden Felder und den Böttcherberg in einen Landschaftspark zu verwandeln. Mit seinen waldartigen Partien folgt der Park einem geographisch geprägten Programm, führt vom dichten nordischen Hochwald in die lichteren südlichen Gehölze. Dem paßt sich auch die Architektur der Gebäude an: das englische Jägertor im Norden, die alpenländische Teufelsbrücke in der Mitte oder das Abruzzenkastell des Maschinenhauses im Süden. Stilistisch ist im topographisch Bestimmbaren der Wandel von der Romantik zum Naturalismus ablesbar.

Hardenberg had already had his property landscaped by Lenné, and this section now makes up the southwestern area of the park. When Prinz Karl acquired Glienicke in 1824, he commissioned Lenné to transform the fields adjacent to the north and east and the Böttcherberg into a landscape park. The park's wooded sections follow a geographically defined programme, leading from the dense Nordic hill forest to the lighter timbers of the south. This also fits in with the architecture of the buildings: the English hunting tower in the north, the Alpine Teufelsbrücke in the middle or the Abruzzi fortress that is the engine house in the south. Stylistically this topographical determination shows the transition from Romanticism to Realism.

R 15 Große Neugierde
Berlin-Wannsee; Königstraße
1835, 1837 • Karl Friedrich Schinkel

Graf Lindenau, damals Besitzer des Gutes Glienicke, ließ sich 1796 vor seinem Haus unmittelbar an der gerade fertiggestellten Landstraße von Potsdam nach Berlin einen kleinen Pavillon errichten, von dem er selbst ungesehen die Passanten beobachten konnte. »Neugierde« nannte er bezeichnenderweise das Häuschen an dem offenbar an Abwechslung und Zerstreuung nicht gerade reichen Ort. Die nächste Stufe dieser Art von Kurzweil verwirklichte Prinz Karl unter dem Motto »sehen und gesehen werden«. Seine »Große Neugierde« wurde zum offenen Rundbau, ein Säulenkranz trug ein einfaches Dach. Zwei Jahre später erhielt der Bau einen Aufsatz nach dem Vorbild des Monuments des Lysikrates in Athen. Der Blick ging von hier aus frei über die Havel nach Potsdam, im Vordergrund die von Schinkel gebaute Steinbrücke, die nach der Jahrhundertwende dem wachsenden Verkehr zugunsten einer neuen Eisenbrücke geopfert werden mußte.

In 1796 Graf Lindenau, at that time owner of the Glienicke estate, had a little pavilion built in front of his house directly on the recently completed road from Potsdam to Berlin, so that he could watch the passers-by unobserved. Typically he called the little building «Neugierde» (curiosity); apparently the place did not provide very much variety and distraction. The next improvement on this method of passing the time was made by Prinz Karl on the principle of «see and be seen». His «Grosse Neugierde» was an open circular building, with a simple roof borne by a ring of columns. Two years later the building acquired a top section modelled on the Lysikrates monument in Athens. This gave way to a view right over the Havel to Potsdam, with the stone bridge built by Schinkel in the foreground; this had to be sacrificed to a new iron bridge after the turn of the century because of increasing traffic.

in der Nähe/nearby:
Kleine Neugierde; Königstraße
1796 (Umbauten 1826-27 und 1848)
Löwenfontäne; Königstraße
1838 • Karl Friedrich Schinkel
Johannitertor; Königstraße
1838/1842 • Karl Friedrich Schinkel, Ludwig Persius
Nach 1862 • August Kiss (Umbau und Greifen)

R 16 Kasino
Berlin-Wannsee; Königstraße
1824-25 • Karl Friedrich Schinkel

Noch vor den Arbeiten am Schloß Glienicke ließ Prinz Karl ein älteres Billardhäuschen am Havelsteilhang zum Kasino umbauen. Am Entwurf war sicher auch der Kronprinz beteiligt. Schinkel – soeben zurückgekehrt von seiner zweiten Italienreise – orientierte sich an italienischen Villenbauten. Auch die Innenarchitektur folgt dem »pompejanischen Stil«. Dem Ergebnis ist aber weder die künstlerische Einengung durch den Umbau noch durch fremde Einmischung anzusehen, das Kasino gilt sogar als eine der besten Schöpfungen Schinkels. Heiter wirkt der Bau, der sich zur Terrasse öffnet und dessen Pergolen beiderseits weit in die Parklandschaft hineingreifen. Antike Spolien und Skulpturen runden den Eindruck des Italienischen ab.

Even before work started on Schloss Glienicke Prinz Karl had a small, old billiard hall on the steep slope to the Havel rebuilt as a casino. The Crown Prince was certainly also involved in the design. Schinkel – just back from his Italian journey – based his design on Italian villas. The interior also follows the «Pompeian style». But the result shows no signs of artistic restriction from the fact that this is a conversion, nor from foreign influence; in fact the Casino is considered to be one of Schinkel's best works. The building makes a lighthearted effect; it opens on to the terrace and its pergolas run deep into the parkland on either side. Ancient spoils and sculptures confirm the Italian impression.

in der Nähe/nearby:
Hirschtor; Westteil des Parks
1841-42 • Ludwig Persius
Hofgärtner- und Maschinenhaus; Westteil des Parks
1837-38 • Ludwig Persius
Teufelsbrücke; Westteil des Parks
1838 • Ludwig Persius
Matrosenhaus; Mitte des Parks
1840 • Ludwig Persius
Jägerhof; Nordwestteil des Parks
1828 • Karl Friedrich Schinkel
Jägertor; Nordwestteil des Parks
1842-43 • Ludwig Persius
Wildparktorhaus; Nikolskoer Weg
1842 • Ferdinand v. Arnim
Obertorhaus; Königstraße
1842 • Ferdinand v. Arnim

R 17 Blockhaus Nikolskoe
Berlin-Wannsee; Nikolskoer Weg
1819 • Snethlage

»Nikolskoe«, das bedeutet »Nikolaus zu eigen« und galt dem russischen Großfürsten und späteren Zaren Nikolaus, der 1817 Charlotte, die Tochter des preußischen Königs Friedrich Wilhelm III. geheiratet hatte. Ein Besuch in Petersburg führte Vater und Tochter auch in ein Bauernhaus, welches so gefiel, daß der König es nach russischen Plänen von seinem Garde-Pionierbataillon unter Hauptmann Snethlage für den Gegenbesuch errichten ließ. Das Blockhaus kam ganz nach dem Geschmack Friedrich Wilhelms III., der dem höfischen Prunk abhold und dem einfachen ländlichen Leben zugetan war. Die Tradition des Gasthauses geht auf den ersten Kastellan und früheren königlichen Leibkutscher Iwan Bockow zurück, der zu seinem Nebenverdienst bald Erfrischungen an Spaziergänger ausschenkte. In seiner Nationaltracht und mit rauschendem Bart war er wohl eine Attraktion eigener Art.

«Nikolskoe» means «Nicholas' own», and refers to the Russian Grand Duke and later Tsar Nicholas, who married Charlotte, daughter of King Friedrich Wilhelm III of Prussia, in 1817. A visit to St. Petersburg took both father and daughter into a farmhouse that they liked so much that the king had a copy built to Russian plans by his batallion of guards and pioneers under Captain Snethlage, in honour of the return visit. The log cabin was entirely to the taste of Friedrich Wilhelm III, who disliked courtly show, and inclined to a rural existence. The guesthouse tradition goes back to Iwan Bockow, the first castellan and former personal coachman to the king, who started providing refreshments for pedestrians to supplement his income. He was probably a very striking feature in his own right, with his national costume and flowing beard.

in der Nähe/nearby:
Königliche Freischule; B-Wannsee; Nikolskoer Weg
1837 • Friedrich August Stüler, Albert Dietrich Schadow
Jägerhaus; B-Wannsee; Moorlake
1841 • Ludwig Persius
Heilandskirche; P-Sacrow; Am Port
1841-42 • Ludwig Persius, Friedrich Wilhelm IV.

R 18 St. Peter und Paul
Berlin-Wannsee; Nikolskoer Weg
1834-37 • Friedrich August Stüler, Albert Dietrich Schadow

Am Hang der Höhe oberhalb der Pfaueninsel mit Blick über die weite Havellandschaft liegt die Kirche Peter und Paul. Es ist eine einschiffige Saalkirche mit flachem quergerichteten Stirntrakt. Gelbe Ziegel verblenden in bodenständiger Tradition die Mauern, nur ein oktogonaler Turmaufsatz mit Zwiebelhaube liefert das russische Element. Die dem russischen Zaren vermählte Tochter des preußischen Königs Friedrich Wilhelm III. hatte einmal voller Gemütstiefe auf einem Spaziergang zu ihrem Vater gesagt: »Wie schön und erbaulich müßte es doch sein, wenn diese Abendstille von Glockengeläut durchtönt würde und hier eine Kapelle zum stillen Abendgebet einlüde!« In einer Mischung aus Religiosität und romantischem Empfinden förderte der König den Bau, schrieb aber auch die Gestalt der Kirche vor.

The church of Peter and Paul is on a slope of the heights above the Pfaueninsel with a view over the broad Havel landscape. It is a single-roomed church with flat transverse end section. The walls are clad in yellow brick in accordance with local tradition, and the only Russian element is an octagonal top to the tower with onion dome. The daughter of King Friedrich Wilhelm III of Prussia, who was married to the Tsar of Russia, had once said, full of emotion, while out walking with her father: «How beautiful and uplifting it must be if this evening peace were to thrill with the sound of bells, and a chapel invite us to say a quiet evening prayer!» In a mixture of piety and Romantic sensibility the king commissioned the building of the church, but also prescribed its design.

in der Nähe/nearby:
Marstall (Gasthaus); Pfaueninselchaussee
Um 1825 • Vermutlich Albert Dietrich Schadow

R 19 Schloß Pfaueninsel
Berlin-Wannsee; Pfaueninsel
1794-95 • Johann Gottlieb David Brendel

Die Lust zu bauen, sich ein Leben voller Überraschungen und skurriler Einfälle zu bereiten, das ist durchaus noch rokokohaft. Die Idee, am Ende einer Kahnfahrt auf einer wilden Insel mit einer verfallenen Burg zu landen, war »chic«. Friedrich Wilhelm II. und seine an dieser Idee maßgeblich beteiligte Geliebte Wilhelmine dürften kaum aus den religiösen Bedürfnissen der Empfindsamkeit heraus die Ruine als Sinnbild weltlicher Vergänglichkeit gewählt haben. So deutet nur ein Caspar David Friedrich die Zeichen. Auch wird sie Rousseaus Ruf »Zurück zur Natur!« weniger überzeugt haben als die sich daraus ableitende Mode, eine andere Welt zu erleben. Das Schloß Pfaueninsel ist illusionistische Architektur. Hinter dem inszenierten Verfall finden sich Räume in erlesener und kostbarer Ausstattung, selbst wenn eines der Zimmer, das »Otaheitische Kabinett«, durch Ausmalung und Requisiten eine primitive Südseehütte vorgaukelt. Wilhelmines Anregungen zur Architektur der »Ruine« gehen auf einen Entwurf für ein Schloß auf dem Potsdamer Pfingstberg von Georg Friedrich Boumann zurück und auf das Bild aus der englischen Kupferstichsammlung »Dekorationen für Park und Garten«.

It is a thoroughly rococo view of life to take delight in building, to make oneself a life full of surprises and comical ideas. The idea of ending a boat trip on a wild island with a ruined castle was «chic». Friedrich Wilhelm II and his mistress Wilhelmine, who was highly involved in the project, could hardly have selected the ruin as a symbol of worldly transience because of religious requirements or sensibilities. Only a Caspar David Friedrich could interpret the signs this way. They will also have been less convinced by Rousseau's cry of «back to nature!» than the fashion derived from it of experiencing another world. The Pfaueninsel castle is illusionistic architecture. Behind the staged decay are rooms of exquisite and costly decoration, even though one of the rooms, the «Otaheitisches Kabinett» is decorated and fitted out in such a way as to give the illusion of being a primitive hut in the South Seas. Wilhelminian stimuli for the architecture of the «ruin» go back to a design for a palace on the Pfingstberg in Potsdam by Georg Friedrich Boumann and to the picture from the English collection of etchings «Decorations for Park and Garden».

in der Nähe/nearby:
Park; Pfaueninsel
1824 • Peter Joseph Lenné

R 20 Kavalierhaus
Berlin-Wannsee; Pfaueninsel
1824-25 • Karl Friedrich Schinkel

Friedrich Wilhelm II. war nach Erwerb der Insel entschlossen, die vorgefundene Wildnis weitgehend zu belassen. Lediglich die nächste Umgebung von Schloß und Meierei durfte gärtnerisch gestaltet werden. Sein Nachfolger Friedrich Wilhelm III. dachte praktischer und ordnete landwirtschaftliche Nutzung an. 1803-04 baute Friedrich Ludwig Carl Krüger ein Gärtner- und Schäferhaus mit zwei Türmen. Dieses veränderte Schinkel dann zwei Jahrzehnte später zum Kavalierhaus. Dazu verwendete er die gotische Sandsteinfassade eines in Danzig abgetragenen Patrizierhauses, die der Kronprinz erworben hatte. Das Haus wurde taktvoll neugotisch ergänzt. Es dokumentiert das zu Beginn des 19. Jahrhunderts erwachende Verständnis für Bau- und Kunstgeschichte als Grundlage einer Denkmalpflege. Die Art und Weise, wie hier Altes und Neues miteinander baulich verschmelzen, wie sich das Haus in die Natur einpaßt, wie aus Fassaden, Bäumen und Wiese ein kleiner idyllischer und stimmungsvoller Ort entsteht, das ist Anliegen des Biedermeier und die Leistung eines seiner großen Architekten.

After acquiring the Pfaueninsel, Friedrich Wilhelm II decided to leave the wilderness he found largely as it was. He only permitted the immediate surroundings of palace and dairy to be designed in garden terms. His successor Friedrich Wilhelm III thought more practically, and ordered agricultural use. In 1803-4 Friedrich Ludwig Karl Krüger built a gardeners' and shepherds' house with two towers, and Schinkel converted this into the Kavalierhaus two decades later. For this purpose he used the Gothic sandstone façade from a patrician house that had been demolished in Danzig and acquired by the Crown Prince. The building was tactfully completed in neo-Gothic style. It documents awakening interest in architectural and art history as a basis for the preservation of monuments in the early nineteenth century. The way in which old and new blend here in architectural terms, the way the house blends with nature, the way façades, trees and lawn create a miniature atmosphere of idyll, was what Biedermeier sought to achieve, achieved here by one of its great architects.

in der Nähe/nearby:
Kastellanshaus; Pfaueninsel, Südspitze
1795-96 • Johann Gottlieb David Brendel
Schweizerhaus; Pfaueninsel, Südspitze
1829-30 • Albert Dietrich Schadow
Fregattenschuppen; Pfaueninsel, Südostufer
1832 • Albert Dietrich Schadow
Maschinenhaus; Pfaueninsel, Südostteil
1824-25 • Voß
Meierei; Pfaueninsel, Nordspitze
1794 • Johann Gottlieb David Brendel

S
Zwischen Teltow und Fläming

Drei größere Landschaftsräume mit unterschiedlicher Wirtschaftsstruktur haben sich in dieser Region der Mark herausgebildet. Im Osten sind es die Seen- und Waldgebiete zwischen Königs Wusterhausen, Teupitz, Märkisch Buchholz und Baruth mit Schwerindustrie und Forstwirtschaft. Auf der Grundmoränenplatte des Teltow im Norden liegen die sandigen Böden, ausgedehnten Ackerflächen im Wechsel mit Kiefernwäldern, mit dem Standort der elektronischen Industrie in Teltow und dem Obstanbaugebiet um Werder. Im Südwesten sind es die flachwelligen, teils kuppig ausgebildeten, bewaldeten Grundmoränengebiete des Fläming mit seinem 201 m hohen Hagelberg als auch die weidewirtschaftlich genutzten, vermoorten Niederungen, wie die von Brück bis zum Fiener Bruch westlich von Ziesar. Ihren besonderen Reiz erhielt die Landschaft durch den Wechsel der Grund-, End- und Stauchmoränen und den uralten Schmelzwassertälern im Verlauf der heutigen Flüsse, Seenketten und Niederungsgebiete, zurückzuführen auf die Verformungen und Ablagerungen der letzten Eiszeit. Durch Funde sind erste längerfristige Siedlungen von Stämmen unterschiedlicher Kultur bis hin zur ersten schriftlich überlieferten Besiedlung germanischer Stämme, von etwa 8000 v.Chr. bis zum 6. Jahrhundert n.Chr. verbürgt. Im 7. Jahrhundert ist keine germanische Bevölkerung mehr nachweisbar. Die slawische Besiedlung des 6. und 7. Jahrhunderts wird durch eine Nachricht aus dem Jahre 798 über den Feldzug des fränkischen Königs Karl des Großen gegen den slawischen Volksstamm der Wilzen schriftlich überliefert. Von den Sprewanen um Mittenwalde bis zum Gau der Ploni um Belzig und der Heveller im erweiterten Havelland erstrecken sich die Stammesgebiete. Dort entstanden Burgen mit Befestigungen aus Holz, Erde und Mauerwerk sowie dazugehörige Siedlungen. Die frühdeutsche Besiedlung seit dem 10. Jahrhundert war mit einer durchgreifenden Siedlungspolitik und der Stiftung zahlreicher Klöster vor allem zur Ansiedlung des Zisterzienserordens verbunden. Im 19. Jahrhundert wirkte die rasche bauliche Entwicklung Berlins stimulierend auf den gewerblichen und industriellen Aufschwung in dieser Region, besonders der Tongruben, der Ziegeleien und der Schiffahrt im südlichen Havelbogen. Mit dem Bau des Teltowkanals gewannen dann seit 1907 auch andere Industriezweige an Bedeutung.

Three relatively large areas of countryside with differing economic structures have formed in this area of the Mark. In the east are the lake and forest districts between Königs Wusterhausen, Teupitz, Märkisch Buchholz and Baruth with heavy industry and forestry. On the base moraine of the Teltow in the north is sandy land, extensive cultivated fields alternating with pine forests, electronics industry in Teltow and a fruit-growing area around Werder. In the south west are the shallow-rolling wooded base moraine areas of the Fläming, sometimes rising to small hills – the Hagelberg is 201 metres high – and also the marshy lowlands used for grazing, like those of Brück to the Fiener Bruch west of Ziesar. The landscape derives its particular charm from the alternating base, terminal and compressed moraines and the ancient meltwater valleys in the course of the present rivers, chains of lakes and lowlands, all caused by distortions and deposits in the last ice age. Archaeological finds confirm long settlement, from about 8000 BC to the sixth century AD, by tribes of differing culture down to the first written evidence of Germanic tribes. No Germanic population can be confirmed in the seventh century. Slavic settlement in the sixth and seventh centuries is confirmed by a report dating from 798 of a campaign by Charlemagne against the Slavic Wilzen tribe. From the Sprevans around Mittenwalde to the area of the Ploni around Belzig and the Hevells in the extended Havelland, the tribal areas spread. Castles were built with fortifications of wood, earth and masonry, and settlements sprang up beside them. Early German settlement from the tenth century was connected with drastic settlement policies and the foundation of numerous monasteries, in particular for the Cistercian Order. In the nineteenth century rapid building in Berlin stimulated the rise of trade and industry in this region. Clay pits, brickmaking and shipping were the principal industries, but others became more important when the Teltow canal was built in 1907.

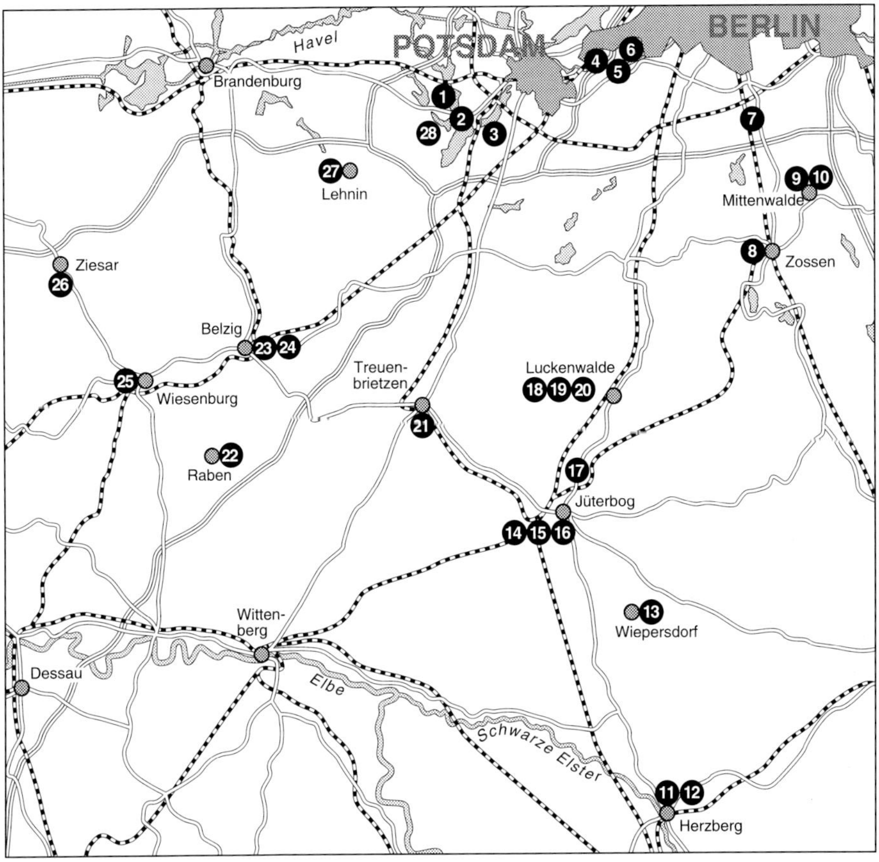

S 1	Inselstadt Werder	S 15	Dammtor Jüterbog
S 2	Schloß Petzow	S 16	Pfarrkirche St. Nikolai
S 3	Wohnhaus Albert Einstein, Caputh	S 17	Siechen- und Gästehaus Zinna
S 4	Grabdenkmal Wissinger, Stahnsdorf	S 18	Stadtkern Luckenwalde
S 5	Schleuse am Teltowkanal, Teltow	S 19	Wohnsiedlung Jänickendorfer Straße
S 6	Haus Bahner, Kleinmachnow	S 20	Hutfabrik
S 7	Wohnhaus Bruno Taut, Dahlewitz	S 21	Stadtkern Treuenbrietzen
S 8	Stadtkern Zossen	S 22	Burg Rabenstein
S 9	Stadtkern Mittenwalde	S 23	Stadtkern Belzig
S 10	Berliner Tor	S 24	Burg Eisenhardt
S 11	Rathaus Herzberg	S 25	Schloß Wiesenburg
S 12	Marienkirche Herzberg	S 26	Burgkapelle Ziesar
S 13	Herrenhaus Wiepersdorf	S 27	Kloster Lehnin
S 14	Stadtkern Jüterbog	S 28	Ziegelei Glindow

S 1 Inselstadt Werder
Werder an der Havel
1317

Die Stadt Werder an dem seenartig verbreiterten Havelfluß ist das Zentrum des schon im Mittelalter beachtlichen Obstanbaugebietes. Die 1317 ersterwähnte, vermutlich aber bereits im 13. Jahrhundert auf einer großen Havelinsel regelmäßig angelegte Landstadt ist durch eine Brücke mit dem nahen Westufer verbunden. Die Erweiterung der Bebauung nach Westen begann Anfang des 15. Jahrhunderts. Der im Mittelalter betriebene Weinanbau wurde durch den in der 2. Hälfte des 19. Jahrhunderts stark geförderten Kernobstanbau abgelöst und begründete den Reiz der »Blütenstadt« Werder. Zu dem seit 1860 stattfindenden »Fest der Baumblüte« kommen alljährlich im Frühjahr tausende Besucher vornehmlich mit Schiffen herbei. Inmitten der Altstadt steht auf einer Anhöhe anstelle eines Vorgängerbaues die 1857 von Friedrich August Stüler errichtete Heiliggeistkirche, ein stattlicher neugotischer Putzbau, von dem Fontane in seinen »Wanderungen« sagt, daß sie »in der Nähe vielleicht mannigfach zu beanstanden, als Landschaftsdekoration aber von seltener Schönheit ist«. Die schlichten ein- und zweigeschossigen Wohnhäuser stammen aus dem 18. und frühen 19. Jahrhundert.

The town of Werder on the Havel, which broadens almost to a lake, is the centre of a fruit-growing district that was significant even in the Middle Ages. This country town was first mentioned in 1317, but was presumably in existence with its regular layout on a large island in the Havel in the thirteenth century. It is connected to the west bank by a bridge. It began to expand westwards in the early fifteenth century. In the Middle Ages grapes were grown, but they were replaced by pomaceous fruits, much in demand in the second half of the nineteenth century; this was the beginning of the attraction of the «blossom town» of Werder. The «festival of fruit trees in bloom» has taken place annually in spring since 1860, and attracts thousands of visitors, most of them coming by boat. The old town is 400 m by 400 m, and in its centre is Friedrich August Stüler's Heiliggeistkirche, built in 1857 on a small hill on the site of an earlier building. It is an imposing neo-Gothic rendered building of which Fontane said in his «Wanderungen» that «from close to there was perhaps a lot to be found fault with, but it is of rare beauty as a decorative feature of the landscape». The plain one- and two-storey houses date from the eighteenth and early nineteenth centuries.

in der Nähe/nearby:
Rathaus; Markt
1742
Heiliggeistkirche
1857 • Friedrich August Stüler
Berufsschule; Hoher Weg 150
1976-79 • Rudolf Schmolke, Wolfgang Geißler

S 2 Schloß Petzow
Werder-Petzow; Zelterstraße
1825 • vermutlich Karl Friedrich Schinkel

Das erstmals 1419/20 erwähnte Gut Petzow entwickelte sich vom Lehnschulzengut 1845 zum landtagsfähigen Rittergut. Als eines der gut erhaltenen ländlichen Ensembles des frühen 19. Jahrhunderts in der Mark mit Schloß, Park, Wirtschaftsgebäuden, Dorf und Kirche bietet es heute vielen Urlaubern Entspannung. Das Schloß, um 1825 vermutlich nach Entwurf von Karl Friedrich Schinkel errichtet, ist ein zweigeschossiger, im Kern neugotischer elfachsiger Putzbau mit vier runden Türmen und Mittelrisalit. Die Türme und die Gartenseite schmücken Zinnenkränze. Die Schmalseiten sind als Staffelgiebel ausgebildet, und Barockgitter zieren einige Fenster des Erdgeschosses. 1955 wurde das Schloß in nördlicher Richtung durch einen Saalanbau erweitert. Der Schloßpark, von Peter Joseph Lenné 1820 als Landschaftspark am Schwielowsee angelegt, bezieht drei neugotische Tore aus der Zeit des Schloßbaues ein. Das Dorfensemble ist durch eingeschossige Wohnhäuser als Putzbauten an der zum Schloß führenden Straße geprägt.

The Petzow estate was first mentioned in 1419/20. It developed from being a feudal mayoralty to a manor with parliamentary rights in 1845. It is now a popular holiday resort as one of the best early nineteenth century rural building ensembles in the Mark with castle, park, working quarters, village and church. The Schloss, built c. 1825, presumably to a design by Karl Friedrich Schinkel, is a two-storey rendered building, essentially neo-Gothic, with eleven axes, four round towers and a projecting central section. The towers and the garden side are decorated with battlements. The narrow sides have stepped gables and some of the ground floor windows have decorative baroque grilles. In 1955 the castle was extended to the north by the addition of a hall. Peter Josef Lenné's park was laid out as a landscaped park by the Schwielowsee in 1820, and includes three neo-Gothic gates from the period when the castle was built. The principal feature of the village are the one-storey rendered houses lining the road to the castle.

in der Nähe/nearby:
Dorfkirche; Werder-Petzow
1841-42 • Friedrich August Stüler, Gustav Emil Prüfer
Aussichtsturm; Geltow; Franzensberg
Um 1830
Chausseehaus; Geltow; Potsdamer Straße 92
2. H. 19. Jh.
Villa; Geltow; Auf dem Franzensberg 1/3
1926-28 • Vermutlich Henry van de Velde
Dorfkirche; Ferch
17. Jh.

S 3 Wohnhaus Albert Einstein
Caputh; Am Waldrand 3-3 a
1928-29 • Konrad Wachsmann

Das alte Fischerdorf Caputh, seit 1317 erwähnt und im 16. Jahrhundert kurfürstliches Gut, wählte Albert Einstein 1928 zu seinem Sommersitz und erteilte dem Architekten Konrad Wachsmann den Auftrag zur Errichtung eines Hauses. Wachsmann, nach Aufenthalt in Holland und Frankreich, arbeitete zu dieser Zeit auf Empfehlung von Hans Poelzig in der Holzbaufirma Christoph & Unmack Niesky. Begeistert von der Arbeit in diesen Werkstätten und Kenner vorgefertigter Holzkonstruktionen, entwarf er das Haus Einsteins in Holzbauweise auf massivem Unterbau. Der zweigeschossige Baukörper mit Walmdach und der eingeschossige Anbau mit als Terrasse ausgebildetem Flachdach sind geschickt dem abschüssigen Gelände eingefügt. Nach Einsteins Austritt aus der preußischen Akademie der Wissenschaften und der Emigration 1933 wurde sein Caputher Besitz enteignet. 1979 wurde das Haus nach einem Entwurf von Horst Kiklas und Peter Herling zur Arbeitsstätte für Wissenschaftler ausgebaut. Konrad Wachsmann äußerte sich bei seinem letzten Besuch in Caputh zustimmend zur gelungenen Rekonstruktion.

The old fishing village of Caputh, mentioned from 1317 and an Electoral estate in the sixteenth century, was chosen by Albert Einstein as his summer residence in 1928. He commissioned a house from architect Konrad Wachsmann. Wachsmann, back from Holland and France, was working at the time on the recommendation of Hans Poelzig for Christoph & Unmack Niesky, a firm who built in wood. He was enthusiastic about the products of these workshops and familiar with prefabricated wooden structures, and so designed Einstein's house in wood, on a solid substructure. The two-storey building with hipped roof and single-storey annexe with a flat roof serving as a terrace are skilfully adapted to the sloping site. When Einstein resigned from the Prussian Academy of Science and emigrated in 1933, his Caputh property was confiscated. In 1979 Horst Kiklas and Peter Herling redesigned the house as a work-place for scientists, and on his last visit to Caputh Konrad Wachsmann pronounced himself satisfied with the successful reconstruction.

in der Nähe/nearby:
Schloß; Caputh; Straße der Einheit
1662 • Philippe de la Chièze
Schloßpark; Caputh
1820 • Peter Joseph Lenné
Dorfkirche; Caputh; Straße der Einheit
1848-52 • Friedrich August Stüler
Gutshaus; Alt Langerwisch
Um 1800
Vierseithof; Michendorf; Schmerbergerstraße 11
18. Jh.

S 4 Grabdenkmal Wissinger
Stahnsdorf; Bahnhofstraße (Südwest-Friedhof)
1922-23 • Max Taut

Der in Stahnsdorf seit 1902 für die Stadt Berlin erschlossene Südwestfriedhof und der Wilmersdorfer Waldfriedhof liegen mit 128 000 Grabstätten und einer Fläche von 237 Hektar in einem ehemaligen Waldgebiet. Wie beim Friedhof Ahrensfelde war aus Kosten- und Platzgründen ein Gelände weit vor den Toren der Stadt gewählt worden. 1911-13 legte man sogar eine eigene Vorortbahn von Wannsee nach Stahnsdorf an, die Friedhofsbahn. Bedeutende Persönlichkeiten haben hier ihre Grabstätten: Lovis Corinth (1858-1925), Heinrich Zille (1858-1929), Hans Baluschek (1870-1935), Engelbert Humperdinck (1854-1921), Wilhelm Murnau (1888-1931), Hans Otto (1900-1933), Joachim Gottschalk (1904-1941). Nur einige Grabmale wie das von August Kraus für Heinrich Zille tragen Reliefbilder oder Büsten. Besonders hervorzuheben ist das Grabdenkmal für das Erbbegräbnis Wissinger. Hier schuf Max Taut ein filigranes Betonrippenwerk als expressionistische Arkatur über der Grabstätte. Taut stand noch ganz unter dem Einfluß der »Gläsernen Kette«, die in einer Art architektonischem Dadaismus ihre utopischen Bauten nach Formen von Kristallen aus Glas errichtete.

The south-west cemetery, established for the city of Berlin from 1902, and the Wilmersdorf Waldfriedhof have 128,000 graves and cover an area of 237 hectares in a former forest. As in the case of the Ahrensfelde cemetery, for reasons of cost and space an area far outside the gates of the city was selected. In 1911-3 a special suburban railway, the Friedhofsbahn, was built from Wannsee to Stahnsdorf. Many famous people are buried here: Lovis Corinth (1858-1925), Heinrich Zille (1858-1929), Hans Baluschek (1870-1935), Engelbert Humperdinck (1854-1921), Wilhelm Murnau (1888-1931), Hans Otto (1900-1933), Joachim Gottschalk (1904-1941). Only a few reliefs, like that of August Kraus for Heinrich Zille, have relief pictures or busts. Particularly striking is the Wissinger family tomb. Here Max Taut created a filigree concrete ribbed structure to form an Expressionist arcature over the tomb. Taut was still heavily influenced by the «Gläserne Kette» group who, in a kind of architectural Dadaism, built utopian glass buildings in the form of crystals.

in der Nähe/nearby:
Dorfkirche; Stahnsdorf; Dorfplatz
13. Jh.
Dorfkirche; Kleinmachnow; Zehlendorfer Damm
15./16. Jh.
Schloß; Gütersfelde; Lindenstraße
1805 • David Gilly (Umbau 1868)

S 5 Schleuse am Teltowkanal
Teltow; Stahnsdorfer Damm
1902-05 • Havestadt & Contag

Mit dem Ausbau des Teltowkanals zwischen Potsdam-Babelsberg und Berlin-Grünau 1900-06 auf einer Länge von 37 km erfolgte auch der Bau einer Schleuse nach dem Entwurf der Ingenieurgemeinschaft Havestadt & Contag. Es ist die einzige Schleuse, die zwischen Spree und Havel den Differenzpegel von knapp drei Metern überwindet. Der Kanal erhielt nahezu kein Gefälle, da der Spree bei Niedrigpegel kein Wasser entnommen werden durfte. So kam es auch an der Schleuse zum Einbau einer leistungsfähigen Pumpe, die für den nötigen Wasserausgleich zu sorgen hatte. Bei der Doppelschleuse ermöglichte ferner ein Querkanal zwischen beiden Kammern, daß im Sparbetrieb jeweils die erste Hälfte des ablaufenden Wassers zur Teilfüllung der anderen Kammer benutzt werden konnte. Diese ursprünglichen zwei Kammern mit Hubtoren wurden 1939 zur Schleusung von 1000-t-Schiffen um eine dritte Kammer erweitert.

When the Teltow canal was extended between Potsdam-Babelsberg and Berlin-Grünau in 1900-6 over a length of 37 km, a lock was also built to designs by the Havestadt and Contag engineering company. It is the only lock to overcome the difference in level of just under three metres between the Spree and the Havel. The canal scarcely sloped, as it was not permissible to remove water from the Spree at low water level. Thus the lock had to include a powerful pump to produce the necessary compensating water. Also, a transverse canal between the two chambers of the double lock made it possible to save water by using the first half of the water flowing out for partial filling of the other chamber. A third chamber was added to the original two with lift gates in 1939, to allow ships displacing 1,000 tons to pass through the lock.

in der Nähe/nearby:
Pfarrkirche; Teltow; Ritterstraße
13. Jh. (Umbau 1811-12 teils nach Schinkel)
Bürogebäude der Gerätewerke; Teltow; Oderstraße
1965 • Wolfgang Hahn, Paul Pöschke, Helmut Wendt
Wohngebäude; Teltow; Ruhlsdorfer Platz
1988-89 • Helmut Janke, Herbert Gödicke

S 6 Haus Bahner
Kleinmachnow; Tucholskyhöhe 11
1933 • Walter Gropius

Das 1375 erstmals erwähnte Machnow »Uffm Sande«, heute mit etwa 13000 Einwohnern Landgemeinde in der Mark, war über sieben Jahrhunderte in Besitzkontinuität derer von Hake. Durch den Ausbau günstiger Verkehrsverbindungen in die Innenstadt Berlins entwickelte sich Kleinmachnow besonders in den dreißiger Jahren unseres Jahrhunderts zu einem bevorzugten Wohnsitz am Stadtrand Berlins. Vor allem Künstler und Intellektuelle siedelten sich hier an. Bekannte Architekten wie Walter Gropius, Egon Eiermann und Hermann Henselmann bauten hier beachtenswerte Einfamilienhäuser. Das von Walter Gropius 1933 auf der Tucholskyhöhe geschaffene Wohnhaus ist ein zweigeschossiger Baukörper mit gegliedertem Grundriß, stark flach geneigtem Satteldach und auskragendem Gesims. Es war eines der letzten von ihm im damaligen Deutschland errichteten Häuser. Seine Erkenntnis, daß unter den seit 1933 herrschenden Verhältnissen eine Weiterführung der Ideen des Neuen Bauens nicht mehr möglich sei, veranlaßte ihn 1934 zur Emigration nach England.

Machnow «Uffm Sande» (on the sand) was first mentioned in 1375; it is now a country community in the Mark, with about 13,000 inhabitants. For over seven centuries it was in continuous possession of the von Hake family. As good connections to central Berlin were built Kleinmachnow, particularly in the 1930s, became a popular place to live on the outskirts of Berlin, attracting artists and intellectuals in particular. Striking detached houses were built here by artists of the eminence of Walter Gropius, Egon Eiermann and Hermann Henselmann. The house built by Walter Gropius on the Tucholskyhöhe in 1933 is a two-storey building with an elaborate ground plan, flat sloping roof and projecting cornice. It was one of the last houses built by him in Germany. Realizing that his ideas on building could no longer be realized under the prevailing circumstances, he emigrated to England in 1934.

in der Nähe/nearby:
Dorfkirche; Kleinmachnow
Bis 1597
Wohnhaus Ihring; Kleinmachnow; Tucholskyhöhe 12
1934 • Hermann Henselmann
Wohnhaus; Kleinmachnow; Am Weinberg 5
1936 • Egon Eiermann
Freibad; Kleinmachnow; Fontanestraße 30
1975-76 • Manfred Thiel

S 7 Wohnhaus Bruno Taut
Dahlewitz; Wiesenstraße 13
1926-29 • Bruno Taut

Zum erstenmal wurde das Dorf Dahlewitz 1305 erwähnt. Heute gehört es zu den typischen Berliner Randsiedlungen. Hierher siedelte der als Reformarchitekt bekannte Bruno Taut nach seiner Zeit als Stadtbaumeister in Magdeburg über und errichtete 1926-28 für sich ein Wohnhaus. Sein neues Schaffensgebiet war nun Berlin, wo er zum wichtigsten Architekten des mit den Gewerkschaften eng verbundenen »Sozialen Bauens« werden sollte. Das Haus, ein über einem viertelkreisförmigen Grundriß errichteter zweigeschossiger Baukörper, krümmt die Rundung mit Eingang und Treppenhaus wie einen Rücken zur Straße. Es orientiert sich mit einem gartensaalartigen Raum und dem Balkon in der Spitze des Hauses zur offenen Landschaft. »Wie ein Schiff mit seinem Bug« taucht es gleichsam in die Natur ein. Taut verschmähte aufwendige Möblierung, sein Haus wirkte nur durch Form und Farbe, darin sah er das Wohnliche.

The village of Dahlewitz was first mentioned in 1305. It is now a typical residential area on the edge of Berlin. Bruno Taut, known as an architect of reform, moved here after his period as city architect in Magdeburg and built a house for himself in 1926-8. His new working area was now Berlin, where he was to become the most important architect of the «social building» movement, which was closely linked with the trade unions. The Dahlewitz house, a two-storey building on a quarter-circle ground plan, presents its curved line with entrance and stairwell like a back to the street. It has a room like a garden room and a balcony at the tip of the house, oriented towards the open countryside. It almost seems to plunge into nature «like a ship with its prow». Taut despised lavish furnishing, his house made its effect simply by shape and colour, and he saw this as what made it liveable in.

in der Nähe/nearby:
Dorfkirche; Dahlewitz
2. H. 13. Jh.; 16./17. Jh.
Dorfkirche; Rangsdorf
1890
Denkmal der Schlacht bei Großbeeren; Großbeeren
1817 • Karl Friedrich Schinkel
Gedenkturm; Großbeeren; Dorfaue
1913 • G. Lange
Dorfkirche; Großbeeren
1818-20 • Nach Plänen von Karl Friedrich Schinkel
Schloß; Märkisch Wilmersdorf
1801

S 8 Stadtkern Zossen
1355

Die an der Notte gelegene Kreisstadt hat etwa 6000 Einwohner. Sie wurde erstmalig 1320 als »Sossen, zu der Szosne« und 1355 als Stadt Zossen erwähnt. Das ursprünglich slawische Zentrum gehörte bis zum 15. Jahrhundert zur Lausitz. Es wies um 1430 im Gegensatz zu den derzeit üblichen Straßendörfern eine Dreiecksform auf. Im 16. Jahrhundert wird die Burg als Grenzfeste gegen Sachsen ausgebaut. Der »märkische Eulenspiegel« Hans Klanert war in dieser Zeit oft Gast in Zossen. Nach den Bränden 1661 und 1671 wurde die Stadt mit ihrem 300 m × 300 m großen Kern und angerartigem Markt mit schlichten zweigeschossigen Wohnhäusern wieder aufgebaut. Vom Wohnhausbau des 18. und den spätklassizistischen Häusern des 19. Jahrhunderts sind – oftmals stark verändert – bemerkenswert und erhalten: Kirchplatz (heute Bibliothek), Puschkinstraße 7, Puschkinstraße Ecke Marktplatz (heute Sparkasse), Leninplatz 17 sowie Bahnhofstraße 56 und 57. Die 1739 von Christoph Gottlieb Hedemann errichtete Pfarrkirche ist ein querorientierter Rechteckbau mit dem Turm mittig an der Südseite und gegenüberliegend die Sakristei an der Nordseite. Das Turmoberteil und das Innere mit seiner umlaufenden Empore erfuhren 1873 Veränderungen.

This district centre on the Notte has about 6,000 inhabitants. It was first mentioned in 1320 as «Sossen, zu der Szosne», and in 1355 as the town of Zossen. Originally a Slavic centre, it was part of the Lausitz until the fifteenth century. Around 1430, unlike the linear villages customary at the time, it was on a triangular plan. The castle was extended in the sixteenth century as a border fortress against Saxony. Hans Klanert, the «Eulenspiegel of the Mark» was a regular visitor to Zossen at this time. After fires in 1661 and 1671 the town with its 300 m × 300 m centre and village-green-like market place with plain two-storey houses was rebuilt. Of the housing dating from the eighteenth and nineteenth centuries, the latter in late classical style, the following have survived, often with much alteration, and are worthy of attention: Kirchplatz (now library), 7 Puschkinstrasse, Puschkinstrasse/Marktplatz corner (now bank), 17 Leninplatz and 56 and 57 Bahnhofstrasse. The parish church, built by Christoph Gottlieb Hedemann in 1739, is a transversely oriented rectangular building with the tower placed centrally on the south side and the sacristy opposite on the north side. The upper part of the tower and the interior with gallery running round it were altered in 1873.

in der Nähe/nearby:
Park mit Bastion (Burgreste) und Torhaus; Zossen
16. Jh.
Kalköfen; Zossen; Wasserstraße 5
vermutlich 1852 und um 1880 • System Lösche
Windmühle; Saalow
1970 restauriert

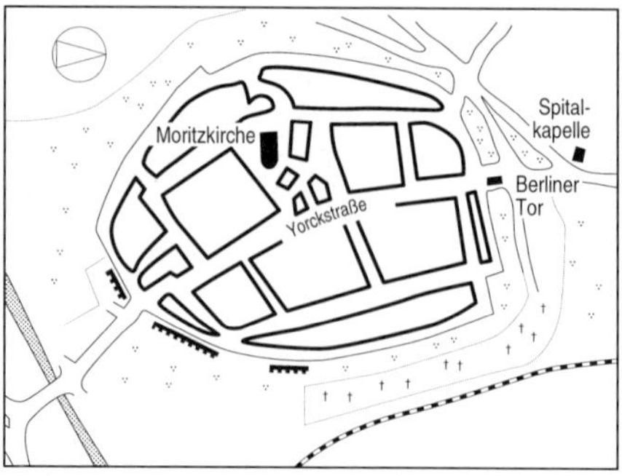

S 9 Stadtkern Mittenwalde
1307

Mit Stammeszentrum in Köpenick besiedelten die Sprewanen im 6. und 7. Jahrhundert die östlichen Teile des Teltow. Die slawische Burg, die auf dem Pennigberg anderthalb Kilometer westlich der Stadt lag, war wohl sprewanisch. Vermutlich mit den Vorstößen der Markgrafen von Meißen aus dem nahen Niederlausitzer Grenzraum Teupitz entstand nach 1180 als frühdeutscher Siedlungsansatz die »Alte Stadt« wohl im Schutze der Burgstelle »Am Hausgrabenberg«. Nach askanischer Eroberung 1245 wurde die Stadtanlage »Middenwalde« planmäßig im Kolonialschema entwickelt und auf Grund ihrer günstigen Lage am Notteübergang des Berlin-Lausitzer Straßenzuges als »Tor der Mark« ausgebaut. Der mittelalterliche ovale Stadtgrundriß mit gitterförmigem Straßennetz und dreieckigem, später überbautem Markt ist nahezu unverändert. Bemerkenswert sind vor allem die zweigeschossigen Putzbauten des 18. Jahrhunderts Yorckstraße 25 und 45, Kirchstraße 4 und das Fachwerkhaus Salzmarkt 5 sowie die in fast ungestörter Reihe erhaltenen eingeschossigen Traufenhäuser des frühen 19. Jahrhunderts in der Katharinen-, Schützen- und Paul-Gerhardt-Straße sowie in der Baruther Vorstadt.

Around their tribal centre in Köpenick the Sprevans settled the eastern parts of Teltow in the sixth and seventh centuries. The Slavic fortress on the Pennigberg one and a half kilometres west of the town was probably Sprevan. It is presumed that the «old town», probably protected by the fortress «Am Hausgrabenberg», came into being as an early German settlement after 1180 as the Margraves of Meissen advanced from the nearby Niederlausitz frontier zone of Teupitz. After being conquered by the Ascanians in 1245 the town of «Middenwalde» was planned and built under the colonial scheme and extended as «Gate of the Mark» because of its favourable position at the Notte crossing of the Berlin-Lausitz road. The medieval oval ground plan with a grid of streets and a triangular market place, later built over, is almost unchanged. Particularly striking are the two-storey eighteenth century rendered buildings at 25 and 45 Yorckstrasse and 4 Kirchstrasse and the half-timbered house at 5 Salzmarkt and the single-storey early nineteenth century houses with eaves which have survived in almost unbroken series in Katharinen-, Schützen- and Paul-Gerhardt-Strasse, and in the suburb of Baruth.

In der Nähe/nearby:
Dorfkirche; Motzen
1755 (Turmhaube 1930)
Bauernhaus (Heimatmuseum); Prieros
18. Jh.
Dorfkirche; Schenkendorf
1713 (restauriert 1910)

S 10 Berliner Tor
Mittenwalde; Yorckstraße
Ende 15. Jahrhundert

Von der Stadtbefestigung sind nur Mauerreste im Südwesten und das Berliner Tor im Norden der Stadt erhalten. Das rechteckige Vortor in Backstein mit runden Ecktürmchen und Blendengiebel an der Feldseite, stammt vom Ende des 15. Jahrhunderts. Von dem wohl zur gleichen Zeit errichteten Haupttor ist der Feldsteinturm erhalten. Der Turm mit seinem backsteinernen Oberteil wurde 1898 restauriert. Ursprünglich waren beide Toranlagen durch eine Zwingermauer, von der nur noch Reste vorhanden sind, verbunden.

All that remains of the town fortifications are fragments of walls in the south-west and the Berlin Gate in the north of the town. The rectangular outer gate in brick with round corner turrets and false gables on the outer side dates from the late fifteenth century. The rubble stone tower of the main gate, probably built at the same time, has survived. The tower with its brick upper section was restored in 1898. Originally the two gates were connected by a bailey wall, of which only fragments have survived.

In der Nähe/nearby:
Pfarrkirche St. Moritz; Kirchplatz
13. bis 15. Jh.
Spitalkapelle St. Georg; Nähe Berliner Tor
1394
Altes Rathaus
1840
Alte Probstei; Yorckstraße 25
Um 1740
Wohnhaus; Yorckstraße 38
1747
Hotel Yorck; Yorckstraße 45
1806
Wohnhaus; Kirchstraße 4
1787

S 11 Rathaus
Herzberg; Markt 1
1616-18

Weit im Süden des Landes Brandenburg liegt Herzberg. Nach dem Wiener Kongreß kam es erst zu Preußen, bis dahin war es sächsisch. Seine jeweilige Randlage konnte es auch nicht durch die Anbindung an wichtige Verkehrswege der Neuzeit ausgleichen, so blieb dem Städtchen eine spürbare Beschaulichkeit erhalten, die auch das Rathaus widerspiegelt. Der verputzte Renaissancebau mit seinen Voutengiebeln, mit Zwerchhaus und Dachreiter zeigt sich in seiner soliden Architektur im Einfluß beschwingter sächsischer Bauweise, überhaucht von der ernsten Sparsamkeit Brandenburgs. Dabei ist dieses Rathaus Zeugnis eines selbstbewußten Bürgertums, das sich gemessen an der Größe der Stadt doch ein repräsentatives Denkmal baulichen Vermögens gesetzt hat, ganz im Sinne der nachmittelalterlichen Zeit.

Herzberg is located in the deep south of the Land Brandenburg. Formerly belonging to Saxony, it became part of Prussia following the Congress of Vienna. Its marginal location could not be improved through the link with important traffic routes in modern times, and thus the town maintained its remarkably contemplative atmosphere which is also reflected in the town hall. The solid architecture of the rendered Renaissance building with its voluted gables, lucarne and ridge turret suggests the influence of a light-hearted Saxonian style with a touch of Brandenburgian austerity. At the same time this town hall is representative of a proud and assertive bourgeoisie which has created for itself an impressive – considering the size of the town – monument to its ability to build, fully in keeping with the post-medieval spirit.

in der Nähe/nearby:
Wohnhaus; Herzberg; Magisterstraße 2
18. Jh.
Wohnhäuser; Herzberg; Torgauer Straße
18./19. Jh.

S 12 Marienkirche
Herzberg
2. Hälfte 14. Jahrhundert

Von beachtlicher Größe ist die spätgotische Herzberger Pfarrkirche, was durch ihre Bauart als Hallenkirche mit dem großen, alle drei Schiffe überspannenden Dach noch betont wird. Der Turm – ohnehin zuletzt fertiggestellter Bauteil der Kirche – fiel dem Stadtbrand von 1483 zum Opfer. Sein Wiederaufbau erfolgte erst 1562, nun im oktogonalen Abschluß, zeitgemäß mit Okuli. Später nochmals erhöht und 1782 mit Barockhaube und Laterne abgeschlossen, läßt sich eine ganze Abfolge von Baustilen an ihm ablesen. Das Innere der Kirche birgt beachtliche Ausstattung wie Altaraufsatz (1765), Kanzel (1658), Taufstein (1624), Altargitter (1769), Bilder und Grabmäler. Beherrscht wird der Raum von einem feinen Netzgewölbe aus Parallelrippen nach Prager Vorbild und Sterngewölben über den Seitenschiffjochen. Die mittelalterliche Gewölbeausmalung, die in vielen Kirchen den Purifizierungen des 19. Jahrhunderts zum Opfer fiel, blieb hier auf Betreiben von Quast und Schinkel erhalten.

The late-Gothic Herzberg parish church is of quite impressive size, emphasized even more by the structure consisting of a hall church with a huge roof spanning the nave and aisles. The tower – the last part of the church to be completed – was destroyed by the town fire of 1483. It was not reconstructed until 1562, this time with the octagonal spire and oculi that were typical of the time. Subsequently raised again and in 1782 covered with a baroque cupola and lantern, it can be seen to illustrate a highly revealing succession of different building styles. The interior of the church contains remarkable features such as altar-piece (1765), pulpit (1658), baptismal font (1624), altar-screen (1769), paintings, and tombs. The space is dominated by delicate reticulated vaults with parallel ribs after the Prague model and stellar vaults above the aisle bays. The medieval painting of the vaults, which in many churches has fallen victim to purification in the nineteenth century, is preserved here, thanks to the efforts of Quast and Schinkel.

in der Nähe/nearby:
Friedhofskapelle; Herzberg; westl. Vorstadt
15. Jh.

S 13 Herrenhaus Wiepersdorf 1731-38

Das seit 1780 im Familienbesitz des Dichterehepaares Achim v. Arnim und seiner Frau Bettina, Schwester des Clemens Brentano, befindliche Gut wurde 1958 Arbeits- und Erholungsstätte für Künstler. Das auf den Fundamenten eines spätmittelalterlichen »Festen Hauses« errichtete Herrenhaus gibt sich preußisch-schlicht. Die kurzen Anbauten sind gegen 1784 hinzugefügt. Um 1880 erhielt die Gartenfront ihre neubarocke Form. Der barocke Park wurde um 1800 durch einen Landschaftspark erweitert. Achim v. Arnim ließ ihn 1880-89 wiederherstellen und fügte die halbkreisförmige Orangerie hinzu. Die im Garten aufgestellten, um 1880 erworbenen barocken Freiplastiken stammen aus Italien und Süddeutschland. Die Grabstätten des Dichterpaares mit Inschrift und Wappen auf Kalksteinplatten über Sandsteinsockel befinden sich an der ehemaligen Gutskirche nördlich des Herrenhauses. Bettina v. Arnim gilt als eine der großen brandenburgischen Persönlichkeiten der Mitte des 19. Jahrhunderts. Ihr engagiertes politisches Auftreten für soziale und frauenrechtliche Fragen machte sie dem Hof unbequem. In Berlin verkehrte sie im Salon von Rahel Varnhagen; dort traf sie zusammen mit Kleist, Heine, den Brüdern Humboldt, Schinkel und auch dem Fürsten Pückler.

Having been in the family of the poets Achim von Arnim and his wife Bettina, a sister of Clemens Brentano, since 1780, the estate was turned into a place of work and recreation for artists in 1958. The mansion in simple Prussian style was built on the foundations of a late medieval fortified house. The short extensions were added c. 1880. The garden façade was rebuilt in neo-baroque style c. 1880. The baroque park itself had been extended by a landscape garden c. 1800. Achim von Arnim had the garden restored in 1880-89 and added the semicircular orangery. The baroque statuary was acquired c. 1800 and came from Italy and south Germany. The tombs of the poet couple, with inscription and coat of arms on limestone slabs set on sandstone plinths, are located at the former estate church north of the mansion. Bettina von Arnim ranks as one of the great personages of mid nineteenth century Brandenburg. Her political commitment to social problems and women's rights caused frequent irritation at Court. In Berlin she was a regular guest in the house of Rahel Varnhagen where she met Kleist, Heine, the brothers Humboldt, Schinkel and even Fürst Pückler.

in der Nähe/nearby:
Gutskirche; Wiepersdorf; Park
1894-95
Bauerngehöfte; Hohenseefeld; Nr. 2, 3 und 18
18./19. Jh.
Dorfkirche; Ihlow
14. Jh. (Doppelhelm 1879)

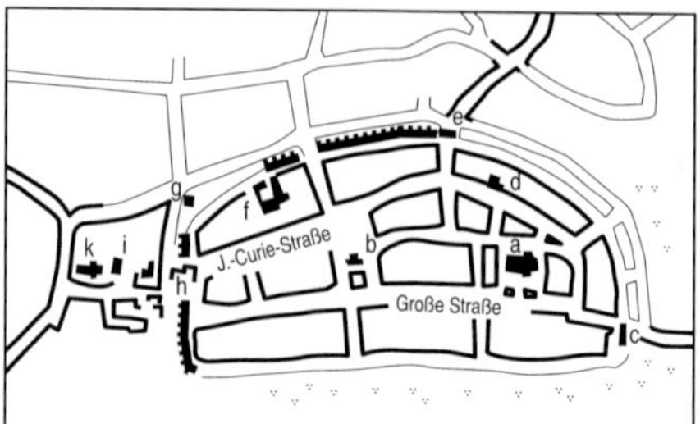

a Nikolaikirche
b Rathaus
c Neumarkter Tor
d Abtshof
e Zinnaer Tor
f Franziskanerkloster
g Wohnhaus, Bleichhag 6
h Dammtor
i Amtshaus
k Marienkirche

S 14 Stadtkern Jüterbog 1174

Die aus drei Siedlungskernen entstandene heutige Kreisstadt mit etwa 13 000 Einwohnern, bei der Ersterwähnung 1007 als »Justriboc« verzeichnet, war wohl slawischer Zentralort im Nuthegebiet. Nach Inbesitznahme des Raumes Jüterbog entschloß sich Erzbischof Wichmann von Magdeburg 1174 zum planmäßigen Aufbau der Stadt. Nach einer zweiten Ausbaustufe Anfang des 13. Jahrhunderts erhielt sie ihre elliptische Form, im Grundriß 870 m × 420 m, mit zwei Längsstraßen, mehreren querenden Nebenstraßen, dazwischengespanntem Markt und einem Kirchplatz. 1174 erhielt Jüterbog Magdeburger Stadtrecht. Die den mittelalterlichen Stadtgrundriß aufnehmende Wohnbebauung, meistens Traufenhäuser aus Fachwerk, vielfach nachträglich verputzt, führt in der Regel in die Zeit um 1800 und in die 1. Hälfte des 19. Jahrhunderts zurück. Die Stadtbefestigung aus dem späten 13. Jahrhundert oder dem frühen 14. Jahrhundert mit Mauer, Wieckhäusern und mehreren Toren ist wegen des noch vorhandenen Bestandes besonders bemerkenswert.

The present district centre has about 13,000 inhabitants, and grew up from three settlements. It was first mentioned as «Justriboc» in 1007, and was probably the central Slav settlement in the Nuthe area. After annexing the Jüterbog district, Archbishop Wichmann of Magdeburg decided to build up the town systematically in 1174. After a second building stage in the early thirteenth century it was given its elliptical form, 870 m × 420 m, with two longitudinal streets, several side streets, a market between them and a church square. Jüterbog was granted a charter by Magdeburg in 1174. Residential accommodation follows the medieval layout of the town and consists mainly of half-timbered houses with eaves, often rendered later, dating generally from the period around 1800 and the first half of the nineteenth century. The surviving late thirteenth century or early fourteenth century town fortifications with wall, towers and several gates are of particular interest.

in der Nähe/nearby:
Bauerngehöft; Dennewitz; Dorfstraße 41
Um 1800
Stallgebäude mit Oberlaube; Werder; Dorfstraße 4
1835
Bockwindmühle; Petkus
1835 (1950 verändert)

S 15 Dammtor
Jüterbog; Am Dammtor
14. Jahrhundert

Die Ausmaße und die künstlerische Qualität der Stadtbefestigung von Jüterbog überliefern vor allem die drei Torbauten Dammtor, Neumarkter Tor und Zinnaer Tor. Teile der aus Feldstein errichteten Stadtmauer sind beiderseits des Dammtores und westlich des Zinnaer Tores bis zur Höhe von 2 bis 3 m ohne Mauerkrone erhalten. Das Dammtor, ebenso wie die beiden weiteren Tore aus dem frühen 14. Jahrhundert, im Unterbau aus Feldstein und mit backsteinernem Oberbau um 1480/90, verband die Dammvorstadt mit der befestigten Stadt. Der vom Haupttor erhaltene Rundturm ist mit Zinnenkranz und Kegelspitzhelm bekrönt. Auch das zweigeschossige Vortor aus Backstein, um 1480/90 entstanden mit runden Ecktürmen, Blenden und Gitterfriesen an der Feldseite, wird durch Zinnen abgeschlossen.

The extent and artistic quality of the Jüterbog town fortifications are conveyed by the three gates, the Dammtor, the Neumarkter Tor and the Zinnaer Tor. Parts of the rubble-stone town wall have survived on both sides of the Dammtor and west of the Zinnaer Tor to a height of 2 to 3 m, without coping. The Dammtor, dating from the early fourteenth century like the other two gates, is built of rubble stone in its lower part with a brick upper section dating from 1480/90; it connected the causeway suburb with the rest of the town. The round tower that has survived of the main gate has battlements and a small conical spire. The three-storey fore-gate in brick, dating from c. 1480/90, has round corner towers, blind windows, and lattice friezes on the outside; it is topped with battlements.

in der Nähe/nearby:
Marienkirche; Dammvorstadt
1. H. 13. Jh.
Amtshaus; Dammvorstadt
1700
Franziskanerkloster und -kirche; Am Dammtor
1480/1510
Wohnhaus mit Arztpraxis; Bleichhag 6
1928-29 • Konrad Wachsmann

S 16 Pfarrkirche St. Nikolai
Jüterbog
14./15. Jahrhundert

Die dreischiffige kreuzrippengewölbte Hallenkirche in Backstein aus der 2. Hälfte des 14. Jahrhunderts erhielt um 1420 mit dem doppeltürmigen Westbau aus Feldstein und mit der Ergänzung um ein Joch nach Westen ihr endgültiges Ausmaß. Der südliche der beiden durch eine Brücke miteinander verbundenen Türme konnte mit seinem spitzen Steinhelm Ende des 15. Jahrhunderts vollendet werden. Der Nordturm dagegen erhielt 1562/63 einen orthogonalen haubenbekrönten Aufsatz. Die beiden zweigeschossigen Kapellen an der südlichen und nördlichen Seite des Schiffes stammen aus den Jahren um 1447 beziehungsweise um 1493. Der bemerkenswerte Staffelgiebel der nördlichen Kapelle ist vermutlich von Meister Merten. Ein reich profiliertes Sandsteinportal schmückt den Haupteingang im Westen. Das Innere besitzt noch Ausmalungen aus der Erbauungszeit, viele mittelalterliche Bildwerke und ist reich an Ausstattungsstücken aus dem 15. bis 18. Jahrhundert. Die letzte Rekonstruktion begann 1973.

This brick-built hall church with rib vaulting, nave and two aisles dates from the second half of the fourteenth century; the rubble-stone twin-towered west end and an extra western bay were added c. 1420. The spire on the south tower, joined to its twin by a bridge, was added in the late fifteenth century, and the upper part of the north tower, topped with a cupola, was added 1562/3. The two two-storey chapels on the south and north sides of the nave date from c. 1447 and c. 1493 respectively. The remarkable stepped gable of the northern chapel is presumed to be by Meister Merten. The west door is a lavishly profiled sandstone portal. The interior still has painting from the time the church was built, many medieval pictures and other pieces dating from the fifteenth to eighteenth centuries. The last reconstruction phase started in 1973.

in der Nähe/nearby:
Rathaus mit Gerichtslaube; Am Markt
1500/26; 1493 • Meister Merten (Gerichtslaube)
Abtshof (Heimatmuseum); Am Abtshof
Um 1500
Zinnaer Tor
2. H. 15. Jh.
Neumarkter Tor
2. H. 15. Jh.

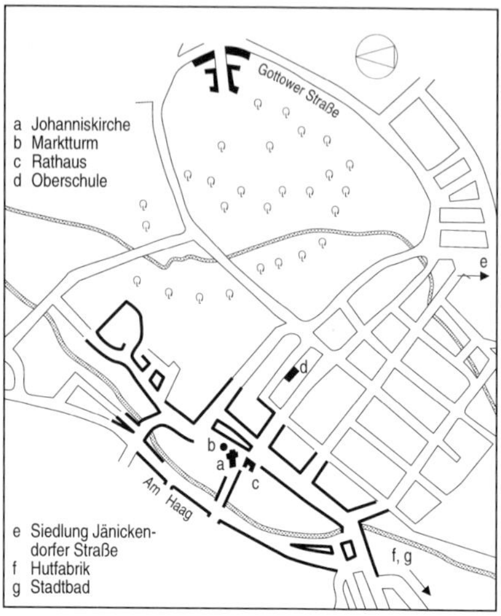

S 17 Siechen- und Gästehaus Kloster Zinna 1. Hälfte 14. Jahrhundert

Nachdem Erzbischof Wichmann von Magdeburg kurz nach 1150 den Raum um Jüterbog in Besitz nahm, wurde von ihm in der Nuthe-Niederung nördlich von Jüterbog 1170/71 das Zisterzienserkloster Zinna gegründet und Mönche aus Altenkamp bei Köln angesiedelt. Als Weber- und Spinnersiedlung durch Friedrich II. für die Zuwanderung von Kolonistenfamilien aus Sachsen bestimmt, legte Bauinspektor Christiani 1764-77 ein 800 m × 580 m großes Dorf mit vier Quartieren an. Zwei sich rechtwinklig kreuzende gerade Straßen mit achteckigem Markt im Kreuzungspunkt markieren die Quartiere. Das in der 1. Hälfte des 14. Jahrhunderts erbaute zweigeschossige Siechen- und Gästehaus, ein rechteckiger Backsteinbau mit Ziergiebel und einem in der 1. Hälfte des 19. Jahrhunderts aufgesetzten Fachwerkdachreiter, bildet mit der Neuen Abtei, dem heutigen Heimatmuseum, eine reizvolle Einheit. Die Neue Abtei, 1440-50 errichtet, ist ebenfalls ein zweigeschossiger Backsteinbau, der mit seinem fein gegliederten Staffelgiebel im wirkungsvollen Kontrast zum Siechenhaus steht.

After Archbishop Wichmann of Magdeburg annexed the region around Jüterbog shortly after 1150 he founded the Cistercian monastery of Zinna in the Nuthe flats north of Jüterbog in 1170/1, and placed monks from Altenkamp near Cologne there. Frederick II designated the area a weaving and spinning centre for immigrating colonists from Saxony, and from 1764-77 building inspector Christiani built an 800 m × 850 m village with four quarters, marked by two roads crossing at right angles with an octagonal market at the point of intersection. The two-storey infirmary and guest house was built in the first half of the fourteenth century, a rectangular brick building with a decorative gable and a timberframe ridge turret added in the first half of the nineteenth century. It forms a charming unit with the Neue Abtei, the present local history museum. This new abbey, built 1440-50, is also a two-storey brick building, and its finely articulated step gable forms an effective contrast with the infirmary.

in der Nähe/nearby:
Klosterkirche und Klausur; Kloster Zinna
Seit 1230
Dorfkirche; Grüna
2. H. 19. Jh.
Dorfkirche; Neuhof
E. 15. Jh.

S 18 Stadtkern Luckenwalde 1285

Die heutige Kreisstadt mit metall-, textil- und holzverarbeitender Industrie und etwa 27 000 Einwohnern entstand im 13. Jahrhundert etwa 1,7 km westlich eines altslawischen Burgwalles im Schutze einer am nordöstlichen Stadtrand gelegenen, 1216 erstmals erwähnten deutschen Burg. Heute erinnert nur noch der Name »Burgstraße« daran. Die unbefestigte Marktsiedlung erweiterte sich mit dem Aufschwung der gewerblichen Wollmanufaktur. Anders als in den benachbarten Städten Jüterbog und Treuenbrietzen ist der Grundriß des Stadtkerns unregelmäßig. Der Markt und die anschließende 1979-80 neugestaltete breite Fußgängerzone bilden den räumlichen und baulichen Mittelpunkt. Der Marktturm, ein quadratischer Feldsteinbau mit backsteinernem Obergeschoß aus der zweiten Hälfte des 15. Jahrhunderts, bildet mit der Johanniskirche aus gleicher Zeit und dem 1844 im Stil der Schinkel-Nachfolge errichteten Rathaus städtebaulich eine räumliche Einheit.

This town, now the regional centre, with metal, textile and wood-processing industry and about 27,000 inhabitants came into being in the thirteenth century about 1.7 km west of an Old Slavic rampart protecting a castle on the north-eastern edge of the town, first mentioned in 1216. Today only the name «Burgstrasse» survives as a reminder of the castle. The unfortified market settlement grew with the upsurge of commercial wool manufacture. Unlike the neighbouring towns of Jüterbog and Treuenbrietzen the town centre is built to an irregular plan. The market and adjacent pedestrian precinct, redesigned in 1979-80, form the spatial and architectural centre. The market tower, a square rubble-stone building with brick upper storey, dates from the second half of the fifteenth century and forms an urban unit with the Johanniskirche, dating from the same period, and the town hall, built in 1844 in the style of Schinkel's successors.

in der Nähe/nearby:
Schloß mit Landschaftspark; Stülpe
1744 (Schloß); 19. Jh. (Park)
Schloß; Blankensee
1701

S 19 Wohnsiedlung
Luckenwalde; Jänickendorfer Straße
Um 1920 • Josef Bischof

Die Ausdehnung der Stadt Luckenwalde als Folge des industriellen Aufschwungs im 19. und 20. Jahrhundert wurde besonders in den zwanziger Jahren und vornehmlich durch die Errichtung von Siedlungen beschleunigt. So entstand 1920 in der südöstlichen Vorstadt die Wohnsiedlung in der Jänickendorfer Straße von Josef Bischof. Die im sogenannten Heimatstil gestalteten ein- bzw. zweigeschossigen Putzbauten sind trauf- oder giebelseitig zur Straße orientiert. Die ausgebauten gekrümmten Bohlenbinderdächer vermitteln der Siedlung ihren eigenen Charakter ebenso wie das angerartige Zentrum und die Betonung der Zufahrtsstraßen durch gemauerte Rundbogen. Es ist eine der malerischen Gartenstädte der Jahre vor und nach dem Ersten Weltkrieg. Die in Luckenwalde reformierte Kommunal- und Siedlungspolitik zog namhafte Architekten jener Zeit an. Unter anderem erhielt Erich Mendelsohn, neben Gropius, den Gebrüdern Taut und Mies van der Rohe Mitbegründer der Berliner Architektenvereinigung »Der Ring«, hier den ersten Großauftrag. Neben der nach seinem Entwurf errichteten Hutfabrik wurde um 1920 von ihm die Wohnsiedlung Gottower Straße am östlichen Stadtrand gebaut.

The town of Luckenwalde expanded as a consequence of the industrial boom in the late nineteenth and early twentieth centuries, and its growth accelerated in the twenties, particularly as a result of estate building. Thus Josef Bischof's residential estate in Jänickendorfer Strasse by Joseph Bischof was built in 1920 in the south-eastern suburbs. The one- or two-storey rendered buildings in the so-called Heimatstil are set some with gables, some with eaves to the street. The protruding curved plank roofs give the estate its particular character, as do the village-green-like centre and the accenting of the access roads with round arches in brick. It is one of the most picturesque garden cities of the period before and after the First World War. Luckenwalde's reformist local government and building policies attracted notable architects of the period. Mendelsohn, with Gropius, the Taut brothers and Mies co-founder of the Berlin architects' association «Der Ring», was one of the architects to get his first major contract here. As well as designing the hat factory he also built the Gottower Strasse estate on the eastern fringes of the town, in about 1920.

in der Nähe/nearby:
Oberschule; Dimitroffstraße 15 a
1928 • Graf
Wohnsiedlung; Gottower Straße, Upstallweg
Um 1920 • Erich Mendelsohn
Waldfriedhof; Straße des Friedens
Um 1920 • Josef Bischof, Richard Neutra

S 20 Hutfabrik
Luckenwalde; Industriestraße
1921-23 • Erich Mendelsohn

Mit der Gründung des »Deutschen Werkbundes« 1907 in Berlin wurde der Industriebau zu einem beliebten Experimentierfeld progressiver Architekten. Die AEG-Turbinenhalle von Peter Behrens in Berlin, die Chemische Fabrik Luban von Hans Poelzig und die Faguswerke von Walter Gropius in Alfeld sind bekannte Zeugen des Aufbruchs in Stahl und Glas. Mendelsohn kannte diese Beispiele, doch für ihn war die Architektur der Zweckmäßigkeit nur Ausgangspunkt und nicht Ziel der Entwicklung. Er dachte an Beton als Gestaltungsmittel und er liebte die Übersteigerung der zweckmäßigen Form. Der Hutfabrik – sie und die Textilfabrik in Leningrad bleiben Mendelsohns einzige Industriebauten – lag von Beginn an der Fabrikationsablauf als Grundrißschema zugrunde: vier parallele Fabrikationshallen zwischen Kraftstation und Färberei. Die Färberei wurde markanter Blickpunkt mit ihrem eigenwilligen Dachaufbau, in dem sich die Lüftungsanlage verbirgt.

When the «Deutscher Werkbund» was founded in 1907 industrial building became a popular area of experimentation for progressive architects. Peter Behrens' AEG turbine hall in Berlin, Hans Poelzig's Luban chemical factory and Walter Gropius' Fagus factory in Alfeld are well-known testaments to the increasing popularity of steel and glass. Mendelsohn knew these examples, but for him architectural expediency was only a starting point and not the end point of the development. The hat factory – this and a textile factory in Leningrad were Mendelsohn's only industrial buildings – was from the beginning based on the manufacturing process as a scheme for its ground plan: four parallel manufacturing shops between power plant and dyeing shop. The dyeing shop was a striking feature: its unconventional roof concealed ventilation equipment.

in der Nähe/nearby:
Stadtbad; Rudolf-Breitscheid-Straße 72
1928
Johanniskirche; Markt
2. H. 15. Jh.
Marktturm; Markt
2. H. 15. Jh.
Rathaus; Markt
1844

S 21 Stadtkern Treuenbrietzen
1290

Die Landstadt an der Nieplitz entstand aus zwei Siedlungskernen. Sie war um 1200 eine eigenständige Kleinherrschaft, wohl begründet durch das Geschlecht der »Buchardiner«, das sich später nach »Brietzen« nannte. Der mittelalterliche ellipsenförmige Stadtgrundriß im Ausmaß von 700 m × 500 m mit angerartiger Hauptstraße ergab sich aus dem Zusammenwachsen der Marktsiedlung um die Marienkirche mit dem Viertel nahe der Nikolaikirche, beiderseits der Handelsstraße Leipzig-Wittenberge-Berlin. Das Stadtbild prägen die Heilig-Geist-Kapelle am südlichen Stadtrand, ein spätgotischer Rundbau mit 1936 ergänztem Fachwerk-Obergeschoß und Kegeldach, das Rathaus in der Mitte der Großstraße, ein dreigeschossiger Putzbau im Kern von 1735, das dritte Geschoß und der quadratische Turmaufsatz später hineingefügt, die Marienkirche, eine dreischiffige spätromanische Gewölbebasilika, begonnen um 1220 aus Feldstein, und die Nikolaikirche, eine frühgotische dreischiffige Gewölbebasilika aus Backstein, entstanden im 2. Drittel des 13. Jahrhunderts. Erwähnenswert sind auch die zweigeschossigen Fachwerk-Wohnhäuser aus dem 18. Jahrhundert in der Großstraße und teilweise in geschlossener Reihe in wenigen Nebenstraßen.

This country town on the Nieplitz developed from two centres of settlement. In about 1200 it was an independent small domain, probably founded by the «Buchardines», who later called themselves after «Brietzen». The medieval elliptical ground plan 700 m × 500 m with village-green-like main street was formed when the market settlement around the Marienkirche and the district by the Nikolaikirche grew together, on both sides of the Leipzig–Wittenberge–Berlin trade route. Principal visual features of the town are the Heilig-Geist-Kapelle on the southern edge of the town, a late Gothic round building with a half-timbered upper storey completed in 1936 and a conical roof, the town hall in the middle of Grossstrasse, a three-storey rendered building with core dating from 1735, third storey and square tower added at a later date, the Marienkirche, a late Romanesque basilica with nave and two aisles, in rubble stone and started c. 1220, and the Nikolaikirche, an early Gothic vaulted basilica with nave and two aisles, built in brick and dating from the second third of the thirteenth century. Also worthy of mention are the eighteenth century half-timbered houses in Grossstrasse, and some complete sets in a few of the side streets.

in der Nähe/nearby:
Posthalterei (Bibliothek); Beelitz; Poststraße 16
1789
Marienkirche; Beelitz; Kirchplatz
13. Jh. (Umbauten 16. Jh. und 1889)

S 22 Burg Rabenstein
Raben
1251

Die erstmals 1251 erwähnte, annähernd ovale Anlage mit Vor- und Hauptburg ist – wie für die brandenburgische Urstrom- und Moränenlandschaft üblich – vorwiegend in Feldstein ausgeführt. Der Zerstörung im Jahre 1395 folgte die Wiederherstellung, im 18. und 19. Jahrhundert kam es mehrfach zu Veränderungen. Die östliche Einfahrt der Hauptburg flankiert der Bergfried aus dem 13. Jahrhundert, ein mächtiger Turm aus Granitmauerwerk, ursprünglich mit einer Einstiegsluke in 15 m Höhe. 1849 wurde der obere Abschluß des Turmes restauriert. In westlicher Richtung schließt ein zweigeschossiger Wohnflügel von 15 Achsen an, der besonders zum Hofraum hin im 18. und 19. Jahrhundert wesentlich verändert wurde. Der Rittersaal im Kern aus dem 13. Jahrhundert schließt die Burganlage nach Westen ab. Er lädt nicht nur die Gäste der Jugendherberge zum Besuch ein.

This approximately oval building, first mentioned in 1251, with outer and inner castle is – as is customary in the glacial valley and moraine landscape of Brandenburg – built mainly of rubble stone. It was destroyed in 1395, then rebuilt, and much altered in the eighteenth and nineteenth centuries. The eastern entrance to the main castle is flanked by the thirteenth century keep, a massive granite masonry tower, originally with an access hatch at a height of 15 m. The top of the tower was restored in 1849. To the west is a two-storey residential wing with 15 axes; its courtyard side was fundamentally rebuilt in the eighteenth and nineteenth centuries. The great hall in the thirteenth century core of the building concludes the complex to the west. Visitors are welcome, and not just those who are staying at the youth hostel.

in der Nähe/nearby:
Dorfkirche; Grubo
1. H. 13. Jh.
Wohnhaus; Buchholz; Dorfstraße 16
1820/30
Dorfkirche; Buchholz
M. 19. Jh.

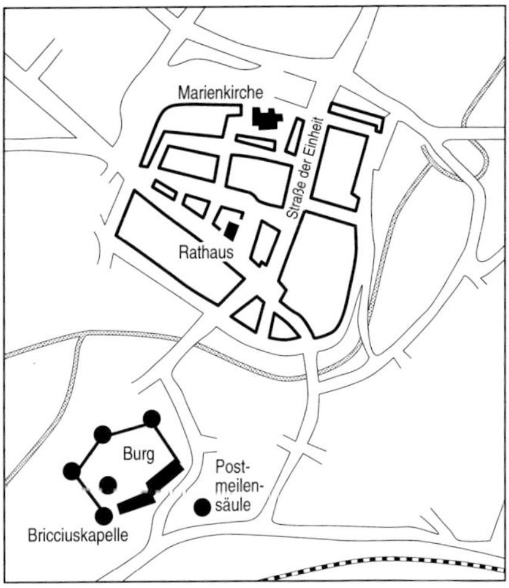

S 23 Stadtkern Belzig
1269

Mit dem 997 als »Burgwardinow Belizi« genannten Ort im Slawengau der Ploni war mit großer Wahrscheinlichkeit Belzig gemeint. Vermutet wird, daß die deutsche Herrschaft mit der Inbesitznahme des Belziger Raumes durch das ostsächsische Geschlecht von Jabilinze begann. Die Marktsiedlung entstand neben der Burg und dem frühdeutschen Suburbium »Sandberg« wohl im 13. Jahrhundert. Da die alte Handelsstraße Zerbst-Brandenburg bald an Bedeutung verlor, erwarb Belzig das volle Stadtrecht erst 1702. Die Altstadt 350 m × 350 m mit viereckigem Markt und unregelmäßigen Quartieren wurde 1547 und 1636 zweimal zerstört. Der Wohnhausbau des 17. und 18. Jahrhunderts wurde durch Putz und im Ausbau verändert. Die meist zweigeschossigen, vereinzelt auch dreigeschossigen Traufen- und Giebelhäuser beleben wirkungsvoll das Straßenbild. Die nördlich bis zur Hacken-Heide der Zauche reichenden Belziger Landschaftswiesen bilden bis heute die weidewirtschaftliche Grundlage der Viehzucht in dem Gebiet.

The place referred to in 997 as «Burgwardinow Belizi» in the Slavic area of the Ploni was in all probability Belzig. It is assumed that German rule began when the Belzig area was annexed by the East Saxon Jabilenze tribe. The market settlement grew up by the castle and the early German suburbium of «Sandberg», probably in the thirteenth century. As the old Zerbst-Brandenburg trade route soon began to wane in importance, Belzig was not granted a full charter until 1702. The old town covers and area of 350 m by 350 m with a square market and irregular quarters, and was destroyed twice, in 1547 and 1636. In the seventeenth and eighteenth centuries residential building was altered by the addition of rendering and in building style. The two- and occasionally thee-storey houses with eaves and gables to the sheet make a striking visual impact. The Belzig landscaped meadows stretch north as far as the Hacken-Heide and are still the principal grazing ground for cattle in the area.

in der Nähe/nearby:
Rathaus Belzig; Marktplatz
1671 (Rekonstruktion 1989-90)
Rathaus Niemegk; Großstraße 6
1570 (Umbau 1933-34)
Johanniskirche Niemegk; Kirchplatz
1853 • Friedrich August Stüler

S 24 Burg Eisenhardt
Belzig
12. Jahrhundert; 1465 erweitert

Die 1161 genannte Burg, heute als Schule, Jugendherberge und Heimatmuseum genutzt, liegt auf einer Anhöhe südlich der Stadt. Von der Anlage des 12. bis frühen 13. Jahrhunderts sind nur noch der 33 m hohe, in geschichtetem Feldsteinmauerwerk errichtete Bergfried und Mauerreste von Gebäuden erhalten. 1465 wurde die Burg unter Kurfürst Ernst v. Sachsen erweitert, von den umfangreichen Backsteinbauten sind wesentliche Teile des Befestigungssystems mit Rundtürmen erhalten. An das rechteckige zweigeschossige Torhaus zwischen zwei massigen Rundtürmen schließt nach Osten ein über der Ringmauer errichtetes Speichergebäude an, das mit seiner Außenansicht einen imposanten Eindruck vermittelt. Unmittelbar vor dem südlichen Burgzugang wurde 1725 die nördlichste sächsische Postmeilensäule, ein mit dem kursächsischen Wappen geschmückter Sandsteinobelisk, aufgestellt.

The castle was mentioned in 1161 and is now used as a school, youth hostel and local history museum. It is on a small hill south of the town. All that has survived of the twelfth to early thirteenth century building are the 33 m high keep, built in layered rubble stone, and remains of walls of other buildings. In 1465 the building was extended under Elector Ernst of Saxony, and substantial parts of the extensive brick-built fortification system with round towers have survived. Adjacent to the east of the rectangular two-storey gatehouse between two massive round towers is an impressive storeroom built over the ring wall. A post office milepost, the most northerly in Saxony, was set up directly outside the southern entrance to the castle in 1725. It is a sandstone obelisk decorated with the arms of the Elector of Saxony.

in der Nähe/nearby:
Briccius-Kapelle; südlich der Burg
15. Jh.
Postmeilensäule
1725
Marienkirche; Kirchplatz
2. V. 13. Jh. (Erweiterung 15. Jh.)
Sitznischenhaus mit Brauhaus; Straße der Einheit 2
A. 18. Jh.
Krankenhaus; Niemegker Straße 45
1959-61 • Gerhard Wachholz, Heribert Scholtysik

S 25 Schloß
Wiesenburg
1547

Der 1160 urkundlich genannte Burgwardvorort »castrum Wiesenburg« sicherte den Übergang im Grenzwald zwischen den Slawengauen der Moraziani und der Ploni. Das Schloß über der alten Burg 1547 nach Brand als zweigeschossige Vierflügelanlage errichtet, erfuhr eine dreimalige Veränderung. Nach der Erweiterung 1730 folgte 1864-66 die Neugestaltung von Oskar Mothes. Den dritten Umbau vollzog der Architekt Hense 1868-80 im Stil der Neorenaissance, in einer Zeit und im Geiste eines erstarkenden deutschen Reiches mit neuem Selbst- und Sendungsbewußtsein. Der Bergfried, ein Rundturm aus Feldstein mit ausladendem, hölzernem Umgang im oberen Drittel, ist aus mittelalterlicher Zeit überliefert. Das Torhaus neben dem Bergfried mit schmückenden Neorenaissancegiebel ist im Kern noch vom Anfang des 13. Jahrhunderts. Die Hofportale schmücken noch originale Reste aus den Jahren 1574 und 1600. Der aufwendig gestalteten Schaufassade im Stil der Spätrenaissance an der Südseite sind großangelegte Terrassen und Parterres vorgelagert. Wertvolle Gehölze beleben den Landschaftspark.

The outlying fortress of «castrum Wiesenburg» was given its first official mention in 1160. It protected the border forest crossing point between the Slav districts of the Moraziani and Ploni tribes. The palace built in 1547 on the site of the old fortress was rebuilt on three occasions. It was extended in 1730, then redesigned by Oskar Molthes from 1864-6. It was rebuilt in neo-Renaissance style by an architect called Hense from 1868-80, at a time and in the spirit of a strengthening German empire with new self-awareness and need to project an image. The keep, a round rubble-stone tower with a projecting wooden walkway in the upper third, has survived from the Middle Ages. The gatehouse by the keep with decorative neo-Renaissance gable is essentially still early thirteenth century. The courtyard portals are till decorated with original fragments dating from 1574 and 1600. The elaborate late Renaissance style façade on the south side has expansive terraces and flower-beds in front of it. The landscaped park has some fine timber.

in der Nähe/nearby:
Gutshaus mit Park; Gräben-Dahlen
M. 19. Jh.
Dorfkirche; Buckau
12./13. Jh.
Dorfkirche; Bücknitz
13. Jh.

S 26 Burg und Burgkapelle
Ziesar
Um 1470

Seit der ersten Christianisierungswelle im 10. Jahrhundert hatte Ziesar schon Bedeutung als Besitz und später als Residenz der Bischöfe von Brandenburg. Der letzte Ausbau einer umfangreichen Burganlage fand im 3. Viertel des 15. Jahrhunderts statt. Vorhanden sind nur noch ein Turm der Vorburg, der Bergfrit und ein vielfach verbauter Trakt der Hauptburg, der in der Burgkapelle endet. Diese gilt als eine der wenigen gut erhaltenen mittelalterlichen Burgkapellen in Norddeutschland. Ihre reiche architektonische Gestaltung und Ausschmückung weist auf die Tätigkeit einer Brandenburger Bauhütte der Brunsberg-Schule hin, die dort an Dom, Gotthardtkirche und Altstädter Rathaus arbeitete. Das Innere schmückt eine einheitliche Ausmalung aus der Bauzeit. Ein Votivrelief aus Kalkstein von 1470 ist in die Nische der fensterlosen Stirnwand über dem Altar eingelassen. Heute dient die Kapelle als katholische Pfarrkirche.

Ever since the first wave of Christianization in the tenth century, Ziesar gained importance first as possession and later as residence of the bishops of Brandenburg. The last expansion of a full-scale castle dates back to the third quarter of the fifteenth century. Today only a tower of the outer castle, the keep and a much-added to wing of the inner castle ending in a chapel which is considered one of the less well preserved medieval castle chapels in North Germany. Its rich architectural design and ornamentation point to the activities of a Brandenburgian masons' lodge of the Brunsberg school which worked on the cathedral, the church of St. Gotthardt and the Altstadt town hall there. The interior was uniformly painted at the time of building and contains a votive relief made of limestone dating from 1470 and inserted into a recess of the windowless end-wall above the altar. Today the chapel serves as Catholic parish church.

in der Nähe/nearby:
Wohnhaus; Ziesar; Mühlentor 16
1775
Pfarrkirche St. Crucis; Ziesar
A. 13. Jh.
Zisterzienserinnen-Kloster; Ziesar
Um 1330

S 27 Klosterkirche und Kloster Lehnin
Lehnin
1190-1270 und 12. bis 15. Jahrhundert

Das 1180 von Markgraf Otto I. gestiftete Zisterzienserkloster Lehnin gilt als erste Niederlassung des Ordens in der askanischen Markgrafschaft. Die landschaftlichen Gegebenheiten entsprachen ganz den Ordensregeln mit ihren Forderungen nach »Waldeinsamkeit« und aktiver Kultivierung. Am Übergang von der Spätromanik zur Frühgotik ist die Kirche einer der ältesten deutschen Backsteinbauten und eines der bedeutendsten Bauwerke der Zisterzienser in der Mark. Gleichzeitig war Lehnin Hauskloster und Begräbnisstätte der märkischen Askanier. Zum reichsten märkischen Kloster aufgestiegen, wurde es 1542 säkularisiert und zum kurfürstlichen Amt mit 25 Ortschaften. Die Kirche und die im späteren Verfall erhalten gebliebenen Bauten wurden zwischen 1872 und 1877 erneuert. Die heutige Architektur der Gebäude des Klosterbezirkes wird davon geprägt. Die mittelalterliche Mauer aus Backstein mit dreipfostigem Tor an der Ostseite und einem quadratischen Wachturm an der Südwestecke umfriedet den gesamten Klosterbezirk.

The Cistercian monastery of Lehnin was founded by Margrave Otto I in 1180. It was the Order's first establishment in the territory of the Ascanian Margrave. The landscape had all the features required by the rules of the Order, which demanded a lonely woodland site and active cultivation. The church stands at the transition from late Romanesque to early Gothic. It is one of the oldest German brick buildings and one of the most important Cistercian buildings in the Mark. Lehnin was also the house monastery and burial place of the Ascanians of the Mark. It rose to be the richest monastery in the Mark, was deconsecrated in 1542 and after that was an Electoral Office covering 25 villages. As well as the monastery church other buildings that survived eihgteenthth century decline were restored between 1872 and 1877, and this is the dominant impression made by the buildings in the monastery precinct. The medieval brick wall with three-post gate on the east side and a square tower in the south-west corner surrounds the whole of the precinct.

in der Nähe/nearby:
Abtshaus und Falkonierhaus; Lehnin; Kloster
15. Jh.
Kornhaus; Lehnin; nordöstlich der Kirche
14. Jh.
Dorfkirche; Rädel
18. Jh. (Turm 1912-13)
Gutshaus (Oberschule); Reckahn
Um 1720 • Schlüter-Umkreis
Gutshaus; Götz
Um 1800
Dorfkirche; Golzow
1750

S 28 Ziegelei
Glindow; Jahnufer
Nach 1858

Das norddeutsche Tiefland mit seinen eiszeitlichen Ablagerungen ist arm an Natursteinen. Die ortsüblichen Baustoffe waren seit alters her eingesammelte Feldsteine oder Ziegelsteine, deren Grundstoff aus heimischen Tongruben stammte. »Glina« – slawisches Wort für Lehm – war für Glindow namensbildend. Mindestens seit dem 15. Jahrhundert wurden hier Ziegel gebrannt. 1856 entwickelte Friedrich Eduard Hoffmann ein neues Brennverfahren, dem in einem halbkontinuierlichen Prozeß unter optimaler Ausnutzung der Heizenergie der Ringofen mit mehreren Brennkammern zugrunde lag. Auch Glindow erhielt solche neuen Ringöfen: Einer mit 12 freiliegenden Kammern und ein fachwerküberdachter mit 14 Kammern sind erhalten. Imposanter baulicher Bestandteil der Anlage ist ein oktogonaler Aufseherturm, gemauert natürlich aus Ziegeln. Glindows wirtschaftlicher Vorteil bestand in der Nähe zu Berlin und im Anschluß an den Schiffahrtsweg der Havel. Über Spree und Landwehrkanal fuhren die ziegelbeladenen Kähne von hier in die großen Neubaugebiete der aufstrebenden Millionenstadt, bis um die Jahrhundertwende die Glindower Gruben erschöpft waren.

The North German lowlands with their glacial deposits have very little natural stones. The vernacular building materials have always been fieldstones gathered around the country or bricks manufactured from clay out of local pits. The name Glindow seems to have had its origin in «Glina», the Slavic word for clay. At least since the fifteenth century, bricks have been manufactured and fired here. In 1856 Friedrich Eduard Hoffmann developed a new method of firing based on circular ovens with several firing chambers which allowed for the greatest utilization of energy in a semi-continuous process. The new ovens were also installed at Glindow, of which one with 12 open-air chambers and a second one with 14 chambers covered by a half-timber roof have survived. Dominating the entire complex is a tall octagonal overseer's tower constructed of brick, of course. Glindow had the great economic advantage of being close to Berlin and thus having access to the waterway of the Havel. From here, countless barges loaded with bricks travelled the Spree and the Landwehrkanal to supply the numerous new construction sites of the up and coming metropolis, until the turn of the century when the Glindow clay-pits were finally exhausted.

in der Nähe/nearby:
Dorfkirche; Glindow
1852-53 • Friedrich August Stüler
Gutshaus; Plessow
1780

T
Brandenburg/Havel

Im Jahre 928 eroberte Kaiser Heinrich I. im Zuge deutscher Ostexpansion Brennabor, die Hauptburg der slawischen Heveller. Die Burg befand sich auf dem Gelände der heutigen Dominsel. 948 gründete Kaiser Otto I. die Bistümer Brandenburg und Havelberg und unterstellte sie dem neu geschaffenen Erzbistum Magdeburg. Die Burginsel sollte zum Kathedralsitz ausgebaut werden, aber schon 983 konnten die Heveller ihre Herrschaft erneuern, der ottonische Dom wurde zerstört und auf dem Marienberg ein Triglaw-Heiligtum errichtet. Erst 1157 fällt Brandenburg durch Erbfolge endgültig an die Askanier. Seit dem 11. Jahrhundert entstand an der Havelfurt der Straße Magdeburg–Brandenburg–Posen ein Handelsplatz. Im Verlauf des 12. Jahrhunderts wuchs aus der Ansiedlung Parduin in Nachbarschaft zur Burginsel die Stadt Brandenburg. Sie erhielt Magdeburger Stadtrecht. Wenig später entwickelte sich auf einer dritten Insel am Kreuzungspunkt zweier Handelsstraßen die Neustadt. Sie modifizierte das Magdeburger Recht zum Brandenburger Stadtrecht. Aus der mittelalterlichen Doppelstadt wurde die »Chur- und Hauptstadt« der Mark Brandenburg. Erst 1715 vereinigten sich die beiden selbständigen Städte. Infolge des Dreißigjährigen Krieges verödete Brandenburg, versank in wirtschaftlicher Bedeutungslosigkeit. Erst im 19. Jahrhundert begann mit der Industrialisierung ein Aufschwung, der durch die Eröffnung der Eisenbahnstrecke Berlin–Potsdam–Magdeburg 1848 noch begünstigt wurde. Bedeutung erlangten Tuchfabrikation und Blechwarenfabrikation. Eisengießereien siedelten sich an. Seit den fünfziger Jahren des 20. Jahrhunderts wurde die Stadt zu einem bedeutenden Industriezentrum ausgebaut und ist nun größter Stahlproduzent im ostdeutschen Raum.

In the year 928 Emperor Henry I, in the course of German expansion to the West, conquered Brennabor, the capital of the Slavic Hevelli. The castle was on the site of the present cathedral island. In 948 Emperor Otto I founded the bishoprics of Brandenburg and Havelberg, and placed them under the new archbishopric of Magdeburg. The castle island was to be developed as a cathedral area, but in 983 the Hevelli conquered the region again, destroyed the Ottonian cathedral and set up a Triglaw shrine on the Marienberg. Brandenburg did not fall to the Ascanians until they inherited it in 1157. A trading area grew up from the eleventh century by the Havel ford on the Magdeburg–Brandenburg–Posen road. The town of Brandenburg grew up from the Parduin settlement in the neighbourhood of the castle island in the course of the twelfth century. It was granted a Magdeburg charter. A little later the new town developed on a third island at the junction of two trade routes. It changed the Magdeburg charter to a Brandenburg charter. The medieval double town became the «Chur- und Hauptstadt» of the Mark Brandenburg. The two independent towns did not unite until 1715. As a result of the Thirty Years' War, Brandenburg became deserted and sank into economic insignificance. It did not start to flourish again until the nineteenth century, when industrialization came, and it was given a further boost by the opening of the Berlin-Potsdam-Magdeburg railway in 1848. Cloth and sheet metal manufacture grew in importance. Iron foundries were established. Since the 1950s the town has been built up into an important industrial centre and is now the largest producer of steel in eastern Germany.

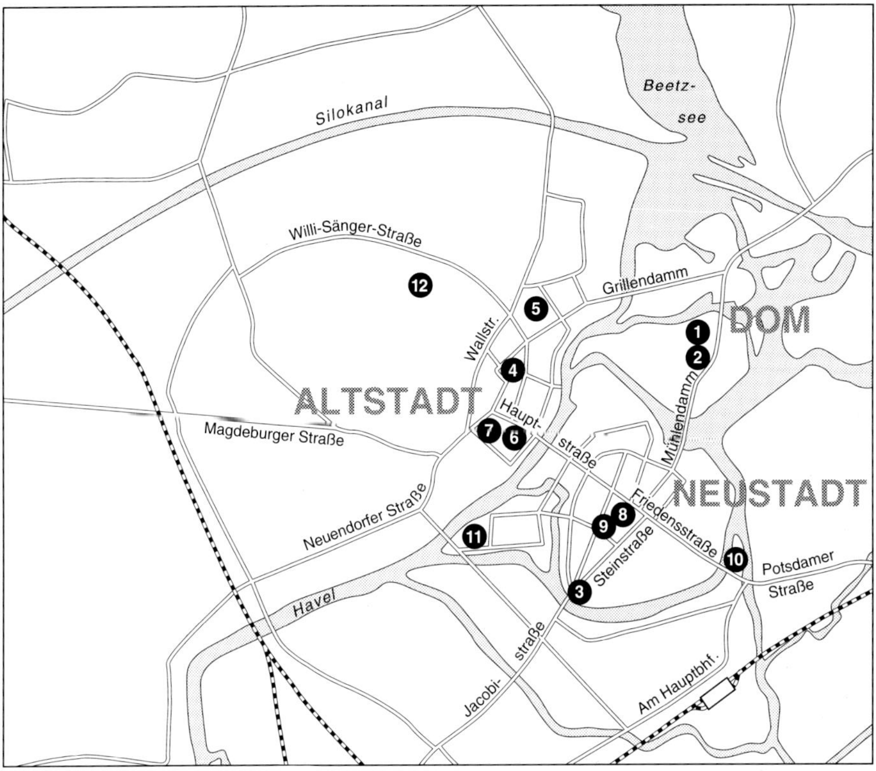

T 1	Dom St. Peter und Paul
T 2	Petrikapelle
T 3	Steintorturm
T 4	Altstädtisches Rathaus
T 5	Gotthardtkirche
T 6	Freyhaus
T 7	Haus Lehmann
T 8	Katharinenkirche
T 9	Gymnasium (Pestalozzischule)
T 10	Wohnhaus (Musikschule)
T 11	Krankenhaus
T 12	Krematorium

T 1 Dom St. Peter und Paul
Brandenburg; Burgweg
1165, 14./15. Jahrhundert

Im Domarchiv liegt die Gründungsurkunde des Bistums Brandenburg zum 1. Oktober 948 mit dem Siegel des deutschen Kaisers Otto I. Ihre geographisch und strategisch günstige Lage macht die Burginsel zum Kathedralsitz. Doch der erste Dombau des 10. Jahrhunderts ist nur urkundlich überliefert. Die Grundsteinlegung für die romanische kreuzförmige Backsteinbasilika erfolgte 1165. Um 1220 wurde unter dem Chor und der Vierung die Krypta errichtet, die sich zu den Kreuzarmen und dem Langhaus in je zwei Rundbögen öffnet, ähnlich wie in der Klosterkirche zu Jerichow. Um 1370 wird der romanische Dom in eine gotische Basilika umgebaut, die Kirche erhält ihr heutiges Aussehen, angefangen mit den höheren Außenmauern über das Chorpolygon bis hin zum Westportal. Neben der Kathedrale gehören zum Dombezirk der Kreuzgang vom 12./13. Jahrhundert, das Kloster aus dem 16./18. und das Stiftsgebäude mit dem Ost- und Nordflügel aus dem 13./14. Jahrhundert, in ihm ist das Dommuseum mit dem wertvollen Domschatz untergebracht.

In the cathedral archive is the certificate of foundation of the bishopric of Brandenburg, dated 1 October 948, with the seal of Emperor Otto I. Its geographical and strategic situation made the castle island the site of the cathedral. The first cathedral, dating from the tenth century, is known only from documents. The foundation stone of the Romanesque cruciform basilica was laid in 1165. The crypt under choir and crossing was built c. 1220. It opens to the arms of the cross and the nave in two round arches each time, similarly to the monastery church in Jerichow. The Romanesque cathedral was rebuilt as a Gothic basilica c. 1370, and the church acquired its present appearance, starting with the high exterior walls, via the choir polygon to the west portal. Aside from the church the cathedral precinct includes the twelfth and thirteenth century cloister, the sixteenth and eighteenth century monastery and the collegiate building with east and north wing dating from the thirteenth and fourteenth centuries and housing the cathedral museum and valuable cathedral treasure.

T 2 Petrikapelle
Brandenburg; Domlinden
1314-20, 1520

In der Burgkapelle wurde im Jahre 1150 der zum Christentum übergetretene Wendenfürst Pribislaw Heinrich beigesetzt. Bis 1183 wird diese Kapelle als »Capella in castro Brandenburgensi« bezeichnet, da der Heilige Peter als Schutzpatron des Domes galt. Als Nachfolgebau der Burgkapelle entsteht ab 1314 die Petrikapelle, ein rechteckiger Backsteinbau mit Wölbung und Strebepfeilern an den Ecken des Außenbaues. Um 1520 wird die zweischiffige Halle umgebaut. Das Tonnengewölbe wird durch ein spätgotisches Ziergewölbe ersetzt: ein Zellengewölbe, das auf sechseckigen Pfeilern ruht. Solche vielteiligen Zellengewölbe sind äußerst selten, verbreitet überwiegend in Böhmen und Sachsen. Zum Ende des 16. Jahrhunderts erhielt die Westgiebelseite einen Turm. Doch auf dem unsicheren Baugrund der Havelinsel senkte und neigte sich der Turm. Bevor er einstürzte, trug man ihn 1848 ab. Ein ähnliches Schicksal drohte auch dem Dom, bis seit 1963 eine neue Pfahlgründung und Sicherungskonstruktionen das Fundament in seiner Stabilität stützen.

The Wendic prince Pribislaw Heinrich, who had been converted to Christianity, was buried in the castle chapel in 1150. Until 1183 this chapel was known as «Capella in castro Brandenburgensi», as St. Peter was patron saint of the cathedral. The Petrikapelle was built from 1314 as a successor to the castle chapel, a rectangular brick building with vaulting and buttresses on the exterior corners. The two-aisled hall was rebuilt c. 1520. The tunnel vault was replaced by a decorative late Gothic vault, a cell vault supported by hexagonal piers. Multipartite cell vaults of this kind are extremely rare, and found largely in Bohemia and Saxony. In the late sixteenth century the tower was added to the west gable end, but it sank and tilted on the shifting Havel land. It was demolished in 1848 before it collapsed. The cathedral was threatened with a similar fate until it was secured with new pile foundations and other reinforcements from 1963.

in der Nähe/nearby:
Kurienhäuser; Burgweg
17./18. Jh.
Seniorenkurie; Burgweg
16. Jh.
Ritterakademie; Burgweg
1869-70

T 3 Steintorturm
Brandenburg; Steinstraße
Mitte 15. Jahrhundert

In der Neustadt Brandenburg sind an verschiedenen Stellen Reste der mittelalterlichen Stadtmauer vom 14./15. Jahrhundert erhalten, so an der St. Annen-Promenade, am Deutschen Dorf, an der Lindenstraße und der Grabenpromenade. Von den ursprünglich vier Stadttoren sind im Norden der Mühltorturm, der 1411 von Nikolaus Krafft aus Stettin erbaut wurde, und im Süden der Steintorturm erhalten. Dieser Rundturm aus rotem Backsteinmauerwerk ist mit spiralförmig angeordneten glasierten Ziegelschichten verziert – nicht nur Befestigung des Tores, sondern auch Schmuck im Stadtbild. Zur ursprünglichen Tor- und Verteidigungsanlage gehörten Zwinger und Vortore. Mit fortschreitender Waffentechnik boten Stadtmauern und Tore bei kriegerischen Angriffen bald keinen hinreichenden Schutz mehr, sie dienten nur noch der öffentlichen Ordnung und der Erhebung von Zöllen. Nach Abschaffung der Mehl- und Schlachtesteuern hatten die Befestigungsanlagen endgültig ihre Funktion verloren und konnten abgetragen werden, störten sie doch zumeist die bauliche Ausbreitung der Stadt und den Verkehr. So wurde 1925 durch den Stadtarchitekten Wolf die städtebauliche Situation durch den Neubau der Steintorbrücke verbessert, die Ausfallstraße verbreitert und in eine Platzgestaltung einbezogen.

Various remnants of the medieval town wall dating from the fourteenth and fifteenth centuries have survived in the new town of Brandenburg, on the St Annen-Promenade, for example, at Deutsches Dorf, in Lindenstrasse and at the Grabenpromenade. There were originally four town gates; the Mühltor tower, built in 1411 by Nikolaus Krafft of Stettin, has survived in the north, and the Steintor tower in the south. This round tower in red brick is decorated with spirals of glazed tiles, not just to reinforce the tower, but as a decorative feature in the townscape as well. The original gate and defensive complex included an outer ward and outer gates. Improving weapon technology meant that town walls and gates no longer offered sufficient protection, they were useful only for the maintenance of public order and the raising of taxes. After flour and slaughtering taxes were abolished the fortifications really were meaningless and could be demolished, as they generally hindered expansion of building in the town and of traffic. And so in 1925 town architect Wolf improved the planning situation by building the Steintor bridge and widening the road out of the town, which was incorporated in a new design for the square.

in der Nähe/nearby:
Jacobskapelle; Jacobistraße
1315

T 4 Altstädtisches Rathaus
Brandenburg; Altstädtischer Markt
1470-80

Neben den Ratsbauten in Frankfurt/Oder, Jüterbog und Wittstock zählt das Rathaus der Altstadt Brandenburg zu den wenigen erhaltenen städtischen Repräsentationsbauten des Mittelalters in der Mark Brandenburg. Der Grundriß ist zeitgemäß rechteckig. Die schmalen Giebelfronten zeigen reichen Maßwerkschmuck und Putzblenden. In der Marktfront dominiert der Turm, die Rückfront ziert ein Stufengiebel. Das schöne Maßwerk über dem Hauptportal ähnelt dem des Dom-Südportals. 1910-12 erneuerte Erich Blunck die Giebel, aus dieser Zeit stammen auch die Sgraffitomalereien in den Blenden. An der Marktfront steht heute der 5,5 Meter hohe steinerne Roland aus dem Jahre 1474 – das erhobene Schwert als Sinnbild städtischer Macht und Unbeugsamkeit. Bis zu dessen Zerstörung hatte er seinen Platz vor dem Neustädtischen Rathaus. Eine Kopie des Brandenburger Roland findet man vor dem Märkischen Museum in Berlin.

The town hall in the old town of Brandenburg is one of the few medieval public buildings in the Mark Brandenburg to have survived. There are others in Frankfurt an der Oder, Jüterbog and Wittstock. The ground plan is rectangular, appropriately for the period. The narrow gable façades have lavish tracery decoration and decorative blind windows. The market place façade is dominated by the tower, and the rear façade has a stepped gable. The fine tracery above the main portal is similar to that on the south portal of the cathedral. Erich Blunck rebuilt the gables in 1910-12, and the sgraffito work in the blind windows also dates from this period. The stone statue of Roland in front of the market façade is 5.5 metres high and dates from 1474. The raised sword is a symbol of municipal power and unbendingness. It stood in front of the Neustädtisches Rathaus until this was destroyed. There is a copy of the Brandenburg Roland outside the Märkisches Museum in Berlin.

In der Nähe/nearby:
Ordonnanzhaus; Schusterstraße 6
M. 15. Jh.
Quitzowhaus; Bäckerstraße 11
2. H. 16. Jh.
Syndikatshaus; Altstädtischer Markt
2. H. 16. Jh.

T 5 Gotthardtkirche
Brandenburg; Gotthardtkirchplatz
2. Hälfte 12. Jahrhundert
1456-76 • Heinrik Reinstorp

Nach dem Slawenaufstand von 983 und der Zerstörung der ersten Domkirche existierte das Bistum im Exil des Klosters Leitzkau weiter. Von dort wurden seit 1138 wieder Mönche in Brandenburg angesiedelt, auf welche die dem Heiligen Godehard geweihte Kirche zurückgeht, das vermutlich älteste Gebäude der Stadt. Der aus Granitquadern errichtete Westbau mit großem Rundfenster und abgetrepptem Rundbogenportal stammt wohl aus der 2. Hälfte des 12. Jahrhunderts. Seine Haube erhielt der mittelalterliche Ziegelturm im ausgehenden Barock 1767. Die dreischiffige gewölbte Hallenkirche mit dem polygonalen Umgangschor und dem Kapellenkranz erbaute als spätgotisches Raumgefüge Henrik Reinstorp. Die Innenausmalung mußte 1972 erneuert werden, die farbige Fassung orientiert sich an den 1904-06 aufgedeckten und restaurierten Wand- und Gewölbemalereien.

After the Slavic revolt of 983 and the destruction of the first cathedral the bishopric went into exile in the monastery of Leitzkau. From there monks were once more sent out into Brandenburg from 1138, and the church dedicated to St. Godehard goes back to these times. It is probably the oldest building in the town. The western section in granite ashlar with staggered round-arched portal and large circular window probably dates from the second half of the twelfth century. The cupola was added to the upper part of the medieval brick building in 1767, at the end of the baroque period. The vaulted hall church with nave and two aisles, polygonal ambulatory choir and radiating chapels was built to a late Gothic spatial pattern by Henrik Reinstorp. The interior had to be redecorated in 1972, and the colour scheme is based on the wall and vault painting which was revealed and restored in 1904-6.

in der Nähe/nearby:
Ehemaliges Schulhaus; Gotthardtkirchplatz 5
1552
Bischofshof (Oberschule); Walter-Rathenau-Platz 1
1799
Rathenower Torturm; Rathenower Straße
15./16. Jh.

T 6 Freyhaus
Brandenburg; Hauptstraße 96
1723-33

Im Jahre 1723 ließ sich Generalmajor Jürgen v. Massow das stattliche barocke Wohnhaus in der Altstadt erbauen. Er hatte sich im preußischen Heer Friedrich Wilhelms I. durch die Einrichtung des Montierungswesens, also der Ausrüstung der Soldaten mit Uniformen, hervorgetan. Deshalb verlieh ihm später auch König Friedrich II. das Privileg »Freyhaus«. Aus der Bauzeit ist im Inneren die Holztreppe erhalten, deren gesägte Brüstungsfelder zwar die barocke Neigung zum Ornament widerspiegeln, aber auch den preußischen Hang zur Sparsamkeit. So ist auch der malerische Innenhof an drei Seiten von Fachwerkbauten eingefaßt. Seit 1923 nutzt den Gebäudekomplex das Heimatmuseum. Zu seinen Beständen zählt die vom Brandenburger Bildhauer August Wredow im 19. Jahrhundert zusammengetragene Grafik europäischer Künstler des 16. bis 19. Jahrhunderts.

In 1723 Major General Jürgen von Massow had this handsome baroque residence built in the old town. He had distinguished himself in the Prussian army of Friedrich Wilhelm I by introducing the provision of uniforms for soldiers. The king also bestowed the «Freyhaus» privilege upon him for this reason at a later date. Inside the wooden staircase has survived from the time when the house was built. Its serrated balustrade fields do show a baroque inclination to ornament, but also a Prussian concern for economy. In the same way the picturesque inner courtyard is surrounded by half-timbered buildings on three sides. The local history museum has been housed in the building since 1923. Its exhibits include prints by sixteenth to nineteenth century European artists collected by the nineteenth century sculptor August Wredow.

in der Nähe/nearby:
Wohnhaus; Hauptstraße 90
1774
Plauer Torturm; Nicolaiplatz
15. Jh.

T 7 Haus Lehmann
Brandenburg; Plauer Straße 5
1901 • Bruno Möhring, Adolf Hartung

1881 wurde die Lehmannsche Blechspielwarenfabrik in Brandenburg gegründet. Die gute Geschäftsentwicklung ließ den Bau eines städtischen Wohnhauses für den Fabrikanten zu. Nach Entwürfen und unter der Leitung von Bruno Möhring, Adolf Hartung und Ernst Spindler entstand ein Haus in gewagten Jugendstilformen. Als provokanter Blickfang beugt sich ein massiger zweigeschossiger Erker mit einem Kranz floralen Zierrates in den Straßenraum vor. Die farbig gefaßte Putzfassade mit einem figürlichen Relief wird von dunkel scharriertem Sockel und ebensolchen Seitenrisaliten gerahmt. Haustür und Hoftor sind mit teigig geformten Kupferblechen beschlagen, eine Arbeit der Berliner Firma Hillmer nach Möhrings Entwurf. Original erhalten sind auch Diele und Treppenhaus.

The Lehmann sheet metal toy factory was founded in Brandenburg in 1881. Business went well, and this meant that the owner was able to build a house for himself in the town. It was designed by and built under the direction of Bruno Möhring, Adolf Hartung and Ernst Spindler using daring Jugendstil forms. A massive two-storey oriel is an eye-catching feature, leaning forward into the street, garlanded with floral decoration. The colourfully framed rendered façade with one figurative relief is framed by a darkly chequered base and side projections of the same kind. Front door and yard gate are embellished with copper sheets in doughy forms, made by Hillmer of Berlin to Möhring's design. Hall and staircase have also survived in their original form.

in der Nähe/nearby:
Ruine der Johanniskirche; Klosterstraße
13./14. Jh.
Altstädtische Stadtmauer; Humboldthain
14./15. Jh.

T 8 Katharinenkirche
Brandenburg; Katharinenkirchplatz
1401 • Hinrich Brunsberg

In der südlichen Westturmfront sind Mauerteile einer Pfarrkirche des 12. Jahrhunderts erhalten. Die heutige dreischiffige Backsteinhallenkirche erbaute nach 1400 der Stettiner Baumeister Brunsberg. Der Umgangschor mit den Randkapellen zeigt eine für die Stadtkirchen dieser Zeit typische Bauform. Die Fronleichnamskapelle vor der Nordwand erhielt einen besonders reich gestalteten Maßwerkgiebel. Durch seine Feingliedrigkeit und die Schichtung roter und grüner Ziegel scheint er vollkommen in Schmuckformen aufgelöst. Georg Dehio bezeichnete die Kirche als das »prächtigste Werk spätgotischer Ziegelkunst«.

Parts of the walls of a twelfth century parish church have survived on the south façade of the west tower. The present brick hall church with nave and two aisles was built by Stettin architect Brunsberg after 1400. The ambulatory choir with peripheral chapels show a style of building typical of urban churches. The Corpus Christi chapel in front of the north wall has a particularly lavish traceried gable. Its delicacy and the layering of red and green bricks seem to make it dissolve completely in decorative shapes. Georg Dehio described the church as «the most splendid work of late Gothic brick art».

in der Nähe/nearby:
Bankgebäude; Neustädtischer Markt 10
1901-02 • Max Hasak
Kaufhaus; Hauptstraße 1-5
1951 • Wilm Stolze

T 9 Gymnasium (Pestalozzischule)
Brandenburg; Am Katharinenkirchplatz 5
1797

Bereits 1386 wird der mittelalterliche Vorgängerbau einer Kirchschule erwähnt. Nach der Reformation übernahm der Neustädtische Rat der Stadt Brandenburg das Patronat über die Schule. 1571 entstand dann an gleicher Stelle die Stadtschule. Das Gebäude zählte zu den bedeutendsten Anlagen in der Mark Brandenburg. Im 18. Jahrhundert war es dann aber in Verfall geraten. Zum Ende des Jahrhunderts wurde ein Neubau ausgeführt, zu dem schon 1787 Entwurfszeichnungen vorlagen. So gibt sich der dreigeschossige Putzbau recht konservativ und eigentlich noch dem barocken Fassadenschema verhaftet, wie Mittelrisalit, Pilaster, Fenstergewände und Mansartdach zeigen, anders als die bereits dem Zopfstil zugehörenden Bürgerhäuser um 1780, beispielsweise das Haus Steinstraße 21. Auch die große Sandsteinkartusche mit dem Neustädtischen Stadtwappen paßt nicht so recht in die Zeit um 1800. In der Altstadt ist das nachreformatorische Schulhaus noch erhalten. Mit seinem Fachwerk über massivem Sockel steht es neben der Gotthardtkirche.

A medieval predecessor, also a church school, was mentioned as early as 1386. After the Reformation the Neustädtischer Rat of the city of Brandenburg took over patronage of the school. The Stadtschule was then built in the same site in 1571, and the building was among the most important in the Mark Brandenburg. But in the eighteenth century it started to decline. Towards the end of the century a new building for which designs had been existant since 1787 was finally realized. Thus the three-storey rendered building seems quite conservative, still attached to the baroque façade scheme including central protrusion, pilasters, window jambs and mansard roof, unlike the houses built c. 1780, which are already rococo in style, like for example the house at Steinstrasse 21. The great sandstone cartouche with the arms of the new town is also quite unsuited to the period around 1800. The post-Reformation school building has survived in the old town. It is half-timbered on a solid base, and stands by the Gotthardkirche.

in der Nähe/nearby:
Karpzowsches Haus; Steinstraße 57
1563
Wohnhaus; Steinstraße 21
1780
Wohnhaus; Gorrenberg 14
Um 1800
Wohnhaus; Neustädtischer Markt 11
Um 1780
Wohnhaus; Neustädtischer Markt 7
1790

T 10 Wohnhaus (Musikschule)
Brandenburg; Potsdamer Straße 2
1906-10 • Paul Schultze-Naumburg

In bevorzugter Lage am Ufer des Schleusenkanals, gegenüber der Neustadt errichtete Paul Schultze-Naumburg diese Fabrikantenvilla. Zur Straße nach Potsdam und zu deren Brücke über den Kanal bildet sie zwei Schauseiten aus, die sich mit übergiebeltem Risalit, Pilastern und Fensterverdachung gar nicht in die Zeit zwischen Jugendstil und Moderne einordnen wollen. Der Rückgriff auf Architekturformen des Biedermeier, wie er in den Jahren um 1910 überall zu beobachten ist, gehört bei Schultze-Naumburg zum ureigenen Anliegen, machte ihn in den zwanziger Jahren zum entschiedenen Gegner des Neuen Bauens und so unversehens zu einem politisch opportunen Architekten »deutscher Baukunst«. Zwischen Heimatgefühl und Behaglichkeit ist auch dieses Gebäude anzusiedeln mit seiner formsicheren Gestaltung und gediegenen handwerklichen Ausstattung. So erscheint es auch passend, daß 1955 eine Musikschule das Haus bezogen hat.

Paul Schultze-Naumburg built this villa for an industrialist in a favoured position on the lock canal opposite the new town. It has two show sides, on the road to Potsdam and its bridge over the canal, and their protruding section with pediment, pilasters and window roofing do not seem at all inclined to fit in with the period between Jugendstil and Modernism. This return to the architectural forms of Biedermeier, very popular in the years around 1910, was profoundly important to Schultze-Naumburg and made him a rigorous opponent of Neues Bauen in the twenties, and thus an unexpected and politically opportune exponent of «German building art». This building, with its formal confidence and solidly crafted fittings, can be classified somewhere between homeland feelings and general cosiness. And so it also seems fitting that a music school moved into the building in 1955.

in der Nähe/nearby:
Dominikanerkirche und -kloster; Paulikirchplatz
1300-40

T 11 Krankenhaus
Brandenburg; Kanalstraße 8-9
1929 • W. Ludewig

In Vorbereitung der Tausendjahrfeier der Stadt Brandenburg 1928 erstellte der Stadtbaurat Wolf für das Gebiet der Innenstadt einen Flächennutzungs- und Bebauungsplan. Die Aufgaben der Stadtgemeinde auf technischem und kulturellem Gebiet wurden darin berücksichtigt. Dazu gehörten der Wohnungsbau mit den Siedlungen, Verbesserung der Verkehrsanlagen, Schulbauten sowie Turnhallen, Kindergärten, Sport- und Erholungstätten, die Neuanlage eines Hauptfriedhofs mit Krematorium und auch die Erweiterung des Krankenhauses. In der Folge finanzierte die Allgemeine Ortskrankenkasse den Bau eines Zentralkrankenhauses auf dem Gelände von Grabenpromenade und Kanalstraße. Mit dem rückwärtig anschließenden Stadtbad am Alfred-Messel-Platz nach dem Entwurf des Architekten Erbs entstand ein funktionell gegliedertes Gebäudeensemble. Die in der Höhe variierenden kubischen Bauglieder sind zu einem Komplex zusammengefügt, der durch einheitliche Klinkerverblendung und durchlaufende Fensterbänder als Ganzes wirkt.

Wolf, the councillor responsible for building, set up a land use and a development plan for the town centre in preparation for the celebrations of a thousand years of the city of Brandenburg in 1928. The community's municipal responsibilities in the technical and cultural fields were taken into account in these plans. These included estates to provide new housing, improved traffic facilities, schools and gymnasia, kindergartens, sports and recreational facilities, a new main cemetery with crematorium, and an extension for the hospital. As a result of this the local health insurance association financed the building of a central hospital on the Grabenpromenade and Kanalstrasse site. This and the municipal baths adjacent to the rear in Alfred-Messel-Platz, designed by Erbs, produced a functionally articulated urban ensemble. The sections of the building are cubic and vary in height, making a complex that works as a whole by means of uniform clinker cladding and continous bands of windows.

in der Nähe/nearby:
Luckenberger Brücke; Bauhofstraße
1923 • Wolf
Grabenpromenade und Schleusenkanal; Kanalstraße
1925 • Wolf

T 12 Krematorium
Brandenburg; Willi-Sänger-Straße
1925 • M. Wolf

In den stadtplanerischen Unterlagen der zwanziger Jahre wird für Neubau und Anlage eines Hauptfriedhofes mit Krematorium ein Grundstücksbedarf von 50 Morgen ausgewiesen. Diese Größe deutet schon die im Vordergrund stehende städtebauliche Aufgabe an: eine Verbindung von Friedhof und öffentlicher Gartenanlage. Bereits seit der Einführung der Feuerbestattung in Preußen im Jahre 1911 lebte die Idee, auf den Kult der großen Grabstellen zu verzichten und Urnenhaine als Parklandschaft zu gestalten. In diesem Sinne setzte sich auch der 1920 in Brandenburg gegründete Verein für Feuerbestattung mit einer Denkschrift an den Magistrat ein, worin er die Förderung und Mitfinanzierung der Anlage anbot. Das Gelände fand sich am Nordhang des 73 Meter hohen Marienberges. Der Mittelpunkt der Anlage ist das langgestreckte Gebäude des Krematoriums. Der Stufengiebel mit der expressionistisch stilisierten Rosette, die an ein basilikales Schema erinnernden Anbauten und die runden Obergadenfenster geben dem Bau bewußt ein klerikales Gepräge. Eine überdachte Rundbogenarkade leitet vom Hauptbau zur Friedhofslandschaft über.

A land requirement of 50 acres was included in the twenties' urban development documents for building and laying out a main cemetery with crematorium. The size indicates the town's principal requirement: a combined cemetery and public park. Ever since the introduction of cremation in Prussia in 1911 the idea had caught on of abandoning the cult of large burial areas and replacing them with groves of urns set in parkland. It was in this spirit that the cremation association founded in Brandenburg in 1920 submitted a memorandum to the municipal authorities, offering to promote the scheme and to help finance it. The site was on the north slope of the 73 metre high Marienberg. At the heart of the complex is the long crematorium building. The stepped gable with expressionistically stylized rose window, the adjacent buildings, reminiscent of a basilican scheme, and the round clerestory windows deliberately give the building an ecclesiastical look. A roofed arcade with round arches leads from the main building to the landscaped cemetery.

in der Nähe/nearby:
Marienbergpark; Triglafweg, Am Mariengrund
1847 (Überformung 1974-75)
Aussichtsturm Friedenswarte; Triglafweg
1974 • Günter Franke, Wolfgang Schoppe
Freilichtbühne; Triglafweg
1956
Volksbad; Triglafweg
1967-69 • Gerhard Baum, Klaus Stehr, Hansjoachim Hamann

U
Havelland und Prignitz

Die vom südlichen Havelbogen bis zum Westen des nördlichen Landrückens, also vom Havelland bis zur Prignitz reichende Region ist durch Moränenareale, Sanderflächen und ausgedehnte Niederungen gekennzeichnet. Durch die ehemaligen Eisrandlagen und die einstigen Abflußbahnen der Schmelzwässer entstanden Platten, Ländchen, Luch- und Seengebiete. Charakteristisch für diese Naturräume sind die Nauener und Prignitzer Platte, das Schollener, Rhinower und Nennhausener Ländchen mit Erhebungen bis über 110 Meter sowie das Havelländische Luch, Nauener Luch und Rhinluch und das Untere Havelseenland im Raum Potsdam, Brandenburg und Rathenow. Aus dem Jahre 789, als eine friesische Flotte zur Unterstützung des Feldzuges Karl des Großen entlang der Havel vordrang, ist ein zusammenhängendes frühslawisches Siedlungsgebiet im südlichen Havelbogen und an Nebenflüssen der Havel schriftlich überliefert. Die zu jener Zeit angelegten slawischen Burgen erweckten damals weite Aufmerksamkeit. Die Schilderungen eines jüdischen Kaufmannes über den slawischen Burgenbau hielt der arabische Gelehrte Abu Obaid Abdallah al Bekri im 11. Jahrhundert für so bedeutsam, daß er sie in seinem »Buch der Wege und Länder« wörtlich wiedergab. Spätere, im Zuge der frühdeutschen Besiedlung errichtete Burgen nutzten oftmals die slawischen Anlagen. Die planmäßige Kultivierung der vermoorten Niederungen des Havelländischen Luchs mit dem Fluß Peene, der bis zur Melioration 1718-24 natürlicher Vorläufer des Havelländischen Hauptkanals war, ermöglichte den Aufbau der Weidewirtschaft. Nach 1945 wurde dieses Kanalsystem wieder erschlossen, es wurden Windschutzstreifen angelegt und landwirtschaftliche Produktions- und Verarbeitungsbetriebe errichtet. Begünstigt durch die Fernhandelsstraße nach Lübeck entwickelten sich in den Prignitzstädten Kyritz, Pritzwalk und Wittstock neben der Landwirtschaft besonders das Tuchmacher- und Gewandschneiderhandwerk. Die heute noch nachvollziehbaren, im Mittelalter planmäßig angelegten Stadtgrundrisse zeugen von früher Blüte dieser Region.

The characteristic features of the region extending from the southern bend of the Havel to the west of the northern ridge, in other words from the Havelland to the Prignitz, are moraines, outwash areas and extended lowlands. Plateaus, uplands, marshes and lakes formed as a result of the former position at the edge of the ice and the courses of the meltwater. Characteristic of these natural areas are the Nauener and the Prignitzer Platte, the Schollener, Rhinower and Nennhausener Ländchen, uplands rising to over 110 metres, marshes like the Havelländisches Luch, the Nauener Luch and the Rhinluch, and the Lower Havelseeland around Potsdam, Brandenburg and Rathenow. There is written evidence of a coherent early Slavic settlement in the southern bend of the Havel and by tributaries of the Havel from the year 789, when a Frisian fleet pushed up the Havel in support of Charlemagne's campaign. The Slavic castles established at the time attracted a lot of attention. An Arab scholar, Abu Obaid Abdallah al Bekri, thought a Jewish merchant's writings on Slavic castle building in the eleventh century so significant that he reproduced them word for word in his «Book of Ways and Lands». Later castles, built in the course of early German settlement, often used the Slavic establishments. Planned cultivation of the moorland lowlands of the Havelländisches Luch and the river Peene, that until improvement in 1718-24 was a natural precursor of the main Havelland canal, made it possible to build up grazing land. After 1945 this canal system was opened up again, wind protection strips were established and agricutural production and processing businesses set up. Because of the main road to Lübeck the textile and garment industry as well as agriculture developed in the Prignitz towns of Kyritz, Pritzwalk and Wittstock. The ground plans of medieval towns can still be made out in the region, showing how it flourished in that period.

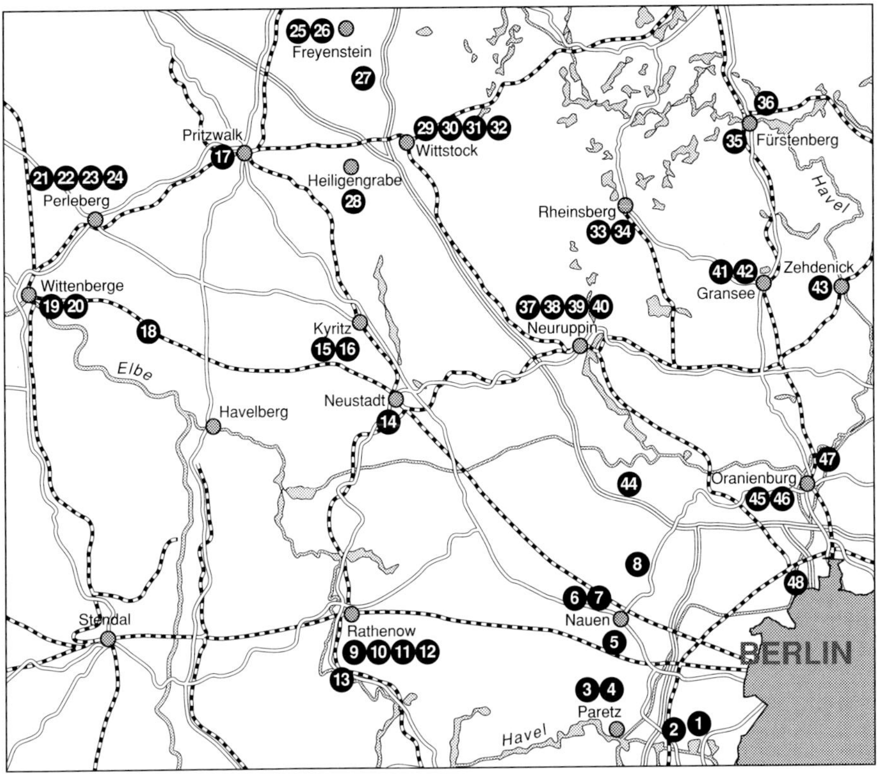

U 1 Mühle Fahrland
U 2 Schloß Marquard
U 3 Dorfkern Paretz
U 4 Schmiede
U 5 Dorfkirche Markee-Markau
U 6 Stadtkern Nauen
U 7 Rathaus Nauen
U 8 Funkamt Nauen
U 9 Stadtkern Rathenow
U 10 Denkmal des Kurfürsten Friedrich Wilhelm I.
U 11 Wohnsiedlung
U 12 Verwaltungsgebäude (Landratsamt)
U 13 Alte Kolonie Premnitz
U 14 Hengstgestüt Neustadt/Dosse
U 15 Stadtkern Kyritz
U 16 Fachwerkhäuser
U 17 Pfarrkirche St. Nikolai Pritzwalk
U 18 Wallfahrtskirche Bad Wilsnack
U 19 Steintor Wittenberge
U 20 Elbbrücke
U 21 Stadtkern Perleberg
U 22 Rathaus
U 23 Stadtkirche St. Jakob
U 24 Wohnhaus
U 25 Stadtkern Freyenstein
U 26 Altes Schloß
U 27 Dorfkirche Wulfersdorf
U 28 Zisterzienser-Nonnenkloster Heiligengrabe
U 29 Stadtkern Wittstock
U 30 Rathaus
U 21 Pfarrkirche St. Marien und St. Martin
U 32 Gröper Torturm
U 33 Stadtkern Rheinsberg
U 34 Schloß Rheinsberg
U 35 Schloß Fürstenberg
U 36 Mahn- und Gedenkstätte Ravensbrück
U 37 Stadtkern Neuruppin
U 38 Pfarrkirche St. Marien
U 39 Wohnhaus August-Bebel-Straße
U 40 Tempelgarten
U 41 Stadtkern Gransee
U 42 Luisendenkmal
U 43 Zisterzienser-Nonnenkloster Zehdenick
U 44 Denkmal der Schlacht von Fehrbellin
U 45 Schloß Oranienburg
U 46 Wohnhaus (Heimatmuseum)
U 47 Mahn- und Gedenkstätte Sachsenhausen
U 48 Kleinhaussiedlung Hennigsdorf

U 1 Mühle
Fahrland; Ketziner Straße
1758 • Aulich

Am nordwestlichen Ortsrand von Fahrland, einer bereits 1197 gemeinsam mit Spandau als Vogteisitz der askanischen Markgrafschaft genannten Siedlung, wurde 1758 die von Architekt Aulich und Mühlenbaumeister Puhlmann errichtete Bockwindmühle in Betrieb genommen. Später als Paltrockmühle ausgebaut und bis 1969 in Betrieb, besitzt sie noch heute ein vollständig erhaltenes, funktionsfähiges Mahlwerk. 1952 wurde die Mühle zum technischen Denkmal erklärt und 1973 vollständig rekonstruiert. Und da die Berührung mit Denkmal und Kultur den Menschen offenbar hungrig und durstig macht, wurde unmittelbar neben der Mühle 1973 die vielbesuchte Gaststätte »Mühlenbaude« mit 90 Plätzen und einer Kegelbahn nach einem Entwurf von Harald Horn und Lothar Böttcher im ländlichen Stil errichtet.

On the north-western edge of Fahrland, a settlement mentioned along with Spandau as early as 1197 as bailiwick of the Ascanian margraves, the post-mill built by architect Aulich and mill-builder Puhlmann was commissioned in 1758. It was later modified and was in use regularly until 1969; its grinding equipment has survived in complete working order. The mill was declared a technical monument in 1952 and completely restored in 1973. And as people are known to feel hungry and thirsty after being exposed to monuments and culture, the popular «Mühlenbaude» restaurant was also established in 1973; it features seating for 90 people and a skittle alley and was built in rustic style to plans by Harald Horn and Lothar Böttcher.

in der Nähe/nearby:
Herrenhaus; Kartzow
Um 1850
Park; Kartzow
1940 • Georg Potente
Gutshaus; Priort
2. V. 19. Jh.
Dorfkirche; Priort
M. 18. Jh.
Oberschule; Wustermark; Berliner Straße
1960 • Felix Hollesch (Sgraffito • Ronald Paris)

U 2 Schloß
Marquardt
Gegen 1910

Mit den repräsentativen Baustilen der Renaissance und später des Barock hatte sich der Typus des Schlosses als angemessene Residenz adeliger, fürstlicher oder königlicher Familien herausgebildet. Seit der Aufklärung und den ersten schweren Erschütterungen der absolutistischen Gesellschaftsform kam es nur noch zögerlich zu Neubauten von Schlössern. Die letzten Bauten dieser Art entstanden in Deutschland kurz vor dem Ersten Weltkrieg, der ja das Ende der Monarchie besiegelte. Marquardt gehört zu diesen letzten baulichen Äußerungen, der Umbau und die Neufassung einer älteren Schloßanlage von 1791. Zeitgemäß bediente man sich nun gegen 1910 wiederum barocker Formen – weniger im historistischen Stilverständnis als im expressiven Sinne, das Zitat ungebrochener Stärke, Restauration in einer Zeit der Reformen. Die alte Gesellschaftsordnung ging unter, nicht aber der Bürgertraum vom Adelsschloß. Und Schloßbewohner auf Zeit kann man im Hotel werden. Das Schloßhotel kam in Mode, und es rettet nun so manches vom Verfall bedrohte Adelsdomizil. Auch Marquardt soll so gerettet werden. Pläne für einen Hotelkomplex unter Einbeziehung des alten Schlosses liegen bereits vor. Die Entwürfe stammen vom Berliner Architekturbüro Nielebock & Partner.

With the imposing building styles of the Renaissance and later the Baroque, the typology of the castle as fitting residence for noble, princely or royal families had emerged. Following the Enlightenment and the first deeply felt tremors that shook the absolutist social order, only a small number of new castles were being built. The last structures of this type in Germany were built shortly before the First World War which marked the end of the monarchy. Marquardt was among the last projects of this kind with the alteration and conversion of an older castle complex dating from 1791. In keeping with the spirit of the times, there was a return to baroque elements, although not so much out of a historicist understanding as in terms of expression: a reference to unbroken strength and restoration in a period of reform. The old social order declined, but not so the bourgeois dream of stately castles. One way of residing in a castle at least temporarily is to stay at a hotel. Thus castle hotels came into fashion and now serve to rescue many a stately manor from falling into decay. Marquardt castle is also to be saved in this way. Plans for a hotel complex incorporating the old castle are already existing. The designs were developed by Berlin architects Nielebock & Partner.

in der Nähe/nearby:
Schloßpark; Marquardt
1823 • Peter Joseph Lenné
Dorfkirche; Falkenrehde
Um 1750

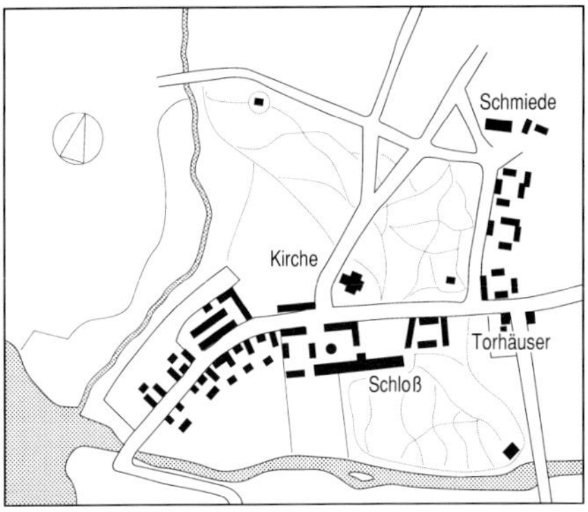

U 3 Dorfkern Paretz
Ketzin-Paretz
1795-1803 • David Gilly

Eine markgräfliche Urkunde bezeichnet 1197 eine Siedlerstelle als »slavika villa«. Das heutige Paretz, inzwischen ein Ortsteil von Ketzin, entstand 1795 bis 1803 nach Plänen von David Gilly als einheitliche Dorfanlage und Sommersitz des Kronprinzen und späteren Königs Friedrich III. Das Gut mit dem ehemaligen Schloß, erbaut 1796-97 von David Gilly, wurde nach 1950 völlig verändert und wird heute von einer wissenschaftlichen Einrichtung genutzt. Die Dorfkirche, wie das Schloß 1797 nach Plänen von Gilly erbaut, ist ein kreuzförmiger neugotischer Putzbau mit Westturm. Die Bauernhöfe beiderseits der Dorfstraße sind im wesentlichen einheitliche eingeschossige klassizistische Putzbauten in Trauf- und Giebelstellung.

In 1197 a document issued by the margrave described a settlement as «slavika villa». Modern Paretz, now part of Ketzin, came into being from 1795-1803. It was built to plans by David Gilly, and intended as the summer residence of the Crown Prince, King Frederick III. The estate with the former palace, built 1796-7 by David Gilly, was completely altered after 1950 and is now used by a scientific institution. The village church, built like the palace to plans by David Gilly in 1797, is a cruciform neo-Gothic rendered building with west tower. The farmhouses on either side of the village street are essentially uniform one-storey classical rendered buildings, placed with eaves and gables to the street.

in der Nähe/nearby:
Gutshaus; Päwesin-Bagow
1545
Schloß; Roskow
1723-27 (Umbau 1880-90 • Hauer)
Gutshaus; Groß Kreuz; Dorfstraße
1765 • Vermutlich Friedrich Wilhelm Dietrichs
Schloß; Plessow
1780 (in jüngerer Zeit verändert)

U 4 Schmiede
Ketzin-Paretz; Parkring 21
Um 1800 • David Gilly

Die ehemalige Schmiede entstand im Zusammenhang mit der Errichtung der gesamten klassizistischen Dorfanlage Paretz im Knickpunkt der nach Ketzin führenden Dorfstraße und schließt im Norden das alte Dorfensemble ab. Der eingeschossige Putzbau in neugotischen Formen, mit Arkadengliederung, gezahnter Gesimsblende und Krüppelwalmdach, auch »Gotisches Haus« genannt, ist heute eine Speisegaststätte, im Sommer mit Gartenbetrieb. Bemerkenswert auch die beiden Torhäuser am südöstlichen Dorfeingang mit quadratischem Grundriß, Putzquadern und Rundbogenblenden aus der Entstehungszeit des Dorfes.

The former smithy was built in the context of the building of the complete classical village of Paretz at the point of the bend in the road to Ketzin and concludes the old village ensemble in the north. It is a single-storey rendered building of neo-Gothic design, articulated by arches, toothed cornice cover and half hip roof; it is also called «Gothic house». It is now a restaurant, with service in the garden in summer. Also noteworthy are the two gatehousses at the south-eastern end of village. They are built on a square ground plan with rendered ashlar and round-arched blind windows, and dated from the time the village was built.

in der Nähe/nearby:
Dorfkirche Paretz; Dorfstraße
1797 • David Gilly
Torhäuser; östlicher Dorfeingang
Um 1800 • David Gilly

U 5 Dorfkirche Markee-Markau 1712

Der 1712 errichtete kreuzförmige Backsteinbau mit aufwendigem Sandsteinportal im Norden und fünfseitigem Ostschluß sowie spätmittelalterlichem Westturm in Feldsteinmauerwerk bezieht Reste des spätgotischen Vorgängerbaues ein. Bemerkenswert ist im Inneren die stuckierte Flachdecke über einer hohen Voute mit schlichter Profileinrahmung, die dreiseitige Empore sowie die wohl niederländisch beeinflußte reiche Ausstattung in Formen des Barock der Schlüter-Nachfolge aus den Jahren 1757-59. Das bezieht sich insbesondere auf den Altaraufsatz mit seinen Plastiken, die Kanzel und die zwei Herrschaftslogen sowie auf das Pfarrgestühl an der nördlichen Wand. Die 1958 ausgeführte räumliche Farbgestaltung in den Tönen blau-weiß-gold besorgte das Institut für Denkmalpflege.

This cruciform brick building with lavish sandstone portal to the north, pentagonal east end and late medieval rubble-stone west tower was built in 1712 and includes remains of its late Gothic predecessor. Striking features of the interior are the stuccoed flat ceiling over a high voute with plain profile framing, the three-sided gallery and the lavish baroque furnishings, probably showing the influence of the Netherlands, which was executed by successors to Schlüter in 1757-9. This shows particularly in the altar with its sculpture, the pulpit and the two loges for the ruling family and the pews for the clergy on the north wall. The interior painting in blue, white and gold was carried out by the Institut für Denkmalpflege in 1958.

in der Nähe/nearby:
Dorfkirche; Tremmen
15. Jh.
Dorfkirche; Wachow
15. Jh. (Umbau um 1700)
Dorfkirche; Ketzür
Ende 14. Jh., 1599, 1793

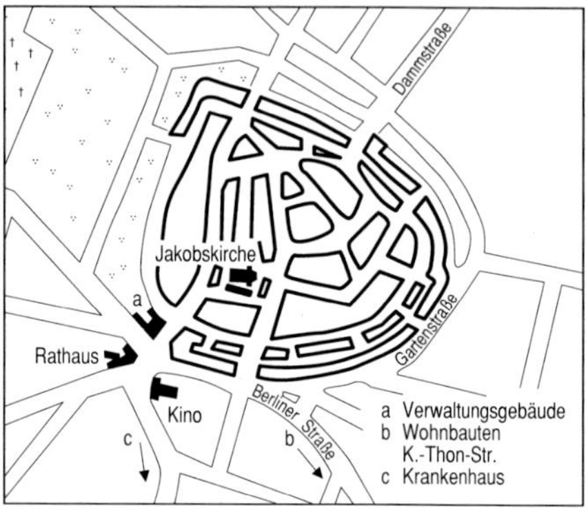

U 6 Stadtkern Nauen 1292

Am Ende des 12. Jahrhunderts entstand Nauen. Die heutige Altstadt entwickelte sich um eine später völlig verschwundene Burg und hatte mit ihrem regellosen Wegenetz und den gebrochenen Straßen im 18. Jahrhundert innerhalb der Stadtmauer eine Ausdehnung von rund 500 m Durchmesser. Früher lag sie abseits von Handelsstraßen, heute berühren sich hier drei wichtige Verkehrswege: die Fernstraße nach Kyritz und Pritzwalk, die Bahnstrecke Berlin-Hamburg und der große Havelländische Hauptkanal. Der Chausseebau Berlin–Nauen–Kyritz und der 1846 erfolgte Anschluß an die Berlin-Hamburger Bahn begünstigten den industriellen Aufschwung. Bekannt wurde Nauen über Landesgrenzen hinaus durch seinen Kurzwellensender. Vom Wohnungsbau des frühen 19. Jahrhunderts ist in einigen Straßenzügen, wie in der Bergstraße, Straße der Jugend und in der Rosenbergstraße, eine verhältnismäßig geschlossene Bebauung mit zweigeschossigen schlichten Traufhäusern aus Fachwerk erhalten.

Nauen came into being in the late twelfth century. The present old town developed around a castle that later disappeared completely. In the eighteenth century its completely irregular pattern of paths and broken streets covered an area about 500 m in diameter within the town wall. Formerly it was off the main trade routes, now three important means of transport are in contact here: the trunk road to Kyritz and Pritzwalk, the Berlin-Hamburg railway and the main Havelland canal. Building of the Berlin-Nauen-Kyritz road and connection to the Berlin-Hamburg railway completed in 1846 favoured industrial expansion. Nauen became known far and wide for its short-wave transmitter. Sections of relatively complete early nineteenth century housing have survived in Bergstrasse, Strasse der Jugend and Rosenbergstrasse nineteenth century residential development in the form of plain, two-storey half-timbered houses with eaves.

in der Nähe/nearby:
Schloß (Altersheim); Ribbeck
1821
Wohnhaus; Falkensee; Hansastraße 64
1935 • Hans Scharoun
Pfarrkirche; Friesack
1841-44 • Schinkel-Schule

U 7 Rathaus
Nauen; Rathausplatz 1
1888-90

Die Erwähnung eines Nauener Rates im Jahre 1320, die Teilnahme an Städtebünden wohl seit 1308, der 1323 vorhandene städtische Grundbesitz von 120 Hufen, die Befreiung von markgräflichen Abgaben 1354 und vor allem der 1302 bezeugte ursprüngliche Rathausbau belegen einen früh ausgereiften städtischen Status. Mit dem industriellen Aufschwung im 19. Jahrhundert nach dem Bau wichtiger Verkehrsverbindungen entstand 1888-90 das neue Rathaus. Im Winkel der Hamburger Straße und der Straße nach Brandenburg steht der neugotische Backsteinbau mit seiner Hauptfront zum örtlichen Verkehrsknotenpunkt. Aus Richtung Wustermark kommend, wird der Blick von der Vorhalle mit ihrem Staffelgiebel und dem Uhrtürmchen angezogen.

Evidence of early town status is provided by mention of a Nauen council in 1320, participation in leagues of towns probably from 1308, the municipal property of 120 hydes of land in 1323, dispensation from the Margrave's taxes in 1354 and above all the building of the original town hall, of which there was evidence in 1302. The new town hall was built in 1888-90 as a result of industrial expansion in the nineteenth century after the building of important traffic connections. The neo-Gothic brick building stands between Hamburger Strasse and the road to Brandenburg, with its main façade facing the local junction. When approaching from Wustermark the eye is drawn by the porch with its stepped gable, and the little clock tower.

in der Nähe/nearby:
Verwaltungsgebäude; Goethestraße 39
1925 • Gebrüder Gran
Kino und Theater; Ketziner Straße 1
1955 • Hans-Peter Richter
Krankenhaus; Ketziner Straße 20
1927-30 • Josef Bischof
Jakobskirche
1742 bzw.1845
Wohnbauten; Karl-Thon-Platz
1929 • Willi Ludewig

U 8 Funkamt Nauen
Nauen; Straße nach Kremmen
1917-20 • Hermann Muthesius

Die 1906 nördlich der Stadt für das Funklaboratorium Graf Arcos errichtete Versuchsanlage wurde 1910 zur Betriebsstation der Firma Telefunken erweitert. Aus ihr entstand über mehrere Ausbau- und Erweiterungsstufen auf einem 250 ha großen Gelände die Großfunkstation Nauen für den Kurzwellenbereich. Sie erlaubte bereits 1924 erste Versuchssendungen nach Argentinien. Das Hauptgebäude, ein symmetrisch gegliederter Klinkerbau mit betontem Mittelteil und kreuzförmiger Maschinenhalle, errichtete Hermann Muthesius, der sich besonders im Bau Berliner Landhäuser hervorgetan hatte. Allein mit der Seidenweberei Nowawes hatte Muthesius bereits 1912 bewiesen, daß seine gestalterischen Elemente auch für den Industriebau taugen. Sein Leitsatz von »Symmetrie, rhythmischer Folge, Proportionalität und Ausdruck der Funktion« ist deutlich an der Funkstation ablesbar. Die 1962-64 montierte dreh- und schwenkbare Kurzwellenrichtantenne ist als weithin sichtbare Gitternetz-Stahlkonstruktion in Teilen vorgefertigt worden und war zur Zeit der Betriebsaufnahme des 100-kW-Rundfunksenders 1964 eine der modernsten Anlagen der Welt. Die mit dem Hauptgebäude gleichzeitig errichtete Werksiedlung in unmittelbarer Nähe des Sendegeländes entstand ebenfalls nach Entwurf des damals im preußischen Staatsdienst stehenden Werkbund-Architekten Hermann Muthesius.

This experimental building for the radio laboratory of Graf von Arcos was built to the north of the town in 1906 and extended in 1910 as an operating station for Telefunken. It was much expanded and extended on a site covering 250 hectares to become the Nauen main short-wave station. The first experimental broadcasts to Argentina were made in 1924. The main building is in brick, symmetrically articulated with stressed central section and cruciform machine shop. It was built by Hermann Muthesius, who had gained a particular reputation for building Berlin villas. The silk mill for Nowawes built in 1912 had been enough to prove that Muthesius' talents were also well suited to industrial design. His guiding principle of «symmetry, rhythmic sequence, proportionality and expression of function» can be read clearly from the radio station. The short-wave directional aerial can be turned and tilted. It is a steel grid structure, visible from a great distance. It was prefabricated and one of the most modern pieces of such equipment in the world when the 100 kw short-wave transmitter became operational in 1964. The workers' accommodation in close proximity to the broadcasting site was built at the same time as the main building, and was also designed by Werkbund architect Hermann Muthesius, who was then in the service of the Prussian state.

in der Nähe/nearby:
Pfarrkirche St. Nikolai; Kremmen
15. Jh.

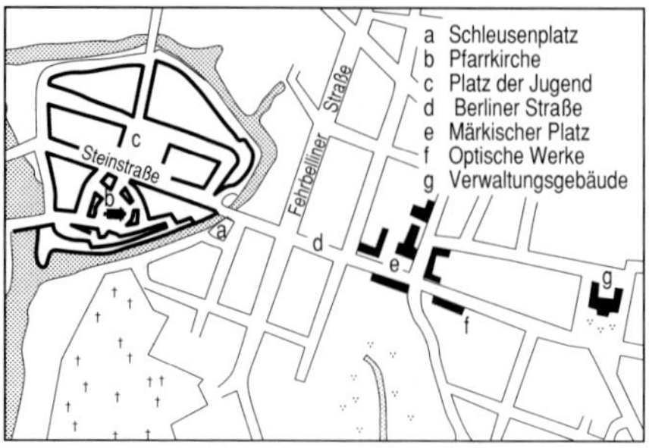

U 9 Stadtkern Rathenow
1288

Mit der Anlage der Planstadt und des Stadtgrabens Mitte des 13. Jahrhunderts entstand eine wehrhafte Insel. Rathenow gehörte durch die städtebauliche Zusammenführung des Oberkietz mit dem Mittel- und dem Jederitzer Kietz zu den wenigen Orten in der Mark mit derartigen Siedlungen. Neben der 420 m × 440 m großen ehemalig ummauerten Altstadt des 13. Jahrhunderts entstand südöstlich anschließend seit 1732 die barocke Neustadt mit gitterförmigem Straßennetz, die bereits 1741 die Größe der Altstadt erreichte. Von der Wohnbebauung in der Altstadt sind die Wohnhäuser der ringförmigen Umbauung des Kirchplatzes aus dem 16. und 18. Jahrhundert, darunter der Putzbau Haus Nr. 16 von 1704 und die ehemalige Superintendantur Haus Nr. 10 aus dem 18. Jahrhundert, erhalten. Von der Neustadtbebauung ist vor allem das Quartier am Schleusenplatz mit den zweigeschossigen barocken Typenhäusern Nr. 1-4 von 1732-40 bemerkenswert. Heute ist die Magistrale mit dem Märkischen Platz das Zentrum der Stadt. Weltbekannt wurde Rathenow durch die von Johannes Heinrich August Duncker 1801 begründete optische Industrie.

When the planned town and town moat were built in the mid thirteenth century this produced a well-fortified island. The upper settlement was joined to the middle and Jederitz settlements, making Rathenow one of the few places in the Mark with a settlement pattern of this kind. The baroque new town with its grid of streets came into being from 1732, alongside the 420 m × 440 m former walled old town dating from the thirteenth century; by 1741 it was already as large as the old town. Of the residential buildings in the old town the houses set in a circle around the church square dating from the sixteenth and eighteenth centuries have survived, including the rendered no. 16, dating from 1704 and the former superintendency at no. 10 dating from the eighteenth century. Most has survived from the new town development in the quarter on Schleusenplatz, with the two-storey baroque houses nos. 1-4 as a remarkable feature. Today the main street and the Märkischer Platz form the centre of the town. Rathenow achieved world fame because of the optical industry founded here by Johannes Heinrich August Duncker in 1801.

in der Nähe/nearby:
Schloß; Hohennauen; Pareystraße
1792
Pfarrkirche; Rhinow; Marktplatz
13. Jh. (Umbau 1734-45)
Otto-Lilienthal-Gedenkstein; Stölln
1953 • Horst Wildebrandt

U 10 Denkmal des Kurfürsten Friedrich Wilhelm I.
Rathenow; Schleusenplatz
1736-38 • Johann Georg Glume

Das Denkmal des Kurfürsten Friedrich Wilhelm I., von Johann Georg Glume aus Sandstein nach einem Modell von Berthold Dammert 1736-38 geschaffen, stellt eine vereinfachte Form des Berliner Kurfürstendenkmals von Andreas Schlüter dar. Die antikisierende Sandsteinfigur wird von einem hohen Sockel mit Schlachtenreliefs getragen. An den Ecken des Sockels Kolossalfiguren gefesselter Sklaven. Die zweigeschossigen barocken Typenhäuser am Schleusenplatz, mit der planmäßigen Anlage der Neustadt 1732-40 erbaut, schließen am Schleusenkanalübergang zwischen Alt- und Neustadt unmittelbar an die Altstadtbebauung an. Das städtebauliche Ensemble Schleusenplatz überzeugt durch die klare horizontale und vertikale Gliederung der fünfachsigen Wohnhäuser mit Walmdach, die gleichzeitig den ruhigen Hintergrund für das reich gegliederte Denkmal bilden.

This monument to Elector Friedrich Wilhelm I, made by Johann Georg Glume in sandstone to a model by Berthold Dammert in 1736-8 is a simplified version of Andreas Schlüter's monument to the Elector in Berlin. The Attic-style sandstone figure is set on a high pedestal carrying reliefs of battles. At the corners of the pedestal are colossal figures of slaves in chains. The two-storey baroque houses on Schleusenplatz, built as part of the planned new town in 1732-40, are immediately adjacent to the old town building at the Schleusenkanal transition point between the old and new towns. Schleusenplatz convinces as an urban group because of the clear horizontal and vertical articulation of the town houses with five axes and hip roofs, which form a peaceful background for the lavishly articulated monument.

in der Nähe/nearby:
Pfarrkirche St. Maria und Andreas; Kirchberg
15. u. 16. Jh.
Wohnbauten; Platz der Jugend
1950-51 • Otto Haesler
Wohnbauten; Berliner Straße
1956-62 • Gerhard Mangelsdorf, Hans-Dieter Bugge

U 11 Wohnsiedlung
Rathenow; Friedrich-Ebert-Ring
1928-29 • Otto Haesler

Die Siedlung am Friedrich-Ebert-Ring ging 1928-29 aus einem Entwurf von Otto Haesler hervor. Das ursprünglich 12 ha große Wohngebiet wurde nur teilweise bebaut. Diese Siedlung ist ein Musterbeispiel für den rationellen Arbeiterwohnungsbau. Die strenge Nord-Süd-Stellung der Blöcke erinnert an die gleichzeitigen Entwürfe zum Wettbewerb der Reichsforschungsgesellschaft für Berlin-Haselhorst. Die dreigeschossigen, durch erkerartige verglaste Treppenhäuser gegliederten Zeilen mit Zwei- bis Vierraum-Wohnungen werden durch Läden als Eckbauten im Bereich des Friedrich-Ebert-Ringes unterbrochen. Die Gestaltung der ausgedehnten Grünflächen zwischen den Wohnzeilen nimmt Rücksicht auf den vorhandenen Waldbestand.

This estate on the Friedrich-Ebert-Ring was built 1928-9 to a design by Otto Haesler. The residential area originally occupied 12 hectares, but only part of this was built upon. The estate is a textbook example of rational building of workers' accommodation. The strict north-south orientation of the blocks is reminiscent of contemporary designs for a competition for the Reichsforschungsgesellschaft for Berlin-Haselhorst. The three-storey terraces are articulated with bay-like glazed stairwells, and contain one- to three-bedroom flats. The lines are broken by shop facilities as corner buildings in the Friedrich-Ebert-Ring area. The extensive green areas between the terraced dwellings are designed to take account of existing woodland.

in der Nähe/nearby:
Ensemble »Märkischer Platz«
1956-58 • Martin Buchsteiner, Wilfried Brennecke
1987-89 • Werner Buricke; Karl-Heinz Birkholz, W. Stelzig
Rathenower Optische Werke; Berliner Straße
1912-13 • Otto Walter
1973-74 • Gerhard Mangelsdorf

U 12 Verwaltungsgebäude (Landratsamt)
Rathenow; Platz der Freiheit 1
1893-95 • Franz Schwechten

Der neugotische Backsteinbau ist mit seinen drei Geschossen und vierzehn Achsen platzbestimmend. Der vierachsige übergiebelte Mittelrisalit mit Balkon über dem vorgezogenen Portal steigert mit seinen architektonischen Details die neugotischen Formen. Die flachbogigen Fenster geschoßweise wechselnd sowie die seitlichen Ziergiebel vervollständigen das Bild eines ausdrucksstarken Gebäudes.

This neo-Gothic brick building with three storeys and fourteen axes dominates the square. The central gabled projection has four axes and a balcony over the protruding portal, and its architectural detail heightens the neo-Gothic effect. The windows have shallow arches changing from storey to storey, and the decorative gables at the sides round off this expressive building.

in der Nähe/nearby:
Zentrum im Wohngebiet »Rathenow-Ost«
1969-77 u. 1984-86 • Werner Buricke, Gerhard Mangelsdorf
Schwesternwohnheim; Friedrich-Ebert-Ring 93-94
1962-63 • Hans-Dieter Bugge

U 13 Alte Kolonie Premnitz
Premnitz; Liebigstraße
1915-20 • Max Stern

Im Zuge des Aufbaus einer Pulverfabrik, die nach der Demontage 1919 auf die Produktion der Stapelfaser »Vistra« umgestellt wurde, errichtete Max Stern zur Ansiedlung von Stammarbeitern 1915-20 die »Alte Kolonie« in der Liebigstraße. Die Bebauung ist angerartig angelegt. Die fünfzig eingeschossigen Einfamilienhäuser sind in kleinen Gebäudegruppen mit mehreren Wohnungen kettenartig aneinandergereiht. Die Mansartdächer wirken mit ihren Zwerchhäusern gestaltend in den Straßenraum. Aber neben dem städtebaulichen Moment spricht der Architekt bewußt auch Stimmungen an. Im Sinne des expressiven Realismus jener Jahre kommt das ländlich oder kleinstädtisch Gemütliche zum Ausdruck, die »gute alte Zeit«.

Max Stern built the «Alte Kolonie» in Liebigstrasse to provide accommodation for permanent workers in 1915-20 while gunpowder manufacture was on the increase; after 1919 it went over to production of the staple fibre «Vistra». The development is laid out like a village green. Fifty single-storey houses for single families are placed in little groups of buildings with several dwellings one next to the other, like chains. The mansard roofs make a considerable visual impact on the street. But the architect is also concerned with mood and atmosphere as well as the urban development element. There is a feeling of rural or small-town comfort, in the spirit of the expressive realism of the period, a sense of the «good old days».

in der Nähe/nearby:
Wohngebiet »Am Dachsberg«; Premnitz
1955-60 • Siegfried Kamke, Karl Kerger
Chemiefaserwerk (Märkische Faser AG); Premnitz; Friedrich-Engels-Straße
Seit 1951 (mehrere Ausbaustufen)
Gesundheitszentrum; Premnitz; Friedrich-Engels-Straße
1969-72 • M. Nießner, G. Haberstroh
Gartenstadt; Plaue
1915-20 • Heinrich Tessenow
Schloß; Plaue
1711-16

U 14 Hengstgestüt
Neustadt/Dosse
1787-90 • Glasewald

Neustadt/Dosse, ein kleiner Flecken, der 1662 an den Landgrafen von Hessen-Homburg fällt, wird 1664 zur Stadt erhoben und um 1800 Zentrum der märkischen Pferdezucht. Den Bedarf an Pferden begründete das preußische Heer. Das Hengstgestüt erbaute 1787-90 Bauinspektor Glasewald. Es ist eine weiträumige, rechteckig bebaute Anlage mit Wohnhaus, Stallanlagen und Wirtschaftsgebäuden. Das spätbarocke zweigeschossige Wohnhaus von sieben Achsen, einem übergiebelten Mittelrisalit und Mansartdach hat seitlich eingeschossige Anbauten und wird von einem Uhrtürmchen bekrönt. Noch heute ist Neustadt/Dosse mit dem Hengstgestüt und dem gleichfalls um 1800 erbauten Hengstdepot Lindenau ein bedeutendes Zentrum der Pferdezucht in der Mark.

Neustadt/Dosse is a little country town that fell to the landgraves of Hessen in 1662; it achieved town status in 1664 and around 1800 became the centre of horse-breeding in the Mark: the Prussian army needed horses. The stud farm was built by Bauinspektor Glasewald in 1787-90. It is a spacious, rectangular complex with residence, stabling and domestic buildings. The late-baroque two-storey residential building has seven axes, a gabled central projection and mansard roof, single-storey buildings at the sides and a small clock tower. Neustadt/Dosse with its stud farm and the Lindau stallion depot also built c. 1800 is still an important centre of horse-breeding in the Mark.

in der Nähe/nearby:
Dorfkirche; Neustadt-Kampehl
M. 13. Jh.
Gaststätte »Zur alten Post«; Plänitz
18.Jh. (erneuert 1988)
Dorfkirche; Plänitz
1709

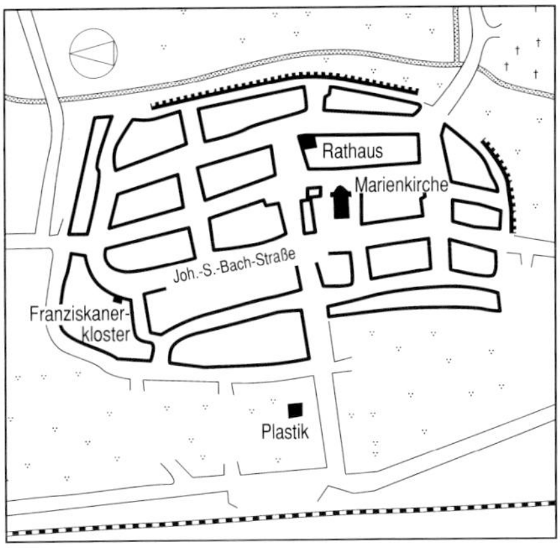

U 15 Stadtkern Kyritz
1273

Beispielgebend für die meisten Prignitzstädte legten die Edlen von Plotho wohl bald nach 1200 Kyritz als Planstadt an. Ausgestattet mit Stendaler Gildenrecht kennzeichnete die Gewandschneidergilde die Stadt als Standort des fernhandelsfähigen Textilgewerbes. Bezeugt ist die Gilde erstmals 1245, Stadtrecht erhält Kyritz 1273. Die Anlage von Kyritz erfolgt in abgerundeter Rechteckform von 625 m × 325 m planmäßig, mit zwei zum Flüßchen Jägelitz parallel verlaufenden, durch den Markt verbundenen Hauptstraßen. Von der spätmittelalterlichen Stadtmauer sind nur noch im Ostteil der Altstadt Reste mit einem halbrunden Weichhaus erhalten. Bemerkenswert ist vor allem die teilweise stattliche, heute noch zahlreich vertretene Fachwerkhausbebauung des 17. bis 19. Jahrhunderts. Das Marktensemble mit seinen platzbeherrschenden Gebäuden, der in der 2. Hälfte des 14. Jahrhunderts errichteten Marienkirche und dem 1879 gebauten Rathaus, wurde 1984-88 wiederhergestellt.

Kyritz, typical of most of the Prignitz towns, was probably built as a planned town by the von Plotho family shortly after 1200. The town's garment-makers' guild had Stendal guild rights, which meant that it provided textiles for long-distance trade. The guild is first recorded in 1245, Kyritz acquired its charter in 1273. The town was built in planned rounded-off rectangular form on an area 625 m × 325 m, with two main streets connected by the market running parallel to the little river Jägelitz. Fragments of the late medieval town wall with a semicircular wash-house have survived only in the eastern part of the old town. The most noteworthy feature is the seventeenth to nineteenth century half-timbered building, of which numerous examples have survived, some of them imposing. The group of buildings in the market place dominate the square: the Marienkirche was built in the second half of the fourteenth century, and the town hall, dating from 1879, was rebuilt in 1984-8.

in der Nähe/nearby:
Pfarrkirche St. Peter und Paul; Wusterhausen
14. und 15. Jh.
Rathaus; Wusterhausen: Markt 20
Um 1840
Fachwerkhäuser; Wusterhausen; Karl-Liebknecht Straße 4, 5, 6, 8, 14, 17/25 und 32/38
17. bis 19. Jh.
Schloß; Dementhin
1604

U 16 Fachwerkhäuser
Kyritz; Johann-Sebastian-Bach-Straße
16. und 17. Jahrhundert

Trotz wiederholter Brände sind bemerkenswerte, zum Teil reiche Fachwerkhäuser aus dem 16. und 17. Jahrhundert erhalten. Sowohl diese als auch die Bebauung aus dem 18. und 19. Jahrhundert folgten durchweg dem ellipsenförmigen Stadtgrundriß aus dem Mittelalter. In der Johann-Sebastian-Bach-Straße sind es die beiden zweistöckigen Giebelhäuser Nr. 36 und Nr. 44, die mit ihren bemalten Schnitzereien zu den stattlichsten Fachwerkhäusern aus der zweiten Hälfte des 17. Jahrhunderts zählen. Die Traufhäuser Nr. 28 von 1677, Nr. 24 aus dem 18. Jahrhundert und Nr. 4 um 1800 sind ähnlich verziert, aber weniger stattlich und im Erdgeschoß verändert. Weitere ein- und zweistöckige Traufhäuser in Fachwerk, teilweise noch in geschlossener Reihe und teilweise als stattliche Doppelhäuser des 19. Jahrhunderts, sind in der Holzhausener und Maxim-Gorki-Straße sowie am Markt zu nennen.

Despite repeated fires remarkable, and in some cases lavish, sixteenth and seventeenth century half-timbered buildings have survived. Both these and the eighteenth and nineteenth century developments follow the medieval elliptical ground plan without exception. In Johann-Sebastian-Bach-Strasse are two two-storey gabled buildings, at nos. 36 and 44, which with their painted carvings are among the most imposing half-timbered buildings dating from the second half of the seventeenth century. The houses with eaves at no. 28, 1677, no. 24, eighteenth century, and no. 4, c. 1800, are similarly decorated, but less imposing, and altered at ground floor level. Other one- and two-storey half-timbered houses with eaves, some in complete series and others as imposing nineteenth century semi-detached houses, are to be found in Holzhausener and Maxim-Gorki-Strasse and in the market place.

in der Nähe/nearby:
Pfarrkirche St. Marien; Bachstraße
2. H. 14. Jh. (Westfassade nach 1849)
Rathaus; Am Markt
1879
Franziskaner-Kloster; Johann-Sebastian-Bach-Straße
14. Jh.
Freiplastik »Die Liegende«; Bahnhofstraße
Nach 1920 • Fritz Klimsch

U 17 Pfarrkirche St. Nikolai
Pritzwalk; Kirchstraße
Mitte 15. Jahrhundert

Den Ort gründeten vermutlich die Edlen Gaus von Putlitz. Er lag im Waldgebiet zwischen den slawischen Stämmen der Linen und Dossanen, als »Siedlung jenseits des Dickichts« gedeutet. 1250 fiel er wahrscheinlich an die Askanier und war um 1305 mit Kyritz zweitgrößte Stadt der Prignitz. Als Übergang wichtiger Fernhandelsstraßen trat die Stadt 1339 der Hanse bei. Die planmäßige Stadtanlage nimmt eine abgerundete Rechteckform mit drei parallel verlaufenden Straßen auf. Verbunden sind diese durch einen langgestreckten Markt. Der Stadtbrand von 1821 vernichtete fast alle mittelalterlichen Bauten. Heute zählt Pritzwalk etwa 12 300 Einwohner. Die Pfarrkirche St. Nikolai ist ein stattlicher dreischiffiger Hallenbau aus Backstein und stammt aus der Mitte des 15. Jahrhunderts. Vom Ursprungsbau aus der Mitte des 13. Jahrhunderts sind Teile des ehemaligen Querschiffes im bestehenden spätgotischen Bau, der 1882 in neugotischen Backsteinformen nach Plänen von Friedrich Adler abgeschlossen wurde, erhalten. Mit ihrem Westturm und ihrem Langhaus beherrscht sie die Silhouette der Stadt. Die Restaurierung im Jahre 1960 besorgte das Institut für Denkmalpflege.

This place was probably founded by the nobility of the Putlitz region. It was in the wooded territory between the Slavic Lini and Dossnai tribes, and was known as the «settlement beyond the thicket». In 1250 it probably fell to the Ascanians, and about 1305 with Kyritz it was the second largest town in the Prignitz. The town joined the Hanseatic League in 1339, as it stood at a crossing point of important trade routes. The planned town is in the form of a rectangle with rounded-off corners with three parallel streets joined by an elongated market. The town fire of 1821 destroyed almost all the medieval buildings. Today Pritzwalk has about 12,300 inhabitants. The parish church of St. Nikolai is an imposing brick-built hall church with nave and two aisles, dating from the mid fifteenth century. Of the original mid thirteenth century church parts of the former transept have survived in the existing late Gothic building, complete in neoGothic style to plans by Friedrich Adler in 1882. The church's west tower and nave dominate the silhouette of the town. The Institut für Denkmalpflege undertook restoration in 1960.

in der Nähe/nearby:
Rathaus; Pritzwalk; Marktstraße 46
Nach 1882
Bibliothek; Pritzwalk; Am Kietz
1977-78 • Hans Stammer
Zahnradwerk; Pritzwalk; Freyensteiner Chaussee
1965-69 • H. Naumann (2. Baustufe • Bernd Schönherr)
Dorfkirche; Porep
Nach 1700

U 18 Wallfahrtskirche St. Nikolaus
Bad Wilsnack
1384-1430

Nach dem Brand einer älteren Dorfkirche und einem »Hostienwunder« kam es 1384 zu einem großzügigen Neubau, der aber immer wieder ins Stocken geriet. Da die Bauarbeiten nie gänzlich abgeschlossen wurden, zeigt sich hier noch deutlich die mittelalterliche Gewohnheit, den meist viel größeren Neubau um den in Gebrauch befindlichen kleinen Vorgängerbau »herumzubauen«. So verstellt der Sockel des alten Westturmes auffällig das Westjoch. Gestalterisches Vorbild für den Neubau war die Lüneburger Johanneskirche, ein Einfluß ging wiederum über auf den Stendaler Dom. Für die Wallfahrtskirche wurde ein Chorumgang gebaut, und auch die emporenartigen Querschiffanbauten stehen mit der besonderen Funktion der Kirche in Zusammenhang. Die reiche Ausstattung stammt überwiegend aus dem 15. Jahrhundert.

Following the burning of an older village church and a «miracle of the host», a lavish new building was begun in 1384. As construction was repeatedly interrupted and never fully completed, one can still recognize the medieval practice of building the new (and usually much bigger) structure «around» a still functional smaller predecessor. Thus the base of the old west tower obviously blocks off the western transept. The new structure was modeled on the Johanneskirche in Lüneburg and in turn influenced the design of the Stendal cathedral. The pilgrimage church was equipped with an ambulatory choir, and the gallery-like additions to the transept reflect the special significance of this church. Most of the lavish furnishings date back to the fifteenth century.

in der Nähe/nearby:
Bischofshaus; Bad Wilsnack
Um 1400

U 19 Steintor
Wittenberge
1. Hälfte 14. Jahrhundert

Wittenberge war schon immer ein wichtiger Elbübergang. Bereits 1226 wird es urkundlich genannt. Im Schutze einer inzwischen untergegangenen Burg legte man ein ellipsenförmiges Städtchen an mit parallelen Nord-Süd-Straßenzügen und einem mittigen Marktplatz. Von der mittelalterlichen Befestigung ist nur das Steintor erhalten: quadratischer Grundriß, Spitzbogen-Durchfahrt und schlichte Blendengiebel. Im 19. Jahrhundert erhielt Wittenberge recht früh mit der Strecke Berlin – Hamburg einen Bahnanschluß und kurz darauf auch über die neue Elbbrücke Verbindung nach Magdeburg. Diese günstigen Voraussetzungen für eine Industrialisierung wurden genutzt, und die Stadt hat heute über 30 000 Einwohner.

Wittenberge has always been an important point of crossing on the Elbe. It is mentioned in official documents as early as 1226. Covered by a no longer extant castle, an ellipse-shaped town with parallel streets running north-south and a central market square was established here. Of the medieval fortifications only the Steintor has survived with its square plan, pointed arch gateway and modest false gables. In the nineteenth century Wittenberge was soon linked to the Berlin-Hamburg railway line, and shortly thereafter a new bridge across the Elbe opened the way to Magdeburg as well. These favourable conditions resulted in rapid industrialization, and today the town has a population of 30,000.

in der Nähe/nearby:
Fachwerkhaus; Wittenberge; Putlitzstraße
1689
Arbeiterwohnhäuser; Wittenberge; Putlitzstraße
1912-15
Rathaus; Wittenberge; August-Bebel-Straße 10
1912-14 • Heinrich Mußfeld
Gymnasium; Wittenberge; August-Bebel-Straße
1914-16 • Heinrich Mußfeld

U 20 Turm des Nähmaschinenwerkes
Wittenberge; Bad Wilsnacker Straße 48
1928 • Felix S. Ascher

1903 gründete die Firma Singer in Wittenberge ein Nähmaschinenwerk. 1922 wurden die Produktionsstätten durch den Architekten Felix S. Ascher erstmals bedeutend erweitert. 1928 folgt wiederum durch Ascher eine erneute Erweiterung. Hierzu gehört auch ein fast 50 m hoher kubischer Wasserturm, der weit sichtbar nach vier Seiten eine Uhr trägt. Es ist mit einem Zifferblattdurchmesser von 7,57 m die größte Turmuhr im östlichen Deutschland. Gestalterisch orientiert sich das Bauwerk an den zwei Treppentürmen des anschließenden sechsgeschossigen Produktionstraktes, hebt sich aber durch Blenden in strenger Pfeilergliederung repräsentativ ab, wagt mit einer dreieckigen Profilierung der Lisenen im Dachkranz sogar expressionistische Äußerungen. Die zwanziger Jahre haben etliche solcher Türme für Industriebauten hervorgebracht: am bekanntesten in Berlin der Ullsteinturm, der Borsigturm, die Türme der Siemensstadt. In ihnen paaren sich technischer Zweck und selbstbewußtes Repräsentieren mit architektonischen Mitteln.

In 1903 the Singer company established a sewing machine factory at Wittenberge. In 1922 the factory complex was extended significantly by the architect Felix S. Ascher, followed by a second extension in 1928, again to designs by Ascher, including an almost 50 m high water-tower in the shape of a cube, equipped with a clock visible from all four sides. The face of the clock has a diameter of 7.57 metres which makes it the largest tower clock in eastern Germany. The formal design of the structure follows the two stair-case towers of the adjoining six-storey production complex; at the same time it asserts a more stately presence with pillars articulating the facing wall and even ventures a touch of expressionism in the triangular profile of the lesenes along the cornice. The 1920s brought forth a variety of such towers for industrial buildings, among the best known in Berlin being the Ullstein tower, the Borsig tower, and the towers of the Siemensstadt. Their design combines functional purpose with proud self-assertiveness achieved with architectonic means.

in der Nähe/nearby:
Bahnhof; Wittenberge
1846 • Friedrich Neuhaus

U 21 Stadtkern Perleberg
1. Hälfte 13. Jahrhundert

Die über fünf Meter hohe Sandsteinfigur des Roland versinnbildlicht die Unabhängigkeit der Stadt. Eine Inschrift verweist auf das Jahr 1546. Die Geschichte von Perleberg geht aber weiter zurück bis auf des Jahr 1239, in dem es die Salzwedeler Stadtrechte erhielt. Die Gründung muß um 1200 erfolgt sein. Zwei Siedlungskerne sind zu erkennen: ein älterer im südlichen Teil der Stepenitz-Insel im Schutze einer Burg und um die inzwischen abgetragene Nikolaikirche, ein jüngerer nach 1239 in der Mitte der Insel um den heutigen Marktplatz und die Jakobikirche. Als Mitglied der Hanse wurde Perleberg eine der bedeutenden Städte Brandenburgs. Von der Stadtmauer des 14. Jahrhunderts sind nur kleine Reste am Wallgebäude und am Schulgang erhalten. Heute hat Perleberg mehr den Charakter eines ländlichen Zentrums.

The more than five metre high sandstone statue of the Roland serves as a symbol to the town's independence. The inscription refers to the year 1546. Yet the history of Perleberg goes back much further to the year 1239 when it was awarded the Salzwedel charter. It was probably founded around 1200. Two settlement cores can be identified: an older one in the southern part of Stepenitz island, protected by a castle, and around the now demolished church of St. Nikolai, and a younger one, dating from after 1239, at the centre of the island around what is now the market square and the church of St. Jacob. As a member of the Hanseatic League, Perleberg became one of the more important towns in Brandenburg. Of the fourteenth century town wall, only a few remnants have survived at the ramparts building and at the Schulgang. Today Perleberg has become more like a rural centre.

in der Nähe/nearby:
Wallgebäude; Puschkinstraße
Vielleicht 1604
Stadtmauerturm; neben Wallgebäude
13./14. Jh.
Schule; Puschkinstraße 13
1861-64 • Friedrich August Stüler

U 22 Rathaus
Perleberg; Großer Markt
Nach 1839 • Friedrich August Stüler

Starr und unvermittelt ragt die neugotische Fassade des Rathauses auf dem Marktplatz empor. Die romantisch-patriotische Baugesinnung des Schinkel-Schülers lehnt sich an das Idealbild des mittelalterlichen Rathauses an, dem hier der Standort und die Kulisse der alten Jakobikirche gerecht werden. Ähnlich wie bei Schramms Kamenzer Rathaus erhielt ein schlanker symmetrischer Bau mit hohem Mittelturm den Vorzug, mehr repräsentierend als gefühlvoll historisierend. So aber, wie der Effekt bedacht ist, wird er auch erreicht. Auf der Rückseite des Neubaues sind die Reste des älteren Rathauses einbezogen: die Gerichtslaube aus dem 15. Jahrhundert mit breiten Spitzbogen, Kreuzgewölben, massigem Rundpfeiler und im Obergeschoß darüber die sterngewölbte Ratsstube.

The neo-Gothic façade of the town hall rises up rigidly and abruptly in the market square. The romantic and patriotic intentions of its architect, a pupil of Schinkel's, takes up the ideal image of a medieval town hall, quite fitting for this location in front of the old church of St. Jacob. As in the case of Schramm's Kamenz town hall, preference was given to a slender symmetrical building with a high central tower. The design is rather imposing as opposed to a sensitive historicism. Yet the calculated effect is indeed achieved quite successfully. At the back of the new building, the remnants of the previous town hall were integrated into the structure: the open-air court, dating back to the fifteenth century, with its broad pointed arches, groin vaults and massive round pillars, and above it the council room with its stellar vaults.

in der Nähe/nearby:
Kaufmannshaus; Großer Markt 4
E. 15. Jh.
Apotheke; Großer Markt 16
E. 18. Jh.

U 23 Stadtkirche St. Jakob
Perleberg; Kirchplatz
14./15. Jahrhundert

Ältester Bauteil ist der polygonale Chor. Mit seinen schlanken Spitzbogen und dem ausgewogenen Rhythmus Fenster–Wand–Pfeiler ist er klar der Hochgotik zuzurechnen. Eine Inschrift weist in das Jahr 1361. Mindestens ein halbes Jahrhundert jünger ist das Langhaus, das sich schon äußerlich durch den weit über die Chorsilhouette hinausragenden Ostgiebel und das gewaltige Dach als Halle zu erkennen gibt. Das deutlich breitere Ostjoch könnte auf die Grundmauern des Querschiffes einer älteren Kirchenanlage hinweisen, von der auch der Feldstein-Unterbau des Turmes herrührt. Beachtenswert sind die Portale, besonders das südöstliche erinnert an spätromanische Trichterportale und kann in seinem Reichtum an Gestaltungsmerkmalen gemessen an der norddeutschen Kirchenbaukunst als üppig gelten. Als Ausstattung findet man eine Kanzel von 1815, Chorgestühl etwa um 1400 und einen schönen fünfarmigen Messingleuchter, den 1475 Harmen Bonstede schuf. 1851 wurde die Kirche – offenbar im Zusammenhang mit dem Rathaus-Neubau – restauriert. Der bauliche Eingriff geschah ganz im Sinne der Zeit, für die Gesamtwirkung aber wenig glücklich.

The oldest part of the building is the polygonal choir. With its slender pointed arches and the well-balanced rhythm of window, wall and pillar it clearly represents the style of the High Gothic. The inscription refers to the year 1361. At least half a century younger is the nave. Even from the outside the church with its huge roof and its east gable projecting far above the silhouette of the choir is clearly recognizable as a hall church. The markedly wider east bay may be an indication of the foundation walls of the transept of an older church; the base of the tower, built of rubble-stone, can also be attributed to this older structure. Especially noteworthy are the portals, particularly the south-east portal which recalls late Romanesque deeply-recessed portals; with its wealth of design elements it can be considered quite lavish in comparison with North German church architecture. Furnishings include a pulpit from 1815, choir pews dating back to about 1400, and a beautiful five-armed brass chandelier created by Harmen Bonstede in 1475. In 1851 the church was restored, probably in conjunction with the building of the new town hall. Although in keeping with the spirit of the time, the architectural intervention was clearly not to the advantage of the overall appearance.

U 24 Wohnhaus
Perleberg; Kirchplatz 11
1584

Markt und Kirchplatz umstehen üblicherweise die prunkvollsten Bürgerhäuser. Nur die reichsten und privilegiertesten Bürger durften hier bauen und wohnen, das waren angesehene Kaufleute oder die führenden Handwerksmeister, also die Repräsentanten des Bürgertums. Das hatte sich im Mittelalter schon in den Reichsstädten, die der Gewalt des Landadels und der Kirchengüter entzogen waren, so herausgebildet, und dieses stadtrepublikanische Modell wurde durch die Reformation noch gestärkt. Architektonisch wird dies in einer Vielzahl wertvoller Renaissance-Bürgerhäuser sichtbar. Auch das Perleberger Haus Kirchplatz 11 gehört in diese Reihe. Es ist verputzt. Den Giebel ziert fächerförmig angelegtes Maßwerk, das in seinem dekorativen Aufwand einen selbstbewußten Anspruch auf Anerkennung dokumentiert. Ein Sitznischenportal erinnert an sächsische Einflüsse.

Market and church square are usually surrounded by the most stately of townhouses. Only the wealthiest, most highly privileged citizens were permitted to build and reside here. Generally they were well-respected merchants or leading master craftsmen, i.e. representatives of the bourgeoisie. Even in the Middle Ages this state of affairs had already been established in the imperial or free cities which were outside the jurisdiction of the rural nobility and the church domains. This model of a civic republic was subsequently strengthened in the Reformation. In terms of architecture this development manifested itself in a multitude of valuable Renaissance town houses. The house at 11 Kirchplatz in Perleberg also belongs to this category. It is a rendered building whose gable is decorated with fan-shaped tracery which illustrates a proud and assertive demand for recognition and respect. A recessed portal with seating niche suggests Saxonian influences.

in der Nähe/nearby:
Wohnhaus; Kirchplatz 9
1616
Wohnhaus; Mühlenstraße 7
1638
Wohnhaus; Schuhstraße 21
17. Jh.
Wohnhaus; Schuhstraße 23
17. Jh.
Wohnhaus; Schuhmarkt 1
17. Jh.

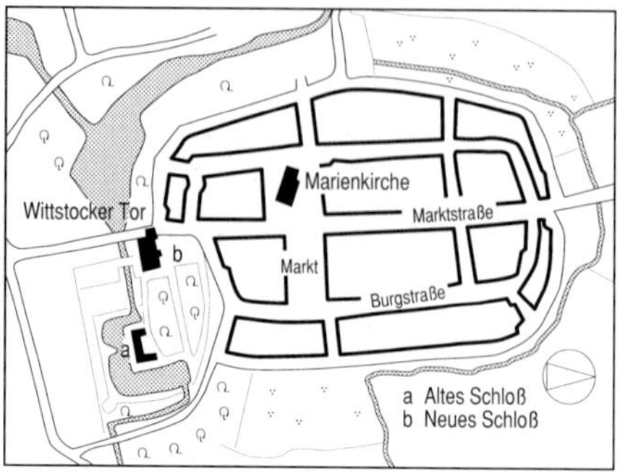

U 25 Stadtkern Freyenstein
1287

Die am nördlichen Rand der Prignitzer Hochfläche gelegene Kleinstadt, mit heute etwa 1400 Einwohnern, gehörte im 12. Jahrhundert zum Besitz der Havelberger Bischöfe. Der Ort war in dieser Zeit wohl an die slawischstämmigen mecklenburgischen Herren von Werle verlehnt und im 13. Jahrhundert als Grenzfeste mit dem Vordringen der brandenburgischen Markgrafen in die Prignitz mehrfach zerstört worden. 1287 legten die askanischen Markgrafen Otto und Conrad Freyenstein nördlich der Burganlage in einem fast elliptischen Stadtgrundriß auf einer Fläche von etwa 300 m × 400 m neu an. Dazu gehörte ein gitterförmiges Straßennetz und ein dazwischengespannter, langgestreckter Markt. Freyenstein erhielt als einzige Stadt der Prignitz Brandenburger Stadtrecht. Die gedrungene Pfarrkirche als frühgotische Feldsteinhalle mit vorgebautem quadratischem Westturm dominiert die ein- bis zweigeschossige Wohnbebauung des 18. und 19. Jahrhunderts, die sich als Fachwerkhäuser in Traufstellung und als geschlossene Reihe in der Marktstraße erhalten hat. Im Laufe der Jahrhunderte verlor die Stadt ihre ehemalige Bedeutung und war 1808 nur noch ein Flecken.

This little town at the edge of the Prignitz heights, with a present population of about 1,400, was a possession of the Havelland bishops in the twelfth century. At this time the place was probably invested to the Slavic Mecklenburg lords of Werle and in the thirteenth century was destroyed on numerous occasions as a result of its position as a border fortress when the princes of Brandenburg pushed forward into the Prignitz. In 1287 the Ascanian margraves Otto and Conrad Freyenstein rebuilt the town north of the castle on an almost elliptical ground plan covering about 300 m × 400 m. This included a grid of streets with an elongated market between them. Freyenstein was the only town in the Prignitz to be granted a Brandenburg charter. The squat parish church is an early Gothic rubble-stone hall with a square west tower in front of it, and dominates the one- and two-storey residential building dating from the eighteenth and nineteenth centuries; they are half-timbered houses placed eaves-on to the street and have survived as a complete row in Marktstrasse. The town lost its former significance in the course of the centuries and in 1808 was reduced to the status of minor town.

in der Nähe/nearby:
Schloß; Meyenburg
16. Jh. (1865 • Friedrich Adler)
Klosterkirche; Stepenitz
2. H. 13. Jh.

U 26 Altes Schloß
Freyenstein; Schloßpark
1556

Die aus Bayern zugewanderte Familie von Rohr, schon 1373 als die »Schloßgesessenen« genannt, stieg mit dem Eintritt in askanische Vasallität an die Spitze des Prignitzadels und trat in das Amt des Vogtes des »terra Prignitz« ein. Vermutlich an der Stelle einer ehemaligen Burg wurde das Alte Schloß als burgähnliche Dreiflügelanlage erbaut. Erhalten ist das jetzt als Heimatmuseum eingerichtete Nordende des Westflügels. Dieser viergeschossige Putzbau, ostseitig mit segmentbogigen Fenstern und Treppenturm, hat an der Stadtseite im Giebelfeld und an den dreigeschossigen flach gerundeten Erkern einen bemerkenswerten Terrakottaschmuck. Dieser erinnert an die mecklenburgischen Schlösser in Gadebusch und Wismar und stammt vermutlich aus der Werkstatt des Statius von Düren. Weitere Teile des Schlosses sind nur als Ruine erhalten. Das Schloß, seit 1974 als Standesamt und Museum genutzt, sowie der Park werden seit 1969 restauriert.

The von Rohr family were immigrants from Bavaria, named as early as 1373 as residents of the castle, and with their entry into Ascanian vassalry rose to the peak of Prignitz nobility and took over the office of steward of the «terra Prignitz». The Altes Schloss was built as a three-winged fortress-like complex, presumably on the site of a former castle. The northern end of the west wing has survived, and is now used as a local history museum. This four-storey rendered building, with segment-arched windows and staircase tower on the eastern side, has remarkable terra cotta decoration on the town side in the tympanum and on the three storeys of shallow-curving oriels. It is reminiscent of Mecklenburg palaces in Gadebusch and Wismar, and probably comes from the workshop of Statius von Düren. Other parts of the Schloss have survived only as ruins. The Schloss, used since 1974 as registry office and local history museum, and the park have been undergoing restoration since 1969.

in der Nähe/nearby:
Pfarrkirche St. Marien
Um 1300
Neues Schloß
A. 17. Jh.
Wittstocker Tor
14./15. Jh. (17. Jh. mit dem Neuen Schloß verbunden)

U 27 Dorfkirche
Wulfersdorf
Um 1520

Unverkennbar war beim Bau dieser Dorfkirche der Blick auf das Vorbild in Heiligengrabe gerichtet. Dort wurde 1512 die Heiliggrabkapelle eingeweiht, deren Westfassade die Wulfersdorfer um ein Blendengeschoß verkürzt nachbauten. Alt Krüssow und Falkenhagen kopierten diesen Giebel ebenso. Im Zuge der ausklingenden Gotik tritt hier wie beim Vorbild schon eine starke horizontale Prägung auf. Nicht mehr allein das Streben in der Senkrechten bestimmt die Gestaltung, sondern der vorrangig geschoßweise Zusammenhalt tritt in den Vordergrund. Der Turm schmückt sich sogar mit deutlichen Renaissanceformen, ist aber wohl auch erst in der zweiten Jahrhunderthälfte vollendet worden.

When this village church was built, it was unmistakably modeled on the Chapel of the Holy Sepulchre at Heiligengrabe which was consecrated In 1512. Its west façade was copied by the Wulfersdorfers, although one of the rows of the tracery was omitted. The same gable was also copied at Alt Krüssow and Falkenhagen. Here as in the original model, the façade is marked by a pronounced horizontal articulation as was typical of the late Gothic. The design is no longer dominated by an emphasis on the vertical alone; instead, attention is focussed primarily on the continuity of individual storeys. The tower is even decorated with obvious Renaissance elements, but then it was probably not completed before the second half of the century.

in der *Nähe/nearby:*
Wohnhaus; Wulfersdorf; Hof 38
Um 1800
Dorfkirche; Halenbeck
M. 17. Jh.
Dorfkirche; Alt Krüssow
Um 1520 (Turm um 1880)

U 28 Zisterzienser-Nonnenkloster
Heiligengrabe
Um 1300

Das auf Veranlassung des Markgrafen Otto 1287 gegründete Zisterzienser-Nonnenkloster in Heiligengrabe ist seit Mitte des 16. Jahrhunderts evangelisches Stift. Bereits im 13. Jahrhundert bestand hier eine Verehrungsstätte des Heiligen Grabes, die dem Ort auch den Namen gab. Die Stiftskirche als zentrales Bauwerk der ausgedehnten Anlage, in Mischbauweise um 1300 errichtet, ist ein gestreckter einschiffiger Rechteckbau mit Kreuzrippengewölbe und Strebepfeilern. Nördlich schließt die mittelalterliche Klausur in Backstein an. Sie erfuhr Umbauten im 15. und 17. bis 20. Jahrhundert, auch durch Friedrich August Stüler. Als Dreiflügelanlage umschließt sie einen vierflügeligen Kreuzgang. Die westlich anschließende Heiliggrabkapelle, ein Backsteinbau mit reich dekoriertem Stufengiebel, wurde 1512 geweiht.

The Cistercian nunnery in Heiligengrabe founded at the behest of Margrave Otto in 1287 has been a Protestant foundation since the mid sixteenth century. Even in the thirteenth century the Holy Sepulchre (Heiliges Grab) was worshipped here, giving the place its name. The collegiate church is the central building in the extensive complex, built in composite construction c. 1300. It is a long, single-aisled rectangular building with rib vaulting and buttresses. The medieval brick enclosure is adjacent to the north. This was rebuilt in the fifteenth and seventeenth to twentieth centuries, also by Friedrich August Stüler. It has three wings enclosing a cloister with four walks. The Chapel of the Sacred Tomb is adjacent to the west, a brick building with a lavishly decorated steped gable, consecrated in 1512.

in der Nähe/nearby:
Dorfkirche
Um 1500 (verändert 2. H. 19. Jh.)
Oberschule; Wittstocker Straße 13
1950 • Siegfried Fehr

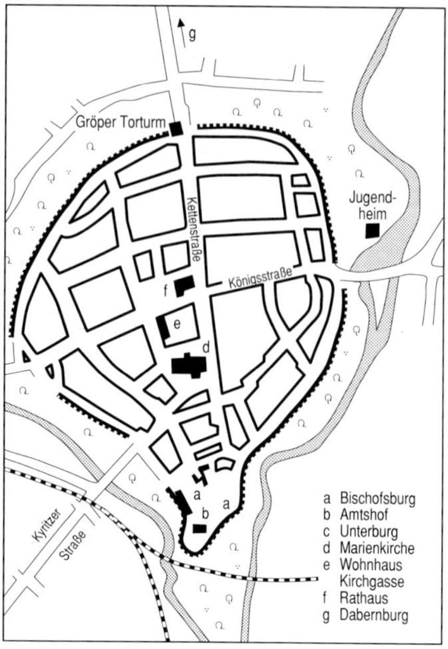

U 29 Stadtkern Wittstock
1248

Dem bereits 946 genannten Ort wird nach einer Kaiserurkunde von 1150 der Beginn der frühdeutschen Besiedlung in der Mark zugeschrieben. Heute hat er etwa 14 400 Einwohner. Stendaler Stadtrecht erhielt Wittstock im Jahre 1248. Seit etwa 1800 ist Wittstock wichtigste Textilstadt in der Prignitz. Namen wie die »Kettenstraße« und der »Bleichwall« weisen auf das alte Tuchmacherhandwerk hin. Der birnenförmige Stadtgrundriß entstand mit der planmäßigen Erweiterung der Siedlung nördlich der Burg um 1240. Das gitterförmige Straßennetz umschließt den rechteckigen Markt. Bemerkenswert sind die Gebäude und Mauern der Bischofsburg aus dem 18. Jahrhundert, die weitgehend erhaltene Stadtmauer aus dem 13. Jahrhundert mit dem Gröper Torturm, das Rathaus und die zweigeschossigen Fachwerkhäuser aus der zweiten Hälfte des 18. und der ersten Hälfte des 19. Jahrhunderts.

The place was first mentioned in 946 and according to an imperial document dated 1150 is ascribed to the initial early German building period in the Mark. Today it has about 14,400 inhabitants. Wittstock was granted a Stendal charter in 1248. It has been the most important textile town in the Prignitz since about 1800. Names like «Kettenstrasse» (warp street) and «Bleichwall» (bleach rampart) suggest the ancient craft of fabric making. The pear-shaped outline of the town was established when the settlement was extended to plan north of the castle c. 1240. The grid of streets surrounds the rectangular market. Notable features are the walls and buildings of the eighteenth century bishop's castle, the largely surviving thirteenth century town wall with the Gröper Torturm, the town hall and the two-storey half-timbered houses dating from the second half of the eighteenth and first half of the nineteenth centuries.

in der Nähe/nearby:
Dorfkirche; Groß Haßlow-Klein Haßlow
M. 19. Jh.
Wohnhaus; Jabel; Hof 7, Hof 9 und Hof 21
18.Jh.

U 30 Rathaus
Wittstock; Markt
1905

Beim Betreten des Marktes zieht das Rathaus als freistehendes, das Ensemble mit seiner giebelgeschmückten Westseite beherrschendes Bauwerk sofort die Blicke auf sich. 1905 wurde es unter Verwendung von Teilen eines mittelalterlichen Baues errichtet. Die Rathausgiebel in ihrer spätgotischen Stilfassung schmücken das in seinem Grundriß nahezu unveränderte, aber durch spätere Bauten ergänzte Marktensemble. Der massig wirkende, im Gegensatz zum Backstein-Baukörper verputzte Turmaufbau wird lediglich im unteren Bereich an den Ecken mit lisenenartigen Ziegelblenden betont. Der schlankere obere Teil trägt eine geschwungene Haube. Das Eingangsportal an der Südseite ist mit einem dreieckigen Schmuckbalkon überdacht. Die in den Neubau einbezogene Gerichtslaube stammt vom Anfang des 15. Jahrhunderts.

The town hall is an immediately arresting feature of the market place. It stands isolated and dominates the rest of the buildings with the gable decoration of its west side. It was built in 1905, using parts of a medieval building. The late Gothic style of the town hall gables enhances the entire market ensemble. Its ground plan is unchanged, although later buildings have been added. The massive-looking top of the tower, rendered in contrast with the brick body of the building, is articulated with pilaster-strip-like tiling only at the corners of its lower section. The more slender upper section has a curved cupola. The entrance portal on the south side is roofed with a triangular decorative balcony. The court area included in the new building dates from the early fifteenth century.

in der Nähe/nearby:
Fachwerkhäuser; Königsstraße, Heilig-Geist-Straße
2. H. 18. bis 19. Jh.
Jugendklub; Am Dossedeich
1983 • Karl-Heinz Rabe
Wohnhaus mit Läden; Am Markt, Kirchgasse
1989 • Bernd Kaiser

U 31 Pfarrkirche St. Marien
Wittstock; Kirchplatz
13. bis 15. Jahrhundert

Die kreuzrippengewölbte Hallenkirche mit breitem Westbau hat einen geraden Chorschluß mit Blendengiebel, ähnlich den Marienkirchen in Prenzlau und Neubrandenburg. Der beeindruckende dreischiffige Backsteinbau entstand in mehreren Bauphasen zwischen dem 13. und 15. Jahrhundert. Das vierjochige Langhaus wurde nach 1451 im System mit einem fünfjochigen Chor, 1484 an der Nordseite mit zweigeschossigen Kapellenbauten und 1498 mit einer Sakristei an der Südseite des Chores ergänzt. Die durch die Anbauten verdeckten Portale gehören zum Ursprungsbau des 13. Jahrhunderts. Die Turmhaube stammt aus dem Jahre 1704. Im Inneren sind unter der reichen Ausstattung die zwei aufeinandergesetzten spätgotischen Schnitzaltäre bemerkenswert, der untere entstand 1530 in der Werkstatt Claus Berg.

This rib-vaulted hall church with broad west building has a straight choir termination with false gable, similarly to the churches dedicated to Mary in Prenzlau and Neubrandenburg. The impressive brick building with nave and two aisles was built in several phases from the thirteenth to the fifteenth century. The nave has four bays and after 1451 was systematically extended by a five-bayed choir, in 1484 by two-storey chapels on the north side and in 1498 by a sacristy on the south side of the choir. The portals are covered by the additional buildings, but were part of the original thirteenth century church. The cupola dates from 1704. The interior is lavishly furnished, with two Gothic carved altars placed one above the other; the lower was made in 1530 in Claus Berg's workshops.

in der Nähe/nearby:
Bischofsburg (Museum); Amtshof
14. Jh.

U 32 Gröper Torturm
Wittstock; Kettenstraße
14. und 16. Jahrhundert

Die mittelalterliche Altstadt ist von einer weitgehend erhaltenen, in Feldstein begonnenen und später in Backstein ergänzten Stadtmauer aus dem 13. bis 16. Jahrhundert mit halbrunden und rechteckigen Weichhäusern, Wall und Graben umgeben. Auf der in Richtung Freyenstein führenden Straße findet die Altstadt mit dem Gröper Torturm im Norden ihren Abschluß. Der im 14. Jahrhundert errichtete gotische Backsteinbau über einer spitzbogigen Durchfahrt hatte ursprünglich stadtein- und stadtauswärts weisende vier- bzw. dreigeschossige Staffelgiebel, die in die im Jahre 1503 erfolgte Erhöhung des Bauwerkes einbezogen wurden. Der abschließende Maßwerkfries und das Pyramidendach stammen aus dem 19. Jahrhundert.

The medieval old town is surrounded by a thirteenth to sixteenth century town wall, started in rubble stone and later completed in brick, with semicircular and rectangular towers, rampart and moat. The northern conclusion of the old town is the Gröper Turm on the road leading to Freyenstein. This fourteenth century brick building over a gateway with a pointed arch originally had three- to four-storey steped gables on the sides facing into and out of town, but these were included in the body of the building when its height was increased in 1503. The tracery at the top and pyramid roof date from the nineteenth century.

in der Nähe/nearby:
Stadtbefestigung
13./14. Jh.
Heiliggeistkirche; Kettenstraße
14./15. Jh.
Erinnerungsmal; Wall
Nach 1813 • G. Marschall
Dabernburg (Heideturm); nördlich der Altstadt
1. H. 15. Jh.

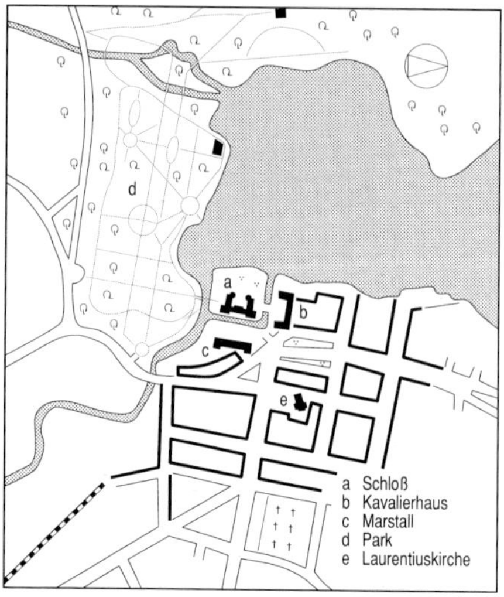

U 33 Stadtkern Rheinsberg
1300

Vermutet wird, daß im Zuge frühdeutscher Besiedlung sich hier Bauern vom Niederrhein an der Ostseite des Grienerick-Sees niederließen. Die bereits um 1300 befestigte Stadt war wohl schon 1291 im Besitz eines arnsteinischen Vasallengeschlechtes, das zur Abwehr werlisch-mecklenburgischer Ansprüche die Stadt zusätzlich befestigen mußte. 1599 erhielt Rheinsberg Marktrechte. In der Mitte der Altstadt ist die im Kern frühgotische, 1568 erweiterte Pfarrkirche St. Laurentius erhalten. Die Stadt, 1733 mit Schloß und Gebiet von König Friedrich Wilhelm I. für den Kronprinzen Friedrich gekauft, wurde nach dem Stadtbrand von 1740 nach Plänen von Georg Wenzeslaus v. Knobelsdorff neu aufgebaut. Auf regelmäßigem Grundriß im rechtwinkligen Straßengitter mit Markt und Kirchplatz entstanden elf Karrees mit barocken Typenhäusern; sie sind im wesentlichen erhalten. Kurt Tucholsky fand hier 1910 Anregungen für seinen Roman »Rheinsberg – Ein Bilderbuch für Verliebte«. Wie im Roman, so auch im Leben, ist die ausgedehnte Seenlandschaft nördlich der Stadt ein beliebtes Ferien- und Erholungsgebiet.

It is presumed that in the course of early German settlement peasants from the Lower Rhine established themselves on the eastern side of the Grienerick Lake. The town was already fortified around 1300 and was probably in the possession of an Arnstein vassal tribe in 1291; they had to build additional town fortifications to ward off Werlish-Mecklenburg claims. Rheinsberg was granted market rights in 1599. In the middle of the old town is the parish church of St. Laurentius, essentially early Gothic, extended in 1568. The town, bought in 1733 with castle and territory by King Friedrich Wilhelm I for Crown Prince Friedrich, was rebuilt after the town fire of 1740 to plans by Georg Wenzeslaus von Knobelsdorff. It consisted of eleven carrées on a regular ground plan with a network of streets at right angles, with market place and church square, and baroque houses in standard types; most of them have survived. In 1910 Kurt Tucholsky found inspiration here for his book «Rheinsberg – ein Bilderbuch für Verliebte». In life as in the novel, the extensive area of lakes north of the town is popular for holidays and recreation.

in der Nähe/nearby:
Pfarrkirche; Lindow
1751-55 • Georg Christoph Berger

U 34 Schloß Rheinsberg
Rheinsberg
1734-40 • Johann Gottfried Kemmeter, Georg Wenzeslaus v. Knobelsdorff

Das aus einer Wasserburg von 1566 hervorgegangene Schloß ist heute Zeugnis früher friderizianischer Architektur. Die heruntergekommene Burg bauten 1734 Kemmeter und von 1737 bis 1740 Knobelsdorff um. Es entstand eine in ihrer Leichtigkeit und in ihrer Harmonie mit der Landschaft bewundernswerte zweigeschossige Dreiflügelanlage. Der landschaftliche Bezug erhöht sich durch den zur Gartenseite geöffneten Ehrenhof mit Säulenkolonnaden und Rundtürmen an den Giebeln, die den Blick über den Grienerick-See zum Park freigeben. Der Mittelrisalit mit Figurenattika und Eingang sowie die beiden 1786 ergänzten Eckpavillons weisen zur Stadtseite. Durch die Bildhauer Johann Carl Scheffler und Friedrich Christian Glume sowie den Maler Antoine Pesne wurde Knobelsdorff meisterlich ergänzt. Die Dekoration der Innenräume aus der Zeit um 1737/40 und ihre teilweise frühklassizistische Veränderung von 1762 und 1769 durch Carl Gotthard Langhans und Carl Wilhelm Hennert ist überwiegend erhalten. Den Schloßpark, seit 1734 durch Knobelsdorff und Friedrich Sello geometrisch angelegt, gestaltete seit 1744 im wesentlichen Carl Wilhelm Hennert zum Landschaftspark mit architektonischen und plastischen Staffagen um.

The Schloss developed from a moated castle dating from 1566 and is an example of the architecture of the early period of Frederick the Great. The castle was in decline, and was rebuilt by Kemmeter in 1734 and from 1737 to 1740 by Knobelsdorff. The two-storey building with three sections they produced is admirable in its lightness and harmony with the landscape. This relationship with the landscape is heightened by the courtyard, open on the garden side with colonnades and round towers on the gable ends, giving a view over the Grienerick lake to the park. The central projection with attica with statues and entrance and the two corner pavilions completed in 1786 face the town. Knobelsdorff was complemented in a masterly fashion by sculptors Friedrich Christian Glume and Johann Carl Scheffler, and painter Antoine Pesne. The decoration of the interior rooms dating from c. 1737/40 and the partial early classical modification of 1762 and 1769 by Carl Gotthard Langhans and Carl Wilhelm Hennert has largely survived. The park, laid out geometrically from 1734 by Knobelsdorff and Friedrich Sello, was redesigned from 1744 largely by Carl Wilhelm Hennert as a landscaped park with architectural and sculptural staffage.

in der Nähe/nearby:
Kavalierhaus; Schloßgelände
1738 • Knobelsdorff (umgestaltet 1774 • Hennert)
Marstall; Schloßgelände
1738 • Knobelsdorff (umgestaltet 1764 • Hennert)

U 35 Schloß Fürstenberg
Fürstenberg
1741 • Christoph Julius Löwe

Fürstenberg, an der Grenze zwischen dem markbrandenburgischen Gransee und dem pommerschen Stargard um 1250 an der Havel im Schutze einer Burg gegründet, war von 1348 bis 1952 mecklenburgisch. Nach dem Brand von 1807 wurde der mittelalterliche Stadtkern begradigt und teilweise durch den Landbaumeister Friedrich Wilhelm Dunkelberg mit klassizistischen Putzbauten ergänzt. Schlichte Fachwerkhäuser aus der gleichen Zeit vervollständigen das Ensemble. Das Schloß errichtete 1741-52 Christoph Julius Löwe als eine monumentale zweigeschossige Dreiflügelanlage. Es wurde 1913 von dem hannoverschen Architekten Brander zum Sanatorium umgebaut. Die Schweifgiebel und die dekorativen historisierenden Rokoko-Ornamente über dem Mittelrisalit des Hauptbaues und an den Stirnseiten der Flügel stammen ebenfalls aus seiner Hand.

Fürstenberg, on the border between the Gransee in Mark Brandenburg and Stargard in Pomerania, was founded c. 1250 by the Havel under the protection of a castle, and belonged to Mecklenburg from 1348 to 1952. After the fire of 1807 the streets in the medieval town centre were straightened, and some classical rendered buildings were added by land architect Friedrich Wilhelm Dunkelberg. The ensemble is completed by plain half-timbered houses dating from the same period. The Schloss was built by Christoph Julius Löwe from 1741-52 as a monumental two-storey complex in three sections. In 1913 it was redesigned as a sanatorium by Brander, a Hannover architect who was also responsible for the curved gable and decorative historicizing rococo ornament on the main building and the faces of the wings.

in der Nähe/nearby:
Pfarrkirche; Fürstenberg
1845-48 • Friedrich Wilhelm Buttel

U 36 Mahn- und Gedenkstätte
Fürstenberg-Ravensbrück
1956-59 • Ludwig Deiters

Zum Gedenken an die in der Zeit von 1939 bis 1945 im Frauenkonzentrationslager Ravensbrück gefangenen 132 000 Frauen, von denen 92 000 ermordet und zu Tode gequält wurden, mahnt diese Stätte. 1956-59 errichteten Ludwig Deiters, Hans Grotewohl, Kurt Tausendschön und Hugo Namslauer diese Anlage am Schwedt-See. Der große, ruhig gestaltete, zum See hin geöffnete Freiraum wird nach Osten begrenzt durch die Lagermauer mit den Namen der dreiundzwanzig Heimatländer der Gefangenen. Dahinter befand sich das Barackenlager. Eine südlich in den See hineinragende Plattform nimmt die von Will Lammert geschaffene Skulptur zweier Frauen auf obeliskartigem Postament auf, Sinnbild für Leiden und Widerstand. Hier wurde die Asche der Ermordeten ins Wasser gestreut. An der Zufahrtsstraße steht die von Fritz Cremer geschaffene Plastik »Die Frauen von Ravensbrück«. Das Lagermuseum befindet sich im ehemaligen Zellenbau.

This monument commemorates the 132,000 women imprisoned in the Ravensbrück concentration camp from 1939 to 1945, of whom 92,000 were murdered and tortured to death. Ludwig Deiters, Hans Grotewohl, Kurt Tausendschön and Hugo Namslauer built this complex on the Schwedtsee from 1956-9. The peaceful open space opening to the lake is bordered on the eastern side by the camp wall with the names of the twenty-three countries from which the prisoners came. Behind this was the hutted camp. A platform jutting into the lake to the south carries Willi Lammert's sculpture of two women on an obelisk-like pedestal, a symbol of suffering and resistance. Here the ashes of the murdered women were strewn on the water. On the access road is Fritz Cremer's sculpture «Die Frauen von Ravensbrück». The camp museum is in the former cell building.

in der Nähe/nearby:
»Festes Haus«; Badingen
2. H. 16. Jh.

U 37 Stadtkern Neuruppin
1256

Mitten im Wald- und Seengebiet der »Ruppiner Schweiz« gelegen, zählt Neuruppin mit 27 000 Einwohnern zu den größeren Städten im Norden der Mark Brandenburg. Namen wie Karl Friedrich Schinkel, Theodor Fontane oder der für die Herstellung der »Neuruppiner Bilderbogen« bekannten Familie Kühn sind mit dieser Stadt eng verbunden. Durch die Grafen von Arnstein vermutlich Anfang des 13. Jahrhunderts begonnen, wurde die planmäßige Stadtanlage mit der Verleihung des Stendaler Stadtrechts 1256 abgeschlossen. Durch den verheerenden Brand 1787 verlor Neuruppin zwei Drittel seiner Bauten, darunter 401 Bürgerhäuser. Der Wiederaufbau in den Jahren 1788/96 prägte auf besondere Weise den heranwachsenden Schinkel. Regelmäßige Karrees, drei rechteckige Plätze, verbunden durch eine breite Hauptstraße mit rechtwinklig kreuzenden Nebenstraßen, bestimmen nach einem Plan von Bernhard Matthias Brasch das neue Stadtbild. Die Neubauten folgen bereits dem frühklassizistischen Zopfstil. Die 25 km lange Seenkette sowie ausgedehnte Natur-und Landschaftsschutzgebiete begründen den landschaftlichen Reiz der nahen und weiteren Umgebung der Stadt.

Neuruppin is centrally placed among the woods and lakes of the «Neuruppin Switzerland». It has 27,000 inhabitants and is one of the larger towns in the north of the Mark Brandenburg. Names like Karl Friedrich Schinkel, Theodor Fontane or the Kühn family, noted for the manufacture of the «Neuruppiner Bilderbogen», are closely associated with this town. The planned town was presumably begun in the early thirteenth century, and concluded with the granting of a Stendal charter in 1256. Neuruppin lost two thirds of its buildings, including 401 citizens' houses, in the devastating fire of 1787. Rebuilding from 1788/96 made a particular impact on the young Schinkel. Regular carrées, three rectangular squares connected by a broad main street with side streets crossing at right angles, determined the image of the new town, designed by Bernhard Matthias Brasch. The new buildings use the early classical rococo style. The 25 km chain of lakes and extensive tracts of countryside under protection for its outstanding natural beauty are the principal attractions of the immediate and further vicinity of the town.

in der Nähe/nearby:
Wohnhaus; Alt Ruppin; Am Zermützelsee
1937 • Hans Scharoun
Schloß Wustrau
M. 18. Jh. (Anbauten 19. Jh.)

U 38 Pfarrkirche St. Marien
Neuruppin; Kirchplatz
1801-04 • Philipp Bernhard Berson, Carl Ludwig Engel

Der langgestreckte klassizistische Putzbau anstelle der mit dem Brand 1787 zerstörten mittelalterlichen Kirche hat vor allem mit seinem turmhaft aufragenden, ovalen Kuppelbau über dem Giebelportikus eine städtebaulich herausragende Wirkung. Die quergelagerte Gestalt des sich nach beiden Seiten des Turmes erstreckenden Saales mit zweigeschossigen Emporen ist für jene Zeit nicht ungewöhnlich, sie entspricht im Zeitalter der Aufklärung der Idee der protestantischen Predigtkirche. Der Raum nimmt den Kanzelaltar und die Orgel auf. Das Interieur stammt aus dem 15. bis 19. Jahrhundert, u. a. das silberne Altarkruzifix aus dem Jahre 1476 sowie das Gemälde »Fußwaschung Christi« aus dem Jahre 1853 von Wilhelm Gentz.

This long classical rendered building on the site of the medieval church destroyed by fire in 1787 makes an outstanding impact principally because of its towerlike oval dome over the gabled portico. The tranverse nature of the building on either side of the tower is not unusual for the period, representing the notion of the Protestant preaching church in the Age of Enlightenment. The interior has two tiers of galleries, and contains a pulpit altar and the organ. The interior furnishings date from the fifteenth to nineteenth centuries, and include the silver altar crucifix dating from 1476 and the painting «Christ washing the disciples' feet» dating from 1853.

in der Nähe/nearby:
Karl-Friedrich-Schinkel-Denkmal; Kirchplatz
1883 • Max Wiese
Predigerwitwenhaus; Fischbänkenstraße 8
1736
Siechenhauskapelle; Siechenhausstraße 4
1401

U 39 Wohnhaus
Neuruppin; August-Bebel-Straße 14-15
1788/90 • Bernhard Matthias Brasch

Mit dem Wiederaufbau der Stadt nach dem Brand von 1787 wurde Neuruppin durch die einheitliche städtebauliche Planung und unter der Oberaufsicht des Berliner Baudepartements neben Potsdam zum bedeutendsten Beispiel spätbarock-frühklassizistischer Stadtbaukunst in der Mark. Besonders der Wohnhausbau, der fast den gesamten zerstörten Bestand an Fachwerkhäusern ersetzen mußte, prägt noch heute das architektonische Gesicht der Stadt. Während aus der Zeit vor dem Brand nur noch wenige Fachwerkhäuser im Süden der Stadt erhalten blieben, ist die 1788/98 errichtete, durchgängig zweigeschossige, traufständige Wohnbebauung massiv ausgeführt. Die Putzbauten tragen zum Teil Fassadengliederung und ornamentalen Dekor. Bemerkenswert ist das Wohnhaus August-Bebel-Straße 14-15. Die einheitliche Fassade des Doppelhauses wird gegliedert durch 16 Fensterachsen, Seitenrisalite mit korinthischen Kolossalpilastern beleben die lange Front und sind bekrönt mit einer Vasenattika. Heute ist das Gebäude als Heimatmuseum genutzt.

When the town was rebuilt after the fire of 1787 Neuruppin, because of uniform urban planning under the supervision of the Berlin building department, became with Potsdam the most important example of late-baroque, early-classical urban architecture in the Mark. Domestic architecture in particular, as almost all the half-timbered earlier buildings had been destroyed, still puts its stamp on the image of the town. Some half-timbered buildings survived in the south of the town. The domestic buildings built 1788/98 are very solid, all two storeys high and set with their eaves to the street. They are rendered, and some of them have articulated façades and ornament. The house at 14-15 August-Bebel-Strasse is remarkable. It is a very large semi-detached house articulated by sixteen axes of windows, and projections with Corinthian colossal pilasters topped with an attica with urns enliven each side of the long façade.

in der Nähe/nearby:
Gymnasium; Karl-Marx-Straße
1790 • Bernhard Matthias Brasch
Spitalhof mit »Uphus«; Siechenhausstraße
Um 1700
Klosterkirche St. Trinitas; Niemöllerplatz
E. 13. Jh. (rest. 1836-41 • Karl Friedrich Schinkel)

U 40 Tempelgarten
Neuruppin; Präsidentenstraße
1732-36 • Georg Wenzeslaus v. Knobelsdorff

Die Anlage des Tempelgartens geht auf den Neuruppiner Aufenthalt des Kronprinzen und späteren König Friedrich II. zurück. Bereits 1688 war die Stadt zu einer der größten Garnisonen in der Mark ausgebaut. Hier wurde dem Kronprinzen Friedrich 1732, schon zwei Tage nach seiner Entlassung aus der Küstriner Haft, als Obrist das Kommando über ein Infanterieregiment übertragen. In diesen für ihn recht sorglosen Jahren gab er sich viel den Musen hin, und für ihn wurde auf dem westlichen Stadtwall der Tempelgarten angelegt. Georg Wenzeslaus v. Knobelsdorff – er gehörte schon damals zum Umkreis des Kronprinzen – schuf hier 1735 mit dem Apollotempel sein frühestes Bauwerk. Der ursprünglich offene Rundtempel mit Kuppeldach über einer Grotte wurde 1791 verändert. Dessen Decken malte 1830 Wilhelm Gentz aus. 1853-56 wurde der Park umgestaltet und eine maurische Villa nach Entwurf von Karl v. Diebitsch errichtet. Zur gleichen Zeit fanden viele barocke Skulpturen Aufstellung. Drei Fürstenstandbilder von 1718-19, Soliman III., Karl V. und Philipp von Spanien, stammen aus dem Benjamin-Thomae-Umkreis und gelten als Hauptwerke sächsischer Barockplastik.

The Temple Garden was laid out as a result of time spent in Neuruppin by the Crown Prince, later Frederick II. By 1688 the town was already one of the largest garrisons of the Mark. Crown Prince Frederick was given command of a regiment of infantry with the rank of colonel here in 1732, just two days after he was released from detention in Küstrin. These were carefree years for him. He was much devoted to the Muses, and the Temple Garden on the western town rampart was laid out for him. Georg Wenzeslaus von Knobelsdorff – already part of the prince's entourage – built the temple of Apollo here as his first building in 1735. It was originally an open circular temple with domed roof over a grotto, altered in 1791. Its ceilings were painted by Wilhelm Gentz in 1830. The park was redesigned from 1853-6 and a Moorish villa built to plans by Karl von Diebitsch. The many baroque sculptures were set up at the same time. Three statues of princes dating from 1718-9, Soliman III, Charles V and Philip of Spain, are by the circle around Benjamin Thomae and are considered major works of Saxon baroque sculpture.

in der Nähe/nearby:
Theodor-Fontane-Denkmal; Franz-Künstler-Straße
1907 • Max Wiese
Geburtshaus Fontanes (Löwenapotheke); Karl-Marx-Straße 84
Gegen 1800

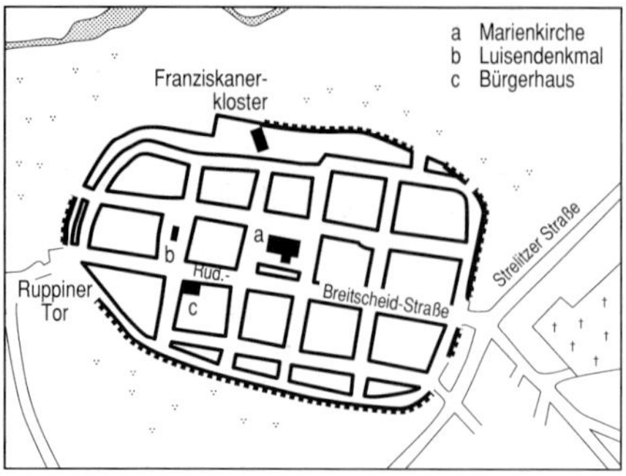

U 41 Stadtkern Gransee
1262

Mit Sicherheit ist anzunehmen, daß das Land um die heutige Kreisstadt bereits in den Jahren 1216/17, da Zehdenick als nordöstlichster Eckpunkt des Archidiakonats Brandenburg genannt wird, im frühdeutschen Herrschaftsraum lag. Der west-östlich ausgerichtete Altstadtgrundriß in Gitterform mit Parallelstraßen und Marktplatz weist das gereifte Stadium hochmittelalterlichen Städtebaues auf. 1262 erhielt Gransee durch den Markgrafen Johann von Brandenburg Stadtrecht. Nach dem Stadtbrand 1711 wurde das Straßennetz begradigt und der Neue Markt, heute Schinkelplatz, angelegt. Die Stadtmauer aus Feldstein vom Ende des 13. und Anfang des 14. Jahrhunderts reicht bis zur eindrucksvollen Höhe von sechs Metern. Mauer und mehrere Weichhäuser sind in großen Teilen erhalten. Weitere Bauteile, wie der Pulverturm aus dem 15. Jahrhundert, ein Rundturm aus Feld- und Backstein mit Zinnenkranz und orthogonalem Spitzhelm sowie am westlichen Stadteingang der Ruppiner Torturm aus Backstein vom zweiten Viertel des 15. Jahrhunderts, ergänzen das Befestigungswerk. Die Wohnhäuser, ein- und zweigeschossige Traufhäuser, stammen im Kern aus dem 18. Jahrhundert.

It can be assumed with certainty that the territory around the present district centre was under early German rule as early as 1216/7, as Zehdenick is named as the north-easternmost corner point of the archdiocese of Brandenburg. The old town is laid out in grid form with parallel streets and market place, an example of the mature stage of urban planning in the high Middle Ages. Gransee was granted a charter by Margrave Johann of Brandenburg in 1262. After the fire of 1711 the network of streets was straightened and the Neuer Markt, now Schinkelplatz, laid out. The rubble-stone town wall dates from the late thirteenth and early fourteenth centuries and attains the impressive height of six metres. The wall and several towers have survived to a large extent. Other buildings like the fifteenth century powder tower, a round tower in brick and rubble stone with battlements and orthogonal spire, and also the Ruppin gate tower in brick at the western entrance to the town, dating from the second half of the fifteenth century, complete the fortifications. The residential buildings are essentially eighteenth century, of one and two storeys and set with their eaves to the street.

in der Nähe/nearby:
Schloß; Hoppenrade
1724 (A. 19. Jh. Aufstockung)
Schloß; Meseberg
1738
Dorfkirche; Altlüdersdorf
1702
Schloß; Dannenwalde
17. Jh. (erweitert 1788)

U 42 Luisendenkmal
Gransee; Schinkelplatz
1811 • Karl Friedrich Schinkel

Anlaß zum Bau des Denkmals war die Übernachtung des Trauerzuges mit dem Sarg der Königin Luise von Preußen am 25./26. Juli 1810 auf dem Weg vom Schloß Hohenzieritz nach Berlin-Charlottenburg und ihre Aufbahrung in Gransee. Wohl gleichzeitig mit dem nicht zur Ausführung gedachten Idealentwurf für eine gotische Grabkapelle für Königin Luise im Charlottenburger Schloßpark entstand 1810-11 Schinkels Entwurf für das Luisendenkmal in Gransee. Dieser romantische Entwurf, ein Sarkophag unter einem Baldachin in neugotischer Architektur, wurde bis auf den Sockel ganz in Eisenguß durch die königliche Eisengießerei ausgeführt und am 19. Oktober 1811 auf dem nach der Königin benannten Luisenplatz eingeweiht. Eine weitere Arbeit Schinkels zu Ehren der verstorbenen Königin war die ebenfalls in Eisenguß vorgesehene, aber nicht ausgeführte Luisenpforte in Paretz.

This monument was built to commemorate the fact that the funeral procession accompanying the coffin of Queen Luise of Prussia stayed the night here on 25/26 July 1810 on its way from Schloss Hohenzieritz to Berlin-Charlottenburg and her lying-in-state in Gransee. Schinkel's design for the monument to Luise in Gransee was conceived in 1810-1, probably at the same time as the ideal design for a Gothic funerary chapel for Queen Luise in the park at Charlottenburg, an idea that was never executed. Schinkel's romantic design, a sarcophagus under a baldacchino in neo-Gothic architecture, was made, with the exception of the base, entirely in cast iron in the royal iron foundry and dedicated on 19 October 1811 in Luisenplatz, which had been named after the queen. Another work by Schinkel in honour of the dead queen was the Luisenpforte in Paretz, also to have been in cast iron, but never executed.

in der Nähe/nearby:
Marienkirche; Kirchplatz
14.-15. Jh.
Franziskanerkloster; Am Klosterplatz
1. H. 14. Jh.
Bürgerhaus; Rudolf-Breitscheid-Straße 59
1. H. 18. Jh.

U 43 Zisterzienser-Nonnenkloster
Zehdenick; im Südosten der Stadt
13. bis 15. Jahrhundert

Das 1216 erstmals erwähnte Zehdenick, vermutlich zu jener Zeit bereits nordöstlicher Burgbezirksmittelpunkt der askanischen Markgrafen, war im städtischen Wachstum begünstigt durch die sich am Havelübergang berührenden Straßen von Ruppin, Prenzlau, Berlin und dem Oderraum. In dieser Landstadt mit einem Grundriß von 500 m × 500 m gründeten die Markgrafen Johann I. und Otto III. im Jahre 1249 nach dem zweitältesten Hostienwunder in der Mark das Zisterzienserinnen-Kloster. Mit dem Übertritt Brandenburgs zum Protestantismus wurde es 1540 in ein adliges Damenstift umgewandelt. Nach starker Zerstörung durch den Stadtbrand 1801 sind aus dem 13. Jahrhundert Teile der Nordmauer und des Chores, von der Klausur die eindrucksvolle Ruine des Ostflügels und aus dem 14./15. Jahrhundert der Nordflügel der Klausur, Reste des Westflügels sowie im Südosten die sogenannte Schule erhalten.

Zehdenick was first mentioned in 1216, and presumably at the time was already the north-easternmost centre of the fortifications of the Ascanian margraves. It grew as a town because the roads from Ruppin, Prenzlau, Berlin and the Oder area met at the Havel crossing. Margraves Johann I and Otto II founded the Cistercian nunnery after the second oldest miracle of the host in the Mark in 1249, and built it in this country town with a ground plan of 500 m × 500 m. The nunnery was transformed into a home for gentlewomen in 1540, when Brandenburg became Protestant. After severe damage in the town fire of 1801, thirteenth century sections of the north wall and the choir, the impressive ruins of the east walk of the cloister and from the fourteenth and fifteenth centuries the north walk of the cloister, remains of the west walk and the so-called school to the south-east have survived.

in der Nähe/nearby:
Amtshaus; westlich des Klosters
Um 1750
Schloß (Altersheim); nördlich der Stadt
18. und 19. Jh.
Rathaus
Nach 1801

U 44 Denkmal der Schlacht von Fehrbellin
Hakenberg; Chaussee Fehrbellin–Nauen
1800

Zur Erinnerung an die Schlacht von Fehrbellin, in der am 28. Juni 1675 das kleine kurbrandenburgische Heer die in Mannschaft und Artillerie weit überlegenen schwedischen Truppen in die Flucht schlug, wurde über hundert Jahre später an der Chaussee von Fehrbellin nach Nauen eine axial orientierte Denkmal-Anlage errichtet. Vom 1800 unmittelbar an der Straße aufgestellten umzäunten Postament mit Vasenaufsatz führt eine Lindenallee zum säulenförmigen, 1875 auf einem künstlichen Hügel errichteten Aussichtsturm. Von der einhundertvierzehn Stufen hohen Plattform öffnet sich der Blick in das weite Luchgebiet. Die Gedenktafel und die monumentale Marmornachbildung von Andreas Schlüters Büste Kurfürst Friedrich-Wilhelms von Brandenburg am Sockel sind 1879 von August Wolff gefertigt. Ebenfalls von Wolff ausgeführt ist der den Aussichtsturm bekrönende Bronzenachguß der Siegesgöttin Viktoria von Christian Daniel Rauch.

In memory of the battle of Fehrbellin, in which the small army of the Elector of Brandenburg put Swedish troops, far superior in manpower and artillery, to flight on 28 June 1675, an axially oriented monument was built beside the road from Fehrbellin to Nauen over a hundred years later. An avenue of limes leads from the pedestal with urn erected in 1800 directly on the side of the road to the viewing tower built in 1875 on an artificial mound. There is a view reaching far into the marshland from the platform to which one hundred and fourteen steps lead. The memorial tablet and monumental marble copy of Andreas Schlüter's bust of Elector Friedrich Wilhelm of Brandenburg on the plinth were made by August Wolff in 1879. Wolff was also responsible for the bronze cast of Christian Daniel Rauch's victory goddess on the top of the viewing tower.

in der Nähe/nearby:
Dorfkirche; Tarmow
1835 • Schinkel-Schule

U 45 Schloß Oranienburg
Oranienburg; Schloßplatz (Platz des Friedens)
1651 • Johann Gregor Memhardt, Michael Matthias Smids

Bötzow, vermutlich ohne spätslawische Vorgängeranlage, 1216 als Burgward genannt, war Ursprungssiedlung der heutigen, etwa 28 900 Einwohner zählenden Kreisstadt Oranienburg. Im Jahre 1650 wurde Bötzow zur Residenz für Kurfürstin Louise Henriette (v. Nassau-Oranien), der ersten Gemahlin des brandenburgischen Kurfürsten Friedrich Wilhelm, erhoben. Sie ließ hier 1651 das repräsentative Schloß »Oranienburg« errichten. 1652 ging der Name »Oranienburg« dann auch auf die Siedlung über. An der Stelle einer ursprünglichen Wasserburg des 15. Jahrhunderts, in den Händen der Quitzows eine gefürchtete mittelmärkische Burg, wurde unter Johann Gregor Memhardt und Michael Matthias Smids die frühbarocke Anlage mit drei Flügeln erbaut. Von 1688 bis 1709 erweiterten Johann Arnold Nering und Martin Grünberg die Anlage zur H-Form. Durch Brand im Jahre 1842 ging der Südostflügel verloren. Die 1945 entstandenen starken Kriegsschäden wurden 1948 bis 1960 behoben. Der zweigeschossige Putzbau orientiert sich mit seiner Eingangsfront, einem fünfachsigen Mittelbau mit vier Geschossen, mit Portalvorbau und bekrönenden Sandsteinfiguren »Vier Jahreszeiten« als dominierender Bauteil über den Ehrenhof zum Schloßplatz.

Bötzow, presumably without a late Slavic preceding settlement, named as Burgward in 1216, was the original settlement which grew into the present district centre of Oranienburg, with about 28,900 inhabitants. In 1650 Bötzow became the residence of Electress Louise Henriette (of Nassau-Oranien), first wife of Elector Friedrich Wilhelm of Brandenburg. She built Schloss Oranienburg here in 1651, and the name was taken by the town as well in 1652. The early baroque complex with three sections was built under Johann Gregor Memhardt and Michael Matthias Smids on the site of an original fifteenth century moated castle, a feared fortress in the central Mark in the hands of the Quitzows. Johann Arnold Nering and Martin Grünberg extended the building into an H-shape from 1688 to 1709. The south-east wing was lost in a fire in 1842. Severe war damage sustained in 1945 was made good from 1948-1960. The two-storey rendered building with its entrance façade, a centrally-planned building with five axes and four storeys, portal porch and sandstones figures on the top representing the «Four Seasons», is placed to dominate the Schlossplatz across the courtyard.

U 46 Wohnhaus (Heimatmuseum)
Oranienburg; Breite Straße 1
1657

Dieser zweigeschossige stattliche Putzbau von 1657 schloß unmittelbar an die damalige halbkreisförmige Bebauung des dem Schloß vorgelagerten Platzes an. Im 18. Jahrhundert Mittelpunkt der barocken Stadtanlage mit drei radial auf den Schloßplatz zulaufenden Straßen, erinnert es an das Vorbild der Piazza del Popolo in Rom. Um 1700 wurde der Bau mit seinen fünf Achsen hofseitig um einen ovalen Saalanbau erweitert. Gleichzeitig wurden die Treppe eingebaut und die Stuckdecken in beiden Geschossen eingebracht. Im Museum selbst ist das Gemälde »Gründung Oranienburgs« von Willem van Honthorst, um 1660, zu sehen.

This imposing two-storey rendered building dating from 1657 was immediately adjacent to the semiciruclar buildings surrounding the square in front of the Schloss at the time. In the eighteenth century it was the central point of the baroque town with three radial streets meeting at the Schlossplatz, reminiscent of the Piazza del Popolo in Rome, upon which it was modelled. In about 1700 an oval room was added on the courtyard side to the building with its five axes, the staircase was put in at the same time and stucco ceilings fixed in both storeys. In the museum itself is the painting «Foundation of Oranienburg» by Willem van Honthorst, c. 1660.

in der Nähe/nearby:
Park mit Parktor; Schloßplatz
17. und 18. Jh.
Standbild »Kurfürstin Louise Henriette«
1858 • Wilhelm Wolff
Plastik »Die Anklagende«
1948/1959 • Fritz Cremer
Bankgebäude; Platz des Friedens 1
1969-71 • Waldemar Gude
Waisenhaus (Gesundheitsamt); Havelstraße 29
2. H. 17. Jh. • Michael Matthias Smids
Nikolaikirche
1864-66 • Friedrich August Stüler

U 47 Mahn- und Gedenkstätte Sachsenhausen
Oranienburg; Straße der Nationen
1956-61 • Ludwig Deiters

1936, auf Befehl des Reichsführers der SS, Himmler, begann vor den Toren von Oranienburg der Aufbau eines der größten faschistischen Konzentrationslager. Zwischen 1936 und 1945 waren hier über 200 000 Menschen aus 47 Nationen gefangen, von denen mehr als 100 000 den Tod fanden. Zur Mahnung an die Opfer wurde auf dem Gelände des ehemaligen Lagers im Eingangsbereich ein Museum errichtet, dahinter eine Gedenkstätte mit dem 40 m hohen Monument der Nationen und einer von René Graetz geschaffenen Plastik angelegt. Die Reste des ehemaligen Krematoriums werden von einer Halle überspannt. Die darunter stehende Plastik wurde von Waldemar Grzimek geschaffen. Die architektonische Gestaltung des Mahnmals geht auf die auch in Buchenwald und Ravensbrück tätige Gruppe unter Ludwig Deiters, Horst Kutzat und Hubert Matthes zurück.

Himmler, Reichsführer of the SS, ordered the establishment of one of the largest Nazi concentration camps here in 1936. Between 1936 and 1945 over 200,000 people from 47 nations were held prisoner here, and more than 100,000 of them died. As a memorial and warning the entrance area with a museum was established on the site of the former prisoners' camp and the memorial area with the 40 m high Monument der Nationen and a sculpture by René Graetz. The remains of the former crematorium are spanned by the memorial hall. The sculpture underneath it was created by Waldemar Grzimek. The architectural design of the memorial was the work of the group that also worked in Buchenwald and Ravensbrück under Ludwig Deiters, with Horst Kutzat and Hubert Matthes.

in der Nähe/nearby:
Kulturhaus; Neuholland
1969 • Klaus Wever, Karl-Heinz Sauer

U 48 Kleinhaussiedlung
Hennigsdorf; Paul-Jordan-Straße 2-8
1919-20 • Peter Behrens

Das bereits 1375 erwähnte ursprüngliche Havel-Fischerdorf ist seit Anfang des 20. Jahrhunderts wegen seiner Lage unmittelbar am nördlichen Rand Berlins gut durch die Eisenbahn und die Havel als Wasserstraße erschlossen. Damit war es Ziel verstärkter Industrieansiedlung. Ab 1911 verlagert die AEG große Teile ihrer Produktion nach Hennigsdorf. Für die Arbeitskräfte entstanden zu jener Zeit Siedlungs- und Werkwohnungsbauten, darunter auch 1919-20 eine Kleinhaussiedlung in der Paul-Jordan-Straße. Peter Behrens, Chefarchitekt der AEG, entwarf sie für Arbeiter des Hennigsdorfer Werkes. Die städtebauliche Anordnung der versetzt errichteten elf zweigeschossigen Reihenhäuser mit vorspringenden eingeschossigen Gebäudeteilen an den Hausecken vermittelt den angerartigen Charakter. Weitere Siedlungen und Werkswohnungen entstanden zu jener Zeit in der Rathenau-, Klingenberg-, Volt-, Watt- und Edisonstraße sowie in der Spandauer Allee. Nach 1945 wuchs die Stadt mit mehreren tausend Wohnungen und Versorgungseinrichtungen westlich des Bahnhofs nach Entwürfen von Horst Kiklas, Günter Vandenherz und in nördlicher Richtung nach Entwürfen von Erich Gassauer, Hansjoachim Hamann, Franz Klinger.

This was originally a Havel fishing village, but has been accessible since the early twentieth century, because of its position close to the northern outskirts of Berlin, via the railway and the Havel as a waterway. It thus became a target for industrial settlement. From 1911 AEG moved large sections of its production to Hennigsdorf. At that time estates and factory accommodation were built for the workforce, including an estate of small houses in Paul-Jordan-Strasse in 1919-20. Peter Behrens, AEG's chief architect, designed them for workers in the Hennigsdorf factory. A village-green character is given by the arrangement in urban development terms of the eleven staggered sets of two-storey terraced houses with protruding single-storey sections of the building on the corners. Other estates or factory houses came into being at the same time in Rathenau-, Klingenberg-, Volt-, Watt- and Edisonstrasse and in Spandauer Allee. After 1945 the town grew by the addition of several thousand dwellings and service institutions west of the station to designs by Horst Kiklas, Günter Vandenherz, and to the north to designs by Erich Gassauer, Hans-Joachim Hamann and Franz Klinger.

in der Nähe/nearby:
Autobahnsee (Badesee); bei Velten
1972 • Fritz Langenickel
Arbeitersiedlung; Leegebruch
1936-39 • Herbert Pimpel
Dorfkrug; Schönfließ; Dorfstraße 26-27
M. 18. Jh. (erweitert 1937-38)

V
Zwischen Uckermark und Oderbruch

Die Uckermark bildet den Nordosten der Mark-Brandenburg. Sie setzt sich fort in Schorfheide und Märkischer Schweiz. Die sanfte Hügellandschaft mit den vielen Gewässern der hier auslaufenden Mecklenburgischen Seenplatte gilt als beliebtes Naherholungsgebiet der Berliner. Die vielen großen und kleinen Becken sowie abflußlosen Seen der Grundmoränenlandschaft sind Ergebnis der Weichsel-Eiszeit. Nach der Völkerwanderung wurden diese Gebiete slawisch besiedelt. Im 12. und 13. Jahrhundert entstanden mit der Ostkolonisation deutscher Feudalherren und mit der Christianisierung durch Prämonstratenser-, Franziskaner- und Zisterziensermönche hervorragende Bauwerke, die als Backsteinbauten heute untrennbar mit Landschaft und Region verwoben sind. Eines der bekanntesten und schönsten Beispiele ist das Kloster Chorin, das erheblichen Einfluß auf die norddeutsche und nordische Gotik ausübte und als ein Symbol für die neuen Landwirtschafts- und Handwerkerschulen sowie für die Städteneugründungen des Mittelalters angesehen werden kann. Wichtige wirtschaftliche Impulse empfing das Land durch den 1605 begonnenen Ausbau des Oder-Havel-Wasserweges und 1842 durch den Bau der Stettiner Eisenbahn. Das Überschwemmungsland des Oderbruchs hat eine weit jüngere Geschichte. Erst zur Mitte des 18. Jahrhunderts ließ Friedrich II. das Gebiet trockenlegen und gegen Hochwasser schützen. Die Siedler aus allen Teilen Deutschlands, aus Böhmen und Schweden brachten ebenso wie die in jenen Jahrzehnten einwandernden Hugenotten Anregungen und neue Ideen mit, etwa den Tabakanbau in der Gegend um Schwedt. Mit dem Aufblühen Brandenburgs und seines kurfürstlichen Herrscherhauses setzte in dieser nordöstlichen Region des Landes auch eine Zeit verstärkter Profanbautätigkeit ein, die über Karl Friedrich Schinkel und August Stüler bis in die jüngste Epoche hineinreicht.

The Uckermark forms the north-eastern part of the Mark Brandenburg and continues in the Schorfheide and the Märkische Schweiz. The gently rolling countryside with its many bodies of water at the extreme edge of the Mecklenburg lake district is a popular recreation area for Berliners. The many large and small pools and lakes without outflow in the base moraine landscape are the product of the Vistula ice age. After the great folk migrations these districts were settled by Slavic peoples. In the twelfth and thirteenth centuries colonization of the east by German feudal lords and Christianization by Premonstratensian, Franciscan and Cistercian monks produced outstanding buildings, and these brick structures have become an inseparable part of the landscape and the region. One of the best-known and most beautiful examples is the monastery at Chorin, which had a considerable influence on the North German and Nordic Gothic; it also stands as a symbol of the new agricultural and craft schools as well as the new towns founded in the Middle Ages. The region was given significant economic impetus by the extension of the Oder-Havel waterway started in 1605 and by the building of the Stettin railway in 1842. The history of the floodlands of the Oderbruch is much younger. It was not before the mid eighteenth century that Frederick II had these lands drained and protected against flooding. Like the Huguenots who also immigrated during those decades, the settlers, coming from all parts of Germany as well as Bohemia and Sweden, brought new stimuli and ideas, like the tobacco plantations in the area around Schwedt. When Brandenburg and its electoral ruling house began to flourish, there came a period of increased secular building activity, extending via Karl Friedrich Schinkel and August Stüler to the most recent times.

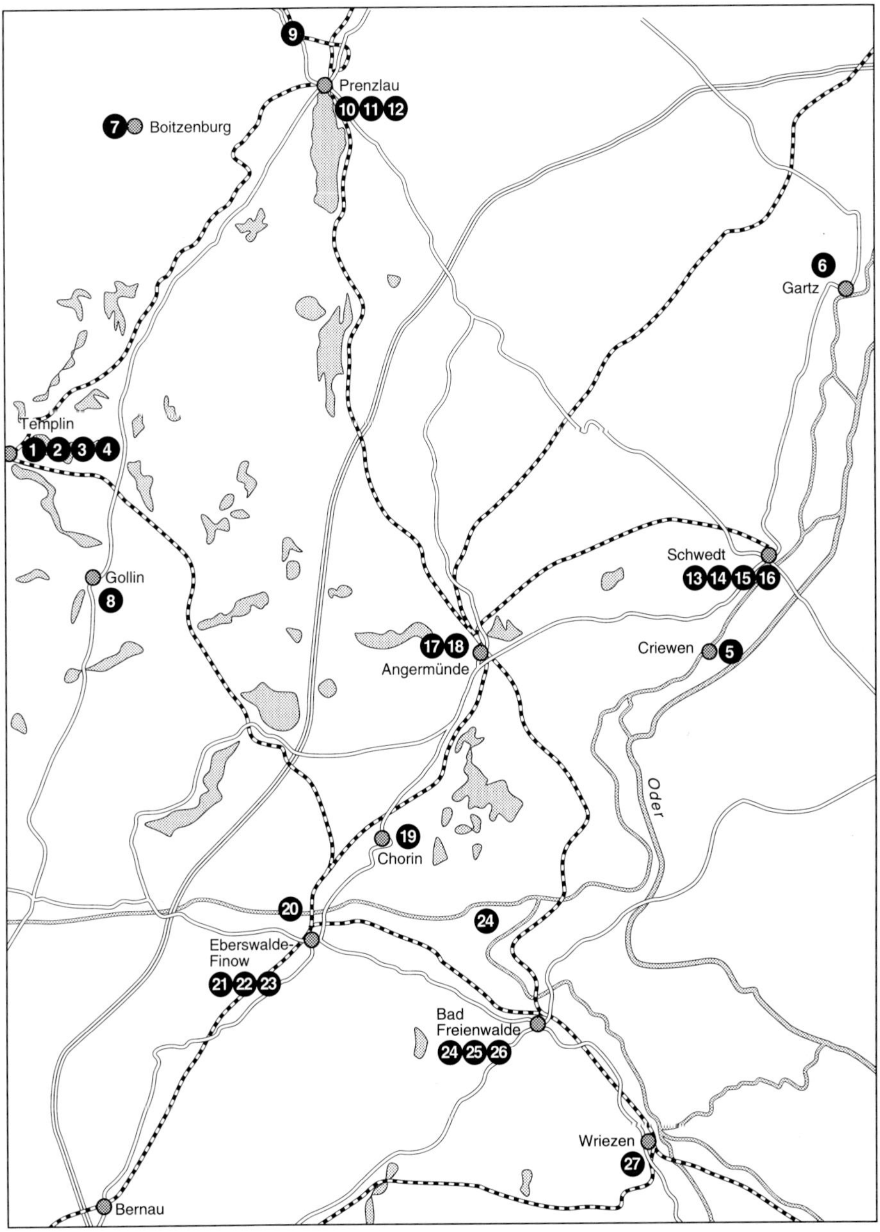

V 1 Stadtkern Templin
V 2 Prenzlauer Tor
V 3 Rathaus
V 4 Fachwerkhaus (Kreissparkasse)
V 5 Gutshaus Criwen
V 6 Stettiner Torturm Gartz
V 7 Schloß Boitzenburg
V 8 Dorfkirche Gollin
V 9 Dorfkirche Dedelow
V 10 Stadtbefestigung Prenzlau
V 11 Marienkirche
V 12 Bahnhof
V 13 Stadt Schwedt
V 14 Frz.-reformierte Kirche (Berlischky-Pavillon)
V 15 Ermelerspeicher
V 16 Ritualbad
V 17 Stadtkern Angermünde
V 18 Ratswaage (heute Feuerwache)
V 19 Zisterzienserkloster Chorin
V 20 Kanalbrücke
V 21 Stadtkern Eberswalde-Finow
V 22 Rathaus
V 23 Alte Forstakademie
V 24 Schiffshebewerk Niederfinow
V 25 Stadtkern Bad Freienwalde
V 26 Pfarrkirche St. Nikolai
V 27 Landhaus Werner-Seelenbinder-Straße
V 28 Kalköfen Wriezen

V 1 Stadtkern Templin
1735

Die Kreisstadt Templin im uckermärkischen Südosten wird heute mit 14 500 Einwohnern von land- und forstwirtschaftsbezogener Industrie geprägt. Unter markgräflich-brandenburgischer Landesherrschaft wurde die Stadt um 1230 am Straßenkreuz Berlin–Prenzlau und Strelitz–Frankfurt auf ovalem Grundriß mit sich rechtwinklig kreuzenden Straßen angelegt, 1270 erstmals genannt. Die heutige geradlinige Straßenführung mit dem etwas dezentral gelegenen Markt und die überwiegende Fachwerkbebauung entstanden erst nach dem Stadtbrand von 1735. Stadtbrände 1492, 1530, 1618 und 1735, ein Luftangriff 1944 sowie Sprengungen in den letzten Kriegstagen hatten jeweils den völligen Wiederaufbau zur Folge. Trotz eifriger wirtschaftlicher Förderung durch die Hohenzollern entwickelte sich Templin seit dem 17. Jahrhundert nur zögernd. Die ursprünglich gute Verkehrslage verschob sich zugunsten anderer Städte. Seit 1895 gewann Templin lediglich für den Schiffsausflugsverkehr aus dem Berliner Raum Bedeutung.

The district capital of Templin in the south-east of Uckermark has 14,500 inhabitants and is largely given over to agriculture and forestry. The town was laid out under the margraves of Brandenburg c. 1230 at the Berlin–Prenzlau Strelitz–Frankfurt crossroads, on an oval ground plan with streets intersecting at right angles; it was first mentioned in 1270. The present linear street pattern with the market place set slightly off centre and a predominance of half-timbered building, dates from after the town fire of 1735. It was repeatedly rebuilt, after town fires in 1492, 1530 and 1618 as well as 1735, and also after a severe air raid in 1944. Despite keen economic encouragement from the Hohenzollerns, Templin developed only hesitantly from the seventeenth century. The transport situation, originally good, gradually declined in relation to other towns. From 1895 Templin was only of importance for boat trips from the Berlin area.

in der Nähe/nearby:
Pfarrkirche St. Johannes; Lychen
2. H. 13. Jh. (Innen 17. und 18. Jh.)
Stargarder Tor und Stadtmauer; Lychen
14. Jh.
Rathaus; Lychen
1748
Dorfkirche; Mittenwalde
2. H. 13. Jh.
Gutshaus; Mittenwalde
2. H. 18. Jh.

V 2 Prenzlauer Tor
Templin; südöstlicher Stadtkern
1325

In Sorgfalt, Aufwand, Ausführung steht die Templiner Stadtbefestigung vergleichbaren Anlagen großer Städte in nichts nach, und sie ist eine der besterhaltenen und geschlossensten einer mittelalterlichen norddeutschen Kleinstadt. Die Stadtmauer vom Ende des 13. Jahrhunderts steht größtenteils noch in ursprünglicher Höhe. Der Pulverturm am Prenzlauer Tor entstand aus einem der über 50 Weichhäuser. Die »Modernisierung« der Befestigung 1325 brachte den Lychener, den Berliner und den Prenzlauer Torturm mit reich gegliederter Stadtseite und Fallgatter-Pfeilervorlagen auf der Feldseite. Die Templiner Tortürme sind frühe sichtbare Beispiele des bürgerlichen Repräsentationsstrebens im 14. und 15. Jahrhundert.

The Templin town fortifications, by no means inferior in terms of expense and careful execution to comparable buildings in large towns, are among the best-preserved and most complete of any north German medieval town. The late thirteenth century town wall still stands largely at its original height. The powder tower at the Prenzlauer Tor was adapted from one of the more than 50 towers in the wall. «Modernization» in 1325 added the Lychen, Berlin and Prenzlau gate-towers, with lavishly articulated town side, and portcullis piers on the outer side. The Templin gate towers are early and conspicuous examples of a bourgeois desire to make a prestigious impression in the fourteenth and fifteenth centuries.

in der Nähe/nearby:
Lychener Torturm (Mühlentorturm); nw. Stadtkern
A. 14. Jh.
Berliner Torturm; südwestlicher Mauerabschnitt
A. 14. Jh.

V 3 Rathaus
Templin; Am Markt 19
Um 1750 • Karl Samuel Schmidt

In der Zeit von etwa 1750 bis 1850, während der in Deutschland nur wenige Rathäuser gebaut wurden, entstanden in den nördlichen und nordöstlichen Teilen der Mark Brandenburg, in Malchow, Lychen, Biesenthal, Angermünde, Strausberg und Templin, einige sich ähnelnde Rathäuser. Es sind meist zweigeschossige, rechteckige, freistehende Baukörper mit sieben Achsen an der Eingangsseite. Das Walm-, Zelt- oder Mansartdach ist oft mit einem Dachreiter als Uhrturm bekrönt. Der in Templin nach dem Stadtbrand von 1735 errichtete dreigeschossige Putzbau in maßvoller Barockform hat einen reichgegliederten quadratischen Dachreiter mit Uhr, dessen Haube vom brandenburgischen Adler bekrönt wird. Den brandenburgischen Adler trägt seit dem 14. Jahrhundert auch das Stadtwappen von Templin. Zwei 1944 durch Kriegseinwirkung zerstörte Achsen des Rathauses sind 1963-66 wiederhergestellt worden.

In the period from about 1750 to 1850, during which very few town halls were built in Germany, several town halls quite similar to each other were actually built in the northern and north-eastern area of the Mark Brandenburg, in Malchow, Lychen, Biesenthal, Angermünde, Strausberg and Templin. Most of them are two-storey, rectangular, free-standing buildings with seven axes on the entrance side. The hipped, pyramid or mansard roof often has a ridge turret as clock tower. The three-storey rendered building erected in Templin to a moderate baroque design after the fire of 1735 has a lavishly articulated square ridge turret with clock, whose cupola is topped by a Brandenburg eagle. The town arms of Templin have also included the Brandenburg eagle since the fourteenth century. Two axes of the town hall were destroyed by the effects of war in 1944, and were restored in 1963-6.

in der Nähe/nearby:
Pfarrkirche St. Maria Magdalena; Steinstraße
1749 (Turm 13. Jh., Kern 15. Jh.) • Karl Samuel Schmidt
Hospitalkapelle St. Georg; Berliner Tor
E. 14. Jh.
Spitalgebäude; Berliner Straße 5
19. Jh.

V 4 Fachwerkhaus (Kreissparkasse)
Templin; Berliner Straße 12, Schinkelstraße
Nach 1735

Nach dem verheerenden Stadtbrand von 1735, der nur das St. Georgen-Hospital und die zugehörige Kirche verschonte, wurde die Stadt neu aufgebaut. Erhebliche Verschiebungen der Häuserfluchten ergaben sich aus der Aufteilung des Stadtgrundrisses in rechtwinklige Häuserblocks und aus der Verkleinerung des Marktplatzes. Die Wohnhäuser wurden nun in geschlossenen Reihen, die Traufseite zur Straße und mit gleicher Firsthöhe, durchweg zweigeschossig in Fachwerk ausgeführt. Hinter jedem Haus befindet sich ein kleiner Hof, der zum dahinter liegenden Garten und zu den Nachbargrundstücken durch Stallungen, Geräte- oder Vorratsgebäude abgegrenzt wird. Bis heute blieben die inneren Flächen der Wohnquartiere im wesentlichen unbebaut, und die Form der Templiner Innenstadt wurde dadurch bewahrt. Dieses praktikable, weit in die Zukunft reichende Konzept jener Zeit wird auch darin deutlich, daß die Scheunen aus Sicherheitsgründen vor dem Lychener Tor konzentriert wurden.

After the disastrous town fire of 1735, in which only the St. Georgen Hospital and the church attached to it were saved, the town was rebuilt. The line of many of the streets was considerably altered because the town ground plan was divided into rectangular blocks of buildings and the market place was reduced in size. Residential buildings were now built in closed rows, with their eaves to the street and with ridges of equal height, all two-storeyed, and all half-timbered. Behind each building is a little courtyard, divided from the garden behind and neighbouring plots by stabling, and buildings for storing tools or domestic use. The internal areas of the residential districts have remained un-built-up until today, thus preserving the shape of the Templin town centre. This practicable plan, well ahead of its time, can also be clearly seen from the fact that for reasons of safety the barns were concentrated outside the Lychen gate.

in der Nähe/nearby:
Joachimsthalsches Gymnasium; Prenzlauer Allee
Um 1910
Wohnhäuser; Martin-Luther-Straße 14-17, Werderstraße
Nach 1735
Wohnhäuser; Weinbergstraße 1, Schinkelstraße 12
18. und 19. Jh.

V 5 Gutshaus
Criewen
18. Jahrhundert

Um seinen Gutspark großflächig erweitern zu können, verlegte O. v. Arnim nach Kauf des Gutes Criewen im Jahre 1816 das gesamte Dorf nach Norden. Nur die Kirche, im Kern ein Feldsteinbau des 13. Jahrhunderts, blieb am alten Ort stehen. Das ehemalige Gutshaus, ein zweigeschossiger Putzbau von elf Achsen mit übergiebeltem Mittelrisalit und hohem Mansartdach, stammt im Kern aus dem 18. Jahrhundert, wurde aber um 1820 sowie grundlegend um 1910 umgebaut. Alle drei Bauzeiten hinterließen deutlich ihre Spuren, und das Schlößchen präsentiert sich heute in vornehmer Schlichtheit getreu preußischer Tradition. Östlich schließt ein Wirtschaftshof an: ein Speicher vom Anfang des 19. Jahrhunderts mit großem hölzernen Rad für eine Winde, etwas jünger ein Gerätehaus und ein Gärtnerhaus, alles Bauten aus gespaltenem Feldstein oder verputztem Backstein. Eine Besonderheit in jener eigenartigen Landschaft sind die Polder zwischen Oder und der Hohensaaten-Friedrichsthaler-Wasserstraße mit kilometerlangen durchgehenden Deichen und reichen Weideflächen.

In order to be able to expand his estate park after purchasing the Criewen estate in 1816, Otto von Arnim had the entire village moved further north. Only the church, originally built in rubble stone in the thirteenth century, was left standing. The core of the former mansion, a two-storey rendered building with eleven axes, gabled central projection and high mansard roof, dates back to the eighteenth century and was remodeled first c. 1820 and again c. 1910. In all three instances the style of the times left clear marks, and today the small castle presents itself as a building of noble simplicity, in keeping with Prussian tradition. To the east is a farmyard with an early-nineteenth century granary with a huge wooden wheel for the winch, a somewhat younger building for storing equipment and a gardener's house, all built of split rubble stone or rendered brickwork. A peculiar feature of this unique landscape are the areas of reclaimed land between the Oder and the Hohensaaten-Friedrichsthal waterway with their continuous dykes, extending for miles, and their rich pastures.

in der Nähe/nearby:
Gutspark; Criewen
Um 1830 • Peter Joseph Lenné
Speicher; Zützen; Wirtschaftshof des Gutes
Um 1800
Park; Zützen
1832 • Peter Joseph Lenné

V 6 Stettiner Torturm
Gartz
14./15. Jahrhundert

Im Mittelalter war die Stadt Gartz pommersche Grenzfeste gegen Brandenburg. Daher erklärt sich die eindrucksvolle Stadtbefestigung, die heute noch in großen Teilen, besonders an der Nord- und Westseite der regelmäßig auf ovalem Grundriß angelegten Stadt, in ursprünglicher Ausbildung erhalten ist. Das Stettiner Tor, ein mehrgeschossiger quadratischer Turm über einer vier Meter breiten spitzbogigen Durchfahrt, stammt ursprünglich aus dem 13. Jahrhundert. Der mehrgeschossige Backsteinoberbau des Turms, der eine stattliche 25 Meter hohe rechteckige Blendwand mit reichem Maßwerk zur Feldseite aufweist, ist dem 15. Jahrhundert zuzuordnen. Wie durch ein Wunder ist der Torturm Anfang April 1945 weitgehend erhalten geblieben, obwohl die Stadt Gartz beim Angriff der Truppen der 2. Belorussischen Front größtenteils zerstört wurde.

In medieval times the town of Gartz was a Pomeranian stronghold on the border with Brandenburg. That explains the impressive fortifications of the town which are still largely extant in their original layout, especially at the north and west sides of the town which was built on a regular oval plan. The Stettiner Tor, a square, multistorey gate-tower above a four meter wide passage, dates back to the thirteenth century. The multi-storey brick upper section of the tower, the field side of which features a 25 meter high rectangular facing wall with rich tracery, is attributed to the fifteenth century. It was something of a miracle that the tower remained largely intact when the town of Gartz was almost completely destroyed in April 1945 during the attack by the armies of the Second Byelorussian Front.

in der Nähe/nearby:
Stadtbefestigung, Türme, Wall und Graben
13./14. Jh.
Storchennest (Wachturm)
14. Jh./15. Jh.
Stadtkirche St. Stephan
2. H. 14. Jh., 15. Jh., E. 18. Jh. (oberer Turm)
Bockwindmühle; Luckow-Petershagen
Vermutlich 1824

**V 7 Schloß
Boitzenburg
Ende 16. Jahrhundert und
1838-42 • Friedrich August Stüler**

Bereits 1276 wird erstmals eine Burg genannt, in deren Schutze sich die Siedlung und der spätere Herrensitz und Marktflecken Boitzenburg in reizvoller Tallage entwickelt hat. Das Schloß mit allen umliegenden Ortschaften erwirbt 1528 Hans v. Arnim, der gleichzeitig auf Lebzeiten als Landvogt der Uckermark eingesetzt wird. Die Säkularisierung des Klosters führt dem Besitz der Arnims noch Güter und Dörfer zu. Der westliche älteste Teil des Schlosses, das Oberhaus, stammt noch aus dem ausgehenden 16. Jahrhundert, Decke und Kamin des Jagdzimmers weisen reiche Stuckverzierungen mit Jagdszenen auf, die aus der Zeit um 1640 stammen. Die beiden anschließenden Schloßflügel, das Unterhaus, wurden 1838-42 durch Friedrich August Stüler im neogotischen Stil erbaut und 1881-84 nochmals in Neorenaissance-Formen umgebaut. 1988 wurde dem Schloßkomplex noch ein Bettenhaus hinzugefügt.

As early as 1276 first mention was made of a stronghold, under the protection of which the settlement and subsequent manorial estate and market-town of Boitzenburg was developed in this charming valley. The castle with all surrounding villages was purchased in 1528 by Hans von Arnim who was simultaneously installed for life as provincial governor of the Uckermark. With the secularization of the monastery a number of additional estates and villages came into the possession of the von Arnims. The oldest part of the castle, the Oberhaus to the west, dates back to the late sixteenth century; the ceiling and chimney of the Jagdzimmer are lavishly decorated with stucco ornaments and hunting scenes dating from c. 1640. The two adjoining wings of the so-called Unterhaus were built in 1838-42 by Friedrich August Stüler in neo-Gothic taste and remodeled in 1881-84 to Renaissance style. In 1988 a new bedroom wing was added to the castle complex.

in der Nähe/nearby:
Schloßpark
Um 1840 • Peter Joseph Lenné
Gedächtnistempel für F. W. v. Arnim; im Park
1804 • Carl Gotthard Langhans
Zisterzienser-Nonnenkloster
Um 1270
Klostermühle
1640
Pfarrkirche
2. H. 13. Jh., 18. Jh.

**V 8 Dorfkirche
Gollin
1817**

Verheerende Kriege und Brände, aber auch Grenzstreitigkeiten und Seuchen haben die uckermärkische Region in ihrer Entwicklung immer wieder zurückgeworfen. Zuletzt der Zweite Weltkrieg hat gerade in diesem Landstrich fürchterliche Zerstörungen hinterlassen, so daß viele wertvolle Bauwerke nur noch stark beschädigt oder als Ruine vorzufinden sind. Bedeutend ist die Palette der sakralen Bauten, die vom Kloster Chorin über die Prenzlauer Marienkirche bis hin zu den kleinen schutzbietenden Wehrkirchen und idyllischen Fachwerkkirchen reicht. Jene Fachwerkbauten sind wohl eine Besonderheit dieser Region. Ähnlich wie die Wehrkirchen sind sie mit sparsamsten Mitteln erbaut, haben meist wenig Schmuckelemente, jedoch einen Dachturm und sind von gedrungener Gestalt. Die Dorfkirche in Gollin ist ein solcher rechteckiger Fachwerkbau mit dreiseitigem Ostschluß und verbrettertem Dachturm. Zur Ausstattung gehört ein Kelch aus dem Jahre 1819, eine Taufschale von 1842 und zwei 1817 und 1818 in der Königlichen Eisengießerei Berlin gegossene Glocken.

Due to the devastations of wars and conflagrations as well as border conflicts and various epidemics, the development of the Uckermark region suffered repeated set-backs. The latest was caused by the Second World War which caused particularly heavy destruction in this part of the country, leaving many valuable buildings largely destroyed or in ruins. Yet there is a wide palette of important ecclesiastical buildings, extending from the Chorin monastery and the Marienkirche in Prenzlau to the numerous small fortified churches and idyllic half-timbered churches. These half-timbered structures are perhaps quite typical for this region. Much like the fortified churches, they were built with the most modest of means and are generally marked by a roof turret and compact, heavy shape bearing very little ornamentation. The village church at Gollin is one of these rectangular half-timbered structures with three-sided east end and boarded roof turret. The furnishings include a chalice from the year 1819, a baptismal font of 1842 and two bells cast in the Royal Foundry Berlin in 1817 and 1818 respectively.

in der Nähe/nearby:
Dorfkirche; Stegelitz
13. Jh.
Grab G. A. v. Arnim; Stegelitz
Nach 1734 • Johann Georg Glume
Burg (Ruine); Gerswalde
14./15. Jh., 1847 (Teilausbau)
Wassermühle; Potzlow
E. 19. Jh.
Kloster (Ruine); Gramzow
Um 1180
Stadtkirche; Gramzow
M. 13. Jh., 1686 (Wiederaufbau)

V 9 Dorfkirche Dedelow
Dedelow
2. Hälfte 13. Jahrhundert

Nur etwa 50 Kilometer Luftlinie beträgt die Entfernung zwischen Dedelow und Chorin, aber welche Kultur-Welten trennen die beiden Bauwerke, die nahezu zur gleichen Zeit errichtet wurden! Die Zisterzienser-Mönche schufen in ihrem Kloster Chorin den Prototyp der gotischen Backsteinkirche in Mittel- und Nordeuropa, der Baumeister des Kirchleins in Dedelow errichtete ein für den Ort bedeutendes Bauwerk mit bescheidensten Mitteln: Feldstein, der überall auf den Äckern zu finden war. Vom Aufbau vergleichbar der Dorfkirche im nahen Schmölln ist der rechteckige Feldsteinbau in Dedelow mit seinem eingezogenen Rechteckchor und dem querrechteckigen Westturm von Schiffsbreite heute noch gut erhalten und weist durch Einbauten und Ausstattung ein sehr stimmungsvolles Innenraumbild auf. Insbesondere tragen dazu die eingeschossigen hölzernen Emporen mit bemalten Brüstungsfeldern aus dem 17. Jahrhundert, das Gestühl, der Logeneinbau, die hölzerne Kanzel und der spätgotische Schnitzaltar mit Mondsichelmadonna zwischen Johannes dem Täufer und Sebastian bei. Im Chor wurden 1963 Reste spätgotischer Wandmalereien freigelegt.

Less than 50 kilometers as the crow flies separate Dedelow from Chorin, and yet these two buildings, constructed roughly at the same time, are worlds apart. With the Chorin monastery the cistercian monks created the prototype of Gothic brick church architecture in Central and Northern Europe, while the builder of the small church at Dedelow erected a building of great significance to the village with the most simple of means: plain rubble stone readily found in the surrounding fields. Comparable in structure to the village church of nearby Schmölln, the rectangular rubble-stone building at Dedelow with its rectangular choir and equally rectangular west tower of the same width as the nave has been quite well-preserved and features a highly impressive interior with numerous furnishings. Particularly noteworthy are the single-storey timber galleries with painted wainscoting from the seventeenth century, the pews, the gallery furnishings, the wooden pulpit and the late-Gothic carved altar with a crescent madonna flanked by figures of St. John the Baptist and St. Sebastian. In the choir, remnants of late-Gothic murals were discovered in 1963.

in der Nähe/nearby:
Mausoleum; nahe der Kirche
M. 19. Jh. • C. G. Cantian nach Entw. von K. F. Schinkel
Dorfkirche; Falkenhagen
2. H. 13. Jh.
Gutshaus; Holzendorf/Zernikow
18. Jh.
Dorfkirche; Holzendorf/Zernikow
13. Jh.

V 10 Mitteltor
Prenzlau; Marktberg
3. Viertel 15. Jahrhundert

Nach einer slawischen Besiedlung und der deutschen Ostkolonisation erwähnen Urkunden bereits 1187/88 die Siedlung Prenzlau mit Markt und Kruggerechtigkeit. Prenzlau bekam 1234 noch vom Pommernherzog Barnim I., der in Stettin residierte, das Stadtrecht verliehen, kam aber bereits 1250 unter brandenburgische Herrschaft. Zum Schutz gegen die Askanier wurde die Stadt ab 1287 mit einer wirkungsvollen Wehranlage befestigt, die die Zeiten teils bis heute überdauert hat. Erhalten sind Teile der Backsteinmauer auf Feldsteinsockel von einst neun Metern Höhe, drei Mauertürme aus Backstein, einige der ursprünglich 60 Wiekhäuser sowie drei der ursprünglich vier Tortürme. Der Blindower Torturm in der nördlichen und der Steintorturm in der südlichen Stadtbefestigung stammen vom Ende des 13. Jahrhunderts, der Oberbau ist jeweils zwei Jahrhunderte jünger. Wohl der eindrucksvollste Turm ist der des Mitteltores aus dem 15. Jahrhundert mit quadratischem Unterbau aus Feld- und Backstein, darüberliegender achteckiger auskragender Galerie auf Granitkonsolen und rundem Abschluß mit Zinnen und Kegelhelm.

Following slavic settlement and German colonization of the east, the earliest records of the settlement of Prenzlau with market and Kruggerechtigkeit date back to 1187/88. In 1234 Prenzlau was awarded a charter by the Pomeranian Duke Barnim I, who resided in Stettin, but soon after fell to Brandenburg in 1250. As protection against the Askanians, the town was equipped, beginning in 1287, with highly effective fortifications some of which have survived to this day. Still extant are parts of the brick wall over a socle of rubble stone which originally reached a height of 9 meters, three brickwork towers, some of the former 60 wall houses, and three of the original four gateway towers. The Blindow gatetower in the northern and the Steintorturm in the southern part of the town fortifications date from the late thirteenth century, the upper structures having been added two centuries later. Probably the most impressive tower is that of the Mitteltor, dating from the fifteenth century, with a square base of rubble stone and brick, an octagonal cantilevering gallery above with granite corbels, and a round top with battlements and conical helm.

V 11 Marienkirche
Prenzlau; Marienkirchstraße
1325-40

Prenzlau, bereits 1465 zur Hauptstadt der Uckermark erklärt, ist immer wieder durch Kriege und Stadtbrände stark in Mitleidenschaft gezogen worden. Darunter litt auch seine wirtschaftliche Entwicklung. Die jüngsten, bis heute noch sichtbaren Narben, stammen aus den letzten Tagen des Zweiten Weltkrieges, als sich im April 1945 die Hauptkampflinie der 2. Belorussischen Front von Stettin und Schwedt kommend über Prenzlau nach Berlin bewegte. Die Stadt wurde dabei zu 85% zerstört, die Marienkirche brannte bis auf die Umfassungsmauern völlig aus. Erst 1970 begann der Wiederaufbau der Kirche und die Arbeiten dauern noch immer an. Die Marienkirche ist eine der bedeutenden gotischen Backsteinkirchen im Norden Deutschlands, bekannt ihre gedrungene Doppelturmfront vor dem hohen Dach der dreischiffigen querhauslosen Halle. Kunsthistorisch besonders wertvoll ist der östliche Schaugiebel, dessen Maßwerkblenden und Rosetten sich frei vor der Giebelwand entfalten.

Prenzlau, capital of the Uckermark since 1465, was repeatedly subject to devastation from wars and town fires. As a result of this, the economic development of the town also suffered heavily. The latest scars, still visible today, stem from the last days of the Second World War when the main line of battle of the Second Byelorussian Front, moving from Stettin and Schwedt in the direction of Berlin, touched Prenzlau in April 1945. In the process 85% of the town was destroyed, the Marienkirche being completely gutted by fire. Reconstruction work did not begin until 1970 and is still in progress. The Marienkirche ranks as one of the greatest Gothic brick churches in North Germany and is well-known with its squat twin-towers adjoining the high roof of the hall with nave and two aisles but lacking a transept. Of particular value for art historians is the east gable with its lavish tracery and rosettes unfolding freely in front of the facing wall.

in der Nähe/nearby:
Franziskaner-Klosterkirche
1235-70
Dominikaner-Kloster; südliche Altstadt
1. H. 14. Jh.
Nikolaikirche (ehem. Dominikaner-Klosterkirche)
1310-43

V 12 Hauptbahnhof
Prenzlau; Pasewalker Straße
Um 1863

Erst im Verlauf der Stein-Hardenbergschen Reformen erhielt Prenzlau nach vielen Jahren der napoleonischen Besatzung 1815 die Selbstverwaltung und wurde 1817 Kreisstadt. Neue Straßen- und Eisenbahnverbindungen begünstigten ab 1830 seine wirtschaftliche Entwicklung. War die Berlin-Stettiner Eisenbahn über Eberswalde und Angermünde bereits 1843 nach drei Jahren Bauzeit und mit bemerkenswertem Engagement ostelbischer Grundbesitzer fertiggestellt worden, so verzögerte sich der Bau der Strecke Angermünde–Prenzlau–Pasewalk–Anklam–Greifswald–Stralsund spürbar, woran die Dominanz des Großgrundbesitzes und die konservative Haltung der Junker nicht unbeteiligt waren. Nach den 1852 durchgeführten Vorarbeiten konnte die Strecke erst 1863 in Betrieb genommen werden. In jene Zeit fällt auch die Fertigstellung des Prenzlauer Hauptbahnhofes, eines funktionsbetonten Klinkerbaues mit Rundbogenfenstern im Erdgeschoß, Rechteckfenstern im Obergeschoß und Drempelgeschoß, der in seiner bescheidenen Gestalt auch gewisse Ähnlichkeiten zum Empfangsgebäude des 1843-45 erbauten Bahnhofs Braunschweig erkennen läßt.

It was only in conjunction with the reforms of Stein and Hardenberg that Prenzlau finally acquired the right to govern itself after the long years of Napoleonic occupation and became district capital in 1817. New road and rail connections led to rapid economic development of the town after 1830. While the railway connecting Berlin with Stettin by way of Eberswalde and Angermünde, was already completed in 1843 after three years of construction and with remarkable support from the East-Elbian estate owners, completion of the line linking Angermünde with Prenzlau, Pasewalk, Anklam, Greifswald and Stralsund continued to be delayed, not least due to the dominating role of large estate-owners and the conservative stance of the Junkers. Following completion of the preliminary work in 1852, the line was finally opened in 1863. It was roughly at the same time that the main station of Prenzlau was also completed, a highly functional clinker building with round-arch windows for the ground floor, rectangular windows for the upper storey and the attic storey. With its unassuming design it shows a certain similarity with the arrival building of the Braunschweig railway station built in 1843-45.

in der Nähe/nearby:
Poliklinik; Grabowstraße 32
1952-53 • Fritz Wollmann, Ernst Magnus
Kreisgericht; Baustraße 346-348
1858
Hotel Uckermark; Friedrichstraße 4
1956-58 • Ernst Magnus, Kurt Sellmer, Fritz Wollmann

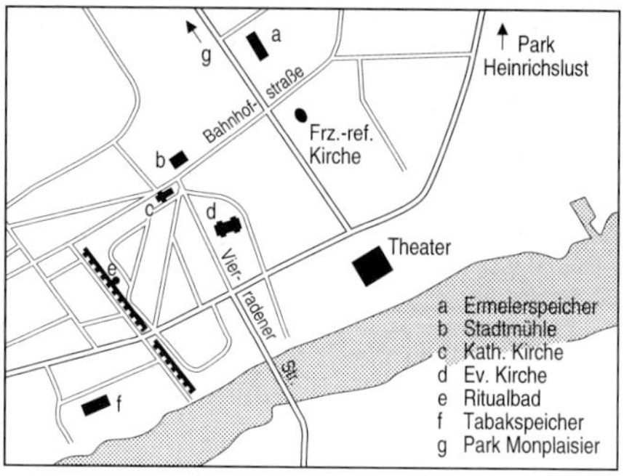

V 13 Stadt Schwedt
Um 1200

Die kreisfreie Stadt mit 52 000 Einwohnern in der östlichen Uckermark – umgeben von Kiefernwäldern und Oderpoldern – ist insbesondere geprägt durch ihre petrochemische Industrie am Ende einer 4300 km langen Erdölleitung aus der Sowjetunion. Die Stadt wurde um 1200 am Oderübergang und Straßenkreuz Berlin–Stettin, Prenzlau–Posen angelegt, 1265 wird sie erstmals erwähnt. Nach verschiedenen Machtwechseln übertrug Kurfürst Friedrich Wilhelm 1670 den Besitz an seine zweite Frau Dorothea von Holstein-Glücksburg. Unter ihrer Herrschaft erfolgte nach dem Stadtbrand 1681 eine barocke Ausrichtung des ursprünglich mittelalterlichen Straßensystems auf den Schloßbereich. Die Schloßachse führte nun zum Park Monplaisier. Die im Februar 1945 zur Festung erklärte Stadt wurde in furchtbaren Kämpfen zu 85 % zerstört. Der Ausbau zur Industriestadt begann Anfang der sechziger Jahre. Neue städtebauliche Ideen entwickelte dabei Selman Selmanagic mit dem Wohnkomplex II, einer viertelkreisförmigen Erweiterung des barocken Stadtkerns. Mit dem Bau von weiteren fünf Wohnkomplexen erlebte die Stadt eine stürmische Entwicklung.

This town in eastern Uckermark, a district in its own right, with 52,000 inhabitants – surrounded by pine woods and Oder polders – is dominated by its petrochemical industry at the end of a 4,300 km long oil pipeline from the Soviet Union. The town was established c. 1200 at the Oder crossing and Berlin-Stettin, Prenzlau-Posen road junction, and was first mentioned in 1265. After various changes of ruler, Elector Friedrich Wilhelm transferred ownership to his second wife, Dorothea von Holstein-Glücksburg, in 1670. Under her, after the fire of 1681, the originally medieval street system was orientated towards the palace, in baroque style. The palace axis now led to the palace of Monplaisir. The town was declared a fortress in February 1945, and 85% of it was destroyed in fierce and terrible fighting. It started to expand as an industrial town in the early sixties. In the course of this, Selman Selmanagic developed new urban development ideas with his Wohnkomplex II, an extension of the baroque core of the town in the form of a quarter circle. The town developed at a tremendous pace with the building of five more residential complexes.

in der Nähe/nearby:
Stadtmühle (Stadtsparkasse); Vierradener Straße 44
Um 1900
Kreisgericht; Paul-Meyer-Straße 8
Um 1900
Katholische Kirche; Vierradener Platz
1895-98 • Max Hasak

V 14 Frz.-reformierte Kirche (Berlischky-Pavillon)
Schwedt; Lindenallee, Bahnhofstraße
1777-79 • Georg Wilhelm Berlischky

Der Berlischky-Pavillon ist unter Markgraf Friedrich Wilhelm als Kirche für die französisch-reformierte Gemeinde und als Mausoleum für die markgräfliche Familie errichtet worden. Die Kirche war nicht gerichtet, der Altar stand im Westen, der Haupteingang lag im Süden zur Allee. Zur Bauzeit hatte sie ihren Platz am Westrand der Schloßfreiheit. Das Schloß – 1945 ausgebrannt und 1961 als Ruine abgetragen – stand an der Stelle des jetzigen Kulturhauses am südöstlichen Ende der Allee. In nordwestlicher Richtung verlief die barocke Achse schnurgerade bis zum Park Monplaisier. 1980-84 erfolgte nach Entwürfen von Eckehard Tattermusch und J. Böhm der Umbau des Pavillons zu einer Konzerthalle. Die vier noch vorhandenen Sarkophage aus dem 18. und 19. Jahrhundert wurden in diesem Zusammenhang in die Berliner Domgruft überführt.

The Berlischky-Pavillon was built under Margrave Friedrich Wilhelm as a church for the French-Reformed congregation and as a mausoleum for the margrave's family. The church stood on no particular line, the altar was in the west, the main entrance was on the avenue to the south. At the time of building its site was on the western edge of the palace precinct. The palace – burned down in 1945 and demolished as a ruin in 1961 – was on the site of the present House of Culture at the south-eastern end of the avenue. The baroque axis ran dead straight in a north-westerly direction to the palace of Monplaisir. The Pavillon was rebuilt as a concert hall in 1980-4 to plans by Eckehard Tattermusch and J. Böhm. In the context of this work the four remaining eighteenth and nineteenth century sarcophagi were taken to the crypt of the Berlin Dom.

in der Nähe/nearby:
Theater; Berliner Straße
1978 • Eckehard Tattermusch, Benes, Josef Konvalina
Evangelische Stadtkirche St. Katharinen; Oderstraße
1887 • Ludwig Dihm

V 15 Ermelerspeicher
Schwedt; Lindenallee
2. Hälfte 19. Jahrhundert

Die Einwanderung der Hugenotten wirkte sich auf die Landwirtschaft ihrer neuen Heimat außerordentlich fruchtbringend aus. Vor allem in der Uckermark bauten die Franzosen Tabak an – eine Kultur, die seit Beginn des 18. Jahrhunderts hier erst von ihnen verbreitet wurde. Insbesondere in und um Schwedt gab es einstmals zahlreiche Tabakspeicher, die sehr gewichtig im Ortsbild in Erscheinung traten. Der erhaltene Ermelerspeicher, ein zweigeschossiger massiver Backsteinbau, diente ebenfalls diesem Zweck. Der Besitzer war Wilhelm Ferdinand Ermeler, ein Tabakfabrikant aus Berlin. Sein Berliner Domizil stand ursprünglich in der Breiten Straße 11, wurde aber 1968-69 zum Märkischen Ufer 10 umgesetzt. Im geräumigen Mansartdach des Gebäudes war ein Trockenboden für die im Hof untergebrachte Tabakfabrik eingerichtet.

Huguenot immigration had a remarkably positive effect on the landscape of their new homeland. In Uckermark in particular, the French planted tobacco – a crop introduced here for the first time by them from the early eighteenth century onwards. In and around Schwedt in particular, there used to be countless tobacco warehouses, which made a very great impression on the appearance of the area. The surviving Ermeler warehouse, a solid, two-storey brick building, was also used for this purpose. The owner was Wilhelm Ferdinand Ermeler, a Berlin tobacco manufacturer. His Berlin domicile was originally at Breite Strasse 11, but was transferred in 1968-9 to Märkisches Ufer 10. The roomy mansard roof of the building was a drying room for the tobacco factory accommodated in the yard downstairs.

in der Nähe/nearby:
Tabakspeicher; Am Kietz
E. 19. Jh.
Petrochemisches Werk; an der B 166
Ab 1959
Amtshaus; Schwedt-Heinersdorf
1794-95 • Georg Wilhelm Berlischky

V 16 Ritualbad
Schwedt; Gartenstraße
1862

Mit zeitweilig mehr als 150 Personen hatte Schwedt bereits im 18. und 19. Jahrhundert neben den Hugenotten einen relativ hohen Anteil jüdischer Bewohner, die nach dem preußischen Edikt von 1812 als Staatsbürger integriert waren. Jede jüdische Gemeinde ist für die Gestaltung ihres gesellschaftlichen und religiösen Lebens selbst verantwortlich. In Schwedt hatte die Gemeinde eine Synagoge in der Gartenstraße – heute zerstört – und einen Friedhof. Zu den Obliegenheiten der Gemeinde gehörte gewohnheitsgemäß auch die Unterhaltung eines Quellbades, dessen Benutzung nach der Bibelvorschrift für Menstruierende vor Wiederaufnahme des ehelichen Verkehrs vorgeschrieben war. Das Ritualbad der Schwedter jüdischen Gemeinde lag ehemals unmittelbar neben der Synagoge. Erhalten ist ein kuppelgewölbter Rundbau von etwa vier Metern Durchmesser, der zum Teil unterirdisch angelegt ist. Von den zwei kleinen, an die Stadtmauer angelehnten, übergiebelten Rechteckbauten vermittelt einer den Zugang zum Kuppelbau durch einen unterirdischen Gang.

Even in the eighteenth and nineteenth century Schwedt had a relatively high proportion of Jewish inhabitants, at times over 150 people, as well as the Huguenots, and they were integrated as citizens of the state after the Prussian edict of 1812. Every Jewish community is responsible for the creation of its own social and religious life. In Schwedt the community had a synagogue in Gartenstrasse – now destroyed – and a cemetery. As a matter of custom it was also incumbent upon the community to maintain a spring-fed bath, the use of which was prescribed by the Bible for menstruating women before returning to marital intercourse. The Schwedt Jewish community's ritual bath used to be directly by the synagogue. All that has survived is a domed circular building about four metres in diameter, some of which is underground. An underground passage from one of the two small gabled rectangular buildings on the town wall gives access to the domed structure.

in der Nähe/nearby:
Denkmal Gustav Adolf v. Schweden; Park Heinrichslust
1788 • B. Chromander
Lustschloß im Park Monplaisier; nordw. d. Stadt
1778-80 • Georg Wilhelm Berlischky

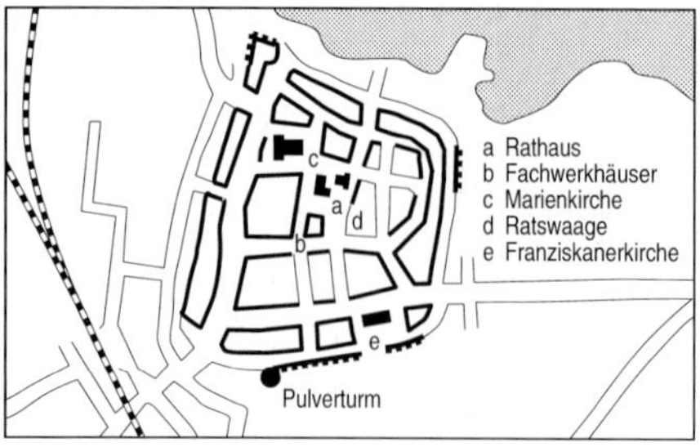

V 17 Stadtkern Angermünde
2. Hälfte 13. Jahrhundert

Die Kreisstadt mit 12 000 Einwohnern im seenreichen und fruchtbaren Hügelland der südlichen Uckermark ist Verkehrsknotenpunkt und wird hauptsächlich durch landwirtschaftlich orientierte Industrie bestimmt. Im Anschluß an eine durch die Markgrafen von Brandenburg um 1230 erbaute Burg wurde die Stadt auf trapezförmigem Grundriß mit sich rechtwinklig kreuzenden Straßen und großem, annähernd rechteckigem Markt mit Rathaus in der 2. Hälfte des 13. Jahrhunderts angelegt, 1284 gab es bereits eine Civitas. Zur gleichen Zeit gründeten die Franziskaner im südlichen Bereich ein Kloster. Fragmentarische Reste der Stadtbefestigung sind nur im Burgbereich und im Süden des Stadtkerns am Pulverturm erhalten. Durch Einwanderung von Hugenotten und Pfälzern Ende des 17. Jahrhunderts bekam Angermünde wirtschaftlichen Auftrieb. Wollweberei, Strumpfwirkerei und vor allem der Tabakanbau kamen damit in die Stadt. Landwirtschaft und darauf ausgerichtete Industrie blieben jedoch Haupterwerbsquelle, auch nachdem die Bahnverbindungen von Berlin nach Stettin 1843 und einige Jahrzehnte später von Angermünde nach Pasewalk, Schwedt und Bad Freienwalde eingerichtet wurden.

This district capital with 12,000 inhabitants amid the lakes and fertile hills of southern Uckermark is a traffic junction, and largely dominated by agriculture. It was laid out in association with a castle built c. 1230 by the margraves of Brandenburg, on a trapezoid ground plan with streets intersecting at right angles and a large, approximately rectangular market place with town hall, in the second half of the thirteenth century, and was a civitas by 1284. At the same time the Franciscans founded a monastery in the southern area. Fragments of the town fortifications have survived only around the castle and in the south of the town core by the powder tower. Angermünde was given an economic boost by Huguenot and Palatinate immigration in the late seventeenth century, bringing weaving, hosiery and above all tobacco plantations to the town. Agriculture and associated industries remained the principal source of income, however, even after rail connections were established from Berlin to Stettin in 1843 and a few decades later from Angermünde to Pasewalk, Schwedt and Bad Freienwalde.

in der Nähe/nearby:
Bergfried; Stolpe; Höhenrücken an der Oder
Um 1200
Giebellaubenhaus; Schmiedeberg
18. Jh.
Steinzeitgrab; Mürow; 1,5 km in Richtung Frauenhagen
Jungsteinzeit
Dorfkirche; Briest
3. V. 13. Jh.
Schloß; Zichow
1745

V 18 Ratswaage (heute Feuerwache)
Angermünde; Brüderstraße 20
18. Jahrhundert

Neben der wirtschaftlichen Entwicklung einer mittelalterlichen Stadt entschied insbesondere die Rats-, Finanz- und Steuerpolitik darüber, ob der Stadtsäckel viel oder wenig Geld enthielt. Von Wichtigkeit waren deshalb regelmäßige Einnahmen aus Grund- und Vermögenssteuer, aus Verpachtung städtischen Grundbesitzes, aus der Besteuerung lebenswichtiger Produkte, wie Getreide, Mehl, Fleisch, Bier, Wein, Salz, sowie aus Benutzungs- und Pachtgebühren für öffentliche Einrichtungen, wie Waage, Mühlen oder Verkaufsstände. Die Finanzpolitik führte im ausgehenden Mittelalter zur Verselbständigung bestimmter Amtsbereiche des Rathauses, in größeren Städten zum Bau repräsentativer Gebäude für die Ratswaage. In der »Waage« wurden Durchgangs-, Kauf-, Stapel- und andere Güter gewogen, gemessen, verzollt, versteuert oder Geleitgebühren festgelegt. Oft befanden sich hier auch andere geeichte Meßinstrumente des Rates, wie die Ratselle oder der Marktscheffel. Die Ratswaage in Angermünde nimmt sich im Vergleich zu Gebäuden in anderen Städten bescheiden aus. Das vorkragende Dach mag die zu behandelnden Waren vor Witterungseinflüssen geschützt haben.

As well as economic development of a medieval town, the main factors affecting whether the municipal coffers were full or empty were council, financial and fiscal policy. Thus regular income was necessary from land and personal wealth taxes, from leasing municipal property, from taxation of essential products like cereals, flour, meat, beer, wine and salt, and also from use and lease fees for public facilities like weights and measures, mills or market stalls. In the late Middle Ages financial policy led to certain branches of the town hall becoming independent, and to the appearance of imposing buildings for the municipal weights and measures department in larger towns. The «Waage» weighed, measured, imposed duty upon and taxed goods in transit, purchases, staple and other goods, or fixed escort charges. It often also housed calibrated council instruments like the council ell or the market bushel. The Angermünde «Ratswaage» is modest in comparison with such buildings in other towns. The overhanging roof may have protected goods, awaiting attention, from the weather.

in der Nähe/nearby:
Rathaus; Marktplatz
1828
Stadtkirche St. Marien; Nähe Marktplatz
M. 13. Jh. (Einwölbung Langhaus E. 15./A. 16. Jh.)
Franziskaner-Klosterkirche; Klosterstraße
1284/1300
Stadtmauer; südlicher und nördlicher Altstadtrand
Um 1300
Pulverturm; südlicher Altstadtrand
15. Jh.

V 19 Zisterzienserkloster
Chorin; am Amtssee
1273 bis Beginn des 14. Jahrhunderts

Eine für die Kolonisation der Mark Brandenburg bedeutende Tochtergründung des Klosters Lehnin war das Zisterzienserkloster Chorin. Das Kloster war der erste gelungene Versuch jener Mönche, die Gebäude nicht wie bis dahin in Haustein, sondern vollständig in gebranntem Stein auszuführen. Mit ihrer schlichten Schönheit und Vielfalt der Formen nehmen die Klostergebäude eine Schlüsselstellung für die Entwicklung und das Verständnis der Backsteingotik in der Umgebung und in ganz Mittel- und Nordeuropa ein. Nach der Säkularisierung des Klosters im Jahre 1542 dienten die Gebäude hauptsächlich als Steinbruch. Erst Karl Friedrich Schinkel erkannte den großen kulturhistorischen Wert des Klosters und setzte sich zusammen mit dem Landschaftsgärtner Peter Joseph Lenné seit 1817 für die Sicherung der Ruine ein.

The Cistercian monastery of Chorin was a daughter foundation, important for the colonization of the Mark Brandenburg, of the monastery of Lehnin. This monastery represents the monks' first successful attempt at building not in cut stone, as had hitherto been the case, but completely in brick. The austere beauty of the monastery buildings and their formal variety give them a key position in the development and understanding of brick Gothic in the region, and throughout central and northern Europe. After the secularization of the monastery in 1542 the building was used mainly as a quarry. Karl Friedrich Schinkel was the first to understand the art-historical value of the monastery, and made efforts to secure the ruins from 1817, with landscape gardner Peter Joseph Lenné.

in der Nähe/nearby:
Kloster Mariensee; Brodowin; Pehlitzwerder
1258
Dorfkirche; Serwest
2. H. 13. Jh. (Fachwerkturm 1728)
Dorfkirche; Golzow
13. Jh.
Löwinghaus; Lüdersdorf
Um 1795

V 20 Kanalbrücke
Eberswalde-Finow; Bahnlinie nach Prenzlau
1906-14

Bereits die Römer bauten gewaltige Brücken, Aquädukte, um beim Wassertransport in offenen Rinnen über große Strecken Geländeunterschiede ausgleichen zu können. Während das Problem des Wassertransports heute mit geschlossenen Röhren und Pumpen gelöst ist, können im Verlauf schiffbarer Kanäle Täler zur Vermeidung von Schleusentreppen nur durch Kanalbrücken überwunden werden. Eine der bekanntesten deutschen Überführungen dieser Art ist wohl das Wasserstraßenkreuz bei Minden, wo die 375 m lange Kanalbrücke des Mittellandkanals in 13 m Höhe die Weser überquert. Auch im Zuge des Oder-Havel-Kanals entstanden bei Eberswalde zwei aufsehenerregende Ingenieurbauwerke. Mit einer 7,90 m breiten Kanalbrücke mußte der Geländeeinschnitt der Berlin-Stettiner-Bahn überspannt werden. Ihr folgt die Überquerung des Ragöser Fließes mit einem bis zu 28 m hohen gedichteten Kanaldamm. Beide Bauwerke erforderten Böschungsbauten auf mehr als 7500 m Länge.

The Romans already built massive bridges, aqueducts, to compensate for differences in terrain when transporting water in open channels over long distances. Today the problem of transporting water is handled by the use of closed pipes and pumps, but valleys in the routes of navigable canals can only be crossed by means of canal bridges if flights of locks are to be avoided. One of the best-known bridges of this kind in Germany is probably the Minden waterway junction, where the 375 m long Mittellandkanal bridge crosses the Weser at a height of 13 m. Construction of the Oder-Havel canal also led to two striking feats of engineering. A canal bridge 7.9 m wide was needed to span the Berlin-Stettin railway cutting. This is followed by the crossing of the Ragöser Fliess by a canal embankment made watertight to a height of 28 m. Both structures needed banking over a length of more than 7,500 m.

in der Nähe/nearby:
Kranbau Eberswalde (ehemals Ardelt-Werke)
1948
Mustersiedlung; Altenhofer Straße
1930 • Robert Krafft
Schlacht- und Verarbeitungskombinat Britz
1975-78

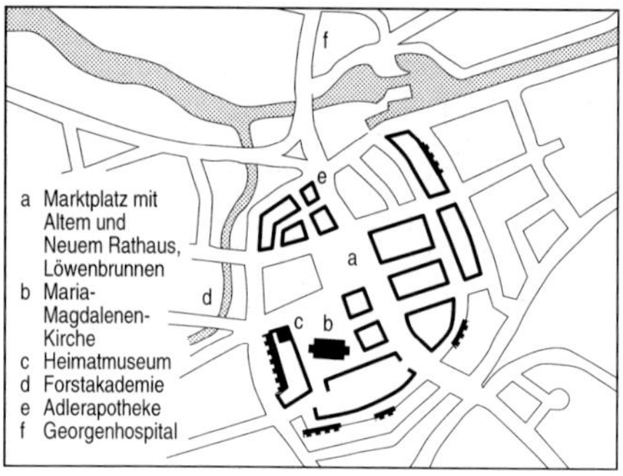

V 21 Stadtkern Eberswalde-Finow
13. Jahrhundert

Die Kreisstadt mit 55 000 Einwohnern im Eberswalder Urstromtal ist mit den Firmen Kranbau Eberswalde, Walzwerk Finow, Schlacht- und Verarbeitungswerk Britz ein wichtiger Industriestandort der östlichen Mark Brandenburg. Die Stadt wurde an einer Furt der Fernstraße Berlin–Stettin im Schutze einer Burg der Markgrafen von Brandenburg als planmäßige Anlage mit gitterförmigem Straßennetz und rechtwinkligem Markt gegründet, 1276 als Civitas erwähnt. Bereits seit dem 15. Jahrhundert entwickelte sich die Region Eberswalde zum frühesten Industriegebiet der Mark. In Eberswalde wurde seit 1440, in Finow seit 1606 in kontinuierlicher Folge die Gründung von verschiedenen Mühlen, Eisen-, Kupfer-, Blech- und Drahthämmern, Gießereien und Walzwerken, Steingutfabriken und Ziegeleien beurkundet. Dazu trugen sowohl der 1620 in Betrieb genommene Finow-Kanal, der Bau der Bahnlinie Berlin–Stettin 1842 wie auch die Gründung einer Vorstadt 1752 auf dem Kienwerder durch Kurfürst Friedrich II. bei, durch die 129 Messer- und Scherenschmiedefamilien aus Ruhla angesiedelt wurden. Große Teile der Innenstadt wurden im April 1945 durch einen Bombenangriff zerstört.

This district capital with 55,000 inhabitants in the Eberswalde glacial valley is an important industrial site in the Mark Brandenburg, home to Kranbau Eberswalde, Walzwerk Finow and Schlacht- und Verarbeitungswerk Britz. The town was founded on a ford on the main road from Berlin to Stettin protected by a castle of the margraves of Brandenburg as a planned complex with street grid and rectangular market place, and mentioned as a civitas in 1276. The Eberswalde region developed to be the Mark's earliest industrial area from as early as the fifteenth century. There is documentary evidence of a continuous sequence of foundations of various mills, iron, copper and wire hammers, foundries and rolling mills, stoneware factories and brickworks, from 1440 in Eberswalde and from 1606 in Finow. This was also boosted by the building of the Finow canal, operative from 1620, the Berlin-Stettin railway line, 1842, and the foundation of a suburb on Kienwerder by Elector Frederick II in 1752, settled by 129 cutlers and scissor-makers from Ruhla. Large parts of the town centre were destroyed by an air raid in April 1945.

in der Nähe/nearby:
Jagdschloß; Groß Schönebeck; Nähe Kirche
Nach 1660 (Instandsetzung und Umbau 1724 u. 19. Jh.)
Pfarrkirche; Joachimsthal
1817-20 (Teile 1735-38) • Schramm, Karl Friedrich Schinkel
Dorfkirche; Tuchen-Klobbicke
M. 13. Jh. (Westturm 1904)

V 22 Rathaus
Eberswalde-Finow; Marktplatz
1903-05 • Ferdinand Kohler, Paul Kranz

Das alte Rathaus an der Ecke Straße der Jugend und Kreuzstraße ist ursprünglich 1775 als Wohnhaus gebaut worden, wurde aber seit 1824 anstelle des bereits 1693 zerstörten gotischen Rathauses für die städtische Verwaltung und das Stadtgericht genutzt. Erst 1903-05 – als der Stadtsäckel wieder gefüllter war – konnte man an den Bau des Neuen Rathauses, unmittelbar neben dem Altbau, denken. Die Architekten folgten dem Formenvokabular der Neorenaissance, deren Wortführer in Deutschland eigentlich Semper war. Bis zum Ende des 19. Jahrhunderts wurden neben Wohnhäusern auch viele öffentliche Bauten wie Theater, Opernhäuser, Museen, Galerien, Rathäuser oder Bahnhöfe in diesem historistischen Stile gebaut, ob in Hamburg, Leipzig, Dresden, Hannover, Wien, Budapest, Paris oder London. Vergleicht man den Rathausbau in Eberswalde-Finow mit dem neuen Leipziger Rathaus, mit dem Hamburger Rathaus oder gar mit dem Schweriner Schloß, dann wird deutlich, daß hier in Eberswalde bei bescheideneren Mitteln nicht nur die Baumasse kleiner, sondern auch der Fassadenzierrat wohltuend schlichter ausfielen.

The old town hall on the corner of Strasse der Jugend and Kreuzstrasse was originally built as a private residence in 1775, but used from 1824 for town administration and as municipal court, instead of the Gothic town hall, destroyed as early as 1693. It was not until 1903-5 – when the town coffers were full again – that building a new town hall could be considered, immediately adjacent to the old building. The architects chose the formal vocabulary of the neo-Renaissance style, the leading exponent of which in Germany was Semper. By the end of the nineteenth century private residences had been built in this historical style, but also public buildings like theatres, opera houses, museums, galleries, town halls or stations, in towns as diverse as Hamburg, Leipzig, Dresden, Hannover, Vienna, Paris or London. If one compares the town hall in Eberswalde-Finow with the new Leipzig town hall, the town hall In Hamburg or the castle in Schwerin, it is clear that here in Eberswalde, with its more modest means, the mass of the building may be smaller, but the façade decoration is pleasingly plainer.

in der Nähe/nearby:
Löwenbrunnen; Marktplatz
1836 • Christian Daniel Rauch
Maria-Magdalenen-Kirche; Kirchstraße
1285-1300 (Restaurierung 1874-76 • Hermann Blankenstein)
Heimatmuseum; Kirchstraße 8
1735-37 • Peter Sucrow

V 23 Alte Forstakademie
Eberswalde-Finow; Schicklerstraße 3
1793

Bereits neun Jahre nach ihrer Gründung war die Berliner Forstakademie 1830 nach Eberswalde verlegt worden, um die forstwirtschaftliche Praxis im wahrsten Sinne des Wortes auch »begreifen« zu können. Mit der Amtsübernahme durch den bekannten Landforstmeister Bernhard Danckelmann – ein Bronzedenkmal für ihn stellte 1905 F. Heinemann im Forstbotanischen Garten auf – wurden neue Lehrstühle eingerichtet. Als neuer Hauptbau kam 1873-76 das Rote Gebäude hinzu, und in den vier Lehrrevieren der Oberförstereien Eberswalde, Biesenthal, Chorin und Freienwalde wurde eine biologisch orientierte Waldwirtschaft, die »Dauerwaldbewegung«, begründet. Auch Lothar Meyer lehrte hier anorganische Naturwissenschaften bis 1868, ein Jahr später stellte er in Tübingen das Periodensystem der chemischen Elemente auf. Die alte Forstakademie – 1793 als Wohnhaus des Bankiers Schickler erbaut – ist im Kern erhalten, jedoch vielfach verändert und erweitert worden. Unter Leitung des Architekten Jennen erfolgte 1913 die Rekonstruktion des Gebäudes und Rückführung auf den ursprünglichen Zustand. Wiederherstellung und Umbau des Roten Gebäudes erfolgten 1964 nach Werner Gräbner und Peter Klinkert.

The Berlin Academy of Forestry was moved to Eberswalde in 1830, just nine years after its foundation, in order to be able to «grasp» the practice of forestry in the true sense of the word. When the well-known master of forestry Bernhard Danckelmann took office – a bronze memorial to him was erected by F. Heinemann in the Forestry Botanical Garden in 1905 – new academic posts were established. The Rotes Gebäude was added in 1873-6 as the new main building, and biologically orientated forestry, the «permanent forest movement», was established in the four teaching areas of the forestry departments of Eberswalde, Biesenthal, Chorin and Freienwalde. Lothar Meyer taught inorganic science here until 1868; a year later he was to draw up the periodic table of chemical elements in Tübingen. The core of the old Forstakademie – built in 1793 as a private residence for the banker Schickler – has survived, but has been much altered and extended. The building was rebuilt and restored to its original condition under the direction of the architect Jennen in 1913. The Rotes Gebäude was restored and rebuilt in 1964 to plans by Werner Gräbner and Peter Klinkert.

in der Nähe/nearby:
Stadtmauer; Nagelstraße, Goethestraße
1. D. 14. Jh.
Adlerapotheke; Steinstraße 3
1499, 1663
Kapelle des Georgenhospitals; Breite Straße
M. 14. Jh. (Umbau zur Konzerthalle 1971)

V 24 Schiffshebewerk
Niederfinow
1926-33 • Kurt Plarre

Das Schiffshebewerk Niederfinow ist wohl der größte Schiffslift der Welt, der 1000-t-Schiffe bei einem Troggewicht von 4300 t – das entspricht dem Gewicht von 75 000 Menschen – in nur fünf Minuten um 36 Meter auf- oder abwärtsbewegt. 60 m hoch, 94 m lang und 27 m breit ist das Liftbauwerk, das mit einer 157 m langen Kanalbrücke an die obere Kanalhaltung angeschlossen ist. Eine erste Verbindung zwischen Oder und Havel gab es bereits nach dem Bau des Finowkanals 1605-1620. Der zweite Finowkanal wurde 1746 eröffnet. Durch Senkung der Oderzölle konnte nun der gesamte Überseehandel Preußens über Stettin gelenkt werden. Die schnelle Entwicklung der Eberswalder Industrie im 19. Jahrhundert und der dafür notwendige Kohle- und Erztransport erforderte einen neuen Wasserweg für 750-t-Kähne. Von 1906-14 wurde auf einer Länge von 64,6 km zwischen Hennigsdorf und Hohensaaten der Oder-Havel-Kanal gebaut. Für die Überwindung des Höhenunterschieds von 36 m zur Oderniederung wurden zunächst vier Schleusen mit einer Schleusungszeit von zwei Stunden benötigt. Das neue Schiffshebewerk bewältigt das in zwanzig Minuten.

The Niederfinow ship lift is probably the largest in the world, moving 1,000 ton ships with a laden weight of 4,300 tons – equivalent to the weight of 75,000 people – upwards or downwards by 36 metres in a mere five minutes. The lifting structure is 60 m high, 94 m long and 27 m wide, and it is connected to the upper canal level by a canal bridge 157 m long. Oder and Havel were first connected by the building of the first Finow canal in 1605-20. The second Finow canal was opened in 1746. Lowering the Oder customs tariffs meant that all Prussia's export trade could now be conducted via Stettin. Rapid development of Eberswalde's industry in the nineteenth century, and the coal and ore transport necessary for this, demanded a new waterway that could take 750 ton barges. The Oder-Havel canal was built in 1906-14 between Hennigsdorf and Hohensaaten, on an overall length of 64.6 km. The difference in height to the Oder plain was first of all tackled by a system of four locks, which took two hours to pass. The new ship lift takes twenty minutes.

in der Nähe/nearby:
Fachwerkhaus; Oderberg; Oberkietz 28
1680 • M. Christian Otte
Dorfkirche; Oderberg-Neuendorf
2. H. 13. Jh.

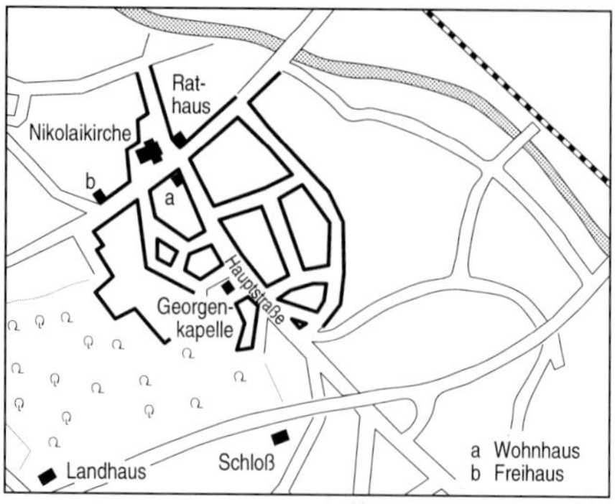

V 25 Stadtkern Bad Freienwalde
13.-17. Jahrhundert

Die Kreisstadt in waldreicher Gegend am Übergang der Barnimhochfläche zum Oderbruch ist mit ihrem Moorbad und Rheumasanatorium seit 1840 hauptsächlich Kur- und Erholungsort. Ursprünglich mag an der Pfarrkirche St. Nikolai um 1200 nahe dem Oderübergang eine deutsche Kaufmannssiedlung bestanden haben, die – 1316 erstmals genannt – sich bis 1632 allmählich nach Südosten an einer Hauptstraße angerartig erweitert hatte. In Freienwalde gab es seit der Mitte des 19. Jahrhunderts reges kulturelles Leben. Im »Aegidischen Kreis«, einem geistigen Zirkel um Karl Julius Aegidi, verkehrten Paul Heyse, Ernst Haeckel, Georg Bleibtreu und Adolf Menzel. Bei dem einflußreichen Politiker Walther Rathenau, jenem Außenminister der Weimarer Republik, der wegen der Unterzeichnung des Rapallovertrages mit der Sowjetunion 1922 ermordet wurde, trafen sich bekannte Schriftsteller wie Gerhart Hauptmann, Stefan Zweig und Fritz v. Unruh. Rathenau hatte 1909 das Schloßgrundstück Kaiser Wilhelms II. erworben. Und es gab schon seit Mitte des 19. Jahrhunderts den »Freienwalder Musenhof« mit den regionalen Dichtern Karl Weise, Julius Dörr und Victor Blüthgen.

This district capital in a densely wooded area at the point of transition from Barnim upland to the Oder marsh has been principally a spa and convalescent town with mud bath and rheumatic sanatorium since 1840. By the parish church of St. Nikolai, c. 1200, near the Oder crossing, there may originally have been a German merchants' settlement, first mentioned in 1316, which gradually extended in village green style in a south-easterly direction on a main road until 1632. There has been lively cultural life in Freienwalde since the mid nineteenth century. Paul Heyse, Ernst Haeckel, Georg Bleibtreu and Adolf Menzel were members of the «Aegidian Circle», a circle of intellectuals that formed around Karl Julius Aegidi. Well-known writers like Gerhart Hauptmann, Stefan Zweig and Fritz von Unruh met at the house of the influential politician Walther Rathenau, the foreign minister under the Weimar Republic who was murdered in 1922 for signing the treaty of Rapallo with the Soviet Union. Rathenau had acquired Kaiser Wilhelm II's palace plot in 1909. And the «Freienwalder Musenhof» with regional poets Karl Weise, Julius Dörr and Victor Blüthgen had existed since the mid nineteenth century.

in der Nähe/nearby:
Schloß; Altranft
16. Jh. (Umbauten E. 17. Jh. und nach 1910)
Chausseehaus; Schiffmühle; an der F 158
1834 • Karl Friedrich Schinkel
Schloß; Neuenhagen b. Bad Freienwalde
E. 16. Jh.

V 26 Pfarrkirche St. Nikolai
Bad Freienwalde; Am Marktplatz
Mitte 15. Jahrhundert; 1867 Turmhelm

Unter Verwendung von Resten des Feldsteinbaus aus dem 13. Jahrhundert wurde Mitte des 15. Jahrhunderts der bestehende Backsteinbau mit einem einschiffigen vierjochigen Langhaus begonnen. Zu jener Zeit war Freienwalde bereits 100 Jahre markgräflich-brandenburgische Zollstätte und blieb bis zu seinem Aussterben 1618 im Besitz des Hauses Uchtenhagen, das zwar den Fährzoll kassierte, die Wirtschaft aber kaum förderte. In der Kirche befinden sich zwei Porträts des C. v. Uchtenhagen aus den Jahren 1597 und 1603 sowie die Begräbnisstätte der Herrschaftsfamilie. Das Freihaus des Stadtherrngeschlechts ist heute Oderlandmuseum.

Work started on the present brick building with a single-aisled nave with four bays in the mid fifteenth century, using remains of the thirteenth century rubble-stone building. At that time Freienwalde had already been a customs post for the margraves of Brandenburg for 100 years, and was owned by the house of Uchtenhagen until it died out in 1618; the Uchtenhagens were happy to take the ferry toll, but did little to encourage the economy. In the church there are two portraits of C. von Uchtenhagen dating from 1597 and 1603, and the family tomb. The Uchtenhagen family house is now the Oderland Museum.

in der Nähe/nearby:
Rathaus; Am Marktplatz
1855
Freihaus Uchtenhagen; Uchtenhagenstraße 2
1557/1760
Wohnhaus; Uchtenhagenstraße 22
1787

V 27 Landhaus
Bad Freienwalde; Heilige Hallen
1789-90 • Carl Gotthard Langhans

Die eisenhaltigen und radioaktiven Quellen waren wohl schon im 14. Jahrhundert bekannt, wurden aber erst seit 1683 intensiver in Anspruch genommen. Die Aufwertung zum höfischen Kurort durch den Großen Kurfürsten und König Friedrich I. förderte die Bautätigkeit beträchtlich. Badehäuser, Moorbäder, ganze Vorstädte wurden errichtet und immer wieder Berliner Architekten, wie Andreas Schlüter, Carl Gotthard Langhans oder Karl Friedrich Schinkel, dazu nach Freienwalde beordert. Von den vielen Bauten ist unverändert nur das frühklassizistische Landhaus erhalten, ursprünglich als Kur- und Badehaus erbaut, heute aber als Internat genutzt. Von den ersten Kurgebäuden, die vermutlich um 1700 von Schlüter, im 18. Jahrhundert von Langhans und um 1820 von Schinkel gebaut wurden, ist nur das völlig veränderte Kurhaus erhalten.

The springs, radioactive and containing iron, were probably known as early as the fourteenth century, but were not intensively used until 1683. Building activity was considerably encouraged by the town's upgrading to the status of spa by the Great Elector and King Frederick I. Bath-houses, mud baths and entire suburbs were built, and Berlin architects like Andreas Schlüter, Carl Gotthard Langhans and Karl Friedrich Schinkel were repeatedly brought to Freienwalde for this purpose. Of these many buildings only the early classical Landhaus has survived unchanged. It was originally built as a spa and bath house, but is now used as a boarding school. Of the first spa buildings, presumably built c. 1700 by Schlüter, in the eighteenth century by Langhans and c. 1820 by Schinkel, only the much-altered Kurhaus has survived.

in der Nähe/nearby:
Schloß; Berliner Straße
1798-99 • David Gilly
Teehäuschen; Schloßpark
1795
Schloßpark
1820 • Peter Joseph Lenné
Georgenkapelle; Hauptstraße
1696-98 • Bernd Nugelahn

V 28 Kalköfen
Wriezen; am ehemaligen Hafen
1860 und 1889

Kalköfen für die Versorgung der örtlichen Baustellen mit Kalk waren vielerorts anzutreffen. Die Lage der Öfen am alten Wriezener Hafen läßt ahnen, daß die Rohstoffe – stückiger Kalkstein und Koks – hier über den Wasserweg kamen. Kunersdorf, südlich von Wriezen, hatte sich seit 1803 unter Peter Alexander Graf v. Itzenplitz den Ruf eines märkischen Musensitzes erworben. Außer dem Landwirtschafts-Reformer Thaer hielten sich hier die Gebrüder Humboldt, der Aufklärer Friedrich Nicolai, Freiherr vom und zum Stein, der Rechtshistoriker Friedrich Karl v. Savigny, die Bildhauer Christian Friedrich Tieck, Johann Gottfried Schadow und Christian Daniel Rauch sowie Adelbert von Chamisso und Theodor Fontane auf. Ebenso wie Wriezen wurde das Schloß, Ort der Zusammenkünfte, 1945 zerstört.

Lime kilns to provide local building sites were to be found in many places. These kilns are sited by the old harbour in Wriezen, which suggests that the raw materials – large lumps of limestone and coke – arrived here by water. Kunersdorf, south of Wriezen, had under Peter Alexander Graf von Itzenplitz acquired a reputation as home of the Muses in the Mark from 1803. Time was spent here by Thaer, the agricultural reformer, the Humboldt brothers, Friedrich Nicolai, the Enlightenment philosopher, Freiherr vom und zum Stein, Friedrich Karl von Savigny, the legal historian, sculptors Christian Friedrich Tieck, Johann Gottfried Schadow and Christian Daniel Rauch, and also Adelbert von Chamisso and Theodor Fontane. Like Wriezen itself, the castle in which they used to meet was destroyed in 1945.

in der Nähe/nearby:
Ruine der Marienkirche; Wriezen
2. H. 15. Jh.
Grabanlage Lestwitz u. Itzenplitz; Kunersdorf
Um 1800 • vermutlich Carl Gotthard Langhans
Ziegelbrennofen; Rathsdorf-Altgaul; Ortsausgang
1. H. 19. Jh.
Schloß; Gusow
17. Jh. (Umbau 3. V. 19. Jh.)

W
Barnim und unteres Spreeland

Östlich von Berlin bildet der Barnim mit der Märkischen Schweiz um Buckow und dem Waldhügelland um Strausberg eine reizvolle Landschaft, die mit landwirtschaftlich genutzten, meist ebenen Flächen abwechselt. Die Moränen der Weichsel-Eiszeit wirkten auch hier gestaltbildend. Abseits der großen Fernverkehrswege und ohne Bodenschätze blieb die Region ein reines Agrargebiet. Eine Ausnahme bildet Rüdersdorf, hier treten Muschelkalkablagerungen der Jura- und Kreidezeit zutage, mit deren Abbau bereits die Zinnaer Klosterbrüder im 13. Jahrhundert begannen und die bis heute zur Ansiedlung einer umfangreichen Baustoffindustrie führten. Die Nähe Berlins spielte hier eine entscheidende Rolle. Der südöstlich von Berlin gelegene Bereich der Mark Brandenburg mit seinem Heide- und Seengebiet und dem unteren Spreewald ist recht dünn besiedelt. Dennoch haben sich einige industrielle Schwerpunkte herausgebildet, so Fürstenwalde und seit den fünfziger Jahren Fürstenberg – das spätere Stalinstadt, zuletzt Eisenhüttenstadt. Die in weiten Teilen anmutige Landschaft mit Wäldern und Seen bietet im Spreewald, im Schlaubetal, in Bad Saarow-Pieskow und den Rauenschen Bergen oder am Scharmützelsee beliebte Ausflugs- und Erholungsziele. Die Markgrafensteine in den Rauenschen Bergen sind Zeugen der eiszeitlichen Entstehungsgeschichte der Landschaft. Wesentliche Einflüsse auf die wirtschaftliche Entwicklung der Region gingen seit 1669 vom Ausbau des Oder-Spree-Wasserweges, seit 1842 bzw. 1867 vom Bau der Märkisch-Niederschlesischen und der Görlitzer Bahn und seit den dreißiger Jahren unseres Jahrhunderts vom Bau der Autobahnen nach Frankfurt und nach Cottbus aus. Die vielfältige Verkehrsanbindung begünstigte besonders in Fürstenwalde die Industrieansiedlung. Wirtschaftliches Autarkiestreben der DDR förderte den schnellen Ausbau einer eigenen Stahlindustrie, für die am Abzweig des Oder-Spree-Kanals von der Oder bei Fürstenberg ein neues Hüttenkombinat mit eigener Wohn- und Geschäftsstadt gebaut wurde. Als vorbildliche sozialistische Stadtgründung erfuhr Eisenhüttenstadt vorrangige staatliche Förderung. Die Stadt ist heute Zeitdokument und bauliches Manifest eines inzwischen vergangenen Abschnittes brandenburgischer und deutscher Geschichte.

To the east of Berlin one finds the Barnim with the Märkische Schweiz – the «Switzerland of the Mark» – around Buckow and the wooded hills around Strausberg. It is a charming stretch of countryside, alternating with areas of flatter land used mostly for agriculture. Here, too, the appearance of the region was affected by the moraines of the Vistula ice age. Off the great long-distance routes and without mineral resources, the area has remained exclusively agricultural. Rüdersdorf is an exception: here there are Jurassic and Cretaceous muschelkalk deposits which were quarried by the monks of the Zinna monastery from the thirteenth century, and a considerable building materials industry has survived until today. The proximity of Berlin was a decisive factor in this. This area of the Mark Brandenburg to the south-east of Berlin with its heath and lake district and the lower Spreewald is thinly populated. Nevertheless there are some focal points for heavy industry, like for example Fürstenwalde and, from the fifties, Fürstenberg – later to be called Stalinstadt and finally Eisenhüttenstadt. Much of the countryside is charming, and the woods and lakes of the Spreewald, Schlaubetal, Bad Saarow-Pieskow and the Rauen hills are popular destinations for excursions and recreation. The Markgrafensteine in the Rauen hills are evidence of the ice age origina of the landscape. Important influences on the economic development of the region were the extension of the Oder-Spree waterway from 1669, the building of the Märkisch-Niederschlesische and Görlitz railways in 1842 and 1867 respectively, and the construction of the autobahns to Frankfurt and Cottbus beginning in the nineteen-thirties. These infrastructural links were a strong stimulus to industry, particularly in Fürstenwalde. The GDR's striving for industrial autonomy led to a rapid development of its own steel industry, and a new iron processing combine complete with residential and business town was built for this purpose at the site where the Oder-Spree canal branches off from the Oder near Fürstenberg. As a model of a new socialist town, Eisenhüttenstadt was given priority in terms of state subsidies. Today the town is a living document of its time and a built manifesto of a period in the history of Brandenburg and Germany that is now part of the past.

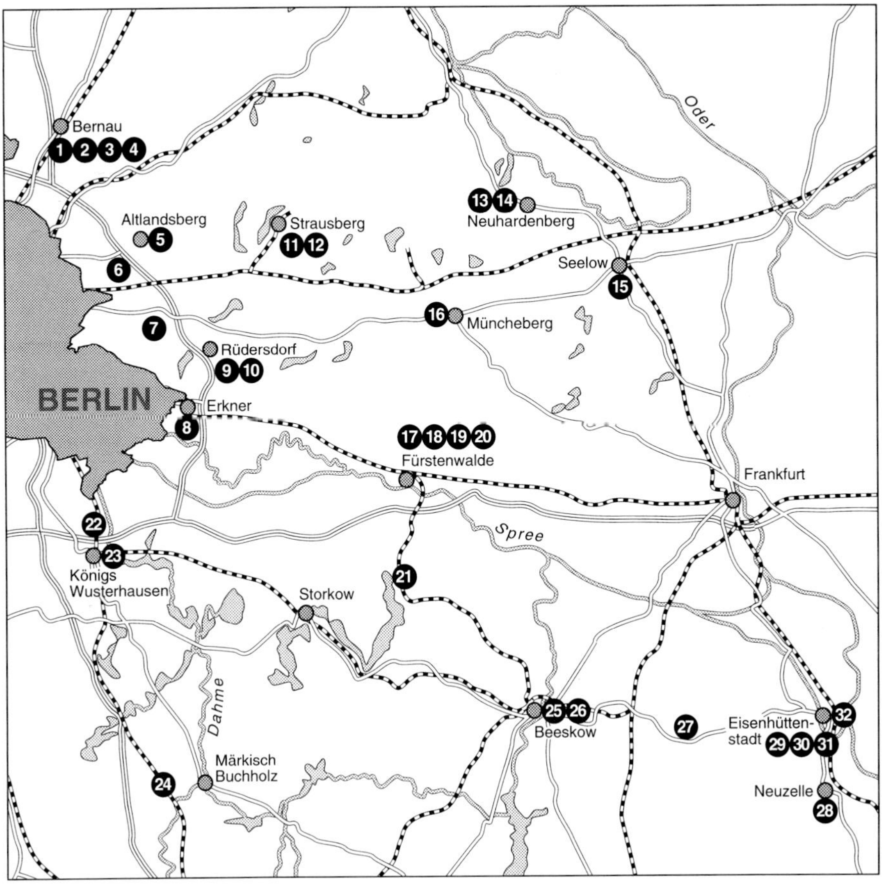

W 1 Stadtkern Bernau
W 2 Pfarrkirche St. Marien
W 3 Stadtbefestigung
W 4 Gewerkschaftshochschule
W 5 Scheunenviertel Altlandsberg
W 6 Rathaus Neuenhagen
W 7 Speicher Schöneiche
W 8 Laßensche Villa, Erkner
W 9 Eingangsportal zum Bülow-Kanal, Rüdersdorf
W 10 Kulturhaus »Martin Andersen Nexö«
W 11 Stadtkern Strausberg
W 12 Pfarrkirche St. Marien
W 13 Dorf Neuhardenberg
W 14 Schloß Neuhardenberg
W 15 Kulturhaus »Erich Weinert«, Seelow
W 16 Pfarrkirche St. Marien Müncheberg
W 17 Stadtkern Fürstenwalde
W 18 Rathaus
W 19 Pfarrkirche St. Marien
W 20 Wohnhäuser Mühlenstraße und Domstraße
W 21 Bahnhof Bad Saarow
W 22 Werksiedlung Wildau
W 23 Schloß Königs Wusterhausen
W 24 Soldatenfriedhof Halbe
W 25 Stadtkern Beeskow
W 26 Wohnhaus Kirchgasse
W 27 Bremsdorfer Mühle
W 28 Kloster Neuzelle
W 29 Eisenhüttenstadt (Fürstenberg)
W 30 Ensemble Leninallee
W 31 Wohngebäude John-Schehr-Straße
W 32 Zwillingsschachtschleuse

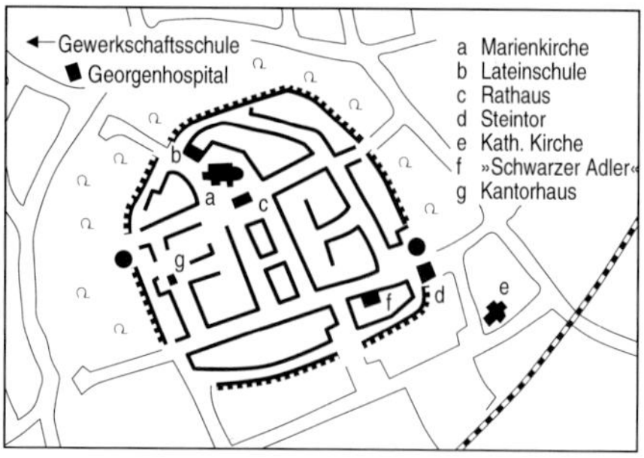

W 1 Stadtkern Bernau
Um 1230

Bernauer Bier wurde bereits seit 1413 in vielen Stadtkellern und Dorfkrügen ausgeschenkt. Bis zum Anfang des 17. Jahrhunderts galt Bernau mit 143 Brauhäusern als wichtigste märkische Braustadt. Die Textil- und Seidenproduktion – seit 1699 durch die Ansiedlung von Hugenotten gefördert – geriet bereits frühzeitig in das Kraftfeld der Berliner Industrialisierung. Seit Bestehen der S-Bahn pendeln viele Einwohner der Kreisstadt als Arbeitskräfte nach Berlin, ein Grund für die zurückhaltende industrielle Entwicklung in Bernau selbst. Um 1230 mögen die Markgrafen von Brandenburg die Stadt am alten Landweg Berlin–Stettin gegründet haben, 1296 wurde sie zur Civitas erhoben. Der kreisförmige Grundriß und das regelmäßige, nahezu rechtwinklige Straßennetz blieben über die Jahrhunderte erhalten. Seit 1975 wurden aber mehr als 80 % der Gebäude im historischen Stadtkern laut staatlichem Beschluß flächenmäßig abgebrochen und durch sterile, maßstablose Plattenbauten in veränderten Straßenfluchten ersetzt, wodurch die historische Identität der Stadt weitgehend verloren ging.

Bernau beer was sold from as early as 1413 in a large number of town cellars and village inns. By the beginning of the seventeenth century Bernau had 143 breweries and was considered the most important brewing town in the Mark. Textile and silk production – boosted from 1699 by the arrival of the Huguenots – soon moved into the force field of Berlin industrialization. As soon as the S-Bahn was built, many inhabitants of Bernau started to commute to work in Berlin, a reason for slow industrial development in Bernau itself. It is possible that the margaves of Brandenburg founded this town on the old road from Berlin to Stettin c. 1230, and it achieved the status of civitas in 1296. The circular ground plan and regular, almost right-angled network of streets survived for centuries. But since 1975 over 80% of the buildings in the historic town centre have been pulled down area by area by state decree, and replaced by sterile slab buildings with no sense of scale, in altered street alignments, which means that the historical identity of the town has largely been lost.

in der Nähe/nearby:
Dorfkirche; Lindenberg
1. H. 13. Jh. (Restauriert 1916)
Bahnhof und Strandbad Wandlitzsee; Wandlitz
1927-28 • Wilhelm Wagner
Evangelische Pfarrkirche; Biesenthal
1764-67
Dorfkirche; Börnicke
13. Jh. (Restauriert 1957)

W 2 Pfarrkirche St. Marien
Bernau; Marktplatz
1230-1519

Die Marienkirche ist eines der spätesten Beispiele der märkischen Hallenkirchen mit Umgangschor. Der erste Bau wurde möglicherweise nach der Stadtgründung um 1230 als Feldsteinbau begonnen und im 14. Jahrhundert durch eine kreuzförmige Basilika ersetzt. Annähernd fixiert ist die Vollendung des überlieferten Baus durch Peter Hinrich von Luckau. Hierzu gibt es eine Gewölbeinschrift von 1519 im Mittelschiff. Der 1490 vollendete breite Westturm wurde auf Grund von Schäden 1846 von Julius Manger durch einen quadratischen Turm ersetzt. Von stattlicher Weite ist das vierschiffige, fast quadratische Langhaus. Die Innenausstattung ist für die Mark von ungewöhnlichem Reichtum. Am kostbarsten scheint der große Hauptaltar mit Schnitzfiguren und gemalten Klappflügeln von 1520, der als Werkstattarbeit von Lucas Cranach d.Ä. angesehen wird. Auf den Emporen der Westseite und im zweiten nördlichen Seitenschiff befinden sich 75 Bilder, die nach 1614 entstanden sind. Bemerkenswert ist auch das Gemeindegestühl, darunter ein Bürgermeisterstuhl aus dem 17. Jahrhundert von nur noch selten anzutreffender Ursprünglichkeit.

The Marienkirche is one of the latest examples in the Mark of a typical hall church with ambulatory choir. It is possible that the first church was built in rubble stone after the foundation of the town in 1230, and replaced by a cruciform basilica in the fourteenth century. Completion of the present building by Peter Hinrich von Luckau is approximately fixed by a vault inscription in the nave, dating from 1519. The broad west tower, completed in 1490, was replaced because of damage by a square tower by Julius Manger in 1846. The nave is of handsome breadth, almost square, with three aisles. For the Mark the interior decoration is unusually lavish. The most valuable item seems to be the large high altar with carved figures and painted folding wings, dating from 1520 and assumed to be from the workshop of Lukas Cranach the Elder. There are 75 pictures dating from after 1614 on the galleries at the west side and in the second north aisle. The pews are also remarkable, including a seventeenth century mayor's pew of rare originality.

in der Nähe/nearby:
Lateinschulhaus; Am Kirchplatz 10
16. Jh. (Umbau 18. Jh.)
Rathaus; Marktplatz 1
1803-05 (mit Teilen von 1485) • Dornstein
Kantorhaus; Tuchmacherstraße 13/15
1582

W 3 Stadtbefestigung
Bernau
13. Jahrhundert

Strausberg und Heckelberg wurden 1402 von den Quitzows und Pommern eingeäschert. Bernaus Befestigung hielt aber stand. Der 1431 von Kurfürst Friedrich I. mit seinem Reichsheer geführte Feldzug gegen die Hussiten endete ein Jahr später mit einem Vergeltungsfeldzug gegen die Mark Brandenburg. Lebus, Müncheberg, Strausberg, Altlandsberg und Eberswalde wurden angegriffen, die Belagerung der stark befestigten Stadt Bernau war jedoch erfolglos. Die Stadtmauer vom späten 13. Jahrhundert aus sauber geschichteten Feldsteinen ist weitgehend und zum Teil in annähernd vollständiger Höhe erhalten. Viele der ursprünglich 42 Weichhäuser, Teile der Wälle und Gräben sind noch vorhanden. Der runde Pulverturm an der Westseite der Stadtmauer stammt aus dem 15. Jahrhundert. Von den einst drei Stadttoren ist nur das Steintor erhalten, ein quadratischer viergeschossiger Torturm aus Backstein mit Mansartdach aus dem späten 15. Jahrhundert, der heute als Heimatmuseum genutzt wird. Das Steintor ist mit zwei übereinander liegenden Wehrgängen mit dem runden Hungerturm verbunden.

Strausberg and Heckelberg were burned to the ground by the Quitzows and the Pomeranians in 1402. The campaign by Elector Frederick I with his imperial army against the Hussites in 1431 ended a year later with a retaliatory campaign against the Mark Brandenburg. Lebus, Müncheberg, Strausberg, Altlandsberg and Eberswalde were attacked, but the siege of the heavily fortified town of Bernau was unsuccessful. The late thirteenth century town wall in cleanly layered rubble stone has survived in good condition to a large extent, in places almost at its full height. Many of the originally 42 towers and parts of the ramparts and moats can still be seen. The round powder tower on the west side of the town wall dates from the fifteenth century. There were originally three gatehouses, of which only the Steintor has survived, a square, four-storey brick gatetower with mansard roof, dating from the fifteenth century, now used as a local history museum. The Steintor is connected to the round Hunger Tower by two fortified passages, one above the other.

in der Nähe/nearby:
Gaststätte am Steintor; Am Steintor
1978 • Wilfried Stallknecht, Lutz Mühlmann, H. Sprenger
Gaststätte »Schwarzer Adler«; Berliner Straße 33
15./16. Jh.
Katholische Pfarrkirche; Nähe Steintor
1907-08 • Ueberholz

W 4 Gewerkschaftshochschule (Bildungszentrum)
Bernau; Wandlitzer Chaussee
1928-30 • Hannes Meyer, Hans Wittwer

Die Verfassung der Weimarer Republik war eine wichtige Grundlage für legale Entfaltungsmöglichkeiten der Gewerkschaften in Deutschland. Die Reformpolitik unter Einfluß der SPD gewann Massenwirksamkeit. Das politische Konzept der Gewerkschaftsführer zur Schaffung einer »Wirtschaftsdemokratie« war mit der Bildungsaufgabe in den Gewerkschaften eng verbunden. Funktionäre und Mitglieder sollten auf Einführungs-, Fortgeschrittenen- und Speziallehrgängen geschult werden. Die Gewerkschaftszeitung schrieb dazu: »Neben der Weckung des Bildungsdranges soll die Schule das Persönlichkeits- und Gemeinschaftsgefühl stärken, durch ihre Raumgestaltung einen Eindruck erstrebenswerter Wohnkultur vermitteln.« Zwei Schulen waren geplant, eine erste in der Mark Brandenburg. Die bereits vorhandenen Tagungs- und Gründungstraditionen für verschiedenste Organisationen mögen den Standort Bernau mitbestimmt haben. Der Anfang 1928 ausgeschriebene Architektur-Wettbewerb, an dem auch Max Berg, Willi Ludewig, Erich Mendelsohn, Max Taut und Aloys Klement teilnahmen, wurde zugunsten des »Musterbeispiels moderner Baukultur« von Hannes Meyer und Hans Wittwer entschieden.

The constitution of the Weimar republic was an important basis for legitimate trade union development in Germany. Reform politics under the influence of the SPD achieved mass effectiveness. The union leaders' political plan of creating an «economic democracy» was closely connected with the educational role of the unions. Functionaries and members were to be trained in introductory, continuation and special courses. The trade union newspaper wrote on this topic: «As well as awakening a thirst for education the school should enhance personal and community awareness, and through the design of its rooms should communicate an impression of a standard of living after which is is worth while to strive.» Two schools were planned, the first in the Mark Brandenburg. The choice of Bernau as a site may have been partly determined by the existing tradition of conferences and foundation of organizations. An architectural competition was announced early in 1928, and Max Berg, Willi Ludewig, Erich Mendelsohn, Max Taut and Aloys Klement took part in it, but the decision went in favour of the «prime example of modern architectural culture» by Hannes Meyer and Hans Wittwer.

in der Nähe/nearby:
Georgenhospital; Mühlenstraße
E. 15. Jh. (Kapelle), 1738 (Spitalgebäude)
Reihenhaussiedlung; Karl-Marx-Straße
1932
Wohngebiet; Zepernicker Straße
1971 • Rudolf Krebs, P. Büttler

W 5 Scheunenviertel
Altlandsberg; Strausberger Straße, Bollersdorfer Weg
2. Hälfte 19. Jahrhundert

Die Kleinstadt Altlandsberg mit ihren nur 3000 Einwohnern hatte bereits vor 1257 brandenburgisches Stadtrecht. Mit der Verlegung der Fernstraßen verlor der Ort seine ursprünglich verkehrsgünstige Lage, was teilweise die gedämpfte wirtschaftliche Entwicklung erklärt. Die vom kurfürstlichen Minister Graf Otto v. Schwerin 1670 hier erstmalig in Brandenburg angesiedelten Hugenotten zogen bereits zwei Jahre später nach Berlin, um sich der französischen Kolonie anzuschließen. Auch die 1709 prachtvoll ausgebaute Residenz König Friedrichs I. verfiel nach seinem Tode. In der 2. Hälfte des 19. Jahrhunderts blühte in Altlandsberg aber offenbar die Landwirtschaft auf, worauf das Scheunenviertel hindeutet. Die starke Konzentration der Scheunen außerhalb der Stadt, die doch sonst einzeln am Bauernhof stehen, läßt Raum für Vermutungen über die Gründe dafür: beschleunigte Entwicklung der deutschen Landwirtschaft seit Mitte des 19. Jahrhunderts oder fehlender Platz im Stadtgebiet, Brandschutz oder erste Bauergebnisse einer deutschen Raiffeisen-Genossenschaft.

The little town of Altlandsberg with only 3,000 inhabitants was granted a Brandenburg charter even before 1257. When the routes of the long-distance roads were altered, the place lost its original favourable situation in terms of traffic, which partially explains its muted economic development. The first Huguenots in Brandenburg were settled here in 1670 by the Elector's minister Graf Otto von Schwerin, but they moved to Berlin two years later to join the French colony there. Frederick I's residence was magnificently extended in 1709, but fell into disrepair after his death. In the second half of the nineteenth century it seems that agriculture thrived in Altlandsberg, as the barn quarter suggests. This great concentration of barns outside the town, rather than building them individually on farms, as is customary, leaves room for speculation as to the reasons for it: accelerated development of German agriculture from the mid nineteenth century, or lack of space inside the town, fire protection, or early buildings by a German farmers' co-operative.

in der Nähe/nearby:
Stadtmauer, Berliner und Strausberger Torturm
14./15. Jh.
Stadtkirche St. Marien; nördl. Teil d. Stadtkerns
M. 13. Jh. (Umbau 1432)
Schloßkirche; nw. d. Stadtmauer
1768

W 6 Rathaus
Neuenhagen; Am Rathaus 1
1925-26 • Wilhelm Wagner

Wassertürme erhielten im 19. Jahrhundert eine architektonisch gegliederte und stilistisch gestaltete Verkleidung, erst in neuerer Zeit werden sie als nackte Konstruktion belassen. In der Bauzeit des Neuenhagener »Ratswasserturms« waren Verkleidungen solcher technischen Anlagen durchaus noch üblich. Sinnigerweise hat der Architekt diesen Aspekt mit den Vorstellungen der Ratsherren verwoben, ein respektables und repräsentatives Amtsgebäude in zeitgemäßen Formen zu errichten. Dazu leisten auch die vertikal- und eckbetonten, dekorativ-ornamentalen Klinkervermauerungen ihren Beitrag. Als Monument im Übergangsstil zwischen Expressionismus und Sachlichkeit wacht das Rathaus seitdem über die Stadt, in der Hans Fallada später »Bauern, Bonzen und Bomben« und »Kleiner Mann, was nun« schrieb.

In the nineteenth century, water towers were still disguised with articulated, highly stylish architecture. It is only recently that they have been left as naked structures, but at the time the Neuenhagen «council water tower» was built it was still customary to cover industrial buildings in this way. Sensibly the architect combined this with the council's request for a respectable and imposing official building of contemporary design. The clinker walls, with stressed corners and verticals, decorative and ornamental, also make a contribution to this. As a monument in the transitional style between Expressionism and Functionalism, the town hall has since that time watched over the town in which Hans Fallada was later to write «Bauern, Bonzen und Bomben» and «Kleiner Mann, was nun».

in der Nähe/nearby:
Pfarrkirche; Werneuchen
1873
Gruftbau; Werneuchen; westlich der Kirche
A. 19. Jh. • Gilly-Schule
Schleuse; Woltersdorf; zw. Kalksee und Flakensee
16. Jh.; 17. Jh.; 1876-82

W 7 Speicher
Schöneiche; An der Reihe
1749

Das bereits 1375 erwähnte Schöneiche, mit seinen heute 9600 Einwohnern immer im »Schatten« von Berlin gelegen, ist im Laufe der Jahrhunderte durch die unterschiedlichen Interessen der hier ansässigen Gutsbesitzer als Dorf weitgehend deformiert worden. Bereits von 1527 bis 1690 zog die Herrschaft von Krummensee sämtliche Bauern- und Kossätenhöfe zum Rittergut zusammen. 1725 hatte der Geheime Rat und spätere Waisenhausbesitzer Severin Schindler das Rittergut erworben und hielt es bis 1747. Bereits 14 Jahre später ging der Besitz an Friedrich Wilhelm Schütze, der neben dem Bankier und Unternehmer Splittgerber der bedeutendste Berliner Kaufmann, Seidenmanufakturist und Hofbankier Friedrichs II. war. Er richtete auf dem Gut eine Wachsmanufaktur ein, die Lichte bis nach Südosteuropa exportierte. Bis 1844 blieb Schöneiche im Besitz der 1786 geadelten Herrschaft Schütze. Das barocke Schloß mit Orangerie und Park aus dem Jahre 1765 wurde 1945-49 unter mysteriösen Umständen beseitigt. Zwei Eisengußvasen der Torpfeiler sind im Heimatmuseum erhalten. Der Speicher, ein eingeschossiger Fachwerkbau mit Aufzugserker, wurde in erster Linie vermutlich als Getreidereservoir genutzt.

Schöneiche was mentioned as early as 1375. It now has 9,600 inhabitants, and has always been in the «shadow» of Berlin. In the course of the centuries it has been largely distorted as a village by the conflicting interests among the resident landowners. From 1527 to 1690 the lords of Krummensee brought all the farmers and cottagers together into the manor. In 1725 Privy Councillor and later orphanage owner Severin Schindler acquired the manor, and retained it until 1747. Fourteen years later it passed to Wilhelm Schütze, who alongside Splittgerber, a banker and entrepreneur, was the most important Berlin merchant, purveyor of silk and court banker to Friedrich II. He established a wax factory on the estate that exported candles as far as southern Europe. Until 1844 Schöneiche remained in the possession of the Schütze family, which had been ennobled in 1786. The baroque Castle with orangery and park dating from 1765 was removed under mysterious circumstances in 1945-9. Two cast-iron urns from the gate pillars have survived in the local history museum. The storehouse, a single-storey half-timbered building with lift bay, was presumably used principally as a grain store.

in derNähe/nearby:
Doppelstubenhaus; Schöneiche-Kleinschönebeck
M. 18. Jh.
Dorfkirche; Schöneiche-Kleinschönebeck
15./16. Jh.
Dorfkirche; Schöneiche
13. Jh. (überformt 1725)

W 8 Laßensche Villa
Erkner; Gerhart-Hauptmann-Straße 1-2
Um 1875

Obwohl bereits 1579 erwähnt, entwickelte sich die heute 8000 »Seelen« zählende Industriegemeinde Erkner erst Mitte des 19. Jahrhunderts. 1860 siedelten sich hier die Rütgerswerke an, die erste Steinkohlenteer-Großdestillation Deutschlands. Bereits drei Jahre nach der Erfindung des Bakelits, des ersten vollsynthetischen Kunststoffs, durch Leo Hendrik Baekeland, begann in Erkner 1910 der Bau eines Bakelitwerkes, in dem die Phenole des Teerwerkes verarbeitet wurden. In dieser Industriegemeinde bezog der lungenkranke Gerhart Hauptmann 1885 die zehn Jahre alte Laßensche Villa – die heutige Gedenkstätte – um in der waldreichen Umgebung Erkners zu gesunden. Der 1912 mit dem Nobelpreis ausgezeichnete Hauptmann sammelte in Erkner Eindrücke für seine Werke »Bahnwärter Thiel«, »Der Biberpelz«, »Die Ratten« und vor allem »Vor Sonnenaufgang« (1889) – das wegen der sozialkritischen Thematik einen der größten Skandale in der deutschen Theatergeschichte auslöste. Als Angehöriger der naturalistischen Generation um Arno Holz pflegte Hauptmann auch Verbindungen mit dem Friedrichshagener Dichterkreis um Wilhelm Bölsche, Bruno Wille und die Brüder Hart.

Although it was mentioned as early as 1579, the Erkner industrial community, then with 8,000 «souls», did not develop until the mid nineteenth century. In 1860 the Rütgers factory moved here, Germany's first large-scale coal tar distillation plant. Only three years after the invention of bakelite, the first completely synthetic manmade material, by Leo Hendrik Baekeland, work started on a bakelite factory in Erkner in 1910, in which phenols from the tar plant were processed. Gerhart Hauptmann, who had a lung disease, moved into the Lassen Villa in 1885, which was ten years old at the time – now the Hauptmann memorial centre – in order to recuperate in the wooded surroundings of Erkner. Hauptmann was awarded the Nobel Prize in 1912. In Erkner he collected material for his «Bahnwärter Thiel», «Der Biberpelz», «Die Ratten» and above all «Vor Sonnenaufgang» (1889), which caused one of the greatest scandals in German theatrical history because of the social criticism inherent in its subject matter. As a member of the naturalistic generation associated with Arno Holz, Hauptmann also maintained connections with the group of Friedrichshagen poets including Wilhelm Bölsche, Bruno Wille and the Hart brothers.

in der Nähe/nearby:
Fachwerkhaus; Erkner; Heinrich-Heine-Straße 17-18
2. H. 18. Jh.
Friderizianisches Kolonistendorf; Gosen
M. 18. Jh.
Doppelhaus; Gosen; Seestraße 28
E. 18. Jh.

W 9 Eingangsportal zum Bülow-Kanal
Rüdersdorf; Heinitzstraße, am Bülow-Kanal
1816 • Johann Gottlieb Schlätzer

Die Industriegemeinde Rüdersdorf mit ihren 12 400 Einwohnern, bekannt durch bedeutende Kalksteinbrüche, entstand 1934 durch Zusammenschluß der Ortsteile Rüdersdorf, Kalkberge und Tassdorf. Der Kalksteinabbau ist bereits aus dem 13. Jahrhundert überliefert. Von 1308 bis 1319 verwalteten hier die Zinnaer Klosterbrüder offenbar ihren Barnimbesitz und den Kalksteinbruch. Nachdem die Kalksteinbrüche 1769 dem Bergwerk- und Hüttendepartement in Berlin unterstellt worden waren, gewann Friedrich II. zu dessen Leitung den erfahrenen kursächsischen Generalbergkommissar Friedrich Anton v. Heinitz. Er und sein Nachfolger Graf v. Reden setzten Sprengpulver zur Kalksteinförderung ein und ließen 1805-16 den Heinitz-, den Bülow- und den Reden-Kanal mit Eingangsportalen für den besseren Transport der Baustoffe nach Berlin anlegen. Die Zementproduktion begann in Rüdersdorf bereits 1855. Seit 1911 mußten sich mehrere Firmen die Produktion teilen, eine davon war die Rittergut-Rüdersdorf-GmbH. Die hochwertigen Portlandzemente eigneten sich besonders für den Deckbeton des Autobahnbaus seit Mitte der dreißiger Jahre.

The industrial community of Rüdersdorf with 12,400 inhabitants, known for important limestone quarries, was created in 1934 when the districts of Rüdersdorf, Kalkberge and Tassdorf were amalgamated. Limestone has been quarried here since the thirteenth century. From 1308 to 1319 the monks of Zinna administered their Barnim possessions and the limestone quarry here. After the quarries 1769 were put under the jurisdiction of the mining and iron and steel department in Berlin, Frederick II appointed the experienced general commissioner of mines from Electoral Saxony, Friedrich Anton von Heinitz, to be director of this department. He and his successor, Graf von Reden, started to use blasting to quarry the limestone, and in 1805-16 built the Heinitz, Bülow and Reden canals, all with entrance portals, to make transporting the materials to Berlin easier. Cement production in Rüdersdorf started as early as 1855. From 1911 several firms had to share production, and one of these was Rittergut-Rüdersdorf-GmbH. The high-quality Portland cement has been particularly suitable for autobahn surfacing since the mid thirtees.

in der Nähe/nearby:
Kalkofen System Rumford; Heinitzstraße
Um 1802
Bergamtsgebäude; Heinitzstraße 10
Um 1820 • Karl Friedrich Schinkel
Uhrturm; Heinitzstraße
Um 1844

W 10 Kulturhaus »Martin Andersen Nexö«
Rüdersdorf; Leninplatz
1954-56 • Emil Leibold

Das »Kulturhaus« wurde für die seinerzeit neu etablierte DDR und ihre gesellschaftlichen Ziele zu einem baulichen Beispiel der vollzogenen politischen Wandlungen. Gegenüber den Volkshäusern im 19. Jahrhundert und den Stadthallen der zwanziger Jahre unterschied es sich durch eine umfassendere Zweckbestimmung und ein entsprechend ausgeklügeltes Raumprogramm. Das Kulturhaus war nicht nur mit einem Mehrzwecksaal, sondern mit Räumen zur künstlerischen Selbstbetätigung, mit einer Bibliothek, mit Spielräumen und Gaststätten ausgestattet. Es gab eine ganze Palette von Kultureinrichtungen und -häusern unterschiedlichster Größe, angefangen bei der »Roten Ecke« in der Gaststätte für nur wenige Personen bis hin zum Kulturpalast mit mehr als 1000 Saalplätzen. Die ersten Kulturhäuser in der DDR, meist in antikisierender Form, sind in den fünfziger Jahren durch große volkseigene Betriebe an Brennpunkten der Wirtschaft errichtet worden, so das Kulturhaus der Maxhütte in Unterwellenborn, das Friedrich-Wolf-Theater in Eisenhüttenstadt und das Kulturhaus in Rüdersdorf.

The «House of Culture» was a solid symbol of the political changes that had taken place in the GDR, newly established at the time, and of its social aims. It differed from the nineteenth century people's halls and the city halls of the twenties by having a more comprehensive set of uses and thus an appropriately more ingenious organization of space. Houses of culture had not only a multi-purpose hall, but also rooms for the people's own artistic activities: library, playrooms and restaurants. There was a whole range of cultural facilities and sections of different sizes, starting with the «Rote Ecke» in the restaurant for only a few people up to the Kulturpalast, a hall seating over a thousand. The first houses of culture in the GDR, usually in classical style, were built in the fifties by large companies owned by the people at economic focal points, like the Maxhütte Kulturhaus in Unterwellenborn, the Friedrich-Wolf-Theater in Eisenhüttenstadt and this Kulturhaus in Rüdersdorf.

in der Nähe/nearby:
Bergarbeitersiedlung »Landhof«; Am Mühlenfließ
Um 1850
Autobahnbrücke; Rüdersdorf-Kalkberge
Um 1935
Zementwerk IV
1963-64 • Werner Gräbner uam.

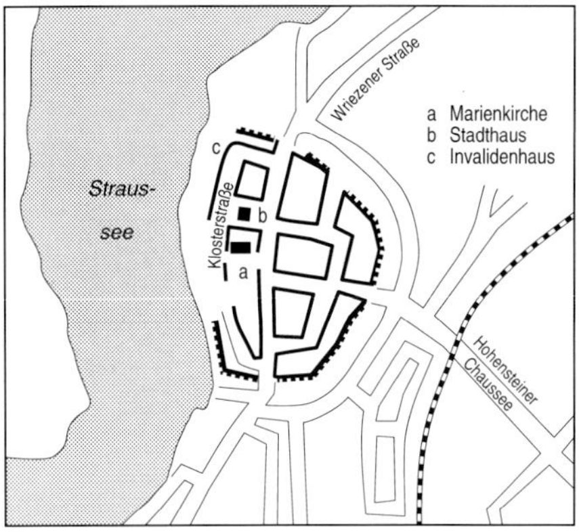

W 11 Stadtkern Strausberg
13. Jahrhundert

Die Kreisstadt mit 28 000 Einwohnern in reizvoller Wald- und Seenlandschaft am Ostufer des Straussees war jahrelang Sitz des DDR-Verteidigungsministeriums. Der Altstadtkern, der im 13. Jahrhundert im Schutze einer wettinischen Burg mit dominierender Marienkirche entstand, war oval und hatte zwei Straßen in Nord-Süd-Richtung, die durch einen breiten Markt verbunden waren. 1232 erhielt Strausberg das Stadtrecht. Trotz Mauerbefestigung wurde die Stadt 1402 von den Quitzows gestürmt und geplündert und nach dem Dreißigjährigen Krieg zum »elendsten Ort der Mark«. Auf königliche Order öffnete 1792 auf dem Gelände des ehemaligen Dominikaner-Klosters ein Landarmen- und Invalidenhaus für »mutwillige Bettler, Zigeuner und andere Vagabunden«. Kriegsinvaliden mit ihren Familien fanden hier Aufnahme, und das Haus füllte sich schnell mit mehr als 300 Personen. Mit der Fabrikation der minderwertigen Tuchsorte »Futterboy« wurde Strausberg vom 18. bis 19. Jahrhundert wichtigster Heereslieferant. Die industrielle Entwicklung blieb aber trotz Eisenbahnanschluß seit 1867 sehr gedämpft.

This district capital with 28,000 inhabitants, set in charming countryside with woods and lakes on the east bank of the Straussee, was for years the administrative centre of the GDR defence ministry. The core of the old town, dominated by the Marienkirche, was built in the thirteenth century under the protection of a Wettin castle. It was oval, and had two streets running north-south, connected by a broad market place. Strausberg was granted a charter in 1232. Despite its fortifying wall the town was stormed and plundered by the Quitzows in 1402 and at the end of the Thirty Years' War was the «most wretched place in the Mark». On the king's orders a local poor-house and infirmary was opened in 1792 on the site of the former Dominican monastery, for «mischievous beggars, gypsies and other vagabonds». War invalids and their families were accepted here, and the building rapidly filled up with over 300 people. From the eighteenth to the nineteenth century Strausberg became the most important army supply centre, manufacturing a low-quality cloth called «Futterboy». Despite the arrival of the railway in 1867 industrial development remained very subdued.

in der Nähe/nearby:
Brecht-Weigel-Haus; Buckow, Bertolt-Brecht-Straße 29
1908
Schloß; Prötzel
1712/1730 • wohl Andreas Schlüter
Dorfkirche; Herzfelde
2. V. 13. Jh. (Glocke 1564 • Michael Kesler)

W 12 Pfarrkirche St. Marien
Strausberg; Predigerstraße
Mitte 13. Jahrhundert

Sie zählt wohl zu den beachtlichen Baudenkmalen der Mark Brandenburg, die Marienkirche. So oder so ähnlich mag auch die erste Berliner Nikolaikirche ausgesehen haben. Das Langhaus und der gestreckte Rechteckchor der gut erhaltenen frühgotischen Pfeilerbasilika aus Feldsteinen waren ursprünglich flach gedeckt und erhielten erst um die Mitte des 15. Jahrhunderts ein Gewölbe, wobei anstelle der rundbogigen neue spitzbogige Fenster eingesetzt wurden. Original erhalten sind allerdings die drei Lanzettfenster in der Ostwand. Zu den Besonderheiten des Innenraumes zählen die Gewölbemalerei des Chores von 1448 – restauriert 1920 – der Schnitzaltar etwa von 1520 und der Orgelprospekt mit reichem Schnitzwerk von 1773. Am mächtigen Westturm fallen das mehrfach abgetreppte breitspitzbogige Portal und die schlanken zweiteiligen spätgotischen Schallfenster auf.

The Marienkirche is probably one of the most important buildings in the Mark Brandenburg. The first Nikolaikirche in Berlin must have looked like this, or very similar. The nave and extended rectangular choir of the well-preserved early Gothic rubble-stone basilica originally had a flat roof, and were not vaulted until the mid fifteenth century, and at the same time new pointed-arched windows replaced the old round-arched ones. The three lancet windows in the east wall are the originals, however. Special interior features are the vault painting in the choir dating from 1448 – restored 1920 – the carved altar of c. 1520 and the organ front with lavish carving dating from 1773. Striking features of the massive west façade are the portal with ribbed, broad, pointed arch and the slender bipartite late Gothic louvres.

in der Nähe/nearby:
Stadtmauer und Weichhäuser; so. und sw. Rand des Stadtkerns
Nach 1254
Stadthaus (Rathaus); Markt
1819-25
Invaliden- und Landarmenhaus; Klosterstraße
1787-92

W 13 Dorf Neuhardenberg
1348 erwähnt

Das Angerdorf, als Quilitz bereits 1348 erwähnt, hat mit 2000 Einwohnern für märkische Verhältnisse die bedeutende Längenausdehnung von zwei Kilometern. Nach starken Zerstörungen durch den Brand von 1801 fand der junge Karl Friedrich Schinkel bei der klassizistischen Neugestaltung des Angerdorfs auch unter Karl August Graf von Hardenberg sein erstes großes Betätigungsfeld. Der Staatskanzler war 1814 vom preußischen König gefürstet und mit dem Dorf Quilitz beschenkt worden, das 1815 in Neuhardenberg umgenannt wurde. Als Nachfolger des Freiherrn vom und zum Stein führte von Hardenberg bis 1822 in Brandenburg-Preußen eine progressive Agrargesetzgebung ein. – Graf Carl Hans v. Hardenberg war als Verschwörer vom 20. Juli 1944 bis April 1945 im KZ Sachsenhausen inhaftiert gewesen. – Der Hardenbergsche Grundbesitz ist im Herbst 1945 enteignet und der Ort 1949 in Marxwalde umgenannt worden.

This village on a village green pattern, mentioned as Quilitz as early as 1348, has 2,000 inhabitants and is an impressive, by Mark standards, two kilometres long. The village was badly damaged by fire in 1801, and the young Karl Friedrich Schinkel found his first major chance of work when he rebuilt the village in classical style under Karl August Graf von Hardenberg. In 1814 the State Chancellor had been raised to the rank of prince by the Prussian king, and presented with the village of Quilitz, which was renamed Neuhardenberg in 1815. As successor to Freiherr vom und zum Stein, Hardenberg introduced progressive agricultural legislation in Brandenburg-Prussia until 1822. Graf Carl Hans von Hardenberg was imprisoned in Sachsenhausen concentration camp from 20 July 1944 to autumn 1945 as a member of the July Plot. The Hardenberg possessions were appropriated in autumn 1945 and the place renamed Marxwalde in 1949.

in der Nähe/nearby:
Verwalterhaus des Vorwerks; Quappendorf-Bärwinkel
1801-03 • Karl Friedrich Schinkel
Turm der ehem. Dorfkirche; Letschin
1812, 1818-19 • Karl Friedrich Schinkel
Dorfkirche; Ringenwalde
M. 13. Jh.

W 14 Schloß
Neuhardenberg; Am Anger
1820-22 • Karl Friedrich Schinkel

Nach dem Aufbau der Dorfkirche von 1815-17 als klassizistischer Saalbau mit dorischer Säulenhalle und Mausoleum des Staatskanzlers Hardenberg erhielt Karl Friedrich Schinkel um 1820 den Auftrag, das Schloß umzubauen. Ursprünglich wohl höher geplant, hatte der Vorbesitzer von Prittwitz auf königlichen Einspruch seinen Bau um 1763 eingeschossig belassen müssen. Deshalb machte es Schinkel wenig Mühe, ein weiteres Geschoß unter Beibehaltung des Grundrisses und der Gliederung aufzubringen. Das Dach mit flacher Neigung, das 1852 zum heutigen Walmdach umgebaut wurde, verschwand hinter einer Brüstung, die über dem Eingang durch einen Adler bekrönt wurde. In der Strenge der Gestaltung war am Schloß und den umliegenden Bauten bereits der spätere Architekt der Berliner Bauakademie spürbar. Die Umgestaltung des Schloßparks zum Landschaftspark 1821 zählte für Peter Joseph Lenné zu seinen ersten Aufgaben. Der Einfluß von Hermann Fürst v. Pückler-Muskau – Hardenbergs Schwiegersohn – war dabei noch wirksam. Im Park befindet sich das erste Denkmal Friedrichs II., 1792 nach Entwürfen von Johann Wilhelm Meil hergestellt.

After extending the village church in 1815-7 as a classical single-roomed building with Doric columned hall and mausoleum for State Chancellor Hardenberg, Karl Friedrich Schinkel was commissioned c. 1820 to rebuild the castle. It was probably originally intended to be higher, but the previous owner of Prittwitz had had to stop building after one single storey in 1763, as a result of a protest from the king. Thus Schinkel had little difficulty in adding another storey, while keeping ground plan and articulation. The shallow slope, rebuilt in 1852 as the present hipped roof, disappeared behind a parapet crowned with an eagle over the entrance. The austere design of castle and surrounding buildings already shows traces of the later architect of the Berlin Bauakademie. Peter Joseph Lenné redesigned the park as a landscaped park as one of his first commissions in 1821. The influence of Hermann Fürst von Pückler-Muskau, Hardenberg's son-in-law, can still be seen here. In the park is the first monument to Frederick II, constructed in 1792 to designs by Johann Wilhelm Meil.

in der Nähe/nearby:
Dorfkirche; Dorfallee
1814-17 • Karl Friedrich Schinkel
Wirtschaftsgebäude; Nähe Schloß
1802-03 • Karl Friedrich Schinkel
Orangerie; östlich vom Schloß
Um 1820

W 15 Kulturhaus
Seelow; Erich-Weinert-Straße 13
1955-57 • Hans-Jürgen Kluge

Oft ist wohl die Geschichte an der alten Kreisstadt Seelow an der Ostkante der Lebuser Hochebene zum Oderbruch vorübergegangen, zweimal nicht. Ein glorreiches Kapitel deutscher Geschichte schlug 1747 König Friedrich II. auf, als er die wohl größte ingenieurtechnische Tat dieser Art und jener Zeit in Europa einleitete: Die wassertechnische Regulierung und Trockenlegung des Oderbruchs, die Neuverlegung und Verkürzung des Oderlaufs von 46 auf 21 km und die Anlage unzähliger Deiche und Entwässerungsgräben brachte fruchtbares Land für Siedler aus ganz Europa. – Ein trauriges Kapitel wurde hier am 16. April 1945 mit der letzten entscheidenden militärischen Operation des Zweiten Weltkrieges eingeleitet, dem sowjetischen Angriff auf die Reichshauptstadt. Bei etwa dreifacher sowjetischer Überlegenheit nahmen an den Kämpfen bei Seelow 3,5 Millionen Soldaten teil, 52 000 Geschütze, 8000 Panzer und 11 000 Flugzeuge. Der Zerstörungsgrad der Region war furchtbar. Der rasche Neubau des Kulturhauses in der vom Krieg schwer gezeichneten Stadt Seelow hatte wohl mehr Symbolcharakter für die vollzogene politische Wandlung.

History often passed by the old district capital of Seelow on the eastern edge of the Lebus plateau as it falls to the low plain of the Oder marsh, but on two occasions it didn't. King Frederick II opened a glorious passage of German history in 1747 when he introduced what was probably the greatest engineering feat of its kind, and for the period, in Europe: water regulation and draining on the Oder marsh, changing and shortening the course of the Oder from 46 to 21 km and constructing countless dikes and drainage ditches, thus creating fertile land for settlers from all over Europe. A sad chapter started here on 16 April 1945 with the last decisive military operation of the Second World War, the Soviet attack on the imperial capital. The Soviets had almost threefold superiority. 3.5 million soldiers were involved in the battle for Seelow, 52,000 pieces of heavy artillery, 8,000 tanks and 11,000 aeroplanes. The level of destruction in the region was terrible. The fact that the House of Culture in the town of Seelow, so badly bruised by the war, was built so rapidly was probably to a large extent a symbol of achieved political change.

in der Nähe/nearby:
Stadtkirche; Seelow
1830-32 • Siedler, Karl Friedrich Schinkel
Gedenkstätte an die Kämpfe 1945; Seelow
1946-47 • Lew Kerbel

W 16 Pfarrkirche St. Marien
Müncheberg; östlich vom Marktplatz
15. Jahrhundert

Bereits 1928 wurde das Forschungszentrum der Landwirtschaftswissenschaften als Institut für Züchtungsforschung der Kaiser-Wilhelm-Gesellschaft Berlin in die Kleinstadt verlegt, wo Erwin Baur 1931 die Süßlupine züchtete. Müncheberg, das um 1225 entstand, wurde 1945 zu 85 Prozent zerstört. Erhalten blieben die Stadtbefestigung von 1310 sowie der Küstriner und der Berliner Torturm aus dem 15. und 14. Jahrhundert. Von der Marienkirche blieben 1945 Westturm und Kirchenschiffumfassung erhalten. Das Kirchenschiff war im 15. Jahrhundert zu einer zweischiffigen Backsteinhalle umgebaut worden. Der »i-Punkt« der Kirche, der hohe Westturm, wurde 1826-29 von Karl Friedrich Schinkel effektvoll mit einem vier Meter langen Zwischenbau über spitzbogiger Öffnung am Kirchenschiff angehängt.

The agricultural science research centre was moved to the little town as early as 1928, as a breeding research institute of the Kaiser-Wilhelm-Gesellschaft in Berlin. Erwin Baur bred the sweet lupin there in 1931. Eighty-five per cent of Müncheberg, which came into being c. 1225, was destroyed in 1945. The 1310 town fortifications survived, and so did the Küstrin and Berlin gate towers, dating from the fifteenth and fourteenth centuries. In 1945 the west tower and outer nave walls of the Marienkiche were still standing. The nave had been rebuilt as a brick hall with nave and one aisle in the fifteenth century. The final striking touch, the high west tower, was attached to the nave by Karl Friedrich Schinkel in 1826-9, using a pointed-arched opening.

in der Nähe/nearby:
Komturei der Templer u. Johanniter; Lietzen-Nord
Um 1244
Speicher; Lietzen-Nord; Wirtschaftshof
Wohl 14. Jh.
Gutshaus (Ambulatorium); Heinersdorf
E. 17. Jh. (Erweiterung 1866)
Gutshof; Heinersdorf-Behlendorf
1802 • Karl Friedrich Schinkel
Schloß, Bibliothek und Dorfkrug; Steinhöfel
1790/1795 • David Gilly
Landschaftspark; Steinhöfel
Um 1795 • vermutlich Johann August Eyserbeck

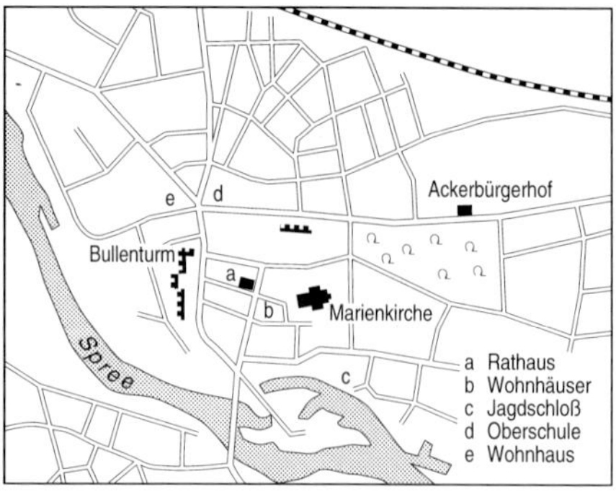

W 17 Stadtkern Fürstenwalde
1252-58

Die Kreisstadt an der schmalsten Stelle des Warschau-Berliner Urstromtales – heute mit 36 000 Einwohnern – ist mit der Reifenproduktion, dem Tankanlagenbau und vielen anderen Betrieben ein wichtiger Industriestandort östlich von Berlin. Die von den Askaniern an einer Spreefurt gegründete Stadt auf annähernd rechteckigem Grundriß mit gitterförmigem Straßennetz, mittig gelegenem Rathaus und am Ostrand befindlicher Kirche und Burg war bereits im 13. Jahrhundert stark befestigt und hatte drei Stadttore. 1285 wurde Fürstenwalde Civitas. Seit Bestehen des Friedrich-Wilhelm-Kanals, der 1669 eine Verbindung zwischen Schlesien und Hamburg herstellte, war die Stadt wichtiger Umschlagplatz für den Handel, im 18. Jahrhundert auch Zentrum der Tuchmacherei. Von 1843 bis 1909 wurden mehr als 100 Betriebe neu gegründet, darunter die Berliner Aktienbrauerei »Tivoli«, die Maschinenbaufirma Pintsch und die Deutsche Kabelwerke-AG. Fürstenwalde war 1842 durch den Bau der Eisenbahn Berlin–Frankfurt und den neuen Oder-Spree-Kanal von 1891 ein attraktiver Industriestandort geworden. Die ansässigen Rüstungswerke wurden aber nach 1945 demontiert.

This district capital at the narrowest point of the Warsaw-Berlin glacial valley – now with 36,000 inhabitants – is an important industrial centre east of Berlin, with tyre production, container tank production and numerous other businesses. The town was founded by the Ascanians at a ford on the Spree on an approximately rectangular ground plan with grid street network, centrally placed town hall and church and castle on the eastern periphery. It was strongly fortified by the thirteenth century and had three town gates. It became a civitas in 1285. From the opening of the Friedrich-Wilhelm-Kanal, which established a connection between Silesia and Hamburg in 1669, the town was an important trade centre, and also a centre for cloth-making in the eighteenth century. From 1843-1909 more than 100 new businesses were founded, including the «Tivoli» brewery, Pintsch, the mechanical engineering firm, and Deutsche Kabelwerke AG. Fürstenwalde had become an attractive industrial site as a result of the building of the Berlin-Frankfurt an der Oder railway in 1842 and the new Oder-Spree canal that opened in 1891. The armament firms were dismantled after 1945, however.

in der Nähe/nearby:
Dorfkirche; Rauen
1. H. 15. Jh.

W 18 Rathaus
Fürstenwalde; Mühlenstraße, Rathausstraße
Um 1500

Eine rege Bautätigkeit, insbesondere bei Rathäusern in Deutschland, kennzeichnet die Entstehungszeit des Gebäudes. Typisch die Raumfolge: Im Erdgeschoß befand sich eine Kaufhalle, darüber Verwaltungs- und Gerichtsräume sowie ein etwas reicher ausgestatteter Saal über dem Durchgang, in dem der Stadtrat tagte und die wohlhabenden Bürger ihre Feste feierten. Der heutige zweijochige Durchgang mit reichem Rippengewölbe und einer Inschrift »1511« am Südbogen war ursprünglich als Gerichtslaube auch nach Osten zum Markt offen. Der zweischiffige Ratskeller mit seinen Stichkappen und spitzbogigen Tonnengewölben dient auch heute noch dem Ausschank von Bier und Wein. 1624 erhielt das Rathaus seinen Turm und den östlichen Giebel. Die gesamte Bebauung der nördlichen Hälfte des Stadtkerns ist in den letzten Kriegstagen 1945 abgebrannt. Auch das Rathaus war davon betroffen, der Abriß der Ruine bereits beschlossen. Proteste aus der Bevölkerung ließen den Wiederaufbau als Ausstellungshalle 1961-68 nach Plänen von Carljürgen Gertler und Christa Heese zur Sache der Stadt und ihrer Umgebung werden.

This building dates from a period of intensive building in Germany, particularly of town halls. The sequence of rooms is typical: there was a market hall on the ground floor, and above this administration and court rooms and a rather more lavishly decorated hall above the entrance in which the council met and well-to-do citizens held their celebrations. The passageway, now with two bays with lavish rib vaulting and an inscription «1511» on the south arch, was originally open to the market place as an open air court. The Ratskeller has two aisles with lunettes and pointed-arched tunnel vaulting, and is still used for the sale of beer and wine. Tower and eastern gable were added to the town hall in 1624. All the development in the northern half of the town centre burned down in the last days of the war in 1945. The town hall was affected as well, and a decision was made to pull down the ruin. Protests from residents made rebuilding as an exhibition hall in 1961-8 to plans by Carljürgen Gertler and Christa Heese into a concern for the town and the entire surrounding area.

in der Nähe/nearby:
Stadtmauer; im Westen und Norden des Stadtkerns
14./15. Jh.
Bullenturm; Nord-West-Ecke des Stadtkerns
15. Jh.
Damastweberkolonie; Dr.-Wilhelm-Külz-Straße 23-31
1774-78

W 19 Pfarrkirche St. Marien
Fürstenwalde; Domstraße
1446

Die stark befestigte Burg Lebus nördlich von Frankfurt war Mittelpunkt des bis ins 13. Jahrhundert polnischen »Landes Lebus«. Nach erneuter Zerstörung ihrer Kathedrale nahmen die Lebuser Bischöfe von 1373 bis 1555 ihren Sitz in Fürstenwalde. Die Kirche St. Marien wurde Domkirche des Bistums Lebus und die Burg südlich davon zur bischöflichen Residenz ausgebaut. Nach Zerstörung der Kirche durch die Hussiten wurde sie als spätgotische Backstein-Hallenkirche Mitte des 15. Jahrhunderts wiedererrichtet und das Innere und die Westturmgruppe 1769-71 durch Johann Boumann d. Ä. barock umgestaltet. Der 1910 gotisch erneuerte Innenraum brannte 1945 restlos aus. Die Wiederherstellung des Äußeren der Kirche erfolgte 1953-70.

The strongly fortified castle of Lebus north of Frankfurt an der Oder was the centre of «Land Lebus», Polish until the thirteenth century. After their cathedral had once more been destroyed the bishops of Lebus made Fürstenwalde their seat from 1373 to 1555. The church of St. Marien became the cathedral church of the bishops of Lebus, and the castle to the south of it was extended as bishop's palace. After destruction of the church by the Hussites it was rebuilt as a late Gothic brick hall church in the mid fifteenth century, and the interior and the west tower group were rebuilt to a baroque design by Johann Boumann the Elder in 1769-71. The interior was renewed in Gothic style in 1910, and burned out completely in 1945. The exterior of the church was restored in 1953-70.

in der Nähe/nearby:
Jagdschloß; Schloßstraße 13
1699-1700 • Martin Grünberg
Fernmeldedienstgebäude; Eisenbahnstraße 160
1961-63 • Ehlert
Kraftfuttermischwerk; Uferstraße 96
Ab 1967 • Wolfgang Roth, Norbert Romers

W 20 Wohnhäuser
Fürstenwalde; Mühlenstraße 26, Domstraße 1
1790 und um 1800

Von dem einst durch Wohnhäuser des 18. und 19. Jahrhunderts geprägten Straßenbild ist wenig erhalten. Die kurz vor Kriegsende zur »Festung Fürstenwalde« erklärte Stadt wurde am 21./22. April 1945 durch die Sowjetarmee eingenommen. Heftige Kämpfe führten zur fast gänzlichen Zerstörung der nördlichen Innenstadt. Weitere Teile der Bausubstanz mußten wegen fehlender Erhaltungsmöglichkeiten im Laufe der letzten zwanzig Jahre abgerissen werden. Bemerkenswert sind das stattliche spätbarocke Eckhaus Mühlenstraße 26 mit seinen korinthischen Kolossalpilastern und stuckierten Girlanden sowie das Haus Domstraße 1 – heute Stadt- und Kreismuseum – mit ursprünglich großer Durchfahrt. Die ständige Ausstellung des Museums enthält u.a. die international bekannte nordische Geschiebesammlung des Fürstenwalder Mineralogen Walter Bennhold sowie Exponate zur ur- und frühgeschichtlichen Besiedlung des Gebietes und zur Geschichte der Stadt von der Gründung bis zur neuesten Zeit.

Little has survived of the former townscape with its eighteenth and nineteenth century houses. The town was declared «Fortress Fürstenwalde» shortly before the end of the war, and it was taken on 21/22 April 1945 by the Soviet army. Fierce fighting led to almost total destruction of the northern part of the town centre. More of the building stock had to be pulled down because of lack of maintenance funds in the past twenty years. A noteable feature is the handsome late baroque corner house at Mühlenstrasse 26 with its Corinthian colossal pilasters and stucco garlands and the house at Domstrasse 1 – now municipal and district museum – with the original large gateway. The museum's permanent exhibition contains among other things Fürstenwalde mineralogist Walter Bennhold's internationally known collection of Nordic glacial deposits and exhibits on pre- and early historical settlement of the area and the history of the town from its foundation to the present day.

in der Nähe/nearby:
Ackerbürgerhof; Frankfurter Straße 88
Um 1840
Oberschule; Eisenbahnstraße 19
1865
Wohnhaus; Dr.-Wilhelm-Külz-Straße 61
1901

W 21 Bahnhof Bad Saarow
Bad Saarow-Pieskow
1911-12

Am Nordende des Scharmützelsees entstand 1905 eine erste Villenkolonie, 1914 erhielt der Ort das Attribut »Moorbad«. 1911 wurde die Eisenbahnstrecke Fürstenwalde–Beeskow gebaut und mit ihr der Bahnhof für den jungen Badeort. Die Architektur des Empfangsgebäudes folgt ländlichen Vorbildern, nicht etwa der ländlichen Umgebung wegen – Bäder zeigten immer einen Hang zum Mondänen –, vielmehr schrieb es der Geschmack der Zeit vor. Es war die Zeit des Landhausstils: der reiche Städter baute sich in den Vororten am See oder vor der Waldkulisse sein ländlich-luxuriöses Domizil, Kronprinz Wilhelm ließ in diesem Stil das Schloß Cecilienhof errichten und Berlin baute fünfgeschossige Miethäuser mit diesen Stilmerkmalen. Sieht man von der technischen Umgebung eines Bahnhofs ab, scheint der neue Stil dennoch hier am passenden Platze mit seinen Fachwerkgiebeln und Fensterläden, mit der laubengangartigen Bahnsteighalle und der verwinkelten Dachlandschaft.

In 1905 a first colony of villas was built on the northern banks of the Scharmützelsee, and in 1914 the town was officially declared a moor bath. In 1911 a railway was built between Fürstenwalde and Beeskow, and the young spa and resort town was given a station of its own. If the architecture of the station building follows rural models, this is not so much because of the rural surroundings – spas always strive to be urbane and stylish – but because this style was dictated by the popular taste of the time. It was the time of the country houses: wealthy people from the cities established their own luxurious rural retreats in the suburbs, either at a lake or near the woods; Crown Prince Wilhelm had the Cecilienhof castle built in the same country-house style, and in Berlin numerous five-storey apartment buildings were erected with the same elements. The technical aspects of a railway station notwithstanding, this new style seems to be quite appropriate here with its half-timber gables and shuttered windows, its arbour-like covered platforms and its roofs with countless angles and corners.

in der Nähe/nearby:
Russisches Blockhaus; Bad Saarow; Ulmenstraße 20
1912
Gutshaus; Saarow Dorf
1723
Doppelstubenhäuser; Saarow Dorf
19. Jh.
Scheune; Saarow Dorf; Hof Driske
A. 18. Jh.

W 22 Werksiedlung
Wildau; Karl-Marx-Straße
1898-1910

Das 1855 zum Ackergut umgewandelte Wildau, seit 1866 mit nahem Eisenbahnanschluß, entwickelt sich mit der Verlagerung von Arbeitsstätten der Berliner Großindustrie an den Stadtrand um 1900 zu einem bedeutenden Industrie- und Wohnstandort. Ein typisches Beispiel zur Ansiedlung von Arbeitskräften ist die von 1898 bis 1910 entstandene Werksiedlung beiderseits der Karl-Marx-Straße. Die mehrgeschossigen Wohnbauten in neugotischen Formen werden durch risalitartig vorgezogene Treppenhäuser mit Blendgiebeln gegliedert. Erdgeschoß, Gebäudeecken und Fensterfaschen sind in Blendmauerwerk ausgeführt im Wechsel mit Putzflächen. Schule und Klubhaus ergänzen die Siedlung zu einer Vorstufe der wenige Jahre später aufkommenden Arbeiter-Gartenstädte, wenn auch in der regelmäßigen Reihung der Bauten und in der Wiederholung gestaltender Elemente noch die stilistische Verhärtung des ausgehenden 19. Jahrhunderts und der Mangel an städtebaulicher Phantasie offenbar wird.

Wildau was turned over to arable farming in 1855, and from 1866, thanks to the nearby railway, it developed into an important industrial and residential area when heavy industry moved to Berlin's boundaries. A typical example of the provision of accommodation for the workforce is the workers' village that was built on either side of Karl-Marx-Strasse from 1898 to 1910. The houses have several storeys and are neo-Gothic; the protruding staircase towers are articulated with false gables. Ground floors, the corners of the buildings and window arches are covered in brick, alternating with rendered surfaces. School and club-house make the estate a forerunner of the workers' garden cities that were to appear a few years later, even if the regular rows of buildings and repetitive design elements still show the stylistic hardening of the latter years of the nineteenth century and a lack of imagination in town-planning terms.

in der Nähe/nearby:
Wohngebiet Hoherlehme; Wildau-Hoherlehme
1952-60 • Georg Labeau
Dorfkirche; Zeuthen-Miersdorf
1710 (1921 Turmaufsatz)
Wohnhaus; Waltersdorf; Straße nach Schulzendorf
Um 1800

W 23 Schloß
Königs Wusterhausen; Schloßplatz
16. Jahrhundert; 1717-18 und 1882 verändert

Die Kreisstadt Königs Wusterhausen mit etwa 18 800 Einwohnern hat ihren Ursprung in einer slawischen Burgsiedlung Wendisch Wusterhausen. Erst mit dem bevorzugten Aufenthalt des Königs Friedrich Wilhelm I. erhielt die ihm bereits als Kurfürst übergebene Herrschaft Wusterhausen 1734 den Namen Königs Wusterhausen. Das Schloß, heute Verwaltungsgebäude, stammt im wesentlichen aus dem 16. Jahrhundert. 1717-18 wurde es zum königlichen Jagdschloß ausgebaut. Hier frönte der »Soldatenkönig« vor allem seinen Leidenschaften, der Jagd und dem Wettrauchen. In Schloß und nahem Gartenhaus tagte das königliche »Tabakkollegium«. Der rechteckige zweigeschossige Putzbau aus Feldstein mit zwei parallelen Gebäudeteilen unter quergerichteten Satteldächern mit Giebelabschluß wurde 1862 verändert. Der hofseitige runde Treppenturm hat einen rechteckigen Aufsatz und ist mit einer geschweiften Haube überdacht. Zwei langgestreckte Flügel mit vorspringenden Kopfbauten von 1703 fassen den Hof ein.

Königs Wusterhausen is a district town with about 18,000 inhabitants; it originated in the Slavic fortress settlement of Wendish Wusterhausen. It was the preferred country residence of King Friedrich Wilhelm I, and the domain of Wusterhausen, already been given over to him as Elector, acquired the name Königs Wusterhausen in 1734. The Schloss, now an adminstrative building, dates essentially from the sixteenth century; in 1717-18 it was extended as a royal hunting lodge and here the Soldier King pursued his twin passions of hunting and competitive smoking. The royal «tobacco college» met in the castle and nearby garden house. The rectangular two-storey rendered building in rubble stone with two parallel sections under saddle roofs at right angles with gables was rebuilt in 1862. The round staircase tower on the courtyard side has an angled upper section and curved cupola. The courtyard is bordered by two long wings with protruding ends.

In der Nähe/nearby:
Kreuzkirche; Kirchplatz
1697 und 1822 • Eytelwein
Blindenschule; Luckenwalder Straße 20
1899-1900 • Gotthilf Ludwig Möckel
Krankenhaus; Köpenicker Straße 29
1963 • Gerhard Wachholz, Heribert Scholtysik, Manfred Kärgel
Dorfkirche; Deutsch Wusterhausen
13 Jh.

W 24 Soldatenfriedhof
Halbe
1951-60 • Walter Funke

Der Waldfriedhof Halbe mit Gräbern von 22 000 deutschen Soldaten ist Mahn- und Gedenkstätte an die Gefallenen der Kesselschlacht vom 25. April bis zum 1. Mai 1945. Die Ablehnung des sowjetischen Kapitulationsangebotes durch General Busse unmittelbar vor dem schon feststehenden Ende des Krieges kostete 60 000 deutsche und sowjetische Soldaten sowie Zivilisten im Waldgebiet von Halbe das Leben. Das 6,5 ha große Areal ist terrassenförmig als Waldfriedhof angelegt. Die Reihen der Massen- und Einzelgräber folgen mit ihren aus rotem Sandstein gefertigten, liegenden Grabsteinen der Bodenbewegung.

The Halbe woodland cemetery with graves of 22,000 soldiers is a memorial to those who died in the battle of encirclement from 25 April to 1 May, 1945. General Busse's refusal of the Soviet offer of capitulation immediately before the already certain end of the war cost the lives of 60,000 German and Soviet soldiers, and also civilians, in the wooded area around Halbe. The burial place covers 6.5 hectares and is laid out in terraces as a woodland cemetery. The rows of mass and individual graves with their flat sandstone gravestones follow the contours of the land.

in der Nähe/nearby:
Burg; Teupitz
1788-91 (1950 umgestaltet)
Kirche; Teupitz
14. bis 17. Jh.
Fachwerkhäuser; Teupitz; Baruther Vorstadt
A. 19. Jh.
Sebastiankirche; Baruth
2. H. 16. Jh.; 1671-78; 1909
Schloß; Baruth
17. Jh.
Schloßpark; Baruth
1838 • Peter Joseph Lenné

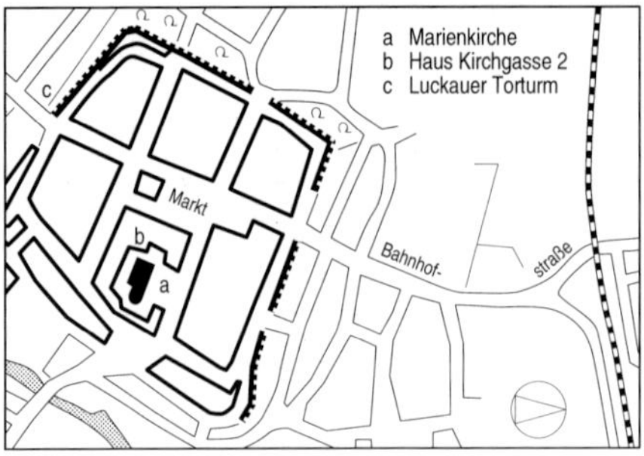

W 25 Stadtkern Beeskow
Mitte 13. Jahrhundert

In der alten märkischen Land- und Kreisstadt Beeskow an der Spree, mit etwa 8400 Einwohnern, haben sich heute einige Betriebe der Leicht- und Lebensmittelindustrie angesiedelt. Nach einer wohl vorhandenen Marktsiedlung folgte Mitte des 13. Jahrhunderts westlich der hier die Spree querenden Handelsstraße von Leipzig nach Frankfurt (Oder) die planmäßige Stadtgründung auf quadratischem Grundriß mit gitterförmigem Straßennetz und zentralem Markt. Seit dieser für den ostelbischen Bereich sehr frühen Zeit waren in Beeskow bereits die verschiedenen Zünfte der Kaufleute, Schuster, Weber, Bäcker, Fleischer, Tuchmacher und Schneider vertreten. Erstmals im Brandenburgischen taucht hier der sogenannte Wendenparagraph, eine Deutschtumsforderung für alle Zunftmitglieder, auf. Beeskow zählte zusammen mit Storkow, Luckau, Lübben, Calau und Lübbenau zu den sechs wendischen Städten des Markgraftums Niederlausitz. Späte Eisenbahnanschlüsse Ende des 19. Jahrhunderts und wenig attraktive Standortbedingungen gaben der Stadt ungünstige Entwicklungsmöglichkeiten für die Industrie. Im April 1945 wurde Beeskow zu zwei Dritteln zerstört.

Some light industry and food manufacturing companies have now established themselves in the old Mark land and district capital of Beeskow, which has approximately 8,400 inhabitants. There was probably already a market settlement here when the town was founded on a square ground plan with street grid and central market place in the mid thirteenth century, west of the trade route from Leipzig to Frankfurt an der Oder, which crosses the Spree here. The various guilds of merchants, shoemakers, weavers, bakers, butchers, cloth-makers and tailors were all represented in Beeskow from this time, which was very early for the eastern Elbe area. This is the first time that the so-called Wendic paragraph crops up in Brandenburg, a requirement that all guild members be German. With Storkow, Luckau, Lübben, Calau annd Lübbenau, Beeskow was one of the six Wendic towns of the margravate of Niederlausitz. The town was unfavourably placed in terms of industry because of late connection to railways in the late nineteenth century and other unattractive site conditions. Two thirds of Beeskow were destroyed in April 1945.

in der Nähe/nearby:
Wasserburg; Storkow
15. Jh. (Umbau 1518)
Schloß; Lindenberg
18./19. Jh.
Schloß; Groß-Rietz
1693-1700

W 26 Wohnhaus
Beeskow; Kirchgasse 2
Nach 1513

Nach den Stadtbränden 1512 und 1513 mußten große Teile der Stadt Beeskow wieder aufgebaut werden. Aus dieser Zeit stammt das Wohnhaus Kirchgasse 2. Es ist sowohl das älteste Fachwerkhaus Beeskows, vermutlich das älteste der ostbrandenburgischen Region. Das Obergeschoß kragt in niedersächsischer Art vor und hat profilierte Konsolen mit einem Treppenfries. Die Gebäudegestalt ordnet sich in die norddeutsche Renaissance ein. Die übrigen noch erhaltenen Fachwerkhäuser, zum Teil im Laufe der Zeit verputzt oder in der Dachform verändert, sind: Kirchplatz 4, eine ehemalige Schule von 1714; Brandstraße 34, Anfang des 18. Jahrhunderts und das Heilig-Geist-Hospital, jetzt Poliklinik, vor dem Luckauer Tor in der Breitscheidstraße 12, erwähnt 1603.

After fires in 1512 and 1513 large parts of the town of Beeskow had to be rebuilt. The house at Kirchgasse 2 dates from this period. It is the oldest half-timbered house in Beeskow and probably the oldest in eastern Brandenburg. The upper storey protrudes in the Lower Saxon manner, and has shaped corbels and a stepped frieze. The building as a whole is in North German Renaissance style. The other surviving half-timbered houses, some now rendered or with altered roofs, are: Kirchplatz 4, a former school dating from 1714; Brandstrasse 34, early eighteenth century; and the Heilig-Geist-Hospital, now an outpatients' department, in front of the Luckauer Tor at Breitscheidstrasse 12, mentioned in 1603.

in der Nähe/nearby:
Stadtbefestigung
Nach 1321 und 15. Jh.
Luckauer Torturm; Berliner Straße
15. Jh.
Ruine der Stadtkirche St. Marien; Breite Straße
1388-1420 Chor, bis 1511 Langhaus

W 27 Bremsdorfer Mühle
Bremsdorf; An der Schlaube
18. Jahrhundert

Von den 10 Landschaftsschutzgebieten dieser Region ist das Schlaubetal mit einer Länge von 20 km und einer Breite von 1,5 km das größte und wichtigste. Findige Köpfe hatten vom 16. bis 19. Jahrhundert in diesem Landstrich die Wasserkraft als Maschinen-Antriebsquelle entdeckt. Die Bremsdorfer Mühle, ein Mühlen- und Wohngebäude an der Schlaube mit einem unterschlächtigen Wasserrad, ist Zeitzeuge. Sieben Kilometer nördlich davon wurde bei Mixdorf am Gasthof Kupferhammer seinerzeit ein Hammerwerk betrieben. Auf Geheiß des Preußischen Königs Friedrich II. wurde 1754 ein Eisenhammer an die neue Schleuse Weißenspring, am Neuen Graben, verlegt, der von 1533 bis Anfang des 18. Jahrhunderts bereits bei Müllrose stand. Knapp ein Jahrzehnt produzierte dieser Hammer Stabeisen für das preußische Heer. Obwohl in dieser Region zu jener Zeit Mahl-, Graupen- und Schneidemühlen arbeiteten und eine Tabakpfeifenmanufaktur, eine Spinnerei, Kalkbrennerei und Gipsmühle existierten, entwickelte sich das Schlaubetal, im Gegensatz zum Finowtal bei Eberswalde, nicht zum Industrierevier weiter, die Anlagen überdauerten das 19. Jahrhundert nicht.

The Schlaubetal, 20 km long and 1.5 km wide, is the largest and most important of the ten nature conservancy areas in this region. Resourceful minds discovered water power as an energy source in this part of the world from the sixteenth to the nineteenth centuries. Bremsdorf Mill, a mill and residential building on the Schlaube with undershot water wheel, stands testimony of these times. Seven kilometres to the north a forge operated near Mixdorf at the Kupferhammer inn. At the behest of the King, Frederick II of Prussia, the forge was moved to the new Weissenspring lock on the Neuer Graben in 1754. The forge had existed near Müllrose from 1533 to the early eighteenth century, and in its new position produced iron bars for the Prussian army for just under a decade. Although at this time the region had grinding, hulling and sawmills and also a tobacco factory, spinning mill, lime works and plaster mill, the Schlaubetal, in contrast with the Finowtal near Eberswalde, did not develop into an industrial region, and the various plants did not outlast the nineteenth century.

in der Nähe/nearby:
Dorfkirche; Mixdorf
1719-20
Dorfkirche; Grunow
18. Jh.
Doppelstubenhaus; Dammendorf; Dorfstraße 11
18. Jh.

W 28 Kloster
Neuzelle
1280-1330

Im Rahmen der wettinisch-meißnischen Kolonisation im nordöstlichen Teil der Lausitz stiftete Markgraf Heinrich der Erlauchte von Meißen 1268 das Zisterzienserkloster Neuzelle. Der Gründungsbau der Klosterkirche aus den Jahren 1280-1330 wurde nach teilweiser Zerstörung im Dreißigjährigen Krieg 1654-58 spätmanieristisch von Johann Bartholomäus Cometa um- und ausgestaltet und von Johannes Vanetti bemalt. Die umfassende Barockisierung führte zwischen 1703 und 1741 die Künstlerfamilie Hennevogel, die Ausmalung Georg Wilhelm Neunhertz durch. Unter böhmischem Einfuß entstand so das in Brandenburg seltene Beispiel eines Barockklosters. Die 1817 säkularisierte Klosterkirche ist heute der bedeutendste Sakralbau der Niederlausitz. Die Klosterbrauerei von 1589 ist der älteste erhaltene Betrieb der Region.

Margrave Heinrich der Erlauchte of Meissen founded the Cistercian monastery of Neuzelle in 1268 in the context of Wettin-Meissen colonization in the north-eastern part of the Lausitz. The original monastery church dating from 1280-1330, was partially destroyed in the Thirty Years' War, then rebuilt and refurbished in 1654-8 in late Mannerist style by Johann Bartholomäus Cometa, and painted by Johannes Vanetti. From 1703 to 1741 the Hennevogel family carried out a complete baroque conversion, with painting by Georg Wilhelm Neunhertz. Thus Bohemian influence led to that rare phenomenon in Brandenburg, a baroque monastery. The monastery church was deconsecrated in 1817, and is now the most important ecclesiastical building in Niederlausitz. The 1589 monastery brewery is the oldest surviving business in the region.

in der Nähe/nearby:
Pfarrkirche zum Heiligen Kreuz; Neuzelle
1728-34 (Umbau 1850 • vermutlich Friedrich August Stüler)
Dorfkirche; Möbiskruge
1. H. 14. Jh. (Umbauten 18. u. 19. Jh.)
Dorfkirche; Steinsdorf
1749

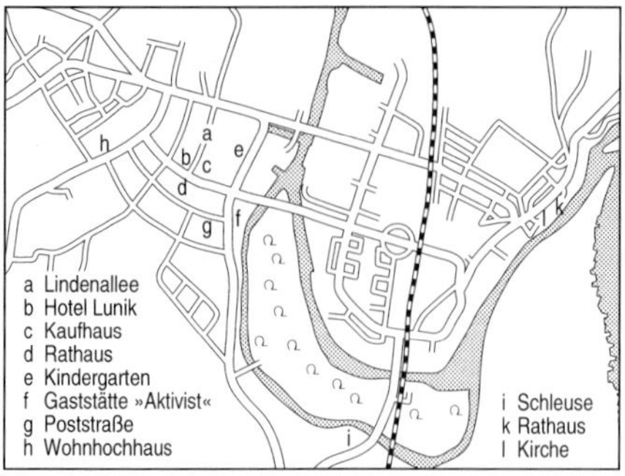

W 29 Eisenhüttenstadt (Fürstenberg)
Nach 1250

Der heutige Stadtkreis mit 53 000 Einwohnern an der Einmündung des Oder-Spree-Kanals in die Oder ist ein wichtiger Standort der brandenburgischen Schwer- und Lebensmittelindustrie. Den eigentlichen Siedlungskern, Fürstenberg, mag der wettinische Markgraf Heinrich der Erlauchte, auch Herr der Lausitz, nach 1250 an der nordöstlichen Grenze seines Herrschaftbereiches mit rechteckigem Grundriß, gitterförmigem Straßennetz und großem rechteckigen Markt gegründet haben. Mit dem Bau der Bahn von Frankfurt (Oder) nach Breslau 1846 und des Oder-Spree-Kanals 1891 begann hier eine industrielle Entwicklung mit Glashütten, Werften und Mühlen. Auf Beschluß der Regierung begann 1950 westlich von Fürstenberg der Aufbau eines Eisenhüttenkombinates. Standortbestimmend dafür waren die günstigen Eisenbahn- und Wasserstraßenverbindungen. Eisenerze sollten aus Kriwoi Rog in der Sowjetunion, Hüttenkoks aus Oberschlesien und Kalkstein aus Rüdersdorf kommen. Bis 1990 wurde hier noch eine Reihe spezieller Stahl- und Walzwerke errichtet. Die 1951 begonnene Neustadt wurde als »Stalinstadt« 1953 zur ersten sozialistischen Stadt der DDR erklärt, bis sie 1961 in Eisenhüttenstadt umbenannt wurde.

The present town, a district in its own right, with 53,000 inhabitants at the junction of the Oder-Spree canal and the Oder, is an important centre for heavy industry and food manufacture in Brandenburg. The actual core of the settlement, Fürstenberg, may have been founded by the Wettin margrave Heinrich der Erlauchte, also Lord of the Lausitz, after 1250 at the north-eastern corner of his territory. It has a rectangular ground plan, a grid of streets and large rectangular market place. Industrial development, including glassworks, shipbuilding and mills, started here in 1846 with the building of the railway from Frankfurt an der Oder to Breslau, and of the Oder-Spree canal in 1891. An iron processing combine was started west of Fürstenberg by government decree in 1950. Choice of site was determined by favourable rail- and waterway connections. Iron ore was to come from Krivoi Rog in the Soviet Union, coke from Upper Silesia and limestone from Rüdersdorf. By 1990 a series of special steel and rolling mills had also been established here. The new town, started in 1951, was declared the first socialist town in the GDR in 1953, and called «Stalinstadt» until it was rechristened Eisenhüttenstadt in 1961.

in der Nähe/nearby:
Ackerbürgerhof; Müllrose; Frankfurter Straße 18
1772
Stadtkirche; Müllrose
1746
Kaisergraben; Müllrose-Kaisermühl
Nach 1556

W 30 Ensemble Leninallee (Lindenallee)
Eisenhüttenstadt; Lindenallee
1953-64 • Kurt W. Leucht, Willi Stamm

In der von Kurt W. Leucht 1951 fast idealstadtartig geplanten Stadtanlage bildete die Magistrale »Leninallee« die zentrale Achse der Stadt. Der in Nord-Süd-Richtung verlaufende repräsentative Straßenzug sollte ein Bindeglied zwischen dem sogenannten Zentralen Platz und dem als monumentale »schloßartige« Anlage konzipierten Haupttor des neuen Hüttenwerkes sein. Nach Entwürfen von Herrmann Enders und Hans Klein entstand 1953-55 jedoch zunächst nur das Theater in einer klassizistisch-volkstümlichen Formensprache. Nach Entwürfen von Härtel u. a. bekam der Straßenzug erst 1959 seine räumliche Fassung durch drei der östlichen Straßenfront vorgelagerte, neungeschossige Punkthäuser, die die Magistrale auch in der Höhe nachdrücklich dominierten sowie kompositorische Bindungen zur ersten Hochofengruppe des Werkes und zu den künftigen Hochbauten am Zentralen Platz herstellen sollten. Obwohl weder diese Gebäude noch das monumentale Werktor realisiert wurden, zählt heute die Lindenallee mit ihren maßstäblich aufeinander abgestimmten Wohn- und Gemeinschaftsbauten zu den bemerkenswertesten Leistungen des DDR-Städtebaus am Ende der fünfziger Jahre.

The town was planned almost as an ideal town by Kurt W. Leucht in 1951, with the main thoroughfare «Leninallee» as the central axis. This imposing street runs north-south and was intended to form a link between the so-called Zentraler Platz and the main gate of the new iron and steel works, conceived as a monumental «castle-like» complex. However, at first only the theatre was built, to a popular-classical design by Herrmann Enders and Hans Klein in 1953-5. It was not until 1959 that the street was organized spatially by the building of three point blocks designed by Härtel. They have nine storeys and stand on the eastern side of the street, and dominate the main thoroughfare emphatically in terms of height. They are intended to make a compositional link with the first group of blast furnaces at the factory and future high-rise buildings in Zentraler Platz. Although neither these buildings nor the monumental gateway to the works were realized, the Lindenallee with its residential and public buildings balanced against each other in terms of scale is among the most remarkable achievements of GDR town planning in the late fifties.

in der Nähe/nearby:
Haus der Organisationen (Rathaus); Zentraler Platz
1954-58 • Harald Wunderlich
Kaufhaus; Lindenallee, Straße der Republik
1958-60 • Ortwin Lopp, Otto Schnabel
Hotel Lunik; Straße der Republik, Lindenallee
1960-63 • Willi Stamm

W 31 Wohngebäude
Eisenhüttenstadt; Saarlouiser Straße, Poststraße
1953-55 • Siegert

Die Wohnkomplexe I bis IV, insbesondere der Wohnkomplex II aus den Jahren 1953-54, waren in ihrer geschlossenen Blockbebauung ganz im Sinne der »16 Grundsätze des Städtebaus« der DDR vom Juli 1950 konzipiert worden. Die Wohngebiete wurden in Wohnbezirke, Wohnkomplexe und Häuserviertel mit eigener Infrastruktur gegliedert. Die Architektur der Gebäude sollte »dem Inhalt nach demokratisch und der Form nach national« sein. Letzteres zielte auf eine volkstümliche Ausdrucksweise, anknüpfend an deutsche wie auch sowjetische Traditionen. Beim 1955 begonnenen Wohnkomplex III sind Architektur und Wohnhäuser merklich vereinfacht, die räumliche Gliederung aber eng angelehnt an den Wohnkomplex II. Der von 1958-61 gebaute IV. Wohnkomplex fügt sich auf Grund der neu entwickelten Plattenbauten nur noch grundrißmäßig in die Konturen des Bebauungsplanes von 1953 ein.

Residential complexes I to IV, and especially residential complex II, dating from 1953-4, were conceived, particularly with respect to their development as complete blocks, entirely within the spirit of the «16 principles of town planning» laid down by the GDR in July 1950. The residential areas were broken down into residential districts, residential complexes and residential quarters with their own infrastructure. The architecture of the buildings was to be «democratic in content and national in form». The latter point aimed at the use of popular means of expression, following both German and Soviet traditions. In residential complex III, started in 1955, architecture and residential buildings are noticeably simplified, but their spatial articulation is closely modelled on residential complex II. Residential complex IV only fits in with outlines of the 1953 development plan in terms of ground plan, because of the newly developed slab building technique.

in der Nähe/nearby:
Kindergarten; Karl-Marx-Straße
1953-55 • Rudolf Nitschke, Friedel Schmidt, Walter Pallocks
Gaststätte »Aktivist«; Karl-Marx-Straße
1953-55 • Herrmann Enders
Wohnhochhaus; Diehloer Straße
1959-62 • Jochen Beige, Werner Hensel

W 32 Zwillingsschachtschleuse
Eisenhüttenstadt; Oder-Spree-Kanal
1921-23 und 1925-29

Einen Schiffahrtsweg zwischen Oder und Elbe – diese Vision hatte Kaiser Karl IV. bereits 1373. Der erste Versuch einer Verwirklichung brachte 1556 nur den »Kaisergraben« bei Müllrose. Im zweiten Anlauf wurde 1662-69 der »Friedrich-Wilhelm-Kanal« zwischen Spree und Oder südlich von Frankfurt fertiggestellt. Das dritte Projekt brachte 1887-91 den Oder-Spree-Kanal, der unter Nutzung von Teilen der Spree bei Fürstenwalde auf 87,6 km eine leistungsfähige Wasserstraße zwischen dem heutigen Eisenhüttenstadt und dem Seddinsee herstellte. Für diesen Kanal wurde zur Überwindung von 15 m Höhenunterschied 1921-29 eine Zwillingsschachtschleuse aus Stahlbeton in 130 m Länge und 12 m Breite errichtet. Das Energiesparprinzip folgt dem früheren Beispiel der Machnower Schleuse im Teltowkanal: in die eine Schleusenkammer fährt vom Oberhafen, in die andere vom Unterhafen her ein Schiff ein. Nach Schließung der Schleusentore sorgen Querstrom-Kanäle für einen Wassergleichstand der Kammern. Anschließend heben oder senken Pumpen den Wasserstand in den Kammern entgegengesetzt, bis er dem – nun vertauscht – des oberen oder unteren Hafens entspricht.

Emperor Charles IV had a vision of shipping between the Oder and the Elbe as early as 1373. The first attempt to realize the dream, in 1556, produced only the «Kaisergraben» at Müllrose. In the second phase the «Friedrich-Wilhelm-Kanal» between the Spree and the Oder south of Frankfurt was completed. The third project, in 1887-91, created the Oder-Spree canal, establishing a link consisting of 87.6 km of effective waterway between the present town of Eisenhüttenstadt and the Seddinsee, using parts of the Spree near Fürstenwalde. In 1921-9 a twin shaft lock in reinforced concrete, 130 m long and 12 m wide, was built for this canal to handle the 15 m height difference. The energy saving principle follows the earlier example of the Machnow lock in the Teltow canal: one ship moves into the lock chamber from the upper harbour, and one from the lower harbour. After the lock gates have been closed, transverse channels balance the water in the chambers equally. Subsequently pumps raise or lower the water level in the chambers, until it corresponds with that in the upper or lower harbour – now reversed.

in der Nähe/nearby:
Rathaus; Eisenhüttenstadt-Fürstenberg; Marktplatz
1900 (Umbau 1934)
Pfarrkirche; Eisenhüttenstadt-Fürstenberg; Kirchplatz
3. V. 15. Jh.

X
Frankfurt/Oder

Mit fast 90 000 Einwohnern ist die einstige Garnison- und Beamtenstadt heute die größte Ansiedlung der östlichen Mark Brandenburg. Das Rückgrat der Wirtschaft bilden die elektronische Industrie, Baustoffbetriebe, Lebensmittelindustrie und der Orgelbau. Die günstigen geografischen Gegebenheiten an einem alten Oderübergang machten das Frankfurter Siedlungsgebiet von jeher zum Streitpunkt für verschiedenste Völkerstämme. Eines der eindrucksvollen archäologischen Denkmäler der Region ist der Burgwall in Lossow, wohl aus der späten Bronzezeit. Ursprünge der heutigen Stadt gehen auf das 12. Jahrhundert zurück, als unter den schlesischen Herzögen um die Nikolaikirche eine Kaufmannssiedlung bestand. Unter dem askanischen Markgrafen Johann I. von Brandenburg erfolgte nach 1253 eine einheitliche Anlage der Stadt mit rechtwinkligem Grundriß, gitterförmigem Straßennetz, Stadtbefestigung und Erweiterung nach Süden mit Marienkirche und Rathaus. Die hohe wirtschaftliche Blüte der Hansestadt Frankfurt im Mittelalter wird durch die Ansiedlung von zwei Klöstern und vier Hospitälern, durch ein großes Rathaus und die eindrucksvolle Ausstattung zweier Kirchen deutlich. Die Rolle als Universitätsstadt von 1506 bis 1811, als Garnison seit 1719 und als Sitz der Preußischen Regierung für Neumark und Niederlausitz seit 1815 brachte Frankfurt unter anderem die Erweiterung um die Gubener Vorstadt und die »Halbe Stadt«. Trotz frühzeitigem Anschluß an wichtige Bahnlinien der östlichen Region – als erste 1842 die Berlin-Frankfurter Bahn – ging die Industrieansiedlung nur zögernd voran. Schwerpunkt der baulichen Entwicklung blieb fortan der Wohnungsbau. Er dehnte sich bald auf die südlichen und westlichen Hochflächen aus, im späten 19. Jahrhundert mit Beresinchen und in den zwanziger Jahren mit den Gartenstädten Paulinenhof und Nuhnen-Vorstadt. Die schweren Zerstörungen am Ende des Zweiten Weltkrieges sind gerade in der Innenstadt noch heute ablesbar. Nicht Wiederaufbau, sondern Neubau und städtebauliche Neuordnung kennzeichnen die betroffenen Stadtteile. Hochhäuser von bewußt ausgeprägter Silhouettenwirkung bestimmen nun das Gesicht des »neuen Frankfurt«.

This former garrison and civil servants' town has almost 90,000 inhabitants, and is thus the largest settlement in the eastern part of the Mark Brandenburg. The backbone of the economy is made up of electronics industry, building material manufacture, food industry and organ building. A favourable geographical situation at an old Oder crossing point made the settlement around Frankfurt a point at which a great variety of tribes clashed from the earliest times. One of the region's most impressive archaeological monuments is the castle rampart in Lossow, probably dating from the Bronze Age. The origins of the present town go back to the twelfth century, when there was a merchants' settlement under the dukes of Silesia around the Nikolaikirche. After 1253, under the Ascanian margrave Johann I of Brandenburg, the town was laid out on a uniform rectangular ground plan, with street grid, town fortifications and an extension to the south including Marienkirche and town hall. The Hanseatic town of Frankfurt obviously flourished in the Middle Ages, acquiring two monasteries and four hospitals, a large town hall and impressive furnishings for two churches. The role as a university town from 1506 to 1811, as a garrison from 1719 and as seat of Prussian government for Neumark and Niederlausitz from 1815 brought Frankfurt further building, including the Gubener Vorstadt and the «Halbe Stadt». Despite early connection to important eastern region railways – the first being the Berlin-Frankfurt railway in 1842 – industry was slow to establish itself. Residential building was the quickest to expand. It soon extended over the high ground to the south and west, with Beresinchen appearing in the late nineteenth century and the garden cities of Paulinenhof and Nuhnen-Vorstadt in the twenties. There is still evidence of severe damage at the end of the Second World War in the town centre. The parts of the town affected have not been rebuilt, but replaced by new buildings and a different style of urban development. High-rise blocks, consciously striking with their silhouettes, are the hallmark of the «new Frankfurt» townscape.

X 1 Rathaus
X 2 Pfarrkirche St. Marien
X 3 Regierungsgebäude
X 4 Hauptpostamt
X 5 Heilig-Geist-Hospital
X 6 Garnisonschule
X 7 Hochhaus »Stadtdominante«
X 8 Franziskaner-Kirche (Konzerthalle)
X 9 Realgymnasium
X 10 Villa für Stadtrat Bauer
X 11 Casino
X 12 Hauptbahnhof
X 13 Georgenkirche
X 14 Wohnsiedlung Paulinenhof
X 15 Musikheim (Kleist-Theater)
X 16 Krematorium auf dem Hauptfriedhof

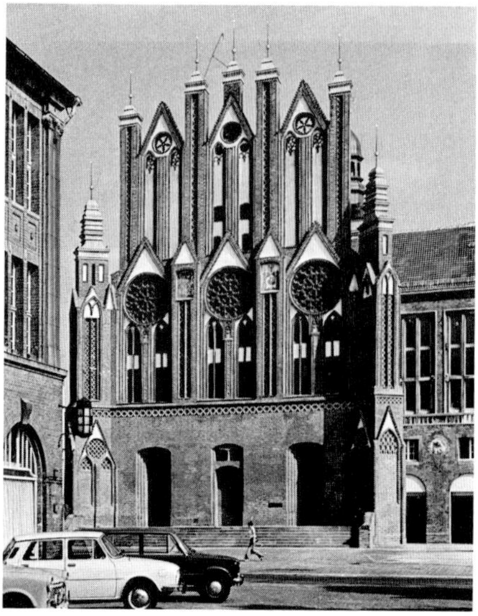

X 1 Rathaus
Frankfurt (Oder); Bischofstraße
2. Hälfte 13. Jahrhundert

Eine markgräfliche Erlaubnis zum Bau eines Kaufhauses enthielt bereits die Gründungsurkunde der Stadt von 1253. Jenes Gebäude dürfte mit dem südlichen Saalbau des heutigen Rathauses identisch sein, drei Keller mit frühgotischen Kreuzrippengewölben sind dabei ohne Zweifel die ältesten Teile. 1348 wird dann das Rathaus erstmals erwähnt. Die heutige Gestalt des Gebäudes hat Thaddäus Paglion geprägt, der 1607-09 umfangreiche Veränderungen im Sinne der Renaissance vornahm. Die Erdgeschoßzone wurde bereits 1864 von den Anbauten der niedrigen, übergiebelten Renaissance-Scharren – mundartlich für Fleisch- und Brotverkaufsstellen – befreit. Neben den Umbauten 1906-07 durch Otto Stiehl und 1912-13 durch Carl Schwatlo entstand 1911-13 auf der Ostseite ein neuer Verwaltungstrakt von Fritz Beyer. Nach den Zerstörungen des Krieges ließen Wiederaufbau 1951-53 und Restaurierung 1976-78 wieder einen ansehnlichen Baukomplex entstehen mit Festsaal, Galerie, Ratskeller und Verwaltungsräumen.

The document certifying the foundation of the city in 1253 contained permission from the margrave to build a trading house. That building may be identical with the south hall of the present town hall, of which three cellars with early Gothic ribbed vaults are indubitably the oldest sections. The town hall was first mentioned in 1348. Thaddäus Paglion determined the present form of the town hall: he made extensive alterations in Renaissance style from 1607-9. The ground floor was made available as early as 1864 for the buildings of the low, gabled Renaissance «Scharren» – the dialect expression for places where bread and meat were sold. As well as rebuilding in 1906-7 by Otto Stiehl and 1912-3 by Carl Schwatlo, a new administrative section was built on the east side by Fritz Beyer from 1911-3. After damage in the war, a handsome set of buildings with ballroom, gallery, Ratskeller and offices reappeared in the course of rebuilding 1951-3 and restoration 1976-8.

in der Nähe/nearby:
Bürgerhaus; Forststraße 1-2
Um 1800 (Umbau 1979-81 • Christian u. Maritta Nülken)
Bürgerhaus; Große Oderstraße 42
Um 1500 u. um 1800

X 2 Pfarrkirche St. Marien
Frankfurt (Oder); Große Scharrnstraße
2. Hälfte 13. Jahrhundert

Als »räumlich bedeutendsten Bau der Mark Brandenburg« stufte der Kunstgeschichtler Georg Dehio die Frankfurter Marienkirche ein. Hauptsächlich zwischen dem 14. und 16. Jahrhundert erreichte sie ihre heutigen Ausmaße. Die dreischiffige Hallenkirche mit Querhaus nach westfälischem Muster ist dem Gründungsbau der Prenzlauer Marienkirche sehr ähnlich. Charakteristisch sind die hohen, gegliederten Attiken über den Langhauswänden, welche ehemals die Pultdächer über den Seitenschiffen verdeckten. Erhebliche Einbußen ihrer Originalität erfuhr die Kirche bei der Restaurierung um 1830 durch Karl Friedrich Schinkel. Die 1945 bis auf die Umfassungsmauern zerstörte Kirche dient nach ihrer baulichen Wiederherstellung seit 1986 als Kunstforum. Ihre einst reiche Ausstattung wird seit 1980 hauptsächlich in der Gertraudenkirche aufbewahrt.

The Marienkirche in Frankfurt was considered the «spatially most significant building in the Mark Brandenburg» by art historian Georg Dehio. It achieved its present size principally between the fourteenth and sixteenth centuries. This hall church with nave and two aisles on the Westphalian pattern is very similar to the original Marienkirche in Prenzlau. It has characteristic high, articulated atticas over the walls of the nave, which originally concealed the penthouse roofs over the aisles. The church sacrificed a great deal of its originality when it was restored by Karl Friedrich Schinkel c. 1830. The church was entirely destroyed in 1945, with the exception of its exterior walls. It has been restored, and used as an art forum, since 1986. Its formerly lavish furnishings have been stored mainly in the Gertraudenkirche since 1980.

in der Nähe/nearby:
Bibliothek; Bischofstraße 17-18
1909-10 • Fritz Beyer
Oderbrunnen; Bischofstraße
1912 • Hans Bernoulli

X 3 Regierungsgebäude (Europa-Universität)
Frankfurt (Oder); Regierungsstraße 1, Logenstraße
1899-1904 • Heinrich Klutmann, Traugott v. Saltzwedel

Bereits 1815 wurde Frankfurt Sitz der Verwaltung eines Regierungsbezirkes. Mit sämtlichen Nachfolgebehörden war Frankfurt nun wie Potsdam Garnison- und Beamtenstadt, was Charakter und Bild der Stadt nachhaltig prägte. Die Konkurrenz zu Potsdam war aber immer vom Fehlen des königlichen Hofs überschattet, und so erhielt Frankfurt auch erst nach 84 Jahren ein eigenes Gebäude für die Bezirksregierung. Dem Geschmack der Zeit folgend wurde der ausgedehnte Geäudekomplex in den Formen des Neubarock gestaltet, nur vereinzelt klingen Elemente des Jugendstils an, der für öffentliche Bauten nicht in das grundsätzlich konservative Denken des Bauherrn paßte. Besonders repräsentativ wirken die Eingangsfront an der Großen Scharrnstraße – leicht geschwungen mit Mittelrisalit und großem Giebelrelief –, die Seite zur Logenstraße mit einem Ehrenhof sowie das Treppenhaus und der Festsaal, der sich in Rokoko-Ornamentik schmückt.

Frankfurt became a regional administrative centre as early as 1815. Frankfurt had then become a soldiers' and civil servants' town, like Potsdam, with all the official organizations these bring in their train, and this made a lasting impression on the character and image of the town. Lack of a royal court always put it in the shade in competition with Potsdam, and so Frankfurt did not have a local government building of its own until 84 years had passed. The extensive complex followed the taste of the times by being neo-baroque, with only isolated Jugendstil elements, which did not fit in with the fundamentally conservative thinking of the commissioning authorities as far as public buildings were concerned. Particularly imposing are the entrance façade on Grosse Scharrnstrasse – slightly curved with protruding central section and pediment relief –, the Logenstrasse side with courtyard and the staircase and ballroom, which has rococo decoration.

in der Nähe/nearby:
Logengebäude (Polizeidirektion); Logenstraße 12
1844-46 • Stüler-Umkreis
Kaufhaus; Logenstraße 7
1933-34 • Winkler, Gütte
Parteischule (Kongreß-Hotel Frankfurter Hof); Logenstraße 2
1976-79 • Manfred Vogler, Jochen Beige, Werner Hensel

X 4 Hauptpostamt
Frankfurt (Oder); Logenstraße 9-10, Lindenstraße 1-7
1899-1902 • Friedrich Anton v. Rechenberg

Angelehnt an historische Vorbilder in der Mark Brandenburg stand beim Bau des Post- und Telegraphengebäudes in Frankfurt die Gotik Pate. Damals war es üblich, daß der Kaiser selbst die Entwürfe für Postbauten überprüfte und auf hinreichend deutschtümelnde Gestaltung achtete. Die Fronten wurden durch Risalite mit Staffelgiebel gegliedert. Frankfurt (Oder) und die Mark blicken auf große Traditionen im Postwesen zurück. Bereits Mitte des 17. Jahrhunderts war das Brandenburgisch-Preußische Postwesen unter der Pflege seiner Landesherren aufgeblüht. Die erste einheitliche Staatspost unter Führung Preußens war die Norddeutsche Bundespost in den Jahren 1868-71, die als unmittelbarer Vorläufer der 1871 gegründeten Reichspost gelten kann. Maßgeblichen Anteil an der Festlegung des Postrechts, Neuregelung der Postgebühren, Vereinheitlichung des Post- und Telegraphenbetriebes sowie an der Vermehrung der Postanstalten hatte der Generalpostmeister und Staatssekretär des Reichspostamtes Heinrich v. Stephan, der seinen Dienst von 1855 bis 1870 in der Oberpostdirektion Frankfurt (Oder) versah. Auf seine Anregung hin trat 1874 der 1. Weltkongreß in Bern zusammen und gründete den Allgemeinen Postverein, der auf dem 2. Weltkongreß 1878 in Paris in Weltpostverein umbenannt wurde

In keeping with historical models in Mark Brandenburg, Gothic was the inspiration behind the design of the post and telegraphy building in Frankfurt an der Oder. It was customary at the time that the Kaiser himself examined designs for postal buildings, to make sure that they had the right degree of Germanness. The façades are articulated with gabled protrusions. Frankfurt an der Oder and the Mark look back on a great postal tradition. The postal service of Brandenburg and Prussia had started to flourish under local rulers as early as the mid seventeenth century. The first united state postal system under Prussian direction was the Norddeutsche Bundespost in 1868-71, which can be seen as the immediate predecessor of the Reichspost, founded in 1871. Heinrich von Stephan, who worked in the Oberpostdirektion in Frankfurt an der Oder from 1855 to 1870, played a great part in establishing postal law, re-regulating postal charges, unifying the postal and telegraph services and increasing the number of post offices. It was at his suggestion that the 1st World Congress met in Bern in 1874 and founded the General Postal Association, renamed World Postal Association in Paris in 1878.

in der Nähe/nearby:
Villa (Galerie Junge Kunst); Heilbronner Straße 19
1895
Filmtheater; Heilbronner Straße 18
1910 (Umbau 1954-55 • Wilhelm Flemming u.a.m.)

X 5 Heilig-Geist-Hospital
Frankfurt (Oder); Lindenstraße 4-7
1787 • Martin Friedrich Knoblauch

Das Franziskaner-Kloster, 1396 außerhalb der Stadt erbaut, wandte sich als erstes Kloster der Versorgung von Kranken zu. Außerdem hatte Frankfurt noch vier Hospitäler, was für die Bedeutung und wirtschaftliche Stärke der Stadt in jener Zeit sprach, denn die Hospitäler übernahmen die Krankenbetreuung in städtischer Regie. Auch das Heilig-Geist-Hospital – 1354 wurde es erstmals erwähnt – lag ursprünglich vor der Stadtmauer am Gubener Tor, hauptsächlich der Ansteckungsgefahr wegen. Für die Stadt ein Schutz, war diese Maßnahme aber in Kriegszeiten ein Nachteil für das Hospital. So wurde es 1432 durch die Hussiten, 1631 durch die Schweden zerstört. Bei dem heutigen langgestreckten Putzbau, der 1820 und 1834 erweitert wurde, sind die Portale in der für Knoblauch typischen, flach-korbbogigen Form ausgebildet. Treppen und Mittelgang im Obergeschoß, mit Kochnischen für die Bewohner, sind zum Teil noch im ursprünglichen Zustand erhalten.

The Franciscan monastery, built outside the town in 1396, was the first monastery to turn to care for the sick. Besides this Frankfurt had four hospitals, which demonstrates the significance and economic strength of the town at the time, as hospitals under municipal management took over care of the sick. The Heilig-Geist-Hospital, mentioned for the first time in 1354, was originally outside the town wall by the Gubener Tor, mainly because of danger of infection. This protected the town, but was a disadvantage for the hospital in times of war, and it was destroyed by the Hussites in 1432 and by the Swedes in 1631. The present long, rendered building, extended in 1820 and 1834, has portals with shallow basket arches typical of Knoblauch. Stairs and central corridor in the upper storey, with cooking niches for occupants, have to an extent survived in their original condition.

in der Nähe/nearby:
Park am Kellenspring (ehem. Gertrauden-Friedhof)
1800
Denkmal Heinrich v. Kleist; Park am Kellenspring
1910 • Gottlieb Elster
Gertraudenkirche; Gertraudenplatz 6
1874-78 • Carl Christ, Wilhelm Kinzel
Reichsbahnsiedlung am Anger; Gertraudenplatz 1-5
1923-24 • Martin Kießling

X 6 Garnisonschule
Frankfurt (Oder); Faberstraße 7
1777 • Martin Friedrich Knoblauch

Der forcierte Ausbau Frankfurts zur Garnisonsstadt im 18. Jahrhundert brachte Probleme für die Kinder mit sich. Der Kommandeur des hiesigen Infanterieregiments und Neffe Friedrichs II., Oberst Leopold v. Braunschweig, stiftete deshalb 1777-78 die Frankfurter Garnisonschule, eine Freischule für verwahrloste Soldatenkinder. Der spätbarocke zweigeschossige Putzbau mit hohem Mansartdach ist heute Kleist-Gedenk- und Forschungsstätte. Seit 1969 beherbergt das Gebäude ein Literaturmuseum, eine Ausstellung zum Werk Kleists, Kleist-Archiv und Präsenzbibliothek. – Heinrich von Kleist, 1777 in Frankfurt (Oder) geboren, 1811 durch Freitod in Berlin-Wannsee aus dem Leben geschieden, wird heute als der bedeutendste Dramatiker und Erzähler zwischen Klassik und Romantik angesehen. Er hörte an der Frankfurter Universität »Viadrina« Vorlesungen über Philosophie, Mathematik, Physik und Kameralistik und geriet bei der Begegnung mit der Kantschen Philosophie in große Widersprüche. Zwei seiner wichtigsten Werke sind das Lustspiel »Der zerbrochene Krug« und das Drama »Prinz Friedrich von Homburg«.

Frankfurt's rapid rise as a garrison town in the eighteenth century brought problems for children. Colonel Leopold von Braunschweig, commander of the local infantry regiment and nephew of Frederick II, therefore endowed the Frankfurt Garrison School in 1777-8; this was a free school for soldiers' children who were neglected. The late baroque two-storey rendered building with high mansard roof is now a Kleist memorial and research centre. Since 1969 the building has housed a literary museum, an exhibition on Kleist's work, Kleist archive and reference library. Heinrich von Kleist was born in Frankfurt an der Oder in 1777 and committed suicide in Berlin-Wannsee in 1811. He is now regarded as the most important dramatist and narrative writer between classicism and Romanticism. He attended lectures at the «Viadrina», the University of Frankfurt, on philosophy, mathematics, physics and cameralistics, and was torn by conflicting interpretations in his encounters with the philosophy of Kant. Two of his most important works are the comedy «Der zerbrochene Krug» and the drama «Der Prinz von Homburg».

in der Nähe/nearby:
Museum Viadrina; Carl-Philipp-Emanuel-Bach-Straße 11
1675 • Cornelius Ryckwaert
Oderpromenade; Hanewald
1970-72 • Rainer Zeletzki, Manfred Vogler
Friedensbrücke; Rosa-Luxemburg-Straße
1892-95 • Malkomess

X 7 Hochhaus »Oderturm«
Frankfurt (Oder); Logenstraße 8
1968-76 • Hans Tulke, Paul Teichmann u.a.m.
1991-93 (Umbau und Erweiterung) • Monika Krebs

Im Gegensatz zu Neubrandenburg mit ähnlich hohem Zerstörungsgrad begann in Frankfurt erst 1956, also vier Jahre später, der Wiederaufbau der Altstadt. Damit stand der hiesige Aufbau im Zeichen der offenen Zeilenbauweise des siedlungsartigen Wohnkomplexes, was sich sehr unvorteilhaft auf Straßen- und Platzräume in der Nähe von Rathaus und Marienkirche auswirkte, ein Phänomen, das sich bei vielen solcher Bauvorhaben in Ost und West beobachten läßt. Auch mit dem Bau eines 24 Geschosse und fast 89 Meter hohen Gebäudes, ursprünglich wohl als Verwaltungshochhaus geplant, dann aber als Jugendhotel genutzt, konnte an der Unausgewogenheit der zentralen Platzräume nichts geändert werden. Erst mit der Verdichtung der Scharrnstraße und ihrem Ausbau zur Fußgängerzone wurde ein erster Bereich der ehemaligen Altstadt mit den vorhandenen Mitteln maßstäblich gefaßt.

In contrast with Neu-Brandenburg, which had been destroyed to an equal degree, Franfurt did not start to rebuild its town centre until 1956. Thus building here was based on open terraces in an estate-like residential complex, which had a deleterious effect on streets and squares near the town hall and the Marienkirche, a phenomenon to be observed in many similar residential ventures in East and West. Even a building with 24 storeys, almost 89 metres high, probably originally planned as an office block, but then used as an hotel for young people, could do nothing to alter the unbalanced nature of the area around the central square. It was not until Scharrnstrasse was closed and extended as a pedestrian precinct that this became the first district of the former old town to be balanced in terms of scale by available means.

in der Nähe/nearby:
Hotel »Stadt Frankfurt«; Karl-Marx-Straße 193
1965-68 • K.-H. Dochow, J. Beige, K.-H. Wohlert u.a.m.
Wohngebäude; Karl-Marx-Straße 7-8
1964-66 • Hans Tulke

X 8 Franziskaner-Kirche (Konzerthalle)
Frankfurt (Oder); Collegienstraße 6
Nach 1270

Der von führenden Männern der Aufklärung hochgeschätzte Carl Philipp Emanuel Bach, zweiter Sohn Johann Sebastian Bachs, von 1738-67 Kammercembalist Friedrichs II. in Ruppin, Berlin und Potsdam, war 1734-38 Jurastudent an der Universität und Kantor an der Marienkirche in Frankfurt (Oder). Nach ihm ist die Konzerthalle benannt worden, die 1966-75 durch Umbau der ehemaligen Franziskaner-Kirche nach Entwürfen von Hans und Sigrid Albeshausen und Mitarbeitern sowie Ernst Wipprecht entstanden ist. Komplettiert wurde die Halle 1970 durch zwei Bronzetüren mit Reliefs von Axel Schulz, 1975 durch eine Konzertorgel der Frankfurter Orgelbaufirma Sauer und in den achtziger Jahren durch Anbauten auf der Nordseite des Gebäudes. Die turmlose dreischiffige Backsteinhalle mit Sterngewölben ist mehrfach umgebaut worden, 1730-40 wurde sie zur Kirche der neuen Garnison Frankfurt eingerichtet. Das hohe Satteldach des Hallenlanghauses ist zusammen mit der Silhouette der benachbarten Friedenskirche für das Stadtbild von Frankfurt (Oder) von besonderer Bedeutung.

Carl Philipp Emanuel Bach, second son of Johann Sebastian Bach and highly esteemed by leading men of the Enlightenment, chamber harpsichordist to Frederick II in Ruppin, Berlin and Potsdam from 1738-67, studied law at the university and was cantor at the Marienkirche in Frankfurt an der Oder from 1734-8. The concert hall, created 1966-75 by converting the former Franciscan church to designs by Hans and Sigrid Albeshausen and colleagues with Ernst Wipprecht, is named after him. The hall was completed by the addition of two bronze doors with reliefs by Axel Schulz in 1970, a concert organ by the Frankfurt organ-building firm of Sauer in 1975, and extensions on the north side of the building in the eighties. The towerless brick hall with three aisles and stellar vaulting has been rebuilt on several occasions. In 1730-40 it became the church for the new Frankfurt garrison. The high saddle roof of the hall nave, together with the silhouette of the neighbouring Friedenskirche, is a particularly important part of the townscape of Frankfurt an der Oder.

in der Nähe/nearby:
Collegienhaus; Collegienstraße 8-9
1737 • Christoph Gottlieb Hedemann
Friedenskirche (St. Nikolai); Große Scharrnstraße
Um 1300 (Restaurierung 1881-83 • Friedrich Adler)
Warenhaus; Berliner Straße 14, Klingestraße
1910-11 • Paul Renner
Georgenhospital; Berliner Straße 23
1794 • Martin Friedrich Knoblauch
Krankenhaus; Seelower Kehre 3
1929-30 • Josef Gesing

X 9 Realgymnasium
Frankfurt (Oder); Wieckestraße 3
1909-11 • Carl Schwatlo

Zwar bildeten sich um die Mitte des 19. Jahrhunderts Schulformen heraus mit neuen Lehrplänen und Unterrichtsmethoden wie die Realschule, die Schulgebäude wiesen aber weiterhin große Mängel auf, weil bis 1870 keinerlei Richtlinien für deren Bau vorlagen. Die Schulpraxis vervollkommnete erst im letzten Drittel des Jahrhunderts das Raumprogramm, indem die Klassenzimmer durch Gesangssaal, Zeichensaal, naturwissenschaftliche Klassen, Werkräume, Turnhalle und Aula ergänzt wurden. Nur in sparsamster, kasernenartiger Ausführung konnten die Baubehörden diesen Mehraufwand bewältigen. Doch um die Jahrhundertwende arrivierte die Schule doch noch zum kommunalen Repräsentationsbau, die Zeit der Schulpaläste brach an. Die Neubauten erhielten bevorzugte Standorte in stadtbildbeherrschender Lage, bekannte Architekten lieferten die Entwürfe, anerkannte Bildhauer den Bauschmuck. Die städtischen Baubeamten hatten sich an diesen Ansprüchen zu messen. In dieser Zeit entstand auch das Frankfurter Realgymnasium. Es folgt in seiner Mischung von Sandstein und roten Ziegeln Vorbildern der holländischen Renaissance, wie sie in den Jahren um 1900 auch Ludwig Hoffmann in seinen Berliner Schulen anwandte.

In the mid nineteenth century, new types of school, curricula and teaching methods emerged, but school buildings continued to have major deficiencies as a result of the fact that until 1870 there were no guidelines for their architecture. It was not until the last third of the century that school practice perfected its design programme, and provided music room, art room, science laboratory, workshop, gymnasium and hall, as well as ordinary classrooms. The building authorities could only deal with these additional needs in very economical, barrack-like form. But around the turn of the century schools started to be provided with imposing municipal buildings: the period of school palaces had arrived. The new buildings were on prime sites from which they could dominate the townscape, they were designed by distinguished architects and decorated by recognized sculptors. Municipal building officials had to adapt to these demands. The Frankfurt Realgymnasium dates from this period. Its mixture of sandstone and red brick follows Dutch Renaissance models, of the kind also used by Ludwig Hoffmann in his Berlin schools built around 1900.

in der Nähe/nearby:
Wohnhäuser; Rosa-Luxemburg-Straße 32-33
1875/80
Wohnhäuser; Sophienstraße 19-21
1879

X 10 Villa für Stadtrat Bauer
Frankfurt (Oder); Rudolf-Breitscheid-Straße 13
1902-03 • Wahlich

Sie wandten sich insbesondere gegen die Nachahmung historischer Stile im 19. Jahrhundert, die Vertreter des Jugendstils, und sie brachten das in ihrer neuen Ornamentik zum Ausdruck, die abstrakte Pflanzenmotive zugrunde legte und flächenhaft dekorativ verbundene, großzügig geschwungene, bewegungsvolle vegetabilische Formen erzeugte. Eigentlich kam dieser sich aufbäumende Gestaltungswille – etwa von 1895 bis 1905 – mehr aus dem Kunstgewerbe, der Innenarchitektur und der Mode, hinterließ aber auch in der Architektur seine Spuren. Man erinnert sich an Architekten wie Henry van de Velde, Peter Behrens, Richard Riemerschmid oder Joseph Maria Olbrich. Daneben gab es aber noch eine Reihe anderer Baumeister, deren Schöpfungen nicht weniger interessant waren. Die von Wahlich für den Frankfurter Stadtrat R. Bauer entworfene Villa mit rundem Eckerker und Zwiebelhaube, mit geschweiftem Giebel und Dachtürmchen läßt sich ins Fach »reizvoll« einordnen. Das wird auch innen durch das große Foyer mit der umlaufenden hölzernen Galerie unterstrichen.

There was a resistance to the imitation of historical styles in the nineteenth century, and devotees of Jugendstil in particular expressed this in their new style of ornamentation based on abstract plant motifs creating extensive, decoratively connected, lavishly curving, highly mobile vegetable forms. In fact this writhing will to design – dominant roughly from 1895-1905 – came more from the realms of applied art, interior design and fashion, but did also make its mark on architecture. One has only to think of architects like Henry van de Velde, Peter Behrens, Richard Riemerschmid or Joseph Maria Olbrich. But there were a number of other builders whose creations were no less interesting. The villa designed by Wahlich for Frankfurt city councillor R. Bauer with round corner oriel and onion dome, shaped gable and small tower on the roof can be placed in the «charming» category. This is also true of the interior, which has a large foyer with a wooden gallery round it.

in der Nähe/nearby:
Wohnzeile; Am Kleistpark 8-12
1902 u. um 1905
Pfarrkirche zum Heiligen Kreuz; Franz-Mehring-Straße
1897-99 • Engelbert Seiberts
Einkaufszentrum; Heilbronner Straße 30
1980-85 • Manfred Vogler, Jochen Beige, Werner Hensel
Wohnkomplex »Halbe Stadt«; Halbe Stadt, Am Kleistpark
1973-78 • Manfred Vogler, Jochen Beige, Bernd Beringschmidt, Günter Hartzsch, Rudolf Krebs, Gudrun Grselka, Franz Klement

X 11 Casino
Frankfurt (Oder); Halbe Stadt 7
Um 1835

Die bereits seit 1816 systematisch betriebene Entfestigung der Stadt hatte zwei wichtige, städtebaulich strukturbestimmende Folgen. Die eine war der Park, der 1833-45 auf den westlich des Altstadtkerns gelegenen Wällen und Gräben von Peter Joseph Lenné angelegt wurde und heute eine beliebte zentrumsnahe Grünoase ist. Die zweite Folge war der Bau der spätklassizistischen Straßenzeile Halbe Stadt, die durch die Einheitlichkeit der einzelnen, verhältnismäßig bescheidenen Wohnhäuser oder Villen zu einem bedeutsamen Ensemble in der Stadt wurde. Um 1835 wurde in diesem Zusammenhang auch das Casino errichtet, ein klassizistischer Putzbau mit dreiachsigem Mittelrisalit, der Mitte des 19. Jahrhunderts zu einer Villa umgebaut wurde. Bei der Restaurierung des Gebäudes, 1983-84 nach Plänen von Christian Nülken, wurde deutlich, daß sich Pflege und Erhaltung dieser Substanz auffallend schwierig gestalten, weil die öffentliche Wertschätzung der Denkmale oft fehlt. Erhalten sind die Gebäude 6-9, 20-24, 30 und 35, herausragend die Gebäude Nr. 8, 9, 22 und 30, saniert und instandgesetzt wurden bisher nur die Gebäude Nr. 7, 10 und 30.

Defortification of the city, carried out systematically from 1816, had two important consequences affecting urban structure. One was the park, laid out 1833-45 on the ramparts and moats west of the old town core by Peter Joseph Lenné and today a popular green oasis near the town centre. The second consequence was the building of the late-classical houses known as Halbe Stadt, which became an important ensemble in the town because of the unity of the individual, relatively modest town houses or villas. The Casino was built in this context c. 1835, a classical rendered building with protruding central section along three axes, rebuilt as a villa in the mid nineteenth century. When the building was restored in 1983-4 to plans by Christian Nülken, it became clear that care and maintenance of this stock was strikingly difficult because often the public do not hold old buildings in high esteem. The surviving buildings are nos. 6-9, 20-24, 30 and 35, outstanding among them nos. 8, 9, 22 and 30. So far only nos. 7, 10 and 30 have been redeveloped and restored.

in der Nähe/nearby:
Wohnhaus (jetzt Ambulanz); Halbe Stadt 8
Um 1835
Lennépark; Halbe Stadt
1833-45 • Peter Joseph Lenné
Heinrich-von-Kleist-Schule; Rosa-Luxemburg-Straße 43
1861-62
Wohnhaus (Kindergarten); Halbe Stadt 30
Um 1835

X 12 Hauptbahnhof
Frankfurt (Oder); Bahnhofsplatz
1922-24 • Behringer

Als Stammbahnhof und Verwaltungsgebäude der 1922 eingerichteten Eisenbahndirektion Osten entstand dieser Gebäudekomplex. Zur Verbesserung des Bahnsteigzuganges wurde das Empfangsgebäude mit dem Hallenniveau unter der Gleisebene angeordnet, was die Treppe zwischen Halle und Bahnsteigunterführung erspart. Noch ganz in der zum Malerischen neigenden Gestaltungsweise der zehner Jahre kam es zu einer geschlossenen städtebaulich-räumlichen Platzlösung. Neben dem Empfangsgebäude des Bahnhofs wurde auch die Wohnbebauung an der östlichen Platzseite in die Planung einbezogen und am anschließenden Kiliansberg für eine Siedlungsgesellschaft in zweigeschossigen Reihenhäusern weitergeführt. Gründe für die einheitliche Konzeption lagen wohl darin, daß für die Unterführung des Gleiskörpers der Bahnhofsvorplatz und die Einmündung der Bahnhofstraße um vier bis fünf Meter abgetragen werden mußten, was bauliche Konsequenzen nach sich zog, aber auch städtebauliche Chancen bot. In der Bahnhofstraße schließen sich seit 1954 viergeschossige Klinkerbauten von Hermann Henselmann an. Mit der Grundsteinlegung am 1. Mai 1951 gelten die Bauten als Beginn des komplexen Wohnungsbaues in der damaligen DDR.

These buildings were put up as headquarters, station and offices of the eastern railway directorate, established in 1922. To improve access to the platforms the reception building was built below platform level, which obviated the need for steps between hall and subway under the platforms. The square became a unified whole in terms of urban style, but its design still inclined to the picturesque of the nineteen-tens. The residential development on the eastern side of the square beside the station reception building was also included in the planning process, and the pattern continued for an estate of two storey terraced houses on the adjacent Kiliansberg. It was probably reasons of unity that led to the excavation of the station square and the junction with Bahnhofstrasse to a depth of four to five metres for the tunnel for the tracks; this had consequences in construction terms but also offered opportunities in terms of urban development. Since 1954 four-storey clinker buildings by Hermann Henselmann have been added in Bahnhofstrasse. The foundation stone was laid on 1 May 1951, meaning that the buildings mark the beginning of complex residential construction in what was then the GDR.

in der Nähe/nearby:
Gymnasium; Gubener Straße 11
1880-82 • Ministerium der öffentlichen Arbeiten
Villa v. Handt; Gubener Straße 14-15
1852 • Friedrich Hitzig, Johann Heinrich Strack
Türmchenhaus; Lindenstraße 28
1785 • (vermutlich) Martin Friedrich Knoblauch

X 13 Georgenkirche
Frankfurt (Oder); Bergstraße
1926-28 • Curt Steinberg

Während das späte 19. Jahrhundert im wesentlichen keinen eigenen Baustil für Kirchenbauten hervorgebracht hat, waren die Architekten in den ersten Jahrzehnten unseres Jahrhunderts bemüht, wie auch auf anderen Gebieten so in der Kirchenbaukunst neue Wege zu gehen. Die Umsetzung der Vorstellungen nach schöpferischem Ausdruck, kubischer Formung, sakral-monumentaler Vereinfachung und sachlicher Ausnutzung der Baustoffe führte zur formal klaren Gestaltung und meist guten städtebaulichen Einfügung. Die neuzeitlichen Konstruktionen und Werkstoffe wie Stahlbeton, Stahl, Glas ermöglichten eine freie Raumbildung ohne störende Stützen. Die Georgenkirche – ein Ersatzbau für die Spitalkirche der Lebuser Vorstadt – entstand in dieser Zeit des Suchens nach neuen Ausdrucksformen. Der Zentralbau aus roten Klinkern mit hohem quadratischen spitzbehelmten Westturm und rundem, flach überkuppeltem Gemeinderaum ist beeindruckend.

While the late nineteenth century essentially produced no new church building style, architects in the first decades of our century were concerned to find new directions for church architecture, as they had in other fields. Implementation of ideas on creative expression, cubic form, ecclesiastical and monumental simplification and functional use of building materials produced formally clear design and buildings that usually fitted into the urban pattern well. Modern construction methods and materials like reinforced concrete, steel and glass made it possible to create free space without distracting supports. The Georgenkirche – a replacement for the Spitalkirche in Lebuser Vorstadt – was built at the time of this search for new expressive forms. The centrally-planned building in red clinker with tall, square west tower with spire, and circular interior with a shallow down, is impressive.

X 14 Wohnsiedlung Paulinenhof
Frankfurt (Oder); Kießlingplatz, Georg-Friedrich-Händel-Straße
1922-23 • Martin Kießling

Nach Abschluß des Versailler Vertrages sollte sich Frankfurt (Oder), rund 80 km von der polnischen Grenze entfernt, zunehmend als »Hauptstadt der mittleren Ostmark« verstehen. In diesem Zusammenhang wurde 1922 auch die Eisenbahndirektion Osten von Berlin nach Frankfurt (Oder) verlegt. Eine ganze Reihe von Baumaßnahmen wurde durch die Verlegung von 1000 Beamten und deren Familien ausgelöst. So entstand 1922-23 nach Entwürfen von Martin Kießling die Eisenbahner-Wohnsiedlung Paulinenhof in Anlehnung an Gartenstädte. Die Bebauung der axialen Anlage zwischen Kießlingplatz und Georg-Friedrich-Händel-Straße mit teilweise gekrümmten Seitenstraßen wurde als niedrige, ein- bis zweigeschossige Bebauung im sogenannten Heimatstil ausgeführt. Der Hauptzugang zur Siedlung am Kießlingplatz wurde mit skulpturgeschmückten Fußgängerpforten seitlich der Fahrbahn betont.

After the conclusion of the Treaty of Versailles, Frankfurt an der Oder, about 80 kilometres from the Polish border, was to see itself increasingly as «capital of the central Ostmark». In this context the eastern railway headquarters was moved from Berlin to Frankfurt an der Oder in 1922. The transfer of 1,000 officials and their families unleashed a great deal of building activity. Thus the Paulinenhof railway workers estate was built in 1922-3 to designs by Martin Kiessling, following garden city ideas. The axial complex between Kiesslingplatz and Georg-Friedrich-Händel-Strasse, including some curving side roads, was developed using low, one- to two-storey buildings in the so-called Heimatstil. The main access to the estate in Kiesslingplatz was emphasized by pedestrian gateways decorated with sculpture on either side of the carriageway.

in der Nähe/nearby:
Pädagogische Akademie; Friedrich-Ebert-Straße 51-52
1930-34 • Adolf Petersen
Wohnhäuser und Schule; August-Bebel-Straße 18-24
1927-28 • Josef Gesing
Wohnzeile; August-Bebel-Straße 104-110
1926 • Behnsen
Wohnzeile; August-Bebel-Straße 111-112
1924-25 • Josef Gesing
Gutshaus (Kinderheim); Rosengarten
1898
Siedlung am Klingetalgraben; Bergstraße 43-45, Grüner Weg 15, 17-19, Karl-Sobkowski-Straße 23-30
1922-23 • Martin Kießling
Wohnkomplex »Hansaviertel«; nördl. Klingetal
1969-76 • Hans Albeshausen, Günter Hartzsch, Dietrich Koch, Gunther Richter, Horst Adler

X 15 Musikheim (Kleist-Theater)
Frankfurt (Oder); Gerhart-Hauptmann-Straße 3-4
1928-29 • Otto Bartning

Das Musikheim entstand als erstes Glied einer geplanten pädagogischen Akademie, getragen vom Preußischen Kultusministerium, bestimmt für die Fortbildung von Lehrern und Jugendpflegern. Idee des Leiters war die Ausübung von Musik, Tanz und Laienspiel in der Gruppe und im Einklang mit dem Rhythmus der Raumfolgen. Bartning ordnete dazu die Bauteile mit ihren Sälen und Zimmern hintereinander, jedoch mehrfach gewinkelt an, so daß lange Flure entstanden, die rhythmisch durchschritten zu eben jener inneren Harmonie in der musischen Übung führen konnten. Diesem Prinzip entspricht auch der asketische Stil von anspruchsloser Zuordnung geometrisch schlichter Baukörper bis hin zu flachen Satteldächern, deren Bohlenbinder innen im offenen Dachraum sichtbar blieben. Die freie Deckenuntersicht des Versammlungsraumes im Rundbau erhielt damit ein eigenwilliges filigranes Linienspiel. Große Glasflächen unterstützen die bewußte Wechselwirkung von Gebäude und Garten, und sogar die Bühne des Theatersaales ist vom Garten aus betretbar und zu bespielen. Bartning übernahm auch die Innenausstattung. Als Leiter der Bauhochschule in Weimar beteiligte er dortige Gestalter: Wilhelm Wagenfeld für die Lampen, Erich Dieckmann für die Möbel.

The Musikheim was built as the first institution of a projected teachers' training academy established by the Prussian Ministry of Culture for the further education of teachers and youth counselors. The director's concept called for music, dance and drama to be practised in groups and in harmony with the rhythm of the spatial sequence of the rooms. For this purpose Bartning arranged the various components of the building complex with their halls and rooms successively one after the other, not in one straight line but with several angles, thus creating long corridors. Moving along to the rhythm of these corridors in the course of a musical exercise was to give rise to the desired sense of inner harmony. The same principle is reflected in the ascetic style, from the unpretentious arrangement of simple geometric volumes to the low gable roofs whose trusses were left visible in the open space of the roof. Thus the ceiling of the assembly hall in the circular building was given a curious filigree pattern. The large glazed areas enhance the purposeful interaction of building and garden, and even the stage of the theatre hall is accessible from the garden. Bartning also designed the interiors. As director of the Weimar school of architecture he commissioned the services of some of the designers working there, e.g. Wilhelm Wagenfeld for the lamps and Erich Dieckmann for the furniture.

in der Nähe/nearby:
Messegaststätte »Grünhof«; August-Bebel-Straße 54
1935-36 • Winkler, Gütte

X 16 Krematorium auf dem Hauptfriedhof
Frankfurt (Oder); Leipziger Straße 154
1929-30 • Josef Gesing

Nach Eröffnung des ersten Krematoriums in Deutschland im Jahre 1878 brauchte es eines gewissen Zeitraums zur Überwindung mancher Schwierigkeiten und Voreingenommenheiten besonders der Kirche, um der Feuerbestattung Akzeptanz zu gewähren. Mit Vermehrung der Anlagen steigerten sich in Deutschland die jährlichen Einäscherungen auch wesentlich. Gab es 1898 erst vier Krematorien mit jährlich 423 Einäscherungen, so wurden 1930 bereits 103 Krematorien mit fast 54 000 Einäscherungen gezählt. – Die Krematoriumsanlage in Frankfurt entstand während des »Baubooms« der zwanziger Jahre und ist als roter Klinkerbau auch in den Formen der Neuen Sachlichkeit beeindruckend. In der Feierhalle befindet sich vor dem Altar die selbsttätig verschließbare Öffnung mit Versenkbühne zur Aufstellung des Sarges für die feierliche Aufbahrung während der Trauerfeier. Dieser Katafalkbereich ist mit einem Mosaik geschmückt. Die zur Einäscherung dienenden Räume liegen unter der Haupthalle, wohin der Sarg über die Versenkbühne gelangt. – Eine Gedenkstätte für die Opfer des Ersten und Zweiten Weltkrieges im Ostteil des Friedhofs wurde von Friedemann Klos gestaltet.

When the first crematorium opened in Germany in 1878, it took some time before difficulties and prejudices were overcome, particularly on the part of the church, and before cremation became accepted. As the number of crematoria grew, the number of cremations in Germany grew substantially as well. In 1898 there were only four crematoria and 423 cremations annually, rising to 103 crematoria and almost 54,000 cremations by 1930. The crematorium in Frankfurt an der Oder dates from the twenties' «building boom», and is a red clinker building, impressive even in its forms of Neue Sachlichkeit. In front of the altar in the interior is the opening, which closes automatically, and a podium that can be lowered for the coffin, for solemn presentation during the ceremony. This catafalque area is decorated with a mosaic. The cremation rooms are under the main hall, and the coffin is taken to them by means of the podium. The memorial to the victims of the First and Second World Wars in the eastern part of the cemetery was designed by Friedemann Klos.

in der Nähe/nearby:
Stadtteil Neuberesinchen
1976-87 • Dietrich Koch, Günter Hartzsch u.a.m.
Richtfunkturm; an der Autobahn
1951-61 • Klaus Thimm, Karl-Heinz Benkert
Baugewerbeschule; Puschkinstraße 7-9
1929-30 • Johannes Müller
Mädchenschule; Beeskower Straße
1930-31 • Josef Gesing

Y
Cottbus (Chośebus)

Cottbus ist mit etwa 126 000 Einwohnern nach Potsdam heute die zweitgrößte Stadt im Land Brandenburg. Obwohl seit dem Mittelalter der wichtigste Ort der Niederlausitz, war es unter dem sorbischen Namen Chośebus weniger bekannt. Durch seine Tuchproduktion hatte Cottbus weit über die Grenzen der Mark Brandenburg hinausreichende Handelsbeziehungen. Doch erst in den letzten Jahrzehnten war es im Zuge der Industrialisierungsbestrebungen der DDR zu einem überregionalen Zentrum der Kohle- und Energiewirtschaft entwickelt worden. Als Verkehrsknotenpunkt gehört zu dieser Stadt ein Eisenbahnausbesserungswerk und seit den dreißiger Jahren bereits der Anschluß an das Autobahnnnetz. Cottbus besitzt eine Universität, ein neues Stadtzentrum, ein Theater aus der Jugendstilzeit und ein Raumflug-Planetarium. Das Grün der vielen Parkanlagen in der Innenstadt setzt sich fort in der Auenlandschaft um Schloß Branitz bis hin zum weitverästelten, wasserreichen Spreewald; doch das ist nur ein spärlicher Rest jener Urlandschaft Germaniens, die der Römer Tacitus beschrieb: »... mit unheimlichen Wäldern bedeckt und mit häßlichen Sümpfen.« Die Lausitz – slawisch Lusici, das heißt so viel wie Sumpfland – gehört in ihrem niederen Teil zum eiszeitlichen Glogau-Baruther Urstromtal in dem zahllose Sandstreifen aufgeworfen wurden; dazwischen schuf zurückgebliebenes Wasser Morast an Morast. In dieser Landschaft erhob sich zwischen dichten Laubwäldern eine hohe, kahle Sandbank mit ihrer höchsten Erhebung am Spreeufer, zum Fluß steil abfallend und mit einem bequemen Aufstieg von Westen. Ihre Besiedlung seit der Steinzeit ist durch Funde bezeugt. Im 6. Jahrhundert siedelten hier Slawen. Der Name Cottbus ist wendischen Ursprungs und heißt Burg des Wachsamen. Im 10. Jahrhundert ist die slawische Wartburg eine deutsche Burgwardei. Anfang des 12. Jahrhunderts gibt es eine Kaufmannssiedlung im Schutze der Burg. 1156 wird Chotibus erstmals erwähnt. Seit der Mitte des 15. Jahrhunderts gehören Cottbus und Peitz zum Eigentum der Brandenburger Kurfürsten, und nach kurzem Besitzwechsel –1807-13 ist es sächsisch – geht die Stadt zusammen mit Brandenburg 1815 in Preußen auf.

With a population of c. 126,000 Cottbus ranks today as the second largest town in the Land Brandenburg after Potsdam. Although already the most important town of the Niederlausitz, it was less well known by its Sorbian name Chośebus. Thanks to its cloth-making industry Cottbus enjoyed trade relations which extended far beyond the boundaries of the Mark Brandenburg. In the context of the industrialization scheme of the GDR it was turned into a supra-regional centre for coal and energy only in the last few decades. As a junction of major traffic routes it also houses a railway maintenance and repair centre and has been connected to the autobahn network since the nineteen-thirties. Cottbus has a university, a new town centre, a theatre from the Jugendstil period, and a modern space-age planetarium. The green area with numerous parks in the town centre is continued in the water meadows around Schloss Branitz and all the way to the extensive, well-watered Spreewald; all this is but a small remainder of the primeval landscape of Germania which Tacitus described as «covered with uncanny forests and ugly swamps.» The lower part of the Lausitz – in Slavic: Lusici, i.e. marshland or swamp – belongs to the Glogau-Baruth glacial valley, dating back to the ice age, with countless sandflats; between them the remaining water created a dense network of bogs. In this landscape with dense deciduous forests rose a high, barren bank of sand which reached its highest elevation at the banks of the Spree, dropping off sharply towards the river and sloping off gently towards the west. It was already settled in the Stone Age as documented by numerous finds. In the sixth century it was Slavs who made this area their home. The name Cottbus is of Wendic origin and means «Castle of the Vigilant». In the tenth century the slavic castle becomes a German stronghold. At the beginning of the twelfth century a trading settlement develops under the protection of the castle. In 1156 Chotibus is mentioned in the documents for the first time. From the mid fifteenth century Cottbus and Peitz belonged to the Elector of Brandenburg, and after falling to Saxony from 1807-1813, the town, along with the Mark Brandenburg, became part of Prussia.

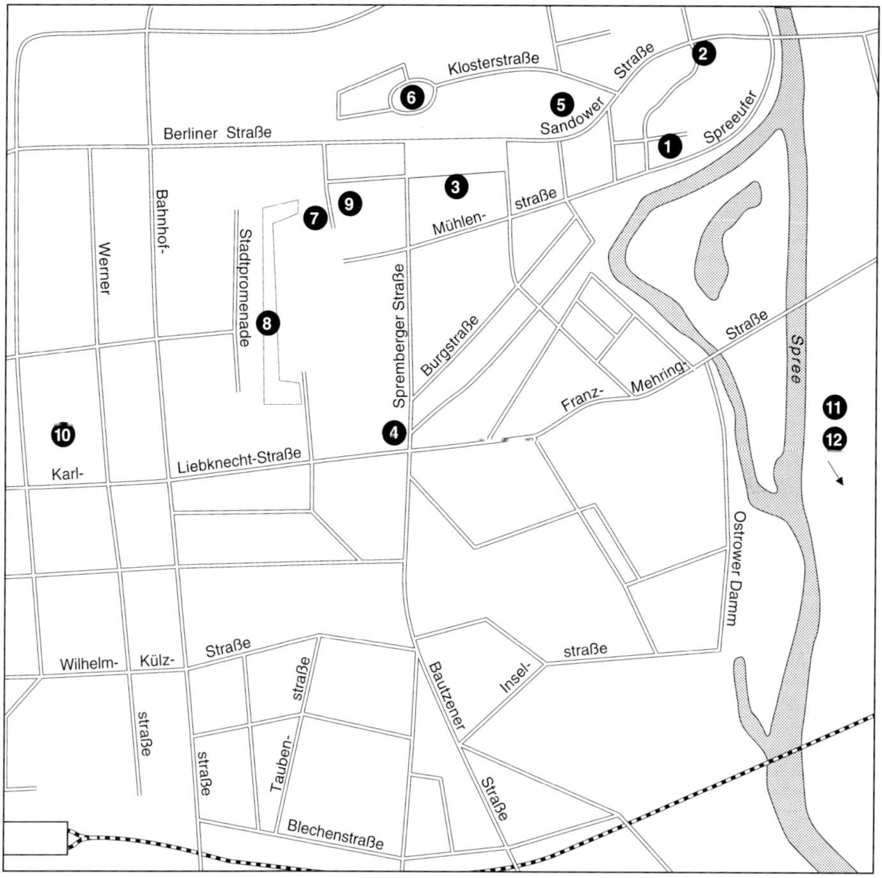

Y 1 Schloßturm
Y 2 Tuchmacherbrunnen
Y 3 Wohnhäuser am Altmarkt
Y 4 Spremberger Turm
Y 5 Oberkirche St. Nikolai
Y 6 Franziskaner-Klosterkirche
Y 7 Mauertürme und Weichhaus
Y 8 Stadtzentrum »Stadtpromenade«
Y 9 Neues Rathaus
Y 10 Stadttheater
Y 11 Schloß Branitz
Y 12 Park Branitz

Y 1 Schloßturm
Cottbus; Gerichtsstraße
Um 1300 und 1876

Am Flußübergang der Salzstraße von Halle nach Schlesien, am linken Ufer, hoch über der Spree, lag wohl schon im 10. Jahrhundert eine deutsche Burg, in deren Schutz sich zu Anfang des 12. Jahrhunderts Kaufleute angesiedelt hatten. – Diese Anlage auf einem Sander gelegen wird damals in die Landschaft gewirkt haben wie heute noch der Schloßberg bei Burg im Spreewald. – Um 1300 gab es zwei Linien der Herren von Cottbus und seitdem auch zwei Schlösser auf der Hochfläche der Burg. Aus dieser Zeit stammt der Unterbau des Schloßturmes, ein ehemaliger Bergfrit, der 1876 aufgestockt und mit Zinnenkranz nebst Aufbau versehen wurde. 1856 brannte die alte Schloßanlage aus. An ihre Stelle trat 1877 das Landgericht, ein Neorenaissancegebäude. Am Gerichtsplatz steht seit 1905 anstelle des ehemaligen Amtshauses das Amtsgericht in Weserrenaissanceformen.

As early as the tenth century, there must have been a German castle at the site where the old salt road from Halle to Silesia crossed the river, high on the left bank of the Spree. Under the protection of this castle, merchants settled here in the early twelfth century. – Located on an outwash, this stronghold must have commanded the countryside in a similar way as the castle mound at Burg in the Spreewald still does today. – Around 1300 there were two lines of the lords of Cottbus and thus two palaces on the high ground of the castle. From that time dates the substructure of the palace tower, a former keep which was heightened and equipped with embattlements and a superstructure in 1876. In 1856 the old castle was gutted by fire and was replaced in 1877 with the Landgericht, a building in neo-Renaissance style. At the Gerichtsplatz the site of the former official building is now occupied by the courthouse, erected in 1905 in the style of the Weser-Renaissance.

in der Nähe/nearby:
Loh- und Weißgerberhaus; Uferstraße 16
Um 1730
Elektrizitätswerk; Uferstraße
1901-03
Dieselkraftwerk; Am Amtsteich
1928 • Walter Klingenberg, Werner Issel

Y 2 Tuchmacherbrunnen
Cottbus; Sandower Straße
Nach 1930 • Richard Kuöhl

Seit dem 12. Jahrhundert wurden die sumpfigen Gebiete der Niederlausitz entwässert. Damit verschwand der Urwald mit den alten Baumriesen, und an die Stelle von Eiche und Linde trat die anspruchslose Kiefer. Die nun sandigen Heideflächen erlaubten aber nur die Schafzucht. Die Wolle und das Wissen der im 12. und 13. Jahrhundert eingewanderten Flamen begründeten hier eine Tuchmacherei, die fortan für die Stadt bestimmend und weltbekannt wurde. An diese Zunft erinnert der Tuchmacherbrunnen mit seinem Spruchband »Ein ehrsam Handwerk wird geehrt / das gute Tuche wirkt und schert«. Richard Kuöhl ist der Bildhauer. Kuöhl arbeitete in Hamburg für Schumacher und Höger. Im dortigen Justizforum baute er 1930 ebenfalls einen Brunnen. Aber auch in Berlin wurde er beschäftigt, etwa bei der plastischen Ausschmückung des U-Bahnhofs Thielplatz.

From the twelfth century on, efforts were made to drain the swamp areas of the Niederlausitz. That was the end of the primeval forest with its ancient giant trees; oak and lime-tree were replaced by the less demanding pine. The now sandy heathland only permitted the raising of sheep. The wool and the knowhow of the Flemish who had come here in the twelfth and thirteenth centuries formed the basis for the manufacture of cloths which soon dominated the town and gained worldwide fame. A reminder to this guild is the Tuchmacherbrunnen. Its inscription reads: «In honour of a noble trade which weaves and shears fine cloths.» The sculptor was Richard Kuöhl who worked in Hamburg for Schumacher and Höger. In 1930 he built another fountain for the forum of justice there and was also commissioned for work in Berlin, for example the sculptured ornaments of the underground station at Thielplatz.

in der Nähe/nearby:
Münzturm; Münzstraße 17-18
15. Jh.; 1903
Biedermeierhaus; Sandower Straße 17
Um 1820
Raumflug-Planetarium; Heinrich-Mosler-Straße 39
1972-74 • G. Müller
Landhaus; Diesterwestraße 2
1910-11 • Hermann Muthesius

Y 3 Wohnhäuser am Markt
Cottbus; Altmarkt
17. bis Anfang 19. Jahrhundert

Um 1230 ist die Kaufmannssiedlung unterhalb der Burg durch die Herren von Cottbus nach Westen und Süden zu einer regelmäßig angelegten mittelalterlichen Gründerstadt erweitert worden. Zwei Straßenzüge, die Berliner und die Spremberger Straße, kreuzen sich an einem großen rechteckigen Marktplatz. Mit den kleineren Nebenstraßen ergeben sie ein annähernd rechtwinkliges Raster. An den beiden Hauptstraßen lagen an besonderen Plätzen die Kirchen, etwas abgelegen das Franziskanerkloster. Das Rathaus wurde 1611 an der Stelle eines Vorgängerbaus mitten auf dem Markt errichtet, 1945 zerstört fehlt es jetzt. Die Fachwerkhäuser aus dem Mittelalter fielen zuletzt dem Stadtbrand von 1671 zum Opfer; nur Kellergewölbe blieben erhalten. Die Bebauung des Altmarktes stammt überwiegend aus der Zeit nach dem Siebenjährigen Krieg, also aus dem letzten Viertel des 18. Jahrhunderts. Dabei zeigen die stattlichen Giebelhäuser Nr. 10, 14 und 16 den Einfluß Sachsens und Schlesiens während die schlichten Traufenhäuser Nr. 21 und 24 mit ihren klassizistischen Formen aus der ersten Hälfte des 19. Jahrhunderts die Ausrichtung auf preußische Vorbilder erkennen lassen.

Around 1230 the merchants' settlement around the castle was moved by the lords of Cottbus to the west and south and expanded into a medieval foundation town on a regular plan. Two streets, the Berliner and Spremberger Strasse, intersect at the large rectangular market square. Together with smaller side streets they form an almost perfect rectangular grid. At prominent points along the main streets churches were located, along with a Franciscan monastery in the vicinity. The townhall was erected in 1611 on the site of its predecessor in the centre of the market square. It was destroyed in 1945 and is no longer extant. The medieval half-timber houses fell victim to the town fire of 1671, only the cellar vaults remain. The majority of buildings at the Altmarkt or old market date back to the time after the Seven Years' War, i.e. the last quarter of the eighteenth century. The stately gabled houses at nos. 10, 14 and 16 show influences from Saxony and Silesia, while the plain houses at nos. 21 and 24, with eaves facing the street, show classicist forms from the first half of the nineteenth century, suggesting the influence of Prussian models.

in der Nähe/nearby:
Wohnhaus; Altmarkt 21
E. 18. Jh. und 1853 (Theatersaal)
Wohnhaus mit Fleischscharren; Altmarkt 22
17. und 18. Jh.
Löwenapotheke (Apothekenmuseum); Altmarkt 24
Um 1800
Marktbrunnen; Altmarkt
1991 • Peter Kittel, Egmar Ponndorf, J. Peschel

Y 4 Spremberger Turm
Cottbus; Spremberger Straße 20
16. Jahrhundert und 1823-25

Die großen Hauptstraßen der mittelalterlichen Gründerstadt führten im Osten, Westen und Süden auf nur drei Tore, da im Norden ein nach wie vor unwegsames Terrain anschloß. Die Sandower Straße mußte zum Tor an der Spree den Burgberg umgehen; an der heutigen Berliner Straße lag das Luckauer Tor. Im Gegensatz zu diesen beiden schlichten Bauten, die im 19 Jahrhundert mit ihren Vortoren verlorengingen, war das Spremberger Tor noch lange durch eine vorgelagerte Bastei des 16. Jahrhunderts geschützt. Das Mühlentor unterhalb des Schlosses diente nur als Zugang zu den Spreemühlen, während das Neustädter Tor erst seit 1733 den Zugang zu der für hugenottische Zuwanderer angelegten Neustadt schützte. Mit der Aufhebung der Mahl- und Schlachtsteuer begann die Abtragung der Stadtmauer und ihrer Tore. 1810 fiel auch ein Teil des Spremberger Turmes. Nach von Karl Friedrich Schinkel genehmigten Plänen erstand er in neuer Gestalt, zwar ohne Barockhaube aber mit einem Zinnenkranz. Er bildet mit dem Wohn- und Geschäftshaus Nr. 16 noch heute ein Torensemble, das den genius loci als Architekturbild bewahrt.

The great mainstreets of the medieval foundation centre ended in only three gates to the east, west and south respectively, as there was still an impassable tract of land to the north. The Sandower Strasse leading to the gate by the Spree had to bypass the castle mount; the Luckau gate was located at the present-day Berliner Strasse. In contrast to these two rather modest buildings, which were lost in the nineteenth century together with their outer gates, the Spremberg gate continued for a long time to be protected by an outer bastion from the sixteenth century. The Mühlentor below the castle merely provided access to the Spree mills, while the Neustädter gate was eventually built in 1733 to guard the way to the new town established for the Huguenot immigrants. When the milling and slaughtering tax was abolished, the town wall and gates were dismantled. In 1810 part of the Spremberg tower also fell. It was rebuilt in new shape to plans authorized by Karl Friedrich Schinkel, complete with embattlements but without the baroque cupola. Together with the residential and commercial building no. 16 it still forms an architectural ensemble which preserves the spirit of the genius loci.

in der Nähe/nearby:
Neustadt; Uferstraße, Freiheitsstraße
1726-30 • Philipp Gerlach
Wohn- und Geschäftshaus; Spremberger Straße 16
1896; um 1905 (Hausecke)
Geschäftshaus Sack; Spremberger Straße 5
Um 1910

Y 5 Oberkirche St. Nikolai
Cottbus; Oberkirchplatz, Sandower Straße
15. Jahrhundert

Die Pfarrkirche der Stadt steht heute frei auf dem Oberkirchplatz, nachdem sie bis 1729 ein Friedhof umgab. Bereits 1156 ist eine Kirche für Cottbus bezeugt. Der Backsteinbau der Nikolaikirche stammt aus dem 15. Jahrhundert. Es ist eine dreischiffige Hallenkirche mit der Besonderheit eines erhöhten Mittelschiffs. Der polygonal geschlossene Umgangschor entstand nach 1468, danach die weiträumige zweijochige Südkapelle (Bild). Der aus der Achse verschobene Westturm aus dem 14. Jahrhundert gehörte zu einem Vorgängerbau; den barocken Turmaufsatz mit Haube und Laterne erhielt er 1685. Der Einbau der Stern- und Netzgewölbe im Innern datiert vom Anfang des 16. Jahrhunderts. Nach Kriegszerstörung 1945 zog sich der Wiederaufbau bis 1989 hin. Verwaiste Ausstattungstücke aus Kirchen zwischen Frankfurt/Oder und Chemnitz zieren nun das Innere.

Today the parish church of the town stands alone on the Oberkirchplatz after being surrounded by a cemetery until 1729. First mention of a church in Cottbus dates back to 1156. The brick structure of the church of St. Nikolai was built in the fifteenth century. It is a hall church with nave and two aisles, remarkable because the nave has a raised floor. The polygonal closed ambulatory choir was added after 1468, followed later by the spacious south chapel (picture) with a vault of two bays. Slightly shifted out of the axis, the west tower dates back to the fourteenth century and was part of an earlier building; the baroque cupola and lantern of the tower were added in 1685. Inside, the reticulated and stellar vaults date back to the early sixteenth century. After war damages in 1945, reconstruction work did not begin until 1989. Salvaged ornaments and furnishings from other churches between Frankfurt an der Oder and Chemnitz found a new place in the interior.

in der Nähe/nearby:
Wohnhaus auf ehem. Burglehen; Oberkirchplatz 11
1785
Wohnhaus; Sandower Straße 54
1698

Y 6 Franziskaner-Klosterkirche
Cottbus; Klosterstraße, Wendenstraße
Anfang 14. Jahrhundert

Um 1300 wurden Kirche und Kloster der Franziskaner gegründet. Nach der Reformation 1537 war sie Pfarrkirche für die Kosterdörfer wie Sandow, Brunschwig oder Ostrow, die späteren Cottbuser Vororte. Als »Wendische Kirche« diente sie bis ins 20. Jahrhundert der sorbischen Bevölkerung im »Wendischen Viertel«, so wie die Oberkirche auch »Deutsche Kirche« hieß und wie ab 1700 die reformierte Schloßkirche lange Zeit nur der hugenottischen Bevölkerung im Tuchmacherviertel zur Verfügung stand. Die Klosterkirche ist ein Backsteinbau aus einem langen Hauptschiff zu zehn Jochen und einem nur vierjochigen Seitenschiff. Die schönen Netzrippengewölbe wurden im 15. Jahrhundert eingezogen. Seit 1307 liegt hier auch der Klostergründer Fredehelm v. Cottbus zusammen mit seiner Gattin Adelheid begraben. Die Hochrelieffiguren zeigen ein fürs Mittelalter seltenes Bild: Der Mann legt den rechten Arm um die Schulter seiner Frau.

The Franciscan church and monastery was established c. 1300. After the Reformation of 1537 it served as parish church for villages like Sandow, Brunschwig and Ostrow, which later became suburbs of Cottbus. Until well into the twentieth century it was called «Wendish Church» and served the Sorbian population of the «Wendish town», just as the Oberkirche was called «German Church», and the reformed Schlosskirche was for a long time open only to the Huguenot population of the Tuchmacherviertel. The monastery church is a brick building with a long middle vessel of ten bays and an aisle of only four bays. The splendid reticulated and ribbed vaults were added in the fifteenth century. Since 1307 the church also contains the graves of the founder of the monastery, Fredehelm von Cottbus, and his consort Adelheid. The high relief figures depict a scene quite rare for the Middle Ages: a man with his arm around the shoulders of his wife.

in der Nähe/nearby:
Jugendherberge; Klosterplatz 3
1719 (Bastei als Malzrösterei) u. 1795 (Neubau)
Klub Töpferturm; Töpferstraße, Klosterplatz
1988/89
Bürgerhaus; Mönchsgasse 1
1804-06 • (vermutlich) Karl Gottlob Kahle
Wohnhaus mit Paulanerbräu; Sandower Straße 57
1781; 1988/89 • Ewald Jantke
Wohn- und Geschäftshaus; Sandower Straße 59
2. H. 18. Jh.

Y 7 Stadtmauer und Weichhaus
Cottbus; Mauerstraße
15. Jahrhundert und 1937

Die Stadt hatte 1429 dem Hussitensturm standgehalten, baute aber die fünf bis sechs Meter hohe Backsteinmauer, die in Teilen noch erhalten ist, wohl erst danach aus. Noch im 18. Jahrhundert bestand die Stadtbefestigung aus Mauer, Innenwall, einem größeren Stadtgraben, Außenwall und dem kleineren Stadtgraben. Die Mauer war mit vielen rechteckigen Weichhäusern besetzt. Das Klostertor im Norden war durch eine Bastei geschützt. Nach dem 30-jährigen Krieg hatte die Mauer nur noch als Zollgrenze Bedeutung; so waren Wälle und Gräben im Süden nach 1726 zur Anlage der Neustadt und am Berliner Platz für einen Viehmarkt eingeebnet worden. Der Münzturm im Nordosten, im unteren Teil mit dunkler Rautenmusterung, ist weitgehend original erhalten. 1937 sind Abschnitte der Mauer im westlichen Teil der Münzstraße und in der Mauerstraße neu aufgeführt worden. Der Turm (Bild) an der Marktstraße erhielt erst 1879 einen Durchgang. Auch der Turm mit dem steilen Spitzhelm, wie ebenfalls die in der Nähe beider Türme gelegenen Weich- und Mauerhäuser sind 1937 neu aufgebaut worden.

In 1429 the town had withstood the onslaught of the Hussites, but the five to six metre high brick wall, still preserved in parts, was probably built some time later. Even in the eighteenth century the fortifications of the town consisted of wall, inner ramparts, a wide town-moat, outer ramparts, and a second, smaller town-moat. The wall was occupied with numerous rectangular wall houses. The Klostertor to the north was protected by a bastion. After the Thirty Years' War the importance of the wall was reduced to a customs line; subsequently, ramparts and moats to the south were razed after 1726 to make way for the new town and, at the Berliner Platz, for a cattle market. The Münzturm to the northeast with its dark lozenge pattern in the lower section has been largely preserved intact. In 1937 some sections of the wall in the western part of Münzstrasse and in Mauerstrasse were reconstructed. Not until 1879 was a gateway constructed in the tower in Marktstrasse (picture). The tower with the steep pointed cupola as well as the wall houses located near the two towers were also reconstructed in 1937.

in der Nähe/nearby:
Schloßkirche; Schloßkirchplatz
1707-14 u. 1870 (Turm)
Herrschaftliches Wohnhaus; Schloßkirchplatz 1
Um 1895
Wohn- und Geschäftshaus; Schloßkirchplatz 3
1909
Wohn- und Geschäftshaus; Schloßkirchplatz 4-5
Um 1928

Y 8 Stadtzentrum »Stadtpromenade«
Cottbus; Stadtpromenade
1964-69 • Gerhard Guder, Martin Röser uam.

Cottbus hatte 1943 lediglich 55 000 Einwohner und war im Zweiten Weltkrieg nur zu etwa zwanzig Prozent zerstört worden. Bis zum 800-jährigen Stadtjubiläum 1956 sollte Cottbus in seiner historischen Gestalt wiederaufgebaut sein. Der Aufstieg zur Hauptstadt des 1952 gebildeten Bezirkes Cottbus und seine Bestimmung zum Ansiedlungsschwerpunkt für das Kraftwerk Jänschwalde und den Braunkohlentagebau der näheren Umgebung lösten zwar die sprunghafte Entwicklung zur Großstadt aus, doch der Aufbau mußte noch warten. Erst 1964 ergab sich die konzeptionelle Planung zur Umgestaltung des Stadtzentrums. Als »Stadtpromenade« ist dieses neue Zentrum im westlichen Grüngürtel, unmittelbar an der Stadtmauer dem denkmalgeschützten Altstadtkern vorgelagert und durch räumlich-funktionelle Querachsen mit ihm verbunden. Heute am Berliner Platz von der Stadthalle und an der Karl-Liebknecht-Straße vom Kaufhaus begrenzt, auf ganzer Länge von der Straßenbahn durchfahren, konnte das Zentrum 1969 in seinen Grundzügen – ohne Planänderungen – mit einer dominierenden 166 Meter langen zehngeschossigen Wohnzeile fertiggestellt werden.

In 1943 Cottbus had a population of no more than 55,000 although only twenty per cent of the town had been destroyed in the war. Plans were made to rebuild the town to its historic shape in time for the 800th anniversary in 1956. In 1952 the town was made capital of the newly created district of Cottbus and became the centre of development for the Jänschwalde power plant and the open-pit lignite mining industry in the area, resulting in the sudden growth of a new large city, but reconstruction still had to wait. A planning concept for redesigning the city centre was only drawn up in 1964. Called «Stadtpromenade», this new centre is located in the western greenbelt, immediately along the town wall, outside the historical old town with which it is linked by a number of functional and spatial transverse axes. Extending today to the Stadthalle at Berliner Platz and the department store at Karl-Liebknecht-Strasse and served by trams along its entire length, the new centre with its 166 metre row of ten-storey apartment buildings was essentially completed in 1969 without plans having been changed.

in der Nähe/nearby:
Galerie »Carl Blechen«; Stadtpromenade
1977-78 • Werner Fichte, Ewald Jantke
Milch-Eis-Mokka-Bar; Stadtpromenade
1968 • Jörg Streitparth, Gerd Wessel
Postamt; Berliner Straße 6
1951 • M. Bergmann
Wohnhaus; Wernerstraße 9
Um 1905

Y 9 Neues Rathaus
Cottbus; Neumarkt 5
1934-36

Außerhalb der mittelalterlichen Stadt lagen im Süden das Dorf Ostrow, im Westen Brunschwig und im Osten Sandow. 1563 kam zu den alten Kämmereidörfern Kolkwitz, Ströbitz und Madlow das Dorf Dissenchen hinzu, Orte, die später eingemeindet wurden. Seit den Befreiungskriegen und mit dem Bau der Berlin-Görlitzer Eisenbahn 1866, nahm die Stadt einen bedeutenden Aufschwung. Von 1818 bis1919 hatte sich die Einwohnerzahl nahezu verzehnfacht, die Bebauung hatte sich über die Bahnhofstraße auf die genannten Vororte ausgedehnt. Schlachthof, Wasserwerk, Kanalisation und Elektrizitätswerk sowie Krankenhaus und Straßenbahn wurden kommunal betrieben. Das alte Rathaus von 1611 reichte zwar für die Zusammenkünfte der Bürgerschaft und der Innungen aus, für die Bewältigung der neuen Verwaltungsaufgaben war es aber zu klein. Ein Neubau mußte her. Er folgte wie auch andere Rathäuser dieser Zeit dem Formenkanon der Sachlichkeit, bediente sich der bewährten Klinkerfassade und schmückte sich dezent mit Bauplastik von P. Horn und Richard Kuöhl.

The medieval town was surrounded by the villages of Ostrow to the south, Brunschwig to the west, and Sandow to the east. In addition to the old wool-combers' villages of Kolkwitz, Ströblitz and Madlow, the village of Dissenchen was also included in 1563. All these villages were later incorporated into the town. After the wars of liberation and the construction of the Berlin-Görlitz railway in 1866 the town enjoyed a rapid economic development. From 1818 to 1919 the population had almost doubled, and the built-up area had expanded beyond the Bahnhofstrasse to the suburbs mentioned above. Water-works, sewage system, power-station, tram system and hospital as well as the slaughter-house were run by the community. Soon the old town-hall of 1611 turned out to be sufficient for the meetings of the townspeople and the guilds but not for taking care of the new administrative needs. A new building was required. Like other town-halls of the time, its architecture adapted the canon of expression of functionalism, making use of the familiar clinker façade and unassuming decoration with building sculpture by P. Horn and Richard Kuöhl.

in der Nähe/nearby:
Stadthalle; Berliner Platz
1975 • Eberhard Kühn
Hotel Lausitzer Hof; Berliner Platz
1992-95 • Wojtek Grabianowski
Wohnhaus; Marktstraße 7
1790
Wohn- und Geschäftshaus; Mühlenstraße 12
A. 19. Jh.
Geschäftshäuser; Spremberger Straße 41-42 u. 43-44
Um 1910

Y 10 Stadttheater
Cottbus; Karl-Liebknecht-Straße 118-121
1907-08 • Bernhard Sehring

Um die Jahrhundertwende erfuhr der Theaterbau einen deutlichen Wandel. Einerseits setzte sich nun endlich der Gedanke des Reformtheaters durch, der seine Wurzeln im Frankreich des 18. Jahrhunderts hatte, bei Gilly, Schinkel und Semper nur als Idee auftauchte und dann bei Wagner in Bayreuth anklang. Andererseits kam es zum Bruch mit der historisierenden Gestaltung falsch verstandener Festlichkeit, mit der auch das konservative Verständnis von der Guckkastenbühne einherging. Der Jugendstil hatte dabei erheblichen Einfluß, wenn ihm auch die Kraft fehlte, die Architektur wie den Theaterbau grundlegend zu reformieren. Sehrings Cottbuser Theater ist ein solches Beispiel. Ihm ist die Befreiung von alten Zwängen anzusehen. Der Umgang mit Baukörper und Detail erfolgt spielerisch-heiter, an die Stelle von ernster Steifheit tritt die übermütige theatralische Geste. Doch was das Äußere mit seinen vielen Überraschungen verspricht, kann das Innere nicht halten: Das Rangtheater der barocken Tradition ist weit vom Reformtheater entfernt. Nur die Tatsache, daß eine selbstbewußte Stadt ihren Bürgern ein Theater von so stattlichem Zuschnitt beschert, ist zeitgemäß und rechnet zum Begriff »Reform«.

Around the turn of the century theatre building saw a marked change. On the one hand, the concept of the reform theatre finally prevailed; it had its roots in eighteenth century France and was first visualized by Gilly, Schinkel and Semper before finding its first expression in Wagner's Bayreuth. On the other hand, there was radical turning away from the historicizing staging of a misinterpreted festiveness associated with the conservative concept of the proscenium stage. The «Jugendstil» proved quite instrumental in all this, although it lacked the power to effect a fundamental revision of theatre building and architecture. An example of this is Sehring's Cottbus Theatre which clearly shows a liberation from old constraints. The treatment of volume and detailing is playful and serene, the former stiff solemnity being replaced with wanton dramatic gestures. Yet the surprises promised by the exterior are not delivered in the interior: The galleried theatre of baroque tradition is far removed from the true reform theatre. Only the fact that a proud and self-assertive town presents its citizens with a stately theatre of this type can be regarded as contemporary and associated with the idea of «reform».

in der Nähe/nearby:
Katholische Kirche St. Maria Friedenskönigin;
Wilhelm-Külz-Straße 60
1932-34; 1976-82 (Innen) • W. Starke, Friedrich Press
Tuchfabrik; Ostrower Straße 15
Um 1860; 1868 • A. Westerkamp; Ch. Hasselbach
Villa; Ostrower Straße 15
1870 • A. Westerkamp, Ch. Hasselbach

Y 11 Schloß Branitz
Cottbus-Branitz
1772; 1846-52 (Innenausbau) • Gottfried Semper

Zwischen Barock und Klassizismus steht dieser bescheidene Schloßbau, den Graf August Heinrich v. Pückler 1772 errichten ließ. Im 19. Jahrhundert verwahrloste der Besitz, bis ihn der Enkel Hermann v. Pückler-Muskau als seine Wohnstätte erkor und Semper ihn von 1846 an um- und ausbaute. Pückler – Lebenskünstler und Genie – hatte ein Jahr zuvor seinen Stammsitz Muskau verkaufen müssen, nachdem ihn dort sein ehrgeiziges Parkprojekt in finanzielle Bedrängnis gebracht hatte. Branitz wurde für den damals sechzigjährigen Fürsten, dessen Schönheitssinn mit Rastlosigkeit gepaart war, zu einem schöpferischen Neubeginn. Vom Schlosse aus leitete er die gewaltigen Arbeiten an seinem zweiten großen Park, was ihn bis zu seinem Tode 1871 ausfüllte. Seine Neigung zum Orientalischen spiegeln die Tapetenzimmer wieder. Heute beherbergt das Schloß ein Museum, das dem bewegten Leben und Werk des ungewöhnlichen Fürsten gewidmet ist. Eine weitere ständige Ausstellung befaßt sich mit dem gleichfalls berühmten Sohn der Stadt Cottbus, mit Carl Blechen, dem Vater der märkischen Landschaftsmalerei.

With an architecture somewhere between Baroque and Classicism, this unassuming castle was built by Graf August Heinrich von Pückler in 1772. In the nineteenth century the estate was largely necglected until Hermann von Pückler-Muskau, a grandson of the builder, took residence here and had the castle remodeled and extended by Semper in 1846. A genius and bon vivant, Pückler had been forced to sell his own ancestral seat of Muskau when his ambitious park project there had led him into financial straits. Branitz marked a kind of creative new beginning for the then sixty-year-old prince whose sense of beauty was accompanied by a continuing restlessness. From the new castle he directed the work on his second great park which occupied him until his death in 1871. His predilection for the oriental is reflected in the tapestry rooms. Today the castle houses a museum dedicated to the eventful life of this unusual personage. A second continuous exhibition is dedicated to another famous Cottbus citizen, Carl Blechen, the father of landscape painting in the Mark.

Y 12 Park Branitz
Cottbus-Branitz
1846-71 • Hermann v. Pückler-Muskau

Sich dem Schönen zuzuwenden, forderte Hermann Fürst v. Pückler-Muskau. Und in seinem Buch über Gartengestaltung beklagte er, daß die ostelbischen Herrensitze nicht den Park, sondern den Dunghaufen kultivieren. Tragisch, aber auch bezeichnend ist der Umstand, daß Pückler an seinem großen Parkprojekt in Muskau finanziell scheiterte. Er ließ sich jedoch nicht davon abbringen, in Branitz wiederum aus einer Sandwüste eine Ideallandschaft zu zaubern. Wasserläufe und Seen wurden angelegt, Täler gegraben und Hügel aufgeschüttet, Gartenarchitektur eingestreut, und es war eine Leidenschaft des Fürsten, in ausgewählten Kostümen durch seine komponierte Welt zu schreiten. Vorbild war der englische Landschaftspark, die Grundidee ein Naturgemälde als Gesamtkunstwerk. Nach Pückler sollte der Park nur den Charakter der freien Natur und Landschaft tragen, die Hand des Menschen durfte sichtbar sein. Sein Plan war aber von romantischen Empfindungen ebenso geprägt wie von einer fast wissenschaftlich herleitbaren Ästhetik des beginnenden Realismus. Die Pyramideninsel und die Landpyramide sind ureigene Bestandteile des Parks; in der einen ist das Herz des Fürsten bestattet, in der zweiten angeblich die Dienerin Machbuba, die Pückler als das »braune geniale Naturkind« auf dem Sklavenmarkt in Khartum erworben hatte.

Hermann Fürst von Pückler-Muskau always demanded that one should turn to beauty, and in his book on garden design he complained that the East-Elbian manorial estates cultivated not their parks but their dung heaps. It is tragic as well as indicative of the situation that Pückler's great park project in Muskau failed due to financial difficulties. That did not prevent him, however, from once again turning a sandy desert into an ideal landscape in Branitz. Waterways and lakes were created, valleys were dug and hills piled up, interspersed with garden architecture, and it became the prince's passion to don fabulous costumes and stroll through this world of his own making. His model was the English landscape park, based on the idea of creating a «Gesamtkunstwerk» resembling a painting after nature. According to Pückler, the character of the park was to resemble that of nature and countryside, although the hand of man was allowed to be visible. Yet his plan was equally influenced both by romantic sentiments as well as an almost scientifically derived aesthetics of an emerging realism. The pyramid island and the land pyramid are essential elements of the park – on the former, the prince's heart lies buried, in the latter rests – supposedly – his maid servant Machbuba whom Pückler once bought on the slave market of Khartoum as a «brown, genial child of nature».

in der Nähe/nearby:
Schmiede; östlicher Parkeingang
1846-50 • Friedrich August Stüler und Ludwig Persius

Z
Spreewald und Niederlausitz

Niederlausitz und Spreewald vermitteln landschaftlich eine Mischung ganz gegensätzlicher Reize, denn fast die halbe Fläche dieser Region ist bewaldet und wechselt mit ausgedehnten Teichlandschaften ab – sechzig Flächenprozent aller Teiche in den neuen Bundesländern befinden sich hier. So unterschiedlich sich die drei Erholungslandschaften des Ober- und des Unterspreewaldes und der Niederlausitz auch heute darstellen lassen, sie haben als Teile des nordeuropäischen Tieflandes einen gemeinsamen Ursprung in der eiszeitlichen Überformung vor etwa 10 000 Jahren. Die weiten west-östlichen Talungen, wie die des südlichen Spreewaldes im Zuge des ehemaligen Glogau-Baruther Urstromtales oder die Grundmoränenflächen, wie der Rücken des Lausitzer Höhenzuges, wechseln mit ebenen Sanderflächen, die beim Abschmelzen der hundert Meter dicken Eismassen angeschwemmt wurden und einfach liegengeblieben sind. Hierin eingestreut fand man aus vulkanischer Tätigkeit früherer Erdzeitalter durch Verwitterung entstandene wertvolle mineralische Vorkommen. Kaolin- und reine Quarzlagerstätten boten Rohstoffe für die vielbegehrten Glas- und Keramikwaren aus der Lausitz; und die weitläufigen Braunkohlenfelder, zunehmend abgebaut während der industriellen Entwicklung der letzten hundert Jahre, erinnern an ausgedehnte wuchskräftige Sumpfwälder voreiszeitlicher Wachstumsprozesse. Die Niederlausitz zwischen Berlin und Dresden, östlich der Elbe gelegen und bis zur Oder reichend, war im Mittelalter umkämpftes Grenzland zwischen slawischen Herzögen und deutschen Markgrafen und wurde im 17. und 18. Jahrhundert ein Streitobjekt zwischen dem erstarkenden Preußenstaat und dem Königreich Sachsen. So blickt dieses Land auf eine wechselvolle und mehr als tausendjährige Geschichte zurück, die bis in die Gegenwart zudem noch durch die kulturelle Eigenständigkeit der hier ansässigen Sorben geprägt ist. In vielen kleineren Orten widerspiegelt sich diese bewegte Entwicklung in bedeutenden Bauten märkischer Backsteinarchitektur, in einfachen, aber sehr alten Dorfkirchen und auch in Hausfassaden des sächsischen Barock oder des reizvollen preußischen Klassizismus.

The landscapes of the Niederlausitz and the Spreewald offer a highly attractive contrast as almost half of this region is covered with woods alternating with extensive areas with ponds – in terms of surface area, almost sixty per cent of all ponds in the new Länder are found here. As different as the three recreational areas of upper and lower Spreewald and Niederlausitz may appear today, they are part of the North European Lowlands that were shaped by the ice age about 10,000 years ago. Wide valleys running from west to east, such as the southern Spreewald, part of the former Glogau-Baruth glacial valley, or the base moraine areas, such as the ridge of the Lausitz hills, alternate with flat outwash areas left behind when the hundred metre high sheet of ice melted. Numerous deposits of valuable mineral resources were found here, brought to the surface by volcanic activity in earlier geological periods and later subject to erosion. Deposits of porcelain clay and pure quartz provided the materials for the highly demanded glass and ceramic products of the Lausitz; and the vast fields of lignite, increasingly mined in the course of the industrial development of the last hundred years, reveal the existence of huge swampy forests and other vegetation before the ice age. In the Middle Ages the Niederlausitz between Berlin and Dresden, east of the Elbe and extending to the Oder, marked a border area contested by Slavic dukes and German margraves; in the seventeenth and eighteenth centuries it became the object of a dispute between the increasingly stronger Prussian state and the kingdom of Saxony. Thus this land looks back on more than a thousand years of an eventful history, which in addition has always been influenced by the cultural autonomy of the Sorb population. In many smaller towns this eventful history is reflected in the characteristic brick architecture of the Mark, from simple but very old village churches to building façades dating from the Saxonian Baroque or the charming classicism of Prussia.

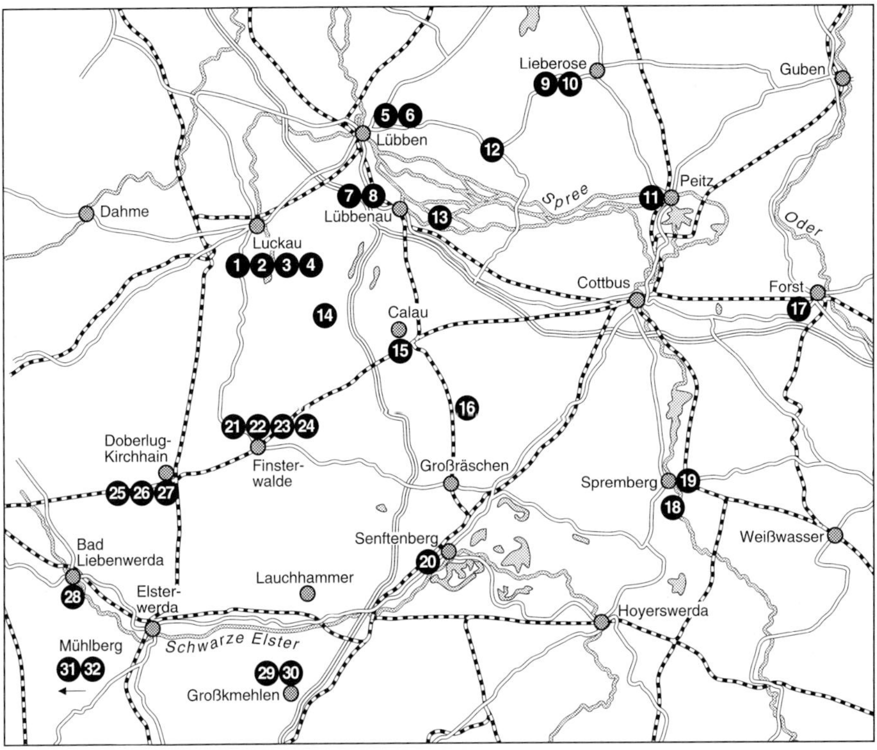

Z 1 Stadtkern Luckau
Z 2 Georgenkapelle mit Hausmannsturm
Z 3 Stadtkirche St. Marien und St. Nicolai
Z 4 Bürgerhaus am Markt
Z 5 Stadtkern Lübben
Z 6 Schloß
Z 7 Schloß Lübbenau
Z 8 Kanzlei
Z 9 Stadtkern Lieberose
Z 10 Schloß
Z 11 Eisenhütte Peitz
Z 12 Kirche Straupitz
Z 13 Museumsdorf Lehde
Z 14 Schloß Drehna
Z 15 Kirche Calau
Z 16 Schloß Alt Döbern
Z 17 Ortskrankenkasse Forst
Z 18 Kraftwerk Trattendorf
Z 19 Rathaus Spremberg
Z 20 Gymnasium Senftenberg
Z 21 Pfarrkirche Finsterwalde
Z 22 Schloß
Z 23 Rathaus
Z 24 Curdsburg
Z 25 Zisterzienserkirche Doberlug
Z 26 Schloß
Z 27 Weißgerbermuseum
Z 28 Kirche Liebenwerda
Z 29 Schloß Großkmehlen
Z 30 Dorfkirche Großkmehlen
Z 31 Kloster Mühlberg
Z 32 Probstei Mühlberg

Z 1 Stadtkern Luckau
12. Jahrhundert

Die heutige Kreisstadt mit etwa 6600 Einwohnern an der Berste im Luckau-Calauer Becken wird hauptsächlich durch landwirtschaftlich orientierte Betriebe geprägt. Um 1000 wurde Luckau mehrfach als Stammeszentrum der slawischen Lusici genannt. Die planmäßige Anlage der Stadt über unregelmäßigem ovalem Grundriß mit dem Straßennetz in Gitterform, rechteckigem Markt, Rathaus und Georgenkapelle in der Mitte mag aus der zweiten Phase der deutschen Ostexpansion stammen. Im späten 12. Jahrhundert hatten wohl die Wettiner an einem Kreuz wichtiger Handelsstraßen die Burg Luckau gegründet, die um 1301 Verwaltungsmittelpunkt der Niederlausitz war. Die Kaufmannssiedlung des 12. Jahrhunderts war 1297 Civitas, hatte eine Kirche, seit 1291 ein Dominikanerkloster und war ummauert. Die Funktion als Hauptstadt des Markgraftums Niederlausitz mußte Luckau im 16. Jahrhundert an Lübben abgeben. Durch Zerstörungen im Dreißigjährigen Krieg und häufige Stadtbrände erfolgte ein starker Niedergang der Stadt, der sich nach 1815, mit Übernahme durch Preußen, fortsetzte. Der späte Bau der Bahnverbindung brachte nur eine bescheidene Industrieentwicklung.

The present district centre with about 6,600 inhabitants on the Berste in the Luckau-Calau basin is largely an agricultural centre. Luckau was often mentioned as a tribal centre for the Slavic Lusici c. 1000. The planned town on an irregular oval ground plan with street grid, rectangular market place, town hall and Georgenkapelle in the middle may date from the second phase of German expansion to the east. In the late twelfth century the castle of Luckau was probably founded by the Wettins at a point where important trade routes met, and c. 1301 it was the administrative centre of Niederlausitz. The twelfth century trade centre was a civitas in 1297, had a church, a Dominican monastery from 1291, and was walled. Luckau had to abandon its function as capital of the margravate of Niederlausitz to Lübben in the sixteenth century. Damage in the Thirty Years' War and frequent town fires led to severe decline, and this continued after 1815, when the town was taken over by Prussia. Connection to the railway came late, and only brought modest industrial development.

in der Nähe/nearby:
Dorfkirche; Görlsdorf-Frankendorf
14. Jh.
Stadtkirche; Golssen
Vor 1820 • Colberg
Schloß und Landschaftspark; Golssen
Um 1720 (Erweiterung nach 1788)

Z 2 Georgenkapelle mit Hausmannsturm
Luckau; Markt
1. Viertel 13. Jahrhundert, 15. und 17. Jahrhundert

Die Stern- und Netzgewölbe der einschiffigen Kapelle stammen aus dem 17. Jahrhundert, der Hausmannsturm aus dem 15. und 17. Jahrhundert. Bereits gegen 1800 wurde der Hausmannsturm als Warte, die Kapelle als städtische Wache genutzt. Nach den Rekonstruktionen 1955 und 1965-67 ist das Kirchlein nun ein Festraum. Auf dem Marktplatz, in der Nähe der Kapelle, erinnert ein ungewöhnliches Denkmal an den Reichstagsabgeordneten Karl Liebknecht, der wegen Teilnahme an einer Antikriegskundgebung am 1. Mai 1916 auf dem Potsdamer Platz in Berlin bis 1918 im Zuchthaus Luckau einsaß. Am 23. Oktober entlassen, proklamierte er am 9. November vom Balkon des Berliner Schlosses die Republik, am 15. Januar 1919 wurde er ermordet.

The stellar and net vaulting of the single-aisled chapel date from the seventeenth century, and the janitor's tower from the fifteenth and seventeenth centuries. From as early as the end of the seventeenth century the janitor's tower was used as a watchtower, and the chapel as town guard-house. After rebuilding in 1955 and 1965-7 the chapel became a festival hall. In the market place, near the chapel, there is an unusual monument to Reichstag deputy Karl Liebknecht, who was imprisoned in Luckau until 1918 for taking part in an anti-war demonstration on 1 May 1916 in Potsdamer Platz in Berlin. He was released on 23 October, and proclaimed the republic from the balcony of the Berliner Schloss on 9 November. He was murdered on 15 January 1919.

in der Nähe/nearby:
Rathaus; Markt
1851-52
Karl-Liebknecht-Denkmal; Markt
1969 • Theo Balden

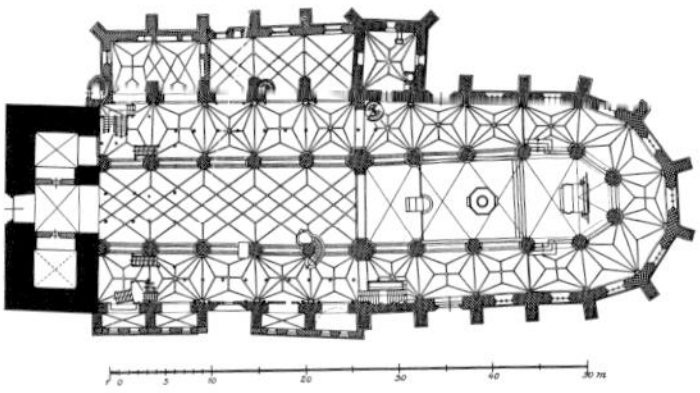

Z 3 Stadtkirche St. Marien und St. Nicolai
Luckau; Kirchplatz
2. Viertel 13. Jahrhundert

Die Hallenkirche aus Backstein ist möglicher Nachfolgebau einer Burgkirche St. Johannes, der nach Vergrößerung der städtischen Gemeinde im zweiten Viertel des 13. Jahrhunderts zur Pfarrkirche mit neuem Doppelpatrozinium erhoben wurde. Der Erstbau war wohl – ähnlich St. Nicolai in Berlin – eine Feldstein-Basilika. Während des Umbaus, der 1375 begann, stiftete Kaiser Karl IV. eine kostbare Reliquie, das Haupt des heiligen Paulinus. Seitdem ist die Kirche Wallfahrtskirche. Der Luckauer Hallenumgangschor des späten 14. Jahrhunderts ist eine der bedeutendsten Architekturschöpfungen der Lausitz und wurde vielleicht von Vorbildern des Hans v. Burghausen in Landshut beeinflußt. Vergleichbar mit dem Prager Dom ist das Langhaus-Mittelschiff mit Parallelrippen-Netzgewölben ausgestattet.

This brick hall church is a possible successor to a castle church of St. Johannes, raised to the status of parish church with two patron saints in the second quarter of the thirteenth century, after the community had grown in size. The first building was probably, like St. Nicolai in Berlin, a rubble-stone basilica. During rebuilding, which started in 1375, Emperor Charles IV donated a precious relic, the head of St. Paul. The church has been a pilgrimage church since then. The Luckau hall ambulatory choir dates from the late fourteenth century and is one of the most important architectural creations in the Lausitz. It may have been influenced by earlier work by Hans von Burghausen in Landshut. The nave has parallel-rib and net vaulting comparable with Prague cathedral.

in der Nähe/nearby:
»Alte Schule«; Kirchplatz
Um 1540
Bürgerhaus; Kirchplatz 6
1832
Heilig-Geist-Hospital; Lindenstraße 22
1727
Dominikaner-Kloster (Zuchthaus); Nähe Markt
1291
Stadtbefestigung
Ab 1290

Z 4 Bürgerhaus
Luckau; Markt 13
Um 1700

Die Zerstörungen von 1644 und die Stadtbrände von 1652 und 1671 hinterließen in der Stadt nur noch einige Reste mittelalterlicher Bausubstanz. Das heutige Stadtbild wird vielfach geprägt von den meist zweigeschossigen Putzbauten aus der 2. Hälfte des 17. Jahrhunderts und vom Anfang des 18. Jahrhunderts. Die geschwungenen Giebel sind auch für Cottbus und andere Städte der Lausitz kennzeichnend. Besonders reizvoll ist die Umbauung des Marktes mit drei prägnanten Beispielen barocker Fassadengestaltung um 1700: die Wohnhäuser Markt 13, Markt 30 und Markt 32. An der Ausformung der flächenfüllenden vegetabilen Ornamentik waren italienische Stukkateure beteiligt.

Damage in 1644 and the fires of 1652 and 1671 left little of the medieval building stock in the town. The present townscape consists largely of rendered buildings, mostly with two storeys, dating from the late seventeenth and early eighteenth centuries. The curved gables are also characteristic of Cottbus and other towns in the Lausitz. A particularly charming feature is the rebuilt market place with striking examples of baroque façace design c. 1700: the houses at Markt 13, Markt 30 and Markt 32. Italian stucco artists were involved in forming the vegetable ornamentation that covers some of the surface of the buildings.

in der Nähe/nearby:
Bürgerhäuser; Markt 6, 16, 29
2. H. 17. Jh.
Bürgerhäuser; Markt 22, 26, 31
18. Jh.
Bürgerhaus; Hauptstraße 16
2. H. 17. Jh.
Bürgerhäuser; Hauptstraße 3a, 52
18. Jh.

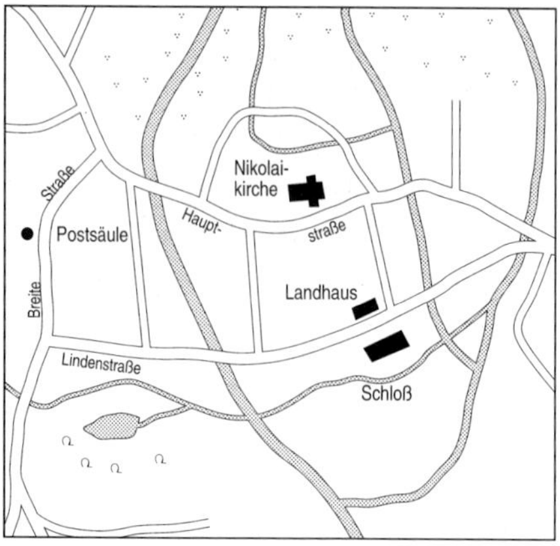

Z 5 Stadtkern Lübben
12. Jahrhundert

Im Verlauf der Straße Leipzig–Frankfurt (Oder) war bereits seit dem 12. Jahrhundert am Südrand einer Spreeinsel eine deutsche Burg vorhanden. Auf dieser Insel entwickelte sich der Ort später als planmäßig angelegte Ackerbürgerstadt mit rechteckigem Grundriß und rippenförmigem Straßennetz. Seit dem 15. Jahrhundert war Lübben Sitz der Landvögte für die Niederlausitz sowie später Hauptstadt des Markgrafentums Niederlausitz und fiel nach dem Wiener Kongreß an Preußen. Im Zweiten Weltkrieg wurde der Ort weitgehend zerstört, was das Gefüge der Altstadt fast unkenntlich machte. Zusammen mit Lübbenau ist Lübben von Bedeutung für die Erschließung des Spreewaldes, der heute noch Siedlungsgebiet der einzigen slawischen Minderheit in Deutschland ist, der Sorben. Trotz der Berichte des Berliner Professors Johann Bernoulli und des märkischen Schriftstellers Theodor Fontane wurde der Spreewald erst ab 1882 touristisch erschlossen, als der Lübbenauer Lehrer und Chronist Paul Fahlisch »Gesellschaftsfahrten« ins Leben rief.

There was a German castle as early as the twelfth century on the road from Leipzig to Frankfurt an der Oder on the southern extremity of an island in the Spree. Lübben later developed on this island as a planned smallholders' town with rectangular ground plan and ribbed street network. From the fifteenth century it was the seat of the Niederlausitz landvogts and later capital of the margravate of Niederlausitz, then fell to Prussia after the Congress of Vienna. It was largely destroyed in the Second World War, which left the structure of the old town almost unrecognizable. With Lübbenau, Lübben played an important role in opening up the Spreewald, today still the home of the only Slavic minority in Germany, the Sorbs. Despite the writings of Berlin professor Johann Bernoulli and Mark writer Theodor Fontane, the Spreewald was not penetrated by tourists until 1882, when the Lübbenau teacher and chronicler Paul Fahlisch started to organize «conducted tours».

in der Nähe/nearby:
Dorf-Kirche; Duben
E. 17. Jh.
Dorf-Kirche; Hohenbrück-Neu Schadow
1856 • Schinkel-Nachfolge
Dorf-Kirche; Schlepzig
1782
Stadtbefestigung mit Weichhaus und Eckturm; Lübben
Um 1480

Z 6 Schloß
Lübben; Heinrich-Heine-Straße
1679-82

Wohl von der Wasserburg um 1368 oder ihrem Vorgänger ist ein mächtiger dreigeschossiger Wohn- und Wehrturm mit 2,5 m dicken Mauern erhalten. In dem großen, zwei Geschosse einnehmenden Wappensaal huldigten einst die Stände der Niederlausitz ihren Herrschern. Die Landstände wurden vom Landvogt einberufen und hatten Aufgabe und Recht, über die politische Sicherheit des Landes zu wachen und landesherrliche Steuerforderungen zu bewilligen. Durch den Bau des Land- oder Ständehauses 1717-22, der Dreiflügelanlage nördlich vom Schloß, wurde der Wappensaal funktionslos. Das eigentliche Schloß ist das dreigeschossige Oberamtshaus, 1679-82 in den Formen der Spätrenaissance erbaut. Hier wohnten und wirkten Burggrafen und Landvögte, später war es auch Sitz der Oberamtsregierung der Niederlausitz.

A massive three-storey keep with walls 2.5 metres thick has survived, probably part of a moated castle dating from c. 1368 or its predecessor. In its emblazoned hall, two storeys high, the Estates of Niederlausitz used to pay homage to their rulers. The rural Estates were summoned by the landvogt and had the duty and the right to watch over the political security of the land and to approve the rulers' tax demands. The hall lost its function when the Land or Estates House was built in 1717-22, a three-winged complex north of the castle. The actual castle is the three-storey Oberamtshaus, built 1679-82 to a late Renaissance design. Here burgraves and landvogts lived and worked, and it was later also the seat of the Niederlausitz government.

in der Nähe/nearby:
Postmeilensäule; am Westabschnitt der Ringmauer
1735
Landhaus oder Ständehaus; Lohmühlengasse 12
1717-22
Hauptsparkasse; Lohmühlengasse
1914-20 • Adolf Zeller
Kreisgericht; Gerichtsstraße 2-3
1930
Pfarrkirche St. Nikolaus (Paul-Gerhardt-Kirche)
Um 1300 (Langhaus 15. Jh.)
Geschäftshaus; Markt
1992 • Ewald Jantke
Wohnhaus; Platz der Märzgefallenen
1929
Goethe-Schule; Berliner Chaussee 2
1913-14 • A. Kippenberg u. F. Beyer
Trüschelkolonie; Frankfurter Straße 2-3 u. 6-15
1920
Wasserturm; Hauptfriedhof
1914 • Wachsning

Z 7 Schloß
Lübbenau; Spreestraße
1817-20 • Karl Benjamin Siegel

Die Ursprünge Lübbenaus reichen bis 1301 zurück, damals gab es eine Burg der Eilenburger, das »castrum lubbenowe«. Es folgten die Geschlechter Köckritz, Kalkreuth und Polenz, bis 1503 die von der Schulenburg den Besitz erwarben, 1621 abgelöst von der Witwe Johann Kasimirs zu Lynar, Sohn des Festungsbaumeisters Rochus Guerrini Graf zu Lynar, der unter anderem die Spandauer Zitadelle ausgebaut hatte. Die zu Lynar waren bis 1945 Standesherren der Niederlausitz und hatten in den Ständeversammlungen des Markgrafentums Sitz und Stimme. Aus der Wasserburg entstand um 1600 ein Renaissance-Schloß, das wiederum wurde 1817-20 klassizistisch überformt. Die beiden neoromanischen Türme am Verbindungsflügel fügte 1839 Homann unter Beteiligung Schinkels hinzu. Der letzte Schloßherr, Wilhelm Friedrich zu Lynar, wurde wegen Beteiligung am Hitler-Attentat vom 20. Juli 1944 in Plötzensee hingerichtet. 1918 wurde das Schloß Museum, 1945 Krankenhaus. 1966 drohte schon der Abriß, doch wurde es zunächst noch für Schulungen genutzt, bis sich 1989 darin ein Hotel etablierte.

The origins of Lübbenau go back to 1301 and the «castrum lubbenowe», a castle belonging to the Eilenburg family. The latter was followed by the Köckritz, Kalkreuth and Polenz families, until the Schulenburgs purchased the domain in 1503. In 1621 they were succeeded by the widow of Johann Kasimir zu Lynar, a son of military architect Rochus Guerrini Graf zu Lynar who had worked on the Spandau Citadel among others. Until 1945 the Lynar family ruled the Niederlausitz and had seat and vote in the assembly of the margravate. About 1600 the moated castle was converted to a Renaissance castle which in turn was rebuilt in classicist style in 1817-20. The two neo-Romanesque towers at the connecting wing were added by Homann, Schinkel participating, in 1839. The last lord of the castle, Graf Wilhelm Friedrich zu Lynar, was executed at Plötzensee on 20 July 1944 for taking part in the attempted assassination of Hitler. The castle was turned into a museum in 1918 and used as hospital in 1945. Threatened with demolition in 1966, it was saved and used for schooling before a hotel was established here in 1989.

in der Nähe/nearby:
Stadtkirche St. Nicolai; Ehm-Welk-Straße
1738-41 • vermutlich Gottfried Findeisen
Kursächsische Postmeilensäule; nw. der Kirche
1740
Rathaus; Ehm-Welk-Straße 15
Um 1840
Wohnhaus; Ehm-Welk-Straße 17
2. H. 18. Jh.
Kreisgericht; Topfmarkt
1850

Z 8 Kanzlei
Lübbenau; Spreestraße (Schloßbezirk)
1745-48

Zu den ältesten Gebäuden im Schloßpark zählen das sogenannte Efeuhaus, ehemals Remise und Marstall, sowie die einstige Kanzlei, architektonisch wohl auch eines der schönsten Gebäude. Bis in die erste Hälfte des 19. Jahrhunderts wurden hier im Auftrage des Standesherren Gerichtsverhandlungen geführt. Zu jener Zeit gehörten den Grafen zu Lynar die Stadt Lübbenau, 30 Dörfer und 13 000 ha Land mit rund 10 000 Untertanen. Nach Aufhebung der grundherrlichen Gerichtsbarkeit beherbergte das Gebäude die gräfliche Bibliothek, seit 1950 das Spreewaldmuseum; ausgestellt sind die Sammlungsbestände des 1899 in Lübbenau gegründeten Heimatmuseums sowie Kunstbesitz und Sammlungen derer zu Lynar, soweit die Gegenstände 1944 den Brand im Schloßmuseum überstanden haben. Als sehr engagierter Museumsleiter wirkte hier noch bis zu seinem Tode Mitte der fünfziger Jahre Wilhelm Graf zu Lynar, der Schwager des letzten Standesherren. Seit 1956 gehört zum Spreewaldmuseum auch das ehemalige Orangeriegebäude, in dem alljährlich insbesondere in der Sommersaison Kunstausstellungen stattfinden.

Among the oldest buildings in the Schloßpark are the so-called Ivy House, a former stables and coach-house, and the former chancery, probably one of the most beautiful buildings. Until well into the nineteenth century legal proceedings were held here by order of the mediatized princes. At that time the counts of Lynar owned the town of Lübbenau, 30 villages and 13,000 hectares of land with c. 10,000 subjects. After landlordly jurisdiction was abolished, the building housed the count's library. Since 1950 it serves as Spreewald museum, exhibiting the collection of the Lübbenau Heimatmuseum, founded in 1899, as well as the works of art and collection of the Lynar family to the extent that it survived the castle museum fire in 1944. Until his death in the mid fifties, Wilhelm Graf zu Lynar, the brother-in-law of the last Standesherr, served here as museum director. Since 1956 the Spreewald museum also includes the former orangery in which art shows are now held every year, particularly in the summer.

in der Nähe/nearby:
Orangerie (Museum)
Um 1820 • vermutl. Karl Benjamin Siegel
Remise u. Marstall (Efeuhaus); Clara-Zetkin-Straße 5
1744/46
Schloßpark
1820 • Johann Erdmann und Heinrich Wilhelm Freschke

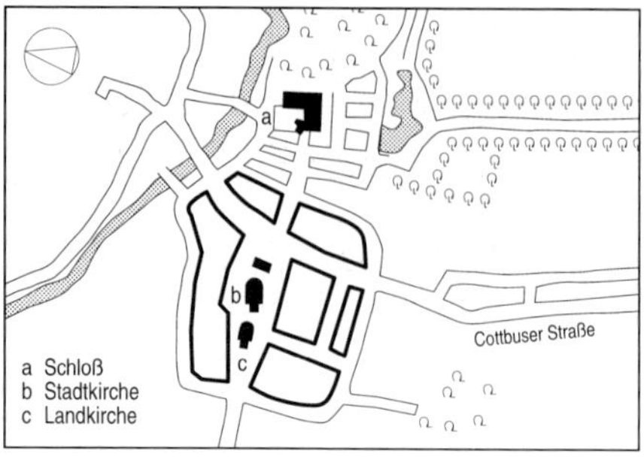

Z 9 Stadtkern Lieberose
1302

Die alte märkische Kleinstadt mit 1700 Einwohnern wird von Betrieben der Leichtindustrie geprägt. Im Schutze einer Wasserburg zur Sicherung des Wegekreuzes Frankfurt–Bautzen und Leipzig–Posen wurde in der zweiten Hälfte des 13. Jahrhunderts eine wendische Siedlung mit etwa quadratischem Grundriß angelegt. Die T-förmige Stadtanlage an der von Nord nach Süd führenden Hauptstraße mit dem rechtwinklig nach Westen abzweigenden langgestreckten Markt, dem Rathaus sowie den beiden Kirchenbauten besaß bereits 1302 deutsches Stadtrecht. Fast in ungebrochener Besitzfolge ging die freie Standesherrschaft von 1519 bis 1945 an die von der Schulenburg über, deren gräfliche Linie des »Schwarzen Stammes« hier ihre Residenz nahm. In der landesherrlich stärker zentralisierten Mark Brandenburg bildete sich eine solche mit der Niederlausitz vergleichbare standesherrschaftliche Struktur nicht heraus. Im nahen Jamlitz befand sich bis Februar 1945 ein Nebenlager des KZ Sachsenhausen.

This is the oldest small town in the Mark with 1700 inhabitants, and is given over mainly to light industry. A Wendic settlement on a roughly square ground plan was established under the protection of a moated castle to secure the Frankfurt an der Oder-Bautzen Leipzig-Posen crossroads in the second half of the thirteenth century. The T-shaped complex on the north-south oriented main road with elongated market place branching off at right angles to the west, town hall and two churches, had a German charter as early as 1302. The free mediatized principality passed in almost unbroken sequence of possession from 1519 to 1945 to the von der Schulenburg family, whose line of counts called the «Schwarzer Stamm» (Black Line) took up residence here. The Mark Brandenburg was more centralized as far as its ruling families were concerned, and a mediatized structure comparable with Niederlausitz did not emerge. There was a subsidiary of the Sachsenhausen concentration camp in nearby Jamlitz until February 1945.

in der Nähe/nearby:
Burg; Friedland
13. Jh. (Umbauten 1623)
Pfarrkirche; Friedland
18. Jh. (Umbau 1846)
Dorfkirche; Ressen-Zaue
Um 1400

Z 10 Schloß
Lieberose; östlich des Marktplatzes
Seit 1557 • Thaddäus Paglion

Der Kern des Schlosses wurde nach 1557 durch Joachim v. d. Schulenburg unter Einbeziehung einer Wasserburg errichtet, jedoch beim Stadtbrand 1657 verwüstet. Von diesem Spätrenaissance-Bau sind in barocker Veränderung nur der Taubenturm auf der Hofseite, die Rundbogenarkaden sowie Gewölbe des Ostflügels erhalten. Nach Einbau reicher Stuckdecken im 17. Jahrhundert bekam das Schloß Mitte des 18. Jahrhundert unter Georg Anton v. d. Schulenburg seine heutige Gestalt in Form einer Vierflügelanlage. 1945 wurden der Nordflügel und Teile des Westflügels beschädigt und abgetragen, 1975 stürzte der Uhrturm aus dem 18. Jahrhundert ein, der Wiederaufbau ist geplant. Die Schulenburgs spielten auch in der jüngeren Geschichte eine Rolle: Erinnert sei an Friedrich Werner Graf v. d. Schulenburg, der 1939 als deutscher Botschafter in Moskau vor Ausbruch des Zweiten Weltkriegs Verhandlungen mit der sowjetischen Regierung führte, und an Fritz Dietlof Graf v. d. Schulenburg, der mit Henning v. Tresckow befreundet und bei der Verschwörung des 20. Juli 1944 gegen Hitler beteiligt war.

The core of the building was erected after 1557 by Joachim von der Schulenburg, to include an old moated castle, but it was destroyed in the fire of 1657. The building was then rebuilt to a baroque design, and only the dovecote on the courtyard side, the round-arched arcade and the vaults of the east wing of the late Renaissance building survived. Lavish stucco ceilings were installed in the seventeenth century, and in the mid eighteenth century the building acquired its present quadripartite form under Georg Anton von der Schulenburg. In 1945 the north wing and parts of the west wing were damaged and demolished, and in 1975 the eighteenth century clock tower collapsed; there are plans to rebuild it. The Schulenburgs also played a part in more recent history: one need only mention Friedrich Werner Graf von der Schulenburg, who conducted negotiations with the Soviet government in Moscow before the outbreak of the Second World War in 1939, and of Fritz Dietlof Graf von der Schulenburg, who was a friend of Henning von Tresckow and also involved in the plot against Hitler on 20 July 1944.

in der Nähe/nearby:
Stadtkirche
1593 • Thaddäus Paglion
Landkirche
1824-26
Postmeilensäule; Cottbuser Straße
1753

Z 11 Eisenhütte
Peitz; Am Hammerstrom
1807-10 • Karl Gottlob Voigtmann

Sieht man von der Braunkohle ab, ist Brandenburg nicht gerade mit Bodenschätzen gesegnet. Die geologischen Bedingungen einer eiszeitlichen Überformung der Landschaft lassen das auch nicht anders erwarten. Lediglich in den Niederungen nördlich von Cottbus fand man Raseneisenerz, eine minderwertige Mineralablagerung aus eisenhaltigem Grundwasser. Dieses wurde – der Not gehorchend – mit Holzkohle aus den umliegenden ausgedehnten Wäldern seit dem 16. Jahrhundert in Peitz verhüttet. 1807 kamen Cottbus und die Niederlausitz zu Sachsen. Die Sachsen, im Hüttenwesen durch den Bergbau im Erzgebirge erfahren, bauten das Werk mit einem neuen Hochofen und einer Gieshalle modern aus. Die Gestalt der heutigen Anlage geht auf diese Zeit zurück. Die technische Ausrüstung mit Abstichöffnungen, Kupolöfen, Winderhitzer und Kran ist erhalten, nur die alten Wasserräder zum Antrieb der Blasebälge sind verschwunden. Sie wurden beizeiten durch ein Zylindergebläse ersetzt, das inzwischen aber auch zum Museumsstück heranreifte.

Apart from the lignite, Brandenburg is not exactly blessed with mineral resources. That is only to be expected in view of the geological conditions of a landscape shaped by the ice age. It was only in the lowlands north of Cottbus that deposits of limonite or bog iron ore, a less valuable mineral sediment from iron-bearing groundwater, were discovered. Nothing else being available, this was smelted in Peitz ever since the sixteenth century, using charcoal from the surrounding vast woodlands. In 1807 Cottbus and the Niederlausitz became part of Saxony. The Saxons, highly experienced in metallurgy with an extensive mining industry in the Erzgebirge, modernized and expanded the works with a new blast furnace and a foundry. The layout of today's facilities in fact goes back to this time. The old technical installations with tapping gates, cupola stoves, heating stove and crane have been preserved, only the old water wheels for driving the bellows are missing, having been replaced in time by a cylinder blower which has also become a museum piece by now.

in der Nähe/nearby:
Rathaus Peitz; Marktplatz
1804 • Johann Gottfried Görn – (Ostgiebel 1850)

Z 12 Dorfkirche
Straupitz
1827-32 • Karl Friedrich Schinkel

Gemessen an den kleinen Schinkelschen Kirchen in den damaligen Berliner Vorstädten entstand nach dem Entwurf des Meisters in Straupitz ein ungewöhnlich großes Gebäude, das so gar nicht mit dem Begriff Dorfkirche in Einklang kommen will. Im Dehio-Handbuch heißt es auch: »Stattlicher Bau von großer Wirkung«. Der Rundbogenstil vermittelt eine von Sparsamkeit geprägte Nüchternheit, die nur durch die gut proportionierte Doppelturmfront gemildert wird. Im Inneren herrscht aber wieder preußische Kargheit. Die fabrikartige Weite der Halle schwört jeder frömmelnden Heimeligkeit ab. In die hohen Pfeilerarkaden ist eine doppelgeschossige Empore eingespannt, im östlichen Joch sieht sich der Besucher gar mit einem dritten Emporengeschoß konfrontiert. 1700 Seelen umfaßte zur Bauzeit die Houwaldsche Herrschaft in Straupitz und den eingepfarrten Dörfern der Umgebung, die auf so staunenswerte Weise hier kirchenbaulich zu versorgen waren.

Compared to the small churches built by Schinkel in what were then suburbs of Berlin, his design for the village of Straupitz resulted in an unusually large building which seems to defy being called a village church. The Dehio Handbuch calls it a «stately building of great impact.» The Romanesque style conveys a sense of thrift and sobriety relieved only by the well proportioned front with its twin towers. The interior is also marked by Prussian austerity. The spacious factory-like hall renounces any suggestion of sanctimonious coziness. Between the high pillared arcades is a two-tiered gallery, and in the east bay the visitor is even confronted with a three-tiered gallery. At the time the domain of the Houwalds in Straupitz and the surrounding villages comprised a total of 1,700 souls which were served by this commanding and impressive example of ecclesiastical architecture.

in der Nähe/nearby:
Gutshaus; Straupitz
1794
Dorfkirche; Neu Zauche
1859-62 • Emil Karl Alexander Flaminius
Spreewald-Dorf; Burg Kauper
18./19. Jh.
Pfarrkirche; Burg
1799-1804

Z 13 Museumsdorf
Lehde
18./19. Jahrhundert

Ergänzend zum Spreewaldmuseum in der Lübbenauer Kanzlei wird seit 1957 in Lehde ein Freilandmuseum aufgebaut. Eine Hofanlage aus dem Dorf Lehde, ein typischer Hof aus dem Spreewalddorf Burg sowie eine Hofanlage aus dem Spreewald-Randgebiet gewähren Einblicke in die einstige Lebens-, Arbeits- und Wohnwelt der Spreewälder. Gezeigt werden hauptsächlich als ortstypischer Baustil der slawische Blockbau mit seinen Schilfrohrdächern und markanten Schlangenkopf-Giebelabschlüssen, unterschiedliche Haustypen sowie Möbel und andere Einrichtungsgegenstände. Neben Wohn- und Stallgebäuden sind Scheunen im Spreewald selten, da das Heu in pyramidenartigen Schobern auf der Wiese bleibt, bis es nach Bedarf eingeholt wird. Dafür erfolgt die Tierhaltung wegen der moorigen Wiesenböden ausschließlich in Ställen. Und nur für den Gemüseanbau wurden wenige Flächen künstlich als sogenannte Horstäcker erhöht. Neben Gemüseanbau und Viehzucht war ursprünglich die Fischerei Haupterwerbsquelle. Seit der Jahrhundertwende ist wohl der Tourismus ebenso wichtig geworden.

As an extension to the Spreewald museum in the Lübbenau chancery, an open-air museum is being built in Lehde since 1957. A farm from the village of Lehde, a typical farm from the Spreewald village of Burg and one from the borderland of the Spreewald show the living, working and dwelling conditions of the old Spreewald population. The exhibits include the vernacular building style of Slavic log structures with reed roof and snake-head gable-top, different types of houses, and furniture and other furnishings. Apart from dwellings and stables, there are very few barns in the Spreewald: the hay is stored in pyramid-like stacks on the land and only brought in as needed. Animal husbandry, however, must rely exclusively on stables because of the marshland. A few limited areas were artificially raised for vegetable gardening only, forming so-called «horst» fields. Next to vegetable farming and animal husbandry, the main source of income was fishery. Ever since the turn of the century tourism has become equally important.

in der Nähe/nearby:
Spreewaldsiedlung; Leipe
1701 (Wiederaufbau nach Brand)
Wendische Kirche; Vetschau
1853
Deutsche Kirche; Vetschau
1690-94
Wasserschloß; Vetschau
1540 • Eustachius v. Schlieben

Z 14 Wasserschloß Fürstlich Drehna
Drehna
2. Hälfte 16. Jahrhundert

Das im Jahre 1447 erst recht spät sicher belegte Drehna war Sitz einer der Niederlausitzer Standesherrschaften. Seit Ende des 15. Jahrhunderts war Drehna im Besitz des landesgeschichtlich sehr aktiven Adelsgeschlechts von Minckwitz, unter dessen Herrschaft das Schloß, möglicherweise unter Einbeziehung eines Vorgängerbaus, errichtet wurde – in der Dorfkirche befinden sich vier Grabsteine derer von Minckwitz aus dem 16. und 17. Jahrhundert. Das Wasserschloß ist eine verhältnismäßig große Vierflügelanlage um einen fast quadratischen Innenhof, zwei Ecken sind durch mächtige Rundtürme, die Nordostecke durch einen quadratischen Turm betont. Interessant sind der kreuzgratgewölbte Laubengang im Hof sowie die Tonnen-, Rippen-, Grat- und Zellengewölbe in den Erdgeschoßräumen. 1697 ging das Schloß an das seit 1621 in Lübbenau ansässige Haus Lynar über, dessen Drehnaer Zweig 1807 in den Fürstenstand erhoben wurde. Das für einen Fürsten gestiegene Repräsentationsbedürfnis führte im gleichen Jahr zur Anlage des Schloßparks, der dann ab 1819 unter Otto Rochus v. Lynar wahrscheinlich unter Mitwirkung von Peter Joseph Lenné und ab 1877 unter dem neuen Besitzer, dem Bremer Reeder Wätjen, weiter zum Landschaftspark vervollkommnet wurde.

First documented in 1447, Drehna was the seat of one of the mediatized princes of the Niederlausitz. From the end of the fifteenth century Drehna was owned by the von Minckwitz family, who played a very active role in regional history. Under their rule the castle was erected, possibly incorporating an earlier building. The village church contains the tombs of four members of the von Minckwitz family from the sixteenth and seventeenth centuries. The moated castle consists of a relatively large four wing complex surrounding an almost square courtyard; two corners are accentuated by massive round towers, the north-east corner with a square tower. Of particular interest are the groin-vaulted arcade in the courtyard as well as the barrel, rib, groin and cell vaults on the ground floor. In 1697 the castle comes into the possession of the Lynar family, residing in Lübbenau since 1621; the Drehna line of this family was promoted to princely rank in 1807. In the same year, the greater need of a prince for prestigious display led to the creation of the castle park which was redesigned into a landscape park after 1819 under Otto Rochus von Lynar, probably with participation by Peter Joseph Lenné, and after 1877 under the new owner, the ship-owner Wätjen from Bremen.

in der Nähe/nearby:
Gasthaus zum Hirschen; südlich vom Schloßeingang
1. H. 18. Jh.

Z 15 Stadtkirche (Deutsche Kirche)
Calau; Nähe Marktplatz
Um 1400, 2. Hälfte 15. Jahrhundert

Im seinerzeit slawischen Kerngebiet am Nordost-Rand des Niederlausitzer Grenzwalls wurde hier wohl schon früh eine Burg der Herren von Eilenburg errichtet und Calau als zugehörige deutsche Siedlung (1279 als civitas urkundlich genannt) auf regelmäßigem, elliptischem Grundriß angelegt. Seit 1815 gehört Calau zu Preußen. Die Stadtkirche, eine dreischiffige spätgotische Backsteinhalle von fünf Jochen mit kapellenlosem Umgangschor und nahezu quadratischem Westturm, wurde, ebenso wie die Stadt, am Ende des Zweiten Weltkrieges weitgehend zerstört. 1950-60 konnte die Kirche notdürftig wiederhergestellt werden, aus jener Zeit stammt auch die Ausstattung.

Quite early in what was at the time the core are of Slavic settlements at the north-eastern edge of the Niederlausitz Grenzwall the Lords of Eilenburg must have established a castle there. The related German settlement of Calau (first mentioned in documents as a civitas in 1279) was built on an elliptical plan and became part of Prussia in 1815. Like the town itself, the church, a late-Gothic brick hall with nave and two aisles and five bays, an ambulatory choir without chapel, and an almost square west tower was largely destroyed towards the end of the World War II. In 1950-60 the church was scantily rebuilt; the furnishings also date from that time.

in der Nähe/nearby:
Wendische Kirche
14./15. Jh.
Katholische Kirche St. Bonifatius
1930 • Hubert Schmid
Rathaus; Marktplatz
1808
Burglehenhaus; Burgplatz
1716
Alte Mädchenschule; Kirchstraße 1
17./18. Jh.

Z 16 Schloß
Altdöbern
1880-91 • Heinrich Kayser und Karl v. Großheim

1717 wurde eine ältere Wasserburg durch einen Schloßneubau ersetzt, den gegen 1749 der frisch geadelte Carl Heinrich Heinecken erwarb. Seine Karriere verdankte der Günstling des Dresdner Grafen Brühl Gemäldespekulationen, seine Wirtschaftskasse füllte er mit Bierbrauerei, Tabakfabrikation und Papierherstellung auf. Damit war er in der Lage, den Besitz 1749-50 durch Christian Conrad Francke um ein drittes Geschoß erweitern zu lassen. Das heutige Erscheinungsbild wird aber wesentlich von einem Umbau unter Graf v. Witzleben geprägt. Die Berliner Architekturfirma Kayser & Großheim verblendete 1880-91 die Fassaden mit historisierenden Dekorelementen, baute eine Vorhalle sowie zwei Türme an und schloß den Hofraum durch eine Galerie mit Terrasse.

In 1717 an older moated castle was replaced with a new castle which was purchased in 1749 by Carl Friedrich Heinecken who had just been raised to noble rank. A favourite of Graf Brühl of Dresden, he owed his career to art speculations and made his money with beer brewing, tobacco processing and paper manufacturing. This enabled him in 1749-50 to have a third storey added to the castle by Christian Conrad Francke. As it stands today, the appearance of the castle owes much to a conversion commissioned by Graf von Witzleben. In 1880-91 the Berlin construction firm of Kayser & Großheim refaced the façades with historicizing decorative elements, adding an entrance hall and two towers and closing off the courtyard with a gallery and terrace.

in der Nähe/nearby:
Kavalierhäuser; Altdöbern; Schloß-Zufahrt
18. Jh.
Landschaftspark; Altdöbern; am Schloß
1881-90 • Eduard Petzold
Wasserparterre; Altdöbern; östlich vom Schloß
1750-55 (Sandsteinfiguren • Gottfried Knöffler)
Pfarrkirche; Altdobern
1918-21 • Curt Steinberg
Schloß; Drebkau
E. 17. Jh.
Pfarrkirche; Drebkau
1810

Z 17 Ortskrankenkasse
Forst; Promenade 9
1924-25 • Rudolf Kühn

Der sozialpolitische Anspruch jener Jahre ließ dieses Gebäude entstehen, das nicht nur den Verwaltungsbedarf der medizinisch zu versorgenden Bevölkerung von Forst zu decken hatte, sondern auch selbst mit Bade- und Massageräumen die gesundheitliche Fürsorge pflegte. Die erstaunliche Größe der Vierflügelanlage hängt nicht zuletzt damit zusammen, daß die seit dem Mittelalter in Forst ansässige Tuchmacherei zu Beginn des 20. Jahrhunderts weit über 10 000 Arbeiter zählte. Der Architekt Rudolf Kühn hatte sich in den zwanziger Jahren in Forst durch etliche öffentliche und Wohnbauten hervorgetan. Hier folgte er – wie die Zeit es gebot – einem expressionistisch ausgerichteten Stil, der im spitzen Zulauf der Pfeiler, im textilen Rippenmuster der Klinkerfronten und in der architektonischen Integration der schelmisch-ausdrucksstarken Plastik »Schmerzensmann« von Johann Ernst Born Beachtung verdient. Auch im Inneren, im Eingangsraum, im Treppenhaus und in den Fluren, finden sich plastische Arbeiten der gleichen Zuordnung als klinkerrote oder blaßblaue keramische Verkleidungen.

The socio-political situation of the period led to the construction of this building which served not only to fill the administrative needs of the medical services in Forst but also to contribute to the health care itself by offering baths and massage facilities. The astonishing size of the four-wing complex is owed not least to the fact that the textile industry, first established in Forst in the Middle Ages, comprised well above 10,000 workers in the early twentieth century. In the nineteen-twenties architect Rudolf Kühl had made a name for himself in Forst with numerous public and private buildings. Here he adhered – in keeping with the times – to an expressionist style noteworthy for the tapering pointed pillars, the textile rib pattern of the clinker façades and the architectural integration of the highly expressive statue of the «Man of Pain» by sculptor Johann Ernst Born. Additional sculptural works are found in the interior, in vestibule, stairwell and corridors in the clinker-red or pale-blue ceramic decor.

in der Nähe/nearby:
Stadtkirche St. Nikolai; Markt
14./17.Jh.; 1750-53 • Johann Christoff Knöffel
Gymnasium; Jahnstraße
1928-29 • Rudolf Kühn
Johann-Sebastian-Bach-Kirche; Südvorstadt
1950 • Otto Bartning
Wohnsiedlung; Forst-Nossdorf; Schwerinstraße
1925-26 • Rudolf Kühn

Z 18 Kraftwerk Trattendorf
Spremberg-Trattendorf
1915-17, um 1925 und nach 1954

Mit der Erfindung der Drehstrommaschine 1889 war die Voraussetzung für die Hochspannungs-Fernübertragung geschaffen. Es dauerte noch über zehn Jahre bis technische Reife der Anlagen und steigender Bedarf an elektrischer Energie zum Bau von Großkraftwerken in den Kohlegebieten führten. Statt des teuren und umständlichen Kohletransportes war es wirtschaftlicher den erzeugten Strom über Fernleitungen in die Industriezentren und Großstädte zu liefern. Die etwa gleichzeitig entstandenen mitteldeutschen Braunkohle-Kraftwerke Zschornewitz, Böhlen, Hirschfelde, Trattendorf und Lauta waren in den zwanziger Jahren durch eine Ringleitung mit Dresden, Leipzig und Berlin verbunden. Aus dieser Zeit stammen auch noch viele Erweiterungsbauten im Werk Trattendorf. Umbauten und Kriegszerstörungen haben von den ersten Gebäuden nur Reste übriggelassen.

The invention of the three-phase machine in 1889 paved the way for long-distance transmission of high voltage electricity. It took another ten years before the technology was sufficiently developed and demand for electricity was so high that large-scale power plants were built in the coal-mining areas. Instead of transporting the coal at great cost and effort, it proved much more economical to deliver electricity to the industrial centres and large cities by way of long-distance powerlines. In the nineteen-twenties the central German lignite-burning power plants at Zschornewith, Böhlen, Hirschfelde, Trattendorf and Lauta, all built about the same time, were linked by way of a loop service feeder system with Dresden, Leipzig and Berlin. Many of the additions to the Trattendorf plant date from this period. Numerous alterations and war damages have left only remnants of the original early buildings.

in der Nähe/nearby:
Wohnsiedlung; Kraftwerkstraße
Um 1925
Bismarckturm; Spremberg
1902-03 • Römmler

Z 19 Rathaus
Spremberg; Markt
1706-20 • C. Auersbach

Spremberg als wichtiger Spreeübergang wechselte in seiner Geschichte oft die Herren. Brandenburgisch war es, sächsisch und auch böhmisch, bis es 1635 für fast zwei Jahrhunderte an Kursachsen kam. Dem scheint auch das Rathaus in seiner Gestalt Rechnung tragen zu wollen. Der Stadtbrand im Jahre 1705 hatte vom Renaissancebau nur die Kreuzgratgewölbe des Erdgeschosses übriggelassen. Auersbach errichtete über diesen Resten in den folgenden Jahren einen Neubau, der 1933-34 durch Einbeziehung angrenzender Wohnhäuser zum heutigen Komplex erweitert wurde. Der barocke Bauteil mit Putz und Werkstein hat wenig gemein mit den märkischen Ziegelbauten, und auch der polygonale Turm mit geschweifter Haube, Laterne und Zwiebel weist auf ein eher süddeutsches Verständnis der Bauaufgabe hin. Die Zutaten der dreißiger Jahre stehen damit im Einklang, wenn flache Stichbogen, schmiedeeiserne Geländer und ein mäßg steiles, auskragendes Dach Bodenständigkeit vermitteln.

Located at an important point of crossing on the Spree, Spremberg had many different lords throughout history. In turn it was part of Brandenburg, Saxony and Bohemia before falling to Kursachsen for almost two decades in 1635. The shape of the town hall seems to try and account for this. All that was left of the Renaissance building after the town fire of 1705 was the cross vaulting of the ground floor. In the following years Auersbach built on these remnants a new structure which was expanded into a larger complex as it stands today by including the adjoining residential buildings. The baroque section with rendering and freestone bears little similarity to the brick buildings of the Mark, and the polygonal tower with shaped cupola, lantern and onion dome reflects a somewhat South German understanding of the task. The characteristic elements of the thirties are clearly harmonious: low segmental arches, wrought-iron railings and a modestly pitched cantilevering roof represent a distinct vernacular touch.

in der Nähe/nearby:
Kreuzkirche
14./15. Jh.
Landkirche (Wendische Kirche); Kirchplatz
1834-35
Schloß
Ab 1680 (Reste von 1290 bis 2. H. 16. Jh.)
Kavalierhaus; Lange Straße 15-16
1706

Z 20 Gymnasium
Senftenberg; Walter-Rathenau-Straße
1931 • Bruno Taut und Max Taut

Der gesellschaftliche Umbruch nach dem Ersten Weltkrieg hatte in Deutschland auch erheblichen Einfluß auf Bildungspolitik und Schulbau. Der Weg zu einem neuen, modernen Schultyp war aber beschwerlich, wie sich am Beispiel von Bruno Tauts Berliner Dammwegschule zeigen sollte, die, revolutionierend in pädagogischer Konzeption und architektonischer Umsetzung, zuletzt doch an ihrem sozialen Anspruch scheiterte und nicht gebaut wurde. Zustande kamen aber mehr oder weniger kompromißbehaftete Schulneubauten, die als Vorzüge alle gemeinsam hatten: großzügige Grundstücke in meist freier Lage, helle und gut belüftbare Klassen, ein zeitgemäßes Angebot an Fachräumen und eine von Leichtigkeit geprägte architektonische Gestaltung fern von der einst obrigkeitsorientierten Bildungsanstalt. Das Senftenberger Gymnasium erinnert in seiner äußerlich asketischen Haltung unübersehbar an Max Tauts Dorotheenschule in Berlin-Köpenick. Sachlichkeit, Funktionalität und hoher Ausrüstungsstandard wurden gleichgesetzt mit Fortschritt, insbesondere mit technischem Fortschritt, der von allen damaligen politischen Richtungen als gültiges Maß anerkannt wurde, während die Definition des sozialen Fortschritts strittig war.

The social upheavals in Germany after the First World War proved of far-reaching signicance for educational policy and the construction of schools. Yet the road towards a new, modern type of school was anything but easy, as the example of the Dammwegschule in Berlin by Bruno Taut demonstrates: Quite revolutionary in terms of educational concept and architectural design, it eventually failed because its social demands proved too high and was never built. In many cases, more or less compromise-ridden new schools were constructed which shared a number of common merits: expansive grounds, usually in an open area; well-lighted and ventilated classrooms; a modern array of technical facilities; and a light touch characterizing the architectural design, much in contrast to the previous authoritarian schools. The ascetic appearance of the Senftenberg Gymnasium shows an undeniable similarity with Max Taut's Dorotheenschule in Berlin-Köpenick. Functionality and furnishings of a high standard were considered as synonymous with progress – particularly technological progress which was then considered to be the valid standard of the day by all factions of the political spectrum, while the definition of social progress remained controversial.

in der Nähe/nearby:
Stadtkirche St. Peter und Paul
15. Jh.
Schloß Senftenberg
M. 16. Jh.
Kaufhaus; Bahnhofstraße 10
Um 1910 und um 1930 (Anbau)
Berufsschule; Calauer Straße 3
Um 1932 • O. Peter

Z 21 Rathaus Finsterwalde
Finsterwalde; Markt
1739 • Georg Christian Haubtmann

Die Kreisstadt Finsterwalde liegt in einer Senke südlich eines großen Endmoränenzuges, des Niederlausitzer Grenzwalles, zwischen zwei Urstromtälern. Im Schutze der nach 1200 angelegten deutschen Sumpfburg an der Salzstraße Torgau–Breslau entstand eine halbkreisförmige Marktsiedlung nördlich des heutigen Schlosses, die bereits 1279 erwähnt wurde. Einen ersten Aufschwung nahm Finsterwalde seit dem 16. Jahrhundert durch das Tuchgewerbe; der Braunkohlenabbau begünstigte die Entwicklung der Textilindustrie. Erst nach 1800 wuchs der Ort über die Altstadt hinaus. Das Rathaus liegt inmitten des Marktes und wurde 1739 von dem Maurermeister Haubtmann aus Kirchhain auf den alten Umfassungsmauern des brandzerstörten Vorgängerbaus von 1492 als zweigeschossiger Putzbau errichtet. Eine besondere Wirkung geht von dem hohen Walmdach aus, das der ebenfalls aus Kirchhain stammende Zimmermeister Martin Günther durch ein Uhrtürmchen mit offener Laterne und Schweifhaube bekrönte. Die beiden Nordportale mit Sitznischen – sie verraten den sächsischen Einfluß – wurden 1928 verändert.

The district capital of Finsterwalde lies in a hollow to the south of a huge base moraine, the Niederlausitz Grenzwall, between two glacial valleys. Protected by the German Sumpfburg dating from after 1200 at the salt road between Torgau and Breslau, a crescent-shaped market town, first mentioned in 1279, was established north of where the castle stands today. Finsterwalde enjoyed a first boom after the sixteenth century with the rise of cloth-making; development of the textile industry was facilitated by the lignite mining. After 1800 the town expanded beyond the Altstadt. The town hall in the centre of the market was erected in 1492 as a two-storey rendered building by contractor Haubtmann from Kirchhain on the old enclosing walls of its burnt-down predecessor. It is noteworthy for its tall hipped roof, which carpenter Martin Günther, also from Kirchhain, crowned with a clock spire with open lantern and shaped cupola. The two north portals with seating niches, suggesting Saxonian influence, were altered in 1928.

in der Nähe/nearby:
Wasserschloß; Sallgast
M. 16. Jh.
Schloßpark; Sallgast
1911 • Bodo Ebhardt
Schloß; Sonnewalde
16./17. Jh.
Autobahn-Raststätte; Freienhufen
1937

Z 22 Wohnhaus »Curdsburg«
Finsterwalde; Schloßstraße 6
1572

Ein einfaches Bürgerhaus ließ Curd v. Dieskau zu einer stattlichen Vierflügelanlage umbauen; jetzt ist es ein versimpelter Putzbau mit einem schönen Sitznischenportal in strenger Ädikularahmung. Das geschnitzte Türblatt aus der Mitte des 17. Jahrhunderts enthält Knorpel- und Ohrmuschelwerk. Im Erdgeschoß sind noch Kreuzgratgewölbe und eine profilierte Balkendecke vorhanden. Offenbar nach diesem Vorbild schmückten sich auch andere Bauten, so das Haus Markt 22 mit einem Sitznischenportal vom Ende des 16. Jahrhunderts in einer Putzrahmung von 1748, in der Durchfahrt ein Kreuzgratgewölbe. Nach mehreren Bränden im 17. und 18. Jahrhundert wurde die Innenstadt zwar immer wieder aufgebaut, doch blieben von den Bürgerhäusern der Renaissance- und frühen Barockzeit nur wenige Beispiele erhalten.

Curd von Dieskau had a simple townhouse converted to a stately four-wing structure; today it is a simplified rendered building with magnificent recessed portal with seating niche and severe aedicule framing. The carved door dating from the mid seventeenth century contains magnificent decorative carvings. The rib vaults and profiled joist ceiling on the ground floor have survived. Apparently the ornamentation was copied in other buildings: the house at Markt no. 22 also has a recessed portal with seating niche from the late sixteenth century with rendered framing of 1748 as well as rib vaults in the gateway. Although the town centre was always rebuilt after several fires in the seventeenth and eighteenth centuries, only a few examples of the townhouses from the Renaissance and Early Baroque have survived.

in der Nähe/nearby:
Bürgerhaus; Külzstraße
M. 19. Jh. und um 1900 (Erdgeschoß)
Gewoba-Wohnsiedlung; Drössiger Straße
1927-28 • Ludewig
Märchenhaus; Friedrich-Hebbel-Straße 16/24
1928-29 • Dassel
Wohngebiet »Langer Haken«;
1960-62 • Kurt Hagemeister, Gerhard Kühnel, Wolfgang Weißpflog, Manfred Lehmann

Z 23 Pfarrkirche St. Trinitatis
Finsterwalde; Markt
1584-93 • Martin Piger

Da bereits 1585, ein Jahr nach Baubeginn, mit der Einwölbung der Trinitatiskirche begonnen wurde, müssen wesentliche Teile der mittelalterlichen Marienkirche übernommen worden sein. Der quadratische Westturm ist schon 1575-78 erbaut worden. Die jetzige Pfarrkirche ist eine dreischiffige Emporenhalle aus Backstein, die Formteile gleichfalls aus Backstein. Im östlichen Seitenschiff liegt die Herrschaftsempore, darunter die Sakristei; sie ist wie die Loge darüber mit schönen Doppelsterngewölben ausgestattet. Vorhalle, Langhaus und Chor haben zeitgemäß Netzgewölbe. Der Altaraufsatz stammt 1594 von Martin Brauer und Samuel Weber; die Kanzel schuf 1613-15 Melchior Kuntze. Im Inneren finden sich auch eine Reihe von Grabsteinen, meist mit Ganzfiguren der Verstorbenen, aber auch mehrere Gemälde-Epitaphien und steinerne Wandepitaphien der Familie von Dieskau.

As the vaulting of St. Trinitatis was begun in 1585, only one year after construction started, it can be assumed that large parts of the medieval Marienkirche must have been incorporated. The square west tower was even erected as early as 1575-78. The current parish church is a galleried hall of brick with nave and two aisles, with moulded elements also of brick. The east aisle contains the loges for the nobility and the sacristy below; like the loges above it, it is furnished with splendid double stellar vaulting. Vestibule, nave and choir were given net vaults in keeping with the time. The altar-piece was created by Martin Brauer and Samuel Weber in 1594, the pulpit by Melchior Kuntze in 1613-15. Inside the church are a number of tombstones, mostly with portrait sculptures of the deceased, as well as several painted epitaphs and stone epitaphs of the von Dieskau family.

in der Nähe/nearby:
Knabenschule; Straße der Jugend
1911-13 • Max Taut
Elektromaschinenbau-Fabrik »Kjellberg«
1924
Krankenhaus; Kirchhainer Straße
1905-08 • P. Droste

Z 24 Schloß
Finsterwalde
1531-97 • Martin Piger

Eine bald nach 1200 an der Salzstraße Torgau–Breslau erbaute Wasserburg diente der nördlich anschließenden Siedlung als Schutz. Im Mittelalter wechselte die Burg mehrfach den Besitzer, ab 1531 gehörte sie den Herren v. Dieskau. In den folgenden Jahren entstand nun als Neubau ein weitläufiger Komplex aus langgestrecktem Vorderschloß mit Wirtschaftsräumen und quadratischem Hinterschloß, dem einstigen Wohnteil der Burg. Die Ähnlichkeit der Sterngewölbe im Erdgeschoß mit denen der Herrenloge in der Trinitatiskirche läßt auf Martin Piger aus Dresden als Baumeister schließen. Das Hinterschloß sichert ein quadratischer Turm. Der Hof verrät böhmischen Einfluß: zwei Wendelsteine, flachbogige Arkaden. Wien, Krakau oder Prag mit ihrer südländischen Leichtigkeit sind hier stilistisch näher als das rauhe Brandenburg.

A moated castle erected shortly after 1200 by the salt road from Torgau to Breslau served to protect the adjoining settlement to the north. In the Middle Ages ownership of the castle changed repeatedly; it belonged to the von Dieskau family since 1531. Between 1531 and 1597 an extensive new complex was built, consisting of an elongated building with domestic facilities in the front, and behind that a square-plan building, the former residential section of the castle. The stellar vaults on the ground floor are similar to those of the gallery in the Trinitatiskirche, suggesting they were also built by Martin Piger from Dresden. The rear section of the castle is protected by a square tower. The courtyard shows Bohemian influences with two staircase-towers and flat-arched arcades. In terms of style, the more southerly lightness of Vienna, Krakow or Prague appear much stronger here than the harshness of Brandenburg.

in der Nähe/nearby:
Stadtsparkasse; Berliner Straße 42
1928 • Kurt Vogler
Doppelturnhalle; August-Bebel-Straße 16
1928 • Kurt Vogeler
Dorfkirche; Finsterwalde-Süd (Nehesdorf)
13.Jh.
Wohngebiet Süd
1963-83

Z 25 Schloß Doberlug
Doberlug-Kirchhain
Nach 1547

In Doberlug an der kleinen Elster lag schon 1005 eine slawische Siedlung. Vor 1165 gründeten hier die Zisterzienser ein Kloster, das 1541 säkularisiert wurde. An der Stelle der Abtei entstand 1547 ein Jagdschloß, das zu seinem Schutz von einem Wassergraben umzogen wurde. Im 17. Jahrhundert erwarb der sächsische Kurfürst das Schloß, 1657 fiel es an Sachsen-Merseburg. Etwa 1661 begann nun der Umbau zu einer trutzigen Vierflügelanlage. Gleichzeitige legte Herzog Christian eine selbständige, planmäßige Stadt an, ohne Rathaus, also dem Schloß unterstellt, aber nach den bitteren Erfahrungen des Dreißigjährigen Krieges durch Mauer, Graben und drei Tore geschützt. Das Schloß erhielt zwei Treppentürme mit Sterngewölben und Schweifgiebel mit Pyramidenaufsätzen ähnlich denen im Merseburger Schloß. Diese Erinnerungsstücke an seine Heimat und andere Steinmetzarbeiten ließ der Herzog von Heinrich Weinhardt aus Pirna arbeiten.

As early as 1005 there was a Slavic settlement at Doberlug on the Kleine Elster. Well before 1165 the Cistercians founded a monastery here which was secularized in 1541. The abbey was replaced with a hunting lodge protected by a moat. In the seventeenth century the Elector of Saxony purchased the castle before it fell to Sachsen-Merseburg. About 1661 it was rebuilt into a defiant four-wing complex. At the same time Duke Christian established a new planned town; having no town hall, it was attached to the castle, but after the bitter experience of the Thirty Years' War it was protected by wall, moat and three gates. The castle was equipped with two staircase towers with stellar vaults and shaped gables with pyramid tops similar to those of Merseburg castle. For these reminders of home and other stonemason's work the Duke commissioned Heinrich Weinhardt from Pirna.

in der Nähe/nearby:
Dorfkirche; Trebbus
13./15. Jh.
Bockwindmühle; Trebbus
1830; 1970 Schauanlage
Mühle; Lichtena
1690

Z 26 Klosterkirche St. Marien
Doberlug-Kirchhain; Zisterzienser-Kloster
12.-13. Jahrhundert

Die Klosterkirche ist neben Lehnin und Chorin der bedeutendste Backsteinbau der Zisterzienser und einer der frühesten gewölbten Großbauten östlich der Elbe. Er wurde vom Ende des 12. bis zur Mitte des 13. Jahrhunderts als kreuzförmige Basilika mit Querschiff errichtet. Das Chorquadrat war ursprünglich von je zwei Nebenchören begleitet. Nach der Säkularisation verkam das Kloster, die Kirche wurde später umgestaltet, 1859 wieder purifiziert. Die Restaurierung von 1905-06 unter Carl Weber hinterließ den Versuch einer Synthese mittelalterlicher und nachmittelalterlicher Stilelemente. Das Westportal erhielt eine Verkleidung in Formen der deutschen Spätrenaissance; auch die rundbogige Fenstergruppe darüber und das große Mittelfenster mit der flachen Blendnische wurden damals erneuert, ebenso wie der Giebel mit seinen Rosetten.

Next to Lehnin and Chorin this monastery church ranks as the most important brick building of the Cistercians and one of the earliest large vaulted structures east of the Elbe. It was built from the late twelfth to the mid thirteenth century as a cruciform basilica with transept. The choir square was originally flanked by two smaller choirs on each side. After secularization the monastery decayed; the church was later altered and again purified in 1859. The restauration of 1905-06 under Carl Weber attempted a synthesis of medieval and post-medieval styles. The west portal was clad, using elements of German late Renaissance; at this time, the round-arched windows above and the great central window with its slight niche were replaced at the time, as was the gable with its rosettes.

in der Nähe/nearby:
Handwerker- u. Hofbedienstetenstadt; Doberlug
1657-64
Gasthof Rautenstock; Doberlug
1665-66
Alte Apotheke; Doberlug
1689

Z 27 Weißgerberei Kirchhain
Doberlug-Kirchhain; Potsdamer Straße 18
1787-88

Kirchhain an der Kleinen Elster – schon im Jahre 1234 erwähnt – wurde als deutsches Angerdorf wohl vom nahen Kloster Dobrilugk gegründet. Die breite Backsteinbasilika stammt aus dieser Zeit, das Rathaus wurde erst gegen Ende des 17. Jahrhunderts errichtet, als der Ort seinen Aufschwung unter Herzog Christian I. von Sachsen-Merseburg durch Ausbreitung des Gerber- und Kürschnerhandwerks nahm. Bereits im 18. Jahrhundert wurde Kirchhainer Weiß- und Glacéleder nach Rußland und Italien exportiert. Die Entwicklung der Lederindustrie – 1897 gab es 98 Gerbereibetriebe – wurde durch das mineralarme, nahezu eisenfreie Wasser der Kleinen Elster begünstigt. Das heutige Weißgerbermuseum ist ein verputzter Fachwerkbau, der von 1787 bis 1957 als Weißgerberei genutzt wurde. 1963 richtete man dieses technische Denkmal als Museum mit Schauanlage her: im Untergeschoß die Wasserwerkstatt, die Trockenwerkstatt im Obergeschoß.

Kirchhain on the Kleine Elster – first documented in 1234 – was probably founded by the nearby Dobrilugk monastery as a German village built around a village green. The wide brick basilica dates from that time, while the town hall was only built in the late seventeenth century when the town began to flourish under Duke Christian I von Sachsen-Merseburg with the expansion of the crafts of tanners and furriers. As early as the eighteenth century white leather and kid from Kirchhain were exported to Russia and Italy. The rise of the leather industry – there were 98 tanneries in 1897 – profited from the low mineral and iron content of the water from the Kleine Elster. The Tanners' Museum is a rendered half-timber building used as tannery from 1787 to 1957. In 1863 this industrial monument was turned into a museum and display, with wet workshop below and dry workshop above.

in der Nähe/nearby:
Stadtkirche St. Marien; Kirchhain
13. Jh. (Umbau 16. Jh.)
Rathaus Kirchhain; Markt
2. H. 17. Jh. (Umbau 1905 • Carl Weber)
Sächsische Postmeilensäule; Karl-Liebknecht-Platz
1736
Wohnhäuser; Potsdamer Straße, Gerberstraße
18. u. 19. Jh.
Wohnhäuser der Lederfabrikanten; Liebknechtstraße
Nach 1930

Z 28 Stadtkirche St. Nikolai
Bad Liebenwerda; Markt
1. Hälfte 15. Jahrhundert

In Liebenwerda waren wie in Mühlberg und anderen Orten der Niederlausitz Burg und Stadt Kolonisationsgründungen. Die Burg, 1231 erwähnt, wurde später zum Renaissanceschloß umgebaut. Die Nikolaikirche, ein spätgotischer Backsteinbau, wurde als Hallenkirche errichtet. Aus älterer Zeit stammt der Westturm, dessen Unterbau auf das 14. Jahrhundert zurückgeht. Nach dem Gewölbeeinsturz von 1513 kam es zu erheblichen Umbauten. Eine Saalkirche mit vergrößerten Fenstern entstand; die erst in der 2. Hälfte des 16. Jahrhunderts fertiggestellten Anbauten folgen schon dem Renaissancestil. Die seltenen Zellengewölbe der Sakristei weisen auf Meißen und böhmische Einflüsse hin. 1898 und 1903 wurden Turm und Kircheninneres nochmals eingreifend verändert, nun in dem für jene Jahre typischen gotisch-historistischen Stil. Damit sollte das Stadtbild des aufstrebenden Eisenmoorbades aufgewertet werden, das seit 1925 im Ortsnamen offiziell den Zusatz »Bad« führt.

As in Mühlberg and elsewhere in the Niederlausitz, castle and town of Liebenwerda originated as colonies. The castle, first recorded in 1231, was later converted to a Renaissance palace. The church of St. Nikolai, a late Gothic brick structure, is a hall church. Somewhat older is the west tower, whose base dates from the fourteenth century. Following the collapse of the vaulting in 1513 there were substantial alterations, resulting in a hall church with enlarged windows. The additions from the second half of the sixteenth century already show Renaissance style. The rare cell vaulting of the sacristy suggests influences from Meissen and Bohemia. In 1898 and 1903 tower and interior were again altered, this time in the Gothic historist style of the day, in order to enhance the townscape of this rising iron-moor bath which officially ranks as a spa since 1925.

in der Nähe/nearby:
Bergfrit, Schloß; Dresdener Straße
13. u. 16. Jh.
Rathaus Bad Liebenwerda; Markt
Um 1800
Wohnhaus; Marktstraße 27-28
Um 1800

Z 29 Schloß
Großkmehlen
Mitte 16. Jahrhundert

Unmittelbar an der Grenze zu Sachsen, schon eher am östlichen Rand der Oberlausitz und nördlich der Großenhainer Pflege, dort wo die Autobahn Berlin–Dresden hinter Ortrand die große Endmoräne erklettert, liegt im Tal bei Großthiemig der Ort Großkmehlen. Hier entstand in der Renaissance ein imposantes Wasserschloß auf quadratischem Grundriß mit drei Ecktürmen. Die zwei Wohnflügel hatten ursprünglich im Inneren keine Verbindung, da das dazugehörige Rittergut seit dem Ende des 16. Jahrhunderts im Besitz geteilt war. Deshalb gab es auch zwei Hauptportale mit Brücken über den Graben. Die Schweifgiebel stammen wohl aus dem 17. Jahrhundert. Das Schloß ist Zeuge der auch in der Niederlausitz nach dem Dreißigjährigen Krieg ausgeprägten Gutsherrschaft mit Erbuntertänigkeit und täglichem unbemessenen Dienst. Und während das Gesinde wegen schlechter Beköstigung klagte, fertigten italienische Stukkateure im Obergeschoß des Schlosses Hermenpilaster und Götter mit Wappenkartuschen oder aus Blüten herauswachsende Halbfiguren zwischen schweren Akanthusranken. Die Großkmehlener Bauernrebellion von 1790 wurde vom Mititär erstickt.

Directly on the border to Saxony, almost at the eastern edge of the Oberlausitz and north of the Grossenhainer Pflege, where the Berlin-Dresden autobahn begins to climb the huge end moraine, lies Grosskmehlen in the valley near Grossthiemig. In the Renaissance a stately moated castle was built here to square plan with three corner towers. The two residential wings were not connected originally, as the estate had been divided among two owners since the late sixteenth century. Thus there were two main portals with bridges over the moat. The shaped gables are probably from the seventeenth century. The castle stands as evidence of the manorial system with serfdom and unlimited daily service, as also dominated the Niederlausitz after the Thirty Years' War. While the domestics complained of insufficient board, in the upper storeys of the castle Italian stuccatori created herm pilasters and deities with armorial cartouches or human half-figures growing out of flowers and heavy acanthus vines. The Grosskmehlen peasant rebellion of 1790 was suppressed by the military.

in der Nähe/nearby:
Haus Menzel; Elsterwerda; Wielandstraße 2
1958-61 • Wolfgang Rauda, Alfred Lohrmann
Garten zum Haus Menzel; Elsterwerda; Wielandstraße 2
1961 • Werner Bauch
Dorfkirche; Hirschfeld
1786

Z 30 Dorfkirche
Großkmehlen
Anfang 16. Jahrhundert (Umbau 1720/30)

Der schlichte Putzbau der Kirche wurde in spätgotischer Zeit errichtet, doch die Kreuzform erhielt er erst durch Anbauten zu Beginn des 18. Jahrhunderts, also teilhabend am Reichtum des Rittergutes: im Norden zwei Herrschaftslogen, im Süden eine Sakristei mit Gruftgewölbe. Auch der Westturm ist eine spätere Anfügung von 1617, als Renaissance-Bauteil erhielt er einen oktogonalen Aufsatz mit Schweifhaube und Laterne. Sehenswert ist vor allem die immer wieder vervollständigte wertvolle Ausstattung des Innenraumes. An der Flachdecke sind Bandelwerk-Stukkaturen zu sehen; die Hufeisenempore mit einer Balusterbrüstung steht auf Stützen mit ionischen Kapitellen. Der Altaraufsatz wurde 1620 aus zwei spätgotischen Schnitzaltären zusammengefügt und mit einer Renaissance-Rahmung aus Skulpturen, Beschlag- und Knorpelwerk versehen. Das Hauptfeld bildet ein Schnitzaltar aus der Werkstatt des Jan Bormann aus Brügge um 1520. Ein spätgotisches Sakramentshaus ist in die Sakristei eingebaut. 1620 wurde die Sandsteinkanzel, 1718 die Taufe gefertigt. 1717 fügte kein geringerer als Gottfried Silbermann die Orgel mit einem dreiteiligen Prospekt hinzu.

The simply rendered structure of the church dates from the late Gothic but the cruciform plan is the result of eighteenth century additions, resulting from the new wealth of the manorial estate: in the north, two galleries for the nobility; in the south, a sacristy with tomb vaults. The west tower was also added in 1617 as a Renaissance element; its octagonal top bears a shaped cupola and lantern. Especially noteworthy are the valuable, repeatedly supplemented furnishings of the interior. The flat ceiling is decorated with banded stucco ornaments; the horse-shoe gallery with balustrade rests on columns with Ionic capitals. The altar-piece was combined from two late Gothic carved altars and given a Renaissance framework with sculptures and splendid carvings. The main panel consists of a carved altar from the Brugge studio of Jan Bormann, c. 1520. The sacristy incorporates a late Gothic sacrament house. The sandstone pulpit dates from 1620, the baptismal font from 1718. In 1717 no other than Gottfried Silbermann built the organ with tripartite prospect.

in der Nähe/nearby:
Schloß; Lindenau
1584; 1783 verändert
Schloßkirche; Lindenau
1686
Stadtkirche; Ortrand
1563; Umbau 1612
Dorfkirche; Kroppen
1718-21 • Balthasar Rumberger

Z 31 Neue Probstei
Mühlberg; Museumsstraße 9
1530-31

Mühlberg liegt an der Elbfurt einer Straße nach Halle und entwickelte sich als Doppelstadt. Die nördliche Altstadt als Suburbium einer wenig älteren Burg und das Kloster blieben bis ins 16. Jahrhundert durch Wall und Graben von der nach der Mitte des 13. Jahrhunderts entstandenen Neustadt getrennt. Trotz oder gerade wegen dieser Trennung, im Wetteifer oder als Ausdruck gemeinsamen Gestaltungswillens taucht im Stadtbild mehrfach ein für Mühlberg typisches Motiv auf: der üppige Maßwerkgiebel mit tiefen Profilen in Kreis- und Gitterschlingen oder engen Bögen. Um 1530 sind diese Giebel jeweils entstanden und zieren heute noch Rathaus, Abtei (Bild Z 32) und Neue Probstei. Die Neue Probstei, inzwischen Stadtmuseum, liegt wie üblich westlich des Klosters, hier jedoch ungewöhnlich weit entfernt. Der winkelförmige verputzte Backsteinbau mit Inschrift 1531 wurde durch zwei prächtige Maßwerkgiebel ausgezeichnet. Die Sandsteingewände der Fenster sind mit gekreuzten Stabprofilen versehen. Den nach 1554 angefügten Südostflügel schließt ein Schweifgiegel in Spätrenaissanceformen ab. Innen findet man Kreuzgratgewölbe im Erdgeschoß und hier wie auch im oberen Konventssaal Decken- und Wandmalereien aus der Bauzeit und aus der Frührenaissance.

Mühlberg, located where the road to Halle crosses the Elbe, originated as a double-town. Until well into the sixteenth century, the northern old town as suburb of a slightly older castle and the monastery were separated from the new town built in the mid thirteenth century. In spite of, or perhaps because of, this separation, out of competition or a sign of a shared design approach, the townscape features a motif that is typical of Mühlberg: lavish traceried gables with deep profiles in circular or gridded loops or narrow arches. These gables date from c. 1530 and still decorate the town hall, abbey (cf. photograph Z 32) and Neue Probstei. As usual, the Neue Probstei (provost's residence), now town museum, lies to the west of the monastery, although in this case remarkably far away. The angled, rendered brick building with the inscription 1531 features two magnificent traceried gables. The sandstone window jambs are fitted with crossed profile bars. The south-east wing added after 1554 ends in a shaped gable in late Renaissance style. The interior contains rib vaults on the ground floor; here as in the convent hall upstairs, the ceilings and walls feature paintings from the time of building and the Early Renaissance.

in der Nähe/nearby:
Schloß; westlich der Stadt
1545-60
Marienkirche
1487-1525

Z 32 Klosterkirche
Mühlberg; Kloster Güldenstern
1227 bis Ende 13. Jahrhundert

Das ehemalige Zisterzienser-Nonnenkloster wurde 1227 gegründet. Es erfreute sich der Förderung des Markgrafen von Meißen und diente seit 1230 den Stiftern, den Grafen von Eilenburg, als Grablege. 1539 säkularisiert, kam das Klostergut an sächsische Adlige; seither ist der Name Güldenstern üblich. Die Klosterkirche ist ein südlicher Ausläufer spätromanischer märkischer Backsteinbaukunst und von großer baugeschichtlicher Bedeutung. Der einschiffige kreuzförmige Bau hat je eine Apsis an Chor und Kreuzarmen. 1539 ausgebrannt, wurde er der Stadt als Pfarrkirche übereignet, 1565-85 wiederhergestellt und seit 1982 zur Nutzung als Konzerthalle umgestaltet. Erste Bauteile sind nördlicher Kreuzarm (1227) und Chor (1280); die spätgotische Westfront entstand wohl 1480.

The former Cistercian nunnery was founded in 1227. It enjoyed support from the margrave of Meissen and served as burial place for the founders, the Counts von Eilenburg, since 1230. After secularization in 1539 the monastery estate fell to noblemen from Saxony; since then, the name Güldenstern is documented. The monastery church is a late outgrowth of late Romanesque brick architecture of the Mark and of great importance for building history. Apses are found at the choir and each of the transept wings of the single-nave cruciform building. Gutted by fire in 1539, it was given to the town as parish church and rebuilt in 1565-85. From 1982 is was converted to a concert hall. The oldest sections are the north transept (1227) and the choir (1280); the late Gothic west façade probably dates from 1480.

in der Nähe/nearby:
Abtei; Kloster Güldenstern
Um 1500 (Umbau 1717)
Rathaus; Neustädtischer Markt
1543-49
Gutsherrenvilla; Rittergut Güldenstern
Um 1900
Historischer Stadtkern; Altstädter Markt
16.-19. Jh.
Archidiakonat; Schulplatz 4
1741

Literatur
Bibliography

Handbücher / *Handbooks*

Die Bau- und Kunstdenkmale in der DDR; hrsg. Institut für Denkmalpflege Berlin; Berlin 1982 ff. (Teilbände: Bezirk Frankfurt/Oder; Bezirk Neubrandenburg; Bezirk Potsdam; Hauptstadt Berlin I u. II)
Die Bauwerke und Kunstdenkmäler von Berlin; Berlin 1955 ff. (Teilbände: Bezirk Tiergarten, bearbeitet von Irmgard Wirth; Stadt und Bezirk Charlottenburg, bearbeitet von Irmgard Wirth; Stadt und Bezirk Spandau, bearbeitet von Gunther Jahn)
Berlin und seine Bauten; hrsg. Architekten- und Ingenieur-Verein zu Berlin (bzw. Vorgänger); 1. Ausgabe Berlin 1877, 2. Ausgabe Berlin 1896, 3. Ausgabe Berlin 1964 ff. (Teilbände: Wohnungsbau A, B und C; Bauten für die Kunst; Schulen; Handel und Gewerbe A und B; Industriebauten u. Bürohäuser; Anlagen und Bauten für den Verkehr 1, 2 und 4; Anlagen und Bauten für Versorgung 1 u. 3; Gartenwesen; sowie bisher unveröffentlichte Manuskripte)
Dehio, Georg: Handbuch der Deutschen Kunstdenkmäler; Berlin 1964 ff. (Teilbände: Bezirke Berlin/DDR und Potsdam; Bezirke Cottbus und Frankfurt a.O.; Bezirke Neubrandenburg, Rostock und Schwerin)
Denkmaltopographie Bundesrepublik Deutschland – Baudenkmale in Berlin, Bezirk Reinickendorf, Ortsteil Reinickendorf; hrsg. Senator für Stadtentwicklung und Umweltschutz Berlin; bearbeitet von Tomisch, Jürgen, u. Schomann, Rainer; Berlin (1988)
Deutsche Kunstdenkmäler – Ein Bildhandbuch – Mark Brandenburg und Berlin; hrsg. Reinhardt Hootz; München/Berlin 1971
Die Kunstdenkmäler der Provinz Brandenburg – Stadt und Dom Brandenburg; hrsg. Brandenburgischer Provinzialverband; Berlin 1912
Die Kunstdenkmäler der Provinz Brandenburg – Kreis Luckau; hrsg. Brandenburgischer Provinzialverband; Berlin 1917
Die Kunstdenkmäler der Provinz Brandenburg – Kreis Niederbarnim; hrsg. Brandenburgischer Provinzialverband; Berlin 1939
Die Kunstdenkmäler der Provinz Brandenburg – Kreis Teltow; hrsg. Brandenburgischer Provinzialverband; Berlin 1941
Die Kunstdenkmäler der Provinz Brandenburg – Kreis Templin; hrsg. Brandenburgischer Provinzialverband; Berlin 1937

Architektur-, Kunst- und Reiseführer / *Architectural, art, and general guides*

Badstübner, Ernst: Stadtkirchen der Mark Brandenburg; Berlin 1982
Bartmann-Kompa, Ingrid, u. Kutschmar, Aribert, u. Karn, Heinz: Architekturführer DDR – Bezirk Potsdam; Berlin 1981
Bauten unter Denkmalschutz – Berlin; hrsg. Berlin-Information; Berlin 1982
Funeck, Gottfried, u. Schönholz, Waltraud, u. Steinwasser, Fritz: Park- und Grünanlagen in Berlin; Berlin 1987
Halbach, Ingrid, u. Rambow, Matthias, u. Büttner, Horst, u. Rätzel, Peter: Architekturführer DDR – Bezirk Frankfurt (Oder); Berlin 1987
Kühne, Günther, u. Stephani, Elisabeth: Evangelische Kirchen in Berlin; Berlin 1978
Rave, Rolf, u. Knöfel, Hans-Joachim: Bauen seit 1900 in Berlin; Berlin 1968
Rave, Rolf, u. Knöfel, Hans-Joachim: Bauen der 70er Jahre in Berlin; Berlin 1981
Schulz, Joachim, u. Gräbner, Werner: Architekturführer DDR – Berlin; Berlin 1974
Wörner, Martin, u. Mollenschott, Doris: Architekturführer Berlin; Berlin 1989

Themenbezogene Monographien / *Monographs on special subjects*

Bau- und Kunstdenkmale in Potsdam; hrsg. Institut für Denkmalpflege Berlin; Berlin 1990
Eckhardt, Götz: Sanssouci; Berlin 1990
Etzold, Alfred, u. Fait, Joachim, u. Kirchner, Peter, u. Knobloch, Heinz: Jüdische Friedhöfe in Berlin; Berlin 1987
Giersberg, Hans-Joachim, u. Scheudel, Adelheid: Potsdamer Veduten; Potsdam 1982
Heydick, Lutz, u. Hoppe, Günther, u. John, Jürgen: Historischer Führer – Stätten und Denkmale der Geschichte in den Bezirken Potsdam, Frankfurt/Oder; Leipzig/Jena/Berlin 1987
Hildebrandt, Werner, u. Lemburg, Peter, u. Wewel, Jörg: Historische Bauwerke der Berliner Industrie; Berlin 1988
Hüter, Karl-Heinz: Architektur in Berlin 1900-1933; Dresden 1987
Internationale Bauausstellung Berlin 1987 – Projektübersicht; Berlin 1989
Krankenhäuser in Berlin; hrsg. Senator für Gesundheit und Soziales Berlin, Berlin 1989
Mielke, Friedrich: Potsdamer Baukunst; Frankfurt/M 1981
Mittenzwei, Ingrid, u. Herzfeld, Erika: Brandenburg-Preußen 1648-1789; Berlin 1987
Natzschka, Werner: Berlin und seine Wasserstraßen; Berlin 1971
Ribbe, Wolfgang: Von der Residenz zur City; Berlin 1980
Ribbe, Wolfgang, u. Schäche, Wolfgang: Die Siemensstadt; Berlin 1985
Schulz, Joachim, u. Gräbner, Werner: Berlin – Architektur von Pankow bis Köpenick; Berlin 1987
Synagogen in Berlin; hrsg. Rolf Bothe; Berlin 1983
Uhlemann, Hans-Joachim: Berlin und die Märkischen Wasserstraßen; Berlin 1987
Vogel, Werner: Führer durch die Geschichte Berlins; Berlin 1989
Volk, Waltraud: Historische Straßen und Plätze heute – Berlin; Berlin 1977
Wagenbreth, Otfried, u. Wächtler, Eberhard: Technische Denkmale in der DDR; Leipzig 1983
Wolff, Karl: Wannsee; Berlin 1972
Wolters, Rudolf: Stadtmitte Berlin; Tübingen 1978

Bildnachweis
Photographs

Architekten / *Architects*

Assmann, Salomon und Scheidt, Berlin H 13
Baller, Berlin E 13, O 14
Fissler & Partner, Berlin (Brian Jennings) B 24, E 6
Kleihues, Berlin D 21, N 23
Libeskind, Berlin B 32
Nalbach, Berlin O 3
Nielebock & Partner, Berlin U 2
Rave & Partner, Berlin D 20
Scholz, Berlin N 21
Spangenberg, Berlin B 25
Steinebach & Weber, Berlin J 2, O 10
Ungers, Köln/Berlin B 16

Archive / *Archives*

ADN-ZB, Berlin B 20
Archiv Bartmann, Berlin P 6-7, P 17-19, Q 2, R 3, T 3, U 44
Archiv Gaffrei, Berlin C 6
Archiv Güttler, Berlin Umschlagseite 1 c, Seite 14 u. 16, B 13, B 17, B 23, B 30, B 33-34, C 15-16, D 7, D 9, D 17-18, E 4-5, E 7, E 9, F 1, F 16, F 20, F 23, F 26-27, F 29, F 32, H 8, H 10-11, H 14-17, H 21, H 24, H 26, J 5, J 7-12, J 14-15, J 18-22, J 29-30, K 1-3, K 9, K 12-13, K 16, L 17, M 7-8, N 5, N 12-13, N 16, O 1-2, O 7-8, O 11, O 18-20, O 22, P 40, Q 3, Q 5, Q 7, Q 10, R 5-6, R 8, R 16, S 20, S 5, T 1, T 4, T 8, T 10, U 8, U 45, V 1-3, W 2, X 2, X 14-15, Y 10, Z 1-4
Archiv Kurt Junghanns, Berlin H 9
Archiv J. Schulz, Berlin A 13, A 21, F 22, S 21, S 28, V 6, V 8, U 21, Z 17, Z 20
Archiv K.-D. Schulz, Berlin W 15, Z 10
Archiv Zoo, Berlin D 3
Bauinformation, Berlin A 5, A 18, B 18 (Mayenfels); A 10, A 15-16 (Baum); A 17, B 6, M 5 (Riemann); B 9 (Gottschalk); B 10, G 9, L 18 (Hartmetz); F 19, G 10 (Schmidt); G 6, G 8, M 3 (-)
Brandenburgisches Amt für Denkmalpflege, Berlin Umschlagseite 1 e, L 1, L 5-8, L 10-11, L 13, P 10, V 18, W 3, W 5-8, W 12, W 14, W 16, W 26 (Leßmann); Seite 10, M 1-2, M 12, N 14, N 19, P 4, P 29, P 33, P 37-39, Q 8, R 2, R 9, S 7, S 13, S 16, S 24-25, T 5, U 4, U 40 (Möller); A 23, B 21, B 38, F 18, G 1, L 2, M 4, N 9-10, U 14, U 16, U 27, W 23 (Hänel); F 7, M 6, T 7, U 26, U 28, U 32, U 47, V 7, W 28 (Fritz); F 13 (Pilgrimm); G 11, P 3, R 7, S 3, S 19, S 26, T 6, T 9, T 12, U 5, U 35, U 42-43, V 5, V 16, W 19 (Worel); L 16, N 1-3, N 6, N 11, V 4, W 9 (Laurentius); P 14, Q 11-12, T 2, V 19 (Meßbildarchiv); P 25, P 31, P 34-36, U 38-39 (Tschilingirov); S 15 (Schröder/Leßmann); U 46 (Schröder)
Debis, Berlin B 39
Dewag, Berlin (Quabbe) F 8
Dewis GmbH, Wittenberge U 20
IRS, Berlin A 7, A 11, F 9
KaDeWe, Berlin D 11
Landesbildstelle Berlin Umschlagseite 1 a, 1 d u. 1 f, Seite 12 u. 18, B 3, B 5, B 15, B 19, B 26, B 28-29, B 31, B 35-37, C 1-2, C 3-4, C 6-14, C 17, C 20-22, D 1-2, D 4-6, D 10, D 12-13, D 14-16, D 22-23, E 1, E 3, E 8, E 10-12, E 15, E 20-23, F 2, F 4-6, F 28, F 30, G 12, G 15-16, H 1-4, H 18-19, H 22-23, H 25, H 27-28, J 1, J 3-4, J 6, J 13, J 16, J 23-26, J 28, K 4-5, K 7-8, K 10-11, K 14-15, N 17, N 22, O 6, O 9, O 15, O 17, O 21, O 23-24, R 11-12, R 14-15, R 17
Landesregierung Berlin (ehem. Magistrat) A 8, A 24, B 11, N 18
Luftbild Interflug G 2, G 7, L 15, N 8, S 22, U 17
Märkisches Museum, Berlin F 14
Sächsische Landesbibliothek (Abt. Dt. Fotothek), Dresden N 7 (Meinecke); S 1 (Handrick); S 11, S 17, Y 2-3, Y 5, Y 8, Z 19, Z 21-26, Z 29-32 (Reinecke); S 12 (Heselbarth); S 27; U 18 (Walther); U 19, V 10-12, Z 28 (Trinks); U 22-23, Z 27 (Richter); U 34 (Nagel); U 36 (Hofert); Y 1, Y 6, Z 11 (Heine); Y 7 (Krause); Y 11, Z 12 (Rous); Z 14 (Hüttel); A 3, L 3 (-)
Senatsverwaltung für Bau- und Wohnungswesen, Berlin J 17
Der Tagesspiegel, Berlin (Stefan Nowak) B 40

Fotografen / *Photographers*

K. W. Anger, Babelsberg U 10
H. v. der Becke, Berlin F 31
Christina Bolduan, Berlin B 22, H 6
Wolfgang Braun, Rathenow U 11
Brumm V 14-15
Horst Büttner, Hamburg W 27
Ernst Otto Denk, Bad Freienwalde V 26-28
Martin Dettloff, Berlin A 14, G 5
E. Dutschmann, Berlin B 14, F 10, F 12
Horst Ende, Schwerin U 24
Joachim Fieguth, Berlin A 6
Reinhard Görner, Berlin D 19
Rudolf Hartmetz, Frankfurt/Oder X 1, X 3-10, X 12-13, X 16
Thomas Helms, Schwerin V 9
Tatjana Herkner, Berlin L 19
Arnold Jacoby, Potsdam R 4, S 4, S 6, S 10, U 12-13, U 30, W 22
Heinz Karn, Kleinmachnow S 2, S 8, W 24
Andres Kilger, Berlin F 15
Klohse V 22, W 4, W 10
Wilmar Koenig, Berlin G 14
Karl-Heinz Kraemer, Berlin A 9, A 19, N 15
Carl Krause, Berlin Seite 8, U 21
Günter Krawutschke, Berlin A 2
K.-H. Müller, Cottbus Y 9
Gerhard Murza, Berlin L 4
Uwe Rau, Berlin Umschlagseite 4
Günter Rinnhofer, Eberswalde V 23
R. Roletschek, Eberswalde V 20
Klaus-Dieter Schulz, Berlin V 24, X 11, W 18, W 20-21, Z 6-8, Z 13, Z 15-16
R. Siebert, Kleinmachnow T 11
Maria Steinfeldt, Berlin, Berlin F 11
Andreas Stirl, Berlin F 21, F 24-25, L 9
Wolfgang Timme, Eisenhüttenstadt W 30-32
Heinrich Trost, Berlin F 17, G 3-4, P 11, P 16, P 22-23, P 32
M. Uelze, Berlin M 9-11
Walter Wawra, Potsdam U 1, U 7
Rainer Weisflog, Cottbus Y 4
Lothar Willmann, Berlin Y 12

Bücher / *Books*

Fritz Eschen: Junges altes Berlin, Berlin 1956 B 8
Fritz Eschen: Unvergessenes Potsdam, Berlin 1963 Q 1
E. M. Hajos u. L. Zahn: Berliner Architektur der Nachkriegszeit; Berlin 1928 B 27, D 8, H 5, H 7, H 12, L 12, L 20, N 4, N 20, O 12, O 16
Hennigsdorfer Siedlungsgesellschaft U 48
Hans Kania: Karl Friedrich Schinkel ; Berlin 1934 P 2, R 10
Kraftwerksbauten; Hrsg. Siemens; Berlin (1930) Z 18
Neubauten der Stadt Berlin, Berlin 1901-1910 F 3, F 26, L 14
Georg Piltz: Sanssouci; Dresden 1954 Q 4, Q 6, Q 9
Paul Ortwin Rave: Berlin in der Geschichte seiner Bauten, Berlin 1960 Umschlagseite 1 b u. 2, A 1, A 4, A 12, A 20, A 22, B 1-2, B 4, B 7, B 12, C 18-19, E 14, E 16-19, H 20, J 27, K 6, O 4-5, O 13, R 13, R 18-20
Otto Zieler: Potsdam; Berlin 1913 P 1, P 5, P 8-9, P 12-13, P 15, P 20-21, P 24, P 26-28, P 30

Objekt-Register
Index of objects

Stadtanlagen, Siedlungsensemble / *Towns and Settlements*

Burgen / *Castles*

Stadtbefestigungen, Schmuckbauten / *Town fortifications, Ornamental buildings*

Denkmale, Ehrenmale / *Monuments*

Brunnen / *Fountains*

Parke und Gärten / *Parks and Gardens*

Brücken / *Bridges*

Anlagen der Bahnen / *Railway facilities*

Anlagen des Wasserverkehrs / *Shipping facilities*

Flughäfen / *Airports*

Elektrizitäts- und Gaswerke / *Power plants and Gasworks*

Wasserwerke und -türme / *Waterworks and Water towers*

Rettungseinrichtungen / *Rescue services*

Schlachthöfe / *Slaughterhouses*

Parlamente, Ministerien / *Parliament buildings, Ministries*

Rathäuser, Ämter / *Town halls, Government offices*

Militär-, Polizei- und Justizbauten / *Military, Police, and Court buildings*

Postgebäude / *Post office buildings*

Funkhäuser, Sendeanlagen / *Broadcasting studios and installations*

Botschaftsgebäude / *Embassies*

Kirchen / *Churches*

Klöster / *Monasteries*

Jüdische Kultbauten / *Jewish religious buildings*

Tempel / *Temples*

Gemeindehäuser / *Parish halls*

Friedhöfe, Krematorien / *Cemeteries, Crematoriums*

Museen / *Museums*

Bibliotheken, Archive / *Libraries, Archives*

Hochschulen, Akademien, Institute / *Universities, Academies, Institutes*

Wissenschaftliche Gärten und Sammlungen / *Scientific gardens and collections*

Schulen / *Schools*

Opernhäuser, Theater, Konzerthäuser / *Opera-houses, Theatres, Concert halls*

Lichtspieltheater / *Cinemas*

Versammlungsbauten / *Assembly halls*

Sportplätze und -hallen / *Sports fields and halls*

Bäder / *Baths*

Heime / *Homes*

Krankenhäuser / *Hospitals*

Büro-, Geschäfts- und Verwaltungsgebäude / *Office, Shop, and Administration buildings*

Banken / *Banks*

Waren- und Kaufhäuser / *Departments stores*

Hotels, Gaststätten / *Hotels, Restaurants*

Industrie und Handwerk / *Industry and Trade*

Landwirtschaftliche Bauten / *Agricultural buildings*

Wirtschaftsgebäude / *Domestic buildings*

Wohnsiedlungen / *Residential estates*

Mehrfamilienhäuser / *Residential buildings*

Doppel- und Reihenhäuser / *Semi-detached houses and Terraces*

Einfamilienhäuser / *Family houses*

Palais / *Palais*

Schlösser, Herrenhäuser / *Palaces, Manor-houses*

Architekten- und Künstler-Register
Index of architects and artists

Bauabteilungen

Ortsregister
Place index